Karen Morrison and Nick Hamshaw

Cambridge IGCSE®

Mathematics

Core and Extended

Coursebook

Revised Edition

CAMBRIDGE
UNIVERSITY PRESS

University Printing House, Cambridge CB2 8BS, United Kingdom

Cambridge University Press is part of the University of Cambridge.

It furthers the University's mission by disseminating knowledge in the pursuit of education, learning and research at the highest international levels of excellence.

www.cambridge.org
Information on this title: education.cambridge.org

First published 2012
Revised Edition First Published 2015

Printed in the United Kingdom by Latimer Trend

A catalogue record for this publication is available from the British Library

ISBN 978-1-316-60563-9 Paperback with CD-ROM

Cover image: Seamus Ditmeyer/Alamy

All examination-style questions, sample mark schemes, solutions and/or comments that appear in this book were written by the authors. In examination, the way marks would be awarded to answers like these may be different.

Contents

Unit 4

Unit 5

Unit 6

Introduction

This highly illustrated coursebook covers the complete *Cambridge IGCSE Mathematics* (0580) syllabus. Core and Extended material is combined in one book, offering a one-stop-shop for all students and teachers. Useful hints are included in the margins for students needing more support, leaving the narrative clear and to the point. The material required for the Extended course is clearly marked using colour panels; Extended students are given access to the parts of the Core syllabus they need without having to use an additional book.

REWIND

You learned how to plot lines from equations in chapter 10. ◀

FAST FORWARD

You will learn much more about sets in chapter 9. For now, just think of a set as a list of numbers or other items that are often placed inside curly brackets. ▶

The coursebook has been written with a clear progression from start to finish, with some later chapters requiring knowledge learned in earlier chapters. There are useful signposts throughout the coursebook that link the content of the chapters, allowing the individual to follow their own course through the book: where the content in one chapter might require knowledge from a previous chapter, a comment is included in a 'Rewind' box; and where content will be covered in more detail later on in the coursebook, a comment is included in a 'Fast forward' box. Examples of both are included here.

Worked examples are used throughout to demonstrate each method using typical workings and thought processes. These present the methods to the students in a practical and easy-to-follow way that minimises the need for lengthy explanations.

There is plenty of practice offered via 'drill' exercises throughout each chapter. The exercises are progressive questions that allow the student to practise methods that have just been introduced. At the end of each chapter there are 'Exam-style' questions and 'Past paper' questions. The 'Exam-style' questions have been written by the authors in the *style* of examination questions. The 'Past paper' questions are *real* questions taken from past exam papers. Both these end of chapter questions typically reflect the kinds of short answer questions that you may face in examinations though you will find some more structured ones in there as well. The answers to *all* of these questions are supplied at the back of the book, allowing self- and/or class- assessment. You can assess your progress as they go along, choosing to do more or less practise as required.

The suggested progression through the coursebook is for Units 1-3 to be covered in the first year of both courses, and units 4-6 to be covered in the second year of both courses. On this basis, there is mixed exam practice at the end of Unit 3 and the end of Unit 6. This is however, only a **suggested** structure and the course can be taught in various different ways; the signposting throughout the coursebook means that it can be used alongside any order of teaching. The end of unit questions represent the longer answer 'structured' examination questions and will use a combination of methods from across all relevant chapters. As with the end of chapter questions, these are a mixture of 'Exam-style' and 'Past paper' questions. The answers to these questions are on the Teacher's resource so that they can be used in classroom tests or for homework, if desired.

The coursebook also comes with a glossary to provide a definition for important / tricky terms.

Helpful guides in the margin of the book include:

Remember 'coefficient' is the *number* in the term.

Clues: these are general comments to remind you of important or key information that is useful to tackle an exercise, or simply useful to know. They often provide extra information or support in potentially tricky topics.

Tip

It is essential that you remember to work out *both* unknowns. Every pair of simultaneous linear equations will have a pair of solutions.

Tip: They cover common pitfalls based on the **authors'** experiences of their students, and give you things to be wary of or to remember.

The accompanying student CD-ROM at the back of the coursebook includes:

- A 'coverage grid' to map the contents of the syllabus to the topics and chapters in the coursebook.
- A 'Calculator support' chapter. This chapter covers the main uses of calculators that students seem to struggle with, and includes some worksheets to provide practice at using your calculator in these situations.
- Revision:
  - Core revision worksheets (and answers) provide extra exercises for each chapter of the book. These worksheets contain only content from the Core syllabus.
  - Extended revision worksheets (and answers) provide extra exercises for each chapter of the book. These worksheets contain the **same** questions as the Core worksheets, **in addition to** some more challenging questions, *and* questions to cover content unique to the Extended syllabus. Students are encouraged to do some (if not all) of the 'Core' questions on these worksheets, as well as the Extended ones (shaded) in order to fully revise the course. If time is limited, you might find it easier to pick two or three 'Core' questions to do before moving on to the 'Extended' questions.
  - Quick revision is a set of interactive questions in the form of multiple choice, drag and drop, or hide and reveal. They are quick-fire questions to test yourself in a different medium to pen and paper, and to get you thinking on the spot. They cover the Core content, with only a few additional screens being specific to the Extended course. There is at least one activity for each chapter. **Students are recommended to use the revision worksheets for a more comprehensive revision exercise.**
  - Worked solutions are interactive hide and reveal screens showing worked solutions to **some** of the end of chapter exam practice questions. Some of these will be 'Exam-style' and some will be 'Past paper' questions but all will be taken from the end of a chapter. There will be at least one for each chapter. The screen includes the question, and the answer, but also includes a series of 'Clue' or 'Tip' boxes. The 'Clue' boxes can be clicked on to reveal a clue to help the student if they are struggling with how to approach the question. The 'Tip' boxes contain tips relating to the exam, just like the 'Tip' boxes in the coursebook.

Also in the *Cambridge IGCSE Mathematics* series are two Practice Books – one for Core and one for Extended – to offer students targeted practice. These follow the chapters and topics of the coursebook to offer additional exercises for those who want more practice. These too, include 'Clues' and 'Tips' to help with tricky topics. There is also a Teacher's resource CD-ROM to offer support and advice

Acknowledgements

The authors and publishers acknowledge the following sources of copyright material and are grateful for the permissions granted.

Past paper examination questions are reproduced by permission of Cambridge International Examinations.

Cover image Seamus Ditmeyer/Alamy; p. 1 © sanderderwilde.com; p. 13 Dmitry Lavruhin/Shutterstock; p. 13 Hadriann/Shutterstock; p. 13 Jason Cox/Shutterstock; p. 13 Ruslan Nabiyev/Shutterstock; p. 46 Ivangott/Shutterstock; p. 47 Claudio Baldini/ Shutterstock; p. 63 akiyoko/Shutterstock; p. 73 INSAGO/Shutterstock; p. 98 © The Trustees of the British Museum; p. 119 Wikipedia; p. 128 Francesco Dazzi/Shutterstock; p. 165 North Wind Picture Archive/Alamy; p. 148 Paolo Gianti/Shutterstock; pp. 153, 347, 495, 537 iStockphoto/ Thinkstock; p. 155 Opachevsky Irina/Shutterstock; p. 156 Chad Littlejohn/Shutterstock; p. 159 sahua d/Shutterstock; p. 210 Photos. com/Thinkstock; pp. 227, 427, 436 Mike van der Wold; p. 239 Picsfive/Shutterstock; p. 255 Vladislav Gurfinkel/Shutterstock; p. 264 Mike Tan C.T./Shutterstock; p. 266 Suzan/Shutterstock; p. 266 R-studio/Shutterstock; p. 269 Galyna Andrushko/Shutterstock; p. 304 Gustavo Miguel Fernandes/Shutterstock; p. 357 Stephanie Fray/Shutterstock; p. 370 Kristina Postnikova/Shutterstock; p. 405 Connors Bros./Shutterstock; p. 449 Philippe Wojazer/AP/Press Association Images

1 Reviewing number concepts

Key words

- Natural number
- Integer
- Prime number
- Symbol
- Multiple
- Factor
- Composite numbers
- Prime factor
- Square root
- Cube
- Directed numbers
- BODMAS

In this chapter you will learn how to:

- identify and classify different types of numbers
- find common factors and common multiples of numbers
- write numbers as products of their prime factors
- calculate squares, square roots, cubes and cube roots of numbers
- work with integers used in real-life situations
- revise the basic rules for operating with numbers
- perform basic calculations using mental methods and with a calculator.

This statue is a replica of a 22 000-year-old bone found in the Congo. The real bone is only 10 cm long and it is carved with groups of notches that represent numbers. One column lists the prime numbers from 10 to 20. It is one of the earliest examples of a number system using tallies.

Our modern number system is called the Hindu-Arabic system because it was developed by Hindus and spread by Arab traders who brought it with them when they moved to different places in the world. The Hindu-Arabic system is decimal. This means it uses place value based on powers of ten. Any number at all, including decimals and fractions, can be written using place value and the digits from 0 to 9.

1.1 Different types of numbers

Make sure you know the correct mathematical words for the types of numbers in the table.

You should already be familiar with most of the concepts in this chapter. It is included here so that you can revise the concepts and check that you remember them.

FAST FORWARD

You will learn about the difference between rational and irrational numbers in chapter 9. ▶

Number	Definition	Example
Natural number	Any whole number from 1 to infinity, sometimes called 'counting numbers'. 0 is not included.	1, 2, 3, 4, 5, . . .
Odd number	A whole number that cannot be divided exactly by 2.	1, 3, 5, 7, . . .
Even number	A whole number that can be divided exactly by 2.	2, 4, 6, 8, . . .
Integer	Any of the negative and positive whole numbers, including zero.	. . . −3, −2, −1, 0, 1, 2, 3, . . .
Prime number	A whole number greater than 1 which has only two factors: the number itself and 1.	2, 3, 5, 7, 11, . . .
Square number	The product obtained when an integer is multiplied by itself.	1, 4, 9, 16, . . .
Fraction	A number representing parts of a whole number, can be written as a common (vulgar) fraction in the form of $\frac{a}{b}$ or as a decimal using the decimal point.	$\frac{1}{2}, \frac{1}{4}, \frac{1}{3}, \frac{1}{8}, \frac{13}{3}, 2\frac{1}{2}$ 0.5, 0.2, 0.08, 1.7

Find the 'product' means 'multiply'. So, the product of 3 and 4 is 12, i.e. 3 × 4 = 12.

Exercise 1.1

FAST FORWARD

You will learn much more about sets in chapter 9. For now, just think of a set as a list of numbers or other items that are often placed inside curly brackets. ▶

1 Here is a set of numbers: {−4, −1, 0, $\frac{1}{2}$, 0.75, 3, 4, 6, 11, 16, 19, 25}

List the numbers from this set that are:

(a) natural numbers
(b) even numbers
(c) odd numbers
(d) integers
(e) negative integers
(f) fractions
(g) square numbers
(h) prime numbers
(i) neither square nor prime.

2 List:

(a) the next four odd numbers after 107
(b) four consecutive even numbers between 2008 and 2030
(c) all odd numbers between 993 and 1007
(d) the first five square numbers
(e) four decimal fractions that are smaller than 0.5
(f) four vulgar fractions that are greater than $\frac{1}{2}$ but smaller than $\frac{3}{4}$.

3 State whether the following will be odd or even:

Remember that a 'sum' is the result of an addition. The term is often used for *any* calculation in early mathematics but its meaning is very specific at this level.

(a) the sum of two odd numbers
(b) the sum of two even numbers
(c) the sum of an odd and an even number
(d) the square of an odd number
(e) the square of an even number
(f) an odd number multiplied by an even number.

Living maths

4 There are many other types of numbers. Find out what these numbers are and give an example of each.

(a) Perfect numbers.
(b) Palindromic numbers.
(c) Narcissistic numbers. (In other words, numbers that love themselves!)

Using symbols to link numbers

Mathematicians use numbers and **symbols** to write mathematical information in the shortest, clearest way possible.

You have used the operation symbols +, –, × and ÷ since you started school. Now you will also use the symbols given in the margin below to write mathematical statements.

Exercise 1.2

= is equal to
≠ is not equal to
≈ is approximately equal to
< is less than
≤ is less than or equal to
> is greater than
≥ is greater than or equal to
∴ therefore
√ the square root of

1 Rewrite each of these statements using mathematical symbols.

(a) 19 is less than 45
(b) 12 plus 18 is equal to 30
(c) 0.5 is equal to $\frac{1}{2}$
(d) 0.8 is not equal to 8.0
(e) –34 is less than 2 times –16
(f) therefore the number x equals the square root of 72
(g) a number (x) is less than or equal to negative 45
(h) π is approximately equal to 3.14
(i) 5.1 is greater than 5.01
(j) the sum of 3 and 4 is not equal to the product of 3 and 4
(k) the difference between 12 and –12 is greater than 12
(l) the sum of –12 and –24 is less than 0
(m) the product of 12 and a number (x) is approximately –40

Remember that the 'difference' between two numbers is the result of a subtraction. The order of the subtraction matters.

2 Say whether these mathematical statements are true or false.

(a) $0.599 > 6.0$
(b) $5 \times 1999 \approx 10\,000$
(c) $8.1 = 8\frac{1}{10}$
(d) $6.2 + 4.3 = 4.3 + 6.2$
(e) $20 \times 9 \geq 21 \times 8$
(f) $6.0 = 6$
(g) $-12 > -4$
(h) $19.9 \leq 20$
(i) $1000 > 199 \times 5$
(j) $\sqrt{16} = 4$
(k) $35 \times 5 \times 2 \neq 350$
(l) $20 \div 4 = 5 \div 20$
(m) $20 - 4 \neq 4 - 20$
(n) $20 \times 4 \neq 4 \times 20$

3 Work with a partner.

(a) Look at the symbols used on the keys of your calculator. Say what each one means in words.
(b) List any symbols that you do not know. Try to find out what each one means.

1.2 Multiples and factors

You can think of the multiples of a number as the 'times table' for that number. For example, the multiples of 3 are $3 \times 1 = \mathbf{3}$, $3 \times 2 = \mathbf{6}$, $3 \times 3 = \mathbf{9}$ and so on.

Multiples

A **multiple** of a number is found when you multiply that number by a positive integer. The first multiple of any number is the number itself (the number multiplied by 1).

Worked example 1

(a) What are the first three multiples of 12?
(b) Is 300 a multiple of 12?

(a)	12, 24, 36	To find these multiply 12 by 1, 2 and then 3. $12 \times 1 = 12$ $12 \times 2 = 24$ $12 \times 3 = 36$
(b)	Yes, 300 is a multiple of 12.	To find out, divide 300 by 12. If it goes exactly, then 300 is a multiple of 12. $300 \div 12 = 25$

Exercise 1.3

1 List the first five multiples of:

(a) 2 (b) 3 (c) 5 (d) 8
(e) 9 (f) 10 (g) 12 (h) 100

2 Use a calculator to find and list the first ten multiples of:

(a) 29 (b) 44 (c) 75 (d) 114
(e) 299 (f) 350 (g) 1012 (h) 9123

3 List:

(a) the multiples of 4 between 29 and 53
(b) the multiples of 50 less than 400
(c) the multiples of 100 between 4000 and 5000.

4 Here are five numbers: 576, 396, 354, 792, 1164. Which of these are multiples of 12?

5 Which of the following numbers are not multiples of 27?

(a) 324 (b) 783 (c) 816 (d) 837 (e) 1116

The lowest common multiple (LCM)

The lowest common multiple of two or more numbers is the smallest number that is a multiple of all the given numbers.

Worked example 2

Find the lowest common multiple of 4 and 7.

$M_4 = 4, 8, 12, 16, 20, 24, \underline{\mathbf{28}}, 32$ $M_7 = 7, 14, 21, \underline{\mathbf{28}}, 35, 42$ LCM = 28	List several multiples of 4. (Note: M_4 means multiples of 4.) List several multiples of 7. Find the lowest number that appears in both sets. This is the LCM.

Exercise 1.4

FAST FORWARD

Later in this chapter you will see how prime factors can be used to find LCMs. ▶

1 Find the LCM of:

(a) 2 and 5 (b) 8 and 10 (c) 6 and 4
(d) 3 and 9 (e) 35 and 55 (f) 6 and 11
(g) 2, 4 and 8 (h) 4, 5 and 6 (i) 6, 8 and 9
(j) 1, 3 and 7 (k) 4, 5 and 8 (l) 3, 4 and 18

2 Is it possible to find the highest common multiple of two or more numbers? Give a reason for your answer.

Factors

A **factor** is a number that divides exactly into another number with no remainder. For example, 2 is a factor of 16 because it goes into 16 exactly 8 times. 1 is a factor of every number. The largest factor of any number is the number itself.

F_{12} means the factors of 12.

To list the factors in numerical order go down the left side and then up the right side of the factor pairs. Remember not to repeat factors.

Worked example 3

Find the factors of:

(a) 12 **(b)** 25 **(c)** 110

(a)	F_{12} = 1, 2, 3, 4, 6, 12	Find pairs of numbers that multiply to give 12: 1 × 12 2 × 6 3 × 4 Write the factors in numerical order.
(b)	F_{25} = 1, 5, 25	1 × 25 5 × 5 Do not repeat the 5.
(c)	F_{110} = 1, 2, 5, 10, 11, 22, 55, 110	1 × 110 2 × 55 5 × 22 10 × 11

Exercise 1.5

1 List all the factors of:

(a) 4 **(b)** 5 **(c)** 8 **(d)** 11 **(e)** 18
(f) 12 **(g)** 35 **(h)** 40 **(i)** 57 **(j)** 90
(k) 100 **(l)** 132 **(m)** 160 **(n)** 153 **(o)** 360

2 Which number in each set is not a factor of the given number?

(a) 14 {1, 2, 4, 7, 14}
(b) 15 {1, 3, 5, 15, 45}
(c) 21 {1, 3, 7, 14, 21}
(d) 33 {1, 3, 11, 22, 33}
(e) 42 {3, 6, 7, 8, 14}

FAST FORWARD

Later in this chapter you will learn more about divisibility tests and how to use these to decide whether or not one number is a factor of another. ▶

3 State true or false in each case.

(a) 3 is a factor of 313 **(b)** 9 is a factor of 99
(c) 3 is a factor of 300 **(d)** 2 is a factor of 300
(e) 2 is a factor of 122 488 **(f)** 12 is a factor of 60
(g) 210 is a factor of 210 **(h)** 8 is a factor of 420

4 What is the smallest factor and the largest factor of any number?

The highest common factor (HCF)

The highest common factor of two or more numbers is the highest number that is a factor of all the given numbers.

Worked example 4

Find the HCF of 8 and 24.

F_8 = 1, 2, 4, 8 F_{24} = 1, 2, 3, 4, 6, 8, 12, 24 HCF = 8	List the factors of each number. Underline factors that appear in both sets. Pick out the highest underlined factor (HCF).

Exercise 1.6

FAST FORWARD

You will learn how to find HCFs by using prime factors later in the chapter. ▶

1 Find the HCF of each pair of numbers.

(a) 3 and 6 **(b)** 24 and 16 **(c)** 15 and 40 **(d)** 42 and 70
(e) 32 and 36 **(f)** 26 and 36 **(g)** 22 and 44 **(h)** 42 and 48

2 Find the HCF of each group of numbers.

(a) 3, 9 and 15 **(b)** 36, 63 and 84 **(c)** 22, 33 and 121

3 Not including the factor provided, find two numbers that have:

(a) an HCF of 2 **(b)** an HCF of 6

4 What is the HCF of two different prime numbers? Give a reason for your answer.

Word problems involving HCF usually involve splitting things into smaller pieces or arranging things in equal groups or rows.

Living maths

5 Simeon has two lengths of rope. One piece is 72 metres long and the other is 90 metres long. He wants to cut both lengths of rope into the longest pieces of equal length possible. How long should the pieces be?

6 Ms Sanchez has 40 canvases and 100 tubes of paint to give to the students in her art group. What is the largest number of students she can have if she gives each student an equal number of canvasses and an equal number of tubes of paint?

7 Indira has 300 blue beads, 750 red beads and 900 silver beads. She threads these beads to make wire bracelets. Each bracelet must have the same number and colour of beads. What is the maximum number of bracelets she can make with these beads?

1.3 Prime numbers

Prime numbers have exactly two factors: one and the number itself.

Composite numbers have more than two factors.

The number 1 has only one factor so it is not prime and it is not composite.

Finding prime numbers

Over 2000 years ago, a Greek mathematician called Eratosthenes made a simple tool for sorting out prime numbers. This tool is called the 'Sieve of Eratosthenes' and the figure on page 7 shows how it works for prime numbers up to 100.

~~1~~	2	3	~~4~~	5	~~6~~	7	~~8~~	~~9~~	~~10~~
11	~~12~~	13	~~14~~	~~15~~	~~16~~	17	~~18~~	19	~~20~~
~~21~~	~~22~~	23	~~24~~	~~25~~	~~26~~	~~27~~	~~28~~	29	~~30~~
31	~~32~~	~~33~~	~~34~~	~~35~~	~~36~~	37	~~38~~	~~39~~	~~40~~
41	~~42~~	43	~~44~~	~~45~~	~~46~~	47	~~48~~	~~49~~	~~50~~
~~51~~	~~52~~	53	~~54~~	~~55~~	~~56~~	~~57~~	~~58~~	59	~~60~~
61	~~62~~	~~63~~	~~64~~	~~65~~	~~66~~	67	~~68~~	~~69~~	~~70~~
71	~~72~~	73	~~74~~	~~75~~	~~76~~	~~77~~	~~78~~	79	~~80~~
~~81~~	~~82~~	83	~~84~~	~~85~~	~~86~~	~~87~~	~~88~~	89	~~90~~
~~91~~	~~92~~	~~93~~	~~94~~	~~95~~	~~96~~	97	~~98~~	~~99~~	~~100~~

Cross out 1, it is not prime.

Circle 2, then cross out other multiples of 2.

Circle 3, then cross out other multiples of 3.

Circle the next available number then cross out all its multiples.

Repeat until all the numbers in the table are either circled or crossed out.

The circled numbers are the primes.

You should try to memorise which numbers between 1 and 100 are prime.

Other mathematicians over the years have developed ways of finding larger and larger prime numbers. Until 1955, the largest known prime number had less than 1000 digits. Since the 1970s and the invention of more and more powerful computers, more and more prime numbers have been found. The graph below shows the number of digits in the largest known primes since 1996.

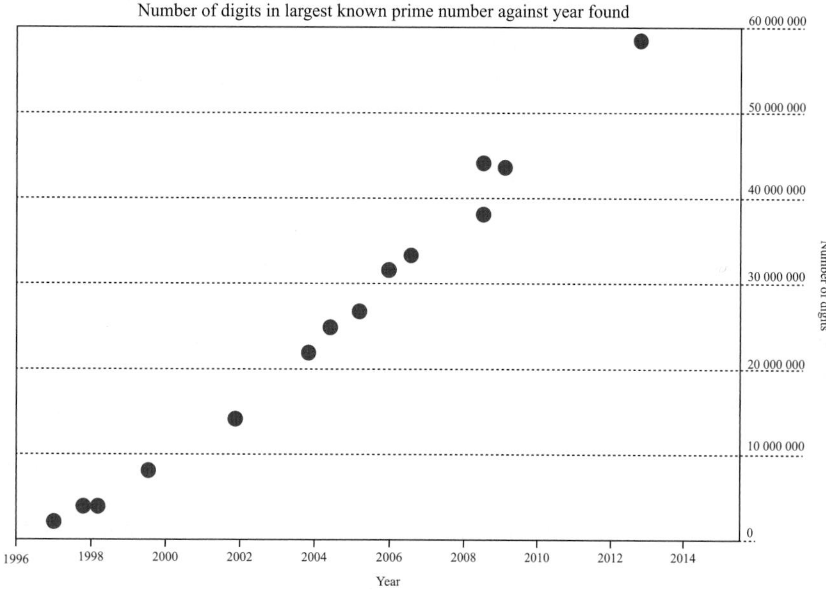

Today anyone can join the Great Internet Mersenne Prime Search. This project links thousands of home computers to search continuously for larger and larger prime numbers while the computer processors have spare capacity.

Exercise 1.7

FAST FORWARD

A good knowledge of primes can help when factorising quadratics in chapter 10. ▶

1. Which is the only even prime number?
2. How many odd prime numbers are there less than 50?
3. (a) List the composite numbers greater than four, but less than 30.
   (b) Try to write each composite number on your list as the sum of two prime numbers. For example: $6 = 3 + 3$ and $8 = 3 + 5$.
4. Twin primes are pairs of prime numbers that differ by two. List the twin prime pairs up to 100.

5 Is 149 a prime number? Explain how you decided.

> **Tip**
> Whilst super-prime numbers are interesting, they are not on the syllabus.

6 Super-prime numbers are prime numbers that stay prime each time you remove a digit (starting with the units). So, 59 is a super-prime because when you remove 9 you are left with 5, which is also prime. 239 is also a super-prime because when you remove 9 you are left with 23 which is prime, and when you remove 3 you are left with 2 which is prime.

(a) Find two three-digit super-prime numbers less than 400.
(b) Can you find a four-digit super-prime number less than 3000?
(c) Sondra's telephone number is the prime number 987-6413. Is her phone number a super-prime?

Prime factors

> Remember a product is the answer to a multiplication. So if you write a number as the product of its prime factors you are writing it using multiplication signs like this: $12 = 2 \times 2 \times 3$.

Prime factors are the factors of a number that are also prime numbers.

Every composite whole number can be broken down and written as the product of its prime factors. You can do this using tree diagrams or using division. Both methods are shown in worked example 5.

Worked example 5

Write the following numbers as the product of prime factors.

(a) 36 **(b)** 48

Using a factor tree

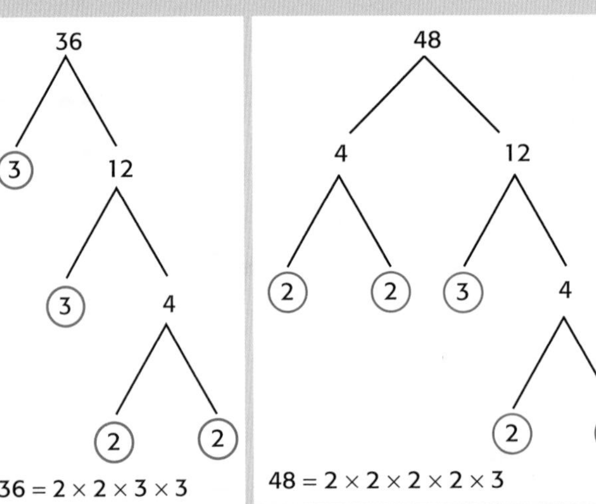

$36 = 2 \times 2 \times 3 \times 3$

$48 = 2 \times 2 \times 2 \times 2 \times 3$

Write the number as two factors.

If a factor is a prime number, circle it.

If a factor is a composite number, split it into two factors.

Keep splitting until you end up with two primes.

Write the primes in ascending order with × signs.

> Prime numbers only have two factors: 1 and the number itself. As 1 is not a prime number, do not include it when expressing a number as a product of prime factors.

Using division

2	36
2	18
3	9
3	3
	1

$36 = 2 \times 2 \times 3 \times 3$

2	48
2	24
2	12
2	6
3	3
	1

$48 = 2 \times 2 \times 2 \times 2 \times 3$

Divide by the smallest prime number that will go into the number exactly. Continue dividing, using the smallest prime number that will go into your new answer each time. Stop when you reach 1. Write the prime factors in ascending order with × signs.

> Choose the method that works best for you and stick to it. Always show your method when using prime factors.

Exercise 1.8

When you write your number as a product of primes, group all occurrences of the same prime number together.

1 Express the following numbers as the product of prime factors.

(a) 30 (b) 24 (c) 100 (d) 225 (e) 360
(f) 504 (g) 650 (h) 1125 (i) 756 (j) 9240

Using prime factors to find the HCF and LCM

FAST FORWARD

You can also use prime factors to find the square and cube roots of numbers if you don't have a calculator. You will deal with this in more detail later in this chapter. ▶

When you are working with larger numbers you can determine the HCF or LCM by expressing each number as a product of its prime factors.

Worked example 6

Find the HCF of 168 and 180.

$168 = \underline{2} \times \underline{2} \times 2 \times \underline{3} \times 7$ $180 = \underline{2} \times \underline{2} \times \underline{3} \times 3 \times 5$ $2 \times 2 \times 3 = 12$ HCF = 12	First express each number as a product of prime factors. Use tree diagrams or division to do this. Underline the factors *common* to both numbers. Multiply these out to find the HCF.

Worked example 7

Find the LCM of 72 and 120.

$72 = \underline{2 \times 2 \times 2} \times \underline{3 \times 3}$ $120 = 2 \times 2 \times 2 \times 3 \times \underline{5}$ $2 \times 2 \times 2 \times 3 \times 3 \times 5 = 360$ LCM = 360	First express each number as a product of prime factors. Use tree diagrams or division to do this. Underline the *largest* set of multiples of each factor. List these and multiply them out to find the LCM.

Exercise 1.9

1 Find the HCF of these numbers by means of prime factors.

(a) 48 and 108 (b) 120 and 216 (c) 72 and 90 (d) 52 and 78
(e) 100 and 125 (f) 154 and 88 (g) 546 and 624 (h) 95 and 120

2 Use prime factorisation to determine the LCM of:

(a) 54 and 60 (b) 54 and 72 (c) 60 and 72 (d) 48 and 60
(e) 120 and 180 (f) 95 and 150 (g) 54 and 90 (h) 90 and 120

3 Determine both the HCF and LCM of the following numbers.

(a) 72 and 108 (b) 25 and 200 (c) 95 and 120 (d) 84 and 60

Living maths

Word problems involving LCM usually include repeating events. You may be asked how many items you need to 'have enough' or when something will happen again at the same time.

4 A radio station runs a phone-in competition for listeners. Every 30th caller gets a free airtime voucher and every 120th caller gets a free mobile phone. How many listeners must phone in before one receives both an airtime voucher *and* a free phone?

5 Lee runs round a track in 12 minutes. James runs round the same track in 18 minutes. If they start in the same place, at the same time, how many minutes will pass before they both cross the start line together again?

Divisibility tests to find factors easily

Sometimes you want to know if a smaller number will divide into a larger one with no remainder. In other words, is the larger number divisible by the smaller one?

These simple divisibility tests are useful for working this out:

A number is exactly divisible by:

2 if it ends with 0, 2, 4, 6 or 8 (in other words is even)
3 if the sum of its digits is a multiple of 3 (can be divided by 3)
4 if the last two digits can be divided by 4
5 if it ends with 0 or 5
6 if it is divisible by both 2 and 3
8 if the last three digits are divisible by 8
9 if the sum of the digits is a multiple of 9 (can be divided by 9)
10 if the number ends in 0.

Tip

Divisibility tests are not part of the syllabus. They are just useful to know when you work with factors and prime numbers.

There is no simple test for divisibility by 7, although multiples of 7 do have some interesting properties that you can investigate on the internet.

Exercise 1.10

23	65	92	10	104	70	500	21	64	798	1223

1 Look at the box of numbers above. Which of these numbers are:

(a) divisible by 5? **(b)** divisible by 8? **(c)** divisible by 3?

2 Say whether the following are true or false.

(a) 625 is divisible by 5 **(b)** 88 is divisible by 3
(c) 640 is divisible by 6 **(d)** 346 is divisible by 4
(e) 476 is divisible by 8 **(f)** 2340 is divisible by 9
(g) 2890 is divisible by 6 **(h)** 4562 is divisible by 3
(i) 40 090 is divisible by 5 **(j)** 123 456 is divisible by 9

3 Can \$34.07 be divided equally among:

(a) two people? **(b)** three people? **(c)** nine people?

4 A stadium has 202 008 seats. Can these be divided equally into:

(a) five blocks? **(b)** six blocks? **(c)** nine blocks?

5 **(a)** If a number is divisible by 12, what other numbers must it be divisible by?
(b) If a number is divisible by 36, what other numbers must it be divisible by?
(c) How could you test if a number is divisible by 12, 15 or 24?

1.4 Powers and roots

Square numbers and square roots

REWIND

In section 1.1 you learned that the product obtained when an integer is multiplied by itself is a square number. ◀

A number is squared when it is multiplied by itself. For example, the **square** of 5 is $5 \times 5 = 25$. The symbol for squared is ^{2}. So, 5×5 can also be written as 5^2.

The **square root** of a number is the number that was multiplied by itself to get the square number. The symbol for square root is $\sqrt{\ }$. You know that $25 = 5^2$, so $\sqrt{25} = 5$.

Cube numbers and cube roots

A number is cubed when it is multiplied by itself and then multiplied by itself again. For example, the **cube** of 2 is $2 \times 2 \times 2 = 8$. The symbol for cubed is ^{3}. So $2 \times 2 \times 2$ can also be written as 2^3.

The cube root of a number is the number that was multiplied by itself to get the cube number. The symbol for cube root is $\sqrt[3]{\ }$. You know that $8 = 2^3$, so $\sqrt[3]{8} = 2$.

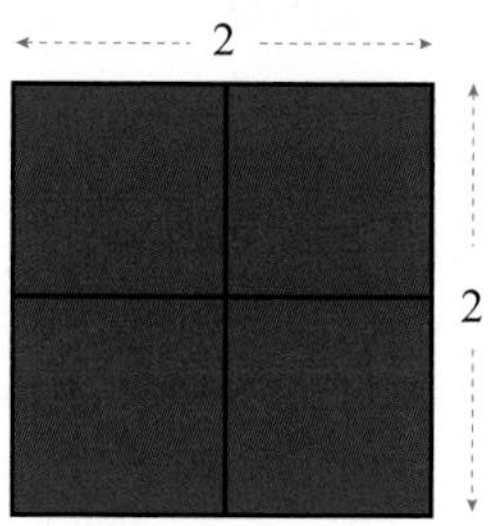

a) Square numbers can be arranged to form a square shape. This is 2^2.

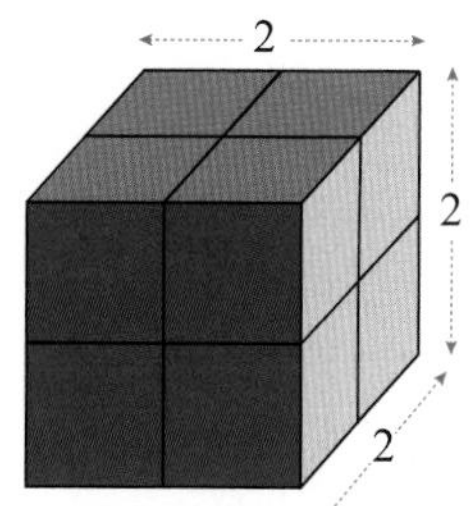

b) Cube numbers can be arranged to form a solid cube shape. This is 2^3.

Finding powers and roots

Not all calculators have exactly the same buttons. [$x^{\square}$] [x^y] and [∧] all mean the same thing on different calculators.

You can use your calculator to square or cube numbers quickly using the [x^2] and [x^3] keys or the [$x^{\square}$] key. Use the [$\sqrt{\ }$] or [$\sqrt[3]{\ }$] keys to find the roots. If you don't have a calculator, you can use the product of prime factors method to find square and cube roots of numbers. Both methods are shown in the worked examples below.

Worked example 8

Use your calculator to find:

(a) 13^2 **(b)** 5^3 **(c)** $\sqrt{324}$ **(d)** $\sqrt[3]{512}$

(a)	$13^2 = 169$	Enter [1] [3] [x^2] [=]
(b)	$5^3 = 125$	Enter [5] [x^3] [=]. If you do not have a [x^3] button then enter [5] [$x^{\square}$] [3] [=]; for this key you have to enter the power.
(c)	$\sqrt{324} = 18$	Enter [$\sqrt{\ }$] [3] [2] [4] [=]
(d)	$\sqrt[3]{512} = 8$	Enter [$\sqrt[3]{\ }$] [5] [1] [2] [=]

Worked example 9

If you do not have a calculator, you can write the integer as a product of primes and group the prime factors into pairs or threes. Look again at parts (c) and (d) of worked example 8:

(c) $\sqrt{324}$ **(d)** $\sqrt[3]{512}$

(c)	$324 = \underbrace{2\times2}_{2}\times\underbrace{3\times3}_{3}\times\underbrace{3\times3}_{3}$	Group the factors into pairs, and write down the square root of each pair.
	$2\times3\times3 = 18$ $\sqrt{324} = 18$	Multiply the roots together to give you the square root of 324.
(d)	$512 = \underbrace{2\times2\times2}_{2}\times\underbrace{2\times2\times2}_{2}\times\underbrace{2\times2\times2}_{2}$	Group the factors into threes, and write the cube root of each threesome.
	$2\times2\times2 = 8$ $\sqrt[3]{512} = 8$	Multiply together to get the cube root of 512.

Exercise 1.11

1 Calculate:

(a) 3^2 (b) 7^2 (c) 11^2 (d) 12^2 (e) 21^2
(f) 19^2 (g) 32^2 (h) 100^2 (i) 14^2 (j) 68^2

2 Calculate:

(a) 1^3 (b) 3^3 (c) 4^3 (d) 6^3 (e) 9^3
(f) 10^3 (g) 100^3 (h) 18^3 (i) 30^3 (j) 200^3

Learn the squares of all integers between 1 and 20 inclusive. You will need to recognise these quickly.

3 Find a value of x to make each of these statements true.

(a) $x \times x = 25$ (b) $x \times x \times x = 8$ (c) $x \times x = 121$
(d) $x \times x \times x = 729$ (e) $x \times x = 324$ (f) $x \times x = 400$
(g) $x \times x \times x = 8000$ (h) $x \times x = 225$ (i) $x \times x \times x = 1$
(j) $\sqrt{x} = 9$ (k) $\sqrt{1} = x$ (l) $\sqrt{x} = 81$
(m) $\sqrt[3]{x} = 2$ (n) $\sqrt[3]{x} = 1$ (o) $\sqrt[3]{64} = x$

4 Use a calculator to find the following roots.

(a) $\sqrt{9}$ (b) $\sqrt{64}$ (c) $\sqrt{1}$ (d) $\sqrt{4}$ (e) $\sqrt{100}$
(f) $\sqrt{0}$ (g) $\sqrt{81}$ (h) $\sqrt{400}$ (i) $\sqrt{1296}$ (j) $\sqrt{1764}$
(k) $\sqrt[3]{8}$ (l) $\sqrt[3]{1}$ (m) $\sqrt[3]{27}$ (n) $\sqrt[3]{64}$ (o) $\sqrt[3]{1000}$
(p) $\sqrt[3]{216}$ (q) $\sqrt[3]{512}$ (r) $\sqrt[3]{729}$ (s) $\sqrt[3]{1728}$ (t) $\sqrt[3]{5832}$

5 Use the product of prime factors given below to find the square root of each number. Show your working.

(a) $324 = 2 \times 2 \times 3 \times 3 \times 3 \times 3$ (b) $225 = 3 \times 3 \times 5 \times 5$
(c) $784 = 2 \times 2 \times 2 \times 2 \times 7 \times 7$ (d) $2025 = 3 \times 3 \times 3 \times 3 \times 5 \times 5$
(e) $19\,600 = 2 \times 2 \times 2 \times 2 \times 5 \times 5 \times 7 \times 7$ (f) $250\,000 = 2 \times 2 \times 2 \times 2 \times 5 \times 5 \times 5 \times 5 \times 5 \times 5$

6 Use the product of prime factors to find the cube root of each number. Show your working.

(a) $27 = 3 \times 3 \times 3$ (b) $729 = 3 \times 3 \times 3 \times 3 \times 3 \times 3$
(c) $2197 = 13 \times 13 \times 13$ (d) $1000 = 2 \times 2 \times 2 \times 5 \times 5 \times 5$
(e) $15\,625 = 5 \times 5 \times 5 \times 5 \times 5 \times 5$
(f) $32\,768 = 2 \times 2 \times 2 \times 2 \times 2 \times 2 \times 2 \times 2 \times 2 \times 2 \times 2 \times 2 \times 2 \times 2 \times 2$

Brackets act as grouping symbols. Work out any calculations inside brackets before doing the calculations outside the brackets.

Root signs work in the same way as a bracket. If you have $\sqrt{25+9}$, you must add 25 and 9 before finding the root.

7 Calculate:

(a) $(\sqrt{25})^2$ (b) $(\sqrt{49})^2$ (c) $(\sqrt[3]{64})^3$ (d) $(\sqrt[3]{32})^3$
(e) $\sqrt{9} + \sqrt{16}$ (f) $\sqrt{9+16}$ (g) $\sqrt{36} + \sqrt{64}$ (h) $\sqrt{36+64}$
(i) $\sqrt{100-36}$ (j) $\sqrt{100} - \sqrt{36}$ (k) $\sqrt{25} \times \sqrt{4}$ (l) $\sqrt{25 \times 4}$
(m) $\sqrt{9 \times 4}$ (n) $\sqrt{9} \times \sqrt{4}$ (o) $\sqrt{\dfrac{36}{4}}$ (p) $\dfrac{\sqrt{36}}{4}$

8 Find the length of the edge of a cube with a volume of:

(a) 1000 cm^3 (b) $19\,683\text{ cm}^3$ (c) $68\,921\text{ mm}^3$ (d) $64\,000\text{ cm}^3$

9 If the symbol * means 'add the square of the first number to the cube of the second number', calculate:

(a) 2 * 3 (b) 3 * 2 (c) 1 * 4 (d) 4 * 1 (e) 2 * 4
(f) 4 * 2 (g) 1 * 9 (h) 9 * 1 (i) 5 * 2 (j) 2 * 5

1.5 Working with directed numbers

Once a direction is chosen to be positive, the opposite direction is taken to be negative. So:

- if up is positive, down is negative
- if right is positive, left is negative
- if north is positive, south is negative
- if above 0 is positive, below 0 is negative.

A negative sign is used to indicate that values are less than zero. For example, on a thermometer, on a bank statement or in an elevator.

When you use numbers to represent real-life situations like temperatures, altitude, depth below sea level, profit or loss and directions (on a grid), you sometimes need to use the negative sign to indicate the direction of the number. For example, a temperature of three degrees below zero can be shown as −3 °C. Numbers like these, which have direction, are called **directed numbers**. So if a point 25 m above sea level is at +25 m, then a point 25 m below sea level is at −25 m.

Exercise 1.12

1 Express each of these situations using a directed number.

(a) a profit of $100
(b) 25 km below sea level
(c) a drop of 10 marks
(d) a gain of 2 kg
(e) a loss of 1.5 kg
(f) 8000 m above sea level
(g) a temperature of 10 °C below zero
(h) a fall of 24 m
(i) a debt of $2000
(j) an increase of $250
(k) a time two hours behind GMT
(l) a height of 400 m
(m) a bank balance of $450.00

Comparing and ordering directed numbers

FAST FORWARD

You will use similar number lines when solving linear inequalities in chapter 14. ▶

In mathematics, directed numbers are also known as integers. You can represent the set of integers on a number line like this:

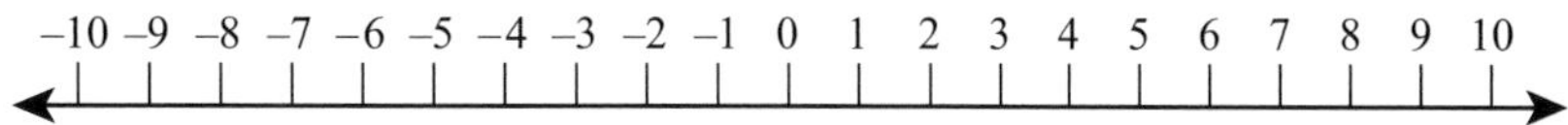

The further to the right a number is on the number line, the greater its value.

Exercise 1.13

It is important that you understand how to work with directed numbers early in your IGCSE course. Many topics depend upon them!

1 Copy the numbers and fill in < or > to make a true statement.

(a) 2□8
(b) 4□9
(c) 12□3
(d) 6□−4
(e) −7□4
(f) −2□4
(g) −2□−11
(h) −12□−20
(i) −8□0
(j) −2□2
(k) −12□−4
(l) −32□−3
(m) 0□−3
(n) −3□11
(o) 12□−89

2 Arrange each set of numbers in ascending order.

(a) −8, 7, 10, −1, −12
(b) 4, −3, −4, −10, 9, −8
(c) −11, −5, −7, 7, 0, −12
(d) −94, −50, −83, −90, 0

Living maths

3 Study the temperature graph carefully.

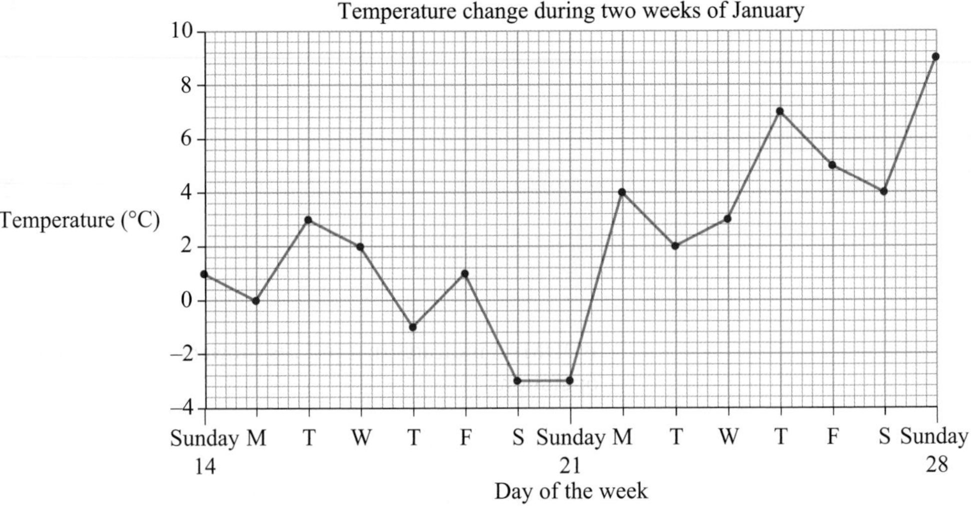

(a) What was the temperature on Sunday 14 January?
(b) By how much did the temperature drop from Sunday 14 to Monday 15?
(c) What was the lowest temperature recorded?
(d) What is the difference between the highest and lowest temperatures?
(e) On Monday 29 January the temperature changed by −12 degrees. What was the temperature on that day?

The difference between the highest and lowest temperature is also called the *range* of temperatures.

4 Matt has a bank balance of \$45.50. He deposits \$15.00 and then withdraws \$32.00. What is his new balance?

5 Mr Singh's bank account is \$420 overdrawn.
(a) Express this as a directed number.
(b) How much money will he need to deposit to get his account to have a balance of \$500?
(c) He deposits \$200. What will his new balance be?

6 A diver 27 m below the surface of the water rises 16 m. At what depth is she then?

7 On a cold day in New York, the temperature at 6 a.m. was –5 °C. By noon, the temperature had risen to 8 °C. By 7 p.m. the temperature had dropped by 11 °C from its value at noon. What was the temperature at 7 p.m.?

8 Local time in Abu Dhabi is four hours ahead of Greenwich Mean Time. Local time in Rio de Janeiro is three hours behind Greenwich Mean Time.
(a) If it is 4 p.m. at Greenwich, what time is it in Abu Dhabi?
(b) If it is 3 a.m. in Greenwich, what time is it in Rio de Janiero?
(c) If it is 3 p.m. in Rio de Janeiro, what time is it in Abu Dhabi?
(d) If it is 8 a.m. in Abu Dhabi, what time is it in Rio de Janeiro?

1.6 Order of operations

At this level of mathematics you are expected to do more complicated calculations involving more than one operation (+, –, × and ÷). When you are carrying out more complicated calculations you have to follow a sequence of rules so that there is no confusion about what operations you should do first. The rules governing the order of operations are:

- complete operations in grouping symbols first (see page 15)
- do division and multiplication next, working from left to right
- do addition and subtractions last, working from left to right.

Many people use the letters **BODMAS** to remember the order of operations. The letters stand for:

Brackets

Of (Sometimes, 'I' for 'indices' is used instead of 'O' for 'of')

Divide **M**ultiply

Add **S**ubtract

BODMAS indicates that indices (powers) are considered after brackets but before all other operations.

Grouping symbols

The most common grouping symbols in mathematics are brackets. Here are some examples of the different kinds of brackets used in mathematics:

$(4 + 9) \times (10 \div 2)$

$[2(4 + 9) - 4(3) - 12]$

$\{2 - [4(2 - 7) - 4(3 + 8)] - 2 \times 8\}$

When you have more than one set of brackets in a calculation, you work out the innermost set first.

Other symbols used to group operations are:

- fraction bars, e.g. $\frac{5-12}{3-8}$
- root signs, such as square roots and cube roots, e.g. $\sqrt{9+16}$
- powers, e.g. 5^2 or 4^3

Worked example 10

Simplify:

(a) $7 \times (3 + 4)$ **(b)** $(10 - 4) \times (4 + 9)$ **(c)** $45 - [20 \times (4 - 3)]$

(a) $7 \times 7 = 49$

(b) $6 \times 13 = 78$

(c) $45 - [20 \times 1] = 45 - 20$
$= 25$

Worked example 11

Calculate:

(a) $3 + 8^2$ **(b)** $\frac{4+28}{17-9}$ **(c)** $\sqrt{36 \div 4} + \sqrt{100 - 36}$

(a) $3 + (8 \times 8)$
$= 3 + 64$
$= 67$

(b) $(4 + 28) \div (17 - 9)$
$= 32 \div 8$
$= 4$

(c) $\sqrt{36 \div 4} + \sqrt{100 - 36}$
$= \sqrt{9} + \sqrt{64}$
$= 3 + 8$
$= 11$

Exercise 1.14

1 Calculate. Show the steps in your working.

(a) $(4+7)\times 3$ (b) $(20-4)\div 4$ (c) $50\div(20+5)$ (d) $6\times(2+9)$
(e) $(4+7)\times 4$ (f) $(100-40)\times 3$ (g) $16+(25\div 5)$ (h) $19-(12+2)$
(i) $40\div(12-4)$ (j) $100\div(4+16)$ (k) $121\div(33\div 3)$ (l) $15\times(15-15)$

2 Calculate:

(a) $(4+8)\times(16-7)$ (b) $(12-4)\times(6+3)$ (c) $(9+4)-(4+6)$
(d) $(33+17)\div(10-5)$ (e) $(4\times 2)+(8\times 3)$ (f) $(9\times 7)\div(27-20)$
(g) $(105-85)\div(16\div 4)$ (h) $(12+13)\div 5^2$ (i) $(56-6^2)\times(4+3)$

A bracket 'type' is always twinned with another bracket of the same type/shape. This helps mathematicians to understand the order of calculations even more easily.

3 Simplify. Remember to work from the innermost grouping symbols to the outermost.

(a) $4+[12-(8-5)]$ (b) $6+[2-(2\times 0)]$
(c) $8+[60-(2+8)]$ (d) $200-[(4+12)-(6+2)]$
(e) $200\{100-[4\times(2+8)]\}$ (f) $\{6+[5\times(2+30)]\}\times 10$
(g) $[(30+12)-(7+9)]\times 10$ (h) $6\times[(20\div 4)-(6-3)+2]$
(i) $1000-[6\times(4+20)-4\times(3+0)]$

4 Calculate:

(a) $6+72$ (b) $29-23$ (c) 8×42
(d) $20-4\div 2$ (e) $\frac{31-10}{14-7}$ (f) $\frac{100-40}{5\times 4}$
(g) $\sqrt{100-36}$ (h) $\sqrt{8+8}$ (i) $\sqrt{90-9}$

5 Insert brackets into the following calculations to make them true.

(a) $3\times 4+6=30$ (b) $25-15\times 9=90$ (c) $40-10\times 3=90$
(d) $14-9\times 2=10$ (e) $12+3\div 5=3$ (f) $19-9\times 15=150$
(g) $10+10\div 6-2=5$ (h) $3+8\times 15-9=66$ (i) $9-4\times 7+2=45$
(j) $10-4\times 5=30$ (k) $6\div 3+3\times 5=5$ (l) $15-6\div 2=12$
(m) $1+4\times 20\div 5=20$ (n) $8+5-3\times 2=20$ (o) $36\div 3\times 3-3=6$
(p) $3\times 4-2\div 6=1$ (q) $40\div 4+1=11$ (r) $6+2\times 8+2=24$

FAST FORWARD

You will apply the order of operation rules to fractions, decimals and algebraic expressions as you progress through the course. ▶

Working in the correct order

Now that you know what to do with grouping symbols, you are going to apply the rules for order of operations to perform calculations with numbers.

Exercise 1.15

1 Simplify. Show the steps in your working.

(a) $5\times 10+3$ (b) $5\times(10+3)$ (c) $2+10\times 3$
(d) $(2+10)\times 3$ (e) $23+7\times 2$ (f) $6\times 2\div(3+3)$
(g) $\frac{15-5}{2\times 5}$ (h) $(17+1)\div 9+2$ (i) $\frac{16-4}{4-1}$
(j) $17+3\times 21$ (k) $48-(2+3)\times 2$ (l) $12\times 4-4\times 8$
(m) $15+30\div 3+6$ (n) $20-6\div 3+3$ (o) $10-4\times 2\div 2$

2 Simplify:

(a) $18-4\times 2-3$ (b) $14-(21\div 3)$ (c) $24\div 8\times(6-5)$
(d) $42\div 6-3-4$ (e) $5+36\div 6-8$ (f) $(8+3)\times(30\div 3)\div 11$

3 State whether the following are true or false.

(a) $(1+4)\times 20+5=1+(4\times 20)+5$ (b) $6\times(4+2)\times 3>(6\times 4)\div 2\times 3$
(c) $8+(5-3)\times 2<8+5-(3\times 2)$ (d) $100+10\div 10>(100+10)\div 10$

4 Place the given numbers in the correct spaces to make a correct number sentence.

(a) 0, 2, 5, 10 □−□÷□=□

(b) 9, 11, 13, 18 □−□÷□=□

(c) 1, 3, 8, 14, 16 □÷(□−□)−□=□

(d) 4, 5, 6, 9, 12 (□+□)−(□−□)=□

Using your calculator

In this section you will use your calculator to perform operations in the correct order. However, you will need to remember the *order of operations* rules and apply them throughout the book as you do more complicated examples using your calculator.

A calculator with algebraic logic will apply the rules for order of operations automatically. So, if you enter $2 + 3 \times 4$, your calculator will do the multiplication first and give you an answer of 14. (Check that your calculator does this!).

When the calculation contains brackets you must enter these to make sure your calculator does the grouped sections first.

Experiment with your calculator by making several calculations with and without brackets. For example: $3 \times 2 + 6$ and $3 \times (2 + 6)$. Do you understand why these are different?

Your calculator might only have one type of bracket (and). If there are two different shaped brackets in the calculation (such as $[4 \times (2 - 3)]$, enter the calculator bracket symbol for each type.

Worked example 12

Use a calculator to find:

(a) $3 + 2 \times 9$ **(b)** $(3 + 8) \times 4$ **(c)** $(3 \times 8 - 4) - (2 \times 5 + 1)$

(a)	21	Enter 3 + 2 × 9 =
(b)	44	Enter (3 + 8) × 4 =
(c)	9	Enter (3 × 8 − 4) − (2 × 5 + 1) =

Exercise 1.16

Some calculators have two '−' buttons: − and (−). The first means 'subtract' and is used to subtract one number from another. The second means 'make negative'. Experiment with the buttons and make sure that your calculator is doing what you expect it to do!

1 Use a calculator to find the correct answer.

(a) $10 - 4 \times 5$
(b) $12 + 6 \div 7 - 4$
(c) $3 + 4 \times 5 - 10$
(d) $18 \div 3 \times 5 - 3 + 2$
(e) $5 - 3 \times 8 - 6 \div 2$
(f) $7 + 3 \div 4 + 1$
(g) $(1 + 4) \times 20 \div 5$
(h) $36 \div 6 \times (3 - 3)$
(i) $(8 + 8) - 6 \times 2$
(j) $100 - 30 \times (4 - 3)$
(k) $24 \div (7 + 5) \times 6$
(l) $[(60 - 40) - (53 - 43)] \times 2$
(m) $[(12 + 6) \div 9] \times 4$
(n) $[100 \div (4 + 16)] \times 3$
(o) $4 \times [25 \div (12 - 7)]$

2 Use your calculator to check whether the following answers are correct. If the answer is incorrect, work out the correct answer.

(a) $12 \times 4 + 76 = 124$
(b) $8 + 75 \times 8 = 698$
(c) $12 \times 18 - 4 \times 23 = 124$
(d) $(16 \div 4) \times (7 + 3 \times 4) = 76$
(e) $(82 - 36) \times (2 + 6) = 16$
(f) $(3 \times 7 - 4) - (4 + 6 \div 2) = 12$

The more effectively you are able to use your calculator, the faster and more accurate your calculations are likely to be. If you have difficulty with this you will find advice and practice exercises on the CD-ROM.

3 Each * represents a missing operation. Work out what it is.

(a) 12 * (28 * 24) = 3
(b) 84 * 10 * 8 = 4
(c) 3 * 7(0.7 * 1.3) = 17
(d) 23 * 11 * 22 * 11 = 11
(e) 40 * 5 * (7 * 5) = 4
(f) 9 * 15 * (3 * 2) = 12

4 Calculate:

(a) $\dfrac{7 \times \sqrt{16}}{2^3 + 7^2 - 1}$ (b) $\dfrac{5^2 \times \sqrt{4}}{1 + 6^2 - 12}$ (c) $\dfrac{2 + 3^2}{5^2 + 4 \times 10 - \sqrt{25}}$

(d) $\dfrac{6^2-11}{2(17+2\times4)}$ (e) $\dfrac{3^2-3}{2\times\sqrt{81}}$ (f) $\dfrac{3^2-5+6}{\sqrt{4}\times5}$

(g) $\dfrac{36-3\times\sqrt{16}}{15-3^2\div3}$ (h) $\dfrac{-30+[18\div(3-12)+24]}{5-8-3^2}$

5 Use a calculator to find the answer.

(a) $\dfrac{0.345}{1.34+4.2\times7}$ (b) $\dfrac{12.32\times0.0378}{\sqrt{16}+8.05}$ (c) $\dfrac{\sqrt{16}\times0.087}{2^2-5.098}$ (d) $\dfrac{19.23\times0.087}{2.45^2-1.03^2}$

FAST FORWARD

In this chapter you are only dealing with square and cube numbers, and the roots of square and cube numbers. When you work with indices and standard form in chapter 5, you will need to apply these skills and use your calculator effectively to solve problems involving any powers or roots. ▶

6 Use your calculator to evaluate.

(a) $\sqrt{64\times125}$ (b) $\sqrt{2^3\times3^2\times6}$

(c) $\sqrt[3]{8^2+19^2}$ (d) $\sqrt{41^2-36^2}$

(e) $\sqrt{3.2^2-1.17^3}$ (f) $\sqrt[3]{1.45^3-0.13^2}$

(g) $\dfrac{1}{4}\sqrt{\dfrac{1}{4}+\dfrac{1}{4}+\sqrt{\dfrac{1}{4}}}$ (h) $\sqrt[3]{2.75^2-\frac{1}{2}\times1.7^3}$

1.7 Rounding numbers

In many calculations, particularly with decimals, you will not need to find an exact answer. Instead, you will be asked to give an answer to a stated level of accuracy. For example, you may be asked to give an answer correct to 2 decimal places, or an answer correct to 3 significant figures.

To round a number to a given decimal place you look at the value of the digit to the right of the specified place. If it is 5 or greater, you round up; if it less than 5, you round down.

Worked example 13

Round 64.839906 to:

(a) the nearest whole number **(b)** 1 decimal place **(c)** 3 decimal places

(a)	64.839906 (4 underlined)	4 is in the units place.
	64.839906 (8 underlined)	The next digit is 8, so you will round up to get 5.
	= 65 (to nearest whole number)	To the nearest whole number.
(b)	64.839906 (8 underlined)	8 is in the first decimal place.
	64.839906 (3 underlined)	The next digit is 3, so the 8 will remain unchanged.
	= 64.8 (1dp)	Correct to 1 decimal place.
(c)	64.839906 (third-place 9 underlined)	9 is in the third decimal place.
	64.839906 (fourth-place 9 underlined)	The next digit is 9, so you need to round up. When you round 9 up, you get 10, so carry one to the previous digit and write 0 in the place of the 9.
	= 64.840 (3dp)	Correct to 3 decimal places.

The first significant digit of a number is the first *non-zero* digit, when reading from left to right. The next digit is the second significant digit, the next the third significant and so on. All zeros *after* the first significant digit are considered significant.

To round to 3 significant figures, find the third significant digit and look at the value of the digit to the right of it. If it is 5 or greater, add one to the third significant digit and lose all of the other digits to the right. If it is less than 5, leave the third significant digit unchanged and lose all the other digits to the right as before. To round to a different number of significant figures, use the same method but find the appropriate significant digit to start with: the fourth for 4sf, the seventh for 7sf etc. If you are rounding to a whole number, write the appropriate number of zeros after the last significant digit as place holders to keep the number the same size.

Worked example 14

Round:

(a) 1.076 to 3 significant figures **(b)** 0.00736 to 1 significant figure

(a)	1.076 = 1.08 (3sf)	The third significant figure is the 7. The next digit is 6, so round 7 up to get 8. Correct to 3 significant figures.
(b)	0.00736 = 0.007 (1sf)	The first significant figure is the 7. The next digit is 3, so 7 will not change. Correct to 1 significant figure.

Exercise 1.17

Remember, the first significant digit in a number is the first *non-zero* digit, reading from left to right. Once you have read past the first non-zero digit, all zeros then become significant.

FAST FORWARD

You will use rounding to a given number of decimal places and significant figures in almost all of your work this year. You will also apply these skills to estimate answers. This is dealt with in more detail in chapter 5. ▶

1 Round each number to 2 decimal places.

(a) 3.185 **(b)** 0.064 **(c)** 38.3456 **(d)** 2.149 **(e)** 0.999
(f) 0.0456 **(g)** 0.005 **(h)** 41.567 **(i)** 8.299 **(j)** 0.4236
(k) 0.062 **(l)** 0.009 **(m)** 3.016 **(n)** 12.0164 **(o)** 15.11579

2 Express each number correct to:

(i) 4 significant figures **(ii)** 3 significant figures **(iii)** 1 significant figure

(a) 4512 **(b)** 12 305 **(c)** 65 238 **(d)** 320.55
(e) 25.716 **(f)** 0.000765 **(g)** 1.0087 **(h)** 7.34876
(i) 0.00998 **(j)** 0.02814 **(k)** 31.0077 **(l)** 0.0064735

3 Change $2\frac{5}{9}$ to a decimal using your calculator. Express the answer correct to:

(a) 3 decimal places **(b)** 2 decimal places **(c)** 1 decimal place
(d) 3 significant figures **(e)** 2 significant figures **(f)** 1 significant figure

Summary

Do you know the following?

- Numbers can be classified as natural numbers, integers, prime numbers and square numbers.
- When you multiply an integer by itself you get a square number (x^2). If you multiply it by itself again you get a cube number (x^3).
- The number you multiply to get a square is called the square root and the number you multiply to get a cube is called the cube root. The symbol for square root is $\sqrt{\ }$. The symbol for cube root is $\sqrt[3]{\ }$.
- A multiple is obtained by multiplying a number by a natural number. The LCM of two or more numbers is the lowest multiple found in all the sets of multiples.
- A factor of a number divides into it exactly. The HCF of two or more numbers is the highest factor found in all the sets of factors.
- Prime numbers have only two factors, 1 and the number itself. The number 1 is not a prime number.
- A prime factor is a number that is both a factor and a prime number.
- All natural numbers that are not prime can be expressed as a product of prime factors.
- Integers are also called directed numbers. The sign of an integer (– or +) indicates whether its value is above or below 0.
- Mathematicians apply a standard set of rules to decide the order in which operations must be carried out. Operations in grouping symbols are worked out first, then division and multiplication, then addition and subtraction.

Are you able to . . . ?

- identify natural numbers, integers, square numbers and prime numbers
- find multiples and factors of numbers and identify the LCM and HCF
- write numbers as products of their prime factors using division and factor trees
- calculate squares, square roots, cubes and cube roots of numbers
- work with integers used in real-life situations
- apply the basic rules for operating with numbers
- perform basic calculations using mental methods and with a calculator.

Examination practice

Exam-style questions

1 Here is a set of numbers: {–4, –1, 0, 3, 4, 6, 9, 15, 16, 19, 20}
Which of these numbers are:

(a) natural numbers? **(b)** square numbers? **(c)** negative integers?
(d) prime numbers? **(e)** multiples of two? **(f)** factors of 80?

2 **(a)** List all the factors of 12. **(b)** List all the factors of 24. **(c)** Find the HCF of 12 and 24.

3 Find the HCF of 64 and 144.

4 List the first five multiples of:

(a) 12 **(b)** 18 **(c)** 30 **(d)** 80

5 Find the LCM of 24 and 36.

6 List all the prime numbers from 0 to 40.

7 **(a)** Use a factor tree to express 400 as a product of prime factors.
(b) Use the division method to express 1080 as a product of prime factors.
(c) Use your answers to find:

(i) the LCM of 400 and 1080 **(ii)** the HCF of 400 and 1080
(iii) $\sqrt{400}$ **(iv)** whether 1080 is a cube number; how can you tell?

8 Calculate:

(a) 26^2 **(b)** 43^3

9 What is the smallest number greater than 100 that is:

(a) divisible by two? **(b)** divisible by ten? **(c)** divisible by four?

10 At noon one day the outside temperature is 4 °C. By midnight the temperature is 8 degrees lower.
What temperature is it at midnight?

11 Simplify:

(a) $6 \times 2 + 4 \times 5$ **(b)** $4 \times (100 - 15)$ **(c)** $(5 + 6) \times 2 + (15 - 3 \times 2) - 6$

12 Add brackets to this statement to make it true.

$7 + 14 \div 4 - 1 \times 2 = 14$

Past paper questions

1 **(a)** Write down a common multiple of 8 and 14. [1]
(b) Complete the list of factors of 81: 1, …, …, …, 81 [2]
(c) Write down the prime factor of 81. [1]

[Cambridge IGCSE Mathematics 0580 Paper 12 Q16 October/November 2011]

2 Calculate:

(a) $\dfrac{0.0548}{1.65 + 5.2 \times 7}$ **(b)** $\dfrac{0.0763}{1.85 + 4.7 \times 8}$ [2]

[Cambridge IGCSE Mathematics 0580 Paper 11 Q2a May/June 2009]

2 Making sense of algebra

Key words

- Algebra
- Variable
- Equation
- Formula
- Substitution
- Expression
- Term
- Power
- Index
- Coefficient
- Exponent
- Base
- Reciprocal

In this chapter you will learn how to:

- use letters to represent numbers
- write expressions to represent mathematical information
- substitute letters with numbers to find the value of an expression
- add and subtract like terms to simplify expressions
- multiply and divide to simplify expressions
- expand expressions by removing grouping symbols
- use index notation in algebra
- learn and apply the laws of indices to simplify expressions.
- EXTENDED: work with fractional indices.

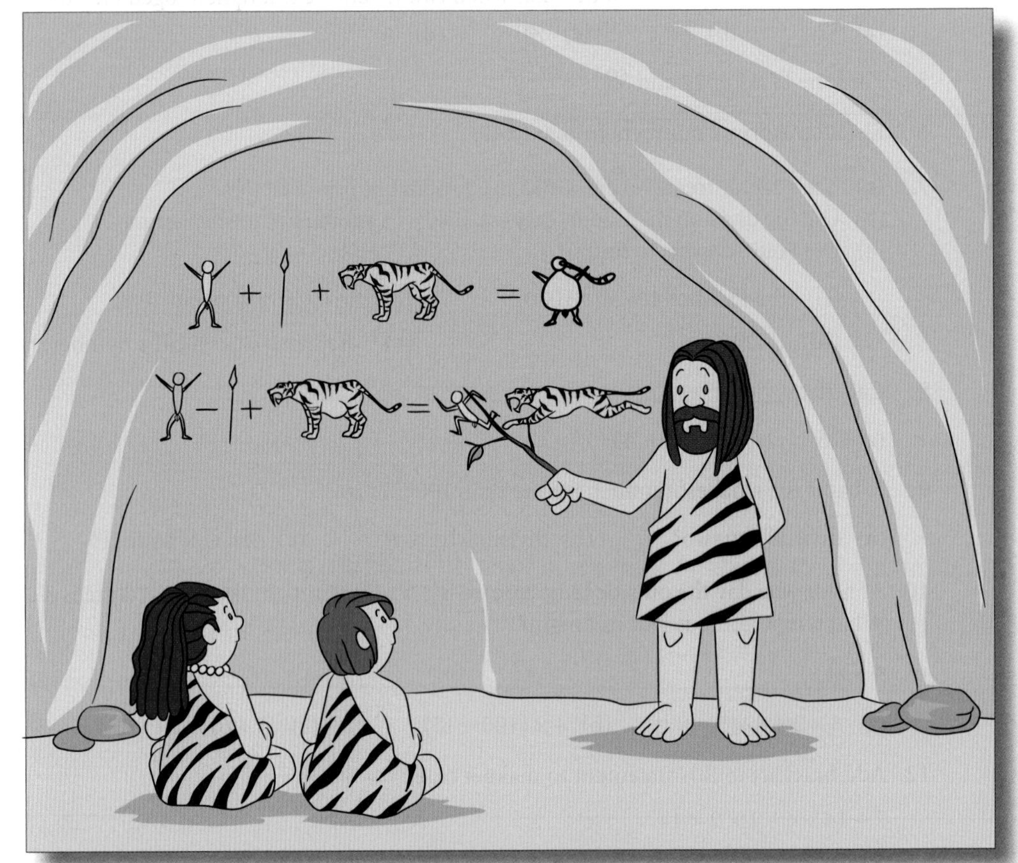

Once you know the basic rules, algebra is very easy and very useful.

You can think of **algebra** as the language of mathematics. Algebra uses letters and other symbols to write mathematical information in shorter ways.

When you learn a language, you have to learn the rules and structures of the language. The language of algebra also has rules and structures. Once you know these, you can 'speak' the language of algebra and mathematics students all over the world will understand you.

At school, and in the real world, you will use algebra in many ways. For example, you will use it to make sense of formulae and spreadsheets and you may use algebra to solve problems to do with money, building, science, agriculture, engineering, construction, economics and more.

2.1 Using letters to represent unknown values

In primary school you used empty shapes to represent unknown numbers. For example, 2 + ▮ = 8 and ▮ + ♦ = 10. If 2 + ▮ = 8, the ▮ can only represent 6. But if ▮ + ♦ = 10, then the ▮ and the ♦ can represent many different values.

In algebra the letters can represent many different values so they are called **variables**.

If a problem introduces algebra, you must not change the 'case' of the letters used. For example, '*n*' and '*N*' can represent *different* numbers in the *same* formula!

In algebra, you use letters to represent unknown numbers. So you could write the number sentences above as: $2 + x = 8$ and $a + b = 10$. Number sentences like these are called **equations**. You can solve an equation by finding the values that make the equation true.

When you worked with area of rectangles and triangles in the past, you used algebra to make a general rule, or **formula**, for working out the area, A:

Area of a rectangle = length × breadth, so $A = lb$

Area of a triangle = $\frac{1}{2}$base × height, so $A = \frac{1}{2}bh$ or $A = \frac{bh}{2}$

Notice that when two letters are multiplied together, we write them next to each other e.g lb, rather than $l \times b$.

To use a formula you have to replace some or all of the letters with numbers. This is called **substitution**.

Writing algebraic expressions

An algebraic **expression** is a group of letter and numbers linked by operation signs. Each part of the expression is called a **term**.

Suppose the average height (in centimetres) of students in your class is an unknown number, h. A student who is 10 cm taller than the average would have a height of $h + 10$. A student who is 3 cm shorter than the average would have a height of $h - 3$.

$h + 10$ and $h - 3$ are algebraic expressions. Because the unknown value is represented by h, we say these are expressions in terms of h.

Worked example 1

Use algebra to write an expression in terms of h for:

(a) a height 12 cm shorter than average
(b) a height $2x$ taller than average
(c) a height twice the average height
(d) a height half the average height.

(a)	$h - 12$	Shorter than means less than, so you subtract.
(b)	$h + 2x$	Taller than means more than, so you add. $2x$ is unknown, but it can still be used in the expression.
(c)	$2 \times h$	Twice means two times, so you multiply by two.
(d)	$h \div 2$	Half means divided by two.

Applying the rules

Algebraic expressions should be written in the shortest, simplest possible way.

- $2 \times h$ is written as $2h$ and $x \times y$ is written as xy
- h means $1 \times h$, but you do not write the 1
- $h \div 2$ is written as $\frac{h}{2}$ and $x \div y$ is written as $\frac{x}{y}$
- when you have the product of a number and a variable, the number is written first, so $2h$ and not $h2$. Also, variables are normally written in alphabetical order, so xy and $2ab$ rather than yx and $2ba$

Mathematicians write the product of a number and a variable with the number first to avoid confusion with powers. For example, $x \times 5$ is written as $5x$ rather than $x5$, which may be confused with x^5.

- $h \times h$ is written as h^2 (h squared) and $h \times h \times h$ is written as h^3 (h cubed). The ^{2} and the ^{3} are examples of a **power** or **index**.
- The power only applies to the number or variable directly before it, so $5a^2$ means $5 \times a \times a$
- When a power is outside a bracket, it applies to everything inside the bracket. So, $(xy)^3$ means $xy \times xy \times xy$

Worked example 2

Write expressions in terms of x to represent:

(a) a number times four **(b)** the sum of the number and five
(c) six times the number minus two **(d)** half the number.

(a)	x times 4 $= 4 \times x$ $= 4x$	Let x represent 'the number'. Replace 'four times' with $4 \times$. Leave out the $\times$ sign, write the number before the variable.
(b)	Sum of x and five $= x + 5$	Let x represent 'the number'. Sum of means +, replace five with 5.
(c)	Six times x minus two $= 6 \times x - 2$ $= 6x - 2$	Let x represent the number. Times means $\times$ and minus means $-$, insert numerals. Leave out the $\times$ sign.
(d)	Half x $= x \div 2$ $= \frac{x}{2}$	Let x represent 'the number'. Half means $\times \frac{1}{2}$ or $\div 2$. Write the division as a fraction.

Exercise 2.1

REWIND

Remember BODMAS in Chapter 1. Work out the bit in brackets first. ◀

REWIND

Remember from Chapter 1 that a 'sum' is the result of an addition. ◀

Also remember that the 'difference' between two numbers is the result of a subtraction. The order of the subtraction matters. ◀

1 Rewrite each expression in its simplest form.

(a) $6 \times x \times y$ **(b)** $7 \times a \times b$ **(c)** $x \times y \times z$
(d) $2 \times y \times y$ **(e)** $a \times 4 \times b$ **(f)** $x \times y \times 12$
(g) $5 \times b \times a$ **(h)** $y \times z \times z$ **(i)** $6 \div x$
(j) $4x \div 2y$ **(k)** $(x + 3) \div 4$ **(l)** $m \times m \times m \div m \times m$
(m) $4 \times x + 5 \times y$ **(n)** $a \times 7 - 2 \times b$ **(o)** $2 \times x \times (x - 4)$
(p) $3 \times (x + 1) \div 2 \times x$ **(q)** $2 \times (x + 4) \div 3$ **(r)** $(4 \times x) \div (2 \times x + 4 \times x)$

2 Let the unknown number be m. Write expressions for:

(a) the sum of the unknown number and 13
(b) a number that will exceed the unknown number by five
(c) the difference between 25 and the unknown number
(d) the unknown number cubed
(e) a third of the unknown number plus three
(f) four times the unknown number less twice the number.

3 Let the unknown number be x. Write expressions for:

(a) three more than x
(b) six less than x
(c) ten times x
(d) the sum of -8 and x
(e) the sum of the unknown number and its square

(f) a number which is twice x more than x
(g) the fraction obtained when double the unknown number is divided by the sum of the unknown number and four.

4 A CD and a DVD cost x dollars.

(a) If the CD costs \$10 what does the DVD cost?
(b) If the DVD costs three times the CD, what does the CD cost?
(c) If the CD costs \$$(x - 15)$, what does the DVD cost?

5 A woman is m years old.

(a) How old will she be in ten years' time?
(b) How old was she ten years ago?
(c) Her son is half her age. How old is the son?

6 Three people win a prize of \$$p$.

(a) If they share the prize equally, how much will each receive?
(b) If one of the people wins three times as much money as the other two, how much will each receive?

2.2 Substitution

When you substitute values you need to write in the operation signs. $5h$ means $5 \times h$, so if $h = 1$, or $h = 6$, you cannot write this in numbers as 51 or 56.

Expressions have different values depending on what numbers you substitute for the variables. For example, let's say casual waiters get paid \$5 per hour. You can write an expression to represent everyone's wages like this: $5h$, where h is the number of hours worked. If you work 1 hour, then you get paid $5 \times 1 = \$5$. So the expression $5h$ has a value of \$5 in this case. If you work 6 hours, you get paid $5 \times 6 = \$30$. The expression $5h$ has a value of \$30 in this case.

'Evaluate' means to find the value of.

REWIND

You will need to keep reminding yourself about the order (BODMAS) of operations from chapter 1. ◀

Worked example 3

Given that $a = 2$ and $b = 8$, evaluate:

(a) ab **(b)** $3b - 2a$ **(c)** $2a^3$ **(d)** $2a(a + b)$

	Working	Explanation
(a)	$ab = a \times b$ $= 2 \times 8$ $= 16$	Put back the multiplication sign. Substitute the values for a and b. Calculate the answer.
(b)	$3b - 2a = 3 \times b - 2 \times a$ $= 3 \times 8 - 2 \times 2$ $= 24 - 4$ $= 20$	Put back the multiplication signs. Substitute the values for a and b. Use the order of operations rules (× before –). Calculate the answer.
(c)	$2a^3 = 2 \times a^3$ $= 2 \times 2^3$ $= 2 \times 8$ $= 16$	Put back the multiplication signs. Substitute the value for a. Work out 2^3 first (grouping symbols first). Calculate the answer.
(d)	$2a(a + b) = 2 \times a \times (a + b)$ $= 2 \times 2 \times (2 + 8)$ $= 4 \times 10$ $= 40$	Put back the multiplication signs. Substitute the values for a and b. In this case you can carry out two steps at the same time: multiplication outside the bracket, and the addition inside. Calculate the answer.

Worked example 4

For each of the shapes in the diagram below:

(i) Write an expression for the perimeter of each shape.
(ii) Find the perimeter in cm if $x = 4$.

(a)

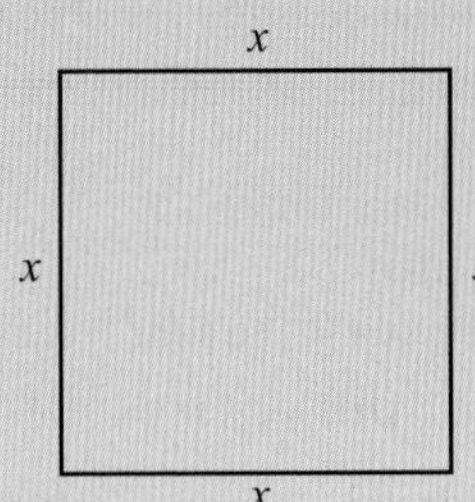

(b)

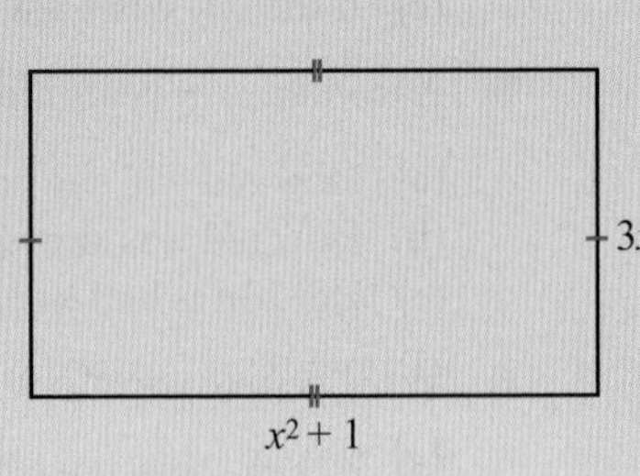

(c)

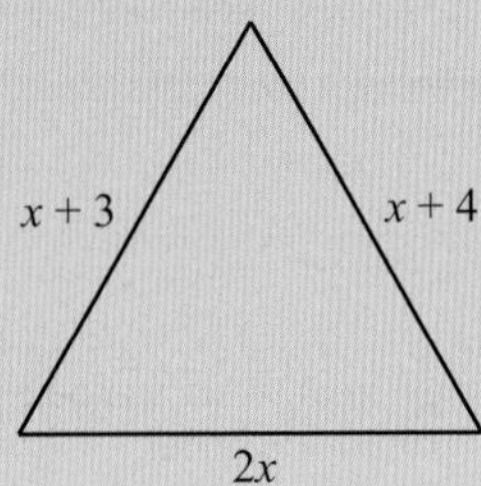

(a)	**(i)**	$x + x + x + x = 4x$	Add the four lengths together.
	(ii)	$4 \times x = 4 \times 4$ $= 16\,\text{cm}$	Substitute 4 into the expression.
(b)	**(i)**	$3x + (x^2 + 1) + 3x + (x^2 + 1) = 2(3x) + 2(x^2 + 1)$	Add the four lengths together and write in its simplest form.
	(ii)	$2 \times (3 \times x) + 2 \times (x^2 + 1) = 2 \times (3 \times 4) + 2 \times (4^2 + 1)$ $= 2 \times 12 + 2 \times (16 + 1)$ $= 24 + 2 \times 17$ $= 24 + 34$ $= 58\,\text{cm}$	Substitute 4 into the expression.
(c)	**(i)**	$x + 3 + x + 4 + 2x$	Add the three lengths together.
	(ii)	$x + 3 + x + 4 + 2 \times x = 4 + 3 + 4 + 4 + 2 \times 4$ $= 4 + 3 + 4 + 4 + 8$ $= 23\,\text{cm}$	Substitute 4 into the expression.

Worked example 5

Complete this table of values for the formula $b = 3a - 3$

a	0	2	4	6
b				

Substitute in the values of a to work out b.

$3 \times 0 - 3 = 0 - 3 = -3$

$3 \times 2 - 3 = 6 - 3 = 3$

$3 \times 4 - 3 = 12 - 3 = 9$

$3 \times 6 - 3 = 18 - 3 = 15$

a	0	2	4	6
b	−3	3	9	15

Exercise 2.2

FAST FORWARD

You will learn more about algebraic fractions in chapter 14. ▶

1 Evaluate the following expressions for $x = 3$.

(a) $3x$ (b) $10x$ (c) $4x - 2$ (d) x^3 (e) $2x^2$

(f) $10 - x$ (g) $x^2 + 7$ (h) $x^3 + x^2$ (i) $2(x - 1)$ (j) $\frac{4x}{2}$

(k) $\frac{6x}{3}$ (l) $\frac{90}{x}$ (m) $\frac{10x}{6}$ (n) $\frac{(4x + 2)}{7}$

Always show your substitution clearly. Write the formula or expression in its algebraic form but with the letters replaced by the appropriate numbers. This makes it clear to your teacher, or an examiner, that you have put the correct numbers in the right places.

2 What is the value of each expression when $a = 3$ and $b = 5$ and $c = 2$?

(a) abc **(b)** a^2b **(c)** $4a + 2c$ **(d)** $3b - 2(a + c)$
(e) $a^2 + c^2$ **(f)** $4b - 2a + c$ **(g)** $ab + bc + ac$ **(h)** $2(ab)^2$
(i) $3(a + b)$ **(j)** $(b - c) + (a + c)$ **(k)** $(a + b)(b - c)$ **(l)** $\frac{3bc}{ac}$
(m) $\frac{4b}{a} + c$ **(n)** $\frac{4b^2}{bc}$ **(o)** $\frac{2(a+b)}{c^2}$ **(p)** $\frac{3abc}{10a}$
(q) $\frac{6b^2}{(a+c)^2}$ **(r)** $(\frac{1}{2}abc)^2$ **(s)** $\frac{8a}{\sqrt[3]{a+b}}$ **(t)** $\frac{6ab}{a^2} - 2bc$

You may need to discuss part (f)(i) with your teacher.

3 Work out the value of y in each formula when:

(i) $x = 0$ **(ii)** $x = 3$ **(iii)** $x = 4$ **(iv)** $x = 10$ **(v)** $x = 50$

(a) $y = 4x$ **(b)** $y = 3x + 1$ **(c)** $y = 100 - x$
(d) $y = \frac{x}{2}$ **(e)** $y = x^2$ **(f)** $y = \frac{100}{x}$
(g) $y = 2(x + 2)$ **(h)** $y = 2(x + 2) - 10$ **(i)** $y = 3x^3$

4 A sandwich costs \$3 and a drink costs \$2.

(a) Write an expression to show the total cost of buying x sandwiches and y drinks.
(b) Find the total cost of:

(i) four sandwiches and three drinks
(ii) 20 sandwiches and 20 drinks
(iii) 100 sandwiches and 25 drinks.

5 The formula for finding the perimeter of a rectangle is $P = 2(l + b)$, where l represents the length and b represents the breadth of the rectangle.

Find the perimeter of a rectangle if:

(a) the length is 12 cm and the breadth is 9 cm
(b) the length is 2.5 m and the breadth is 1.5 m
(c) the length is 20 cm and the breadth is half as long
(d) the breadth is 2 cm and the length is the cube of the breadth.

2.3 Simplifying expressions

Remember, terms are not separated by × or ÷ signs. A fraction line means divide, so the parts of a fraction are all counted as one term, even if there is a + or – sign in the numerator or denominator.

So, $\frac{a+b}{c}$ is one term.

Remember, the number in a term is called a **coefficient**. In the term $2a$, the coefficient is 2; in the term $-3ab$, the coefficient is -3. A term with only numbers is called a constant. So in $2a + 4$, the constant is 4.

The parts of an algebraic expression are called *terms*. Terms are separated from each other by + or – signs. So $a + b$ is an expression with two terms, but ab is an expression with only one term and $2 + \frac{3a}{b} - \frac{ab}{c}$ is an expression with three terms.

Adding and subtracting like terms

Terms with exactly the same variables are called *like terms*. $2a$ and $4a$ are like terms; $3xy^2$ and $-xy^2$ are like terms.

The variables and any indices attached to them have to be identical for terms to be like terms. Don't forget that variables in a different order mean the same thing, so xy and yx are like terms ($x \times y = y \times x$).

Like terms can be added or subtracted to simplify algebraic expressions.

Note that a '+' or a '–' that appears within an algebraic expression, is attached to the term that sits to its right. For example: $3x - 4y$ contains two terms, $3x$ and $-4y$. If a term has no symbol written before it then it is taken to mean that it is '+'.

Worked example 6

Simplify:

(a) $4a + 2a + 3a$ **(b)** $4a + 6b + 3a$ **(c)** $5x + 2y - 7x$
(d) $2p + 5q + 3q - 7p$ **(e)** $2ab + 3a^2b - ab + 3ab^2$

(a)	$4a + 2a + 3a$ $= 9a$	Terms are all like. Add the coefficients, write the term.
(b)	$4a + 6b + 3a$ $= 7a + 6b$	Identify the like terms ($4a$ and $3a$). Add the coefficients of like terms. Write terms in alphabetical order.
(c)	$5x + 2y - 7x$ $= -2x + 2y$	Identify the like terms ($5x$ and $-7x$). Subtract the coefficients, remember the rules. Write the terms. (This could also be written as $2y - 2x$.)
(d)	$2p + 5q + 3q - 7p$ $= -5p + 8q$	Identify the like terms ($2p$ and $-7p$; $5q$ and $3q$). Add and subtract the coefficients. Write the terms.
(e)	$2ab + 3a^2b - ab + 3ab^2$ $= ab + 3a^2b + 3ab^2$	Identify like terms; pay attention to terms that are squared because a and a^2 are not like terms. Remember that ab means $1ab$.

Notice that you can rearrange the terms provided that you remember to take the '–' and '+' signs with the terms to their right. For example:

$3x - 2y + 5z$
$= 3x + 5z - 2y$
$= 5z + 3x - 2y$
$= -2y + 3x + 5z$

Exercise 2.3

1 Identify the like terms in each set.

(a) $6x, -2y, 4x, x$ (b) $x, -3y, \frac{3}{4}y, -5y$ (c) $ab, 4b, -4ba, 6a$
(d) $2, -2x, 3xy, 3x, -2y$ (e) $5a, 5ab, ab, 6a, 5$ (f) $-1xy, -yx, -2y, 3, 3x$

2 Simplify by adding or subtracting like terms.

(a) $2y + 6y$ (b) $9x - 2x$ (c) $10x + 3x$
(d) $21x + x$ (e) $7x - 2x$ (f) $4y - 4y$
(g) $9x - 10x$ (h) $y - 4y$ (i) $5x - x$
(j) $9xy - 2xy$ (k) $6pq - 2qp$ (l) $14xyz - xyz$
(m) $4x^2 - 2x^2$ (n) $9y^2 - 4y^2$ (o) $y^2 - 2y^2$
(p) $14ab^2 - 2ab^2$ (q) $9x^2y - 4x^2y$ (r) $10xy^2 - 8xy^2$

3 Simplify:

(a) $2x + y + 3x$ (b) $4y - 2y + 4x$ (c) $6x - 4x + 5x$
(d) $10 + 4x - 6$ (e) $4xy - 2y + 2xy$ (f) $5x^2 - 6x^2 + 2x$
(g) $5x + 4y - 6x$ (h) $3y + 4x - x$ (i) $4x + 6y + 4x$
(j) $9x - 2y - x$ (k) $12x^2 - 4x + 2x^2$ (l) $12x^2 - 4x^2 + 2x^2$
(m) $5xy - 2x + 7xy$ (n) $xy - 2xz + 7xy$ (o) $3x^2 - 2y^2 - 4x^2$
(p) $5x^2y + 3x^2y - 2xy$ (q) $4xy - x + 2yx$ (r) $5xy - 2 + xy$

FAST FORWARD

You will need to be very comfortable with the simplification of algebraic expressions when solving equations, inequalities and simplifying expansions throughout the course. ▶

4 Simplify as far as possible:

(a) $8y - 4 - 6y - 4$ (b) $x^2 - 4x + 3x^2 - x$ (c) $5x + y + 2x + 3y$
(d) $y^2 + 2y + 3y - 7$ (e) $x^2 - 4x - x + 3$ (f) $x^2 + 3x - 7 + 2x$
(g) $4xyz - 3xy + 2xz - xyz$ (h) $5xy - 4 + 3yx - 6$ (i) $8x - 4 - 2x - 3x^2$

5 Write an expression for the perimeter (P) of each of the following shapes and then simplify it to give P in the simplest possible terms.

(a) $2x$

(b)

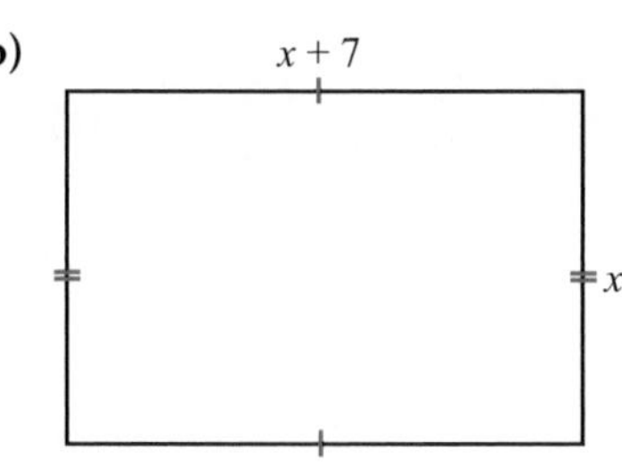

(c)

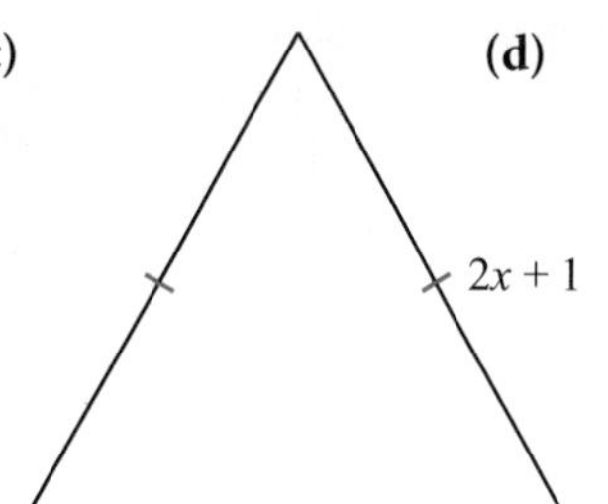

(d)

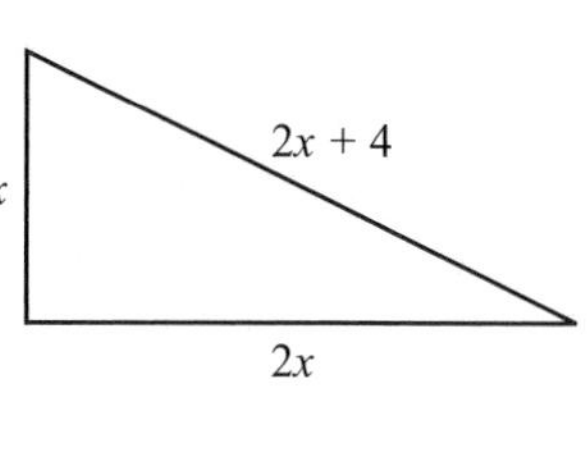

(e)

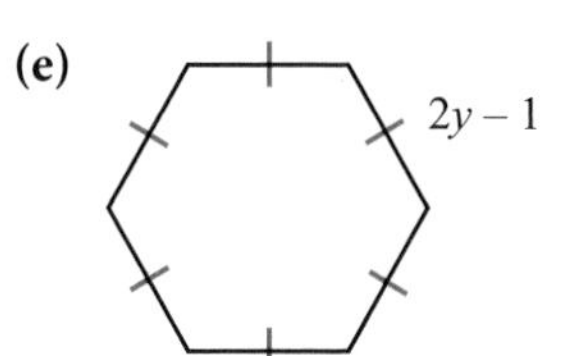

(f)

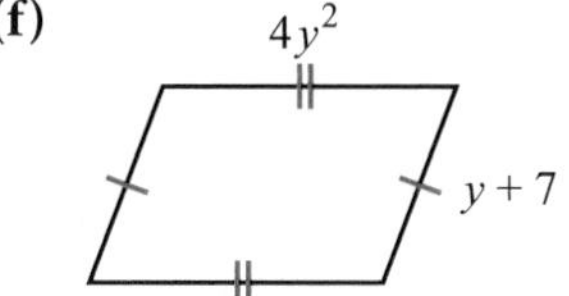

(g)

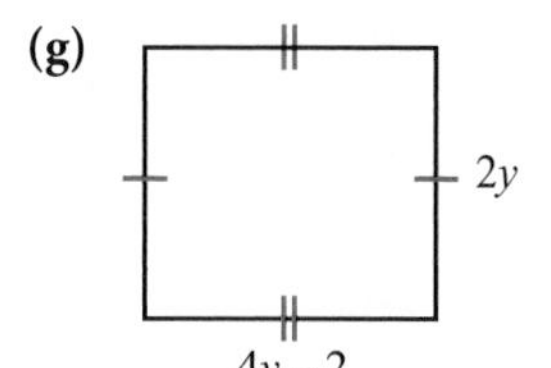

(h)

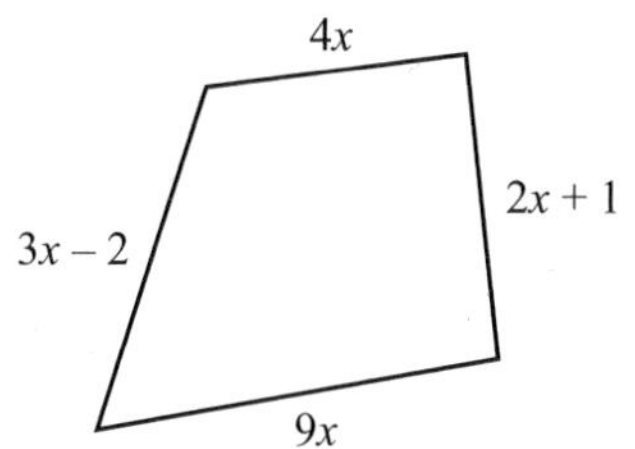

Multiplying and dividing in expressions

Although terms are not separated by × or ÷ they still need to be written in the simplest possible way to make them easier to work with.

In section 2.1 you learned how to write expressions in simpler terms when multiplying and dividing them. Make sure you understand and remember these important rules:

- $3x$ means $3 \times x$ and $3xy$ means $3 \times x \times y$
- xy means $x \times y$
- x^2 means $x \times x$ and x^2y means $x \times x \times y$ (only the x is squared)
- $\frac{2a}{4}$ means $2a \div 4$

Worked example 7

Simplify:

(a) $4 \times 3x$ **(b)** $4x \times 3y$ **(c)** $4ab \times 2bc$ **(d)** $7x \times 4yz \times 3$

(a)	$4 \times 3x = 4 \times 3 \times x$ $= 12 \times x$ $= 12x$	Insert the missing × signs. Multiply the numbers first. Write in simplest form.
(b)	$4x \times 3y = 4 \times x \times 3 \times y$ $= 12 \times x \times y$ $= 12xy$	Insert the missing × signs. Multiply the numbers. Write in simplest form.
(c)	$4ab \times 2bc = 4 \times a \times b \times 2 \times b \times c$ $= 8 \times a \times b \times b \times c$ $= 8ab^2c$	Insert the missing × signs. Multiply the numbers, then the variables. Write in simplest form.
(d)	$7x \times 4yz \times 3 = 7 \times x \times 4 \times y \times z \times 3$ $= 84 \times x \times y \times z$ $= 84xyz$	Insert the missing × signs. Multiply the numbers. Write in simplest form.

You can multiply numbers first and variables second because the order of any multiplication can be reversed without changing the answer.

FAST FORWARD

You will learn more about cancelling and equivalent fractions in chapter 5. ▶

Worked example 8

Simplify:

(a) $\frac{12x}{3}$ **(b)** $\frac{12xy}{3x}$ **(c)** $\frac{7xy}{70y}$ **(d)** $\frac{2x}{3} \times \frac{4x}{2}$

(a) $\frac{12x}{3} = \frac{\cancel{12}^{4}x}{\cancel{3}_{1}} = \frac{4x}{1} = 4x$	Divide both top and bottom by 3 (making the numerator and denominator smaller so that the fraction is in its simplest form is called *cancelling*).
(b) $\frac{12xy}{3x} = \frac{\cancel{12}^{4}\cancel{x}y}{\cancel{3x}_{1}} = \frac{4 \times y}{1} = 4y$	Cancel and then multiply.
(c) $\frac{7xy}{70y} = \frac{\cancel{7}^{1}x\cancel{y}}{\cancel{70}_{10}\cancel{y}} = \frac{x}{10}$	Cancel.
(d) $\frac{2x}{3} \times \frac{4x}{2} = \frac{2 \times x \times 4 \times x}{3 \times 2}$	Insert signs and multiply.
$= \frac{\cancel{8}^{4}x^2}{\cancel{6}_{3}}$	Cancel.
$= \frac{4x^2}{3}$	
or $\frac{\cancel{2}^{1}x}{3} \times \frac{4x}{\cancel{2}_{1}} = \frac{1x}{3} \times \frac{4x}{1} = \frac{4x^2}{3}$	Cancel first, then multiply.

Exercise 2.4

1 Multiply:

(a) $2 \times 6x$ (b) $4y \times 2$ (c) $3m \times 4$
(d) $2x \times 3y$ (e) $4x \times 2y$ (f) $9x \times 3y$
(g) $8y \times 3z$ (h) $2x \times 3y \times 2$ (i) $4xy \times 2xy$
(j) $4xy \times 2x$ (k) $9y \times 3xy$ (l) $4y \times 2x \times 3y$
(m) $2a \times 4ab$ (n) $3ab \times 4bc$ (o) $6abc \times 2a$
(p) $8abc \times 2ab$ (q) $4 \times 2ab \times 3c$ (r) $12x^2 \times 2 \times 3y^2$

2 Simplify:

(a) $3 \times 2x \times 4$ (b) $5x \times 2x \times 3y$ (c) $2x \times 3y \times 2xy$
(d) $xy \times xz \times x$ (e) $2 \times 2 \times 3x \times 4$ (f) $4 \times 2x \times 3x^2y$
(g) $x \times y^2 \times 4x$ (h) $2a \times 3ab \times 2c$ (i) $10x \times 2y \times 3$
(j) $4 \times x \times 2 \times y$ (k) $9 \times x^2 \times xy$ (l) $4xy^2 \times 2x^2y$
(m) $7xy \times 2xz \times 3yz$ (n) $4xy \times 2x^2y \times 7$ (o) $9 \times xyz \times 4xy$
(p) $3x^2y \times 2xy^2 \times 3xy$ (q) $9x \times 2xy \times 3x^2$ (r) $2x \times xy^2 \times 3xy$

3 Simplify:

(a) $\frac{15x}{3}$ (b) $\frac{40x}{10}$ (c) $\frac{21x}{7}$ (d) $\frac{12xy}{2x}$
(e) $\frac{14xy}{2y}$ (f) $\frac{18x^2y}{9x^2}$ (g) $\frac{10xy}{40x}$ (h) $\frac{15x}{60xy}$
(i) $\frac{7xyz}{14xy}$ (j) $\frac{6xy}{x}$ (k) $\frac{x}{4x}$ (l) $\frac{x}{9x}$

4 Simplify:

(a) $8x \div 2$ (b) $12xy \div 2x$ (c) $16x^2 \div 4xy$ (d) $24xy \div 3xy$
(e) $14x^2 \div 2y^2$ (f) $24xy \div 8y$ (g) $8xy \div 24y$ (h) $9x \div 36xy$
(i) $\frac{77xyz}{11xz}$ (j) $\frac{45xy}{20x}$ (k) $\frac{60x^2y^2}{15xy}$ (l) $\frac{100xy}{25x^2}$

5 Simplify these as far as possible.

(a) $\frac{x}{2}\times\frac{y}{3}$ (b) $\frac{x}{3}\times\frac{x}{4}$ (c) $\frac{xy}{2}\times\frac{5x}{3}$ (d) $\frac{2x}{3}\times\frac{5}{y}$
(e) $\frac{2x}{4}\times\frac{3y}{4}$ (f) $\frac{5x}{2}\times\frac{5x}{2}$ (g) $\frac{x}{y}\times\frac{2y}{x}$ (h) $\frac{xy}{3}\times\frac{x}{y}$
(i) $5y\times\frac{2x}{5}$ (j) $4\times\frac{2x}{3}$ (k) $\frac{x}{6}\times\frac{3}{2x}$ (l) $\frac{5x}{2}\times\frac{4x}{10}$

2.4 Working with brackets

FAST FORWARD

In this section you will focus on simple examples. You will learn more about removing brackets and working with negative terms in chapters 6 and 10. You will also learn a little more about why this method works. ▶

When an expression has brackets, you normally have to remove the brackets before you can simplify the expression. Removing the brackets is called expanding the expression.

To remove brackets you multiply each term inside the bracket by the number (and/or variables) outside the bracket. When you do this you need to pay attention to the positive and negative signs in front of the terms:

$x(y+z) = xy + xz$

$x(y-z) = xy - xz$

Removing brackets is really just multiplying, so the same rules you used for multiplication apply in these examples.

Worked example 9

Remove the brackets to simplify the following expressions.

(a) $2(2x + 6)$ **(b)** $4(7 - 2x)$ **(c)** $2x(x + 3y)$ **(d)** $xy(2 - 3x)$

(a)
$2(2x+6) = 2\times 2x + 2\times 6$
$= 4x + 12$

(b)
$4(7-2x) = 4\times 7 - 4\times 2x$
$= 28 - 8x$

(c)
$2x(x+3y) = 2x\times x + 2x\times 3y$
$= 2x^2 + 6xy$

(d)
$xy(2-3x) = xy\times 2 - xy\times 3x$
$= 2xy - 3x^2y$

For parts (a) to (d) write the expression out, or do the multiplication mentally.

Follow these steps when multiplying by a term outside a bracket:

- Multiply the term on the left-hand inside of the bracket first - shown by the red arrow labelled i.
- Then multiply the term on the right-hand side – shown by the blue arrow labelled ii.
- Then add the answers together.

Exercise 2.5

1 Expand:

(a) $2(x+6)$	**(b)** $3(x+2)$	**(c)** $4(2x+3)$
(d) $10(x-6)$	**(e)** $4(x-2)$	**(f)** $3(2x-3)$
(g) $5(y+4)$	**(h)** $6(4+y)$	**(i)** $9(y+2)$
(j) $7(2x-2y)$	**(k)** $2(3x-2y)$	**(l)** $4(x+4y)$
(m) $5(2x-2y)$	**(n)** $6(3x-2y)$	**(o)** $3(4y-2x)$
(p) $4(y-4x^2)$	**(q)** $9(x^2-y)$	**(r)** $7(4x+x^2)$

2 Remove the brackets to expand these expressions.

(a) $2x(x+y)$	**(b)** $3y(x-y)$	**(c)** $2x(x+2y)$
(d) $4x(3x-2y)$	**(e)** $xy(x-y)$	**(f)** $3y(4x+2)$
(g) $2xy(9-4y)$	**(h)** $2x^2(3-2y)$	**(i)** $3x^2(4-4x)$
(j) $4x(9-2y)$	**(k)** $5y(2-x)$	**(l)** $3x(4-y)$
(m) $2x^2y(y-2x)$	**(n)** $4xy^2(3-2x)$	**(o)** $3xy^2(x+y)$
(p) $x^2y(2x+y)$	**(q)** $9x^2(9-2x)$	**(r)** $4xy^2(3-x)$

3 Given the formula for area, $A = \text{length} \times \text{breadth}$, write an expression for A in terms of x for each of the following rectangles. Expand the expression to give A in simplest terms.

(a)

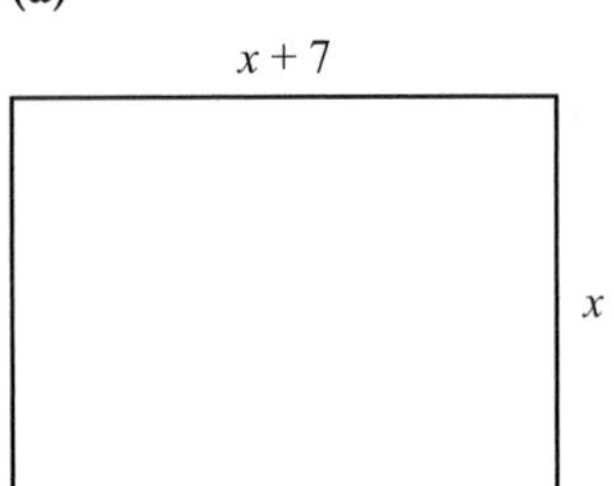

(b)

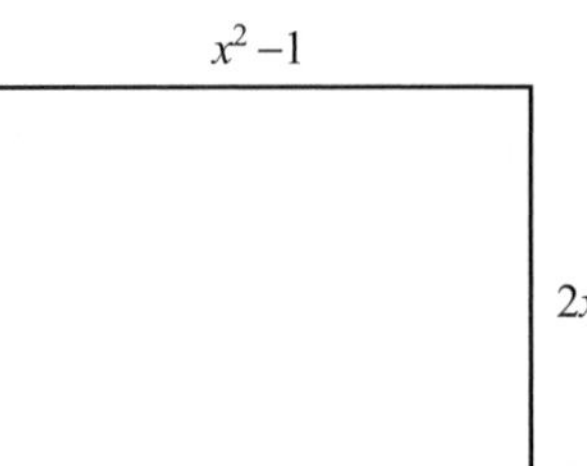

(c)

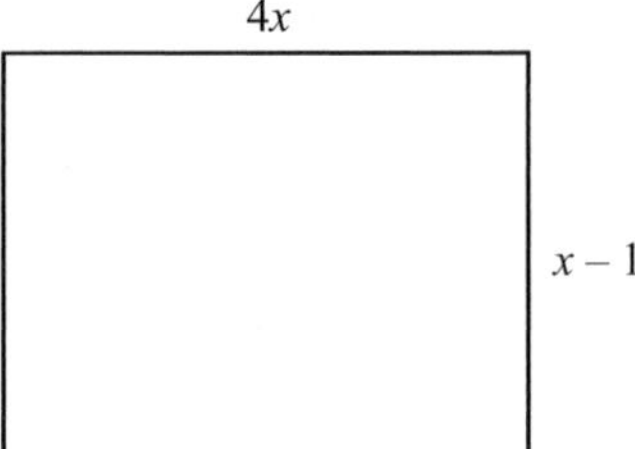

Expanding and collecting like terms

When you remove brackets and expand an expression you may end up with some like terms. When this happens, you collect the like terms together and add or subtract them to write the expression in its simplest terms.

Worked example 10

Expand and simplify where possible.

(a) $6(x+3)+4$ **(b)** $2(6x+1)-2x+4$ **(c)** $2x(x+3)+x(x-4)$

(a)	$6(x+3)+4 = 6x+18+4$ $= 6x+22$	Remove the brackets. Add like terms.
(b)	$2(6x+1)-2x+4 = 12x+2-2x+4$ $= 10x+6$	Remove the brackets. Add or subtract like terms.
(c)	$2x(x+3)+x(x-4) = 2x^2+6x+x^2-4x$ $= 3x^2+2x$	Remove the brackets. Add or subtract like terms.

Exercise 2.6

1 Expand and simplify:

(a) $2(5+x)+3x$	**(b)** $3(y-2)+4y$	**(c)** $2x+2(x-4)$
(d) $4x+2(x-3)$	**(e)** $2x(4+x)-5$	**(f)** $4(x+2)-7$

(g) $6+3(x-2)$ (h) $4x+2(2x+3)$ (i) $2x+3+2(2x+3)$
(j) $3(2x+2)-3x-4$ (k) $6x+2(x+3)$ (l) $7y+y(x-4)-4$
(m) $2x(x+4)-4$ (n) $2y(2x-2y+4)$ (o) $2y(5-4y)-4y^2$
(p) $3x(2x+4)-9$ (q) $3y(y+2)-4y^2$ (r) $2(x-1)+4x-4$

2 Simplify these expressions by removing brackets and collecting like terms.

(a) $4(x+40)+2(x-3)$ (b) $2(x-2)+2(x+3)$ (c) $3(x+2)+4(x+5)$
(d) $8(x+10)+4(3-2x)$ (e) $4(x^2+2)+2(4-x^2)$ (f) $4x(x+1)+2x(x+3)$
(g) $3x(4y-4)+4(3xy+4x)$ (h) $2x(5y-4)+2(6x-4xy)$ (i) $3x(4-8y)+3(2xy-5x)$
(j) $3(6x-4y)+x(3-2y)$ (k) $3x^2(4-x)+2(5x^2-2x^3)$ (l) $x(x-y)+3(2x-y)$
(m) $4(x-2)+3x(4-y)$ (n) $x(x+y)+x(x-y)$ (o) $2x(x+y)+2(x^2+3xy)$
(p) $x(2x+3)+3(5-2x)$ (q) $4(2x-3)+(x-5)$ (r) $3(4xy-2x)+5(3x-xy)$

2.5 Indices

Revisiting index notation

The plural of 'index' is 'indices'.

You already know how to write powers of two and three using indices:

$2\times 2=2^2$ and $y\times y=y^2$

$2\times 2\times 2=2^3$ and $y\times y\times y=y^3$

Exponent is another word sometimes used to mean 'index' or 'power'. These words can be used interchangeably but 'index' is more commonly used for IGCSE.

When you write a number using indices (powers) you have written it in index notation. Any number can be used as an index including 0, negative integers and fractions. The index tells you how many times the **base** has been multiplied by itself. So:

$3\times 3\times 3\times 3=3^4$ 3 is the base, 4 is the index

$a\times a\times a\times a\times a=a^5$ a is the base, 5 is the index

When you write a power out in full as a multiplication you are writing it in expanded form.

Worked example 11

Write each expression using index notation.

(a) $2\times 2\times 2\times 2\times 2\times 2$ (b) $x\times x\times x\times x$ (c) $x\times x\times x\times y\times y\times y\times y$

(a)	$2\times 2\times 2\times 2\times 2\times 2=2^6$	Count how many times 2 is multiplied by itself to give you the index.
(b)	$x\times x\times x\times x=x^4$	Count how many times x is mulitplied by itself to give you the index.
(c)	$x\times x\times x\times y\times y\times y\times y=x^3y^4$	Count how many times x is mulitplied by itself to get the index of x; then work out the index of y in the same way.

When you *evaluate* a number raised to a power, you are carrying out the multiplication to obtain a single value.

Worked example 12

Use your calculator to evaluate:

(a) 2^5 (b) 2^8 (c) 10^6 (d) 7^4

(a)	$2^5=32$	Enter [2] [$x^{[]}$] [5] [=]
(b)	$2^8=256$	Enter [2] [$x^{[]}$] [8] [=]
(c)	$10^6=1\,000\,000$	Enter [1] [0] [$x^{[]}$] [6] [=]
(d)	$7^4=2401$	Enter [7] [$x^{[]}$] [4] [=]

REWIND

Quickly remind yourself, from chapter 1, how a composite number can be written as a product of primes. ◀

Index notation and products of prime factors

Index notation is very useful when you have to express a number as a product of its prime factors because it allows you to write the factors in a short form.

Worked example 13

Express these numbers as products of their prime factors in index form.

(a) 200 **(b)** 19683

The diagrams below are a reminder of the factor tree and division methods for finding the prime factors.

(a)

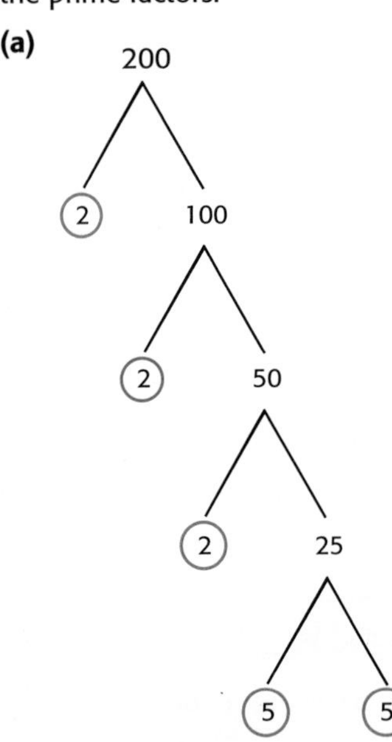

$= 2 \times 2 \times 2 \times 5 \times 5$

(b)

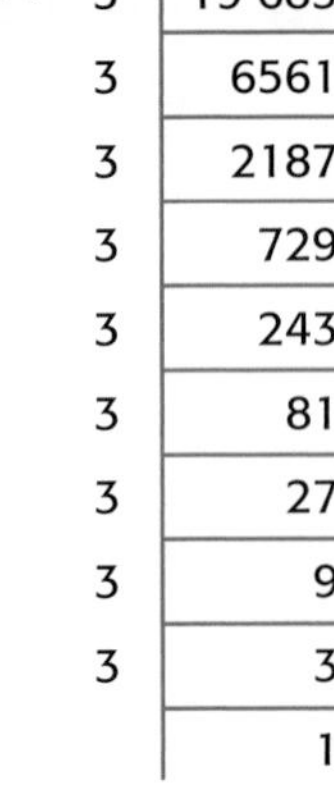

$= 3 \times 3 \times 3 \times 3 \times 3 \times 3 \times 3 \times 3 \times 3$

(a) $200 = 2^3 \times 5^2$ **(b)** $19683 = 3^9$

Exercise 2.7

1 Write each expression using index notation.

(a) $2\times2\times2\times2\times2$ (b) $3\times3\times3\times3$ (c) 7×7
(d) $11\times11\times11$ (e) $10\times10\times10\times10\times10$ (f) $8\times8\times8\times8\times8$
(g) $a\times a\times a\times a$ (h) $x\times x\times x\times x\times x\times x$ (i) $y\times y\times y\times y\times y\times y$
(j) $a\times a\times a\times b\times b$ (k) $x\times x\times y\times y\times y\times y$ (l) $p\times p\times p\times q\times q$
(m) $x\times x\times x\times x\times y\times y\times y$ (n) $x\times y\times x\times y\times y\times x\times y$ (o) $a\times b\times a\times b\times a\times b\times c$

2 Evaluate:

(a) 10^4 (b) 7^3 (c) 6^7 (d) 4^9 (e) 10^5
(f) 1^{12} (g) 2^{10} (h) 9^4 (i) 2^6 (j) $2^3\times3^4$
(k) $5^2\times3^8$ (l) $4^5\times2^6$ (m) $2^6\times3^4$ (n) $2^8\times3^2$ (o) $5^3\times3^5$

3 Express the following as products of prime factors, in index notation.

(a) 64 (b) 243 (c) 400 (d) 1600 (e) 16 384
(f) 20 736 (g) 59 049 (h) 390 625

4 Write several square numbers as products of prime factors, using index notation. What is true about the index needed for each prime?

The laws of indices

The laws of indices are very important in algebra because they give you quick ways of simplifying expressions. You will use these laws over and over again as you learn more and more algebra, so it is important that you understand them and that you can apply them in different situations.

Multiplying the same base number with different indices

Look at these two multiplications:

$3^2 \times 3^4$ $\quad$ $x^3 \times x^4$

In the first multiplication, 3 is the 'base' number and in the second, x is the 'base' number.

You already know you can simplify these by expanding them like this:

$3\times3\times3\times3\times3\times3=3^6$ $\quad$ $x\times x\times x\times x\times x\times x\times x=x^7$

In other words:

$3^2 \times 3^4 = 3^{2+4}$ and $x^3 \times x^4 = x^{3+4}$

This gives you the law of indices for multiplication:

> When you multiply index expressions with the same base you can add the indices: $x^m \times x^n = x^{m+n}$

Worked example 14

Simplify:

(a) $4^3 \times 4^6$ **(b)** $x^2 \times x^3$ **(c)** $2x^2y \times 3xy^4$

(a)	$4^3 \times 4^6 = 4^{3+6} = 4^9$	Add the indices.
(b)	$x^2 \times x^3 = x^{2+3} = x^5$	Add the indices.
(c)	$2x^2y \times 3xy^4 = 2\times3\times x^{2+1}\times y^{1+4} = 6x^3y^5$	Multiply the numbers first, then add the indices of like variables.

Remember every letter or number has a power of 1 (usually unwritten). So x means x^1 and y means y^1.

Dividing the same base number with different indices

FAST FORWARD

The multiplication and division rules will be used more when you study standard form in chapter 5. ▶

Look at these two divisions:

$3^4 \div 3^2$ and $x^6 \div x^2$

You already know you can simplify these by writing them in expanded form and cancelling like this:

$\dfrac{3\times3\times\cancel{3}\times\cancel{3}}{\cancel{3}\times\cancel{3}}$ $\quad$ $\dfrac{x\times x\times x\times x\times\cancel{x}\times\cancel{x}}{\cancel{x}\times\cancel{x}}$

$=3\times3$ $\quad$ $=x\times x\times x\times x$

$=3^2$ $\quad$ $=x^4$

In other words:

$3^4 \div 3^2 = 3^{4-2}$ and $x^6 \div x^2 = x^{6-2}$

This gives you the law of indices for division:

> When you divide index expressions with the same base you can subtract the indices: $x^m \div x^n = x^{m-n}$

Worked example 15

Simplify:

(a) $\frac{x^6}{x^2}$ **(b)** $\frac{6x^5}{3x^2}$ **(c)** $\frac{10x^3y^2}{5xy}$

(a) $\frac{x^6}{x^2} = x^{6-2} = x^4$	Subtract the indices.
(b) $\frac{6x^5}{3x^2} = \frac{6}{3} \times \frac{x^5}{x^2} = \frac{2}{1} \times x^{5-2} = 2x^3$	Divide (cancel) the coefficients. Subtract the indices.
(c) $\frac{10x^3y^2}{5xy} = \frac{10}{5} \times \frac{x^3}{x} \times \frac{y^2}{y}$ $= \frac{2}{1} \times x^{3-1} \times y^{2-1}$ $= 2x^2y$	Divide the coefficients. Subtract the indices.

Remember 'coefficient' is the *number* in the term.

The power 0

You should remember that any value divided by itself gives 1.

So, $3 \div 3 = 1$ and $x \div x = 1$ and $\frac{x^4}{x^4} = 1$.

If we use the law of indices for division we can see that:

$$\frac{x^4}{x^4} = x^{4-4} = x^0$$

This gives us the law of indices for the power 0.

Technically, there is an awkward exception to this rule when $x = 0$. 0^0 is usually defined to be 1!

> Any value to the power 0 is equal to 1. So $x^0 = 1$.

Raising a power

Look at these two examples:

$(x^3)^2 = x^3 \times x^3 = x^{3+3} = x^6$ $(2x^3)^4 = 2x^3 \times 2x^3 \times 2x^3 \times 2x^3 = 2^4 \times x^{3+3+3+3} = 16x^{12}$

If we write the examples in expanded form we can see that $(x^3)^2 = x^6$ and $(2x^3)^4 = 16x^{12}$

This gives us the law of indices for raising a power to another power:

> When you have to raise a power to another power you multiply the indices: $(x^m)^n = x^{mn}$

Worked example 16

Simplify:

(a) $(x^3)^6$ **(b)** $(3x^4y^3)^2$ **(c)** $(x^3)^4 \div (x^6)^2$

(a) $(x^3)^6 = x^{3\times 6}$ $= x^{18}$	Multiply the indices.

A common error is to forget to take powers of the numerical terms. For example in part (b), the '3' needs to be squared to give '9'.

(b)	$(3x^4y^3)^2$ $= 3^2 \times x^{4\times2} \times y^{3\times2}$ $= 9x^8y^6$	Square each of the terms to remove the brackets and multiply the indices.
(c)	$(x^3)^4 \div (x^6)^2$ $= x^{3\times4} \div x^{6\times2}$ $= x^{12} \div x^{12}$ $= x^{12-12}$ $= x^0$ $= 1$	Expand the brackets first by multiplying the indices. Divide by subtracting the indices.

Exercise 2.8

1 Simplify:

(a) $3^2 \times 3^6$ **(b)** $4^2 \times 4^9$ **(c)** $8^2 \times 8^0$ **(d)** $x^9 \times x^4$

(e) $y^2 \times y^7$ **(f)** $y^3 \times y^4$ **(g)** $y \times y^5$ **(h)** $x \times x^4$

(i) $3x^4 \times 2x^3$ **(j)** $3y^2 \times 3y^4$ **(k)** $2x \times x^3$ **(l)** $3x^3 \times 2x^4$

(m) $5x^3 \times 3$ **(n)** $8x^4 \times x^3$ **(o)** $4x^6 \times 2x$ **(p)** $x^3 \times 4x^5$

2 Simplify:

(a) $x^6 \div x^4$ **(b)** $x^{12} \div x^3$ **(c)** $y^4 \div y^3$ **(d)** $x^3 \div x$ **(e)** $\frac{x^5}{x}$

(f) $\frac{x^6}{x^4}$ **(g)** $\frac{6x^5}{2x^3}$ **(h)** $\frac{9x^7}{3x^4}$ **(i)** $\frac{12y^2}{3y}$ **(j)** $\frac{3x^4}{6x^3}$

(k) $\frac{15x^3}{5x^3}$ **(l)** $\frac{9x^4}{3x^3}$ **(m)** $\frac{3x^3}{9x^4}$ **(n)** $\frac{16x^2y^2}{4xy}$ **(o)** $\frac{12xy^2}{12xy^2}$

3 Simplify:

(a) $(x^2)^2$ **(b)** $(x^2)^3$ **(c)** $(x^2)^6$ **(d)** $(y^3)^2$ **(e)** $(2x^2)^5$

(f) $(3x^2y^2)^2$ **(g)** $(x^4)^0$ **(h)** $(5x^2)^3$ **(i)** $(x^2y^2)^3$ **(j)** $(x^2y^4)^5$

(k) $(xy^4)^3$ **(l)** $(4xy^2)^2$ **(m)** $(3x^2)^4$ **(n)** $(xy^6)^4$ **(o)** $\left(\frac{x^2}{y}\right)^0$

4 Use the appropriate laws of indices to simplify these expressions.

When there is a mixture of numbers and letters, deal with the numbers first and then apply the laws of indices to the letters in alphabetical order.

(a) $2x^2 \times 3x^3 \times 2x$ **(b)** $4 \times 2x \times 3x^2y$ **(c)** $4x \times x \times x^2$

(d) $(x^2)^2 \div 4x^2$ **(e)** $11x^3 \times 4(a^2b)^2$ **(f)** $4x(x^2+7)$

(g) $x^2(4x - x^3)$ **(h)** $x^8 \div (x^3)^2$ **(i)** $7x^2y^2 \div (x^3y)^2$

(j) $\frac{(4x^2 \times 3x^4)}{6x^4}$ **(k)** $\left(\frac{x^4}{y^2}\right)^3$ **(l)** $\frac{x^8 \times (xy^2)^4}{(2x^2)^4}$

(m) $(8x^2)^0$ **(n)** $4x^2 \times 2x^3 \div (2x)^0$ **(o)** $\frac{(4x^2y^3)^2}{(2xy)^3}$

Negative indices

At the beginning of this unit you read that negative numbers can also be used as indices. But what does it mean if an index is negative?

Look at the two methods of working out $x^3 \div x^5$ below.

Using expanded notation:

$$x^3 \div x^5 = \frac{x \times x \times x}{x \times x \times x \times x \times x} = \frac{1}{x \times x} = \frac{1}{x^2}$$

Using the law of indices for division:

$$x^3 \div x^5 = x^{3-5} = x^{-2}$$

This shows that $\frac{1}{x^2} = x^{-2}$. And this gives you a rule for working with negative indices:

In plain language you can say that when a number is written with a negative power, it is equal to 1 over the number to the same positive power. Another way of saying '1 over' is **reciprocal**, so a^{-2} can be written as the reciprocal of a^2, i.e. $\frac{1}{a^2}$.

$$x^{-m} = \frac{1}{x^m} \text{ (when } x \neq 0\text{)}$$

When an expression contains negative indices you apply the same laws as for other indices to simplify it.

FAST FORWARD

These are simple examples. Once you have learned more about working with directed numbers in algebra in chapter 6, you will apply what you have learned to simplify more complicated expressions. ▶

Worked example 17

1 Find the value of:

(a) 4^{-2} **(b)** 5^{-1}

(a) $4^{-2} = \frac{1}{4^2} = \frac{1}{16}$

(b) $5^{-1} = \frac{1}{5^1} = \frac{1}{5}$

2 Write these with a positive index.

(a) x^{-4} **(b)** y^{-3}

(a) $x^{-4} = \frac{1}{x^4}$

(b) $y^{-3} = \frac{1}{y^3}$

3 Simplify. Give your answers with positive indices.

(a) $\frac{4x^2}{2x^4}$ **(b)** $2x^{-2} \times 3x^{-4}$ **(c)** $(3y^2)^{-3}$

(a) $\frac{4x^2}{2x^4} = \frac{4}{2} \times x^{2-4} = 2x^{-2} = \frac{2}{x^2}$

(b) $2x^{-2} \times 3x^{-4} = \frac{2}{x^2} \times \frac{3}{x^4} = \frac{6}{x^{2+4}} = \frac{6}{x^6}$

(c) $(3y^2)^{-3} = \frac{1}{(3y^2)^3} = \frac{1}{3^3 \times y^{2\times3}} = \frac{1}{27y^6}$

Exercise 2.9

1 Evaluate:

(a) 4^{-1} (b) 3^{-1} (c) 8^{-1} (d) 5^{-3} (e) 6^{-4} (f) 2^{-5}

2 State whether the following are true or false.

(a) $4^{-2} = \frac{1}{16}$ (b) $8^{-2} = \frac{1}{16}$ (c) $x^{-3} = \frac{1}{3x}$ (d) $2x^{-2} = \frac{1}{x}$

3 Write each expression so it has only positive indices.

(a) x^{-2} (b) y^{-3} (c) $(xy)^{-2}$ (d) $2x^{-2}$
(e) $12x^{-3}$ (f) $7y^{-3}$ (g) $8xy^{-3}$ (h) $12x^{-3}y^{-4}$

4 Simplify. Write your answer using only positive indices.

(a) $x^{-3} \times x^4$ (b) $2x^{-3} \times 3x^{-3}$ (c) $4x^3 \div 12x^7$ (d) $\frac{x^{-7}}{x^4}$

(e) $(2x^2)^{-3}$ (f) $(x^{-2})^3$ (g) $\frac{x^{-3}}{x^{-4}}$ (h) $\frac{x^{-2}}{x^3}$

Summary of index laws

$x^m \times x^n = x^{m+n}$ When multiplying terms, add the indices.

$x^m \div x^n = x^{m-n}$ When dividing, subtract the indices.

$(x^m)^n = x^{mn}$ When finding the power of a power, multiply the indices.

$x^0 = 1$ Any value to the power 0 is equal to 1

$x^{-m} = \frac{1}{x^m}$ (when $x \neq 0$).

Fractional indices

The laws of indices also apply when the index is a fraction. Look at these examples carefully to see what fractional indices mean in algebra:

- $x^{\frac{1}{2}} \times x^{\frac{1}{2}}$

  $= x^{\frac{1}{2}+\frac{1}{2}}$ Use the law of indices and add the powers.

  $= x^1$

  $= x$

  In order to understand what $x^{\frac{1}{2}}$ means, ask yourself: what number multiplied by itself will give x?

  $\sqrt{x} \times \sqrt{x} = x$

  So, $x^{\frac{1}{2}} = \sqrt{x}$

- $y^{\frac{1}{3}} \times y^{\frac{1}{3}} \times y^{\frac{1}{3}}$

  $= y^{\frac{1}{3}+\frac{1}{3}+\frac{1}{3}}$ Use the law of indices and add the powers.

  $= y^1$

  $= y$

  What number multiplied by itself and then by itself again will give y?

  $\sqrt[3]{y} \times \sqrt[3]{y} \times \sqrt[3]{y} = y$

  So $y^{\frac{1}{3}} = \sqrt[3]{y}$

This shows that any root of a number can be written using fractional indices. So, $x^{\frac{1}{m}} = \sqrt[m]{x}$.

Worked example 18

1 Rewrite using root signs.

(a) $y^{\frac{1}{2}}$ **(b)** $x^{\frac{1}{5}}$ **(c)** $x^{\frac{1}{y}}$

(a) $y^{\frac{1}{2}} = \sqrt{y}$ **(b)** $x^{\frac{1}{5}} = \sqrt[5]{x}$ **(c)** $x^{\frac{1}{y}} = \sqrt[y]{x}$

2 Write in index notation.

(a) $\sqrt{90}$ **(b)** $\sqrt[3]{64}$ **(c)** $\sqrt[4]{x}$ **(d)** $\sqrt[5]{(x-2)}$

(a) $\sqrt{90} = 90^{\frac{1}{2}}$ **(b)** $\sqrt[3]{64} = 64^{\frac{1}{3}}$ **(c)** $\sqrt[4]{x} = x^{\frac{1}{4}}$ **(d)** $\sqrt[5]{(x-2)} = (x-2)^{\frac{1}{5}}$

A non-unit fraction has a numerator (the number on top) that is not 1. For example, $\frac{2}{3}$ and $\frac{5}{7}$ are non-unit fractions.

Dealing with non-unit fractions

Sometimes you may have to work with indices that are non-unit fractions. For example $x^{\frac{2}{3}}$ or $y^{\frac{3}{4}}$. To find the rule for working with these, you have to think back to the law of indices for raising a power to another power. Look at these examples carefully to see how this works:

$x^{\frac{2}{3}} = (x^{\frac{1}{3}})^2 \qquad \frac{1}{3}\times 2 \text{ is } \frac{2}{3}$

$y^{\frac{3}{4}} = (y^{\frac{1}{4}})^3 \qquad \frac{1}{4}\times 3 = \frac{3}{4}$

You already know that a unit-fraction gives a root. So we can rewrite these expressions using root signs like this:

$(x^{\frac{1}{3}})^2 = (\sqrt[3]{x})^2$ and $(y^{\frac{1}{4}})^3 = (\sqrt[4]{y})^3$

So, $(x^{\frac{2}{3}}) = (\sqrt[3]{x})^2$ and $(y^{\frac{3}{4}}) = (\sqrt[4]{y})^3$.

It is possible that you would want to reverse the order of calculations here and the result will be the same. $x^{\frac{m}{n}} = (\sqrt[n]{x})^m = \sqrt[n]{x^m}$, but the former tends to work best.

In general terms: $x^{\frac{m}{n}} = x^{m\times\frac{1}{n}} = (x^{\frac{1}{n}})^m = (\sqrt[n]{x})^m$

Worked example 19

Work out the value of:

(a) $27^{\frac{2}{3}}$ **(b)** $25^{1.5}$

(a)	$27^{\frac{2}{3}} = (\sqrt[3]{27})^2$ $= (3)^2$ $= 9$	$\frac{2}{3} = 2\times\frac{1}{3}$ so you square the cube root of 27.
(b)	$25^{1.5} = 25^{\frac{3}{2}}$ $= (\sqrt{25})^3$ $= (5)^2$ $= 125$	Change the decimal to a vulgar fraction. $\frac{3}{2} = 3\times\frac{1}{2}$, so you need to cube the square root of 25.

REWIND

You saw in chapter 1 that a 'vulgar' fraction is in the form $\frac{a}{b}$. ◀

Sometimes you are asked to find the value of the power that produces a given result. You have already learned that another word for power is exponent. An equation that requires you to find the exponent is called an *exponential* equation.

Worked example 20

If $2^x = 128$ find the value of x.

$2^x = 128$ $2^7 = 128$ $\therefore x = 7$	Remember this means $2 = \sqrt[x]{128}$. Find the value of x by trial and improvement.

Exercise 2.10

1 Evaluate:

(a) $8^{\frac{1}{3}}$ **(b)** $32^{\frac{1}{5}}$ **(c)** $8^{\frac{4}{3}}$ **(d)** $216^{\frac{2}{3}}$ **(e)** $256^{0.75}$

2 Find the value of x in each of these equations.

(a) $2^x = 64$ **(b)** $196^x = 14$ **(c)** $x^{\frac{1}{5}} = 7$

(d) $(x-1)^{\frac{3}{4}} = 64$ **(e)** $3^x = 81$ **(f)** $4^x = 256$

(g) $2^{-x} = \frac{1}{64}$ **(h)** $3^{x-1} = 81$ **(i)** $9^{-x} = \frac{1}{81}$

(j) $3^{-x} = 81$ **(k)** $64^x = 2$ **(l)** $16^x = 8$ **(m)** $4^{-x} = \frac{1}{64}$

3 Simplify:

(a) $x^{\frac{1}{3}} \times x^{\frac{1}{3}}$ **(b)** $x^{\frac{1}{2}} \times x^{\frac{2}{3}}$ **(c)** $\left(\frac{x^4}{x^{10}}\right)^{\frac{1}{2}}$ **(d)** $\left(\frac{x^6}{y^2}\right)^{\frac{1}{2}}$

(e) $\frac{x^{\frac{6}{7}}}{x^{\frac{2}{7}}}$ **(f)** $\frac{7}{8}x^{\frac{1}{2}} \div \frac{1}{2}x^{-\frac{3}{2}}$ **(g)** $\frac{2x^{\frac{2}{3}}}{x^{\frac{8}{3}}}$ **(h)** $\frac{9x^{\frac{1}{3}}}{12x^{\frac{4}{3}}}$

(i) $\frac{1}{2}x^{\frac{1}{2}} \div 2x^2$ **(j)** $-\frac{1}{2}x^{\frac{3}{4}} \div -2x^{-\frac{1}{4}}$ **(k)** $\frac{3}{4}x^{\frac{1}{2}} \div \frac{1}{2}x^{-\frac{1}{4}}$ **(l)** $-\frac{1}{4}x^{\frac{3}{4}} \div -2x^{-\frac{1}{4}}$

Remembers, simplify means to write in its simplest form. So if you were to simplify $x^{\frac{1}{5}} \times x^{-\frac{1}{2}}$ you would write:

$= x^{\frac{1}{5}-\frac{1}{2}}$

$= x^{\frac{2}{10}-\frac{5}{10}}$

$= x^{-\frac{3}{10}}$

$= \frac{1}{x^{\frac{3}{10}}}$

Summary

Do you know the following?

- Algebra has special conventions (rules) that allow us to write mathematical information is short ways.
- Letters in algebra are called variables, the number before a letter is called a coefficient and numbers on their own are called constants.
- A group of numbers and variables is called a term. Terms are separated by + and – signs, but not by × or ÷ signs.
- Like terms have exactly the same combination of variables and powers. You can add and subtract like terms. You can multiply and divide like and unlike terms.
- The order of operations rules for numbers (BODMAS) apply in algebra as well.
- Removing brackets (multiplying out) is called expanding the expression. Collecting like terms is called simplifying the expression.
- Powers are also called indices. The index tells you how many times a number or variable is multiplied by itself. Indices only apply to the number or variable immediately before them.
- The laws of indices are a set of rules for simplifying expressions with indices. These laws apply to positive, negative, zero and fractional indices.

Are you able to . . . ?

- use letters to represent numbers
- write expressions to represent mathematical information
- substitute letters with numbers to find the value of an expression
- add and subtract like terms to simplify expressions
- multiply and divide to simplify expressions
- expand expressions by removing brackets and getting rid of other grouping symbols
- use and make sense of positive, negative and zero indices
- apply the laws of indices to simplify expressions
- work with fractional indices
- solve exponential equations using fractional indices.

Examination practice

Exam-style questions

1 Write an expression in terms of n for:
(a) the sum of a number and 12
(b) twice a number minus four
(c) a number multiplied by x and then squared
(d) the square of a number cubed.

2 Simplify:
(a) $9xy+3x+6xy-2x$
(b) $6xy-xy+3y$

3 Simplify:
(a) $\frac{a^3b^4}{ab^3}$
(b) $2(x^3)^2$
(c) $3x\times 2x^3y^2$
(d) $(4ax^2)^0$
(e) $4x^2y\times x^3y^2$

4 What is the value of x, when:
(a) $2^x=32$
(b) $3^x=\frac{1}{27}$

5 Expand each expression and simplify if possible.
(a) $5(x-2)+3(x+2)$
(b) $5x(x+7y)-2x(2x-y)$

6 Find the value of $(x+5)-(x-5)$ when:
(a) $x=1$
(b) $x=0$
(c) $x=5$

7 Simplify and write the answers with positive indices only.
(a) $x^5\times x^{-2}$ (b) $\frac{8x^2}{2x^4}$ (c) $(2x-2)^{-3}$

8 If $x\neq 0$ and $y\neq 0$, simplify:
(a) $3x^{\frac{1}{2}}\times 5x^{\frac{1}{2}}$ (b) $(81y^6)^{\frac{1}{2}}$ (c) $(64x^3)^{\frac{1}{3}}$

Past paper questions

1 Simplify:
(a) $32x^8\div 8x^{32}$, [2]
(b) $\left(\frac{x^3}{64}\right)^{\frac{2}{3}}$. [2]

[Cambridge IGCSE Mathematics 0580 Paper 22 Q17 May/June 2011]

3 Lines, angles and shapes

Key words

- Line
- Parallel
- Angle
- Perpendicular
- Acute
- Right
- Obtuse
- Reflex
- Vertically opposite
- Corresponding
- Alternate
- Co-interior
- Triangle
- Quadrilateral
- Polygon
- Circle
- Perpendicular bisector

In this chapter you will learn how to:

- use the correct terms to talk about points, lines, angles and shapes
- classify, measure and construct angles
- calculate unknown angles using angle relationships
- talk about the properties of triangles, quadrilaterals, circles and polygons.
- use a ruler and a pair of compasses to bisect lines and angles
- use instruments to construct triangles and other geometrical figures.
- EXTENDED: calculate unknown angles in irregular polygons

In this photo white light is bent by a prism and separated into the different colours of the spectrum. When scientists study the properties of light they use the mathematics of lines and angles.

Geometry is one of the oldest known areas of mathematics. Farmers in Ancient Egypt knew about lines and angles and they used them to mark out fields after floods. Builders in Egypt and Mesopotamia used knowledge of angles and shapes to build huge temples and pyramids.

Today geometry is used in construction, surveying and architecture to plan and build roads, bridges, houses and office blocks. We also use lines and angles to find our way on maps and in the software of GPS devices. Artists use them to get the correct perspective in drawings, opticians use them to make spectacle lenses and even snooker players use them to work out how to hit the ball.

3.1 Lines and angles

Mathematicians use specific terms and definitions to talk about geometrical figures. You are expected to know what the terms mean and you should be able to use them correctly in your own work.

FAST FORWARD

You will use these terms throughout the course but especially in chapter 14, where you learn how to solve simultaneous linear equations graphically. ▶

Terms used to talk about lines and angles

Term	What it means	Examples
Point	A point is shown on paper using a dot (·) or a cross (×). Most often you will use the word 'point' to talk about where two lines meet. You will also talk about points on a grid (positions) and name these using ordered pairs of co-ordinates (x, y). Points are normally named using capital letters.	
Line	A line is a straight (one-dimensional) figure that extends to infinity in both directions. Normally though, the word 'line' is used to talk about the shortest distance between two points. Lines are named using starting point and end point letters.	
Parallel	A pair of lines that are the same distance apart all along their length are parallel. The symbol $\|\|$ (or $/\!/$) is used for parallel lines, e.g. $AB \| CD$. Lines that are parallel are marked on diagrams with arrows.	
Angle	When two lines meet at a point, they form an angle. The meeting point is called the vertex of the angle and the two lines are called the arms of the angle. Angles are named using three letters: the letter at the end of one arm, the letter at the vertex and the letter at the end of the other arm. The letter in the middle of an angle name always indicates the vertex. The symbol $\angle$ or ^ is used to indicate an angle.	
Perpendicular	When two lines meet at right angles they are perpendicular to each other. The symbol $\perp$ is used to show that lines are perpendicular, e.g. $MN \perp PQ$.	

Term	What it means	Examples
Acute angle	An acute angle is > 0° but < 90°.	$A\hat{B}C < 90°$ $D\hat{E}F < 90°$ $M\hat{N}P < 90°$
Right angle	A right angle is an angle of exactly 90°. A square in the corner is usually used to represent 90°. A right angle is formed between perpendicular lines.	$X\hat{Y}Z = 90°$; $XY \perp YZ$
Obtuse angle	An obtuse angle is > 90° but < 180°.	$A\hat{B}C > 90°$ $P\hat{Q}R > 90°$
Straight angle	A straight angle is an angle of 180°. A line is considered to be a straight angle.	$M\hat{N}O = 180°$ MO = straight line
Reflex angle	A reflex angle is an angle that is > 180° but < 360°.	$A\hat{B}C > 180°$ $D\hat{E}F > 180°$
Revolution	A revolution is a complete turn; an angle of exactly 360°.	360°

Measuring and drawing angles

The size of an angle is the amount of turn from one arm of the angle to the other. Angle sizes are measured in degrees (°) from 0 to 360 using a protractor.

Always take time to measure angles carefully. If you need to make calculations using your measured angles, a careless error can lead to several wrong answers.

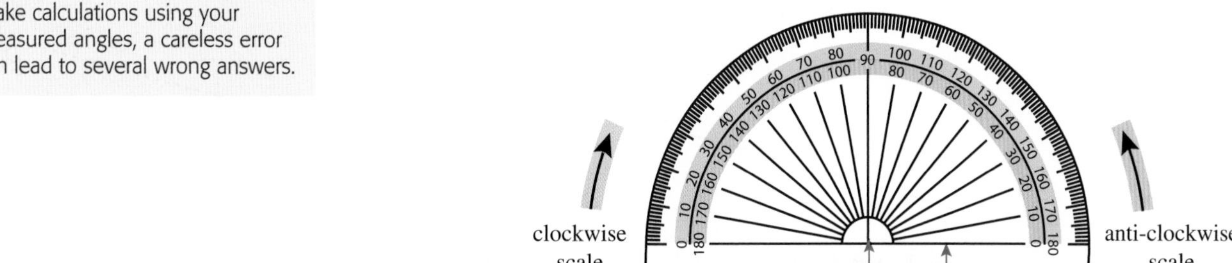

A 180° protractor has two scales. You need to choose the correct one when you measure an angle.

> If the arm of the angle does not extend up to the scale, lengthen the arm past the scale. The length of the arms of the angle does not affect the size of the angle.

Measuring angles < 180°

Put the centre of the protractor on the vertex of the angle. Align the baseline so it lies on top of one arm of the angle.

Using the scale that starts with 0° to read off the size of the angle, move round the scale to the point where it crosses the other arm of the angle.

Worked example 1

Measure angles $A\hat{B}C$ and $P\hat{Q}R$.

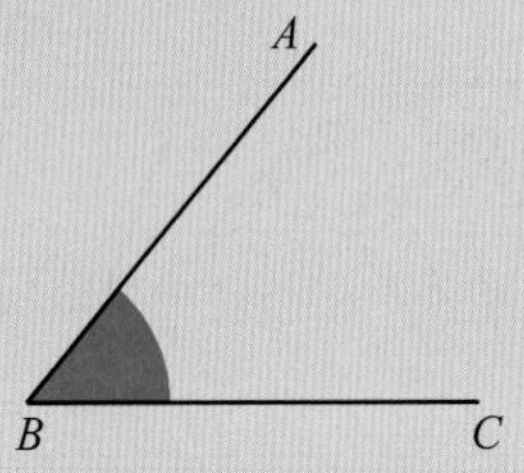

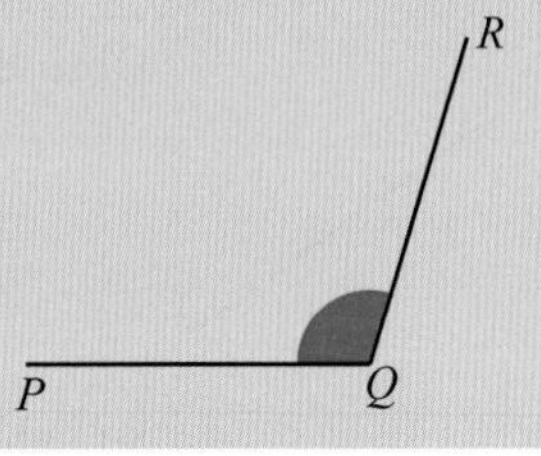

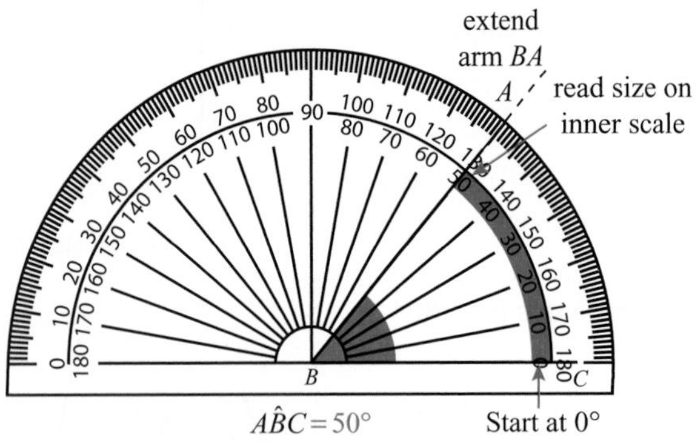

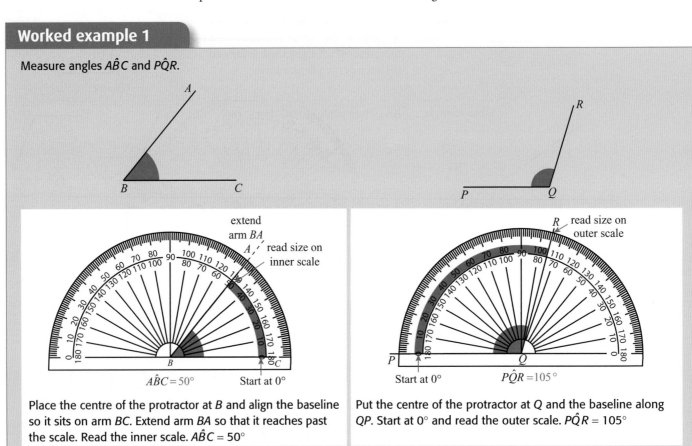

extend arm BA

read size on inner scale

$A\hat{B}C = 50°$ Start at 0°

read size on outer scale

Start at 0° $P\hat{Q}R = 105°$

Place the centre of the protractor at B and align the baseline so it sits on arm BC. Extend arm BA so that it reaches past the scale. Read the inner scale. $A\hat{B}C = 50°$

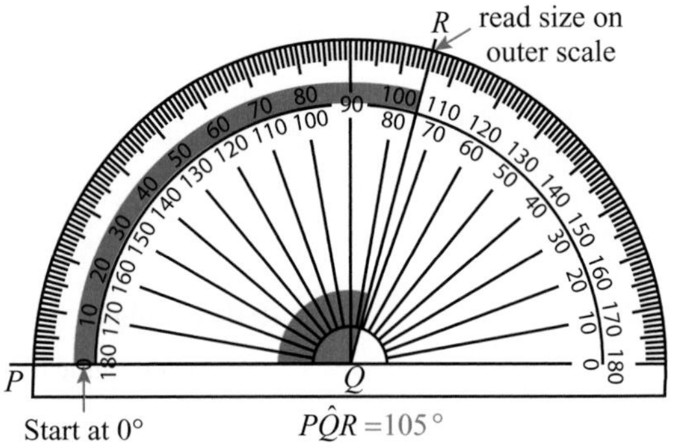

Put the centre of the protractor at Q and the baseline along QP. Start at 0° and read the outer scale. $P\hat{Q}R = 105°$

Measuring angles > 180°

Here are two different methods for measuring a reflex angle with a 180° protractor. You should use the method that you find easier to use. Suppose you had to measure the angle $A\hat{B}C$:

Method 1: Extend one arm of the angle to form a straight line (180° angle) and then measure the 'extra bit'. Add the 'extra bit' to 180° to get the total size.

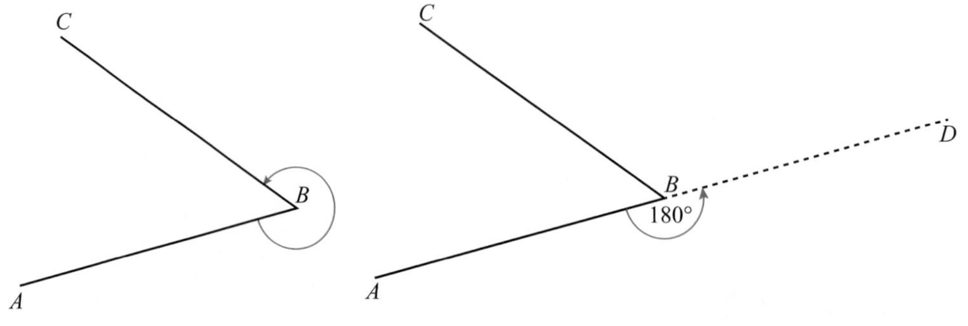

Angle $A\hat{B}C$ is >180°.

Extend AB to point D. You know the angle of a straight line is 180°. So $A\hat{B}D = 180°$.

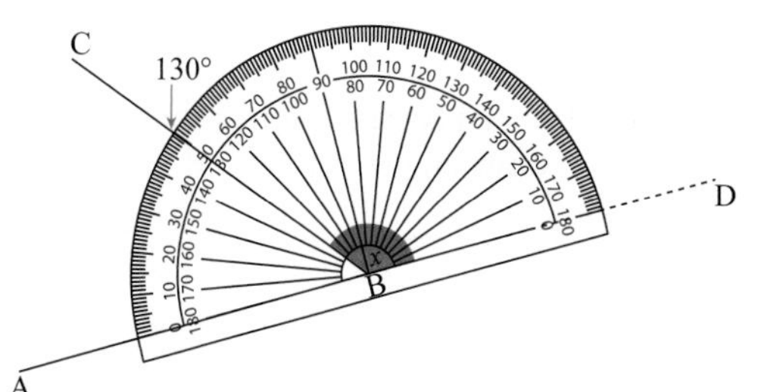

Use the protractor to measure the other piece of the angle, $D\hat{B}C$ (marked x). Add this to 180° to find $A\hat{B}C$.

$180° + 180° = 310°$

$\therefore A\hat{B}C = 310°$

Method 2: Measure the inner (non-reflex) angle and subtract it from 360° to get the size of the reflex angle.

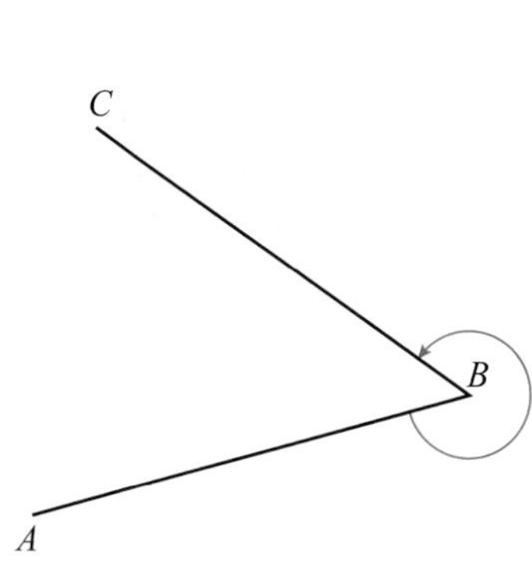

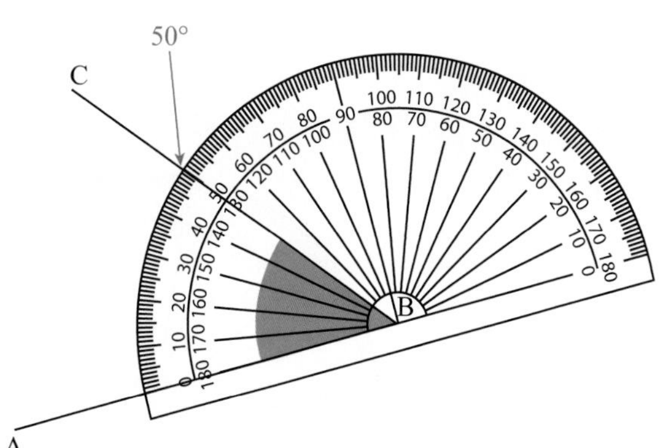

You can see that the angle $A\hat{B}C$ is almost 360°.

Measure the size of the angle that is < 180° (non-reflex) and subtract from 360°.

$360° - 50° = 310°$

$\therefore A\hat{B}C = 310°$

Exercise 3.1

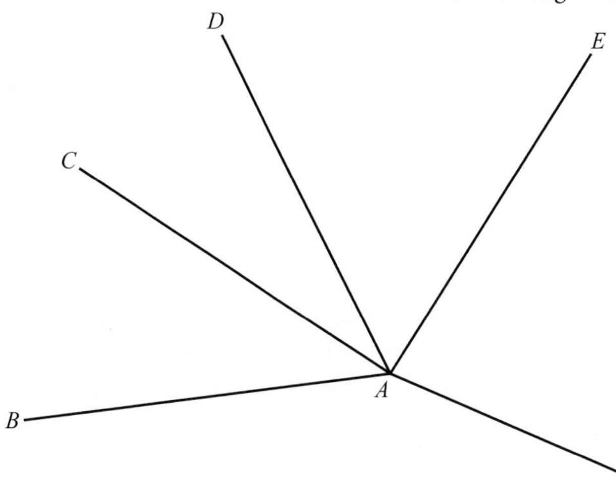

1 For each angle listed:

(i) $\angle BAC$	**(ii)** $\angle BAD$	**(iii)** $\angle BAE$
(iv) $\angle CAD$	**(v)** $\angle CAF$	**(vi)** $\angle CAE$
(vii) $\angle DAB$	**(viii)** $\angle DAE$	**(ix)** $\angle DAF$

(a) state what type of angle it is (acute, right or obtuse)
(b) estimate its size in degrees
(c) use a protractor to measure the actual size of each angle to the nearest degree.
(d) What is the size of reflex angle $D\hat{A}B$?

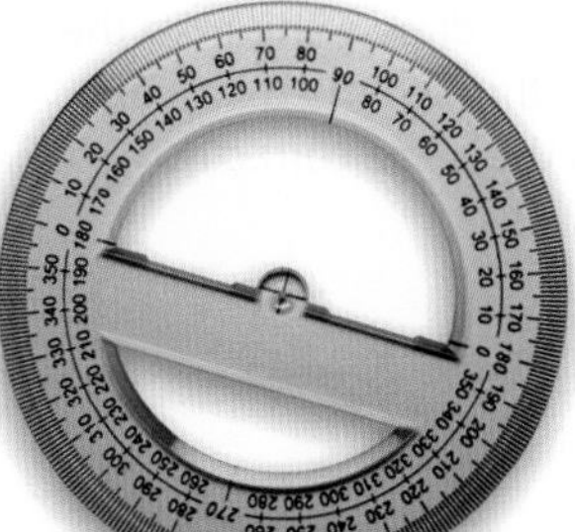

Living maths

2 Some protractors, like the one shown on the left, are circular.

(a) How is this different from the 180° protractor?
(b) Write instructions to teach someone how to use a circular protractor to measure the size of an obtuse angle.
(c) How would you measure a reflex angle with a circular protractor?

Drawing angles

It is fairly easy to draw an angle of a given size if you have a ruler, a protractor and a sharp pencil. Work through this example to remind yourself how to draw angles < 180° and > 180°.

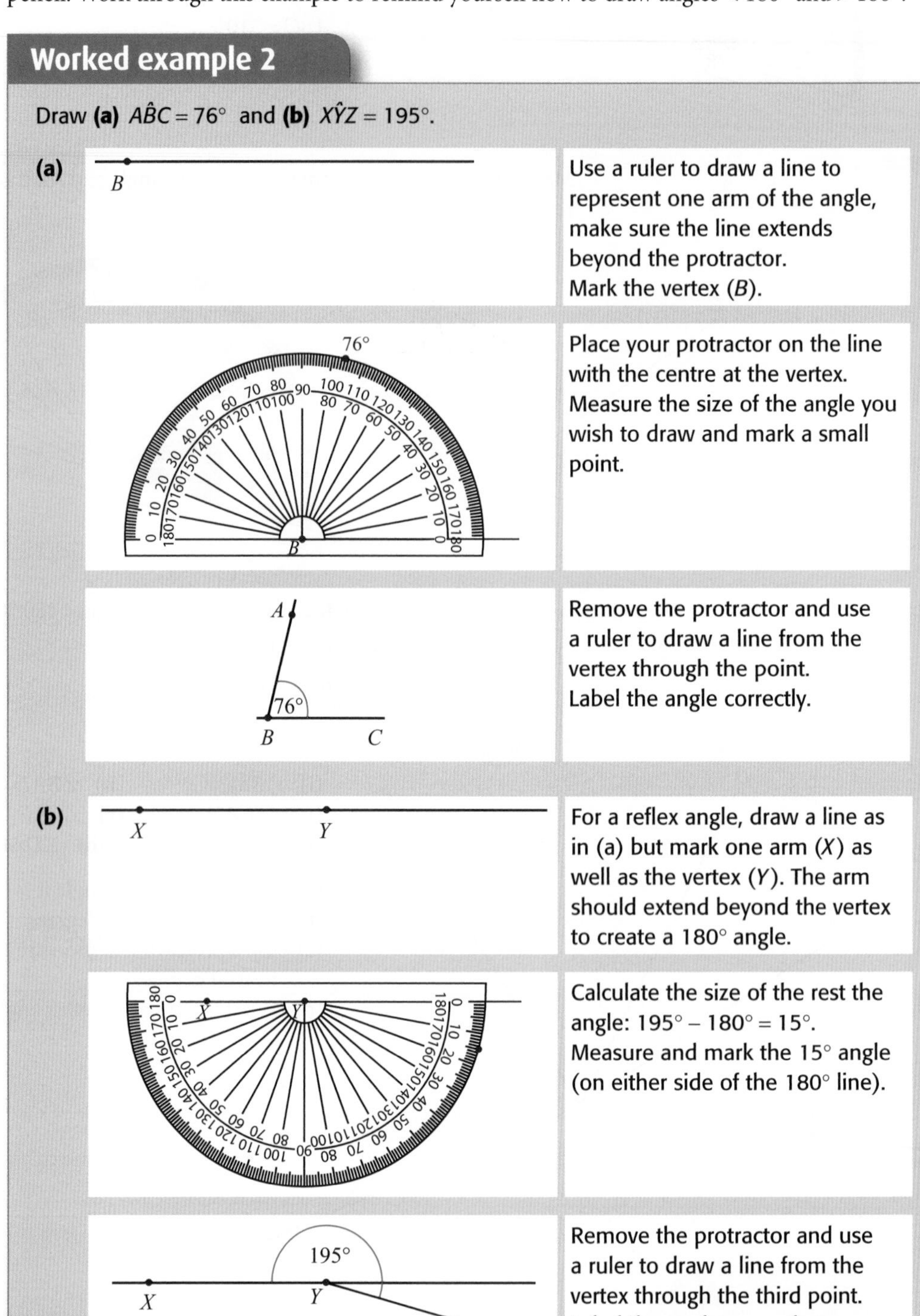

Worked example 2

Draw **(a)** $A\hat{B}C = 76°$ and **(b)** $X\hat{Y}Z = 195°$.

(a)

Use a ruler to draw a line to represent one arm of the angle, make sure the line extends beyond the protractor.
Mark the vertex (*B*).

Place your protractor on the line with the centre at the vertex. Measure the size of the angle you wish to draw and mark a small point.

Remove the protractor and use a ruler to draw a line from the vertex through the point.
Label the angle correctly.

(b)

For a reflex angle, draw a line as in (a) but mark one arm (*X*) as well as the vertex (*Y*). The arm should extend beyond the vertex to create a 180° angle.

Calculate the size of the rest the angle: 195° – 180° = 15°.
Measure and mark the 15° angle (on either side of the 180° line).

Remove the protractor and use a ruler to draw a line from the vertex through the third point.
Label the angle correctly.

To draw a reflex angle, you could also work out the size of the inner angle and simply draw that. 360° – 195° = 165°. If you do this, remember to mark the reflex angle on your sketch and not the inner angle!

Exercise 3.2

Use a ruler and a protractor to accurately draw the following angles:

(a) $\angle ABC = 80°$ **(b)** $\angle PQR = 30°$ **(c)** $\angle XYZ = 135°$

(d) $\angle EFG = 90°$ **(e)** $\angle KLM = 210°$ **(f)** $\angle JKL = 355°$

Angle relationships

Make sure you know the following angle facts:

Complementary angles

Angles in a right angle add up to 90°.
When the sum of two angles is 90° those two angles are complementary angles.

> **Tip**
>
> In general terms:
>
> for complementary angles, if one angle is $x°$, the other must be $90° - x°$ and vice versa.
>
> For supplementary angles, if one angle is $x°$, the other must be $180° - x°$ and vice versa.

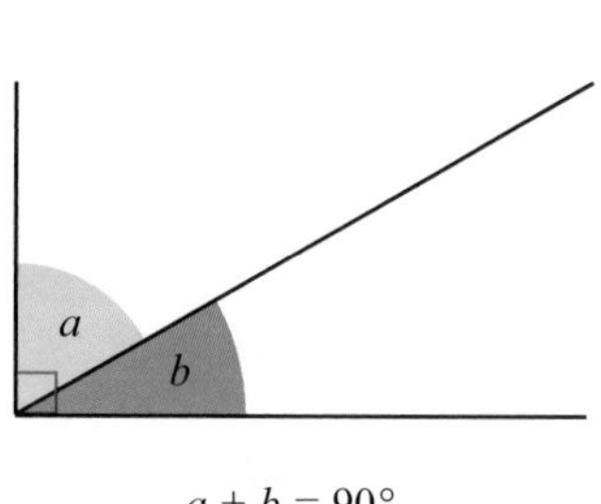

$a + b = 90°$

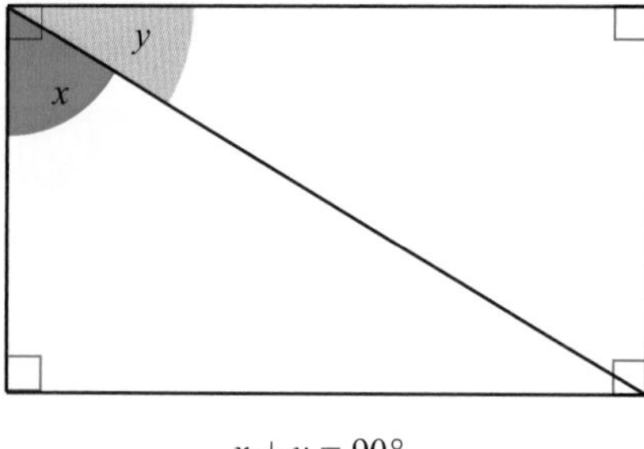

$x + y = 90°$

Supplementary angles

Angles on a straight line add up to 180°.

When the sum of two angles is 180° those two angles are supplementary angles.

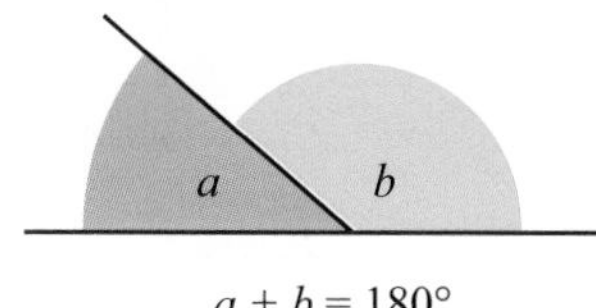

$a + b = 180°$

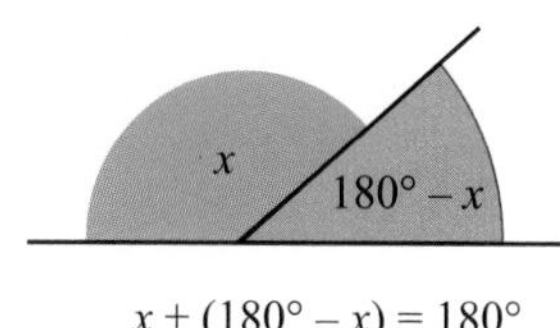

$x + (180° - x) = 180°$

Angles round a point

Angles at a point make a complete revolution.

The sum of the angles at a point is 360°.

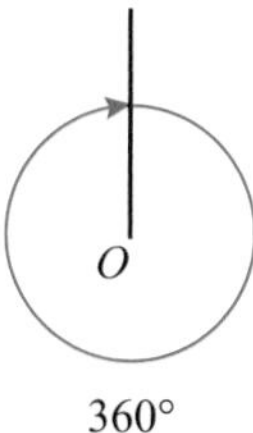

360°

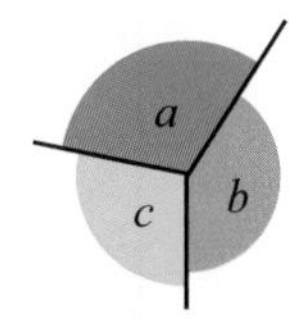

$a + b + c = 360°$

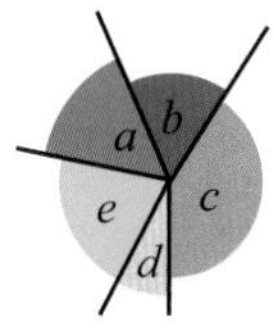

$a + b + c + d + e = 360°$

Vertically opposite angles

The adjacent angle pairs in vertically opposite angles form pairs of supplementary angles because they are also angles on a straight line.

When two lines intersect, two pairs of **vertically opposite** angles are formed.

Vertically opposite angles are equal in size.

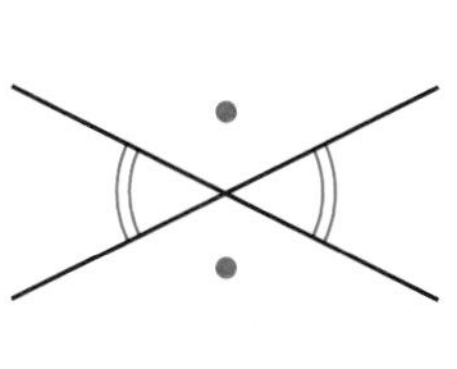

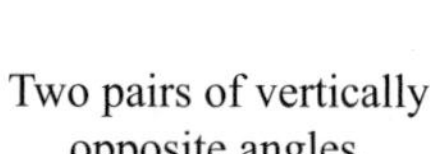

Two pairs of vertically opposite angles.

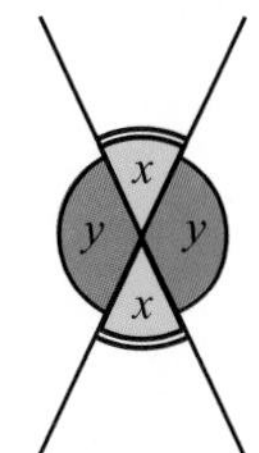

The angles marked x are equal to each other. The angles marked y are also equal to each other.

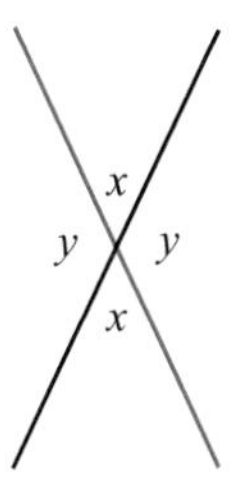

$x + y = 180°$

Using angle relationships to find unknown angles

The relationships between angles can be used to work out the size of unknown angles. Follow these easy steps:

- identify the relationship
- make an equation
- give reasons for statements
- solve the equation to find the unknown value.

You will usually be expected to give reasons when you are finding the size of an unknown angle. To do this, state the relationship that you used to find the unknown angle after your statements. You can use these abbreviations to give reasons:

- comp ∠s
- supp ∠s
- ∠s on line
- ∠s round point

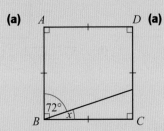

Worked example 3

Find the size of the angle marked x in each of these figures. Give reasons.

(a)	**(a)** $72° + x = 90°$ ($\angle ABC = 90°$, comp ∠s) $x = 90° - 72°$ $x = 18°$	You are told that $A\hat{B}C$ is a right angle, so you know that 72° and x are complementary angles. This means that $72° + x = 90°$, so you can rearrange to make x the subject.
(b) 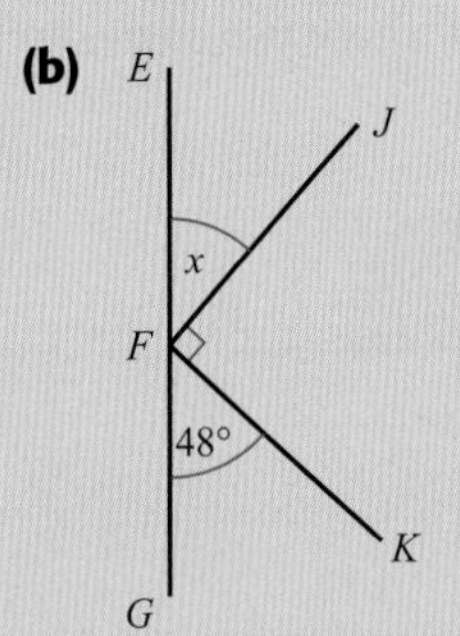	**(b)** $48° + 90° + x = 180°$ (∠s on line) $x = 180° - 90° - 48°$ $x = 42°$	You can see that 48°, the right angle and x are angles on a straight line. Angles on a straight line add up to 180°. So you can rearrange to make x the subject.
(c) 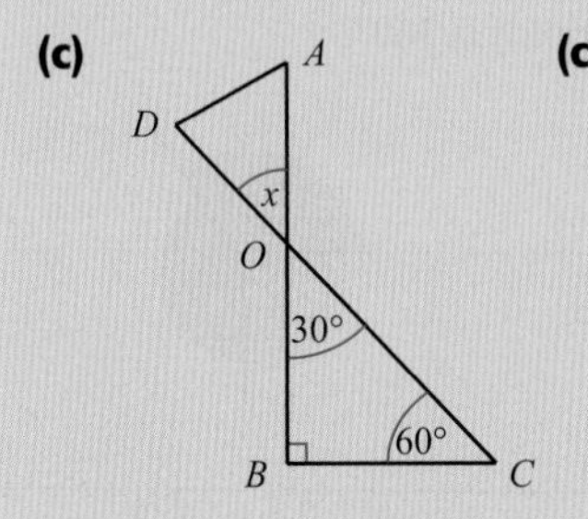	**(c)** $x = 30°$ (vertically opposite ∠s)	You know that when two lines intersect, the resulting vertically opposite angles are equal. x and 30° are vertically opposite, so $x = 30°$.

Exercise 3.3

1 In the following diagram, name:

(a) a pair of complementary angles
(b) a pair of equal angles
(c) a pair of supplementary angles
(d) the angles on line DG
(e) the complement of angle EBF
(f) the supplement of angle EBC.

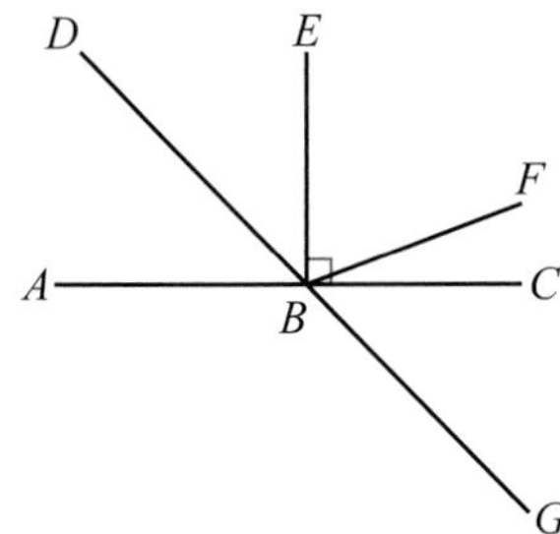

2 In each diagram, find the value of the angles marked with a letter.

(a)

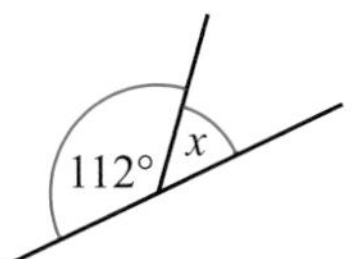

(b)

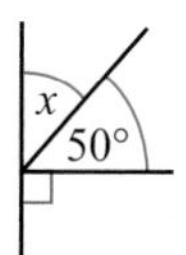

(c)

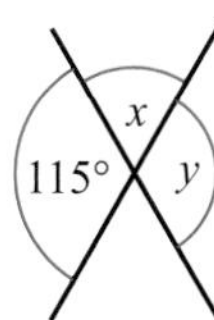

(d)

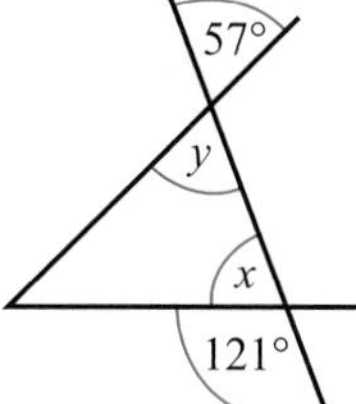

(e)

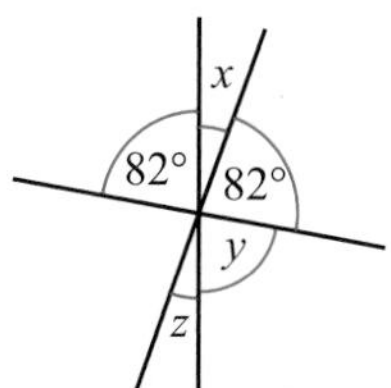

(f)

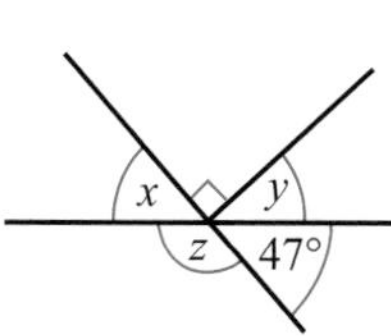

(g)

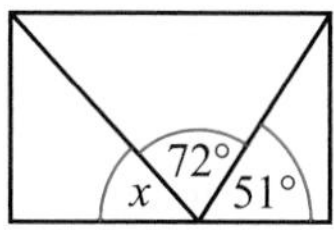

(h)

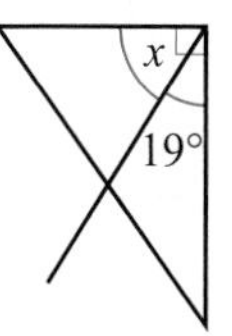

(i)

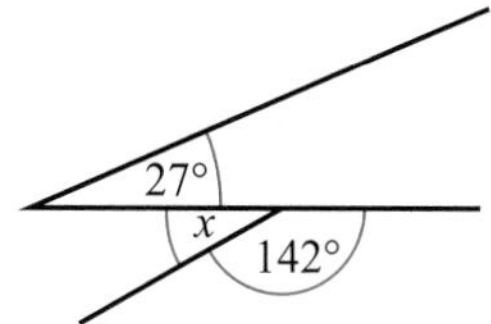

3 Find the value of x in each of the following figures.

(a)

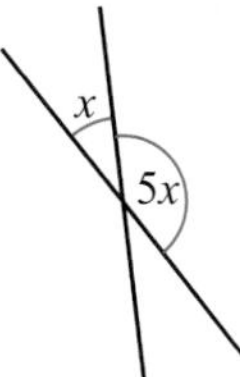

(b)

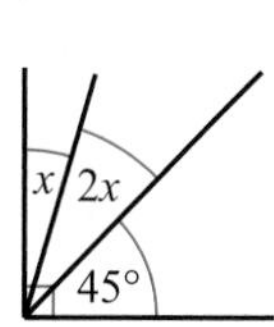

(c)

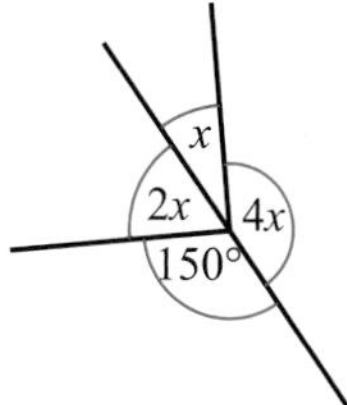

4 Two angles are supplementary. The first angle is twice the size of the second. What are their sizes?

5 One of the angles formed when two lines intersect is 127°. What are the sizes of the other three angles?

Angles and parallel lines

When two parallel lines are cut by a third line (the transversal) eight angles are formed. These angles form pairs which are related to each other in specific ways.

Corresponding angles ('*F*'-shape)

When two parallel lines are cut by a transversal four pairs of **corresponding** angles are formed. Corresponding angles are equal to each other.

> **Tip**
> Although '*F*', '*Z*' and '*C*' shapes help you to remember these properties, you must use the terms 'corresponding', 'alternate' and 'co-interior' to describe them when you answer a question.

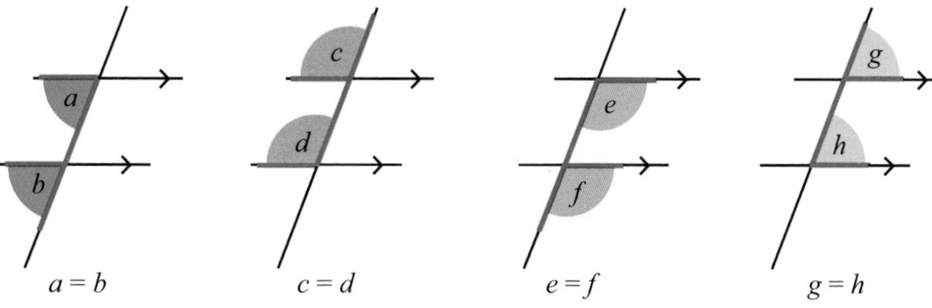

$a = b$ $c = d$ $e = f$ $g = h$

Alternate angles ('Z'-shape)

When two parallel lines are cut by a transversal two pairs of **alternate** angles are formed. Alternate angles are equal to each other.

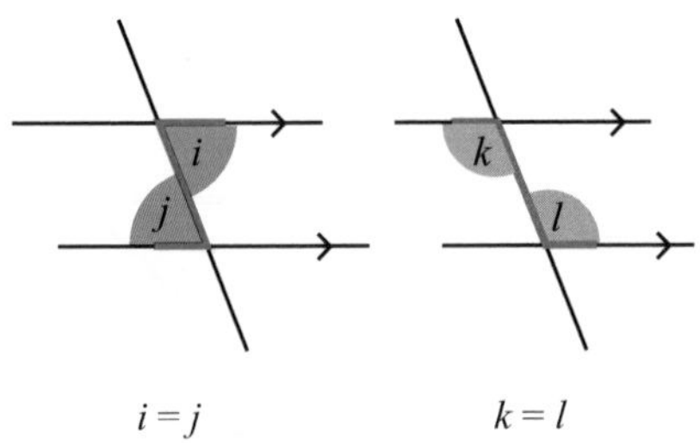

$i = j$ $\qquad$ $k = l$

> Co-interior angles will only be equal if the transversal is perpendicular to the parallel lines (when they will both be 90°).

> 'Co-' means together. Co-interior angles are found together on the same side of the transversal.

Co-interior angles ('C'-shape)

When two parallel lines are cut by a transversal two pairs of **co-interior** angles are formed. Co-interior angles are supplementary (together they add up to 180°).

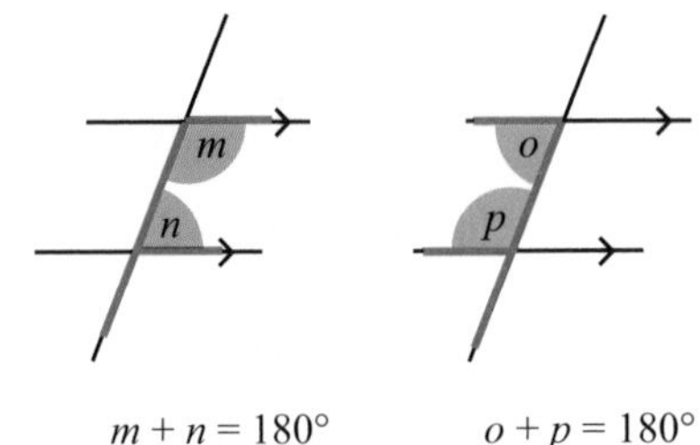

$m + n = 180°$ $\qquad$ $o + p = 180°$

> **FAST FORWARD**
> You will use the angle relationships in this section again when you deal with triangles, quadrilaterals, polygons and circles. ▶

These angle relationships around parallel lines, combined with the other angle relationships from earlier in the chapter, are very useful for solving unknown angles in geometry.

Worked example 4

Find the size of angles *a*, *b* and *c* in this figure.

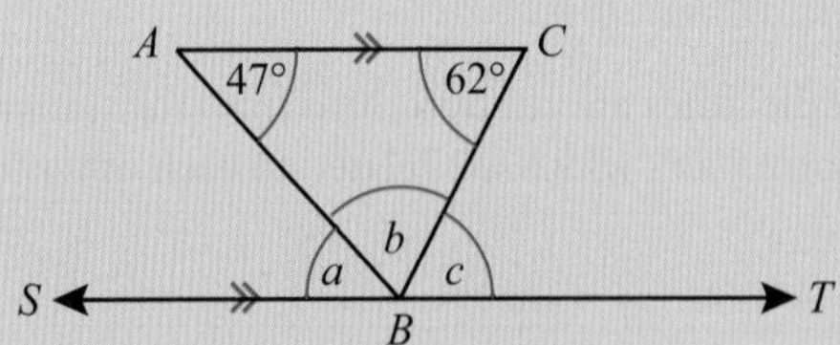

$a = 47°(\angle CAB \text{ alt } \angle SBA)$ $c = 62° \ (\angle ACB \text{ alt } \angle CBT)$ $a + b + c = 180° \ (\angle\text{s on line})$ $\therefore b = 180° - 47° - 62°$ $b = 71°$	$\angle CAB$ and $\angle SBA$ are alternate angles and therefore are equal in size. $\angle ACB$ and $\angle CBT$ are alternate angles and so equal in size. Angles on a straight line = 180°. You know the values of *a* and *c*, so can use these to find *b*.

Exercise 3.4

1 Calculate the size of all angles marked with variables in the following diagrams. Give reasons.

(a)
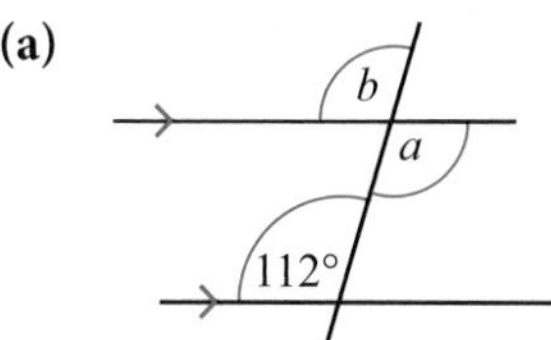

(b)
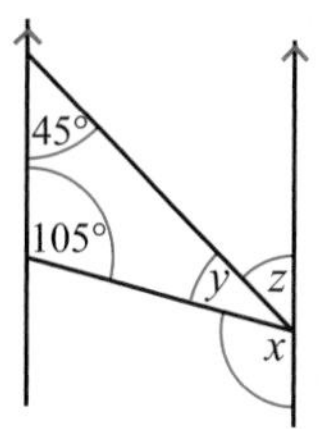

(c)
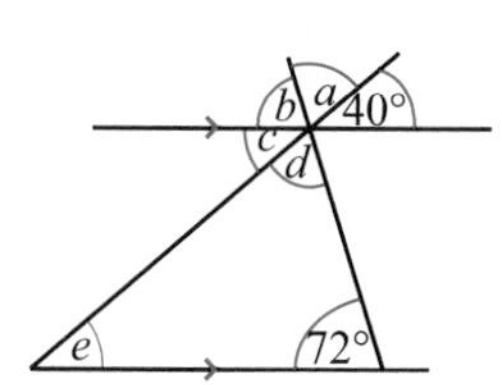

(d)
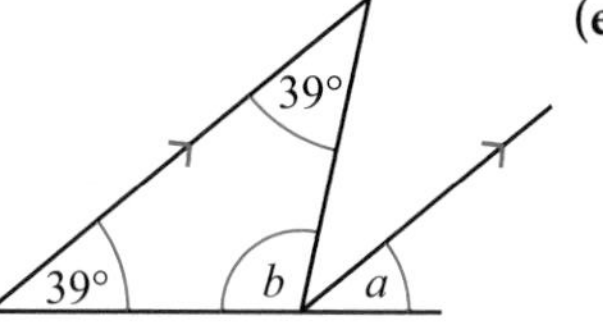

(e)
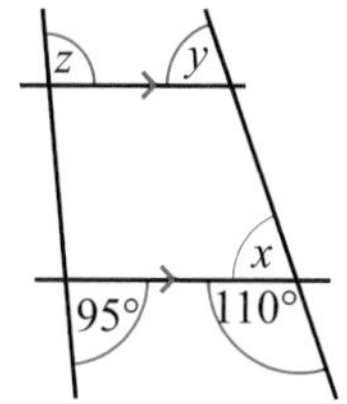

(f)
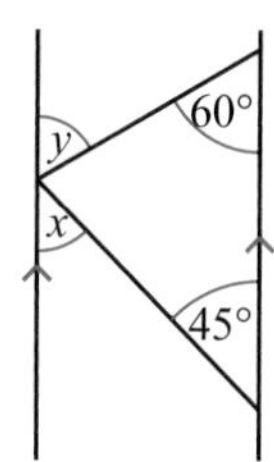

(g)
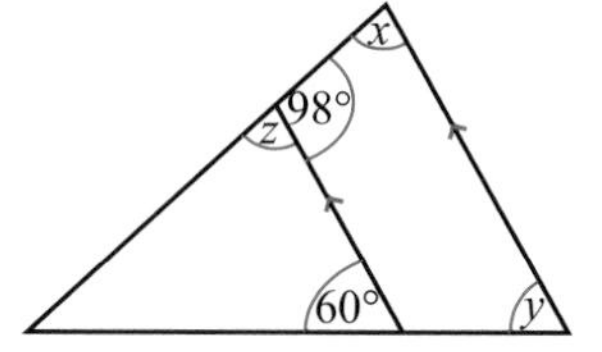

(h)
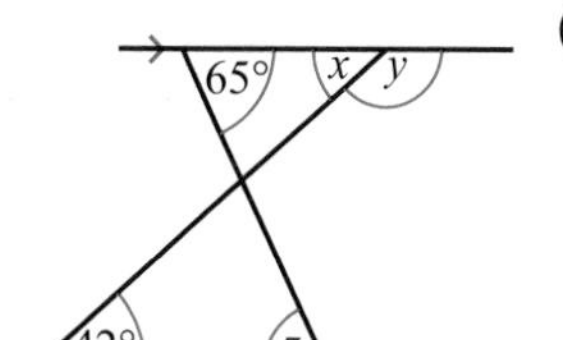

(i)
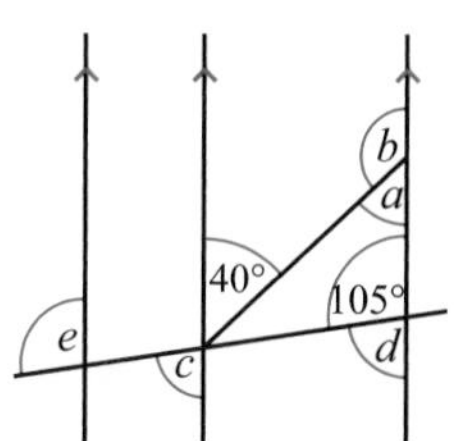

2 Decide whether $AB \parallel DC$ in each of these examples. Give a reason for your answer.

(a)
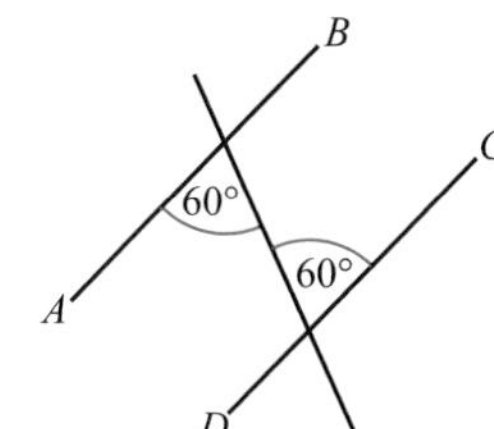

(b)
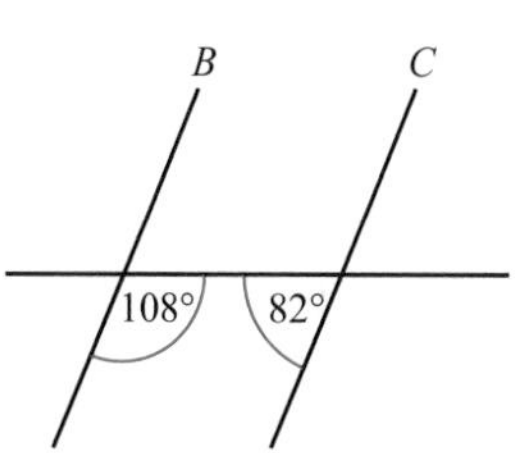

(c)
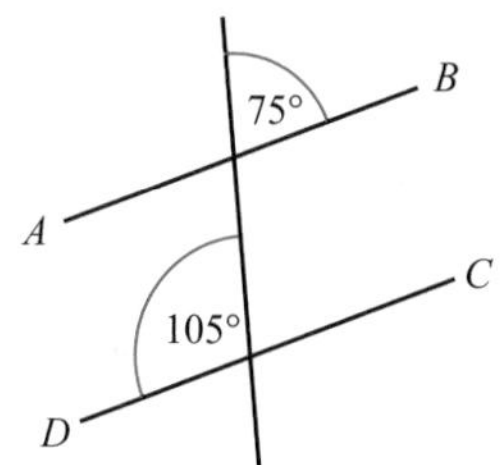

3.2 Triangles

Plane means flat. Plane shapes are flat or two-dimensional shapes.

A **triangle** is a plane shape with three sides and three angles.

Triangles are classified according to the lengths of their sides and the sizes of their angles (or both).

FAST FORWARD

You will need these properties in chapter 11 on Pythagoras' theorem and similar triangles, and in chapter 15 for trigonometry. ▶

Scalene triangle

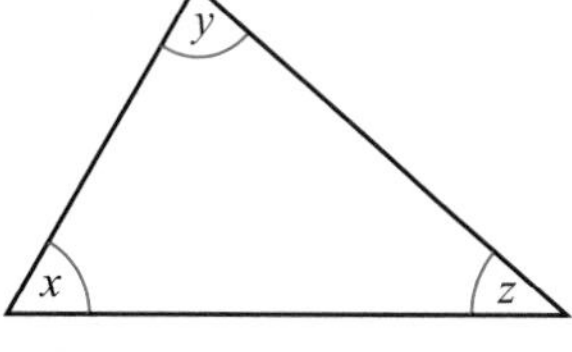

Scalene triangles have no sides of equal length and no angles that are of equal sizes.

Isosceles triangle

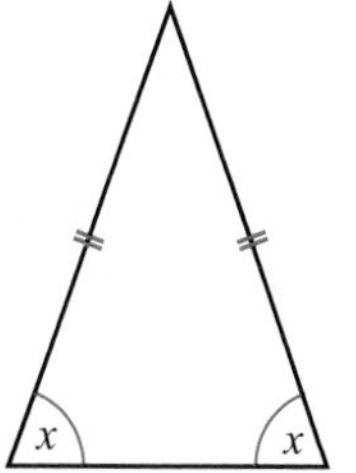

Isosceles triangles have two sides of equal length. The angles at the bases of the equal sides are equal in size.

Equilateral triangle

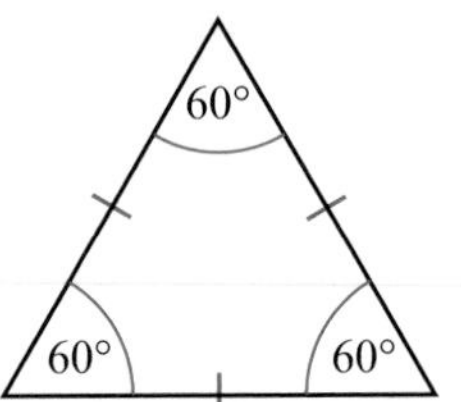

Equilateral triangles have three equal sides and three equal angles (each being 60°).

Other triangles

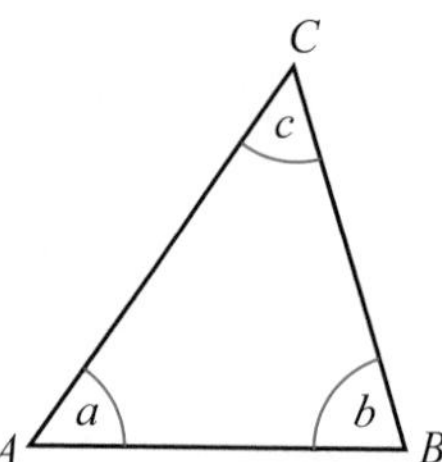

Acute-angled triangles have three angles each < 90°.

A
90°
B
C

Right-angled triangles have one angle = 90°.

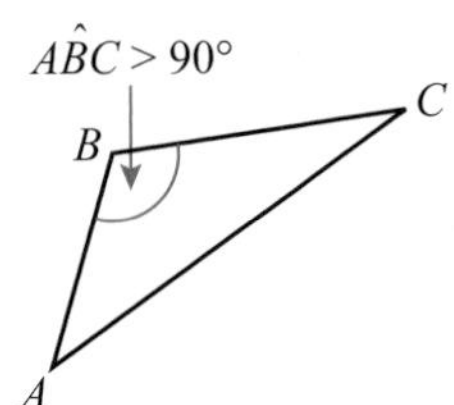

Obtuse-angled triangles have one angle > 90°.

Angle properties of triangles

The three angles inside a triangle are called interior angles.

If you extend a side of a triangle you make another angle outside the triangle. Angles outside the triangle are called exterior angles.

Look at the diagram below carefully to see two important angle properties of triangles.

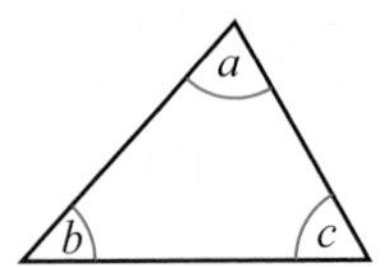

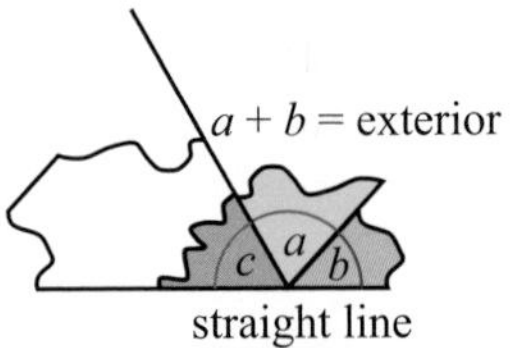

The diagram shows two things:

- The three interior angles of a triangle add up to 180°.
- Two interior angles of a triangle are equal to the opposite exterior angle.

You don't need to know these proofs, but you do need to remember the rules associated with them.

If you try this yourself with any triangle you will get the same results. But why is this so? Mathematicians cannot just show things to be true, they have to prove them using mathematical principles. Read through the following two simple proofs that use the properties of angles you already know, to show that angles in a triangle will always add up to 180° and that the exterior angle will always equal the sum of the opposite interior angles.

Angles in a triangle add up to 180°

To prove this you have to draw a line parallel to one side of the triangle.

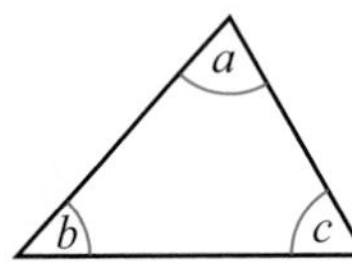

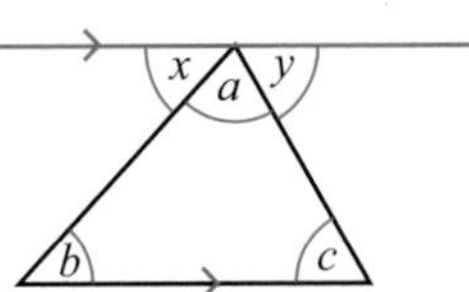

$x + a + y = 180°$ (angles on a line)

but:

$b = x$ and $c = y$ (alternate angles are equal)

so $a + b + c = 180°$

The exterior angle is equal to the sum of the opposite interior angles

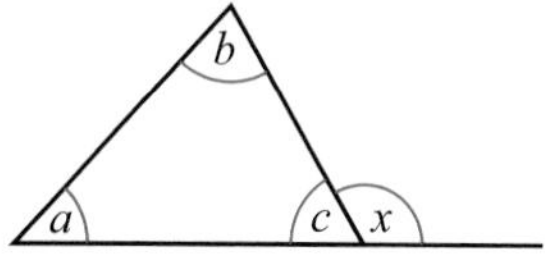

FAST FORWARD

Some of the algebraic processes used here are examples of the solutions to linear equations. You've done this before, but it is covered in more detail in chapter 14. ▶

$c + x = 180°$ (angles on a line)

so, $c = 180° - x$

$a + b + c = 180°$ (angle sum of triangle)

$c = 180° - (a + b)$

so, $180° - (a + b) = 180° - x$

hence, $a + b = x$

These two properties allow us to find the missing angles in triangles and other diagrams involving triangles.

Worked example 5

FAST FORWARD

Many questions on trigonometry require you to make calculations like these before you can move on to solve the problem. ▶

Find the value of the unknown angles in each triangle. Give reasons for your answers.

(a)

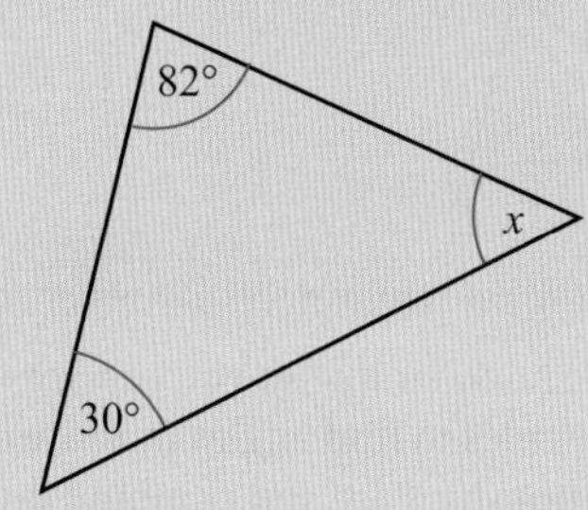

(a) $82° + 30° + x = 180°$ (angle sum of triangle)

$x = 180° - 82° - 30°$

$x = 68°$

(b)

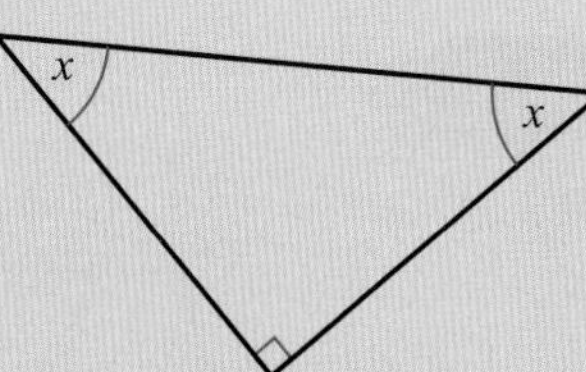

(b) $2x + 90° = 180°$ (angle sum of triangle)

$2x = 180° - 90°$

$2x = 90°$

$x = 45°$

(c)

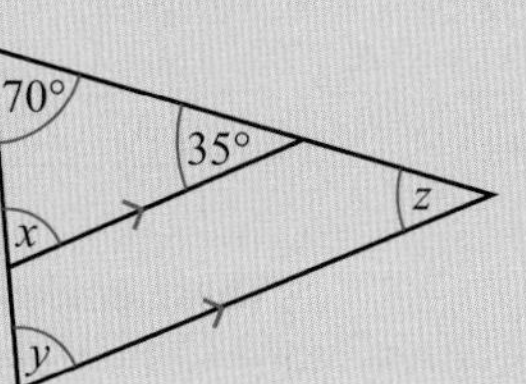

(c) $70° + 35° + x = 180°$ (angle sum of triangle)

$x = 180° - 70° - 35°$

$x = 75°$

$y = 75°$ (corresponding angles)

$70° + y + z = 180°$

$70° + 75° + z = 180°$ (angle sum of triangle)

$z = 180° - 75° - 70°$

$z = 35°$

or $z = 35°$ (corresponding angles)

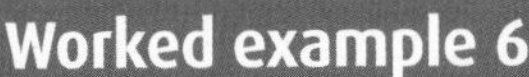

Worked example 6

Find the size of angles *x*, *y* and *z*.

(a)

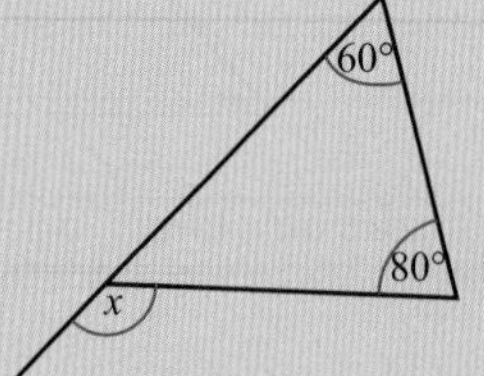

(a) $x = 60° + 80°$
$x = 140°$

(exterior angle of triangle)

(b)

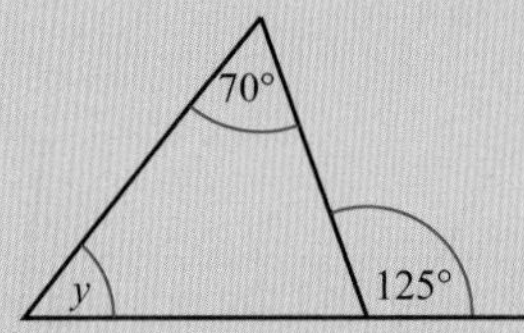

(b) $y + 70° = 125°$
$y = 125° - 70°$
$y = 55°$

(exterior angle of triangle)

(c)

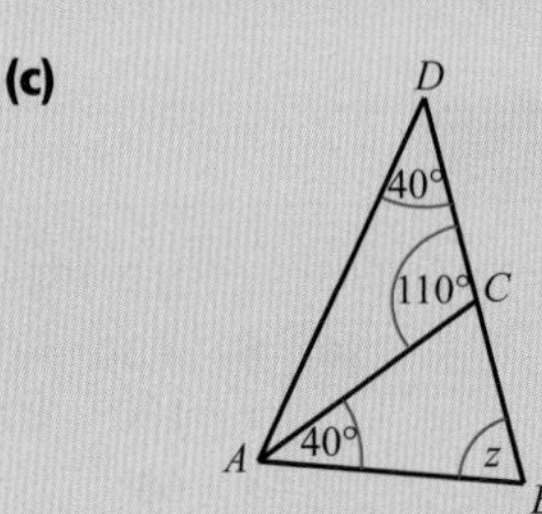

(c) $40° + z = 110°$
$z = 110° - 40°$
$z = 70°$

(exterior angle triangle *ABC*)

The exterior angle of one triangle may be inside another triangle as in worked example 6, part (c).

The examples above are fairly simple so you can see which rule applies. In most cases, you will be expected to apply these rules to find angles in more complicated diagrams. You will need to work out what the angle relationships are and combine them to find the solution.

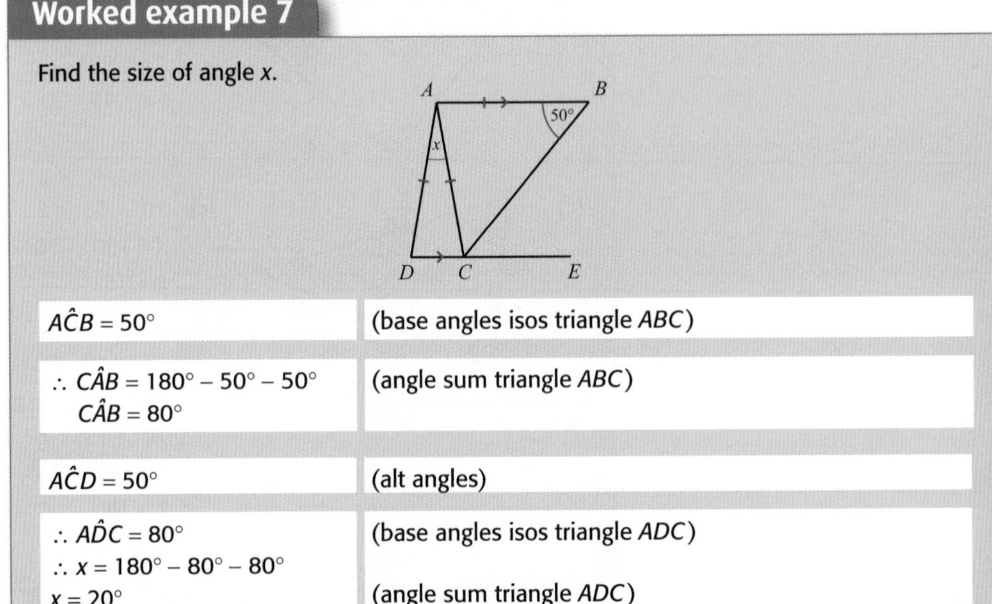

Worked example 7

Find the size of angle *x*.

$A\hat{C}B = 50°$	(base angles isos triangle *ABC*)
$\therefore C\hat{A}B = 180° - 50° - 50°$ $C\hat{A}B = 80°$	(angle sum triangle *ABC*)
$A\hat{C}D = 50°$	(alt angles)
$\therefore A\hat{D}C = 80°$ $\therefore x = 180° - 80° - 80°$ $x = 20°$	(base angles isos triangle *ADC*) (angle sum triangle *ADC*)

REWIND

An isosceles triangle has two sides and two angles equal, so if you know that the triangle is isosceles you can mark the two angles at the bases of the equal sides as equal. ◀

Exercise 3.5

1 Find the size of the marked angles. Give reasons.

(a)

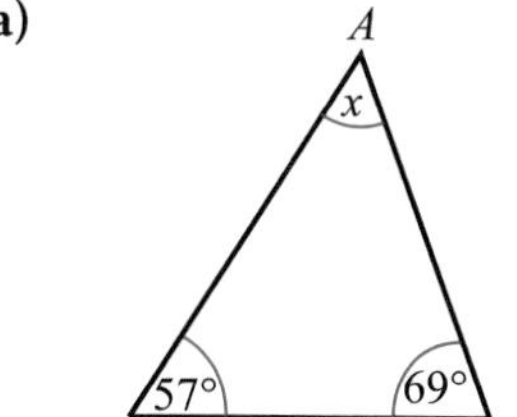

(b) M, 48°, x, N, O

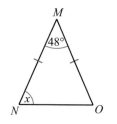

(c)

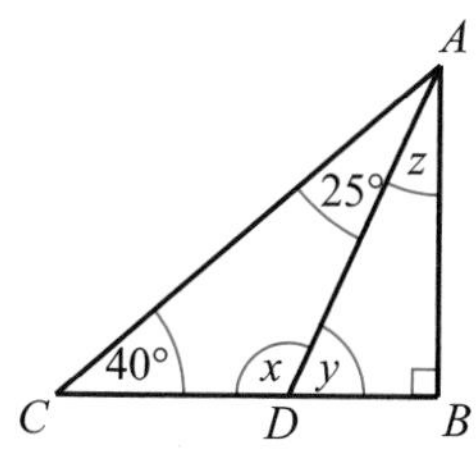

2 Calculate the value of x in each case. Give reasons.

(a)

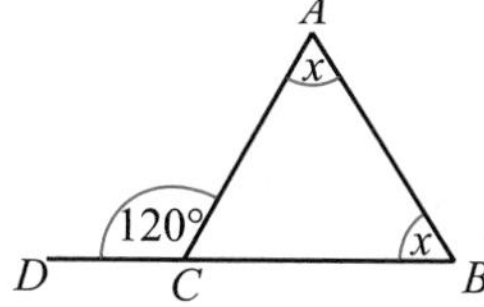

(b)

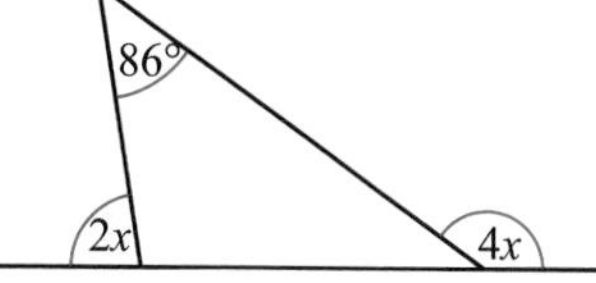

3 What is the size of the angle marked x in these figures? Show all steps and give reasons.

(a)

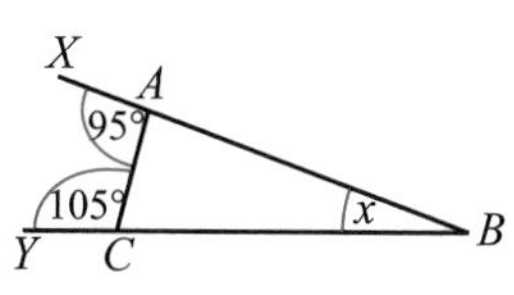

(b)

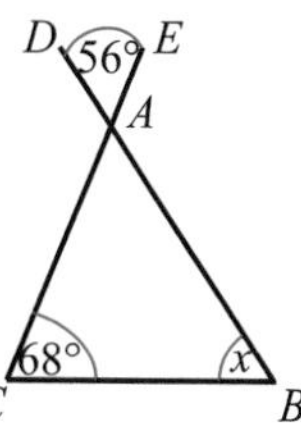

(c)

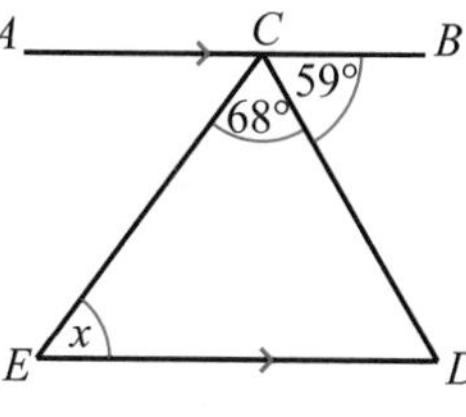

(d)

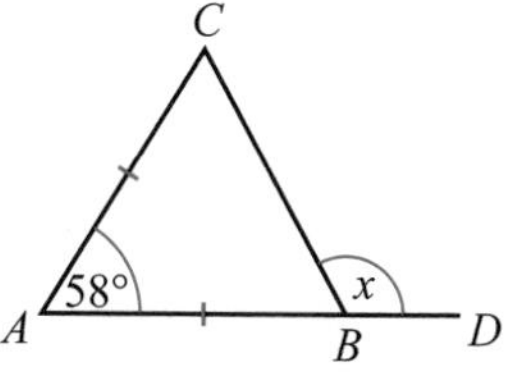

(e)

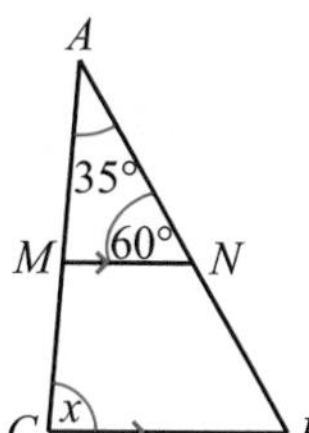

(f)

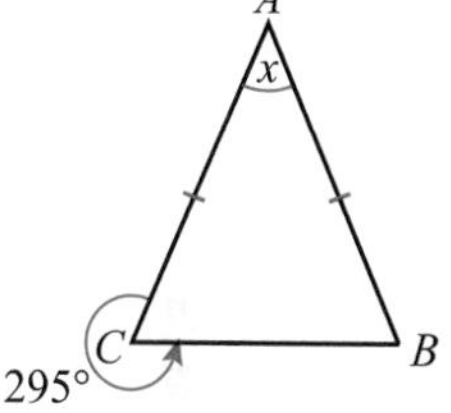

3.3 Quadrilaterals

Quadrilaterals are plane shapes with four sides and four interior angles. Quadrilaterals are given special names according to their properties.

Some of these shapes are actually 'special cases' of others. For example, a square is also a rectangle because opposite sides are equal and parallel and all angles are 90°. Similarly, any rhombus is also a parallelogram. In both of these examples the converse is not true! A rectangle is not also a square. Which other special cases can you think of?

Type of quadrilateral	Examples	Summary of properties
Parallelogram	$a = c \quad b = d$	Opposite sides parallel and equal. Opposite angles are equal. Diagonals bisect each other.
Rectangle		Opposite sides parallel and equal. All angles = 90°. Diagonals are equal. Diagonals bisect each other.
Square		All sides equal. All angles = 90°. Diagonals equal. Diagonals bisect each other at 90°. Diagonals bisect angles.

Type of quadrilateral	Examples	Summary of properties
Rhombus	$a = c \quad b = d$	All sides equal in length. Opposite sides parallel. Opposite angles equal. Diagonals bisect each other at 90°. Diagonals bisect angles.
Trapezium		One pair of sides parallel.
Kite	$a = b \quad c = d$	Two pairs of adjacent sides equal. One pair of opposite angles is equal. Diagonals intersect at 90°. Diagonals bisect angles.

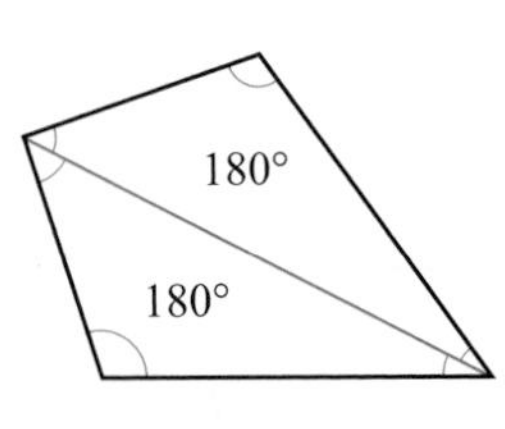

180°
180°

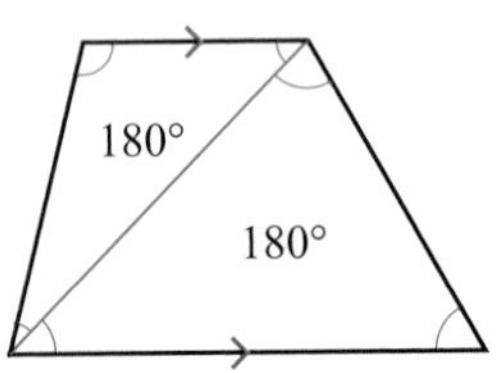

The angle sum of a quadrilateral

All quadrilaterals can be divided into two triangles by drawing one diagonal. You already know that the angle sum of a triangle is 180°. Therefore, the angle sum of a quadrilateral is 180° + 180° = 360°.

This is an important property and we can use it together with the other properties of quadrilaterals to find the size of unknown angles.

Worked example 8

Find the size of the marked angles in each of these figures.

(a) Parallelogram

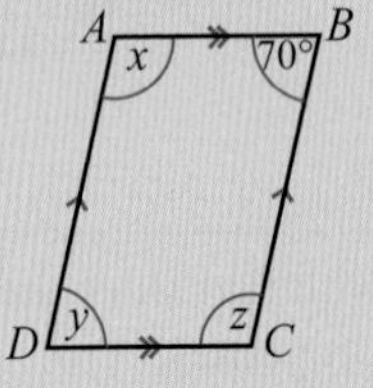

(a) $x = 110°$ (co-interior ∠s)
$y = 70°$ (opposite ∠s of || gram)
$z = 110°$ (opposite ∠s of || gram)

(b) Rectangle

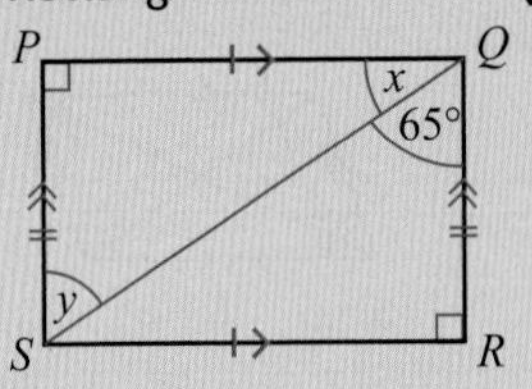

(b) $x + 65° = 90°$ (right angle of rectangle)
$\therefore x = 90° - 65°$
$x = 25°$
$y = 65°$ (alt angles)

(c) Quadrilateral

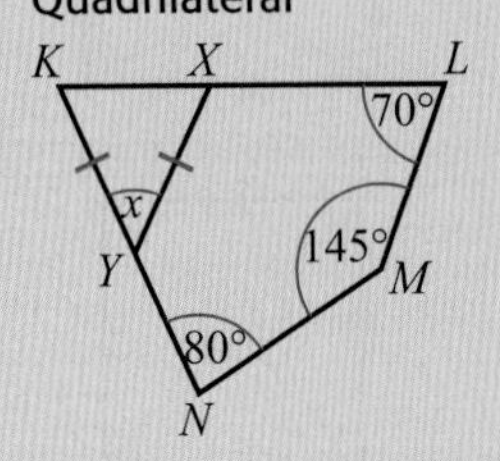

(c) $L\hat{K}N = 360° - 70° - 145° - 80°$ (angle sum of quad)
$L\hat{K}N = 65°$
$\therefore K\hat{X}Y = 65°$ (base angles isos triangle)
$\therefore x = 180° - 65° - 65°$ (angle sum triangle KXY)
$x = 50°$

Exercise 3.6

1 A quadrilateral has two diagonals that intersect at right angles.
   (a) What quadrilaterals could it be?
   (b) The diagonals are not equal in length. What quadrilaterals could it NOT be?

2 Find the value of x in each of these figures. Give reasons.

(a)
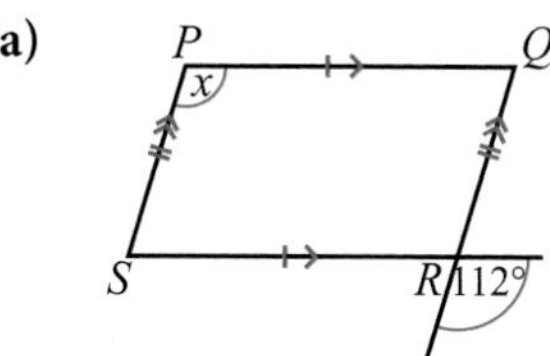

(b)
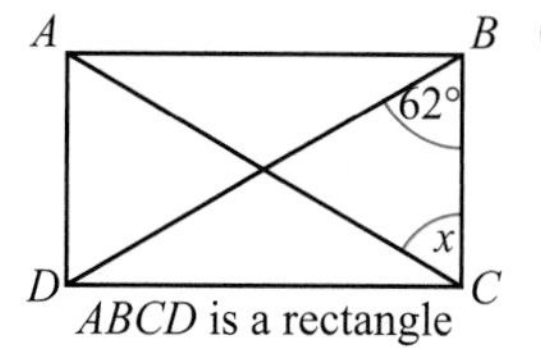

(c)
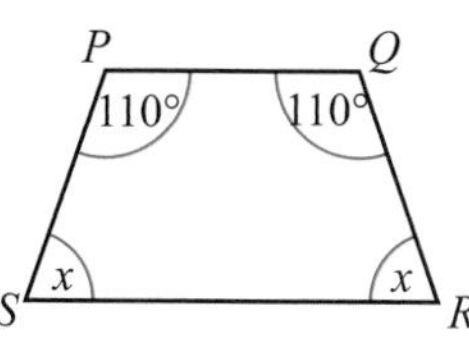

(d)
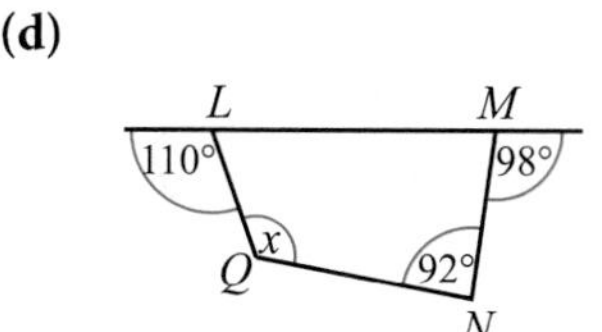

(e)
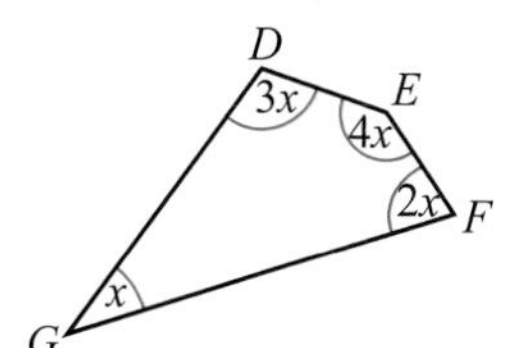

(f)
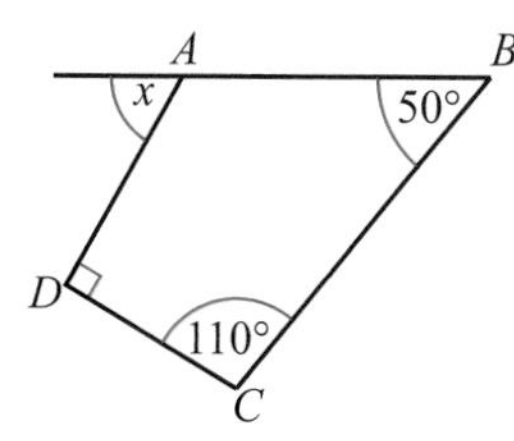

You may need to find some other unknown angles before you can find x. If you do this, write down the size of the angle that you have found and give a reason.

3 Find the value of x in each of these figures. Give reasons.

(a)
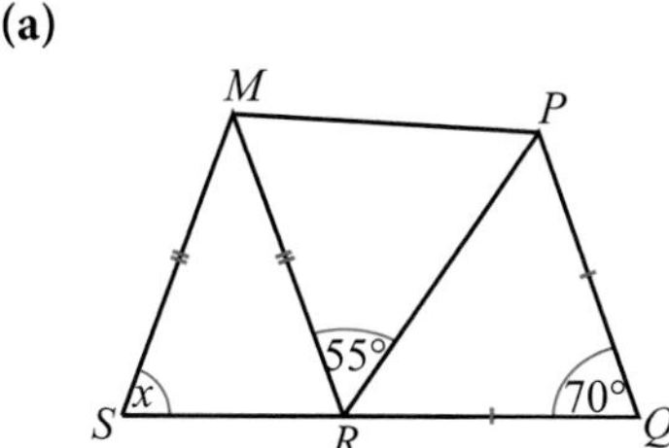

(b)
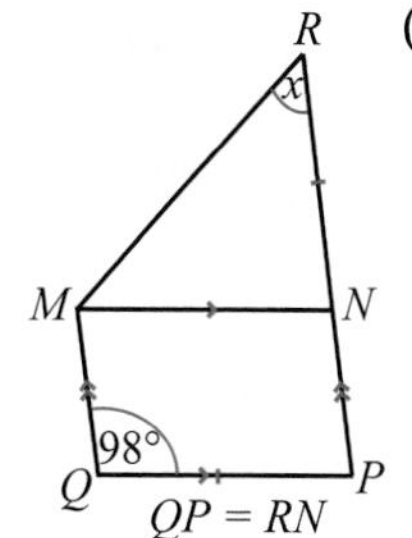

(c)
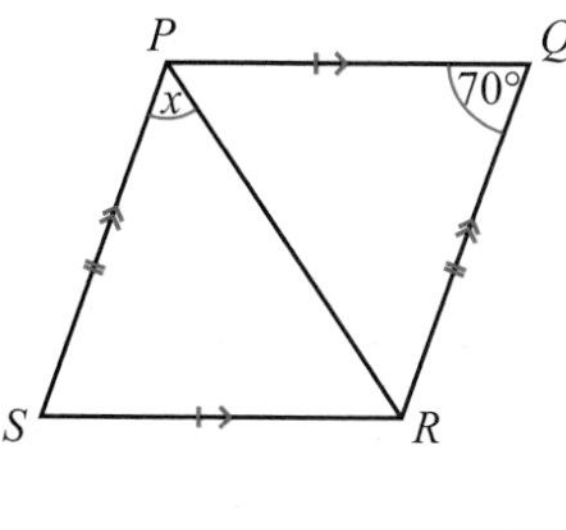

3.4 Polygons

A **polygon** is a plane shape with three or more straight sides. Triangles are polygons with three sides and quadrilaterals are polygons with four sides. Other polygons can also be named according to the number of sides they have. Make sure you know the names of these polygons:

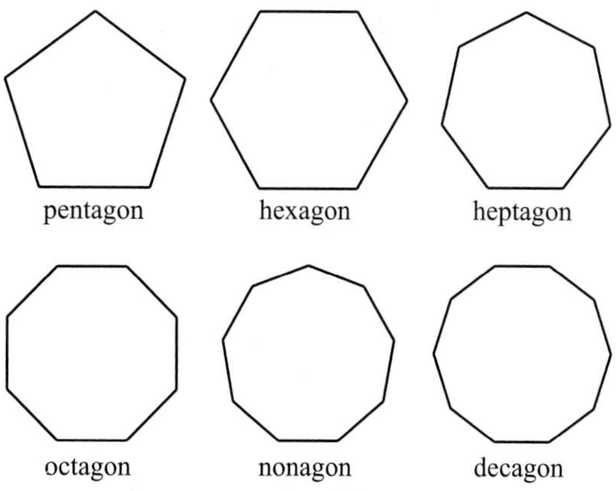

If a polygon has any reflex angles, it is called a concave polygon.

All other polygons are convex polygons.

A polygon with all its sides and all its angles equal is called a regular polygon.

Angle sum of a polygon

By dividing polygons into triangles, we can work out the sum of their interior angles.

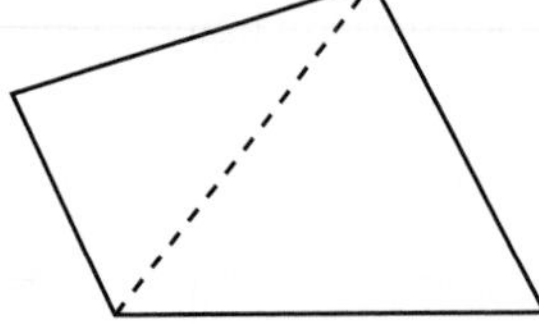
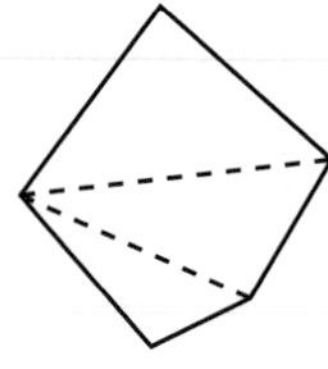
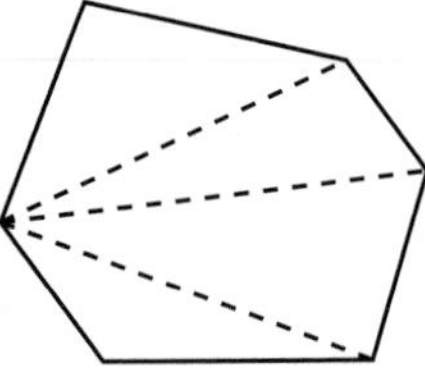

Can you see the pattern that is forming here?

The number of triangles you can divide the polygon into is always two less than the number of sides. If the number of sides is n, then the number of triangles in the polygon is $(n - 2)$.

The angle sum of the polygon is $180° \times$ the number of triangles. So for any polygon, the angle sum can be worked out using the formula:

sum of interior angles $= (n - 2) \times 180°$

Worked example 9

Find the angle sum of a decagon and state the size of each interior angle if the decagon is regular.

sum of interior angles $= (n - 2) \times 180°$	Sum of angles
$= (10 - 2) \times 180°$	A decagon has 10 sides, so $n = 10$.
$= 1440°$	
$= \frac{1440}{10}$	A regular decagon has 10 equal angles.
$= 144°$	Size of one angle

Worked example 10

A polygon has an angle sum of 2340°. How many sides does it have?

$2340° = (n - 2) \times 180°$	Put values into angle sum formula.
$\frac{2340}{180} = n - 2$	
$13 = n - 2$	Rearrange the formula to get n.
$13 + 2 = n$	
$\therefore\ 15 = n$	So the polygon has 15 sides.

The sum of exterior angles of a convex polygon

The sum of the exterior angles of a convex polygon is always 360°, no matter how many sides it has. Read carefully through the information about a hexagon that follows, to understand why this is true for every polygon.

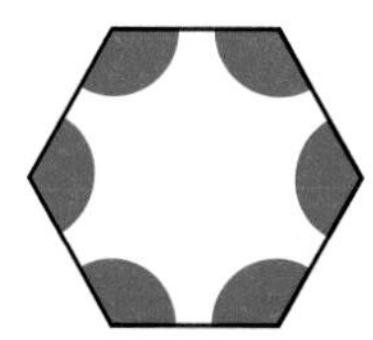

A hexagon has six interior angles.

$$\text{The angle sum of the interior angles} = (n-2)\times 180^\circ = 4\times 180^\circ = 720^\circ$$

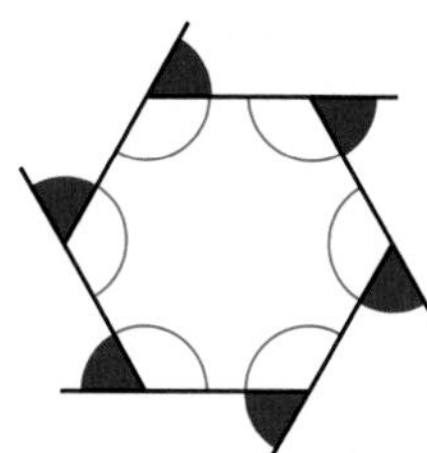

If you extend each side you make six exterior angles; one next to each interior angle.
Each pair of interior and exterior angles adds up to 180° (angles on line).
There are six vertices, so there are six pairs of interior and exterior angles that add up to 180°.

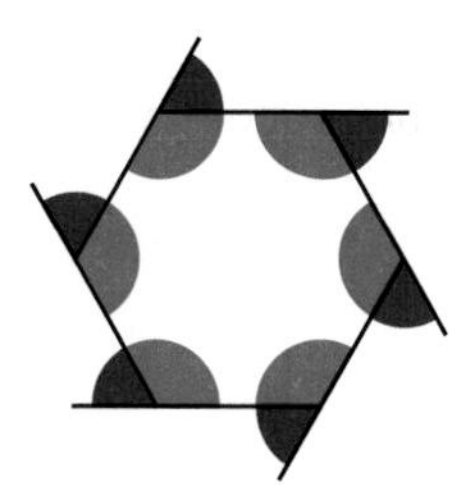

$$\therefore \text{ sum of (interior + exterior angles)} = 180\times 6 = 1080^\circ$$

$$\text{But, sum of interior angles} = (n-2)\times 180 = 4\times 180 = 720^\circ$$

$$\text{So, } 720^\circ + \text{sum of exterior angles} = 1080$$

$$\text{sum of exterior angles} = 1080 - 720$$

$$\text{sum of exterior angles} = 360^\circ$$

Tip

You do not have to remember this proof, but you must remember that the sum of the exterior angles of any convex polygon is 360°.

This can be expressed as a general rule like this:

If I = sum of the interior angles, E = sum of the exterior angles and n = number of sides of the polygon

$$I+E=180n$$

$$E=180n-I$$

but $I=(n-2)\times 180$

so $E=180n-(n-2)\times 180$

$$E=180n-180n+360$$

$$E=360^\circ$$

Exercise 3.7

A regular polygon has all sides equal and all angles equal. An irregular polygon does *not* have all equal sides and angles.

1 Copy and complete this table.

Number of sides in the polygon	5	6	7	8	9	10	12	20
Angle sum of interior angles								

2 Find the size of one interior angle for each of the following regular polygons.

(a) pentagon **(b)** hexagon **(c)** octagon
(d) decagon **(e)** dodecagon (12 sides) **(f)** a 25-sided polygon

3 A regular polygon has 15 sides. Find:

(a) the sum of the interior angles
(b) the sum of the exterior angles
(c) the size of each interior angle
(d) the size of each exterior angle.

4 A regular polygon has n exterior angles of 15°. How many sides does it have?

The rule for the sum of interior angles, and for the sum of exterior angles is true for both regular and irregular polygons. *But* with irregular polygons, you can't simply divide the sum of the interior angles by the number of sides to find the size of an interior angle: all interior angles may be different.

5 Find the value of x in each of these irregular polygons.

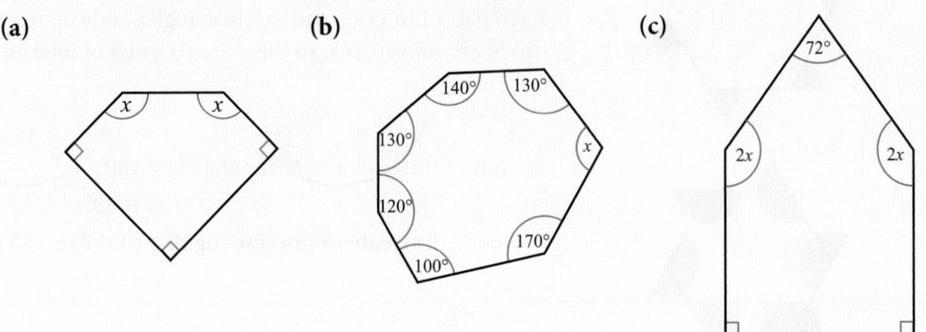

3.5 Circles

In mathematics, a **circle** is defined as a set of points which are all the same distance from a given fixed point. In other words, every point on the outside curved line around a circle is the same distance from the centre of the circle.

There are many mathematical terms used to talk about circles. Study the following diagrams carefully and then work through exercise 3.8 to make sure you know and can use the terms correctly.

Parts of a circle

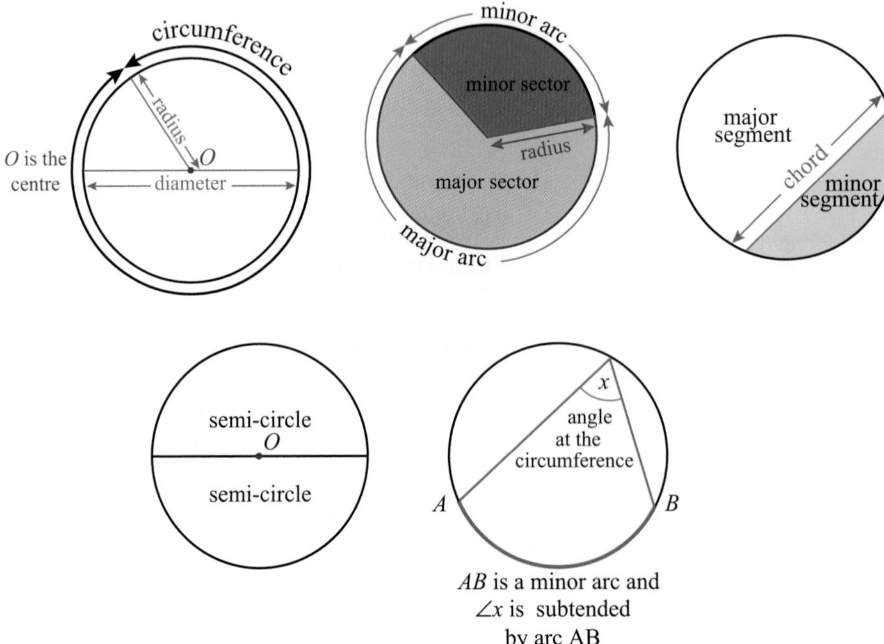

The angle x is subtended at the circumference. This means that it is the angle formed by two chords passing through the end points of the arc and meeting again at the edge of the circle.

Exercise 3.8

1 Name the features shown in blue on these circles.

(a) (b)

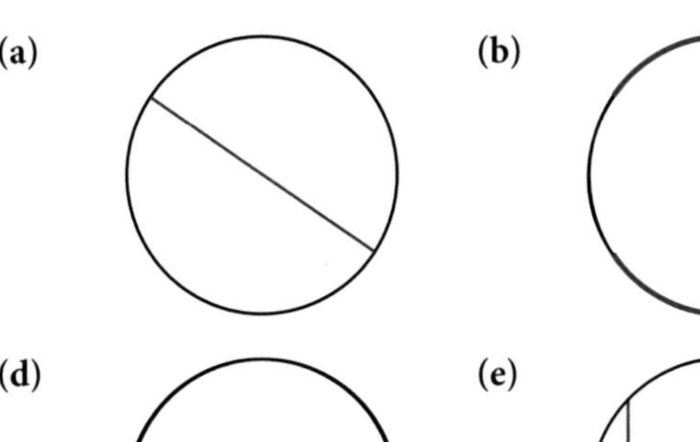

(c)

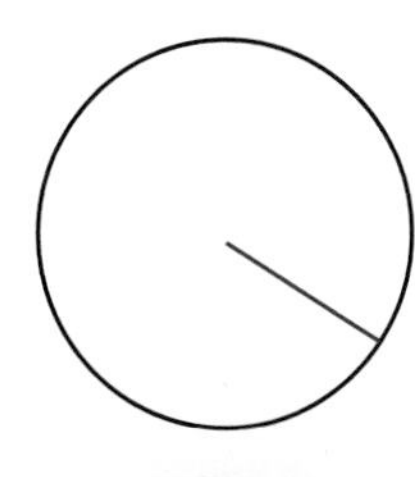

(d)

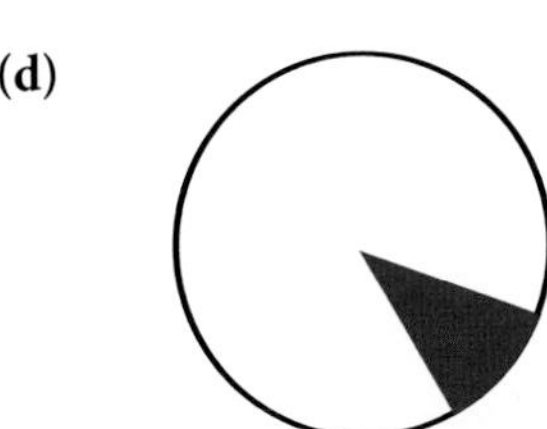

(e)

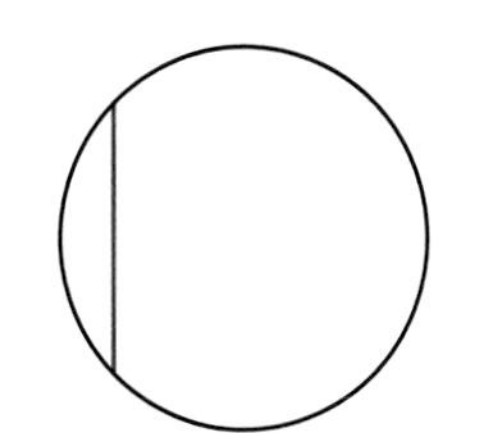

(f)

2 Draw four small circles. Use shading to show:

(a) a semi-circle
(b) a minor segment
(c) a tangent to the circle
(d) angle y subtended by a minor arc MN.

FAST FORWARD

You will learn more about circles and the angle properties in circles when you deal with circle symmetry and circle theorems in chapter 19. ▶

3 Circle 1 and circle 2 have the same centre (O). Use the correct terms or letters to copy and complete each statement.

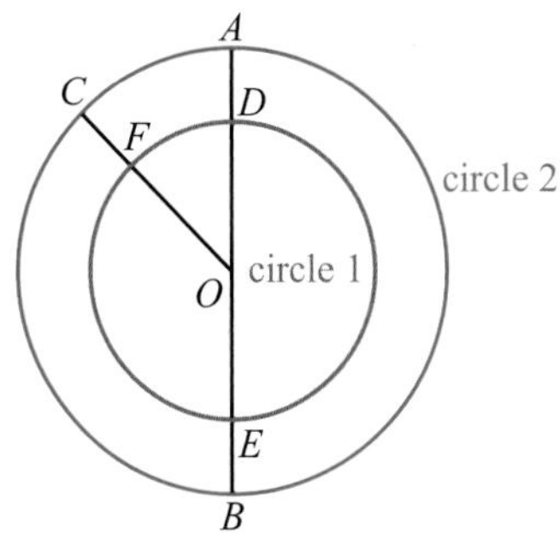

(a) OB is a __ of circle 2.
(b) DE is the __ of circle 1.
(c) AC is a __ of circle 2.
(d) __ is a radius of circle 1.
(e) CAB is a __ of circle 2.
(f) Angle FOD is the vertex of a __ of circle 1 and circle 2.

3.6 Construction

In geometry, constructions are accurate geometrical drawings. You use mathematical instruments to construct geometrical drawings.

The photograph shows you the basic equipment that you are expected to use.

It is important that you use a sharp pencil and that your pair of compasses are not loose.

Using a ruler and a pair of compasses

Your ruler (sometimes called a straight-edge) and a pair of compasses are probably your most useful construction tools. You use the ruler to draw straight lines and the pair of compasses to measure and mark lengths, draw circles and bisect angles and lines.

Once you can use a ruler and pair of compasses to measure and draw lines, you can easily construct triangles and other geometric shapes.

Do you remember how to use a pair of compasses to mark a given length? Here is an example showing you how to construct line *AB* that is 4.5 cm long. (Diagrams below are NOT TO SCALE.)

- Use a ruler and sharp pencil to draw a straight line that is longer than the length you need. Mark point *A* on the line with a short vertical dash (or a dot).

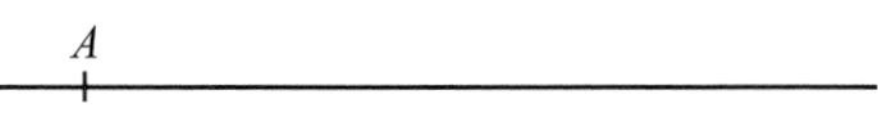

- Open your pair of compasses to 4.5 cm by measuring against a ruler.

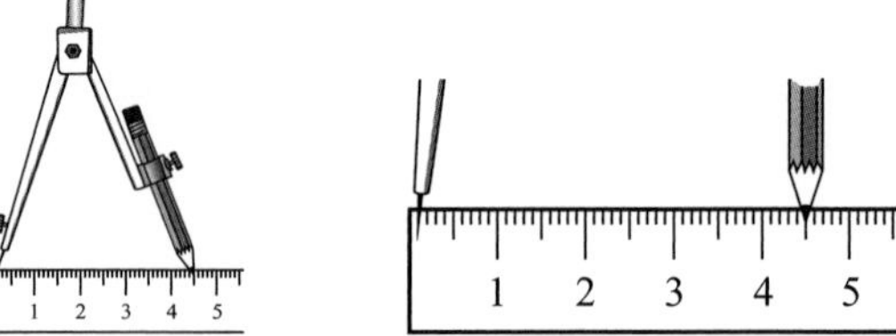

- Put the point of the pair of compasses on point *A*. Twist the pair of compasses lightly to draw a short arc on the line at 4.5 cm. Mark this as point *B*. You have now drawn the line *AB* at 4.5 cm long.

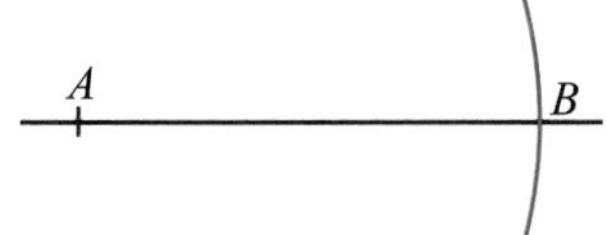

Bisecting a line

Bisect means cut in half. You can use your pair of compasses to bisect any line without measuring. Follow these steps:

- Start with a line. Make sure that points *A* and *B* are marked clearly.

- Open your pair of compasses to any width (but it must be more than half the length of the line).
- Put the point of the pair of compasses on *A*. Draw an arc above and below the line as shown.

- Put the point of the pair of compasses on *B*. Draw an arc above and below the line as shown.

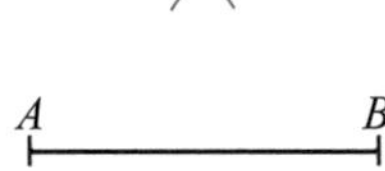

If the arcs don't cross, you have not opened the compasses enough.

- Use a ruler to draw a line through the points where the arcs cross. This line cuts *AB* in half.

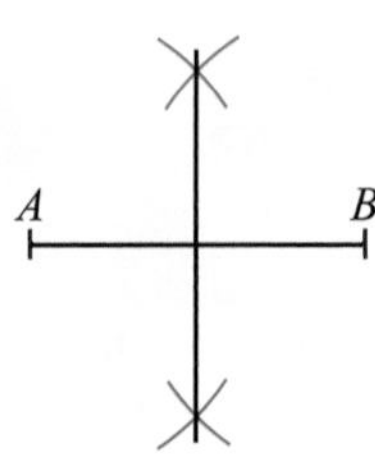

The point where the line cuts *AB* is called the midpoint of the line.

The line you have drawn is perpendicular to *AB*. We call it a **perpendicular bisector**.

Bisecting an angle

Follow these steps to bisect any angle:

- Start with an angle.

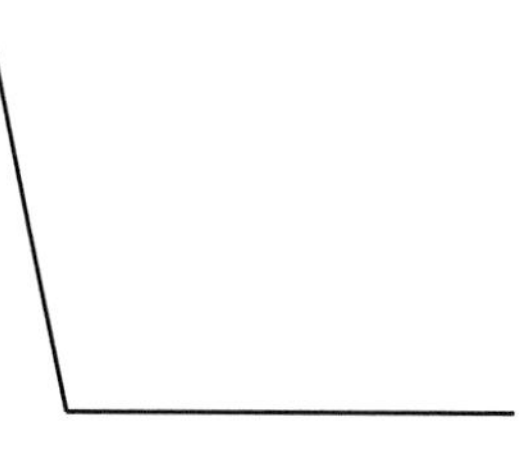

- Open the pair of compasses and put the point on the vertex of the angle. Draw an arc that cuts both arms of the angle.

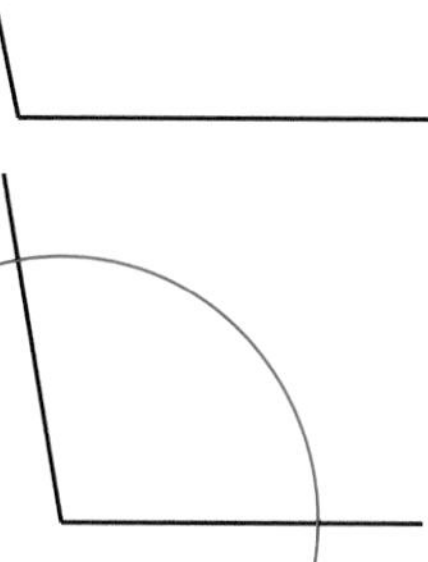

- Put the point of the compasses where the arc cuts one arm. Draw an arc.

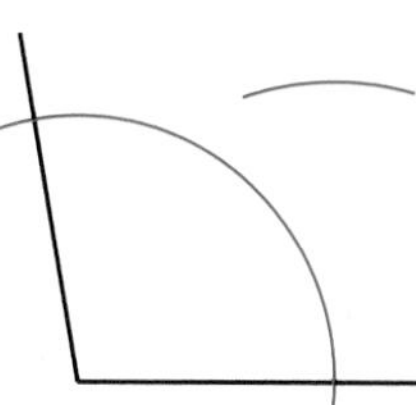

- Repeat this with for the other arm.

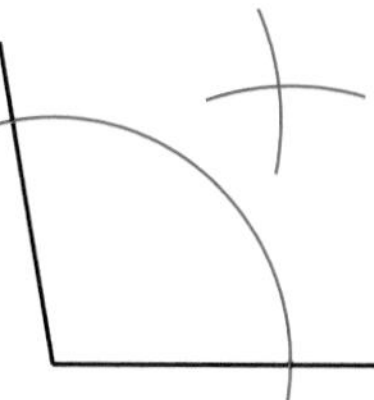

- Draw a line from the vertex through the point where the arcs cross.
- The angle has now been bisected.

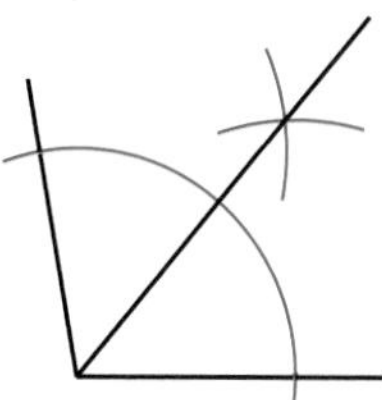

Exercise 3.9

1 Construct these lines.

(a) $AB = 6\,\text{cm}$ (b) $CD = 75\,\text{mm}$ (c) $EF = 5.5\,\text{cm}$

2 Bisect *AB*, *CD* and *EF*.

3 Draw any triangle *ABC*.

(a) Bisect each side of the triangle.
(b) Use the point where the perpendicular bisectors meet as the centre and draw a circle that passes through vertex *A* of the triangle.
(c) What do you notice about this circle?

4 Use a ruler and protractor to measure and draw these angles.

(a) $A\hat{B}C = 60°$ (b) $D\hat{E}F = 125°$ (c) $K\hat{L}M = 45°$

5 Bisect each angle drawn in question **4**.

Constructing triangles

If you are given enough information you can construct an accurate triangle. You can draw a triangle if you know:

- the lengths of three sides
- the lengths of two sides and the size of the angle between them
- the size of two angles and the length of the side between them.

Read through these worked examples carefully to see how to construct a triangle given each set of information.

Worked example 11

Construct ΔABC with $AB = 5$ cm, $BC = 6$ cm and $CA = 4$ cm.

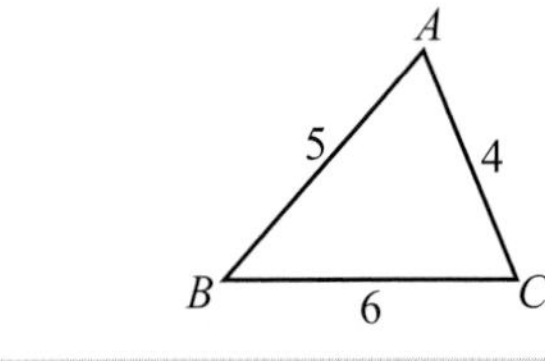

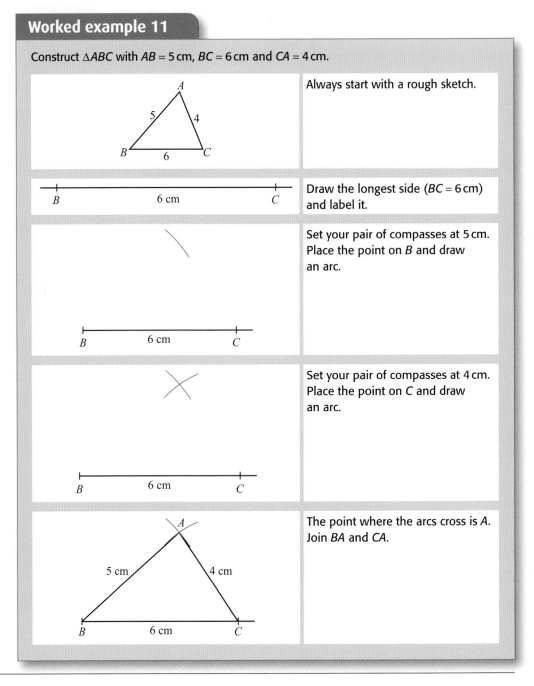

Always start with a rough sketch.

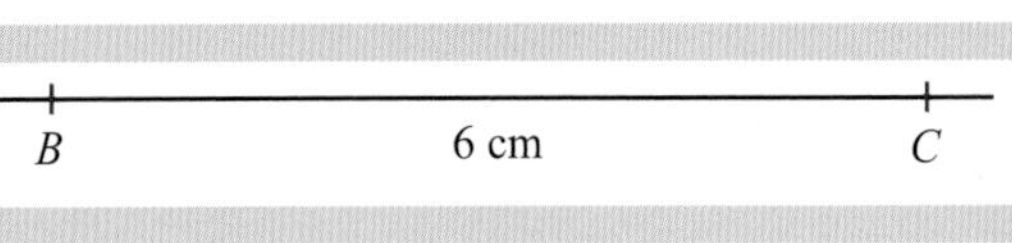

Draw the longest side ($BC = 6$ cm) and label it.

It is a good idea to draw the line longer than you need it and then measure the correct length along it. When constructing a shape, it can help to mark points with a thin line to make it easier to place the point of the pair of compasses.

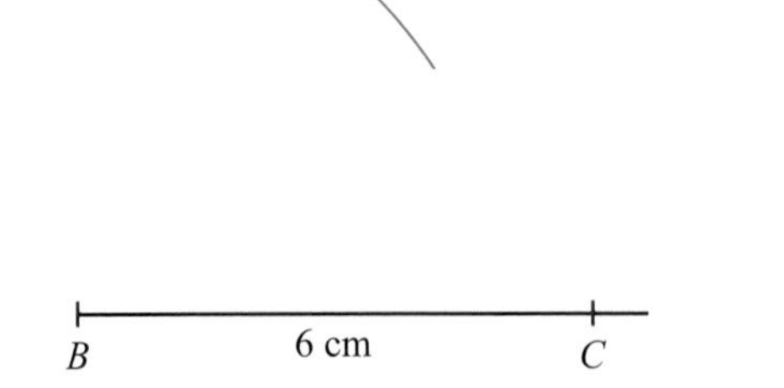

Set your pair of compasses at 5 cm. Place the point on B and draw an arc.

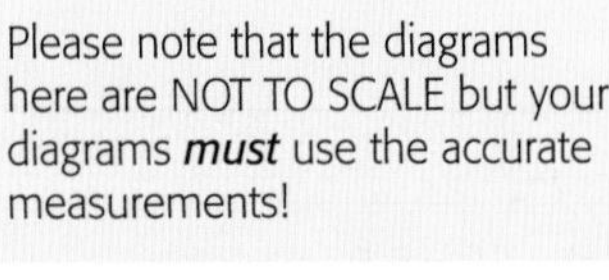

Please note that the diagrams here are NOT TO SCALE but your diagrams ***must*** use the accurate measurements!

Set your pair of compasses at 4 cm. Place the point on C and draw an arc.

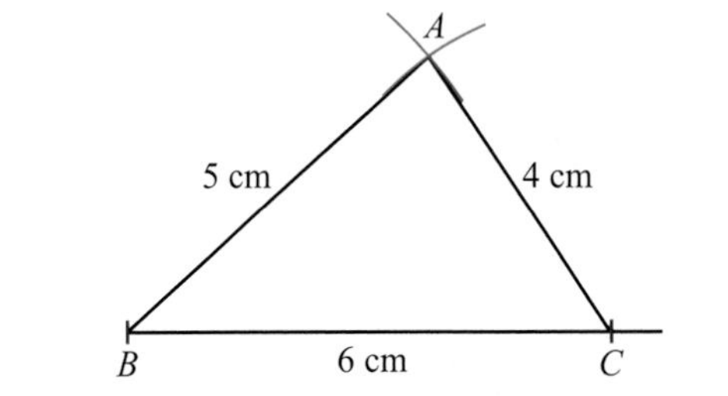

The point where the arcs cross is A. Join BA and CA.

REWIND

Remind yourself how to use a protractor from earlier in this chapter. ◀

Please note that the diagrams here are NOT TO SCALE but your diagrams ***must*** use the accurate measurements!

Worked example 12

Construct ΔXYZ with $Z\hat{X}Y = 40°$, $XY = 33$ mm and $XZ = 21$ mm.

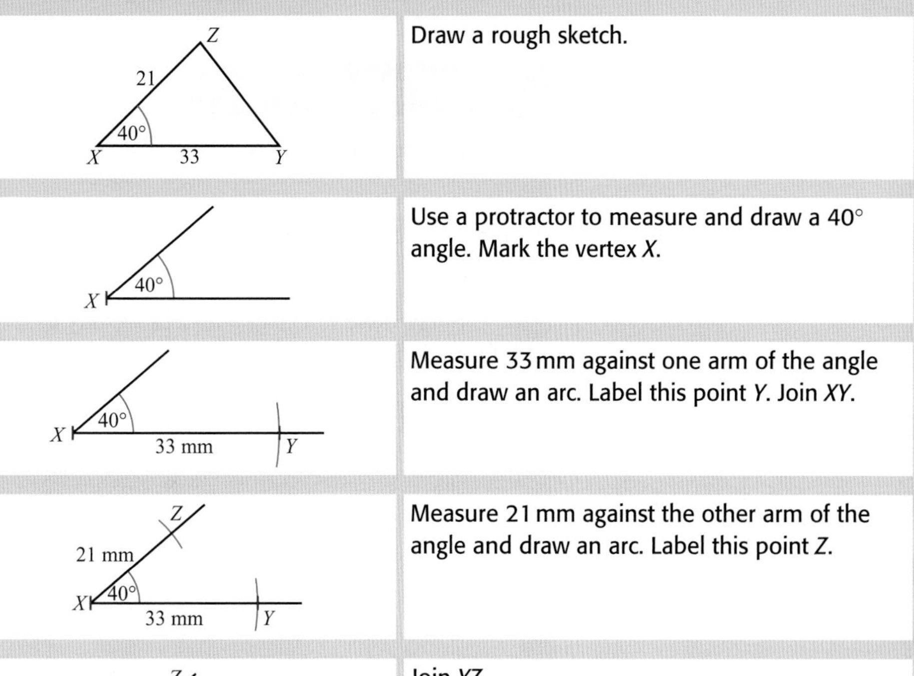

Draw a rough sketch.

Use a protractor to measure and draw a 40° angle. Mark the vertex *X*.

Measure 33 mm against one arm of the angle and draw an arc. Label this point *Y*. Join *XY*.

Measure 21 mm against the other arm of the angle and draw an arc. Label this point *Z*.

Join *YZ*.

Please note that the diagrams here are NOT TO SCALE but your diagrams ***must*** use the accurate measurements!

Worked example 13

Construct ΔPQR with $PQ = 4$ cm, $Q\hat{P}R = 80°$ and $R\hat{Q}P = 45°$.

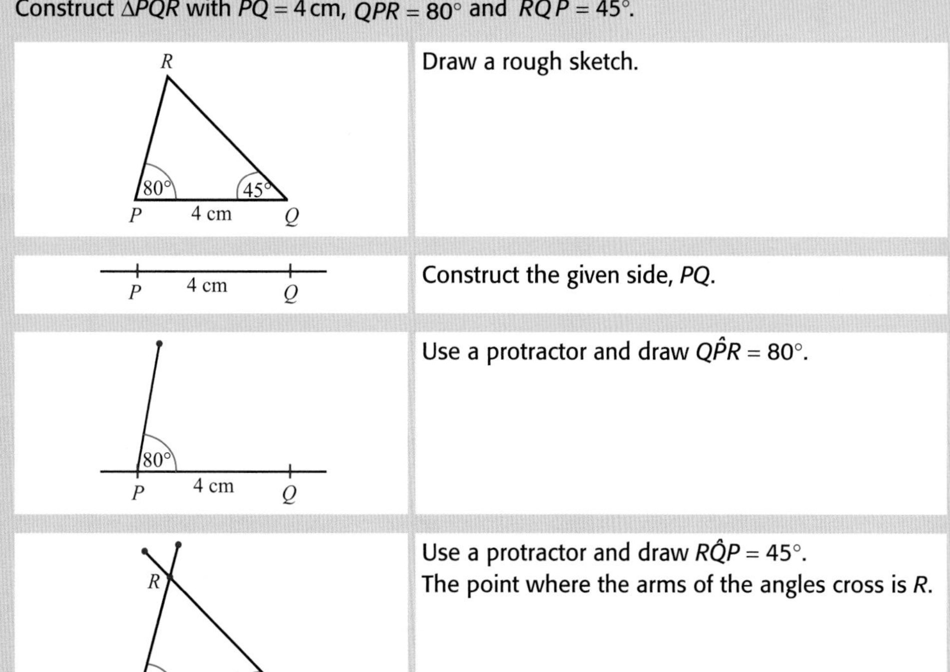

Draw a rough sketch.

Construct the given side, *PQ*.

Use a protractor and draw $Q\hat{P}R = 80°$.

Use a protractor and draw $R\hat{Q}P = 45°$.
The point where the arms of the angles cross is *R*.

Constructing other figures

You can combine what you have learned about drawing lines, angles and shapes to construct other geometrical figures. Worked example 14 shows you how to construct a square.

Please note that the diagrams here are NOT TO SCALE but your diagrams ***must*** use the accurate measurements!

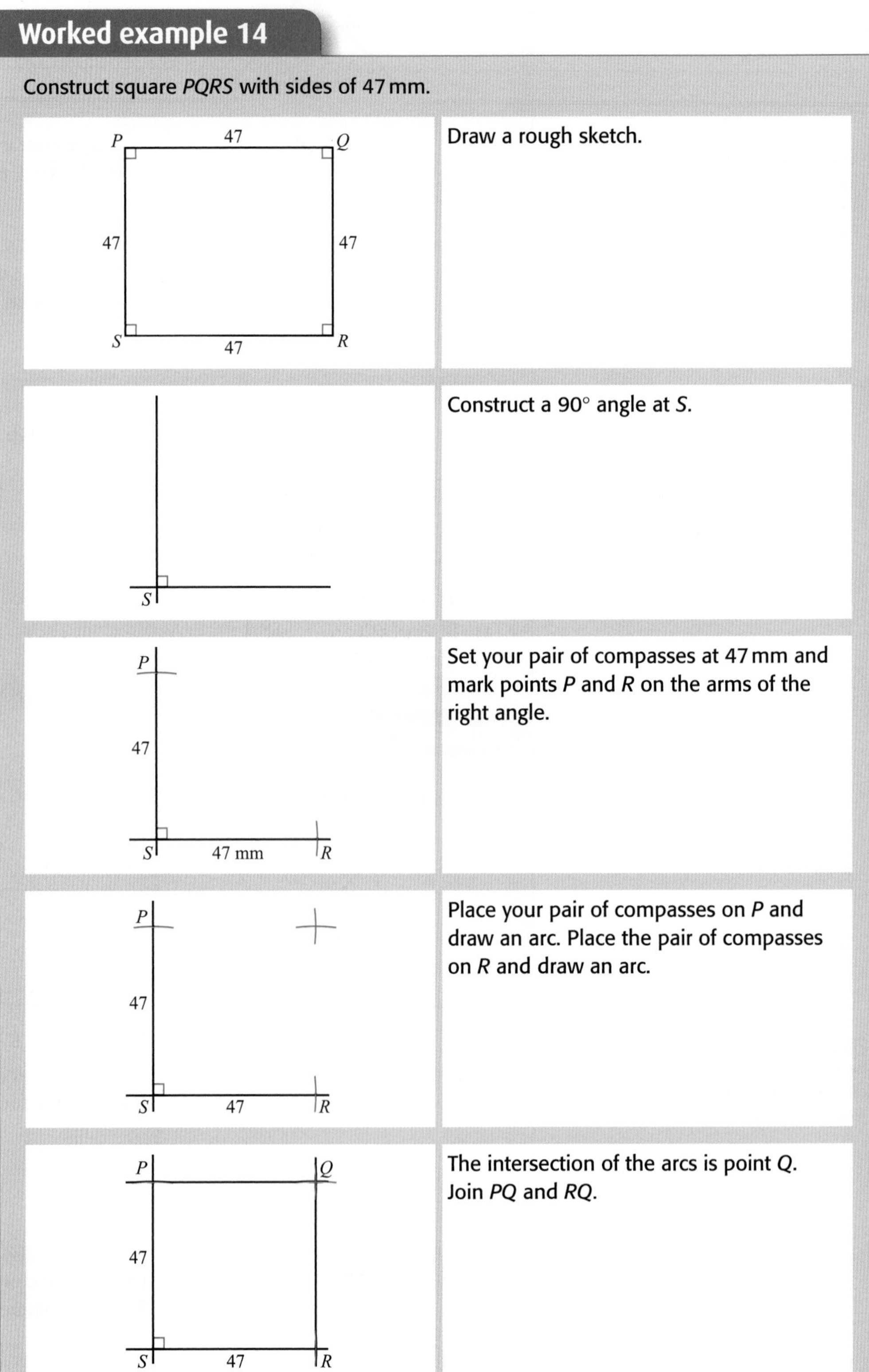

Worked example 14

Construct square *PQRS* with sides of 47 mm.

Draw a rough sketch.

Construct a 90° angle at *S*.

Set your pair of compasses at 47 mm and mark points *P* and *R* on the arms of the right angle.

Place your pair of compasses on *P* and draw an arc. Place the pair of compasses on *R* and draw an arc.

The intersection of the arcs is point *Q*. Join *PQ* and *RQ*.

Exercise 3.10

1 Accurately construct these triangles.

(a)

A, B, C, 2.4 cm, 1.7 cm, 3.2 cm

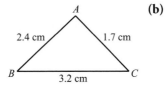

(b)

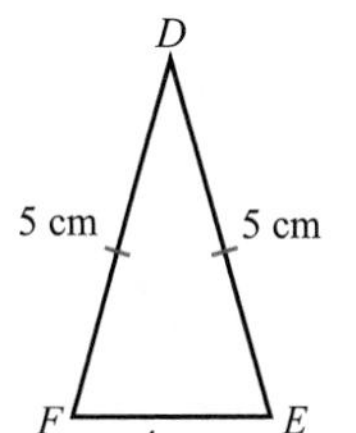

(c)

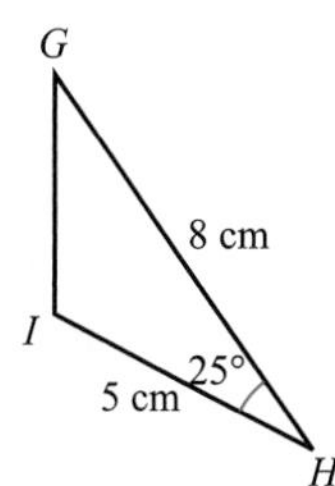

(d)

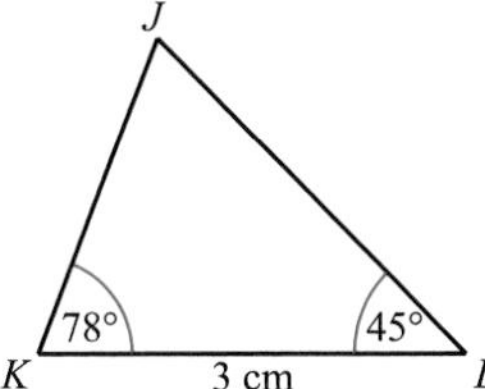

(e)

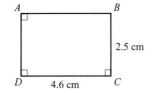

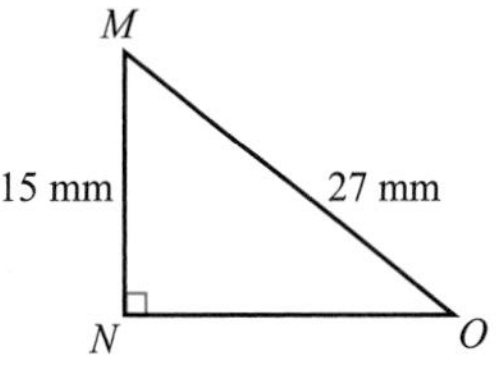

(f)

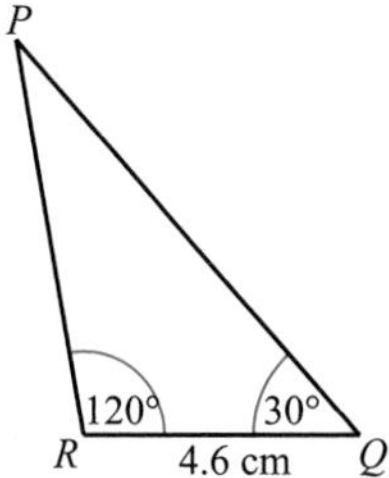

2 Construct these triangles.

(a) ΔABC with $BC = 8.5$ cm, $AB = 7.2$ cm and $AC = 6.9$ cm.
(b) ΔXYZ with $YZ = 86$ mm, $XY = 120$ mm and $XZ = 66$ mm.
(c) Equilateral triangle DEF with sides of 6.5 cm.
(d) Isosceles triangle PQR with a base of 4 cm and $PQ = PR = 6.5$ cm.

3 Construct ΔABC with $AB = 9$ cm, $BC = 55$ mm and $AC = 62$ mm.

(a) Bisect each angle. Label the point of intersection of the bisectors X.
(b) Measure AX, BX and CX.

4 Construct ΔDEF with $D\hat{E}F = 100°$, $E\hat{D}F = 50°$ and $DE = 57$ mm.

(a) Bisect angles EDF and DFE. Let the bisectors intersect at O.
(b) Join EO and measure its length.

5 Construct $JKLM$, a square of side 6 cm.

(a) Bisect angle JKL.
(b) Does the bisector of angle JKL bisect angle JML? How can you check?

Exercise 3.11

Accurately construct the figures shown.

(a)

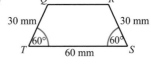

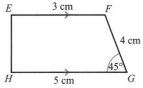

A, B, C, D, 2.5 cm, 4.6 cm

(b)

E, F, G, H, 3 cm, 4 cm, 45°, 5 cm

(c)

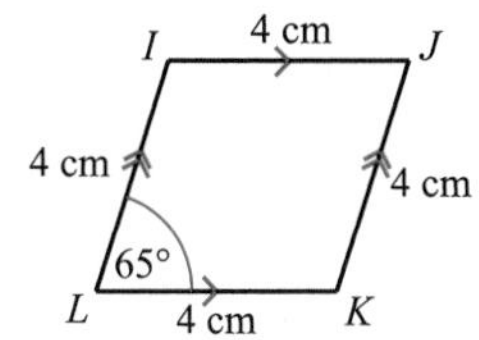

(d)

M, N, O, P, 52 mm, 36 mm, 50°

(e)

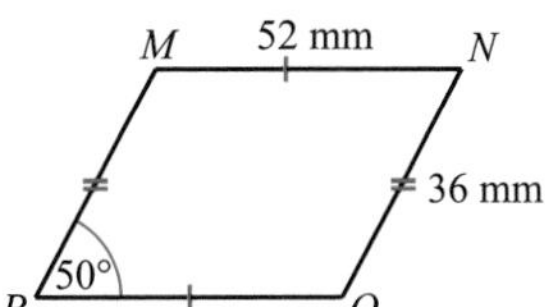

(f)

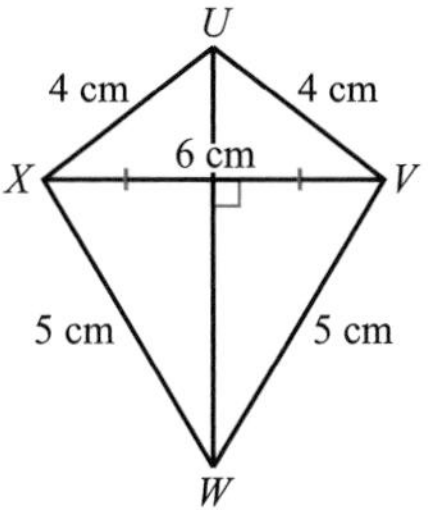

Summary

Do you know the following?

- A point is position and a line is the shortest distance between two points.
- Parallel lines are equidistant along their length.
- Perpendicular lines meet at right angles.
- Acute angles are < 90°, right angles are exactly 90°, obtuse angles are > 90° but < 180°. Straight angles are exactly 180°. Reflex angles are > 180° but < 360°. A complete revolution is 360°.
- Scalene triangles have no equal sides, isosceles triangles have two equal sides and a pair of equal angles, and equilateral triangles have three equal sides and three equal angles.
- Complementary angles have a sum of 90°. Supplementary angles have a sum of 180°.
- Angles on a line have a sum of 180°.
- Angles round a point have a sum of 360°.
- Vertically opposite angles are formed when two lines intersect. Vertically opposite angles are equal.
- When a transversal cuts two parallel lines various angle pairs are formed. Corresponding angles are equal. Alternate angles are equal. Co-interior angles are supplementary.
- The angle sum of a triangle is 180°.
- The exterior angle of a triangle is equal to the sum of the two opposite interior angles.
- Quadrilaterals can be classified as parallelograms, rectangles, squares, rhombuses, trapeziums or kites according to their properties.
- The angle sum of a quadrilateral is 360°.
- Polygons are many-sided plane shapes. Polygons can be named according to the number of sides they have: e.g. pentagon (5); hexagon (6); octagon (8); and decagon (10).
- Regular polygons have equal sides and equal angles.
- Irregular polygons have unequal sides and unequal angles.
- The angle sum of a polygon is $(n - 2) \times 180°$, where n is the number of sides.
- The angle sum of exterior angles of any convex polygon is 360°.

Are you able to ... ?

- calculate unknown angles on a line and round a point
- calculate unknown angles using vertically opposite angles and the angle relationships associated with parallel lines
- calculate unknown angles using the angle properties of triangles, quadrilaterals and polygons
- accurately measure and construct lines and angles
- construct the perpendicular bisector of a line
- bisect an angle using only a pair of compasses
- construct a triangle using given measurements
- apply construction skills to construct other geometrical figures.

Examination practice

Exam-style questions

1 Find x in each figure. Give reasons.

(a)

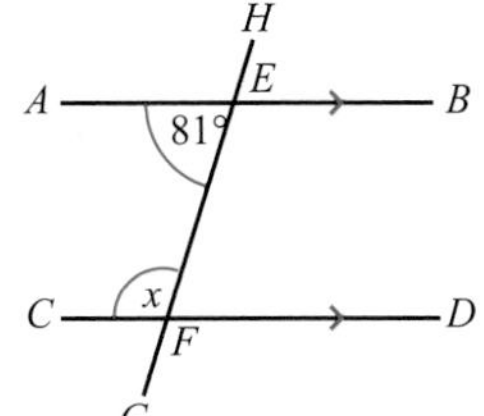

(b)

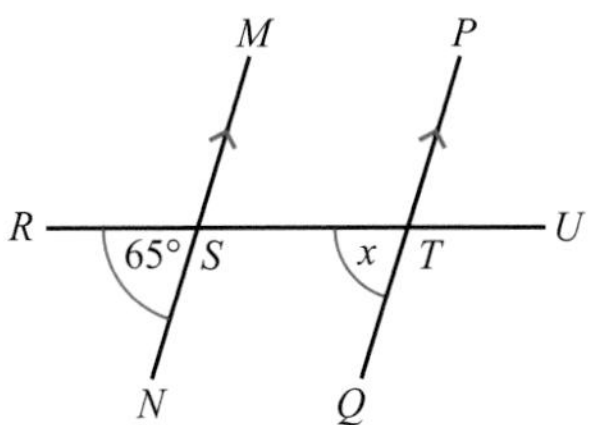

(c)

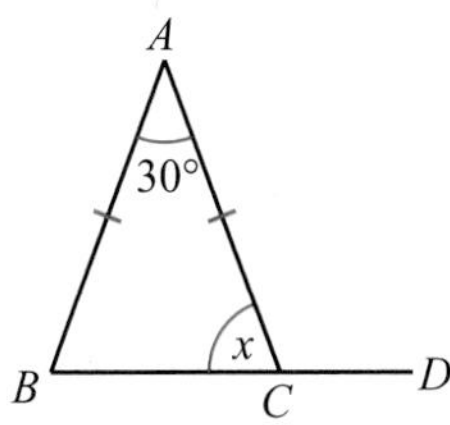

(d)

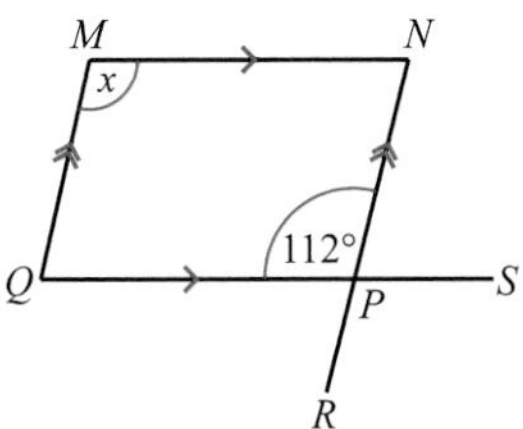

(e)

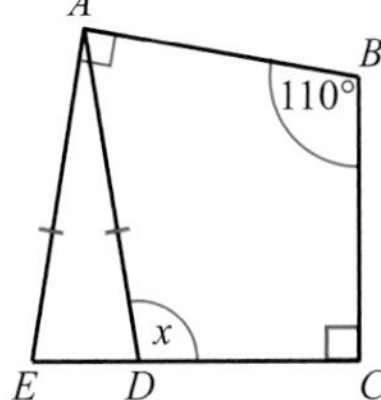

(f)

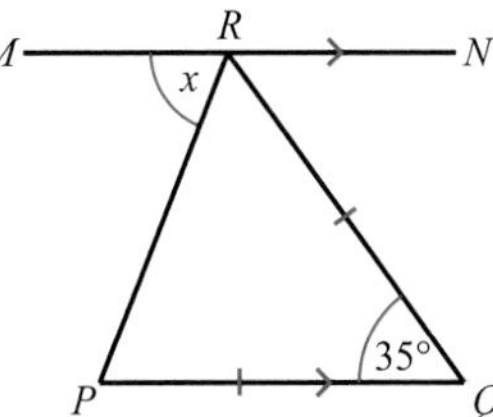

2 Study the triangle.

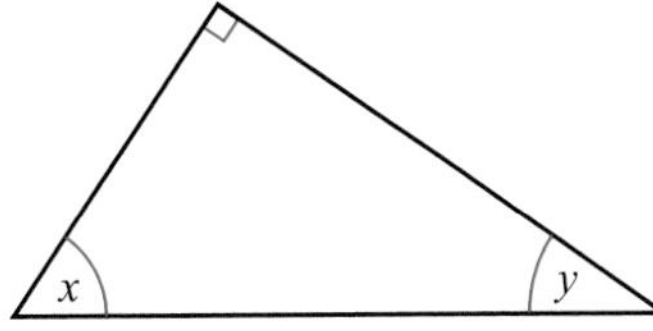

(a) Explain why $x + y = 90°$.
(b) Find y if $x = 37°$.

3 What is the sum of interior angles of a regular hexagon?

4 (a) What is the sum of exterior angles of a convex polygon with 15 sides?
(b) What is the size of each exterior angle in this polygon?
(c) If the polygon is regular, what is the size of each interior angle?

5 Explain why $x = y$ in the following figures.

(a)

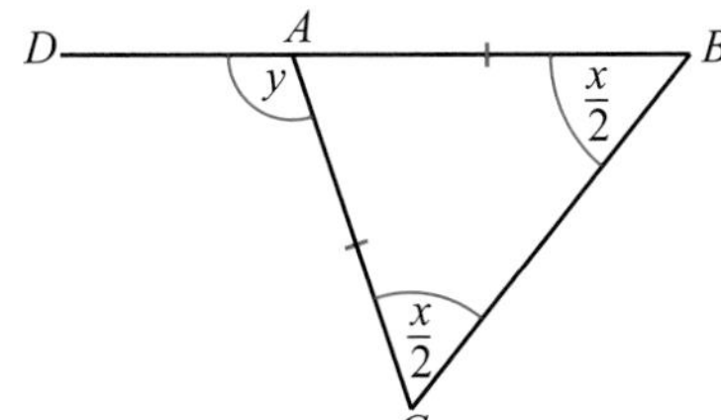

(b)

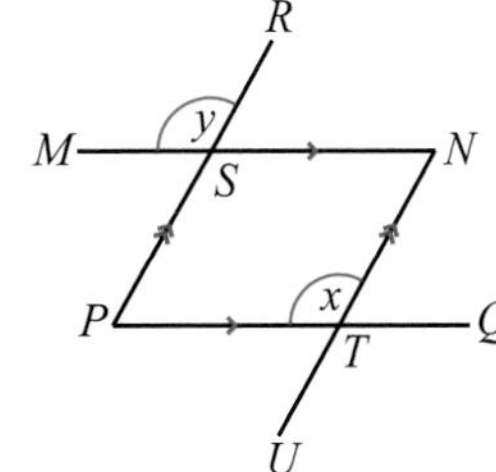

6 **(a)** Measure this line and construct *AB* the same length in your book using a ruler and compasses.

A ____ *B*

(b) At point *A*, measure and draw $B\hat{A}C$, a 75° angle.
(c) Bisect angle $B\hat{A}C$.

7 **(a)** Construct triangle *PQR* with sides *PQ* = 4.5 cm, *QR* = 5 cm and *PR* = 7 cm.

Past paper questions

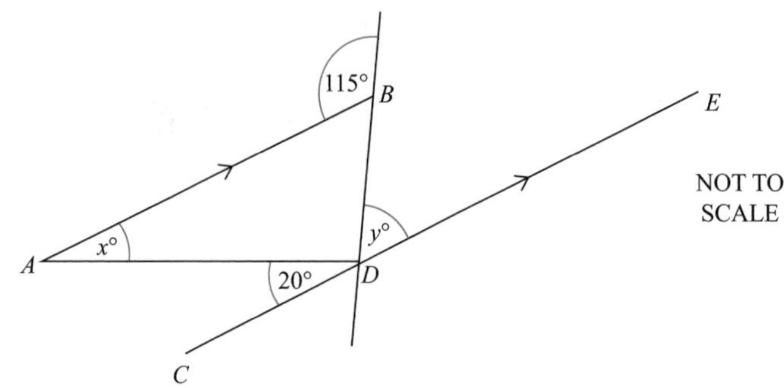

1 In the diagram, *AB* is parallel to *CDE*. Find the value of
(a) *x*, [1]
(b) *y*. [2]

[Cambridge IGCSE Mathematics 0580 Paper 12 Q10 October/November 2011]

4

Collecting, organising and displaying data

Key words

- Data
- Categorical data
- Qualitative
- Numerical data
- Quantitative
- Discrete
- Continuous
- Primary data
- Secondary data
- Frequency table
- Grouped
- Two-way table
- Pictogram
- Bar graph
- Pie chart
- Line graph

In this chapter you will learn how to:

- collect data and classify different types of data
- organise data using tally tables, frequency tables and two-way tables
- draw pictograms, bar graphs, and pie charts to display data and answer questions about it.

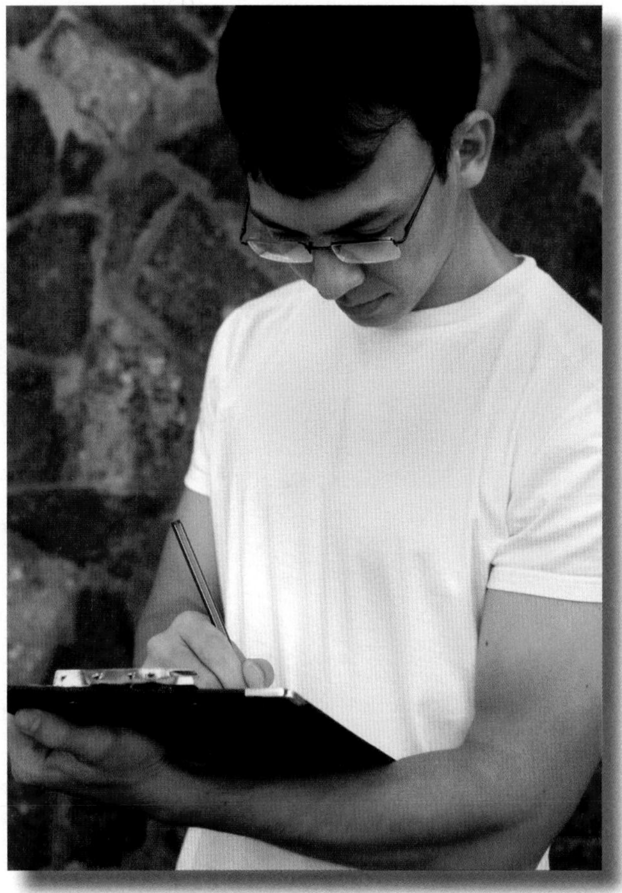

This person is collecting information to find out whether people in his village know what government aid is available to them.

People collect information for many different reasons. We collect information to answer questions, make decisions, predict what will happen in the future, compare ourselves with others and understand how things affect our lives. A scientist might collect information from experiments or tests to find out how well a new drug is working. A businesswoman might collect data from business surveys to find out how well her business is performing. A teacher might collect test scores to see how well his students perform in an examination and an individual might collect data from magazines or the internet to decide which brand of shoes, jeans, make-up or car to buy. The branch of mathematics that deals with collecting data is called statistics. At this level, you will focus on asking questions and then collecting information and organising or displaying it so that you can answer questions.

4.1 Collecting and classifying data

Data is actually the plural of the Latin word datum, but in modern English the word data is accepted and used as a singular form, so you can talk about a set of data, this data, two items of data or a lot of data.

Data is a set of facts, numbers or other information. Statistics involves a process of collecting data and using it to try and answer a question. The flow diagram shows the four main steps involved in this process of statistical investigation:

The information that is stored on a computer hard-drive or CD is also called data. In computer terms, data has nothing to do with statistics, it just means stored information.

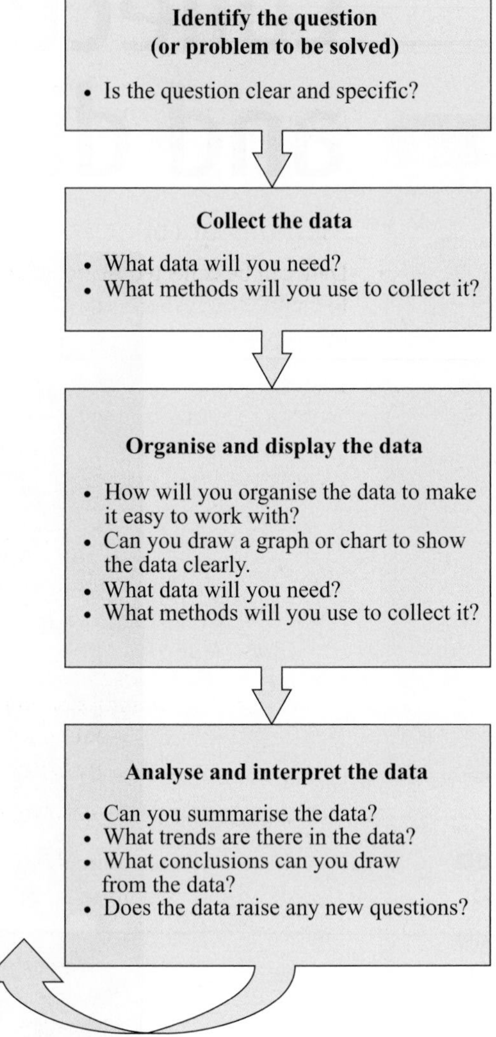

Different types of data

Answer these two questions:

- Who is your favourite singer?
- How many brothers and sisters do you have?

Your answer to the first question will be the name of a person. Your answer to the second question will be a number. Both the name and the number are types of data.

Categorical data is non-numerical data. It names or describes something without reference to number or size. Colours, names of people and places, yes and no answers, opinions and choices are all categorical. Categorical data is also called **qualitative** data.

Numerical data is data in number form. It can be an amount, a measurement, a time or a score. Numerical data is also called **quantitative** data (from the word quantity).

FAST FORWARD

You will need to fully understand continuous data when you study histograms in chapter 20. ▶

Numerical data can be further divided into two groups:

- **discrete data** – this is data that can only take certain values, for example, the number of children in a class, goals scored in a match or red cars passing a point. When you count things, you are collecting discrete data.
- **continuous data** – this is data that could take any value between two given values, for example, the height of a person who is between 1.5 m and 1.6 m tall could be 1.5 m, 1.57 m, 1.5793 m, 1.5793421 m or any other value between 1.5 m and 1.6 m depending on the degree of accuracy used. Heights, masses, distances and temperatures are all examples of continuous data. Continuous data is normally collected by measuring.

One way to decide if data is continuous is to ask whether it is possible for the values to be fractions or decimals. If the answer is yes the data is usually continuous. But be careful:

- age may seem to be discrete, because it is often given in full years, but it is actually continuous because we are getting older all the time
- shoe sizes are discrete, even though you can get shoes in half sizes, because you cannot get shoes in size $7\frac{1}{4}$ or $7\frac{3}{4}$ or $7\frac{8}{9}$.

Methods of collecting data

Data can be collected from primary sources by doing surveys or interviews, by asking people to complete questionnaires, by doing experiments or by counting and measuring. Data from primary sources is known as **primary data**.

Data can also be collected from secondary sources. This involves using existing data to find the information you need. For example, if you use data from an internet site or even from these pages to help answer a question, to you this is a secondary source. Data from secondary sources is known as **secondary data**.

Exercise 4.1

1 Copy this table into your book.

Categorical data	Numerical data
Hair colour	*Number of brothers and sisters*

(a) Add five examples of categorical data and five examples of numerical data that could be collected about each student in your class.
(b) Look at the numerical examples in your table. Circle the ones that will give discrete data.

2 State whether the following data would be discrete or continuous.

(a) Mass of each animal in a herd.
(b) Number of animals per household.
(c) Time taken to travel to school.
(d) Volume of water evaporating from a dam.
(e) Number of correct answers in a spelling test.
(f) Distance people travel to work.
(g) Foot length of each student in a class.
(h) Shoe size of each student in a class.
(i) Head circumference of newborn babies.
(j) Number of children per family.
(k) Number of TV programmes watched in the last month.
(l) Number of cars passing a zebra crossing per hour.

3 For each of the following questions state:

(i) one method you could use to collect the data
(ii) whether the source of the data is primary or secondary
(iii) whether the data is categorical or numerical
(iv) If the data is numerical, state whether it is discrete or continuous.

(a) How many times will you get a six if you throw a dice 100 times?
(b) Which is the most popular TV programme among your classmates?
(c) What are the lengths of the ten longest rivers in the world?

(d) What is the favourite sport of students in your school?
(e) How many books are taken out per week from the local library?
(f) Is it more expensive to drive to work than to use public transport?
(g) Is there a connection between shoe size and height?
(h) What is the most popular colour of car?
(i) What is the batting average of the national cricket team this season?
(j) How many pieces of fruit do you eat in a week?

4.2 Organising data

FAST FORWARD

You will use these methods and extend them in later chapters. Make sure that you understand them now. ▶

When you collect a large amount of data you need to organise it in some way so that it becomes easy to read and use. Tables (tally tables, frequency tables and two-way tables) are the most commonly used methods of organising data.

Tally tables

Tallies are little marks (////) that you use to keep a record of items you count. Each time you count five items you draw a line across the previous four tallies to make a group of five (~~////~~). Grouping tallies in fives makes it much easier to count and get a total when you need one.

A tally table is used to keep a record when you are counting things.

Look at this tally table. A student used this to record how many cars of each colour there were in a parking lot. He made a tally mark in the second column each time he counted a car of a particular colour.

Colour	Number of cars
White	~~////~~ ~~////~~ ///
Red	~~////~~ ~~////~~ ~~////~~ ~~////~~ /
Black	~~////~~ ~~////~~ ~~////~~ ~~////~~ ~~////~~ ~~////~~ ~~////~~ //
Blue	~~////~~ ~~////~~ ~~////~~ ~~////~~ ~~////~~ //
Silver	~~////~~ ~~////~~ ~~////~~ ~~////~~ ~~////~~ ~~////~~ ~~////~~ ~~////~~ ///
Green	~~////~~ ~~////~~ ~~////~~ /

(The totals for each car are shown after Exercise 4.2 on page 78.)

Worked example 1

Anita wanted to find out what people thought about smoking in public places. She did a survey of 100 people. Each person chose an answer A, B C or D.

What do you think about this statement? Please choose one response.
Public places should be totally smoke free. Smoking should be totally banned in public places at all times.
A I strongly agree
B I agree
C I disagree
D I strongly disagree

She recorded these results:

A B A C A C C D A C
C C D A D D C C C A
B B A C D B B A C C
A B C A D B C D A B
A C C D A C C C D A
D D C C C A B B A C
D C C D A C A B D B
C C D A D D C C C A
B B A C D B B C C C
A B C A D B C D A B

(a) Draw a tally table to organise the results.
(b) What do the results of her survey suggest people think about smoking in public places?

(a)

Response	Tally
A	~~||||~~ ~~||||~~ ~~||||~~ ~~||||~~ ||||
B	~~||||~~ ~~||||~~ ~~||||~~ ||||
C	~~||||~~ ~~||||~~ ~~||||~~ ~~||||~~ ~~||||~~ ~~||||~~ ~~||||~~ ||
D	~~||||~~ ~~||||~~ ~~||||~~ ~~||||~~

Count each letter. Make a tally each time you count one.
It may help to cross the letters off the list as you count them.
Check that your tallies add up to 100 to make sure you have included all the scores. (You could work across the rows or down the columns, putting a tally into the correct row in your table, rather than just counting one letter at a time.)

(b) The results suggest that people generally don't think smoking should be banned in public places. 57 people disagreed or strongly disagreed. Only 24 of the 100 people strongly agreed with Anita's statement.

Exercise 4.2

1 Julie threw a dice 50 times. These are her scores. Draw a tally table to organise her data.

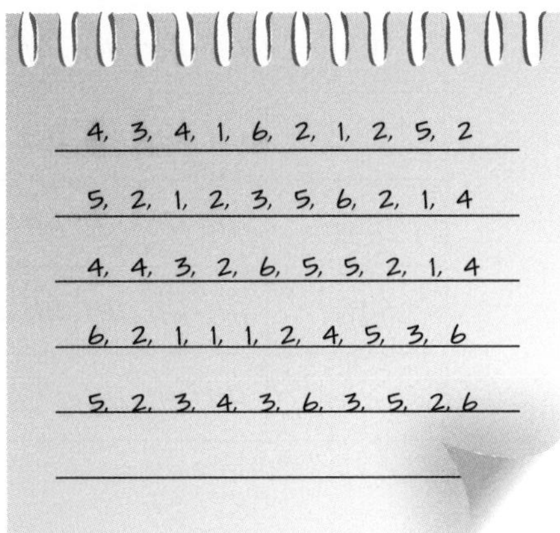

4, 3, 4, 1, 6, 2, 1, 2, 5, 2
5, 2, 1, 2, 3, 5, 6, 2, 1, 4
4, 4, 3, 2, 6, 5, 5, 2, 1, 4
6, 2, 1, 1, 1, 2, 4, 5, 3, 6
5, 2, 3, 4, 3, 6, 3, 5, 2, 6

2 Do a quick survey among your class to find out how many hours each person usually spends doing his or her homework each day. Draw your own tally table to record and organise your data.

3 Faizel threw two dice together 250 times and recorded the score he got using a tally table. Look at the tally table and answer the questions about it.

Score	Tally
2	𝍸 ||
3	𝍸 𝍸 𝍸
4	𝍸 𝍸 𝍸 𝍸 |||
5	𝍸 𝍸 𝍸 𝍸 𝍸 ||||
6	𝍸 𝍸 𝍸 𝍸 𝍸 𝍸 |||
7	𝍸 𝍸 𝍸 𝍸 𝍸 𝍸 𝍸 𝍸 |
8	𝍸 𝍸 𝍸 𝍸 𝍸 𝍸 𝍸
9	𝍸 𝍸 𝍸 𝍸 𝍸 |||
10	𝍸 𝍸 𝍸 𝍸 |
11	𝍸 𝍸 ||
12	𝍸 |

(a) Which score occurred most often?
(b) Which two scores occurred least often?
(c) Why do you think Faizel left out the score of one?
(d) Why do you think he scored six, seven and eight so many times?

Frequency tables

A **frequency table** shows the totals of the tally marks. Some frequency tables include the tallies.

This frequency table is the same as the tally table the student used to record car colours (page 76). It has another column added with the totals (frequencies) of the tallies.

Colour	Number of cars	Frequency
White	𝍸 𝍸 |||	13
Red	𝍸 𝍸 𝍸 𝍸 |	21
Black	𝍸 𝍸 𝍸 𝍸 𝍸 𝍸 𝍸 ||	37
Blue	𝍸 𝍸 𝍸 𝍸 𝍸 ||	27
Silver	𝍸 𝍸 𝍸 𝍸 𝍸 𝍸 𝍸 𝍸 |||	43
Green	𝍸 𝍸 𝍸 |	16
		Total 157

The frequency table has space to write a total at the bottom of the frequency column. This helps you to know how many pieces of data were collected. In this example the student recorded the colours of 157 cars.

Most frequency tables will not include tally marks. Here is a frequency table without tallies. It was drawn up by the staff at a clinic to record how many people were treated for different diseases in one week.

The frequency column tells you how often (how frequently) each result appeared in the data and the data is discrete.

Illness	Frequency
Diabetes	30
HIV/Aids	40
TB	60
Other	50
Total	180

Grouping data in class intervals

FAST FORWARD

You will soon use these tables to construct bar charts and other frequency diagrams. These diagrams give a clear, visual impression of the data. ▶

Sometimes numerical data needs to be recorded in different groups. For example, if you collected test results for 40 students you might find that students scored between 40 and 84 (out of 100). If you recorded each individual score (and they could all be different) you would get a very large frequency table that is difficult to manage. To simplify things, the collected data can be arranged in groups called class intervals. A frequency table with results arranged in class intervals is called a **grouped** frequency table. Look at the example below:

In this example, the test does not allow for fractions of a mark, so all test scores are integers and the data is discrete.

Points scored	Frequency
40–44	7
45–49	3
50–54	3
55–59	3
60–64	0
65–69	5
70–74	3
75–79	7
80–84	9
Total	40

The range of scores (40–84) has been divided into class intervals. Notice that the class intervals do not overlap so it is clear which data goes in what class.

Exercise 4.3

1 Sheldon did a survey to find out how many coins the students in his class had on them (in their pockets or purses). These are his results:

0	2	3	1	4	6	3	6	7	2
1	2	4	0	0	6	5	4	8	2
6	3	2	0	0	0	2	4	3	5

(a) Copy this frequency table and use it to organise Sheldon's data.

Number of coins	0	1	2	3	4	5	6	7	8
Frequency									

(b) What is the highest number of coins that any person had on them?
(c) How many people had only one coin on them?

(d) What is the most common number of coins that people had on them?
(e) How many people did Sheldon survey altogether? How could you show this on the frequency table?

2 Penny works as a waitress in a fast food restaurant. These are the amounts (in dollars) spent by 25 customers during her shift.

Note that currency (money) is discrete data because you cannot get a coin (or note) smaller than one cent.

43.55	4.45	17.60	25.95	3.75
12.35	55.00	12.90	35.95	16.25
25.05	2.50	29.35	12.90	8.70
12.50	13.95	6.50	39.40	22.55
20.45	4.50	5.30	15.95	10.50

(a) Copy and complete this grouped frequency table to organise the data.

Amount ($)	0–9.99	10–19.99	20–29.99	30–39.99	40–49.99	50–59.99
Frequency						

(b) How many people spent less than $20.00?
(c) How many people spent more than $50.00?
(d) What is the most common amount that people spent during Penny's shift?

3 Leonard records the length in minutes and whole seconds, of each phone call he makes during one day. These are his results:

3 min 29 s	4 min 12 s	4 min 15 s	1 min 29 s	2 min 45 s
1 min 32 s	1 min 09 s	2 min 50 s	3 min 15 s	4 min 03 s
3 min 04 s	5 min 12 s	5 min 45 s	3 min 29 s	2 min 09 s
1 min 12 s	4 min 15 s	3 min 45 s	3 min 59 s	5 min 01 s

Use a grouped frequency table to organise the data.

Two-way tables

A **two-way table** shows the frequency of certain results for two or more sets of data. Here is a two way table showing how many men and woman drivers were wearing their seat belts when they passed a check point.

	Wearing a seat belt	**Not wearing a seat belt**
Men	10	4
Women	6	3

The headings at the top of the table give you information about wearing seat belts. The headings down the side of the table give you information about gender.

You can use the table to find out:

- how many men were wearing seat belts
- how many women were wearing seat belts
- how many men were not wearing seat belts
- how many women were not wearing seat belts.

You can also add the totals across and down to work out:

- how many men were surveyed
- how many women were surveyed
- how many people (men + women) were wearing seat belts or not wearing seat belts.

Here are two more examples of two-way tables:

Drinks and crisps sold at a school tuck shop during lunch break

	Sweet chilli	Plain	Cheese and onion
Cola	9	6	23
Fruit juice	10	15	12

How often male and female students use Facebook

	Never use it	Use it sometimes	Use it every day
Male	35	18	52
Female	42	26	47

Exercise 4.4

1 A teacher did a survey to see how many students in her class were left-handed. She drew up this two-way table to show the results.

	Left-handed	Right-handed
Girls	9	33
Boys	6	42

(a) How many left-handed girls are there in the class?
(b) How many of the girls are right-handed?
(c) Are the boys mostly left-handed or mostly right-handed?
(d) How many students are in the class?

2 Do a quick survey in your own class to find out whether girls and boys are left- or right-handed. Draw up a two-way table of your results.

3 Nancy asked her friends whether they liked algebra or geometry best. Here are the responses.

Name	Algebra	Geometry
Sheldon		✓
Leonard	✓	
Raj	✓	
Penny		✓
Howard	✓	
Zarah		✓
John		✓

Name	Algebra	Geometry
Ahmed	✓	
Jenny	✓	
Samantha		✓
Anne		✓
Ellen	✓	

FAST FORWARD

Make sure you understand how to draw up and read a two-way table. You will use them again in chapter 8 when you deal with probability. ▶

(a) Draw a two-way table using these responses.
(b) Write a sentence to summarise what you can learn from the table.

Two-way tables in everyday life

Two-way tables are often used to summarise and present data in real life situations. You need to know how to read these tables so that you can answer questions about them.

Worked example 2

This table shows world population data for 2008 with estimated figures for 2025 and 2050.

Region	Population in 2008	Projected population 2025	Projected population 2050
World	6705000000	8000000000	9352000000
Africa	967000000	1358000000	1932000000
North America	338000000	393000000	480000000
Latin America and the Caribbean	577000000	678000000	778000000
Asia	4052000000	4793000000	5427000000
Europe	736000000	726000000	685000000
Oceania	35000000	42000000	49000000

(Data from Population Reference Bureau.)

(a) What was the total population of the world in 2008?
(b) By how much is the population of the world expected to grow by 2025?
(c) What percentage of the world's population lived in Asia in 2008? Give your answer to the closest whole per cent.
(d) Which region is likely to experience a decrease in population between 2008 and 2025?
(i) What.is the population of this region likely to be in 2025?
(ii) By how much is the population expected to decrease by 2050?

(a)	6705000000	Read this from the table.
(b)	8000000000 − 6705000000 = 1295000000	Read the value for 2025 from the table and subtract the smaller figure from the larger.
(c)	$\frac{4052000000}{6705000000} \times 100 = 60.4352\% \approx 60\%$	Read the figures from the table and then calculate the percentage.
(d)	Europe **(i)** 726000000 **(ii)** 736000000 − 685000000 = 51000000	Look to see which numbers are decreasing across the row. Read this from the table. Read the values from the table and subtract the smaller figure from the larger.

Exercise 4.5 *Living maths*

This distance table shows the flying distance (in miles) between some major world airports.

	Mumbai	Hong Kong	London	Montreal	Singapore	Sydney
Dubai	1199	3695	3412	6793	3630	7580
Hong Kong	2673		8252	10 345	1605	4586
Istanbul	2992	7016	1554	5757	5379	11 772
Karachi	544	3596	5276	8888	2943	8269
Lagos	5140	8930	3098	6734	7428	11 898
London	4477	8252		3251	6754	10 564
Singapore	2432	1605	6754	9193		3912
Sydney	6308	4586	10 564	12 045	3916	

(a) Find the flying distance from Hong Kong to:

(i) Dubai **(ii)** London **(iii)** Sydney

(b) Which is the longer flight: Istanbul to Montreal or Mumbai to Lagos?

(c) What is the total flying distance for a return flight from London to Sydney and back?

(d) If the plane flies at an average speed of 400 miles per hour, how long will it take to fly the distance from Singapore to Hong Kong to the nearest hour?

(e) Why are there some blank blocks on this table?

4.3 Using charts to display data

FAST FORWARD

You also need to be able to draw and use frequency distributions and histograms. These are covered in chapter 20. ▶

Charts are useful for displaying data because you can see patterns and trends easily and quickly. You can also compare different sets of data easily. In this section you are going to revise what you already know about how to draw and make sense of pictograms, bar charts and pie charts.

Pictograms

Pictograms are fairly simple charts. Small symbols (pictures) are used to represent quantities. The meaning of the symbol and the amount it represents (a 'key') must be provided for the graph to make sense.

Worked example 3

The table shows how many books five different students have finished reading in the past year.

Student	Number of books read
Amina	12
Bheki	14
Dabilo	8
Saul	16
Linelle	15

Draw a pictogram to show this data.

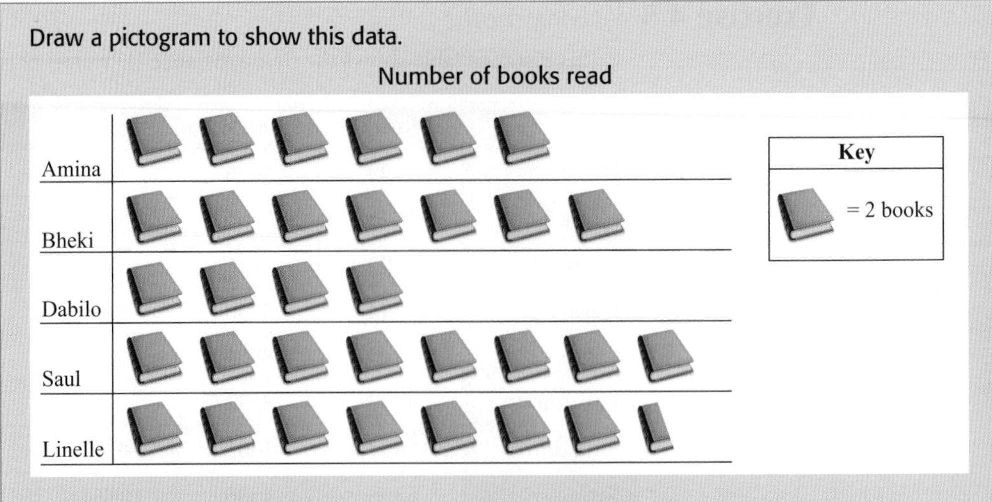

Worked example 4

This pictogram shows the amount of time that five friends spent talking on their phones during one week.

(a) Who spent the most time on the phone that week?
(b) How much time did Isobel spend on the phone that week?
(c) Who spent $3\frac{1}{2}$ hours on the phone this week?
(d) Draw the symbols you would use to show $2\frac{1}{4}$ hours.

(a)	Anna	The person with the most clocks.
(b)	$3\frac{3}{4}$ hours	There are three whole clocks; the key shows us each one stands for 1 hour. The fourth clock is only three-quarters, so it must be $\frac{3}{4}$ of an hour.
(c)	Tara	She has three full clocks, each worth 1 hour, and one half clock.
(d)	 	Two full clocks to represent two hours, and a quarter of a clock to represent $\frac{1}{4}$ hours.

Exercise 4.6

1 A pictogram showing how many tourists visit the top five tourist destinations uses this symbol.

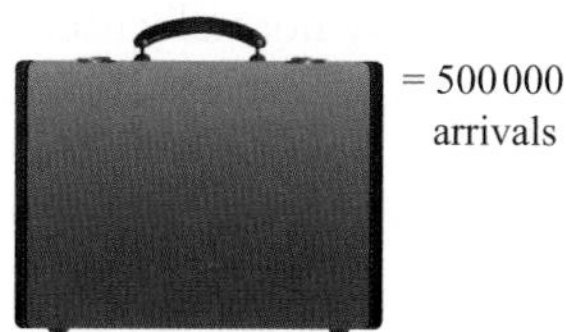

How many tourists are represented by each of these symbols?

The number of arrivals represented by the key should be an integer that is easily divided into the data; you may also need to round the data to a suitable degree of accuracy.

2 Here is a set of data for the five top tourist destination countries (2008). Use the symbol from question **1** with your own scale to draw a pictogram to show this data.

Most tourist arrivals

Country	France	USA	Spain	China	Italy
Number of tourists	79 300 000	58 030 000	57 316 000	53 049 000	42 734 000

3 This pictogram shows the number of fish caught by five fishing boats during one fishing trip.

Number of fish caught per boat

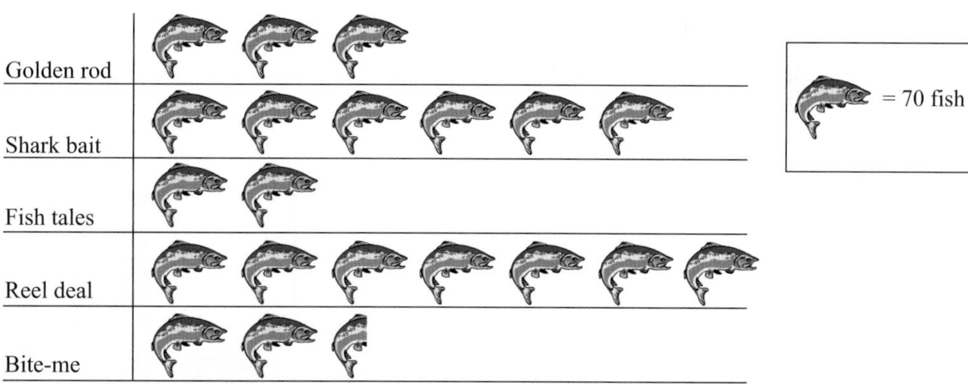

(a) Which boat caught the most fish?
(b) Which boat caught the least fish?
(c) How many fish did each boat catch?
(d) What is the total catch for the fleet on this trip?

Bar charts

Bar charts are normally used to display discrete data. The chart shows information as a series of bars plotted against a scale on the axis. The bars can be horizontal or vertical.

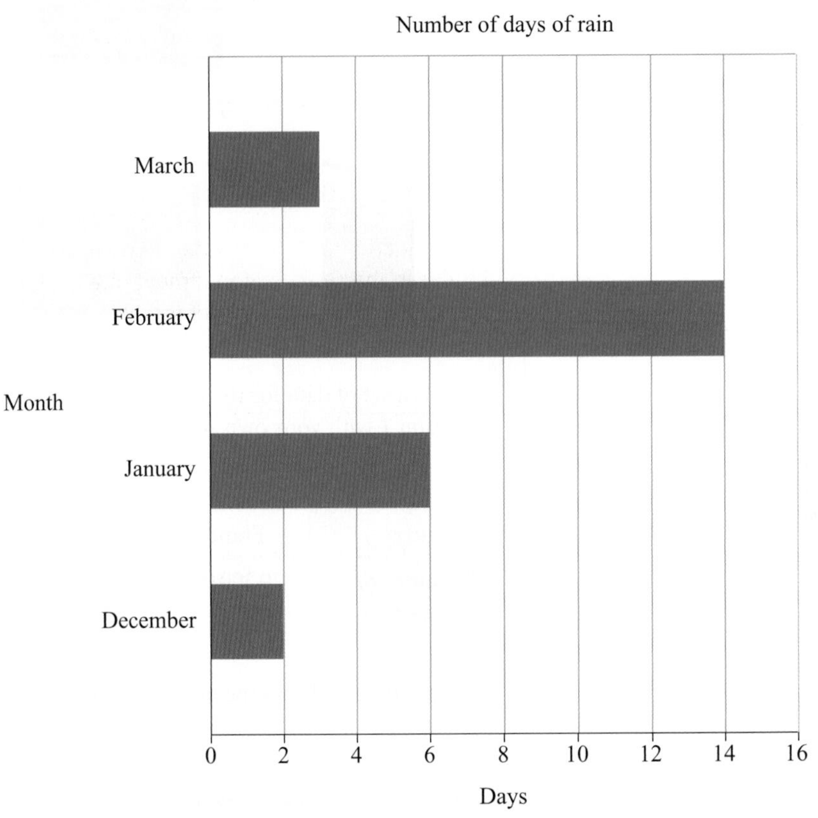

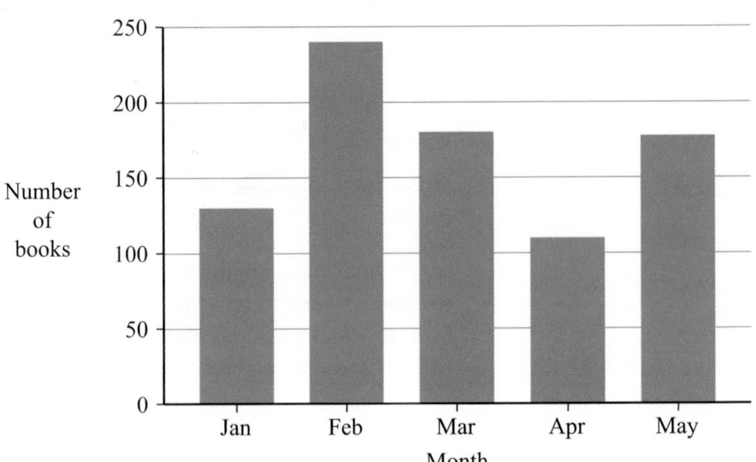

The bars should not touch for qualitative or discrete data.

There are different methods of drawing bar charts, but all bar charts should have:

- a title that tells what data is being displayed
- a number scale or axis (so you can work out how many are in each class) and a label on the scale that tells you what the numbers stand for
- a scale or axis that lists the categories displayed
- bars that are equally wide and equally spaced.

Worked example 5

The frequency table shows the number of people who were treated for road accident injuries in the casualty department of a large hospital in the first six months of the year. Draw a bar chart to represent the data.

Patients admitted as a result of road accidents	
Month	**Number of patients**
January	360
February	275
March	190
April	375
May	200
June	210

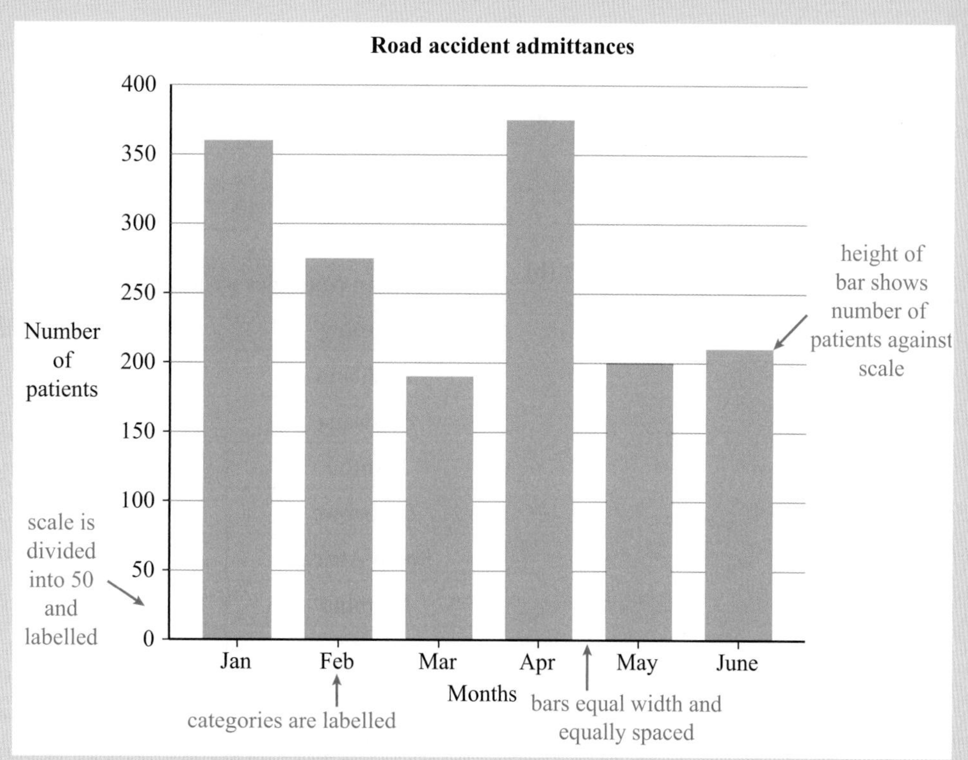

FAST FORWARD

A bar chart is not the same as a histogram. A histogram is normally used for continuous data. You will learn more about histograms in chapter 20. ▶

Compound bar charts

A compound bar chart displays two or more sets of data on the same set of axes to make it easy to compare the data. This chart compares the growth rates of children born to mothers with different education levels.

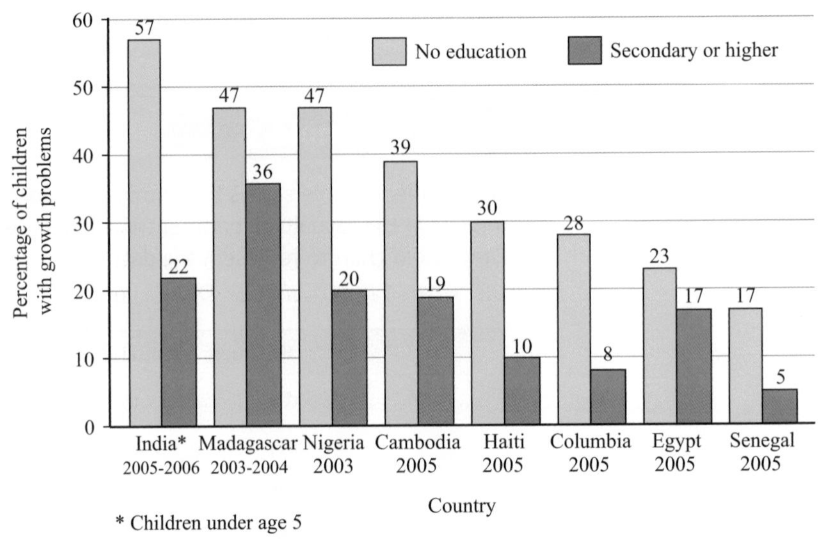

(Adapted from 'Demographic and Health Surveys': www.measuredhs.com).

You can see that children born to mothers with secondary education are less likely to experience growth problems because their bars are shorter than the bars for children whose mothers have only primary education. The aim of this graph is to show that countries should pay attention to the education of women if they want children to develop in healthy ways.

Exercise 4.7 *Living maths*

1 Draw a bar chart to show each of these sets of data.

(a)

Favourite take-away food	Burgers	Noodles	Fried chicken	Hot chips	Other
No. of people	40	30	84	20	29

(b)

African countries with the highest HIV/AIDS infection rates (2013 est)	
Country	**% of adults (aged 15 to 49) infected**
Swaziland	26.5
Botswana	23.0
Lesotho	23.1
Zimbabwe	14.7
South Africa	17.9
Namibia	13.3
Zambia	12.7
Malawi	10.8
Kenya	6.2
Mozambique	11.1

(Data taken from www.avert.org)

REWIND
Look at the earlier sections of this chapter to remind yourself about grouped frequency tables if you need to. ◀

In this example, the temperature groups/class intervals will be displayed as 'categories' with gaps between each bar. As temperature is continuous, a better way to deal with it is to use a histogram with equal class intervals; you will see these in chapter 20.

3 Here is a set of raw data showing the average summer temperature (in °C) for 20 cities in the Middle East during one year.

32	42	36	40	35	36	33	32	38	37
34	40	41	39	42	38	37	42	40	41

(a) Copy and complete this grouped frequency table to organise the data.

Temperature (°C)	32–34	35–37	38–40	41–43
Frequency				

(b) Draw a horizontal bar chart to represent this data.

4 The tourism organisation on a Caribbean island records how many tourists visit from the region and how many tourists visit from international destinations. Here is their data for the first six months of this year. Draw a compound bar chart to display this data.

	Jan	Feb	Mar	Apr	May	Jun
Regional visitors	12 000	10 000	19 000	16 000	21 000	2 000
International visitors	40 000	39 000	15 000	12 000	19 000	25 000

Pie charts

A **pie chart** is a circular chart which uses slices or sectors of the circle to show the data. The circle in a pie chart represents the 'whole' set of data. For example, if you surveyed the favourite sports played by everyone in a school then the total number of students would be represented by the circle. The sectors would represent groups of students who played each sport.

Like other charts, pie charts should have a heading and a key. Here are some fun examples of pie charts:

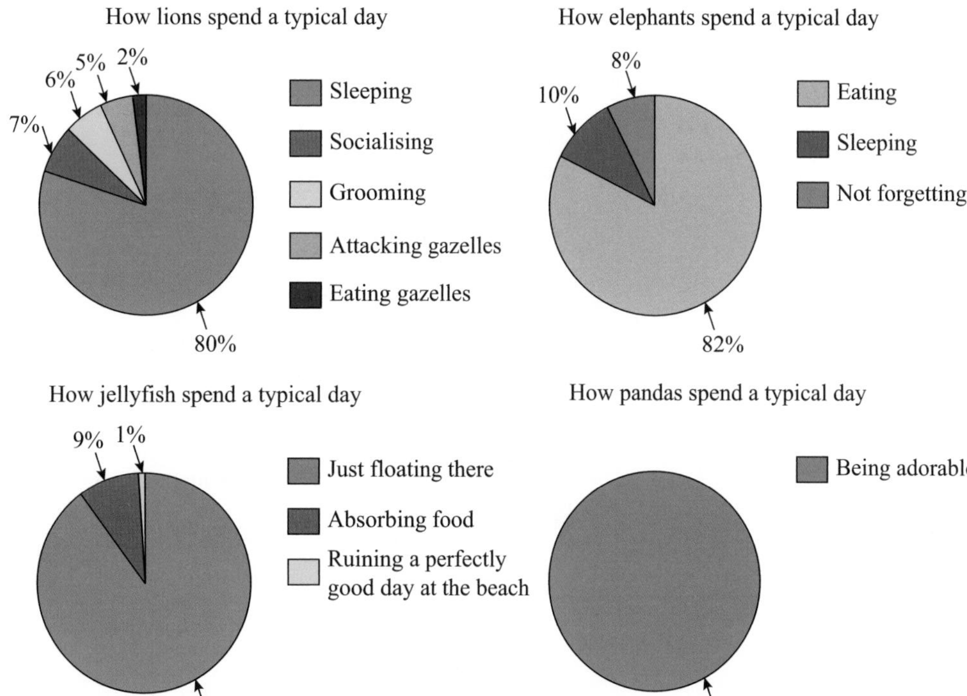

Worked example 6

The table shows how a student spent her day.

Activity	School	Sleeping	Eating	Online	On the phone	Complaining about stuff
Number of hours	7	8	1.5	3	2.5	2

Draw a pie chart to show this data.

$7 + 8 + 1.5 + 3 + 2.5 + 2 = 24$ First work out the total number of hours.

Then work out each category as a fraction of the whole and convert the fraction to degrees:

	(as a fraction of 24)	(convert to degrees)
School	$= \frac{7}{24}$	$= \frac{7}{24} \times 360 = 105°$
Sleeping	$= \frac{8}{24}$	$= \frac{8}{24} \times 360 = 120°$
Eating	$= \frac{1.5}{24} = \frac{15}{240}$	$= \frac{15}{240} \times 360 = 22.5°$
Online	$= \frac{3}{24}$	$= \frac{3}{24} \times 360 = 45°$
On the phone	$= \frac{2.5}{24} = \frac{25}{240}$	$= \frac{25}{240} \times 360 = 37.5°$
Complaining	$= \frac{2}{24}$	$= \frac{2}{24} \times 360 = 30°$

It is possible that your angles, once rounded, don't quite add up to 360°. If this happens, you can add or subtract a degree to or from the largest sector (the one with the highest frequency).

Activity	School	Sleeping	Eating	Online	On the phone	Complaining about stuff
Number of hours	7	8	1.5	3	2.5	2
Angle	105°	120°	22.5°	45°	37.5°	30°

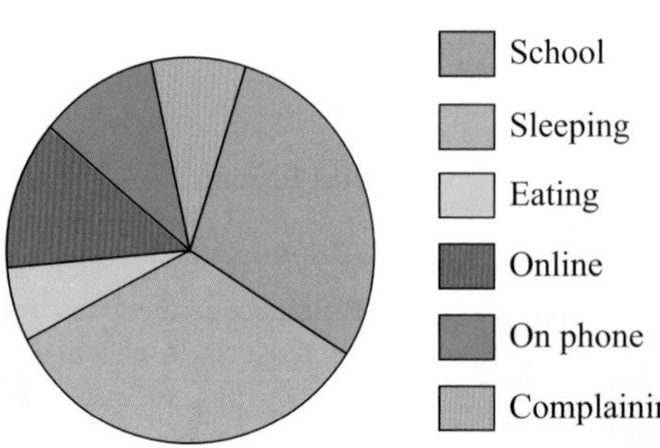

- Draw a circle to represent the whole day.
- Use a ruler and a protractor to measure each sector.
- Label the chart and give it a title.

Worked example 7

This pie chart shows how Henry spent one day of his school holidays.

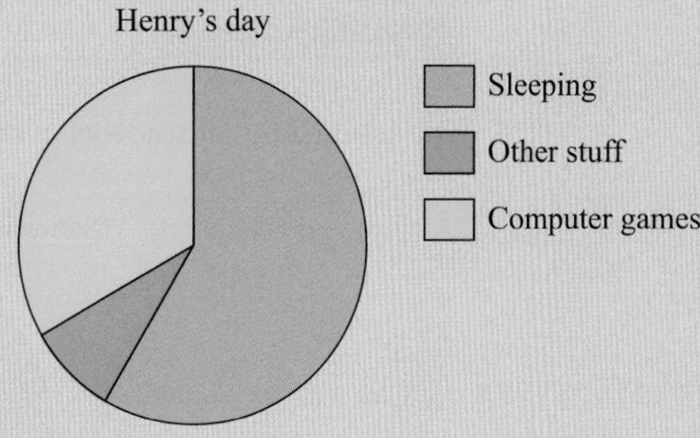

(a) What fraction of his day did he spend playing computer games?
(b) How much time did Henry spend sleeping?
(c) What do you think 'other stuff' involved?

(a)	$\frac{120}{360} = \frac{1}{3}$	Measure the angle and convert it to a fraction. The yellow sector has an angle of 120°. Convert to a fraction by writing it over 360 and simplify.
(b)	$\frac{210}{360} \times 24 = 14$ hours	Measure the angle, convert it to hours.
(c)	Things he didn't bother to list. Possibly eating, showering, getting dressed.	

Exercise 4.8

1 The table shows the results of a survey carried out on a university campus to find out about smoking habits among students. Draw a pie chart to illustrate this data.

Category	Number of students
Never smoked	180
Smoked in the past	120
Smoke at present	100

2 The table shows the home language of a number of people passing through an international airport. Display this data as a pie chart.

Language	Frequency
English	130
Spanish	144
Chinese	98
Italian	104
French	24
German	176
Japanese	22

3 The amount of land used to grow different vegetables on a farm is shown below. Draw a pie chart to show the data.

Vegetable	Squashes	Pumpkins	Cabbages	Sweet potatoes
Area of land (km²)	1.4	1.25	1.15	1.2

4 The nationalities of students in an international school is shown on this pie chart.

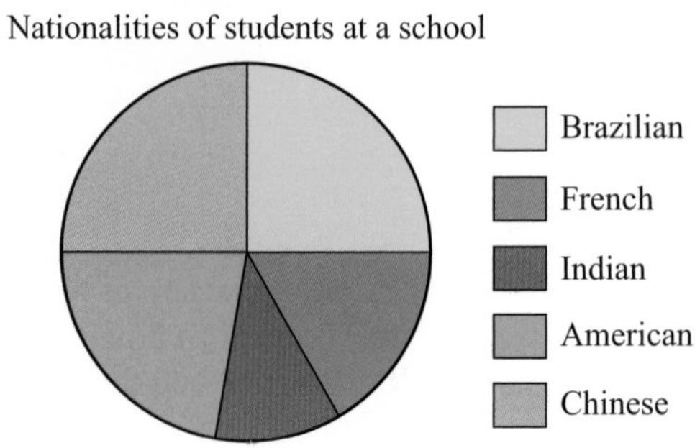

(a) What fraction of the students are Chinese?
(b) What percentage of the students are Indian?
(c) Write the ratio of Brazilian students : total students as a decimal.
(d) If there are 900 students at the school, how many of them are:
(i) Chinese? **(ii)** Indian? **(iii)** American? **(iv)** French?

FAST FORWARD

Graphs that can be used for converting currencies or systems of units will be covered in chapter 13. Graphs dealing with time, distance and speed are covered in chapter 21. ▶

Line graphs

Some data that you collect changes with time. Examples are the average temperature each month of the year, the number of cars each hour in a supermarket car park or the amount of money in your bank account each week.

The following **line graph** shows how the depth of water in a garden pond varies over a year. The graph shows that the water level is at its lowest between June and August.

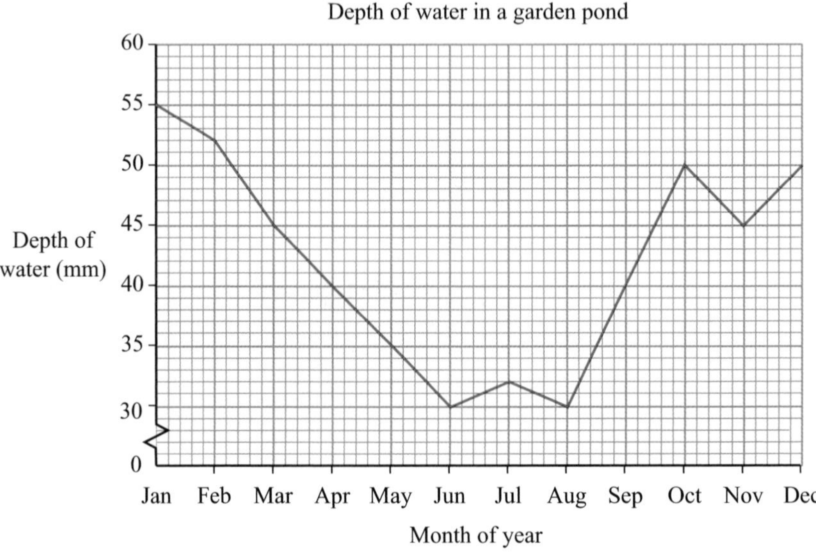

When time is one of your variables it is always plotted on the horizontal axis.

Choosing the most appropriate chart

You cannot always say that one type of chart is better than another – it depends very much on the data and what you want to show. However, the following guidelines are useful to remember:

- Use pie charts or bar charts (single bars) if you want to compare different parts of a whole, if there is no time involved, and there are not too many pieces of data.
- Use bar charts for discrete data that does not change over time.
- Use compound bar charts if you want to compare two or more sets of discrete data.
- Use line graphs for numerical data when you want to show how something changes over time.

The table summarises the features, advantages and disadvantages of each different types of chart/graph. You can use this information to help you decide which type to use.

Tip

You may be asked to give reasons for choosing a particular type of chart. Be sure to have learned the advantages and disadvantages in the table.

Tip

Before you draw a chart decide:

- how big you want the chart to be
- what scales you will use and how you will divide these up
- what title you will give the chart
- whether you need a key or not.

Chart/graph and their features	Advantages	Disadvantages
Pictogram Data is shown using symbols or pictures to represent quantities. The amount represented by each symbol is shown on a key.	Attractive and appealing, can be tailored to the subject. Easy to understand. Size of categories can be easily compared.	Symbols have to be broken up to represent 'in-between values' and may not be clear. Can be misleading as it does not give detailed information.
Bar chart Data is shown in columns measured against a scale on the axis. Double bars can be used for two sets of data. Data can be in any order. Bars should be labelled and the measurement axis should have a scale and label.	Clear to look at. Easy to compare categories and data sets. Scales are given, so you can work out values.	Chart categories can be reordered to emphasise certain effects. Useful only with clear sets of numerical data.
Pie charts Data is displayed as a fraction, percentage or decimal fraction of the whole. Each section should be labelled. A key and totals for the data should be given.	Looks nice and is easy to understand. Easy to compare categories. No scale needed. Can shows percentage of total for each category.	No exact numerical data. Hard to compare two data sets. 'Other' category can be a problem. Total is unknown unless specified. Best for three to seven categories.
Line graph Values are plotted against 'number lines' on the vertical and horizontal axes, which should be clearly marked and labelled.	Shows more detail of information than other graphs. Shows patterns and trends clearly. Other 'in-between' information can be read from the graph. Has many different formats and can be used in many different ways (for example conversion graphs, curved lines).	Useful only with numerical data. Scales can be manipulated to make data look more impressive.

FAST FORWARD

You will work with line graphs when you deal with frequency distributions in chapter 20. ▶

Exercise 4.9

1 Which type of graph would you use to show the following information? Give a reason for your choice.

(a) The number of people in your country looking for jobs each month this year.
(b) The favourite TV shows of you and nine of your friends.
(c) The number of people using a gym at different times during a day.
(d) The favourite subjects of students in a school.
(e) The reasons people give for not donating to a charity.
(f) The different languages spoken by people in your school.
(g) The distance you can travel on a tank of petrol in cars with different sized engines.

Living maths

2 Collect ten different charts from newspapers, magazines or other sources.

Stick the charts into your book.
For each graph:

(a) write the type of chart it is
(b) write a short paragraph explaining what each chart shows
(c) identify any trends or patterns you can see in the data.
(d) Is there any information missing that makes it difficult to interpret the chart? If so what is missing?
(e) Why do you think the particular type and style of chart was used in each case?
(f) Would you have chosen the same type and style of chart in each case? Why?

Summary

Do you know the following?

- In statistics, data is a set of information collected to answer a particular question.
- Categorical (qualitative) data is non-numerical. Colours, names, places and other descriptive terms are all categorical.
- Numerical (quantitative) data is collected in the form of numbers. Numerical data can be discrete or continuous. Discrete data takes a certain value; continuous data can take any value in a given range.
- Primary data is data you collect yourself from a primary source. Secondary data is data you collect from other sources (previously collected by someone else).
- Unsorted data is called raw data. Raw data can be organised using tally tables, frequency tables and two-way tables to make it easier to work with.
- Data in tables can be displayed as graphs to show patterns and trends at a glance.
- Pictograms are simple graphs that use symbols to represent quantities.
- Bar charts have rows of horizontal bars or columns of vertical bars of different lengths. The bar length (or height) represents an amount. The actual amount can be read from a scale.
- Compound bar charts are used to display two or more sets of data on the same set of axes.
- Pie charts are circular charts divided into sectors to show categories of data.
- The type of graph you draw depends on the data and what you wish to show.

Are you able to … ?

- collect data to answer a statistical question
- classify different types of data
- use tallies to count and record data
- draw up a frequency table to organise data
- use class intervals to group data and draw up a grouped frequency table
- draw up and use two-way tables to organise two or more sets of data
- construct and interpret pictograms
- construct and interpret bar charts and compound bar charts
- construct and interpret pie charts.

Examination practice

Exam-style questions

1 Salma is a quality control inspector. She randomly selects 40 packets of biscuits at a large factory. She opens each packet and counts the number of broken biscuits it contains. Her results are as follows:

0	0	2	1	3	0	0	2	3	1
1	1	2	3	0	1	2	3	4	2
0	0	0	0	1	0	0	1	2	3
3	2	2	2	1	0	1	2	1	2

(a) Is this primary or secondary data to Salma? Why?
(b) Is the data discrete or continuous? Give a reason why.
(c) Copy and complete this frequency table to organise the data.

No. of broken biscuits	Tally	Frequency
0		
1		
2		
3		
4		

(d) What type of graph should Salma draw to display this data? Why?

2 The number of aircraft movements in and out of five main London airports during August 2010 is summarised in the table.

Airport	Gatwick	Heathrow	London City	Luton	Stansted
Total flights	24 585	41 428	5423	8727	15 161

(a) Which airport handled most aircraft movement?
(b) How many aircraft moved in and out of Stansted Airport?
(c) Round each figure to the nearest thousand.
(d) Use the rounded figures to draw a pictogram to show this data.

3 This table shows the percentage of people who own a laptop and a mobile phone in four different districts in a large city.

District	Own a laptop	Own a mobile phone
A	45	83
B	32	72
C	61	85
D	22	68

(a) What kind of table is this?
(b) If there are 6000 people in District A, how many of them own a mobile phone?
(c) One district is home to a University of Technology and several computer software manufacturers. Which district do you think this is? Why?
(d) Draw a compound bar chart to display this data.

4 This table shows how a sample of people in the Hong Kong travel to work.

Mode of transport	Percentage
Metro	36
Bus	31
Motor vehicle	19
Cycle	14

Represent this data as a pie chart.

5 Study this pie chart and answer the questions that follow.

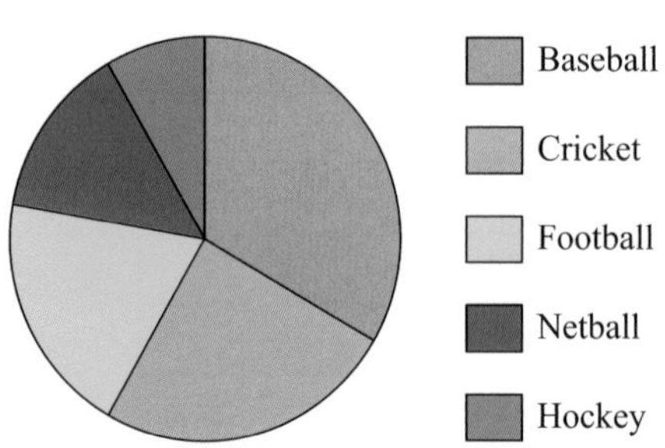

The data was collected from a sample of 200 students.

(a) What data does this graph show?
(b) How many different categories of data are there?
(c) Which was the most popular sport?
(d) What fraction of the students play cricket?
(e) How many students play netball?
(f) How many students play baseball or hockey?

Past paper questions

1 **(d)** The table shows the number of goals scored in each match by Mathsletico Rangers.

Number of goals scored	Number of matches
0	4
1	11
2	6
3	3
4	2
5	1
6	2

Draw a bar chart to show this information.
Complete the scale on the frequency axis. [3] 

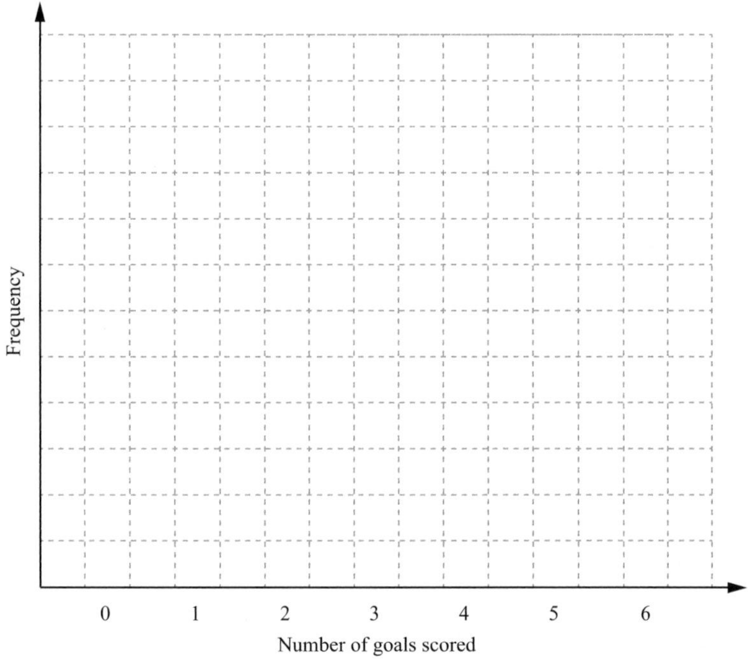

[Cambridge IGCSE Mathematics 0580 Paper 33 Q1 d(i) October/November 2012]

Fractions

Key words

- Fraction
- Vulgar fraction
- Numerator
- Denominator
- Equivalent fraction
- Simplest form
- Lowest terms
- Mixed number
- Common denominator
- Reciprocal
- Percentage
- Percentage increase
- Percentage decrease
- Reverse percentage
- Standard form
- Estimate

In this chapter you will learn how to:

- find equivalent fractions
- simplify fractions
- add, subtract, multiply and divide fractions and mixed numbers
- find fractions of numbers
- find one number as a percentage of another
- find a percentage of a number
- calculate percentage increases and decreases
- increase and decrease by a given percentage
- EXTENDED: handle reverse percentages (undoing increases and decreases)
- work with standard form
- make estimations without a calculator.

The Rhind Mathematical Papyrus is one of the earliest examples of a mathematical document. It is thought to have been written sometime between 1600 and 1700 BC by an Egyptian scribe called Ahmes, though it may be a copy of an older document. The first section of it is devoted to work with fractions.

Fractions are not only useful for improving your arithmetic skills. You use them, on an almost daily basis, often without realising it. How far can you travel on half a tank of petrol? If your share of a pizza is two-thirds will you still be hungry? If three-fifths of your journey is complete how far do you still have to travel? A hairdresser needs to mix her dyes by the correct amount and a nurse needs the correct dilution of a drug for a patient.

5.1 Equivalent fractions

REWIND

Before reading this next section you should remind yourself about Highest Common Factors (HCFs) in chapter 1. ◀

A **fraction** is part of a whole number.

Common fractions (also called **vulgar fractions**) are written in the form $\frac{a}{b}$. The number on the top, a, can be any number and is called the **numerator**. The number on the bottom, b, can be any number except 0 and is called the **denominator**. The numerator and the denominator are separated by a horizontal line.

If you multiply or divide both the numerator and the denominator by the same number, the new fraction still represents the same amount of the whole as the original fraction. The new fraction is known as an **equivalent fraction**.

For example, $\frac{2}{3}=\frac{2\times 4}{3\times 4}=\frac{8}{12}$ and $\frac{25}{35}=\frac{25\div 5}{35\div 5}=\frac{5}{7}$.

REWIND

You have come across simplifying in chapter 2 in the context of algebra. ◀

Notice in the second example that the original fraction $\left(\frac{25}{35}\right)$ has been divided to smaller terms and that as 5 and 7 have no common factor other than 1, the fraction cannot be divided any further. The fraction is now expressed in its **simplest form** (sometimes called the **lowest terms**). So, simplifying a fraction means expressing it using the lowest possible terms.

Worked example 1

Express each of the following in the simplest form possible.

(a) $\frac{3}{15}$ **(b)** $\frac{16}{24}$ **(c)** $\frac{21}{28}$ **(d)** $\frac{5}{8}$

(a) $\frac{3}{15}=\frac{3\div 3}{15\div 3}=\frac{1}{5}$

(b) $\frac{16}{24}=\frac{16\div 8}{24\div 8}=\frac{2}{3}$

(c) $\frac{21}{28}=\frac{21\div 7}{28\div 7}=\frac{3}{4}$

(d) $\frac{5}{8}$ is already in its simplest form (5 and 8 have no common factors other than 1).

Notice that in each case you divide the numerator and the denominator by the HCF of both.

Worked example 2

Which two of $\frac{5}{6}, \frac{20}{25}$ and $\frac{15}{18}$ are equivalent fractions?

Simplify each of the other fractions: $\frac{5}{6}$ is already in its simplest form.

$\frac{20}{25}=\frac{20\div 5}{25\div 5}=\frac{4}{5}$

$\frac{15}{18}=\frac{15\div 3}{18\div 3}=\frac{5}{6}$

So $\frac{5}{6}$ and $\frac{15}{18}$ are equivalent.

You could have written:

$\frac{\overset{5}{\cancel{15}}}{\underset{6}{\cancel{18}}}=\frac{5}{6}$

This is called *cancelling* and is a shorter way of showing what you have done.

Exercise 5.1

1 By multiplying or dividing both the numerator and denominator by the same number, find three equivalent fractions for each of the following.

(a) $\frac{5}{9}$ (b) $\frac{3}{7}$ (c) $\frac{12}{18}$ (d) $\frac{18}{36}$ (e) $\frac{110}{128}$

2 Express each of the following fractions in its simplest form.

(a) $\frac{7}{21}$ (b) $\frac{3}{9}$ (c) $\frac{9}{12}$ (d) $\frac{15}{25}$ (e) $\frac{500}{2500}$ (f) $\frac{24}{36}$ (g) $\frac{108}{360}$

5.2 Operations on fractions

Multiplying fractions

When multiplying two or more fractions together you can simply multiply the numerators and then multiply the denominators. Sometimes you will then need to simplify your answer. It can be faster to cancel the fractions before you multiply.

Worked example 3

Calculate:

(a) $\frac{3}{4}\times\frac{2}{7}$ (b) $\frac{5}{7}\times 3$ (c) $\frac{3}{8}$ of $4\frac{1}{2}$

(a) $\frac{3}{4}\times\frac{2}{7}=\frac{3\times 2}{4\times 7}=\frac{6}{28}=\frac{3}{14}$

Multiply the numerators to get the new numerator value. Then do the same with the denominators. Then express the fraction in its simplest form.

Notice that you can also cancel before multiplying:

$\frac{3}{\cancel{4}_2}\times\frac{\cancel{2}^1}{7}=\frac{3\times 1}{2\times 7}=\frac{3}{14}$

Divide the denominator of the first fraction, and the numerator of the second fraction, by two.

To multiply a fraction by an integer you only multiply the numerator by the integer. For example, $\frac{5}{7}\times 3=\frac{5\times 3}{7}=\frac{15}{7}$.

(b) $\frac{5}{7}\times 3=\frac{5\times 3}{7\times 1}=\frac{15}{7}$

15 and 7 do not have a common factor other than 1 and so cannot be simplified.

(c) $\frac{3}{8}$ of $4\frac{1}{2}$

Here, you have a **mixed number** ($4\frac{1}{2}$). This needs to be changed to an improper fraction (sometimes called a top heavy fraction), which is a fraction where the numerator is larger than the denominator. This allows you to complete the multiplication.

To change a mixed number to a vulgar fraction, multiply the whole number part (in this case 4) by the denominator and add it to the numerator. So: $4\frac{1}{2}=\frac{4\times 2+1}{2}=\frac{9}{2}$

$\frac{3}{8}\times 4\frac{1}{2}=\frac{3}{8}\times\frac{9}{2}=\frac{27}{16}$ Notice that the word 'of' is replaced with the $\times$ sign.

Exercise 5.2

Evaluate each of the following.

1 (a) $\frac{2}{3}\times\frac{5}{9}$ (b) $\frac{1}{2}\times\frac{3}{7}$ (c) $\frac{1}{4}\times\frac{8}{9}$ (d) $\frac{2}{7}\times\frac{14}{16}$

2 (a) $\frac{50}{128}\times\frac{256}{500}$ (b) $1\frac{1}{3}\times\frac{2}{7}$ (c) $2\frac{2}{7}\times\frac{7}{8}$ (d) $\frac{4}{5}$ of $3\frac{2}{7}$

(e) $1\frac{1}{3}$ of 24 (f) $5\frac{1}{2}\times 7\frac{1}{4}$ (g) $8\frac{8}{9}\times 20\frac{1}{4}$ (h) $7\frac{2}{3}\times 10\frac{1}{2}$

Adding and subtracting fractions

REWIND

You will need to use the lowest common multiple (LCM) in this section. You met this in chapter 1. ◀

You can only add or subtract fractions that are the same type. In other words, they must have the same denominator. This is called a **common denominator**. You must use what you know about equivalent fractions to help you make sure fractions have a common denominator.

The following worked example shows how you can use the LCM of both denominators as the common denominator.

Worked example 4

Write each of the following as a single fraction in its simplest form.

(a) $\frac{1}{2}+\frac{1}{4}$ **(b)** $\frac{3}{4}+\frac{5}{6}$ **(c)** $2\frac{3}{4}-1\frac{5}{7}$

Notice that, once you have a common denominator, you only add the numerators. *Never* add the denominators!

(a)

$\frac{1}{2}+\frac{1}{4}$ $=\frac{2}{4}+\frac{1}{4}$ $=\frac{3}{4}$	Find the common denominator. The LCM of 2 and 4 is 4. Use this as the common denominator and find the equivalent fractions. Then add the numerators.

You will sometimes find that two fractions added together can result in an improper fraction (sometimes called a top-heavy fraction). Usually you will re-write this as a mixed number.

(b)

$\frac{3}{4}+\frac{5}{6}$ $=\frac{9}{12}+\frac{10}{12}$ $=\frac{19}{12}$ $=1\frac{7}{12}$	Find the common denominator. The LCM of 4 and 6 is 12. Use this as the common denominator and find the equivalent fractions. Add the numerators. Change an improper fraction to a mixed number.

The same rules apply for subtracting fractions as adding them.

(c)

$2\frac{3}{4}-1\frac{5}{7}$ $=\frac{11}{4}-\frac{12}{7}$ $=\frac{77}{28}-\frac{48}{28}$ $=\frac{77-48}{28}$ $=\frac{29}{28}$ $=1\frac{1}{28}$	Change mixed numbers to improper fractions to make them easier to handle. The LCM of 4 and 7 is 28, so this is the common denominator. Find the equivalent fractions. Subtract one numerator from the other. Change an improper fraction to a mixed number.

Tip

Egyptian fractions are a good example of manipulating fractions but they are not in the syllabus.

Egyptian fractions

An Egyptian fraction is the sum of any number of *different* fractions (different denominators) each with numerator one. For example $\frac{1}{2}+\frac{1}{3}$ is the Egyptian fraction that represents $\frac{5}{6}$. Ancient Egyptians used to represent single fractions in this way but in modern times we tend to prefer the single fraction that results from finding a common denominator.

Exercise 5.3

Evaluate the following.

1 (a) $\frac{1}{3}+\frac{1}{3}$ (b) $\frac{3}{7}+\frac{2}{7}$ (c) $\frac{5}{8}-\frac{3}{8}$ (d) $\frac{5}{9}+\frac{8}{9}$

(e) $\frac{1}{6}+\frac{1}{5}$ (f) $\frac{2}{3}-\frac{5}{8}$ (g) $2\frac{5}{8}-1\frac{3}{4}$ (h) $5\frac{1}{8}-3\frac{1}{16}$

2 (a) $4-\frac{2}{3}$ (b) $6+\frac{5}{11}$ (c) $11+7\frac{1}{4}$ (d) $11-7\frac{1}{4}$

(e) $3\frac{1}{2}-4\frac{1}{3}$ (f) $5\frac{1}{4}+3\frac{1}{16}+4\frac{3}{8}$ (g) $5\frac{1}{8}-3\frac{1}{16}+4\frac{3}{4}$ (h) $1\frac{1}{3}+2\frac{2}{5}-1\frac{1}{4}$

(i) $\frac{3}{7}+\frac{2}{3}\times\frac{14}{8}$ (j) $3\frac{1}{2}-2\frac{1}{4}\times\frac{4}{3}$ (k) $3\frac{1}{6}-1\frac{1}{2}+7\frac{3}{4}$ (l) $2\frac{1}{4}-3\frac{1}{3}+4\frac{1}{5}$

Remember to use BODMAS here.

3 Find Egyptian fractions for each of the following.

(a) $\frac{3}{4}$ (b) $\frac{2}{3}$ (c) $\frac{5}{8}$ (d) $\frac{3}{16}$

Think which two fractions with a numerator of 1 might have an LCM equal to the denominator given.

FAST FORWARD

The multiplication, division, addition and subtraction of fractions will be revisited in chapter 14 when *algebraic* fractions are considered. ▶

Dividing fractions

Before describing how to divide two fractions, the **reciprocal** needs to be introduced. The reciprocal of any fraction can be obtained by swapping the numerator and the denominator.

So, the reciprocal of $\frac{3}{4}$ is $\frac{4}{3}$ and the reciprocal of $\frac{7}{2}$ is $\frac{2}{7}$.

Also the reciprocal of $\frac{1}{2}$ is $\frac{2}{1}$ or just 2 and the reciprocal of 5 is $\frac{1}{5}$.

If any fraction is multiplied by its reciprocal then the result is always 1. For example:

$\frac{1}{3}\times\frac{3}{1}=1$, $\frac{3}{8}\times\frac{8}{3}=1$ and $\frac{a}{b}\times\frac{b}{a}=1$

To divide one fraction by another fraction, you simply multiply the first fraction by the reciprocal of the second.

Look at the example below:

$$\frac{a}{b}\div\frac{c}{d}=\frac{\left(\frac{a}{b}\right)}{\left(\frac{c}{d}\right)}$$

Now multiply both the numerator and denominator by bd and cancel:

$$\frac{a}{b}\div\frac{c}{d}=\frac{\left(\frac{a}{b}\right)}{\left(\frac{c}{d}\right)}=\frac{\left(\frac{a}{\not b}\right)\times \not bd}{\left(\frac{c}{\not d}\right)\times b\not d}$$

$$=\frac{ad}{bc}=\frac{a}{b}\times\frac{d}{c}$$

Worked example 5

Evaluate each of the following.

(a) $\frac{3}{4}\div\frac{1}{2}$ **(b)** $1\frac{3}{4}\div 2\frac{1}{3}$ **(c)** $\frac{5}{8}\div 2$ **(d)** $\frac{6}{7}\div 3$

(a) $\frac{3}{4}\div\frac{1}{2}=\frac{3}{\not 4_{2}}\times\frac{\not 2^{1}}{1}=\frac{3}{2}=1\frac{1}{2}$

Multiply by the reciprocal of $\frac{1}{2}$. Use the rules you have learned about multiplying fractions.

(b)	$1\frac{3}{4} \div 2\frac{1}{3} = \frac{7}{4} \div \frac{7}{3}$ $= \frac{\cancel{7}^1}{4} \times \frac{3}{\cancel{7}_1}$ $= \frac{3}{4}$	Convert the mixed fractions to improper fractions. Multiply by the reciprocal of $\frac{7}{3}$.
(c)	$\frac{5}{8} \div 2 = \frac{5}{8} \div \frac{2}{1}$ $= \frac{5}{8} \times \frac{1}{2}$ $= \frac{5}{16}$	Write 2 as an improper fraction. Multiply by the reciprocal of $\frac{2}{1}$.
(d)	$\frac{6}{7} \div 3 = \frac{\cancel{6}^2}{7} \times \frac{1}{\cancel{3}_1}$ $= \frac{2}{7}$	

To divide a fraction by an integer you can either just multiply the denominator by the integer, *or* divide the numerator by the same integer.

Exercise 5.4

Evaluate each of the following.

1 $\frac{1}{7} \div \frac{1}{3}$ **2** $\frac{2}{5} \div \frac{3}{7}$ **3** $\frac{4}{9} \div 7$ **4** $\frac{10}{11} \div 5$

5 $4\frac{1}{5} \div \frac{1}{7}$ **6** $3\frac{1}{5} \div 5\frac{2}{3}$ **7** $7\frac{7}{8} \div 5\frac{1}{12}$ **8** $3\frac{1}{4} \div 3\frac{1}{2}$

Fractions with decimals

Sometimes you will find that either the numerator or the denominator, or even both, are *not* whole numbers! To express these fractions in their simplest forms you need to

- make sure both the numerator and denominator are converted to an integer by finding an equivalent fraction
- check that the equivalent fraction has been simplified.

Worked example 6

Simplify each of the following fractions.

(a) $\frac{0.1}{3}$ **(b)** $\frac{1.3}{2.4}$ **(c)** $\frac{36}{0.12}$

(a)	$\frac{0.1}{3} = \frac{0.1 \times 10}{3 \times 10} = \frac{1}{30}$	Multiply 0.1 by 10 to convert 0.1 to an integer. To make sure the fraction is equivalent, you need to do the same to the numerator and the denominator, so multiply 3 by 10 as well.
(b)	$\frac{1.3}{2.4} = \frac{1.3 \times 10}{2.4 \times 10} = \frac{13}{24}$	Multiply both the numerator and denominator by 10 to get integers. 13 and 24 do not have a HCF other than 1 so cannot be simplified.
(c)	$\frac{36}{0.12} = \frac{36 \times 100}{0.12 \times 100} = \frac{3600}{12} = 300$	Multiply 0.12 by 100 to produce an integer. Remember to also multiply the numerator by 100, so the fraction is equivalent. The final fraction can be simplified by cancelling.

Exercise 5.5

Remember that any fraction that contains a decimal in either its numerator or denominator will not be considered to be simplified.

What fraction can be used to represent 0.3?

Simplify each of the following fractions.

1 $\frac{0.3}{12}$ **2** $\frac{0.4}{0.5}$ **3** $\frac{6}{0.7}$ **4** $\frac{0.7}{0.14}$

5 $\frac{36}{1.5}$ **6** $0.3\times\frac{5}{12}$ **7** $0.4\times\frac{1.5}{1.6}$ **8** $\frac{2.8}{0.7}\times\frac{1.44}{0.6}$

Further calculations with fractions

You can use fractions to help you solve problems.

Remember for example, that $\frac{2}{3}=2\times\frac{1}{3}$ and that, although this may seem trivial, this simple fact can help you to solve problems easily.

Worked example 7

Suppose that $\frac{2}{5}$ of the students in a school are girls. If the school has 600 students, how many girls are there?

Remember in worked example 3, you saw that 'of' is replaced by ×.

$\frac{2}{5}$ of $600=\frac{2}{5}\times 600=\frac{2}{\cancel{5}_1}\times\frac{\cancel{600}^{120}}{1}=2\times 120=240$ girls

Worked example 8

Now imagine that $\frac{2}{5}$ of the students in another school are boys, and that there are 360 boys. How many students are there in the whole school?

$\frac{2}{5}$ of the total is 360, so $\frac{1}{5}$ of the total must be half of this, 180. This means that $\frac{5}{5}$ of the population, that is all of it, is $5\times 180=900$ students in total.

Exercise 5.6

1 $\frac{3}{4}$ of the people at an auction bought an item. If there are 120 people at the auction, how many bought something?

2 An essay contains 420 sentences. 80 of these sentences contain typing errors. What fraction (given in its simplest form) of the sentences contain errors?

3 28 is $\frac{2}{7}$ of which number?

4 If $\frac{3}{5}$ of the people in a theatre buy a snack during the interval, and of those who buy a snack $\frac{5}{7}$ buy ice cream, what fraction of the people in the theatre buy ice cream?

5 Andrew, Bashir and Candy are trying to save money for a birthday party. If Andrew saves $\frac{1}{4}$ of the total needed, Bashir saves $\frac{2}{5}$ and Candy saves $\frac{1}{10}$, what fraction of the cost of the party is left to pay?

5.3 Percentages

A **percentage** is a fraction with a denominator of 100. The symbol used to represent percentage is %.

To find 40% of 25, you simply need to find $\frac{40}{100}$ of 25. Using what you know about multiplying fractions:

$$\frac{40}{100}\times 25=\frac{\overset{2}{\cancel{40}}}{_{5}\cancel{100}}\times\frac{25}{1}$$
$$=\frac{2}{_{1}\cancel{5}}\times\frac{\cancel{25}^{5}}{1}$$
$$=\frac{2}{1}\times\frac{5}{1}=10$$

$\therefore$ 40% of 25 = 10

Equivalent forms

This works because the decimal point is moved two places to the left when you divide by 100.

A percentage can be converted into a decimal by dividing by 100 (notice that the decimal point moves two places to the left). So, $45\%=\frac{45}{100}=0.45$ and $3.1\%=\frac{3.1}{100}=0.031$.

A decimal can be converted to a percentage by multiplying by 100 (notice that the decimal point moves two places to the right). So, $0.65=\frac{65}{100}=65\%$ and $0.7\times 100=70$.

Converting percentages to vulgar fractions (and vice versa) involves a few more stages.

Worked example 9

Convert each of the following percentages to fractions in their simplest form.

(a) 25% **(b)** 30% **(c)** 3.5%

Remember that a fraction that contains a decimal is not in its simplest form.

(a)	$25\%=\frac{25}{100}=\frac{1}{4}$	Write as a fraction with a denominator of 100, then simplify.
(b)	$30\%=\frac{30}{100}=\frac{3}{10}$	Write as a fraction with a denominator of 100, then simplify.
(c)	$3.5\%=\frac{3.5}{100}=\frac{35}{1000}=\frac{7}{200}$	Write as a fraction with a denominator of 100, then simplify.

Worked example 10

Convert each of the following fractions into percentages.

(a) $\frac{1}{20}$ **(b)** $\frac{1}{8}$

(a)	$\frac{1}{20}=\frac{1\times 5}{20\times 5}=\frac{5}{100}=5\%$	Find the equivalent fraction with a denominator of 100. (Remember to do the same thing to both the numerator and denominator). $\left(\frac{5}{100}=0.05,\ 0.05\times 100=5\%\right)$

(b) $\frac{1}{8} = \frac{1 \times 12.5}{8 \times 12.5}$ $= \frac{12.5}{100} = 12.5\%$

Find the equivalent fraction with a denominator of 100. (Remember to do the same thing to both the numerator and denominator).

$\left(\frac{12.5}{100} = 0.125,\ 0.125 \times 100 = 12.5\%\right)$

Although it is not always easy to find an equivalent fraction with a denominator of 100, any fraction can be converted into a percentage by multiplying by 100 and cancelling.

Worked example 11

Convert the following fractions into percentages:

(a) $\frac{3}{40}$ **(b)** $\frac{8}{15}$

(a) $\frac{3}{40} \times \frac{100}{1} = \frac{30}{4} = \frac{15}{2} = 7.5,$

so $\frac{3}{40} = 7.5\%$

(b) $\frac{8}{15} \times \frac{100}{1} = \frac{160}{3} = 53.3$ (1 d.p.),

so $\frac{8}{15} = 53.3\%$ (1d.p.)

Exercise 5.7

Later in the chapter you will see that a percentage can be greater than 100.

1 Convert each of the following percentages into fractions in their simplest form.

(a) 70% (b) 75% (c) 20% (d) 36% (e) 15% (f) 2.5%
(g) 215% (h) 132% (i) 117.5% (j) 108.4% (k) 0.25% (l) 0.002%

2 Express the following fractions as percentages.

(a) $\frac{3}{5}$ (b) $\frac{7}{25}$ (c) $\frac{17}{20}$ (d) $\frac{3}{10}$ (e) $\frac{8}{200}$ (f) $\frac{5}{12}$

Finding one number as a percentage of another

To write one number as a percentage of another number, you start by writing the first number as a fraction of the second number then multiply by 100.

Worked example 12

(a) Express 16 as a percentage of 48.

$\frac{16}{48} = \frac{16}{48} \times 100 = 33.3\%$ (1d.p.)

First, write 16 as a fraction of 48, then multiply by 100.

$\frac{16}{48} = \frac{1}{3} \times 100 = 33.3\%$ (1d.p.)

This may be easier if you write the fraction in its simplest form first.

(b) Express 15 as a percentage of 75.

$\frac{15}{75} \times 100$

$= \frac{1}{5} \times 100 = 20\%$

Write 15 as a fraction of 75, then simplify and multiply by 100. You know that 100 divided by 5 is 20, so you don't need a calculator.

(c) Express 18 as a percentage of 23.

You need to calculate $\frac{18}{23} \times 100$, but this is not easy using basic fractions because you cannot simplify it further, and 23 does not divide neatly into 100. Fortunately, you can use your calculator. Simply type:

[1] [8] [÷] [2] [3] [×] [1] [0] [0] [=] 78.26%

Exercise 5.8 Where appropriate, give your answer to 3 significant figures.

1. Express 14 as a percentage of 35.
2. Express 3.5 as a percentage of 14.
3. Express 17 as a percentage of 63.
4. 36 people live in a block of flats. 28 of these people jog around the park each morning. What percentage of the people living in the block of flats go jogging around the park?
5. Jack scores $\frac{19}{24}$ in a test. What percentage of the marks did Jack get?
6. Express 1.3 as a percentage of 5.2.
7. Express 0.13 as a percentage of 520.

Percentage increases and decreases

Suppose the cost of a book increases from \$12 to \$15. The actual increase is \$3. As a fraction of the original value, the increase is $\frac{3}{12} = \frac{1}{4}$. This is the fractional change and you can write this fraction as 25%. In this example, the value of the book has increased by 25% of the original value. This is called the **percentage increase**. If the value had reduced (for example if something was on sale in a shop) then it would have been a **percentage decrease**.

Note carefully: whenever increases or decreases are stated as percentages, they are stated as percentages of the *original* value.

Worked example 13

(a) The value of a house increases from \$120 000 to \$124 800 between August and December. What percentage increase is this?

$\$124\,800 - \$120\,000 = \$4800$	First calculate the increase.
$\%\text{increase} = \frac{\text{increase}}{\text{original}} \times 100\%$	Write the increase as a fraction of the original and multiply by 100.
$= \frac{4800}{120\,000} \times 100\% = 4\%$	Then do the calculation (either in your head or using a calculator).

(b) The United States Census Bureau found the population of New Orleans, Louisiana to be 484 674 in 2000 and 223 388 in 2006 following Hurricane Katrina. What percentage decrease does this represent?

$484\,674 - 223\,388 = 261\,286$	First calculate the decrease.
$\%\text{decrease} = \frac{\text{decrease}}{\text{original}} \times 100\%$	Write the decrease as a fraction of the original, and multiply by 100.
$= \frac{261286}{484\,674} \times 100\% = 53.9\%$	Use a calculator to find the answer. (This answer is rounded to 3sf)

Exercise 5.9 *Living maths*

Where appropriate, give your answer to the nearest whole percent.

1. Between 2000 and 2006, the population of the state of Louisiana in the United States of America decreased from 4 468 976 to 4 287 768. Find the percentage decrease in the population of Louisiana between 2000 and 2006.
2. Barney bought 38 CDs during 2009 and 46 during 2010. Find the percentage increase.

3 A theatre has enough seats for 450 audience members. After renovation it is expected that this number will increase to 480. Find the percentage increase.

4 Sally works in an electrical component factory. On Monday she makes a total of 363 components but on Tuesday she makes 432. Calculate the percentage increase.

5 Inter Polation Airlines carried a total of 383 402 passengers in 2008 and 287 431 in 2009. Calculate the percentage decrease in passengers carried by the airline.

6 A liquid evaporates steadily. In one hour the mass of liquid in a laboratory container decreases from 0.32 kg to 0.18 kg. Calculate the percentage decrease.

Increasing and decreasing by a given percentage

If you know what percentage you want to increase or decrease an amount by, you can find the actual increase or decrease by finding a percentage of the original. If you want to know the new value you either add the increase to or subtract the decrease from the original value.

Remember that you are always considering a percentage of the *original* value.

Worked example 14

Increase 56 by: **(a)** 10% **(b)** 15% **(c)** 4%

(a) $10\%\text{ of }56 = \frac{10}{100} \times 56$

$= \frac{1}{10} \times 56 = 5.6$

$56 + 5.6 = 61.6$

First of all, you need to calculate 10% of 56 to work out the size of the increase.

To increase the original by 10% you need to add this to 56.

If you don't need to know the actual increase but just the final value, you can use this method:

If you consider the original to be 100% then adding 10% to this will give 110% of the original. So multiply 56 by $\frac{110}{100}$, which gives 61.6.

(b) $\frac{115}{100} \times 56 = 64.4$

A 15% increase will lead to 115% of the original.

(c) $\frac{104}{100} \times 56 = 58.24$

A 4% increase will lead to 104% of the original.

Worked example 15

In a sale all items are reduced by 15%. If the normal selling price for a bicycle is \$120 calculate the sale price.

$100 - 15 = 85$

$\frac{85}{100} \times \$120 = \$102$

Note that reducing a number by 15% leaves you with 85% of the original. So you simply find 85% of the original value.

Exercise 5.10

1 Increase 40 by:

(a) 10% (b) 15% (c) 25% (d) 5% (e) 4%

2 Increase 53 by:

(a) 50% (b) 84% (c) 13.6% (d) 112% (e) $\frac{1}{2}\%$

3 Decrease 124 by:

(a) 10% **(b)** 15% **(c)** 30% **(d)** 4% **(e)** 7%

4 Decrease 36.2 by:

(a) 90% **(b)** 35.4% **(c)** 0.3% **(d)** 100% **(e)** $\frac{1}{2}$%

Living maths

The remaining questions in this exercise show how percentages may appear in real-life problems.

5 Shajeen usually works 30 hours per week but decides that he needs to increase this by 10% to be sure that he can save enough for a holiday. How many hours per week will Shajeen need to work?

6 12% sales tax is applied to all items of clothing sold in a certain shop. If a T-shirt is advertised for $12 (before tax) what will be the cost of the T-shirt once tax is added?

7 The Oyler Theatre steps up its advertising campaign and manages to increase its audiences by 23% during 2010. If 21 300 people watched plays at the Oyler Theatre during 2009, how many people watched plays during 2010?

8 The population of Trigville was 153 000 at the end of 2011. Following a flood, 17% of the residents of Trigville moved away during 2012. What was the population of Trigville at the end of 2012?

9 Anthea decides that she is watching too much television. If Anthea watched 12 hours of television in one week and then decreased this by 12% the next week, how much time did Anthea spend watching television in the second week? Give your answer in hours and minutes.

Reverse percentages

Sometimes you are given the value or amount of an item *after* a percentage increase or decrease has been applied to it and you need to know what the original value was. To solve this type of **reverse percentage** question it is important to remember that you are always dealing with percentages of the *original* values. The method used in worked example 14 (b) and (c) is used to help us solve these type of problems.

Worked example 16

A store is holding a sale in which every item is reduced by 10%. A jacket in this sale is sold for $108. How can you find the original price of the Jacket?

$\frac{90}{100} \times x = 108$	If an item is reduced by 10%, the new cost is 90% of the original (100–10). If x is the original value of the jacket then you can write a formula using the new price.
$x = \frac{100}{90} \times 108$	Notice that when the $\times\frac{90}{100}$ was moved to the other side of the = sign it became its
original price = $120.	reciprocal, $\frac{100}{90}$.

Important: Undoing a 10% decrease is *not* the same as increasing the reduced value by 10%. If you *increase* the sale price of $108 by 10% you will get $\frac{110}{100} \times \$108 = \$118.80$ which is a different *(and incorrect)* answer.

Exercise 5.11

1 If 20% of an amount is 35, what is 100%?

2 If 35% of an amount is 127, what is 100%?

3 245 is 12.5% of an amount. What is the total amount?

4 The table gives the sale price and the % by which the price was reduced for a number of items. Copy the table, then complete it by calculating the original prices.

Sale price ($)	% reduction	Original price ($)
52.00	10	
185.00	10	
4700.00	5	
2.90	5	
24.50	12	
10.00	8	
12.50	7	
9.75	15	
199.50	20	
99.00	25	

5 A shop keeper marks up goods by 22% before selling them. The selling price of ten items are given below. For each one, work out the cost price (the price before the mark up).

(a) $25.00 **(b)** $200.00 **(c)** $14.50 **(d)** $23.99 **(e)** $15.80
(f) $45.80 **(g)** $29.75 **(h)** $129.20 **(i)** $0.99 **(j)** $0.80

6 Seven students were absent from a class on Monday. This is 17.5% of the class.

(a) How many students are there in the class in total?
(b) How many students were present on Monday?

7 A hat shop is holding a 10% sale. If Jack buys a hat for $18 in the sale, how much did the hat cost before the sale?

8 Nick is training for a swimming race and reduces his weight by 5% over a 3-month period. If Nick now weighs 76 kg how much did he weigh before he started training?

9 The water in a pond evaporates at a rate of 12% per week. If the pond now contains 185 litres of water, approximately how much water was in the pond a week ago?

5.4 Standard form

When numbers are very small, like 0.0000362, or very large, like 358 000 000, calculations can be time consuming and it is easy to miss out some of the zeros. **Standard form** is used to express very small and very large numbers in a compact and efficient way. In standard form, numbers are written as a number multiplied by 10 raised to a given power.

Remember that digits are in place order:

1000s	100s	10s	units		10ths	100ths	1000ths
3	0	0	0	•	0	0	0

Standard form for large numbers

The key to standard form for large numbers is to understand what happens when you multiply by powers of 10. Each time you multiply a number by 10 each digit within the number moves one place order to the left (notice that this *looks* like the decimal point has moved one place to the right).

3.2

$3.2 \times 10 = 32.0$ The digits have moved one place order to the left.

$3.2 \times 10^2 = 3.2 \times 100 = 320.0$ The digits have moved two places.

$3.2 \times 10^3 = 3.2 \times 1000 = 3200.0$ The digits have moved three places.

... and so on. You should see a pattern forming.

Any large number can be expressed in standard form by writing it as a number between 1 and 10 multiplied by a suitable power of 10. To do this write the appropriate number between 1 and 10 first (using the non-zero digits of the original number) and then count the number of places you need to move the first digit to the left. The number of places tells you by what power, 10 should be multiplied.

Worked example 17

Write 320 000 in standard form.

3.2	Start by finding the number between 1 and 10 that has the same digits in the same order as the original number. Here, the extra 4 zero digits can be excluded because they do not change the size of your new number.
5 4 3 2 1 3 2 0 0 0 0.0 3.2	Now compare the position of the first digit in both numbers: '3' has to move 5 place orders to the left to get from the new number to the original number.
$320\,000 = 3.2 \times 10^5$	The first digit, '3', has moved five places. So, you multiply by 10^5.

Calculating using standard form

REWIND

The laws of indices can be found in chapter 2. ◀

Having converted large numbers into standard form, calculations involving multiplication and division can be carried out using the laws of indices.

Worked example 18

Solve and give your answer in standard form.

(a) $(3\times10^5)\times(2\times10^6)$ **(b)** $(2\times10^3)\times(8\times10^7)$

(c) $(2.8\times10^6)\div(1.4\times10^4)$ **(d)** $(9\times10^6)+(3\times10^8)$

(a) $(3\times10^5)\times(2\times10^6) = (3\times2)\times(10^5\times10^6)$
$= 6\times10^{5+6}$
$= 6\times10^{11}$

Simplify by putting like terms together. Use the laws of indices where appropriate.

Write the number in standard form.

You may be asked to convert your answer to an ordinary number. To convert 6×10^{11} into an ordinary number, the '6' needs to move 11 places to the left:

6.0×10^{11}

11 10 9 8 7 6 5 4 3 2 1

= 6 0 0 0 0 0 0 0 0 0 0 0.0

Although it is the place order that is changing; it looks like the decimal point moves to the right.

(b) $(2\times10^3)\times(8\times10^7) = (2\times8)\times(10^3\times10^7)$
$= 16\times10^{10}$

$16\times10^{10} = 1.6\times10\times10^{10}$
$= 1.6\times10^{11}$

The answer 16×10^{10} is numerically correct but it is not in standard form because 16 is not between 1 and 10. You can change it to standard form by thinking of 16 as 1.6×10.

(c) $(2.8\times10^6)\div(1.4\times10^4) = \dfrac{2.8\times10^6}{1.4\times10^4} = \dfrac{2.8}{1.4}\times\dfrac{10^6}{10^4}$
$= 2\times10^{6-4}$
$= 2\times10^2$

Simplify by putting like terms together. Use the laws of indices.

Tip

Always be sure to check that your final answer is in standard form. Check that all conditions are satisfied. Make sure that the number part is between 1 and 10.

To make it easier to add up the ordinary numbers make sure they are lined up so that the place values match:

300 000 000
+ 9 000 000

(d) $(9\times10^6)+(3\times10^8)$

When adding or subtracting numbers in standard form it is often easiest to re-write them both as ordinary numbers first, then convert the answer to standard form.

$9\times10^6 = 9\,000\,000$

$3\times10^8 = 300\,000\,000$

So $(9\times10^6)+(3\times10^8) = 300\,000\,000 + 9\,000\,000$

$= 309\,000\,000$

$= 3.09\times10^8$

Exercise 5.12

1 Write each of the following numbers in standard form.

(a) 380 **(b)** 4 200 000 **(c)** 45 600 000 000 **(d)** 65 400 000 000 000
(e) 20 **(f)** 10 **(g)** 10.3 **(h)** 5

When converting standard form back to an ordinary number, the power of 10 tells you how many places the first digit moves to the left (or decimal point moves to the right), not how many zeros there are.

2 Write each of the following as an ordinary number.

(a) 2.4×10^6 **(b)** 3.1×10^8 **(c)** 1.05×10^7 **(d)** 9.9×10^3 **(e)** 7.1×10^1

3 Simplify each of the following, leaving your answer in standard form.

(a) $(2\times10^{13})\times(4\times10^{17})$ **(b)** $(1.4\times10^8)\times(3\times10^4)$ **(c)** $(1.5\times10^{13})^2$
(d) $(12\times10^5)\times(11\times10^2)$ **(e)** $(0.2\times10^{17})\times(0.7\times10^{16})$ **(f)** $(9\times10^{17})\div(3\times10^{16})$
(g) $(8\times10^{17})\div(4\times10^{16})$ **(h)** $(1.5\times10^8)\div(5\times10^4)$ **(i)** $(2.4\times10^{64})\div(8\times10^{21})$
(j) $(1.44\times10^7)\div(1.2\times10^4)$ **(k)** $\dfrac{(1.7\times10^8)}{(3.4\times10^5)}$ **(l)** $(4.9\times10^5)\times(3.6\times10^9)$

Remember that you can write these as ordinary numbers before adding or subtracting.

4 Simplify each of the following, leaving your answer in standard form.

(a) $(3\times10^4)+(4\times10^3)$ **(b)** $(4\times10^6)-(3\times10^5)$ **(c)** $(2.7\times10^3)+(5.6\times10^5)$
(d) $(7.1\times10^9)-(4.3\times10^7)$ **(e)** $(5.8\times10^9)-(2.7\times10^3)$

Standard form for small numbers

You have seen that digits move place order to the left when multiplying by powers of 10. If you *divide* by powers of 10 move the digits in place order to the right and make the number *smaller*.

Consider the following pattern:

2300

$2300 \div 10 = 230$

$2300 \div 10^2 = 2300 \div 100 = 23$

$2300 \div 10^3 = 2300 \div 1000 = 2.3$

. . . and so on.

The digits move place order to the right (notice that this looks like the decimal point is moving to the left). You saw in chapter 1 that if a direction is taken to be positive, the opposite direction is taken to be negative. Since moving place order to the left raises 10 to the power of a *positive* index, it follows that moving place order to the right raises 10 to the power of a *negative* index.

Also remember from chapter 2 that you can write negative powers to indicate that you divide, and you saw above that with small numbers, you divide by 10 to express the number in standard form.

Worked example 19

Write each of the following in standard form.

(a) 0.004 **(b)** 0.000 000 34 **(c)** $(2\times10^{-3})\times(3\times10^{-7})$

(a)

1 2 3
0.0 0 4
4.0
$= 4\times10^{-3}$

Start with a number between 1 and 10, in this case 4.

Compare the position of the first digit: '4' needs to move 3 place orders to the right to get from the new number to the original number. In worked example 17 you saw that moving 5 places to the *left* meant multiplying by 10^5, so it follows that moving 3 places to the *right* means multiply by 10^{-3}.

Notice also that the first non-zero digit in 0.004 is in the 3rd place after the decimal point and that the power of 10 is –3.

Alternatively: you know that you need to divide by 10 three times, so you can change it to a fractional index and then a negative index.

$0.004 = 4\div10^3$

$= 4\times10^{\frac{1}{3}}$

$= 4\times10^{-3}$.

(b) $0.000\,000\,34 = 3.4\div10^7$

$= 3.4\times10^{-7}$

1 2 3 4 5 6 7
0. 0 0 0 0 0 0 3 4 $= 3.4\times10^{-7}$

Notice that the first non-zero digit in 0.000 000 34 is in the 7th place after the decimal point and that the power of 10 is –7.

(c) $(2\times10^{-3})\times(3\times10^{-7})$

$= (2\times3)\times(10^{-3}\times10^{-7})$

$= 6\times10^{-3+-7}$

$= 6\times10^{-10}$

Simplify by gathering like terms together.

Use the laws of indices.

Exercise 5.13

When using standard form with negative indices, the power to which 10 is raised tells you the position of the first *non-zero* digit after (to the right of) the decimal point.

For some calculations, you might need to change a term into standard form before you multiply or divide.

Remember that you can write these as ordinary numbers before adding or subtracting.

1 Write each of the following numbers in standard form.

(a) 0.004 **(b)** 0.00005 **(c)** 0.000032 **(d)** 0.0000000564

2 Write each of the following as an ordinary number.

(a) 3.6×10^{-4} **(b)** 1.6×10^{-8} **(c)** 2.03×10^{-7} **(d)** 8.8×10^{-3} **(e)** 7.1×10^{-1}

3 Simplify each of the following, leaving your answer in standard form.

(a) $(2\times10^{-4})\times(4\times10^{-16})$ **(b)** $(1.6\times10^{-8})\times(4\times10^{-4})$
(c) $(1.5\times10^{-6})\times(2.1\times10^{-3})$ **(d)** $(11\times10^{-5})\times(3\times10^{2})$
(e) $(9\times10^{17})\div(4.5\times10^{-16})$ **(f)** $(7\times10^{-21})\div(1\times10^{16})$
(g) $(4.5\times10^{8})\div(0.9\times10^{-4})$ **(h)** $(11\times10^{-5})\times(3\times10^{2})\div(2\times10^{-3})$

4 Simplify each of the following, leaving your answer in standard form.

(a) $(3.1\times10^{-4})+(2.7\times10^{-2})$ **(b)** $(3.2\times10^{-1})-(3.2\times10^{-2})$
(c) $(7.01\times10^{3})+(5.6\times10^{-1})$ **(d)** $(1.44\times10^{-5})-(2.33\times10^{-6})$

Living maths

The remainder of this exercise will focus on real-life problems that relate to standard form.

5 Find the number of seconds in a day, giving your answer in standard form.

6 The speed of light is approximately 3×10^8 metres per second. How far will light travel in:

(a) 10 seconds **(b)** 20 seconds **(c)** 102 seconds

7 Data storage (in computers) is measured in gigabytes. One gigabyte is 2^{30} bytes.

(a) Write 2^{30} in standard form correct to 1 significant figure.
(b) There are 1024 gigabytes in a terabyte. How many bytes is this? Give your answer in standard form correct to one significant figure.

5.5 Your calculator and standard form

Standard form is also called scientific notation or exponential notation.

On modern scientific calculators you can enter calculations in standard form. Your calculator will also display numbers with too many digits for screen display in standard form.

Keying in standard form calculations

You will need to use the $\times 10^x$ button or the Exp or EE button on your calculator. These are known as the exponent keys. All exponent keys work in the same way, so you can follow the example below on your own calculator using whatever key you have and you will get the same result.

When you use the exponent function key of your calculator, you do NOT enter the '× 10' part of the calculation. The calculator does that part automatically as part of the function.

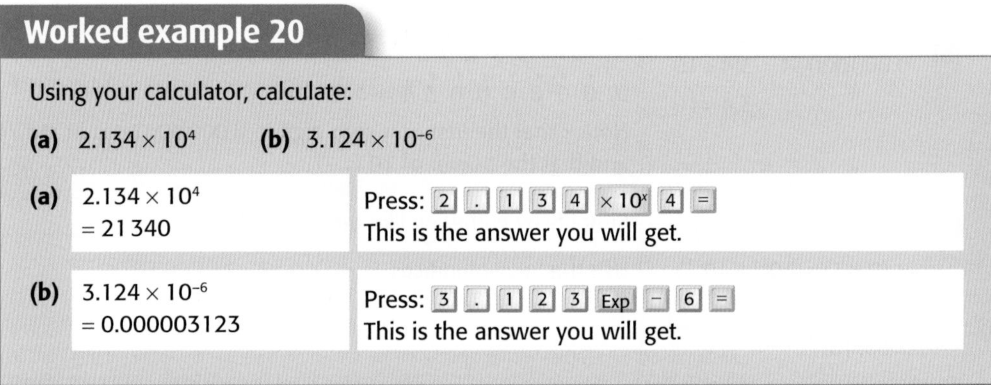

Worked example 20

Using your calculator, calculate:

(a) 2.134×10^4 **(b)** 3.124×10^{-6}

(a)	2.134×10^4 $= 21\,340$	Press: 2 . 1 3 4 $\times 10^x$ 4 = This is the answer you will get.
(b)	3.124×10^{-6} $= 0.000003123$	Press: 3 . 1 2 3 Exp − 6 = This is the answer you will get.

Making sense of the calculator display

Different calculators work in different ways and you need to understand how your own calculator works. Make sure you know what buttons to use to enter standard form calculations and how to interpret the display and convert your calculator answer into decimal form.

Depending on your calculator, answers in scientific notation will be displayed on a line with an exponent like this:

5.98E-06 This is 5.98×10^{-06}

or on two lines with the calculation and the answer, like this:

6.23E23*4.11
2.56E24 This is 2.56×10^{24}

If you are asked to give your answer in standard form, all you need to do is interpret the display and write the answer correctly. If you are asked to give your answer as an ordinary number (decimal), then you need to apply the rules you already know to write the answer correctly.

Exercise 5.14

1 Enter each of these numbers into your calculator using the correct function key and write down what appears on your calculator display.

(a) 4.2×10^{12}	**(b)** 1.8×10^{-5}	**(c)** 2.7×10^6
(d) 1.34×10^{-2}	**(e)** 1.87×10^{-9}	**(f)** 4.23×10^7
(g) 3.102×10^{-4}	**(h)** 3.098×10^9	**(i)** 2.076×10^{-23}

2 Here are ten calculator displays giving answers in standard form.

(i) `1.09 05` (ii) `2.876 -06` (iii) `4.012 09` (iv) `1.89 07`

(v) `3.123E13` (vi) `2.876E-04` (vii) `9.02E15` (viii) `8.076E-12`

(ix) `8.124E-11` (x) `5.0234 19`

(a) Write out each answer in standard form.
(b) Arrange the ten numbers in order from smallest to largest.

3 Use your calculator. Give the answers in standard form correct to 5 significant figures.

(a) 4234^5 **(b)** $0.0008 \div 9200^3$ **(c)** $(1.009)^5$
(d) $123\,000\,000 \div 0.00076$ **(e)** $(97 \times 876)^4$ **(f)** $(0.0098)^4 \times (0.0032)^3$
(g) $\dfrac{8543 \times 9210}{0.000034}$ **(h)** $\dfrac{9754}{(0.0005)^4}$

4 Use your calculator to find the answers correct to 4 significant figures.

(a) $9.27 \times (2.8 \times 10^5)$ **(b)** $(4.23 \times 10^{-2})^3$ **(c)** $(3.2 \times 10^7) \div (7.2 \times 10^9)$
(d) $(3.2 \times 10^{-4})^2$ **(e)** $231 \times (1.5 \times 10^{-6})$ **(f)** $(4.3 \times 10^5) + (2.3 \times 10^7)$
(g) $\sqrt{3.24 \times 10^7}$ **(h)** $\sqrt[3]{4.2 \times 10^{-8}}$ **(i)** $\sqrt[3]{4.126 \times 10^{-9}}$

5.6 Estimation

REWIND

For this section you will need to remember how to round an answer to a specified number of significant figures. You covered this in chapter 1.◀

It is important that you know whether or not an answer that you have obtained is at least roughly as you expected. This section demonstrates how you can produce an approximate answer to a calculation easily.

To **estimate**, the numbers you are using need to be rounded *before* you do the calculation. Although you can use any accuracy, usually the numbers in the calculation are rounded to one significant figure:

$3.9 \times 2.1 \approx 4 \times 2 = 8$

Notice that $3.9 \times 2.1 = 8.19$, so the estimated value of 8 is not too far from the real value!

Worked example 21

Estimate the value of:

(a) $\dfrac{4.6 + 3.9}{\sqrt{398}}$ **(b)** $\sqrt{42.2 - 5.1}$

(a)

$\dfrac{4.6 + 3.9}{\sqrt{398}} \approx \dfrac{5 + 4}{\sqrt{400}}$ $= \dfrac{9}{20} = \dfrac{4.5}{10} = 0.45$	Round the numbers to 1 significant figure.
Check the estimate: $\dfrac{4.6 + 3.9}{\sqrt{398}} = 0.426$ (3sf)	Now if you use a calculator you will find the exact value and see that the estimate was good.

Tip

Note that the '≈' symbol is *only* used at the point where an approximation is made. At other times you should use '=' when two numbers are exactly equal.

(b) $\sqrt{42.2-5.1} \approx \sqrt{40-5}$ $= \sqrt{35}$ $\approx \sqrt{36}$ $= 6$	In this question you begin by rounding each value to one significant figure but it is worth noting that you can only easily take the square root of a square number! Round 35 up to 36 to get a square number.

A good starting point for the questions in the following exercise will be to round the numbers to 1 significant figure. Remember that you can sometimes make your calculation even simpler by modifying your numbers again.

Exercise 5.15

1 Estimate the value of each of the following. Show the rounded values that you use.

(a) $\dfrac{23.6}{6.3}$ **(b)** $\dfrac{4.3}{0.087 \times 3.89}$ **(c)** $\dfrac{7.21 \times 0.46}{9.09}$

(d) $\dfrac{4.82 \times 6.01}{2.54 + 1.09}$ **(e)** $\dfrac{\sqrt{48}}{2.54 + 4.09}$ **(f)** $(0.45 + 1.89)(6.5 - 1.9)$

(g) $\dfrac{23.8 + 20.2}{4.7 + 5.7}$ **(h)** $\dfrac{109.6 - 45.1}{19.4 - 13.9}$ **(i)** $(2.52)^2 \times \sqrt{48.99}$

(j) $\sqrt{223.8 \times 45.1}$ **(k)** $\sqrt{9.26} \times \sqrt{99.87}$ **(l)** $(4.1)^3 \times (1.9)^4$

2 Work out the actual answer for each part of question **1**, using a calculator.

Summary

Do you know the following?

- An equivalent fraction can be found by multiplying or dividing the numerator and denominator by the same number.
- Fractions can be added or subtracted, but you must make sure that you have a common denominator first.
- To multiply two fractions you multiply their numerators and multiply their denominators.
- To divide by a fraction you find its reciprocal and then multiply.
- Percentages are fractions with a denominator of 100.
- Percentage increases and decreases are always percentages of the original value.
- You can use reverse percentages to find the *original* value.
- Standard form can be used to write very large or very small numbers quickly.
- Estimations can be made by rounding the numbers in a calculation to one significant figure.

Are you able to. . . ?

- find a fraction of a number
- find a percentage of a number
- find one number as a percentage of another number
- calculate a percentage increase or decrease
- find a value before a percentage change
- do calculations with numbers written in standard form
- find an estimate to a calculation.

Examination practice

Exam-style questions

1 Calculate $\frac{5}{6}\left(\frac{1}{4}+\frac{1}{8}\right)$ giving your answer as a fraction in its lowest terms.

2 93 800 students took an examination.
19% received grade A.
24% received grade B.
31% received grade C.
10% received grade D.
11% received grade E.
The rest received grade U.

(a) What percentage of the students received grade U?
(b) What fraction of the students received grade B? Give your answer in its lowest terms.
(c) How many students received grade A?

3 During one summer there were 27 500 cases of *Salmonella* poisoning in Britain. The next summer there was an increase of 9% in the number of cases. Calculate how many cases there were in the second year.

4 Abdul's height was 160 cm on his 15th birthday. It was 172 cm on his 16th birthday. What was the percentage increase in his height?

Past paper questions

1 **(a)** Rewrite this calculation with all the numbers rounded to 1 significant figure.

$$\frac{77.8}{21.9-3.8\times4.3}.$$ [1]

(b) Use your answer to **part (a)** to work out an estimate for the calculation. [1]
(c) Use your calculator to find the **actual** answer to the calculation in **part (a)**.
Give your answer correct to 1 decimal place. [2]

[Cambridge IGCSE Mathematics 0580 Paper 12 Q13 May/June 2011]

2 $\frac{3}{5}<p<\frac{2}{3}$

Which of the following could be a value of p?

$\frac{16}{27}$ 0.67 60% $(0.8)^2$ $\sqrt{\frac{4}{9}}$ [2]

[Cambridge IGCSE Mathematics 0580 Paper 22 Q4 May/June 2011]

3 **Do not use a calculator in this question and show all the steps of your working.**
Give each answer as a fraction in its lowest terms.
Work out

(a) $\frac{3}{4}-\frac{1}{12}$ [2]

(b) $2\frac{1}{2}\times\frac{4}{25}$ [2]

[Cambridge IGCSE Mathematics 0580 Paper 11 Q21 October/November 2013]

4 Calculate 17.5% of 44 kg. [2]

[Cambridge IGCSE Mathematics 0580 Paper 11 Q10 October/November 2013]

5 **Without using your calculator,** work out

$5\frac{3}{8} - 2\frac{1}{5}$.

Give your answer as a fraction in its lowest terms.
You must show all your working. [3]

[Cambridge IGCSE Mathematics 0580 Paper 13 Q17 October/November 2012]

6 Samantha invests $600 at a rate of 2% per year simple interest.
Calculate the interest Samantha earns in 8 years. [2]

[Cambridge IGCSE Mathematics 0580 Paper 13 Q5 October/November 2012]

7 Show that $\left(\frac{1}{10}\right)^2 + \left(\frac{2}{5}\right)^2 = 0.17$

Write down all the steps in your working. [2]

[Cambridge IGCSE Mathematics 0580 Paper 13 Q6 October/November 2012]

8 Maria pays $84 rent.
The rent is increased by 5%. Calculate Maria's new rent. [2]

[Cambridge IGCSE Mathematics 0580 Paper 13 Q10 October/November 2012]

9 Huy borrowed $4500 from a bank at a rate of 5% per year compound **interest**.
He paid back the money and **interest** at the end of 2 years.
How much **interest** did he pay? [3]

[Cambridge IGCSE Mathematics 0580 Paper 13 Q13 May/June 2013]

6 Equations and transforming formulae

Key words

- Expansion
- Linear equation
- Solution
- Common factor
- Factorisation
- Variable
- Subject

In this chapter you will learn how to:

- expand brackets that have been multiplied by a negative number
- solve a linear equation
- factorise an algebraic expression where all terms have common factors
- rearrange a formula to change the subject.

Leonhard Euler (1707–1783), pictured here on a Swiss bank note, was a great Swiss mathematician. He created much of the algebraic terminology and notation that is used today.

Equations are a shorthand way of recording and easily manipulating many problems. Straight lines or curves take time to draw and change but their equations can quickly be written. How to calculate areas of shapes and volumes of solids can be reduced to a few, easily remembered symbols. A formula can help you work out how long it takes to cook your dinner, how well your car is performing or how efficient the insulation is in your house.

6.1 Further expansions of brackets

REWIND

You dealt with expanding brackets in chapter 2. ◀

You have already seen that you can re-write algebraic expressions that contain brackets by expanding them. The process is called **expansion**. This work will now be extended to consider what happens when negative numbers appear before brackets.

The key is to remember that a '+' or a '−' is attached to the number immediately following it and should be included when you multiply out brackets.

Worked example 1

Expand and simplify the following expressions.

(a) $-3(x + 4)$ **(b)** $4(y - 7) - 5(3y + 5)$ **(c)** $8(p + 4) - 10(9p - 6)$

(a)	$-3(x + 4)$	Remember that you must multiply the number on the outside of the bracket by everything inside *and* that the negative sign is attached to the 3.
	$-3(x + 4) = -3x - 12$	Because $-3 \times x = -3x$ and $-3 \times 4 = -12$.
(b)	$4(y - 7) - 5(3y + 5)$ $4(y - 7) = 4y - 28$ $-5(3y + 5) = -15y - 25$	Expand each bracket first and remember that the '−5' must keep the negative sign when it is multiplied through the second bracket.
	$4(y - 7) - 5(3y + 5) = 4y - 28 - 15y - 25$ $= -11y - 53$	Collect like terms and simplify.
(c)	$8(p + 4) - 10(9p - 6)$ $8(p + 4) = 8p + 32$ $-10(9p - 6) = -90p + 60$	It is important to note that when you expand the second bracket '−10' will need to be multiplied by '−6', giving a positive result for that term.
	$8(p + 4) - 10(9p - 6) = 8p + 32 - 90p + 60$ $= -82p + 92$	Collect like terms and simplify.

Tip

Watch out for negative numbers in front of brackets because they always require extra care. Remember:

$+ \times + = +$

$+ \times - = -$

$- \times - = +$

Exercise 6.1

1 Expand each of the following and simplify your answers as far as possible.

(a) $-10(3p + 6)$ **(b)** $-3(5x + 7)$ **(c)** $-5(4y + 0.2)$
(d) $-3(q - 12)$ **(e)** $-12(2t - 7)$ **(f)** $-1.5(8z - 4)$

2 Expand each of the following and simplify your answers as far as possible.

(a) $-3(2x + 5y)$ **(b)** $-6(4p + 5q)$ **(c)** $-9(3h - 6k)$
(d) $-2(5h + 5k - 8j)$ **(e)** $-4(2a - 3b - 6c + 4d)$ **(f)** $-6(x^2 + 6y^2 - 2y^3)$

3 Expand each of the following and simplify your answers as far as possible.

(a) $2 - 5(x + 2)$ **(b)** $2 - 5(x - 2)$ **(c)** $14(x - 3) - 4(x - 1)$
(d) $-7(f + 3) - 3(2f - 7)$ **(e)** $3g - 7(7g - 7) + 2(5g - 6)$ **(f)** $6(3y - 5) - 2(3y - 5)$

Try not to carry out too many steps at once. Show every term of your expansion and then simplify.

4 Expand each of the following and simplify your answers as far as possible.

(a) $4x(x - 4) - 10x(3x + 6)$ **(b)** $14x(x + 7) - 3x(5x + 7)$
(c) $x^2 - 5x(2x - 6)$ **(d)** $5q^2 - 2q(q - 12) - 3q^2$
(e) $18pq - 12p(5q - 7)$ **(f)** $12m(2n - 4) - 24n(m - 2)$

5 Expand each expression and simplify your answers as far as possible.

(a) $8x - 2(3 - 2x)$ **(b)** $11x - (6 - 2x)$ **(c)** $4x + 5 - 3(2x - 4)$
(d) $7 - 2(x - 3) + 3x$ **(e)** $15 - 4(x - 2) - 3x$ **(f)** $4x - 2(1 - 3x) - 6$
(g) $3(x + 5) - 4(5 - x)$ **(h)** $x(x - 3) - 2(x - 4)$ **(i)** $3x(x - 2) - (x - 2)$
(j) $2x(3 + x) - 3(x - 2)$ **(k)** $3(x - 5) - (3 + x)$ **(l)** $2x(3x + 1) - 2(3 - 2x)$

You will now look at solving linear equations and return to these expansions a little later in the chapter.

6.2 Solving linear equations

REWIND

It is important to remind yourself about BODMAS before working through this section. (Return to chapter 1 if you need to.) ◀

I think of a number. My number is x. If I multiply my number by three and then add one, the answer is 13. What is my number?

To solve this problem you first need to understand the stages of what is happening to x and then undo them in reverse order:

This diagram (sometimes called a function machine) shows what is happening to x, with the reverse process written underneath. Notice how the answer to the problem appears quite easily:

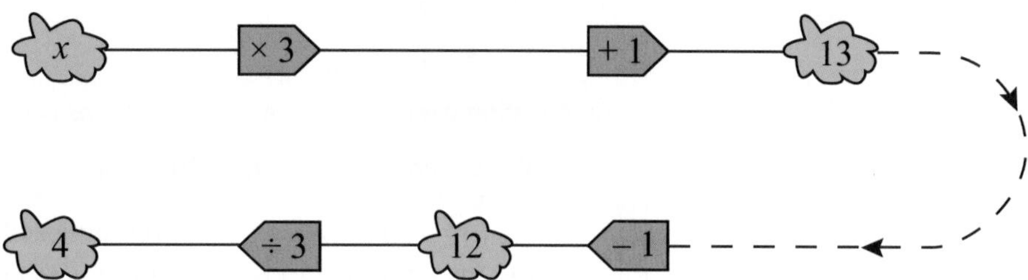

So $x = 4$

A more compact and efficient solution can be obtained using algebra. Follow the instructions in the question:

Even if you can see what the solution is going to be easily you *must* show working.

1	The number is x:	x
2	Multiply this number by three:	$3x$
3	Then add one:	$3x + 1$
4	The answer is 13:	$3x + 1 = 13$

This is called a **linear equation**. 'Linear' refers to the fact that there are no powers of x other than one.

The next point you must learn is that you can change this equation without changing the **solution** (the value of x for which the equation is true) *provided* you do the same to both sides at the same time.

Follow the reverse process shown in the function machine above but carry out the instruction on both sides of the equation:

$$3x + 1 = 13$$

$$3x + 1 - 1 = 13 - 1 \qquad \text{(Subtract one from both sides.)}$$

$$3x = 12$$

$$\frac{3x}{3} = \frac{12}{3} \qquad \text{(Divide both sides by three.)}$$

$$x = 4$$

Always line up your '=' signs because this makes your working much clearer.

Sometimes you will also find that linear equations contain brackets, and they can also contain unknown values (like x, though you can use any letter or symbol) on *both* sides.

The following worked example demonstrates a number of possible types of equation.

Worked example 2

An equation with x *on both sides and all x terms with the same sign:*

(a) Solve the equation $5x - 2 = 3x + 6$

$5x - 2 = 3x + 6$ $5x - 2 - 3x = 3x + 6 - 3x$ $2x - 2 = 6$	Look for the *smallest* number of x's and subtract this from both sides. So, subtract $3x$ from both sides.
$2x - 2 + 2 = 6 + 2$ $2x = 8$	Add two to both sides.
$\frac{2x}{2} = \frac{8}{2}$ $x = 4$	Divide both sides by two.

An equation with x *on both sides and x terms with different sign:*

(b) Solve the equation $5x + 12 = 20 - 11x$

$5x + 12 = 20 - 11x$	This time add the negative x term to both sides.
$5x + 12 + 11x = 20 - 11x + 11x$ $16x + 12 = 20$	Add $11x$ to both sides.
$16x + 12 - 12 = 20 - 12$ $16x = 8$	Subtract 12 from both sides.
$\frac{16x}{16} = \frac{8}{16}$ $x = \frac{1}{2}$	Divide both sides by 16.

By adding $11x$ to both sides you will see that you are left with a *positive* x term. This helps you to avoid errors with '–' signs!

An equation with *brackets on at least one side:*

(c) Solve the equation $2(y - 4) + 4(y + 2) = 30$

$2(y - 4) + 4(y + 2) = 30$	Expand the brackets and collect like terms together.
$2y - 8 + 4y + 8 = 30$	Expand.
$6y = 30$	Collect like terms.
$\frac{6y}{6} = \frac{30}{6}$ $y = 5$	Divide both sides by 6.

An equation that contains fractions:

(d) Solve the equation $\frac{6}{7}p = 10$

$\frac{6}{7}p \times 7 = 10 \times 7$ $6p = 70$	Multiply both sides by 7.
$p = \frac{70}{6} = \frac{35}{3}$	Divide both sides by 6. Write the fraction in its simplest form.

Unless the question asks you to give your answer to a specific degree of accuracy, it is perfectly acceptable to leave it as a fraction.

Exercise 6.2

1 Solve the following equations.

(a) $4x + 3 = 31$ (b) $8x + 42 = 2$
(c) $6x - 1 = 53$ (d) $7x - 4 = -66$
(e) $9y + 7 = 52$ (f) $11n - 19 = 102$
(g) $12q - 7 = 14$ (h) $206t + 3 = 106$
(i) $\frac{2x+1}{3} = 8$ (j) $\frac{2x}{3} + 1 = 8$
(k) $\frac{3}{5}x + 11 = 21$ (l) $\frac{x+3}{2} = x$
(m) $\frac{2x-1}{3} = 3x$ (n) $\frac{3x}{2} + 5 = 2x$

2 Solve the following equations.

(a) $12x + 1 = 7x + 11$ (b) $6x + 1 = 7x + 11$ (c) $6y + 1 = 3y - 8$
(d) $11x + 1 = 12 - 4x$ (e) $8 - 8p = 9 - 9p$ (f) $\frac{1}{2}x - 7 = \frac{1}{4}x + 8$

3 Solve the following equations.

(a) $4(x + 1) = 12$ (b) $2(2p + 1) = 14$
(c) $8(3t + 2) = 40$ (d) $5(m - 2) = 15$
(e) $-5(n - 6) = -20$ (f) $2(p - 1) + 7(3p + 2) = 7(p - 4)$
(g) $2(p - 1) - 7(3p - 2) = 7(p - 4)$ (h) $3(2x + 5) - (3x + 2) = 10$

4 Solve for x.

(a) $7(x + 2) = 4(x + 5)$ (b) $4(x - 2) + 2(x + 5) = 14$
(c) $7x - (3x + 11) = 6 - (5 - 3x)$ (d) $-2(x + 2) = 4x + 9$
(e) $3(x + 1) = 2(x + 1) + 2x$ (f) $4 + 2(2 - x) = 3 - 2(5 - x)$

6.3 Factorising algebraic expressions

You have looked in detail at expanding brackets and how this can be used when solving some equations. It can sometimes be helpful to carry out the opposite process and put brackets back into an algebraic expression.

REWIND

If you need to remind yourself how to find HCFs, return to chapter 1. ◀

Consider the algebraic expression $12x - 4$. This expression is already simplified but notice that 12 and 4 have a **common factor**. In fact the HCF of 12 and 4 is 4.

Now, $12 = 4 \times 3$ and $4 = 4 \times 1$.

So, $12x - 4 = 4 \times 3x - 4 \times 1$
$= 4(3x - 1)$

Notice that the HCF has been 'taken out' of the bracket and written at the front. The terms inside are found by considering what you need to multiply by 4 to get $12x$ and -4.

The process of writing an algebraic expression using brackets in this way is known as **factorisation.** The expression, $12x - 4$, has been factorised to give $4(3x-1)$.

Some factorisations are not quite so simple. The following worked example should help to make things clearer.

Worked example 3

Factorise each of the following expressions as fully as possible.

(a) $15x + 12y$ **(b)** $18mn - 30m$ **(c)** $36p^2q - 24pq^2$ **(d)** $15(x - 2) - 20(x - 2)^3$

(a)	$15x + 12y$	The HCF of 12 and 15 is 3, but x and y have no common factors.
	$15x + 12y = 3(5x + 4y)$	Because $3 \times 5x = 15x$ and $3 \times 4y = 12y$.
(b)	$18mn - 30m$	The HCF of 18 and 30 = 6 and HCF of mn and m is m.
	$18mn - 30m = 6m(3n - 5)$	Because $6m \times 3n = 18mn$ and $6m \times 5 = 30m$.
(c)	$36p^2q - 24pq^2$	The HCF of 36 and 24 = 12 and p^2q and pq^2 have common factor pq.
	$36p^2q - 24pq^2 = 12pq(3p - 2q)$	Because $12pq \times 3p = 36p^2q$ and $12pq \times -2q = -24pq^2$.

Sometimes, the terms can have an expression in brackets that is common to both terms.

(d)	$15(x - 2) - 20(x - 2)^3$	The HCF of 15 and 20 is 5 and the HCF of $(x - 2)$ and $(x - 2)^3$ is $(x - 2)$.
	$15(x - 2) - 20(x - 2)^3 = 5(x - 2)[3 - 4(x - 2)^2]$	Because $5(x - 2) \times 3 = 15(x - 2)$ and $5(x - 2) \times 4(x - 2)^2 = 20(x - 2)^3$.

Make sure that you have taken out *all* the common factors. If you don't, then your algebraic expression is not *fully* factorised.

Take care to put in all the bracket symbols.

Exercise 6.3

1 Factorise.

(a) $3x + 6$ (b) $15y - 12$ (c) $8 - 16z$ (d) $35 + 25t$
(e) $2x - 4$ (f) $3x + 7$ (g) $18k - 64$ (h) $33p + 22$
(i) $2x + 4y$ (j) $3p - 15q$ (k) $13r - 26s$ (l) $2p + 4q + 6r$

2 Factorise as fully as possible.

(a) $21u - 49v + 35w$ (b) $3xy + 3x$ (c) $3x^2 + 3x$ (d) $15pq + 21p$
(e) $9m^2 - 33m$ (f) $90m^3 - 80m^2$ (g) $36x^3 + 24x^5$ (h) $32p^2q - 4pq^2$

Once you have taken a common factor out, you may be left with an expression that needs to be simplified further.

3 Factorise as fully as possible.

(a) $14m^2n^2 + 4m^3n^3$ (b) $17abc + 30ab^2c$ (c) $m^3n^2 + 6m^2n^2(8m + n)$
(d) $\frac{1}{2}a + \frac{3}{2}b$ (e) $\frac{3}{4}x^4 + \frac{7}{8}x$ (f) $3(x - 4) + 5(x - 4)$
(g) $5(x + 1)^2 - 4(x + 1)^3$ (h) $6x^3 + 2x^4 + 4x^5$ (i) $7x^3y - 14x^2y^2 + 21xy^2$
(j) $x(3 + y) + 2(y + 3)$

6.4 Transformation of a formula

FAST FORWARD

You will look again at transforming formulae in chapter 22. ▶

Very often you will find that a formula is expressed with one **variable** written alone on one side of the '=' symbol (usually on the left but not always). The variable that is written alone is known as the **subject** of the formula.

Consider each of the following formulae:

$s = ut + \frac{1}{2}at^2$ (s is the subject)

$F = ma$ (F is the subject)

$x = \frac{-b \pm \sqrt{b^2 - 4ac}}{2a}$ (*x* is the subject)

Now that you can recognise the subject of a formula, you must look at how you *change* the subject of a formula. If you take the formula $v = u + at$ and note that v is currently the subject, you can change the subject by rearranging the formula.

Another word sometimes used for changing the subject is 'transposing'.

To make a the subject of this formula:

Remember that what you do to one side of the formula must be done to the other side. This ensures that the formula you produce still represents the same relationship between the variables.

$v = u + at$ Write down the starting formula.

$v - u = at$ Subtract u from both sides (to isolate the term containing a).

$\frac{v-u}{t} = a$ Divide both sides by t (notice that everything on the left is divided by t).

You now have a on its own and it is the new subject of the formula.

This is usually re-written so that the subject is on the left:

$a = \frac{v-u}{t}$

Notice how similar this process is to solving equations.

Worked example 4

Make the variable shown in brackets the subject of the formula in each case.

(a) $x + y = c$ (y) **(b)** $\sqrt{x} + y = z$ (x) **(c)** $\frac{a-b}{c} = d$ (b)

⇒ is a symbol that can be used to mean 'implies that'.

(a)	$x + y = c$	
	$\Rightarrow y = c - x$	Subtract x from both sides.
(b)	$\sqrt{x} + y = z$	
	$\Rightarrow \sqrt{x} = z - y$	Subtract y from both sides.
	$\Rightarrow x = (z - y)^2$	Square both sides.
(c)	$\frac{a-b}{c} = d$	
	$\Rightarrow a - b = cd$	Multiply both sides by c to clear the fraction.
	$\Rightarrow a = cd + b$	Make the number of b's positive by adding b to both sides.
	$\Rightarrow a - cd = b$	Subtract cd from both sides.
	So $b = a - cd$	Re-write so the subject is on the left.

Exercise 6.4

Make the variable shown in brackets the subject of the formula in each case.

1 **(a)** $a + b = c$ (a) **(b)** $p - q = r$ (r) **(c)** $fh = g$ (h)
(d) $ab + c = d$ (b) **(e)** $\frac{a}{b} = c$ (a) **(f)** $an - m = t$ (n)

2 **(a)** $an - m = t$ (m) **(b)** $a(n - m) = t$ (a) **(c)** $\frac{xy}{z} = t$ (x)
(d) $\frac{x-a}{b} = c$ (x) **(e)** $x(c - y) = d$ (y) **(f)** $a - b = c$ (b)

3 **(a)** $p - \frac{r}{q} = t$ (r) **(b)** $\frac{x-a}{b} = c$ (b) **(c)** $a(n - m) = t$ (m)
(d) $\frac{a}{b} = \frac{c}{d}$ (a) **(e)** $\frac{x-a}{b} = c$ (a) **(f)** $\frac{xy}{z} = t$ (z)

4 (a) $\sqrt{b}=c$ (b) (b) $\sqrt{ab}=c$ (b) (c) $a\sqrt{b}=c$ (b)

(d) $\sqrt{b+c}=c$ (b) (e) $\sqrt{x-b}=c$ (b) (f) $\frac{x}{\sqrt{y}}=c$ (y)

Living maths

5 A rocket scientist is trying to calculate how long a Lunar Explorer Vehicle will take to descend towards the surface of the moon. He knows that if u = initial speed and v = speed at time t seconds, then:

$v = u + at$

where a is the acceleration and t is the time that has passed.

If the scientist wants to calculate the time taken for any given values of u, v, and a, he must rearrange the formula to make a the subject. Do this for the scientist.

6 Geoff is the Headmaster of a local school, who has to report to the board of Governors on how well the school is performing. He does this by comparing the test scores of pupils across an entire school. He has worked out the mean but also wants know the spread about the mean so that the Governors can see that it is representative of the whole school. He uses a well-known formula from statistics for the upper bound b of a class mean:

$$b=a+\frac{3s}{\sqrt{n}}$$

where s = sample spread about the mean, n = the sample size, a = the school mean and b = the mean maximum value.

If Geoff wants to calculate the standard deviation (diversion about the mean) from values of b, n and a he will need to rearrange this formula to make s the subject. Rearrange the formula to make s the subject to help Geoff.

7 If the length of a pendulum is l metres, the acceleration due to gravity is g m s^{-2} and T is the period of the oscillation in seconds then:

$$T=2\pi\sqrt{\frac{l}{g}}$$

Rearrange the formula to make l the subject.

Summary

Do you know the following?

- Expanding brackets means to multiply all the terms inside the bracket by the term outside.
- A variable is a letter or symbol used in an equation or formula that can represent many values.
- A linear equation has no variable with a power greater than one.
- Solving an equation with one variable means to find the value of the variable.
- When solving equations you must make sure that you always do the same to *both* sides.
- Factorising is the reverse of expanding brackets.
- A formula can be rearranged to make a different variable the subject.
- A recurring fraction can be written as an exact fraction.

Are you able to . . . ?

- expand brackets, taking care when there are negative signs
- solve a linear equation
- factorise an algebraic expressions by taking out any common factors
- rearrange a formulae to change the subject by treating the formula as if it is an equation

Examination practice

Exam-style questions

1 Given that $T = 3p - 5$, calculate T when $p = 12$.

2 In mountaineering, in general, the higher you go, the colder it gets. This formula shows how the height and temperature are related.

$$\text{Temperature drop (°C)} = \frac{\text{height increase (m)}}{200}$$

(a) If the temperature at a height of 500 m is 23 °C, what will it be when you climb to 1300 m?
(b) How far would you need to climb to experience a temperature drop of 5 °C?

3 The formula $e = 3n$ can be used to relate the number of sides (n) in the base of a prism to the number of edges (e) that the prism has.
(a) Make n the subject of the formula.
(b) Find the value of n for a prism with 21 edges.

Past paper questions

1 **(a)** Expand the brackets and simplify. $3(2x - 5y) - 4(x - y)$ [2]
(b) Factorise completely. $6x^2 - 9xy$ [2]

[Cambridge IGCSE Mathematics 0580 Paper 12 Q15 May/June 2011]

2 Rearrange the formula $c = \frac{4}{a - b}$ to make a the subject. [3]

[Cambridge IGCSE Mathematics 0580 Paper 22 Q11 May/June 2011]

3 Expand the brackets. $y(3 - y^3)$ [2]

[Cambridge IGCSE Mathematics 0580 Paper 13 Q9 October/November 2012]

4 Factorise completely. $4xy + 12yz$ [2]

[Cambridge IGCSE Mathematics 0580 Paper 13 Q13 October/November 2012]

5 Solve the equation. $5(2y - 17) = 60$ [3]

[Cambridge IGCSE Mathematics 0580 Paper 22 Q12 May/June 2013]

6 Solve the equation $(3x - 5) = 16$. [2]

[Cambridge IGCSE Mathematics 0580 Paper 13 Q5 May/June 2013]

7 Factorise completely. $6xy^2 + 8y$ [2]

[Cambridge IGCSE Mathematics 0580 Paper 13 Q9 May/June 2013]

7

Perimeter, area and volume

Key words

- Perimeter
- Area
- Irrational number
- Sector
- Arc
- Semi-circle
- Solid
- Net
- Vertices
- Face
- Surface area
- Volume
- Apex
- Slant height

In this chapter you will learn how to:

- calculate areas and perimeters of two-dimensional shapes
- calculate areas and perimeters of shapes that can be separated into two or more simpler polygons
- calculate areas and circumferences of circles
- EXTENDED: calculate perimeters and areas of circular sectors
- understand nets for three-dimensional solids
- calculate volumes and surface areas of solids
- EXTENDED: calculate volumes and surface area of pyramids, cones and spheres.

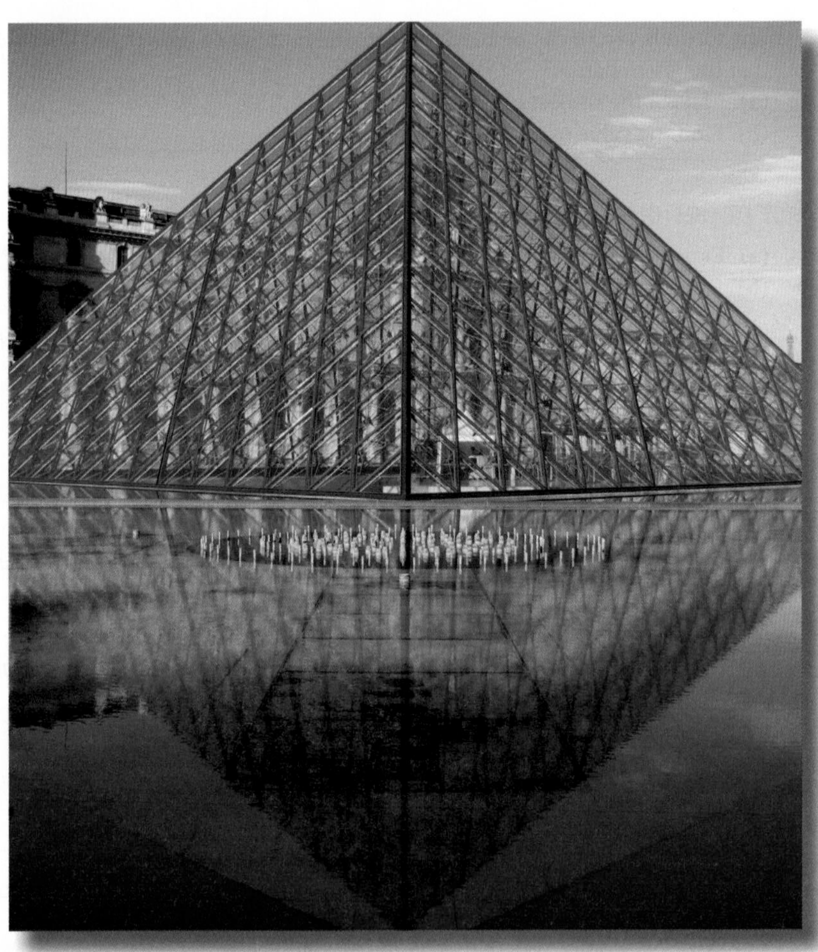

The glass pyramid at the entrance to the Louvre Art Gallery in Paris. Reaching to a height of 20.6 m, it is a beautiful example of a three-dimensional object. A smaller pyramid – suspended upside down – acts as a skylight in an underground mall in front of the museum.

When runners begin a race around a track they do not start in the same place because their routes are not the same length. Being able to calculate the perimeters of the various lanes allows the officials to stagger the start so that each runner covers the same distance.

A can of paint will state how much area it should cover, so being able to calculate the areas of walls and doors is very useful to make sure you buy the correct size can.

How much water do you use when you take a bath instead of a shower? As more households are metered for their water, being able to work out the volume used will help to control the budget.

7.1 Perimeter and area in two dimensions

Polygons

A polygon is a flat (two-dimensional) shape with three or more straight **sides**. The **perimeter** of a polygon is the sum of the lengths of its sides. The perimeter measures the total distance around the outside of the polygon.

The **area** of a polygon measures how much space is contained inside it.

Two-dimensional shapes	**Formula for area**
Quadrilaterals with parallel sides 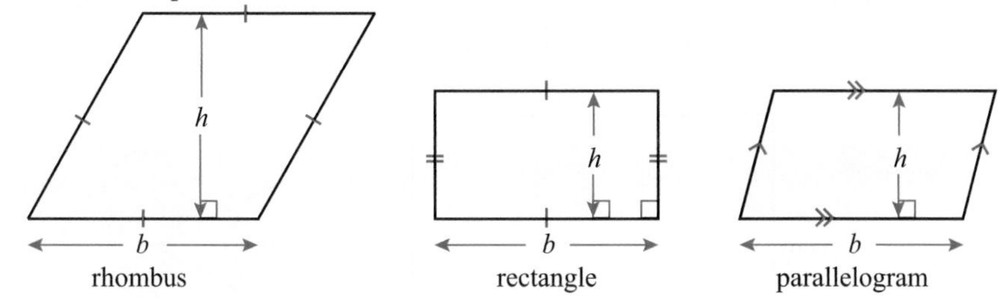 rhombus, rectangle, parallelogram (base b, height h)	Area = bh
Triangles 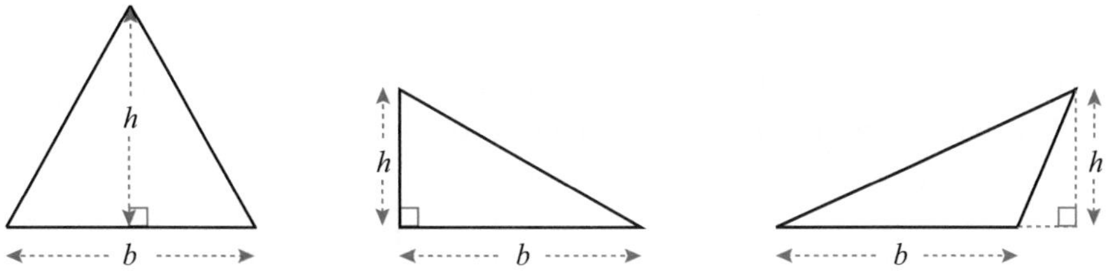 (base b, height h)	Area $= \frac{1}{2}bh$ or $\frac{bh}{2}$
Trapezium 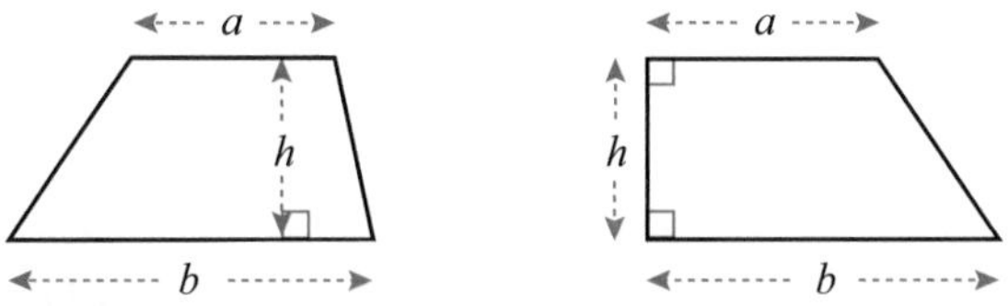 (parallel sides a and b, height h)	Area $= \frac{1}{2}(a+b)h$ or $\frac{(a+b)h}{2}$
Here are some examples of other two-dimensional shapes. 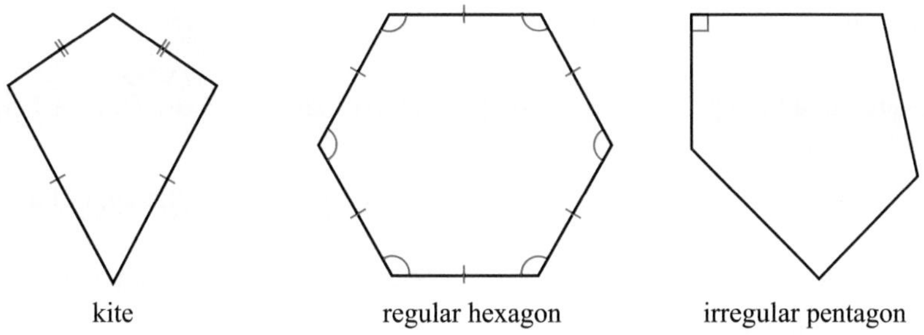 kite, regular hexagon, irregular pentagon	It is possible to find areas of other polygons such as those on the left by dividing the shape into other shapes such as triangles and quadrilaterals.

Tip

You should always give units for a final answer if it is appropriate to do so. It can, however, be confusing if you include units throughout your working.

Units of area

If the dimensions of your shape are given in cm, then the units of area are square centimetres and this is written cm². For metres, m² is used and for kilometres, km² is used and so on. Area is always given in square units.

The formula for the area of a triangle can be written in different ways:

$$\frac{1}{2}\times b\times h=\frac{bh}{2}$$

$$\text{OR } =\left(\frac{1}{2}b\right)\times h$$

$$\text{OR } = b\times\left(\frac{1}{2}h\right)$$

Choose the way that works best for you, but make sure you write it down as part of your method.

You do not usually have to redraw the separate shapes, but you might find it helpful.

REWIND

At this point you may need to remind yourself of the work you did on transformation of formulae in chapter 6. ◀

Worked example 1

(a) Calculate the area of the shape shown in the diagram.

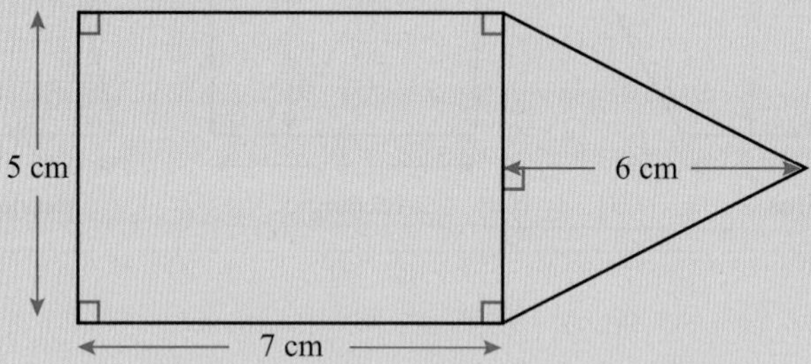

This shape can be divided into two simple polygons: a rectangle and a triangle. Work out the area of each shape and then add them together.

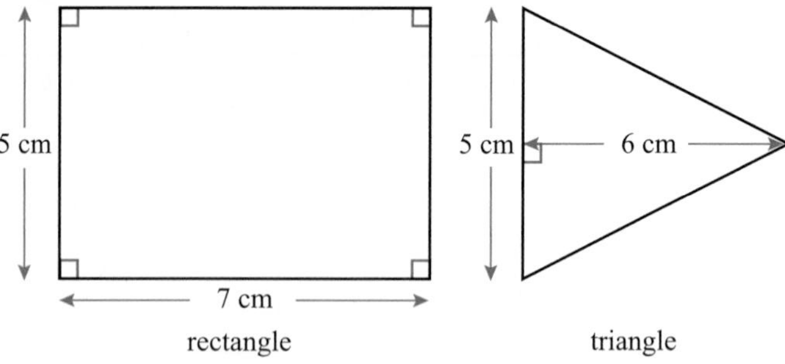

Area of rectangle $= bh = 7\times 5 = 35\,\text{cm}^2$ (substitute values in place of b and h)

Area of triangle $=\frac{1}{2}bh=\frac{1}{2}\times 5\times 6=\frac{1}{2}\times 30 = 15\,\text{cm}^2$

Total area $= 35 + 15 = 50\,\text{cm}^2$

(b) The area of a triangle is 40 cm². If the base of the triangle is 5 cm, find the height.

$A=\frac{1}{2}\times b\times h$	Use the formula for the area of a triangle.
$40=\frac{1}{2}\times 5\times h$	Substitute all values that you know.
$\Rightarrow 40\times 2 = 5\times h$	
$\Rightarrow h=\frac{40\times 2}{5}=\frac{80}{5}=16\,\text{cm}$	Rearrange the formula to make h the subject.

Exercise 7.1

1 By measuring the lengths of each side and adding them together, find the perimeter of each of the following shapes.

(a)

(b)

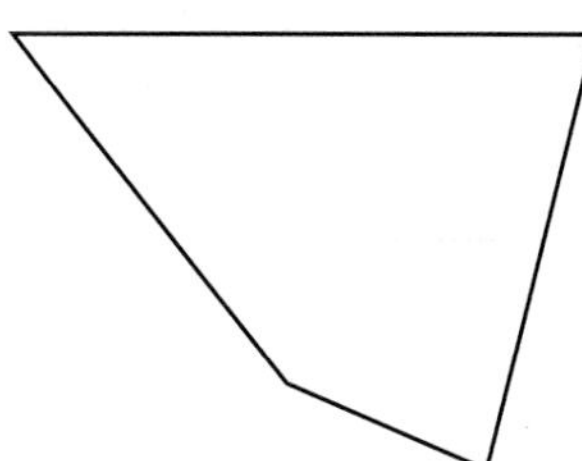

(c)

(d)

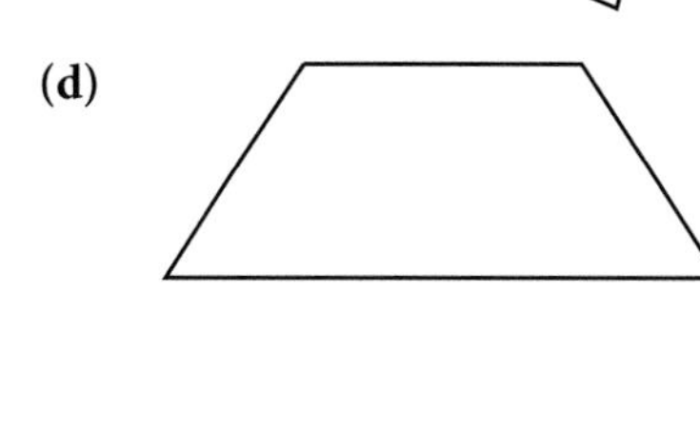

2 Calculate the perimeter of each of the following shapes.

(a)

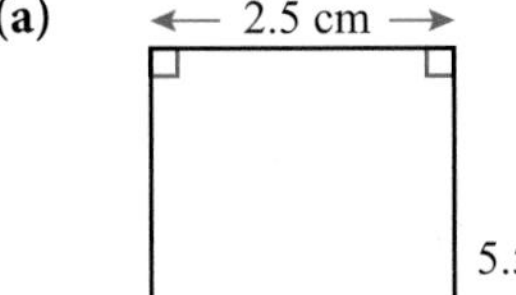

(b)

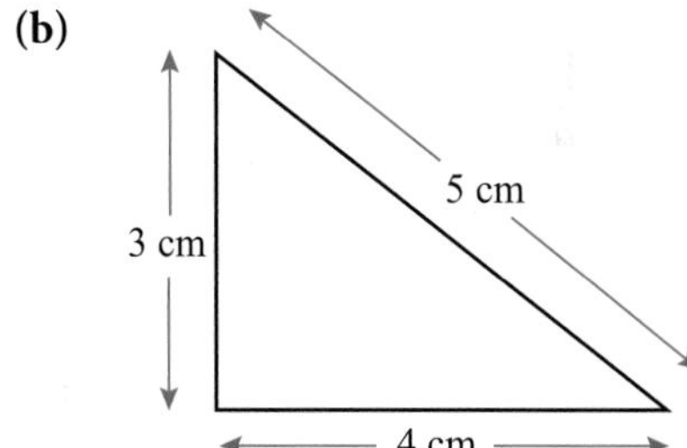

(c)

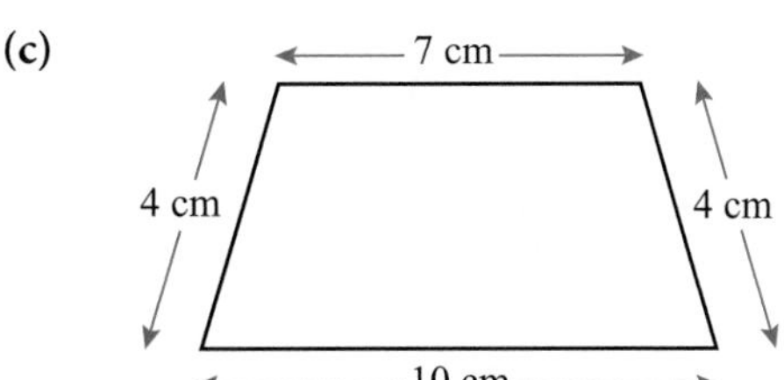

(d)

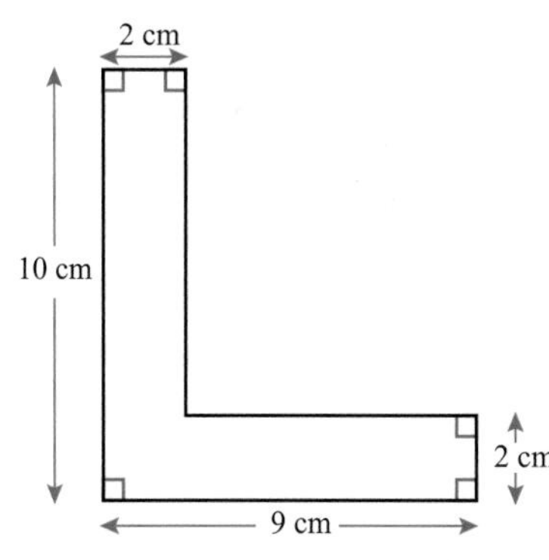

(e)

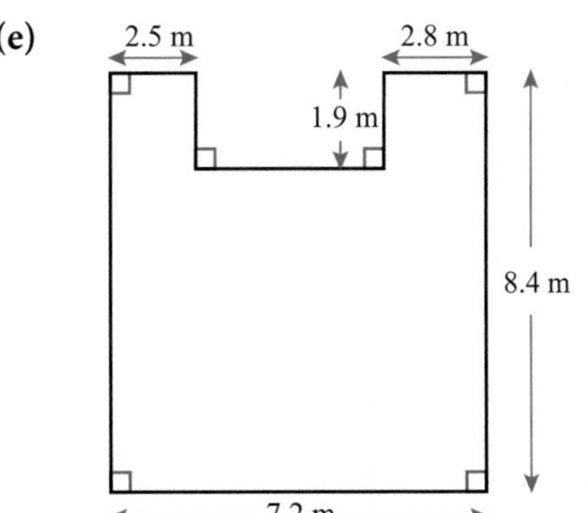

(f)

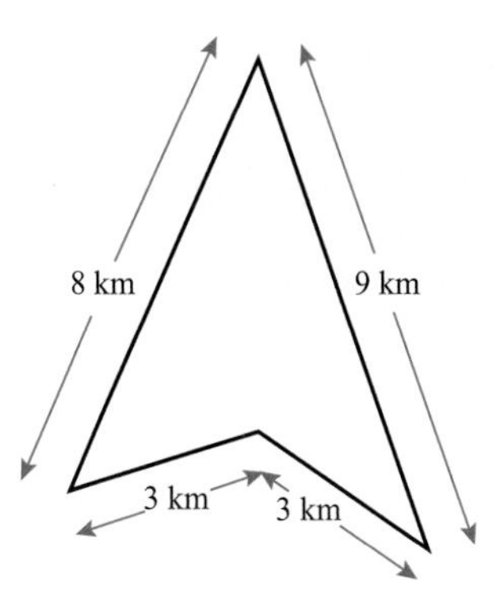

3 Calculate the area of each of the following shapes.

(a)

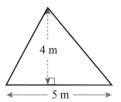

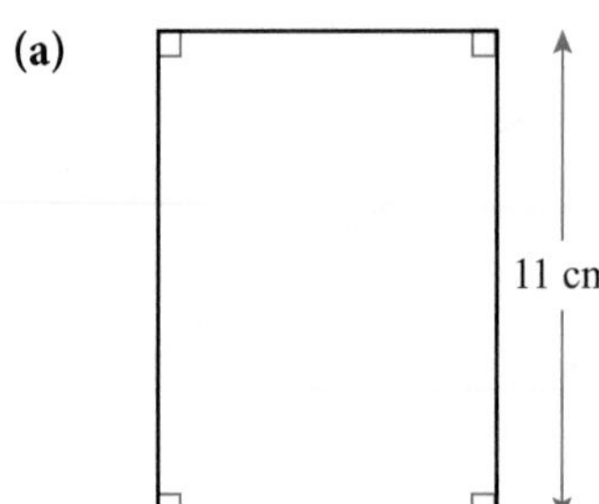

(b)

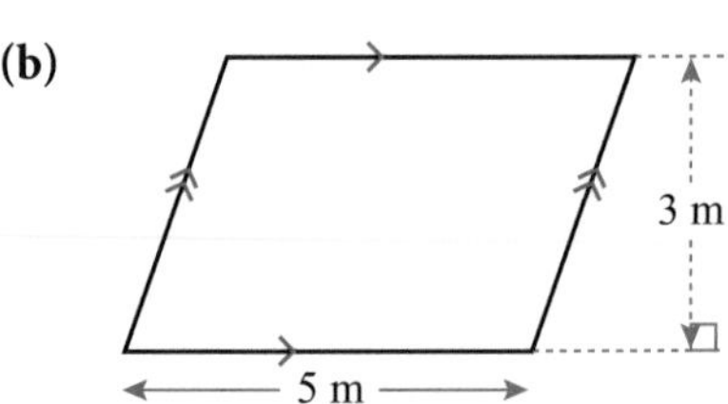

(c)

4 m
5 m

(d)

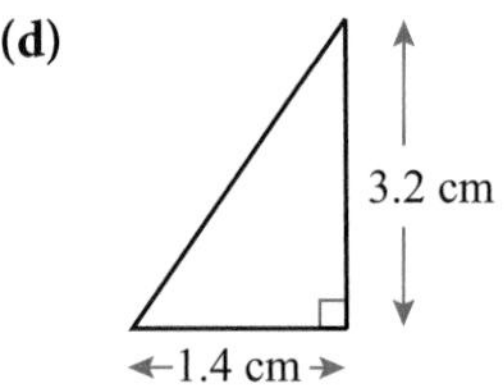

(e)

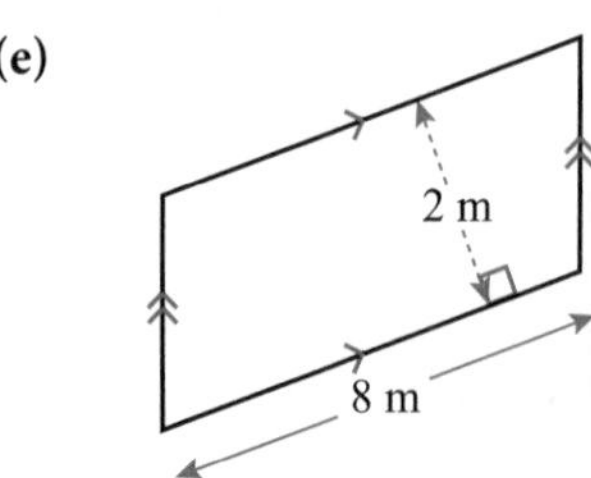

(f)

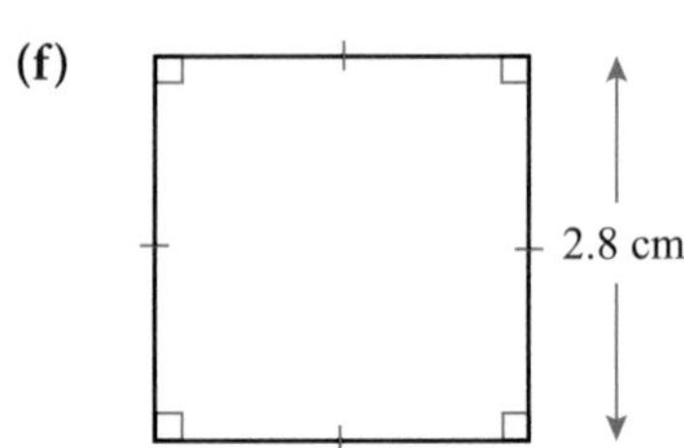

(g)

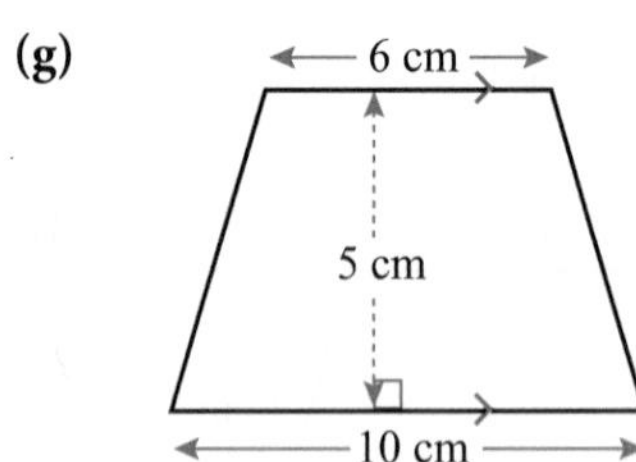

(h)

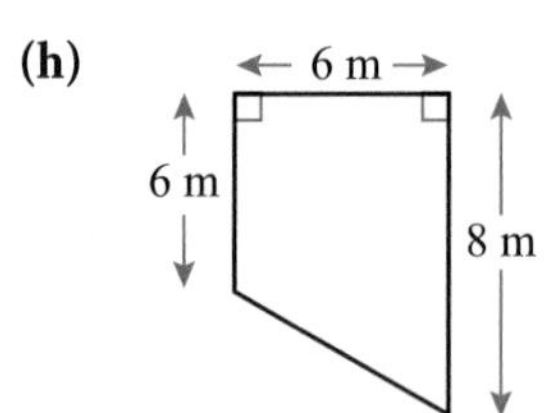

(i)

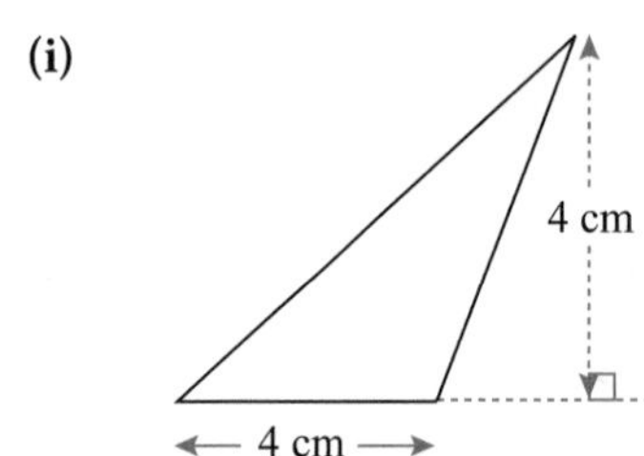

(j)

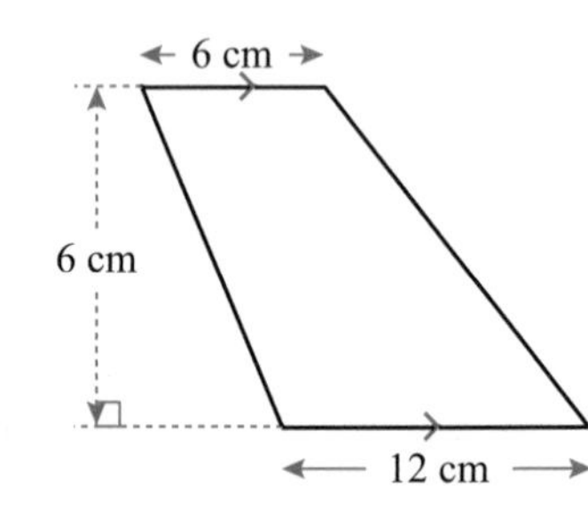

Draw the simpler shapes separately and then calculate the individual areas, as in worked example 1.

4 The following shapes can all be divided into simpler shapes. In each case find the total area.

(a)

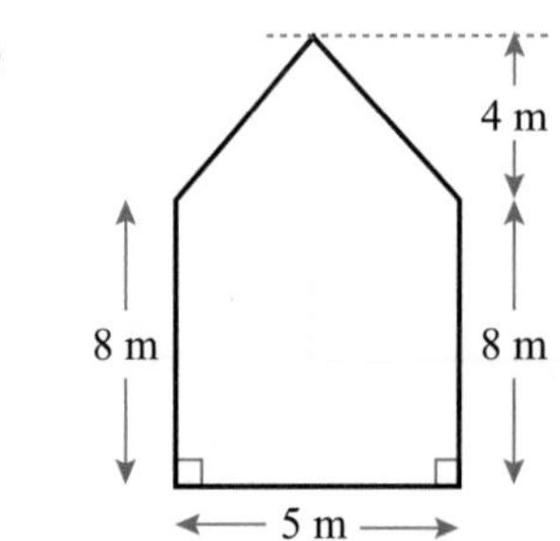

(b)

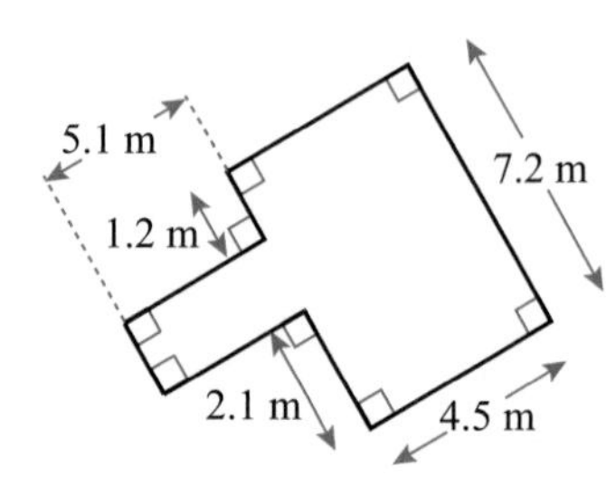

(c)

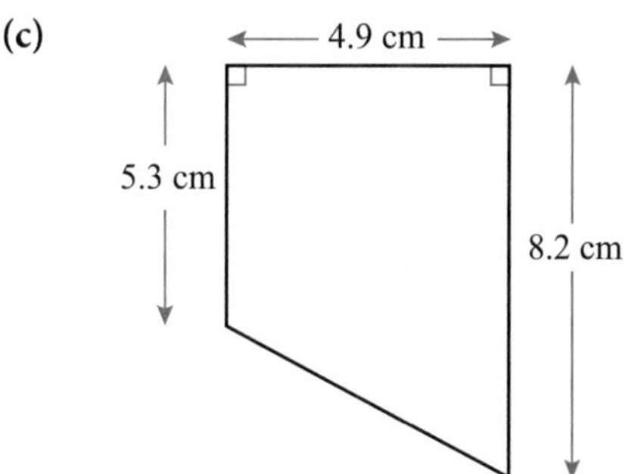

(d)

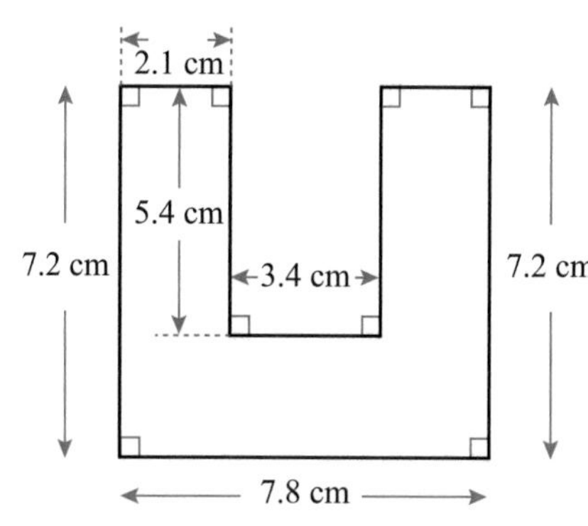

(e)

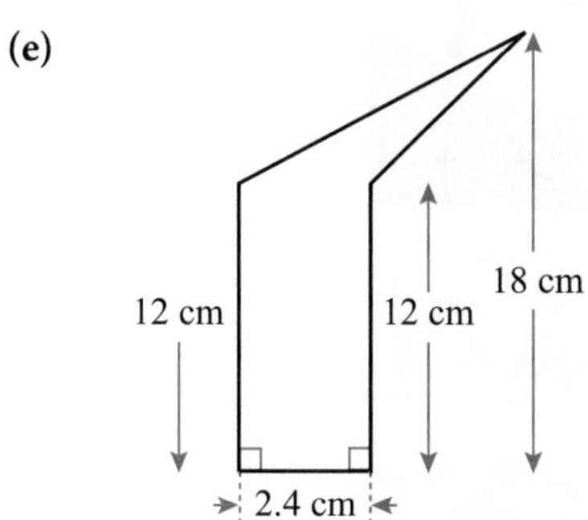

(f)

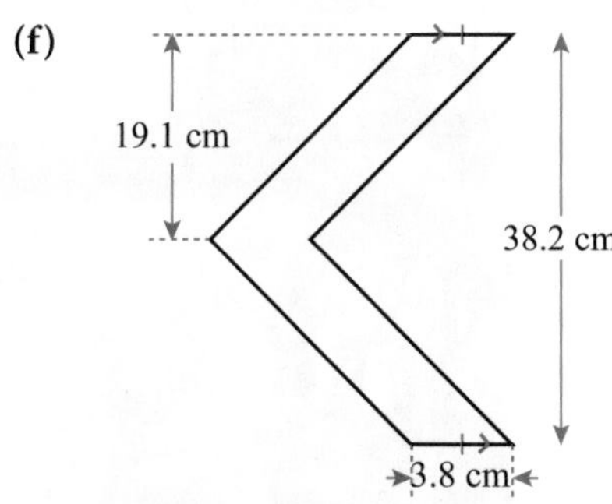

(g)

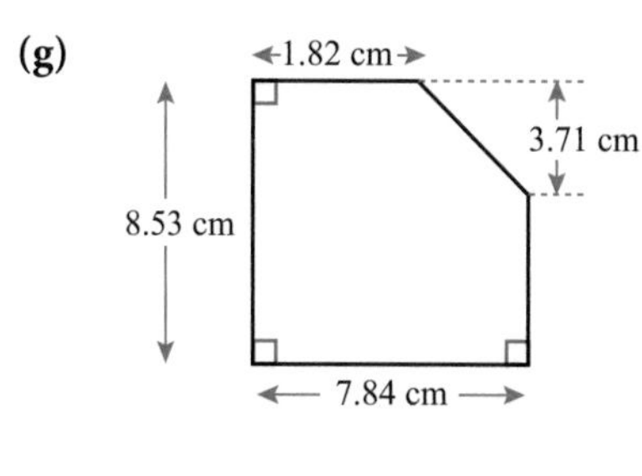

Write down the formula for the area in each case. Substitute into the formula the values that you already know and then rearrange it to find the unknown quantity.

5 For each of the following shapes you are given the area and one other measurement. Find the unknown length in each case.

(a)

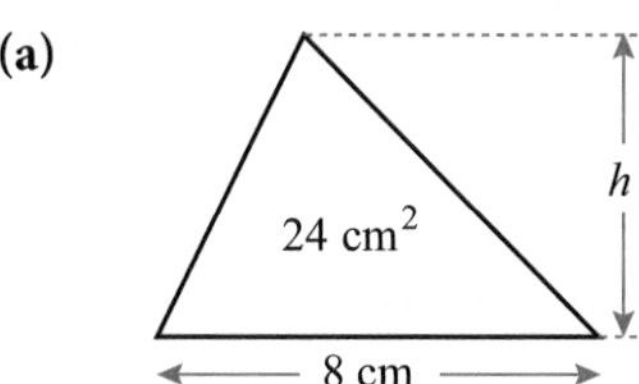

(b)

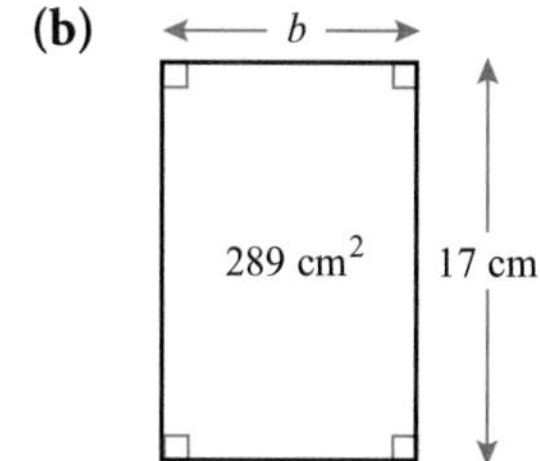

(c)

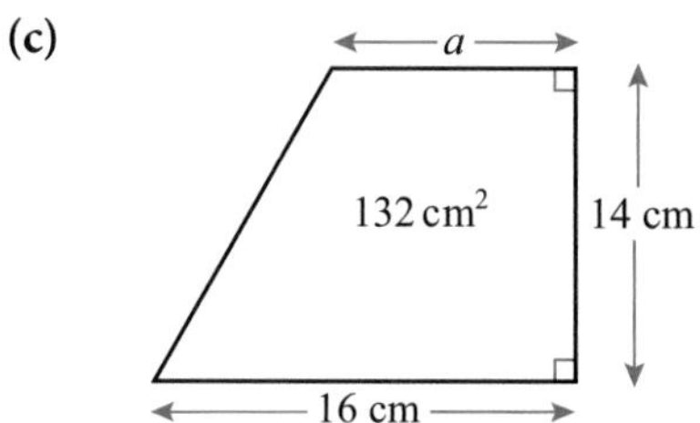

(d)

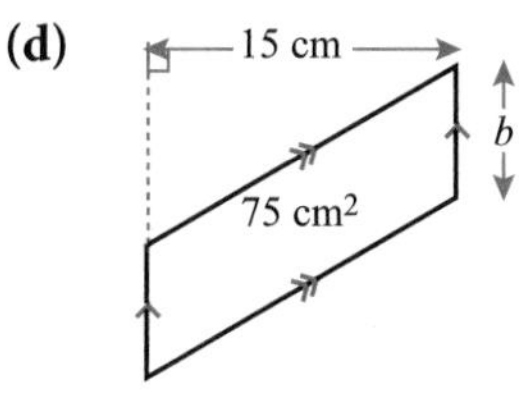

(e)

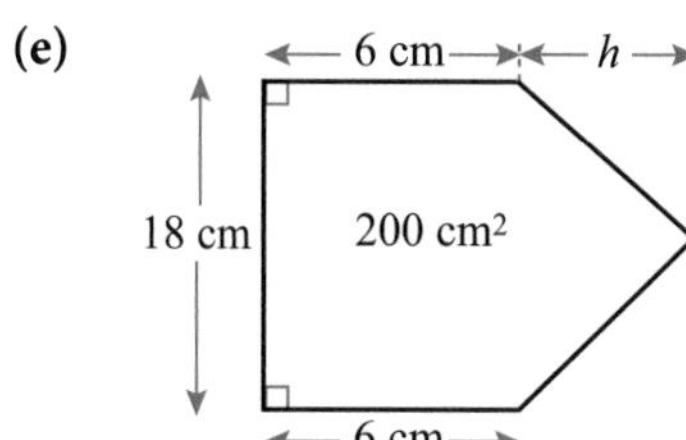

6 How many 20 cm by 30 cm rectangular tiles would you need to tile the outdoor area shown below?

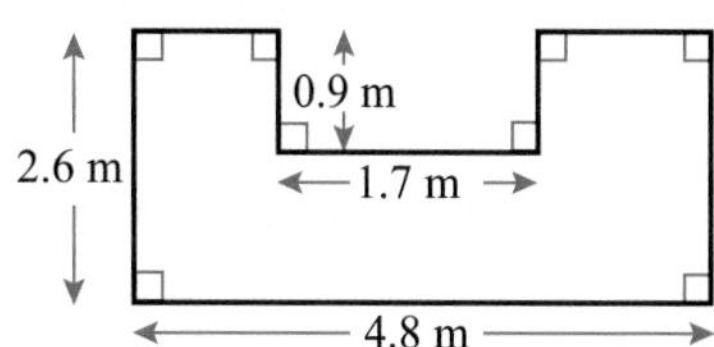

7 Sanjay has a square mirror measuring 10 cm by 10 cm. Silvie has a square mirror which covers twice the area of Sanjay's mirror. Determine the dimensions of Silvie's mirror correct to 2 decimal places.

8 For each of the following, draw rough sketches and give the dimensions:
 (a) two rectangles with the same perimeter but different areas
 (b) two rectangles with the same area but different perimeters
 (c) two parallelograms with the same perimeter but different areas
 (d) two parallelograms with the same area but different perimeters.

Circles

'Inscribing' here means to draw a circle inside a polygon so that it just touches every edge. 'Circumscribing' means to draw a circle outside a polygon that touches every vertex.

Archimedes worked out the formula for the area of a circle by inscribing and circumscribing polygons with increasing numbers of sides.

The circle seems to appear everywhere in our everyday lives. Whether driving a car, running on a race track or playing basketball, this is one of a number of shapes that are absolutely essential to us.

REWIND

You learned the names of the parts of a circle in chapter 3. The diagram on the right is a reminder of some of the parts. The diameter is the line that passes through a circle and splits it into two equal halves. ◀

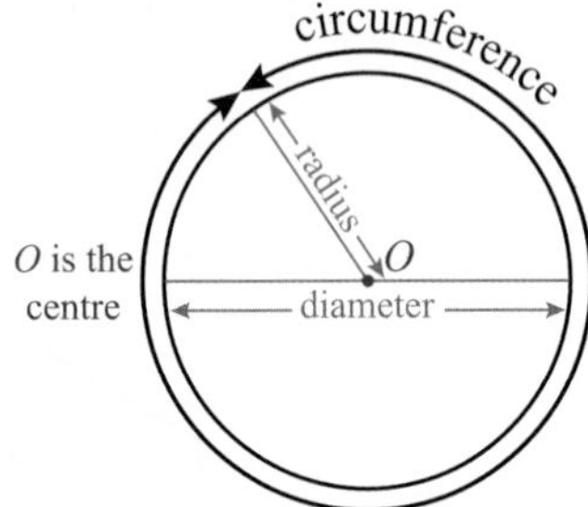

Finding the circumference of a circle

FAST FORWARD

π is an example of an **irrational number**. The properties of irrational numbers will be discussed later in chapter 9. ▶

Circumference is the word used to identify the perimeter of a circle. Note that the diameter = $2 \times$ radius ($2r$). The Ancient Greeks knew that they could find the circumference of a circle by multiplying the diameter by a particular number. This number is now known as 'π' (which is the Greek letter 'p'), pronounced 'pi' (like apple *pie*). π is equal to 3.141592654. . .

The circumference of a circle can be found using a number of formulae that all mean the same thing:

Circumference $= \pi \times$ diameter
$= \pi d$ (where $d =$ diameter)
$= 2\pi r$ (where $r =$ radius)

Finding the area of a circle

There is a simple formula for calculating the area of a circle. Here is a method that shows how the formula can be worked out:

Consider the circle shown in the diagram below. It has been divided into 12 equal parts and these have been rearranged to give the diagram on the right.

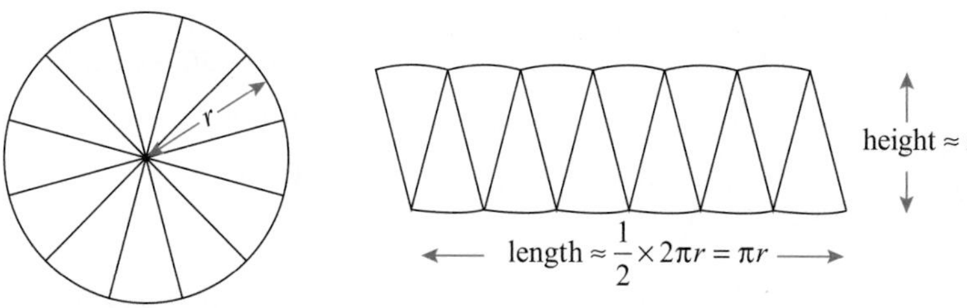

Because the parts of the circle are narrow, the shape almost forms a rectangle with height equal to the radius of the circle and the length equal to half of the circumference.

Now, the formula for the area of a rectangle is Area = bh so,

$$\text{Area of a circle} \approx \frac{1}{2} \times 2\pi r \times r \quad \text{(Using the values of } b \text{ and } h \text{ shown above)}$$

$$= \pi r^2 \quad \text{(Simplify)}$$

If you try this yourself with a greater number of even narrower parts inside a circle, you will notice that the right-hand diagram will look even more like a rectangle.

This indicates (but does not prove) that the area of a circle is given by: $A = \pi r^2$.

You will now look at some examples so that you can see how to apply these formulae.

REWIND

BODMAS in chapter 1 tells you to calculate the square of the radius before multiplying by π. ◀

Note that in (a), the diameter is given and in (b) only the radius is given. Make sure that you look carefully at which measurement you are given.

Tip

Your calculator should have a π button. If it does not, use the approximation 3.142, but make sure you write this in your working. Make sure you record the final calculator answer before rounding and then state what level of accuracy you rounded to.

Worked example 2

For each of the following circles calculate the circumference and the area. Give each answer to 3 significant figures.

(a)

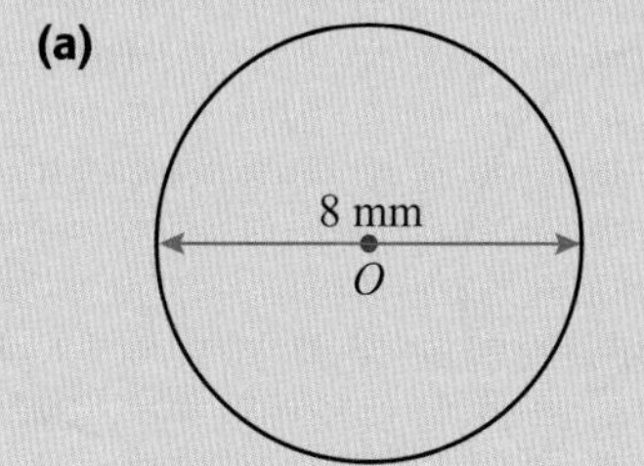

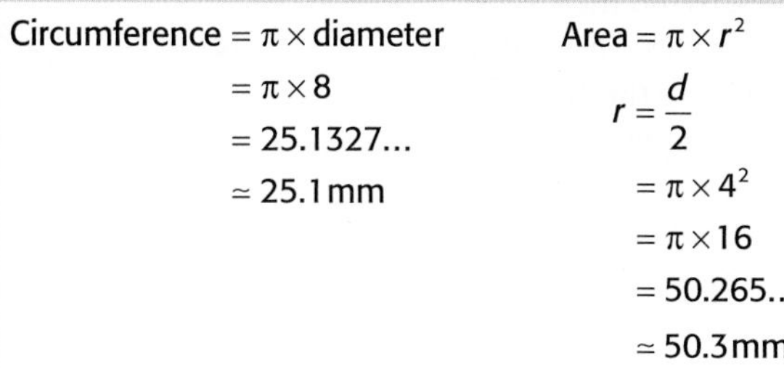

(a) Circumference = π × diameter
$= \pi \times 8$
$= 25.1327...$
≈ 25.1 mm

Area $= \pi \times r^2$
$r = \frac{d}{2}$
$= \pi \times 4^2$
$= \pi \times 16$
$= 50.265...$
$\approx 50.3\text{ mm}^2$

(b)

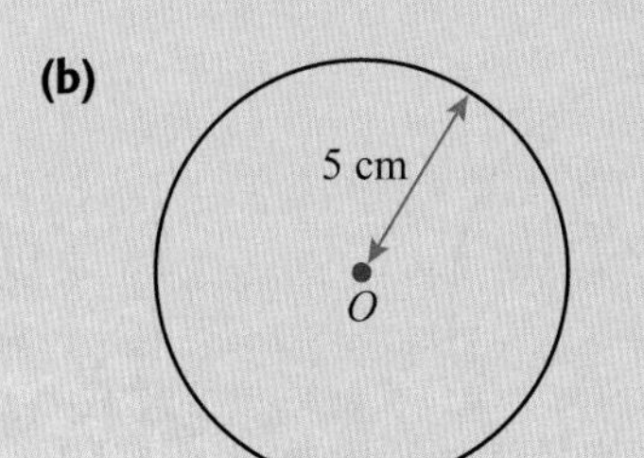

(b) Circumference = π × diameter
$= \pi \times 10 \quad (d = 2 \times r)$
$= 31.415...$
≈ 31.4 cm

Area $= \pi \times r^2$
$= \pi \times 5^2$
$= \pi \times 25$
$= 78.539...$
$\approx 78.5\text{ cm}^2$

Worked example 3

Calculate the area of the shaded region in the diagram.

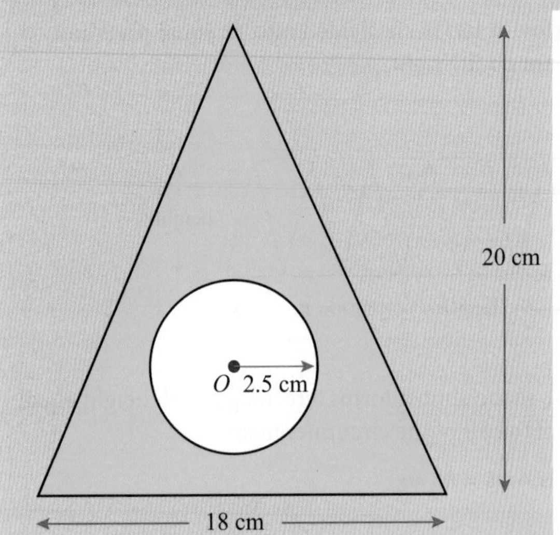

Shaded area = area of triangle – area of circle.

$$\text{Area} = \frac{1}{2}bh - \pi r^2$$

$$= \frac{1}{2} \times 18 \times 20 - \pi \times 2.5^2$$

$$= 160.365\ldots$$

$$\simeq 160\,\text{cm}^2$$

Substitute in values of b, h and r.
Round the answer. In this case it has been rounded to 3 significant figures.

Exercise 7.2

Tip

Some calculators might leave the answer in terms of π e.g 3π. If this happens, you should convert it to a decimal: using the S↔D button on your calculator and round the answer. If your calculator does not have this button, or an equivalent, you could workout the calculation using the π key: e.g $3 \times \pi = 9.42$(3sf).

In some cases you may find it helpful to find a decimal value for the radius and diameter before going any further, though you can enter exact values easily on most modern calculators. If you know how to do so, then this is a good way to avoid the introduction of rounding errors.

1 Calculate the area and circumference in each of the following.

(a)

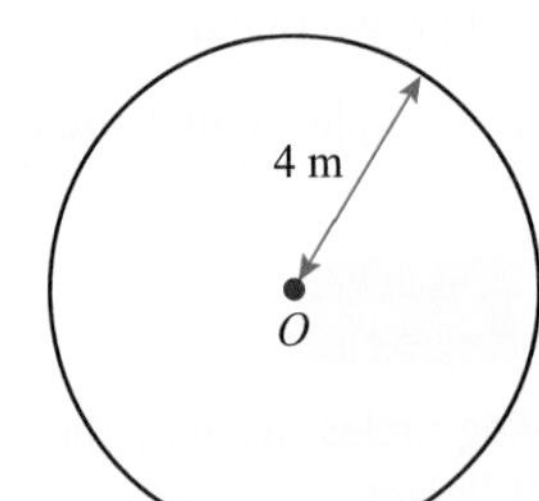

(b)

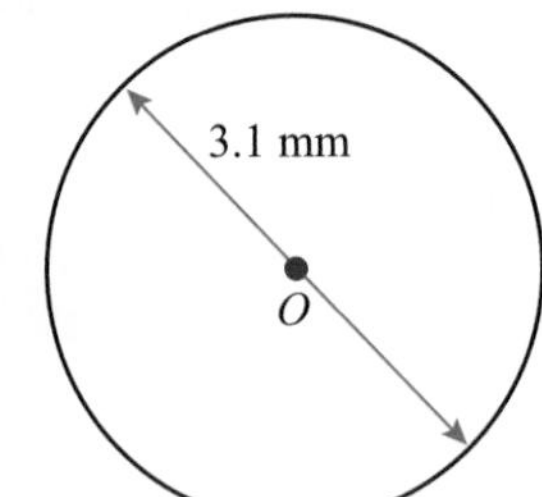

(c)

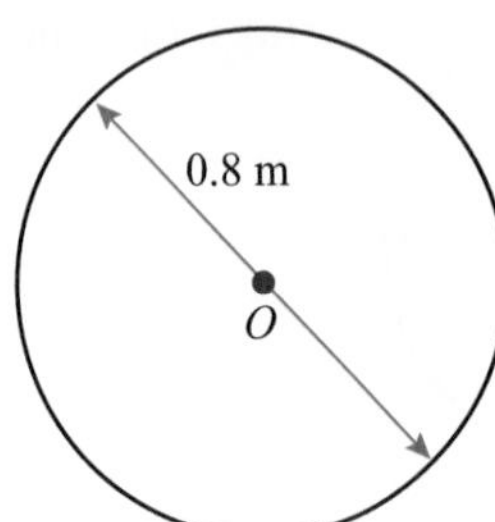

(d)

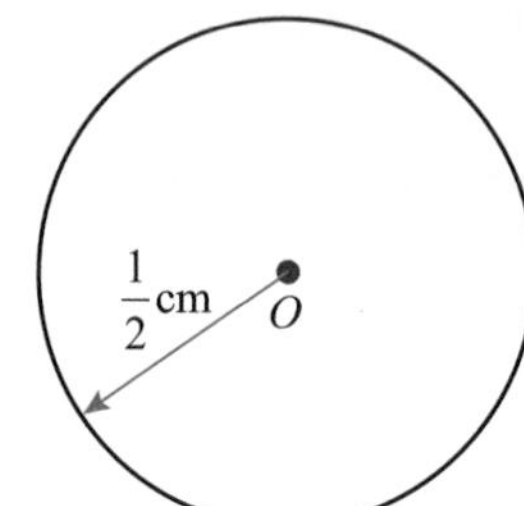

(e)

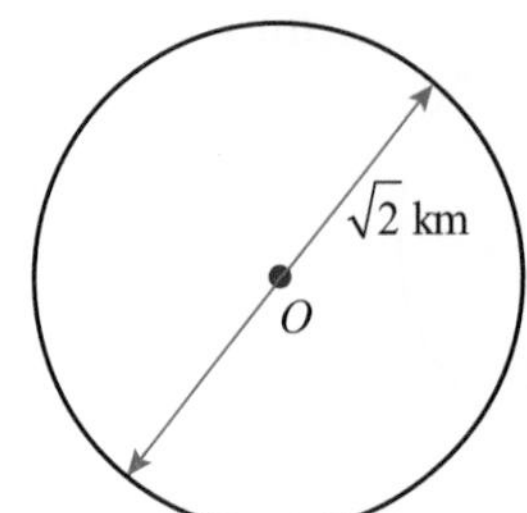

(f)

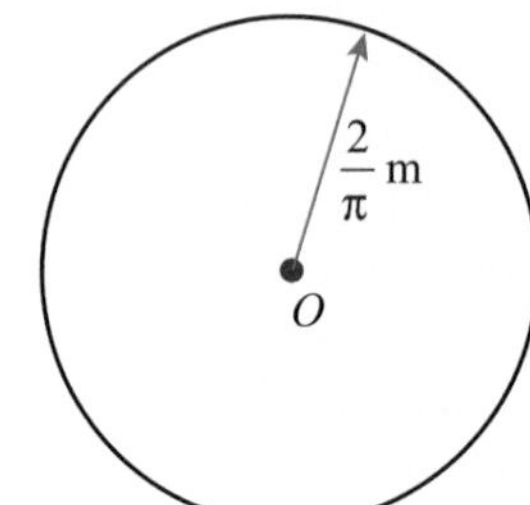

2 Calculate the area of the shaded region in each case.

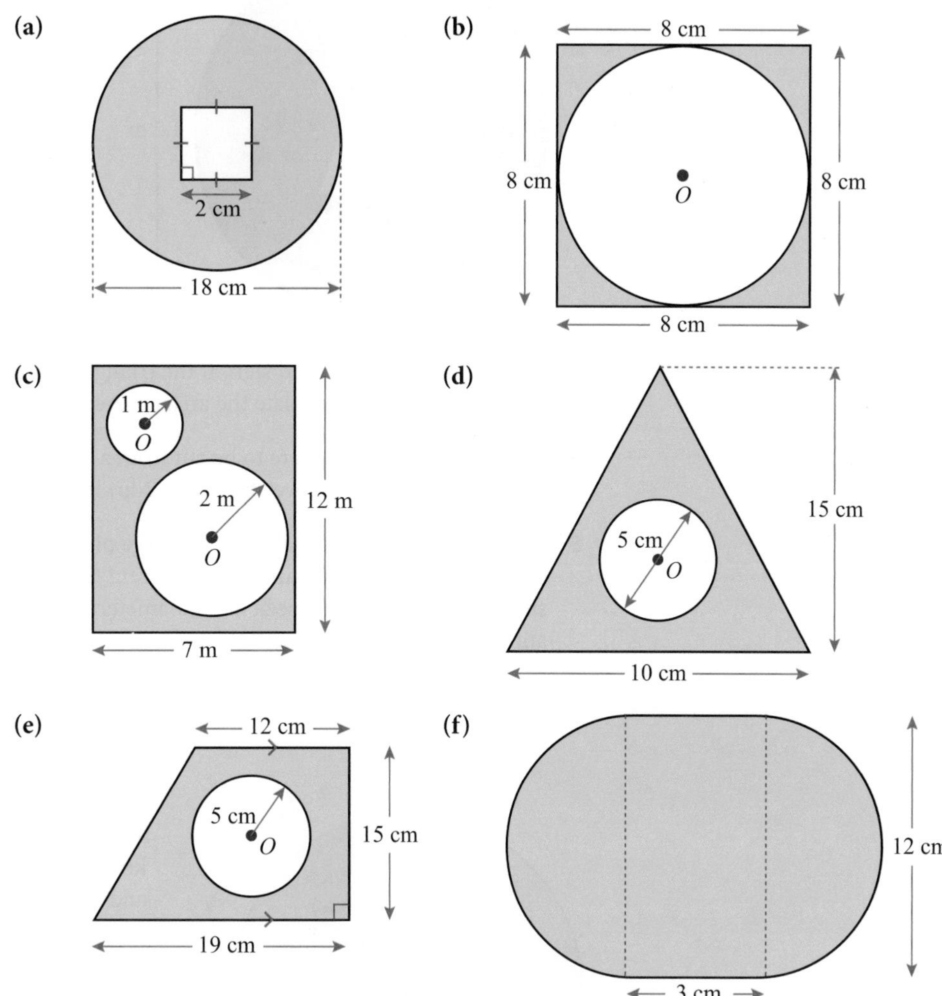

Living maths

3

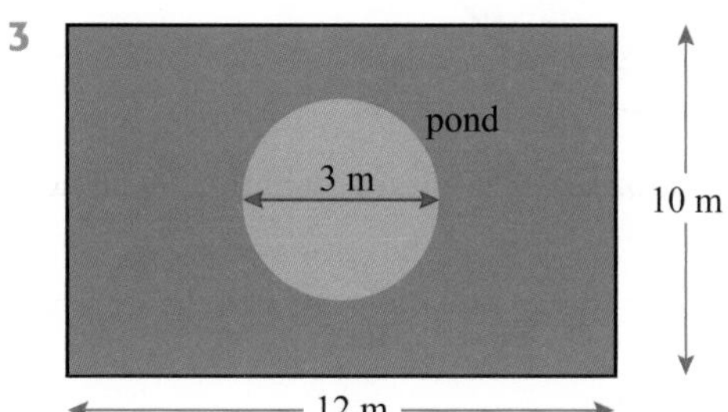

The diagram shows a plan for a rectangular garden with a circular pond. The part of the garden not covered by the pond is to be covered by grass. One bag of grass seed covers five square metres of lawn. Calculate the number of bags of seed needed for the work to be done.

4

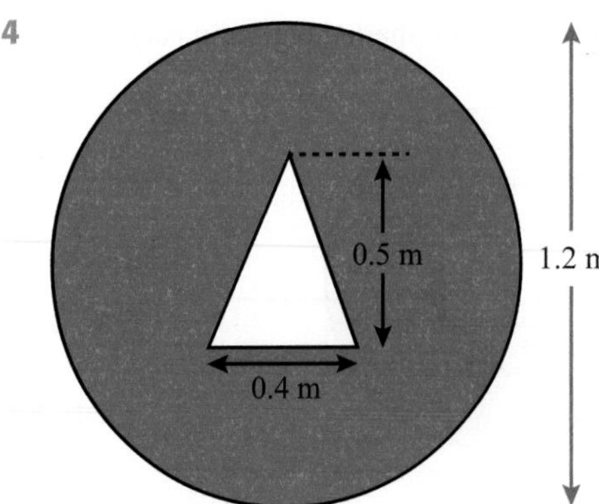

The diagram shows a road sign. If the triangle is to be painted white and the rest of the sign will be painted red, calculate the area covered by each colour to 1 decimal place.

5 Sixteen identical circles are to be cut from a square sheet of fabric whose sides are 0.4 m long. Find the area of the leftover fabric (to 2dp) if the circles are made as large as possible.

6 Anna and her friend usually order a large pizza to share. The large pizza has a diameter of 24 cm. This week they want to eat different things on their pizzas, so they decide to order two small pizzas. The small pizza has a diameter of 12 cm. They want to know if there is the same amount of pizza in two small pizzas as in one large. Work out the answer.

Arcs and sectors

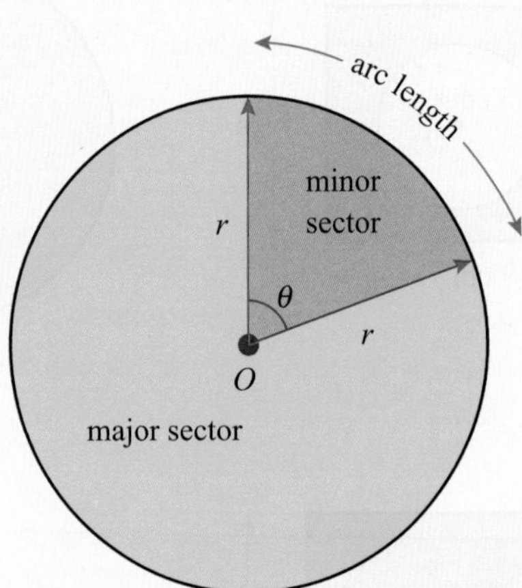

The diagram shows a circle with two radii (plural of radius) drawn from the centre.

The region contained in-between the two radii is known as a **sector**. Notice that there is a *major* sector and a *minor* sector.

A section of the circumference is known as an **arc.**

The Greek letter θ represents the angle *subtended* at the centre.

Notice that the minor sector is a fraction of the full circle. It is $\frac{\theta}{360}$ of the circle.

Area of a circle is πr^2. The sector is $\frac{\theta}{360}$ of a circle, so replace 'of' with '×' to give:

Sector area $= \frac{\theta}{360} \times \pi r^2$

Circumference of a circle is $2\pi r$. If the sector is $\frac{\theta}{360}$ of a circle, then the length of the arc of a sector is $\frac{\theta}{360}$ of the circumference. So;

Arc length $= \frac{\theta}{360} \times 2\pi r$

Make sure that you remember the following two special cases:

- If $\theta = 90°$ then you have a quarter of a circle. This is known as a *quadrant*.
- If $\theta = 180°$ then you have a half of a circle. This is known as a **semi-circle.**

Worked example 4

Find the area and perimeter of shapes **(a)** and **(b)**, and the area of shape **(c)**. Give your answer to 3 significant figures.

(a)

$\text{Area} = \frac{\theta}{360} \times \pi r^2$	$\text{Perimeter} = \frac{\theta}{360} \times 2\pi r + 2r$
$= \frac{30}{360} \times \pi \times 5^2$	$= \frac{30}{360} \times 2 \times \pi \times 5 + 2 \times 5$
$= 6.544...$	$= 12.617...$
$\approx 6.54\,\text{m}^2$	$\approx 12.6\,\text{m}$

Note that for the perimeter you need to add 5 m twice. This happens because you need to include the two straight edges.

(b)

$\text{Area} = \frac{\theta}{360} \times \pi r^2$	$\text{Perimeter} = \frac{\theta}{360} \times 2\pi r + 2r$
$= \frac{360 - 65}{360} \times \pi \times 4^2$	$= \frac{295}{360} \times 2 \times \pi \times 4 + 2 \times 4$
$= \frac{295}{360} \times \pi \times 16$	$= 28.594...$
$= 41.189...$	$\approx 28.6\,\text{cm}$
$\approx 41.2\,\text{cm}^2$	

Note that the size of θ has not been given. You need to calculate it ($\theta = 360 - 65$).

(c)

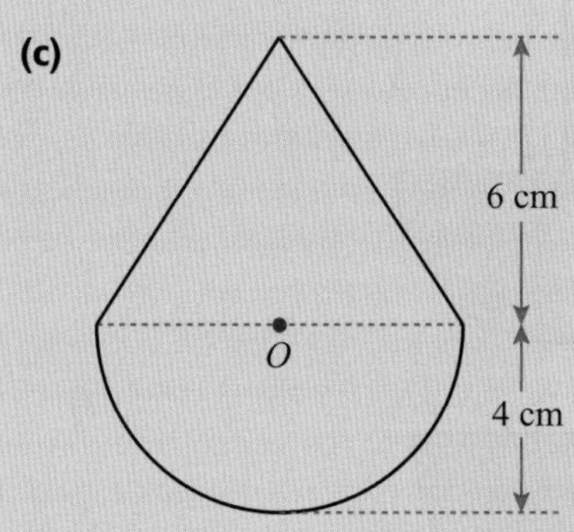

Total area = area of triangle + area of a semi-circle.

$\text{Area} = \frac{1}{2}bh + \frac{1}{2}\pi r^2$ (Semi-circle is half of a circle so divide circle area by 2).

$= \frac{1}{2} \times 8 \times 6 + \frac{1}{2}\pi \times 4^2$

$= 49.132...$

$\approx 49.1\,\text{cm}^2$

You should have spotted that you do not have enough information to calculate the perimeter of the top part of the shape using the rules you have learned so far.

FAST FORWARD

You will be able to find the perimeter of this third shape after completing the work on Pythagoras' theorem in chapter 11. ▶

Note that the base of the triangle is the diameter of the circle.

Exercise 7.3

1 Find the area of the coloured region and find the arc length l in each of the following.

(a)

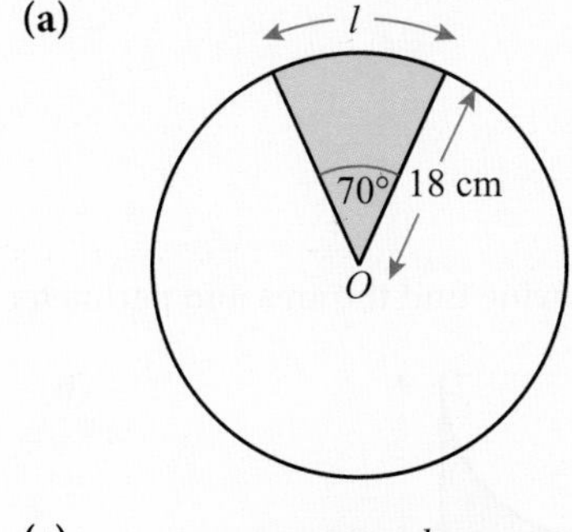

(b)

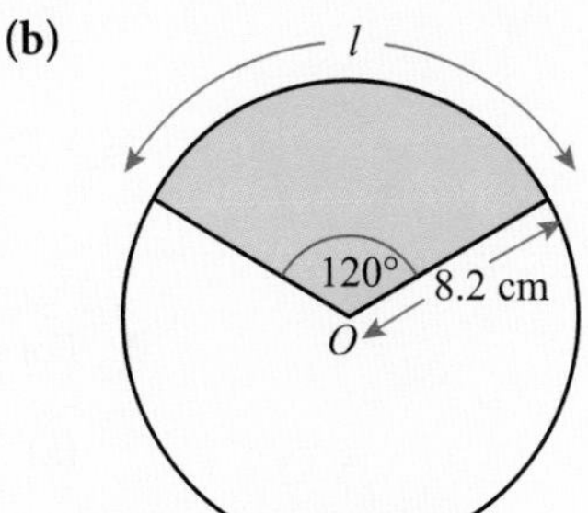

(c)

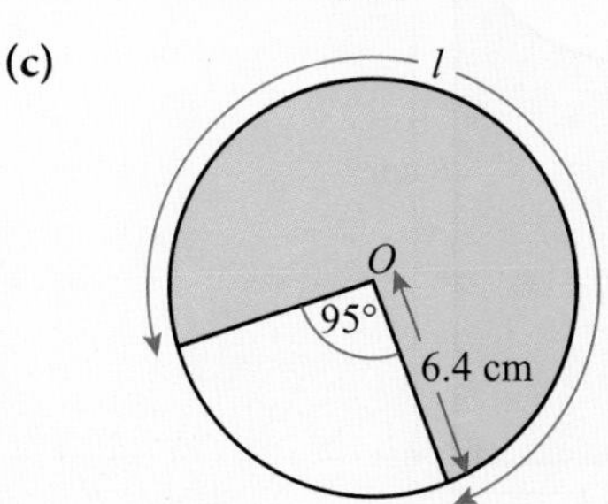

(d)

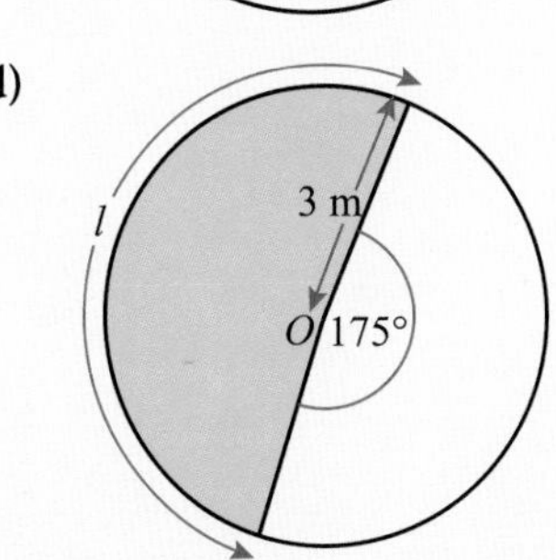

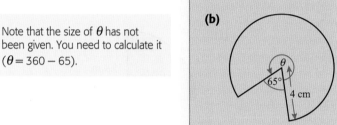

2 For each of the following shapes find the area *and* perimeter.

(a)

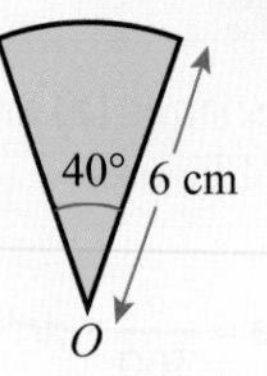

(b)

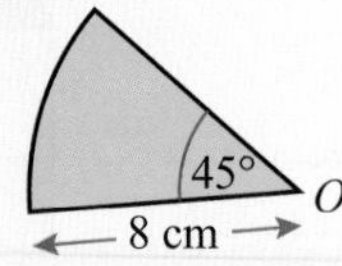

(c)

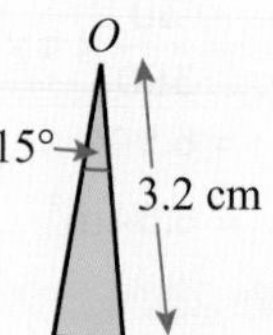

(d)

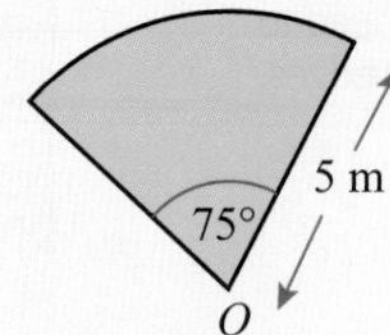

(e)

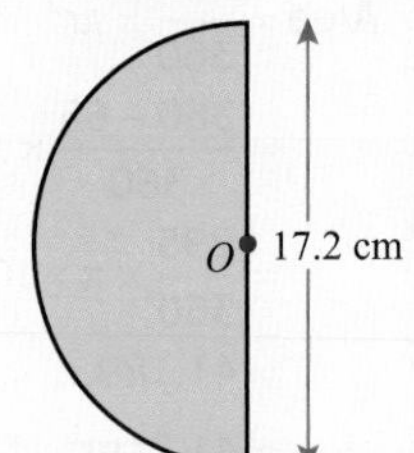

(f)

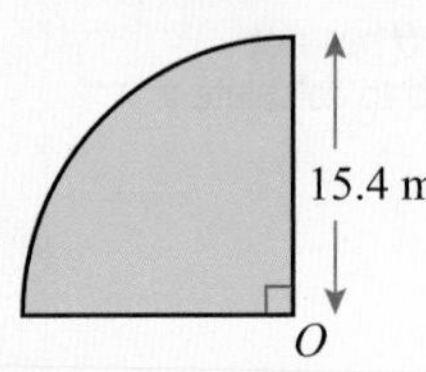

(g)

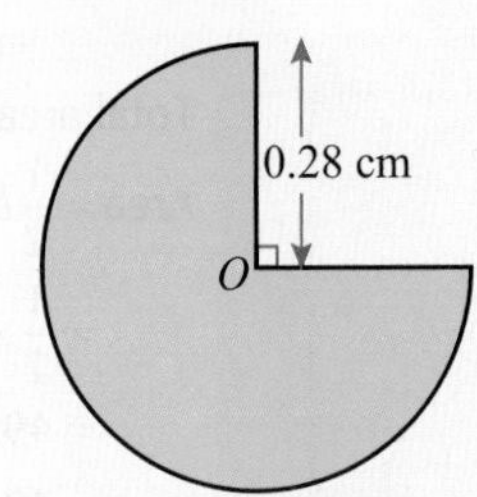

(h)

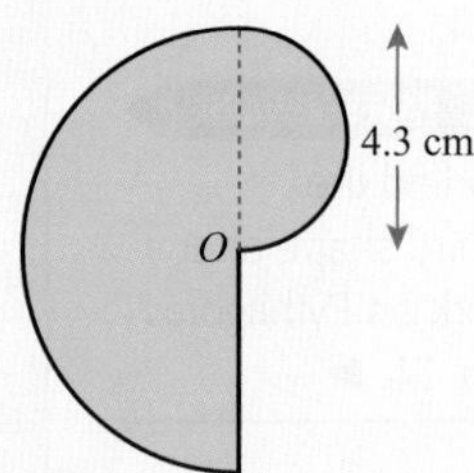

(i)

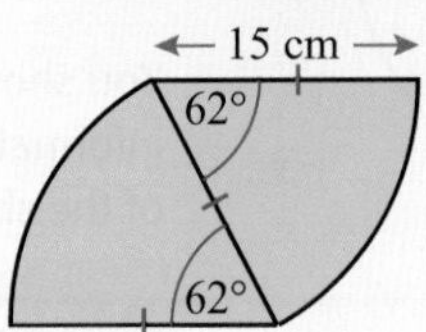

(j)

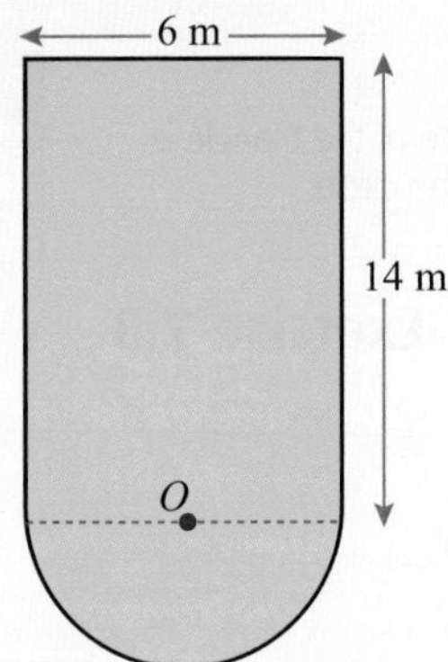

3 For each of the following find the area and perimeter of the coloured region.

(a)

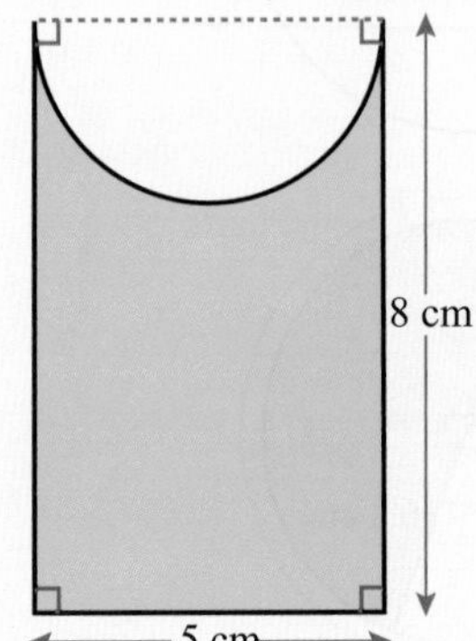

(b)

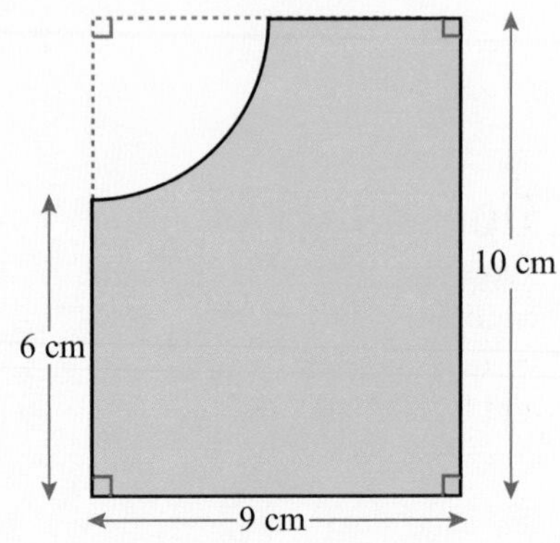

(c)

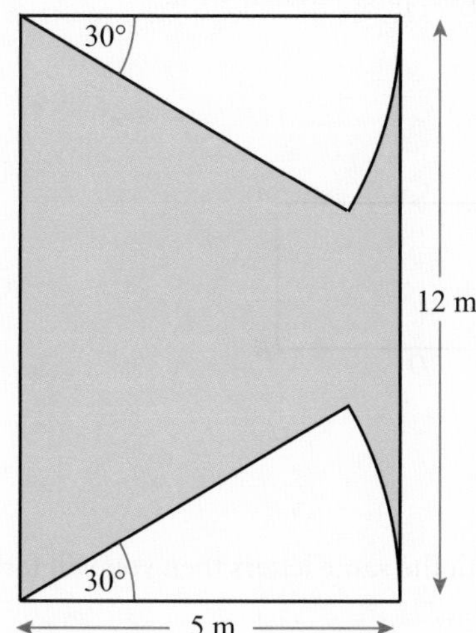

(d)

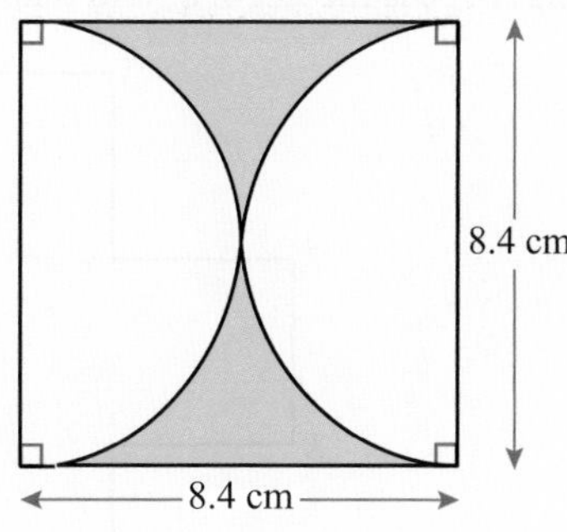

(e)

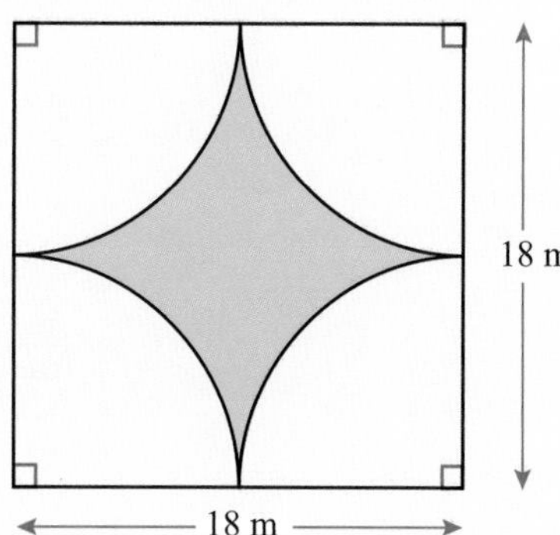

4 Each of the following shapes can be split into simpler shapes.
In each case find the perimeter and area.

(a)

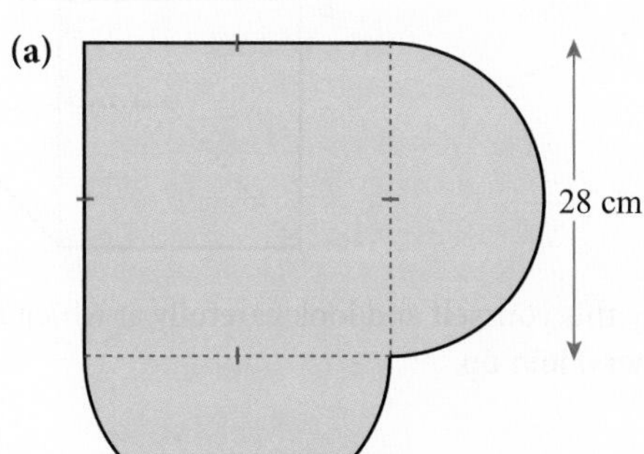

(b)

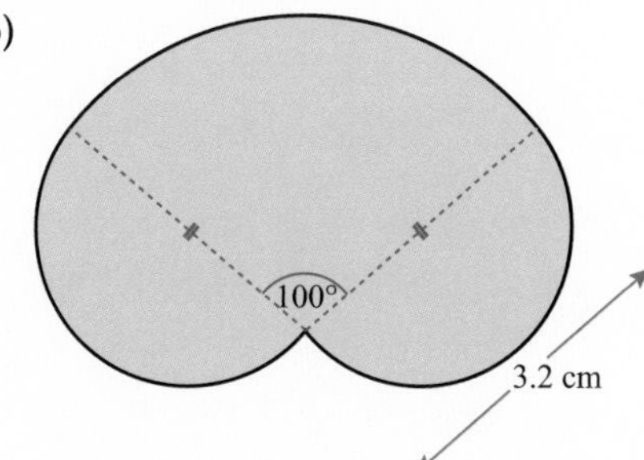

(c)

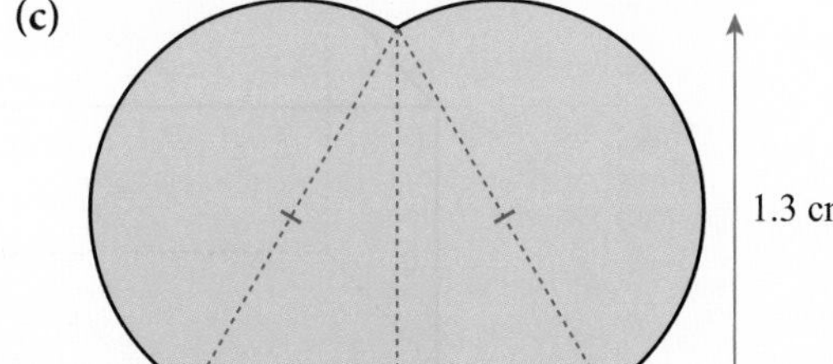

(d)

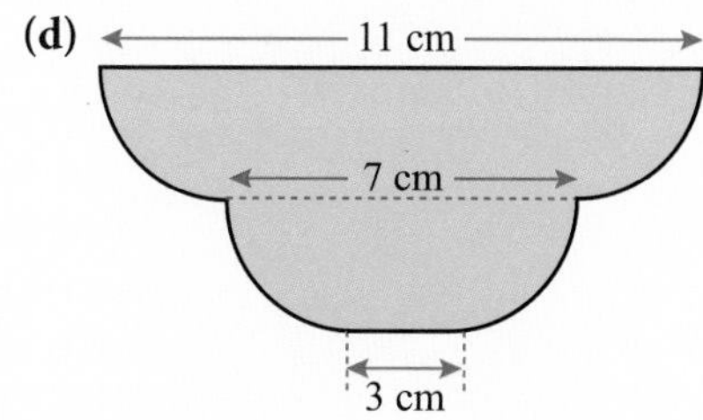

7.2 Three-dimensional objects

> **Tip**
> You might be asked to count the number of vertices (corners), edges and faces that a solid has.

We now move into three dimensions but will use many of the formulae for two-dimensional shapes in our calculations. A three-dimensional object is called a **solid**.

Nets of solids

A **net** is a two-dimensional shape that can be drawn, cut out and folded to form a three-dimensional solid.

The following shape is the net of a solid that you should be quite familiar with.

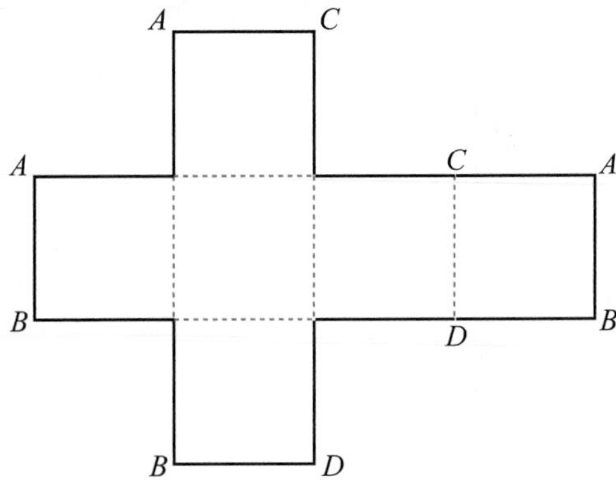

If you fold along the dotted lines and join the points with the same letters then you will form this cube:

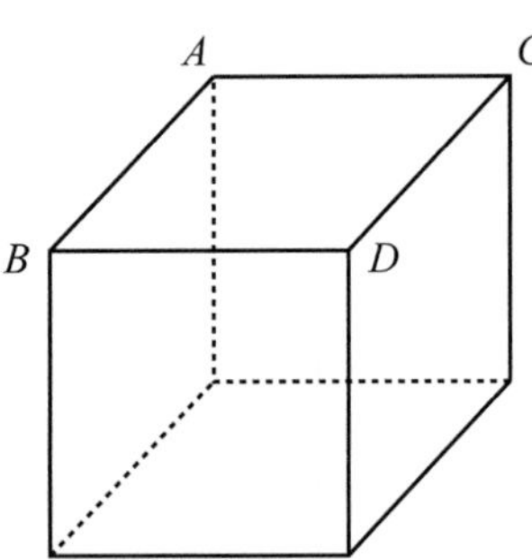

You should try this yourself and look carefully at which edges (sides) and which **vertices** (the points or corners) join up.

Exercise 7.4

1 The diagram shows a cuboid. Draw a net for the cuboid.

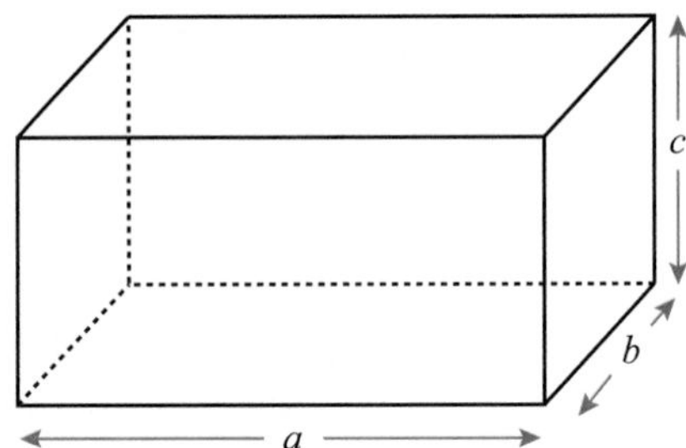

2 The diagram shows the net of a solid.

(a) Describe the solid in as much detail as you can.

(b) Which two points will join with point M when the net is folded?

(c) Which edges are certainly equal in length to PQ?

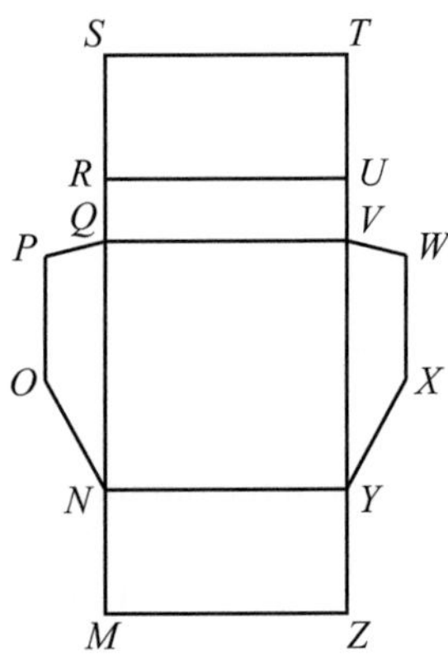

3 A teacher asked her class to draw the net of a cuboid cereal box. These are the diagrams that three students drew. Which of them is correct?

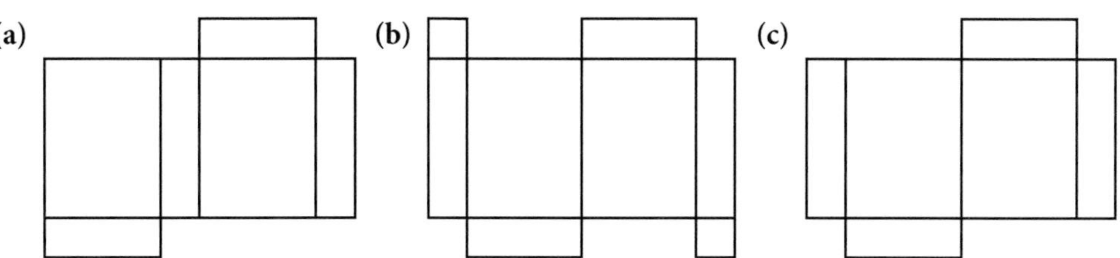

4 How could you make a cardboard model of this octahedral dice? Draw labelled sketches to show your solution.

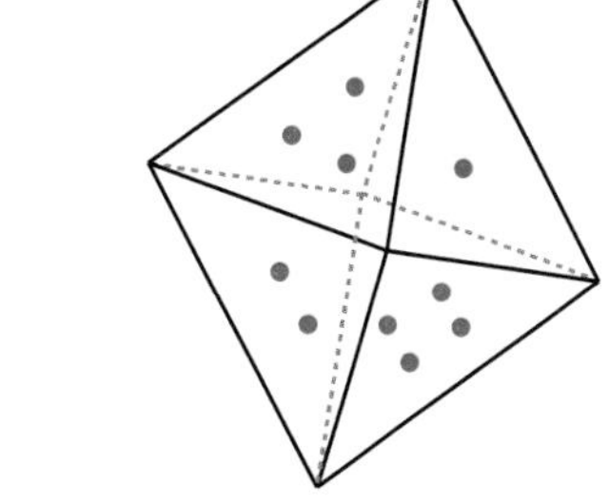

7.3 Surface areas and volumes of solids

It can be helpful to draw the net of a solid when trying to find its surface area.

The flat, two-dimensional surfaces on the outside of a solid are called **faces**. The area of each face can be found using the techniques from earlier in this chapter. The total area of the faces will give us the **surface area** of the solid.

The **volume** is the amount of space contained inside the solid. If the units given are cm, then the volume is measured in cubic centimetres (cm^3) and so on.

Some well known formulae for surface area and volume are shown below.

Cuboids

A cuboid has six rectangular faces, 12 edges and eight vertices.

If the length, breadth and height of the cuboid are a, b and c (respectively) then the surface area can be found by thinking about the areas of each rectangular face.

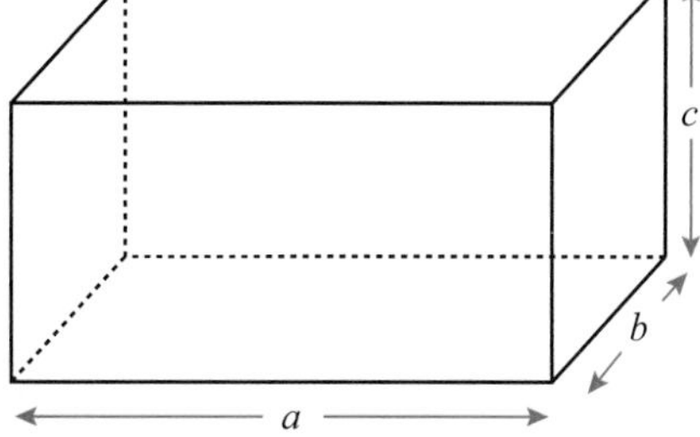

Notice that the surface area is exactly the same as the area of the cuboid's net.

Surface area of cuboid $= 2(ab + ac + bc)$

Volume of cuboid $= a \times b \times c$

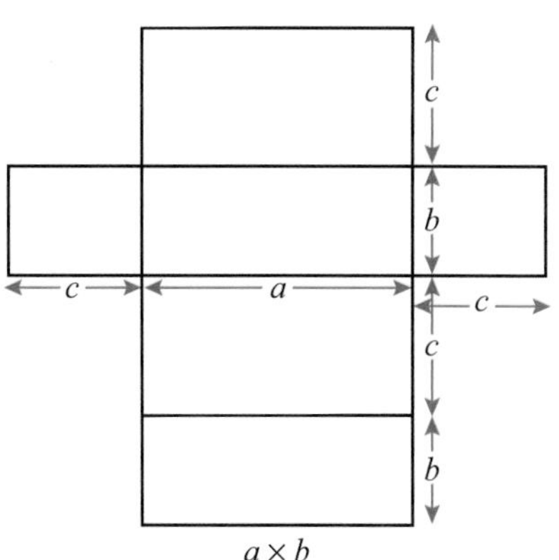

The volume of a cuboid is its length × breadth × height.

So, volume of cuboid $= a \times b \times c$.

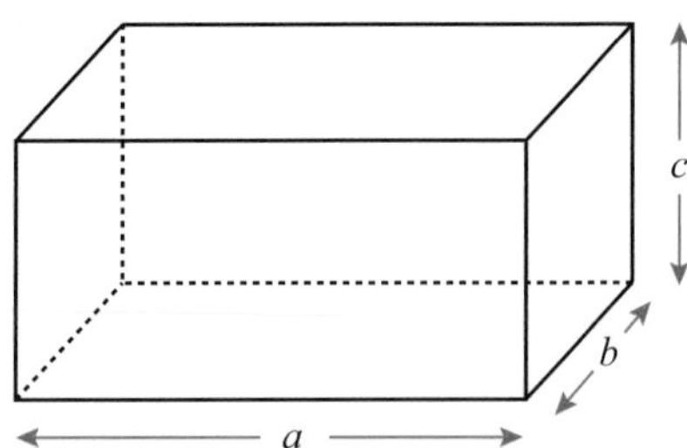

Prisms

A prism is a solid whose cross-section is the same all along its length. (A cross-section is the surface formed when you cut parallel to a face.)

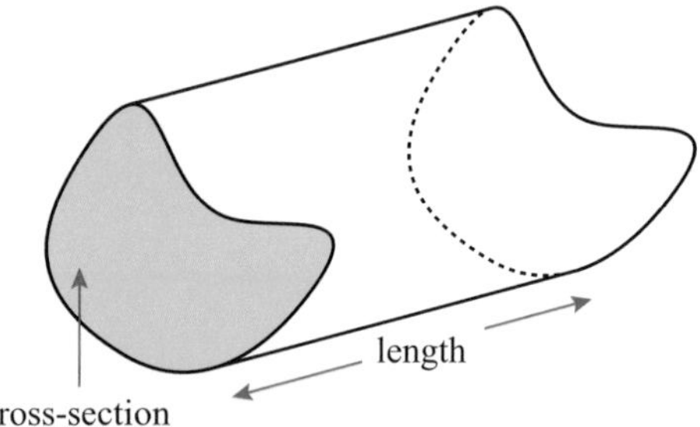

The cuboid is a special case of a prism with a rectangular cross-section. A triangular prism has a triangular cross-section.

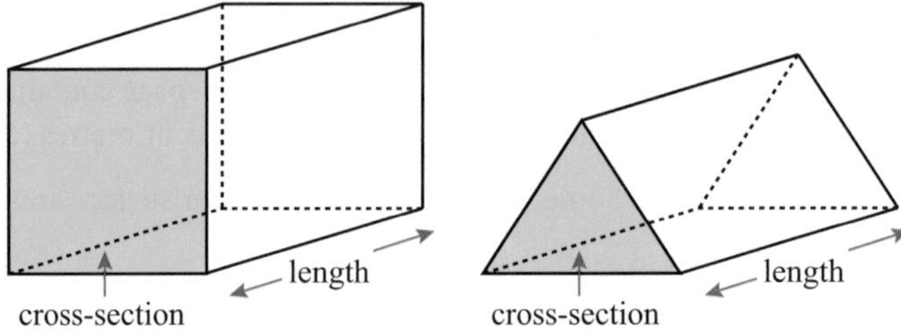

The surface area of a prism is found by working out the area of each face and adding the areas together. There are two ends with area equal to the cross-sectional area. The remaining sides are all the same length, so their area is equal to the perimeter of the cross-section multiplied by the length:

surface area of a prism = 2 × area of cross-section + perimeter of cross-section × length

The volume of a prism is found by working out the area of the cross-section and multiplying this by the length.

volume of a prism = area of cross-section × length

Cylinders

A cylinder is another special case of a prism. It is a prism with a circular cross-section.

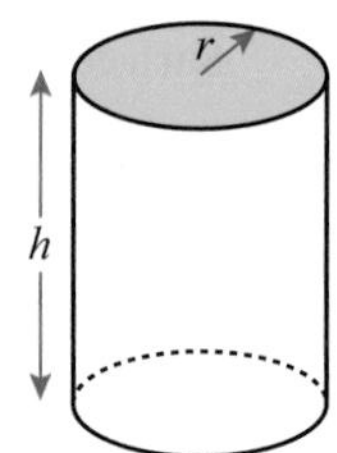

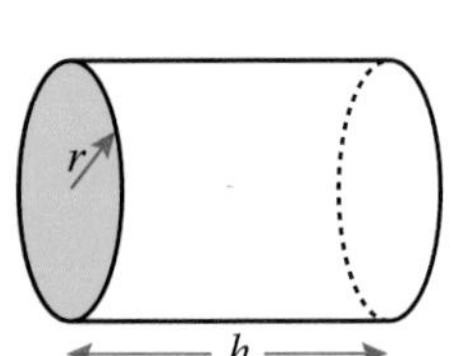

A cylinder can be 'unwrapped' to produce its net. The surface consists of two circular faces and a curved face that can be flattened to make a rectangle.

Curved surface area of a cylinder = $2\pi rh$

and

Volume = $\pi r^2 h$.

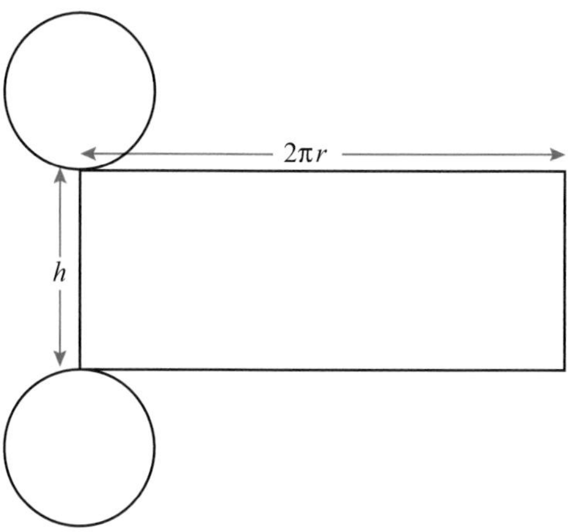

Exercise 7.5

1 Find the volume and surface area of the solid with the net shown in the diagram.

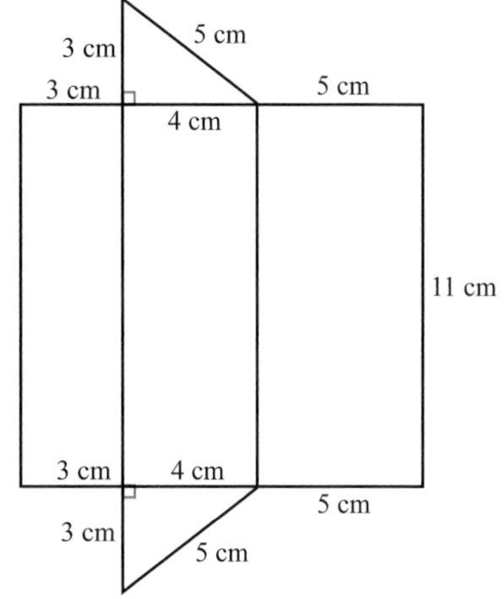

2 Find **(i)** the volume and **(ii)** the surface area of the cuboids with the following dimensions:

(a) length = 5 cm, breadth = 8 cm, height = 18 cm
(b) length = 1.2 mm, breadth = 2.4 mm, height = 4.8 mm

Living maths

3 The diagram shows a bottle crate. Find the volume of the crate.

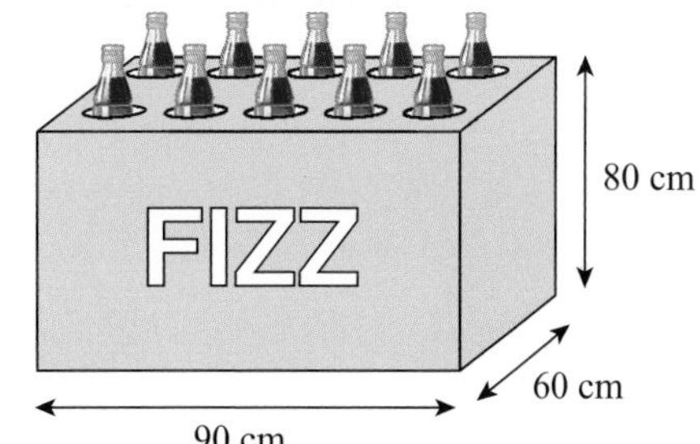

4 The diagram shows a pencil case in the shape of a triangular prism.

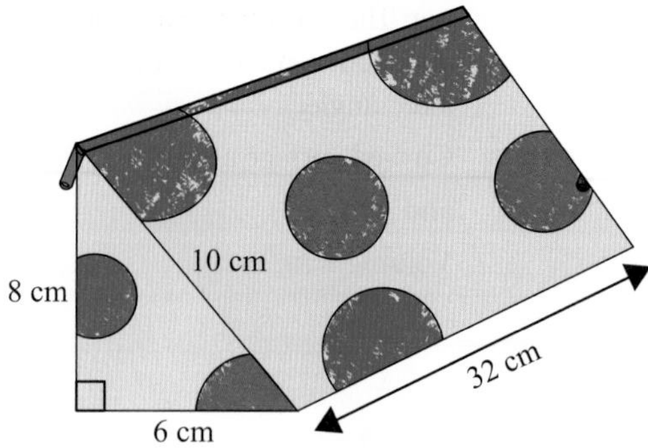

Calculate:
(a) the volume and **(b)** the surface area of the pencil case.

5 The diagram shows a cylindrical drain. Calculate the volume of the drain.

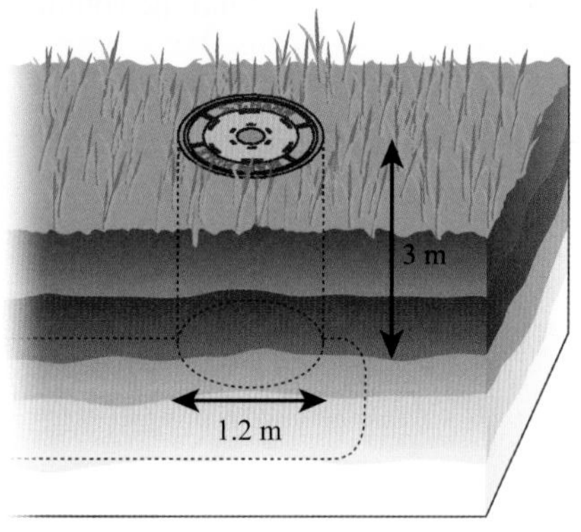

Don't forget to include the circular faces.

6 The diagram shows a tube containing chocolate sweets. Calculate the *total* surface area of the tube.

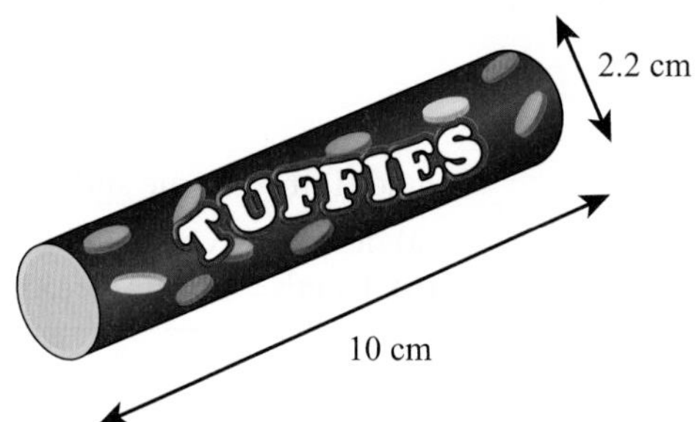

7 The diagram shows the solid glass case for a clock. The case is a cuboid with a cylinder removed (to fit the clock mechanism). Calculate the volume of glass required to make the clock case.

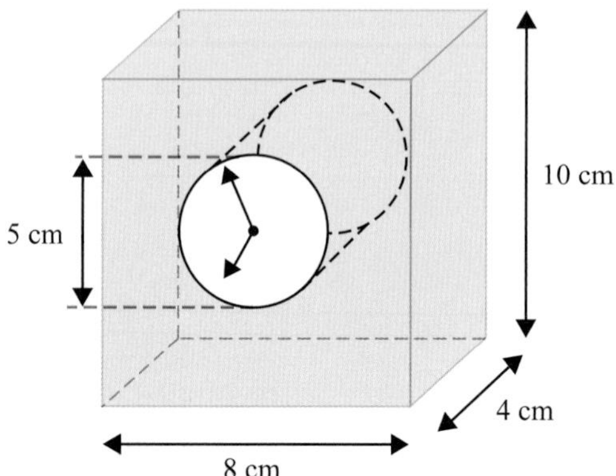

8 A storage company has a rectangular storage area 20 m long, 8 m wide and 2.8 m high.

(a) Find the volume of the storage area.

(b) How many cardboard boxes of dimensions 1 m × 0.5 m × 2.5 m can fit into this storage area?

(c) What is the surface area of each cardboard box?

9 Vuyo is moving to Brazil for his new job. He has hired a shipping container of dimensions 3 m × 4 m × 4 m to move his belongings.

(a) Calculate the volume of the container.

(b) He is provided with crates to fit the dimensions of the container. He needs to move eight of these crates, each with a volume of 5 m³. Will they fit into one container?

Pyramids

A pyramid is a solid with a polygon-shaped base and triangular faces that meet at a point called the **apex**.

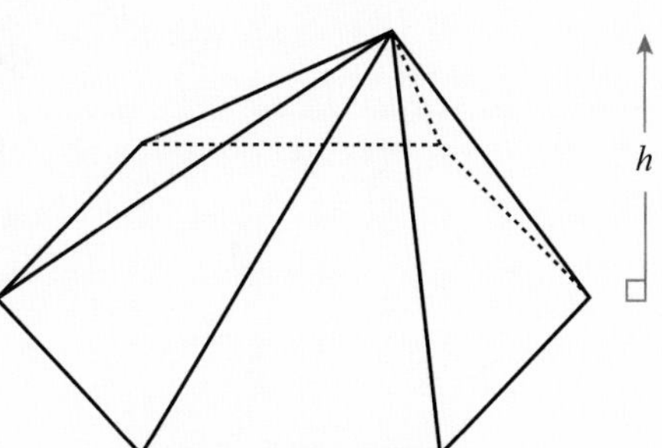

If you find the area of the base and the area of each of the triangles, then you can add these up to find the total surface area of the pyramid.

The perpendicular height is the shortest distance from the base to the apex.

The volume can be found by using the following formula:

$$\text{Volume} = \frac{1}{3} \times \text{base area} \times \text{perpendicular height}$$

Cones

FAST FORWARD

The slant height can be calculated by using Pythagoras' theorem, which you will meet in chapter 11. ▶

A cone is a special pyramid with a circular base. The length l is known as the **slant height.** h is the perpendicular height.

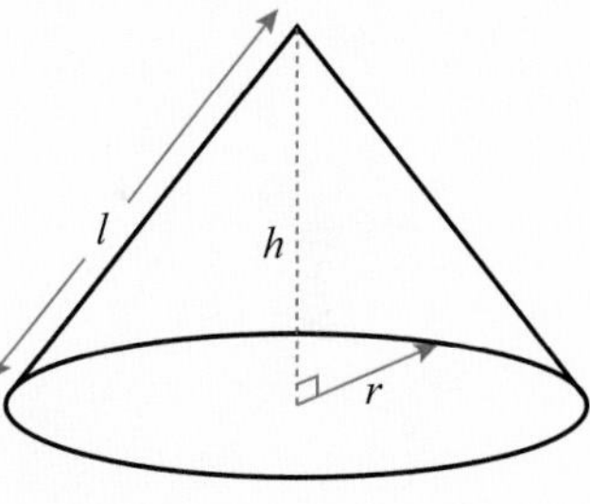

If you are asked for the total surface area of a cone, you must work out the area of the circular base and add it to the curved surface area.

The curved surface of the cone can be opened out and flattened to form a sector of a circle.

Curved surface area = πrl

and

$$\text{Volume} = \frac{1}{3}\pi r^2 h$$

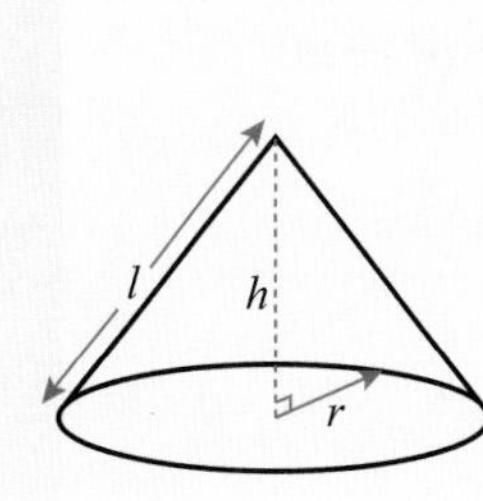

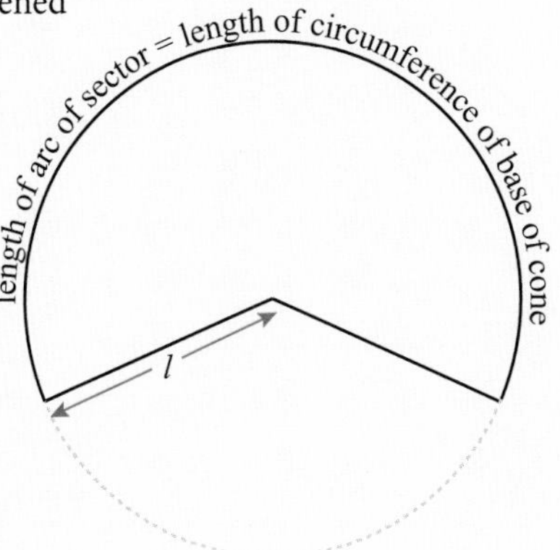

Spheres

The diagram shows a sphere with radius r.

Surface area $= 4\pi r^2$

and

Volume $= \frac{4}{3}\pi r^3$

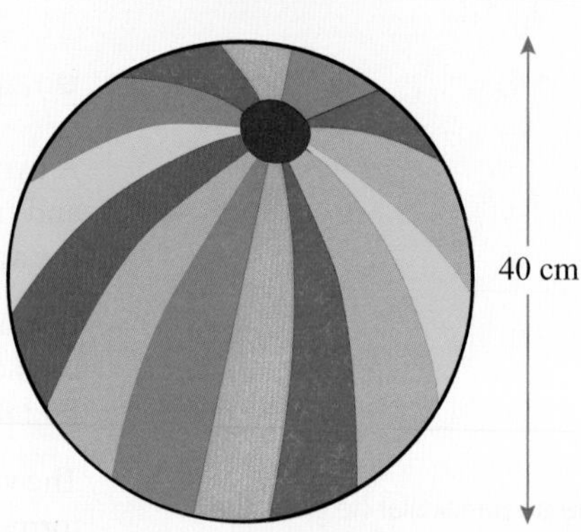

Exercise 7.6

1 The diagram shows a beach ball.

(a) Find the surface area of the beach ball.

(b) Find the volume of the beach ball.

40 cm

2 The diagram shows a metal ball bearing that is completely submerged in a cylinder of water. Find the volume of water in the cylinder.

The volume of the water is the volume in the cylinder minus the displacement caused by the metal ball. The displacement is equal to the volume of the metal ball.

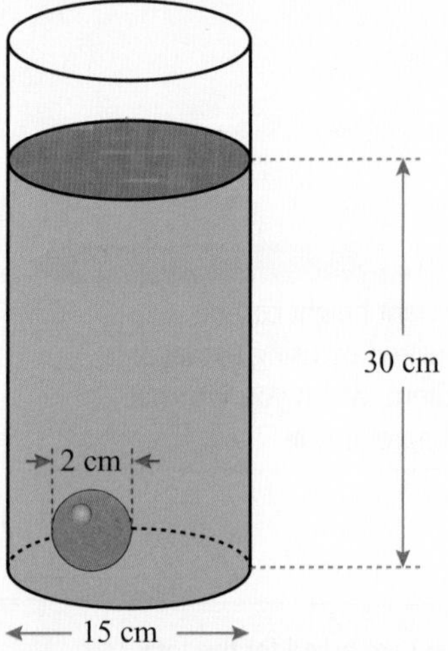

3 The Great Pyramid at Giza has a square base of side 230 m and perpendicular height 146 m.

Find the volume of the Pyramid.

4 The diagram shows a rocket that consists of a cone placed on top of a cylinder.

(a) Find the surface area of the rocket.

(b) Find the volume of the rocket.

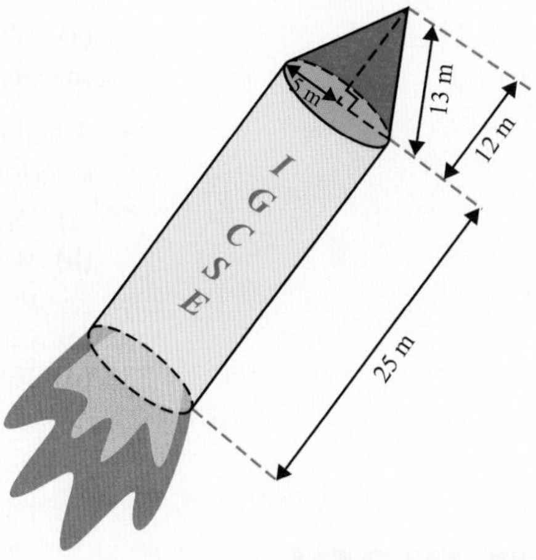

5 The diagram shows a child's toy that consists of a hemisphere (half of a sphere) and a cone.

(a) Find the volume of the toy.

(b) Find the surface area of the toy.

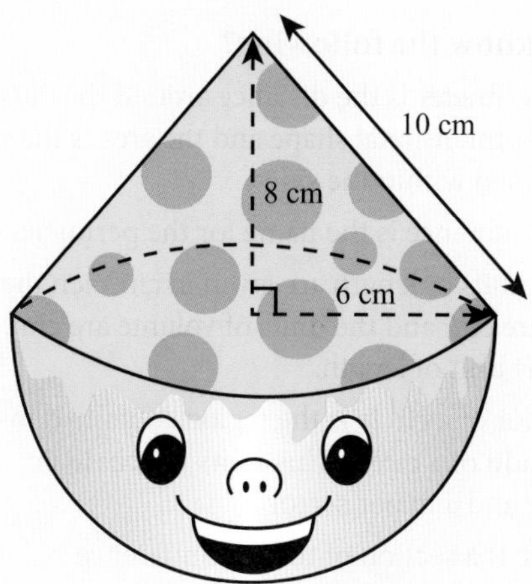

6 The sphere and cone shown in the diagram have the same volume.

Find the radius of the sphere.

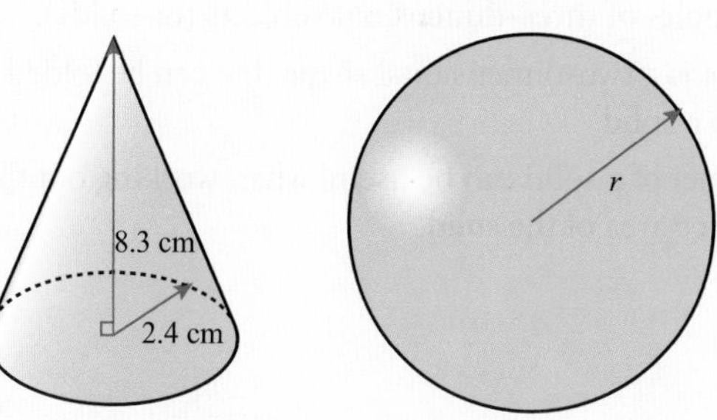

7 The volume of the larger sphere (of radius R) is twice the volume of the smaller sphere (of radius r).

Find an equation connecting r to R.

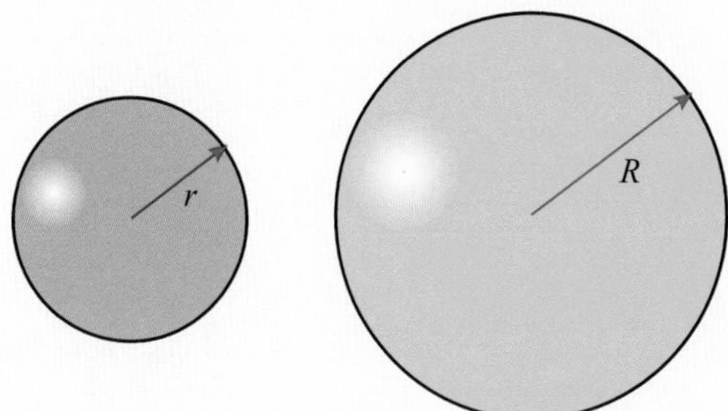

8 A 32 cm long cardboard postage tube has a radius of 2.5 cm.

(a) What is the volume of the tube?

(b) For posting the tube is sealed at both ends. What is the surface area of the sealed tube?

9 A hollow metal tube is made using a 5 mm metal sheet. The tube is 35 cm long and has an exterior diameter of 10.4 cm.

(a) Draw a rough sketch of the tube and add its dimensions

(b) Write down all the calculations you will have to make to find the volume of metal in the tube.

(c) Calculate the volume of metal in the tube.

(d) How could you find the total surface area of the outside plus the inside of the tube?

Summary

Do you know the following?

- The perimeter is the distance around the outside of a two-dimensional shape and the area is the space contained within the sides.
- Circumference is the name for the perimeter of a circle.
- If the units of length are given in cm then the units of area are cm^2 and the units of volume are cm^3. This is true for any unit of length.
- A sector of a circle is the region contained in-between two radii of a circle. This splits the circle into a minor sector and a major sector.
- An arc is a section of the circumference.
- Prisms, pyramids, spheres, cubes and cuboids are examples of three-dimensional objects (or solids).
- A net is a two-dimensional shape that can be folded to form a solid.
- The net of a solid can be useful when working out the surface area of the solid.

Are you able to . . . ?

- recognise different two-dimensional shapes and find their areas
- give the units of the area
- calculate the areas of various two-dimensional shapes
- divide a shape into simpler shapes and find the area
- find unknown lengths when some lengths and an area are given
- calculate the area and circumference of a circle
- calculate the perimeter, arc length and area of a sector
- recognise nets of solids
- fold a net correctly to create its solid
- find the volumes and surface areas of a cuboid, prism and cylinder
- find the volumes of solids that can be broken into simpler shapes
- find the volumes and surface areas of a pyramid, cone and sphere.

Examination practice

Exam-style questions

1 A piece of rope is wound around a cylindrical pipe 18 times. If the diameter of the pipe is 600 mm, how long is the rope?

2 Find the perimeter and area of this shape.

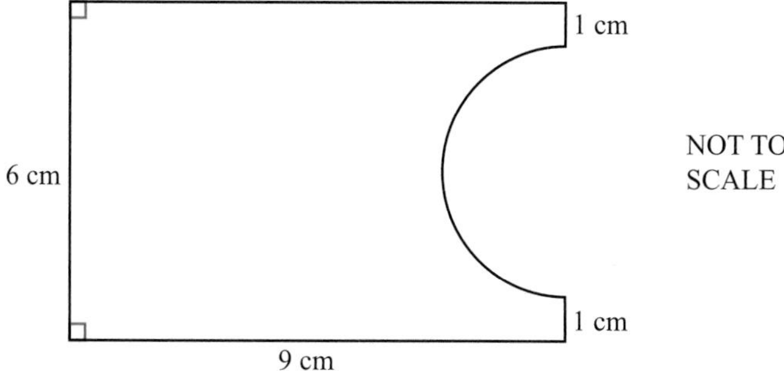

3 A cylindrical rainwater tank is 1.5 m tall with a diameter of 1.4 m. What is the maximum volume of rainwater it can hold?

Past paper questions

1 This diagram shows the plan of a driveway to **a** house.

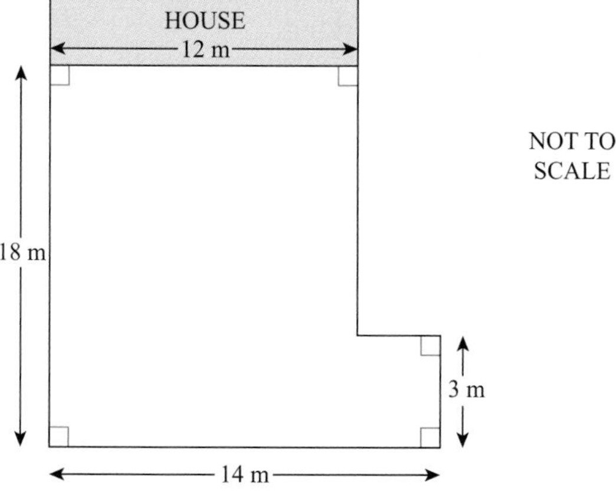

(d) Work out the perimeter of the driveway. [2]

(e) The driveway is made from concrete. The concrete is 15 cm thick. Calculate the volume of concrete used for the driveway. Give your answer in cubic metres. [4]

Cambridge IGCSE Mathematics 0580 Paper 33 Q8 d, e October/November 2012

2

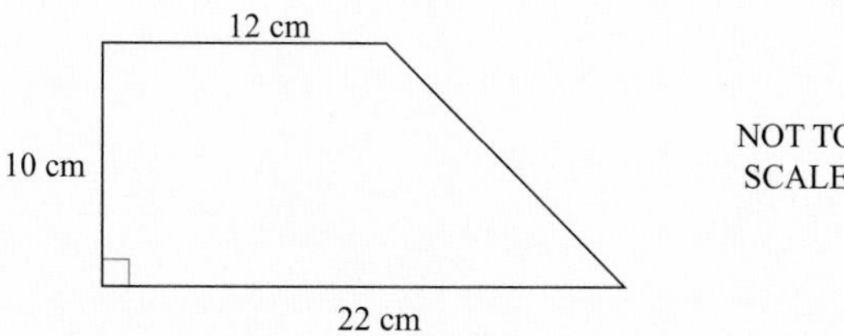

Find the area of the trapezium. [2]

[Cambridge IGCSE Mathematics 0580 Paper 22 Q7 October/November 2013]

3

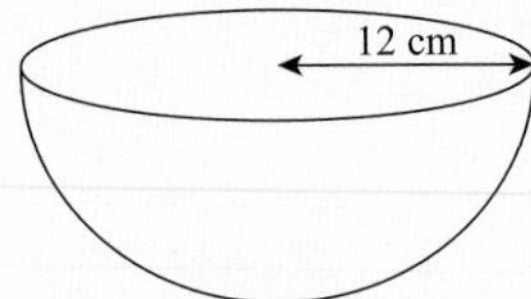

A **hemisphere** has a radius of 12 cm.
Calculate its volume.
[The volume, V, of a sphere with radius r is $V = \frac{4}{3}\pi r^3$.] [2]

[Cambridge IGCSE Mathematics 0580 Paper 22 Q8 October/November 2013]

4 A large conference table is made from four rectangular sections and four corner sections. Each rectangular section is 4 m long and 1.2 m wide. Each corner section is a quarter of circle, radius 1.2 m.

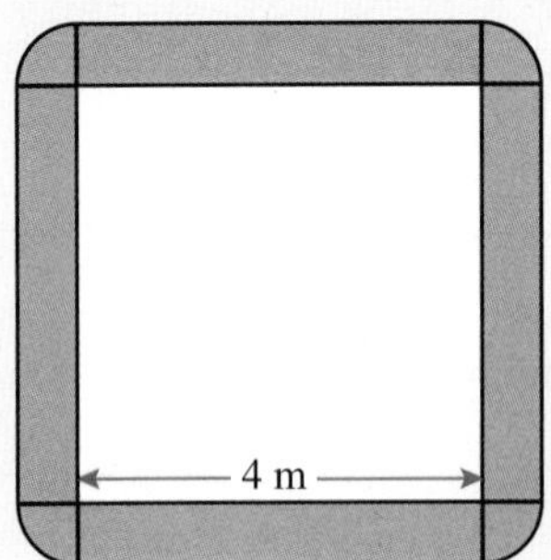

NOT TO SCALE

Each person sitting at the conference table requires one metre of its outside perimeter. Calculate the greatest number of people who can sit around the **outside** of the table. Show all your working. [3]

[Cambridge IGCSE Mathematics 0580 Paper 02 Q11 October/November 2005]

5

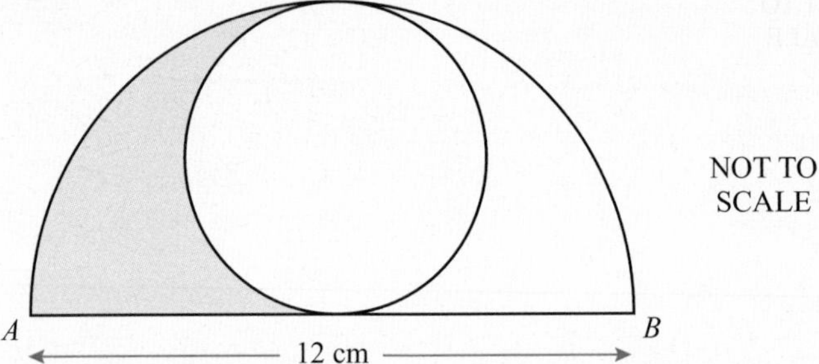

NOT TO SCALE

The largest possible circle is drawn inside a semi-circle, as shown in the diagram. The distance AB is 12 centimetres.

(a) Find the shaded area. [4]

(b) Find the perimeter of the shaded area. [2]

[Cambridge IGCSE Mathematics 0580 Paper 02 Q23 May/June 2007]

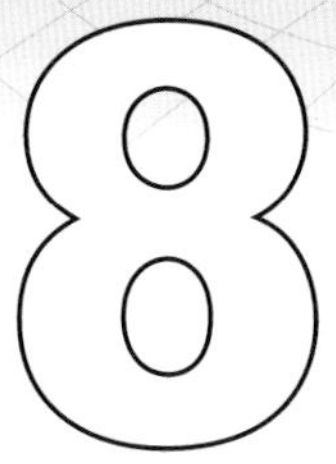

Introduction to probability

Key words

- Event
- Probability
- Probability scale
- Trial
- Experimental probability
- Outcome
- Theoretical probability
- Favourable outcomes
- Bias
- Possibility diagram
- Independent
- Mutually exclusive

In this chapter you will learn how to:

- express probabilities mathematically
- calculate probabilities associated with simple experiments
- use possibility diagrams to help you calculate probability of combined events
- identify when events are independent
- identify when events are mutually exclusive

EXTENDED

Blaise Pascal was a French mathematician and inventor. In 1654, a friend of his posed a problem of how the stakes of a game may be divided between the players even though the game had not yet ended. Pascal's response was the beginning of the mathematics of probability.

What is the chance that it will rain tomorrow? If you take a holiday in June, how many days of sunshine can you expect? When you flip a coin to decide which team will start a match, how likely is it that you will get a head?

Questions of chance come into our everyday life from what is the weather going to be like tomorrow to who is going to wash the dishes tonight. Words like 'certain', 'even' or 'unlikely' are often used to roughly describe the chance of an event happening but probability refines this to numbers to help make more accurate predictions.

8.1 Basic probability

A die is the singular of dice.

When you roll a die, you may be interested in throwing a prime number. When you draw a name out of a hat, you may want to draw a boy's name. Throwing a prime number or drawing a boy's name are examples of **events**.

Probability is a measure of how likely an event is to happen. Something that is impossible has a value of zero and something that is certain has a value of one. The range of values from zero to one is called a **probability scale**. A probability cannot be negative or be greater than one.

The smaller the probability, the closer it is to zero and the less likely the associated event is to happen. Similarly, the higher the probability, the more likely the event.

Performing an experiment, such as rolling a die, is called a **trial**. If you repeat an experiment, by carrying out a number of trials, then you can find an **experimental probability** of an event happening: this fraction is often called the **relative frequency**.

P(A) means the probability of event A happening.

$$P(A) = \frac{\text{number of times desired event happens}}{\text{number of trials}}$$

or, sometimes:

$$P(A) = \frac{\text{number of successes}}{\text{number of trials}}$$

Worked example 1

Suppose that a blindfolded man is asked to throw a dart at a dartboard.

If he hits the number six 15 times out of 125 throws, what is the probability of him hitting a six on his next throw?

$$P(\text{six}) = \frac{\text{number times a six obtained}}{\text{number of trials}}$$
$$= \frac{15}{125}$$
$$= 0.12$$

8.2 Theoretical probability

In some countries, theoretical probability is referred to as 'expected probability'. This is a casual reference and does *not* mean the same thing as mathematical 'expectation'.

When you flip a coin you may be interested in the event 'obtaining a head' but this is only one possibility. When you flip a coin there are two possible **outcomes**: 'obtaining a head' or 'obtaining a tail.'

You can calculate the **theoretical** (or expected) probability easily if all of the possible outcomes are *equally likely*, by counting the number of **favourable outcomes** and dividing by the number of possible outcomes. Favourable outcomes are any outcomes that mean your event has happened.

Never assume that a die or any other object is unbiased unless you are told that this is so.

For example, if you throw an unbiased die and need the probability of an even number, then the favourable outcomes are two, four or six. There are three of them.

Under these circumstances the event A (obtaining an even number) has the probability:

$$P(A) = \frac{\text{number of favourable outcomes}}{\text{number of possible outcomes}} = \frac{3}{6} = \frac{1}{2}$$

Of course a die may be weighted in some way, or imperfectly made, and indeed this may be true of any object discussed in a probability question. Under these circumstances a die, coin or other object is said to be **biased.** The outcomes will no longer be equally likely and you may need to use experimental probability.

Worked example 2

An unbiased die is thrown and the number on the upward face is recorded. Find the probability of obtaining:

(a) a three **(b)** an even number **(c)** a prime number.

(a) $P(3) = \frac{1}{6}$

There is only one way of throwing a three, but six possible outcomes (you could roll a 1, 2, 3, 4, 5, 6).

(b) $P(\text{even number}) = \frac{3}{6} = \frac{1}{2}$

There are three even numbers on a die, giving three favourable outcomes.

(c) $P(\text{prime number}) = \frac{3}{6} = \frac{1}{2}$

The prime numbers on a die are 2, 3 and 5, giving three favourable outcomes.

Worked example 3

A card is drawn from an ordinary 52 card pack. What is the probability that the card will be a king?

$P(\text{King}) = \frac{4}{52} = \frac{1}{13}$

Number of possible outcomes is 52.

Number of favourable outcomes is four, because there are four kings per pack.

Worked example 4

Jason has 20 socks in a drawer.

8 socks are red, 10 socks are blue and 2 socks are green. If a sock is drawn at random, what is the probability that it is green?

$P(\text{green}) = \frac{2}{20} = \frac{1}{10}$

Number of possible outcomes is 20.

Number of favourable outcomes is two.

Worked example 5

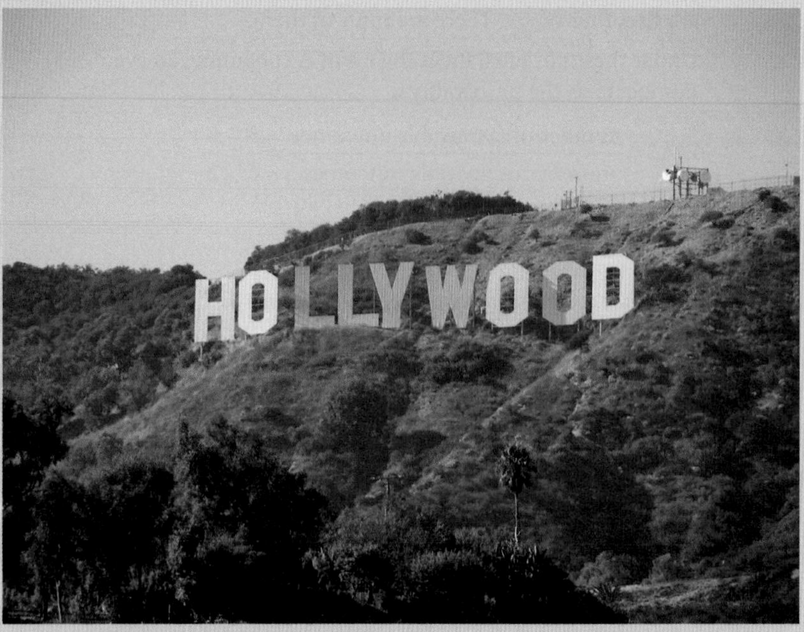

The picture shows the famous Hollywood sign in Los Angeles, USA.

Nine painters are assigned a letter from the word HOLLYWOOD for painting at random. Find the probability that a painter is assigned:

(a) the letter 'Y' **(b)** the letter 'O' **(c)** the letter 'H' or the letter 'L' **(d)** the letter 'Z'.

For each of these the number of possible outcomes is 9.

(a)	$P(Y) = \frac{1}{9}$	Number of favourable outcomes is one (there is only one 'Y').
(b)	$P(O) = \frac{3}{9} = \frac{1}{3}$	Number of favourable outcomes is three.
(c)	$P(H \text{ or } L) = \frac{3}{9} = \frac{1}{3}$	Number of favourable outcomes = number of letters that are *either* H or L = 3, since there is one H and two L's in Hollywood.
(d)	$P(Z) = \frac{0}{9} = 0$	Number of favourable outcomes is zero (there are no 'Z's)

8.3 The probability that an event does not happen

Something may happen or it may not happen. The probability of an event happening may be different from the probability of the event not happening but the two combined probabilities will always sum up to one.

If A is an event, then $\overline{A}$ is the event that A does *not* happen and $P(\overline{A}) = 1 - P(A)$

$\overline{A}$ is usually just pronounced as 'not A'.

Worked example 6

The probability that Jasmine passes her driving test is $\frac{2}{3}$. What is the probability that Jasmine fails?

$P(\text{failure}) = 1 - \frac{2}{3} = \frac{1}{3}$	P(failure) = P(not passing) = 1 − P(passing)

Exercise 8.1

The first two questions in this exercise are about experimental probability.

1 A simple die is thrown 100 times and the number five appears 14 times. Find the experimental probability of throwing a five, giving your answer as a fraction in its lowest terms.

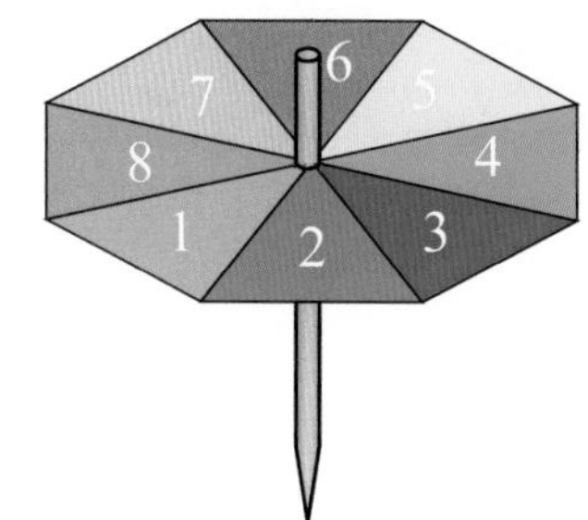

2 The diagram shows a spinner that is divided into exactly eight equal sectors.

Ryan spins the spinner 260 times and records the results in a table:

Number	1	2	3	4	5	6	7	8
Frequency	33	38	26	35	39	21	33	35

Calculate the experimental probability of spinning:

(a) the number three **(b)** the number five **(c)** an odd number **(d)** a factor of eight.

The remaining questions are about theoretical probability.

3 A flower enthusiast collected 385 examples of a *Polynomialus mathematicus* flower in deepest Peru. Just five of the flowers were blue.

One flower is chosen at random.
Find the probability that:

(a) it is blue
(b) it is not blue.

4 A bag contains nine equal sized balls. Four of the balls are coloured blue and the remaining five balls are coloured red.

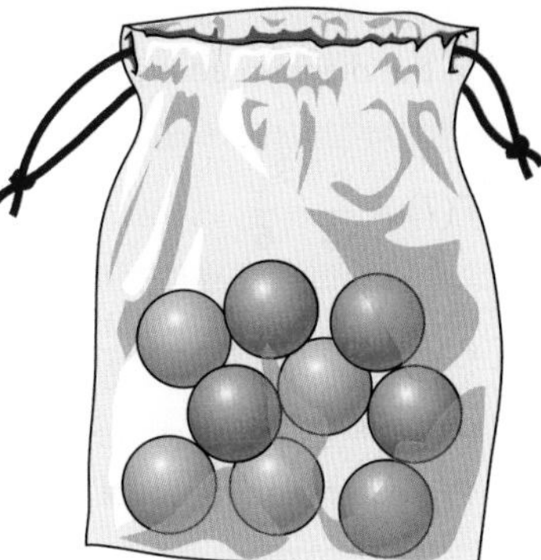

What is the probability that, when a ball is drawn from the bag:

(a) it is blue?
(b) it is red?
(c) it neither blue nor red?
(d) it is either blue or red?

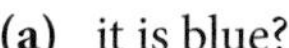

5 A bag contains 36 balls. The probability that a ball drawn at random is blue is $\frac{1}{4}$. How many blue balls are there in the bag?

6 Oliver shuffles an ordinary pack of 52 playing cards. If he then draws a single card at random, find the probability that the card is:

(a) a king **(b)** a spade **(c)** a black card **(d)** a prime-numbered card.

8.4 Possibility diagrams

In some countries, these might be called 'probability space diagrams'.

The probability space is the set of all possible outcomes. It can sometimes simplify our work if you draw a **possibility diagram** to show all outcomes clearly.

See how drawing a possibility diagram helps solve problems in the following worked example.

Worked example 7

Two dice, one red and one blue, are thrown at the same time and the numbers showing on the dice are added together. Find the probability that:

(a) the sum is 7
(b) the sum is less than 5
(c) the sum is greater than or equal to 8
(d) the sum is less than 8.

Red (columns), Blue (rows)

+	1	2	3	4	5	6
1	2	3	4	5	6	7
2	3	4	5	6	7	8
3	4	5	6	7	8	9
4	5	6	7	8	9	10
5	6	7	8	9	10	11
6	7	8	9	10	11	12

In the diagram above there are 36 possible sums, so there are 36 equally likely outcomes in total.

(a) $P(7) = \frac{6}{36} = \frac{1}{6}$

There are six 7s in the grid, so six favourable outcomes.

(b) $P(\text{less than } 5) = \frac{6}{36} = \frac{1}{6}$

The outcomes that are less than 5 are 2, 3 and 4. These numbers account for six favourable outcomes.

(c) $P(\text{greater than or equal to } 8) = \frac{15}{36} = \frac{5}{12}$

The outcomes greater than or equal to 8 (which includes 8) are 8, 9, 10, 11 or 12, accounting for 15 outcomes.

(d) $P(\text{less than } 8) = 1 - \frac{5}{12} = \frac{7}{12}$

P(less than 8) = P(not greater than or equal to 8)

= 1 − P(greater than or equal to 8)

Exercise 8.2

1 An unbiased coin is thrown twice and the outcome for each is recorded as H (head) or T (tail). A possibility diagram could be drawn as shown.

First throw

Second throw

	H	T
H		T H
T		

(a) Copy and complete the diagram.
(b) Find the probability that:

(i) the coins show the same face
(ii) the coins both show heads
(iii) there is at least one head
(iv) there are no heads.

2 Two dice are thrown and the product of the two numbers is recorded.

(a) Draw a suitable possibility diagram to show all possible outcomes.
(b) Find the probability that:

(i) the product is 1
(ii) the product is 7
(iii) the product is less than or equal to 4
(iv) the product is greater than 4
(v) the product is a prime number
(vi) the product is a square number.

3

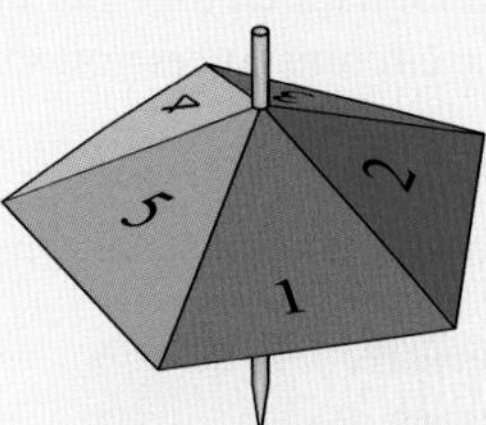

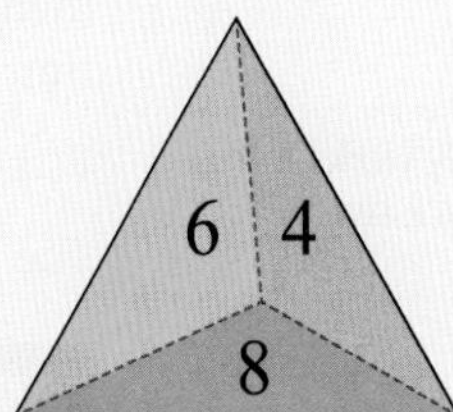

The diagram shows a spinner with five equal sectors numbered 1, 2, 3, 4 and 5, and an unbiased tetrahedral die with faces numbered 2, 4, 6 and 8. The spinner is spun and the die is thrown and the *higher* of the two numbers is recorded. If both show the same number then that number is recorded.

(a) Draw a possibility diagram to show the possible outcomes.
(b) Calculate the probability that:

(i) the higher number is even
(ii) the higher number is odd
(iii) the higher number is a multiple of 3
(iv) the higher number is prime
(v) the higher number is more than twice the smaller number.

REWIND

You learnt about HCF in chapter 1.◀

4 An unbiased cubical die has six faces numbered 4, 6, 10, 12, 15 and 24. The die is thrown twice and the highest common factor (HCF) of both results is recorded.

(a) Draw a possibility diagram to show the possible outcomes.
(b) Calculate the probability that:

(i) the HCF is 2
(ii) the HCF is greater than 2
(iii) the HCF is not 7
(iv) the HCF is not 5
(v) the HCF is 3 or 5
(vi) the HCF is equal to one of the numbers thrown.

8.5 Combining independent and mutually exclusive events

If you flip a coin once the probability of it showing a head is 0.5. If you flip the coin a second time the probability of it showing a head is still 0.5, regardless of what happened on the first flip. Events like this, where the first outcome has no influence on the next outcome, are called **independent** events.

Sometimes there can be more than one stage in a problem and you may be interested in what combinations of outcomes there are. If A and B are independent events then:

Note that this formula is only true if A and B are independent.

P(A happens and then B happens) = P(A) × P(B)

or

P(A and B) = P(A) × P (B)

There are situations where it is impossible for events A and B to happen at the same time. For example, if you throw a normal die and let:

A = the event that you get an even number

and

B = the event that you get an odd number

then A and B cannot happen together because no number is both even and odd at the same time. Under these circumstances you say that A and B are **mutually exclusive** events and

Note, this formula only works if A and B are mutually exclusive.

P(A or B) = P(A) + P(B).

The following worked examples demonstrate how these simple formulae can be used.

Worked example 8

James and Sarah are both taking a music examination independently. The probability that James passes is $\frac{3}{4}$ and the probability that Sarah passes is $\frac{5}{6}$.
What is the probability that:

(a) both pass **(b)** neither passes **(c)** at least one passes
(d) either James or Sarah passes (not both)?

Use the formula for combined events in each case.

Sarah's success or failure in the exam is independent of James' outcome and vice versa.

(a) P(both pass) = P(James passes and Sarah passes) $= \frac{3}{4} \times \frac{5}{6} = \frac{15}{24} = \frac{5}{8}$

(b) P(neither passes) = P(James fails and Sarah fails)

$$= (1 - \frac{3}{4}) \times (1 - \frac{5}{6})$$
$$= \frac{1}{4} \times \frac{1}{6}$$
$$= \frac{1}{24}$$

(c) P(at least one passes) = 1 − P(neither passes) $= 1 - \frac{1}{24} = \frac{23}{24}$

The events, 'James passes and Sarah fails' and, 'James fails and Sarah passes,' are mutually exclusive because no-one can both pass and fail at the same time. This is why you can add the two probabilities here.

(d) P(either Sarah or James passes)

= P(James passes and Sarah fails or James fails and Sarah passes)

$= \frac{3}{4} \times \frac{1}{6} + \frac{1}{4} \times \frac{5}{6}$

$= \frac{3}{24} + \frac{5}{24}$

$= \frac{8}{24}$

$= \frac{1}{3}$

Worked example 9

Simone and Jon are playing darts. The probability that Simone throws a bull's-eye is 0.1. The probability that Jon throws a bull's-eye is 0.2. Simone and Jon throw one dart each. Find the probability that:

(a) both throw a bull's-eye

(b) Simone throws a bull's-eye but Jon does not

(c) exactly one bull's-eye is thrown.

Simone's success or failure at hitting the bull's-eye is independent of Jon's and vice versa.

(a) P(both throw a bull's-eye) $= 0.1 \times 0.2 = 0.02$

(b) P(Simone throws a bull's-eye but Jon does not) $= 0.1 \times (1 - 0.2) = 0.1 \times 0.8 = 0.08$

(c) P(exactly one bull's-eye is thrown)

= P(Simone throws a bull's-eye and Jon does not or Simone does not throw a bull's-eye and Jon does)

$= 0.1 \times 0.8 + 0.9 \times 0.2$

$= 0.08 + 0.18$

$= 0.26$

Exercise 8.3

Usually 'AND' in probability means you will need to multiply probabilities. 'OR' usually means you will need to add them.

1 A standard cubical die is thrown twice. Calculate the probability that:

(a) two sixes are thrown
(b) two even numbers are thrown
(c) the same number is thrown twice
(d) the two numbers thrown are different.

2 A bag contains 12 coloured balls. Five of the balls are red and the rest are blue. A ball is drawn at random from the bag. It is then replaced and a second ball is drawn. The colour of each ball is recorded.

(a) List the possible outcomes of the experiment.
(b) Calculate the probability that:

(i) the first ball is blue
(ii) the second ball is red
(iii) the first ball is blue and the second ball is red
(iv) the two balls are the same colour
(v) the two balls are a different colour
(vi) neither ball is red
(vii) at least one ball is red.

FAST FORWARD

You will learn how to calculate probabilities for situations where objects are *not* replaced in chapter 24. ▶

3 Devin and Tej are playing cards. Devin draws a card, replaces it and then shuffles the pack. Tej then draws a card. Find the probability that:

(a) both draw an ace
(b) both draw the king of Hearts
(c) Devin draws a spade and Tej draws a queen
(d) exactly one of the cards drawn is a heart
(e) both cards are red or both cards are black
(f) the cards are different colours.

4 Kirti and Justin are both preparing to take a driving test. They each learned to drive separately, so the results of the tests are independent. The probability that Kirti passes is 0.6 and the probability that Justin passes is 0.4. Calculate the probability that:

(a) both pass the test
(b) neither passes the test
(c) Kirti passes the test, but Justin doesn't pass
(d) at least one of Kirti and Justin passes
(e) exactly one of Kirti and Justin passes.

Summary

Do you know the following?

- Probability measures how likely something is to happen.
- An outcome is the single result of an experiment.
- An event is a collection of favourable outcomes.
- Experimental probability can be calculated by dividing the number of favourable outcomes by the number of trials.
- Favourable outcomes are any outcomes that mean your event has happened.
- If outcomes are equally likely then theoretical probability can be calculated by dividing the number of favourable outcomes by the number of possible outcomes.
- The probability of an event happening and the probability of that event ***not*** happening will always sum up to one. If $\overline{A}$ is an event, then A is the event that A does ***not*** happen and $P(A) = 1 - P(A)$
- Independent events do not affect one another.
- Mutually exclusive events cannot happen together.

Are you able to . . . ?

- find an experimental probability given the results of several trials
- find a theoretical probability
- find the probability that an event will not happen if you know the probability that it will happen
- draw a possibility diagram
- recognise independent and mutually exclusive events
- do calculations involving combined probabilities.

Examination practice

Exam-style questions

1 Rooms in a hotel are numbered from 1 to 19. Rooms are allocated at random as guests arrive.

(a) What is the probability that the first guest to arrive is given a room which is a prime number? (Remember: 1 is not a prime number.)
(b) The first guest to arrive is given a room which is a prime number. What is the probability that the second guest to arrive is given a room which is a prime number?

2 A bowl of fruit contains three apples, four bananas, two pears and one orange. Aminata chooses one piece of fruit at random. What is the probability that she chooses:

(a) a banana?
(b) a mango?

3 The probability that it will rain in Switzerland on 1 September is $\frac{5}{12}$. State the probability that it will *not* rain in Switzerland on 1 September.

4 Sian has three cards, two of them black and one red. She places them side by side, in random order, on a table. One possible arrangement is red, black, black.

(a) Write down all the possible arrangements.
(b) Find the probability that the two black cards are next to one another. Give your answer as a fraction.

5 A die has the shape of a tetrahedron. The four faces are numbered 1, 2, 3 and 4. The die is thrown on the table. The probabilities of each of the four faces finishing flat on the table are as shown.

Face	1	2	3	4
Probability	$\frac{2}{9}$	$\frac{1}{3}$	$\frac{5}{18}$	$\frac{1}{6}$

(a) Copy the table and fill in the four empty boxes with the probabilities changed to fractions with a common denominator.
(b) Which face is most likely to finish flat on the table?
(c) Find the sum of the four probabilities.
(d) What is the probability that face 3 does not finish flat on the table?

6 Josh and Soumik each take a coin at random out of their pockets and add the totals together to get an amount. Josh has two \$1 coins, a 50c coin, a \$5 coin and three 20c coins in his pocket. Soumik has three \$5 coins, a \$2 coin and three 50c pieces.

(a) Draw up a possibility diagram to show all the possible outcomes for the sum of the two coins.
(b) What is the probability that the coins will add up to \$6?
(c) What is the probability that the coins add up to less than \$2?
(d) What is the probability that the coins will add up to \$5 or more?

Past paper questions

1 A letter is chosen at random from the following word.

S T A T I S T I C S

Write down the probability that the letter is

(a) **A** or **I**, [1]

(b) **E**. [1]

[Cambridge IGCSE Mathematics 0580 Paper 12 Q3 May/June 2011]

2 Felix rolls two fair dice, each numbered from 1 to 6, and adds the numbers shown.
He repeats the experiment 70 times and records the results in a frequency table.
The first 60 results are shown in the tally column of the table.
The last 10 results are 6, 8, 9, 2, 6, 4, 7, 9, 6, 10.

Total	Tally	Frequency
2	|	
3	卌	
4	卌 ||||	
5	|||	
6	卌 卌 ||||	
7	卌 卌	
8	卌 |||	
9	卌 |	
10	||	
11	|	
12	|	

(a) (i) Complete the frequency table to show all his results. [2]
(ii) Write down the relative frequency of a total of 5. [3]

[Cambridge IGCSE Mathematics 0580 Paper 33 Q6 a May/June 2013]

3 **S** **P** **A** **C** **E** **S**

One of the 6 letters is taken at random.

(a) Write down the probability that the letter is S. [1]

(b) The letter is replaced and again a letter is taken at random. This is repeated 600 times.
How many times would you expect the letter to be S? [1]

[Cambridge IGCSE Mathematics 0580 Paper 11 Q14 October/November 2013]

Sequences and sets

Key words

- Sequence
- Term
- n^{th} term
- Rational number
- Terminating decimals
- Recurring decimals
- Set
- Element
- Empty set
- Universal set
- Complement
- Union
- Intersection
- Subset
- Venn diagram
- Set builder notation

In this chapter you will learn how to

- describe the rule for continuing a sequence
- find the nth term of some sequences
- use the nth term to find terms from later in a sequence
- generate and describe sequences from patterns of shapes

EXTENDED

- list the elements of a set that have been described by a rule
- find unions and intersections of sets
- find complements of sets
- represent sets and solve problems using Venn diagrams
- express recurring decimals as fractions

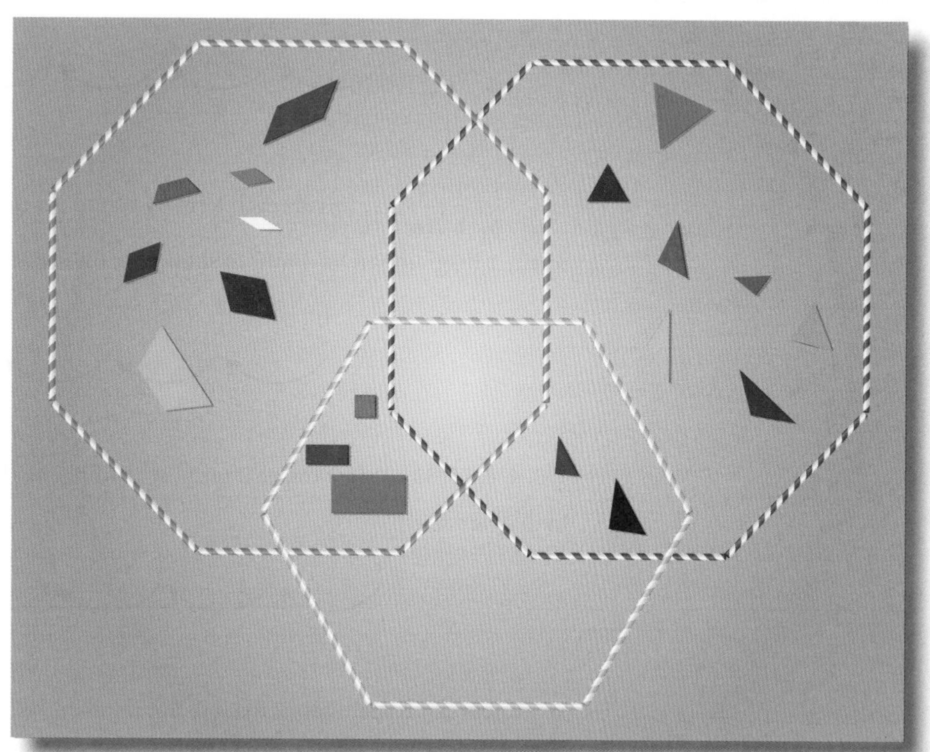

Collecting shapes with the same properties into groups can help to show links between groups. Here, three-sided and four-sided shapes are grouped as well as those shapes that have a right angle.

How many students at your school study History and how many take French? If an event was organised that was of interest to those students who took either subject, how many would that be? If you chose a student at random, what is the probability that they would be studying both subjects? Being able to put people into appropriate sets can help to answer these types of questions!

9.1 Sequences

REWIND

In chapter 1 you learned that a set is a list of numbers or other items. ◀

When trying to spot the pattern followed by a sequence, keep things simple to start with. You will often find that the simplest answer is the correct one.

A **sequence** can be thought of as a set whose elements (items in the list) have been listed in a particular order, with some connection between the elements. Sets are written using curly brackets { }, whereas sequences are generally written without the brackets and there is usually a rule that will tell you which number, letter, word or object comes next. Each number, letter or object in the sequence is called a **term**. Any two terms that are next to each other are called consecutive terms.

Here are some sequences with the rule that tells you how to keep the sequence going:

2, 8, 14, 20, 26, 32, . . . (get the next term by adding six to the previous term).

The pattern can be shown by drawing it in this way:

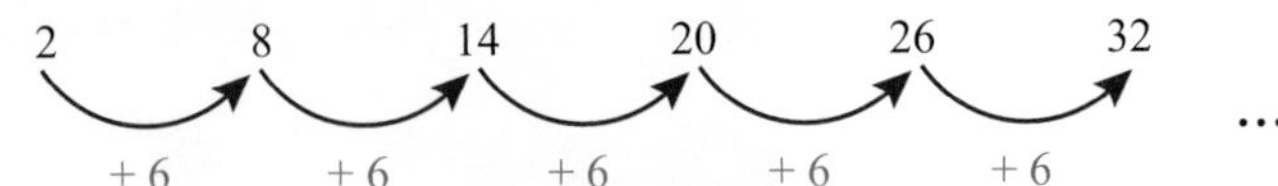

$1, \frac{1}{2}, \frac{1}{4}, \frac{1}{8}, \frac{1}{16}, \ldots$ (divide each term by two to get the next term).

Again, a diagram can be drawn to show how the sequence progresses:

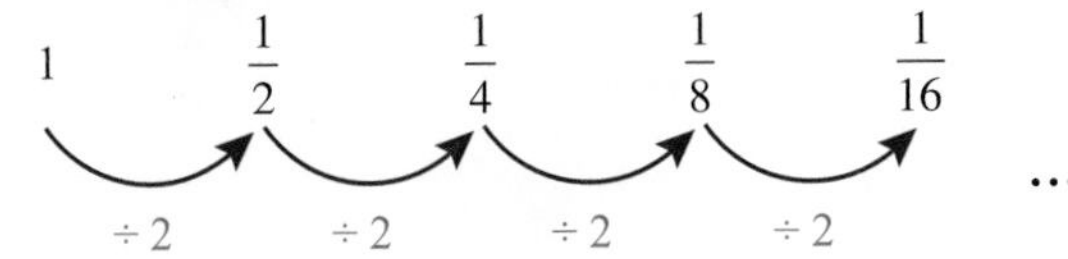

1, 2, 4, 8, 16, 32, . . . (get the next term by multiplying the previous term by two).

In diagram form:

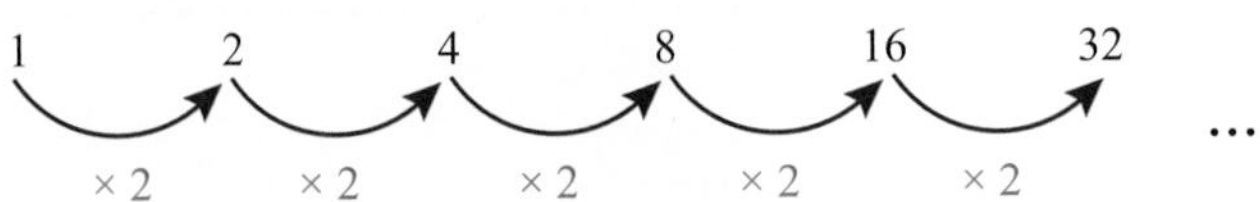

Sequences can contain terms that are not numbers. For example, the following sequence is very well known:

a, b, c, d, e, f, g, h, i, . . .

In this last example, the sequence stops at the 26th element and is, therefore, a *finite* sequence. The previous three sequences do not necessarily stop, so they may be *infinite* sequences (unless you choose to stop them at a certain point).

Exercise 9.1

1 Draw a diagram to show how each of the following sequences continues and find the next three terms in each case.

(a) 5, 7, 9, 11, 13, . . .
(b) 3, 8, 13, 18, 23, . . .
(c) 3, 9, 27, 81, 243, . . .
(d) 0.5, 2, 3.5, 5, 6.5, . . .
(e) 8, 5, 2, −1, −4, . . .
(f) 13, 11, 9, 7, 5, . . .
(g) 6, 4.8, 3.6, 2.4, 1.2, . . .
(h) 2.3, 1.1, −0.1, −1.3, . . .

2 Find the next three terms in each of the following sequences and explain the rule that you have used in each case.

(a) 1, −3, 9, −27, . . .
(b) Mo, Tu, We, Th, . . .
(c) a, c, f, j, o, . . .
(d) 1, 2, 2, 4, 3, 6, 4, 8, . . .

Relating a term to its position in the sequence

Think about the following sequence:

1, 4, 9, 16, 25, . . .

You should have recognised these as the first five square numbers, so:

first term $= 1 \times 1 = 1^2 = 1$

second term $= 2 \times 2 = 2^2 = 4$

third term $= 3 \times 3 = 3^3 = 9$

and so on.

You could write the sequence in a table that also shows the position number of each term:

Term number (n)	1	2	3	4	5	6	7	8	9
Term value (n^2)	1	4	9	16	25	36	49	64	81

Notice that the term number has been given the name 'n'. This means, for example, that $n = 3$ for the third term and $n = 100$ for the hundredth term. The rule that gives each term from its position is:

term in position $n = n^2$

An expression for the term in position n is called the **n^{th} term**. So for this sequence:

n^{th} term $= n^2$

FAST FORWARD

You will carry out similar calculations when you study equations of straight lines in chapter 10. ▶

Now think about a sequence with n^{th} term $= 3n + 2$

For term 1, $n = 1$ so the first term is $3 \times 1 + 2 = 5$

For term 2, $n = 2$ so the second term is $3 \times 2 + 2 = 8$

For term 3, $n = 3$ so the third term is $3 \times 3 + 2 = 11$

Continuing this sequence in a table you will get:

n	1	2	3	4	5	6	7	8	9
Term	5	8	11	14	17	20	23	26	29

You should always try to include a diagram like this. It will remind you what to do and will help anyone reading your work to understand your method.

If you draw a diagram to show the sequence's progression, you get:

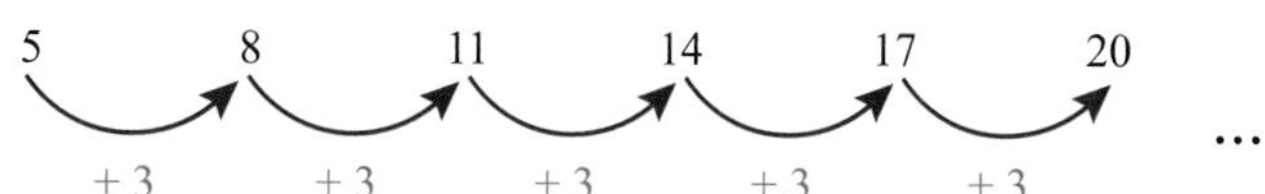

Notice that the number *added* to each term in the diagram appears in the nth term formula (it is the value that is multiplying n, or the *coefficient* of n).

This happens with any sequence for which you move from one term to the next by adding (or subtracting) a fixed number. This fixed number is known as the *common difference.*

For example, if you draw a sequence table for the sequence with n^{th} term $= 4n - 1$, you get:

n	1	2	3	4	5	6	7	8	9
Term	3	7	11	15	19	23	27	31	35

Here you can see that 4 is added to get from one term to the next and this is the coefficient of n that appears in the nth term formula.

The following worked example shows you how you can find the nth term for a sequence in which a common difference is added to one term to get the next.

Worked example 1

(a) Draw a diagram to show the rule that tells you how the following sequence progresses and find the nth term.

2, 6, 10, 14, 18, 22, 26, . . .

(b) Find the 40th term of the sequence.
(c) Explain how you know that the number 50 is in the sequence and work out which position it is in.
(d) Explain how you know that the number 125 is *not* in the sequence.

(a)

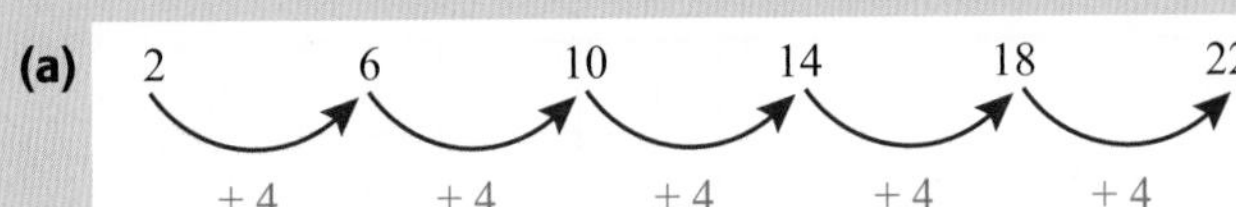

Notice that 4 is added on each time, this is the common difference. This means that the coefficient of n in the nth term will be 4. This means that '$4n$' will form part of your n^{th} term rule.

If $n = 3$

Then

$4n = 4 \times 3 = 12$

Now think about any term in the sequence, for example the third (remember that the value of n gives the position in the sequence). Try $4n$ to see what you get when $n = 3$. You get an answer of 12 but you need the third term to be 10, so you must subtract 2.

It appears that the nth term rule should be $4n - 2$.

You should check this.

Try for $n = 5$

$4n - 2 = 4 \times 5 - 2 = 18$

So the nth term $= 4n - 2$

Test it using any term, say the 5th term. Substitute $n = 5$ into the rule. Notice that the 5th term is indeed 18.

(b) 40th term $\therefore n = 40$

$4 \times 40 - 2 = 158$

To find the 40th term in the sequence you simply need to let $n = 40$ and substitute this into the nth term formula.

(c) $4n - 2 = 50$

If the number 50 is in the sequence there must be a value of n for which $4n - 2 = 50$. Rearrange the rule to make n the subject:

$4n - 2 = 50$

$4n = 52$ — Add 2 to both sides

$n = \frac{52}{4} = 13$ — Divide both sides by 4

Since this has given a whole number, 50 must be the 13th term in the sequence.

(d) $4n - 2 = 125$

If the number 125 is in the sequence then there must be a value of n for which $4n - 2 = 125$. Rearrange to make n the subject.

$4n = 127$ — Add 2 to both sides

$n = \frac{127}{4} = 31.75$ — Divide both sides by 4

Since n is the position in the sequence it must be a whole number and it is not in this case. This means that 125 cannot be a number in the sequence.

Exercise 9.2

1 Find the **(i)** 15th and **(ii)** n^{th} term for each of the following sequences.

(a) 5, 7, 9, 11, 13, . . .
(b) 3, 8, 13, 18, 23, . . .
(c) 3, 9, 27, 81, 243, . . .
(d) 0.5, 2, 3.5, 5, 6.5, . . .
(e) 8, 5, 2, −1, −4, . . .
(f) 13, 11, 9, 7, 5, . . .
(g) 6, 4.8, 3.6, 2.4, 1.2, . . .
(h) 2, 8, 18, 32, 50, ...

2 Consider the sequence:

4, 12, 20, 28, 36, 44, 52, . . .

Remember that 'n' is always going to be a positive integer in n^{th} term questions.

(a) Find the nth term of the sequence.
(b) Find the 500th term.
(c) Which term of this sequence has the value 236? Show full working.
(d) Show that 154 is not a term in the sequence.

Not all sequences progress in the same way. You will need to use your imagination to find the nth terms for each of these.

Questions 3 to 6 involve much more difficult n^{th} terms.

3 **(a)** $\frac{1}{2}, \frac{1}{4}, \frac{1}{8}, \frac{1}{16}, \frac{1}{32}, \ldots$
(b) $\frac{3}{8}, \frac{7}{11}, \frac{11}{14}, \frac{15}{17}, \ldots$
(c) $\frac{9}{64}, \frac{49}{121}, \frac{121}{196}, \frac{225}{289}, \ldots$
(d) $-\frac{2}{3}, -\frac{1}{6}, \frac{1}{3}, \frac{5}{6}, \frac{4}{3}, \ldots$

4 List the first three terms and find the 20th term of the number patterns given by the following rules, where T = term and n = the position of the term.

(a) $T_n = 4 - 3n$
(b) $T_n = 2 - n$
(c) $T_n = \frac{1}{2}n^2$
(d) $T_n = n(n + 1)(n - 1)$
(e) $T_n = \frac{3}{1+n}$
(f) $T_n = 2n^3$

5 If $x + 1$ and $-x + 17$ are the second and sixth terms of a sequence with a common difference of 5, find the value of x.

6 If $x + 4$ and $x - 4$ are the third and seventh terms of a sequence with a common difference of −2, find the value of x.

Generating sequences from patterns

The diagram shows a pattern using matchsticks.

The table shows the number of matchsticks for the first five patterns.

Pattern number (n)	1	2	3	4	5
Number of matches	3	5	7	9	11

Notice that the pattern number can be used as the position number, n, and that the numbers of matches form a sequence, just like those considered in the previous section.

The number added on each time is two but you could also see that this was true from the original diagrams. This means that the number of matches for pattern n is the same as the value of the nth term of the sequence.

The nth term will therefore be: $2n \pm$ something.

Use the ideas from the previous section to find the value of the 'something'.

Taking any term in the sequence from the table, for example the first:

$n = 1$, so $2n = 2 \times 1 = 2$. But the first term is 3, so you need to add 1.

So, n^{th} term $= 2n + 1$

Which means that, if you let 'p' be the number of matches in pattern n then,

$p = 2n + 1$.

Worked example 2

The diagram shows a pattern made with squares.

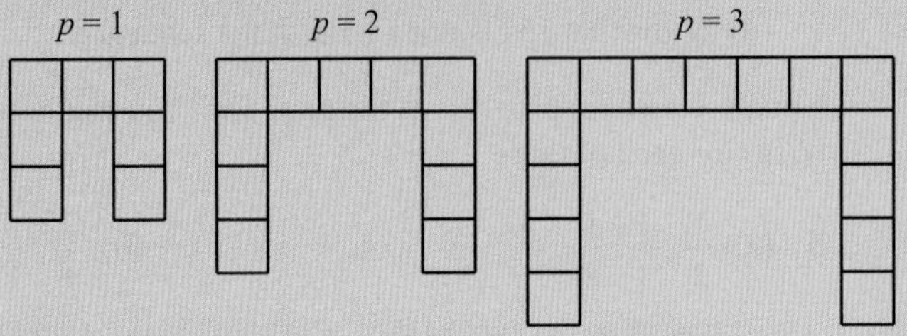

(a) Construct a sequence table showing the first six patterns and the number of squares used.
(b) Find a formula for the number of squares, s, in terms of the pattern number 'p'.
(c) How many squares will there be in pattern 100?

Notice that 'p' has been used for the pattern number rather than 'n' here. You can use any letters that you like – it doesn't have to be n every time.

(a)

Pattern number (p)	1	2	3	4	5	6
Number of squares (s)	7	11	15	19	23	27

(b)

$4p$ is in the formula	Notice that the number of squares increases by 4 from shape to shape. This means that there will be a term '$4p$' in the formula.
If $p = 1$ then $4p = 4$ $4 + 3 = 7$	Now, if $p = 1$ then $4p = 4$. The first term is seven, so you need to add three.
so, $s = 4p + 3$	This means that $s = 4p + 3$.
If $p = 5$ then $4p + 3 = 20 + 3 = 23$, the rule is correct.	Check: if $p = 5$ then there should be 23 squares, which is correct.

(c) For pattern 100, $p = 100$ and $s = 4 \times 100 + 3 = 403$.

Exercise 9.3

For each of the following shape sequences:

(i) draw a sequence table for the first six patterns, taking care to use the correct letter for the pattern number and the correct letter for the number of shapes
(ii) find a formula for the number of shapes used in terms of the pattern number
(iii) use your formula to find the number of shapes used in the 300th pattern.

(a)

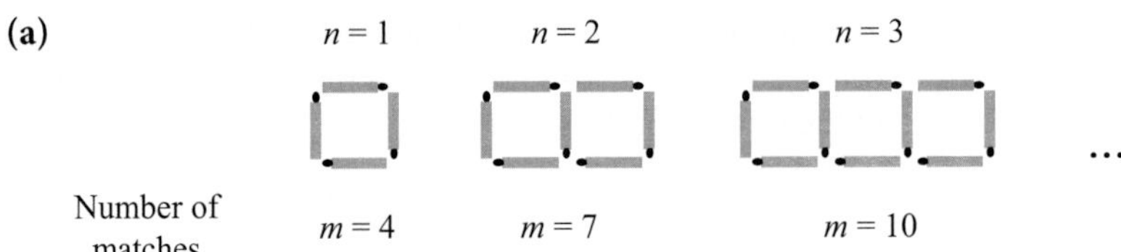

(b)

	$p = 1$	$p = 2$	$p = 3$	
Number of circles	$c = 1$	$c = 3$	$c = 5$	...

(c)

	$p = 1$	$p = 2$	$p = 3$	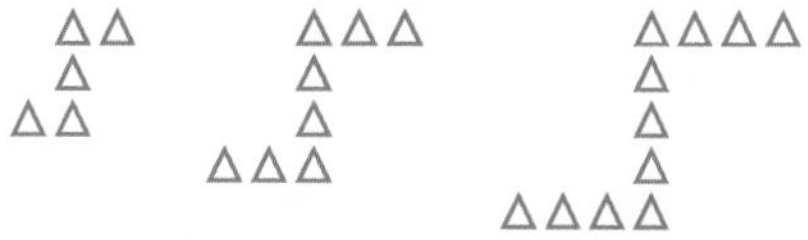
Number of triangles	$t = 5$	$t = 8$	$t = 11$	...

(d)

	$n = 1$	$n = 2$	$n = 3$	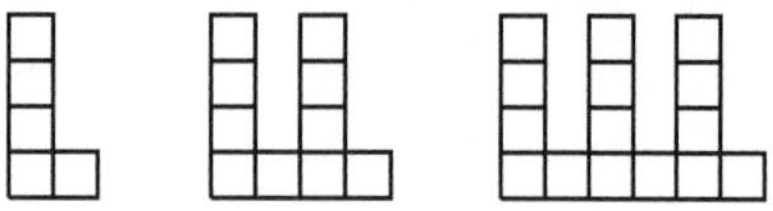
Number of squares	$s = 5$	$s = 10$	$s = 15$	...

9.2 Rational and irrational numbers

Rational numbers

You already know about decimals and how they are used to write down numbers that are not whole. Some of these numbers can be expressed as fractions, for example:

$0.5 = \frac{1}{2}$ $\quad 2.5 = \frac{5}{2}$ $\quad 0.125 = \frac{1}{8}$ $\quad 0.33333333\ldots = \frac{1}{3}$

. . . and so on.

Any number that can be expressed as a fraction in its lowest terms is known as a **rational number**.

Notice that there are two types of rational number: **terminating decimals** (i.e. those with a decimal part that doesn't continue forever) and **recurring decimals** (the decimal part continues forever but repeats itself at regular intervals).

Recurring decimals can be expressed by using a dot above the repeating digit(s):

$0.333333333\ldots = 0.\dot{3}$ $\quad 0.302302302302\ldots = 0.\dot{3}0\dot{2}$

$0.454545454\ldots = 0.\dot{4}\dot{5}$

Converting recurring decimals to fractions

What can we do with a decimal that continues forever but *does* repeat? Is this kind of number rational or irrational?

Remember that the dot above one digit means that you have a *recurring* decimal. If more than one digit repeats we place a dot above the first and last repeating digit. For example $0.\dot{4}1\dot{8}$ is the same as 0.418418418418418... and $0.34\dot{2} = 0.3422222222\ldots$.

As an example we will look at the number $0.\dot{4}$.

We can use algebra to find another way of writing this recurring decimal:

Let

$$x = 0.\dot{4} = 0.444444\ldots$$

Then

$$10x = 4.444444\ldots$$

We can then subtract x from $10x$ like this:

$$10x = 4.444444...$$
$$x = 0.444444...$$
$$9x = 4$$
$$\Rightarrow x = \frac{4}{9}$$

Every recurring decimal is a rational number. It is always possible to write a recurring decimal as a fraction.

Notice that this shows how it is possible to write the recurring decimal $0.\dot{4}$ as a fraction. This means that $0.\dot{4}$ is a rational number. Indeed all recurring decimals can be written as fractions, and so are rational.

Worked example 3

Use algebra to write each of the following as fractions. Simplify your fractions as far as possible.

(a) $0.\dot{3}$ **(b)** 0.24 **(c)** $0.\dot{9}3\dot{4}$ **(d)** $0.52\dot{4}$

(a)

$x = 0.33333...$ $10x = 3.33333...$	Write your recurring decimal in algebra. It is easier to see how the algebra works if you write the number out to a handful of decimal places.
Subtract $10x = 3.33333...$ $x = 0.33333...$	Multiply by 10, so that the recurring digits still line up
$9x = 3$	Subtract
$\Rightarrow x = \frac{3}{9} = \frac{1}{3}$	Divide by 9

(b)

Let $x = 0.\dot{2}\dot{4}$	(1)
then, $100x = 24.\dot{2}\dot{4}$	(2) Multiply by 100
$99x = 24.\dot{2}\dot{4} - 0.\dot{2}\dot{4}$	Subtract (2) – (1)
$99x = 24$	
so, $x = \frac{24}{99} = \frac{8}{33}$	Divide both sides by 99

Notice that you start by multiplying by 100 to make sure that the '2's and '4's started in the correct place after the decimal point.

(c)

$x = 0.934934...$ $1000x = 934.934934...$	This time we have three recurring digits. To make sure that these line up we multiply by 1000, so that all digits move three places.
$1000x = 934.934934...$ $x = 0.934934...$ $999x = 934$ $\Rightarrow x = \frac{934}{999}$	Notice that the digits immediately after the decimal point for both x and 1000x are 9, 3 and 4 in the same order.

(d)

$x = 0.52444444...$ $100x = 52.4444444...$	Multiply by 100 so that the recurring digits begin immediately after the decimal point.
$1000x = 524.444444...$ $1000x = 524.444444...$ $100x = 52.4444444...$	Then proceed as in the first example, multiplying by a further 10 to move the digits one place.
$900x = 472$ $\Rightarrow x = \frac{472}{900} = \frac{118}{225}$	Subtract and simplify.

Tip

Once you have managed to get the recurring decimals to start immediately after the decimal point you will need to multiply again, by another power of 10. The power that you choose should be the same as the number of digits that recur. In the second example the digits 9, 3 and 4 recur, so we multiply by $10^3 = 1000$.

The key point is that you need to subtract two different numbers, but in such a way that the recurring part disappears. This means that sometimes you have to multiply by 10, sometimes by 100, sometimes by 1000, depending on how many digits repeat.

Exercise 9.4

1 Copy and complete each of the following by filling in the boxes with the correct number or symbol.

(a) Let $x = 0.\dot{6}$

Then $10x = \square$

Subtracting:

$10x = \square$

$-x = 0.\dot{6}$

$\square\, x = \square$

So $\square\, x = \square$

Simplify:

$x = \square$

(b) Let $x = 0.\dot{1}\dot{7}$

Then $100x = \square$

Subtracting:

$100x = \square$

$-x = 0.\dot{1}\dot{7}$

$\square\, x = \square$

So $\square\, x = \square$

Simplify:

$x = \square$

2 Write each of the following recurring decimals as a fraction in its lowest terms.

(a) $0.\dot{5}$	**(b)** $0.\dot{1}$	**(c)** $0.\dot{8}$	**(d)** $0.\dot{2}\dot{4}$
(e) $0.\dot{6}\dot{1}$	**(f)** $0.\dot{3}\dot{2}$	**(g)** $0.\dot{6}1\dot{8}$	**(h)** $0.\dot{2}3\dot{3}$
(i) $0.\dot{2}0\dot{8}$	**(j)** $0.0\dot{2}$	**(k)** $0.1\dot{8}$	**(l)** $0.0\dot{3}\dot{1}$
(m) $2.\dot{4}\dot{5}$	**(n)** $3.\dot{1}0\dot{5}$	**(o)** $2.\dot{5}\dot{0}$	**(p)** $5.\dot{4} + 4.\dot{5}$
(q) $2.\dot{3}\dot{6} + 3.\dot{6}\dot{3}$	**(r)** $0.\dot{1}\dot{7} + 0.\dot{7}\dot{1}$	**(s)** $0.\dot{9}$	

3 **(a)** Write down the numerical value of each of the following

(i) $1 - 0.9$ **(ii)** $1 - 0.99$ **(iii)** $1 - 0.999$ **(iv)** $1 - 0.999999999$

(b) Comment on your answers to (a). What is happening to the answer as the number of digits in the subtracted number increases? What is the answer getting closer to? Will it ever get there?

(c) Use algebra to express $0.\dot{6}$ and $0.\dot{2}$ as fractions in their simplest form.

(d) Express $0.\dot{6} + 0.\dot{2}$ as a recurring decimal.

(e) Use your answer to (c) to express $0.\dot{6} + 0.\dot{2}$ as a fraction in its lowest terms.

(f) Now repeat parts c, d and e using the recurring decimals $0.\dot{4}$ and $0.\dot{5}$.

(g) Explain how your findings for part f relate to your answers in parts a and b.

4 Jessica's teacher asks a class to find the largest number that is smaller than 4.5. Jessica's friend Jeevan gives the answer 4.4.

(a) Why is Jeevan not correct?

Jessica's friend Ryan now suggests that the answer is 4.49999.

(b) Why is Ryan not correct?

Jessica now suggests the answer $4.4\dot{9}$

(c) Is Jessica correct? Give full reasons for your answer, including any algebra that helps you to explain. Do you think that there is a better answer than Jessica's?

Exercise 9.5

1 Say whether each number is rational or irrational.

(a) $\frac{1}{4}$ (b) 4 (c) −7 (d) 3.147

(e) π (f) $\sqrt{3}$ (g) $\sqrt{25}$ (h) 0

(i) 0.45 (j) −0.67 (k) −232 (l) $\frac{3}{8}$

(m) $9.\dot{4}\dot{5}$ (n) $\sqrt{123}$ (o) 2π (p) $3\sqrt{2}$

2 Show that the following numbers are rational.

(a) 6 (b) $2\frac{3}{8}$ (c) $1.\dot{1}\dot{2}$ (d) $0.\dot{8}$ (e) 0.427 (f) $3.\dot{1}\dot{4}$

3 Find a number in the interval $-1 < x < 3$ so that:

(a) x is rational (b) x is a real number but not rational

(c) x is an integer (d) x is a natural number

4 Which set do you think has more members: rational numbers or irrational numbers? Why?

5 Mathematicians also talk about imaginary numbers. Find out what these are and give one example.

9.3 Sets

A **set** is a list or collection of objects that share a characteristic. The objects in a set can be anything from numbers, letters and shapes to names, places or paintings, but there is usually something that they have in common.

The list of members or **elements** of a set is placed inside a pair of curly brackets { }.

Some examples of sets are:

When writing sets, never forget to use the curly brackets on either side.

{2, 4, 6, 8, 10} – the set of all even integers greater than zero but less than 11

{a, e, i, o, u} – the set of vowels

{Red, Green, Blue} – the set containing the colours red, green and blue.

Capital letters are usually used as names for sets:

If A is the set of prime numbers less than 10, then: $A = \{2, 3, 5, 7\}$

Notice, for set B, that elements of a set are not repeated.

If B is the set of letters in the word 'HAPPY', then: $B = \{H, A, P, Y\}$.

Two sets are equal if they contain exactly the same elements, even if the order is different, so:

$\{1, 2, 3, 4\} = \{4, 3, 2, 1\} = \{2, 4, 1, 3\}$ and so on.

A set that contains no elements is known as the **empty set**. The symbol $\varnothing$ is used to represent the empty set.

For example:

{odd numbers that are multiples of two} = $\varnothing$ because no odd number is a multiple of two.

Now, if x is a member (an element) of the set A then it is written: $x \in A$.

If x is *not* a member of the set A, then it is written: $x \notin A$.

For example, if H = {Spades, Clubs, Diamonds, Hearts}, then:

Spades $\in H$ but Turtles $\notin H$.

Some sets have a number of elements that can be counted. These are known as *finite* sets. If there is no limit to the number of members of a set then the set is *infinite*.

If A = {letters of the alphabet}, then A has 26 members and is finite.

If B = {positive integers}, then $B = \{1, 2, 3, 4, 5, 6, \ldots\}$ and is infinite.

The number of elements in set A is written as $n(A)$. For the set A = {letters of the alphabet}, $n(A) = 26$.

So, to summarise:

- sets are listed inside curly brackets { }
- $\varnothing$ means it is an empty set
- $a \in B$ means a is an element of the set B
- $a \notin B$ means a is not an element of the set B
- $n(A)$ is the number of elements in set A

The following exercise requires you to think about things that are outside of mathematics. In each case you might like to see if you can find out ALL possible members of each set.

Exercise 9.6 *Living maths*

1 List all of the elements of each set.

(a) {days of the week}
(b) {months of the year}
(c) {factors of 36}
(d) {colours of the rainbow}
(e) {multiples of seven less than 50}
(f) {primes less than 30}
(g) {ways of arranging the letters in the word 'TOY'}

2 Find two more members of each set.

(a) {rabbit, cat, dog, . . .}
(b) {carrot, potato, cabbage, . . .}
(c) {London, Paris, Stockholm, . . .}
(d) {Nile, Amazon, Loire, . . .}
(e) {elm, pine, oak, . . .}
(f) {tennis, cricket, football, . . .}
(g) {France, Germany, Belgium, . . .}
(h) {Bush, Obama, Truman, . . .}
(i) {Beethoven, Mozart, Sibelius, . . .}
(j) {rose, hyacinth, poppy, . . .}
(k) {3, 6, 9, . . .}
(l) {Husky, Great Dane, Boxer, . . .}
(m) {Mercury, Venus, Saturn, . . .}
(n) {happy, sad, angry, . . .}
(o) {German, Czech, Australian, . . .}
(p) {hexagon, heptagon, triangle, . . .}

3 True or false?

(a) If $A = \{1, 2, 3, 4, 5\}$ then $3 \notin A$
(b) If $B = \{\text{primes less than } 10\}$, then $n(B) = 4$
(c) If $C = \{\text{regular quadrilaterals}\}$, then square $\in C$
(d) If $D = \{\text{paint primary colours}\}$, then yellow $\notin D$
(e) If $E = \{\text{square numbers less than } 100\}$, then $64 \in E$

4 Describe each set fully in words.

(a) $\{1, 4, 9, 16, 25, \ldots\}$
(b) {Asia, Europe, Africa, . . .}
(c) $\{2, 4, 6, 8\}$
(d) $\{2, 4, 6, 8, \ldots\}$
(e) $\{1, 2, 3, 4, 6, 12\}$

Universal sets and complements

The following sets all have a number of things in common:

$M = \{1, 2, 3, 4, 5, 6, 7, 8\}$
$N = \{1, 5, 9\}$
$O = \{4, 8, 21\}$

All three are contained within the set of whole numbers. They are also all contained in the set of integers less than 22.

When dealing with sets there is usually a 'largest' set which contains all of the sets that you are studying. This set can change according to the nature of the problem you are trying to solve.

Here, the set of integers contains all elements from M, N or O. But then so does the set of all positive integers less than 22.

Both these sets (and many more) can be used as a **universal set**. A universal set contains all possible elements that you would consider for a set in a particular problem. The symbol $\mathscr{E}$ is used to mean the universal set.

The **complement** of the set A is the set of all things that are in $\mathscr{E}$ but NOT in the set A. The symbol A' is used to denote the complement of set A.

For example, if: $\mathscr{E} = \{1, 2, 3, 4, 5, 6, 7, 8, 9, 10\}$

and $F = \{2, 4, 6\}$

then the complement of F would be $F' = \{1, 3, 5, 7, 8, 9, 10\}$.

So, in summary:
- $\mathscr{E}$ represents a universal set
- A' represents the complement of set A.

Unions and intersections

The **union** of two sets, A and B, is the set of all elements that are members of A or members of B or members of both. The symbol $\cup$ is used to indicate union so, the union of sets A and B is written:

$A \cup B$

The **intersection** of two sets, A and B, is the set of all elements that are members of *both* A and B. The symbol $\cap$ is used to indicate intersection so, the intersection of sets A and B is written:

$A \cap B$.

For example, if $C = \{4, 6, 8, 10\}$ and $D = \{6, 10, 12, 14\}$, then:

$C \cap D =$ the set of all elements common to both $= \{6, 10\}$

$C \cup D =$ the set of all elements that are in C or D or both $= \{4, 6, 8, 10, 12, 14\}$.

Tip

Note that taking the union of two sets is rather like adding the sets together. You must remember, however, that you do not repeat elements within the set.

Subsets

Let the set A be the set of all quadrilaterals and let the set B be the set of all rectangles. A rectangle is a type of quadrilateral. This means that every element of B is also a member of A and, therefore, B is *completely* contained within A. When this happens B is called a **subset** of A, and is written: $B \subseteq A$. The $\subseteq$ symbol can be reversed but this does not change its meaning. $B \subseteq A$ means B is a subset of A, but so does $A \supseteq B$. If B is not a subset of A, we write $B \not\subseteq A$. If B is not equal to A, then B is known as a *proper subset*. If it is possible for B to be equal to A, then B is not a proper subset and you write: $B \subset A$. If A is not a proper subset of B, we write $A \not\subset B$.

Note that the symbol, $\subset$, has a open end and a closed end. The subset goes at the closed end.

So in summary:

- $\cup$ is the symbol for union
- $\cap$ is the symbol for intersection
- $B \subset A$ indicates that B is a proper subset of A
- $B \subseteq A$ indicates that B is a subset of A but also equal to A i.e. it is *not* a proper subset of A.
- $B \not\subset A$ indicates that B is not a proper subset of A.
- $B \not\subseteq A$ indicates that B is not a subset of A.

Worked example 4

If $W = \{4, 8, 12, 16, 20, 24\}$ and $T = \{5, 8, 20, 24, 28\}$.

(i) List the sets:

(a) $W \cup T$ **(b)** $W \cap T$

(ii) Is it true that $T \subset W$?

(i) **(a)** $W \cup T$ = set of all members of W or of T or of both = $\{4, 5, 8, 12, 16, 20, 24, 28\}$.

(b) $W \cap T$ = set of all elements that appear in both W and $T = \{8, 20, 24\}$.

(ii) Notice that $5 \in T$ but $5 \notin W$. So it is not true that every member of T is also a member of W. So T is not a subset of W.

Exercise 9.7

Unions and intersections can be reversed without changing their elements, for example $A \cup B = B \cup A$ and $C \cap D = D \cap C$.

1 $A = \{2, 4, 6, 8, 10\}$ and $B = \{1, 3, 5, 6, 8, 10\}$.

(a) List the elements of:

(i) $A \cap B$ (ii) $A \cup B$

(b) Find:

(i) $n(A \cap B)$ (ii) $n(A \cup B)$

2 $C = \{a, b, g, h, u, w, z\}$ and $D = \{a, g, u, v, w, x, y, z\}$.

(a) List the elements of:

(i) $C \cap D$ (ii) $C \cup D$

(b) Is it true that $u \in C \cap D$? Explain your answer.

(c) Is it true that $g \notin C \cup D$? Explain your answer.

3 F = {equilateral triangles} and G = {isosceles triangles}.

(a) Explain why $F \subset G$.

(b) What is $F \cap G$? Can you simplify $F \cap G$ in any way?

4 $T = \{1, 2, 3, 6, 7\}$ and $W = \{1, 3, 9, 10\}$.

(a) List the members of the set:

(i) $T \cup W$ (ii) $T \cap W$

(b) Is it true that $5 \notin T$? Explain your answer fully.

5 If $\mathscr{E}$ = {rabbit, cat, dog, emu, turtle, mouse, aardvark} and H = {rabbit, emu, mouse} and J = {cat, dog}:

(a) list the members of H'

(b) list the members of J'

(c) list the members of $H' \cup J'$

(d) what is $H \cap J$?

(e) find $(H')'$

(f) what is $H \cup H'$?

Venn diagrams

In 1880, mathematician John Venn began using overlapping circles to illustrate connections between sets. These diagrams are now referred to as **Venn diagrams.**

For example, if $\mathscr{E} = \{1, 2, 3, 4, 5, 6, 7, 8, 9, 10\}$, $A = \{1, 2, 3, 4, 5, 6, 7\}$ and $B = \{4, 5, 8\}$ then the Venn diagram looks like this:

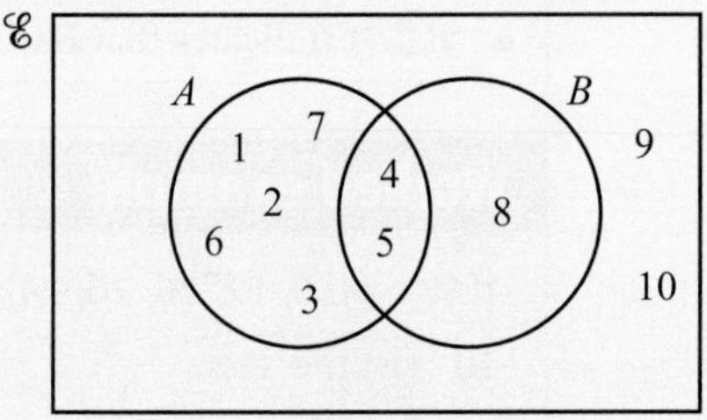

Always remember to draw the box around the outside and mark it, $\mathscr{E}$, to indicate that it represents the universal set.

Notice that the universal set is shown by drawing a rectangle and then each set within the universal set is shown as a circle. The intersection of the sets A and B is contained within the overlap of the circles. The union is shown by the region enclosed by at least one circle. Here are some examples of Venn diagrams and shaded regions to represent particular sets:

The rectangle represents $\mathscr{E}$.

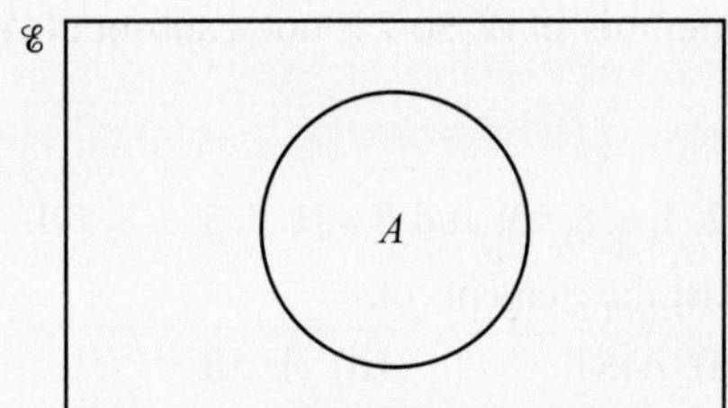

The circle represents set A.

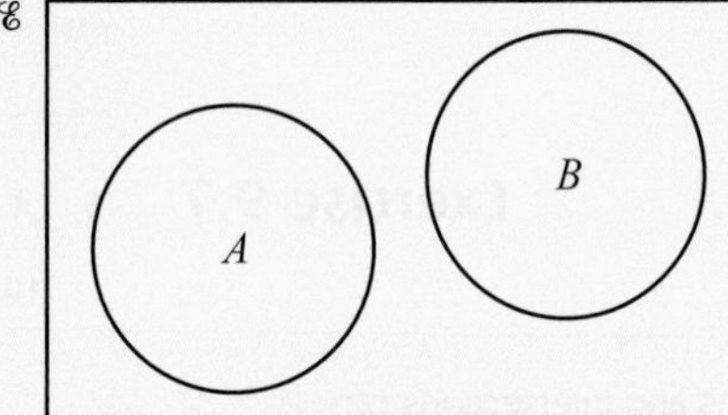

Set A and set B are disjoint, they have no common elements.

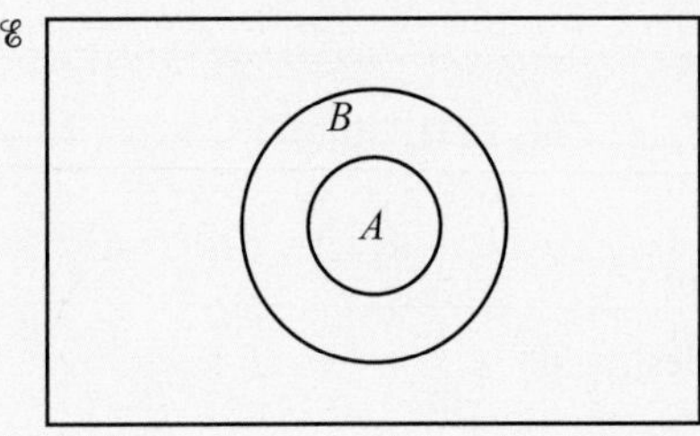

$A \subset B$

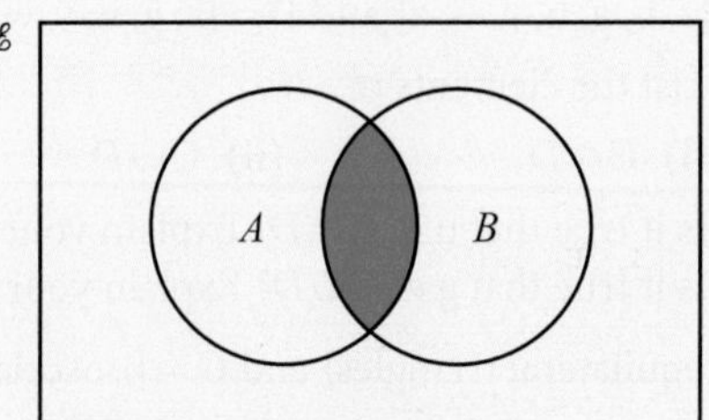

$A \cap B$ is the shaded portion.

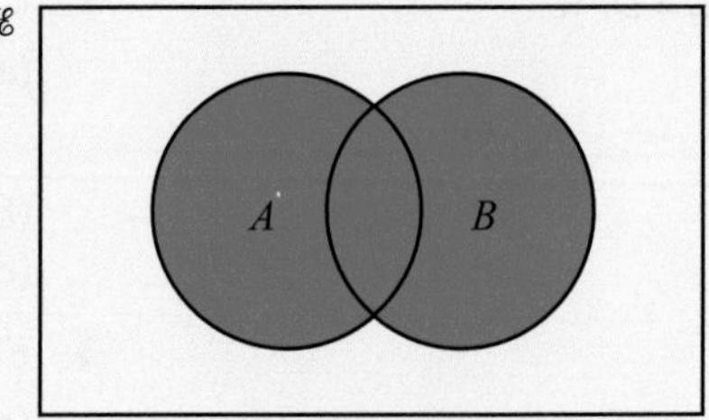

$A \cup B$ is the shaded portion.

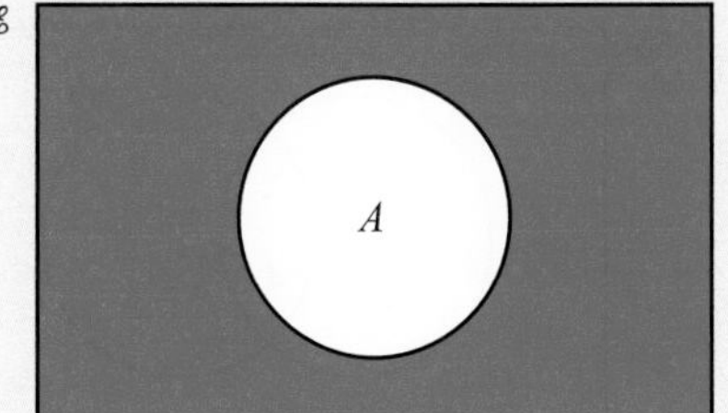

A' is the shaded portion.

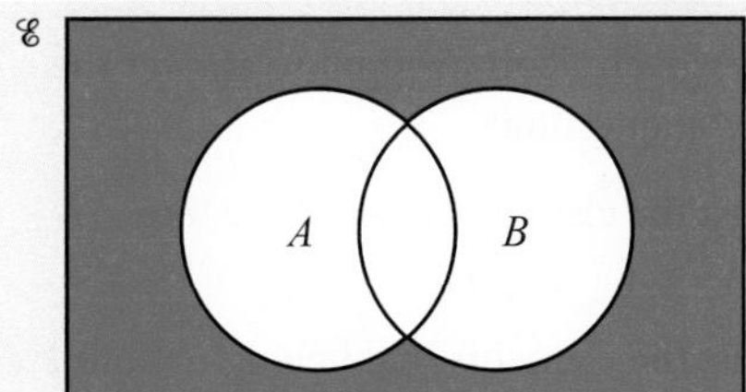

$(A \cup B)'$ is the shaded portion.

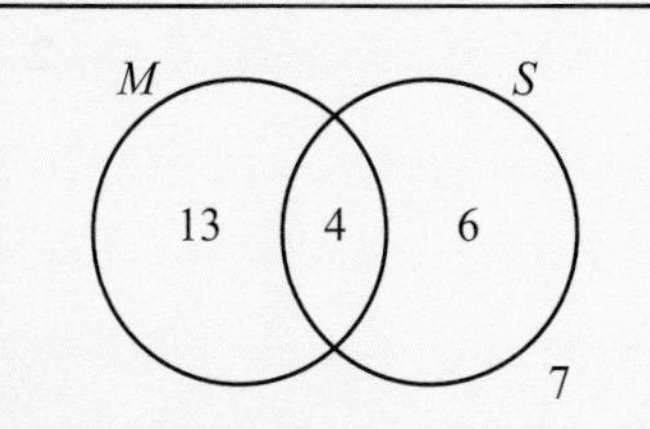

Venn diagrams can also be used to show the number of elements n(A) in a set.
In this case:
M = {students doing Maths},
S = {students doing Science}.

Worked example 5

For the following sets:

ℰ = {a, b, c, d, e, f, g, h, i, j, k}
A = {a, c, e, h, j}
B = {a, b, d, g, h}

(a) illustrate these sets in a Venn diagram
(b) list the elements of the set $A \cap B$
(c) find n($A \cap B$)
(d) list the elements of the set $A \cup B$
(e) find n($A \cup B$)
(f) list the set $A \cap B'$.

(a)

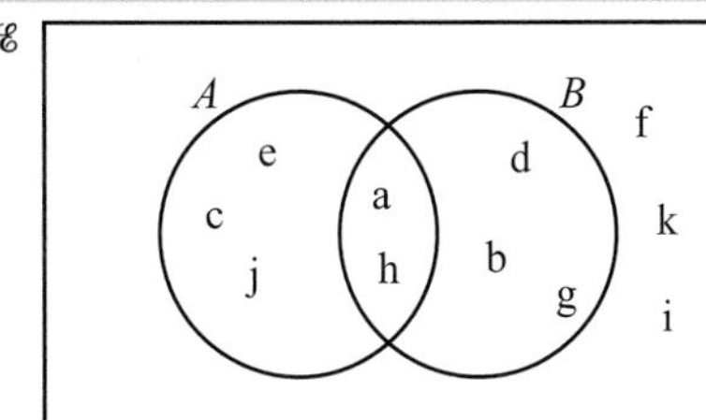

(b) Look in the region that is contained within the overlap of both circles. This region contains the set {a, h}. So $A \cap B$ = {a, h}.
(c) n($A \cap B$) = 2 as there are two elements in the set $A \cap B$.
(d) $A \cup B$ = set of elements of A or B or both = {a, b, c, d, e, g, h, j}.
(e) n($A \cup B$) = 8
(f) $A \cap B'$ = set of all elements that are both in set A and not in set B = {c, e, j}

Exercise 9.8

1 Use the given Venn diagram to answer the following questions.

(a) List the elements of A and B
(b) List the elements of $A \cap B$.
(c) List the elements of $A \cup B$.

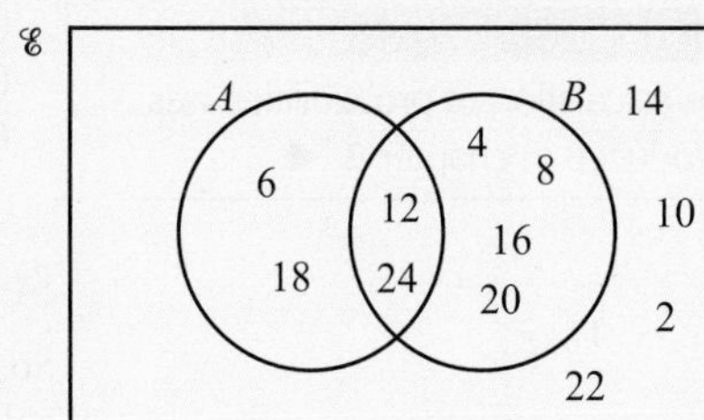

2 Use the given Venn diagram to answer the following questions.

(a) List the elements that belong to:

(i) P **(ii)** Q

(b) List the elements that belong to both P and Q.

(c) List the elements that belong to:

(i) neither P nor Q

(ii) P but not Q.

3 Draw a Venn diagram to show the following sets and write each element in its correct space.

(a) The universal set is {a ,b, c, d, e, f, g, h}.
A = {b, c, f, g} and B = {a, b, c, d, f}.

(b) $\mathscr{E}$ = {whole numbers from 20 to 36 inclusive}.
A = {multiples of four} and B = {numbers greater than 29}.

4 The universal set is: {students in a class}.
V = {students who like volleyball}.
S = {students who play soccer}.
There are 30 students in the class.
The Venn diagram shows numbers of students.

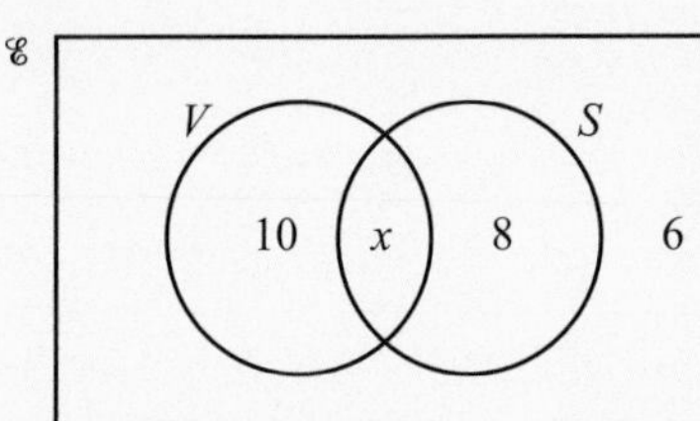

(a) Find the value of x.

(b) How many students like volleyball?

(c) How many students in the class do not play soccer?

5 Copy the Venn diagram and shade the region which represents the subset $A \cap B'$.

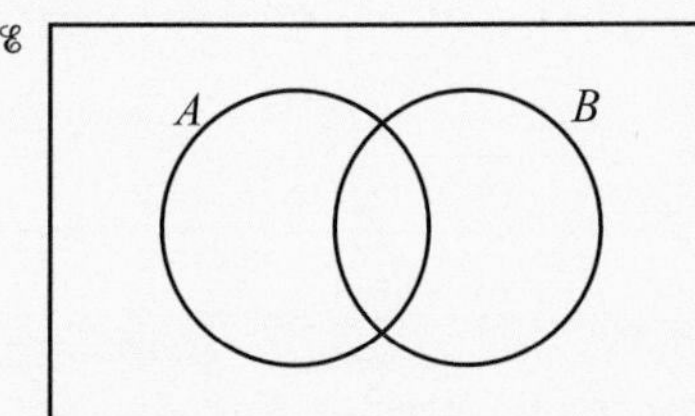

6 A survey into which cat food is enjoyed by cats is undertaken.
24 cats are tested to see whether they like *Fluffy* or *Bouncer*.
Some of the results are shown in the Venn diagram.

$\mathscr{E}$ = {all cats tested}
F = {cats who like *Fluffy*}
B = {cats who like *Bouncer*}

(a) How many cats like both *Fluffy* and *Bouncer*?

(b) How many cats do not like either food?

(c) Write down the value of $n(F \cup B)$.

(d) Write down the value of $n(F \cap B)$.

(e) A tested cat is selected at random. What is the probability that this cat likes *Bouncer*?

(f) A cat that likes *Fluffy* is chosen at random. What is the probability that this cat likes *Bouncer*?

REWIND

The calculation of probabilities was introduced in chapter 8. ◄

Set builder notation

So far the contents of a set have either been given as a list of the elements or described by a rule (in words) that defines whether or not something is a member of the set. Think about the following set:

A = {integers greater than zero but less than 20}.

This is quite a lot to write so, sometimes, an alternative presentation is used:

$A = \{x : x \text{ is an integer}, 0 < x < 20\}$

This is read as: 'A is the set of all x such that x is an integer and x is greater than zero but less than 20'. This notation is called **set builder notation**.

The following examples should help you to get used to the way in which this notation is used.

Worked example 6

List the members of the set C if: $C = \{x : x \in \text{primes}, 10 < x < 20\}$.

Read the set as: 'C is the set of all x such that x is a member of the set of primes and x is greater than 10 but less than 20'.

The prime numbers greater than 10 but less than 20 are 11, 13, 17 and 19.

So, $C = \{11, 13, 17, 19\}$

Worked example 7

Express the following set in set builder notation:

$D = \{\text{right-angled triangles}\}$.

So, $D = \{x : x \text{ is a triangle}, x \text{ has a right-angle}\}$	If D is the set of all right-angled triangles then D is the set of all x such that x is a triangle and x is right-angled.

As you can see from this last example, set builder notation can sometimes force you to write more, but this isn't always the case, as you will see in the following exercise.

Exercise 9.9

1 List the members of each of the following sets.

(a) $\{x : x \text{ is an integer}, 40 < x < 50\}$
(b) $\{x : x \text{ is a regular polygon and } x \text{ has no more than six sides}\}$
(c) $\{x : x \text{ is a multiple of } 3, 16 < x < 32\}$

2 Express each of the following in set builder notation.

(a) {2, 3, 4, 5, 6, 7, 8}
(b) {a, e, i, o, u}
(c) {n, i, c, h, o, l, a, s}
(d) {2, 4, 6, 8, 10, 12, 14, 16, 18, 20}
(e) {1, 2, 3, 4, 6, 9, 12, 18, 36}

3 If $A = \{x : x \text{ is a multiple of three}\}$ and $B = \{y : y \text{ is a multiple of five}\}$, express $A \cap B$ in set builder notation.

4 $\mathscr{E} = \{y : y \text{ is a positive}, y \text{ is an integer less than } 18\}$.
$A = \{w : w > 5\}$ and $B = \{x : x \leq 5\}$.

(a) List the members of the set:

(i) $A \cap B$ (ii) A' (iii) $A' \cap B$ (iv) $A \cap B'$ (v) $(A \cap B')'$

(b) What is $A \cup B$?
(c) List the members of the set in part (b).

Summary

Do you know the following?

- A sequence is the elements of a set arranged in a particular order, connected by a rule.
- A term is a value (element) of a sequence.
- If the position of a term in a sequence is given the letter n then a rule can be found to work out the value of the nth term.
- A rational number is a number that can be written as a fraction.
- An irrational number has a decimal part that continues forever without repeating.
- A set is a list or collection of objects that share a characteristic.
- An element is a member of a set.
- A set that contains no elements is called the empty set ($\varnothing$).
- A universal set ($\mathscr{E}$) contains all the possible elements appropriate to a particular problem.
- The complement of a set is the elements that are not in the set ($'$).
- The elements of two sets can be combined (without repeats) to form the union of the two sets ($\cup$).
- The elements that two sets have in common is called the intersection of the two sets ($\cap$).
- The elements of a subset that are all contained within a larger set are a proper subset ($\subseteq$).
- If it is possible for a subset to be equal to the larger set, then it is not a proper subset ($\subset$).
- A Venn diagram is a pictorial method of showing sets.
- A shorthand way of describing the elements of a set is called set builder notation.

Are you able to ...?

- continue sequences
- describe a rule for continuing a sequence
- find the nth term of a sequence
- use the nth term to find later terms
- find out whether or not a specific number is in a sequence
- generate sequences from shape patterns
- find a formula for the number of shapes used in a pattern
- write a recurring decimal as a fraction in its lowest terms
- describe a set in words
- find the complement of a set
- represent the members of set using a Venn diagram
- solve problems using a Venn diagram
- describe a set using set builder notation.

Examination practice

Exam-style questions

1 Pattern 1 Pattern 2 Pattern 3

The first three patterns in a sequence are shown above.

(a) Copy and complete the table.

Pattern number (*n*)	1	2	3	4
Number of dots (*d*)	5			

(b) Find a formula for the number of dots, d, in the nth pattern.
(c) Find the number of dots in the 60th pattern.
(d) Find the number of the pattern that has 89 dots.

2 The diagram below shows a sequence of patterns made from dots and lines.

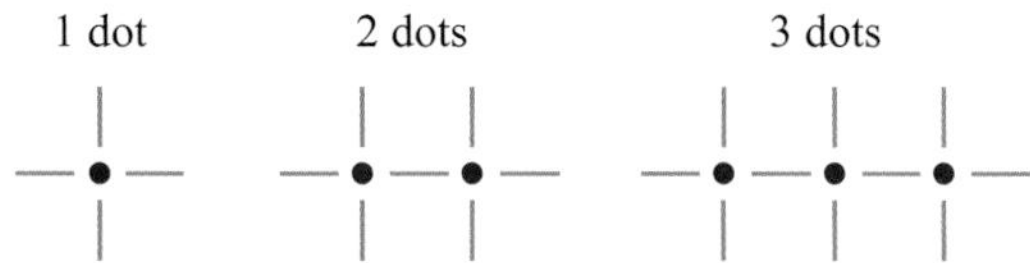

(a) Draw the next pattern in the sequence.
(b) Copy and complete the table for the numbers of dots and lines.

Dots	1	2	3	4	5	6
Lines	4	7	10			

(c) How many lines are in the pattern with 99 dots?
(d) How many lines are in the pattern with n dots?
(e) Complete the following statement:

There are 85 lines in the pattern with . . . dots.

Past paper questions

1 **(a)** Here are the first four terms of a sequence:
27 23 19 15
(i) Write down the next term in the sequence. [1]
(ii) Explain how you worked out your answer to **part (a)(i)**. [1]
(b) The nth term of a different sequence is $4n - 2$.
Write down the first three terms of this sequence. [1]
(c) Here are the first four terms of another sequence:
−1 2 5 8
Write down the nth term of this sequence. [2]

[Cambridge IGCSE Mathematics 0580 Paper 11 Q23 October/November 2013]

2 Shade the required region on each Venn diagram. [2] 

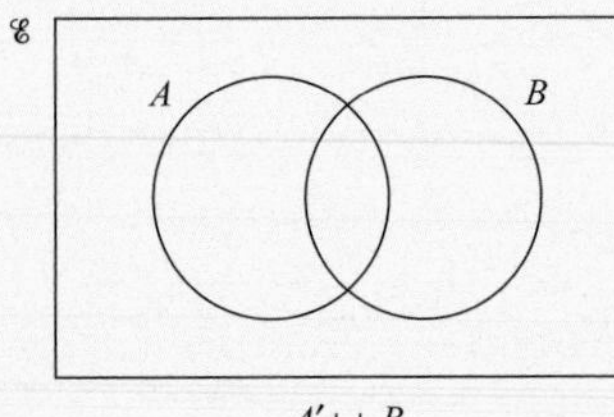

$A' \cup B$

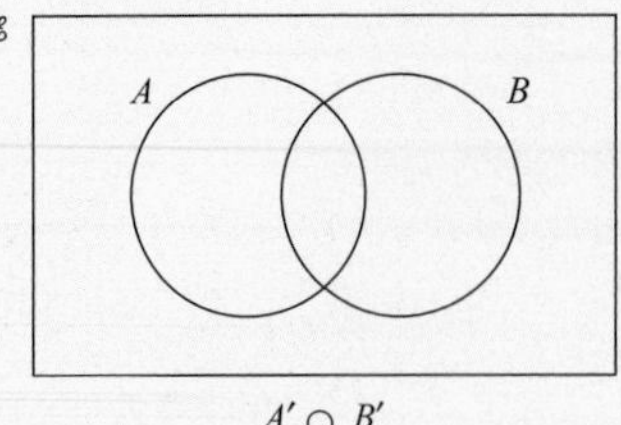

$A' \cap B'$

[Cambridge IGCSE Mathematics 0580 Paper 22 Q1 May/June 2013]

3 The first five terms of a sequence are shown below.
13 9 5 1 −3
Find the nth term of this sequence. [2]

[Cambridge IGCSE Mathematics 0580 Paper 22 Q3 May/June 2013]

4 Shade the required region in each of the Venn diagrams. [2] 

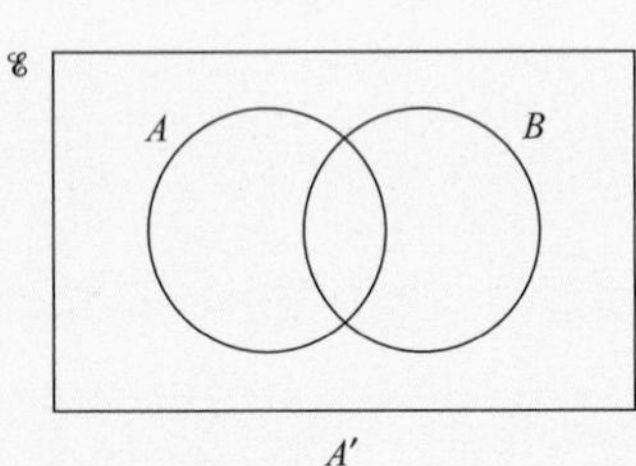

A'

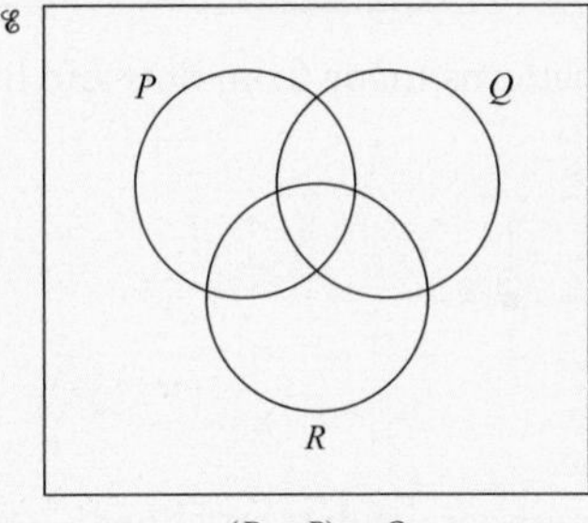

$(P \cap R) \cup Q$

[Cambridge IGCSE Mathematics 0580 Paper 23 Q9 October/November 2012]

5 **(a)** ℰ = {25 students in a class}
F = {students who study French}
S = {students who study Spanish}
16 students study French and 18 students study Spanish.
2 students study neither of these.

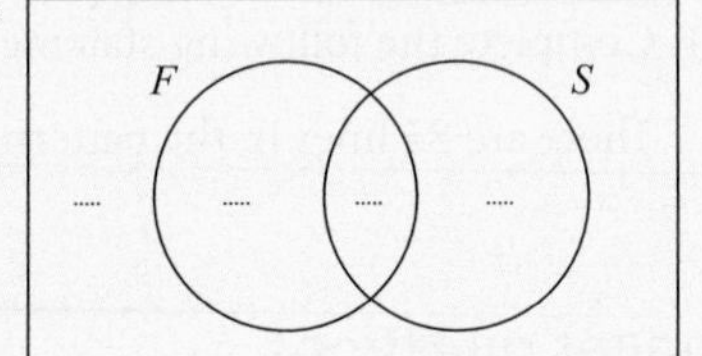

(i) Complete the Venn diagram to show this information. [2]
(ii) Find $n(F')$. [1]
(iii) Find $n(F \cap S)'$. [1]
(iv) One student is chosen at random.
Find the probability that this student studies both French and Spanish. [1]
(v) Two students are chosen at random without replacement.
Find the probability that they both study only Spanish. [2]

(b) In another class the students all study at least one language from French, German and Spanish.
No student studies all three languages.
The set of students who study German is a proper subset of the set of students who study French.
4 students study both French and German.
12 students study Spanish but not French.
9 students study French but not Spanish.
A total of 16 students study French.
(i) Draw a Venn diagram to represent this information. [4]
(ii) Find the total number of students in this class. [1]

[Cambridge IGCSE Mathematics 0580 Paper 42 Q9 October/November 2012]

10 Straight lines and quadratic equations

Key words

- Equation of a line
- Gradient
- *y*-intercept
- Constant
- *x*-intercept
- Line segment
- Midpoint
- Expand
- Constant term
- Quadratic expression
- Factorisation
- Difference between two squares
- Quadratic equation

In this chapter you will learn how to:

- construct a table of values and plot points to draw graphs
- find the gradient of a straight line graph
- recognise and determine the equation of a line
- determine the equation of a line parallel to a given line

EXTENDED

- calculate the gradient of a line using co-ordinates of points on the line
- find the gradient of parallel and perpendicular lines
- find the length of a line segment and the co-ordinates of its midpoint
- expand products of algebraic expressions
- factorise quadratic expressions
- solve quadratic equations by factorisation

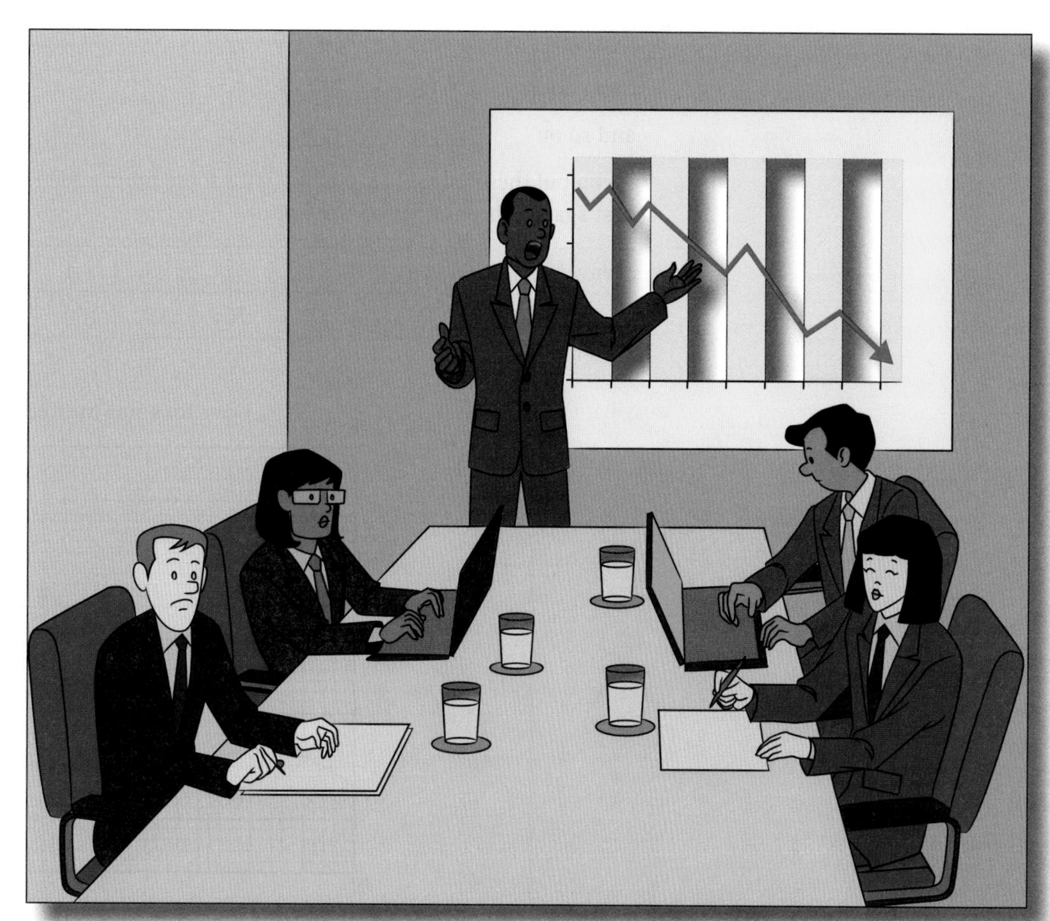

Geoff wishes he had paid more attention when his teacher talked about negative and positive gradients.

On 4 October 1957, the first artificial satellite, Sputnik, was launched. This satellite orbited the Earth but many satellites that do experiments to study the upper atmosphere fly on short, sub-orbital flights. The flight path can be described with a quadratic equation, so scientists know where the rocket will be when it deploys its parachute and so they know where to recover the instruments. The same equation can be used to describe any thrown projectile including a baseball!

10.1 Straight lines

Using equations to plot lines

Mr Keele owns a boat hire company. If Mr Keele makes a flat charge of \$40 and then another \$15 per hour of hire, you can find a formula for the total cost \$$y$ after a hire time of x hours.

Total cost = flat charge + total charge for all hours

$y = 40 + 15 \times x$

or (rearranging)

$y = 15x + 40$

REWIND

You will recognise that the formulae used to describe n^{th} terms in chapter 9 are very similar to the equations used in this chapter. ◀

Now think about the total cost for a range of different hire times:

one hour: cost = $15 \times 1 + 40 =$ \$55

two hours: cost = $15 \times 2 + 40 =$ \$70

three hours: cost = $15 \times 3 + 40 =$ \$85

and so on.

If you put these values into a table (with some more added) you can then plot a graph of the total cost against the number of hire hours:

Number of hours (x)	1	2	3	4	5	6	7	8	9
Total cost (y)	55	70	85	100	115	130	145	160	175

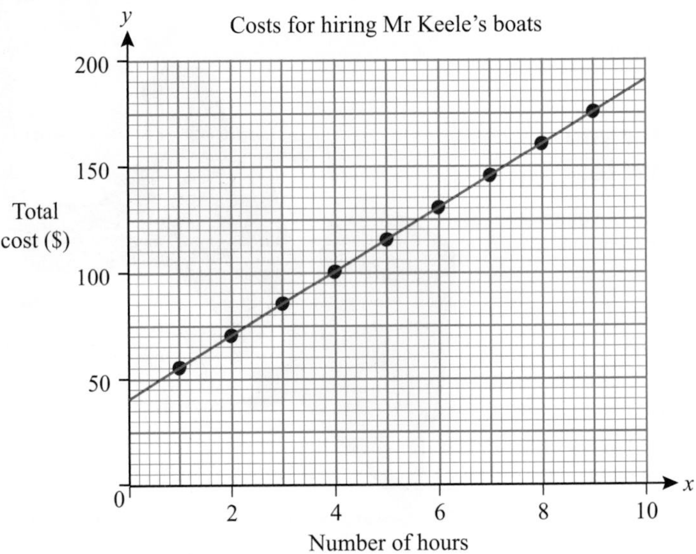

The graph shows the total cost of the boat hire (plotted on the vertical axis) against the number of hire hours (on the horizontal axis). Notice that the points all lie on a straight line.

The formula $y = 15x + 40$ tells you how the y-co-ordinates of all points on the line are related to the x-co-ordinates. This formula is called an **equation of the line.**

The following worked examples show you how some more lines can be drawn from given equations.

Worked example 1

A straight line has equation $y = 2x + 3$. Construct a table of values for x and y and draw the line on a labelled pair of axes. Use integer values of x from –3 to 2.

Substituting the values –3, –2, –1, 0, 1 and 2 into the equation gives the values in the following table:

x	–3	–2	–1	0	1	2
y	–3	–1	1	3	5	7

Notice that the y-values range from –3 to 7, so your y-axis should allow for this.

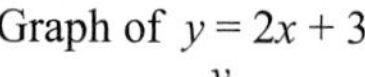

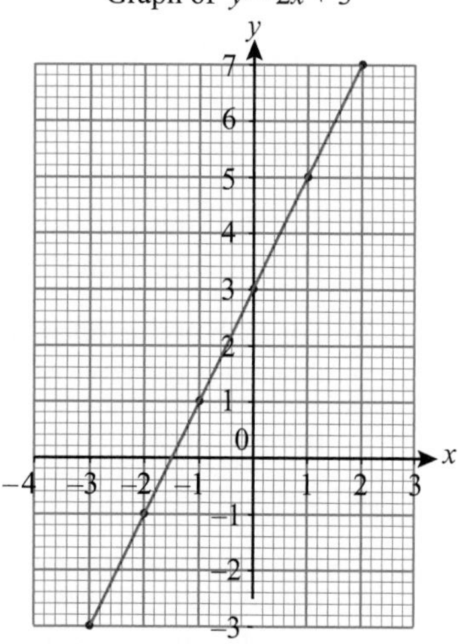

Worked example 2

Draw the line with equation $y = -x + 3$ for x-values between –2 and 5 inclusive.

The table for this line would be:

x	–2	–1	0	1	2	3	4	5
y	5	4	3	2	1	0	–1	–2

Graph of $y = -x + 3$

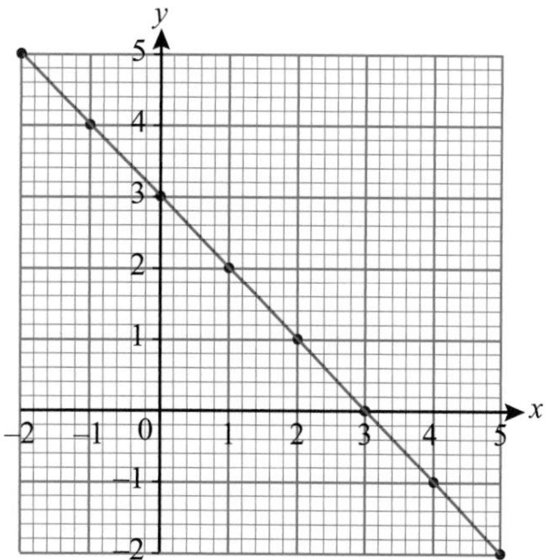

To draw a graph from its equation:

- draw up a table of values and fill in the x- and y-co-ordinates of at least three points (although you may be given more)
- draw up and label your set of axes for the range of y-values you have worked out
- plot each point on the number plane
- draw a straight line to join the points (use a ruler).

Before drawing your axes, always check that you know the range of y-values that you need to use.

Exercise 10.1

1 Make a table for x-values from –3 to 3 for each of the following equations.
Plot the co-ordinates on separate pairs of axes and draw the lines.

(a) $y = 3x + 2$ (b) $y = x + 2$ (c) $y = 2x - 1$ (d) $y = 5x - 4$

(e) $y = -2x + 1$ (f) $y = -x - 2$ (g) $y = 6 - x$ (h) $y = 3x + \frac{1}{2}$

(i) $y = \frac{1}{2}x + 1$ (j) $y = 4x$ (k) $y = -3$ (l) $y = -1 - x$

(m) $x + y = 4$ (n) $x - y = 2$ (o) $y = x$ (p) $y = -x$

2 Plot the lines $y = 2x$, $y = 2x + 1$, $y = 2x - 3$ and $y = 2x + 2$ on the same pair of axes.
Use x-values from –3 to 3. What do you notice about the lines that you have drawn?

3 For each of the following equations, draw up a table of x-values for –3, 0 and 3.
Complete the table of values and plot the graphs on the same set of axes.

(a) $y = x + 2$ (b) $y = -x + 2$ (c) $y = x - 2$ (d) $y = -x - 2$

4 Use your graphs from question **3** above to answer these questions.

(a) Where do the graphs cut the x-axis?
(b) Which graphs slope up to the right?
(c) Which graphs slope down to the right?
(d) Which graphs cut the y-axis at (0, 2)?
(e) Which graphs cut the y-axis at (0, –2)?
(f) Does the point (3, 3) lie on any of the graphs? If so, which?
(g) Which graphs are parallel to each other?
(h) Compare the equations of graphs that are parallel to each other. How are they similar? How are they different?

Gradient

The **gradient** of a line tells you how steep the line is. For every one unit moved to the right, the gradient will tell you how much the line moves up (or down). When graphs are parallel to each other, they have the same gradient.

Vertical and horizontal lines

Look at the two lines shown in the following diagram:

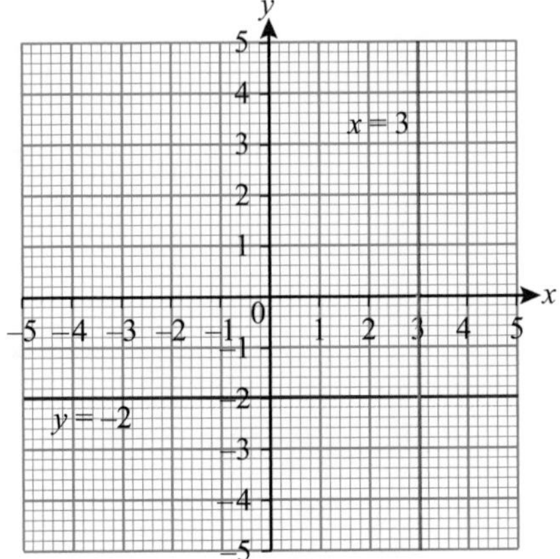

Every point on the vertical line has x-co-ordinate = 3. So the equation of the line is simply $x = 3$.

Every point on the horizontal line has y-co-ordinate = −2. So the equation of this line is $y = -2$.

All vertical lines are of the form: x = a number.

All horizontal lines are of the form: y = a number.

The gradient of a horizontal line is zero (it does not move up or down when you move to the right).

Exercise 10.2

1 Write down the equation of each line shown in the diagram.

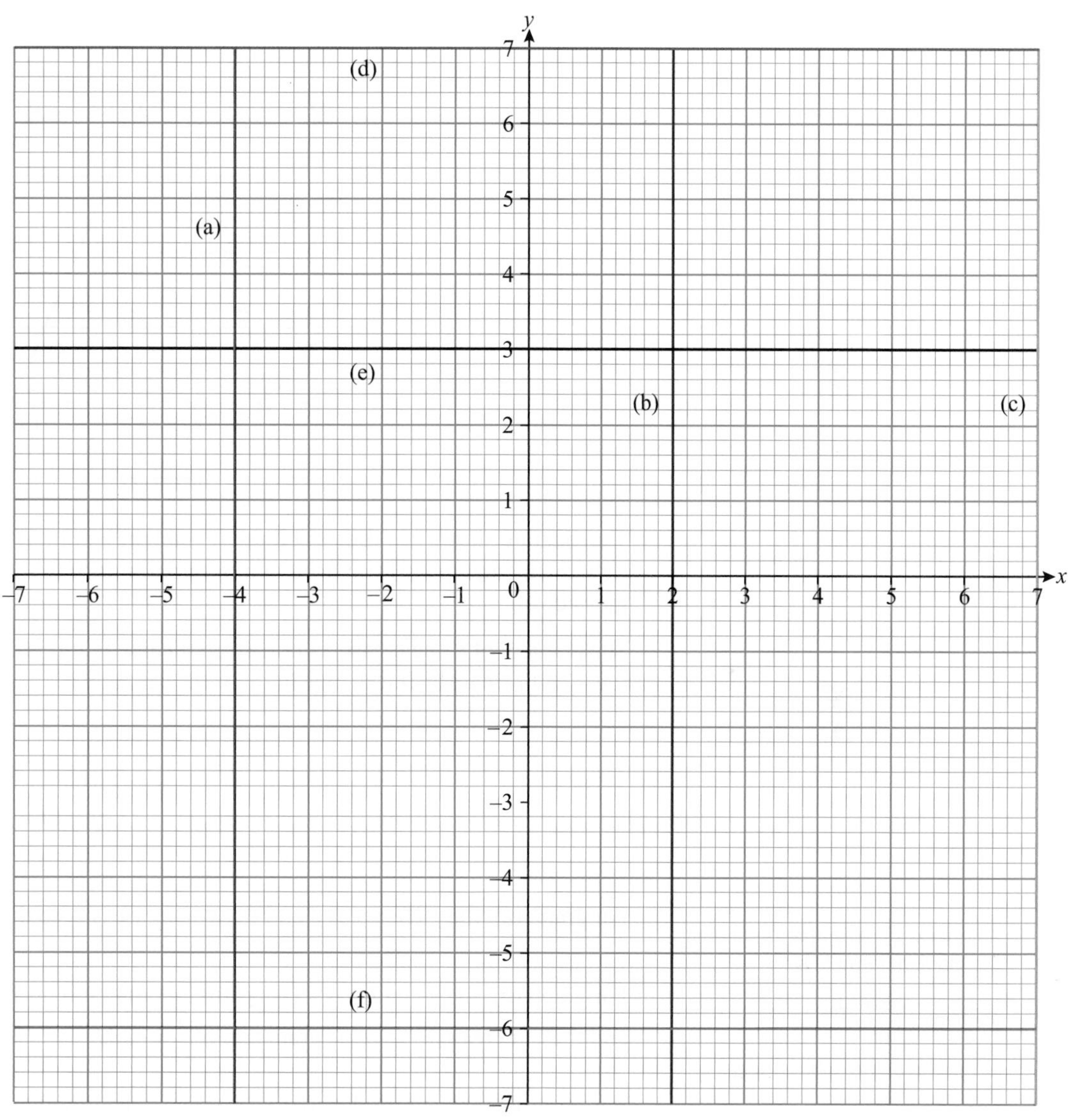

2 Draw the following graphs on the same set of axes without plotting points or drawing up a table of values.

(a) $y = 3$ **(b)** $x = 3$ **(c)** $y = -1$ **(d)** $x = -1$

(e) $y = -3$ **(f)** $y = 4$ **(g)** $x = \frac{1}{2}$ **(h)** $x = \frac{-7}{2}$

(i) a graph parallel to the x-axis which cuts the y-axis at (0, 4)

(j) a graph parallel to the y-axis which goes through the point (−2, 0)

Lines that are neither vertical nor horizontal

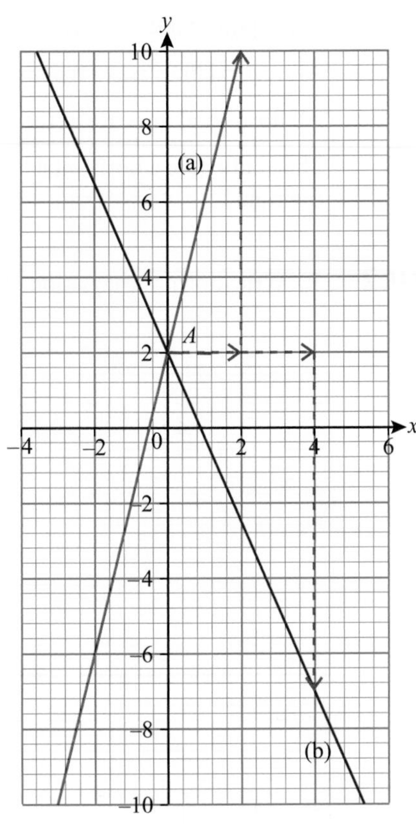

The diagram shows two different lines. If you take a point A on the line and then move *to the right* then, on graph (a) you need to move up to return to the line, and on graph (b) you need to move down.

The gradient of a line measures how steep the line is and is calculated by dividing the change in the y-co-ordinate by the change in the x-co-ordinate:

$$\text{gradient} = \frac{y\text{-change}}{x\text{-increase}}$$

Another good way of remembering the gradient formula is $\text{gradient} = \frac{\text{'rise'}}{\text{'run'}}$. The 'run' must always be to the right (increase x).

For graph (a): the y-change is 8 and the x-increase is 2, so the gradient is $\frac{8}{2} = 4$

For graph (b): the y-change is -9 (negative because you need to move *down* to return to the line) and the x-increase is 4, so the gradient is $\frac{-9}{4} = -2.25$.

It is essential that you think about *x-increases* only. Whether the y-change is positive or negative tells you what the sign of the gradient will be.

Worked example 3

Calculate the gradient of each line. Leave your answer as a whole number or fraction in its lowest terms.

(a)

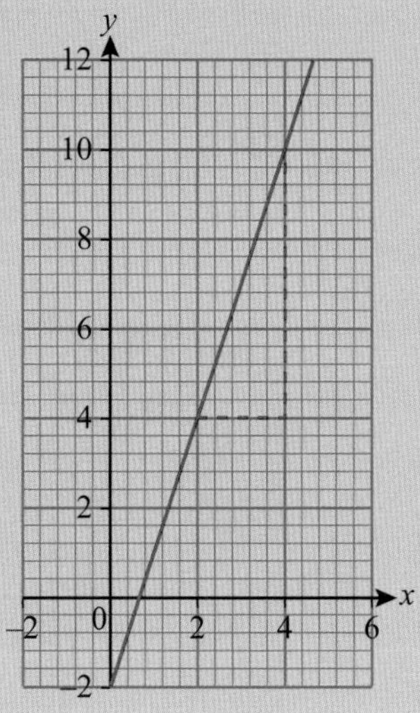

(b)

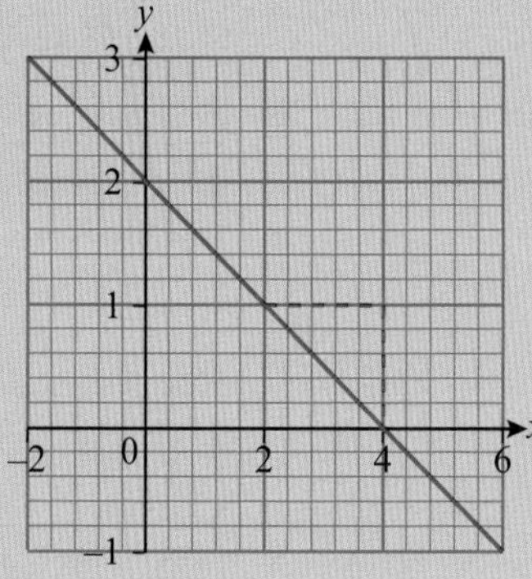

(a) Notice that the graph passes through the points (2, 4) and (4, 10).

$$\text{gradient} = \frac{y\text{-change}}{x\text{-increase}} = \frac{10-4}{4-2} = \frac{6}{2} = 3$$

(b) Notice that the graph passes through the points (2, 1) and (4, 0).

$$\text{gradient} = \frac{y\text{-change}}{x\text{-increase}} = \frac{0-1}{4-2} = -\frac{1}{2}$$

Worked example 4

Calculate the gradient of the line that passes through the points (3, 5) and (7, 17).

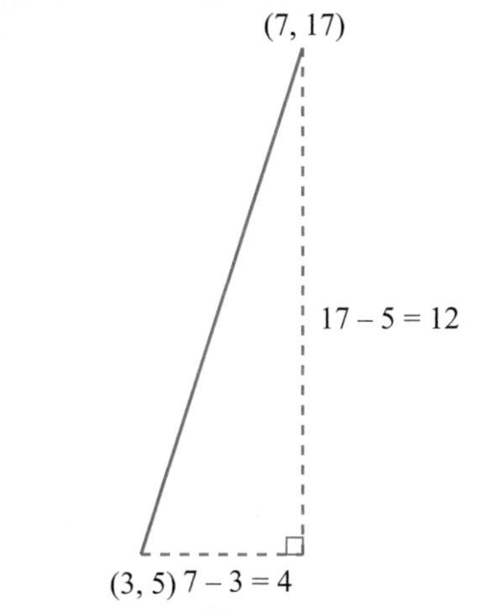

$$\text{gradient} = \frac{y\text{-change}}{x\text{-increase}} = \frac{17-5}{7-3} = \frac{12}{4} = 3$$

Think about where the points would be, in relation to each other, on a pair of axes. You don't need to draw this accurately but the diagram will give you an idea of how it may appear.

Exercise 10.3

1 Calculate the gradient of each line. Leave your answers as a fraction in its lowest terms.

(a)

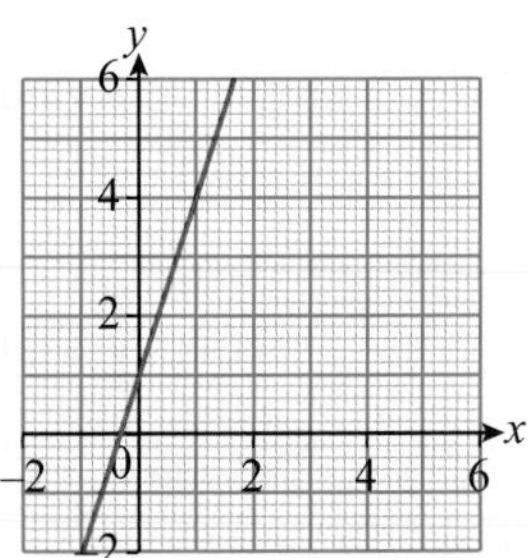

(b)

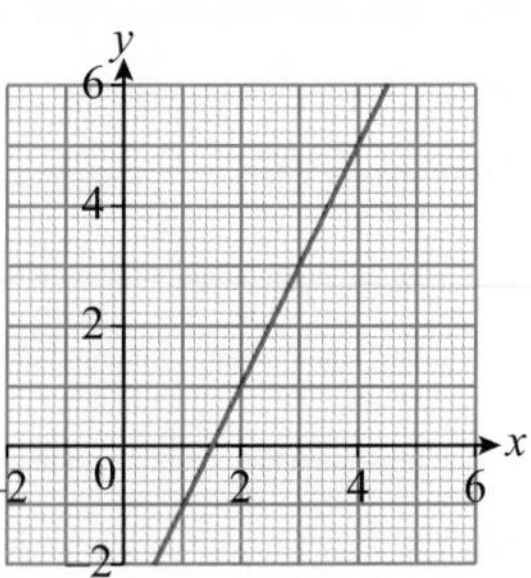

(c)

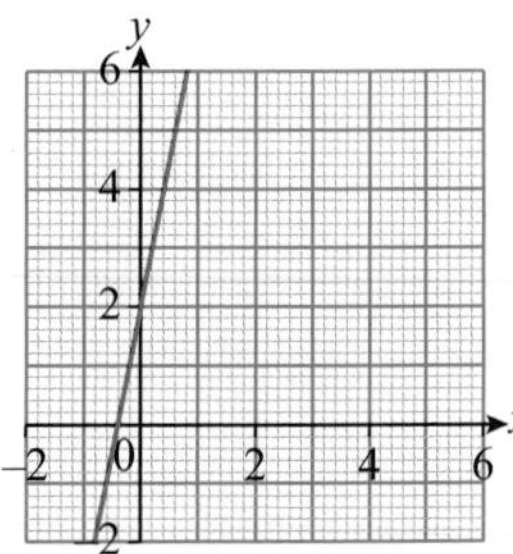

(d)

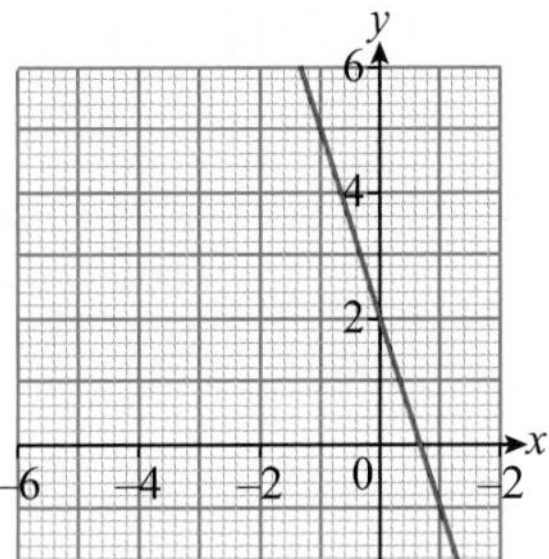

(e)

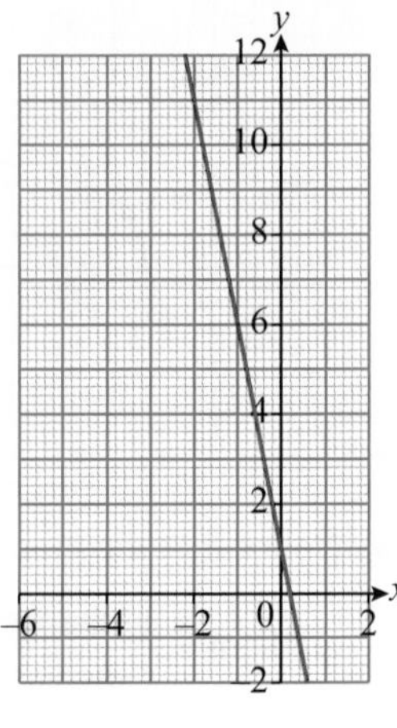

(f)

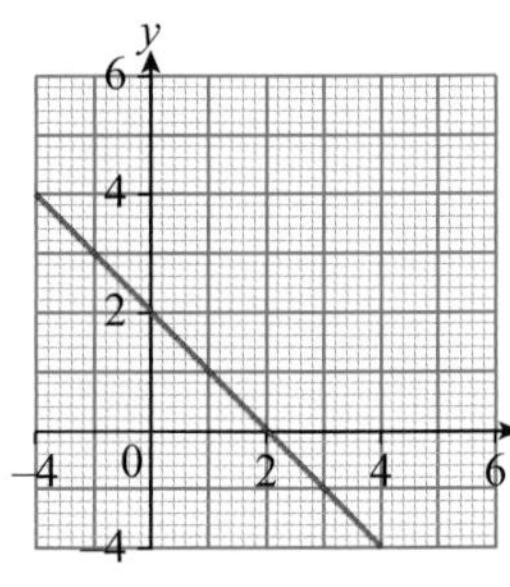

(g)

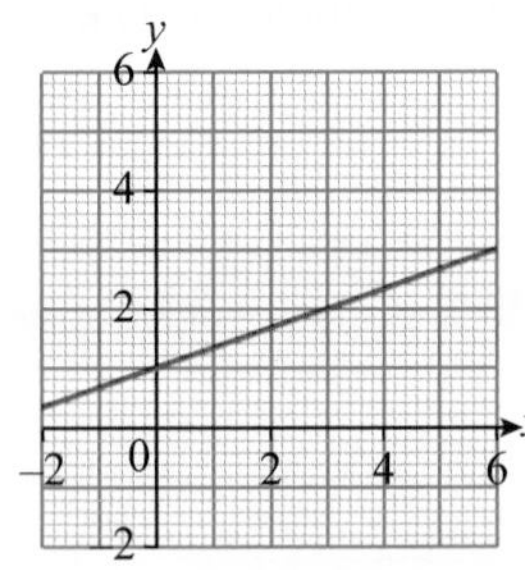

(h)

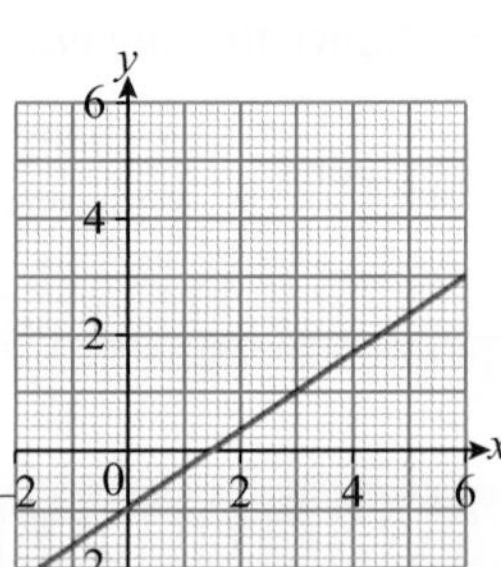

(i)

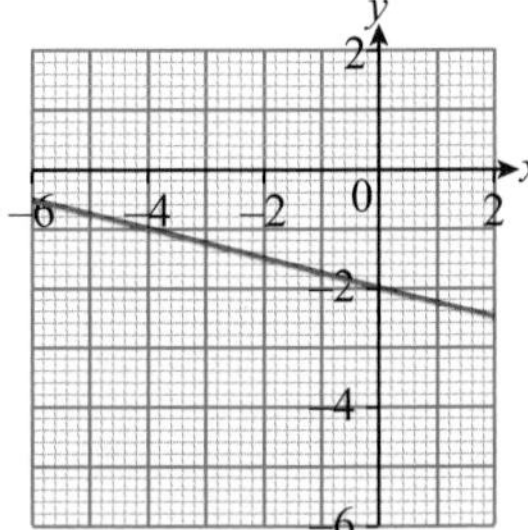

Think carefully about whether you expect the gradient to be positive or negative.

2 Calculate the gradient of the line that passes through both points in each case. Leave your answer as a whole number or a fraction in its lowest terms.

(a) A (1, 2) and B (3, 8) **(b)** A (0, 6) and B (3, 9)
(c) A (2, −1) and B (4, 3) **(d)** A (3, 2) and B (7, −10)
(e) A (−1, −4) and B (−3, 2) **(f)** A (3, −5) and B (7, 12)

Living maths

3 If the car climbs 60 m vertically how far must the car have travelled *horizontally*?

Finding the equation of a line

Look at the three lines shown below.

(a)

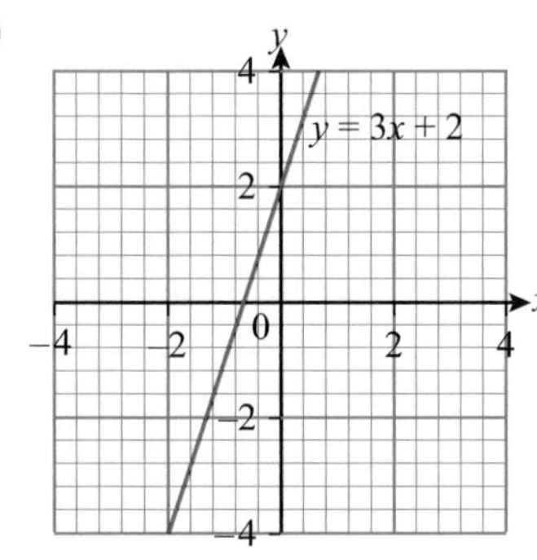

(b)

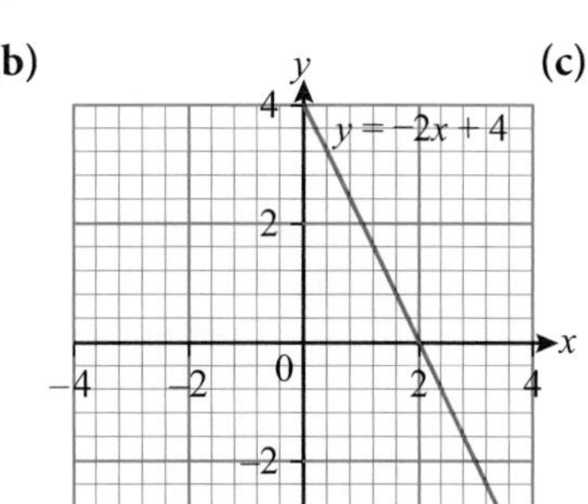

(c)

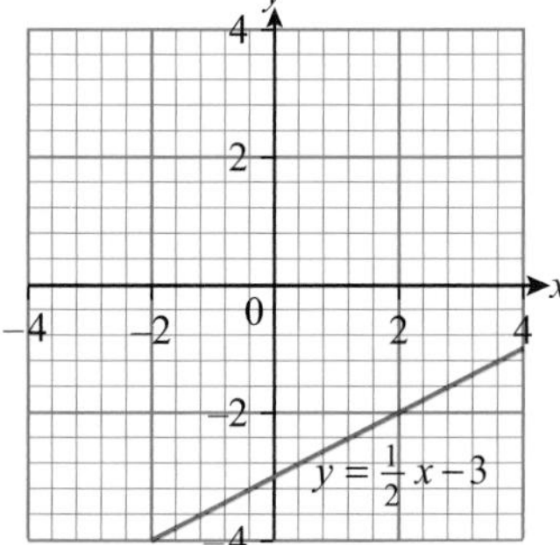

Check for yourself that the lines have the following gradients:

- gradient of line (a) = 3
- gradient of line (b) = −2
- gradient of line (c) = $\frac{1}{2}$

REWIND

You met the coefficient in chapter 2. ◀

Notice that the gradient of each line is equal to the coefficient of x in the equation and that the point at which the line crosses the y-axis (known as the ***y*-intercept**) has a y-co-ordinate that is equal to the **constant** term.

In fact this is always true when y is the subject of the equation:

$$y = mx + c$$

y is the subject of the equation; m: gradient; c: y-intercept

In summary:

- equations of a straight line graphs can be written in the form of $y = mx + c$
- c (the constant term) tells you where the graph cuts the y-axis (the y-intercept)
- m (the coefficient of x) is the gradient of the graph; a negative value means the graph slopes down the to the right, a positive value means it slopes up to the right. The higher the value of m, the steeper the gradient of the graph
- graphs which have the same gradient are parallel to each other (therefore graphs that are parallel have the same gradient).

Worked example 5

Find the gradient and y-intercept of the lines given by each of the following equations.

(a) $y = 3x + 4$ **(b)** $y = 5 - 3x$ **(c)** $y = \frac{1}{2}x + 9$ **(d)** $x + y = 8$

(e) $3x + 2y = 6$

(a) $y = 3x + 4$ Gradient = 3 y-intercept = 4	The coefficient of x is 3. The constant term is 4.
(b) $y = 5 - 3x$ Gradient = −3 y-intercept = 5	Re-write the equation as $y = -3x + 5$. The coefficient of x is −3. The constant term is 5.

(c) $y = \frac{1}{2}x + 9$ Gradient $= \frac{1}{2}$ y-intercept $= 9$	The gradient can be a fraction.
(d) $x + y = 8$ Gradient $= -1$ y-intercept $= 8$	Subtracting x from both sides, so that y is the subject, gives $y = -x + 8$.
(e) $3x + 2y = 6$ Gradient $= \frac{-3}{2}$ y-intercept $= 3$	Make y the subject of the equation. $3x + 2y = 6$ $2y = -3x + 6$ $y = \frac{-3}{2}x + \frac{6}{2}$ $y = \frac{-3}{2}x + 3$

Worked example 6

Find the equation of each line shown in the diagrams.

(a)

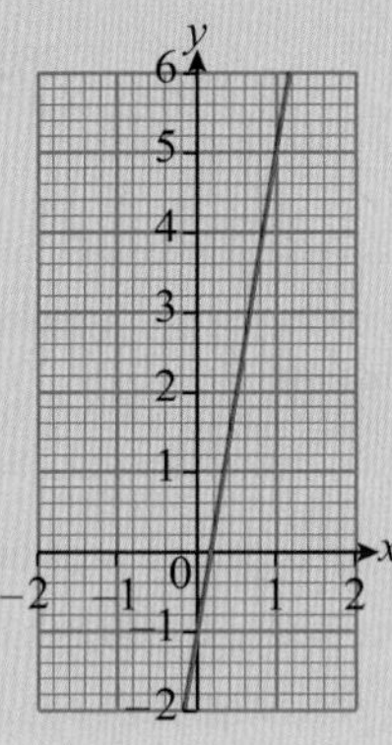

(b)

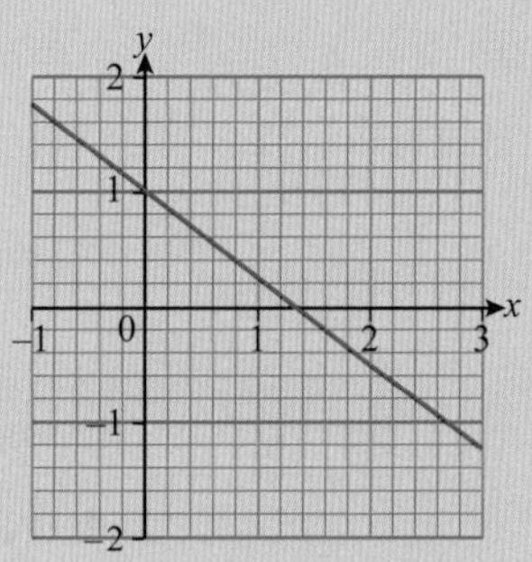

(a) Gradient $= 6$ and the y-intercept $= -1$ So the equation is $y = 6x - 1$	Gradient $= \frac{6}{1} = 6$ Graph crosses y-axis at -1
(b) Gradient $= \frac{-3}{4}$ and the y-intercept $= 1$ So the equation is $y = -\frac{3}{4}x + 1$	Gradient $= \frac{-1.5}{2} = \frac{-3}{4}$ Graph crosses y-axis at 1.

You should always label your axes x and y when drawing graphs – even when they are sketches.

Exercise 10.4

Look carefully at your sketches for answers 1(d) and 1(g). If you draw them onto the same axes you will see that they are parallel. These lines have the same gradient but they cut the y-axis at different places. If two or more lines are parallel, they will have the same gradient.

1 Find the gradient and y-intercept of the lines with the following equations. Sketch the graph in each case, taking care to show where the graph cuts the y-axis.

(a) $y = 4x - 5$ **(b)** $y = 2x + 3$ **(c)** $y = -3x - 2$ **(d)** $y = -x + 3$

(e) $y = \frac{1}{3}x + 2$ **(f)** $y = 6 - \frac{1}{4}x$ **(g)** $x + y = 4$ **(h)** $x + 2y = 4$

(i) $x + \frac{y}{2} = 3$ **(j)** $x = 4y - 2$ **(k)** $x = \frac{y}{4} + 2$ **(k)** $2x - 3y = -9$

2 Rearrange each equation so that it is in the form $y = mx + c$ and then find the gradient and y-intercept of each graph.

(a) $2y = x - 4$ **(b)** $2x + y - 1 = 0$ **(c)** $x = \frac{y}{2} - 2$ **(d)** $2x - y - 5 = 0$

(e) $2x - y + 5 = 0$ **(f)** $x + 3y - 6 = 0$ **(g)** $4y = 12x - 8$ **(h)** $4x + y = 2$

(i) $\frac{y}{2} = x + 2$ **(j)** $\frac{y}{3} = 2x - 4$ **(k)** $\frac{x}{2} - 4y = 12$ **(l)** $\frac{-y}{3} = 4x - 2$

3 Find the equation (in the form of $y = mx + c$) of a line which has:

(a) a gradient of 2 and a y-intercept of 3
(b) a gradient of -3 and a y-intercept of -2
(c) a gradient of 3 and a y-intercept of -1
(d) a gradient of $-\frac{3}{2}$ and a y-intercept at $(0, -0.5)$
(e) a y-intercept of 2 and a gradient of $-\frac{3}{4}$
(f) a y-intercept of -3 and a gradient of $\frac{4}{8}$
(g) a y-intercept of -0.75 and a gradient of 0.75
(h) a y-intercept of -2 and a gradient of 0
(i) a gradient of 0 and a y-intercept of 4

4 Find an equation for each line.

(a)

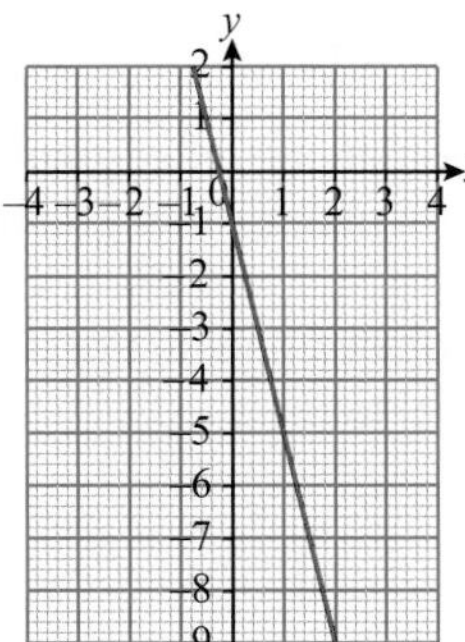

(b)

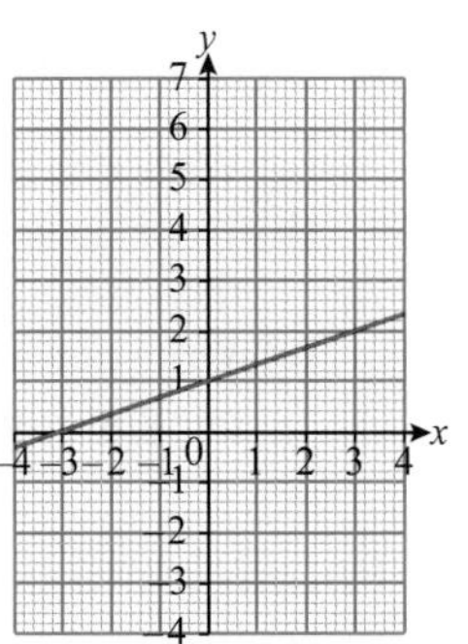

(c)

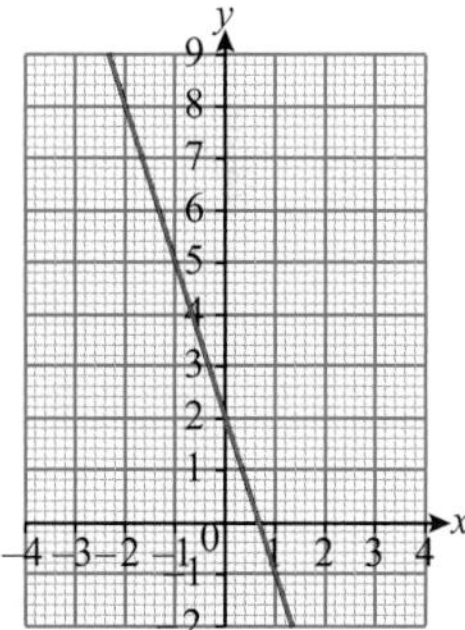

(d)

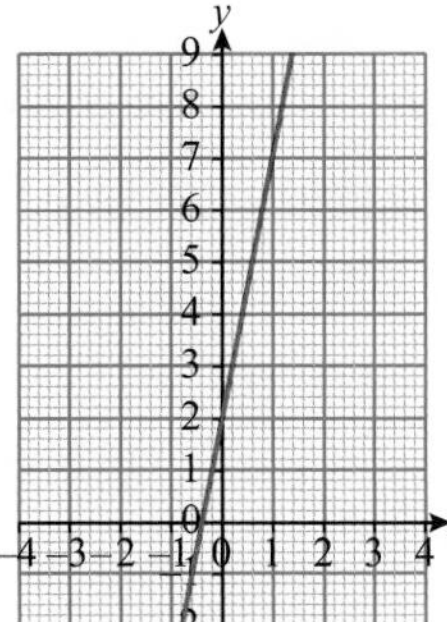

(e)

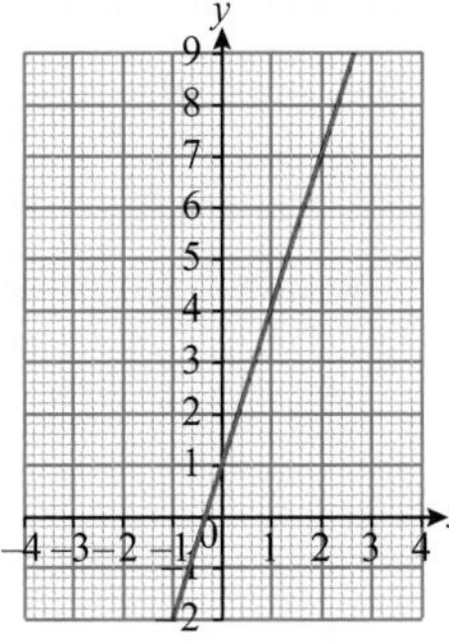

(f)

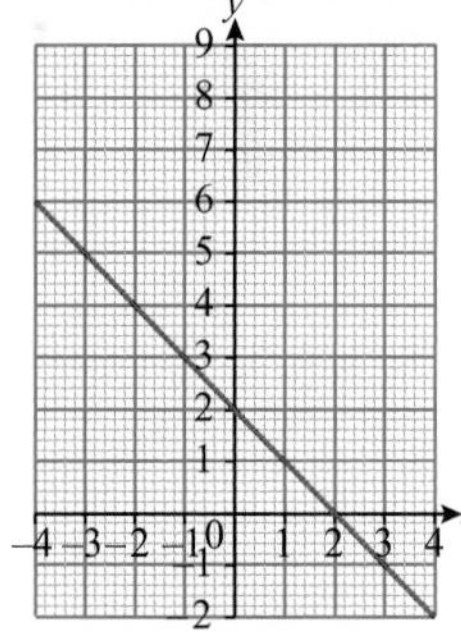

(g)

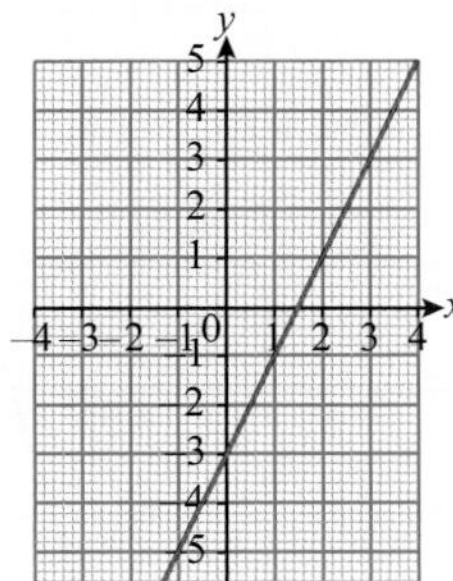

(h)

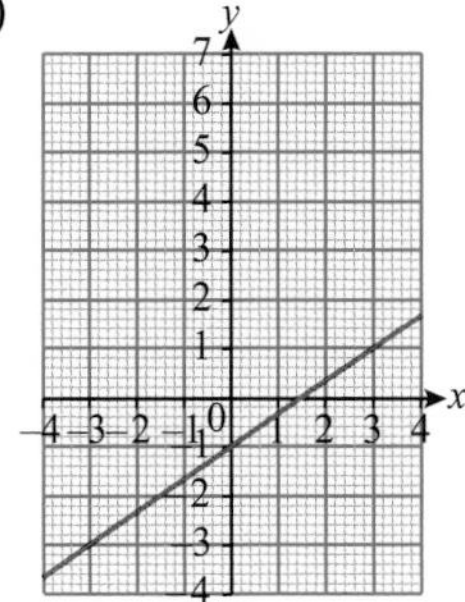

(i)

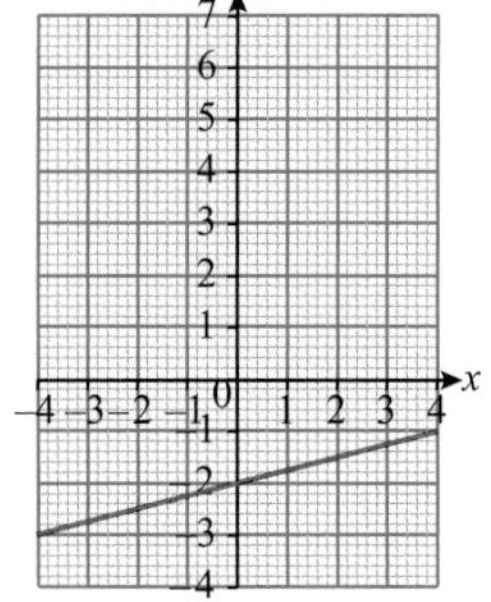

5 Find the equation of the line which passes through both points in each case.

(a) A (2, 3) and B (4, 11) **(b)** A (4, 5) and B (8, –7)
(c) A (–1, –3) and B (4, 6) **(d)** A (3, –5) and B (7, 12)

6 Write down the equation of a line that is parallel to:

(a) $y = -3x$ **(b)** $y = 2x - 3$ **(c)** $y = \frac{x}{2} + 4$
(d) $y = -x - 2$ **(e)** $x = 8$ **(f)** $y = -6$

7 Which of the following lines are parallel to $y = \frac{1}{2}x$?

(a) $y = \frac{1}{2}x + 1$ **(b)** $y = 2x$ **(c)** $y + 1 = \frac{1}{2}x$ **(d)** $2y + x = -6$ **(e)** $y = 2x - 4$

8 Find the equation of a line parallel to $y = 2x + 4$ which:

(a) has a y-intercept of –2
(b) passes through the origin
(c) passes through the point (0, –4)
(d) has a y-intercept of $\frac{1}{2}$

9 A graph has the equation $3y - 2x = 9$.

(a) Write down the equation of one other graph that is parallel to this one.
(b) Write down the equation of one other graph that crosses the y-axis at the same point as this one.
(c) Write down the equation of a line that passes through the y-axis at the same point as this one and which is parallel to the x-axis.

If the product of the gradients of two lines is equal to –1, it follows that the lines are perpendicular to each other.

Parallel and perpendicular lines

You have already seen that parallel lines have the same gradient and that lines with the same gradient are parallel.

Perpendicular lines meet at right angles. The product of the gradients is –1.

So, $m_1 \times m_2 = -1$, where m is the gradient of each line.

The sketch shows two perpendicular graphs.

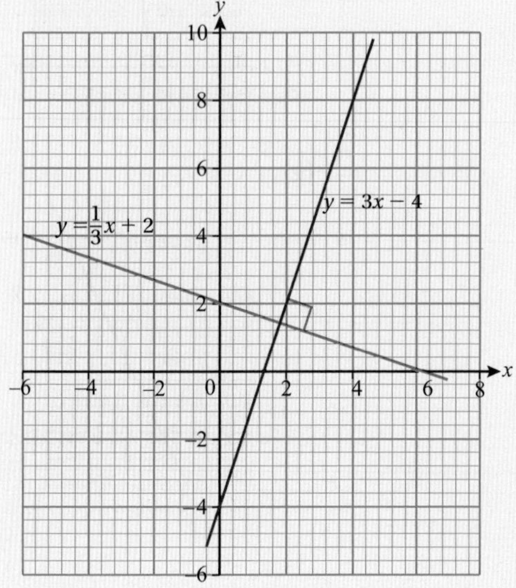

$y = -\frac{1}{3}x + 2$ has a gradient of $-\frac{1}{3}$

$y = 3x - 4$ has a gradient of 3

The product of the gradients is $-\frac{1}{3} \times 3 = -1$.

Worked example 7

Given that $y = \frac{2}{3}x + 2$, determine the equation of the straight line that is:

(a) perpendicular to this line and which passes through the origin

(b) perpendicular to this line and which passes through the point (–3, 1).

(a)

$y = mx + c$

$m = -\frac{3}{2}$ The gradient is the negative reciprocal of $\frac{2}{3}$

$c = 0$

The equation of the line is $y = -\frac{3}{2}x$.

(b)

$y = -\frac{3}{2}x + c$	Using $m = -\frac{3}{2}$ from part (a) above.
$x = -3$ and $y = 1$	
$1 = -\frac{3}{2}(-3) + c$	Substitute the values of x and y for the given point to solve for c.
$1 = \frac{9}{2} + c$	
$c = -3\frac{1}{2}$	
$y = -\frac{3}{2}x - 3\frac{1}{2}$	

Exercise 10.5

1 A line perpendicular to $y = \frac{x}{5} + 3$ passes through (1, 3). What is the equation of the line?

2 Show that the line through the points $A(6, 0)$ and $B(0, 12)$ is:

(a) perpendicular to the line through $P(8, 10)$ and $Q(4, 8)$

(b) perpendicular to the line through $M(-4, -8)$ and $N(-1, -\frac{13}{2})$

3 Given $A(0, 0)$ and $B(1, 3)$, find the equation of the line perpendicular to AB with a y-intercept of 5.

4 Find the equation of the following lines:

(a) perpendicular to $2x - y - 1 = 0$ and passing through $(2, -\frac{1}{2})$

(b) perpendicular to $2x + 2y = 5$ and passing through (1, –2)

5 Line A joins the points (6, 0) and (0, 12) and Line B joins the points (8, 10) and (4, 8). Determine the gradient of each line and state whether A is perpendicular to B.

6 Line MN joins points (7, 4) and (2, 5). Find the equation of AB, the perpendicular bisector of MN.

7 Show that points $A(-3, 6)$, $B(-12, -4)$ and $C(8, -5)$ could not be the vertices of a rectangle $ABCD$.

Intersection with the x-axis

So far only the y-intercept has been found, either from the graph or from the equation. There is, of course, an **x-intercept** too. The following sketch shows the line with equation $y = 3x - 6$.

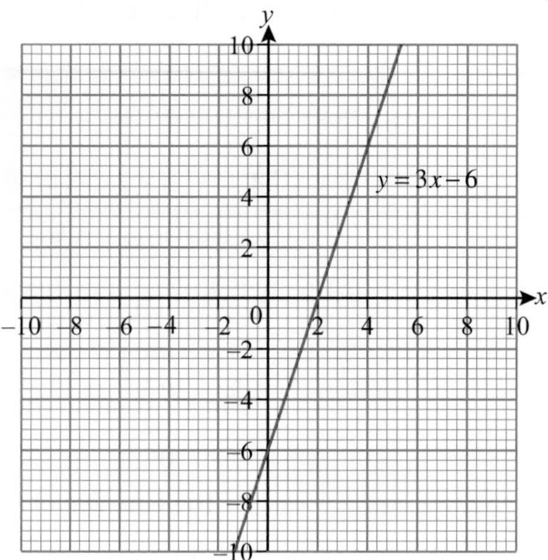

Notice that the line crosses the x-axis at the point where $x = 2$ and, importantly, $y = 0$. In fact, all points on the x-axis have y-co-ordinate = 0. If you substitute $y = 0$ into the equation of the line:

FAST FORWARD

You will need to understand this method when solving simultaneous equations in chapter 14. ▶

$y = 3x - 6$

$0 = 3x - 6$ (putting $y = 0$)

$3x = 6$ (add 6 to both sides)

$x = 2$ (dividing both sides by 3)

this is exactly the answer that you found from the graph.

You can also find the y-intercept by putting $x = 0$. The following worked examples show calculations for finding both the x- and y-intercepts.

Worked example 8

Find the x- and y-intercepts for each of the following lines. Sketch the graph in each case.

(a) $y = 6x - 12$ **(b)** $y = -x + 3$ **(c)** $2x + 5y = 20$

(a) $y = 6x - 12$

$x = 0 \Rightarrow y = -12$

$y = 0 \Rightarrow 6x - 12 = 0$

$\Rightarrow x = 2$

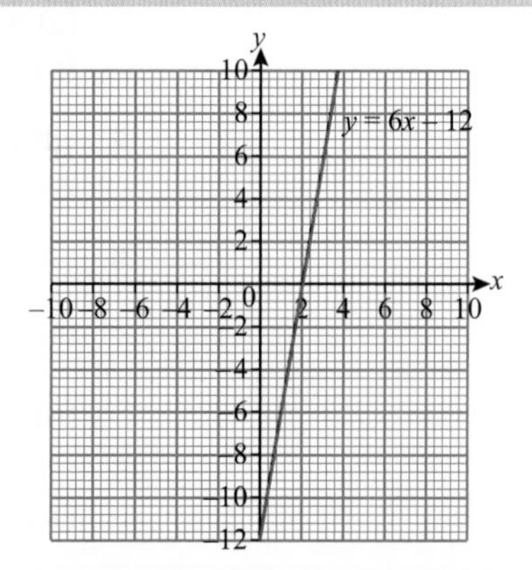

(b) $y = -x + 3$

$x = 0 \Rightarrow y = 3$

$y = 0 \Rightarrow -x + 3 = 0$

$\Rightarrow x = 3$

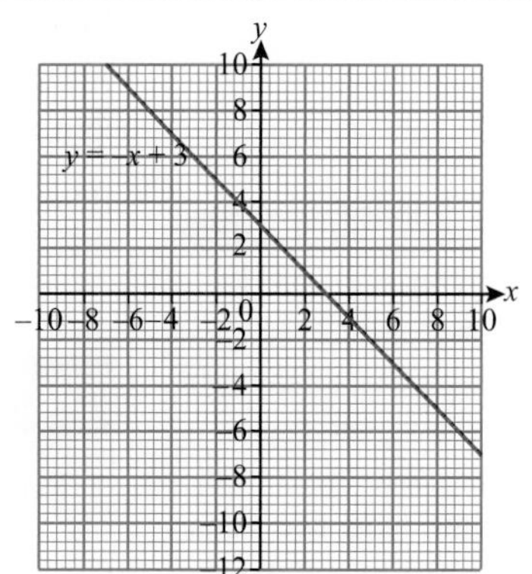

(c) $2x + 5y = 20$

$x = 0 \Rightarrow 5y = 20$

$\Rightarrow y = 4$

$y = 0 \Rightarrow 2x = 20$

$\Rightarrow x = 10$

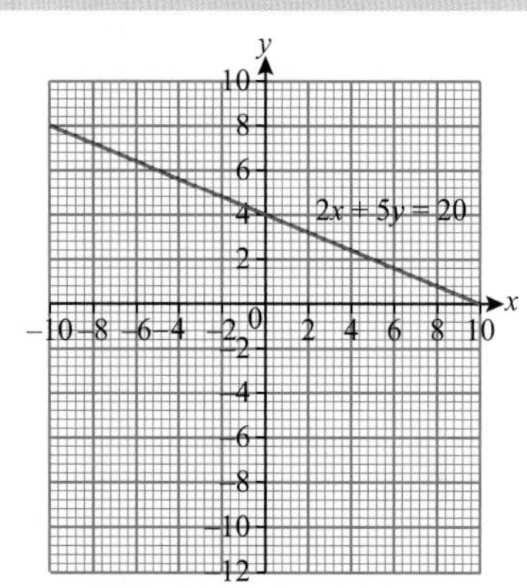

Exercise 10.6

1 Find the x- and y-intercepts for each of the following lines. Sketch the graph in each case.

(a) $y = -5x + 10$ (b) $y = \frac{x}{3} - 1$ (c) $y = -3x + 6$ (d) $y = 4x + 2$

(e) $y = 3x + 1$ (f) $y = -x + 2$ (g) $y = 2x - 3$ (h) $y = \frac{2x}{3} - 1$

(i) $y = \frac{x}{4} - 2$ (j) $y = \frac{2x}{5} + 1$ (k) $-2 + y = \frac{x}{4}$ (l) $\frac{-y}{3} = 4x - 2$

2 For each equation, find c, if the given point lies on the graph.

(a) $y = 3x + c$ (1, 5) (b) $y = 6x + c$ (1, 2)

(c) $y = -2x + c$ (−3, −3) (d) $y = \frac{3}{4}x + c$ (4, −5)

(e) $y = \frac{1}{2}x + c$ (−2, 3) (f) $y = c - \frac{1}{2}x$ (−4, 5)

(g) $y = c + 4x$ (−1, −6) (h) $\frac{2}{3}x + c = y$ (3, 4)

Finding the length of a straight line segment

Although lines are infinitely long, usually just a part of a line is considered. Any section of a line joining two points is called a **line segment**.

If you know the co-ordinates of the end points of a line segment you can use Pythagoras' theorem to calculate the length of the line segment.

FAST FORWARD

Pythagoras' theorem is covered in more detail in chapter 11. Remember though, that in any right-angled triangle the square on the hypotenuse is equal to the sum of the squares on the other two sides. We write this as $a^2 + b^2 = c^2$. ▶

Worked example 9

Find the distance between the points (1, 1) and (7, 9)

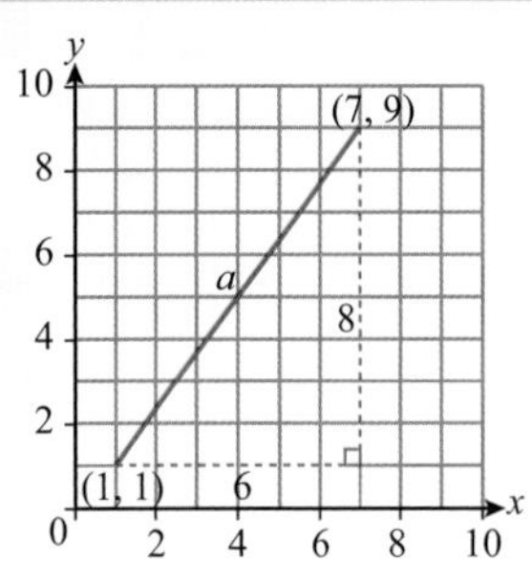

$a^2 = 8^2 + 6^2$ $a^2 = 64 + 36$ $a^2 = 100$ $\therefore a = \sqrt{100}$ $a = 10$ units	$a^2 = b^2 + c^2$ (Pythagoras' theorem) Work out each expression. Undo the square by taking the square root of both sides.

Worked example 10

Given that $A(3, 6)$ and $B(7, 3)$, find the length of AB.

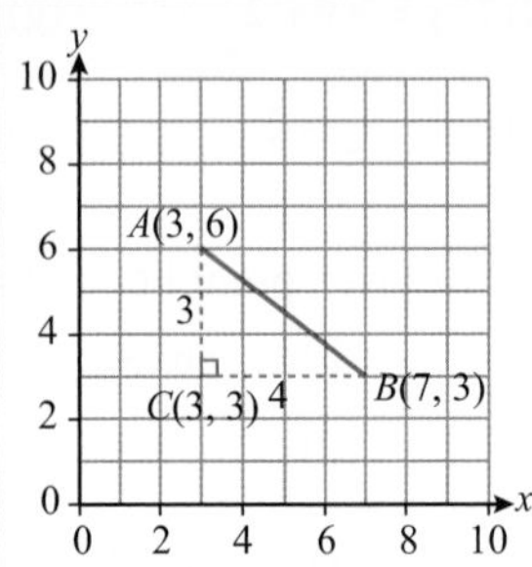

$AB^2 = AC^2 + CB^2$ $AB^2 = 3^2 + 4^2$ $= 9 + 16$ $= 25$ $\therefore AB = \sqrt{25} = 5$ units	$a^2 = b^2 + c^2$ (Pythagoras' theorem) Work out each expression.

Midpoints

It is possible to find the co-ordinates of the **midpoint** of the line segment (i.e. the point that is exactly halfway between the two original points).

Consider the following line segment and the points $A(3, 4)$ and $B(5, 10)$.

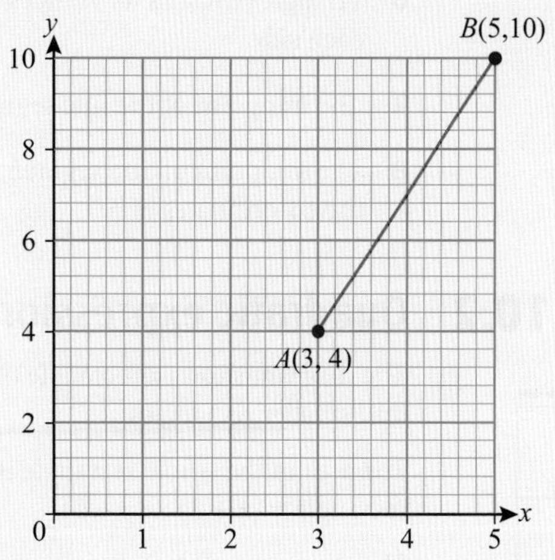

FAST FORWARD

In chapter 12 you will learn about the *mean* of two or more numbers. The midpoint uses the mean of the *x* co-ordinates and the mean of the *y* co-ordinates. ▶

If you add both *x*-co-ordinates and then divide by two you get $\frac{(3+5)}{2} = \frac{8}{2} = 4$.

If you add both *y*-co-ordinates and then divide by two you get $\frac{(4+10)}{2} = \frac{14}{2} = 7$.

This gives a new point with co-ordinates (4, 7). This point is exactly half way between *A* and *B*.

Exercise 10.7

REWIND

Check that you remember how to deal with negative numbers when adding. ◀

1 Find the length and the co-ordinates of the midpoint of the line segment joining each pair of points.

(a) (3, 6) and (9, 12) **(b)** (4, 10) and (2, 6) **(c)** (8, 3) and (4, 7)
(d) (5, 8) and (4, 11) **(e)** (4, 7) and (1, 3) **(f)** (12, 3) and (11, 4)
(g) (−1, 2) and (3, 5) **(h)** (4, −1) and (5, 5) **(i)** (−2, −4) and (−3, 7)

2 Use the graph to find the length and the midpoint of each line segment.

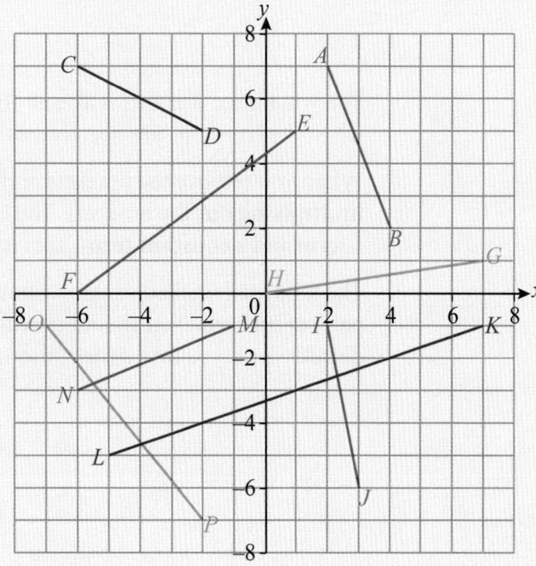

3 Find the distance from the origin to point (–3, –5).

4 Which of the points $A(5, 6)$ or $B(5, 3)$ is closer to point $C(-3, 2)$?

5 Which is further from the origin, $A(4, 2)$ or $B(-3, -4)$?

6 Triangle ABC has its vertices at points $A(0, 0)$, $B(4, -5)$ and $C(-3, -3)$. Find the length of each side.

7 The midpoint of the line segment joining $(10, a)$ and $(4, 3)$ is $(7, 5)$. What is the value of a?

8 The midpoint of line segment DE is $(-4, 3)$. If point D has the co-ordinates $(-2, 8)$, what are the co-ordinates of E?

10.2 Quadratic expressions

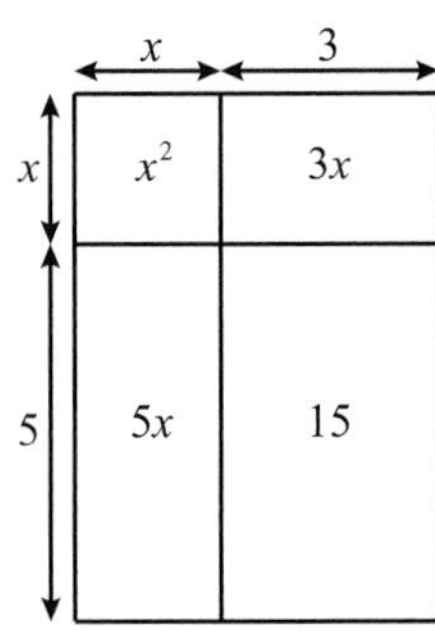

The diagram shows a rectangle of length $(x + 3)$ cm and width $(x + 5)$ cm that has been divided into smaller rectangles.

The area of the whole rectangle is equal to the sum of the smaller areas, so the area of whole rectangle = $(x + 3) \times (x + 5)$.

The sum of smaller rectangle areas: $x^2 + 3x + 5x + 15 = x^2 + 8x + 15$.

This means that $(x + 3) \times (x + 5) = x^2 + 8x + 15$ and this is true for *all* values of x.

Notice what happens if you multiply every term in the second bracket by every term in the first:

$(x+3)(x+5)$ → x^2 $(x+3)(x+5)$ → $5x$ $(x+3)(x+5)$ → $3x$ $(x+3)(x+5)$ → 15

Notice that the four terms in boxes are exactly the same as the four smaller areas that were calculated before.

Another way to show this calculation is to use a grid:

	x	3
x	x^2	$3x$
5	$5x$	15

You will notice that this is almost the same as the areas method above but it can also be used when the constants are negative, as you will see in the worked examples shortly.

When you remove the brackets and re-write the algebraic expression you are **expanding** or **multiplying out** the brackets. The resulting algebraic expression contains an x^2 term, an x term and a **constant term**. This is called a **quadratic expression.**

The following worked example shows these two methods and a third method for expanding pairs of brackets. You should try each method when working through the next exercise and decide which you find easiest, though you will begin to notice that they are all, in fact, the same.

Worked example 11

Expand and simplify:

(a) $(x + 2)(x + 9)$ **(b)** $(x - 7)(x + 6)$ **(c)** $(2x - 1)(x + 9)$

(a)

$(x + 2)(x + 9)$

$x^2 + 9x + 2x + 18$
$= x^2 + 11x + 18$

In this version of the method you will notice that the arrows have not been included and the multiplication 'arcs' have been arranged so that they are symmetrical and easier to remember.

You need to choose which method works best for you but ensure that you show all the appropriate stages of working clearly.

(b)

	x	-7
x	x^2	$-7x$
$+6$	$6x$	-42

$x^2 - 7x + 6x - 42$
$= x^2 - x - 42$

The grid method with a negative value.

(c) $(2x - 1)(x + 9)$

Firsts: $2x \times x = 2x^2$
Outsides: $2x \times 9 = 18x$
Insides: $-1 \times x = -x$
Lasts: $-1 \times 9 = -9$

$2x^2 + 18x - x - 9$
$= x^2 + 17x - 9$

A third method that you can remember using the mnemonic '**FOIL**' which stands for **F**irst, **O**utside, **I**nside, **L**ast. This means that you multiply the first term in each bracket together then the 'outside' pair together (i.e. the first term and last term), the 'inside' pair together (i.e. the second term and third term) and the 'last' pair together (i.e. the second term in each bracket).

Exercise 10.8

REWIND

You will need to remember how to multiply fractions. This was covered in chapter 5. ◀

1 Expand and simplify each of the following.

(a) $(x + 3)(x + 1)$ **(b)** $(x + 6)(x + 4)$ **(c)** $(x + 9)(x + 10)$
(d) $(x + 3)(x + 12)$ **(e)** $(x + 1)(x + 1)$ **(f)** $(x + 5)(x + 4)$
(g) $(x + 4)(x - 7)$ **(h)** $(x - 3)(x + 8)$ **(i)** $(x - 1)(x + 1)$
(j) $(x - 9)(x + 8)$ **(k)** $(x - 6)(x - 7)$ **(l)** $(x - 13)(x + 4)$
(m) $(y + 3)(y - 14)$ **(n)** $(z + 8)(z - 8)$ **(o)** $(t + 17)(t - 4)$
(p) $(h - 3)(h - 3)$ **(q)** $(g - \frac{1}{2})(g + 4)$ **(r)** $(d + \frac{3}{2})(d - \frac{3}{4})$

2 Find the following products.

(a) $(4 - x)(3 - x)$ **(b)** $(3 - 2x)(1 + 3x)$ **(c)** $(3m - 7)(2m - 1)$
(d) $(2x + 1)(3 - 4x)$ **(e)** $(4a - 2b)(2a + b)$ **(f)** $(2m - n)(-3n - 4m)$
(g) $\left(x + \frac{1}{2}\right)\left(x + \frac{1}{4}\right)$ **(h)** $\left(2x + \frac{1}{3}\right)\left(x - \frac{1}{2}\right)$ **(i)** $(2x^2 - 4y)(y - x^2)$
(j) $(7 - 9b)(4b + 6)$ **(k)** $(x + y)(2y^2 - 4x^3)$ **(l)** $(3x - 3)(5 + 2x)$

3 Expand and simplify each of the following.

(a) $(2x + 3)(x + 3)$ **(b)** $(3y + 7)(y + 1)$ **(c)** $(7z + 1)(z + 2)$
(d) $(t + 5)(4t - 3)$ **(e)** $(2w - 7)(w - 8)$ **(f)** $(4g - 1)(4g + 1)$
(g) $(8x - 1)(9x + 4)$ **(h)** $(20c - 3)(18c - 4)$ **(i)** $(2m - 4)(3 - m)$

REWIND

Refer to chapter 2 to remind you how to multiply different powers of the same number together. ◀

4 Expand and simplify each of the following.

(a) $(3x^2+1)(2x+3)$ (b) $(5x^2-1)(3x^2-3)$ (c) $(3x^2-y)(2x+3y)$

Squaring a binomial

$(x+y)^2$ means $(x+y)(x+y)$

To find the product, you can use the method you learned earlier.

$(x+y)(x+y) = x^2 + xy + xy + y^2 = x^2 + 2xy + y^2$

However, if you think about this, you should be able to solve these kinds of expansions by inspection. Look at the answer. Can you see that:

- the first term is the square of the first term (x^2)
- the middle term is twice the product of the middle terms ($2xy$)
- the last term is the square of the last term (y^2)?

Exercise 10.9

1 Find the square of each binomial. Try to do this by inspection first and then check your answers.

(a) $(x-y)^2$ (b) $(a+b)^2$ (c) $(2x+3y)^2$ (d) $(3x-2y)^2$

(e) $(x+2y)^2$ (f) $(y-4x^2)^2$ (g) $(x^2-y^2)^2$ (h) $(2+y^3)^2$

(i) $(-2x-4y^2)^2$ (j) $\left(\frac{1}{2x}-\frac{1}{4y}\right)^2$ (k) $\left(\frac{3x}{4}-\frac{y}{2}\right)^2$ (l) $\left(a+\frac{1}{2}b\right)^2$

(m) $(-ab-c^4)^2$ (n) $(3x^2y-1)^2$ (o) $\left(\frac{2x}{3}+4y\right)^2$ (p) $[-(x-3)]^2$

2 Simplify.

(a) $(x-2)^2-(x-4)^2$ (b) $(x+2)(x-2)-(3-x)(5+x)$

(c) $(y+2x)^2+(2x-y)(-y+2x)$ (d) $\frac{1}{2}(3x-2)\left(\frac{x}{3}+2\right)$

(e) $3(x+2)(2x+0.6)$ (f) $(\sqrt{2x}-y)(\sqrt{2x}+y)-(4x-y)^2$

(g) $(x+4)(x-5)-2(x-1)^2$ (h) $(2x-y)^2+(x-2y)(x+2y)-(x+4y)^2$

(i) $-2x(x+1)^2-(x-5)(-3x)$ (j) $(3+2x)^2-5(5x+2)$

3 Evaluate each expression when $x = 4$.

(a) $(x+7)(x-7)-x^2$ (b) $x^2-(x-3)(x+3)$

(c) $(3+2x)^2-(2x+3)(2x-3)$ (d) $(x+2)^2$

(e) $(x^2+3)(x-4)$ (f) $(2x+3)^2-4(x+1)(2-3x)$

Factorising quadratic expressions

Look again at the expansion of $(x+2)(x+9)$, which gave $x^2+11x+18$:

$$(x+2)(x+9) = x^2 + 11x + 18$$

$2+9=11$

$2\times 9=18$

Here the two numbers add to give the coefficient of x in the final expression and the two numbers multiply to give the constant term.

This works whenever there is just one x in each bracket.

Worked example 12

Expand and simplify: **(a)** $(x + 6)(x + 12)$ **(b)** $(x + 4)(x - 13)$

(a)	$(x + 6)(x + 12) = x^2 + 18x + 72$	$6 + 12 = 18$ and $6 \times 12 = 72$ so this gives $18x$ and 72.
(b)	$(x + 4)(x - 13) = x^2 - 9x - 52$	$4 + -13 = -9$ and $4 \times -13 = -52$ so this gives $-9x$ and -52.

If you use the method in worked example 11 and work backwards you can see how to put a quadratic expression back into brackets. Note that the coefficient of x^2 in the quadratic expression must be 1 for this to work.

REWIND

1×72 and 6×12 are the factor pairs of 72. You learned about factor pairs in chapter 1. ◀

Consider the expression $x^2 + 18x + 72$ and suppose that you want to write it in the form $(x + a)(x + b)$.

From the worked example you know that $a + b = 18$ and $a \times b = 72$.

Now $72 = 1 \times 72$ but these two numbers don't add up to give 18.

However, $72 = 6 \times 12$ and $6 + 12 = 18$.

So, $x^2 + 18x + 72 = (x + 6)(x + 12)$.

The process of putting a quadratic expression *back* into brackets like this is called **factorisation**.

Worked example 13

Factorise completely:

(a) $x^2 + 7x + 12$ **(b)** $x^2 - 6x - 16$ **(c)** $x^2 - 8x + 15$

List the factor pairs of 12.
(If you spot which pair of numbers works straight away then you don't need to write out all the other factor pairs.)

(a)		You need two numbers that multiply to give 12 and add to give 7.
	$12 = 1 \times 12$	These don't add to give 7.
	$12 = 2 \times 6$	These don't add to give 7.
	$12 = 3 \times 4$ and $3 + 4 = 7$	These multiply to give 12 and add to give 7.
	So, $x^2 + 7x + 12 = (x + 3)(x + 4)$	
(b)	$-8 \times 2 = -16$ and $-8 + 2 = -6$ So, $x^2 - 6x - 16 = (x - 8)(x + 2)$.	You need two numbers that multiply to give -16 and add to give -6. Since they multiply to give a negative answer, one of the numbers must be negative and the other must be positive. (Since they add to give a negative, the larger of the two numbers must be negative.)
(c)	$-5 \times -3 = 15$ and $-5 + -3 = -8$ So, $x^2 - 8x + 15 = (x - 3)(x - 5)$.	You need two numbers that multiply to give 15 and add to give -8. Since they multiply to give a positive value but add to give a negative then both must be negative.

Exercise 10.10

When looking for your pair of integers, think about the factors of the constant term first. Then choose the pair which adds up to the x term in the right way.

1 Factorise each of the following.

(a) $x^2 + 14x + 24$ **(b)** $x^2 + 3x + 2$ **(c)** $x^2 + 7x + 12$
(d) $x^2 + 12x + 35$ **(e)** $x^2 + 12 + 27$ **(f)** $x^2 + 7x + 6$
(g) $x^2 + 11x + 30$ **(h)** $x^2 + 10x + 16$ **(i)** $x^2 + 11x + 10$
(j) $x^2 + 8x + 7$ **(k)** $x^2 + 24x + 80$ **(l)** $x^2 + 13x + 42$

2 Factorise each of the following.

(a) $x^2 - 8x + 12$ **(b)** $x^2 - 9x + 20$ **(c)** $x^2 - 7x + 12$
(d) $x^2 - 6x + 8$ **(e)** $x^2 - 12x + 32$ **(f)** $x^2 - 14x + 49$
(g) $x^2 - 8x - 20$ **(h)** $x^2 - 7x - 18$ **(i)** $x^2 - 4x - 32$
(k) $x^2 + x - 6$ **(l)** $x^2 + 8x - 33$ **(m)** $x^2 + 10x - 24$

3 Factorise each of the following.

(a) $y^2 + 7y - 170$ **(b)** $p^2 + 8p - 84$ **(c)** $w^2 - 24w + 144$
(d) $t^2 + 16t - 36$ **(e)** $v^2 + 20v + 75$ **(f)** $x^2 - 100$

Difference between two squares

The very last question in the previous exercise was a special kind of quadratic. To factorise $x^2 - 100$ you must notice that $x^2 - 100 = x^2 + 0x - 100$.

Now, proceeding as in worked example 12:

$10 \times -10 = -100$ and $-10 + 10 = 0$ so, $x^2 + 0x - 100 = (x - 10)(x + 10)$.

Now think about a more general case in which you try to factorise $x^2 - a^2$. Notice that $x^2 - a^2 = x^2 + 0x - a^2$.

Since $a \times -a = -a$ and $a + -a = 0$, this leads to: $\boxed{x^2 - a^2 = (x - a)(x + a).}$

You must remember this special case. This kind of expression is called a **difference between two squares.**

Worked example 14

Factorise the following using the difference between two squares:

(a) $x^2 - 49$ **(b)** $x^2 - \frac{1}{4}$ **(c)** $16y^2 - 25w^2$

(a) $49 = 7^2$ $x^2 - 49 = x^2 - 7^2$ $= (x - 7)(x + 7)$	Use the formula for the difference between two squares: $x^2 - a^2 = (x - a)(x + a)$. You know that $\sqrt{49} = 7$ so you can write 49 as 7^2. This gives you a^2. Substitute 7^2 into the formula.
(b) $\left(\frac{1}{2}\right)^2 = \frac{1}{4}$ $x^2 - \frac{1}{4} = x^2 - \left(\frac{1}{2}\right)^2$ $= (x - \frac{1}{2})(x + \frac{1}{2})$	$\sqrt{\frac{1}{4}}$ is $\frac{1}{2}$ so you can rewrite $\frac{1}{4}$ as $\left(\frac{1}{2}\right)^2$ and substitute it into the formula for the difference between two squares.

(c) $(4y)^2 = 4y \times 4y = 16y^2$	The $\sqrt{16y^2} = (4y)^2$.
and	
$(5w)^2 = 5w \times 5w = 25w^2$	$\sqrt{25w^2} = (5w)^2$
$16y^2 - 25w^2 = (4y)^2 - (5w)^2$ $= (4y - 5w)(4y + 5w)$	Substitute in $(4y)^2$ and $(5w)^2$.

Exercise 10.11

From question (l) you should notice that the numbers given are not square. Try taking a common factor out first.

1 Factorise each of the following.

(a) $x^2 - 36$ (b) $p^2 - 81$ (c) $w^2 - 16$ (d) $q^2 - 9$
(e) $k^2 - 400$ (f) $t^2 - 121$ (g) $x^2 - y^2$ (h) $81h^2 - 16g^2$
(i) $16p^2 - 36q^2$ (j) $144s^2 - c^2$ (k) $64h^2 - 49g^2$ (l) $27x^2 - 48y^2$
(m) $200q^2 - 98p^2$ (n) $20d^2 - 125e^2$ (o) $x^4 - y^4$ (p) $xy^2 - x^3$

2 Factorise and simplify $36^2 - 35^2$ without using a calculator.

3 Factorise and simplify $(6\frac{1}{4})^2 - (5\frac{3}{4})^2$ without using a calculator.

Using factors to solve quadratic equations

You can now use the factorisation method to solve some **quadratic equations**. A quadratic equation is an equation of the form $ax^2 + bx + c = 0$. The method is illustrated in the following worked examples.

Worked example 15

Solve each of the following equations for x.

(a) $x^2 - 3x = 0$ **(b)** $x^2 - 7x + 12 = 0$ **(c)** $x^2 + 6x - 4 = 12$

(d) $x^2 - 8x + 16 = 0$

(a) Notice that both terms of the left-hand side are multiples of x so you can use common factorisation.

$x^2 - 3x = 0$
$x(x - 3) = 0$

Now the key point:

If two or more quantities multiply to give zero, then at least one of the quantities must be zero.
So either $x = 0$ or $x - 3 = 0 \Rightarrow x = 3$.
Check: $0^2 - 3 \times 0 = 0$ (this works).
$3^2 - 3 \times 3 = 9 - 9 = 0$ (this also works).
In fact both $x = 0$ and $x = 3$ are solutions.

(b) Use the factorisation method of worked example 12 on the left-hand side of the equation.

$x^2 - 7x + 12 = 0$
$(x - 4)(x - 3) = 0$

Therefore either $x - 4 = 0 \Rightarrow x = 4$
or $x - 3 = 0 \Rightarrow x = 3$.
Again, there are two possible values of x.

When solving quadratic equations they should be rearranged so that a zero appears on one side, i.e. so that they are in the form $ax^2 + bx + c = 0$

(c) $x^2 + 6x - 4 = 12$

$\Rightarrow x^2 + 6x - 16 = 0$ (subtract 12 from both sides)

Factorising, you get $(x + 8)(x - 2) = 0$

So either $x + 8 = 0 \Rightarrow x = -8$

or $x - 2 = 0 \Rightarrow x = 2$.

There are still two solutions here, but they are identical.

(d) Factorising, $x^2 - 8x + 16 = 0$

$(x - 4)(x - 4) = 0$

So either $x - 4 = 0 \Rightarrow x = 4$

or $x - 4 = 0 \Rightarrow x = 4$

Of course these are both the same thing, so the only solution is $x = 4$.

Exercise 10.12

1 Solve the following equations by factorisation.

(a) $x^2 - 9x = 0$	**(b)** $x^2 + 7x = 0$	**(c)** $x^2 - 21x = 0$
(d) $x^2 - 9x + 20 = 0$	**(e)** $x^2 + 8x + 7 = 0$	**(f)** $x^2 + x - 6 = 0$
(g) $x^2 + 3x + 2 = 0$	**(h)** $x^2 + 11x + 10 = 0$	**(i)** $x^2 - 7x + 12 = 0$
(j) $x^2 - 8x + 12 = 0$	**(k)** $x^2 - 100 = 0$	**(l)** $t^2 + 16t - 36 = 0$
(m) $y^2 + 7y - 170 = 0$	**(n)** $p^2 + 8p - 84 = 0$	**(o)** $w^2 - 24w + 144 = 0$

Summary

Do you know the following?

- The equation of a line tells you how the x- and y-co-ordinates are related for all points that sit on the line.
- The gradient of a line is a measure of its steepness.
- The x- and y-intercepts are where the line crosses the x- and y-axes respectively.
- The value of m in $y = mx + c$ is the gradient of the line.
- The value of c in $y = mx + c$ is the y-intercept.
- The x-intercept can be found by substituting $y = 0$ and solving for x.
- The y-intercept can be found by substituting $x = 0$ and solving for y.
- Two lines with the same gradient are parallel.
- The gradients of two perpendicular lines will multiply to give -1.
- There is more than one way to expand brackets.
- Some quadratic expressions can be factorised to solve quadratic equations.
- Quadratic equations usually have two solutions, though these solutions may be equal to one another.

Are you able to …?

- draw a line from its equation by drawing a table and plotting points
- find the gradient, x-intercept and y-intercept from the equation of a line
- calculate the gradient of a line from its graph
- find the equation of a line if you know its gradient and y-intercept
- find the equation of a vertical or horizontal line
- calculate the gradient of a line from the co-ordinates of two points on the line
- find the length of a line segment and the co-ordinates of its midpoint
- expand double brackets
- factorise a quadratic expression
- factorise an expression that is the difference between two squares
- solve a quadratic equation by factorising.

Examination practice

Exam-style questions

1 Expand and simplify each of the following.

(a) $(x + 2)(x + 18)$ **(b)** $(2x + 3)(2x - 3)$ **(c)** $(4y^2 - 3)(3y^2 + 1)$

2 **(a)** Factorise each of the following.

(i) $12x^2 - 6x$ **(ii)** $y^2 - 13y + 42$ **(iii)** $d^2 - 196$

(b) Solve the following equations.

(i) $12x^2 - 6x = 0$ **(ii)** $y^2 - 13y + 30 = -12$ **(iii)** $d^2 - 196 = 0$

Past paper questions

1

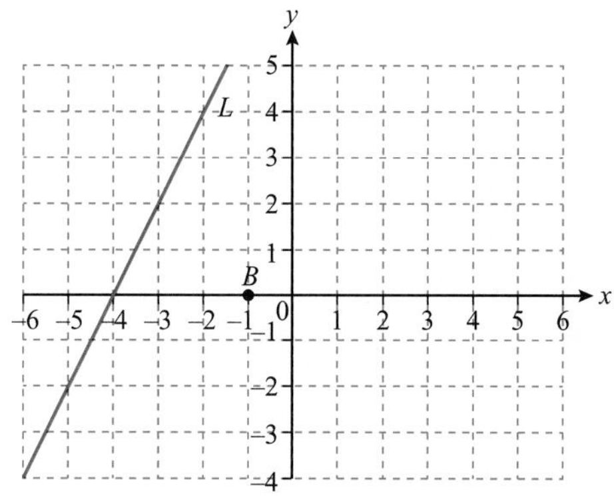

(a) On the grid mark the point (5, 1). Label it A. [1]

(b) Write down the co-ordinates of the point B. [1]

(c) Find the gradient of the line L. [2]

[Cambridge IGCSE Mathematics 0580 Paper 13 Q19 October/November 2012]

11 Pythagoras' theorem and similar shapes

Key words

- Right angle
- Hypotenuse
- Similar
- Corresponding sides
- Corresponding angles
- Scale factor of lengths
- Scale factor of volumes
- Scale factor of areas
- Congruent
- Included side
- Included angle

In this chapter you will learn how to:

- use Pythagoras' theorem to find unknown sides of a right-angled triangles
- learn how to use Pythagoras' theorem to solve problems
- decide whether or not triangles are mathematically similar
- use properties of similar triangles to solve problems

EXTENDED

- find unknown lengths in similar figures
- use the relationship between sides and areas of similar figures to find missing values
- recognise similar solids
- calculate the volume and surface area of similar solids

- decide whether or not triangles are congruent.

One man – Pythagoras of Samos – is usually credited with the discovery of the Pythagorean theorem, but there is evidence to suggest that an entire group of religious mathematicians would have been involved.

Right-angled triangles appear in many real-life situations, including architecture, engineering and nature. Many modern buildings have their sections manufactured off-site and so it is important that builders are able to accurately position the foundations on to which the parts will sit so that all the pieces will fit smoothly together.

Many properties of right-angled triangles were first used in ancient times and the study of these properties remains one of the most significant and important areas of Mathematics.

11.1 Pythagoras' theorem

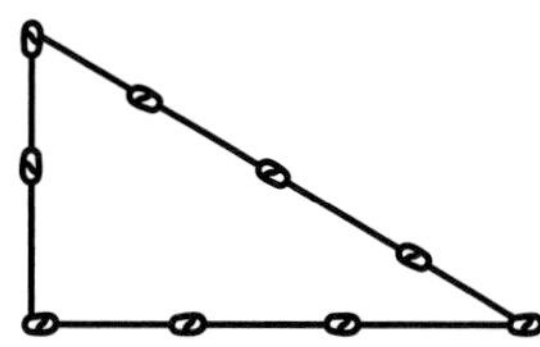

Centuries before the theorem of right-angled triangles was credited to Pythagoras, the Egyptians knew that if they tied knots in a rope at regular intervals, as in the diagram on the left, then they would produce a perfect **right angle**.

In some situations you may be given a right-angled triangle and then asked to calculate the length of an unknown side. You can do this by using Pythagoras' theorem if you know the lengths of the other two sides.

Learning the rules

Pythagoras' theorem describes the relationship between the sides of a right-angled triangle.

The longest side – the side that does not touch the right angle – is known as the **hypotenuse**.

c = hypotenuse

a

b

For this triangle, Pythagoras' theorem states that: $a^2 + b^2 = c^2$

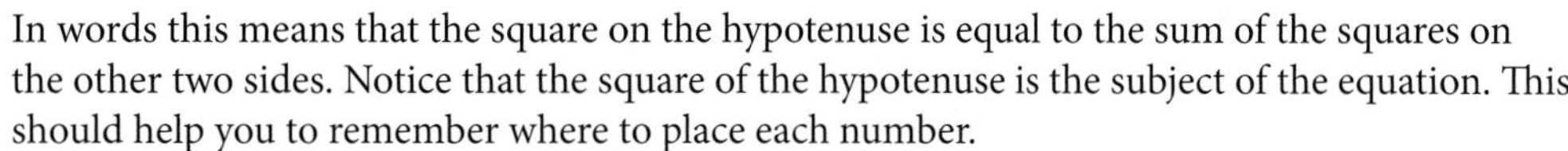

In words this means that the square on the hypotenuse is equal to the sum of the squares on the other two sides. Notice that the square of the hypotenuse is the subject of the equation. This should help you to remember where to place each number.

Tip

You will be expected to remember Pythagoras' theorem.

Worked example 1

Find the value of x in each of the following triangles, giving your answer to one decimal place.

(a)

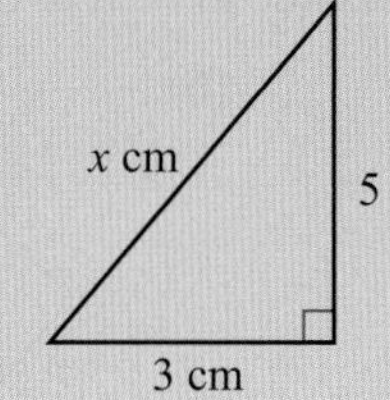

(b)

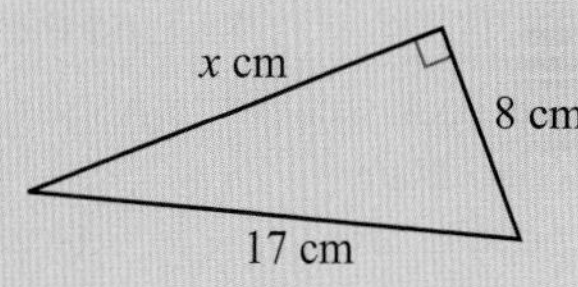

(a)

$a^2 + b^2 = c^2$

$3^2 + 5^2 = x^2$

$9 + 25 = x^2$

$\Rightarrow x^2 = 34$

$x = \sqrt{34} = 5.8309...$

$\approx 5.8\text{ cm (1dp)}$

Notice that the final answer needs to be rounded.

(b)

$a^2 + b^2 = c^2$

$8^2 + x^2 = 17^2$

$64 + x^2 = 289$

$x^2 = 289 - 64$

$x^2 = 225$

$x = \sqrt{225} = 15\text{ cm (1dp)}$

Notice that a shorter side needs to be found so, after writing the Pythagoras formula in the usual way, the formula has to be rearranged to make x^2 the subject.

Checking for right-angled triangles

You can also use the theorem to determine if a triangle is right-angled or not. Substitute the values of a, b and c of the triangle into the formula and check to see if it fits. If $a^2 + b^2$ does not equal c^2 then it is *not* a right-angled triangle.

Notice here the theorem is written as $c^2 = a^2 + b^2$; you will see it written like this or like $a^2 + b^2 = c^2$ in different places but it means the same thing.

The symbol '≠' means 'does not equal'.

Worked example 2

Use Pythagoras' theorem to decide whether or not the triangle shown below is right-angled.

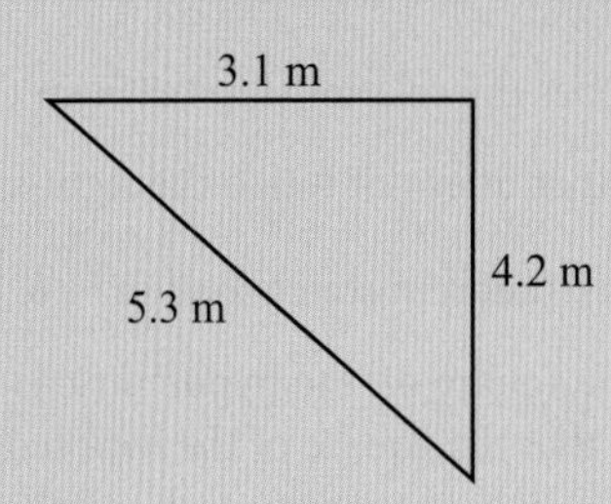

Check to see if Pythagoras' theorem is satisfied:

$c^2 = a^2 + b^2$

$3.1^2 + 4.2^2 = 27.25$

$5.3^2 = 28.09 \neq 27.25$

Pythagoras' theorem is not satisfied, so the triangle is not right-angled.

Exercise 11.1

For all the questions in this exercise, give your final answer correct to three significant figures where appropriate.

REWIND

You will notice that some of your answers need to be rounded. Many of the square roots you need to take produce irrational numbers. These were mentioned in chapter 9. ◀

1 Find the length of the hypotenuse in each of the following triangles.

(a) 6 cm, 8 cm, x cm

(b) 12 cm, 6 cm

(c) 1.2 cm, 2.3 cm, h cm

(d) 1.5 cm, 0.6 cm, p cm

(e)

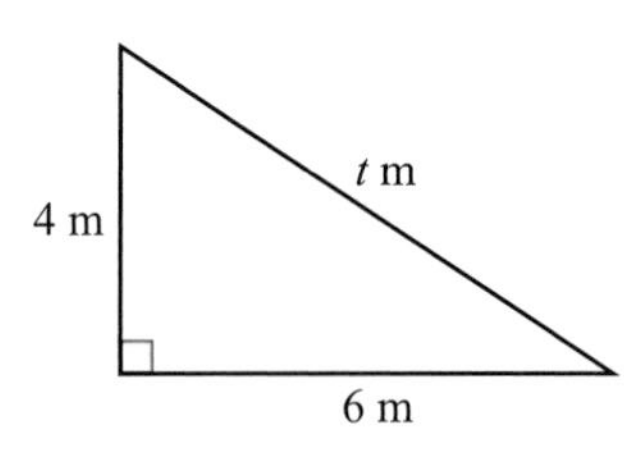

2 Find the values of the unknown lengths in each of the following triangles.

(a)

3 m
8 m
x m

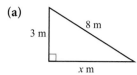

(b)

(c)

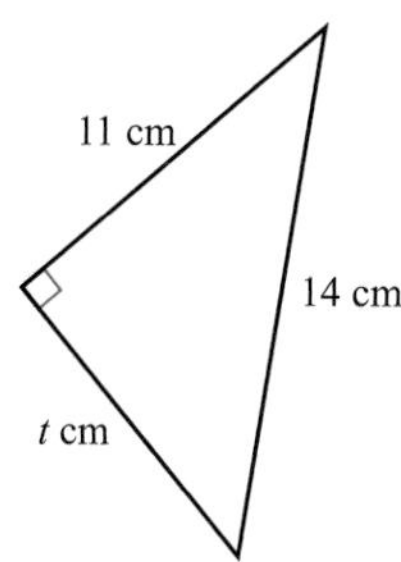

(d)

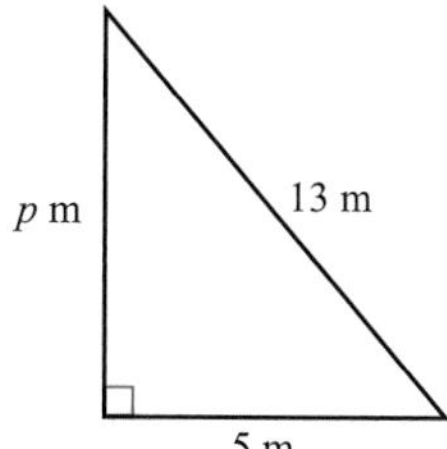

(e)

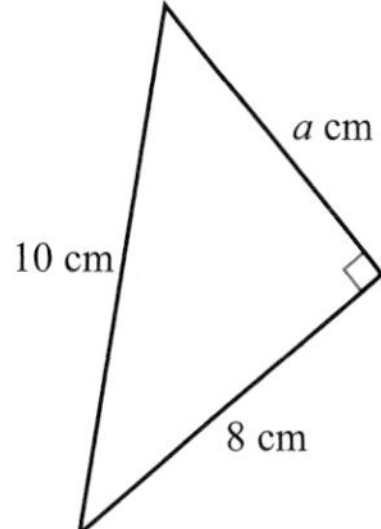

3 Find the values of the unknown lengths in each of the following triangles.

(a)

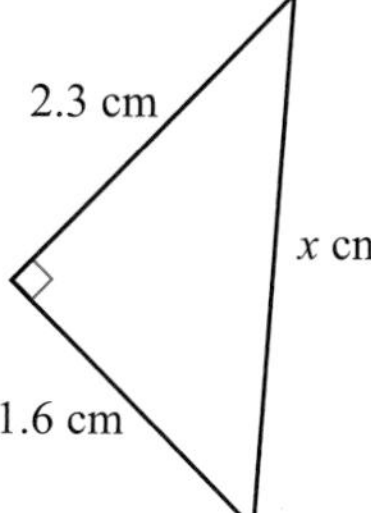

(b)

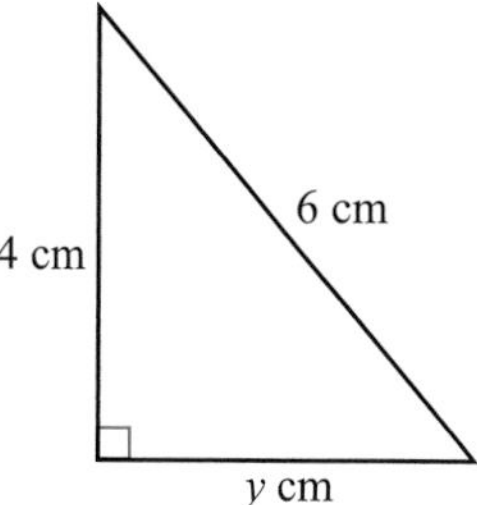

(c)

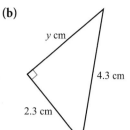

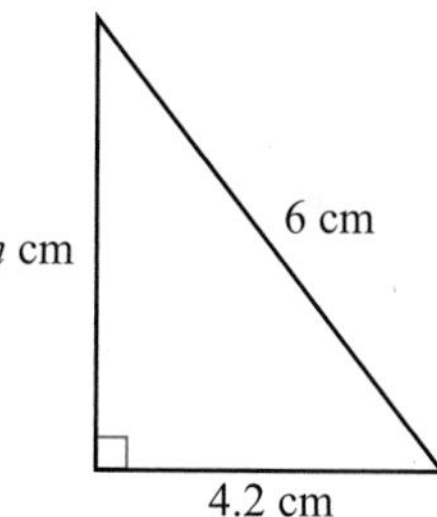

(d)

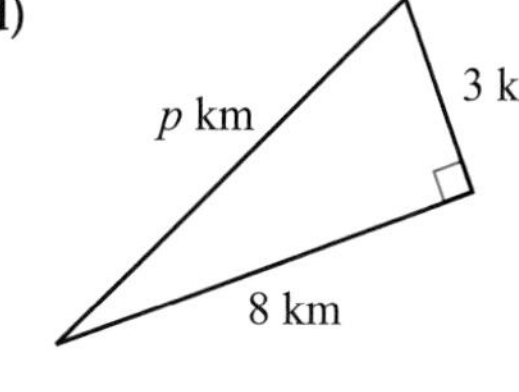

(e)

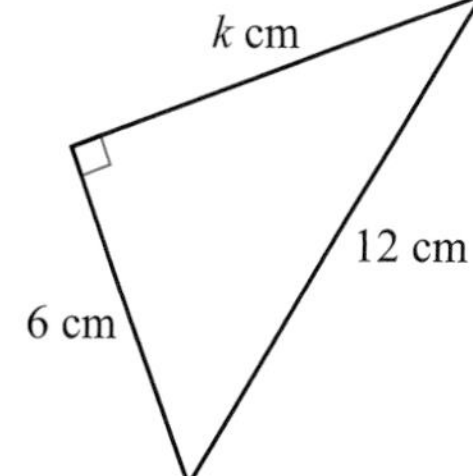

(f)

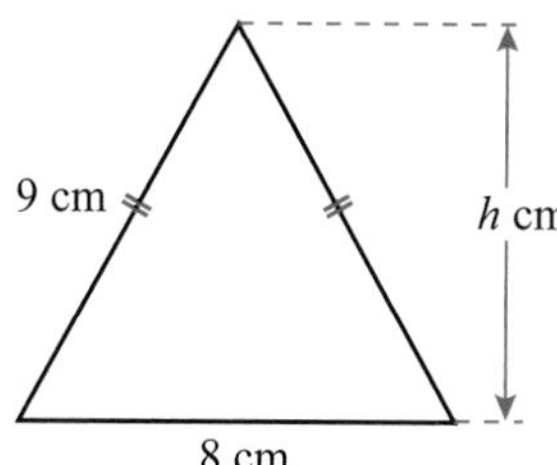

(g)

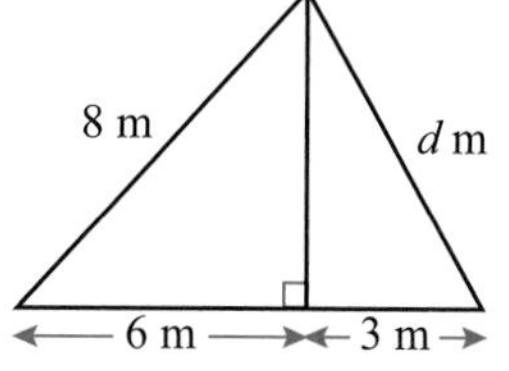

(h)

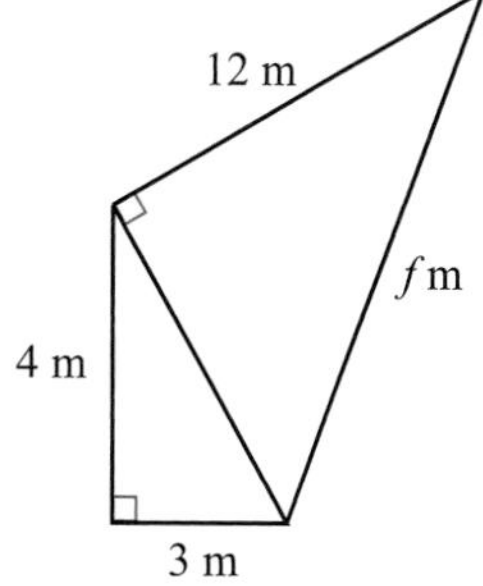

4 Use Pythagoras' theorem to help you decide which of the following triangles are right-angled.

(a)

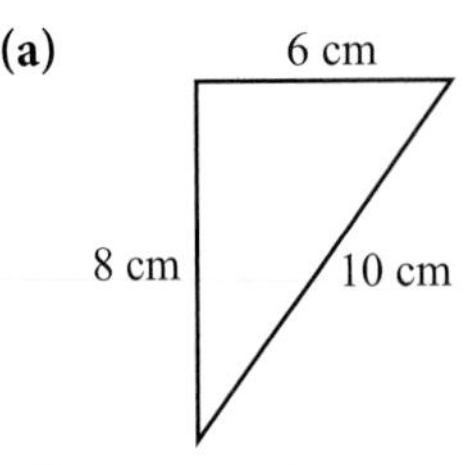

(b)

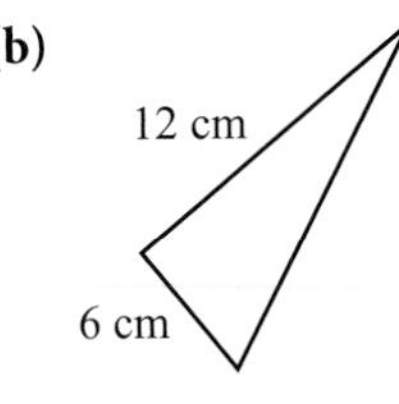

(c)

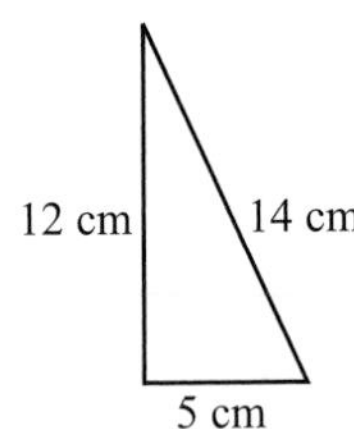

(d)

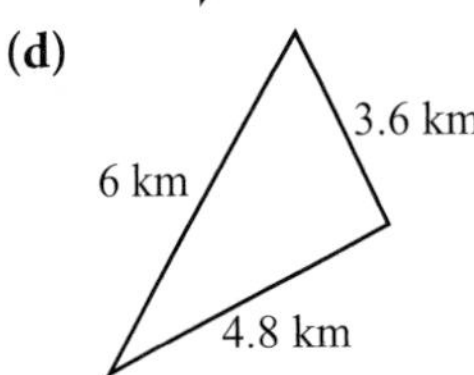

(e)

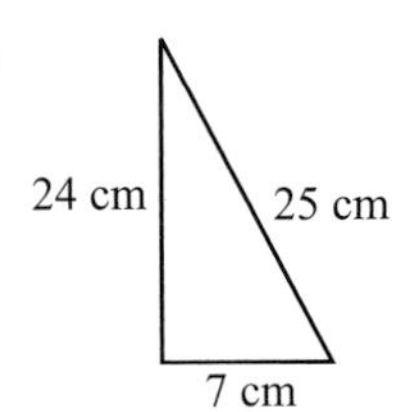

Applications of Pythagoras' theorem

This section looks at how Pythagoras' theorem can be used to solve real-life problems. In each case look carefully for right-angled triangles and draw them separately to make the working clear.

Worked example 3

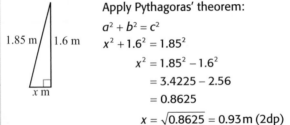

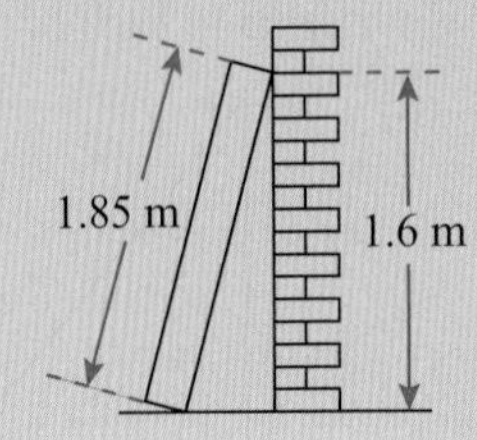

The diagram shows a bookcase that has fallen against a wall. If the bookcase is 1.85 m tall, and it now touches the wall at a point 1.6 m above the ground, calculate the distance of the foot of the bookcase from the wall. Give your answer to 2 decimal places.

It is usually useful to draw the triangle that you are going to use as part of your working.

Apply Pythagoras' theorem:

$a^2 + b^2 = c^2$

$x^2 + 1.6^2 = 1.85^2$

$x^2 = 1.85^2 - 1.6^2$

$= 3.4225 - 2.56$

$= 0.8625$

$x = \sqrt{0.8625} = 0.93\text{m (2dp)}$

Think what triangle the situation would make and then draw it. Label each side and substitute the correct sides into the formula.

Worked example 4

Find the distance between the points $A(3, 5)$ and $B(-3, 7)$.

It can be helpful to draw diagrams when you are given co-ordinates.

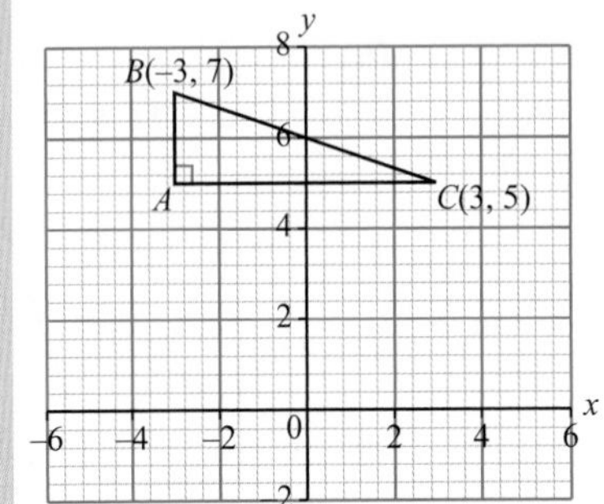

$AB = 7 - 5 = 2$ units — Difference between y-co-ordinates.

$AC = 3 - -3 = 6$ units — Difference between x-co-ordinates.

$BC^2 = 2^2 + 6^2$ — Apply Pythagoras' theorem.

$= 4 + 36$

$= 40$

So $BC = \sqrt{40}$

$= 6.32$ units (3sf)

Exercise 11.2

1 The size of a television screen is its longest diagonal. The diagram shows the length and breadth of a television set. Find the distance AB.

A B 21.6 inches 48.6 inches

2 The diagram shows a ladder that is leaning against a wall. Find the length of the ladder.

3 m 0.4 m

3 Sarah stands at the corner of a rectangular field. If the field measures 180 m by 210 m, how far would Sarah need to walk to reach the opposite corner in a straight line?

4 The diagram shows the side view of a shed. Calculate the height of the shed.

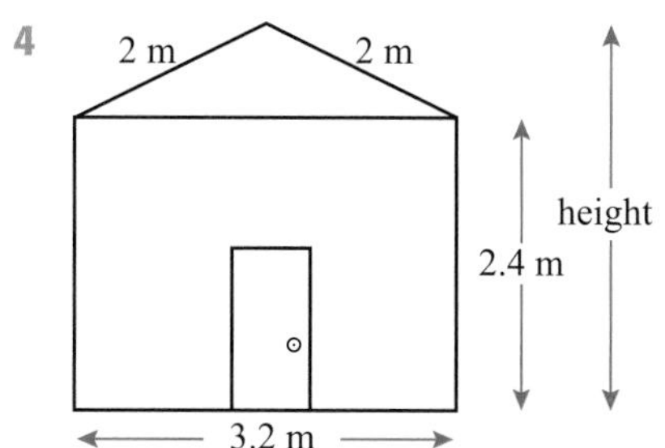

5 The diagram shows a bridge that can be lifted to allow ships to pass below. What is the distance AB when the bridge is lifted to the position shown in the diagram?
(Note that the bridge divides exactly in half when it lifts open.)

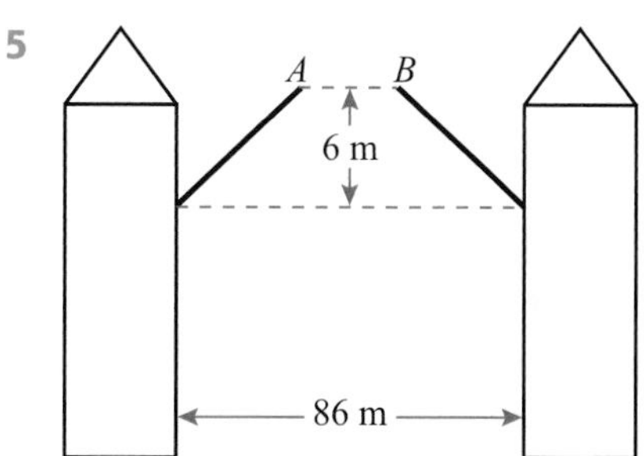

6 Find the distance between the points A and B with co-ordinates:

(a) $A(3, 2)$ $B(5, 7)$
(b) $A(5, 8)$ $B(6, 11)$
(c) $A(-3, 1)$ $B(4, 8)$
(d) $A(-2, -3)$ $B(-7, 6)$

7 The diagonals of a square are 15 cm. Find the perimeter of the square.

11.2 Understanding similar triangles

Two mathematically **similar** objects have exactly the same shape and proportions, but may be different in size.

When one of the shapes is enlarged to produce the second shape, each part of the original will *correspond* to a particular part of the new shape. For triangles, **corresponding sides** join the same angles.

All of the following are true for similar triangles:

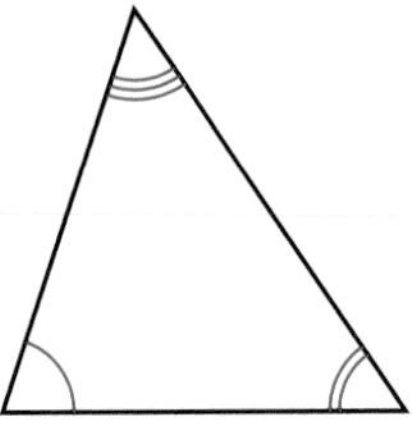
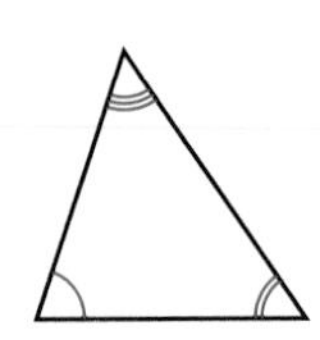

Corresponding angles are equal.

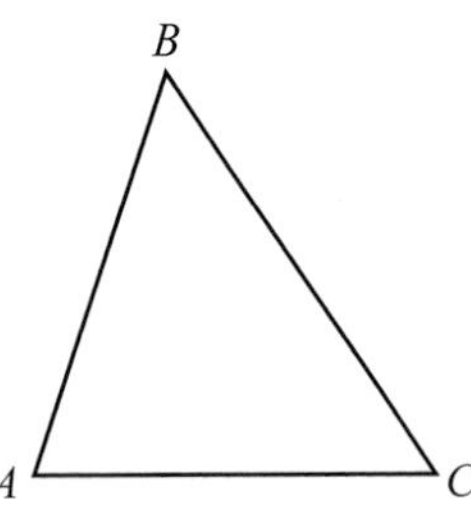

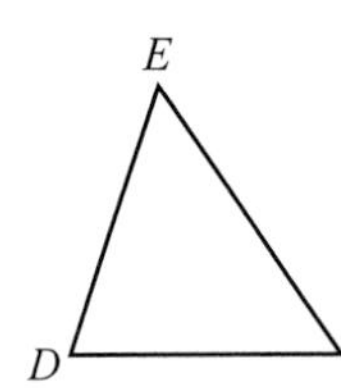

'Internal' ratios of sides are the same for both triangles. For example:

$\frac{AB}{BC} = \frac{DE}{EF}$

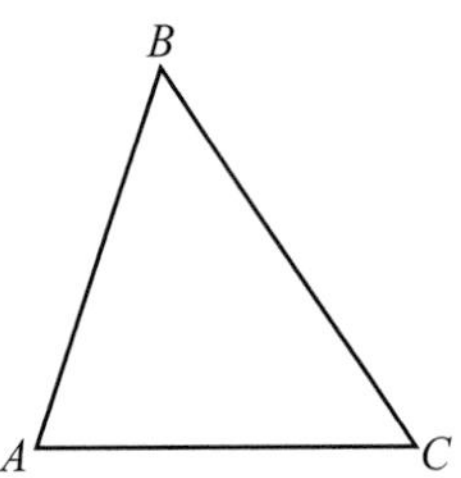

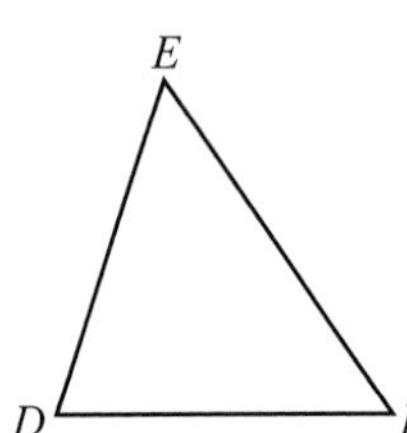

Ratios of corresponding sides are equal:

$\frac{AB}{DE} = \frac{BC}{EF} = \frac{AC}{DF}$

If any of these things are true about two triangles, then all of them will be true for both triangles.

Worked example 5

Explain why the two triangles shown in the diagram are similar and work out x and y.

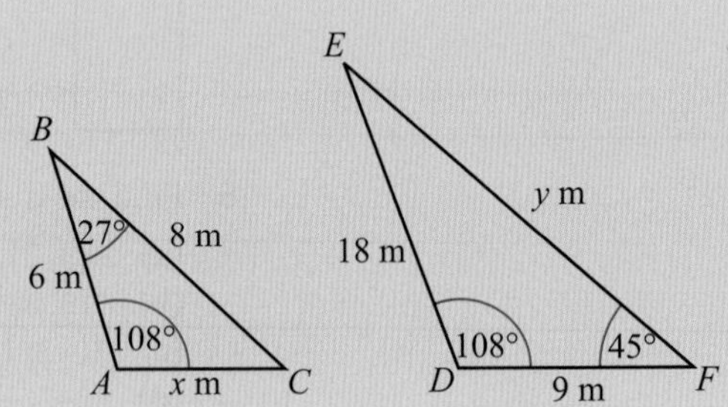

$A\hat{C}B = 180° - 27° - 108° = 45°$
$F\hat{E}D = 180° - 45° - 108° = 27°$

So both triangles have exactly the same three angles and are, therefore, similar.

Since the triangles are similar: $\frac{DE}{AB} = \frac{EF}{BC} = \frac{DF}{AC}$

So : $\frac{y}{8} = \frac{18}{6} = 3 \Rightarrow y = 24\text{m}$

and: $\frac{9}{x} = \frac{18}{6} = 3 \Rightarrow x = 3\text{m}$

REWIND

You learned in chapter 2 that the angle sum in a triangle is always 180°. ◀

Worked example 6

The diagram shows a tent that has been attached to the ground using ropes *AB* and *CD*. *ABF* and *DCF* are straight lines. Find the height of the tent.

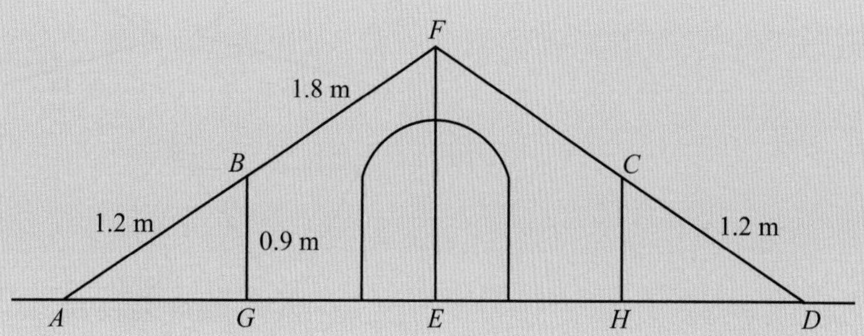

Consider triangles *ABG* and *AEF*:

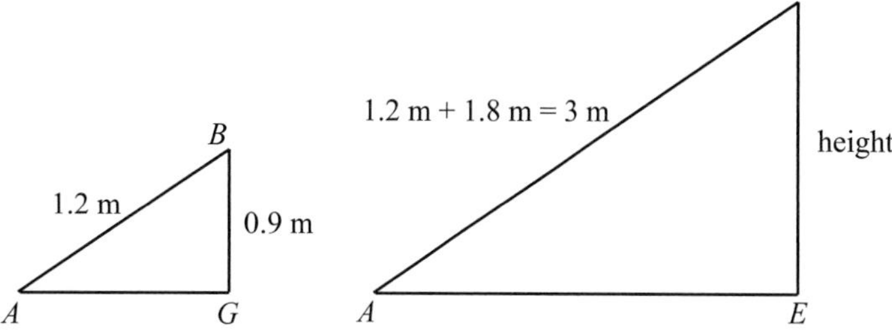

$B\hat{A}G = F\hat{A}E$ Common to both triangles.

$A\hat{G}B = A\hat{E}F = 90°$

$A\hat{B}G = A\hat{F}E$ *BG* and *FE* are both vertical, hence parallel lines. Angles correspond.

Therefore triangle *ABG* is similar to triangle *AEF*.

So: $\frac{\text{height}}{0.9} = \frac{3}{1.2} \Rightarrow \text{height} = \frac{0.9 \times 3}{1.2} = 2.25\,\text{m}$

Exercise 11.3

Always look for corresponding sides (sides that join the same angles).

1 For each of the following decide whether or not the triangles are similar in shape. Each decision should be explained fully.

(a)

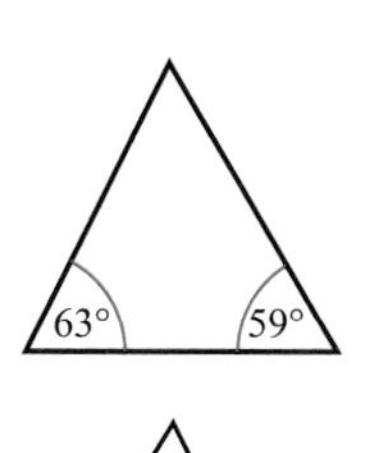

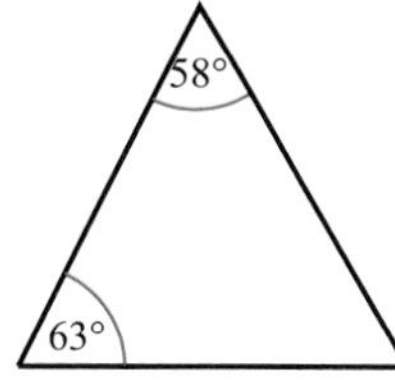

(b)

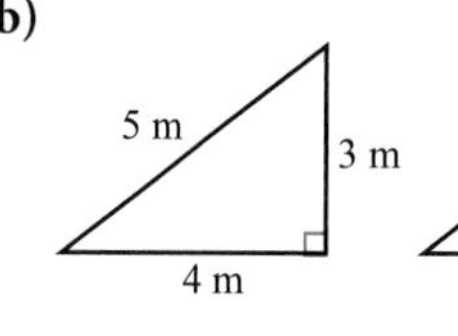

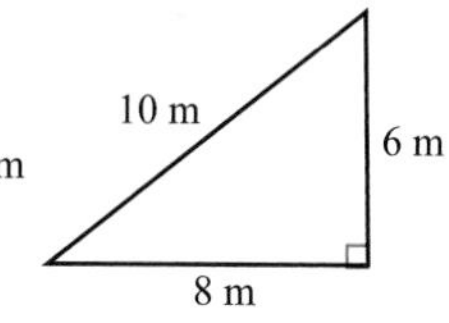

(c)

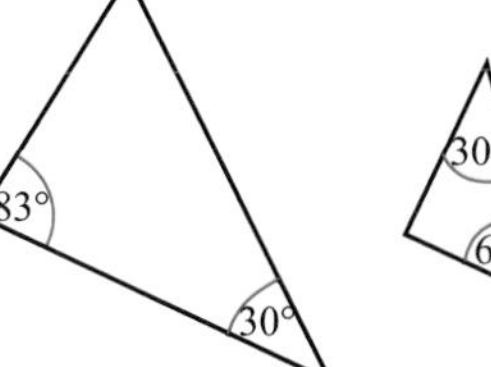

(d)

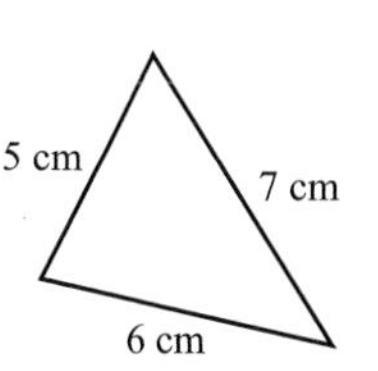

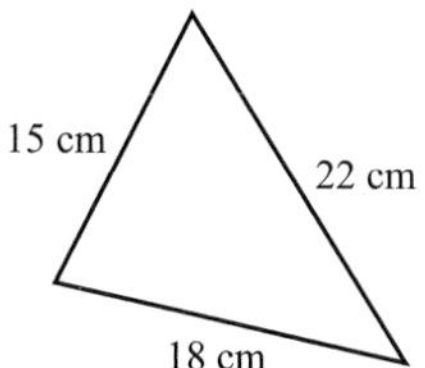

(e)

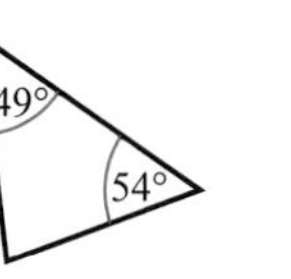

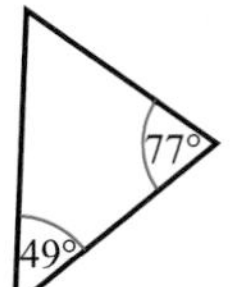

(f)

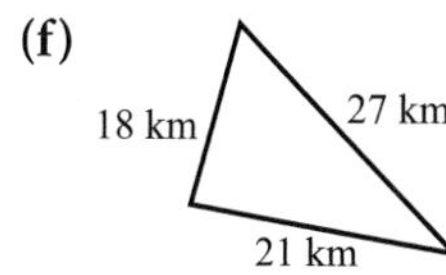

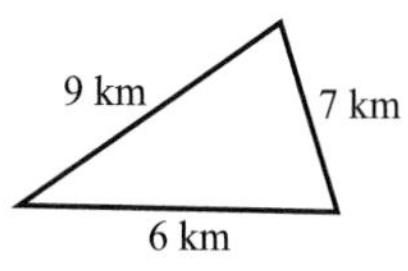

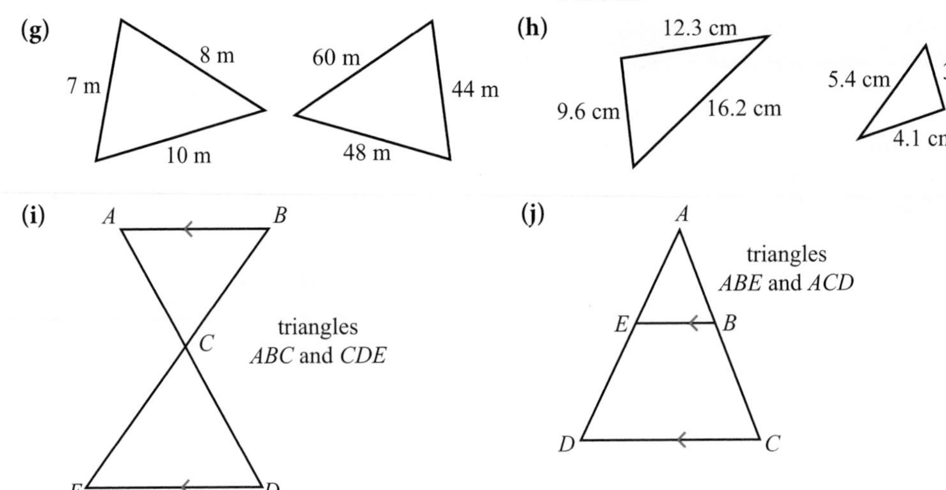

2 The pairs of triangles in this question are similar. Calculate the unknown (lettered) length in each case.

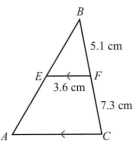

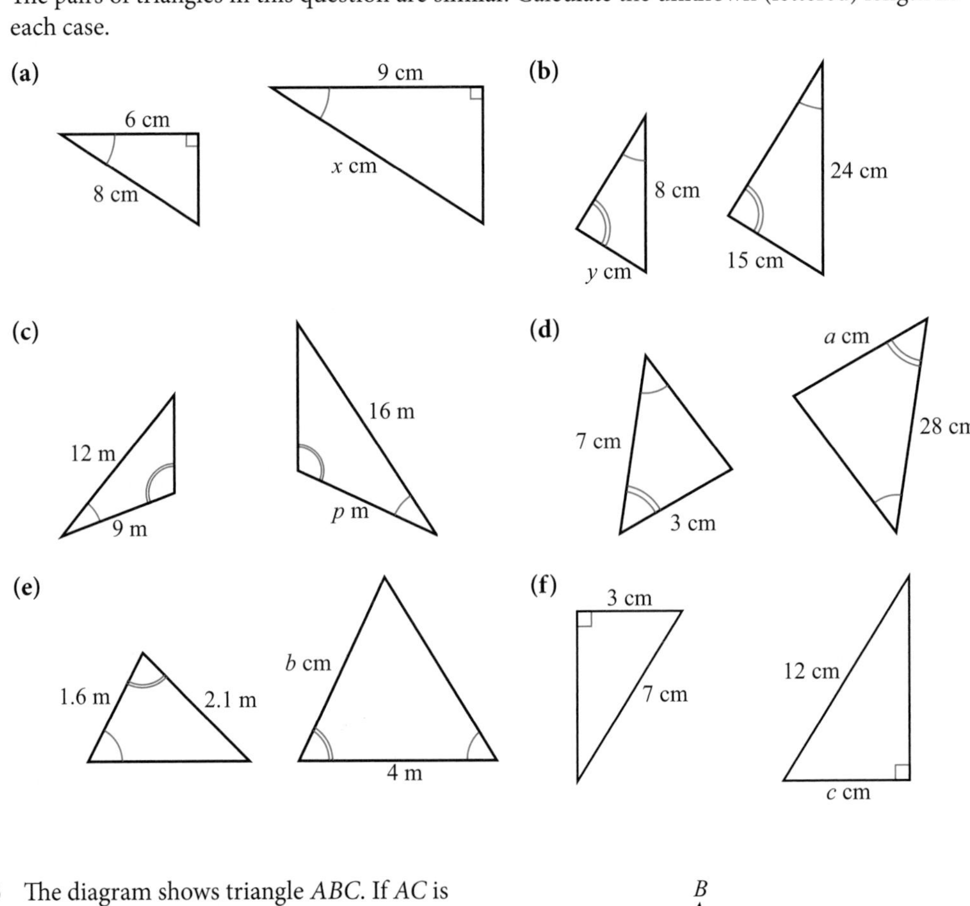

3 The diagram shows triangle *ABC*. If *AC* is parallel to *EF*, find the length of *AC*.

B
5.1 cm
E
F
3.6 cm
7.3 cm
A
C

4 In the diagram AB is parallel to DE. Explain why triangle ABC is mathematically similar to triangle CDE and find the length of CE.

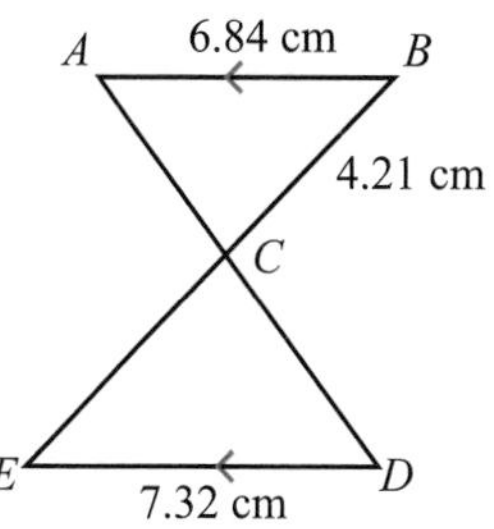

5 The diagram shows a part of a children's climbing frame. Find the length of BC.

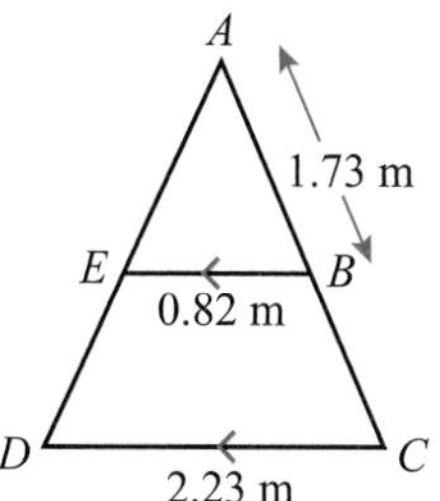

6 Swimmer A and boat B, shown in the diagram, are 80 m apart, and boat B is 1200 m from the lighthouse C. The height of the boat is 12 m and the swimmer can just see the top of the lighthouse at the top of the boat's mast when his head lies at sea level. What is the height of the lighthouse?

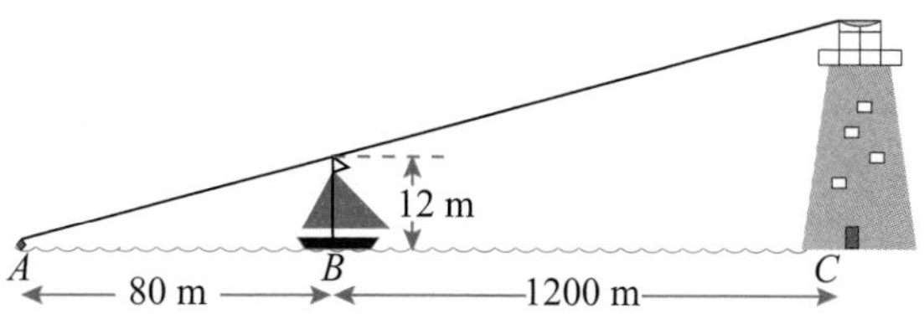

7 The diagram shows a circular cone that has been filled to a depth of 18 cm. Find the radius r of the top of the cone.

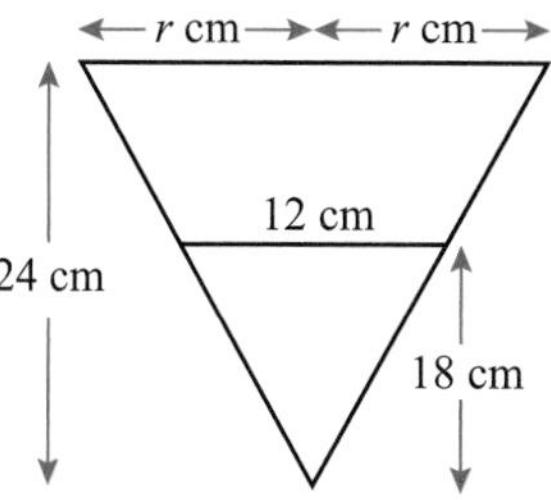

8 The diagram shows a step ladder that is held in place by an 80 cm piece of wire. Find x.

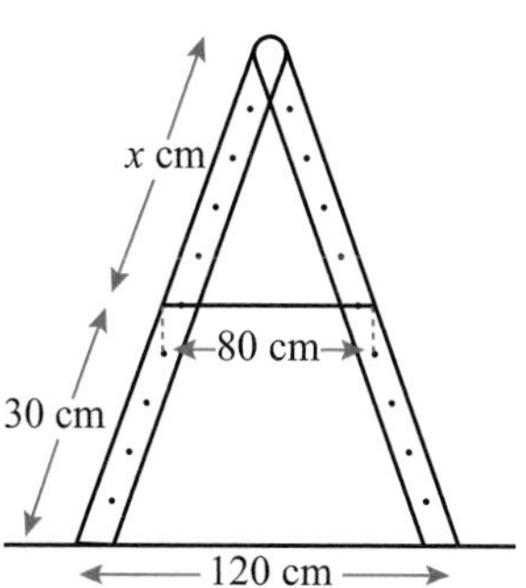

11. 3 Understanding similar shapes

In the previous section you worked with similar triangles, but any shapes can be similar. A shape is similar if the ratio of corresponding sides is equal and the corresponding angles are equal. Similar shapes are therefore identical in shape, but they differ in size.

You can use the ratio of corresponding sides to find unknown sides of similar shapes just as you did with similar triangles.

Worked example 7

Ahmed has two rectangular flags. One measures 1000 mm by 500 mm, the other measures 500 mm by 350 mm. Are the flags similar in shape?

$\frac{1000}{500} = 2$ and $\frac{500}{350} = 1.43$ (Work out the ratio of corresponding sides.)

$\frac{1000}{500} \neq \frac{500}{350}$

The ratio of corresponding sides is not equal, therefore the shapes are not similar.

Worked example 8

Given that the two shapes in the diagram are mathematically similar, find the unknown length x.

8 m
12 m
20 m
x m

Using the ratios of corresponding sides: $\frac{x}{12} = \frac{20}{8} = 2.5$

$\Rightarrow x = 12 \times 2.5 = 30\text{m}$

Exercise 11.4

1 Establish whether each pair of shapes is similar or not. Show your working.

(a)

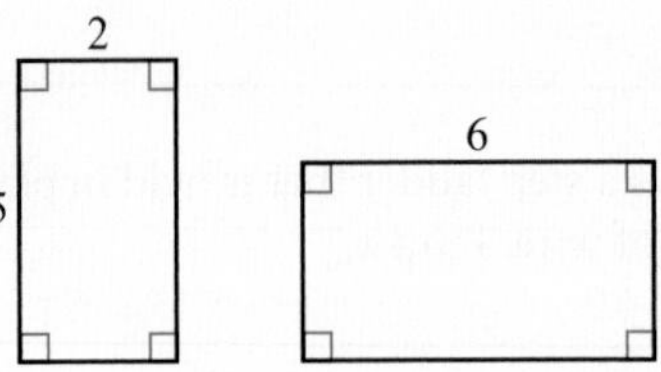

(b)

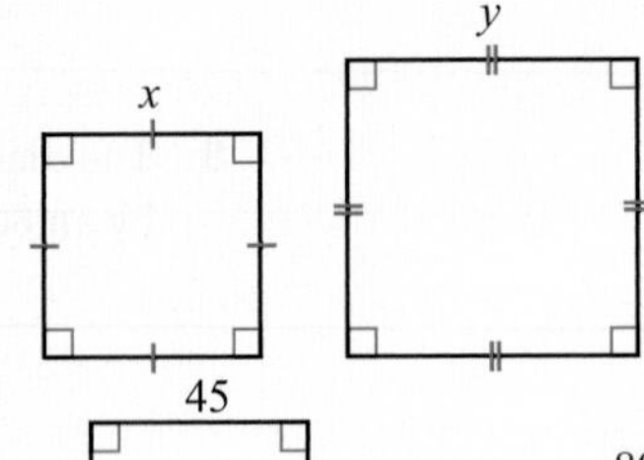

(c)

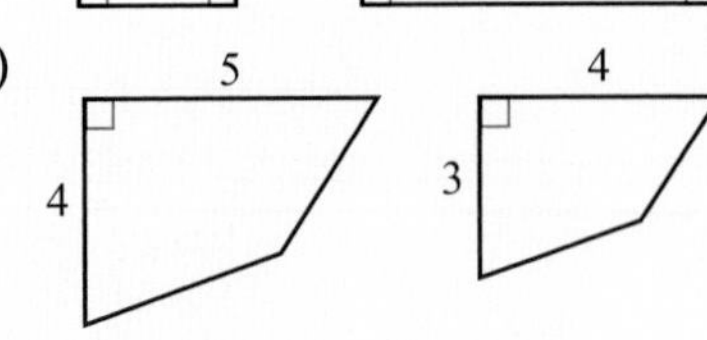

(d)

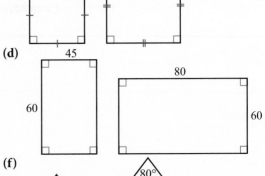

45
60
80
60

(e)

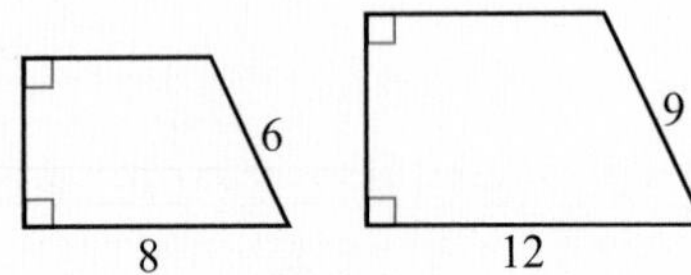

(f)

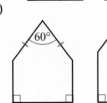

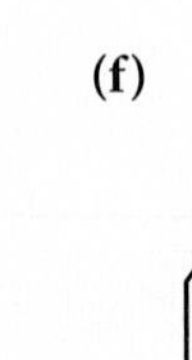

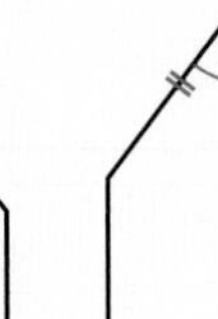

2 In each part of this question the two shapes given are mathematically similar to one another. Calculate the unknown lengths in each case.

(a)

5 cm
3 cm
15 cm
x cm

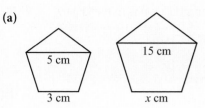

(b)

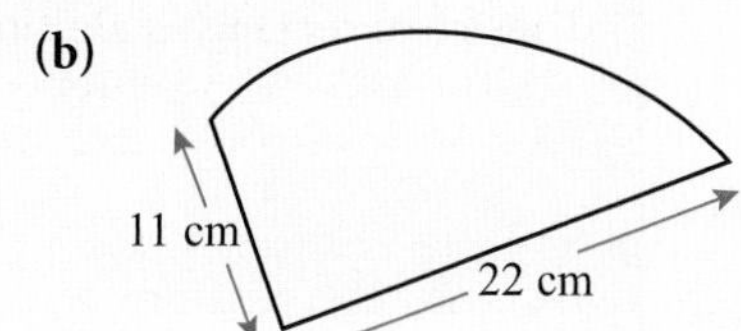

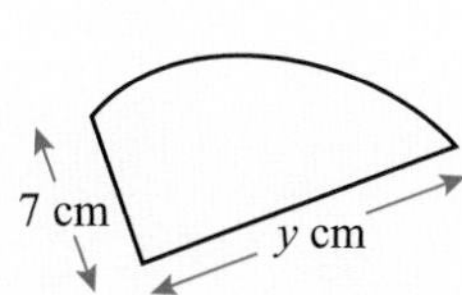

(c)

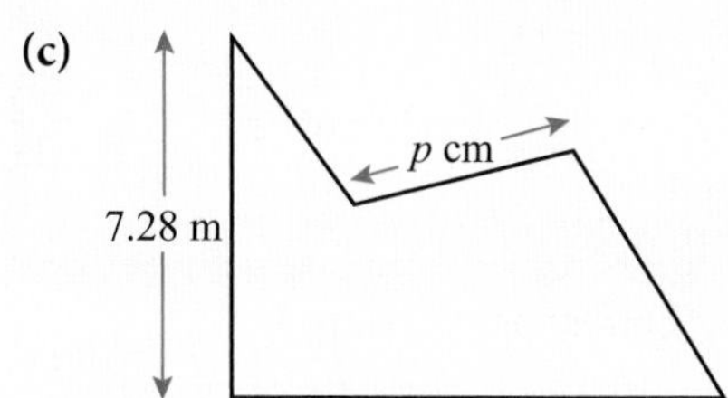

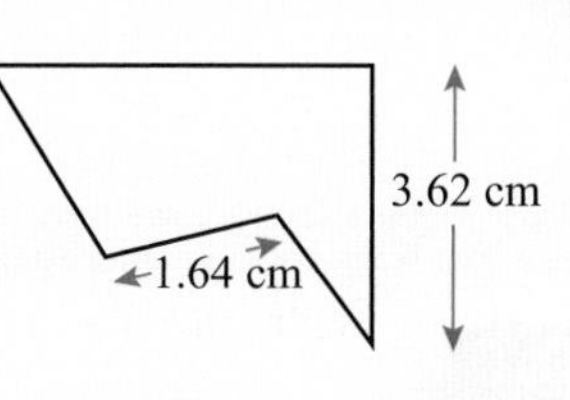

(d)

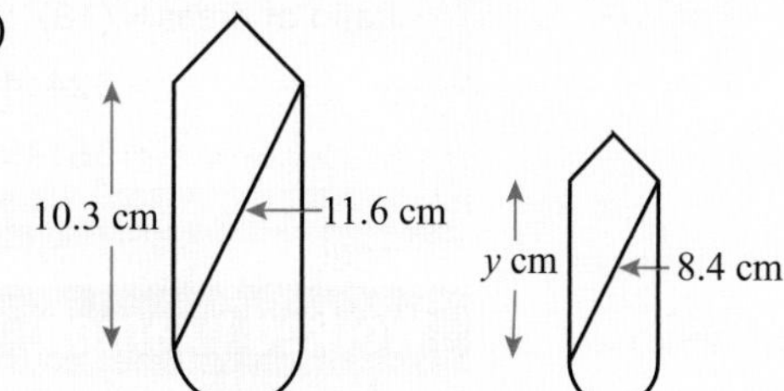

(e)

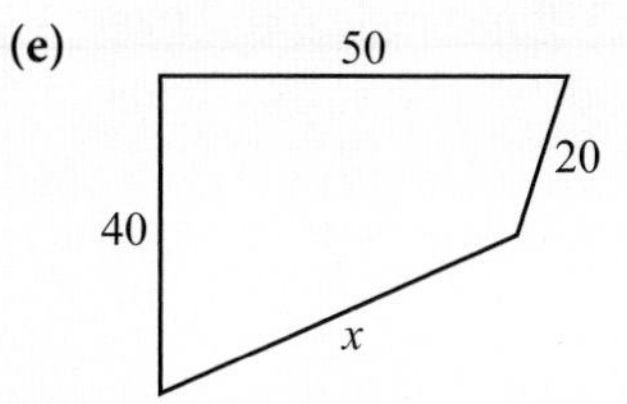

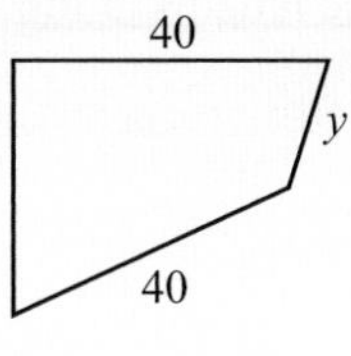

(f)

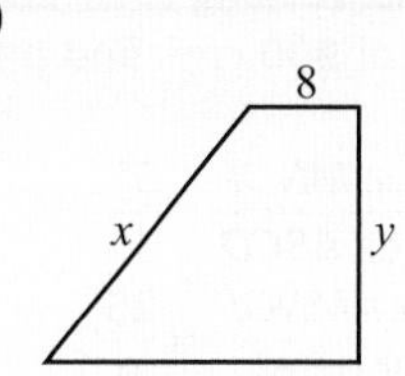

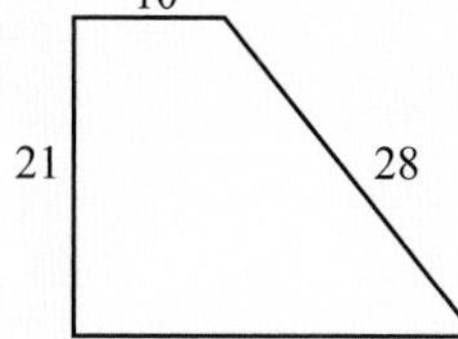

(g)

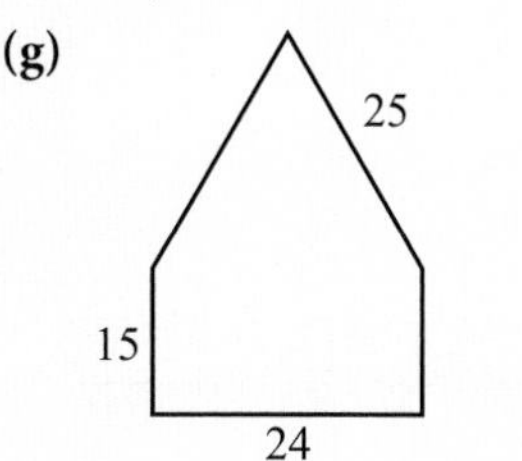

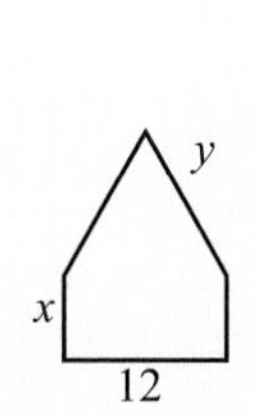

(h)

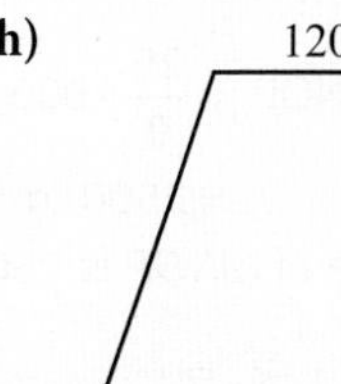

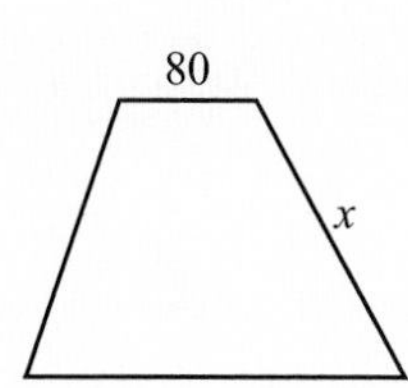

Area of similar shapes

Each pair of shapes below is similar:

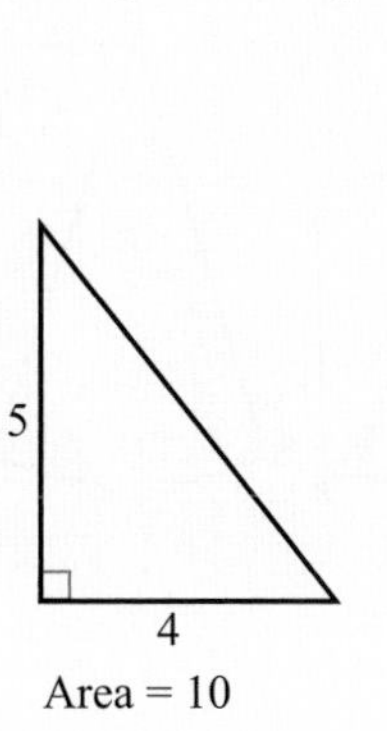

Area = 10

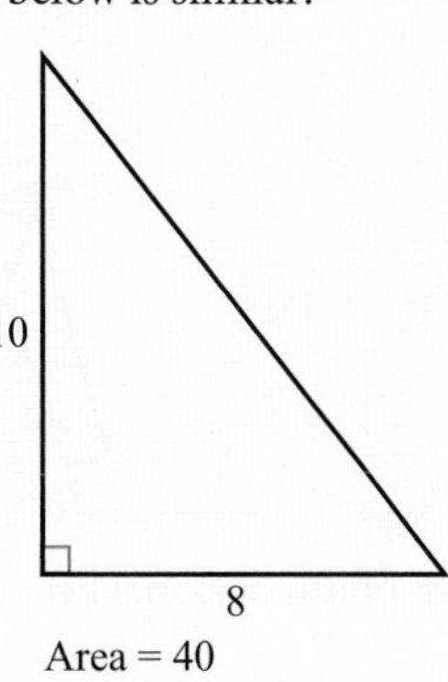

Area = 40

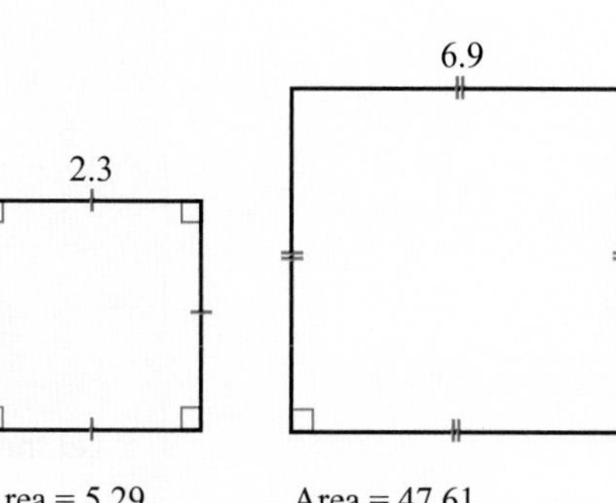

Area = 5.29

Area = 47.61

The ratio that compares the measurements of two similar shapes is called the **scale factor**.

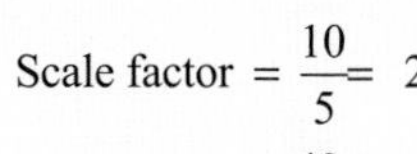

Scale factor $= \dfrac{10}{5} = 2$

Area factor $= \dfrac{40}{10} = 4$

Scale factor $= \dfrac{6.9}{2.3} = 3$

Area factor $= \dfrac{47.61}{5.29} = 9$

If you look at the diagrams and the dimensions you can see that there is a relationship between the corresponding sides of similar figures and the areas of the figures.

In similar figures where the ratio of corresponding sides is $a : b$, the ratio of areas is $a^2 : b^2$.

In other words, **scale factor of areas** = (scale factor of lengths)^2

Worked example 9

These two rectangles are similar. What is the ratio of the smaller area to the larger?

18 21

Ratio of sides = 18 : 21

Ratio of areas $= (18)^2 : (21)^2$

$= 324 : 441$

$= 36 : 49$

Worked example 10

Similar rectangles *ABCD* and *MNOP* have lengths in the ratio 3 : 5. If rectangle *ABCD* has area of 900 cm², find the area of *MNOP*.

$$\frac{\text{Area } MNOP}{\text{Area } ABCD} = \frac{5^2}{3^2}$$

$$\frac{\text{Area } MNOP}{900\,\text{cm}^2} = \frac{25}{9}$$

$$\text{Area MNOP} = \frac{25}{9} \times 900$$

$$= 2500\,\text{cm}^2$$

The area of *MNOP* is 2500 cm².

Worked example 11

The shapes below are similar. Given that the area of *ABCD* = 48 cm² and the area of *PQRS* = 108 cm², find the diagonal *AC* in *ABCD*.

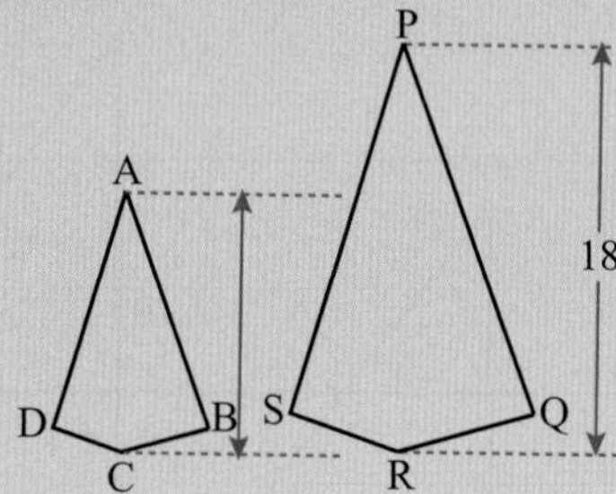

Let the length of the diagonal be x cm.

$$\frac{48}{108} = \frac{x^2}{18^2}$$

$$\frac{48}{108} = \frac{x^2}{324}$$

$$\frac{48}{108} \times 324 = x^2$$

$x^2 = 144$

$x = 12$

Diagonal *AC* is 12 cm long.

Exercise 11.5

1 In each part of this question, the two figures are similar. The area of one figure is given. Find the area of the other.

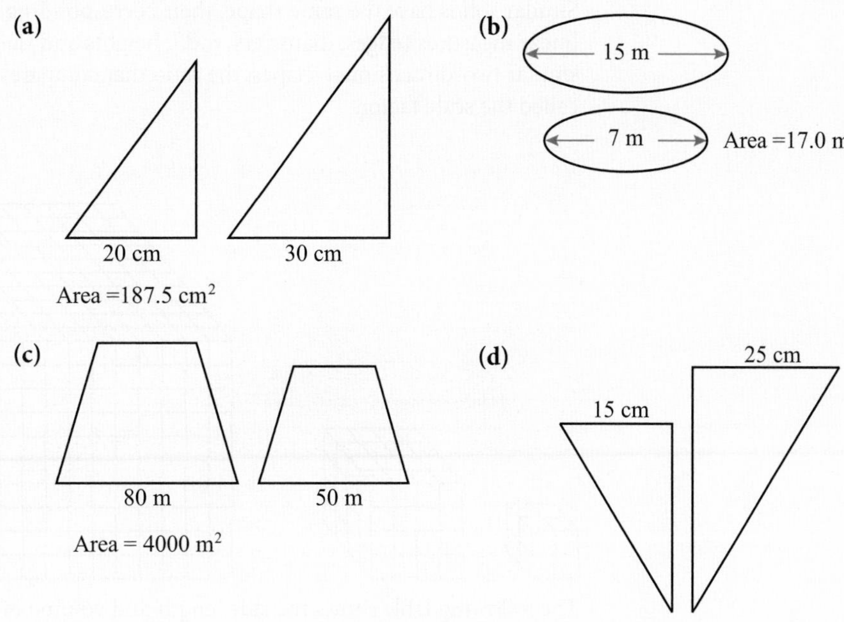

2 In each part of this question the areas of the two similar figures are given. Find the length of the side marked x in each.

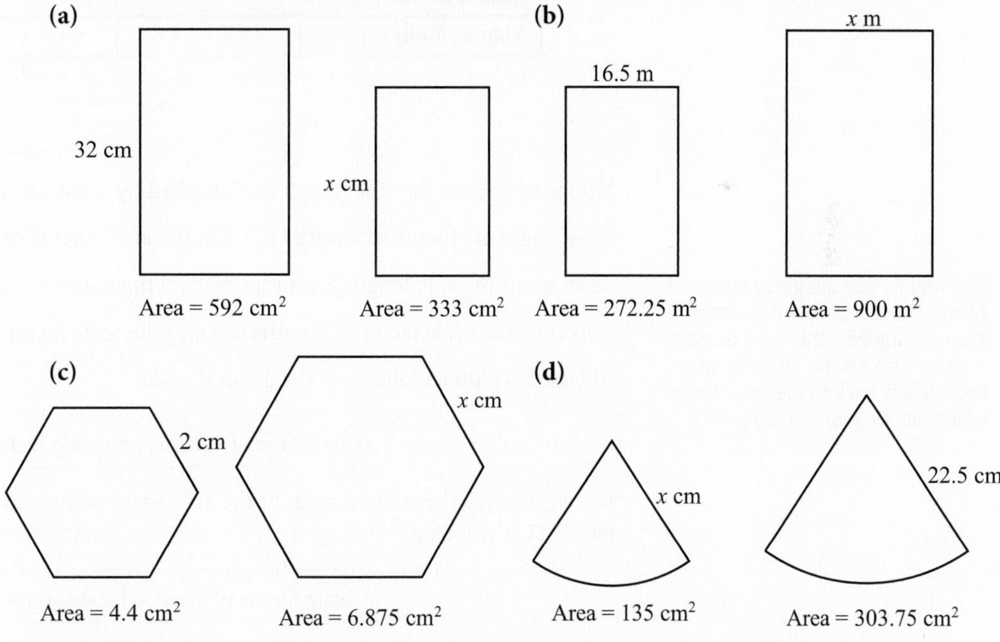

3 Clarissa is making a pattern using a cut out regular pentagon. How will the area of the pentagon be affected if she:

(a) doubles the lengths of the sides?
(b) trebles the lengths of the sides?
(c) halves the lengths of the sides?

4 If the areas of two similar quadrilaterals are in the ratio 64 : 9, what is the ratio of matching sides?

Similar solids

Three-dimensional shapes (solids) can also be similar.

Similar solids have the same shape, their corresponding angles are equal and all corresponding linear measures (edges, diameters, radii, heights and slant heights) are in the same ratio. As with similar two-dimensional shapes, the ratio that compares the measurements on the two shapes is called the scale factor.

Volume and surface area of similar solids

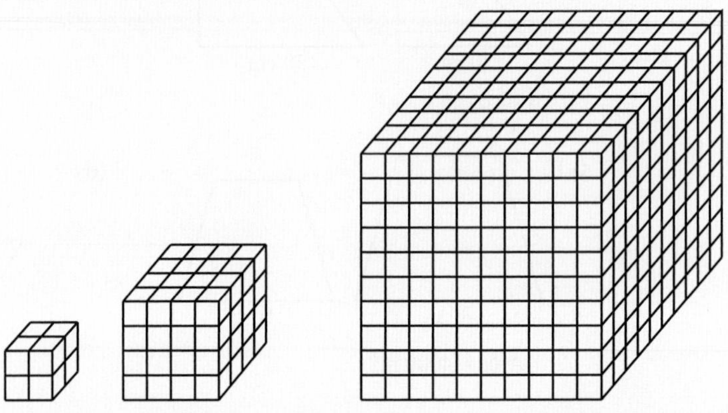

The following table shows the side length and volume of each of the cubes above.

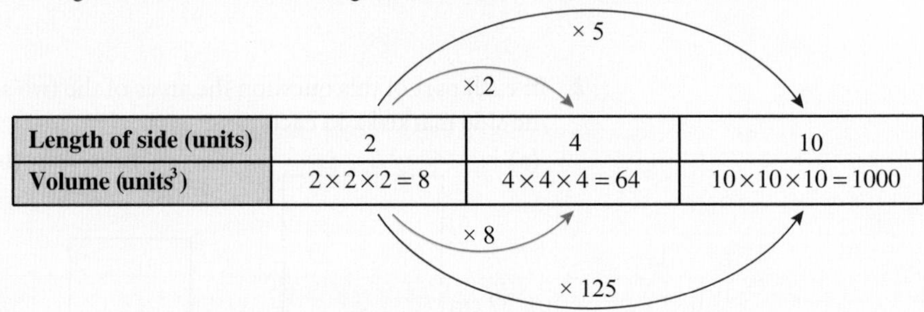

Length of side (units)	2	4	10
Volume (units^3)	$2 \times 2 \times 2 = 8$	$4 \times 4 \times 4 = 64$	$10 \times 10 \times 10 = 1000$

Notice that when the side length is multiplied by 2 the volume is multiplied by $2^3 = 8$

Here, the **scale factor of lengths** is 2 and the **scale factor of volumes** is 2^3.

Also, when the side length is multiplied by 5 the volume is multiplied by $5^3 = 125$.

This time the scale factor of lengths is 5 and the scale factor of volumes is 5^3.

In fact this pattern follows in the general case:

> Sometimes you are given the scale factor of areas or volumes rather than starting with the scale factor of lengths. Use square roots or cube roots to get back to the scale factor of lengths as your starting point.

$$\text{scale factor of volumes} = (\text{scale factor of lengths})^3$$

By considering the surface areas of the cubes you will also be able to see that the rule from page 221 is still true:

$$\text{scale factor of areas} = (\text{scale factor of lengths})^2$$

In summary, if two solids (A and B) are similar:

- the ratio of their volumes is equal to the cube of the ratio of corresponding linear measures (edges, diameter, radii, heights and slant heights). In other words: Volume $A \div$ Volume $B = \left(\frac{a}{b}\right)^3$
- the ratio of their surface areas is equal to the square of the ratio of corresponding linear measures. In other words: Surface area $A \div$ Surface area $B = \left(\frac{a}{b}\right)^2$

The following worked examples show how these scale factors can be used.

Worked example 12

The cones shown in the diagram are mathematically similar. If the smaller cone has a volume of 40 cm³ find the volume of the larger cone.

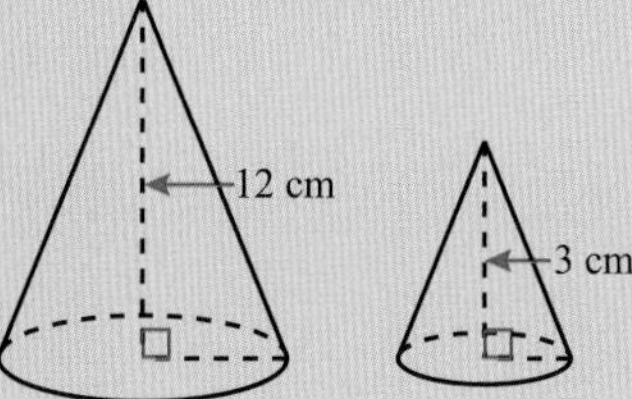

Scale factor of lengths $= \frac{12}{3} = 4$

$\Rightarrow$ Scale factor of volumes $= 4^3 = 64$

So the volume of the larger cone $= 64 \times 40 = 2560\,\text{cm}^3$

Worked example 13

The two shapes shown in the diagram are mathematically similar. If the area of the larger shape is 216 cm², and the area of the smaller shape is 24 cm², find the length x in the diagram.

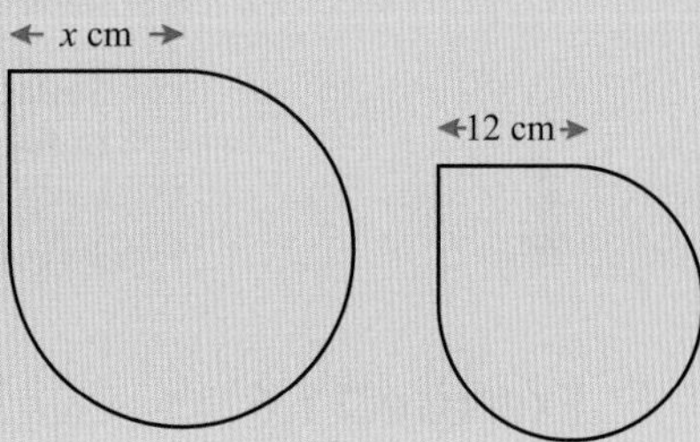

Scale factor of areas $= \frac{216}{24} = 9$

$\Rightarrow$ (Scale factor of lengths)$^2 = 9$

$\Rightarrow$ Scale factor of lengths $= \sqrt{9} = 3$

So: $x = 3 \times 12 = 36$ cm

Worked example 14

A shipping crate has a volume of 2000 cm³. If the dimensions of the crate are doubled, what will its new volume be?

$$\frac{\text{Original volume}}{\text{New volume}} = \left(\frac{\text{original dimensions}}{\text{new dimensions}}\right)^3$$

$$\frac{2000}{\text{New volume}} = \left(\frac{1}{2}\right)^3$$

$$\frac{2000}{\text{New volume}} = \frac{1}{8}$$

New volume $= 2000 \times 8$

New volume $= 16\,000\text{ cm}^3$

Worked example 15

The two cuboids A and B are similar. The larger has a surface area of 608 cm². What is the surface area of the smaller?

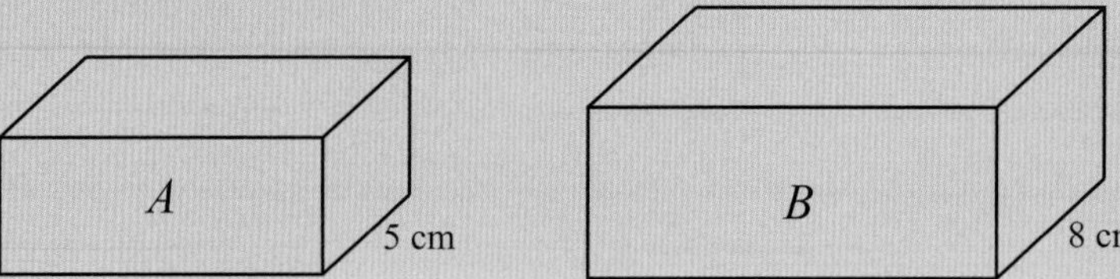

$$\frac{\text{Surface area } A}{\text{Surface area } B} = \left(\frac{\text{width } A}{\text{width } B}\right)^2$$

$$\frac{\text{Surface area } A}{608} = \left(\frac{5}{8}\right)^2$$

$$\frac{\text{Surface area } A}{608} = \frac{25}{64}$$

$$\text{Surface area } A = \frac{25}{64} \times 608$$

Surface area A = 237.5 cm²
Cuboid A has a surface area of 237.5 cm²

Exercise 11.6

1 Copy and complete the statement.

When the dimensions of a solid are multiplied by k, the surface area is multiplied by __ and the volume is multiplied by __.

2 Two similar cubes A and B have sides of 20 cm and 5 cm respectively.

(a) What is the scale factor of A to B?
(b) What is the ratio of their surface areas?
(c) What is the ratio of their volumes?

3 Pyramid A and pyramid B are similar. Find the surface area of pyramid A.

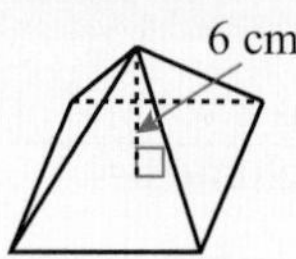

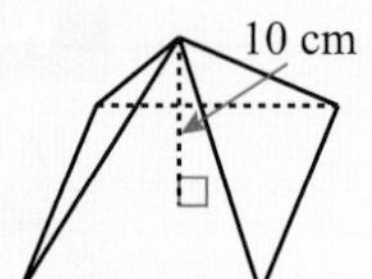

Surface area = 600 cm²

4 Sam has two similar cylindrical metal rods. The smaller rod has a diameter of 4 cm and a surface area of 110 cm². The larger rod has a diameter of 5 cm. Find the surface area of the larger rod.

5 Cuboid X and cuboid Y are similar. The scale factor X to Y is $\frac{3}{4}$.

(a) If a linear measure in cuboid X is 12 mm, what is the length of the corresponding measure on cuboid Y?
(b) Cuboid X has a surface area of 88.8 cm². What is the surface area of cuboid Y?
(c) If cuboid X has a volume of 35.1 cm³, what is the volume of cuboid Y?

6 For each part of this question, the solids are similar. Find the unknown volume.

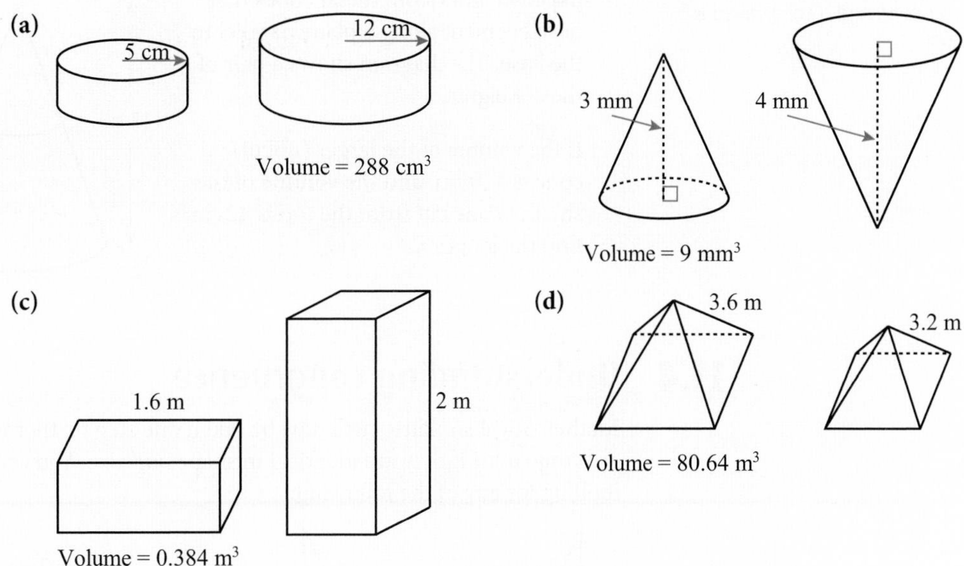

7 Find the unknown quantity for each of the following pairs of similar shapes.

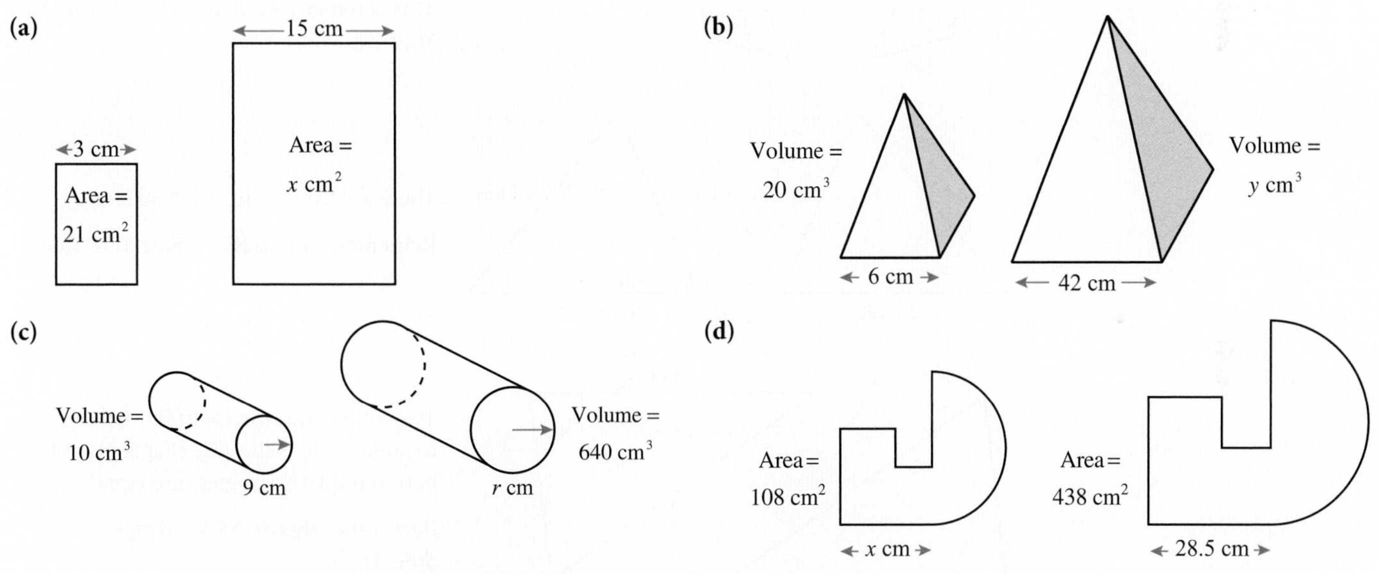

Living maths

8 Karen has this set of three Russian dolls. The largest doll is 13 cm tall, the next one is 2 cm shorter and the third one is 4 cm shorter. Draw up a table to compare the surface area and volume of the three dolls in algebraic terms.

A cone cut in this way produces a smaller cone and a solid called a frustum.

9 A manufacturer is making pairs of paper weights from metal cones that have been cut along a plane parallel to the base. The diagram shows a pair of these weights.

If the volume of the larger (uncut) cone is $128\,cm^3$ and the volume of the smaller cone cut from the top is $42\,cm^3$ find the length x.

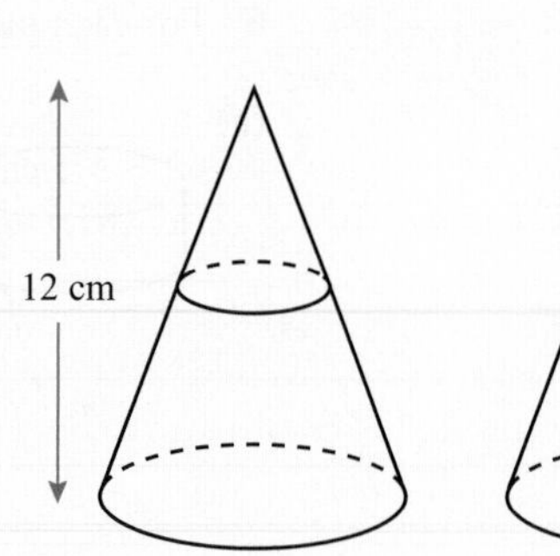

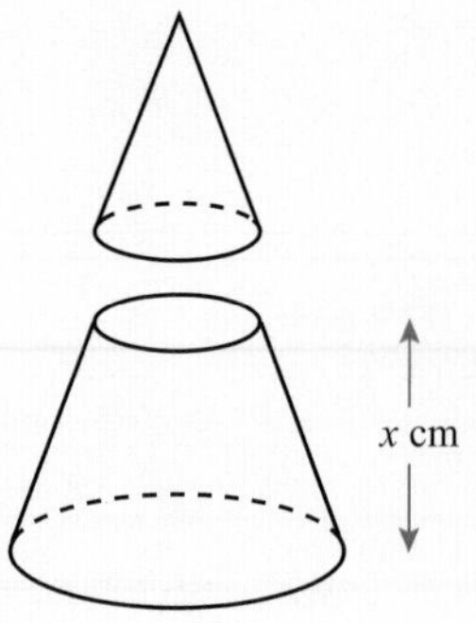

11.4 Understanding congruence

Mathematical similarity will now be taken one step further to look at congruence. Two shapes are **congruent** if they are identical in shape *and* size. You can test for congruent triangles by looking for any of the following:

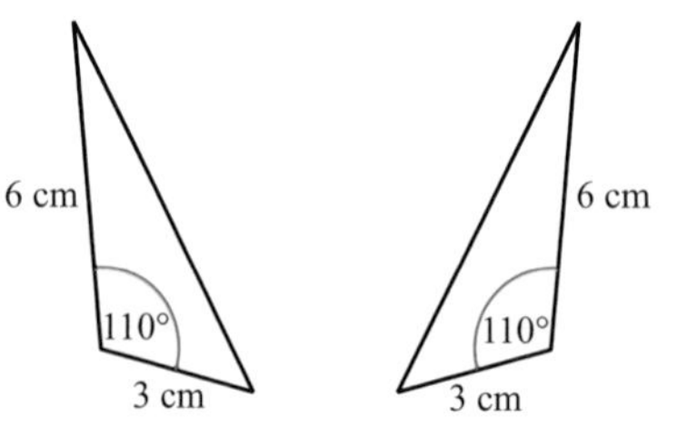

Two sides and the **included angle** (this is the angle that sits between the two given sides) are equal.

This is remembered as SAS – **S**ide **A**ngle **S**ide.

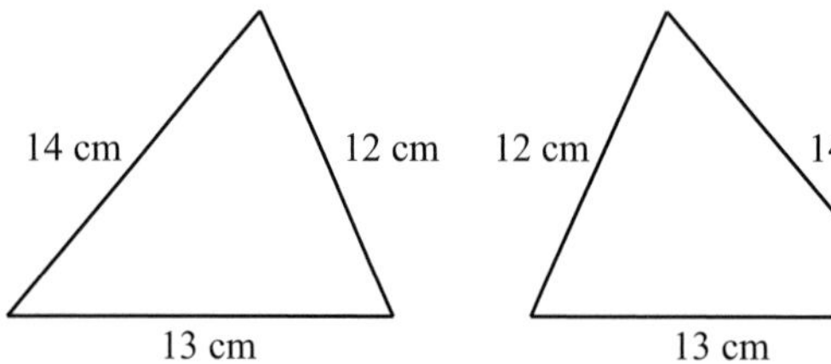

There are three pairs of equal sides.

Remember this as SSS – **S**ide **S**ide **S**ide.

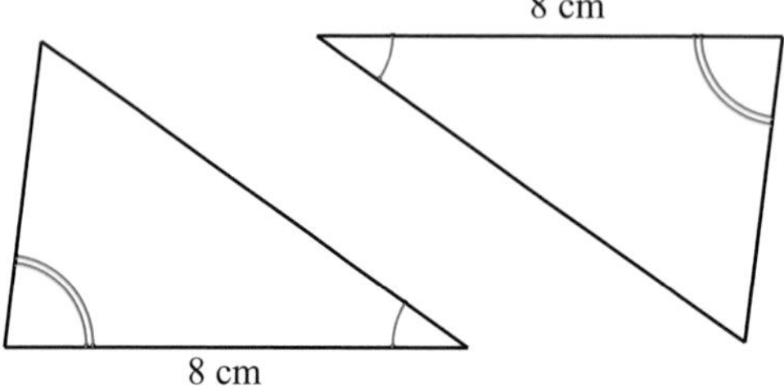

Two angles and the **included side** (the included side is the side that is placed between the two angles) are equal.

Remember this as ASA – **A**ngle **S**ide **A**ngle.

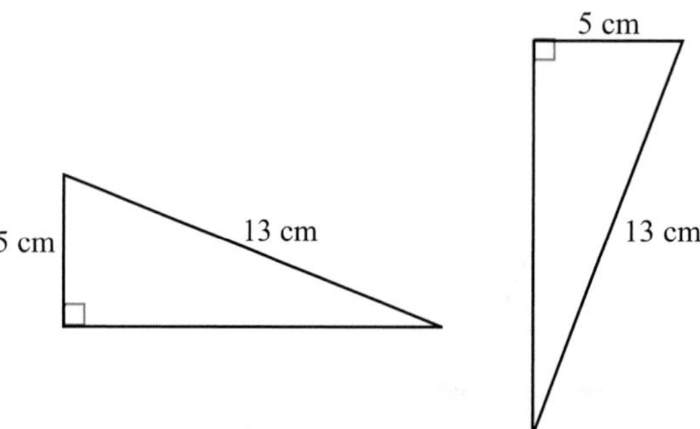

If you have right-angled triangles, the angle does not need to be included for the triangles to be congruent. The triangles must have the same length of hypotenuse and one other side equal.

Remember this as RHS – ***R**ight-angle* ***S**ide* ***H**ypotenuse*.

If any one of these conditions is satisfied then you have two congruent triangles.

Worked example 16

For each of the following pairs of triangles, show that they are congruent.

(a)

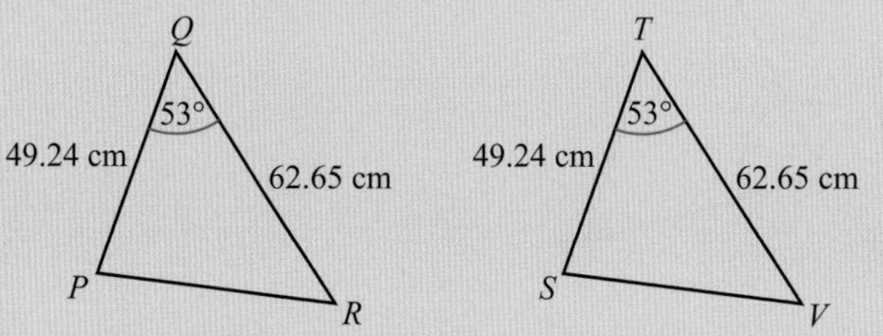

(a) Length *PQ* = Length *ST*

$P\hat{Q}R = S\hat{T}V$

Length *QR* = Length *TV*

So the condition is SAS and the triangles are congruent.

(b)

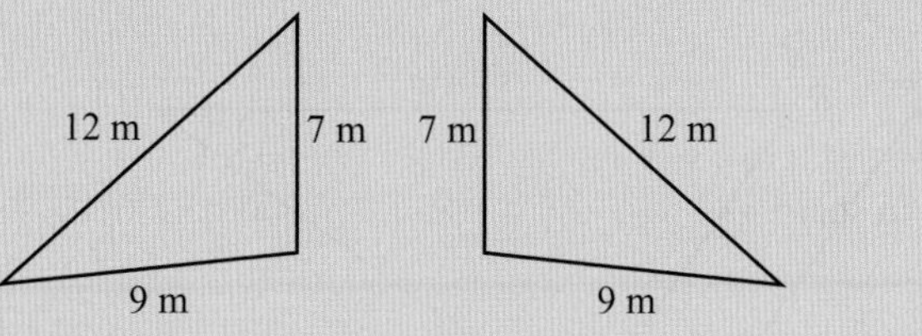

(b) There are three pairs of equal sides.

So the condition is SSS and the triangles are congruent.

(c)

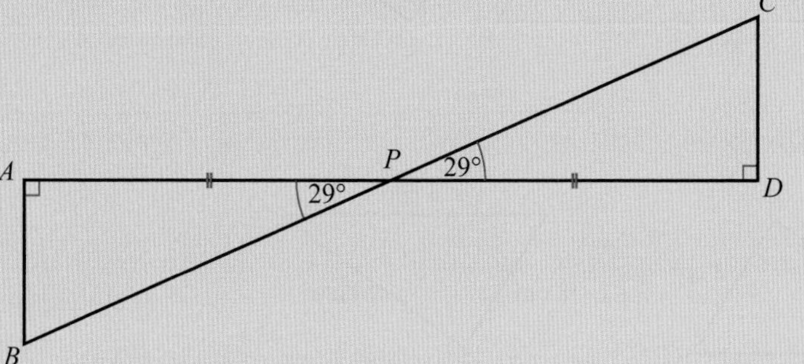

(c) $B\hat{A}P = C\hat{D}P$ (both are right angles)

$AP = PD$ (given on diagram)

$A\hat{P}B = C\hat{P}D$ (vertically opposite)

So the condition is ASA and the triangles are congruent.

(d)

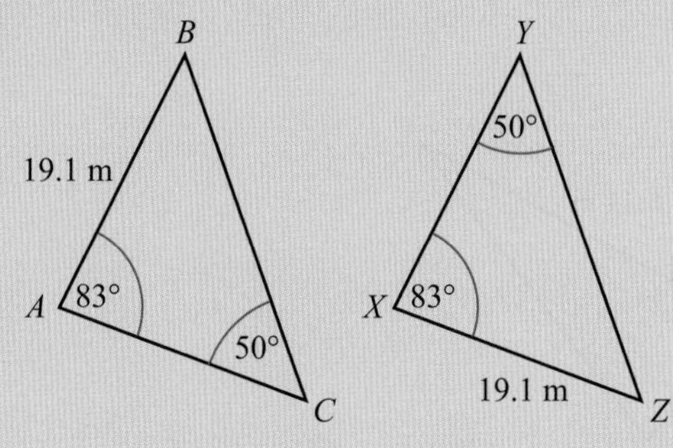

(d) $B\hat{A}C = Y\hat{X}Z = 83°$

$B\hat{C}A = Z\hat{Y}X = 50°$

$A\hat{B}C = X\hat{Z}Y = 47°$ (angles in a triangle)

Length *AB* = Length *XZ*

So the condition is ASA and the triangles are congruent.

Exercise 11.7

For each question show that the pair of shapes are congruent to one another. Explain each answer carefully and state clearly which of SAS, SSS, ASA or RHS you have used.

1

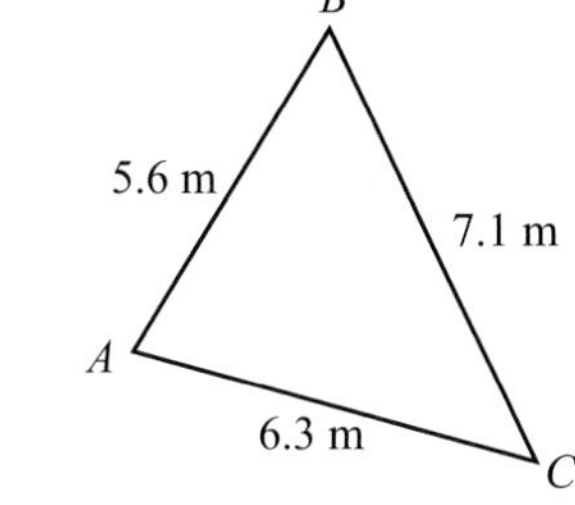

2

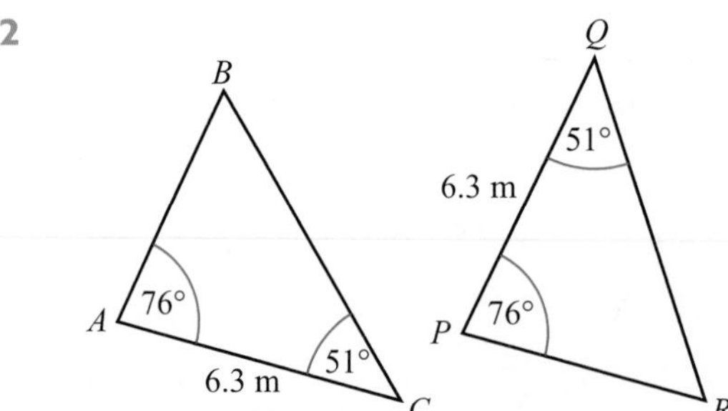
B
A
C
76°
51°
6.3 m
Q
P
R
51°
6.3 m
76°

3

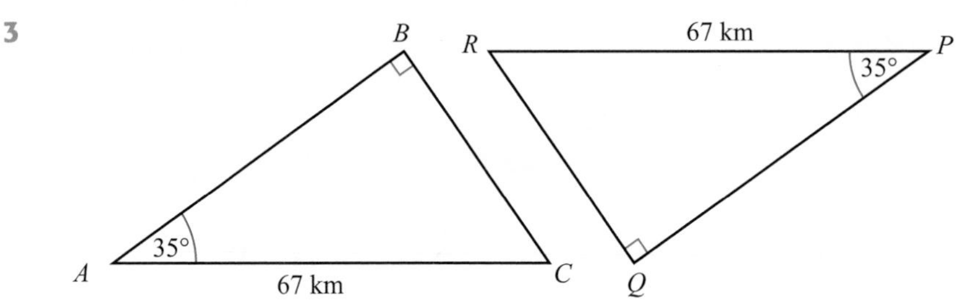
B
A
C
35°
67 km
R
P
Q
67 km
35°

4

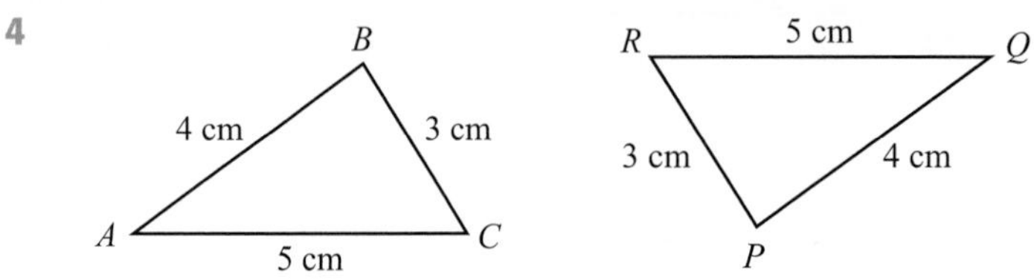
B
A
C
4 cm
3 cm
5 cm
R
Q
P
5 cm
3 cm
4 cm

5

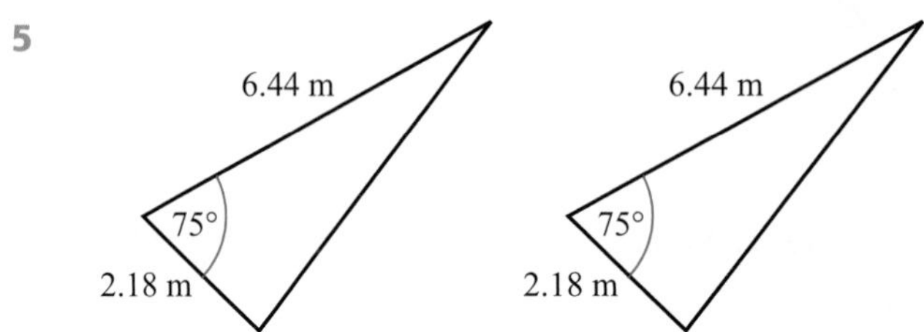
6.44 m
75°
2.18 m
6.44 m
75°
2.18 m

6

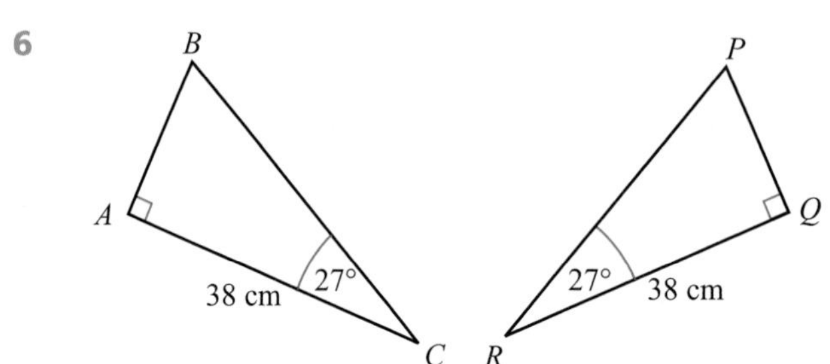
B
A
C
27°
38 cm
P
Q
R
27°
38 cm

7

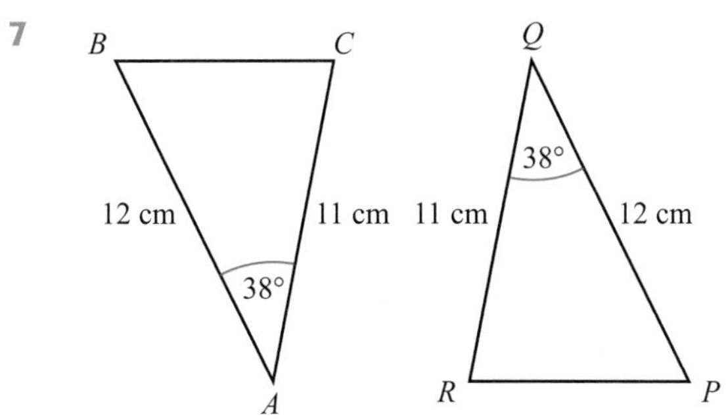

8

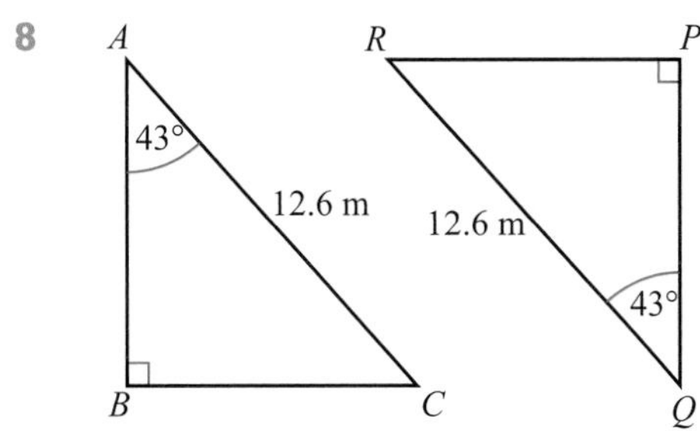

Summary

Do you know the following?

- The longest side of a right-angled triangle is called the hypotenuse.
- The square of the hypotenuse is equal to the sum of the squares of the two shorter sides of the triangle.
- Similar shapes have equal corresponding angles and the ratios of corresponding sides are equal.
- If shapes are similar and the lengths of one shape are multiplied by a scale factor of n:
  - then the areas are multiplied by a scale factor of n^2
  - and the volumes are multiplied by a scale factor of n^3.
- Congruent triangles are exactly equal to each other.

Are you able to ...?

- use Pythagoras' theorem to find an unknown side of a right-angled triangle
- use Pythagoras' theorem to solve real-life problems
- decide whether or not two objects are mathematically similar
- use the fact that two objects are similar to calculate:
  - unknown lengths
  - areas or volumes
- decide whether or not two triangles are congruent.

Examination practice

Exam-style questions

1 Mohamed takes a short cut from his home (H) to the bus stop (B) along a footpath HB.

How much further would it be for Mohamed to walk to the bus stop by going from H to the corner (C) and then from C to B?

Give your answer in metres.

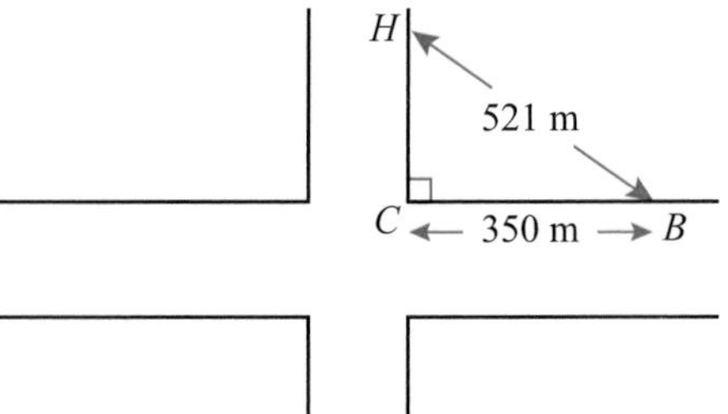

2 A ladder is standing on horizontal ground and rests against a vertical wall. The ladder is 4.5 m long and its foot is 1.6 m from the wall. Calculate how far up the wall the ladder will reach. Give your answer correct to 3 significant figures.

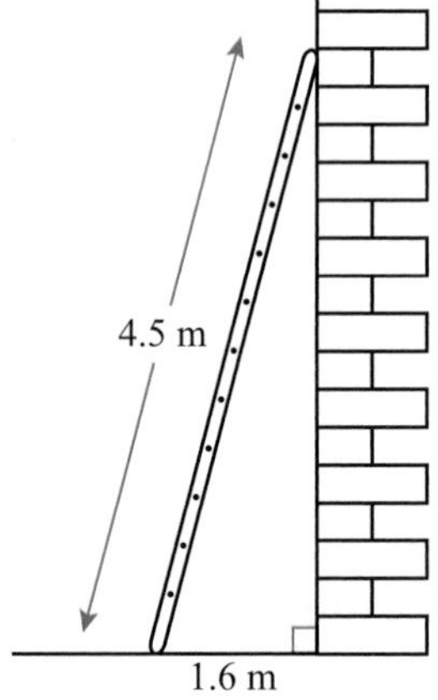

3 A rectangular box has a base with internal dimensions 21 cm by 28 cm, and an internal height of 12 cm. Calculate the length of the longest straight thin rod that will fit:

(a) on the base of the box

(b) in the box.

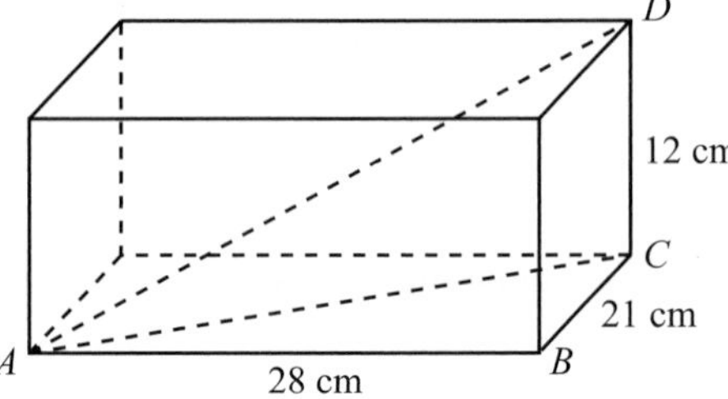

4

NOT TO SCALE

7x cm

150 cm

24x cm

The right-angled triangle in the diagram has sides of length $7x$ cm , $24x$ cm and 150 cm.

(a) Show that $x^2 = 36$

(b) Calculate the perimeter of the triangle.

Past paper questions

1

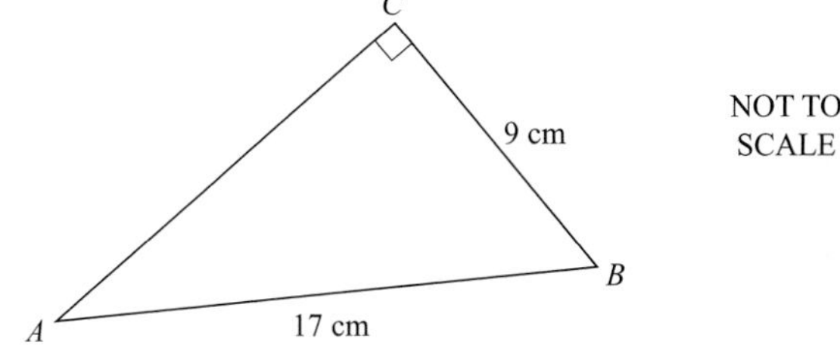

In the triangle ABC, $AB = 17$ cm, $BC = 9$ cm and angle $ACB = 90°$. Calculate AC. [3]

[Cambridge IGCSE Mathematics 0580 Paper 12 Q10 May/June 2011]

12 Averages and measures of spread

Key words

- Average
- Mode
- Mean
- Spread
- Median
- Range
- Discrete
- Continuous
- Grouped data
- Estimated mean
- Modal class
- Percentiles
- Upper quartile
- Lower quartile
- Interquartile range

In this chapter you will learn how to:

- calculate the mean, median and mode of sets of data
- calculate and interpret the range as a measure of spread
- interpret the meaning of each result and compare data using these measures

EXTENDED

- construct and use frequency distribution tables for grouped data
- identify the class that contains the median of grouped data
- calculate and work with quartiles
- divide data into quartiles and calculate the interquartile range
- identify the modal class from a grouped frequency distribution.

The newspaper headline is just one example of a situation in which statistics have been badly misunderstood. It is important to make sure that you fully understand the statistics before you use it to make any kind of statement!

Sometimes you need to summarise data to make sense of it. You do not always need to draw a diagram; instead you can calculate numerical summaries of average and spread. Numerical summaries can be very useful for comparing different sets of data but, as with all statistics, you must be careful when interpreting the results.

12.1 Different types of average

> **Tip**
>
> There is more than one 'average', so you should never refer to *the* average. Always specify *which* average you are talking about: the *mean, median* or *mode*.

An **average** is a single value used to represent a set of data. There are three types of average used in statistics and the following shows how each can be calculated.

The shoe sizes of 19 students in a class are shown below:

4 7 6 6 7 4 8 3 8 11 6 8 6 3 5 6 7 6 4

How would you describe the shoe sizes in this class?

If you count how many size fours, how many size fives and so on, you will find that the most common (most frequent) shoe size in the class is six. This average is called the **mode**.

What most people think of as the average is the value you get when you add up all the shoe sizes and divide your answer by the number of students:

$$\frac{\text{total of shoe sizes}}{\text{number of students}} = \frac{115}{19} = 6.05\,(2\text{d.p.})$$

> If you take the mean of *n* items and multiply it by *n*, you get the total of all *n* values.

This average is called the **mean**. The mean value tells you that the shoe sizes appear to be **spread** in some way around the value 6.05. It also gives you a good impression of the general 'size' of the data. Notice that the value of the mean, in this case, is not a possible shoe size.

The mean is sometimes referred to as the measure of 'central tendency' of the data. Another measure of central tendency is the middle value when the shoe sizes are arranged in ascending order.

3 3 4 4 4 5 6 6 6 6 6 6 7 7 7 8 8 8 11

If you now think of the first and last values as one pair, the second and second to last as another pair, and so on, you can cross these numbers off and you will be left with a single value in the middle.

~~3~~ ~~3~~ ~~4~~ ~~4~~ ~~4~~ ~~5~~ ~~6~~ ~~6~~ ~~6~~ $\boxed{6}$ ~~6~~ ~~6~~ ~~7~~ ~~7~~ ~~7~~ ~~8~~ ~~8~~ ~~8~~ ~~11~~

This middle value, (in this case six), is known as the **median**.

Crossing off the numbers from each end can be cumbersome if you have a lot of data. You may have noticed that, counting from the left, the median is the 10th value. Adding one to the number of students and dividing the result by two, $\frac{(19+1)}{2}$, also gives 10 as the median position.

What if there had been 20 students in the class? For example, add an extra student with a shoe size of 11. Crossing off pairs gives this result:

~~3~~ ~~3~~ ~~4~~ ~~4~~ ~~4~~ ~~5~~ ~~6~~ ~~6~~ ~~6~~ $\boxed{6\ 6}$ ~~6~~ ~~7~~ ~~7~~ ~~7~~ ~~8~~ ~~8~~ ~~8~~ ~~11~~ ~~11~~

You are left with a middle pair rather than a single value. If this happens then you simply find the mean of this middle pair: $\frac{(6+6)}{2} = 6$.

Notice that the position of the first value in this middle pair is $\frac{20}{2} = 10$.

Adding an extra size 11 has not changed the median or mode in this example, but what will have happened to the mean?

In summary:

Mode The value that appears in your list more than any other. There can be more than one mode but if there are no values that occur more often than any other then there is no mode.

Mean $\frac{\text{total of all data}}{\text{number of values}}$. The mean may not be one of the actual data values.

Median

1. Arrange the data into ascending numerical order.
2. If the number of data is n and n is odd, find $\frac{n+1}{2}$ and this will give you the position of the median.
3. If n is even, then calculate $\frac{n}{2}$ and this will give you the position of the first of the middle pair. Find the mean of this pair.

Dealing with extreme values

Sometimes you may find that your collection of data contains values that are extreme in some way. For example, if you were to measure the speeds of cars as they pass a certain point you may find that some cars are moving unusually slowly or unusually quickly. It is also possible that you may have made a mistake and measured a speed incorrectly, or just written the wrong numbers down!

Suppose the following are speeds of cars passing a particular house over a five minute period (measured in kilometres per hour):

67.2 58.3 128.9 65.0 49.0 55.7

One particular value will catch your eye immediately. 128.9 km/h seems somewhat faster than any other car. How does this extreme value affect your averages?

You can check yourself that the mean of the above data *including* the extreme value is 70.7 km/h.

Tip

You could be asked to give reasons for choosing the mean or median as your average.

This is *larger* than all but one of the values and is not representative. Under these circumstances the mean can be a poor choice of average. If you discover that the highest speed was a mistake, you can exclude it from the calculation and get the much more realistic value of 59.0 km/h (try the calculation for yourself).

If the extreme value is genuine and cannot be excluded, then the median will give you a better impression of the main body of data. Writing the data in rank order:

49.0 55.7 58.3 65.0 67.2 128.9

As there is an even number of 'speeds', the median is the mean of the 3rd and 4th data points.

The median is the mean of 58.3 and 65.0, which is 61.7. Notice that the median reduces to 58.3 if you remove the highest value, so this doesn't change things a great deal.

There is no mode for these data.

Worked example 1

After six tests, Graham has a mean average score of 48. He takes a seventh test and scores 83 for that test.

(a) What is Graham's total score after six tests?
(b) What is Graham's mean average score after seven tests?

(a) Since $\text{mean} = \frac{\text{total of all data}}{\text{number of values}}$

then, total of all data $= \text{mean} \times \text{number of values}$

$= 48 \times 6$

$= 288$

(b) Total of all seven scores $=$ total of first six plus seventh

$= 288 + 83$

$= 371$

$\text{mean} = \frac{371}{7} = 53$

Exercise 12.1

1 For each of the following data sets calculate:

(i) the mode (ii) the median (iii) the mean.

(a)	12	2	5	6	9	3	12	13	10	
(b)	5	9	7	3	8	2	5	8	8	2
(c)	2.1	3.8	2.4	7.6	8.2	3.4	5.6	8.2	4.5	2.1
(d)	12	2	5	6	9	3	12	13	43	

2 Look carefully at the lists of values in parts (a) and (d) above. What is different? How did your mean, median and mode change?

3 Andrew and Barbara decide to investigate their television watching patterns and record the number of minutes that they watch the television for 8 days:

Andrew:	38	10	65	43	125	225	128	40
Barbara:	25	15	10	65	90	300	254	32

(a) Find the median number of minutes spent watching television for each of Andrew and Barbara.

(b) Find the mean number of minutes spent watching television for each of Andrew and Barbara.

4 Find a list of five numbers with a mean that is larger than all but one of the numbers.

5 A keen ten pin bowler plays five rounds in one evening. His scores are 98, 64, 103, 108 and 109. Which average (mode, mean or median) will he choose to report to his friends at the end of the evening? Explain your answer carefully, showing all your calculations clearly.

6 If the mean height of 31 children is 143.6 cm, calculate the total height of the children.

7 The mean mass of 12 bags of potatoes is 2.4 kg. If a 13th bag containing 2.2 kg of potatoes is now included, what would the new mean mass of the 13 bags be?

8 The mean temperature of 10 cups of coffee is 89.6 °C. The mean temperature of a different collection of 20 cups of coffee is 92.1 °C. What is the mean temperature of all 30 cups of coffee?

9 Find five numbers with mean five, median four and mode four.

10 Find five *different* whole numbers with mean five and median four.

11 The mean mass of a group of m boys is X kg and the mean mass of a group of n girls is Y kg. Find the mean mass of all of the children combined.

12.2 Making comparisons using averages and ranges

Having found a value to represent your data (an average) you can now compare two or more sets of data. However, just comparing the averages can sometimes be misleading.

It can be helpful to know how *consistent* the data is and you do this by thinking about how spread out the values are. A simple measure of spread is the **range**.

Range = largest value − smallest value

The larger the range, the more spread out the data is and the less consistent the values are with one another.

Worked example 2

Two groups of athletes want to compare their 100 m sprint times. Each person runs once and records his or her time as shown (in seconds).

Team Pythagoras	14.3	16.6	14.3	17.9	14.1	15.7
Team Socrates	13.2	16.8	14.7	14.7	13.6	16.2

(a) Calculate the mean 100 m time for each team.
(b) Which is the smaller mean?
(c) What does this tell you about the 100 m times for Team Pythagoras in comparison with those for Team Socrates?
(d) Calculate the range for each team.
(e) What does this tell you about the performance of each team?

(a) Team Pythagoras:

$$\text{Mean} = \frac{14.3+16.6+14.3+17.9+14.1+15.7}{6} = \frac{92.9}{6} = 15.48 \text{ seconds}$$

Team Socrates:

$$\text{Mean} = \frac{13.2+16.8+14.7+14.7+13.6+16.2}{6} = \frac{89.2}{6} = 14.87 \text{ seconds}$$

(b) Team Socrates have the smaller mean 100 m time.

(c) The smaller time means that Team Socrates are slightly faster as a team than Team Pythagoras.

(d) Team Pythagoras' range = 17.9 − 14.1 = 3.8 seconds
Team Socrates' range = 16.8 − 13.2 = 3.6 seconds

(e) Team Socrates are slightly faster as a whole and they are slightly more consistent. This suggests that their team performance is not improved significantly by one or two fast individuals but rather all team members run at more or less similar speeds. Team Pythagoras is less consistent and so their mean is improved by individuals.

Tip
When comparing means or ranges, make sure that you refer to the original context of the question.

Exercise 12.2

1 Two friends, Ricky and Oliver, are picking berries. Each time they fill a carton its mass, in kg, is recorded. The masses are shown below:

Ricky	0.145	0.182	0.135	0.132	0.112	0.155	0.189	0.132	0.145	0.201	0.139
Oliver	0.131	0.143	0.134	0.145	0.132	0.123	0.182	0.134	0.128		

(a) For each boy calculate:
  (i) the mean mass of berries collected per box **(ii)** the range of masses.
(b) Which boy collected more berries per load?
(c) Which boy was more consistent when collecting the berries?

2 The marks obtained by two classes in a Mathematics test are show below. The marks are out of 20.

Class Archimedes	12	13	4	19	20	12	13	13	16	18	12
Class Bernoulli	13	6	9	15	20	20	13	15	17	19	3

(a) Calculate the median score for each class.
(b) Find the range of scores for each class.
(c) Which class did better in the test overall?
(d) Which class was more consistent?

3 Three shops sell light bulbs. A sample of 100 light bulbs is taken from each shop and the working life of each is measured in hours. The following table shows the mean time and range for each shop:

Shop	Mean (hours)	Range (hours)
Brightlights	136	18
Footlights	145	36
Backlights	143	18

Which shop would you recommend to someone who is looking to buy a new light bulb and why?

12.3 Calculating averages and ranges for frequency data

So far, the lists of data that you have calculated averages for have been quite small. Once you start to get more than 20 pieces of data it is better to collect the data with the same value together and record it in a table. Such a table is known as a *frequency distribution table* or just a *frequency distribution*.

Data shown in a frequency distribution table

If you throw a single die 100 times, each of the six numbers will appear several times. You can record the number of times that each appears like this:

Number showing on the upper face	1	2	3	4	5	6
Frequency	16	13	14	17	19	21

Mean

You need to find the total of all 100 throws. Sixteen 1s appeared giving a sub-total of $1 \times 16 = 16$, thirteen 2s appeared giving a sub-total of $13 \times 2 = 26$ and so on. You can extend your table to show this:

Tip

You can add columns to a table given to you! It will help you to organise your calculations clearly.

Number showing on the upper face	Frequency	Frequency × number on the upper face
1	16	$1 \times 16 = 16$
2	13	$2 \times 13 = 26$
3	14	$3 \times 14 = 42$
4	17	$17 \times 4 = 68$
5	19	$19 \times 5 = 95$
6	21	$21 \times 6 = 126$

REWIND

Sometimes you will need to retrieve the data from a diagram like a bar chart or a pictogram and then calculate a mean. These charts were studied in chapter 4. ◀

The total of all 100 die throws is the sum of all values in this third column:

$$= 16 + 26 + 42 + 68 + 95 + 126$$
$$= 373$$

So the mean score per throw $= \dfrac{\text{total score}}{\text{total number of throws}} = \dfrac{373}{100} = 3.73$

Median

There are 100 throws, which is an even number, so the median will be the mean of a middle pair.

The first of this middle pair will be found in position $\dfrac{100}{2} = 50$

The table has placed all the values in order. The first 16 are ones, the next 13 are twos and so on. Notice that adding the first three frequencies gives 16 + 13 + 14 = 43. This means that the first 43 values are 1, 2 or 3. The next 17 values are all 4s, so the 50th and 51st values will both be 4. The mean of both 4s is 4, so this is the median.

Mode

For the mode you simply need to find the die value that has the highest frequency. The number 6 occurs most often (21 times), so 6 is the mode.

Range

The highest and lowest values are known, so the range is 6 – 1 = 5

In summary:

- **Mode** The value that has the highest frequency will be the mode. If more than one value has the same highest frequency then there is no single mode.
- **Mean** $\frac{\text{total of all data}}{\text{number of values}} = \frac{\text{sum of frequency} \times \text{value}}{\text{total frequency}}$

  (Remember to extend the table so that you can fill in a column for calculating frequency × value in each case.)
- **Median**
  - If the number of data is n and n is odd, find $\frac{n+1}{2}$ and this will give you the position of the median.
  - If n is even, then calculate $\frac{n}{2}$ and this will give you the position of the first of the middle pair. Find the mean of this pair.
  - Add the frequencies in turn until you find the value whose frequency makes you exceed (or equal) the value from one or two above. This is the median.

Exercise 12.3

1 Construct a frequency table for the following data and calculate:

(a) the mean **(b)** the median **(c)** the mode **(d)** the range.

3	4	5	1	2	8	9	6	5	3	2	1	6	4	7	8	1
1	5	5	2	3	4	5	7	8	3	4	2	5	1	9	4	5
6	7	8	9	2	1	5	4	3	4	5	6	1	4	4	8	

2 Tickets for a circus were sold at the following prices: 180 at \$6.50 each, 215 at \$8 each and 124 at \$10 each.

(a) Present this information in a frequency table.
(b) Calculate the mean price of tickets sold (give your answer to 3 significant figures).

3 A man kept count of the number of letters he received each day over a period of 60 days. The results are shown in the table below.

Number of letters per day	0	1	2	3	4	5
Frequency	28	21	6	3	1	1

For this distribution, find:

(a) the mode **(b)** the median **(c)** the mean **(d)** the range.

4 A survey of the number of children in 100 families gave the following distribution:

Number of children in family	0	1	2	3	4	5	6	7
Number of families	4	36	27	21	5	4	2	1

For this distribution, find:

(a) the mode **(b)** the median **(c)** the mean.

5 The distribution of marks obtained by the students in a class is shown in the table below.

Mark obtained	0	1	2	3	4	5	6	7	8	9	10
Number of students	1	0	3	2	2	4	3	4	6	3	2

Find:

(a) the mode **(b)** the median **(c)** the mean.

(d) The class teacher is asked to report on her class's performance and wants to show them to be doing as well as possible. Which average should she include in her report and why?

12.4 Calculating averages and ranges for grouped continuous data

Some data is **discrete** and can only take on certain values. For example, if you throw an ordinary die then you can only get one of the numbers 1, 2, 3, 4, 5 or 6. If you count the number of red cars in a car park then the result can only be a whole number.

Some data is **continuous** and can take on *any* value in a given range. For example, heights of people, or the temperature of a liquid, are continuous measurements.

Continuous data can be difficult to process effectively unless it is summarised. For instance, if you measure the heights of 100 children you could end up with 100 different results. You can group the data into frequency tables to make the process more manageable – this is now **grouped data**. The groups (or classes) can be written using *inequality* symbols. For example, if you want to create a class for heights (h cm) between 120 cm and 130 cm you could write:

$120 \leq h < 130$

This means that h is greater than or equal to 120 but strictly less than 130. The next class could be:

$130 \leq h < 140$

Notice that 130 is not included in the first class but is included in the second. This is to avoid any confusion over where to put values at the boundaries.

The following worked example shows how a grouped frequency table is used to find the **estimated mean** and range, and also to find the **modal class** and the median classes (i.e. the classes in which the mode and median lie).

Tip

You may be asked to explain why your calculations only give an estimate. Remember that you don't have the exact data, only frequencies and classes.

Worked example 3

The heights of 100 children were measured in cm and the results recorded in the table below:

Height in cm (h)	Frequency (f)
$120 \le h < 130$	12
$130 \le h < 140$	16
$140 \le h < 150$	38
$150 \le h < 160$	24
$160 \le h < 170$	10

Find an estimate for the mean height of the children, the modal class, the median class and an estimate for the range.

None of the children's heights are known exactly, so you use the *midpoint* of each group as a best estimate of the height of each child in a particular class. For example, the 12 children in the $120 \le h < 130$ class have heights that lie between 120 cm and 130 cm, and that is all that you know. Halfway between 120 cm and 130 cm is $\frac{(120+130)}{2} = 125\,\text{cm}$.

A good estimate of the total height of the 12 children in this class is 12×125 (= frequency × midpoint).

So, extend your table to include midpoints and then totals for each class:

Height in cm (h)	Frequency (f)	Midpoint	Frequency × midpoint
$120 \le h < 130$	12	125	$12 \times 125 = 1500$
$130 \le h < 140$	16	135	$16 \times 135 = 2160$
$140 \le h < 150$	38	145	$38 \times 145 = 5510$
$150 \le h < 160$	24	155	$24 \times 155 = 3720$
$160 \le h < 170$	10	165	$10 \times 165 = 1650$

An estimate for the mean height of the children is then:

$$\frac{1500+2160+5510+3720+1650}{12+16+38+24+10} = \frac{14540}{100} = 145.4\,\text{cm}$$

To find the median class you need to find where the 50th and 51st tallest children would be placed. Notice that the first two frequencies add to give 28, meaning that the 28th child in an ordered list of heights would be the tallest in the $130 \le h < 140$ class. The total of the first *three* frequencies is 66, meaning that the 50th child will be somewhere in the $140 \le h < 150$ class. This then, makes $140 \le h < 150$ the median class.

The class with the highest frequency is the modal class. In this case it is the same class as the median class: $140 \le h < 150$.

The shortest child could be as small as 120 cm and the tallest could be as tall as 170 cm. The best estimate of the range is, therefore, $170 - 120 = 50\,\text{cm}$.

Exercise 12.4

The symbol Σ is the Greek letter capital 'sigma'. It is used to mean 'sum'. So, Σf simply means, 'the sum of all the frequencies'.

1 The table shows the heights of 50 sculptures in an art gallery. Find an estimate for the mean height of the sculptures.

Heights (h cm)	Frequency (f)
$130 < h \leq 135$	7
$135 < h \leq 140$	13
$140 < h \leq 145$	15
$145 < h \leq 150$	11
$150 < h \leq 155$	4
Total	$\Sigma f = 50$

2 The table shows the lengths of 100 telephone calls.

Time (t minutes)	Frequency (f)
$0 < t \leq 1$	12
$1 < t \leq 2$	14
$2 < t \leq 4$	20
$4 < t \leq 6$	14
$6 < t \leq 8$	12
$8 < t \leq 10$	18
$10 < t \leq 15$	10

(a) Calculate an estimate for the mean time, in minutes, of a telephone call.
(b) Write your answer in minutes and seconds, to the nearest second.

3 The table shows the temperatures of several test tubes during a Chemistry experiment.

Temperature (T °C)	Frequency (f)
$45 \leq T < 50$	3
$50 \leq T < 55$	8
$55 \leq T < 60$	17
$60 \leq T < 65$	6
$65 \leq T < 70$	2
$70 \leq T < 75$	1

Calculate an estimate for the mean temperature of the test tubes.

4 Two athletics teams – the *Hawks* and the *Eagles* – are about to compete in a race. The masses of the team members are shown in the table below.

Hawks

Mass (M kg)	Frequency (f)
$55 \leq M < 65$	2
$65 \leq M < 75$	8
$75 \leq M < 85$	12
$85 \leq M < 100$	3

Eagles

Mass (M kg)	Frequency (f)
$55 \leq M < 65$	1
$65 \leq M < 75$	7
$75 \leq M < 85$	13
$85 \leq M < 100$	4

(a) Calculate an estimate for the mean mass of each team.
(b) Calculate the range of masses of each team.
(c) Comment on your answers for (a) and (b).

5 The table below shows the lengths of 50 pieces of wire used in a Physics laboratory. The lengths have been measured *to the nearest centimetre*. Find an estimate for the mean.

Length	26–30	31–35	36–40	41–45	46–50
Frequency (f)	4	10	12	18	6

Be careful when calculating the midpoints here. Someone who is just a day short of 31 will still be in the 21–30 class. What difference does this make?

6 The table below shows the ages of the teachers in a secondary school to the nearest year.

Age in years	21–30	31–35	36–40	41–45	46–50	51–65
Frequency (f)	3	6	12	15	6	7

Calculate an estimate for the mean age of the teachers.

12.5 Percentiles and quartiles

Fashkiddler's accountancy firm is advertising for new staff to join the company and has set an entrance test to examine the ability of candidates to answer questions on statistics. In a statement on the application form the company states that, *'All those candidates above the 80th percentile will be offered an interview.'* What does this mean?

FAST FORWARD

You will do further work with percentiles in chapter 20 when you learn about cumulative frequency curves. You will also find the solution to *Fashkiddler's* problem. ▶

The median is a very special example of a **percentile**. It is placed exactly half way through a list of ordered data so that 50% of the data is smaller than the median. Positions other than the median can, however, also be useful.

The tenth percentile, for example, would lie such that 10% of the data was smaller than its value. The 75th percentile would lie such that 75% of the values are smaller than its value.

Quartiles

Two very important percentiles are the **upper** and **lower quartiles.** These lie 25% and 75% of the way through the data respectively.

Use the following rules to estimate the positions of each quartile within a set of ordered data:

Q_1 = lower quartile = value in position $\frac{1}{4}(n+1)$

Q_2 = median (as calculated earlier in the chapter)

Q_3 = upper quartile = value in position $\frac{3}{4}(n+1)$

If the position does not turn out to be a whole number, you simply find the mean of the pair of numbers on either side. For example, if the position of the lower quartile turns out to be 5.25, then you find the mean of the 5th and 6th pair.

Interquartile range

As with the *range*, the **interquartile range** gives a measure of how spread out or consistent the data is. The main difference is that the interquartile range (IQR) avoids using extreme data by finding the difference between the lower and upper quartiles. You are, effectively, measuring the spread of the central 50% of the data.

$$\text{IQR} = Q_3 - Q_1$$

If one set of data has a smaller IQR than another set, then the first set is more consistent and less spread out. This can be a useful comparison tool.

FAST FORWARD

In chapter 20 you will learn about *cumulative frequency* graphs. These enable you to calculate estimates for the median when there are too many data to put into order, or when you have grouped data. ▶

Worked example 4

For each of the following sets of data calculate the median, upper and lower quartiles. In each case calculate the interquartile range.

(a) 13 12 8 6 11 14 8 5 1 10 16 12
(b) 14 10 8 19 15 14 9

(a) First *sort the data into ascending order*.

1 5 6 8 8 10 11 12 12 13 14 16

There is an even number of items (12). So for the median, you find the value of the middle pair, the first of which is in position $\frac{12}{2} = 6$. So the median is $\frac{(10+11)}{2} = 10.5$

There are 12 items so, for the quartiles, you calculate the positions

$\frac{1}{4}(12+1) = 3.25$ and $\frac{3}{4}(12+1) = 9.75$

Notice that these are not whole numbers, so the lower quartile will be the mean of the 3rd and 4th values, and the upper quartile will be the mean of the 9th and 10th values.

$Q_1 = \frac{(6+8)}{2} = 7$ and $Q_3 = \frac{(12+13)}{2} = 12.5$

Thus, the IQR $= 12.5 - 7 = 5.5$

(b) The ordered data is:

8 9 10 14 14 15 19

The number of data is odd, so the median will be in position $\frac{(7+1)}{2} = 4$. The median is 14.

There are seven items, so calculate $\frac{1}{4}(7+1) = 2$ and $\frac{3}{4}(7+1) = 6$

These are whole numbers so the lower quartile is in position two and the upper quartile is in position six.

So $Q_1 = 9$ and $Q_3 = 15$.

IQR $= 15 - 9 = 6$

Worked example 5

Two companies sell sunflower seeds. Over the period of a year, seeds from Allbright produce flowers with a median height of 98 cm and IQR of 13 cm. In the same year seeds from Barstows produce flowers with a median height of 95 cm and IQR of 4 cm. Which seeds would you buy if you wanted to enter a competition for growing the tallest sunflower and why?

I would buy Barstows' seeds. Although Allbright sunflowers seem taller (with a higher median) they are less consistent. So, whilst there is a chance of a very big sunflower there is also a good chance of a small sunflower. Barstows' sunflowers are a bit shorter, but are more consistent in their heights so you are more likely to get flowers around the height of 95 cm.

Exercise 12.5

1 Find the median, quartiles and interquartile range for each of the following. Make sure that you show your method clearly.

(a) 5 8 9 9 4 5 6 9 3 6 4
(b) 12 14 12 17 19 21 23
(c) 4 5 12 14 15 17 14 3 18 19 18 19 14 4 15
(d) 3.1 2.4 5.1 2.3 2.5 4.2 3.4 6.1 4.8
(e) 13.2 14.8 19.6 14.5 16.7 18.9 14.5 13.7 17.0 21.8 12.0 16.5

Living maths

Try to think about what the calculations in each question tell you about each situation.

2 Gideon walks to work when it is not raining. Each week for 15 weeks Gideon records the number of walks that he takes and the results are shown below:

5	7	5	8	4
2	9	9	4	7
6	4	6	12	4

Find the median, quartiles and interquartile range for this data.

3 Paavan is conducting a survey into the traffic on his road. Every Monday for eight weeks in the summer Paavan records the number of cars that pass by his house between 08.00 a.m. and 09.00 a.m. He then repeats the experiment during the winter. Both sets of results are shown below:

Summer:	18	15	19	25	19	26	17	13
Winter:	12	9	14	11	13	9	12	10

(a) Find the median number of cars for each period.
(b) Find the interquartile range for each period.
(c) What differences do you notice? Try to explain why this might happen.

4 Julian and Aneesh are reading articles from different magazines. They count the number of words in a random selection of sentences from their articles and the results are recorded below:

Julian

(reading the *Statistician*): 23 31 12 19 23 13 24

Aneesh

(reading the *Algebraist*): 19 12 13 16 18 15 18 21 22

(a) Calculate the median for each article.
(b) Calculate the interquartile range for each article.
(c) Aneesh claims that the editor of the *Algebraist* has tried to control the writing and seems to be aiming it at a particular audience. What do your answers from (a) and (b) suggest about this claim?

Summary

Do you know the following?

- Averages – the mode, median and mean – are used to summarise a collection of data.
- There are two main types of numerical data – discrete and continuous.
- Discrete data can be listed or arranged in a frequency distribution.
- Continuous data can be listed or arranged into groups
- The mean is affected by extreme data.
- The median is less affected by extreme data.
- The median is a special example of a percentile.
- The lower quartile (Q_1) lies 25% of the way through the data.
- The upper quartile (Q_3) lies 75% of the way through the data.
- The interquartile range ($IQR = Q_3 - Q_1$) gives a measure of how spread out or consistent the data is. It is a measure of the spread of the central 50% of the data.

Are you able to ...?

- calculate the mean, median, mode and range of data given in a list
- calculate the mean, median, mode and range of data given in a frequency distribution
- calculate an estimate for the mean of grouped data
- find the median class for grouped data
- find the modal class for grouped data
- compare sets of data using summary averages and ranges
- find the quartiles of data arranged in ascending order
- find the interquartile range for listed data.

Examination practice

Past paper questions

1 8 15 7 8 7 15 4 13 4 3 10 2 9 4 5

(a) Write down the mode. [1]

(b) Work out the median. [2]

[Cambridge IGCSE Mathematics 0580 Paper 11 Q16 October/November 2013]

2 30 students took a vocabulary test.
The marks they scored are shown below.

7	8	5	8	3	2
6	6	3	3	6	2
7	1	5	10	2	6
6	5	8	1	2	7
3	1	5	3	10	3

(a) Complete the frequency table below.
The first five frequencies have been completed for you.
You may use the tally column to help you. [3]

Mark	Tally	Frequency
1		3
2		4
3		6
4		0
5		4
6		
7		
8		
9		
10		

(b) **(i)** Find the range. [1]

(ii) Write down the mode. [1]

(iii) Find the median. [2]

(iv) Calculate the mean. [3]

[Cambridge IGCSE Mathematics 0580 Paper 31 Q8 a, b May/June 2011]

3 (a) A farmer takes a sample of 158 potatoes from his crop.
He records the mass of each potato and the results are shown in the table.

Mass (m grams)	Frequency
$0 < m \le 40$	6
$40 < m \le 80$	10
$80 < m \le 120$	28
$120 < m \le 160$	76
$160 < m \le 200$	22
$200 < m \le 240$	16

Calculate an estimate of the mean mass.
Show all your working. [4]

(b) A new frequency table is made from the results shown in the table in **part (a)**.

Mass (m grams)	Frequency
$0 < m \le 80$	
$80 < m \le 200$	
$200 < m \le 240$	16

(i) Complete the table above. [2]

(ii) On the grid, complete the histogram to show the information in this new table.

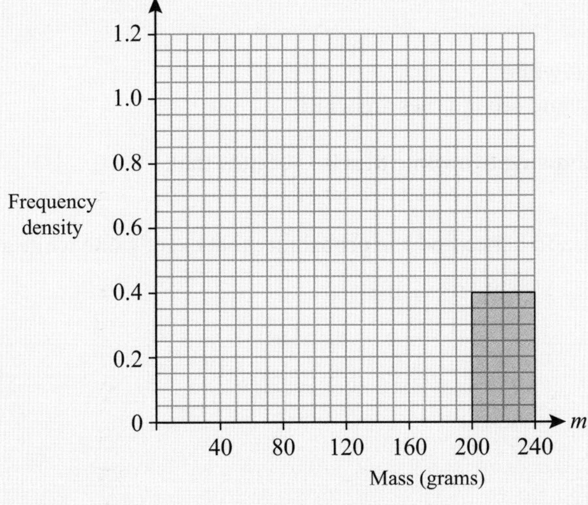

[3]

(c) A bag contains 15 potatoes which have a mean mass of 136 g.
The farmer puts 3 potatoes which have a mean mass of 130 g into the bag.
Calculate the mean mass of all the potatoes in the bag. [3]

[Cambridge IGCSE Mathematics 0580 Paper 42 Q5 October/November 2012]

Examination practice: structured questions for Units 1–3

Exam-style questions

1 **(a)** Factorise the expression $5x^2 + 4x - 57$.

(b) The shaded regions in diagrams *A* (a rectangle) and *B* (a square with a section cut out) are equal in area.

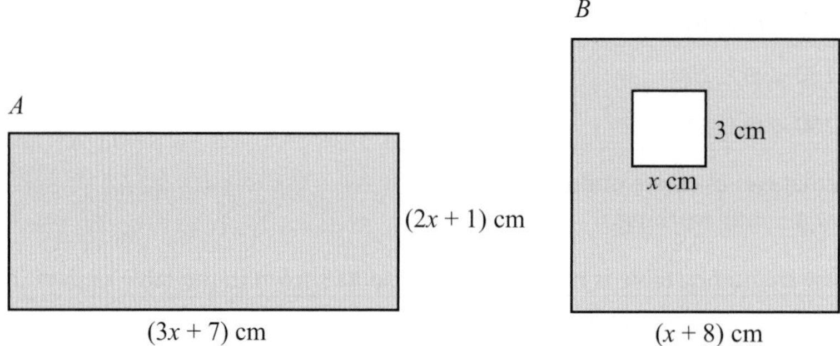

(i) Show that the area of the shaded region in *A* is $6x^2 + 17x + 7$ cm².
(ii) Show that the area of the shaded region in *B* is $x^2 + 13x + 64$ cm².
(iii) Use your answers in (i) and (ii) to show that $5x^2 + 4x - 57 = 0$.
(iv) Hence find the dimensions of rectangle *A*.

2 A bag contains n white tiles and five black tiles. The tiles are all equal in shape and size. A tile is drawn at random and is replaced. A second tile is then drawn.

(a) Find:

(i) the probability that the first tile is white
(ii) the probability that both the first and second tiles are white.

(b) You are given that the probability of drawing two white tiles is $\frac{7}{22}$. Show that:

$3n^2 - 17n - 28 = 0$.

(c) Solve the equation, $3n^2 - 17n - 28 = 0$, and hence find the probability that exactly one white and exactly one black tile is drawn.

3 $p = 2^x$ and $q = 2^y$.

(a) Find, in terms of p and q:

(i) 2^{x+y}
(ii) 2^{x+y-2}
(iii) 2^{3x}.

(b) You are now given that:

$$p^2q = 16 \text{ and } \frac{q^2}{p} = 32.$$

Find the values of x, y, p, and q.

4

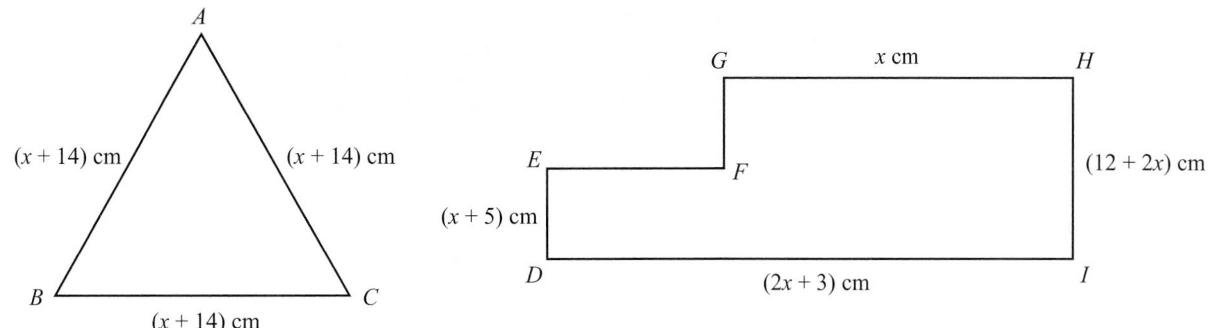

(a) Find the perimeter of triangle ABC. Simplify your answer as fully as possible.
(b) Find the distance EF in terms of x.
(c) Find the distance FG in terms of x.
(d) Find the perimeter of shape $DEFGHI$ in terms of x. Simplify your answer.
(e) You are given that the perimeters of both shapes are equal. Form an equation and solve it for x.
(f) Find the perimeters of both shapes and the area of $DEFGHI$.

5

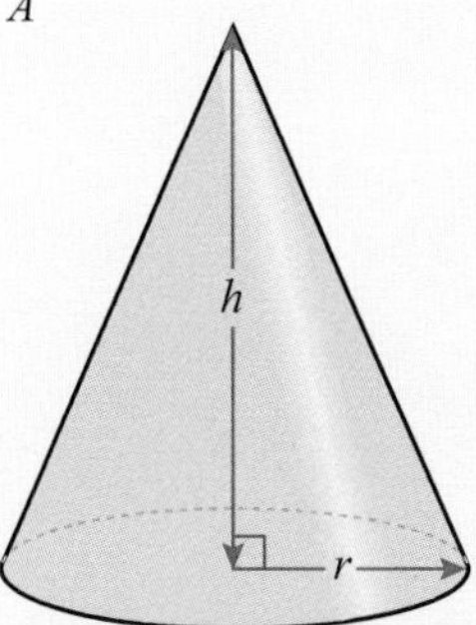

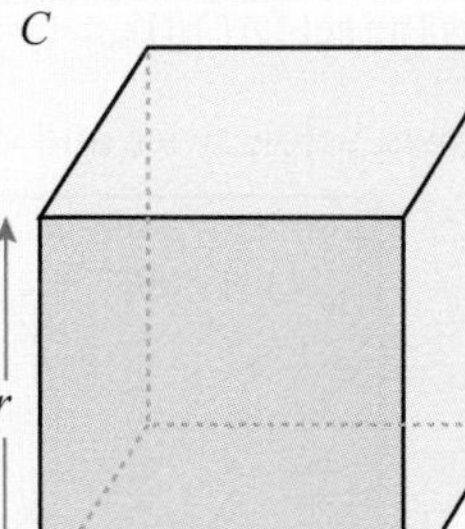

The right cone, A, has perpendicular height h cm and base radius r cm.

The sphere, B, has a radius of r cm.

The cuboid, C, measures $r\text{ cm} \times r\text{ cm} \times h\text{ cm}$.

(a) You are given that cone A and sphere B are equal in volume. Write down an equation connecting r and h, and show that $h = 4r$.

(b) The surface area of cuboid C is 98 cm^2. Form a second equation connecting r and h.

(c) Combine your answers to **(a)** and **(b)** to show that $r = \frac{7}{3}$.

(d) Find h and, hence, the volume of the cuboid.

6 **(a)** Express 60 and 36 as products of primes.
(b) Hence find the LCM of 60 and 36.
(c) Planet Carceron has two moons, Anderon and Barberon. Anderon completes a full orbit of Carceron every 60 days, and Barberon completes a full single orbit of Carceron in 36 days.
If Anderon, Barberon and Carceron lie on a straight line on 1 March 2010 on which date will this next be true?

7 **(a)** Factorise the expression $x^2 - 50x + 609$.
(b) Hence or otherwise solve the equation $2x^2 - 100x + 1218 = 0$.

A farmer wants to use 100 m of fencing to build three sides of the rectangular pen shown in the diagram:

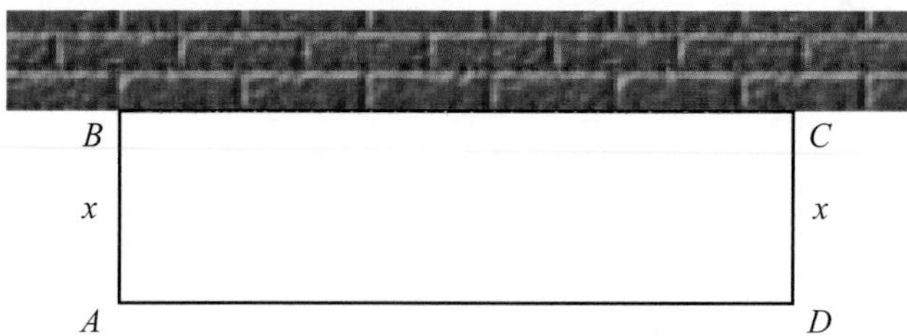

(c) Find an expression for the length AD in terms of x.
(d) Find an expression for the area of the pen in terms of x.
(e) The farmer wants the area of the pen to be exactly 1218 square metres. Using your answer to **(d)**, find and solve an equation for x and determine all possible dimensions of the pen.

8 If $\mathscr{E}$ = {integers}, $A = \{x : x \text{ is an integer and } -4 < x < 7\}$ and $B = \{x : x \text{ is a positive multiple of three}\}$:

(a) list the elements of set A
(b) find $n(A \cap B)$
(c) describe in words the set $(A \cap B)'$.

9 Copy the diagram shown below twice and shade the sets indicated.

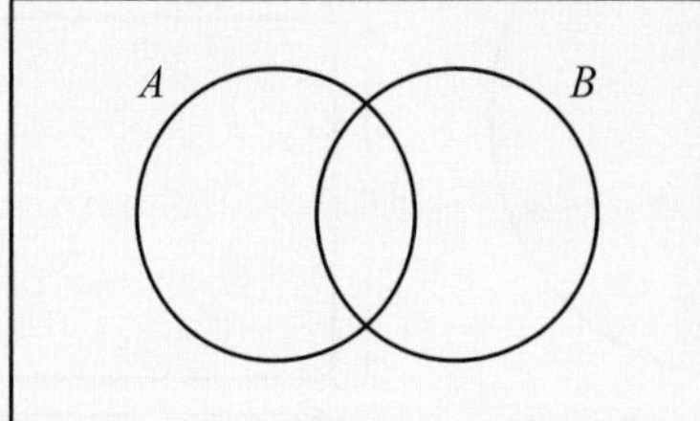

(a) $(A \cap B)'$
(b) $(A \cup B')' \cup (A \cap B)$

10 Mr Dane took a walk in the park and recorded the various types of birds that he saw. The results are shown in the pie chart below.

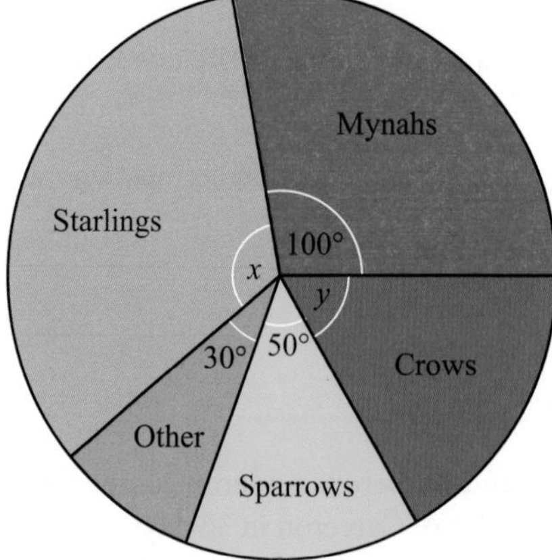

There were 30 Sparrows and 72 Starlings in the park.

(a) Calculate the number of Mynahs in the park.
(b) Calculate the angle x.
(c) Calculate the angle y.
(d) Calculate the number of Crows in the park.

Past paper questions

1

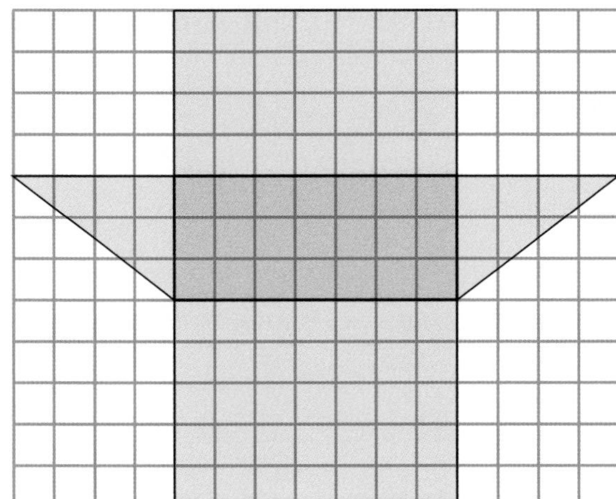

The shape above is the net of a solid drawn on a 1 cm square grid.

(a) Write down the geometrical name of the solid. [1]

(b) Find the perimeter of the net. [1]

(c) Work out

(i) the area of one of the triangles, [2]

(ii) the volume of the solid. [2]

(d) A cuboid of length 4 cm and width 3 cm has the same volume as the solid.
Calculate the height of the cuboid. [2]

[Cambridge IGCSE Mathematics 0580 Paper 31 Q02 May/June 2011]

2 Here is a sequence of patterns made using identical polygons.

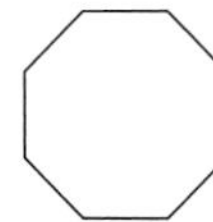

Pattern 1

Pattern 2

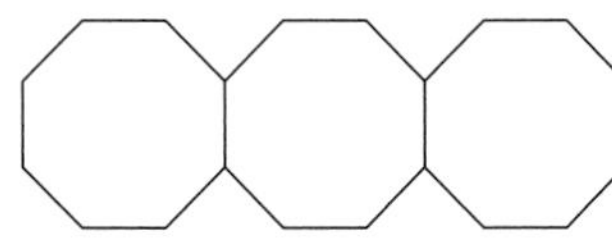

Pattern 3

(a) Write down the mathematical name of the polygon in Pattern 1. [1]

(b) Complete the table for the number of vertices (corners) and the number of lines in Pattern 3, Pattern 4 and Pattern 7. [5]

Pattern	1	2	3	4		7
Number of vertices	8	14				
Number of lines	8	15				

(c) (i) Find an expression for the number of **vertices** in Pattern n. [2]

(ii) Work out the number of vertices in Pattern 23. [1]

(d) Find an expression for the number of **lines** in Pattern n. [2]

(e) Work out an expression, in its simplest form, for
(number of lines in Pattern n) – (number of vertices in Pattern n). [2]

[Cambridge IGCSE Mathematics 0580 Paper 33 Q08 October/November 2013]

3 **(a)** Using only the integers from 1 to 50, find

(i) a multiple of both 4 and 7, [1]

(ii) a square number that is odd, [1]

(iii) an even prime number, [1]

(iv) a prime number which is one less than a multiple of 5. [1]

(b) Find the value of

(i) $\left(\sqrt{5}\right)^2$, [1]

(ii) $2^{-3} \times 6^3$. [2]

[Cambridge IGCSE Mathematics 0580 Paper 33 Q03 October/November 2013]

13 Understanding measurement

Key words

- Metric
- Lower bound
- Upper bound
- Imperial
- Conversion
- Exchange rate

In this chapter you will learn how to:

- convert between units in the metric system
- find lower and upper bounds of numbers that have been quoted to a given accuracy
- EXTENDED: Solve problems involving upper and lower bounds
- use conversion graphs to change units from one measuring system to another
- use exchange rates to convert currencies.

Weather systems are governed by complex sets of rules. The mathematics that describes these rules can be highly sensitive to small changes or inaccuracies in the available numerical data. We need to understand how accurate our predictions may or may not be.

The penalties for driving an overloaded vehicle can be expensive, as well as dangerous for the driver and other road users. If a driver is carrying crates that have a rounded mass value, he needs to know what the maximum mass could be before he sets off and, if necessary, put his truck onto a weighbridge as a precaution against fines and, worse, an accident.

13.1 Understanding units

REWIND

You encountered these units in chapter 7 when working with perimeters, areas and volumes. ◀

Vishal has a 1 m × 1 m × 1 m box and has collected a large number of 1 cm × 1 cm × 1 cm building blocks. He is very tidy and decides to stack all of the cubes neatly into the box.

Try to picture a 1 m × 1 m × 1 m box:

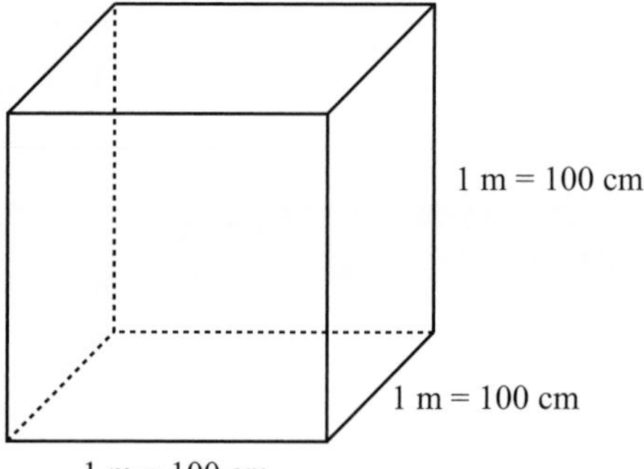

The lengths of each side will be 1 m = 100 cm. The total number of 1 cm × 1 cm × 1 cm cubes that will fit inside will be 100 × 100 × 100 = 1 000 000.

The main point of this example is that if you change the units with which a quantity is measured, the actual numerical values can be wildly different.

Here, you have seen that one cubic metre is equivalent to one million cubic centimetres!

Centimetres and metres are examples of **metric** measurements, and the table below shows some important conversions. You should work through the table and make sure that you understand *why* each of the conversions is as it is.

Capacity is measured in terms of what something *can* contain, not how much it *does* contain. A jug can have a capacity of 1 litre but only contain 500 ml. In the latter case, you would refer to the volume of the liquid in the container.

Measure	Units used	Equivalent to . . .
Length – how long (or tall) something is.	Millimetres (mm) Centimetres (cm) Metres (m) Kilometres (km)	10 mm = 1 cm 100 cm = 1 m 1000 m = 1 km 1 km = 1 000 000 mm
Mass – the amount of material in an object, (sometimes incorrectly called weight).	Milligrams (mg) Grams (g) Kilograms (kg) Tonnes (t)	1000 mg = 1 g 1000 g = 1 kg 1000 kg = 1 t 1 t = 1 000 000 g
Capacity – the inside volume of a container; how much it can hold.	Millilitres (ml) Centilitres (cl) Litres (ℓ)	10 ml = 1 cl 100 cl = 1 ℓ 1 ℓ = 1000 ml
Area – the amount of space taken up by a flat (two-dimensional) shape, always measured in square units.	Square millimetre (mm^2) Square centimetre (cm^2) Square metre (m^2) Square kilometre (km^2) Hectare (ha)	100 mm^2 = 1 cm^2 10 000 cm^2 = 1 m^2 1 000 000 m^2 = 1 km^2 1 km^2 = 100 ha 1 ha = 10 000 m^2
Volume – the amount of space taken up by a three-dimensional object, always measured in cubic units (or their equivalent liquid measurements, e.g. ml).	Cubic millimetre (mm^3) Cubic centimetre (cm^3) Cubic metre (m^3) Millilitre (mℓ)	1000 mm^3 = 1 cm^3 1 000 000 cm^3 = 1 m^3 1 m^3 = 1000 ℓ 1 cm^3 = 1 mℓ

The example on page 257 shows how these conversions can be used.

Worked example 1

Express:

(a) 5 km in metres **(b)** 3.2 cm in mm **(c)** 2 000 000 cm^2 in m^2.

(a) 1 km = 1000 m
So, 5 km = 5 × 1000 m = 5000 m

(b) 1 cm = 10 mm
So, 3.2 cm = 3.2 × 10 = 32 mm

(c) 1 m^2 = 100 cm × 100 cm = 10 000 cm^2
So, 2 000 000 $cm^2 = \frac{2\,000\,000}{10\,000} = 200\,m^2$

Exercise 13.1

1 Express each quantity in the unit given in brackets.

(a) 4 kg (g) (b) 5 km (m) (c) 35 mm (cm)
(d) 81 mm (cm) (e) 7.3 g (mg) (f) 5760 kg (t)
(g) 2.1 m (cm) (h) 2 t (kg) (i) 140 cm (m)
(j) 2024 g (kg) (k) 121 mg (g) (l) 23 m (mm)
(m) 3 cm 5 mm (mm) (n) 8 km 36 m (m) (o) 9 g 77 mg (g)

2 Arrange in ascending order of size.

3.22 m, $3\frac{2}{9}$ m, 32.4 cm

3 Write the following volumes in order, starting with the smallest.

$\frac{1}{2}$ litre, 780 ml, 125 ml, 0.65 litres

4 How many 5 ml spoonfuls can be obtained from a bottle that contains 0.3 litres of medicine?

5 Express each quantity in the units given in brackets.

(a) 14.23 m (mm, km) (b) 19.06 g (mg, t) (c) $2\frac{3}{4}$ litres (ml, cl)

(d) 4 m^2 (mm^2, ha) (e) 13 cm^2 (mm^2, ha) (f) 10 cm^3 (mm^3, m^3)

REWIND

You will need to remind yourself how to calculate volumes of three-dimensional shapes in chapter 7. You also need to remember what you learned about standard form in chapter 5. ◄

6 A cube has sides of length 3 m. Find the volume of the cube in:

(a) m^3 (b) cm^3 (c) mm^3 (give your answer in standard form).

7 The average radius of the Earth is 6378 km. Find the volume of the Earth, using each of the following units. Give your answers in standard form to 3 significant figures. The volume of a sphere $= \frac{4}{3}\pi r^3$

(a) km^3
(b) m^3
(c) mm^3

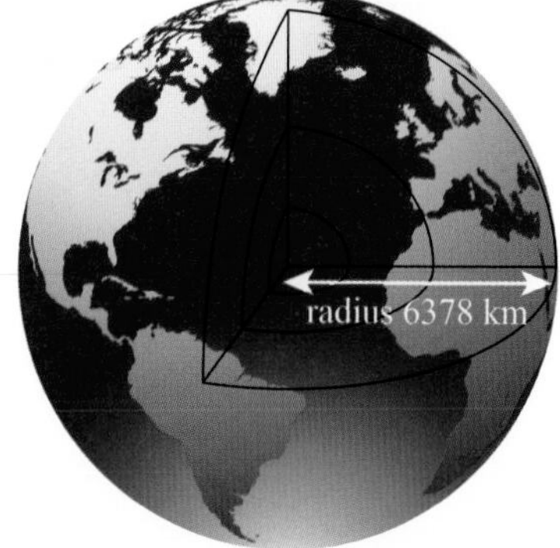

You were given the formula for the volume of a cone in chapter 7:
Volume $= \frac{1}{3}\pi r^2 h$.

8 The dimensions of the cone shown in the diagram are given in cm. Calculate the volume of the cone in:

(a) cm^3
(b) mm^3
(c) km^3

Give your answers in standard form to 3 significant figures.

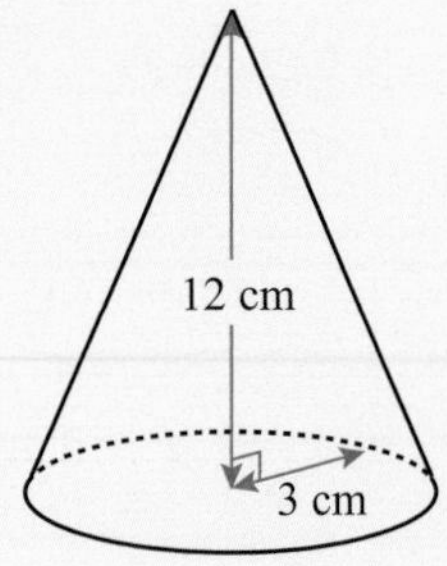

Living maths

9 Miss Molly has a jar that holds 200 grams of flour.

(a) How many 30 gram measures can she get from the jar?
(b) How much flour will be left over?

10 This is a lift in an office building.

The lift won't start if it holds more than 300 kg.

(a) Tomas (105 kg), Shaz (65 kg), Sindi (55 kg), Rashied (80 kg) and Mandy (70 kg) are waiting for the lift. Can they all ride together?
(b) Mandy says she will use the stairs. Can the others go safely into the lift?
(c) Rashied says he will wait for the lift to come down again. Can the other four go together in the lift?

13.2 Time

You have already learned how to tell the time and you should know how to read and write time using the 12-hour and 24-hour system.

The clock dial on the left shows you the times from 1 to 12 (a.m. and p.m. times). The inner dial shows what the times after 12 p.m. are in the 24-hour system.

Always remember that time is written in hours and minutes and that there are 60 minutes in an hour. This is very important when calculating time – if you put 1.5 hours into your calculator, it will assume the number is decimal and work with parts of 100, not parts of 60. So, you need to treat minutes and hours separately.

Worked example 2

Sara and John left home at 2.15 p.m. Sara returned at 2.50 p.m. and John returned at 3.05 p.m. How long was each person away from home?

Sara: 2 hours 50 minutes – 2 hours 15 minutes = 0 h 35 min 2 hours – 2 hours = 0 hours 50 min – 15 min = 35 min Sara was away for 35 minutes.	Think about how many hours you have, and how many minutes. 2.50 p.m. is the same as 2 hours and 50 minutes after 12 p.m., and 2.15 p.m. is the same as 2 hours and 15 minutes after 12 p.m. Subtract the hours separately from the minutes.
John: 3 h 5 min = 2 h 65 min 2 h 65 min – 2 h 15 min = 0 h 50 min John was away for 50 minutes.	3.05 p.m. is the same as 2 hours and 65 minutes after 12 p.m.; do a subtraction like before. Note both times are p.m. See the next example for when one time is a.m. and the other p.m.

You cannot subtract 15 min from 5 min in the context of time (you can't have negative minute) so carry one hour over to the minutes so that 3 h 5min becomes 2 h 65 mins.

Worked example 3

Again note that you cannot simply do 18.20 – 05.35 because this calculation would not take into account that with time you work in jumps of 60 not 100.

A train leaves at 05.35 and arrives at 18.20. How long is the journey?

18.20 is equivalent to 17 hours and 80 minutes after 12 a.m.	Again, 20–35 is not meaningful in the context of time, so carry one hour over to give 17 h 80 min.
17h – 5h = 12h 80 min – 35 min = 45 min	Now you can subtract the earlier time from the later time as before (hours and minutes separately).
The journey took 12 hours and 45 minutes.	Then add the hours and minutes together.

The methods in examples 1–3 are best used when you are dealing with time within the same day. But what happens when the time difference goes over one day?

Worked example 4

How much time passes from 19.35 on Monday to 03.55 on Tuesday?

19.35 to 24.00 is one part and 00.00 to 03.55 the next day is the other part.	The easiest way to tackle this problem is to divide the time into parts.
Part one: 19.35 to 24.00. 24 h = 23 h 60 min (past 12 a.m.) 23 h 60 min – 19 h 35 min = 4 h 25 min	00–35 is not meaningful in time, so carry one hour over so that 24.00 becomes 23 h 60 min. Then do the subtraction as before (hours and minutes separately).

Part two: 0.00 to 03.55 3h 55 min − 0 h 0 min = 3 h 55 min	03.55 is 3 hours and 55 minutes past 12 a.m. (or 0.00) so this is simply a difference of + 3 hours and 55 minutes
4 h 25 min + 3 h 55 min = 7 h 80 min 80 min = 1 h 20 min 7 h 0 min + 1 h 20 min = 8 h 20 min 8 hours and 20 min passes.	Add the result of the two parts together. Change the 80 minutes into hours and minutes. Add together.

Exercise 13.2 *Living maths*

1. Gary started a marathon race at 9.25 a.m. He finished at 1.04 p.m. How long did he take? Give your answer in hours and minutes.

2. Nick has a satellite TV decoder that shows time in 24-hour time. He wants to program the machine to record some programmes. Write down the timer settings for starting and finishing each recording.
   (a) 10.30 p.m. to 11.30 p.m.
   (b) 9.15 a.m. to 10.45 a.m.
   (c) 7.45 p.m. to 9.10 p.m.

3. Yasmin's car odometer shows distance travelled in kilometres. The odometer dial showed these two readings before and after a journey:

   (a) How far did she travel?
   (b) The journey took $2\frac{1}{2}$ hours. What was her average speed in km/h?

4. Yvette records three songs onto her MP4 player. The time each of them lasts is three minutes 26 seconds, three minutes 19 seconds and two minutes 58 seconds. She leaves a gap of two seconds between each of the songs. How long will it take to play the recording?

5. A journey started at 17:30 hours on Friday, 7 February, and finished 57 hours later. Write down the time, day and date when the journey finished.

6. Samuel works in a bookshop. This is his time sheet for the week.

Day	Mon	Tues	Wed	Thurs	Fri
Start	8:20	8:20	8:20	8:22	8:21
Lunch	12:00	12:00	12:30	12:00	12:30
Back	12:45	12:45	1:15	12:45	1:15
End	5:00	5:00	4:30	5:00	5:30
Total time worked					

(a) Complete the bottom row of the time sheet.
(b) How many hours in total did Samuel work this week?
(c) Samuel is paid $5.65 per hour. Calculate how much he earned this week.

Reading timetables

Most travel timetables are in the form of tables with columns representing journeys. The 24-hour system is used to give the times.

Here is an example:

	SX	D	D	D	MO	D	SX
Anytown	06:30	07:45	12:00	16:30	17:15	18:00	20:30
Beecity	06:50	08:05	12:25	16:50	17:35	18:25	20:50
Ceeville	07:25	08:40	13:15	17:25	18:15	19:05	21:25

D – daily including Sundays, SX – daily except Saturdays, MO – Mondays only

Make sure you can see that each column represents a journey. For example, the first column shows a bus leaving at 06:30 every day except Saturday (six times per week). It arrives at the next town, Beecity, at 06:50 and then goes on to Ceeville, where it arrives at 07:25.

Exercise 13.3 *Living maths*

1 The timetable for evening trains between Mitchell's Plain and Cape Town is shown below.

Mitchell's Plain	18:29	19:02	19:32	20:02	21:04
Nyanga	18:40	19:13	19:43	20:13	21:15
Pinelands	19:01	19:31	20:01	20:31	21:33
Cape Town	19:17	19:47	20:17	20:47	21:49

(a) Shaheeda wants to catch a train at Mitchell's Plain and get to Pinelands by 8.45 p.m. What is the time of the latest train she should catch?
(b) Calculate the time the 19:02 train from Mitchell's Plain takes to travel to Cape Town.
(c) Thabo arrives at Nyanga station at 6.50 p.m. How long will he have to wait for the next train to Cape Town?

2 The timetable for a bus service between Aville and Darby is shown below.

Aville	10:30	10:50	and	18:50
Beeston	11:05	11:25	every	19:25
Crossway	11:19	11:39	20 minutes	19:39
Darby	11:37	11:57	until	19:57

(a) How many minutes does a bus take to travel from Aville to Darby?
(b) Write down the timetable for the first bus on this service to leave Aville after the 10:50 bus.
(c) Ambrose arrives at Beeston bus station at 2.15 p.m. What is the time of the next bus to Darby?

3 The tides for a two-week period are shown on this tide table.

February	High tide		Low tide	
	Morning	Afternoon	Morning	Afternoon
1 Wednesday	1213	--	0518	1800
2 Thursday	0017	1257	0614	1849
3 Friday	0109	1332	0700	1930
4 Saturday	0152	1404	0740	2004
5 Sunday	0229	1434	0815	2038
6 Monday	0303	1505	0848	2111
7 Tuesday	0336	1537	0922	2143
8 Wednesday	0411	1610	0957	2215
9 Thursday	0448	1644	1030	2245
10 Friday	0528	1718	1104	2316
11 Saturday	0614	1757	1140	2354
12 Sunday	0706	1845	1222	--
13 Monday	0808	1948	0041	1315
14 Tuesday	0917	2111	0141	1425

(a) What is the earliest high tide in this period?
(b) How long is it between high tides on day two?
(c) How long is it between the first high tide and the first low tide on day seven?
(d) Mike likes to go surfing an hour before high tide.
  (i) At what time would this be on Sunday 5 February?
  (ii) Explain why it would unlikely to be at 01:29.

(e) Sandra owns a fishing boat.
  (i) She cannot go out in the mornings if the low tide occurs between 5 a.m. and 9 a.m. On which days did this happen?
  (ii) Sandra takes her boat out in the afternoons if high tide is between 11 a.m. and 2.30 p.m. On which days could she go out in the afternoons?

13.3 Upper and lower bounds

Raeman has ordered a sofa and wants to work out whether or not it will fit through his door. He has measured both the door (47 cm) and the sofa (46.9 cm) and concludes that the sofa should fit with 1 mm to spare. Unfortunately, the sofa arrives and doesn't fit. What went wrong?

Looking again at the value 47 cm, Raeman realises that he rounded the measurement to the nearest cm. A new, more accurate measurement reveals that the door frame is, in fact, closer to 46.7 cm wide. Raeman also realises that he has rounded the sofa measurement to the nearest mm. He measures it again and finds that the actual value is closer to 46.95 cm, which is 2.5 mm wider than the door!

Finding the greatest and least possible values of a rounded measurement

Consider again, the width of Raeman's door. If 47 cm has been rounded to the nearest cm it can be useful to work out the greatest and least possible values of the *actual* measurement.

If you place the measurement of 47 cm on a number line, then you can see much more clearly what the range of possible values will be:

Notice at the upper end, that the range of possible values stops at 47.5 cm. If you round 47.5 cm to the nearest cm you get the answer 48 cm. Although 47.5 cm does not round to 47 (to the nearest cm), it is still used as the upper value. But, you should understand that the *true* value of the width could be anything up to *but not including* 47.5 cm. The lowest possible value of the door width is called the **lower bound**. Similarly, the largest possible value is called the **upper bound.**

Letting w represent the width of the sofa, the range of possible measurements can be expressed as:

$46.5 \leq w < 47.5$

This shows that the true value of w lies between 46.5 (including 46.5) and 47.5 (not including 47.5).

Worked example 5

Find the upper and lower bounds of the following, taking into account the level of rounding shown in each case.

(a) 10 cm, to the nearest cm **(b)** 22.5, to 1 decimal place

(c) 128 000, to 3 significant figures.

If you get confused when dealing with upper and lower bounds, draw a number line to help you.

(a) Show 10 cm on a number line with the two nearest whole number values.

The real value will be closest to 10 cm if it lies between the lower bound of 9.5 cm and the upper bound of 10.5 cm.

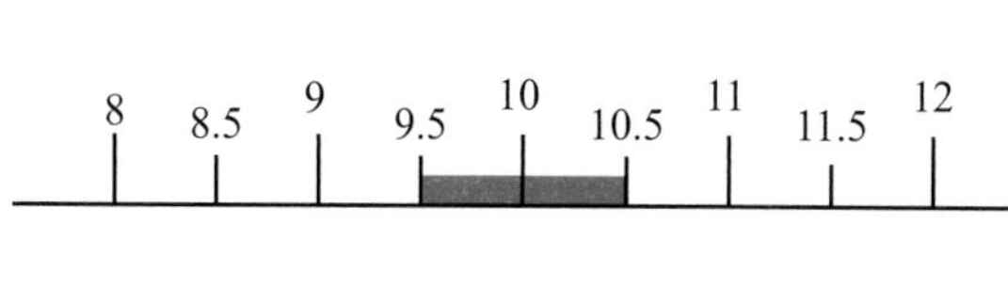

(b) Look at 22.5 on a number line.

The real value will be closest to 22.5 if it lies between the lower bound of 22.45 and the upper bound of 22.55.

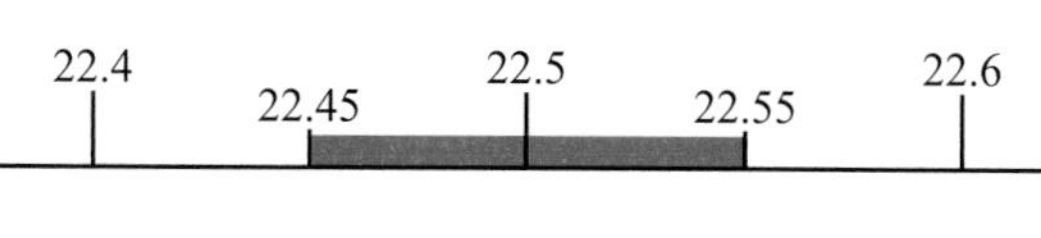

(c) 128 000 is shown on a number line.

128 000 lies between the lower bound of 127 500 and the upper bound of 128 500.

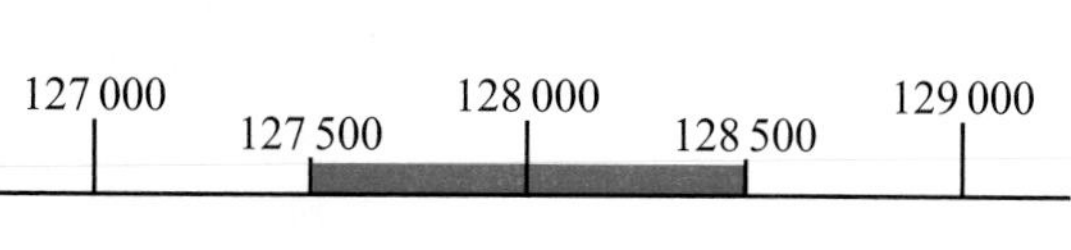

Exercise 13.4

1 Each of the following numbers is given to the nearest whole number. Find the lower and upper bounds of the numbers.

(a) 12 (b) 8 (c) 100 (d) 9 (e) 72 (f) 127

2 Each of the following numbers is correct to 1 decimal place. Write down the lower and upper bounds of the numbers.

(a) 2.7 (b) 34.4 (c) 5.0 (d) 1.1 (e) −2.3 (f) −7.2

3 Each of the numbers below has been rounded to the degree of accuracy shown in the brackets. Find the upper and lower bounds in each case.

(a) 132 (nearest whole number)
(b) 300 (nearest one hundred)
(c) 405 (nearest five)
(d) 15 million (nearest million)
(e) 32.3 (1dp)
(f) 26.7 (1dp)
(g) 0.5 (1dp)
(h) 12.34 (2dp)
(i) 132 (3sf)
(j) 0.134 (3sf)

Living maths

4 Anne estimates that the mass of a lion is 300 kg. Her estimate is correct to the nearest 100 kg. Between what limits does the actual mass of the lion lie?

5 In a race, Nomatyala ran 100 m in 15.3 seconds. The distance is correct to the nearest metre and the time is correct to one decimal place. Write down the lower and upper bounds of:

(a) the actual distance Nomatyala ran (b) the actual time taken.

6 The length of a piece of thread is 4.5 m to the nearest 10 cm. The actual length of the thread is L cm. Find the range of possible values for L, giving you answer in the form $\ldots \leq L < \ldots$

Problem solving with upper and lower bounds

Some calculations make use of more than one rounded value. Careful use of the upper and lower bounds of each value, will give correct upper and lower bounds for the calculated answer.

Worked example 6

If $a = 3.6$ (to 1 dp) and $b = 14$ (to the nearest whole number), find the upper and lower bounds for each of the following:

(a) $a + b$ (b) ab (c) $b - a$ (d) $\frac{a}{b}$ (e) $\frac{a+b}{a}$

Firstly, find the upper and lower bounds of a and b:

$3.55 \leq a < 3.65$ and $13.5 \leq b < 14.5$

(a) Upper bound for $(a+b)$ = upper bound of a + upper bound of b

$= 3.65 + 14.5$

$= 18.15$

Lower bound for $(a+b)$ = lower bound for a + lower bound for b

$= 3.55 + 13.5$

$= 17.05$

This can be written as: $17.05 \leq (a+b) < 18.15$

(b) Upper bound for ab = upper bound for a × upper bound for b

$= 3.65 \times 14.5$

$= 52.925$

Lower bound for ab = lower bound for a × lower bound for b

$= 3.55 \times 13.5$

$= 47.925$

This can be written as: $47.925 \leq ab < 52.925$

(c) Think carefully about $b - a$. To find the upper bound you need to subtract as small a number as possible from the largest possible number. So:

Upper bound for $(b-a)$ = upper bound for b lower bound for a

$= 14.5 - 3.55$

$= 10.95$

Similarly, for the lower bound:

Lower bound $(b-a)$ = lower bound for b upper bound for a

$= 13.5 - 3.65$

$= 9.85$

This can be written as: $9.85 \leq (b-a) < 10.95$

(d) To find the upper bound of $\frac{a}{b}$ you need to divide the largest possible value of a by the smallest possible value of b:

$$\text{Upper bound} = \frac{\text{upper bound for } a}{\text{lower bound for } b} = \frac{3.65}{13.5} = 0.2703\ldots = 0.270 \text{ (3sf)}$$

$$\text{Lower bound} = \frac{\text{lower bound for } a}{\text{upper bound for } b} = \frac{3.55}{14.5} = 0.2448\ldots = 0.245 \text{ (3sf)}$$

This can be written as: $0.245 \leq \frac{a}{b} < 0.270$

(e)

$$\text{Upper bound of} = \frac{a+b}{a} = \frac{\text{upper bound of } a+b}{\text{lower bound of } a} = \frac{18.15}{3.55} = 5.1126\ldots = 5.11 \text{ (3sf)}$$

$$\text{Lower bound of} = \frac{a+b}{a} = \frac{\text{lower bound of } a+b}{\text{upper bound of } a} = \frac{17.05}{3.65} = 4.6712\ldots = 4.67 \text{ (3sf)}$$

This can be written as: $4.67 \leq \frac{a+b}{a} < 5.11$

Exercise 13.5

1 You are given that:

$a = 5.6$ (to 1dp) $b = 24.1$ (to 1dp) $c = 145$ (to 3sf) $d = 0.34$ (to 2dp)

Calculate the upper and lower bounds for each of the following to 3 significant figures:

(a) a^2 (b) b^3 (c) cd^3 (d) $a^2 + b^2$ (e) $\frac{c}{b^2}$

(f) $\frac{ab}{cd}$ (g) $\frac{c}{a} - \frac{b}{d}$ (h) $\frac{a}{d} \div \frac{c}{b}$ (i) $dc + \sqrt{\frac{a}{b}}$ (j) $dc - \sqrt{\frac{a}{b}}$

Living maths

2 Jonathan and Priya want to fit a new washing machine in their kitchen. The width of a washing machine is 79 cm to the nearest cm. To fit in the machine, they have to make a space by removing cabinets. They want the space to be as small as possible.

(a) What is the smallest space into which the washing machine can fit?
(b) What is the largest space they might need for it to fit?

3 12 kg of sugar are removed from a container holding 50 kg. Each measurement is correct to the nearest kilogram. Find the lower and upper bounds of the mass of sugar left in the container.

4 The dimensions of a rectangle are 3.61 cm and 2.57 cm, each correct to 3 significant figures.

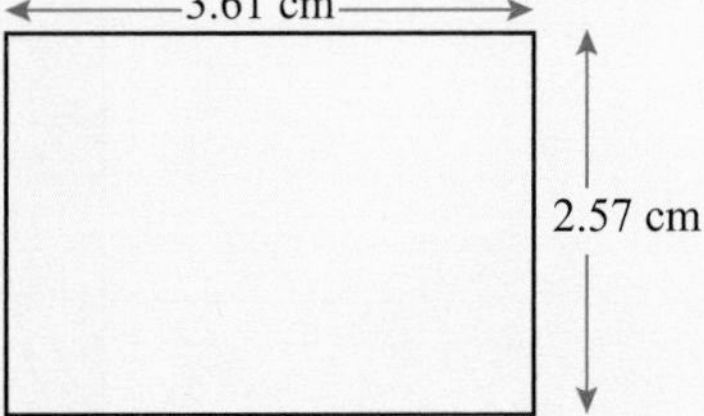

(a) Write down the upper and lower bounds for each dimension.
(b) Find the upper and lower bounds of the area of the rectangle.
(c) Write down the upper and lower bounds of the area correct to 3 significant figures.

REWIND

Look back at chapter 7 to remind yourself about calculating areas. ◀

5 The mean radius of the Earth is 6378 km, to the nearest km. Assume that the Earth is a sphere. Find upper and lower bounds for:

(a) the surface area of the Earth in km^2
(b) the volume of the Earth in km^3.

6 A cup holds 200 ml to the nearest ml, and a large container holds 86 litres to the nearest litre. What is the largest possible number of cupfuls of water needed to fill the container? What is the smallest possible number of cupfuls?

REWIND

Gradient was covered in chapter 10. ◀

7 A straight road slopes steadily upwards. If the road rises 8 m (to the nearest metre) over a horizontal distance of 120 m (given to the nearest 10 m), what is the maximum possible gradient of the road? What is the minimum possible gradient? Give your answers to 3 significant figures.

REWIND

Remind yourself about Pythagoras' theorem from chapter 11. ◀

8 The two short sides of a right-angled triangle are 3.7 cm (to nearest mm) and 4.5 cm (to nearest mm). Calculate upper and lower bounds for:

(a) the area of the triangle

(b) the length of the hypotenuse.

Give your answers to the nearest mm.

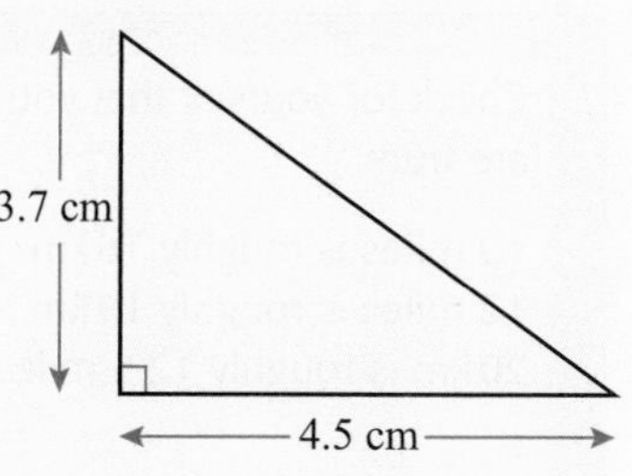

9 The angles in a triangle are $x°$, 38.4° (to 1 d.p.) and 78.1° (to 1 d.p.). Calculate upper and lower bounds for x.

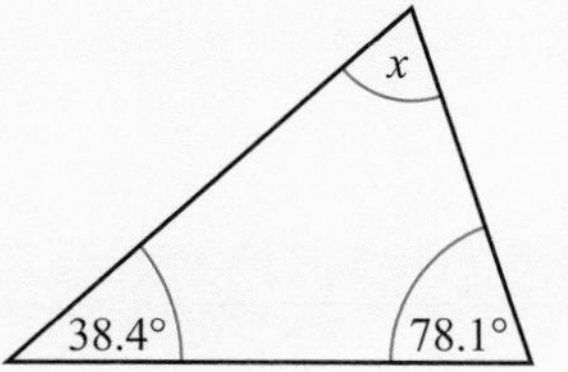

10 Quantity x is 45 to the nearest integer. Quantity y is 98 to the nearest integer. Calculate upper and lower bounds for x as a percentage of y to 1 decimal place.

11 The following five masses are given to 3 significant figures.

138 kg 94.5 kg 1090 kg 345 kg 0.354 kg

Calculate upper and lower bounds for the *mean* of these masses.

12 Gemma is throwing a biased die. The probability that she throws a five is 0.245 to 3 decimal places. If Gemma throws the die exactly 480 times, calculate upper and lower bounds for the number of fives Gemma *expects* to throw. Give your answer to 2 decimal places.

13.4 Conversion graphs

Generally speaking, the imperial equivalents of common metric units are shown below:

metric	imperial
mm/cm	inches
metres	feet/yards
kilometres	miles

So far in this chapter, you have seen that it is possible to convert between different units in the metric system. Another widely used measuring system is the **imperial** system. Sometimes you might need to convert a measurement from metric to imperial, or the other way around. Similarly different countries use different currencies: dollars, yen, pounds, euros. When trading, it is important to accurately convert between them.

Conversion graphs can be used when you need to convert from one measurement to another. For example from miles (imperial) to kilometres (metric) or from dollars to pounds (or any other currency!).

Worked example 7

8 km is approximately equal to five miles. If you travel no distance in kilometres then you also travel no distance in miles. These two points of reference enable you to draw a graph for converting between the two measurements.

If the line is extended far enough you can read higher values. Notice, for example, that the line now passes through the point with co-ordinates (25, 40), meaning that 25 miles is approximately 40 km.

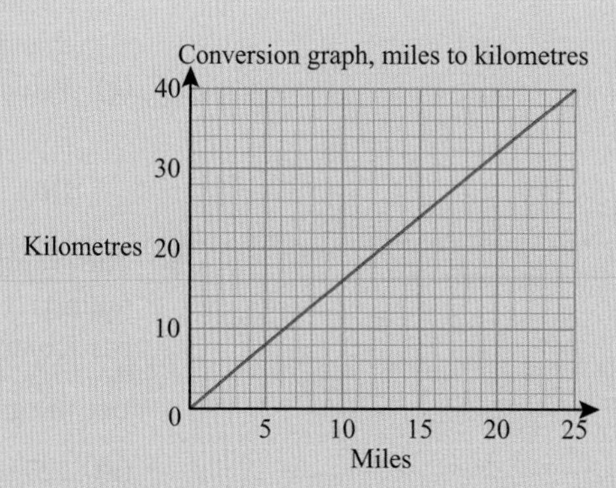

Check for yourself that you can see that the following are true:

10 miles is roughly 16 km
12 miles is roughly 19 km
20 km is roughly 12.5 miles, and so on.

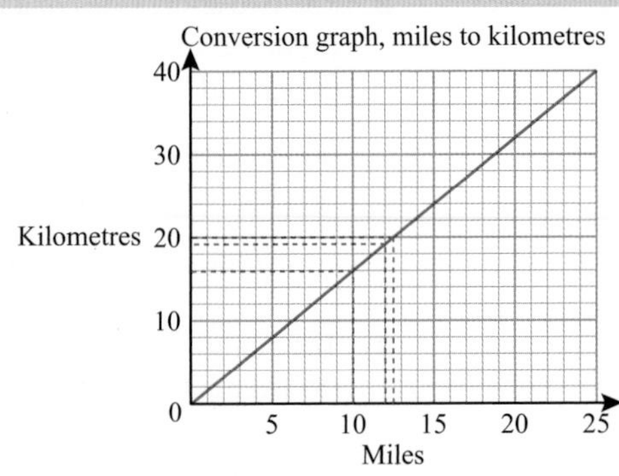

Exercise 13.6 *Living maths*

1 The graph shows the relationship between temperature in degrees Celsius (°C) and degrees Fahrenheit (°F).

Use the graph to convert:

(a) 60 °C to °F
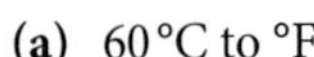
(b) 16 °C to °F
(c) 0 °F to °C
(d) 100 °F to °C.

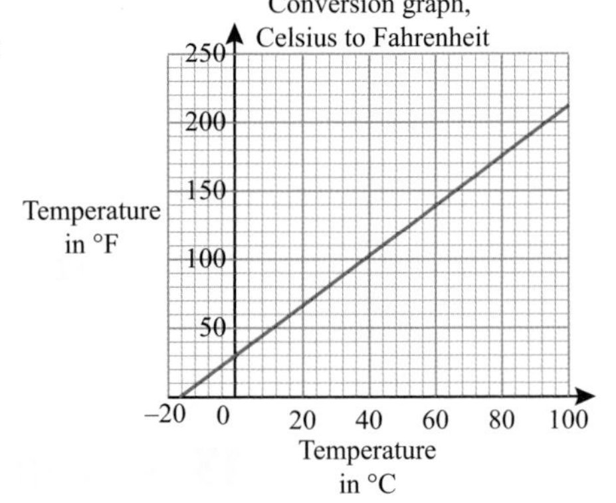

The unit symbol for the imperial mass, pounds, is lb.

2 The graph is a conversion graph for kilograms and pounds. Use the graph to answer the questions below.

Conversion graph, pounds to kilograms
Kilograms
60
40
20
0
40
80
120
160
Pounds

(a) What does one small square on the horizontal axis represent?
(b) What does one small square on the vertical axis represent?
(c) Change 80 pounds to kilograms
(d) The minimum mass to qualify as an amateur lightweight boxer is 57 kg. What is this in pounds?
(e) Which of the following conversions are incorrect? What should they be?

(i) 30 kg = 66 pounds (ii) 18 pounds = 40 kg
(iii) 60 pounds = 37 kg (iv) 20 pounds = 9 kg

3 The graph shows the conversion between UK pounds (£) and US dollars ($), as shown on a particular website in February, 2011.

Use the graph to convert:

(a) £25 to $
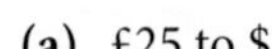
(b) £52 to $
(c) $80 to £
(d) $65 to £.

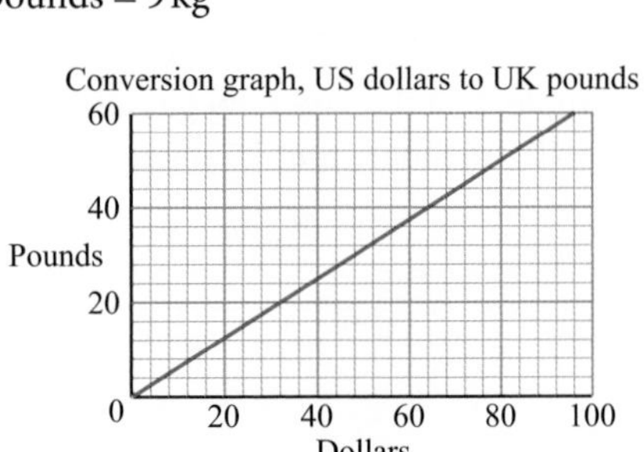

4 The cooking time (in minutes) for a joint of meat (in kilograms) can be calculated by multiplying the mass of the joint by 40 and then adding 30 minutes. The graph shows the cooking time for different masses of meat.

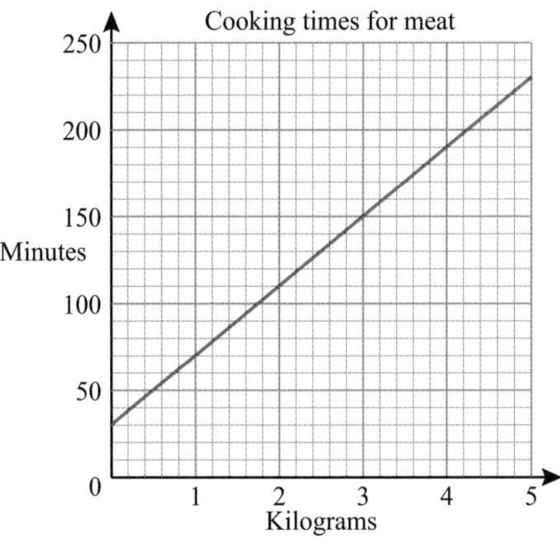

Use the graph to answer the following questions.

(a) If a joint of this meat has a mass of 3.4 kg, approximately how long should it be cooked?
(b) If a joint of meat is to be cooked for 220 minutes, approximately how much is its mass?
(c) By calculating the mass of a piece of meat that takes only 25 minutes to cook, explain carefully why it is not possible to use this graph for every possible joint of meat.

ft is the abbreviation for the imperial unit foot (plural, feet). One foot is a little over 30 cm.

5 You are told that Mount Everest is approximately 29 000 ft high, and that this measurement is approximately 8850 m.

(a) Draw a conversion graph for feet and metres on graph paper.
(b) You are now told that Mount Snowdon is approximately 1085 m high. What is this measurement in feet? Use your graph to help you.
(c) A tunnel in the French Alps is 3400 feet long. Approximately what is the measurement in metres?

Mount Everest.

6 Mount Rubakumar, on the planet Ktorides is 1800 *Squidges* high. This measurement is equivalent to 3450 *Splooges.*

(a) Draw a conversion graph for *Squidges* and *Splooges.*
(b) If Mount Otsuki, also on planet Ktorides, is 1200 *Splooges* high, what is this measurement in *Squidges*?
(c) There are, in fact, 80 *Ploggs* in a *Splooge*. If Mount Adil on planet Ktorides is 1456 *Squidges* high, what is the measurement in *Ploggs* ?

13.5 More money

You have used graphs to convert from one currency to another. However, if you know the **exchange rate**, then you can make conversions without a graph.

Working with money is the same as working with decimal fractions, because most money amounts are given as decimals. Remember though, that when you work with money you need to include the units ($ or cents) in your answers.

REWIND

Before trying this section it will be useful to remind yourself about working with fractions from chapter 5. ◀

Foreign currency

The money a country uses is called its currency. Each country has its own currency and most currencies work on a decimal system (100 small units are equal to one main unit). The following table shows you the currency units of a few different countries.

Country	Main unit	Smaller unit
USA	Dollar ($)	= 100 cents
Japan	Yen (¥)	= 100 sen
UK	Pound (£)	= 100 pence
Germany	Euro (€)	= 100 cents
Eurozone	Euro (€)	= 100 cents

Worked example 8

Convert £50 into Botswana pula, given that £1 = 9.83 pula.

£1 = 9.83 pula
£50 = 9.83 pula × 50 = 491.50 pula

Worked example 9

Convert 803 pesos into British pounds given that £1 = 146 pesos.

146 pesos = £1

So 1 peso = $£\frac{1}{146}$

803 pesos = $£\frac{1}{146} \times 803 = £5.50$

Exercise 13.7 *Living maths*

1 Find the cost of eight apples at 50c each, three oranges at 35c each and 5 kg of bananas at $2.69 per kilogram.

2 How much would you pay for: 240 textbooks at $15.40 each, 100 pens at $1.25 each and 30 dozen erasers at 95c each?

3 If 1 Bahraini dinar = £2.13, convert 4000 dinar to pounds.

4 If US $1 = £0.9049, how many dollars can you buy with £300?

R is the symbol for Rands.

5 An American tourist visits South Africa with $3000. The exchange rate when she arrives is $1 = R8.20. She changes all her dollars into rands and then spends R900 per day for seven days. She changes the rands she has left back into dollars at a rate of $1 = R8.25. How much does she get in dollars?

Summary

Do you know the following?

- There are several measuring systems, the most widely used being metric and imperial.
- Every measurement quoted to a given accuracy will have both a lower bound and an upper bound. The actual value of a measurement is greater than or equal to the lower bound, but strictly less than the upper bound.
- You can draw a graph to help convert between different systems of units.
- Countries use different currencies and you can convert between them if you know the exchange rate.

Are you able to …?

- convert between various metric units
- calculate upper and lower bounds for numbers rounded to a specified degree of accuracy
- calculate upper and lower bounds when more than one rounded number is used in a problem
- draw a conversion graph
- use a conversion graph to convert between different units
- convert between currencies when given the exchange rate.

Examination practice

Exam-style questions

1 A cuboid has dimensions 14.5 cm, 13.2 cm and 21.3 cm. These dimensions are all given to 1 decimal place. Calculate the upper and lower bounds for the volume of the cuboid in:

(a) cm^3 **(b)** mm^3

Give your answers in standard form.

2 The graph shows the relationship between speeds in mph and km/h.

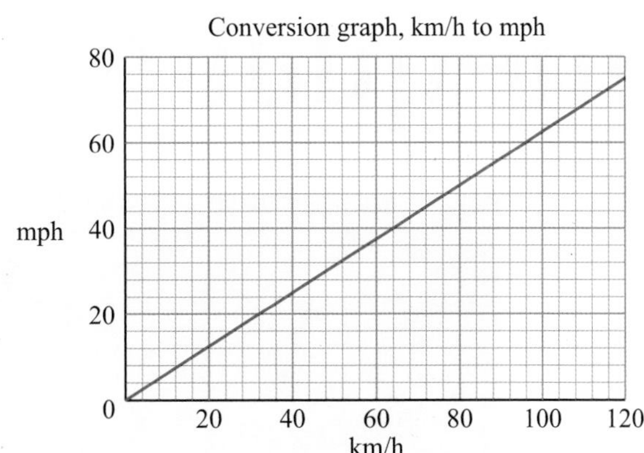

Use the graph to estimate:

(a) the speed, in km/h, of a car travelling at 65 mph
(b) the speed, in mph, of a train travelling at 110 km/h.

3 You are given that $a = 6.54$ (to 3 significant figures) and $b = 123$ (to 3 significant figures).
Calculate upper and lower bounds for each of the following, give your answers to 3 significant figures:

(a) $a + b$ **(b)** ab **(c)** $\frac{a}{b}$ **(d)** $b - \frac{1}{a}$

Past paper questions

1 A carton contains 250 ml of juice, correct to the nearest millilitre.
Complete the statement about the amount of juice, j ml, in the carton.
...... $\leq j <$ ..... [2]

[Cambridge IGCSE Mathematics 0580 Paper 13 Q11 October/November 2012]

2 George and his friend Jane buy copies of the same book on the internet.
George pays \$16.95 and Jane pays £11.99 on a day when the exchange rate is \$1 = £0.626.
Calculate, in dollars, how much more Jane pays. [2]

[Cambridge IGCSE Mathematics 0580 Paper 22 Q6 May/June 2013]

3 Joe measures the side of a square correct to 1 decimal place.
He calculates the **upper** bound for the area of the square as 37.8225 cm^2.
Work out Joe's measurement for the side of the square. [2]

[Cambridge IGCSE Mathematics 0580 Paper 22 Q8 May/June 2013]

14 Further solving of equations and inequalities

Key words

- Intersection
- Simultaneous
- Linear inequalities
- Region
- Linear programming
- Quadratic

In this chapter you will learn how to:

- solve simultaneous linear equations graphically and algebraically

EXTENDED

- solve linear inequalities algebraically
- find regions in a plane
- solve quadratic equations by completing the square
- solve quadratic equations by using the quadratic formula
- factorise quadratics where the coefficient of x^2 is not 1
- simplify algebraic fractions.

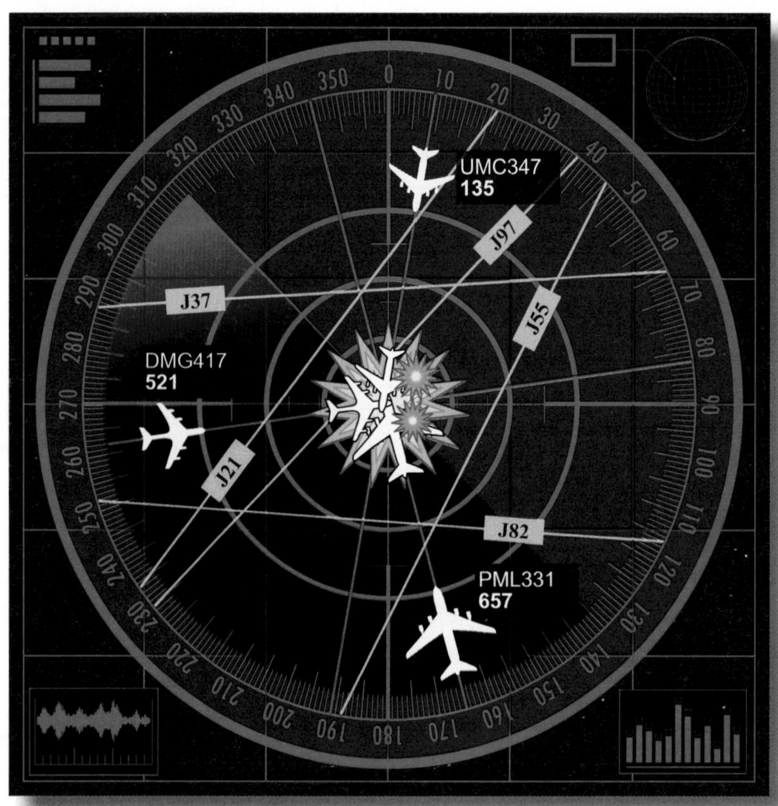

Any two airliners must be kept apart by air traffic controllers. An understanding of how to find meeting points of straight paths can help controllers to avoid disaster!

Businesses have constraints on the materials they can afford, how many people they can employ and how long it takes to make a product. They wish to keep their cost low and their profits high. Being able to plot their constraints on graphs can help to make their businesses more cost effective.

14.1 Simultaneous linear equations

Graphical solution of simultaneous linear equations

A little girl looks out of her window and notices that she can see some goats and some geese. From the window she can see some heads and then, when she looks out of the cat flap, she can see some feet. She knows that each animal has one head, goats have four feet and geese have two feet. Suppose that the girl counts eight heads and 26 feet. How many goats are there? How many geese are there?

If you let $x =$ the number of goats and $y =$ the number of geese, then the number of heads must be the same as the total number of goats and geese.

So, $x + y = 8$

Each goat has four feet and each goose has two feet. So the total number of feet must be $4x + 2y$ and this must be equal to 26.

So you have,

$$x + y = 8$$
$$4x + 2y = 26$$

REWIND

You plotted and drew straight line (linear) graphs in chapter 10. ◀

The information has two unknown values and two different equations can be formed. Each of these equations is a linear equation and can be plotted on the same pair of axes. There is only one point where the values of x and y are the same for both equations – this is where the lines cross (the **intersection**). This is the **simultaneous** solution.

Simultaneous means, 'at the same time.' With simultaneous linear equations you are trying to find the point where two lines cross. i.e. where the values of ***x*** and ***y*** are the same for both equations.

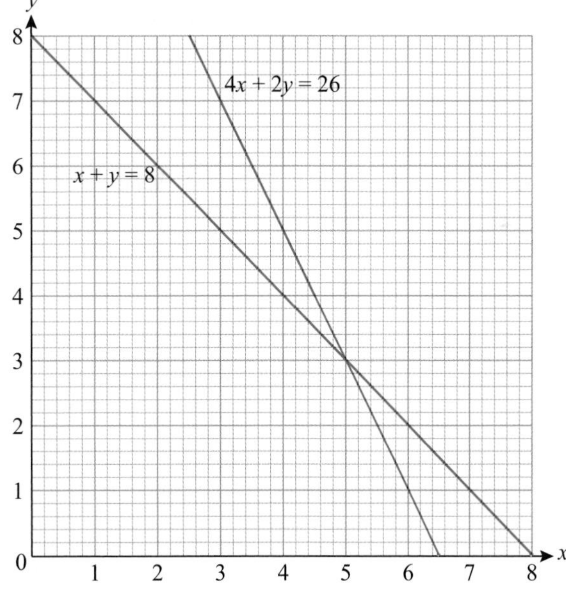

Notice that the point with co-ordinates (5, 3) lies on *both* lines so, $x = 5$ and $y = 3$ satisfy *both* equations. You can check this by substituting the values into the equations:

$$x + y = 5 + 3 = 8$$

and

$$4x + 2y = 4(5) + 2(3) = 20 + 6 = 26$$

This means that the girl saw five goats and three geese.

Tip

It is essential that you remember to work out *both* unknowns. Every pair of simultaneous linear equations will have a pair of solutions.

REWIND

You learned how to plot lines from equations in chapter 10. ◀

REWIND

Throughout this chapter you will need to solve basic linear equations as part of the method. Remind yourself of how this was done in chapter 6. ◀

Worked example 1

By drawing the graphs of each of the following equations on the same pair of axes, find the simultaneous solutions to the equations.

$x - 3y = 6$

$2x + y = 5$

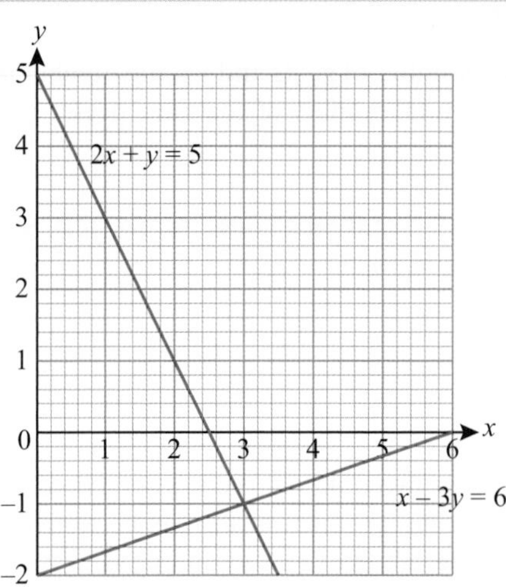

For the first equation:

if $x = 0, -3y = 6 \Rightarrow y = -2$
and, if $y = 0, x = 6$

So this line passes through the points (0, −2) and (6, 0).

For the second equation:

if $x = 0, y = 5$

and, if $y = 0, 2x = 5 \Rightarrow x = \frac{5}{2}$

So this line passes through the points (0, 5) and $\left(\frac{5}{2}, 0\right)$.

Plot the pairs of points and draw lines through them.
Notice that the two lines meet at the point with co-ordinates (3, −1)
So, the solution to the pair of equations is $x = 3$ and $y = -1$

Exercise 14.1

1 Draw the lines for each pair of equations and then use the point of intersection to find the simultaneous solution. The axes that you should use are given in each case.

(a) $x + 2y = 11$ (x from 0 to 11 and y from 0 to 10)
$2x + y = 10$

(b) $x - y = -1$ (x from −2 to 3 and y from 0 to 4)
$2x + y = 4$

(c) $5x - 4y = -1$ (x from −1 to 5 and y from 0 to 10)
$2x + y = 10$

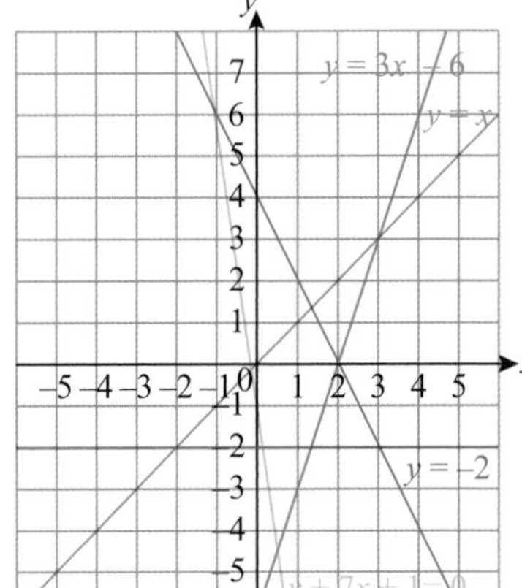

2 Use the graphs supplied to find the solutions to the following pairs of simultaneous equations.

(a) $y = x$
$y = -2$

(b) $y = x$
$y = 3x - 6$

(c) $y = 4 - 2x$
$y = -2$

(d) $y = 4 - 2x$
$y + 7x + 1 = 0$

(e) $y = -2$
$y + 7x + 1 = 0$

(f) $y = x$
$y = 4 - 2x$

3 For each pair of equations, find three points on each line and draw the graphs on paper. Use your graphs to estimate the solution of each pair of simultaneous equations.

(a) $3y = -4x + 3$
$x = 2y + 1$

(b) $2 - x = -y$
$8x + 4y = 7$

(c) $4x = 1 + 6y$
$4x - 4 = 3y$

(d) $3x + 2y = 7$
$4x = 2 + 3y$

4 **(a)** Explain why the graphical method does not always give an accurate and correct answer.
(b) How can you check whether a solution you obtained graphically is correct or not?

Algebraic solution of simultaneous linear equations

The graphical method is suitable for whole number solutions but it can be slow and, for non-integer solutions, may not be as accurate as you need. You have already learned how to solve linear equations with one unknown using algebraic methods. You now need to look at how to solve a pair of equations in which there are two unknowns.

You are going to learn two methods of solving simultaneous equations:

- solving by substitution
- solving by elimination.

Solving by substitution

You can solve the equations by substitution when one of the equations can be solved for one of the variables (i.e. solved for x or solved for y). The solution is then substituted into the other equation so it can be solved.

The equations have been numbered so that you can identify each equation efficiently. You should always do this.

Worked example 2

Solve simultaneously by substitution.

$3x - 2y = 29$ (1)
$4x + y = 24$ (2)

$4x + y = 24$ $y = 24 - 4x$ (3)	Solve equation (2) for y. Label the new equation (3).
$3x - 2y = 29$ (1) $3x - 2(24 - 4x) = 29$	Substitute (3) into (1) by replacing y with $24 - 4x$.
$3x - 48 + 8x = 29$	Remove brackets.
$3x + 8x = 29 + 48$	Subtract $8x$ and add 48 to both sides.
$11x = 77$	Add like terms.
$x = 7$	Divide both sides by 11.
So, $x = 7$	
$y = 24 - 4(7)$ $y = 24 - 28$ $y = -4$	Now, substitute the value of x into any of the equations to find y. Equation (3) will be easiest, so use this one.
$x = 7$ and $y = -4$	Write out the solutions.

Solving by elimination

You can also solve the equations by eliminating (getting rid of) one of the variables by adding the two equations together.

Worked example 3

Solve the following pair of equations using elimination:

$x - y = 4$ (1)

$x + y = 6$ (2)

$x - y = 4$ (1) $x + y = 6$ (2) $2x = 10$	You can add the two equations together by adding the left-hand sides and adding the right-hand sides.
$2x = 10$ $\Rightarrow x = \frac{10}{2} = 5$	Notice that the equation that comes from this addition no longer contains a '*y*' term, and that it is now possible to complete the calculation by solving for *x*.
$x = 5$ $x + y = 6$ $\Rightarrow 5 + y = 6$ $y = 1$	As you saw in the previous section you will need a *y* value to go with this. Substitute *x* into equation (2).
$x - y = 5 - 1 = 4$	Check that these values for *x* and *y* work in equation (1).

Both equations are satisfied by the pair of values $x = 5$ and $y = 1$.

The following worked examples look at different cases where you may need to subtract, instead of add, the equations or where you may need to multiply one, or both, equations before you consider addition or subtraction.

Worked example 4

Solve the following pairs of simultaneous equations:

$2x - 3y = -8$ (1)

$5x + 3y = 1$ (2)

$2x - 3y = -8$ $5x + 3y = 1$ $7x = -7$ $\Rightarrow x = -1$	(1) + (2)	Notice that these equations have the same coefficient of *y* in both equations, though the signs are different. If you add these equations together, you make use of the fact that $-3y + 3y = 0$
$2x - 3y = -8$ $\Rightarrow 2(-1) - 3y = -8$ $6 - 3y = 0$ $3y = 6$ $y = 2$	Substitute in (1)	Now that you have the value of *x*, you can substitute this into either equation and then solve for *y*.
$5x + 3y = 5(-1) + 3(2)$ $= -5 + 6 = 1$		Now you should check these values in equation (2) to be sure.

The second equation is also satisfied by these values so $x = -1$ and $y = 2$.

Always 'line up' '*x*'s with '*x*'s, '*y*'s with '*y*'s and '=' with '='. It will make your method clearer.

REWIND

Remind yourself about dealing with directed numbers from chapter 1. ◀

Always make it clear which equation you have chosen to subtract from which.

Here, you have used the fact that $-4 - (-1) = -3$.

Worked example 5

Solve simultaneously:

$4x + y = -1$ (1)

$7x + y = -4$ (2)

$7x + y = -4$ (2) − (1) $4x + y = -1$ $3x = -3$ $\Rightarrow x = -1$	Notice this time that you have the same coefficient of y again, but this time the 'y' terms have the same sign. You now make use of the fact that $y - y = 0$ and so *subtract* one equation from the other. There are more 'x's in (2) so, consider (2) − (1).
$4x + y = -1$ $\Rightarrow 4(-1) + y = -1$ $y = 3$	Substitute in (1)
$7x + y = 7(-1) + = -7 + 3 = -4$	Now check that the values $x = -1$ and $y = 3$ work in equation (2).

Equation (2) is also satisfied by these values, so $x = -1$ and $y = 3$.

Manipulating equations before solving them

Sometimes you need to manipulate or rearrange one or both of the equations before you can solve them simultaneously by elimination. Worked examples 6 to 8 show you how this is done.

Worked example 6

Solve simultaneously:

$2x - 5y = 24$ (1)

$4x + 3y = -4$ (2)

$2 \times (1)\ 4x - 10y = 48$ (3) $4x + 3y = -4$ (2) $4x - 10y = 48$ (3)	With this pair of simultaneous equations notice that neither the coefficient of x nor the coefficient of y match. But, if you multiply equation (1) by equation (2), you can make the coefficient of x the same in each. This equation, now named (3), has the same coefficient of x as equation (2) so write both of these equations together and solve as before.
$4x + 3y = -4$ $4x - 10y = 48$ $13y = -52$ $\Rightarrow y = -4$	(2) − (3)
$2x - 5y = 24$ $\Rightarrow 2x - 5(-4) = 24$ $2x + 20 = 24$ $x = 2$	Substitute in (1)
$4x + 3y = 4(2) + 3(-4) = 8 - 12 = -4$	Check using equation (2).

So the pair of values $x = 2$ and $y = -4$ satisfy the pair of simultaneous equations.

Worked example 7

Solve simultaneously:
$2x - 21 = 5y$
$3 + 4y = -3x$

Working	Explanation
$2x - 5y = 21$ (1) $3x + 4y = -3$ (2)	Before you can work with these equations you need to rearrange them so they are in the same form. In this pair, not only is the coefficient of x different but so is the coefficient of y. It is not possible to multiply through just one equation to solve this problem.
$4 \times (1) \Rightarrow 8x - 20y = 84$ (3) $5 \times (2) \Rightarrow 15x + 20y = -15$ (4)	Here, you need to multiply each equation by a different value so that the coefficient of x *or* the coefficient of y match. It is best to choose to do this for the 'y' terms here because they have different signs and it is simpler to add equations rather than subtract!
$8x - 20y = 84$ $15x + 20y = -15$ $23x = 69$	(3) + (4)
$x = 3$ $2x - 5y = 21$ $\Rightarrow 2(3) - 5y = 21$ $5y = -15$ $y = -3$	Substitute for x in (1).
$3x + 4y = 3(3) + 4(-3) = 9 - 12 = -3$	Check using equation (2).

So $x = 3$ and $y = -3$ satisfy the pair of simultaneous equations.

Worked example 8

Solve simultaneously:

$\frac{3x - 4y}{2} = 10$ (1)

$\frac{3x + 2y}{4} = 2$ (2)

Working	Explanation
$3x - 4y = 20$ (3)	In this pair of equations it makes sense to remove the fractions before you work with them. Multiply both sides of equation (1) by 2.
$3x + 2y = 8$ (4)	Multiply both sides of equation (2) by 4.
$3x - 4y = 20$ (3) $3x + 2y = 8$ (4) $-6y = 12$ $y = -2$	Subtract equation (4) from equation (3).
$3x - 4(-2) = 20$ $3x + 8 = 20$ $3x = 12$ $x = 4$	Substitute the value for y into equation (3).
$3(4) + 2(-2) = 12 - 4 = 8$ So $x = 4$ and $y = -2$	Check using equation (4).

Exercise 14.2

REWIND

Remember from chapter 1 that adding a negative is the same as subtracting a positive. ◀

Remember that you need either the same coefficient of x or the same coefficient of y. If both have the *same* sign, you should then subtract one equation from the other. If they have a *different* sign, then you should add.

1 Solve for x and y by substitution. Check each solution.

(a) $y+x=7$, $y=x+3$
(b) $y=1-x$, $x-5=y$
(c) $2x+y=-14$, $y=6$
(d) $x-8=2y$, $x+y=-2$
(e) $3x-2=-2y$, $2x-y=-8$
(f) $3x+y=6$, $9x+2y=1$
(g) $4x-1=2y$, $x+1=3y$
(h) $3x-4y=1$, $2x=4-3y$

2 Solve for x and y by elimination. Check each solution.

(a) $2x-y=4$, $5x+y=24$
(b) $-3x+2y=6$, $3x+5y=36$
(c) $2x+5y=12$, $2x+3y=8$
(d) $5x-2y=27$, $3x+2y=13$
(e) $x+2y=11$, $x+3y=15$
(f) $-2x+5y=13$, $2x+3y=11$
(g) $4x+y=27$, $3x-y=15$
(h) $4x-y=16$, $6x-y=26$
(i) $6x-5y=9$, $2x+5y=23$
(j) $6x-y=18$, $4x-y=10$
(k) $x+y=12$, $5x-y=24$
(l) $4x+3y=22$, $4x+y=18$

3 Solve simultaneously. Use the method you find easiest. Check all solutions.

(a) $5x+3y=22$, $10x-y=16$
(b) $4x+3y=25$, $x+9y=31$
(c) $-3x+y=5$, $-6x+5y=-20$
(d) $x+y=10$, $3x+5y=40$
(e) $5x+y=11$, $-2x+2y=1$
(f) $4x-3y=11$, $5x-9y=-2$
(g) $6x+2y=9$, $7x+4y=12$
(h) $12x-13y=34$, $3x-26y=19$
(i) $5x-17y=-3$, $25x-19y=-45$
(j) $3x-3y=13$, $4x-12y=-6$
(k) $10x=2-2y$, $2y=-7x-1$
(l) $-2y=1-7x$, $4x=4+2y$
(m) $x=12+y$, $2x=3-y$
(n) $3x+4y=-1$, $3x+10=2y$
(o) $2x+y=7$, $11+x=2y$

4 Solve simultaneously.

(a) $3x+7y=37$, $5x+6y=39$
(b) $2x-5y=-16$, $3x-5y=-14$
(c) $-7x+4y=41$, $-5x+6y=45$
(d) $7x+4y=54$, $2x+3y=21$
(e) $2x-y=1$, $3x+5y=34$
(f) $3x-4y=25$, $x-3y=15$
(g) $7x-4y=23$, $4x+5y=35$
(h) $3x-y=2$, $3x+5y=26$
(i) $2x+7y=25$, $x+y=5$
(j) $x+3=y$, $4x+y=-7$
(k) $3x+11=-y$, $-2x+y=4$
(l) $y=6x-1$, $4x-3y=-4$
(m) $2x+3y-8=0$, $4x+5=y$
(n) $y=\frac{2}{3}x+6$, $2y-4x=20$
(o) $8x-5y=0$, $13x=8y+1$

If an equation contains fractions, you can make everything much easier by multiplying each term by a suitable number (a common denominator). 'Clear' the fractions first.

5 Solve each pair of equations simultaneously.

(a) $\frac{1}{2}x+\frac{2}{3}y=6\frac{1}{5}$

$\frac{3}{4}x-\frac{1}{7}y=13\frac{3}{5}$

(b) $\frac{3}{7}x-\frac{5}{8}y=33\frac{1}{3}$

$64x-17y=12\frac{1}{2}$

(c) $456\frac{2}{17}x+987\frac{3}{4}y=1$

$233\frac{13}{22}x-94\frac{2}{3}y=4$

(d) $3x+\frac{2y}{3}=0$

$2x-\frac{y}{4}=14$

(e) $4y+x+5=0$

$y=x-5$

(f) $3y+\frac{6}{2}=-3$

$y-\frac{x}{2}=2$

(g) $2x+\frac{y}{2}=3$

$6x=-2y$

(h) $y=3x-6$

$2x+\frac{3y}{7}=-5$

(i) $\frac{3x}{7}-\frac{2y}{13}=5$

$x+\frac{1}{3}y=\frac{3}{5}$

6 Form a pair of simultaneous equations for each situation below, and use them to solve the problem. Let the unknown numbers be x and y.

(a) The sum of two numbers is 120 and one of the numbers is 3 times the other. Find the value of the numbers.
(b) The sum of two numbers is –34 and their difference is 5. Find the numbers.
(c) A pair of numbers has a sum of 52 and a difference of 11. Find the numbers.
(d) The combined ages of two people is 34. If one person is 6 years younger than the other, find their ages.

7 A computer store sold 4 hard drives and 10 pen drives for \$200. and 6 hard drives and 14 pen drives for \$290. Find the cost of a hard drive and the cost of a pen drive.

8 A large sports stadium has 21 000 seats. The seats are organised into blocks of either 400 or 450 seats. There are three times as many blocks of 450 seats as there are blocks of 400 seats. How many blocks are there?

14.2 Linear inequalities

The work earlier in the book on linear equations led to a single solution for a single variable. Sometimes however, there are situations where there are a range of possible solutions. This section extends the previous work on linear equations to look at **linear inequalities.**

Number lines

REWIND

Remind yourself how inequality symbols were used for grouped data in chapter 12. ◀

Suppose you are told that $x < 4$. You will remember from chapter 1 that this means each possible value of x must be less than 4. Therefore, x can be 3, 2, 1, 0, –1, –2 . . . but that is not all. 3.2 is also less than 4, as is 3.999, 2.43, –3.4, –100 . . .

If you draw a number line, you can use an arrow to represent the set of numbers:

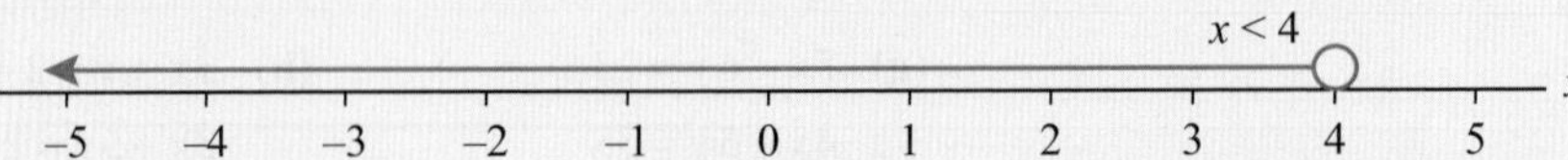

FAST FORWARD

You will find it useful to review inequalities before you tackle histograms in chapter 20. ▶

This allows you to show the possible values of x neatly without writing them all down (there is an infinite number of values, so you can't write them all down!). Notice that the 'open circle' above the four is not filled in. This symbol is used because it is not possible for x to be *equal* to four.

Now suppose that $x \geq -2$. This now tells you that x can be greater than, *or equal to* –2. You can show that that x can be equal to –2 by 'filling in' the circle above –2 on the number line:

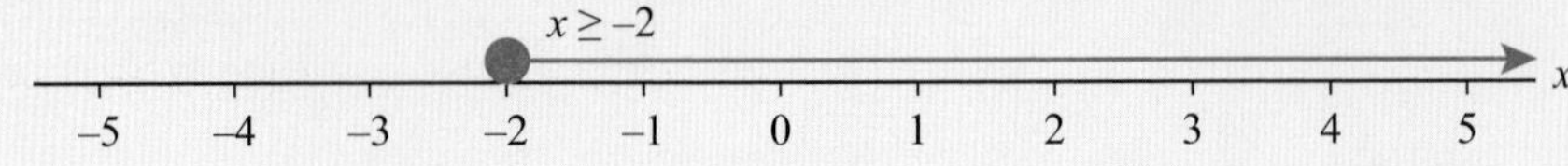

The following worked examples show that more than one inequality symbol can appear in a question.

Worked example 9

Show the set of values that satisfy each of the following in equalities on a number line.

(a) $x > 3$ **(b)** $4 < y < 8$ **(c)** $-1.4 < x \leq 2.8$
(d) List all integers that satisfy the inequality $4.2 < x \leq 10.4$

(a) The values of x have to be larger than 3. x cannot be equal to 3, so do not fill in the circle. 'Greater than' means 'to the right' on the number line.

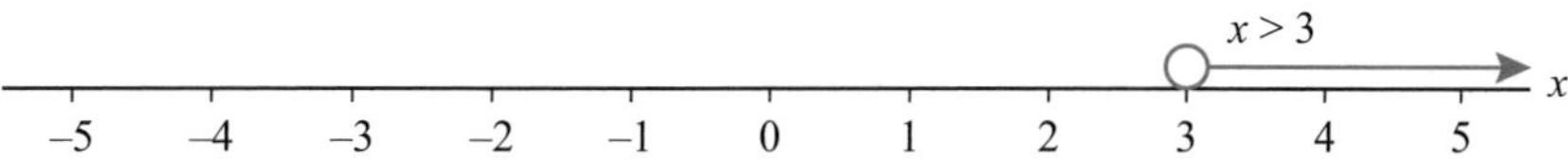

(b) Notice that y is now being used as the variable and this should be clearly labelled on your number line. Also, two inequality symbols have been used. In fact there are two inequalities, and *both* must be satisfied.

$4 < y$ tells you that y is greater than (but not equal) to 4.

$y < 8$ tells you that y is also less than (but not equal to) 8.

So y lies between 4 and 8 (not inclusive):

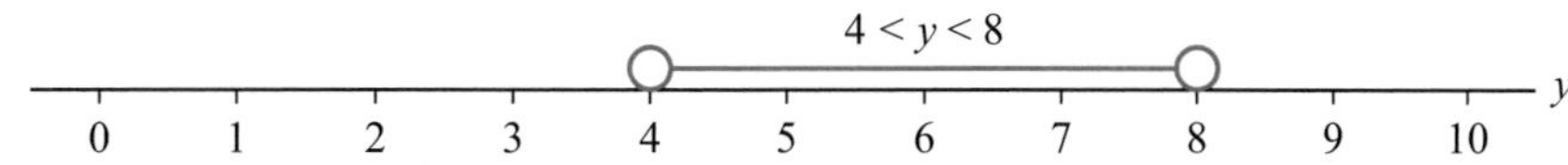

(c) This example has two inequalities that must both be satisfied. x is greater than (but not equal to) -1.4, and x is less than or equal to 2.8:

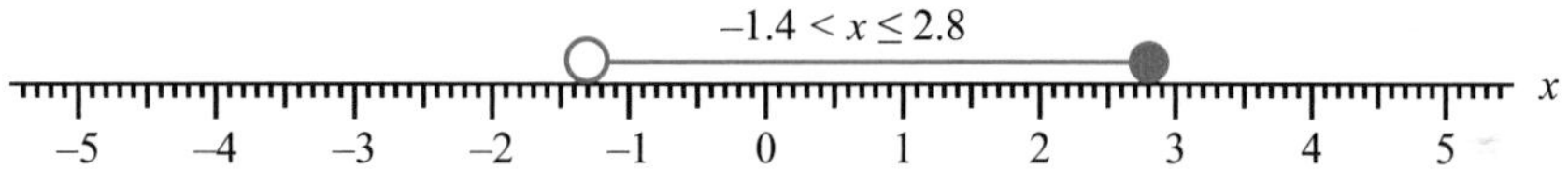

(d) Here x must be greater than, but not equal to 4.2. So the smallest possible value of x is 5. x must also be less than or equal to 10.4. The largest that x can be is therefore 10.

So the possible values of x are 5, 6, 7, 8, 9 or 10.

Exercise 14.3

1 Draw a number line to represent the possible values of the variable in each case.

(a) $x < 5$ (b) $x > 2$ (c) $p \leq 6$
(d) $y > -8$ (e) $q \geq -5$ (f) $x < -4$
(g) $1.2 < x < 3.5$ (h) $-3.2 < x \leq 2.9$ (i) $-4.5 \leq k \leq -3.1$

2 Write down all *integers* that satisfy each of the following inequalities.

(a) $3 < b < 33$ (b) $7 < h \leq 19$ (c) $18 \leq e \leq 27$
(d) $-3 \leq f < 0$ (e) $-3 \geq f \leq 0$ (f) $2.5 < m < 11.3$
(g) $-7 < g \leq -4$ (h) $\pi < r < 2\pi$ (i) $\sqrt{5} < w < \sqrt{18}$

Solving inequalities algebraically

Consider the inequality $3x > 6$.

Now, suppose that $x = 2$, then $3x = 6$ but this doesn't quite satisfy the inequality! *Any* value of x that is *larger* than 2 *will* work however. For example:

If $x = 2.1$, then $3x = 6.3$, which *is* greater than 6.

In the same way that you could divide both sides of an equation by 3, both sides of the inequality can be divided by 3 to get the solution:

$$3x > 6$$
$$\frac{3x}{3} > \frac{6}{3}$$
$$x > 2$$

Notice that this solution is a range of values of x rather than a single value. Any value of x that is greater than 2 works!

In fact you can solve any linear inequality in much the same way as you would solve a linear equation, though there are important exceptions, and this is shown in the 'warning' section on page 283. Most importantly, you should simply remember that what you do to one side of the inequality you must do to the other.

Worked example 10

Find the set of values of x for which each of the following inequalities holds.

(a) $3x - 4 < 14$ **(b)** $4(x - 7) \geq 16$ **(c)** $5x - 3 \leq 2x + 18$ **(d)** $4 - 7x \leq 53$

	Working	Explanation
(a)	$3x - 4 < 14$	
	$3x < 18$	Add 4 to both sides.
	$\frac{3x}{3} < \frac{18}{3}$	Divide both sides by 3.
	So, $x < 6$	
(b)	$4(x - 7) \geq 16$	
	$4x - 28 \geq 16$	Expand the brackets.
	$4x \geq 44$	Add 28 to both sides.
	$\frac{4x}{4} \geq \frac{44}{4}$	Divide both sides by 4.
	So, $x \geq 11$	
	$4(x - 7) \geq 16$	Notice that you can also solve this inequality by dividing both sides by 4 at the beginning:
	$x - 7 \geq 4$	Divide both sides by 4.
	$x \geq 11$	Add 7 to both sides to get the same answer as before.
(c)	$5x - 3 \leq 2x + 18$	
	$5x - 3 - 2x \leq 2x + 18 - 2x$	Subtract the smaller number of 'x's from both sides ($2x$).
	$3x - 3 \leq 18$	Simplify.
	$3x \leq 21$	Add 3 to both sides.
	$x \leq 7$	Divide both sides by 3.

(d)	$4 - 7x \le 53$	
	$4 \le 53 + 7x$	Add $7x$ to both sides
	$-49 \le 7x$	Subtract 53 from both sides.
	$-7 \le x$	Divide both sides by 7.
		Notice that the x is on the right-hand side of the inequality in this answer. This is perfectly acceptable. You can reverse the entire inequality to place the x on the left without changing its meaning, but you must
	And, $x \ge -7$.	remember to reverse the actual inequality symbol!

A warning

Before working through the next exercise you should be aware that there is one further rule to remember. Consider this inequality:

$$3 - 5x > 18$$
$$\Rightarrow -5x > 15$$

If you divide both sides of this by -5 it *appears* that the solution will be,

$$x > -3$$

If you can avoid negatives, by adding or subtracting terms, then try to do so.

This is satisfied by any value of x that is greater than -3, for example $-2, -1, 2.4, 3.5, 10 \ldots$

If you calculate the value of $3 - 5x$ for each of these values you get $13, 8, -14.5, -47 \ldots$ and not one of these works in the original inequality as they are all smaller than 18.

But here is an alternate solution:

$$3 - 5x > 18$$
$$\Rightarrow \quad 3 > 18 + 5x$$
$$-15 > 5x$$
$$-3 > x$$

or, $\quad x < -3$

This is a correct solution, and the final answer is very similar to the 'wrong' one above. The only difference is that the inequality symbol has been reversed. You should remember the following:

> If you multiply or divide both sides of an inequality by a *negative* number then you must *reverse* the direction of the inequality.

Exercise 14.4

Solve each of the following inequalities. Some of the answers will involve fractions. Leave your answers as fractions in their simplest form where appropriate.

1 **(a)** $18x < 36$ **(b)** $13x > 39$ **(c)** $15y \le 14$ **(d)** $7y > -14$
(e) $4 + 8c \ge 20$ **(f)** $2x + 1 < 9$ **(g)** $\frac{x}{3} < 2$ **(h)** $5p - 3 > 12$
(i) $\frac{x}{3} + 7 > 2$ **(j)** $12g - 14 \ge 34$ **(k)** $22(w - 4) < 88$ **(l)** $10 - 10k > 3$

2 **(a)** $\frac{y+6}{4} > 9$ **(b)** $10q - 12 < 48 + 5q$ **(c)** $3g - 7 \ge 5g - 18$ **(d)** $3(h - 4) > 5(h - 10)$
(e) $\frac{y+6}{4} \le 9$ **(f)** $\frac{1}{2}(x+5) \le 2$ **(g)** $3 - 7h \le 6 - 5h$ **(h)** $2(y-7) + 6 \le 5(y+3) + 21$
(i) $6(n - 4) - 2(n + 1) < 3(n + 7) + 1$ **(j)** $5(2v - 3) - 2(4v - 5) \ge 8(v + 1)$

(k) $\frac{z-2}{3}-7>13$ (l) $\frac{3k-1}{7}-7>7$ (m) $\frac{2e+1}{9}>7-6e$

3 (a) $2t-\frac{2t+1}{3}>12$ (b) $\frac{2}{3}t-\frac{2t+1}{9}>12$ (c) $\frac{2}{7}t-\frac{2t+1}{9}>12$

(d) $\frac{r}{2}+\frac{1}{3}<2$ (e) $\frac{3}{8}(2d-\frac{1}{3})-\frac{2}{9}(7-3d)\geq\frac{1}{4}d+\frac{2(d-8)}{7}$

14.3 Regions in a plane

So far, you have only considered one variable and inequalities along a number line. You can, however, have two variables connected with an inequality, in which case you end up with a **region** on the Cartesian plane.

Diagram A shows a broken line that is parallel to the x-axis. Every point on the line has a y co-ordinate of 3. This means that the equation of the line is $y = 3$.

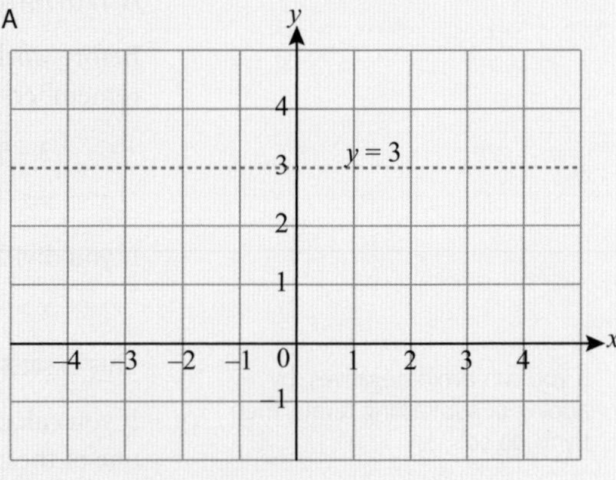

All of the points above the line $y = 3$ have y co-ordinates that are greater than 3. The region above the line thus represents the inequality $y > 3$. Similarly, the region below the line represents the inequality $y < 3$. These regions are shown on diagram B.

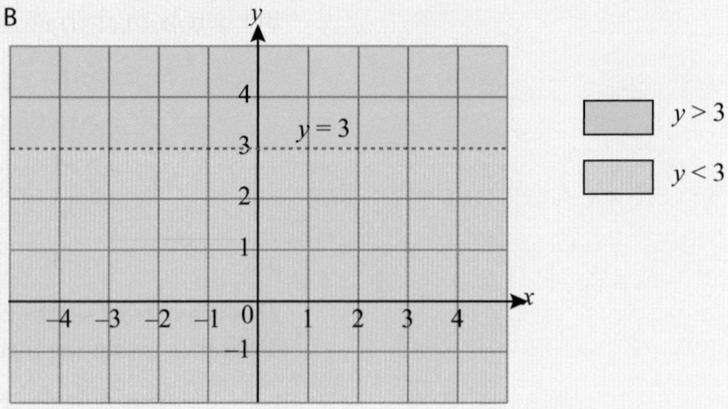

In diagram C, the graph of $y = 2x + 1$ is shown as a broken line. Every point on the line has co-ordinates (x, y) which satisfy $y = 2x + 1$.

Q is a point on the line. Point P has a y co-ordinate that is greater than the y co-ordinate of Q. P and Q have the same x co-ordinate. This means that for any point P in the region above the line, $y > 2x + 1$.

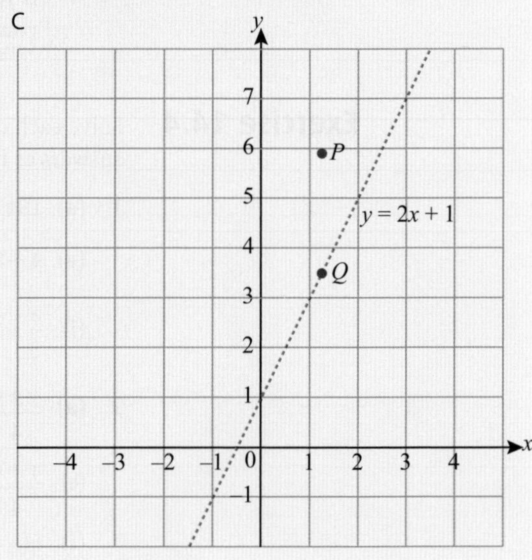

The region above the line represents the inequality $y > 2x + 1$.

Similarly the region below the line represents the inequality $y < 2x + 1$.

You can see this on diagram D.

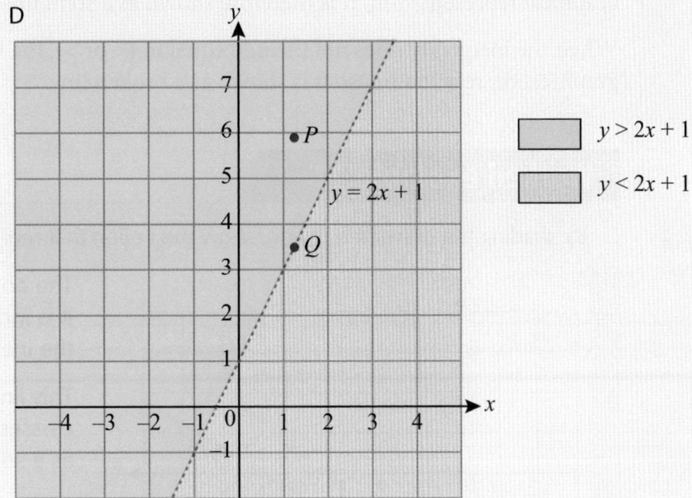

If the equation of the line is in the form $y = mx + c$, then:

- the inequality $y > mx + c$ is above the line
- the inequality $y < mx + c$ is below the line.

If the equation is not in the form $y = mx + c$, you have to find a way to check which region represents which inequality.

Worked example 11

In a diagram, show the regions that represent the inequalities $2x - 3y < 6$ and $2x - 3y > 6$.

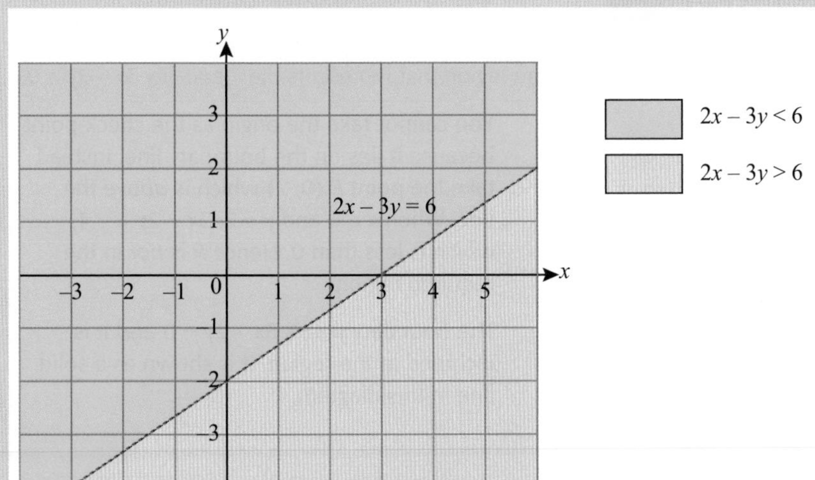

The boundary between the two required regions is the line $2x - 3y = 6$.

This line crosses the x-axis at (3, 0) and the y-axis at (0, −2). It is shown as a broken line in this diagram.

Consider any point in the region above the line. The easiest point to use is the origin (0, 0). When $x = 0$ and $y = 0$, $2x - 3y = 0$. Since 0 is less than 6, the region above the line represents the inequality $2x - 3y < 6$.

Rules about boundaries and shading of regions

You have already seen inequalities are not always < or >. They may also be ≤ or ≥. Graphical representations have to show the difference between these variations.

When the inequality includes equal to (≤ or ≥), the boundary line must be included in the graphical representation. It is therefore shown as a solid line.

When the inequality does not include equal to (< or >), the boundary line is not included in the graphical representation, so it is shown as a broken line.

Sometimes it is better to shade out the *unwanted* region.

Worked example 12

By shading the *unwanted* region, show the region that represents the inequality $3x - 5y \leq 15$.

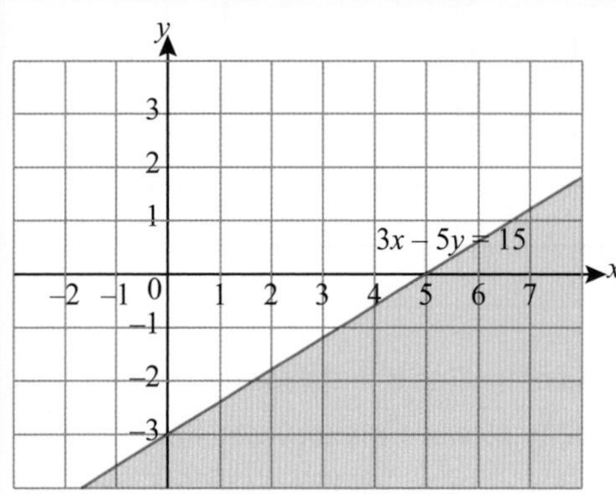

The boundary line is $3x - 5y = 15$ and it is included in the region (because the inequality includes *equal to*).

This line crosses the x-axis at (5, 0) and crosses the y-axis at (0, −3). It is shown as a solid line in this diagram.

When $x = 0$ and $y = 0$, $3x - 5y = 0$. Since 0 is less than 15, the origin (0, 0) is in the required region. (Alternatively, rearrange $3x - 5y \leq 15$ to get $y \geq \frac{3}{5}x - 3$ and deduce that the required region is above the line.)

The unshaded region in this diagram represents the inequality, $3x - 5y \leq 15$.

Worked example 13

By shading the *unwanted* region, show the region that represents the inequality $3x - 2y \geq 0$.

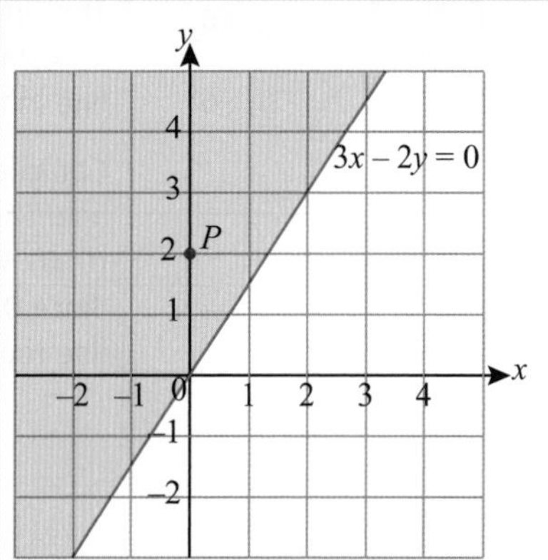

You cannot take the origin as the check-point because it lies on the boundary line. Instead take the point P (0, 2) which is *above* the line. When $x = 0$ and $y = 2$, $3x - 2y = -4$, which is less than 0. Hence P is *not* in the required region.

The boundary line is $3x - 2y = 0$ and it is included in the region. It is shown as a solid line in this diagram.

Worked example 14

Find the inequality that is represented by the *unshaded* region in this diagram.

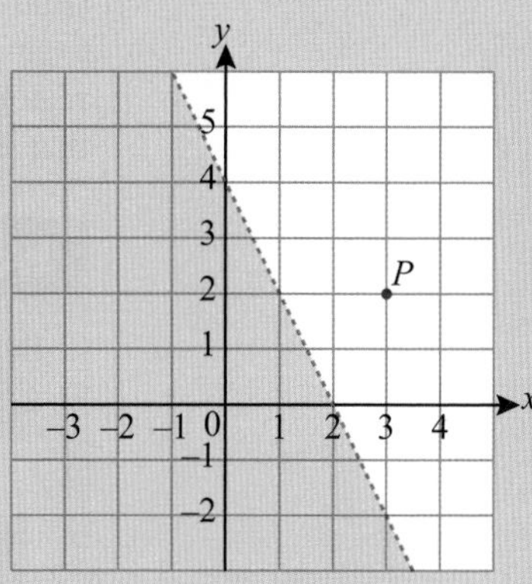

First find the equation of the boundary. Its gradient $= \frac{-4}{2} = -2$ and its intercept on the y-axis is $y = 4$. Hence the boundary line is $y = -2x + 4$ or this can be re-written as $y + 2x = 4$. Take P (3, 2) in the unshaed region as the check-point: $2 + 6 = 8$. Note that 8 is greater than 4, hence, the *unshaded* region represents $y + 2x > 4$. As the boundary is a broken line, it is not included, and thus the sign is not $\geq$.

Exercise 14.5

For questions 1 to 3, show your answers on a grid with x- and y-axes running from –3 to +4.

1. By shading the unwanted region, show the region that represents the inequality $2y - 3x \geq 6$.
2. By shading the unwanted region, show the region that represents the inequality $x + 2y < 4$.
3. By shading the unwanted region, show the region that represents the inequality $x - y \geq 0$.
4. Shade the region that represents each inequality.

   (a) $y > 3 - 3x$ **(b)** $3x - 2y \geq 6$ **(c)** $x \leq 5$ **(d)** $y > 3$
   (e) $x + 3y \leq 10$ **(f)** $-3 < x < 5$ **(g)** $0 \leq x \leq 2$

5. Copy and complete these statements by choosing the correct option:

   (a) If $y < mx + c$, shade the unwanted region **above/below** the graph of $y = mx + c$.
   (b) If $y > mx + c$, shade the unwanted region **above/below** the graph of $y = mx + c$.
   (c) For $y < m_1x + c_1$ and $y > m_2x + c_2$, shade the unwanted region **above/below** the graph of $y = m_1x + c_1$ **and/or above/below** the graph of $y = m_2x + c_2$.

6. For each of the following diagrams, find the inequality that is represented by the *unshaded* region.

(a)

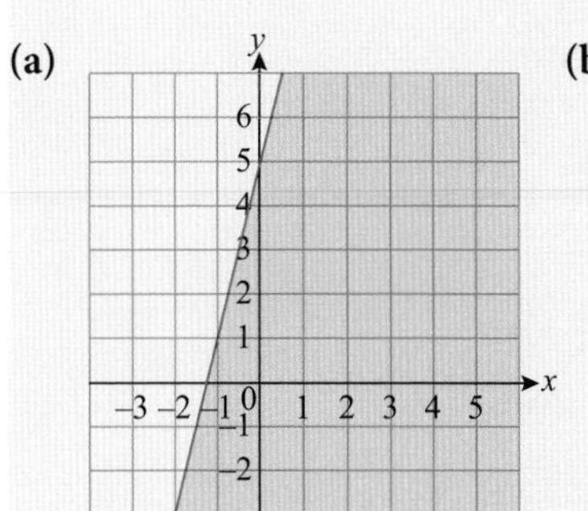

(b)

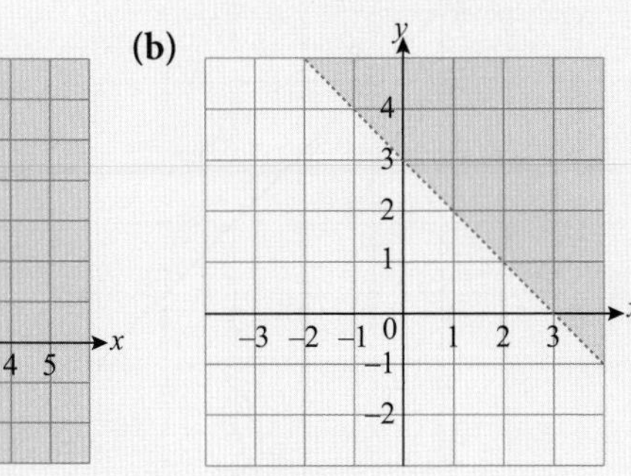

(c)

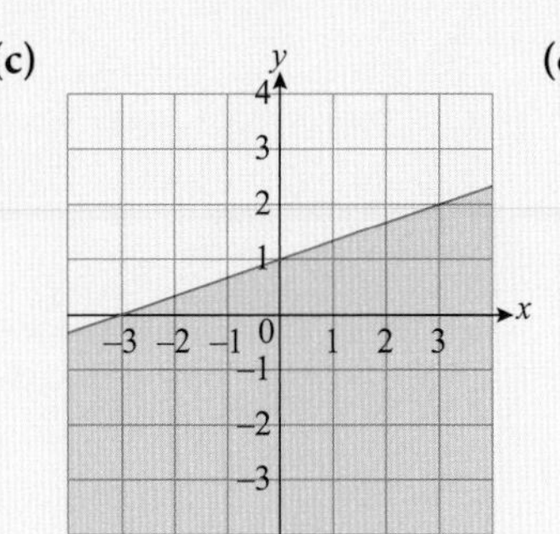

(d)

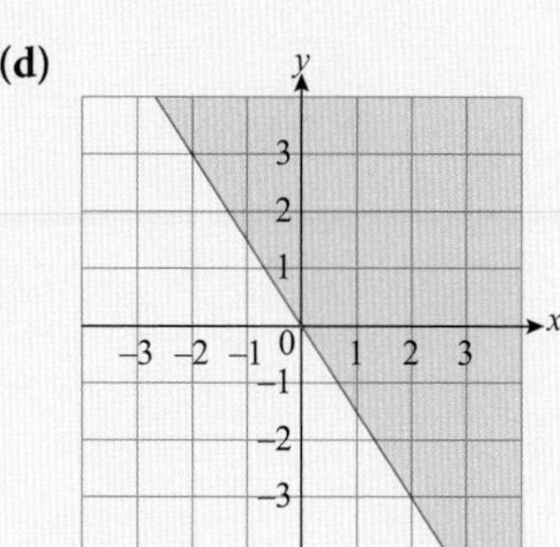

Representing simultaneous inequalities

When two or more inequalities have to be satisfied at the same time, they are called simultaneous inequalities. These can also be represented graphically. On the diagram in worked example 15 the inequalities are represented by regions on the same diagram. The unwanted regions are shaded or crossed out. The unshaded region will contain all the co-ordinates (x, y) that satisfy all the inequalities simultaneously.

Worked example 15

By shading the unwanted regions, show the region defined by the set of inequalities $y < x + 2$, $y \leq 4$ and $x \leq 3$.

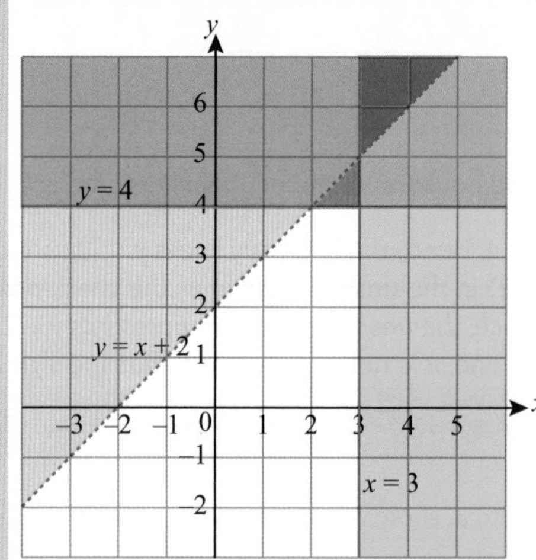

The boundaries of the required region are $y = x + 2$ (broken line), $y = 4$ (solid line) and $x = 3$ (solid line).

The unshaded region in the diagram represents the set of inequalities $y < x + 2$, $y \leq 4$ and $x \leq 3$.

Notice that this region does not have a finite area – it is not 'closed'.

Exercise 14.6

1 By shading the unwanted regions, show the region defined by the set of inequalities $x + 2y \geq 6$, $y \leq x$ and $x < 4$.

2 By shading the unwanted regions, show the region defined by the set of inequalities $x + y \geq 5$, $y \leq 2$ and $y \geq 0$.

3 (a) On a grid, draw the lines $x = 4$, $y = 3$ and $x + y = 5$.

(b) By shading the unwanted regions, show the region that satisfies all the inequalities $x \leq 4$, $y \leq 3$ and $x + y \geq 5$. Label the region R.

4 Write down the three inequalities that define the unshaded triangular region R.

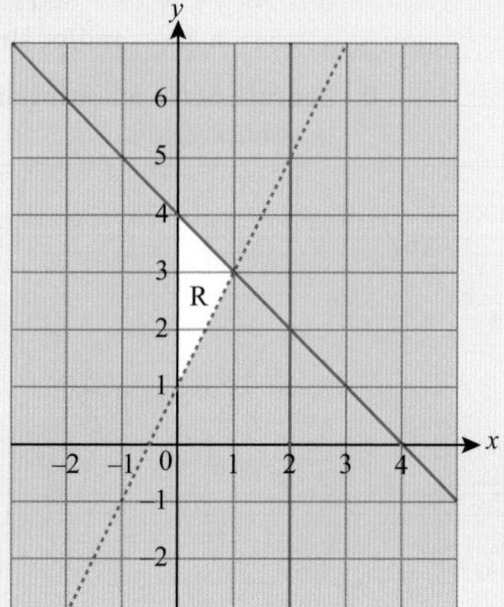

5 The unshaded region in diagram represents the set of inequalities $y \geq 0$, $y + 2x \geq 2$ and $x + y < 4$. Write down the pairs of integers (x, y) that satisfy all the inequalities.

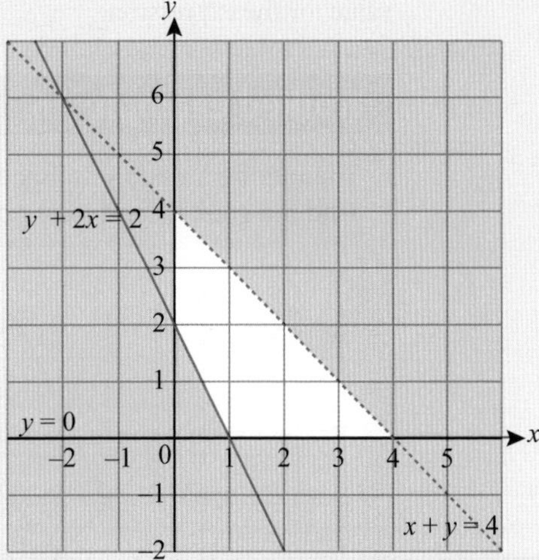

6 Draw graphs to show the solution sets of these inequalities: $y \leq 4$, $y \geq x + 2$ and $3x + y \geq 4$. Write down the integer co-ordinates (x, y) that satisfy all the inequalities in this case.

14.4 Linear programming

Many of the applications of mathematics in business and industry are concerned with obtaining the greatest profits or incurring the least cost subject to constraints (restrictions) such as the number of workers, machines available or capital available.

When these constraints are expressed mathematically, they take the form of inequalities. When the inequalities are linear (such as $3x + 2y < 6$), the branch of mathematics you would use is called **linear programming**.

Greatest and least values.

The expression $2x + y$ has a value for every point (x, y) in the Cartesian plane. Values of $2x + y$ at some grid points are shown in the diagram.

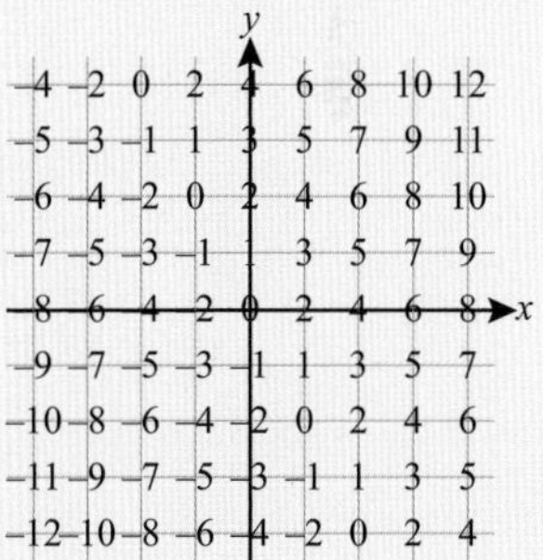

If points that give the same value of $2x + y$ are joined, they result in a set of contour lines. These contour lines are straight lines; their equations are in the form $2x + y = k$ (k is the constant).

You can see that as k increases, the line $2x + y$ moves parallel to itself towards the top right-hand side of the diagram. As k decreases, the line moves parallel to itself towards the bottom left-hand side of the diagram. (Only the even numbered contours are shown here.)

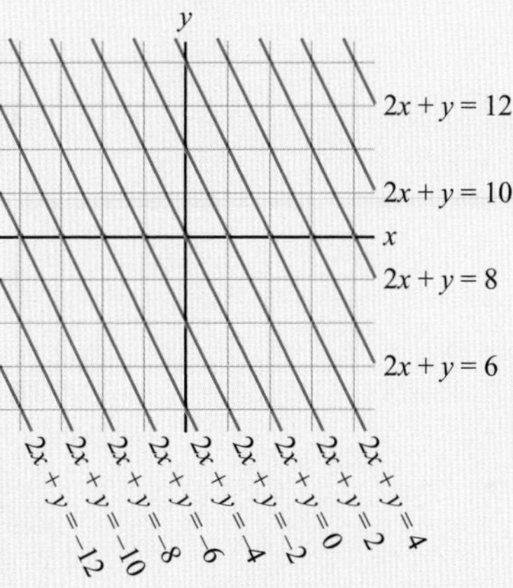

The expression $2x + y$ has no greatest or least value if there are no restrictions on the values of x and y. When there are restrictions on the values, there is normally a greatest and/or a least value for the expression.

Worked example 16

The numbers x and y satisfy all the inequalities $x + y \leq 4$, $y \leq 2x - 2$ and $y \geq x - 2$. Find the greatest and least possible values of the expression $2x + y$.

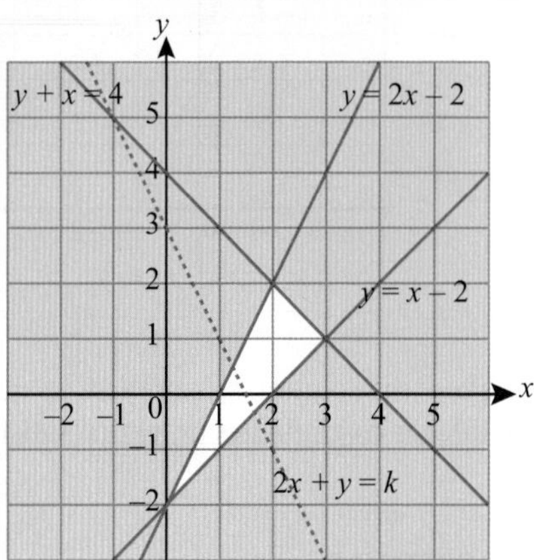

You only have to consider the values of $2x + y$ for points in the unshaded region. If $2x + y = k$, then $y = -2x + k$. Draw a line with gradient equal to −2. (The dashed line in this example has $k = 3$.)

Using a set square and a ruler, place one edge of your set square on the dashed line you have drawn and your ruler against one of the other sides. If you slide your set square along the ruler, the original side will remain parallel to your dashed line.

Moving to the right, when your set square is just about to leave the unshaded region (at the point (3, 1)), $2x + y$ will have its greatest value. Substituting $x = 3$ and $y = 1$ into $2x + y$ gives a greatest value of 7.

Similarly, moving to the left will give a least value of −2 (at co-ordinates (0, −2)).

Exercise 14.7

1 In the diagram, the unshaded region represents the set of inequalities $x \leq 6$, $0 \leq y \leq 6$ and $x + y \geq 4$. Find the greatest and least possible values of $3x + 2y$ subject to these inequalities.

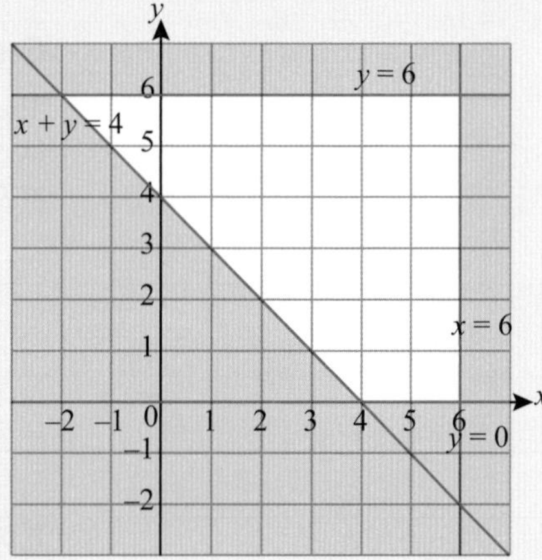

2 **(a)** On a grid, shade the unwanted regions to indicate the region satisfying all the inequalities $y \leq x$, $x + y \leq 6$ and $y \geq 0$.

(b) What is the greatest possible value of $2x + y$ if x and y satisfy all these inequalities?

3 The whole numbers x and y satisfy all the inequalities $y \geq 1$, $y \leq x + 3$ and $3x + y \leq 6$. Find the greatest and least possible values of the expression, $x + y$.

4 An IGCSE class is making school flags and T-shirts to sell to raise funds for the school. Due to time constraints, the class is able to make at most 150 flags and 120 T-shirts. The fabric is donated and they have enough to make 200 items in total. A flag sells for \$2 and a T-shirt sells for \$5. How many of each item should they make to maximise their income from sales?

5 A school principal wants to buy some book cases for the school library. She can choose between two types of book case. Type A costs \$10 and it requires 0.6 m^2 of floor space and holds 0.8 m^3 of books. Type B costs \$20 and it requires 0.8 m^2 of floor space and holds 1.2 m^3 of books. The maximum floor space available is 7.2 m^2 and the budget is \$140 (but the school would prefer to spend less). What number and type of book cases should the principal buy to get the largest possible storage space for books?

14.5 Completing the square

REWIND

Quadratic expressions contain an x^2 term as the highest power. You learned how to solve quadratic equations by factorising in chapter 10. ◀

It can be helpful to re-write **quadratic** expressions in a slightly different form. Although this first method will be used to solve quadratic equations, it can be used to find the co-ordinates of maximums or minimums in a quadratic. An application of this method to the general form of a quadratic will produce the quadratic formula that is used in the next section.

Remember that when you expand $(x+a)^2$ you get:

$$(x+a)(x+a) = x^2 + 2ax + a^2$$

Most importantly you will see that the value of 'a' is doubled and this gives the coefficient of x in the final expansion. This is the key to the method.

The completing the square method can only be used when the coefficient of $x^2 = 1$. Use this method when the trinomial (expression with three terms) cannot be factorised.

Now consider $x^2 + 6x + 1$ and compare with $(x+3)^2 = (x+3)(x+3) = x^2 + 6x + 9$.

The '3' has been chosen as it is half of the number of 'x's in the original expression.

This latter expression is similar, but there is constant term of 9 rather than 1. So, to make the new expression equal to the original, you must subtract 8.

$$x^2 + 6x + 1 = (x+3)^2 - 8$$

This method of re-writing the quadratic is called *completing the square.*

Worked example 17

Rewrite the expression $x^2 - 4x + 11$ in the form $(x+a)^2 + b$.

The number of 'x's is –4. Half of this is –2.

$(x-2)^2 = x^2 - 4x + 4$

The constant term is too small by 7, so $x^2 - 4x + 11 = (x-2)^2 + 7$

In chapter 10 you solved quadratic equations like $x^2 - 7x + 12 = 0$ by factorisation. But some quadratic equations cannot be factorised. In such cases, you can solve the equation by completing the square.

Worked example 18

Solve $x^2 + 4x - 6 = 0$, giving your answer to two decimal places.

$x^2 + 4x - 6 = 0$	This equation cannot be factorised.
$x^2 + 4x = 6$	Add 6 to both sides.

A $\sqrt{\ }$ can have both a positive and negative value, which leads to the two solutions for a quadratic.

$(x+2)^2-4=6$	Complete the square by writing x^2+4x in the form $(x+a)^2+b$. Half of 4 is 2 so try $(x+2)^2 = x^2+4x+4$. The constant of +4 is too big, so it becomes $(x+2)^2-4$.
$(x+2)^2=10$	Add 4 to both sides.
$x+2=\pm\sqrt{10}$	Take the square root of both sides.
$x=-2\pm\sqrt{10}$	Subtract 2 from each side.
$x=1.1622\ldots$ or $-5.1622\ldots$	Solve for both options.
$x=1.16$ or -5.16 (2 d.p.)	Round your solutions.

Exercise 14.8

1 Write each of the following expressions in the form $(x+a)^2+b$.

(a) $x^2+6x+14$ (b) x^2+8x+1 (c) $x^2+12x+20$
(d) x^2+6x+5 (e) $x^2-4x+12$ (f) $x^2-2x-17$
(g) x^2+5x+1 (h) x^2+7x-2 (i) x^2-3x-3
(j) x^2+7x-8 (k) $x^2-13x+1$ (l) $x^2-20x+400$

2 Solve the following quadratic equations by the method of completing the square, giving your final answer to 2 decimal places.

(a) $x^2+6x-5=0$ (b) $x^2+8x+4=0$ (c) $x^2-4x+2=0$
(d) $x^2+5x-7=0$ (e) $x^2-3x+2=0$ (f) $x^2-12x+1=0$

3 Solve each equation by completing the square.

(a) $x^2-x-10=0$ (b) $x^2+3x-6=0$ (c) $x(6+x)=1$
(d) $2x^2+x=8$ (e) $5x=10-\frac{1}{x}$ (f) $x-5=\frac{2}{x}$
(g) $(x-1)(x+2)-1=0$ (h) $(x-4)(x+2)=-5$ (i) $x^2=x+1$

14.6 Quadratic formula

REWIND

You saw in chapter 2 that the coefficient of a variable is the number that multiplies it. This is still true for quadratic equations: a is the coefficient of x^2 and b is the coefficient of x. c is the constant term. ◀

In the previous section the coefficient of x^2 was always 1. Applying the completing the square method when the coefficient of x^2 is not 1 is more complex but if you do apply it to the general form of a quadratic equation ($ax^2+bx+c=0$), the following result is produced:

$$\text{If } ax^2+bx+c=0 \text{ then } x=\frac{-b\pm\sqrt{b^2-4ac}}{2a}$$

This is known as the quadratic formula.

Notice the '±' symbol. This tells you that you should calculate two values: one with a '+' and one with a '–' in the position occupied by the '±'. The quadratic formula can be used for all quadratic equations that have real solutions even if the quadratic expression cannot be factorised.

The advantage of the quadratic formula over completing the square is that you don't have to worry when the coefficient of x^2 is not 1.

Worked example 19

Solve the following quadratic equations, giving your answers to 3 significant figures.

(a) $x^2+4x+3=0$ **(b)** $x^2-7x+11=0$ **(c)** $3x^2-2x-1=0$

(a) Compare the quadratic equation $x^2+4x+3=0$ with $ax^2+bx+c=0$.
From this you should see that $a=1$, $b=4$ and $c=3$.

$$x=\frac{-b\pm\sqrt{b^2-4ac}}{2a}=\frac{-4\pm\sqrt{4^2-4\times1\times3}}{2\times1}$$
$$=\frac{-4\pm\sqrt{16-12}}{2}$$
$$=\frac{-4\pm\sqrt{4}}{2}$$
$$=\frac{-4\pm2}{2}$$

So, $x=\frac{-4+2}{2}=\frac{-2}{2}=-1$ or $x=\frac{-4-2}{2}=\frac{-6}{2}=-3$

Notice that the original quadratic equation can be factorised to give $(x+1)(x+3)=0$ and the same solutions. If you can factorise the quadratic then you should because the method is much simpler.

(b) $x^2-7x+11=0$, $a=1$, $b=-7$ and $c=11$.

$$x=\frac{-(-7)\pm\sqrt{(-7)^2-4\times1\times11}}{2\times1}=\frac{7\pm\sqrt{49-44}}{2}$$
$$=\frac{7\pm\sqrt{5}}{2}$$

So, $x=\frac{7+\sqrt{5}}{2}=4.6180\ldots$ or $x=\frac{7-\sqrt{5}}{2}=2.3819\ldots$

$x\approx4.62$ or 2.38 (3sf)

(c) For this example you should note that a is not 1!
$3x^2-2x-1=0$, $a=3$, $b=-2$ and $c=-1$.

$$x=\frac{-(-2)\pm\sqrt{(-2)^2-4\times3\times(-1)}}{2\times3}=\frac{2\pm\sqrt{4+12}}{6}$$
$$=\frac{2\pm\sqrt{16}}{6}$$
$$=\frac{2\pm4}{6}$$

So, $x=\frac{2+4}{6}=\frac{6}{6}=1$ or $x=\frac{2-4}{6}=\frac{-2}{6}=\frac{-1}{3}$

Tip

Here you need to take particular care. BODMAS always applies and you should check the order of your working, and your solution, carefully.

Notice that there are brackets around the –7. If you miss these the calculation becomes $-7^2=-49$ rather than +49.

If b is negative ALWAYS use brackets to make sure that you square it correctly.

Most modern calculators will allow you to input these fractions exactly as they appear here.

Exercise 14.9

1 Each of the following quadratics will factorise. Solve each of them by factorisation and then use the quadratic formula to show that you get the same answers in both cases.

(a) $x^2+7x+12=0$ (b) $x^2+8x+12=0$ (c) $x^2+11x+28=0$
(d) $x^2+4x-5=0$ (e) $x^2+6x-16=0$ (f) $x^2+12x-160=0$
(g) $x^2-6x+8=0$ (h) $x^2-3x-28=0$ (i) $x^2-5x-24=0$
(j) $x^2-12x+32=0$ (k) $x^2-2x-99=0$ (l) $x^2-9x-36=0$
(m) $x^2-10x+24=0$ (n) $x^2-12x+35=0$ (o) $x^2+9x-36=0$

2 Solve each of the following equations by using the quadratic formula. Round your answers to 3 significant figures where necessary. These quadratic expressions do not factorise.

(a) $x^2+6x-1=0$ (b) $x^2+5x+5=0$ (c) $x^2+7x+11=0$
(d) $x^2+4x+2=0$ (e) $x^2-3x-1=0$ (f) $x^2-4x+2=0$
(g) $x^2-8x+6=0$ (h) $x^2-2x-2=0$ (i) $x^2-6x-4=0$
(j) $x^2-8x-2=0$ (k) $x^2-9x+7=0$ (l) $x^2+11x+7=0$

3 Solve each of the following equations by using the quadratic formula. Round your answers to 3 significant figures where necessary. Take particular note of the coefficient of x^2.

(a) $2x^2-4x+1=0$ (b) $3x^2-3x-1=0$ (c) $4x^2+2x-5=0$
(d) $-2x^2+3x+4=0$ (e) $-2x^2-2x+1=0$ (f) $5x^2+x-3=0$

4 Solve each of the following equations by using the quadratic formula. Round your answers to 3 significant figures where necessary. You must make sure that your equation takes the form of a quadratic expression *equal to zero*. If it does not, then you will need to collect all terms on to one side so that a zero appears on the other side!

(a) $2x^2-x+6=4x+5$ (b) $7x^2-3x-6=3x-7$ (c) $x(6x-3)-2=0$
(d) $0.5x^2+0.8x-2=0$ (e) $(x+7)(x+5)=9$ (f) $\frac{1}{x}+x=7$

5 A rectangle has area 12 cm^2. If the length of the rectangle is $(x+1)$ cm and the width of the rectangle is $(x+3)$ cm, find the possible value(s) of x.

14.7 Factorising quadratics where the coefficient of x^2 is not 1

The quadratic equation in worked example 19 (c) gave two solutions that could have been obtained by factorisation. It turns out that $(x-1)(3x+1)=3x^2-2x-1$ (you can check this by expanding the brackets).

In general, if the coefficient of x^2 in a quadratic is a number other than 1 it is harder to factorise, but there are some tips to help you.

Worked example 20

Factorise each of the following expressions:

(a) $2x^2+3x+1$ (b) $3x^2-14x+8$ (c) $10x^2+11x-8$

(a) $2x^2+3x+1$

$2x^2+3x+1=(2x\quad)(x\quad)$

The only way to produce the term $2x^2$ is to multiply $2x$ and x. These two terms are placed at the front of each bracket. There are blank spaces in the brackets because you don't yet know what else needs to be included. The clue lies in the constant term at the end, which is obtained by multiplying these two unknown values together.

The constant term is 1, so the only possible values are +1 or −1. Since the constant term is positive, the unknown values must be either both −1 or both +1.

Try each of these combinations systematically:

$(2x-1)(x-1)=2x^2-3x+1$ The coefficient of x is wrong.

$(2x+1)(x+1)=2x^2+3x+1$ This is correct.

So, $2x^2+3x+1=(2x+1)(x+1)$

(b) $3x^2-14x+8$

Start by writing $3x^2-14x+8=(3x\quad)(x\quad)$.

The two unknown terms must multiply to give 8. Since the constant term is positive, the unknowns must have the same sign. The possible pairs are:

8 and 1 2 and 4 –8 and –1 –2 and –4

Try each pair in turn, remembering that you can reverse the order:

$(3x+8)(x+1)=3x^2+3x+8x+8=3x^2+11x+8$ Incorrect

$(3x+1)(x+8)=3x^2+24x+x+8=3x^2+25x+8$ Incorrect

$(3x+2)(x+4)=3x^2+12x+2x+8=3x^2+14x+8$ Incorrect

This last one is very close. You just need to change the sign of the 'x' term. This can be done by jumping to the last pair: –2 and –4.

$(3x-2)(x-4)=3x^2-12x-2x+8=3x^2-14x+8$ Correct

So, $3x^2-14x+8=(3x-2)(x-4)$

(c) $10x^2+11x-8$

This question is rather more difficult because there is more than one way to multiply two expressions to get $10x^2$:

$2x$ and $5x$ or $10x$ and x.
Each possibility needs to be tried.

Start with $10x^2+11x-8=(10x\quad)(x\quad)$.

Factor pairs that multiply to give –8 are:

–8 and 1 8 and –1 2 and –4 –2 and 4

Remember that you will need to try each pair with the two values in either order.
For this particular quadratic you will find that none of the eight possible combinations works!

Instead, you must now try: $10x^2+11x-8=(5x\quad)(2x\quad)$.
Trying the above set of pairs once again you will eventually find that:

$10x^2+11x-8=(5x+8)(2x-1)$

This process does appear to be long but with practice you will find ways of making the process faster. After the following exercise is another worked example. This shows an alternative, systematic method of solving these more complex quadratics, but you should try to get a feel for the problems before you use it.

Exercise 14.10

1 Factorise each of the following expressions.

(a) $3x^2+14x+8$ (b) $2x^2+x-3$ (c) $6x^2+x-2$
(d) $3x^2+14x+16$ (e) $2x^2-x-10$ (f) $16x^2+32x-9$
(g) $3x^2+16x+5$ (h) $8x^2+2x-1$ (i) $2x^2-x-6$
(j) $2x^2+9x+9$ (k) $3x^2+2x-16$ (l) $10x^2-x-3$
(m) $5x^2+6x+1$ (n) $2x^2-19x+9$ (o) $12x^2+8x-15$

Here is another method for factorising a quadratic like those in the previous exercise.

Worked example 21

Factorise $10x^2+11x-8$.

$10\times-8=-80$	Multiply the coefficient of x^2 by the constant term.
$-1, 80$ (no) $-2, 40$ (no) $-4, 20$ (no) $-5, 16$ (yes)	List the factor pairs of -80 until you obtain a pair that totals the coefficient of x (11) (note as 11 is positive and -80 is negative, the larger number of the pair must be positive and the other negative).
$10x^2-5x+16x-8$	Re-write the x term using this factor pair.
$5x(2x-1)+8(2x-1)$	Factorise pairs of terms. (Be careful with signs here so that the second bracket is the same as the first bracket.)
$(5x+8)(2x-1)$	Factorise, using the bracket as the common term.

Exercise 14.11

1 Now go back to Exercise 14.10 and try to factorise the expressions using this new method.

2 Factorise completely. You may need to remove a common factor before factorising the trinomials.

(a) $6x^2-5x-21$ (b) $-2x^2-13x-15$ (c) $4x^2+12xy+9y^2$
(d) $6x^2-19xy-7y^2$ (e) x^4-13x^2+36 (f) $6x^2-38xy+40y^2$
(g) $6x^2+7x+2$ (h) $3x^2-13x+12$ (i) $3x^2-39x+120$
(j) $(x+1)^2-5(x+1)+6$ (k) $(2x+1)^2-8(2x+1)+15$ (l) $3(2x+5)^2-17(2x+5)+10$

A trinomial is an algebraic expression that contains three terms: an x^2 term, an x term and a constant term.

14.8 Algebraic fractions

You will now use several of the techniques covered so far in this chapter to simplify complex algebraic fractions.

You already know that you can simplify fractions by dividing the numerator and denominator by a common factor. This can also be done with algebraic fractions.

Worked example 22

Simplify each of the following fractions as far as possible:

(a) $\frac{3x}{6}$ (b) $\frac{y^2}{y^5}$ (c) $\frac{12p^3}{16p^7}$ (d) $\frac{x^2-4x+3}{x^2-7x+12}$

(a) $\frac{3x}{6}$	
$\frac{3x}{6}=\frac{3x\div 3}{6\div 3}=\frac{x}{2}$	The highest common factor of 3 and 6 is 3.
(b) $\frac{y^2}{y^5}$	The highest common factor of y^2 and y^5 is y^2.
$\frac{y^2}{y^5}=\frac{y^2\div y^2}{y^5\div y^2}=\frac{1}{y^3}$	
(c) $\frac{12p^3}{16p^7}$	
$\frac{12p^3}{16p^7}=\frac{3p^3}{4p^7}$	Consider the constants first. The HCF of 12 and 16 is 4, so you can divide both 12 and 16 by 4.
$\frac{12p^3}{16p^7}=\frac{3p^3}{4p^7}=\frac{3}{4p^4}$	Now note that the HCF of p^3 and p^7 is p^3. You can divide both the numerator and the denominator by this HCF.
(d) $\frac{x^2-4x+3}{x^2-7x+12}$	
$\frac{x^2-4x+3}{x^2-7x+12}=\frac{(x-3)(x-1)}{(x-3)(x-4)}$	Notice that you can factorise both the numerator and the denominator.
$=\frac{\cancel{(x-3)}(x-1)}{\cancel{(x-3)}(x-4)}$	You can see that $(x-3)$ is a factor of both the numerator and the denominator, so you can cancel this common factor.
$=\frac{(x-1)}{(x-4)}$	

REWIND

You might need to recap the laws of indices that you learned in chapter 2. ◀

Exercise 14.12

Simplify each of the following fractions by dividing both the numerator and the denominator by their HCF.

1 (a) $\frac{2x}{4}$ (b) $\frac{3y}{12}$ (c) $\frac{5x}{x}$ (d) $\frac{10y}{y}$ (e) $\frac{6t}{36}$

(f) $\frac{9u}{27}$ (g) $\frac{5t}{50}$ (h) $\frac{4y}{8}$ (i) $\frac{15z}{20}$ (j) $\frac{16t}{12}$

2 (a) $\frac{5xy}{15}$ (b) $\frac{3x}{12y}$ (c) $\frac{17ab}{34ab}$ (d) $\frac{9xy}{18x}$ (e) $\frac{25x^2}{5x}$

(f) $\frac{21b^2}{7b}$ (g) $\frac{14x^2}{21xy}$ (h) $\frac{12ab^2}{4ab}$ (i) $\frac{20de}{30d^2e^2}$ (j) $\frac{5a}{20ab^2}$

3 (a) $\frac{7a^2b^2}{35ab^3}$ (b) $\frac{(ab)^2}{ab}$ (c) $\frac{18abc}{36ac}$ (d) $\frac{13a^2bc}{52ab}$ (e) $\frac{12a^2b^2c^2}{24abc}$

(f) $\frac{36(ab)^2c}{16a^2bc^2}$ (g) $\frac{(abc)^3}{abc}$ (h) $\frac{9x^2y^3}{12x^3y^2}$ (i) $\frac{20x^3y^2z^2}{15xy^3z}$ (j) $\frac{(3y)^3}{3y^3}$

4 (a) $\frac{18(xy)^2z^3}{17(xyz^3)^2}$ (b) $\frac{334x^4y^7z^3}{668xy^8z^2}$ (c) $\frac{249u(vw)^3}{581u^3v^2w^7}$ (d) $\frac{x^2+3x}{x^2+4x}$ (e) $\frac{x^2+3x}{x^2+7x+12}$

(f) $\frac{y^3+y^4}{y^2+2y+1}$ (g) $\frac{x^2-8x+12}{x^2-6x+8}$ (h) $\frac{x^2+9x+20}{x^2+x-12}$ (i) $\frac{24x^2+8x}{3x^2+x}$ (j) $\frac{3x^2-10x-8}{3x^2-14x+8}$

(k) $\frac{x^2-9}{x^2+5x-24}$ (l) $\frac{2x^2-x-3}{x^2+2x+1}$ (m) $\frac{7x^2-29x+4}{x^2-8x+16}$ (n) $\frac{10y^2-3y-4}{2y^2-13y-7}$ (o) $\frac{6x^2-11x-7}{10x^2-3x-4}$

5 (a) $\frac{6x^2-35x+36}{14x^2-61x-9}$ (b) $\frac{(x^2)^2-(y^2)^2}{(x-y)(x+y)}$ (c) $\frac{\sqrt{x}}{(\sqrt{x})^3}$

(d) $\frac{x^4+2x^2+1}{x^2+1}$ (e) $\frac{(x^2+7x+12)(x^2+8x+12)}{(x^2+9x+18)(x^2+6x+8)}$ (f) $\frac{\left(\sqrt{x^3+y^3}\right)^3}{x^3+y^3}$

Multiplying and dividing algebraic fractions

You can use the ideas explored in the previous section when multiplying or dividing algebraic fractions. Consider the following multiplication: $\frac{x}{y^2}\times\frac{y^4}{x^3}$

You already know that the numerators and denominators can be multiplied in the usual way: $\frac{x}{y^2}\times\frac{y^4}{x^3}=\frac{xy^4}{y^2x^3}$

Now you can see that the HCF of the numerator and denominator will be xy^2. If you divide through by xy^2 you get: $\frac{x}{y^2}\times\frac{y^4}{x^3}=\frac{y^2}{x^2}$

The following worked examples will help you to understand the process for slightly more complicated multiplications and divisions.

Worked example 23

Simplify each of the following.

(a) $\frac{4}{3x^2}\times\frac{14x^3}{16y^2}$ (b) $\frac{3(x+y)^3}{16z^2}\times\frac{12z}{9(x+y)^7}$ (c) $\frac{14x^4y^3}{9}\div\frac{7x^2y}{18}$

(a) $\frac{4}{3x^2}\times\frac{14x^3}{16y^2}$

$\frac{4}{3x^2}\times\frac{14x^3}{16y^2}=\frac{4\times14x^3}{3x^2\times16y^2}=\frac{56x^3}{48x^2y^2}=\frac{7x}{6y^2}$

You can simply multiply numerators and denominators and then simplify using the methods in the previous section.

(b) $\frac{3(x+y)^3}{16z^2}\times\frac{12z}{9(x+y)^7}$

$\frac{3(x+y)^3}{16z^2}\times\frac{12z}{9(x+y)^7}=\frac{36(x+y)^3z}{144(x+y)^7z^2}=\frac{1}{4(x+y)^4z}$

(c) $\dfrac{14x^4y^3}{9} \div \dfrac{7x^2y}{18}$

$$\frac{14x^4y^3}{9} \div \frac{7x^2y}{18} = \frac{14x^4y^3}{9} \times \frac{18}{7x^2y} = \frac{14x^4y^3 \times 18}{9 \times 7x^2y} = 4x^2y^2$$

Exercise 14.13

Write each of the following as a single fraction in its lowest terms.

1 (a) $\dfrac{2x}{3} \times \dfrac{3x}{8}$ (b) $\dfrac{3y}{4} \times \dfrac{2y}{7}$ (c) $\dfrac{2z}{7} \times \dfrac{3z}{4}$ (d) $\dfrac{5t}{9} \times \dfrac{9t}{15}$

(e) $\dfrac{2x^2}{5} \times \dfrac{5}{2x^2}$ (f) $\dfrac{7x^2}{12} \times \dfrac{4}{14x^2}$ (g) $\dfrac{12e^2}{11f} \times \dfrac{33f^2}{24e^3}$ (h) $\dfrac{18g^4}{16h^2} \times \dfrac{h^4}{36g^3}$

(i) $\dfrac{3y}{4} \div \dfrac{3y}{8}$ (j) $\dfrac{3y}{8} \div \dfrac{3y^3}{4}$ (k) $\dfrac{4cd}{7} \div \dfrac{16c^2}{8}$ (l) $\dfrac{8pq}{r} \div \dfrac{16p^2q^2}{r^2}$

2 (a) $\dfrac{24zt^3}{x^2} \div \dfrac{8xt}{z}$ (b) $\dfrac{8}{12} \times \dfrac{x^3}{t^2} \times \dfrac{t^3}{x^2}$ (c) $\dfrac{9}{27} \times \dfrac{3x^2}{12y^3} \times \dfrac{81}{27} \times \dfrac{9y^2}{3x^3}$

(d) $\left(\dfrac{3}{8} \times \dfrac{64t^3y^2}{27t}\right) \div \left(\dfrac{3}{8} \times \dfrac{y^2}{t^3} \times \dfrac{t}{y^4}\right)$ (e) $\dfrac{(x+y)^2}{(x-y)^3} \times \dfrac{33(x-y)^2}{44(x+y)^7}$

(f) $\dfrac{3(a+b)(a-b)}{(a+b)^2} \div \dfrac{12(a-b)^2}{(a+b)}$ (g) $\dfrac{3\sqrt{x^2+y^2}}{24\sqrt{z^2+t^2}} \times \dfrac{(z^2+t^2)^2}{18\left(\sqrt{x^2+y^2}\right)^3}$

(h) $\dfrac{3(x+y)^{10}}{18(z-t)^{19}} \times \dfrac{10(x+y)(z-t)^4}{12(x+y)^3(z-y)} \times \dfrac{108(x+y)^2(z-t)^{20}}{15(z-t)^4(x+y)^{10}}$

Adding and subtracting algebraic fractions

You can use *common denominators* when adding together algebraic fractions, just as you do with ordinary fractions.

Worked example 24

Write as a single fraction in its lowest terms, $\dfrac{1}{x} + \dfrac{1}{y}$.

$$\frac{1}{x} + \frac{1}{y} = \frac{y}{xy} + \frac{x}{xy} = \frac{y+x}{xy}$$

The lowest common multiple of x and y is xy. This will be the common denominator.

Worked example 25

Write as a single fraction in its lowest terms, $\frac{1}{x+1}+\frac{1}{x+2}$.

The lowest common multiple of $(x + 1)$ and $(x + 2)$ is $(x + 1)(x + 2)$

$$\begin{aligned}\frac{1}{x+1}+\frac{1}{x+2} &= \frac{x+2}{(x+1)(x+2)}+\frac{x+1}{(x+1)(x+2)}\\ &= \frac{x+2+x+1}{(x+1)(x+2)}\\ &= \frac{2x+3}{(x+1)(x+2)}\end{aligned}$$

Worked example 26

Write as a single fraction in its lowest terms, $\frac{3x+4}{x^2+x-6}-\frac{1}{x+3}$.

First you should factorise the quadratic expression:

$$\frac{3x+4}{x^2+x-6}-\frac{1}{x+3}=\frac{3x+4}{(x+3)(x-2)}-\frac{1}{(x+3)}$$

The two denominators have a common factor of $(x + 3)$, and the lowest common multiple of these two denominators is $(x + 3)(x - 2)$:

$$\begin{aligned}\frac{3x+4}{x^2+x-6}-\frac{1}{x+3} &= \frac{3x+4}{(x+3)(x-2)}-\frac{1}{(x+3)}\\ &= \frac{3x+4}{(x+3)(x-2)}-\frac{(x-2)}{(x+3)(x-2)}\\ &= \frac{3x+4-(x-2)}{(x+3)(x-2)}\\ &= \frac{3x+4-x+2}{(x+3)(x-2)}\\ &= \frac{2x+6}{(x+3)(x-2)}\end{aligned}$$

This may appear to be the final answer but if you factorise the numerator you will find that more can be done!

$$\begin{aligned}\frac{3x+4}{x^2+x-6}-\frac{1}{x+3} &= \frac{2x+6}{(x+3)(x-2)}\\ &= \frac{2(x+3)}{(x+3)(x-2)}\\ &= \frac{2}{(x-2)}\end{aligned}$$

Always check to see if your final numerator factorises. If it does, then there may be more stages to go.

Exercise 14.14

Write each of the following as a single fraction in its lowest terms.

1 (a) $\frac{y}{2}+\frac{y}{4}$ (b) $\frac{t}{3}+\frac{t}{5}$ (c) $\frac{u}{7}+\frac{u}{5}$ (d) $\frac{z}{7}-\frac{z}{14}$ (e) $\frac{(x+y)}{3}+\frac{(x+y)}{12}$

(f) $\frac{2x}{3}+\frac{5x}{6}$ (g) $\frac{3y}{4}+\frac{5y}{8}$ (h) $\frac{2a}{5}-\frac{3a}{8}$ (i) $\frac{2a}{7}+\frac{3a}{14}$ (j) $\frac{x}{9}+\frac{2y}{7}$

2 (a) $\frac{5(x+1)^2}{7}-\frac{3(x+1)^2}{8}$ (b) $\frac{10pqr}{17}-\frac{3pqr}{8}$ (c) $\frac{3p}{5}+\frac{3p}{7}+\frac{3p}{10}$

(d) $\frac{2x}{3}+\frac{3x}{7}-\frac{x}{4}$ (e) $\frac{8x^2}{9}+\frac{3x^2}{7}-\frac{x^2}{3}$ (f) $\frac{5-x}{2}-\frac{3-x}{3}+\frac{3-x}{9}$

3 (a) $\frac{x}{a}+\frac{3}{a}$ (b) $\frac{2}{3a}+\frac{5}{4a}$ (c) $\frac{3x}{2y}+\frac{5x}{3y}$

(d) $\frac{3}{a}+\frac{2}{a^2}$ (e) $\frac{3}{2x}+\frac{4}{3x}$ (f) $\frac{5}{4e}+\frac{3}{20e}$

4 (a) $\frac{1}{x+1}+\frac{1}{x+4}$ (b) $\frac{3}{x-2}+\frac{2}{x-1}$ (c) $\frac{5}{x+2}+\frac{2}{x+7}$

(d) $\frac{3}{x}-\frac{1}{2x}$ (e) $\frac{5}{2xy}-\frac{4}{3xy}$ (f) $\frac{2}{x}+x$

(g) $\frac{x+1}{2}+\frac{2}{x+1}$ (h) $\frac{3(x^2-1)}{7y}-\frac{2(x^2-1)}{9y^2}$ (i) $\frac{1}{x^2}-\frac{x}{2y}$

(j) $\frac{x+1}{3z^2}-\frac{y+z}{12xy}$ (k) $\frac{1}{(x+2)}-\frac{1}{(x+3)(x+2)}$ (l) $\frac{2}{x+1}-\frac{2}{x^2+3x+2}$

Summary

Do you know the following?

- Simultaneous means at the same time.
- The intersection of two straight lines is the simultaneous solution of their equations.
- Simultaneous linear equations can be solved graphically or algebraically.
- Inequalities represent a range of solutions.
- Inequalities in one variable can be represented on a number line and in two variables as a region on a plane.
- A quadratic expression, x^2+bx+c can be written in the completed square form, $\left(x+\frac{b}{2}\right)^2-\left(\frac{b}{2}\right)^2+c$.
- Quadratic equations that do not factorise can be solved by the method of completing the square or by use of the quadratic formula.
- Complex algebraic fractions can be simplified by factorising and cancelling like terms.

Are you able to …?

- solve simultaneous linear equations graphically
- solve simultaneous linear equations algebraically
- show an inequality in one variable on a number line
- show an inequality in two variables as a region in the Cartesian plane
- show a region in the Cartesian plane that satisfies more than one inequality
- use linear programming to find the great and least values to an expression in a region
- rewrite a quadratic in completed square form
- solve a quadratic using the completed square or the quadratic formula
- simplify complex algebraic fractions.

Examination practice

Exam-style questions

1 The quadratic equation $x^2 - 5x - 3 = 0$ has solutions a and b. Find the value of:

(i) $a - b$
(ii) $a + b$
Leave your answers in exact form.

2 **(a)** By shading the unwanted regions on a diagram, show the region that satisfies all the inequalities $y \geq \frac{1}{2}x + 1$, $5x + 6y \leq 30$ and $y \leq x$.
(b) Given that x and y satisfy these three inequalities, find the greatest possible value of $x + 2y$.

Past paper questions

1 Solve the simultaneous equations.
$x - 5y = 0$
$15x + 10y = 17$ [3]

[Cambridge IGCSE Mathematics 0580 Paper 22 Q12 May/June 2011]

2 Find the co-ordinates of the point of intersection of the two lines.
$2x - 7y = 2$
$4x + 5y = 42$ [3]

[Cambridge IGCSE Mathematics 0580 Paper 22 Q15 October/November 2013]

3 x is a positive integer and $15x - 43 < 5x + 2$.
Work out the possible values of x. [3]

[Cambridge IGCSE Mathematics 0580 Paper 22 Q6 May/June 2012]

4 Write the following as a single fraction in its simplest form. [3]

$$\frac{x+2}{3} - \frac{2x-1}{4} + 1$$

[Cambridge IGCSE Mathematics 0580 Paper 23 Q13 October/November 2012]

5 Jay makes wooden boxes in two sizes. He makes x small boxes and y large boxes.
He makes at least 5 **small** boxes.
The greatest number of **large** boxes he can make is 8.
The greatest total number of boxes is 14.
The number of **large** boxes is at least half the number of **small** boxes.

(a) **(i)** Write down four inequalities in x and y to show this information. [4]

(ii) Draw four lines on the grid and write the letter R in the region which represents these inequalities.

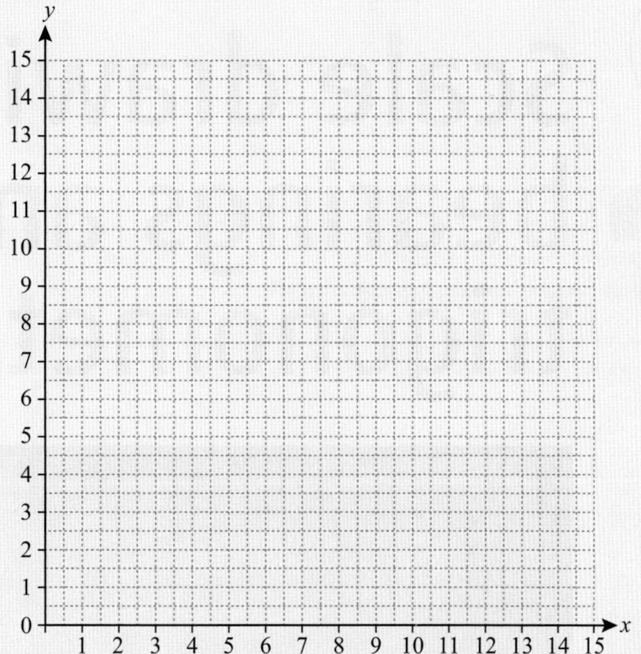

[5]

(b) The price of the small box is $20 and the price of the large box is $45.

(i) What is the greatest amount of money he receives when he sells all the boxes he has made? [2]

(ii) For this amount of money, how many boxes of each size did he make? [1]

[Cambridge IGCSE Mathematics 0580 Paper 42 Q7 October/November 2012]

6 Simplify the following. $\dfrac{h^2-h-20}{h^2-25}$ [4]

[Cambridge IGCSE Mathematics 0580 Paper 23 Q21 October/November 2012]

15 Scale drawings, bearings and trigonometry

Key words

- Scale drawing
- Bearing
- Hypotenuse
- Adjacent
- Opposite
- Tangent ratio
- Inverse function
- Sine ratio
- Cosine ratio
- Sine rule
- Cosine rule
- Projection

In this chapter you will learn how to:

- make scale drawings
- interpret scale drawings
- calculate bearings
- calculate sine, cosine and tangent ratios for right-angled triangles
- use sine, cosine and tangent ratios to calculate the lengths of sides and angles of right-angled triangles

EXTENDED

- calculate sine and cosine values between 90° and 180°
- apply the sine and cosine rules to calculate unknown sides and angles in triangles that are not right-angled
- calculate the area of a triangle that is not right-angled using the sine ratio
- use the sine, cosine and tangent ratios, together with Pythagoras' theorem in three-dimensions.

A full understanding of how waves strengthen or destroy one another can help to save countless lives. Such an understanding begins with the study of trigonometry.

To 'get your bearings' is to find out the direction you need to move from where you are. Sat Navs and the GPS can take a lot of the effort out of finding where you are going but their software uses the basic mathematical principles of calculating angles.

15.1 Scale drawings

Later in this chapter you will be learning how to use the trigonometric ratios to accurately calculate missing angles and sides. For this you will need the use of a calculator. Missing lengths and angles can also be found using **scale drawings**; although this is less accurate, it is still valid. For scale drawings you will need a ruler, a protractor and a sharp pencil.

Sometimes you have to draw a diagram to represent something that is much bigger than you can fit on the paper or so small that it would be very difficult to make out any detail. Examples include a plan of a building, a map of a country or the design of a microchip. These accurate diagrams are called a scale drawings.

The lines in the scale drawing are all the same fraction of the lines they represent in reality. This fraction is called the *scale* of the drawing.

The scale of a diagram, or a map, may be given as a fraction or a ratio such as $\frac{1}{50000}$ or 1 : 50 000.

REWIND

Some of the construction skills from chapter 3 will be useful for scale drawings. ◀

A scale of $\frac{1}{50000}$ means that every line in the diagram has a length which is $\frac{1}{50000}$ of the length of the line that it represents in real life. Hence, 1 cm in the diagram represents 50 000 cm in real life. In other words, 1 cm represents 500 m or 2 cm represents 1 km.

Worked example 1

A rectangular field is 100 m long and 45 m wide. A scale drawing of the field is made with a scale of 1 cm to 10 m. What are the length and width of the field in the drawing?

10 m is represented by 1 cm

∴ 100 m is represented by (100 ÷ 10) cm = 10 cm
and 45 m is represented by (45 ÷ 10) cm = 4.5 cm

So, the dimensions on the drawing are: length = 10 cm and width = 4.5 cm.

Exercise 15.1

1 On the plan of a house, the living room is 3.4 cm long and 2.6 cm wide. The scale of the plan is 1 cm to 2 m. Calculate the actual length and width of the room.

2 The actual distance between two villages is 12 km. Calculate the distance between the villages on a map whose scale is:

(a) 1 cm to 4 km   (b) 1 cm to 5 km.

3 A car ramp is 28 m long and makes an angle of 15° with the horizontal. A scale drawing is to be made of the ramp using a scale of 1 cm to 5 m.

(a) How long will the ramp be on the drawing?
(b) What angle will the ramp make with the horizontal on the drawing?

Angle of elevation and angle of depression

Angles of elevation are *always* measured from the *horizontal.*

Scale drawing questions often involve the observation of objects that are higher than you or lower than you, for example, the top of a building, an aeroplane or a ship in a harbour. In these cases, the angle of elevation or depression is the angle between the horizontal and the line of sight of the object.

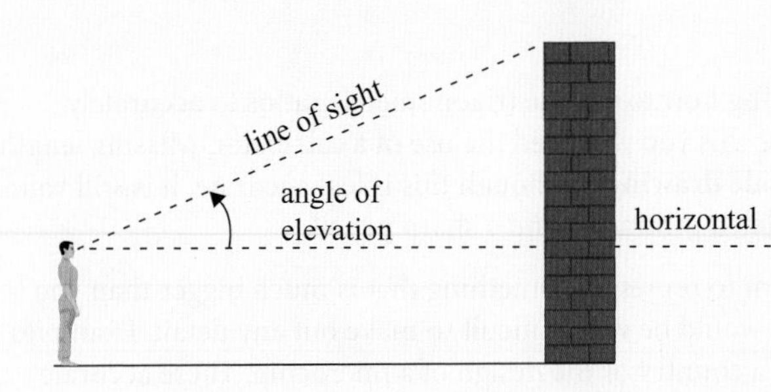

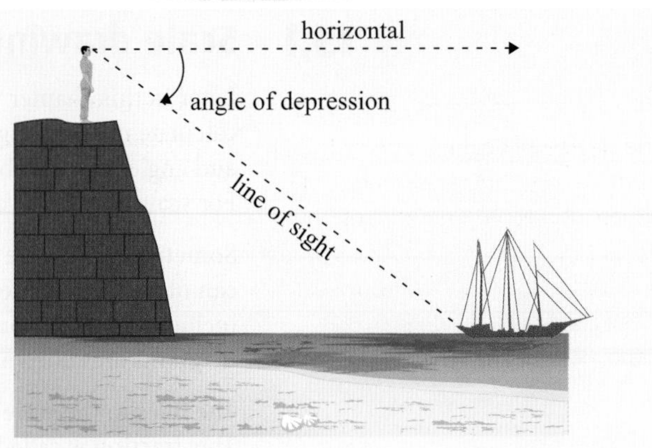

Drawing a scale diagram

Here are some clues and tips for drawing diagrams to scale:

- Draw a rough sketch, showing all details as given in the question.
- If you are told to use a particular scale you must use it! If you are not given a scale try to choose one that will make your diagram fit neatly onto a page.
- Make a clean, tidy and accurate scale drawing using appropriate geometrical instruments. Show on it the given lengths and angles. Write the scale next to the drawing.
- Measure lengths and angles in the drawing to find the answers to the problem. Remember to change the lengths to *full size* using the scale. Remember that the full size angles are the same as the angles in the scale drawing.

A scale drawing is *similar* to the real object, so the sides are in proportion and corresponding angles are equal.

Exercise 15.2

1 The diagram is a rough sketch of a field $ABCD$.

(a) Using a scale of 1 cm to 20 m, make an accurate scale drawing of the field.
(b) Find the sizes of $B\hat{C}D$ and $A\hat{D}C$ at the corners of the field.
(c) Find the length of the side CD of the field.

2 A ladder of length 3.6 m stands on horizontal ground and leans against a vertical wall at an angle of 70° to the horizontal (see diagram).

(a) What is the size of the angle that the ladder makes with the wall (a)?
(b) Draw a scale drawing using a scale of 1 cm to 50 cm, to find how far the ladder reaches up the wall (b).

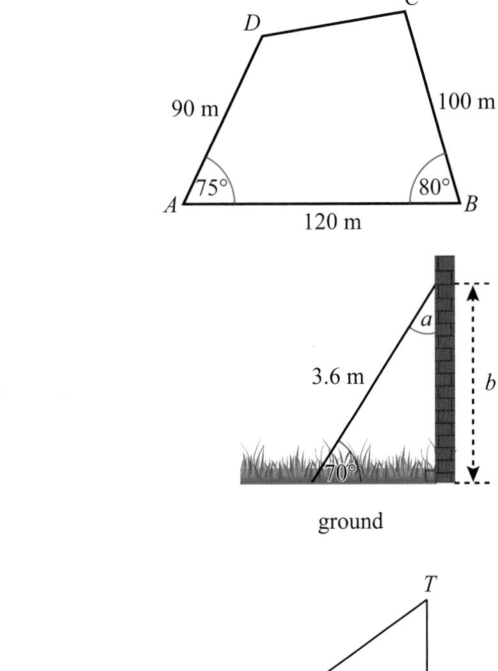

3 The *accurate* scale diagram represents the vertical wall TF of a building that stands on horizontal ground. It is drawn to a scale of 1 cm to 8 m.

(a) Find the height of the building.
(b) Find the distance from the point A to the foot (F) of the building.
(c) Find the angle of elevation of the top (T) of the building from the point A.

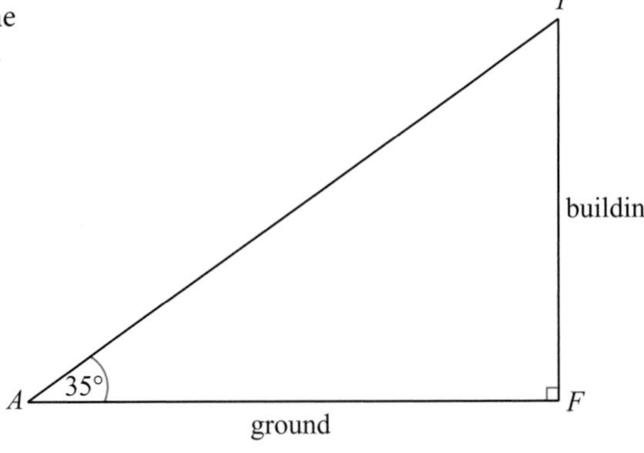

15.2 Bearings

FAST FORWARD

One degree of bearing does not seem like a lot but it can represent a huge distance in the real world. This is why you will need to use the trigonometry you will learn later in this chapter to calculate angles accurately. ▶

You have now used scale drawings to find distances between objects and to measure angles. When you want to move from one position to another, you not only need to know how far you have to travel but you need to know the direction. One way of describing directions is the **bearing**. This description is used around the world.

The angle 118°, shown in the diagram, is measured clockwise from the north direction. Such an angle is called a bearing.

All bearings are measured clockwise from the north direction.

Here the bearing of P from O is 118°.

If the angle is less than 100° you still use three figures so that it is clear that you mean to use a bearing.

Here the bearing of Q from O is 040°.

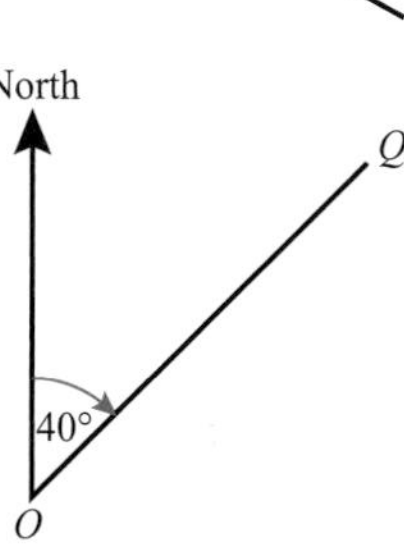

REWIND

You saw in chapter 3 that a reflex angle is >180° but < 360°. ◀

Since you *always* measure clockwise from north it is possible for your bearing to be a reflex angle.

Here the bearing of R from O is 315°.

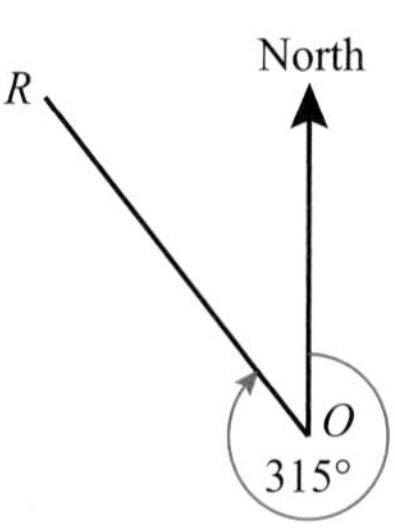

You may sometimes need to use angle properties from previous chapters to solve bearings problems.

Always make sure that you draw a clear diagram and mark all north lines clearly.

REWIND

You should remind yourself how to deal with alternate and corresponding angles from chapter 3. ◀

Worked example 2

The bearing of town B from city A is 048°. What is the bearing of city A from town B?

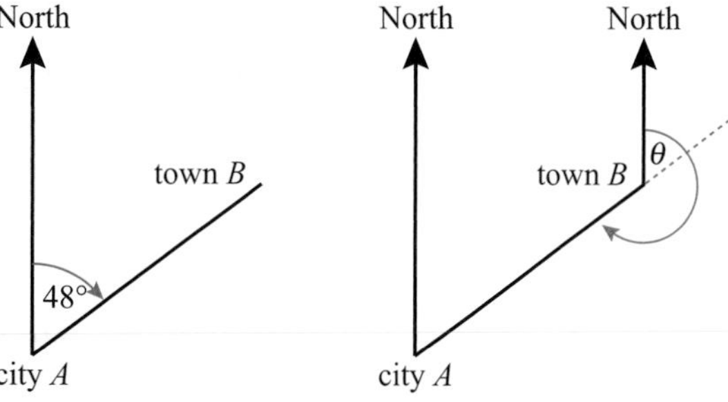

In the second diagram, the two north lines are parallel. Hence angle $\theta = 48°$ (using the properties of corresponding angles).

The bearing of city A from town B = 48°+180° = 228°.

Notice that the difference between the two bearings (48° and 228°) is 180°.

This is an example of a 'back' bearing. If you know the bearing of point X from point Y then, to find the bearing to return to point Y from point X, you add 180° to the original bearing (or subtract 180° if adding would give a value greater than 360°).

Exercise 15.3

1 Give the three-figure bearing corresponding to:

(a) west (b) south-east (c) north-east

2 Write down the three figure bearings of *A* from *B* for each of the following:

(a)

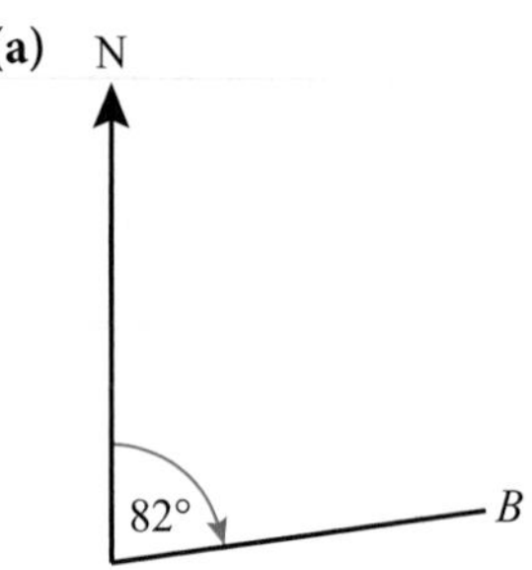

(b)

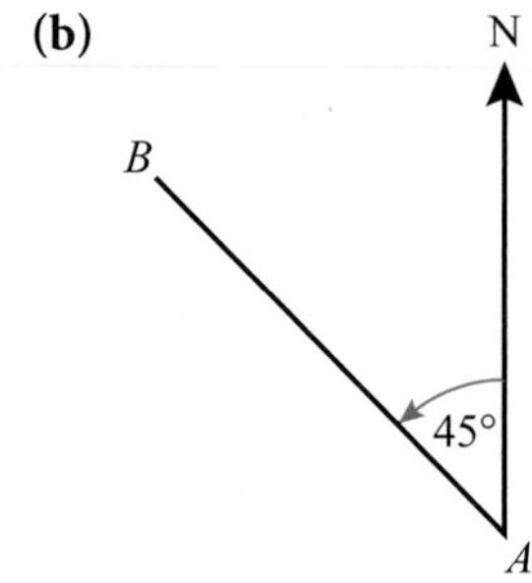

3 Use the map of Southern Africa to find the three-figure bearing of:

(a) Johannesburg from Windhoek
(b) Johannesburg from Cape Town
(c) Cape Town from Johannesburg
(d) Lusaka from Cape Town
(e) Kimberley from Durban.

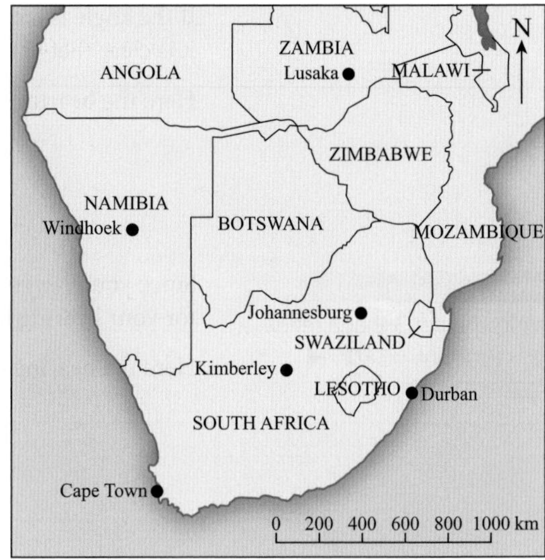

4 Townsville is 140 km west and 45 km north of Beeton. Using a scale drawing with a scale of 1 cm to 20 km, find:

(a) the bearing of Beeton from Townsville
(b) the bearing of Townsville from Beeton
(c) the direct distance from Beeton to Townsville.

5 Village *Q* is 7 km from village *P* on a bearing of 060°. Village *R* is 5 km from village *P* on a bearing of 315°. Using a scale drawing with a scale of 1 cm to 1 km, find:

(a) the direct distance from village *Q* to village *R*
(b) the bearing of village *Q* from village *R*.

15.3 Understanding the tangent, cosine and sine ratios

Trigonometry is the use of the ratios of the sides of right-angled triangles. The techniques covered in the following sections will help you to make much more precise calculations with bearings.

Throughout the remainder of this chapter you must make sure that your calculator is set in degrees mode. A small letter '*D*' will usually be displayed. If this is not the case, or if your calculator displays a '*G*' or an '*R*', then please consult your calculator manual.

REWIND

The hypotenuse was introduced with the work on Pythagoras' theorem in chapter 11. ◀

Labelling the sides of a right-angled triangle

You will have already learned that the longest side of a right-angled triangle is called the **hypotenuse.** If you take one of the two non right-angles in the triangle for reference then you can also 'name' the two shorter sides:

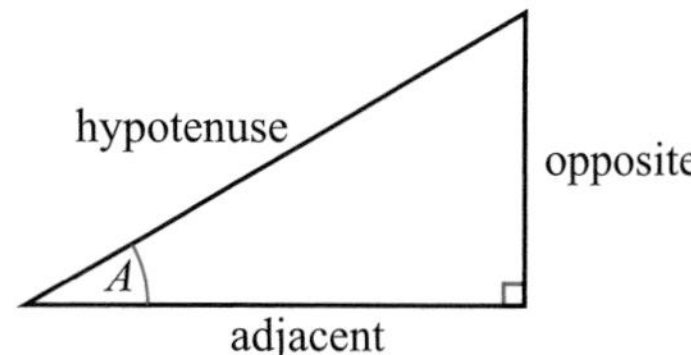

Notice that the **adjacent** is the side of the triangle that touches the angle A, but is not the hypotenuse. The third side does not meet with angle A at all and is known as the **opposite.** Throughout the remainder of the chapter, opp(A) will be used to mean the length of the opposite side, and adj(A) to mean the length of the adjacent. The hypotenuse does not depend upon the position of angle A, so is just written as 'hypotenuse' (or hyp).

Exercise 15.4

1 For each of the following triangles write down the letters that correspond to the length of the hypotenuse and the values of opp(A) and adj(A).

(a)

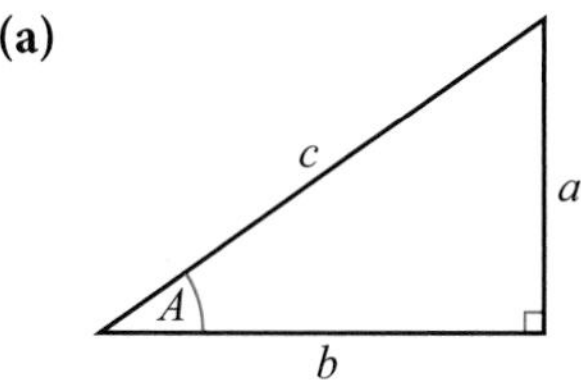

(b)

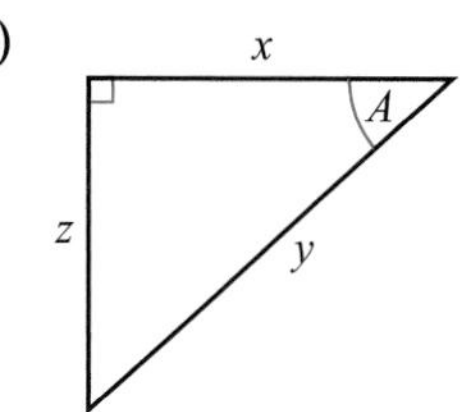

(c)

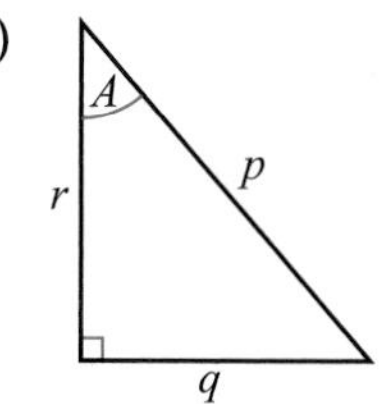

(d)

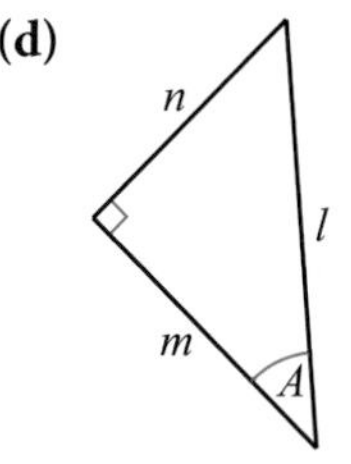

(e)

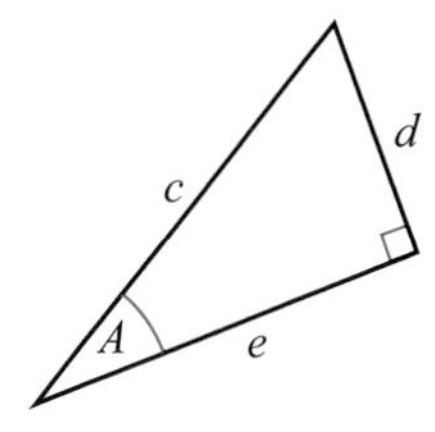

(f)

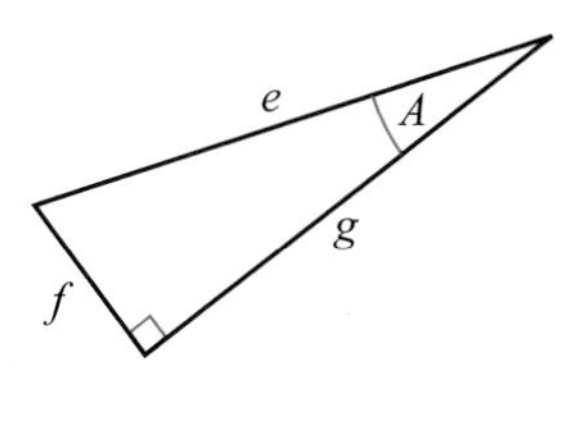

2 In each case copy and complete the statement written underneath the triangle.

(a)

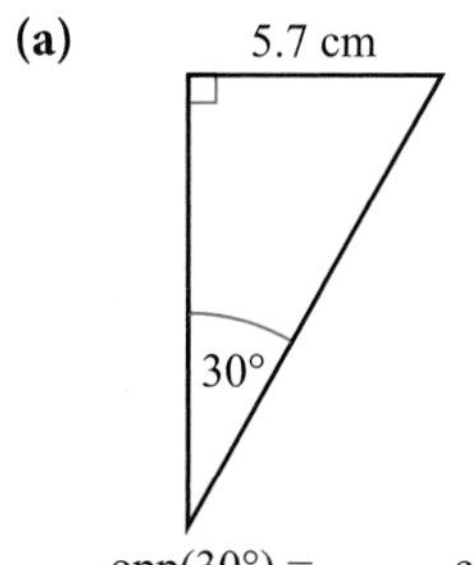

opp(30°) = ... cm

(b)

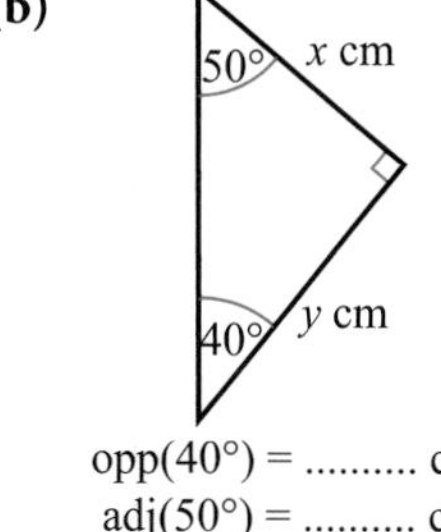

opp(40°) = ... cm
adj(50°) = ... cm

(c)

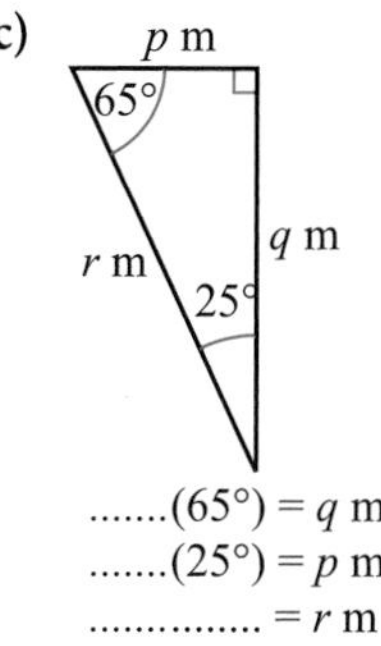

.......(65°) = q m
.......(25°) = p m
.... = r m

Investigation

REWIND

You will need to use the skills you learned for constructing accurate drawings of triangles in chapter 3. ◀

You will now explore the relationship between the opposite, adjacent and hypotenuse and the angles in a right-angled triangle.

For this investigation you will need to draw four *different* scale copies of the diagram opposite. The right angle and 30° angle must be drawn as accurately as possible, and all four triangles should be of different sizes. Follow the instructions listed on the next page.

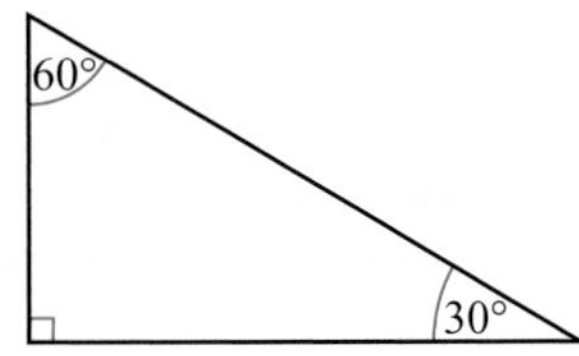

1 Label the opp(30°), adj(30°) and hypotenuse clearly.

2 Measure the length of opp(30°) and write it down.

3 Measure the length of the adj(30°) and write it down.

4 Calculate $\frac{\text{opp}(30°)}{\text{adj}(30°)}$ in each case.

5 What do you notice about your answers?

6 Ask a friend to draw some triangles (with the same angles) and make the same calculations. What do you notice?

7 Now repeat the investigation using a triangle with different angles. Record any observations that you make.

REWIND

Look back at the work on calculating gradients in chapter 10 and compare it with the tangent ratio. What connection do you notice? ◀

Tangent ratio

It turns out that $\frac{\text{opp}(A)}{\text{adj}(A)}$ is constant for any given angle A. $\frac{\text{opp}(A)}{\text{adj}(A)}$ depends on the angle only, and not the actual size of the triangle. The ratio $\frac{\text{opp}(A)}{\text{adj}(A)}$ is called the **tangent ratio** and you write:

$$\tan A = \frac{\text{opp}(A)}{\text{adj}(A)}$$

Your calculator can work out the tangent ratio for any given angle and you can use this to help work out the lengths of unknown sides of a right-angled triangle.

For example, if you wanted to find the tangent of the angle 22° you enter:

tan 2 2 = 0.404026225835157

Notice that the answer has many decimal places. When using this value you must make sure that you don't round your answers too soon.

Now, consider the right-angled triangle shown below.

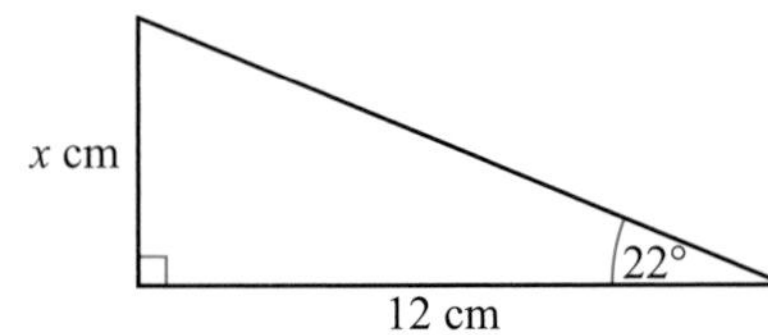

You can find the *unknown side*, x cm, by writing down what you know about the tangent ratio:

$$\tan 22° = \frac{\text{opp}(22°)}{\text{adj}(22°)} = \frac{x}{12}$$

$$\Rightarrow x = 12\tan(22°)$$

$$\therefore\ x = 4.848314...$$

$$x \approx 4.8\,\text{cm}\ (1\text{dp})$$

Worked example 3

Calculate the value of:

(a) $\tan 40°$ **(b)** $\tan 15.4°$

(a)

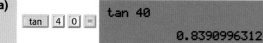

tan 40
0.8390996312

(b)

tan 1 5 . 4 =

tan (15.4)
0.2754458909

Worked example 4

Find the value of x in the diagram. Give your answer to the nearest mm.

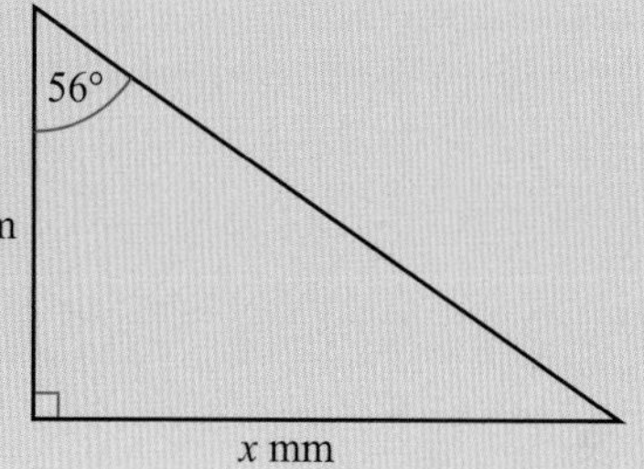

Opp(56°) = x
Adj 56° = 22.1 mm

$$\tan 56° = \frac{x}{22.1}$$

$$\Rightarrow x = 22.1 \tan(56°)$$
$$= 32.76459\ldots$$
$$\approx 33 \text{ mm (nearest mm)}$$

REWIND

Remind yourself how to deal with equations that involve fractions from chapter 6. ◀

Worked example 5

The angle of approach of an airliner should be 3°. If a plane is 305 metres above the ground, how far should it be from the airfield?

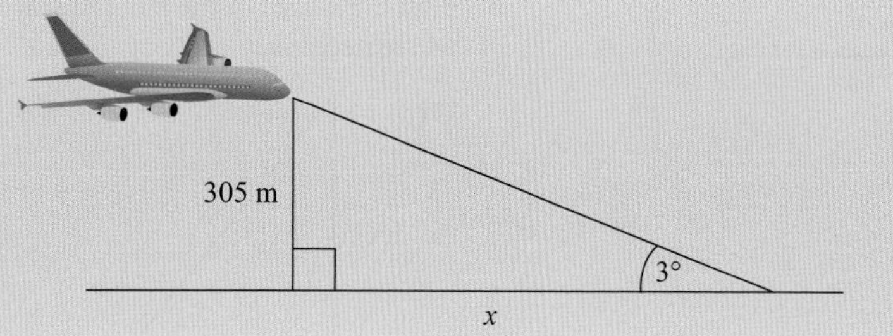

$$\tan 3° = \frac{305}{x}$$
$$\Rightarrow x \tan 3° = 305$$
$$\Rightarrow x = \frac{305}{\tan 3°}$$
$$= 5819.74\ldots$$
$$\approx 5820 \text{ (nearest metre)}$$

Exercise 15.5

1 Calculate the value of these tangent ratios, giving your answers to 3 significant figures where necessary.

(a) tan 35° **(b)** tan 46° **(c)** tan 18° **(d)** tan 45°
(e) tan 15.6° **(f)** tan 17.9° **(g)** tan 0.5° **(h)** tan 0°

2 For each of the following triangles find the required tangent ratio as a fraction in the lowest terms.

(a) tan A =

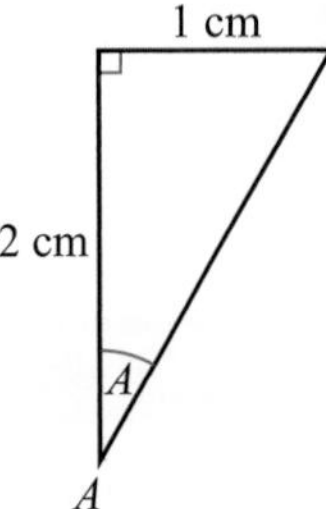

(b) tan A =

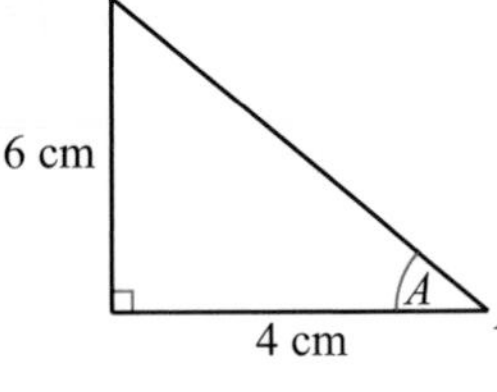

(c) tan A =
tan B =

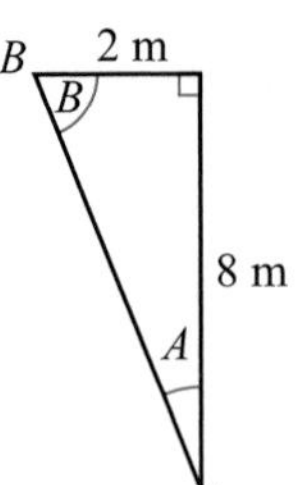

(d) tan x =

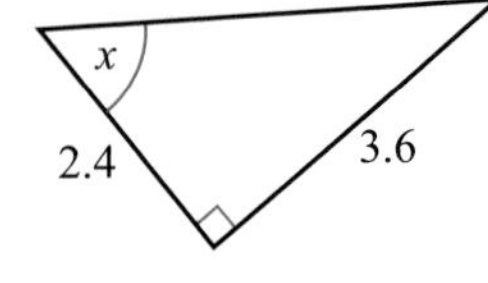

(e) tan z =
tan y =

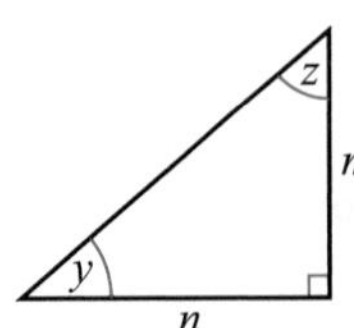

(f) tan C =

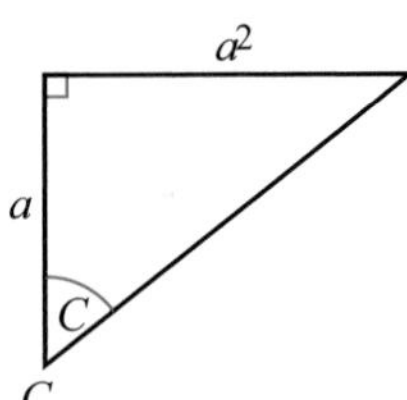

(g) tan D =

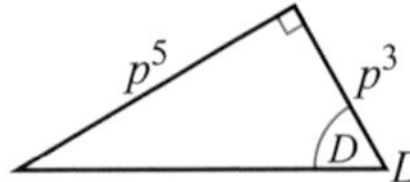

3 Find the length of the lettered side in each case. Give your answers to 3 significant figures where necessary.

(a)

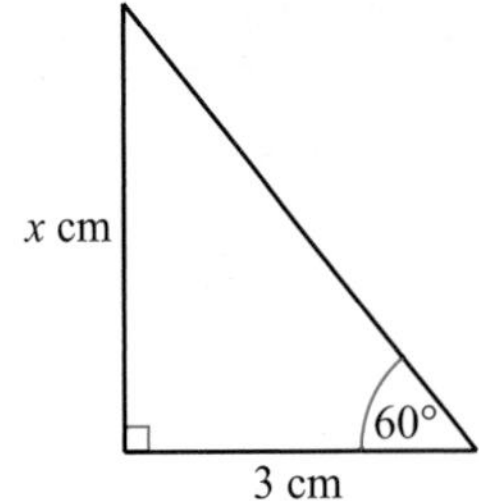

(b)

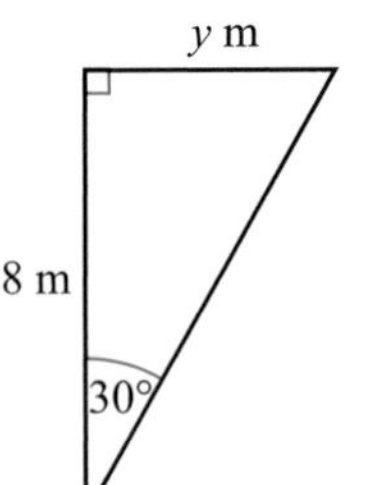

(c)

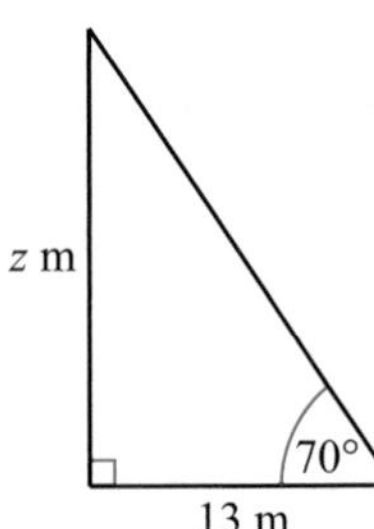

(d)

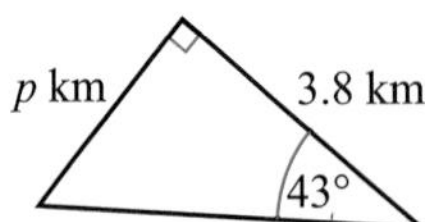

(e)

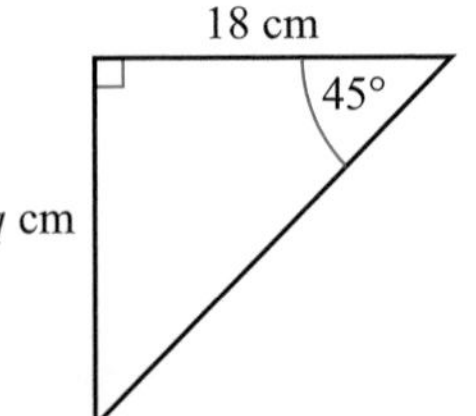

(f)

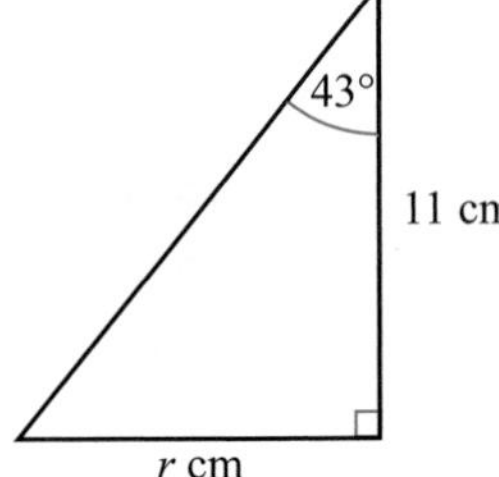

4 Calculate the lettered length in each case. In some cases you are expected to calculate the length of the adjacent. Make sure that you are careful when substituting lengths into the tangent ratio formula.

(a)

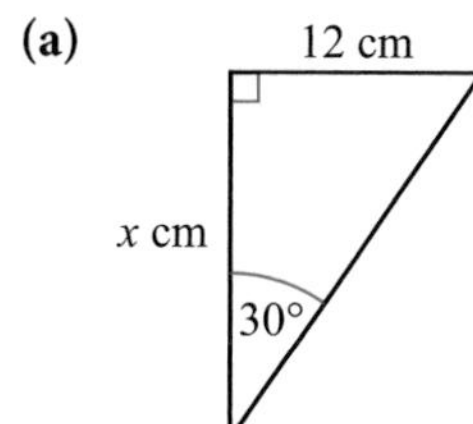

(b)

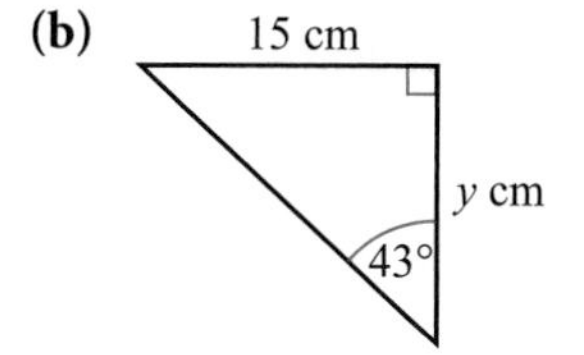

(c)

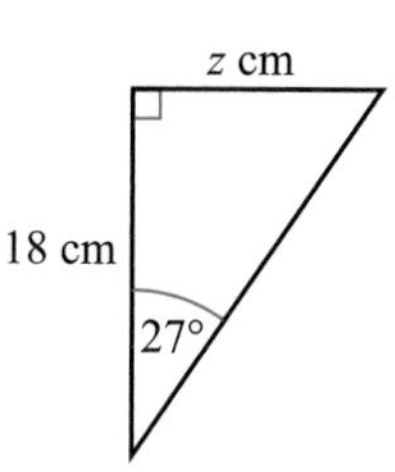

(d)

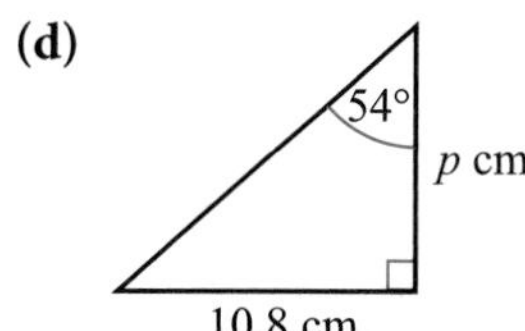

(e)

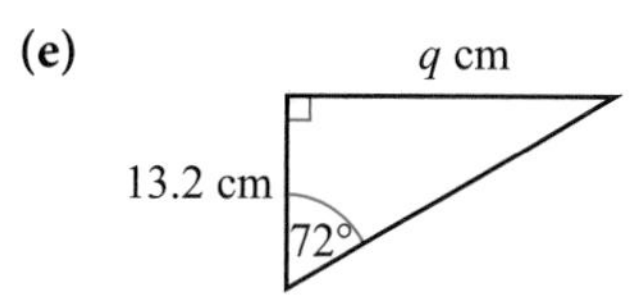

(f)

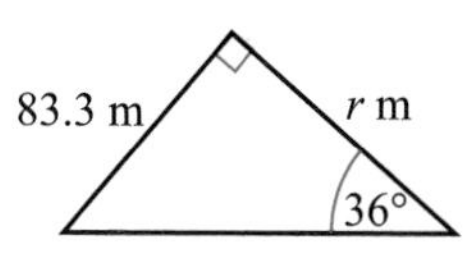

(g)

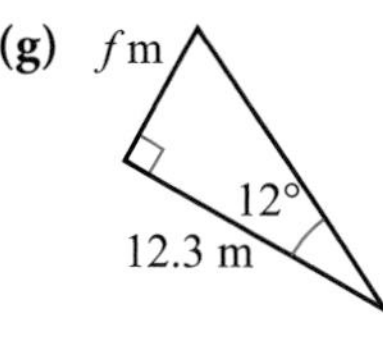

(h)

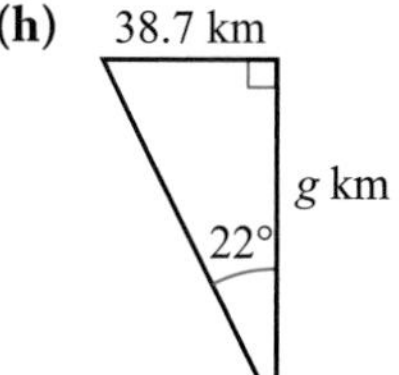

(i)

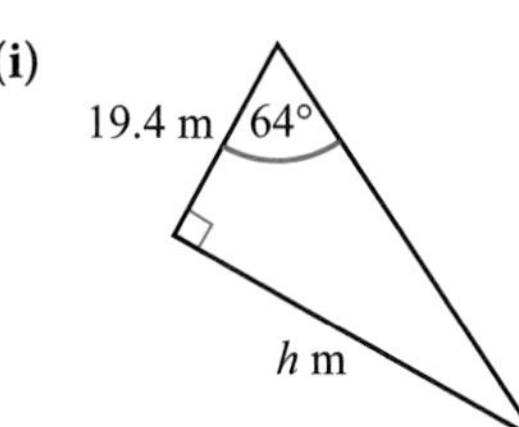

5

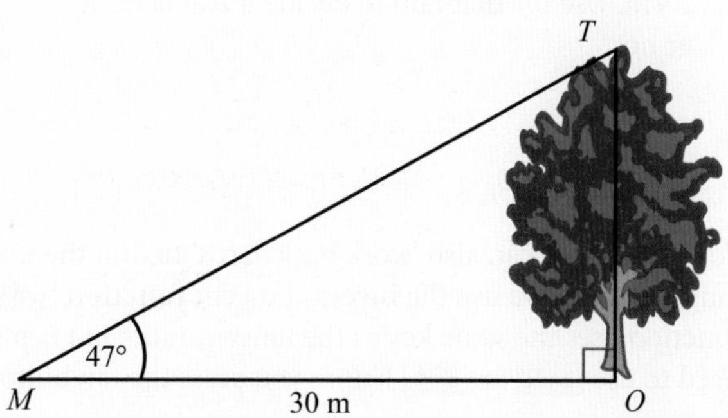

(a) Use your calculator to find the value of tan 47° correct to 4 decimal places.

(b) The diagram shows a vertical tree, OT, whose base, O, is 30 m horizontally from point M. The angle of elevation of T from M is 47°. Calculate the height of the tree.

6 Devon wants to estimate the width of a river which has parallel banks. He starts at point A on one bank directly opposite a tree on the other bank. He walks 80 m along the bank to point B and then looks back at the tree. He finds that the line between B and the tree makes an angle of 22° with the bank. Calculate the width of the river.

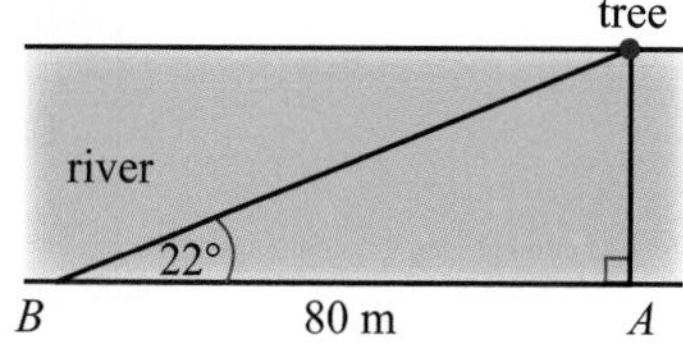

7 The right-angled ΔABC has $B\hat{A}C = 30°$. Taking the length of BC to be one unit:

(a) work out the length of AC

(b) use Pythagoras' theorem to obtain the length of AB.

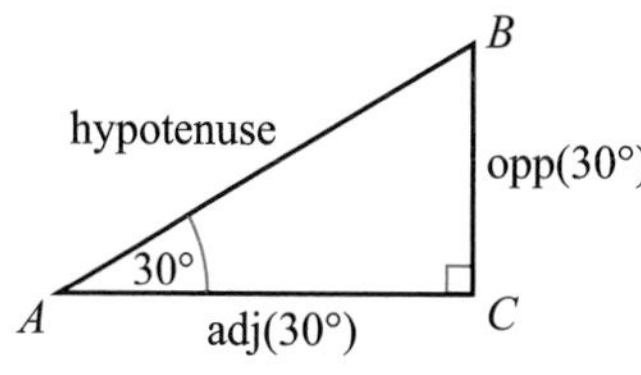

8 The diagram shows a ladder that leans against a brick wall. If the angle between the ladder and the floor is 82°, and the ladder reaches 3.2 m up the wall, find the distance d m of the foot of the ladder from the bottom of the wall. Give your answer to the nearest cm.

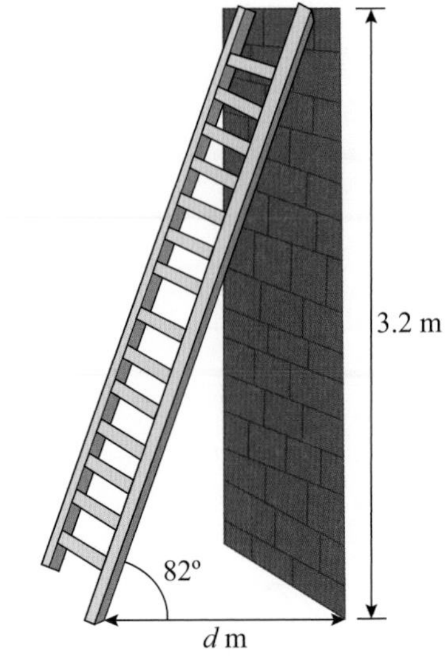

9 Adi and Sarah are taking part in a Maypole dance. Adi claims that the pole is 4 metres tall but Sarah thinks he is wrong. Adi and Sarah each pull a piece of maypole ribbon tight and pin it to the ground. The points A and B represent where the ribbon was pinned to the ground; Adi and Sarah measure this distance as 2.4 m. Use the diagram to decide if Adi is right or not.

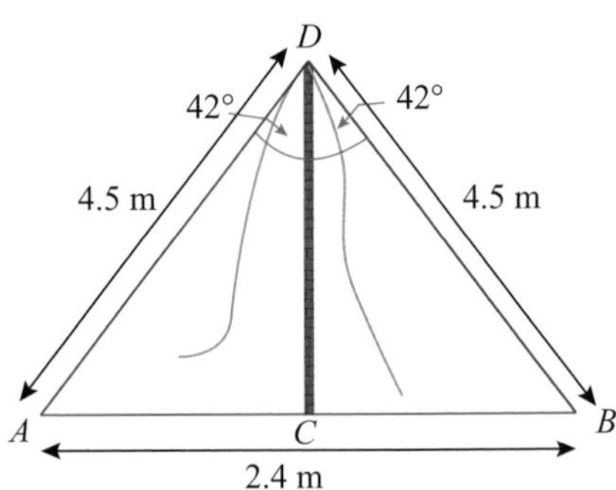

FAST FORWARD

'Functions' are dealt with more thoroughly in chapter 22. ▶

Calculating angles

Your calculator can also 'work backwards' to find the *unknown angle* associated with a particular tangent ratio. You use the **inverse** tangent **function** $\tan^{-1}$ on the calculator. Generally this function uses the same key as the tangent ratio, but is placed above. If this is the case you will need to use 2ndF or shift before you press the tan button.

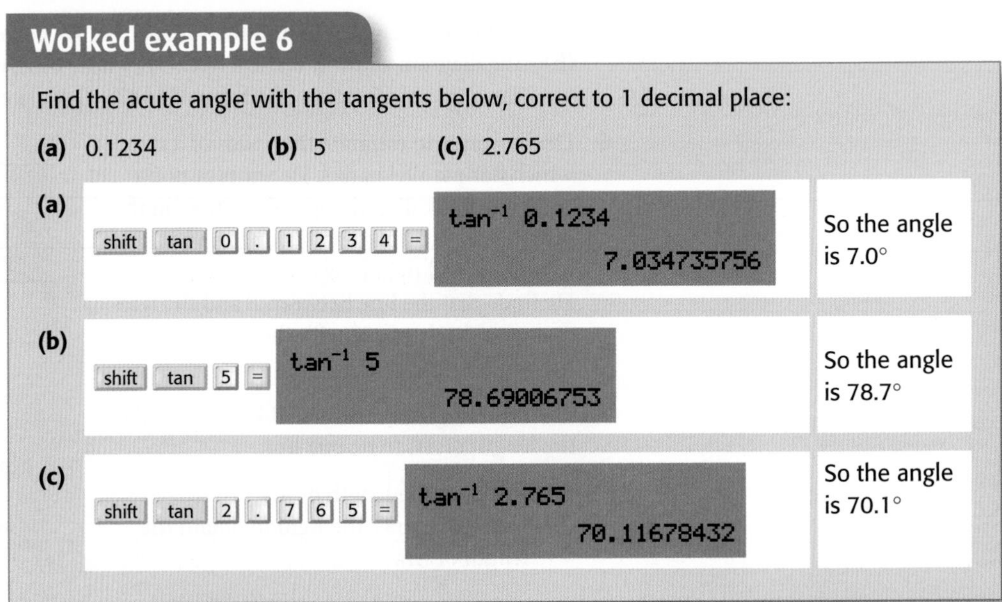

Worked example 6

Find the acute angle with the tangents below, correct to 1 decimal place:

(a) 0.1234 **(b)** 5 **(c)** 2.765

(a) shift tan 0 . 1 2 3 4 =

$\tan^{-1}$ 0.1234
7.034735756

So the angle is 7.0°

(b) shift tan 5 =

$\tan^{-1}$ 5
78.69006753

So the angle is 78.7°

(c) shift tan 2 . 7 6 5 =

$\tan^{-1}$ 2.765
70.11678432

So the angle is 70.1°

Worked example 7

Calculate, correct to 1 decimal place, the lettered angles.

(a)

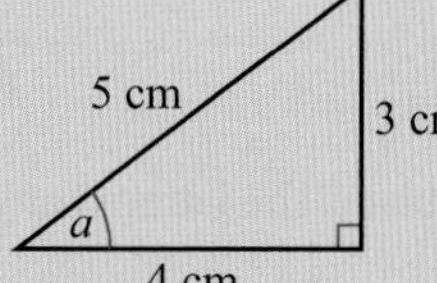

(b)

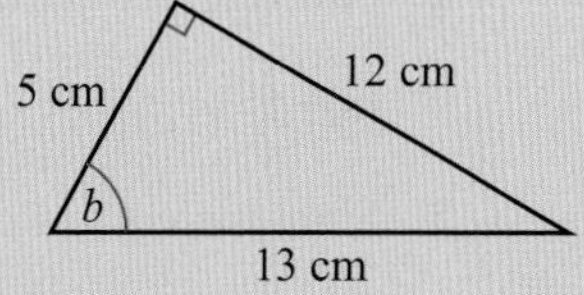

(c)

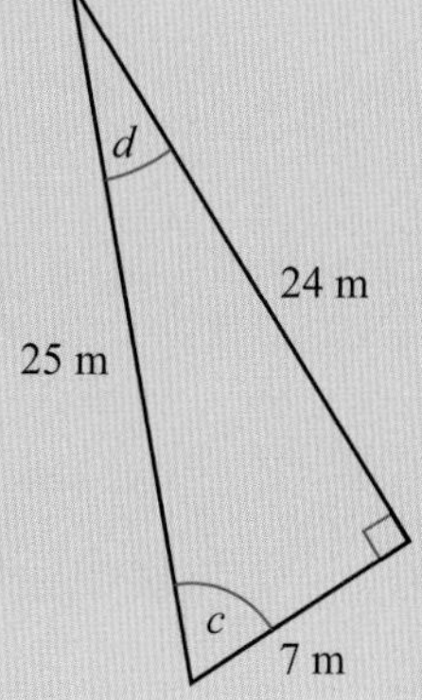

(a)

$\tan a = \frac{\text{opp}(a)}{\text{adj}(a)} = \frac{3}{4} = 0.75$

$a = \tan^{-1}(0.75)$

$= 36.869897...$

$a = 36.9°$ (1dp)

(b)

$\tan b = \frac{\text{opp}(b)}{\text{adj}(b)} = \frac{12}{5} = 2.4$

$b = \tan^{-1}(2.4)$

$= 67.380135...$

$b = 67.4°$ (1dp)

(c)

$\tan c = \frac{\text{opp}(c)}{\text{adj}(c)} = \frac{24}{7}$

$c = \tan^{-1}\left(\frac{24}{7}\right)$

$= 73.739795...$

$c = 73.7°$ (1dp)

To find the angle d, you could use the fact that the angle sum in a triangle is 180°. This gives $d = 180° - (90° + 73.7°) = 16.3°$.

Alternatively, you could use the tangent ratio again but with the opp and adj re-assigned to match this angle:

$\tan d = \frac{\text{opp}(d)}{\text{adj}(d)} = \frac{7}{24}$

$d = \tan^{-1}\left(\frac{7}{24}\right)$

$= 16.260204...$

$d = 16.3°$ (1dp)

Exercise 15.6

1 Find, correct to 1 decimal place, the acute angle that has the tangent ratio:

(a) 0.85 **(b)** 1.2345 **(c)** 3.56 **(d)** 10.

2 Find, correct to the nearest degree, the acute angle that has the tangent ratio:

(a) $\frac{2}{5}$ **(b)** $\frac{7}{9}$ **(c)** $\frac{25}{32}$ **(d)** $2\frac{3}{4}$

3 Find, correct to 1 decimal place, the lettered angles in these diagrams.

(a)

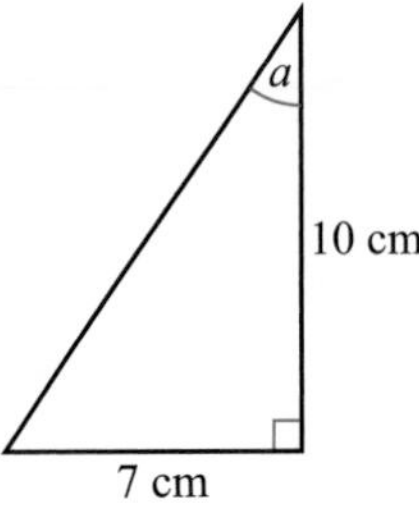

(b) **(c)**

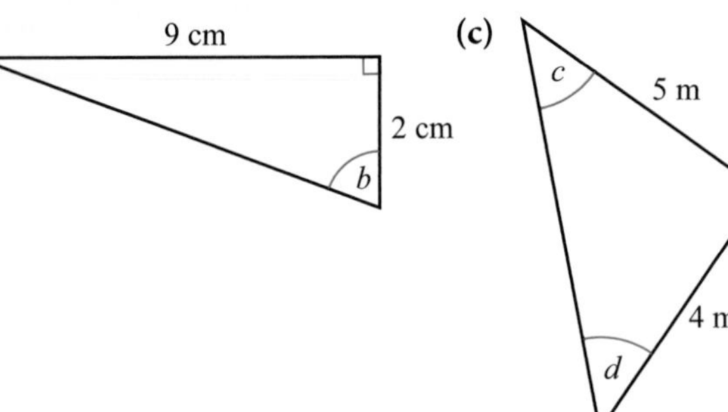

(d)

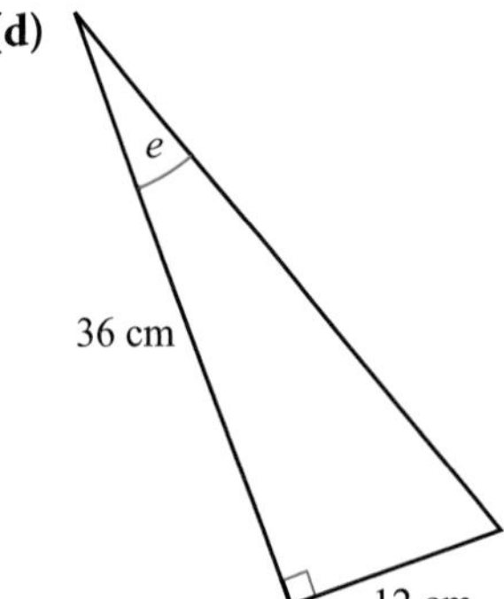

(e)

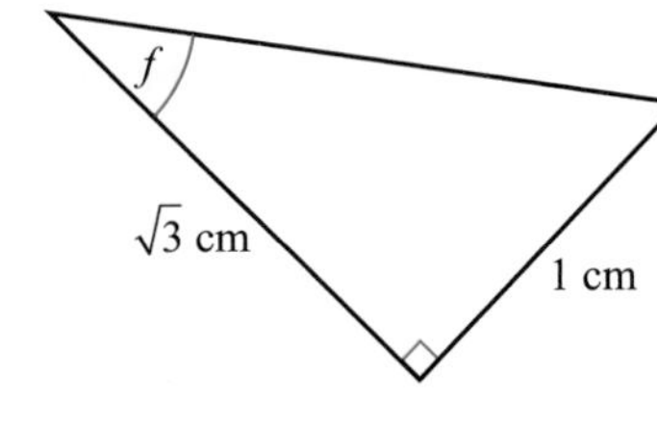

4 A ladder stands on horizontal ground and leans against a vertical wall. The foot of the ladder is 2.8 m from the base of the wall and the ladder reaches 8.5 m up the wall. Calculate the angle the ladder makes with the ground.

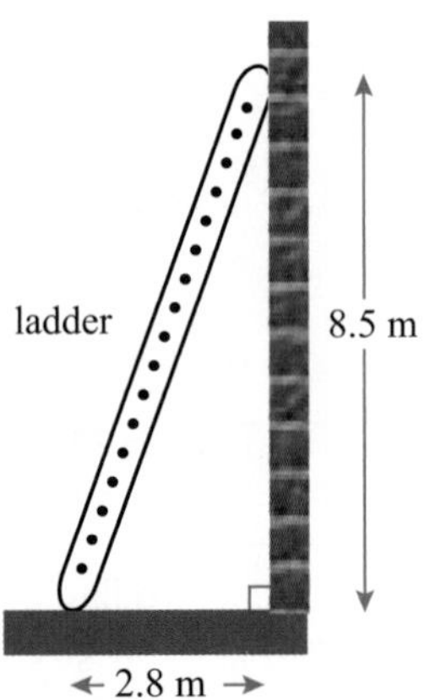

Draw a clear diagram.

5 The top of a vertical cliff is 68 m above sea level. A ship is 175 m from the foot of the cliff. Calculate the angle of elevation of the top of the cliff from the ship.

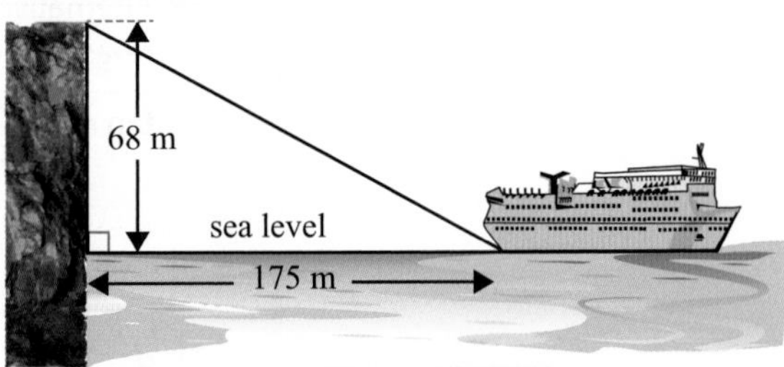

6 O is the centre of a circle with $OM = 12$ cm.

(a) Calculate AM.
(b) Calculate AB.

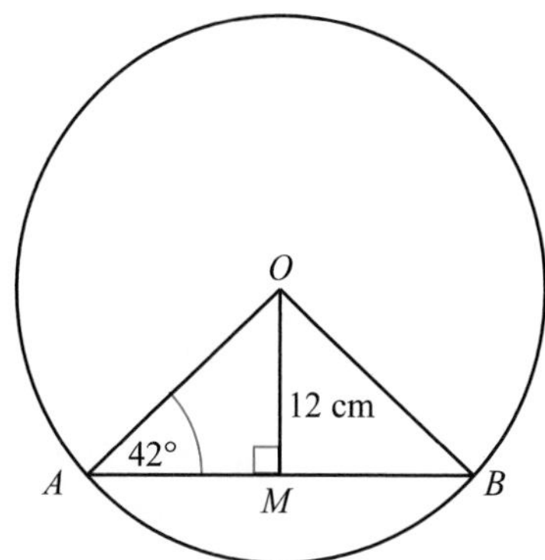

7 The right-angled triangle ABC has hypotenuse $AC = 7$ cm and side $BC = 3$ cm. Calculate the length AB and hence the angle $A\hat{C}B$.

Sine and cosine ratios

You will have noticed that the tangent ratio only makes use of the opposite and adjacent sides. What happens if you need to use the hypotenuse? In fact, there are three possible pairs of sides that you could include in a ratio:

- opposite and adjacent (already used with the tangent ratio)
- opposite and hypotenuse
- or adjacent and hypotenuse.

This means that you need two more ratios:

the **sine ratio** is written as $\sin(A) = \dfrac{\text{opp}(A)}{\text{hyp}}$

the **cosine ratio** is written as $\cos(A) = \dfrac{\text{adj}(A)}{\text{hyp}}$.

The abbreviation 'cos' is pronounced 'coz' and the abbreviation 'sin' is pronounced 'sine' or 'sign'.

As with the tangent ratio, you can use the sin and cos keys on your calculator to find the sine and cosine ratios associated with given angles. You can also use the shift sin or $\sin^{-1}$ and shift cos or $\cos^{-1}$ 'inverse' functions to find angles.

Before looking at some worked examples you should note that with three possible ratios you need to know how to pick the right one! 'SOHCAHTOA' might help you to remember:

S = sine
O = opposite
H = hypotenuse
C = cosine
A = adjacent
T = tan

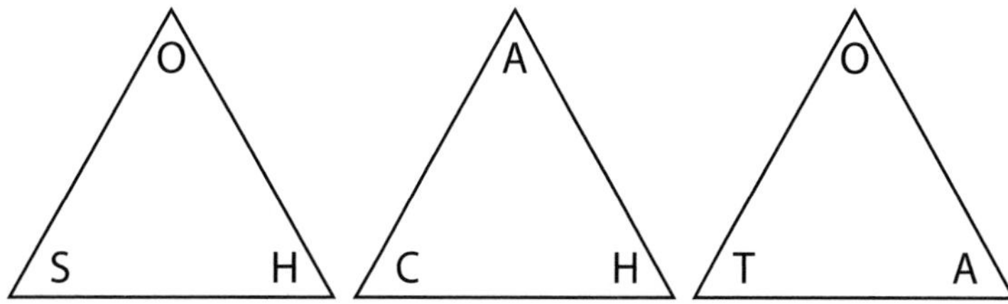

The word 'SOHCAHTOA' has been divided into three triangles of letters, each representing one of the three trigonometric ratios. The first letter in each trio tells you which ratio it represents (sine, cosine or tangent), the second letter (at the top) tells you which side's length goes on the top of the ratio, and the third letter tells you which side's length goes on the bottom.

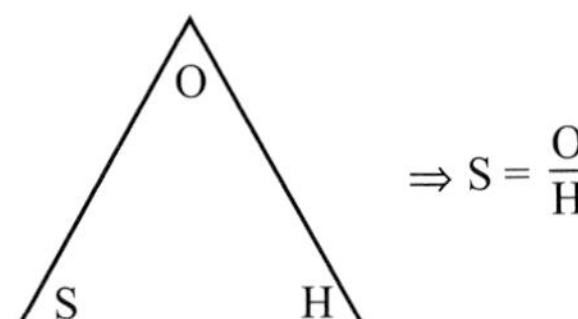

$\Rightarrow S = \frac{O}{H}$

For example, if a problem involves the opposite and hypotenuse you simply need to find the triangle of letters that includes 'O' and 'H': SOH.

The 'S' tells you that it is the sine ratio, the 'O' at the top of the triangle sits on top of the fraction, and the lower 'H' sits on the bottom.

The use of 'SOHCAHTOA' is shown clearly in the following worked examples. The tangent ratio has been included again in these examples to help show you how to decide which ratio should be used.

Worked example 8

Find the length of the sides lettered in each of the following diagrams.

(a)

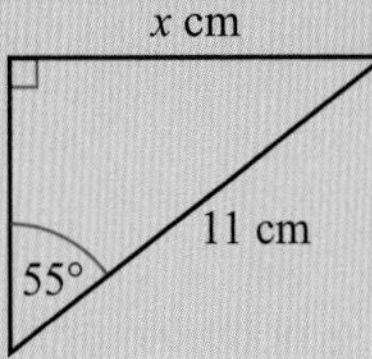

(b)

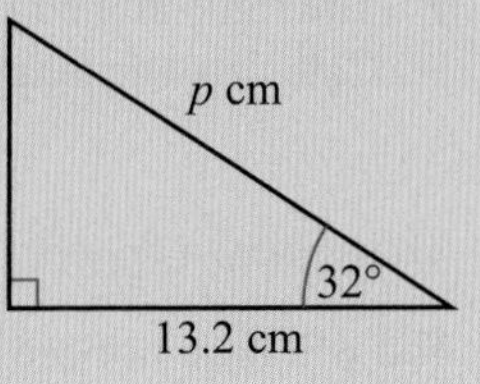

(c)

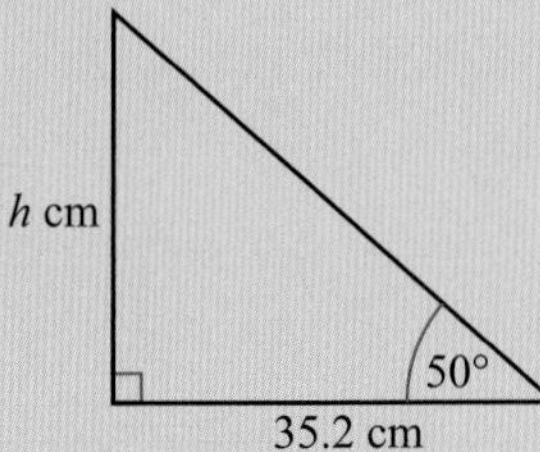

(a) opp(55°) = x
hyp = 11 cm

So $\sin 55° = \frac{\text{opp}(55°)}{\text{hyp}} = \frac{x}{11}$

$\Rightarrow x = 11 \sin 55°$
$\Rightarrow x = 9.0$ cm (to 1dp)

Identify the sides that you are going to consider clearly:

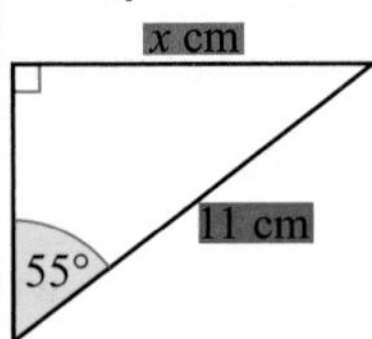

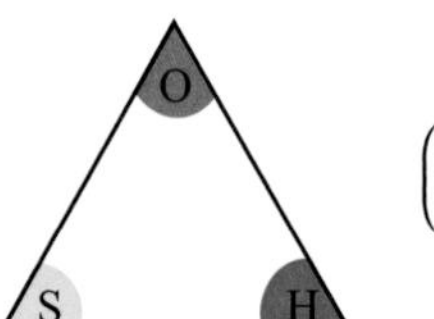

$\left(S = \frac{O}{H}\right)$

(b) adj(32°) = 13.2 cm
hyp = p cm

So $\cos 32° = \frac{\text{adj}(32°)}{\text{hyp}} = \frac{13.2}{p}$

$\Rightarrow p \cos 32° = 13.2$

$\Rightarrow p = \frac{13.2}{\cos 32°}$

$\Rightarrow p = 15.6$ cm (to 1dp)

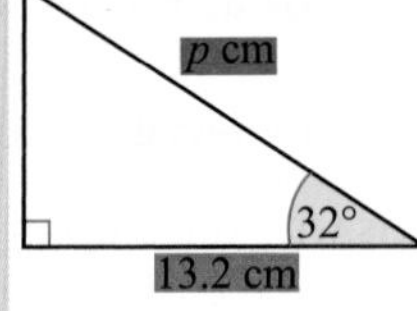

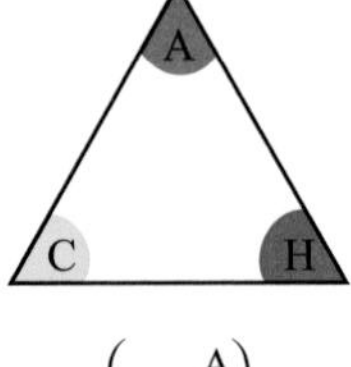

$\left(C = \frac{A}{H}\right)$

(c) opp(50°) = h cm

adj(50°) = 35.2 cm

So $\tan 50° = \frac{\text{opp}(50°)}{\text{adj}(50°)} = \frac{h}{35.2}$

$\Rightarrow h = 35.2 \tan 50°$
$\Rightarrow h = 41.9$ cm (to 1dp)

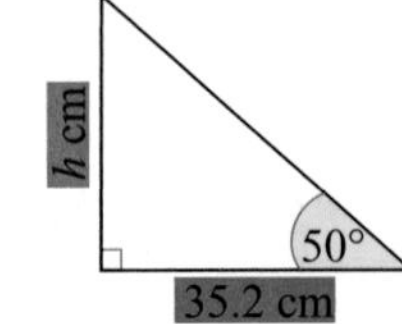

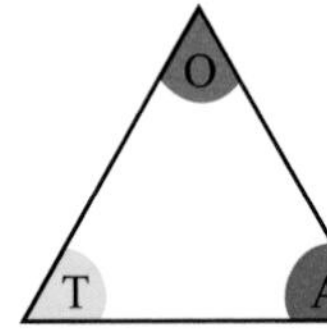

$\left(T = \frac{O}{A}\right)$

Worked example 9

Find the size of the lettered angles in each of the following diagrams.

(a)

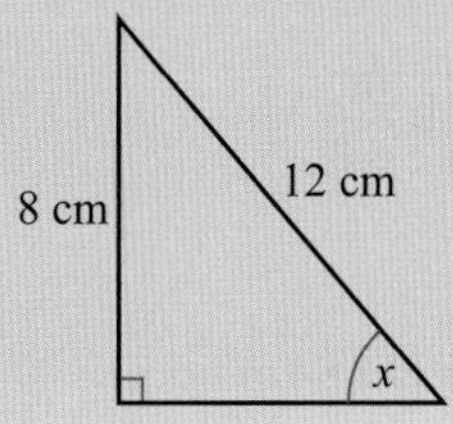

(b)

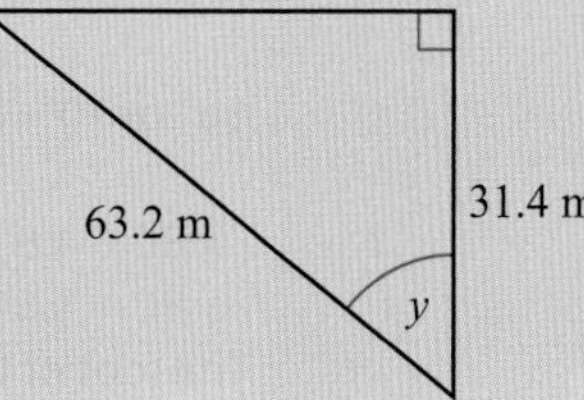

(a) opp(x) = 8 cm
hyp = 12 cm

So $\sin x = \frac{\text{opp}(x)}{\text{hyp}} = \frac{8}{12}$

$\Rightarrow x = \sin^{-1}\left(\frac{8}{12}\right)$

$\Rightarrow x = 41.8°$ (1dp)

Once again, clearly identify the sides and ratio to be used:

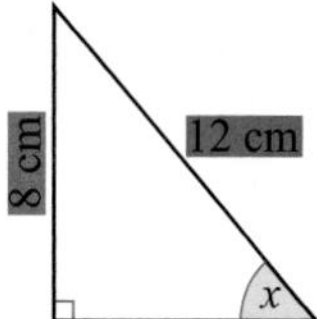

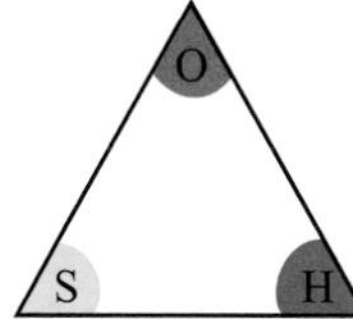

(b) adj(y) = 31.4 m
hyp = 63.2 m

So $\cos y = \frac{\text{adj}(y)}{\text{hyp}} = \frac{31.4}{63.2}$

$\Rightarrow y = \cos^{-1}\left(\frac{31.4}{63.2}\right)$

$\Rightarrow y = 60.2°$ (1dp)

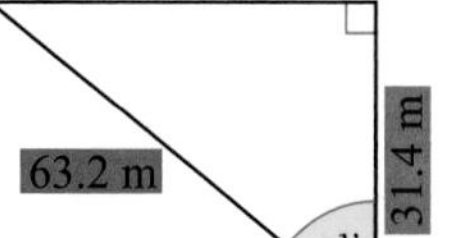

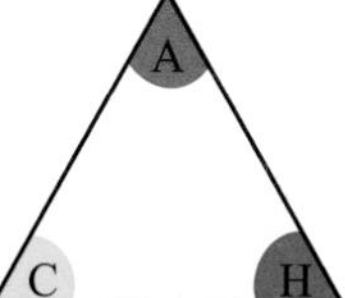

Worked example 10

A ladder 4.8 m long leans against a vertical wall with its foot on horizontal ground. The ladder makes an angle of 70° with the ground.

(a) How far up the wall does the ladder reach?
(b) How far is the foot of the ladder from the wall?

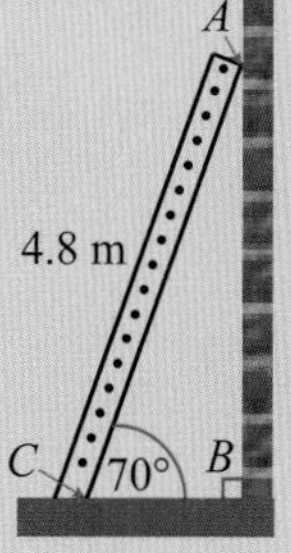

(a) In the diagram, AC is the hypotenuse of the right-angled $\triangle ABC$. AB is the distance that the ladder reaches up the wall.

opp(70°) = AB
hyp = 4.8 m

So $\sin 70° = \frac{\text{opp}(70°)}{\text{hyp}} = \frac{AB}{4.8}$

$\Rightarrow AB = 4.8 \sin 70°$
$\Rightarrow AB = 4.5$ m (1dp)
So the ladder reaches 4.5 m up the wall.

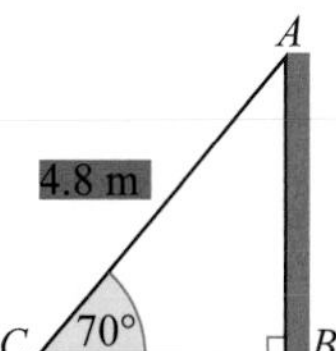

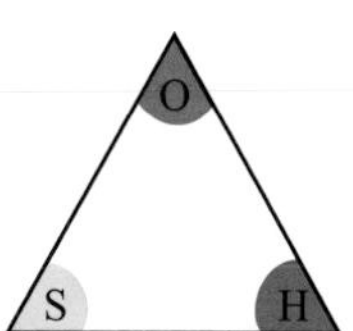

(b) The distance of the foot of the ladder from the wall is BC.

adj(70°) = BC

hyp = 4.8 m

So $\cos 70° = \frac{\text{adj}(70°)}{\text{hyp}} = \frac{BC}{4.8}$

$\Rightarrow BC = 4.8 \cos 70°$

$\Rightarrow BC = 1.64$ m (2dp)

The foot of the ladder is 1.64 m from the wall.

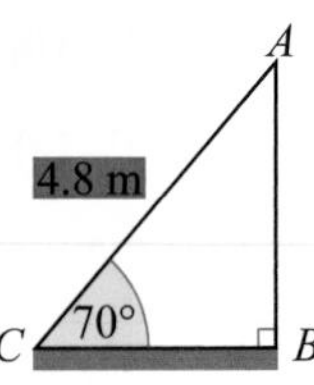

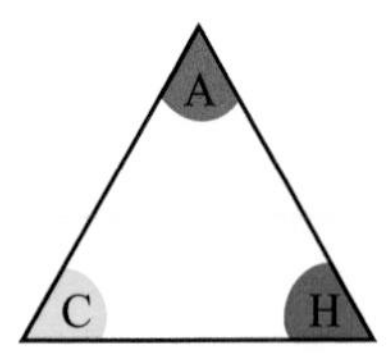

Exercise 15.7

1 For each of the following triangles write down the value of:

(i) $\sin A$ **(ii)** $\cos A$ **(iii)** $\tan A$

(a) **(b)** 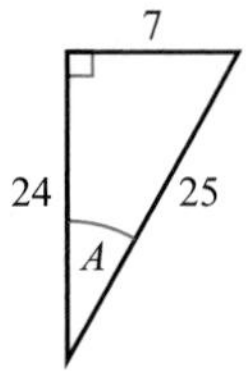 **(c)** 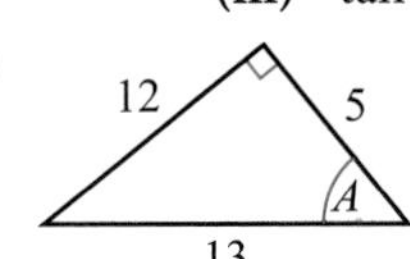

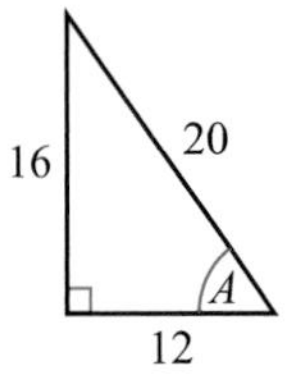

(d) 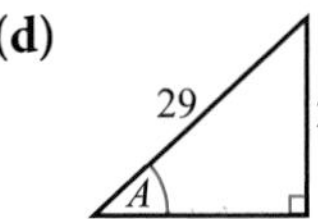

(e) 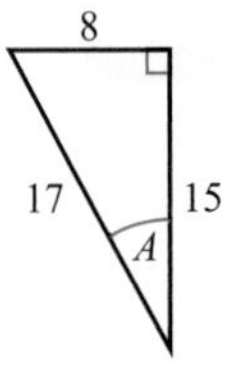 **(f)** 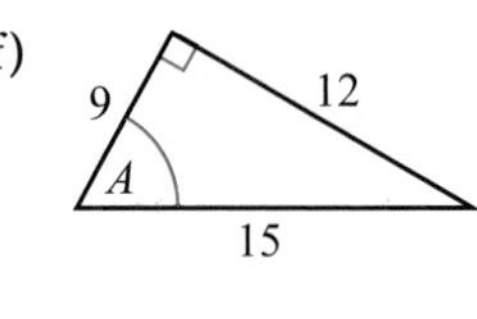

(g) 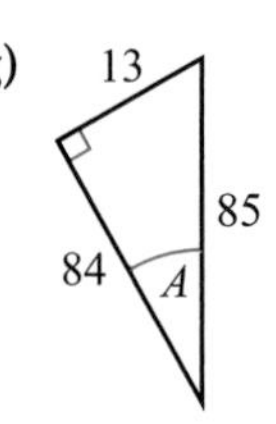

Remember to check that your calculator is in degrees mode. There should be a small 'D' on the screen.

2 Use your calculator to find the value of each of the following. Give your answers to 4 decimal places.

(a) sin 5° **(b)** cos 5° **(c)** sin 30° **(d)** cos 30°
(e) sin 60° **(f)** cos 60° **(g)** sin 85° **(h)** cos 85°

3 For each of the following triangles, use the letters of the sides to write down the given trigonometric ratio.

(a) 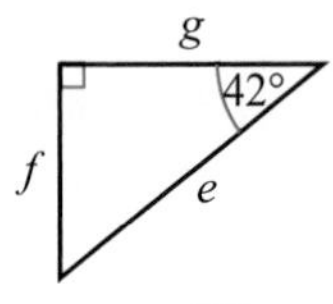

cos 42°

(b) 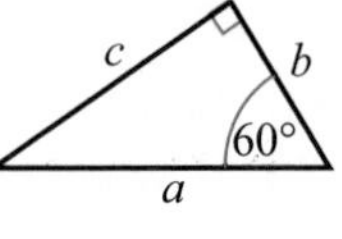

sin 60°

(c) 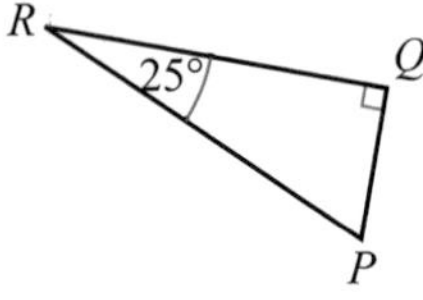

cos 25°

(d) 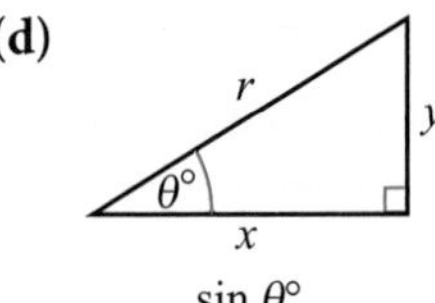

sin θ°

(e) 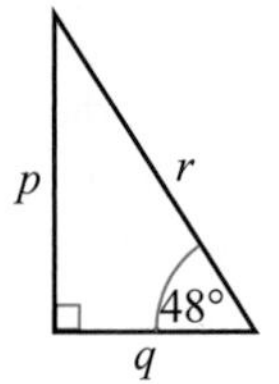

cos 48°

(f) 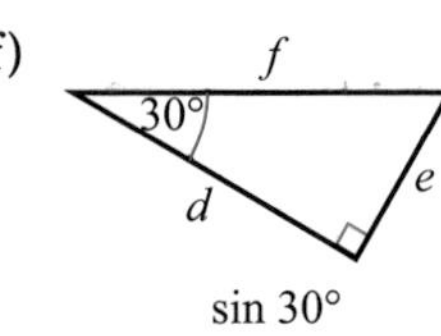

sin 30°

(g) 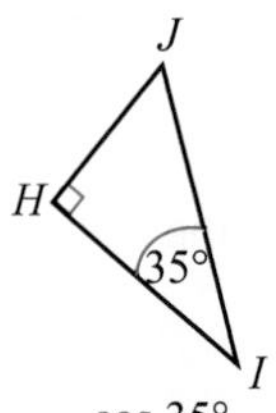

cos 35°

(h) 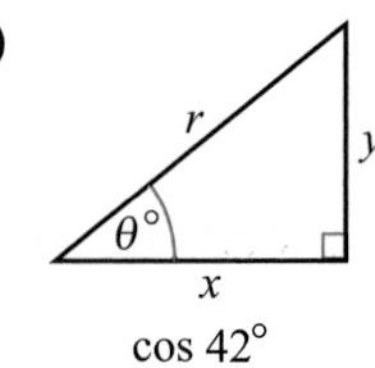

cos 42°

4 For each of the following triangles find the length of the unknown, lettered side. (Again, some questions that require the tangent ratio have been included. If you use SOHCAHTOA carefully you should spot these quickly!)

(a)

2.0 m
a m
25°

(b)

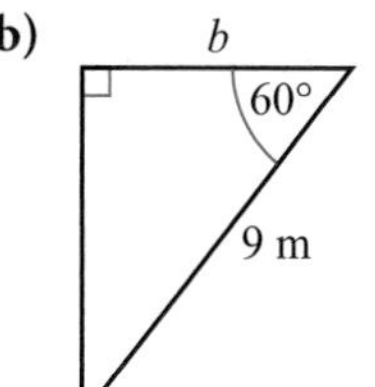

(c)

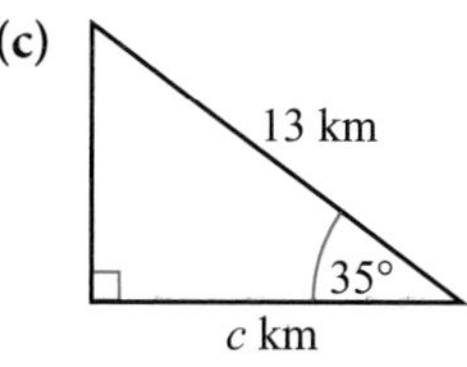

(d)

d cm
27°
10 cm

(e)

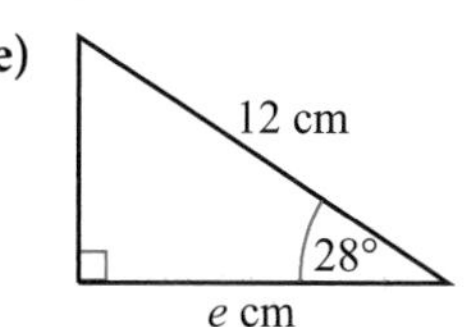

(f)

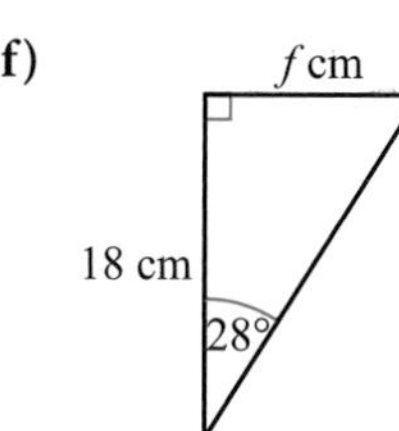

(g)

g cm
15 cm
70°

(h)

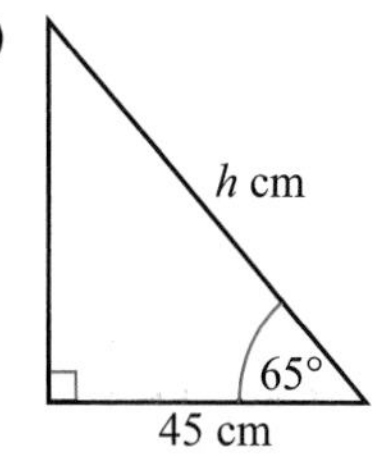

(i)

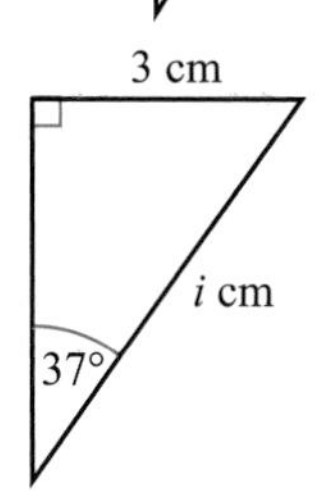

(j)

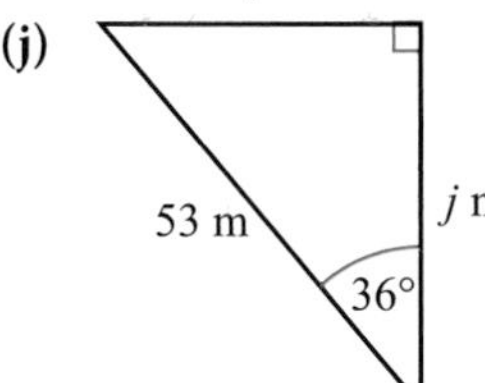

(k)

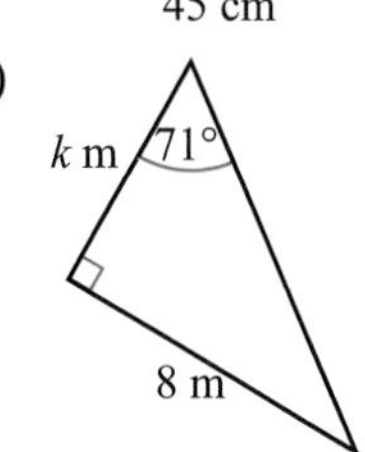

(l)

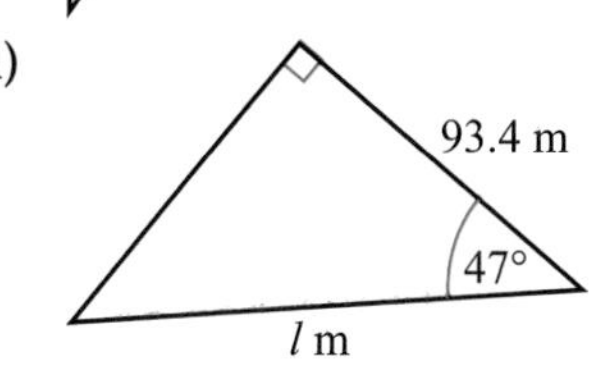

5 Use your calculator to find, correct to 1 decimal place:

(a) an acute angle whose sine is 0.99
(b) an acute angle whose cosine is 0.5432
(c) an acute angle whose sine is $\frac{3}{8}$
(d) an acute angle whose cosine is $\frac{\sqrt{3}}{2}$.

6 Find, to 1 decimal place, the lettered angle in each of the following triangles.

(a)

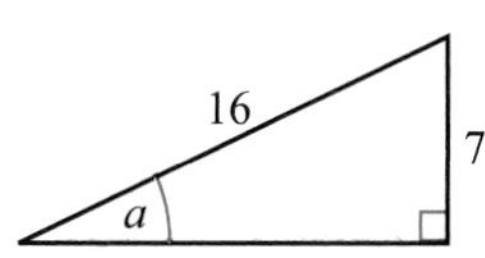

(b)

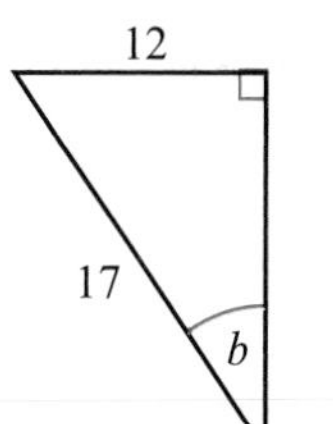

(c)

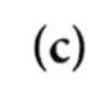
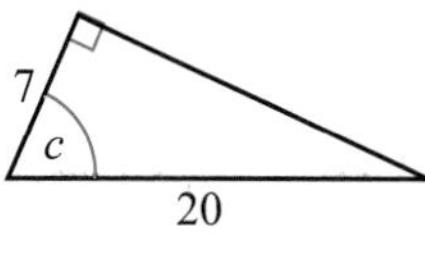

(d)

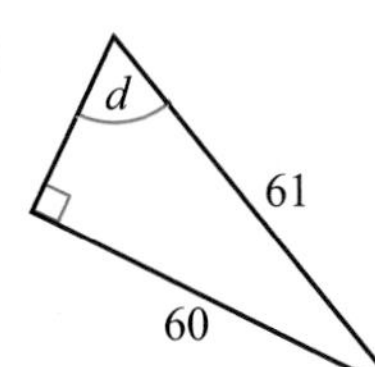

(e)

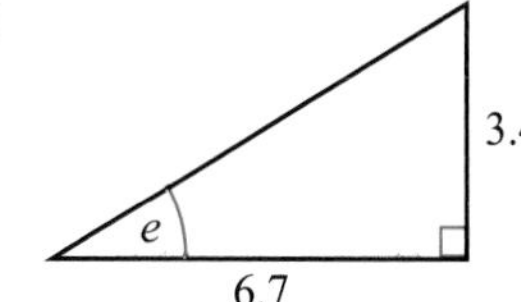

(f)

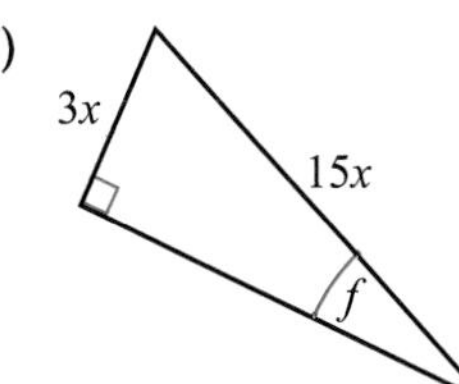

7 The diagram shows a ramp, AB, which makes an angle of 18° with the horizontal. The ramp is 6.25 m long. Calculate the difference in height between A and B (this is the length BC in the diagram).

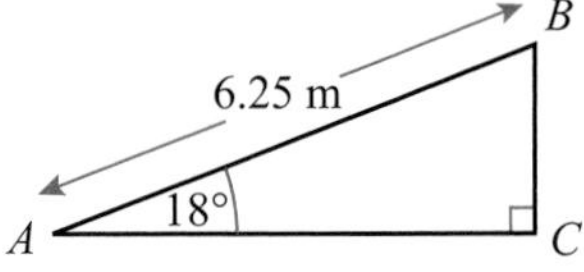

8 Village Q is 18 km from village P, on a bearing of 056°.

(a) Calculate the distance Q is north of P.
(b) Calculate the distance Q is east of P.

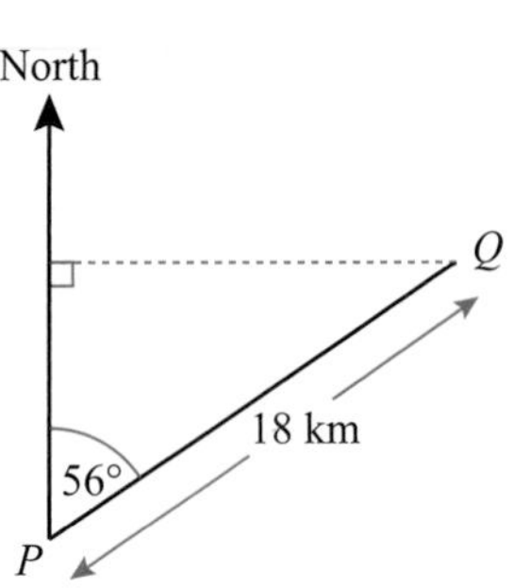

9 A 15 m beam is resting against a wall. The base of the beam forms an angle of 70° with the ground.

(a) At what height is the top of the beam touching the wall?
(b) How far is the base of the beam from the wall?

10 A mountain climber walks 380 m along a slope that is inclined at 65° to the horizontal, and then a further 240 m along a slope inclined at 60° to the horizontal.

Calculate the total vertical distance through which the climber travels.

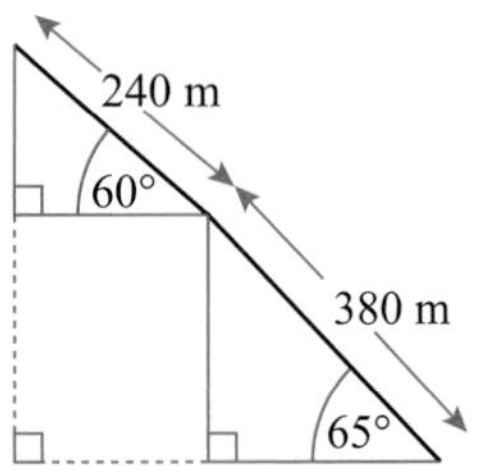

11 Calculate the unknown, lettered side(s) in each of the following shapes. Give your answers to 2 decimal places where necessary.

(a)

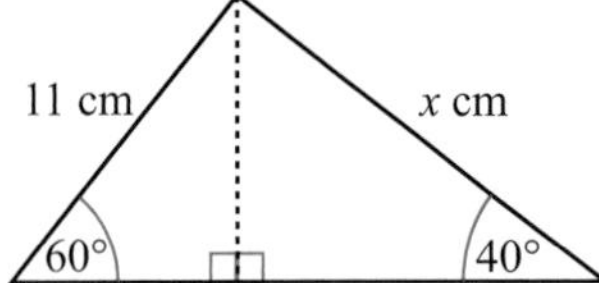

(b)

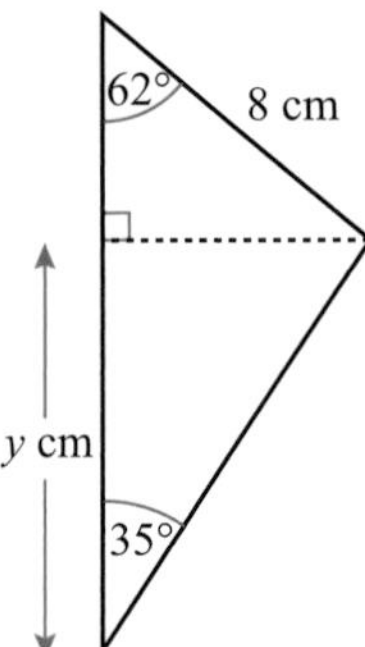

(c)

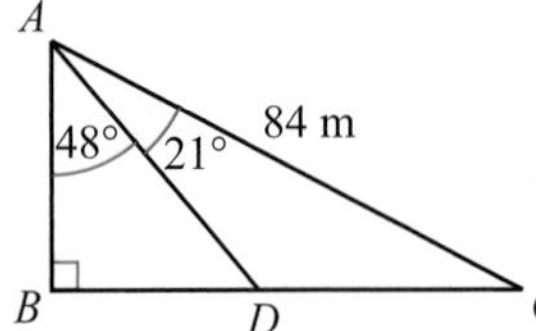

Find length AD.

(d)

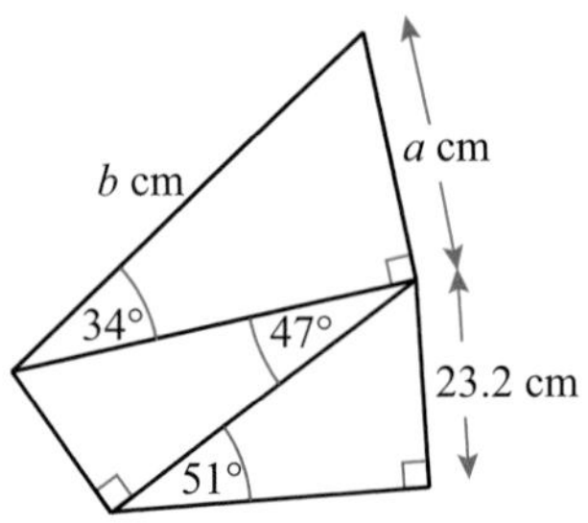

12 For each of the following angles calculate:

(i) $\tan x$ **(ii)** $\dfrac{\sin x}{\cos x}$

(a) $x = 30°$ **(b)** $x = 48°$ **(c)** $x = 120°$ **(d)** $x = 194°$

What do you notice?

13 Calculate:

(a) $(\sin 30°)^2 + (\cos 30°)^2$
(b) $(\sin 48°)^2 + (\cos 48°)^2$.
(c) Choose another angle and repeat the calculation.
(d) What do you notice?

14 The diagrams show a right-angled isosceles triangle and an equilateral triangle.

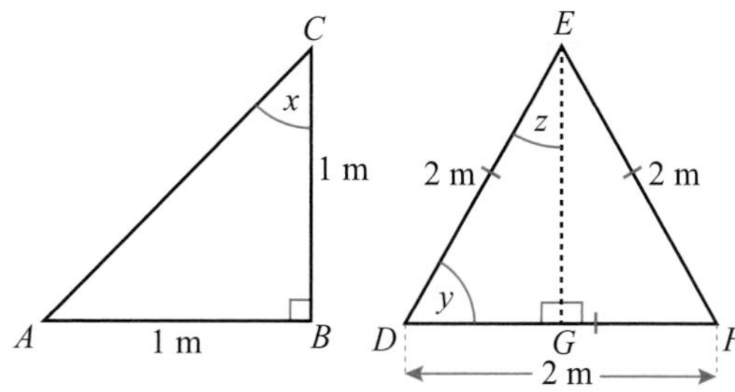

(a) Write down the value of angle $A\hat{C}B$.
(b) Use Pythagoras' theorem to calculate length AC, leaving your answer in exact form.
(c) Copy triangle ABC, including your answers to **(a)** and **(b)**.
(d) Use your diagram to find the exact values of sin 45°, cos 45° and tan 45°.
(e) Write down the value of angle y.
(f) Write down the value of angle z.
(g) Use Pythagoras' theorem to calculate the length EG, leaving your answer in exact form.
(h) Copy the diagram, including your answers to **(e)**, **(f)** and **(g)**.
(i) Use your diagram to find the exact values of sin 30°, cos 30°, tan 30°, sin 60°, cos 60°, tan 60°.
(j) Copy and complete the table below, using your answers from previous parts of this question.

Angle x	$\sin x$	$\cos x$	$\tan x$
30°			
60°			
45°			

Exact form

You have already met irrational numbers in chapter 9. An example was $\sqrt{2}$. This is called a 'surd'. Written like this it is exact, but if you put it through a calculator and then use a rounded value, your answer is an approximation. The same is true for recurring decimals like $\frac{2}{3}$.

When a question asks for an answer in exact form it intends you to leave any surds in root form and any recurring decimals as fractions. So, $5\sqrt{2}$ is exact but putting it through a calculator and writing 7.07 (2 d.p.) is not. Similarly $\frac{2}{3}$ is exact but 0.67 (2 d.p.) is not.

15.4 Solving problems using trigonometry

REWIND

It will be useful to remind yourself about general angle properties of triangles from chapter 3. ◀

You may need to make use of more than one trigonometric ratio when solving problems that involve right-angled triangles. To make it clear which ratio to use and when, you should follow these guidelines.

- If the question does not include a diagram, draw one. Make it clear and large.
- Draw any triangles that you are going to use separately and clearly label angles and sides.
- Identify any right-angled triangles that may be useful to you.
- Identify any sides or angles that you already know.
- Write down which of the opposite, adjacent and hypotenuse are going to be used, and then use SOHCAHTOA to help you decide which ratio to use.
- Write down the ratio and solve, either for an angle or a side.
- If you need to use a side or angle that you have calculated for another part of a question, try hard to use the unrounded value that you have in your calculator memory. This will help to avoid rounding errors later on.

The following worked example shows you how the solution to a trigonometry problem could be set out.

Worked example 11

The diagram shows an isosceles trapezium *ABDC*.
Calculate the area of the trapezium.

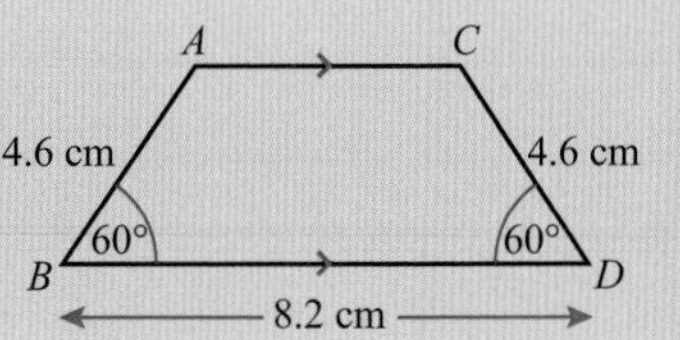

The area of a trapezium = (mean of the parallel sides) × (perpendicular distance between them)

In this diagram, perpendiculars have been added to form right-angled triangles so that trigonometry can be used.

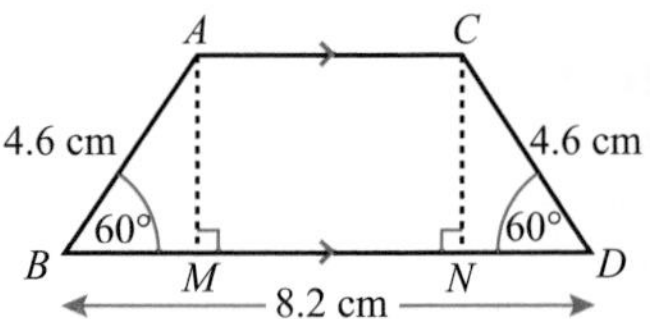

$AC = MN$ and you can find the length of MN if you calculate the lengths of BM and ND.

In ΔABM, $\sin 60° = \frac{\text{opp}(60°)}{\text{hyp}} = \frac{AM}{4.6}$ and $\cos 60° = \frac{\text{adj}(60°)}{\text{hyp}} = \frac{BM}{4.6}$

Hence, $AM = 4.6 \times \sin 60°$ and $BM = 4.6 \times \cos 60°$
$AM = 3.983716\ldots$ cm and $BM = 2.3$ cm

By symmetry, $ND = BM = 2.3$ cm
and $\therefore MN = 8.2 - (2.3 + 2.3) = 3.6$ cm

Hence, $AC = 3.6$ cm and $AM = CN = 3.983716\ldots$ cm

$$\text{The area of } ABDC = \left(\frac{AC + BD}{2}\right) \times AM$$
$$= \left(\frac{3.6 + 8.2}{2}\right) \times 3.983716\ldots \text{cm}^2$$
$$= 23.503929\ldots \text{cm}^2$$

Area of $ABDC = 23.5\text{ cm}^2$ (to 3sf)

Tip

Give your answer to 3 significant figures if no degree of accuracy is specified.

Worked example 12

The span between the towers of Tower Bridge in London is 76 m. When the arms of the bridge are raised to an angle of 35°, how wide is the gap between their ends?

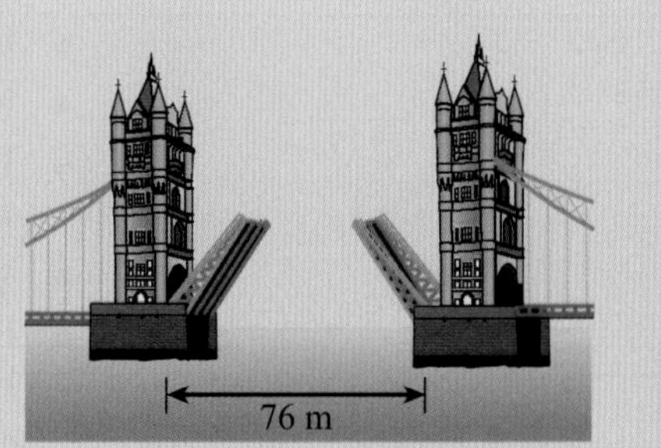

Here is a simplified labelled drawing of the bridge, showing the two halves raised to 35°.

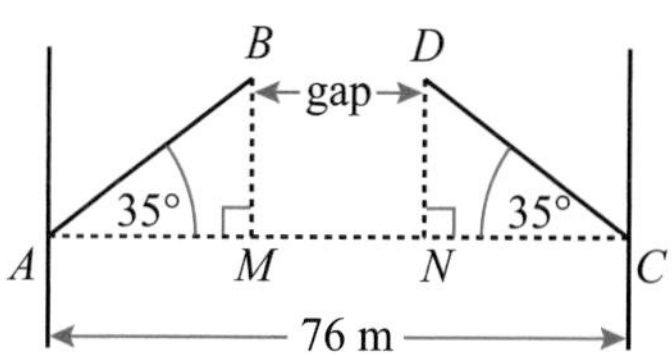

The gap = $BD = MN$ and $MN = AC - (AM + NC)$.

The right-angled triangles ABM and CDN are congruent, so $AM = NC$.
When the two halves are lowered, they must meet in the middle.

$\therefore AB = CD = \frac{76}{2} = 38\,\text{m}$

In ΔABM, $\cos 35° = \frac{\text{adj}(35°)}{\text{hyp}} = \frac{AM}{38}$

$AM = 38 \times \cos 35°$
$= 31.1277...\text{m}$

$\therefore MN = 76 - (31.1277... + 31.1277...)$
$= 13.744...\text{m}$

The gap $BD = 13.7\,\text{m}$ (to 3sf)

Exercise 15.8 *Living maths*

1 The diagram represents a ramp AB for a lifeboat. AC is vertical and CB is horizontal.

(a) Calculate the size of $A\hat{B}C$ correct to 1 decimal place.
(b) Calculate the length of BC correct to 3 significant figures.

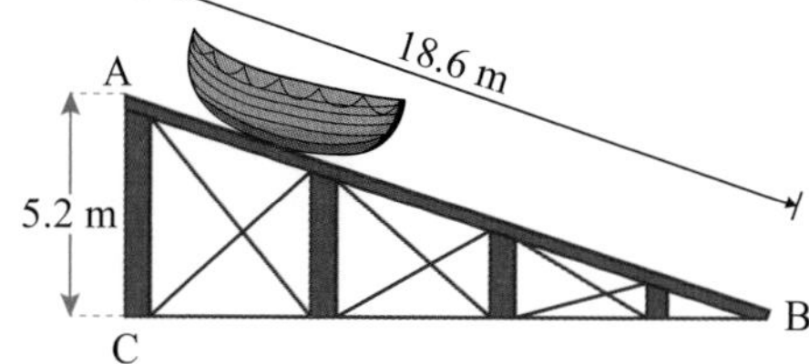

2 AB is a chord of a circle, centre O, radius 8 cm. $A\hat{O}B = 120°$.

Calculate the length of AB.

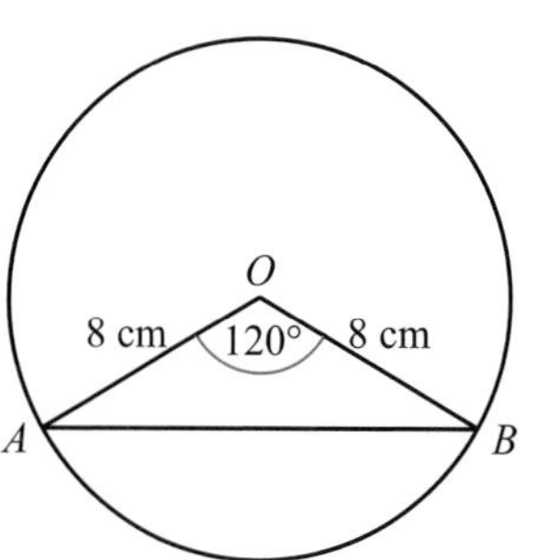

REWIND
Look at chapter 7 and remind yourself about the formula for the volume of a prism. ◀

3 The diagram represents a tent in the shape of a triangular prism. The front of the tent, ABD, is an isosceles triangle with $AB = AD$.

The width, BD, is 1.8 m and the supporting pole AC is perpendicular to BD and 1.5 m high. The tent is 3 m long.

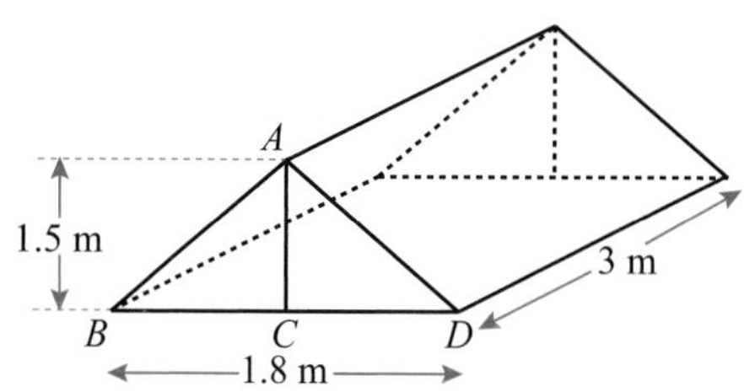

Calculate:

(a) the angle between AB and BD
(b) the length of AB
(c) the capacity inside the tent (i.e. the volume).

4 Calculate the angles of an isosceles triangle that has sides of length 9 cm, 9 cm and 14 cm.

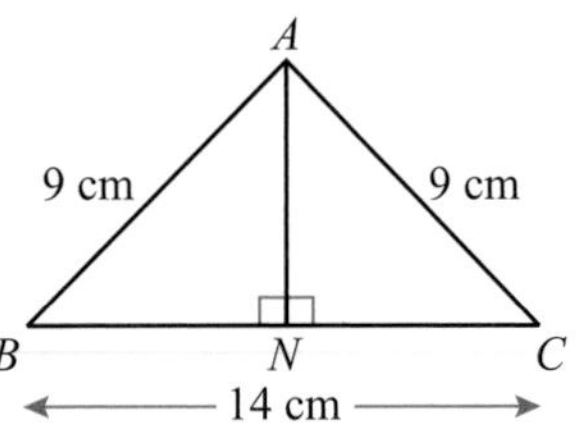

5 The sketch represents a field $PQRS$ on level ground.

The sides PQ and SR run due east.

(a) Write down the bearing of S from P.
(b) Calculate the shortest distance between SR and PQ.
(c) Calculate, in square metres, the area of the field $PQRS$.

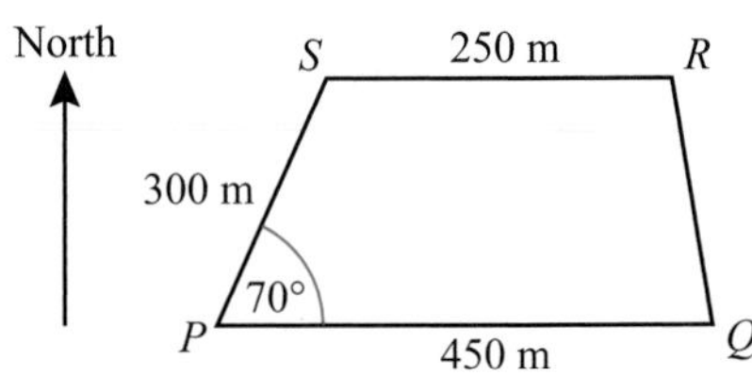

6 In the isosceles triangle DEF, $\hat{E} = \hat{F} = 35°$ and side $EF = 10$ m.

(a) Calculate the perpendicular distance from D to EF.
(b) Calculate the length of the side DE.

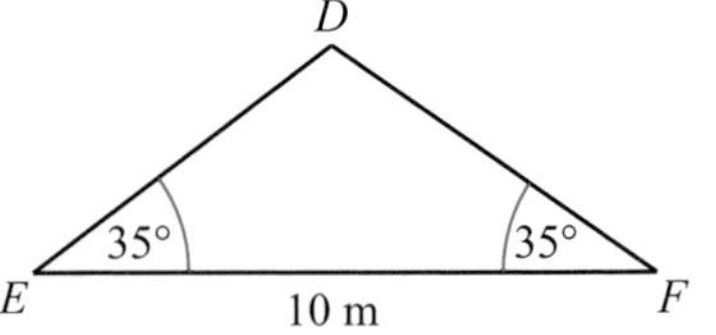

7 Find the length of a diagonal (QT) of a regular pentagon that has sides of length 10 cm. Give your answer to the nearest whole number.

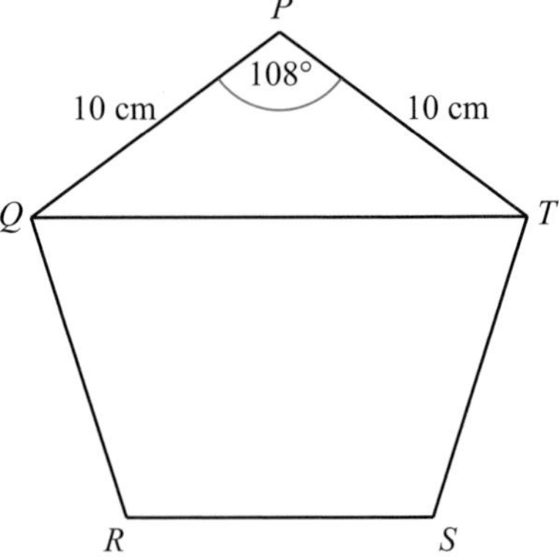

REWIND

Areas of two-dimensional shapes were covered in chapter 7. ◀

8 The diagram shows a regular pentagon with side 2 cm. O is the centre of the pentagon.

(a) Find angle $A\hat{O}E$.
(b) Find angle $A\hat{O}M$.
(c) Use trigonometry on triangle AOM to find the length OM.
(d) Find the area of triangle AOM.
(e) Find the area of the pentagon.

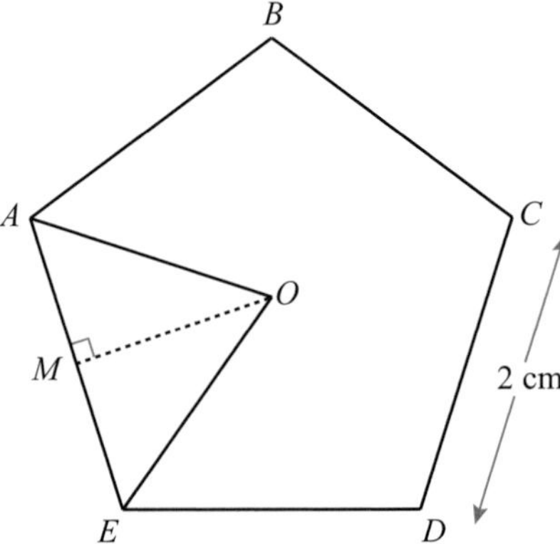

9 Using a similar method to that described in question 8 find the area of a regular octagon with side 4 cm.

10 Find the area of a regular pentagon with side $2a$ metres.

11 Find the area of a regular polygon with n sides, each of length $2a$ metres.

15.5 Angles between 90° and 180°

When you work with a right-angled triangle, the other two angles have to be acute (<90°). If the triangle you want to work with is not right-angled, you may need to find an angle that is obtuse ($90° < x < 180°$). In this section you are going to learn how the sine and cosine ratios can be extended to work with angles that are greater than 90° but less than 180°.

Worked example 13

Village *Q* is *D* kilometres from village *P* on a bearing of *A*°. How far east and how far north is *Q* from *P*?

If *A* is acute, then you work out sin *A* and cos *A*.

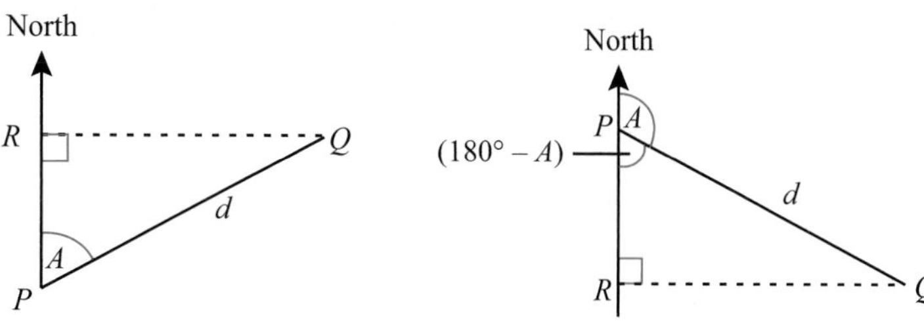

From the diagrams, you can see that:

$\sin A = \frac{RQ}{d}$ and $\cos A = \frac{PR}{d}$

$\therefore RQ = d \sin A$ and $PR = d \cos A$

Now suppose *A* is obtuse.

$QPR = 180° - A$

$\therefore \sin(180° - A) = \frac{RQ}{d}$ and $\cos(180° - A) = \frac{PR}{d}$

$\therefore RQ = d \sin(180° - A)$ and $PR = d \cos(180° - A)$

This gives you a rule for working with the sine and cosine of obtuse angles:

If θ is obtuse, then:

$\sin \theta = +\sin(180° - \theta)$

$\cos \theta = -\cos(180° - \theta)$ (This is the same as $-\cos \theta = \cos(180° - \theta)$).

In practice, you would use a calculator to find the trig ratios. The rules for obtuse angles are programmed into all scientific calculators.

Use your calculator to check that:

$\sin 100° = +0.984807753 = \sin 80°$

$\cos 100° = -0.173648177 = -\cos 80°$

$\sin 150° = +0.5 = \sin 30°$

$\cos 150° = -0.866025403 = -\cos 30°$

In effect, this means that an angle and its supplement have the same sine value. For the cosine of an angle and its supplement, the signs will differ.

Worked example 14

Which acute angle has the same sine as 120°?

$\sin(180° - \theta) = \sin\theta$ But in this case, $\theta = 120°$

$180° - \theta = 120$

$180° - 120° = \theta$

$60° = \theta$

$\sin 60° = \sin 120°$

Worked example 15

Express each of the following in terms of another angle between 0° and 180°.

(a) cos 100° **(b)** −cos 35°

(a) $\cos(180° - \theta) = -\cos\theta$ In this case $\theta = 100°$

$\cos 100° = -\cos(180° - 100°) = -\cos 80°$

(b) $-\cos\theta = \cos(180° - \theta)$

$-\cos 35° = \cos 145°$

Exercise 15.9

1 Express each of the following in terms of the same trig ratio of another angle between 0° and 180°.

(a) cos 120° **(b)** sin 35° **(c)** cos 136° **(d)** sin 170° **(e)** cos 88°
(f) −cos 140° **(g)** sin 121° **(h)** sin 99° **(i)** −cos 45° **(j)** −cos 150°

2 θ is the angle of a triangle. Find all possible values of θ between 0° and 180° (to the nearest degree) if:

(a) $\cos\theta = 0.71$ **(b)** $\cos\theta = -0.71$ **(c)** $\sin\theta = 0.5$ **(d)** $\sin\theta = 0.33$ **(e)** $\cos\theta = -0.82$
(f) $\cos\theta = 0.57$ **(g)** $\cos\theta = 0.94$ **(h)** $\sin\theta = 0.64$ **(i)** $\cos\theta = 0$ **(j)** $\sin\theta = 0$

15.6 The sine and cosine rules

The sine and cosine ratios are not only useful for right-angled triangles. To understand the following rules you must first look at the standard way of labelling the angles and sides of a triangle. Look at the triangle shown in the diagram.

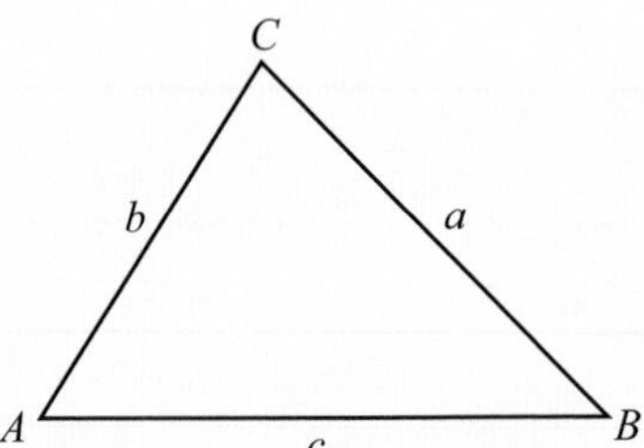

Notice that the sides are labelled with lower case letters and the angles are labelled with upper case letters. The side that is placed opposite angle A is labelled 'a', the side that is placed opposite angle B is labelled 'b' and so on.

The sine rule

For the triangle shown above, the following are true:

$$\frac{\sin A}{a} = \frac{\sin B}{b} \quad \text{and} \quad \frac{\sin A}{a} = \frac{\sin C}{c} \quad \text{and} \quad \frac{\sin B}{b} = \frac{\sin C}{c}$$

These relationships are usually expressed in one go:

$$\frac{\sin A}{a} = \frac{\sin B}{b} = \frac{\sin C}{c}$$

Remember, the sine rule is used when you are dealing with pairs of opposite sides and angles.

This is the **sine rule**. This version of the rule, with the sine ratios placed on the tops of the fractions, is normally used to calculate angles.

The formulae can also be turned upside down when you want to calculate lengths:

$$\frac{a}{\sin A} = \frac{b}{\sin B} = \frac{c}{\sin C}$$

You should remember that this represents *three* possible relationships.

Notice that in each case, both the upper and lower case form of each letter is used. This means that each fraction that you use requires an angle and the length of its opposite side.

Worked example 16

In ΔABC, $\hat{A} = 80°$, $\hat{B} = 30°$ and side $BC = 15$ cm.

Calculate the size of $\hat{C}$ and the lengths of the sides AB and AC.

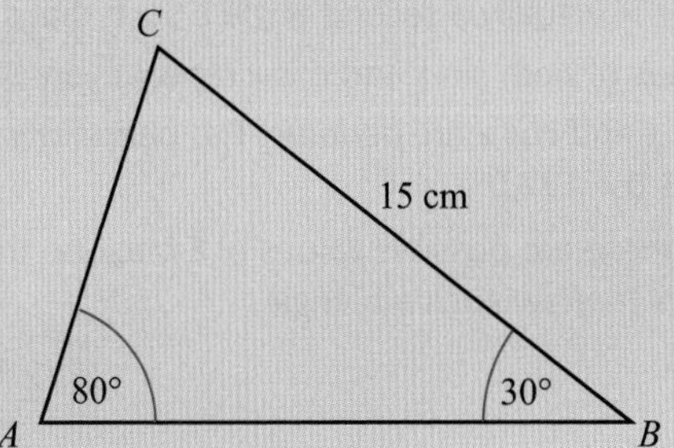

To calculate the angle C, use the fact that the sum of the three angles in a triangle is always 180°.

So, $C + 80 + 30 = 180 \Rightarrow C = 180 - 30 - 80 = 70°$

Now think about the side AB. AB is opposite the angle C (forming an 'opposite pair') and side BC is opposite angle A, forming a second 'opposite pair'.

So, write down the version of the sine rule that uses these pairs:

$$\frac{a}{\sin A} = \frac{c}{\sin C} \Rightarrow \frac{BC}{\sin A} = \frac{AB}{\sin C}$$

So, $\frac{15}{\sin 80°} = \frac{AB}{\sin 70°} \Rightarrow AB = \frac{15}{\sin 80°} \times \sin 70° = 14.3\text{ cm (3sf)}$

Similarly:

AC forms an opposite pair with angle B, so once again use the pair BC and angle A:

$$\frac{a}{\sin A} = \frac{b}{\sin B} \Rightarrow \frac{BC}{\sin A} = \frac{AC}{\sin B}$$

So, $\frac{15}{\sin 80°} = \frac{AC}{\sin 30°} \Rightarrow AC = \frac{15}{\sin 80°} \times \sin 30° = 7.62\text{ cm (3sf)}$

The ambiguous case of the sine rule

The special properties of the sine function can lead to more than one possible answer. The following example demonstrates how this may happen.

Worked example 17

In $\triangle DEF$, $DF = 10$ cm, $EF = 7$ cm and $\hat{D} = 34°$.

Calculate, to the nearest degree, the possible size of:

(a) angle $\hat{E}$ **(b)** angle $\hat{F}$.

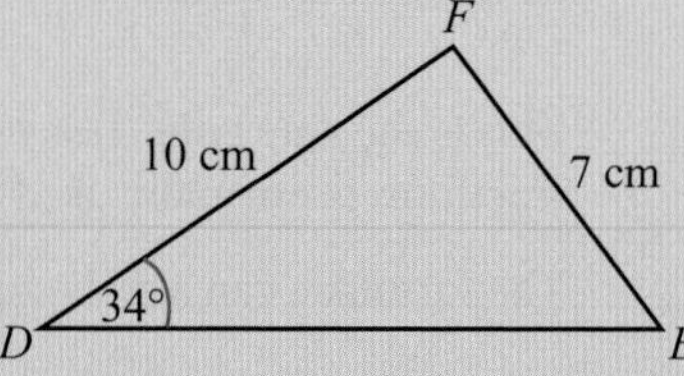

(a) Angle $\hat{E}$ is opposite a side of length 10 cm. This forms one pair.
Angle $\hat{D}$ is opposite a side of length 7 cm. This forms the second pair.
You are trying to find an angle, so choose the version of the sine rule with the value of sine ratios in the numerators:

$$\frac{\sin 34°}{7} = \frac{\sin E}{10} \Rightarrow \sin E = 10 \times \frac{\sin 34°}{7}$$

$$\text{So, } \hat{E} = \sin^{-1}\left(10 \times \frac{\sin 34°}{7}\right) = 53.0°$$

But there is actually a second angle E such that $\sin E = 10 \times \frac{\sin 34°}{7}$. You can see this if you consider the sine graph. The values of both sin x and cos x repeat every 360°. This property of both functions is called 'periodicity', i.e., both sin x and cos x are *periodic*. The periodicity of the function tells you that the second possible value of $\hat{E}$ is $180 - 53.0 = 127.0°$.

Both of these are possible values of $\hat{E}$ because there are two ways to draw such a triangle.

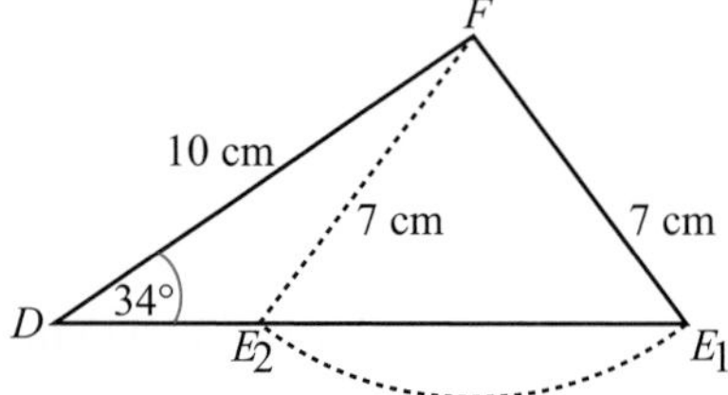

(b) Of course, the answers to part (a) must lead to two possible answers for part (b).
If $\hat{E} = 127.0°$, then $\hat{F} = 180 - 127 - 34 = 19°$ (shown as E_1 in the diagram).
If $\hat{E} = 53.0°$, then $\hat{F} = 180 - 53 - 34 = 93°$ (shown as E_2 in the diagram).
(If asked for, this would also have led to two possible solutions for the length DE).
You absolutely must take care to check that all possible answers have been calculated. Bear this in mind as you work through the following exercise.

Exercise 15.10

1 Find the value of x in each of the following equations.

(a) $\frac{x}{\sin 50} = \frac{9}{\sin 38}$ (b) $\frac{x}{\sin 25} = \frac{20}{\sin 100}$ (c) $\frac{20.6}{\sin 50} = \frac{x}{\sin 70}$ (d) $\frac{\sin x}{11.4} = \frac{\sin 63}{16.2}$

2 Find the length of the side marked x in each of the following triangles.

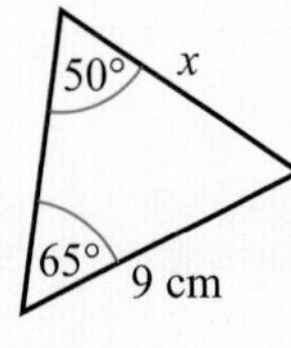

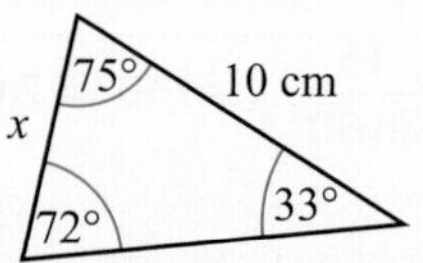

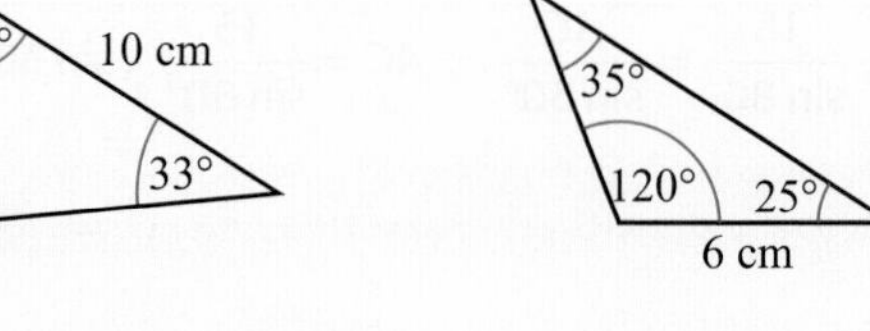

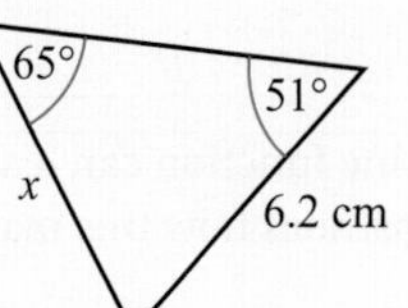

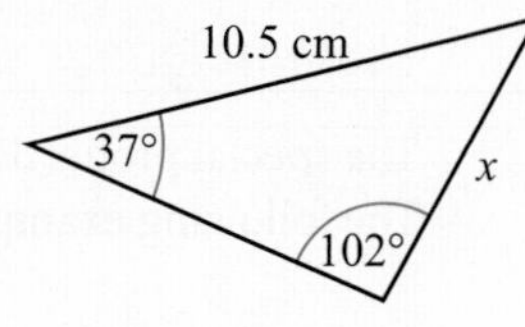

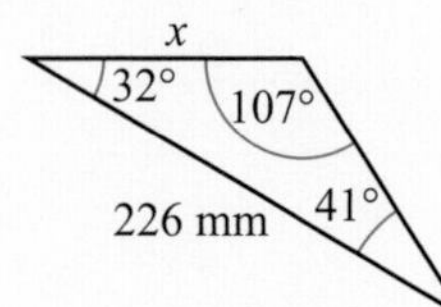

3 Find the size of the angle marked θ in the following triangles. Give your answers correct to 1 decimal place.

(a)

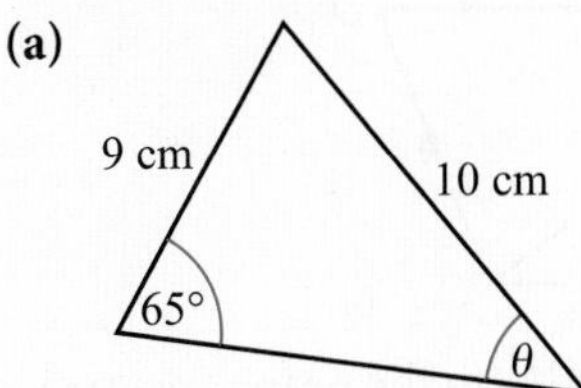

(b)

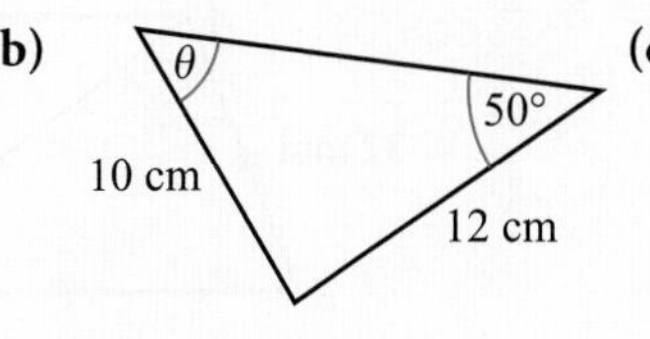

(c)

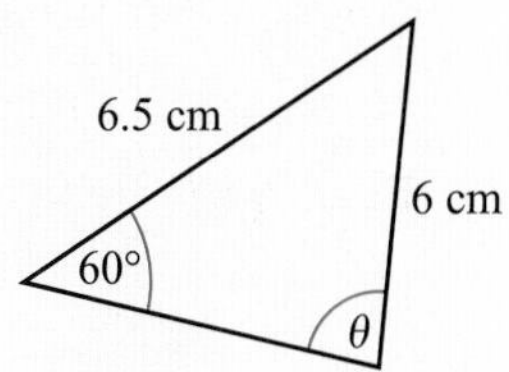

(d)

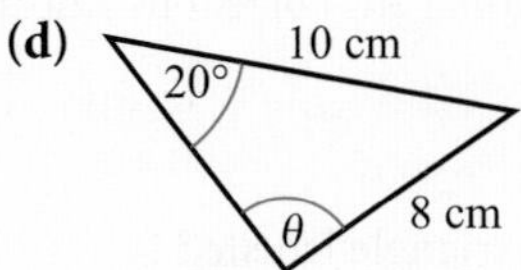

(e)

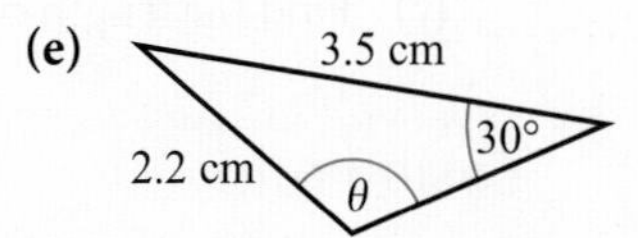

(f)

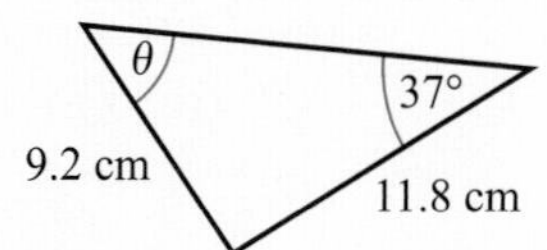

4 In ΔABC, $\hat{A} = 72°$, $\hat{B} = 45°$ and side $AB = 20$ cm.

Calculate the size of C and the lengths of the sides AC and BC.

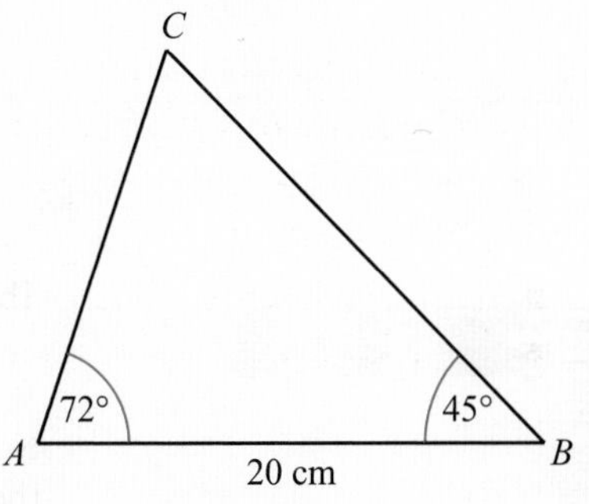

5 In ΔDEF, $\hat{D} = 140°$, $\hat{E} = 15°$ and side $DF = 6$ m.

Calculate the size of $\hat{F}$ and the lengths of the sides DE and EF.

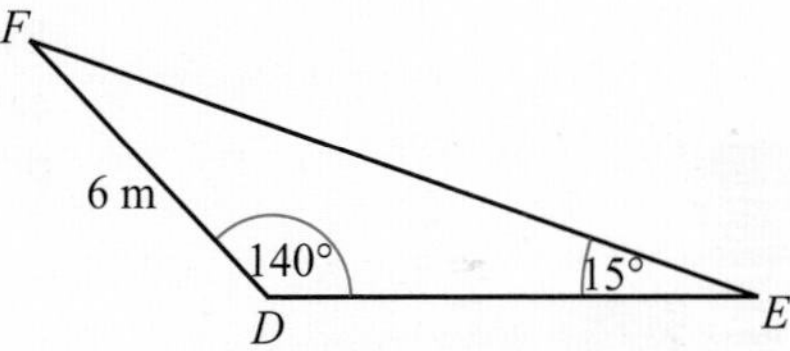

6 In ΔPQR, $\hat{Q} = 120°$, side $PQ = 8$ cm and side $PR = 13$ cm. Calculate the size of $\hat{R}$, the size of $\hat{P}$, and the length of side QR.
Give your answers to the nearest whole number.

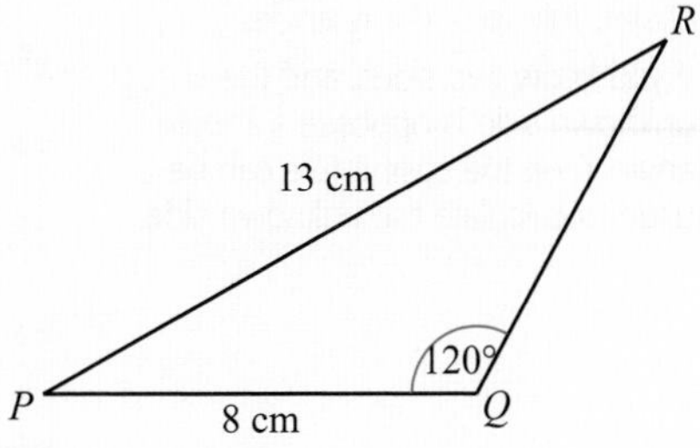

7 In ΔXYZ, $\hat{X} = 40°$, side $XZ = 12$ cm and side $YZ = 15$ cm.

(a) Explain why $\hat{Y}$ must be less than 40°.
(b) Calculate, correct to 1 decimal place, $\hat{Y}$ and $\hat{Z}$.
(c) Calculate the length of the side XY.

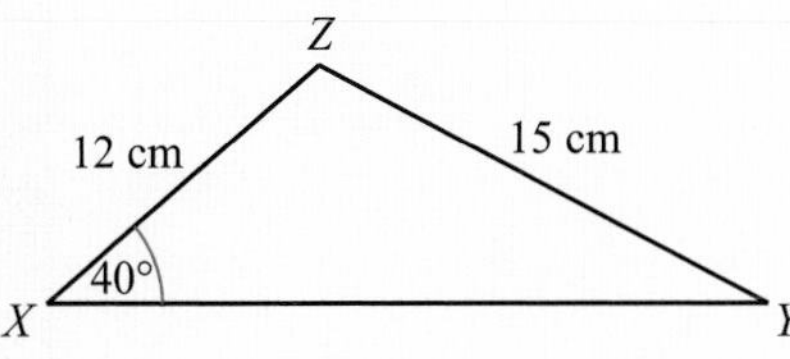

8 *ABCD* is a parallelogram with $AB = 32$ mm and $AD = 40$ mm and $\angle BAC = 77°$.

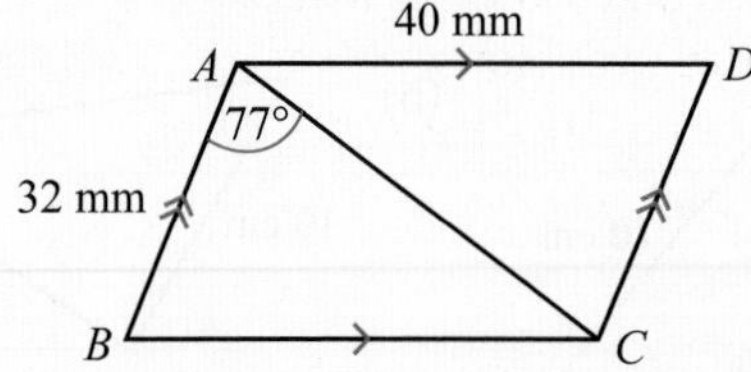

(a) Find the size of $\angle BCA$ (to the nearest degree)
(b) Find the size of $\angle ABC$ (to the nearest degree)
(c) Find the length of diagonal *AC* correct to 2 decimal places.

Cosine rule

For the **cosine rule**, consider a triangle labelled in exactly the same way as that used for the sine rule.

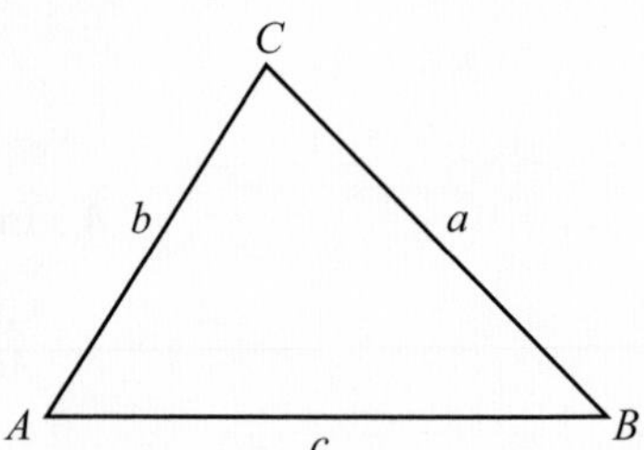

The cosine rule is stated as a single formula:

$$a^2 = b^2 + c^2 - 2bc\cos A$$

Notice the all three sides are used in the formula, and just one angle. The side whose square is the subject of the formula is opposite the angle used (hence they have the same letter but in a different case). This form of the cosine rule is used to find unknown sides.

By rearranging the labels of angles (but making sure that opposite sides are still given the lower case version of the same letter for any given angle) the cosine rule can be stated in two more possible ways:

$$b^2 = a^2 + c^2 - 2ac\cos B \quad \text{or} \quad c^2 = a^2 + b^2 - 2ab\cos C$$

Remember, if you know all three sides of a triangle, you can use the cosine rule to find any angle.

If you know two sides, and the unknown side is opposite a *known* angle, then the cosine rule can be used to calculate the unknown side.

Notice, also, that you can take any version of the formula to make the cosine ratio the subject.

This version can be used to calculate angles:

$$a^2 = b^2 + c^2 - 2bc\cos A$$

$$\Rightarrow a^2 + 2bc\cos A = b^2 + c^2$$

$$\Rightarrow 2bc\cos A = b^2 + c^2 - a^2$$

$$\Rightarrow \cos A = \frac{b^2 + c^2 - a^2}{2bc}$$

Worked example 18

In $\triangle ABC$, $\hat{B} = 50°$, side $AB = 9$ cm and side $BC = 18$ cm.

Calculate the length of *AC*.

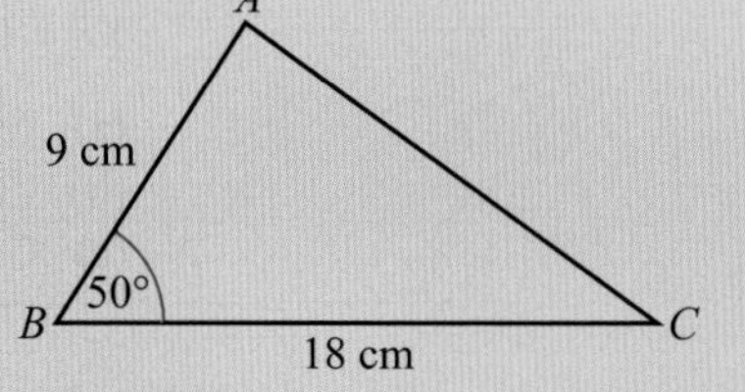

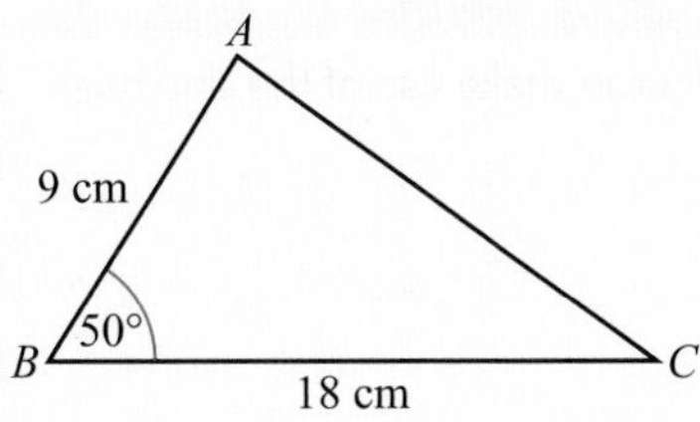

Notice that $AC = b$ and you know that $\hat{B} = 50°$.
Use the cosine rule in the form, $b^2 = a^2 + c^2 - 2ac \cos B$

$$b^2 = 9^2 + 18^2 - (2 \times 9 \times 18 \times \cos 50°)$$
$$= 81 + 324 - (208.2631...)$$
$$= 196.7368...$$
$$\therefore b = \sqrt{196.7368...}$$
$$= 14.0262...$$

Length of AC = 14.0 cm (to 3 s.f.)

Worked example 19

In ΔDEF, $\hat{F} = 120°$, side $EF = 25$ m and side $FD = 34$ m.

Calculate the length of side DE.

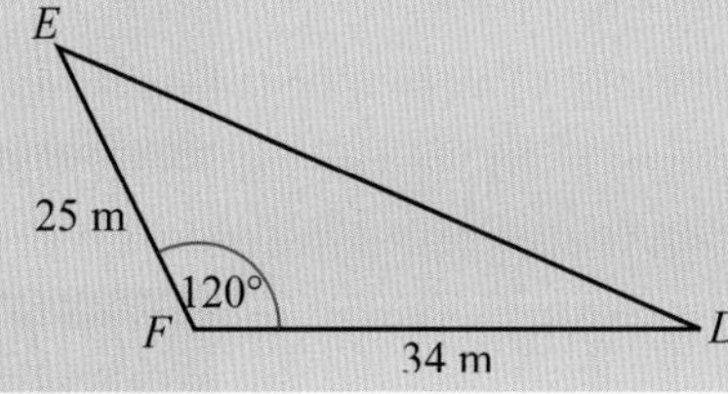

$DE = f$, so use the cosine rule in the form, $f^2 = d^2 + e^2 - 2de \cos F$.

$$f^2 = 25^2 + 34^2 - (2 \times 25 \times 34 \times \cos 120°)$$
$$= 625 + 1156 - (-850) \text{ (notice that cos 120° is negative)}$$
$$= 625 + 1156 + 850$$
$$= 2631$$
$$\therefore f = \sqrt{2631}$$
$$= 51.2932...$$

Length of DE = 51.3 m (to 3 s.f.)

Combining the sine and cosine rules

The following worked examples show how you can combine the sine and cosine rules to solve problems.

Worked example 20

Combining the sine and cosine rules

In ΔPQR, $\hat{R} = 100°$, side $PR = 8$ cm and side $RQ = 5$ cm.

(a) Calculate the length of side PQ.
(b) Calculate, correct to the nearest degree, $\hat{P}$ and $\hat{Q}$.

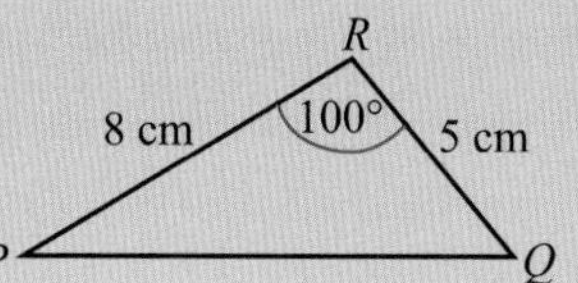

(a) $PQ = r$, so use the cosine rule in the form, $r^2 = p^2 + q^2 - 2pq \cos R$.

$$r^2 = 5^2 + 8^2 - (2 \times 5 \times 8 \times \cos 100°)$$
$$= 25 + 64 - (-13.8918...) \text{ (notice that cos 100° is negative)}$$
$$= 102.8918...$$
$$\therefore r = \sqrt{102.8918...}$$
$$= 10.1435...$$

Length of PQ = 10.1 cm (to 3 s.f.)

If you need to use a previously calculated value for a new problem, leave unrounded answers in your calculator to avoid introducing rounding errors.

(b) Now you know the value of r as well as the value of $\hat{R}$, you can make use of the sine rule:

$$\frac{\sin P}{p} = \frac{\sin Q}{q} = \frac{\sin R}{r}$$

$$\frac{\sin P}{5} = \frac{\sin Q}{8} = \frac{\sin 100^\circ}{10.1435...}$$

Using the first and third fractions, $\sin P = \frac{5 \times \sin 100^\circ}{10.1435...} = 0.4853...$

$\hat{R}$ is obtuse so P is acute, and $\hat{P} = 29.0409...^\circ$
$\hat{P} = 29^\circ$ (to the nearest degree)
To find Q you can use the angle sum of a triangle = 180°:

$Q = 180 - (100 + 29)$
$\therefore Q = 51^\circ$ (to the nearest degree)

Worked example 21

(a) Change the subject of the formula $c^2 = a^2 + b^2 - 2ab\cos C$ to $\cos C$.
(b) Use your answer to part (a) to find the smallest angle in the triangle which has sides of length 7 m, 8 m and 13 m.

(a) $c^2 = a^2 + b^2 - 2ab\cos C$

$2ab\cos C = a^2 + b^2 - c^2$

$$\cos C = \frac{a^2 + b^2 - c^2}{2ab}$$

(b) The smallest angle in a triangle is opposite the shortest side. In the given triangle, the smallest angle is opposite the 7 m side. Let this angle be C. Then $c = 7$ and take $a = 8$ and $b = 13$.
Using the result of part (a):

$$\cos C = \frac{8^2 + 13^2 - 7^2}{2 \times 8 \times 13}$$
$$= \frac{64 + 169 - 49}{208}$$
$$= \frac{184}{208}$$
$$\hat{C} = \cos^{-1}\frac{184}{208}$$
$$= 29.7957...^\circ$$

The smallest angle of the triangle = 27.8° (to 1 d.p.)

Exercise 15.11

1 In ΔABC, $\hat{B} = 45°$, side $AB = 10$ cm and side $BC = 12$ cm. Calculate the length of side AC.

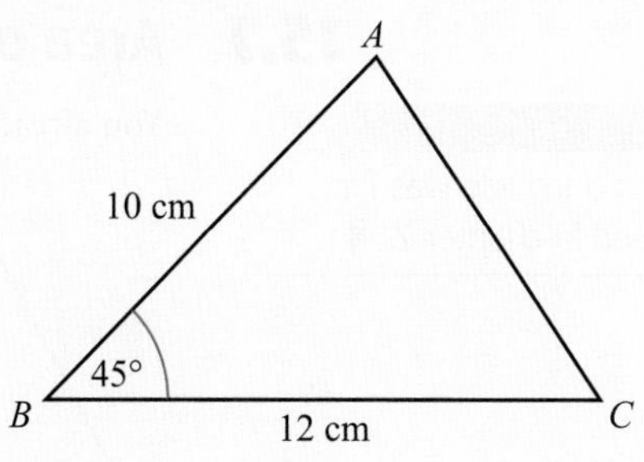

2 In ΔDEF, $\hat{F} = 150°$, side $EF = 9$ m and side $FD = 14$ m. Calculate the length of side DE.

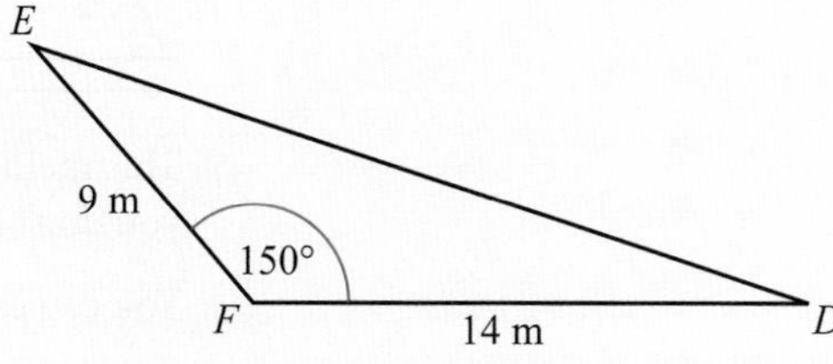

3 In ΔPQR, side $PQ = 11$ cm, side $QR = 9$ cm and side $RP = 8$ cm.

Calculate the size of p correct to 1 decimal place.

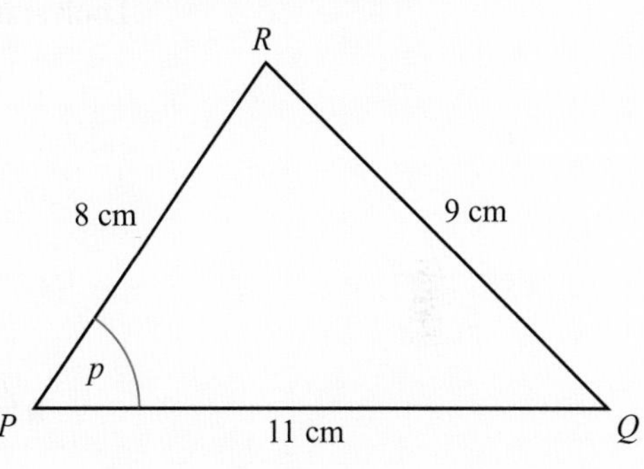

4 In ΔSTU, $S = 95°$, side $ST = 10$ m and side $SU = 15$ m.

(a) Calculate the length of side TU.
(b) Calculate $\hat{U}$.
(c) Calculate $\hat{T}$.

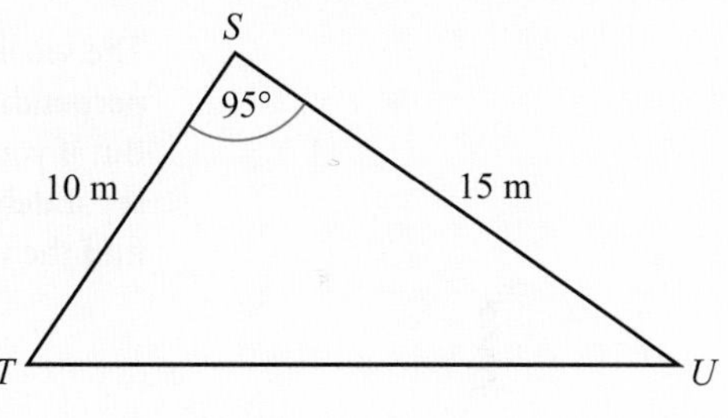

5 In ΔXYZ, side $XY = 15$ cm, side $YZ = 13$ cm and side $ZX = 8$ cm. Calculate the size of:

(a) $\hat{X}$
(b) $\hat{Y}$
(c) $\hat{Z}$.

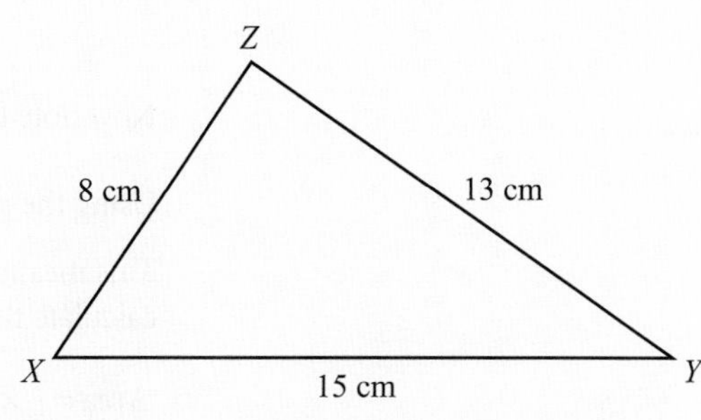

REWIND

Look back at the beginning of this chapter and remind yourself about bearings. ◀

6 A boat sails in a straight line from Aardvark Island on a bearing of 060°. When the boat has sailed 8 km it reaches Beaver Island and then turns to sail on a bearing of 150°. The boat remains on this bearing until it reaches Crow Island, 12 km from Beaver Island. On reaching Crow Island the boat's pilot decides to return directly to Aardvark Island.

Calculate:

(a) The length of the return journey.
(b) The bearing on which the pilot must steer his boat to return to Aardvark Island.

15.7 Area of a triangle

REWIND

The area of a triangle was first encountered in chapter 7. ◀

You already know that the area of a triangle is given by the following formula:

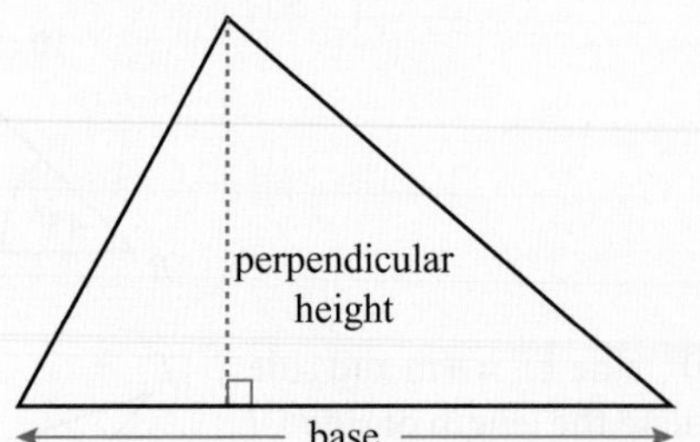

$$\text{Area} = \frac{1}{2} \times \text{base} \times \text{perpendicular height}$$

This method can be used if you know both the length of the base and perpendicular height but if you don't have these values you need to use another method.

You can calculate the area of any triangle by using trigonometry.

Look at the triangle ABC shown in the diagram:

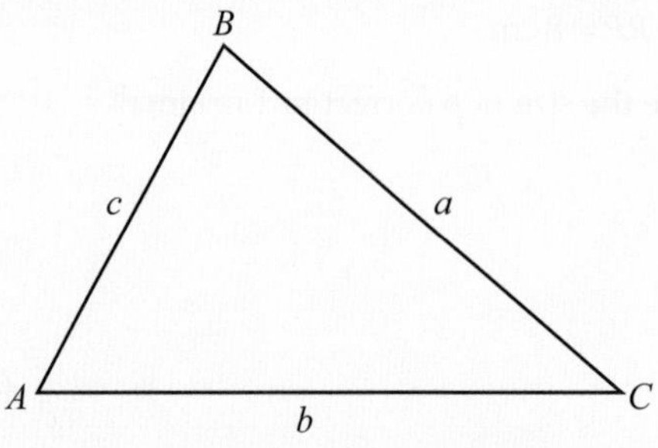

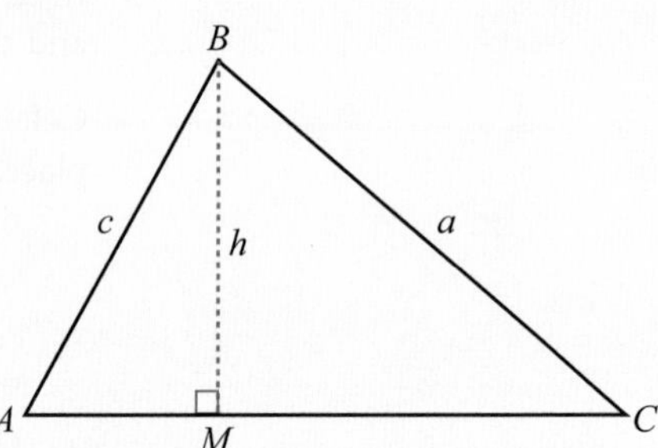

The second copy of the triangle is drawn with a perpendicular height that you don't yet know. But if you draw the right-angled triangle BCM separately, you can use basic trigonometry to find the value of h.

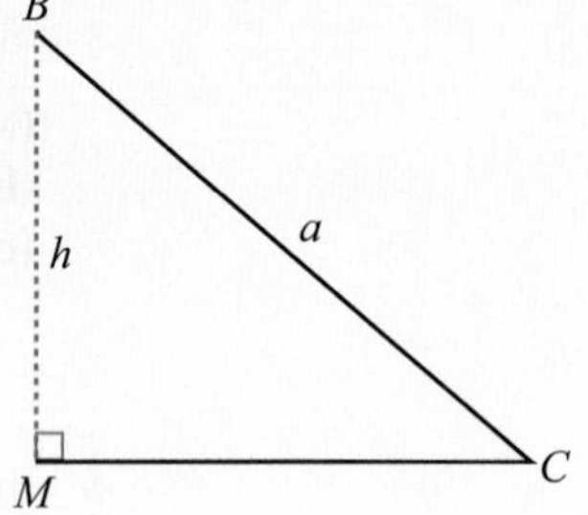

Now note that opp(C) $= h$ and the hypotenuse $= a$.

Using the sine ratio: $\sin C = \frac{h}{a} \Rightarrow h = a \sin C$

This means that you now know the perpendicular height and can use the base length b to calculate the area:

$$\text{Area} = \frac{1}{2} \times \text{base} \times \text{perpendicular height}$$

$$= \frac{1}{2} \times b \times a \sin C$$

$$\text{Area} = \frac{1}{2} ab \sin C$$

In fact you could use any side of the triangle as the base and draw the perpendicular height accordingly. This means that the area can also be calculated with:

$$\text{Area} = \frac{1}{2} ac \sin B \qquad \text{or} \qquad \text{Area} = \frac{1}{2} bc \sin A$$

In each case the sides used meet at the angle that has been included.

Worked example 22

Calculate the areas of each of the following shapes.

(a)

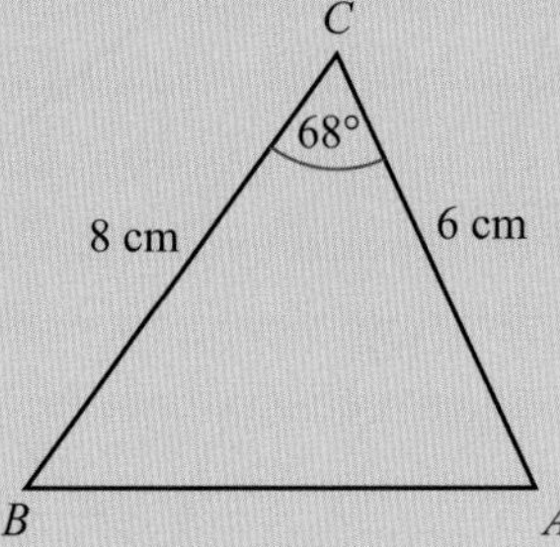

(b)

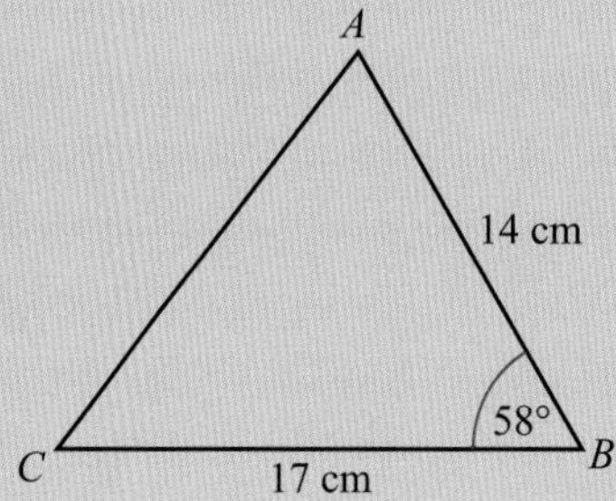

(a)

$$\text{Area} = \frac{1}{2}ab\sin C$$

$$= \frac{1}{2} \times 8 \times 6 \times \sin 68°$$

$$= 22.3\,\text{cm}^2 \text{ (to 1dp)}$$

(b)

$$\text{Area} = \frac{1}{2}ac\sin B$$

$$= \frac{1}{2} \times 17 \times 14 \times \sin 58°$$

$$= 100.9\,\text{cm}^2 \text{ (to 1dp)}$$

Worked example 23

The diagram shows a triangle with area $20\,\text{cm}^2$.

Calculate the size of angle $\hat{F}$.

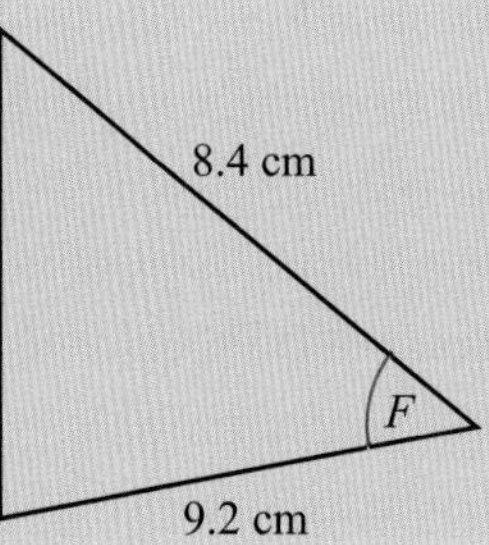

Notice that the area $= \frac{1}{2} \times 8.4 \times 9.2 \times \sin F = 20$

$$\sin F = \frac{2 \times 20}{8.4 \times 9.2}$$

$$\text{So } \hat{F} = \sin^{-1}\left(\frac{2 \times 20}{8.4 \times 9.2}\right)$$

$$= 31.2° \text{ (to 1dp)}$$

Exercise 15.12

1 Find the area of each triangle.

(a)

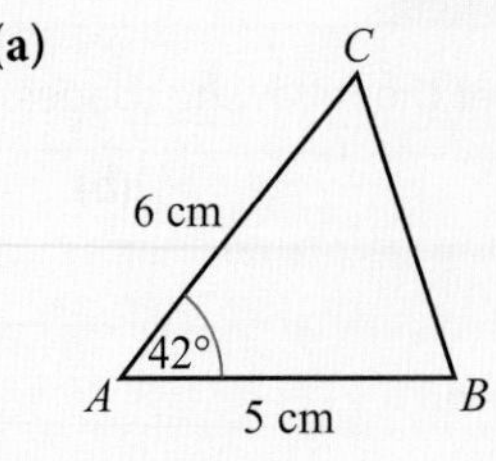

(b)

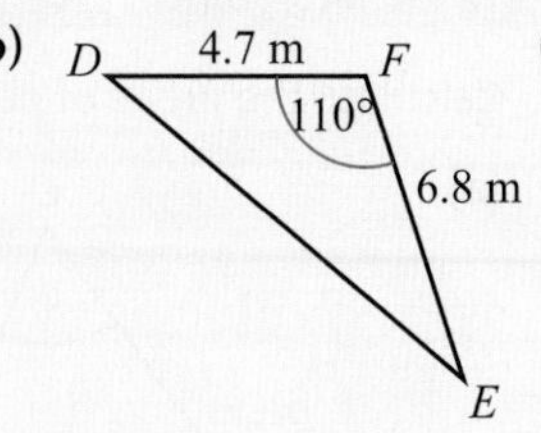

(c)

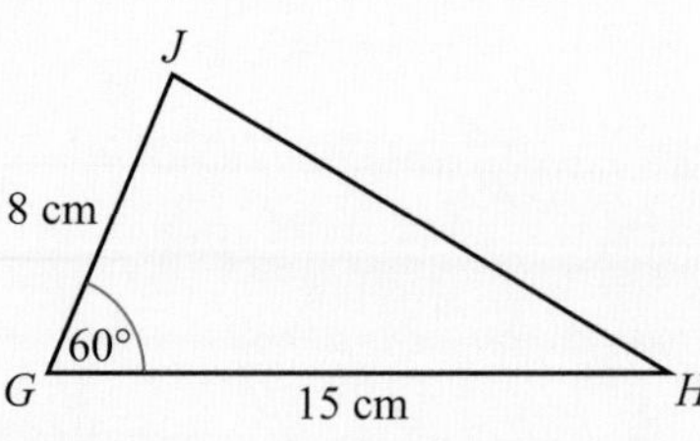

(d)

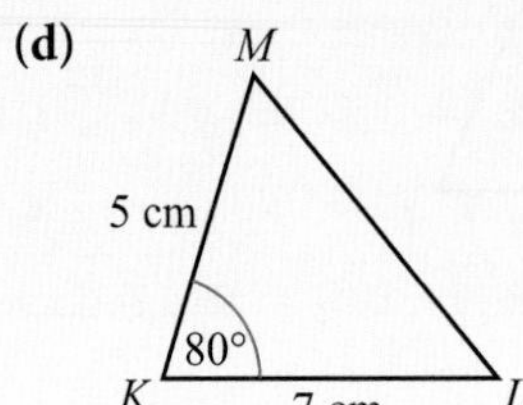

(e)

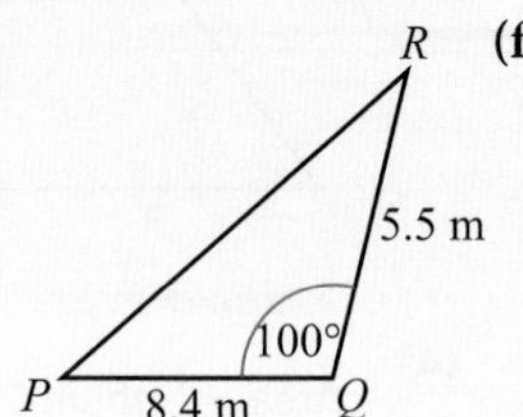

(f)

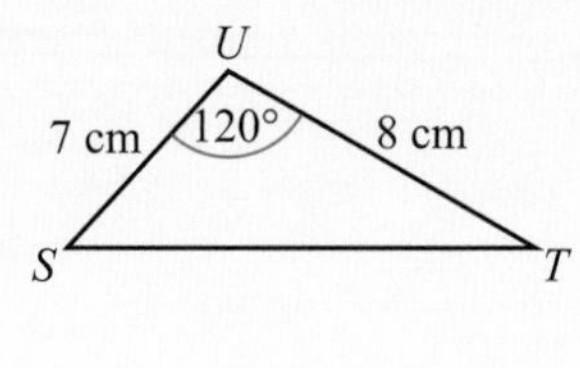

2 Find the area of the parallelogram shown in the diagram.

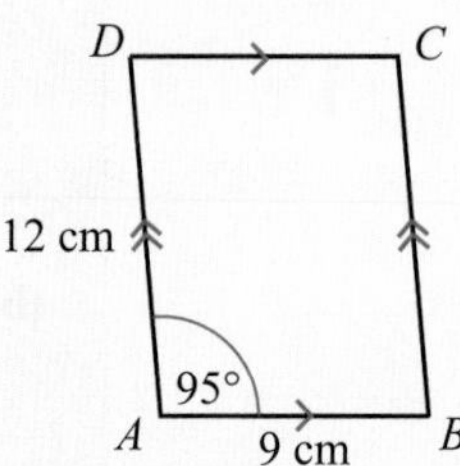

3 The diagram shows the dimensions of a small herb garden. Find the area of the garden. Give your answer correct to two decimal places.

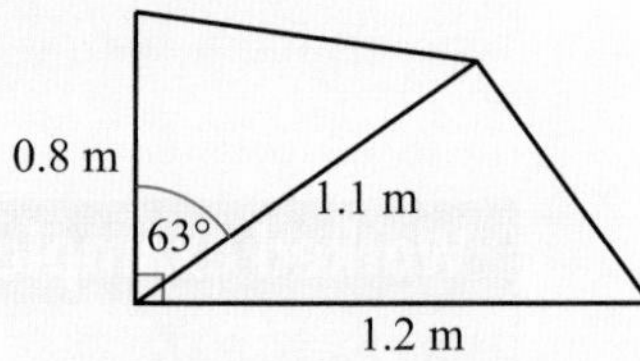

4 Find the area of *PQRS*.

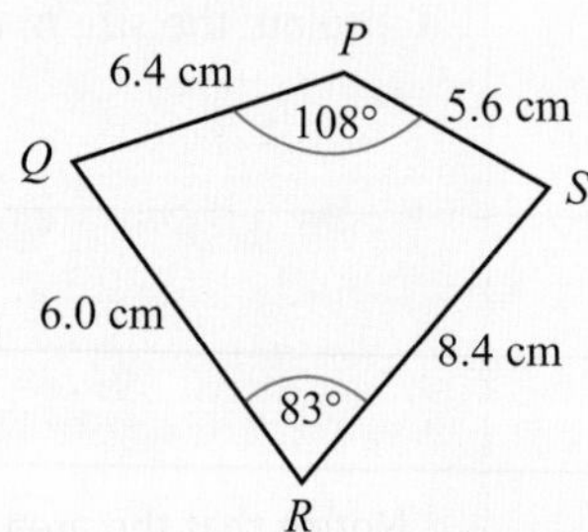

5 Find the area of each polygon. Give your answers to 1 decimal place.

(a)

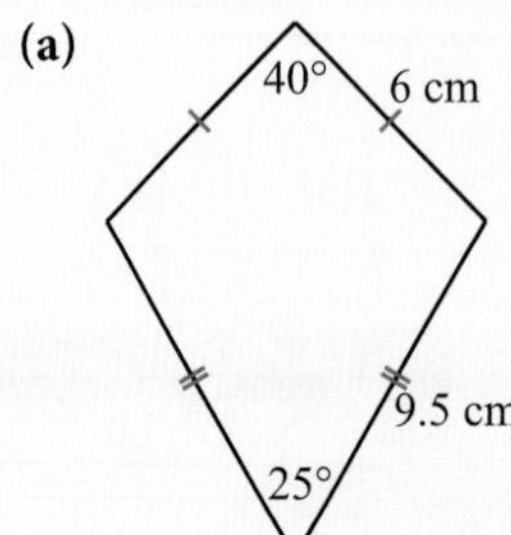

(b)

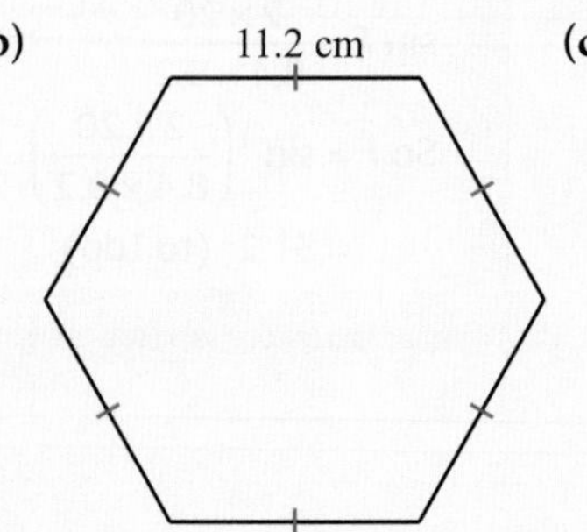

(c)

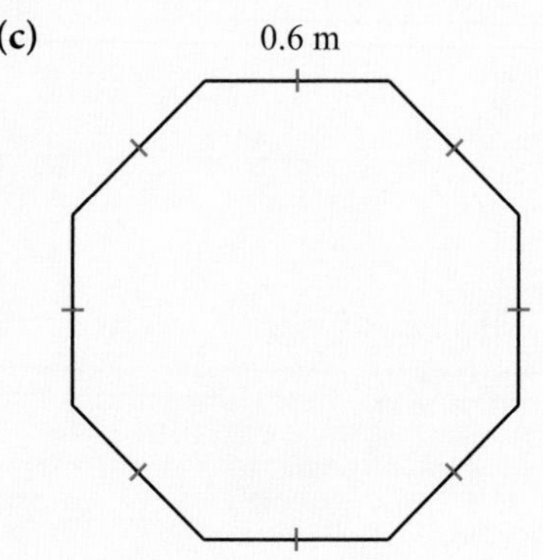

6 The diagonals of a parallelogram bisect each other at an angle of 42°. If the diagonals are 26 cm and 20 cm long, find:

(a) the area of the parallelogram
(b) the lengths of the sides.

7 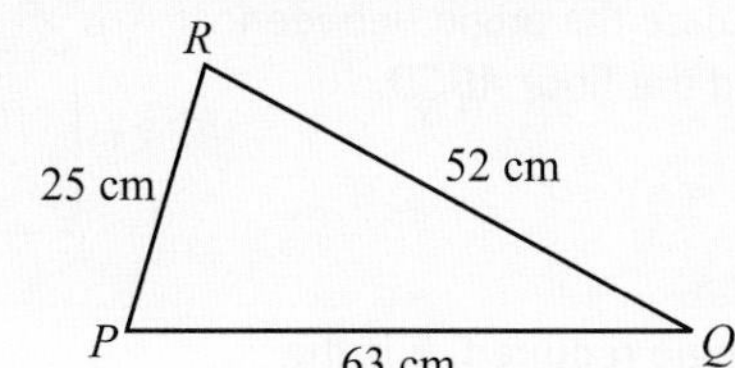

The diagrams shows ΔPQR, which has an area of $630\,\text{cm}^2$.

(a) Use the formula Area $= \frac{1}{2}pr\sin Q$ to find $\hat{Q}$ correct to 1 decimal place.

(b) Find $\hat{P}$ correct to 1 decimal place.

15.8 Trigonometry in three dimensions

The final part of the trigonometry chapter looks at how to use the ratios in three dimensions. With problems of this kind you must draw and label each triangle as you use it. This will help you to organise your thoughts and keep your solution tidy.

When you work with solids you may need to calculate the angle between an edge, or a diagonal, and one of the faces. This is called the angle between a line and a plane.

Consider a line PQ, which meets a plane $ABCD$ at point P. Through P draw lines PR_1, PR_2, PR_3, … in the plane and consider the angles QPR_1, QPR_2, QPR_3…

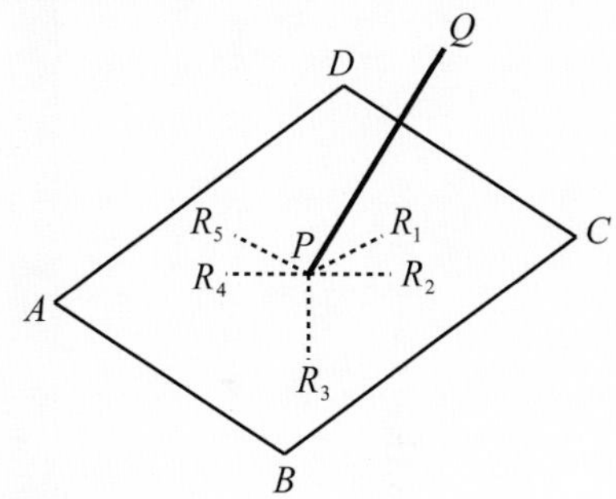

- If PQ is perpendicular to the plane, all these angles will be right angles.
- If PQ is not perpendicular to the plane, these angles will vary in size.

It is the smallest of these angles which is called the angle between the line PQ and the plane $ABCD$.

To identify this angle, do the following:

- From Q draw a perpendicular to the plane. Call the foot of this perpendicular R.
- The angle between the line PQ and the plane is $Q\hat{P}R$.

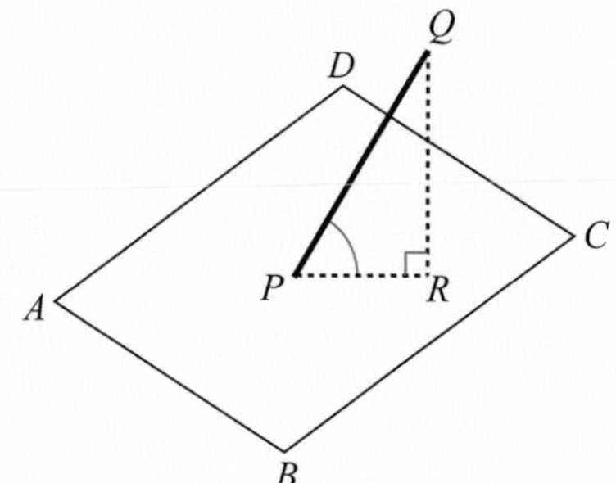

PR is called the **projection** of PQ on the plane $ABCD$.

The following worked example shows how a problem in three dimensions might be tackled.

Worked example 24

The diagram represents a room which has the shape of a cuboid. $AB = 6\,\text{m}$, $AD = 4\,\text{m}$, and $AP = 2\,\text{m}$. Calculate the angle between the diagonal BS and the floor $ABCD$.

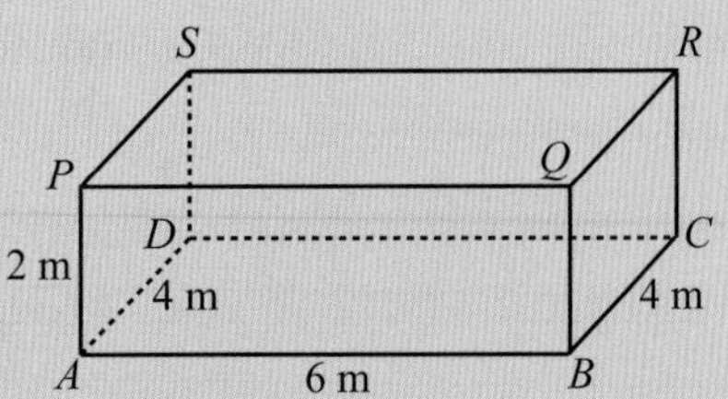

First identify the angle required. B is the point where the diagonal BS meets the plane $ABCD$.

SD is the perpendicular from S to the plane $ABCD$ and so DB is the projection of SB onto the plane.

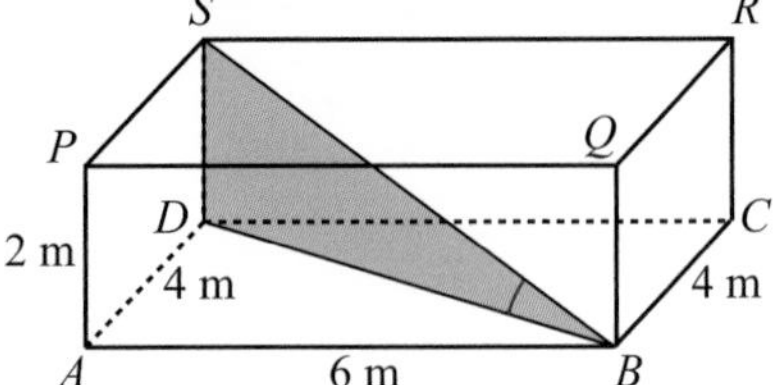

The angle required is $S\hat{B}D$.

You know that ΔSBD has a right angle at D and that $SD = 2\,\text{m}$ (equal to AP).

To find $S\hat{B}D$, you need to know the length of DB or the length of SB. You can find the length of BD by using Pythagoras' theorem in ΔABD.

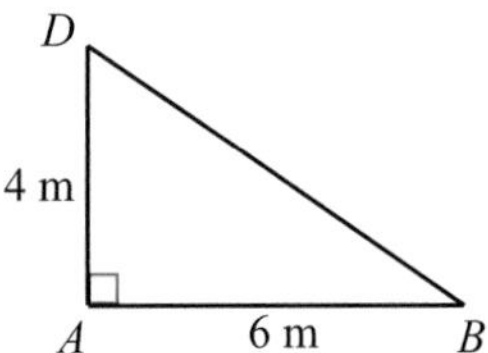

$$BD^2 = 6^2 + 4^2 = 36 + 16 = 52$$

$$BD = \sqrt{52}$$

So, using right-angled triangle SBD:

$$\tan B = \frac{\text{opp}(B)}{\text{adj}(B)} = \frac{SD}{BD} = \frac{2}{\sqrt{52}}$$

$$S\hat{B}D = \tan^{-1}\left(\frac{2}{\sqrt{52}}\right) = 15.5013\ldots$$

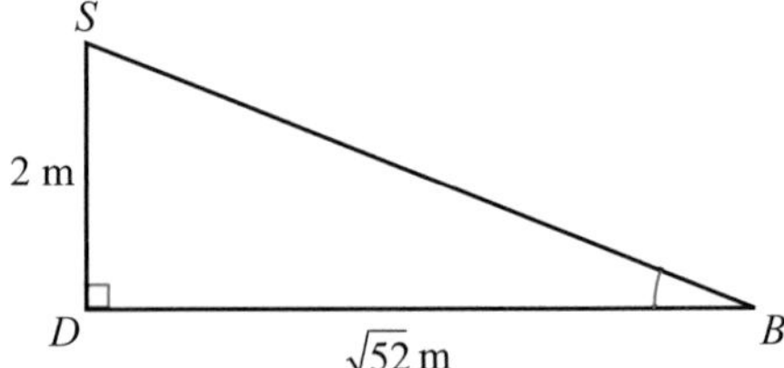

The angle between diagonal BS and the floor $ABCD = 15.5°$ (to 1 d.p.)

Exercise 15.13

1 The diagram represents a triangular prism. The rectangular base, $ABCD$, is horizontal.

$AB = 20\,\text{cm}$ and $BC = 15\,\text{cm}$.
The cross-section of the prism, BCE, is right-angled at C and $E\hat{B}C = 41°$.

(a) Calculate the length of AC.
(b) Calculate the length of EC.
(c) Calculate the angle which the line AE makes with the horizontal.

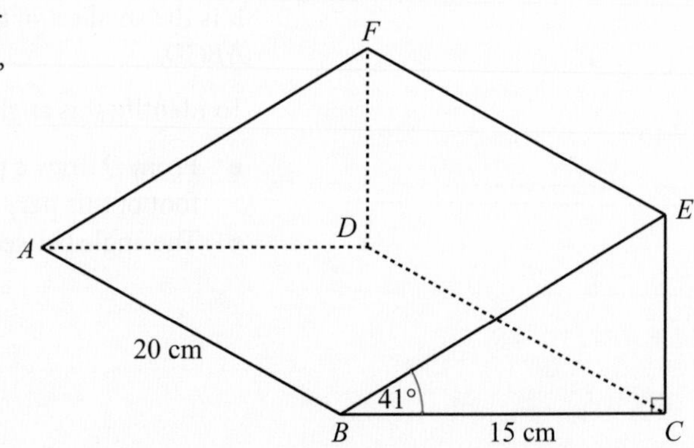

2 The cube shown in the diagram has sides of 5 m.

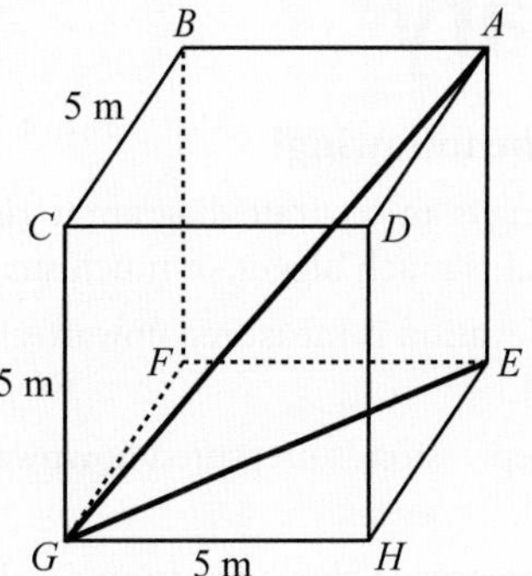

(a) Use Pythagoras' theorem to calculate the distance *EG*. Leave your answer in exact form.
(b) Use Pythagoras' theorem to calculate the distance *AG*. Leave your answer in exact form.
(c) Calculate the angle between the line *AG* and the plane *EFGH*. Give your answer to 1 decimal place.

3 The diagram shows a tetrahedron *ABCD*. *M* is the mid-point of *CD*. *AB* = 4 m, *AC* = 3 m, *AD* = 3 m.

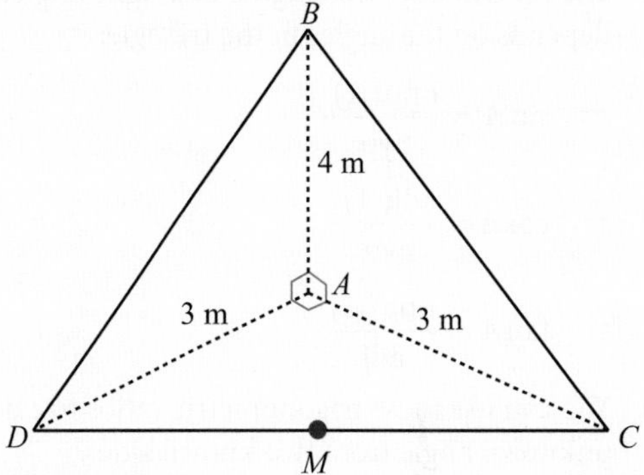

(a) Calculate angle $A\hat{C}B$.
(b) Calculate *BC*.
(c) Calculate *CD*.
(d) Calculate the length of *BM*.
(e) Calculate the angle $B\hat{C}D$.

4 A cuboid is 14 cm long, 5 cm wide and 3 cm high. Calculate:

(a) the length of the diagonal on its base
(b) the length of its longest diagonal
(c) the angle between the base and the longest diagonal.

5 *ABCD* is a tetrahedral drinks carton. Triangle *ABC* is the base and *B* is a right angle. *D* is vertically above *A*.

Calculate the following in terms of the appropriate lettered side(s):

(a) the length of *AC*
(b) length of *DA*
(c) the length of *DC*
(d) the size of angle $D\hat{A}B$
(e) the size of angle $B\hat{D}C$
(f) the size of angle $A\hat{D}C$.

Summary

Do you know the following?

- A scale drawing is an accurate diagram to represent something that is much bigger, or much smaller.
- An angle of elevation is measured upwards from the horizontal.
- An angle of depression is measured downwards from the horizontal.
- Bearings are measured clockwise from north.
- The ratio of any two lengths in a right-angled triangle depends on the angles in the triangle:
  - $\sin A = \dfrac{\text{opp}(A)}{\text{hyp}}$.
  - $\cos A = \dfrac{\text{adj}(A)}{\text{hyp}}$.
  - $\tan A = \dfrac{\text{opp}(A)}{\text{adj}}$.
- You can use these trigonometric ratios to calculate an unknown angle from two known sides.
- You can use these trigonometric ratios to calculate an unknown side from a known side and a known angle.
- The sine, cosine and tangent function can be extended beyond the angles in triangles.
- The sine and cosine rules can be used to calculate unknown sides and angles in triangles that are not right-angled.
- The sine rule is used for calculating an angle from another angle and two sides, or a side from another side and two known angles. The sides and angles must be arranged in opposite pairs.
- The cosine rule is used for calculating an angle from three known sides, or a side from a known angle and two known sides.
- You can calculate the area of a non right-angled triangle by using the sine ratio.

Are you able to.....?

- calculate angles of elevation
- calculate angles of depression
- use trigonometry to calculate bearings
- identify which sides are the opposite, adjacent and hypotenuse
- calculate the sine, cosine and tangent ratio when given lengths in a right-angled triangle
- use the sine, cosine and tangent ratios to find unknown angles and sides
- solve more complex problems by extracting right-angled triangles and combining sine, cosine and tangent ratios
- use the sine and cosine rules to find unknown angles and sides in right-angled triangles
- use sine and cosine rules to find unknown angles and sides in triangles that are not right-angled
- use trigonometry in three dimensions
- find the area of a triangle that is not right-angled.

Examination practice

Exam-style questions

1 The diagram shows the cross-section of the roof of Mr Haziz's house. The house is 12 m wide, $C\hat{A}B = 35°$ and $A\hat{C}B = 90°$.

Calculate the lengths of the two sides of the roof, AC and BC.

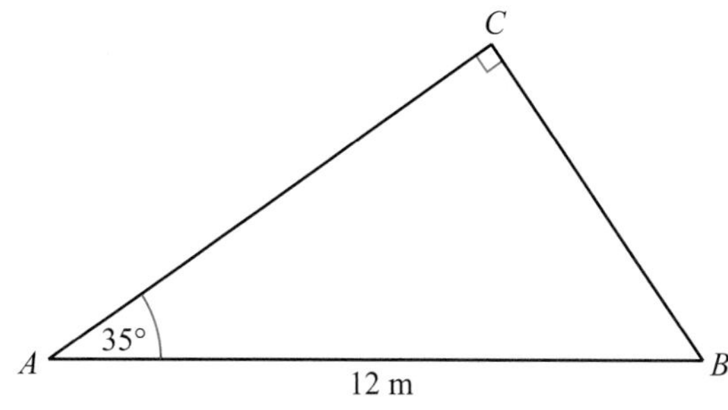

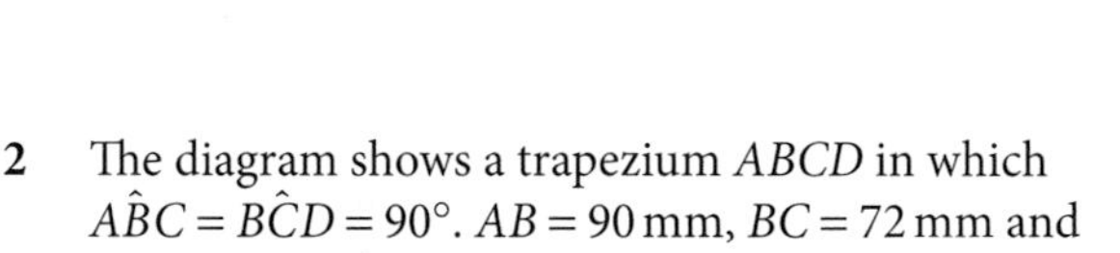

2 The diagram shows a trapezium $ABCD$ in which $A\hat{B}C = B\hat{C}D = 90°$. $AB = 90$ mm, $BC = 72$ mm and $CD = 25$ mm.

Calculate the angle $D\hat{A}B$.

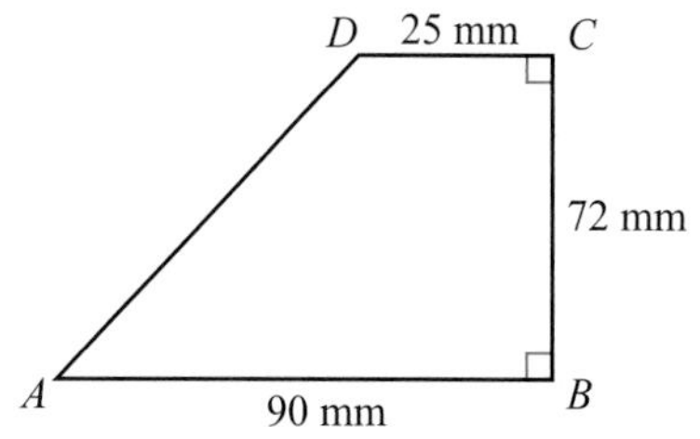

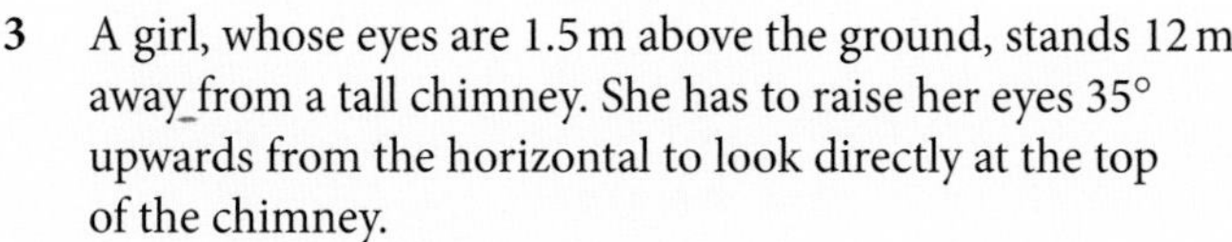

3 A girl, whose eyes are 1.5 m above the ground, stands 12 m away from a tall chimney. She has to raise her eyes 35° upwards from the horizontal to look directly at the top of the chimney.

Calculate the height of the chimney.

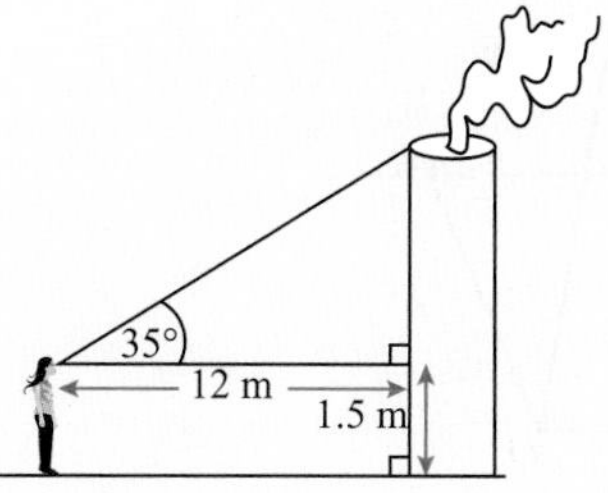

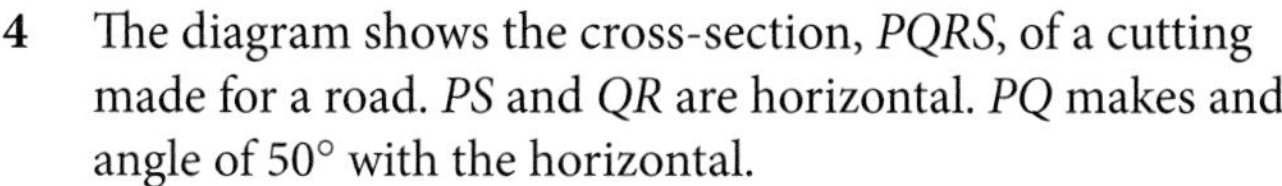

4 The diagram shows the cross-section, $PQRS$, of a cutting made for a road. PS and QR are horizontal. PQ makes and angle of 50° with the horizontal.

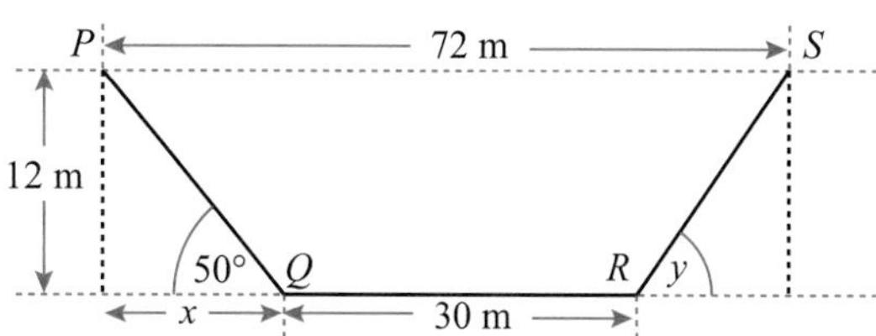

(a) Calculate the horizontal distance between P and Q (marked x in the diagram).

(b) Calculate the angle which RS makes with the horizontal (marked y in the diagram).

5 A game warden is standing at a point P alongside a road which runs north–south. There is a marker post at the point X, 60 m north of his position. The game warden sees a lion at Q on a bearing of 040° from him and due east of the marker post.

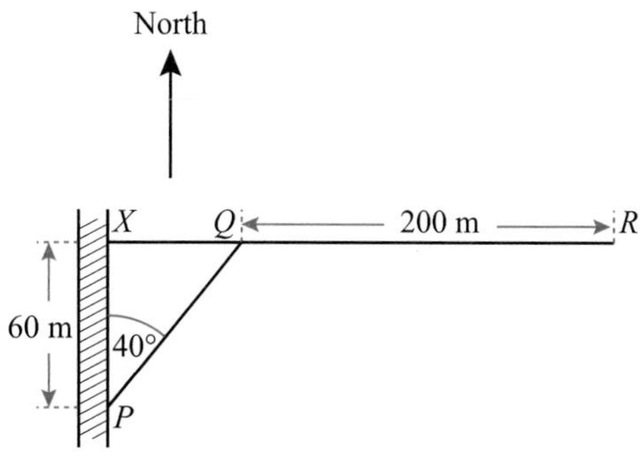

(a) (i) Show by calculation that the distance, QX, of the lion from the road is 50.3 m, correct to 3 significant figures.

(ii) Calculate the distance, PQ, of the lion from the game warden.

(b) Another lion appears at R, 200 m due east of the first one at Q.

(i) Write down the distance XR.

(ii) Calculate the distance, PR, of the second lion from the game warden.

(iii) Calculate the bearing of the second lion from the game warden, correct to the nearest degree.

6 In the ΔOAB, $A\hat{O}B = 15°$, $OA = 3$ m and $OB = 8$ m.
Calculate, correct to 2 decimal places:

(a) the length of AB

(b) the area of ΔOAB.

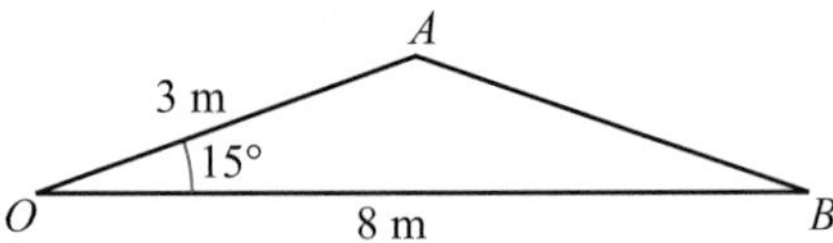

7 A pyramid, $VPQRS$, has a square base, $PQRS$, with sides of length 8 cm. Each sloping edge is 9 cm long.

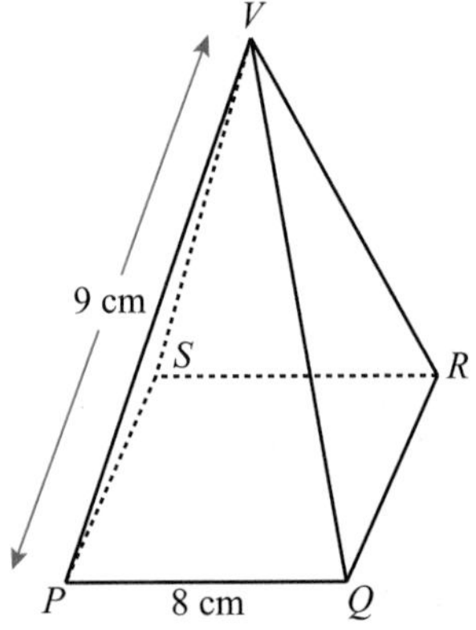

(a) Calculate the perpendicular height of the pyramid.

(b) Calculate the angle the sloping edge VP makes with the base.

8 The diagram shows the graph of $y = \sin x$ for $0 \leq x \leq 360$.

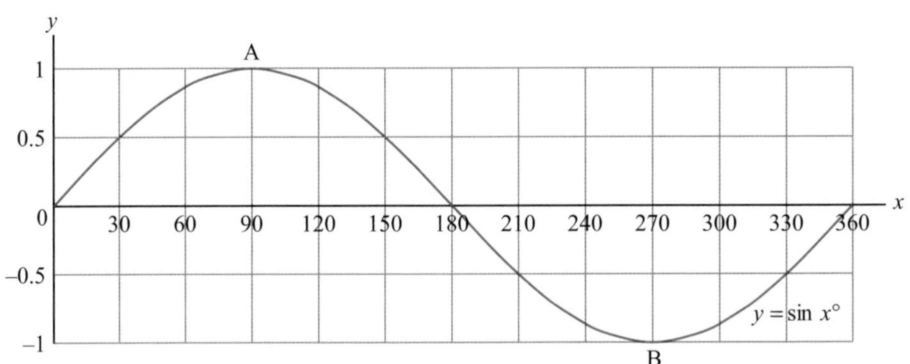

(a) Write down the co-ordinates of A, the point on the graph where $x = 90°$.

(b) Find the value of $\sin 270°$.

(c) On a copy of the diagram, draw the line $y = -\frac{1}{2}$ for $0 \leq x \leq 360$.

(d) How many solutions are there for the equation $\sin x = -\frac{1}{2}$ for $0 \leq x \leq 360$?

9 Two ships leave port P at the same time. One ship sails 60 km on a bearing of 030° to position A. The other ship sails 100 km on a bearing of 110° to position B.

(a) Calculate:

(i) the distance AB

(ii) $P\hat{A}B$

(iii) the bearing of B from A.

(b) Both ships took the same time, t hours, to reach their positions. The speed of the *faster* ship was 20 km/h. Write down:

(i) the value of t

(ii) the speed of the slower ship.

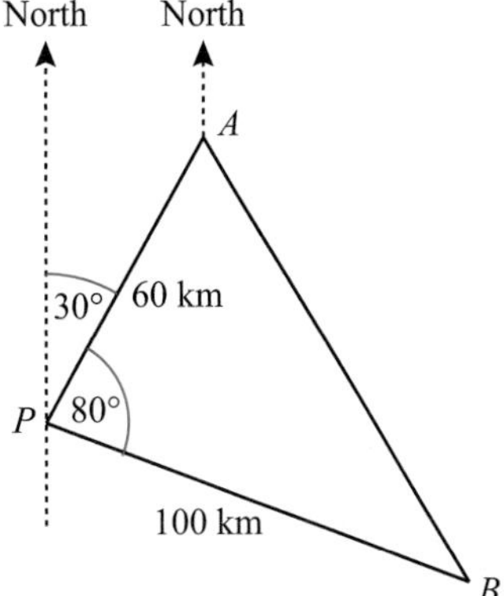

Past paper questions

1 The diagram shows a ladder of length 8 m leaning against a vertical wall.

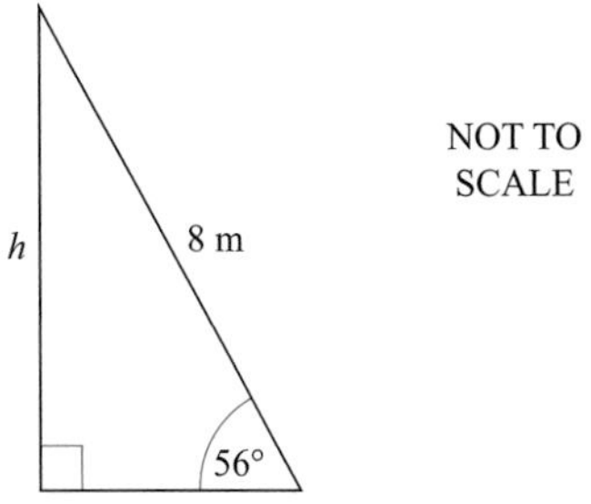

Use trigonometry to calculate h.
Give your answer correct to 2 significant figures. [3]

[Cambridge IGCSE Mathematics 0580 Paper 11 Q19 October/November 2013]

2

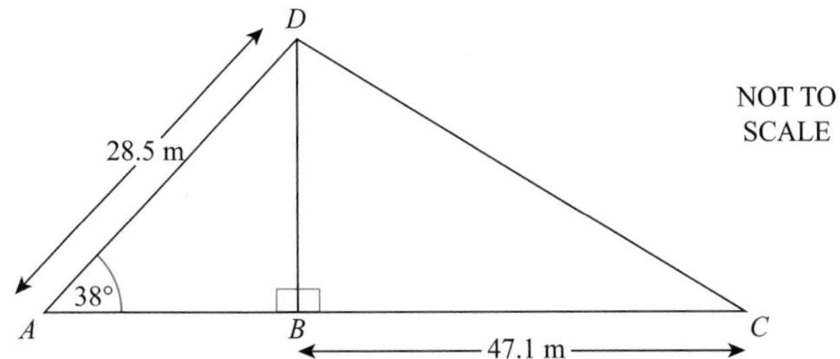

A flagpole, BD, is attached to level horizontal ground by ropes, AD and CD.
$AD = 28.5$ m, $BC = 47.1$ m and angle $DAB = 38°$.
Calculate

(a) BD, the height of the flagpole, [2]

(b) angle BCD. [2]

[Cambridge IGCSE Mathematics 0580 Paper 12 Q16 May/June 2011]

3

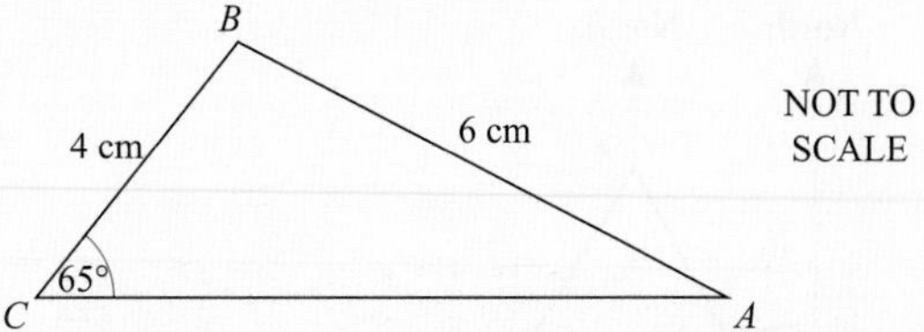

In triangle ABC, $AB = 6$ cm, $BC = 4$ cm and angle $BCA = 65°$.

Calculate

(a) angle CAB, [3]

(b) the area of triangle ABC. [3]

[Cambridge IGCSE Mathematics 0580 Paper 22 Q21 October/November 2013]

4

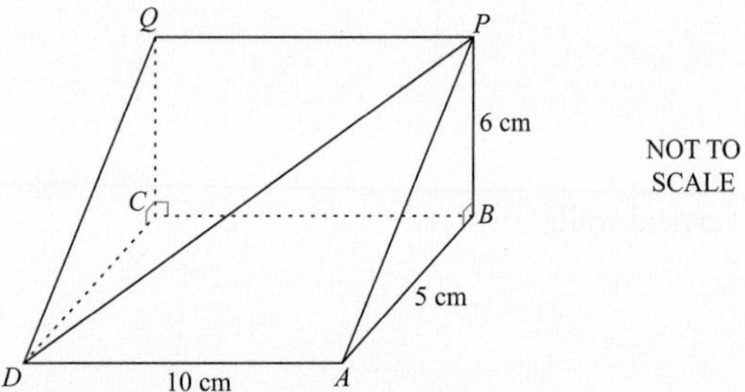

The diagram shows a triangular prism.

$ABCD$ is a horizontal rectangle with $DA = 10$ cm and $AB = 5$ cm.

$BCQP$ is a vertical rectangle and $BP = 6$ cm.

Calculate

(a) the length of DP, [3]

(b) the angle between DP and the horizontal rectangle $ABCD$. [3]

[Cambridge IGCSE Mathematics 0580 Paper 23 Q24 October/November 2012]

5 The diagram shows the positions of three towns A, B and C. The scale is 1 cm represents 2 km.

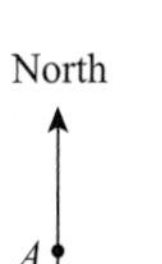

Scale: 1cm = 2 km

(a) **(i)** Find the distance in kilometres from A to B. [2]

(ii) Town D is 9 km from A on a bearing of 135°. Mark the position of town D on the diagram. [2]

(iii) Measure the bearing of A from C. [1]

[Cambridge IGCSE Mathematics 0580 Paper 33 Q10 October/November 2012]

16 Scatter diagrams and correlation

Key words

- Correlation
- Bivariate data
- Scatter diagram
- Dependent variable
- Positive correlation
- Trend
- Negative correlation
- No correlation
- Line of best fit
- Extrapolation

In this chapter you will learn how to:

- draw a scatter diagram for bivariate data
- identify whether or not there is a positive or negative correlation between the two variables
- decide whether or not a correlation is strong or weak
- draw a line of best fit
- use a line of best fit to make predictions
- decide how reliable your predictions are
- recognise the common errors that are often made with scatter diagrams.

The term 'supply and demand' may be something that you have already heard about. Manufacturers are more likely to deliver efficient services if they fully understand the connections between the demands of customers and the quantities of goods that must be produced to make the best profit.

On a hot day it can be frustrating to go for an ice cream and find that the vendor has run out. Vendors know that there is a good link between the hours of sunshine and the number of ice creams they will need. A knowledge of how good the **correlation** is will help them ensure they have enough stock to keep everyone happy.

16.1 Introduction to bivariate data

REWIND

You learned how to summarise data and draw conclusions on it in chapters 4 and 12. ◀

So far you have seen how to summarise data and draw conclusions based on your calculations. In all cases the data has been a collection of single measurements or observations. Now think about the following problem.

An ice cream parlour sells its good throughout the year and the manager needs to look into how sales change as the daily temperature rises or falls. He chooses 10 days at random, records the temperature and records the total takings at the tills. The results are shown in the table:

Day	A	B	C	D	E	F	G	H	I	J
Temperature (°C)	4	18	12	32	21	−3	0	10	22	31
Total takings (sales) ($)	123	556	212	657	401	23	45	171	467	659

Notice that *two measurements* are taken on each day and are recorded as *pairs*. This type of data is known as **bivariate data**. You can see this data much more clearly if you plot the values on a **scatter diagram**.

Drawing a scatter diagram

To draw a scatter diagram you first must decide which variable is the **dependent variable**. In other words, which variable depends on the other. In this case it seems sensible that the total takings will depend on the temperature because people are more likely to buy an ice cream if it is hot!

The scatter diagram will have a pair of axes, as shown below, with the dependent variable represented by the vertical axis. If the data in the table are treated as if they are co-ordinates, then the diagram begins to take shape:

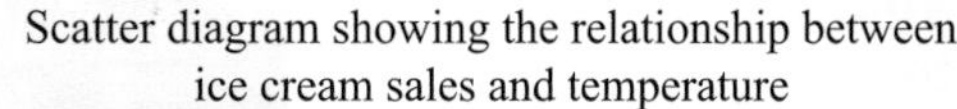

Scatter diagram showing the relationship between ice cream sales and temperature

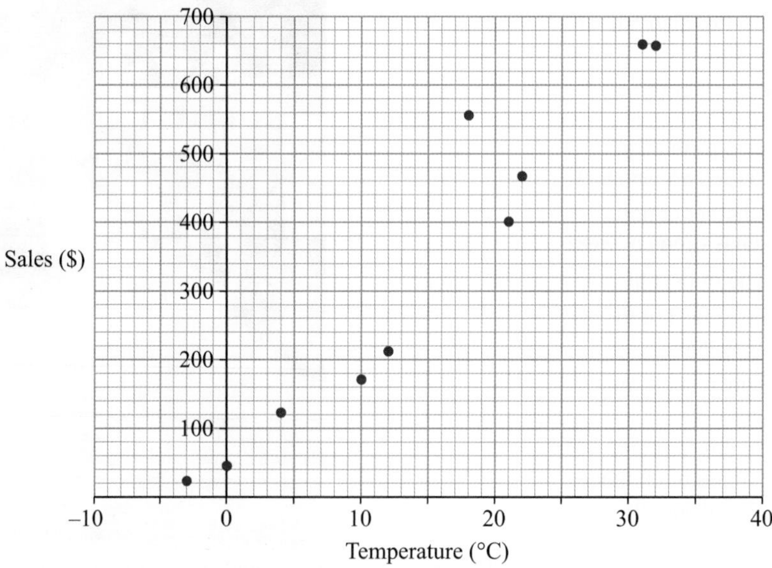

Notice that there seems to be a relationship between the ice cream sales and the temperature. In fact, the sales rise as the temperature rises. This is called a **positive correlation**. The **trend** seems to be that the points roughly run from the bottom left of the diagram to the top right. Had the points been placed from the top left to bottom right you would conclude that the sales decrease as the temperature increases. Under these circumstances you would have a **negative correlation**. If there is no obvious pattern then you have **no correlation**. The clearer the pattern, the stronger the correlation.

Examples of the 'strength' of the correlation:

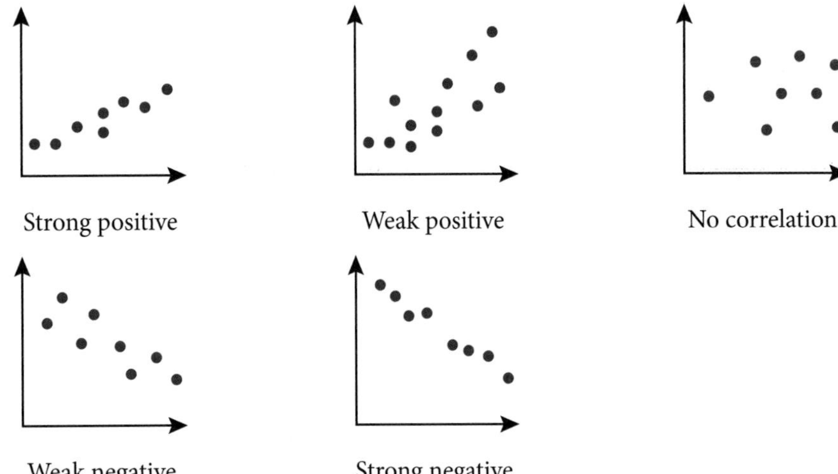

You should always be ready to state whether or not a correlation is positive, negative, strong or weak.

Notice on the graph of ice cream sales that one of the results seems to stand outside of the general pattern. Unusually high sales were recorded on one day. This may have been a special event or just an error. Any such points should be noted and investigated.

You can also show the general trend by drawing a **line of best fit**. In the diagram below a line has been drawn so that it passes as close to as many points as possible.

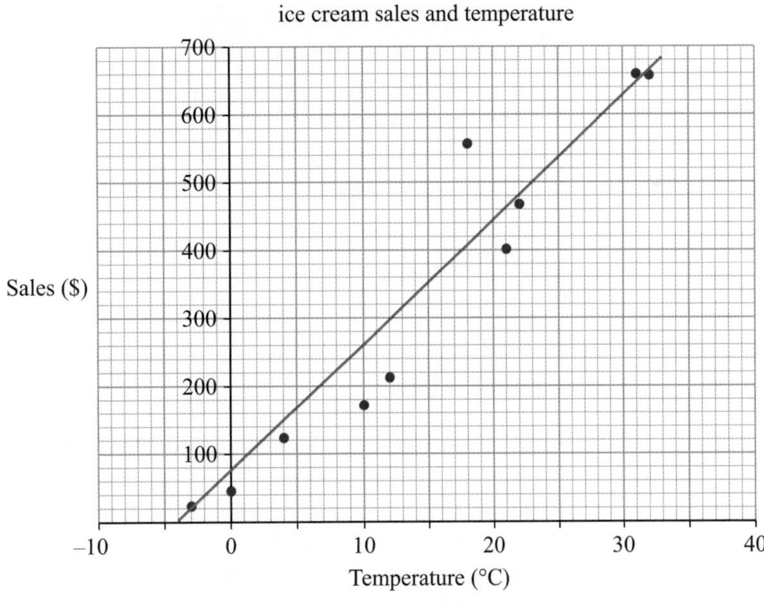

This is the line of best fit and can be used to make predictions based on the collected data.

For example, if you want to try to predict the ice cream sales on a day with an average temperature of 27°, you carry out the following steps:

1 Locate 27° on the temperature axis.

2 Draw a clear line vertically from this point to the line of best fit.

3 Draw a horizontal line to the sales axis from the appropriate point on the line of best fit.

4 Read the sales value from the graph.

The diagram now looks like this:

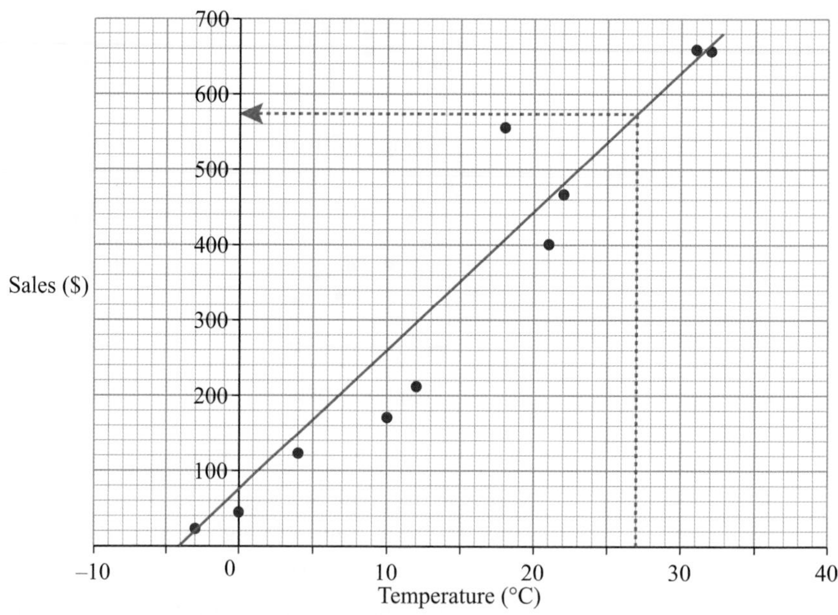

Here, the estimated value is approximately $575.

Worked example 1

Mr. Leatherfoot owns a shoe shop and is trying to help his staff work more efficiently. He claims that a person's height, in cm, can give a very good idea of the length of their foot. To investigate this claim, Mr. Leatherfoot collects the heights and foot lengths of 10 people and records the results in the table below:

Person	A	B	C	D	E	F	G	H	I	J
Foot length (cm)	28.2	31.1	22.5	28.6	25.4	13.2	29.9	33.4	22.5	19.4
Height (cm)	156.2	182.4	165.3	155.1	165.2	122.9	176.3	183.4	163.0	143.1

(a) Draw a scatter diagram, with Height on the horizontal axis and Foot length on the vertical axis.
(b) State what type of correlation the diagram shows.
(c) Draw a line of best fit.
(d) Estimate the foot length of a person with height 164 cm.
(e) Estimate the height of a person with foot length 17 cm.
(f) Comment on the likely accuracy of your estimates in parts **(d)** and **(e)**.

(a)

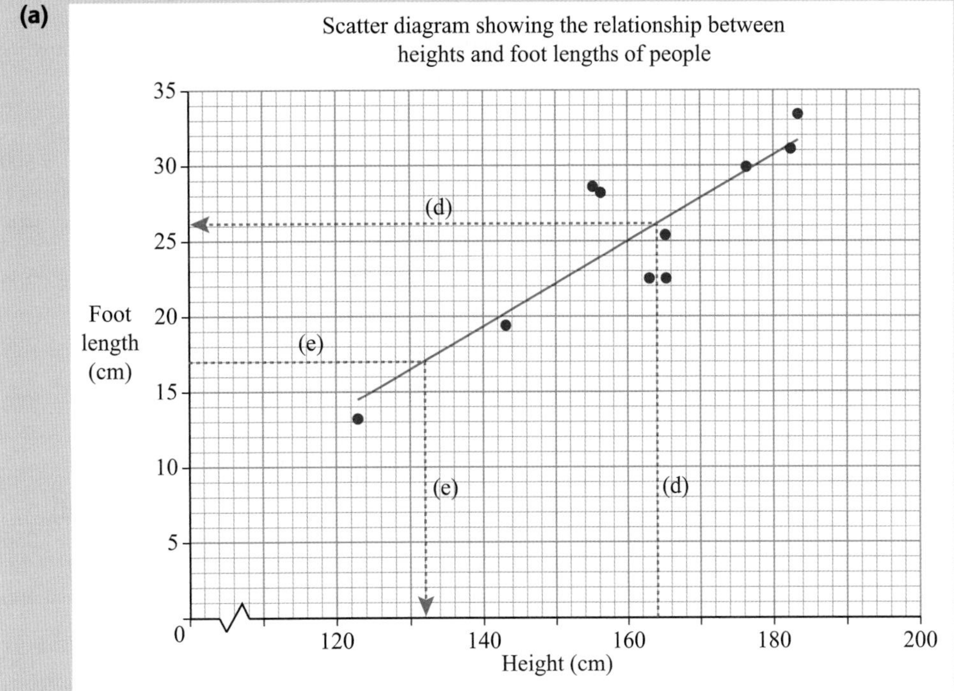

(b) This is a strong positive correlation because foot length generally increases with height.

(c) The line of best fit is drawn on the diagram.

(d) The appropriate lines are drawn on the diagram. A height of 164 cm corresponds to a foot length of approximately 26 cm.

(e) A foot length of 17 cm corresponds to a height of approximately 132 cm.

(f) Most points are reasonably close to the line, so the correlation is fairly strong. This means that the line of best fit will allow a good level of accuracy when estimates are made.

When commenting on correlation, always make sure that you refer back to the original context of the question.

Golden rule

Before you try to draw and interpret some scatter diagrams for yourself you should be aware of an important rule:

- never use a diagram to make predictions *outside* of the range of the collected data.

For example, in the foot length/height diagram above, the data does not include any heights above 183.4 cm. The trend may not continue or may change 'shape' for greater heights, so you should not try to predict the foot length for a person of height, say, 195 cm without collecting more data.

The process of extending the line of best fit beyond the collected data is called **extrapolation.**

Prediction when correlation is weak

If you are asked to comment on a prediction that you have made, always keep in mind the strength of the correlation as shown in the diagram. If the correlation is weak you should say that your prediction may not be very reliable.

Stating answers in context

It is good to relate all conclusions back to the original problem. Don't just say 'strong positive correlation'. Instead you might say that 'it is possible to make good predictions of height from foot length' or 'good estimates of ice cream sales can be made from this data'.

Exercise 16.1 *Living maths*

1 What is the correlation shown by each of the following scatter diagrams? In each case you should comment on the strength of correlation.

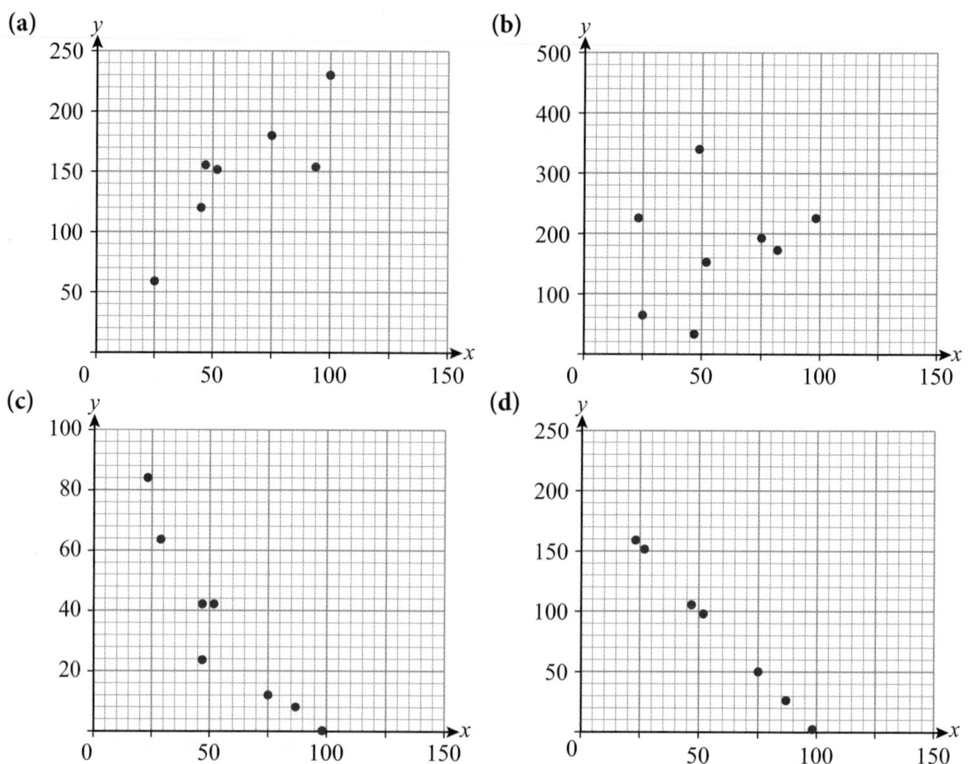

2 The widths and lengths of the leaves (both measured in cm) on a particular tree are recorded in the table below.

Width (cm)	14	25	67	56	26	78	33	35	14	36	13	36	25	62	25
Length (cm)	22	63	170	141	76	201	93	91	24	91	23	67	51	151	79

(a) Draw a scatter diagram for this data with the lengths of the leaves shown on the vertical axis.
(b) Comment on the strength of correlation.
(c) Draw a line of best fit for this data.
(d) Estimate the length of a leaf that has width 20 cm.

3 Emma is conducting a survey into the masses of dogs and the duration of their morning walk in minutes. She presents the results in the table below.

Duration of walk (min)	23	45	12	5	18	67	64	15	28	39
Mass (kg)	22	5	12	32	13	24	6	38	21	12

(a) Draw a scatter diagram to show the mass of each dog against the duration of the morning walk in minutes. (Plot the mass of the dog on the vertical axis.)

(b) How strong is the correlation between the masses of the dogs and the duration of their morning walks?

(c) Can you think of a reason for this conclusion?

4 Mr. Bobby is investigating the relationship between the number of sales assistants working in a department store and the length of time (in seconds) he spends waiting in a queue to be served. His results are shown in the table below.

Number of sales assistants	12	14	23	28	14	11	17	21	33	21	22	13	7
Waiting time (seconds)	183	179	154	150	224	236	221	198	28	87	77	244	266

(a) Draw a scatter diagram to show the length of time Mr. Bobby spends queuing and the number of sales assistants working in the store.

(b) Describe the correlation between the number of sales assistants and the time spent queuing.

(c) Draw a line of best fit for this data.

(d) Mr. Bobby visits a very large department store and counts 45 sales assistants. What happens when Mr Bobby tries to extend and use his scatter diagram to predict his queuing time at this store?

5 Eyal is investigating the relationship between the amount of time spent watching television during a week and the score on a maths test taken a week later. The results for 12 students are shown on the scatter diagram below.

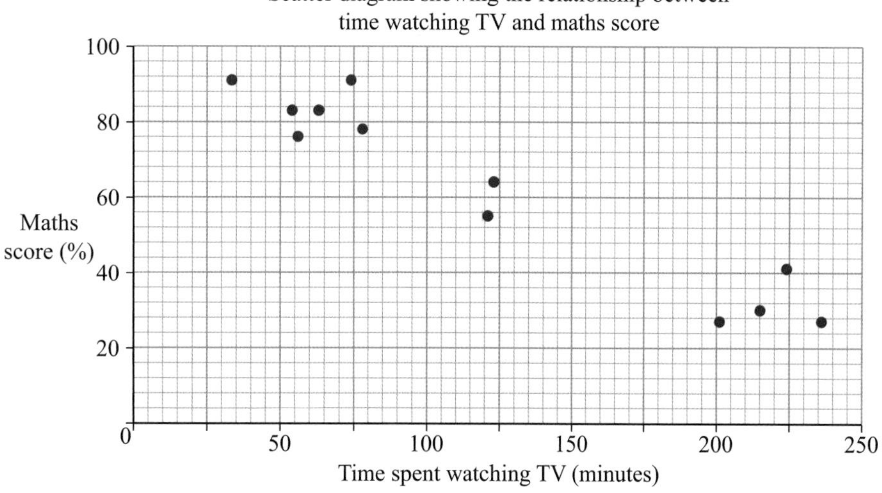

The table shows some of Eyal's results, but it is incomplete.

TV watching (min)		34	215	54		78	224	236	121	74	63	
Maths score (%)	64		30	83	76	78	41		55	91	83	27

(a) Copy the table and use the scatter diagram to fill in the missing values.

(b) Comment on the correlation between the length of time spent watching television and the maths score.

(c) Copy the diagram and draw a line of best fit.

(d) Aneesh scores 67% on the maths test. Estimate the amount of time that Aneesh spent watching television.

(e) Comment on the likely accuracy of your estimate in part **(d)**.

Summary

Do you know the following?

- You can use a scatter diagram to assess the strength of any relationship between two variables.
- If one of the variables generally increases as the other variable increases, then you say that there is a positive correlation.
- If one of the variables generally decreases as the other variable increases, then you say that there is a negative correlation.
- The clearer the relationship, the stronger the correlation.
- You can draw a line of best fit if the points seem to lie close to a straight line.
- The line of best fit can be used to predict values of one variable from values of the other.
- You should only make predictions using a line of best fit that has been drawn within the range of the data.

Are you able to.....?

- draw a scatter diagram
- describe the relationship between the variables shown
- use a scatter diagram to make predictions.

Examination practice

Exam-style questions

1 The table below shows the sizes (in square metres) and prices (in UK pounds) of several paintings on display in a gallery.

Painting	A	B	C	D	E	F	G	H
Painting area (m^2)	1.4	2.3	0.8	0.1	0.7	2.2	3.4	2.6
Price (£)	2400	6565	1800	45	8670	4560	10 150	8950

Painting	I	J	K	L	M	N	O
Painting area (m^2)	1.1	1.3	3.7	1.5	0.4	1.9	0.6
Price (£)	3025	4560	11230	4050	1450	5420	1475

(a) Draw a scatter diagram for this data. The price should be represented by the vertical axis.
(b) Which painting is unusually expensive? Explain your answer clearly.
(c) *Assuming that the unusually expensive painting is not to be included* draw a line of best fit for this data.
(d) A new painting is introduced to the collection. The painting measures 1.5 m by 1.5 m. Use your graph to estimate the price of the painting.
(e) Another painting is introduced to the collection. The painting measures 2.1 m by 2.1 m. Explain why you should not try to use your scatter diagram to estimate the price of this painting.

2 A particular type of printing machine has been sold with a strong recommendation that regular maintenance takes place even when the machine appears to be working properly.

Several companies are asked to provide the machine manufacturer with two pieces of information: (x) the number of hours spent maintaining the machine in the first year and (y) the number of minutes required for repair in the second year. The results are shown in the table below.

Maintenance hours (x)	42	71	22	2	60	66	102
Repairs in second year (y) (minutes)	4040	2370	4280	4980	4000	3170	940

Maintenance hours (x)	78	33	39	111	45	12
Repairs in second year (y) (minutes)	1420	3790	3270	500	3380	4420

(a) Draw a scatter diagram to show this information. You should plot the second year repair times on the vertical axis.
(b) Describe the correlation between maintenance time in the first year and repair time needed in the second year.
(c) Draw a line of best fit on your scatter diagram.
(d) Another company schedules 90 hours of maintenance for the first year of using their machine. Use your graph to estimate the repair time necessary in the second year.
(e) Another company claims that they will schedule 160 hours of maintenance for the first year. Describe what happens when you try to predict the repair time for the second year of machine use.
(f) You are asked by a manager to work out the maintenance time that will reduce the repair time to zero. Use your graph to suggest such a maintenance level and comment on the reliability of your answer.

Past paper questions

1 On the first day of each month, a café owner records the midday temperature (°C) and the number of hot meals sold.

Month	J	F	M	A	M	J	J	A	S	O	N	D
Temperature (°C)	2	4	9	15	21	24	28	27	23	18	10	5
Number of hot meals	38	35	36	24	15	10	4	5	12	20	18	32

(a) Complete the scatter diagram.
The results for January to June have been plotted for you.

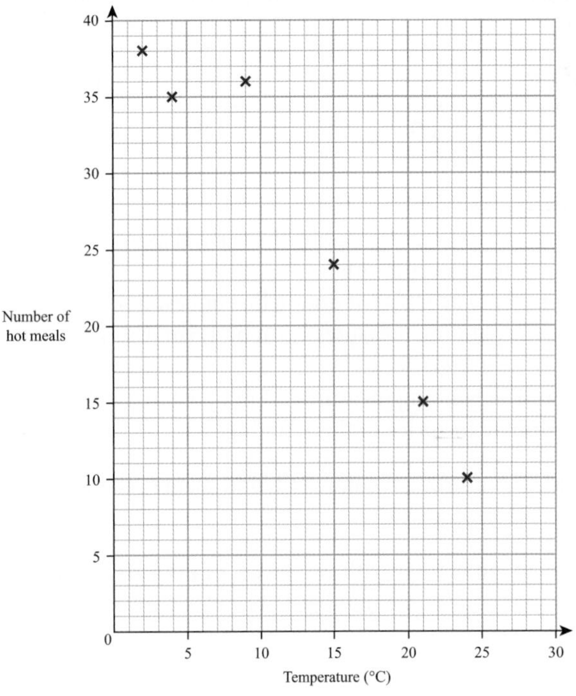

[2]

(b) On the grid, draw the line of best fit. [1]

(c) What type of correlation does this scatter diagram show? [1]

[Cambridge IGCSE Mathematics 0580 Paper 13 Q18 May/June 2013]

17 Managing money

Key words

- Earnings
- Wages
- Salary
- Commission
- Gross income
- Deductions
- Net income
- Tax threshold
- Interest
- Simple interest
- Interest rate
- Principal
- Compound interest
- Cost price
- Selling price
- Profit
- Loss
- Discount

In this chapter you will learn how to:

- calculate earnings (wages and salaries) in different situations
- use and manipulate a formula to calculate simple interest payable and due on a range of loans and investments
- solve problems related to simple and compound interest
- apply what you already know about percentages to work out discounts, profit and loss in everyday contexts
- use a calculator effectively to perform financial calculations
- read and interpret financial data provided in tables and charts.

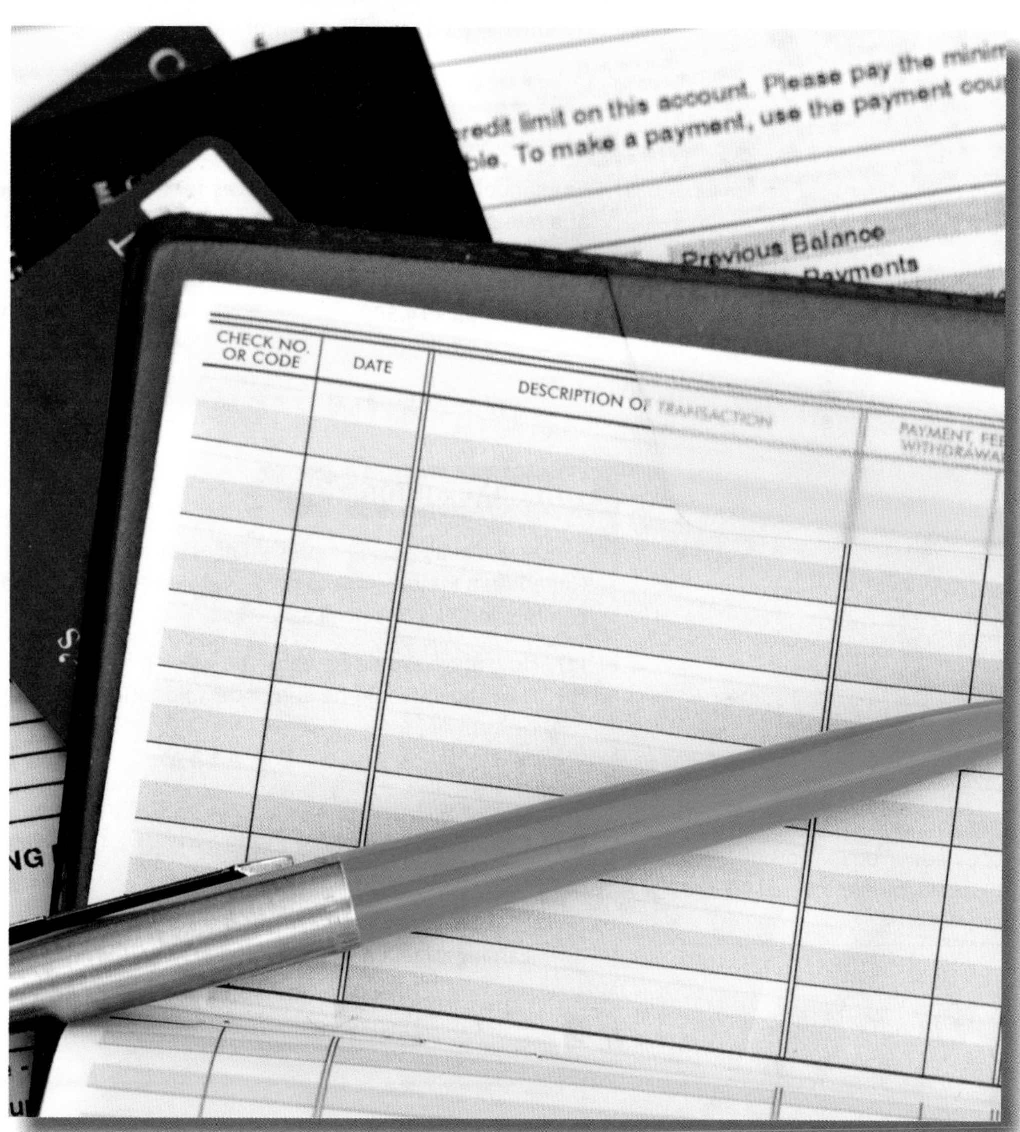

Knowing how to work well with money is an important skill that you will use again and again throughout your life.

During your life so far, you will have solved problems relating to money on a daily basis. You will continue to do this as you get older but the problems you have to solve may become more complicated as you start earning and spending money, borrowing money and saving money.

In this chapter you will apply some of the maths skills you have already learned to solve real world problems. You will use your calculator to find the answers quickly and efficiently.

17.1 Earning money

When you are employed you earn money (get paid) for the work you do. **Earnings** can be worked out in different ways. Make sure you understand these terms:

- **Wages** – pay based on a fixed number of hours worked, usually paid weekly. Extra hours of work are called overtime and these are paid at a higher rate.
- **Salary** – pay based on a fixed yearly amount, usually paid monthly. Overtime may be paid, or workers may be given time off in exchange.
- Piece work – pay based on the number of items produced.
- **Commission** – pay is based on a percentage of sales made; sometimes a low wage, called a retainer, is paid as well as commission.

Worked example 1

Emmanuel makes beaded necklaces for a curio stand. He is paid in South African rand at a rate of R14.50 per completed necklace. He is able to supply 55 necklaces per week. Calculate his weekly income.

Income = 55×14.50 = R797.50	Multiply items produced by the rate paid.

Worked example 2

Sanjay works as a sales representative for a company that sells mobile phones in the United Arab Emirates. He is paid a retainer of 800 dirhams (Dhs) per week plus a commission of 4.5% of all sales.

(a) How much would he earn in a week if he made no sales?
(b) How much would he earn if he sold four phones at Dhs3299 each in a week?

(a)	Dhs800	If he made no sales, he would earn no commission, only his retainer.
(b)	Commission = 4.5% of (3299×4) = $0.045 \times 13\,196$ = 593.82 Earnings = retainer + commission = Dhs800 + Dhs593.82 = Dhs1393.82	Calculate 4.5% of the total sales Sanjay made. Add this to the retainer of Dhs 800.

REWIND

The decimal equivalents of percentage were covered in chapter 5. ◀

Worked example 3

Josh's hourly rate of pay is \$12.50. He is paid 'time-and-a-half' for work after hours and on Saturdays and 'double-time' for Sundays and Public Holidays.

One week he worked 5.5 hours on Saturday and 3 hours on Sunday. How much overtime pay would he earn?

Saturday overtime $= 1.5 \times \$12.50 \times 5.5$ $= \$103.13$	(time-and-a-half = $1.5 \times$ normal time)
Sunday overtime $= 2 \times \$12.50 \times 3$ $= \$75$	(double-time = $2 \times$ normal time)
Total overtime $= \$103.13 + \$75.00$ $= \$178.13$	

Exercise 17.1 *Living maths*

1 A waiter earns $8.25 per hour. How much would she earn for a six-hour shift?

2 How much would a receptionist earn for working a 35-hour week if her rate of pay is $9.50 per hour?

3 Calculate the hourly rate for each of the following:

(a) $67.50 for five hours
(b) $245.10 for a 38-hour week
(c) $126.23 for 13.5 hours
(d) $394.88 for five $6\frac{1}{2}$-hour shifts
(e) $71.82 for working five hours and 15 minutes.

4 A truck driver is paid $15.45 per tonne of wood pulp delivered to a factory in Malaysia. If he delivers 135 tonnes to the factory, how much will he earn?

5 A team of workers in a factory is paid $23.25 per pallet of goods produced. If a team of five workers produces 102 pallets in a shift, how much will each person in the team have earned that shift?

REWIND

Look for a connection between these questions and percentage increases in chapter 5. ◄

6 An estate agent is paid a retainer of $150 per week plus a commission on sales. The rate of commission is 2.5% on sales up to $150 000 and 1.75% on amounts above that. How much would she earn in a week if she sold a house for $220 000 and an apartment for $125 000?

7 Here is the time sheet for five workers in a factory. Calculate each person's income for the week if their standard rate of pay is $8.40 per hour.

Worker	Normal hours worked	Hours overtime at time-and-a-half	Hours overtime at double-time
Annie	35	2	0
Bonnie	25	3	4
Connie	30	1.5	1.75
Donny	40	0	4
Elizabeth	20	3.75	2

8 The *Sunday Times* newspaper in South Africa published a list of the annual earnings in Rands (R) of ten prominent businessmen in December 2010. Here is the list:

Name	What they earned in a year (R million)
Pine Pienaar	63.1
Norbert Platt	58.1
Marius Kloppers	54.4
Paul Adams	47.4
Carl Grim	44.0
Jabu Mabuza	41.1
Timothy McClure	41.1
Johan Rupert	41.0
Graham Mackay	37.2
Julian Roberts	32.3

(a) Calculate each person's earnings per month.
(b) Assuming a tax rate of 35%, work out how much tax each person would pay on these earnings.
(c) How much would they earn per month after tax is deducted?
(d) If the average working week is 40 hours long and each person took three weeks leave during the year, what did the highest and lowest earning person earn on average per working hour (before tax)?

Deductions from earnings

Gross earnings, deductions and net income are normally shown on a payment advice (slip) which is given to each worker when they get paid.

Gross income (earnings) refers to the total amount a person earns.

Deductions, such as income tax, pension contributions, unemployment and health insurance and union dues are often taken from the gross earnings before the person is paid. The amount that is left over after deductions is called the **net income**.

Net income = Gross income – deductions

Exercise 17.2

1 For each person shown in the table:
(a) calculate their net income
(b) calculate what percentage their net income is of their gross income. Give your answers to the nearest whole percent.

Employee	Gross weekly earnings ($)	Tax ($)	Other deductions ($)
B Willis	675.90	235.45	123.45
M Freeman	456.50	245.20	52.41
J Malkovich	1289.00	527.45	204.35
H Mirren	908.45	402.12	123.20
M Parker	853.30	399.10	90.56

REWIND
Look for a connection between these questions and percentage increases in chapter 5. ◀

2 Use the gross weekly earnings to work out:
(a) the mean weekly earnings
(b) the median weekly earnings
(c) the range of earnings.

Living maths

3 Study the two pay advice slips below. For each worker, calculate:

(a) the difference between gross and net income
(b) the percentage of gross income that each takes home as net income.

Poovan's Plastics Pty Ltd PAYMENT ADVICE				
EMPLOYEE DETAILS			**SEPTEMBER**	
M Badru Employee no: MBN 0987			Income tax no. Bank details Account no.	0987654321A Big Bucks Bank 9876598
EARNINGS			**DEDUCTIONS**	
Details	Taxable Amount	Payable Amount	Description	Amount
Salary Medical Car allowance	12 876.98 650.50 1 234.99	12 876.98 0.00 0.00	UIF Funeral plan Group life insurance Union membership PAYE	89.35 9.65 132.90 32.00 3 690.62
	14 762.47	12 876.98		3 954.52
			NET PAY:	**8 922.46**

Nehru–Kapoor Network Services		Employee name: B Singh Job title: Clerk		ID number: 630907000000	
Hours/Days		**Earnings**		**Deductions**	
Normal hours O/time @ 1.5 hours	84.00 11.00	Wages Overtime @ 1.5	1402.80 275.55	Income tax UIF Pension fund Loan Sickpay	118.22 18.94 105.21 474.00 8.42
Deduct tools × 2 Deduct cellphone × 2					
Year-to-date Taxable Benefits Tax paid	 22 881.40 0.00 509.30				
Current period Company Contributions	 358.12	TOTAL EARNINGS	1678.35	TOTAL DEDUCTIONS NET PAY	724.79 953.56

If you earn less than a certain amount each year you don't have to pay income tax. This amount is called the **tax threshold**.

In some Islamic countries, tax is not deducted from earnings. Instead people pay a portion of their earnings as a religious obligation (Zakat).

Getting information from tax tables

In most countries, employers have to take taxes from earnings and pay them over to the government's tax authority. The tax authority publishes a table of tax rates every year so that employers can work out how much tax to deduct. Here is a portion of a tax table:

TAXABLE INCOME (in $)	RATES OF TAX
0 – 132 000	18% of each $1
132 001 – 210 000	$23 760 + 25% of the amount above $132 000
210 001 – 290 000	$43 260 + 30% of the amount above $210 000
290 001 – 410 000	$67 260 + 35% of the amount above $290 000
410 001 – 525 000	$109 260 + 38% of the amount above $410 000
525 001 and above	$152 960 + 40% of the amount above $525 000

Worked example 4

Mr Smith's taxable income is $153 772.00 p.a. How much tax must he pay

(a) per year? **(b)** per month?

(a) To work out the yearly tax, find his tax bracket on the table. His income is in row two because it is between $132 001 and $210 000.

He has to pay $23 760 + 25% of his earnings above $132 000.

$153 772 − $132 000 = $21 772
25% of $21 772 = $5443

Tax payable = $23 760 + $5443 = $29 203 per year

(b) $29 203 ÷ 12 = $2433.58

To find the monthly tax, divide the total from part (a) by 12.

Exercise 17.3 *Living maths*

1 Use the tax table above to work out the annual tax payable and the monthly tax deductions for each of the following taxable incomes.

(a) $98 000 **(b)** $120 000 **(c)** $129 000 **(d)** $135 000 **(e)** $178 000

2 Use the tax table below to answer the questions that follow.

Single person (no dependants)	
Taxable income	**Income tax payable**
$0–$8375	10% of the amount over $0
$8375–$34 000	$837.50 plus 15% of the amount over $8375
$34 000–$82 400	$4681.25 plus 25% of the amount over $34 000
$82 400–$171 850	$16 781.25 plus 28% of the amount over $82 400
$171 850–$373 650	$41 827.25 plus 33% of the amount over $171 850
$373 650+	$108 421.25 plus 35% of the amount over $373 650

(a) Li-Gon has a taxable income of \$40 000 for this tax year. He tells his friends that he is in the 25% tax bracket.
   (i) Is this correct?
   (ii) Does it mean that he pays \$10 000 in income tax? Explain why or why not.
   (iii) When Li-Gon checks his tax return, he finds that he only has to pay \$6181.25 income tax. Show how this amount is calculated by the revenue services.

(b) How much tax would a person earning \$250 000 pay in this tax year?
(c) Cecelia earned \$30 000 in taxable income in this year. Her employer deducts \$320.25 income tax per month from her salary.
   (i) Will Cecelia have to pay in additional tax at the end of the tax year or will she be due for a tax refund as a result of overpaying?
   (ii) How much is the amount due in **(i)** above?

3 Income tax is one form of direct taxation. Carry out some research of your own to find out about each type of tax below, who pays this tax, how it is paid, and the rate/s at which it is charged.

(a) Value-Added-Tax
(b) General sales tax
(c) Customs and Excise duties
(d) Capital Gains Tax
(e) Estate duties

17.2 Borrowing and investing money

In Islam, interest (*riba*) is forbidden so Islamic banks do not charge interest on loans or pay interest on investments. Instead, Islamic banks charge a fee for services which is fixed at the beginning of the transaction (*murabaha*). For investments, the bank and its clients share any profits or losses incurred over a given period in proportion to their investment (*musharaka*). Many banks in Islamic countries have the responsibility of collecting *Zakat* on behalf of the government. *Zakat* is a religious tax which all Muslims are obliged to pay. It is usually calculated at about 2.5% of personal wealth.

When you borrow money or you buy things on credit, you are normally charged **interest** for the use of the money. Similarly, when you save or invest money, you are paid interest by the bank or financial institution in return for allowing them to keep and use your money.

Simple interest

Simple interest is a fixed percentage of the original amount borrowed or invested. In other words, if you borrow \$100 at an **interest rate** of 5% per year, you will be charged \$5 interest for every year of the loan.

Simple interest involves adding the interest amount to the original amount at regular intervals. The formula used to calculate simple interest is:

$I = \frac{PRT}{100}$, where:

P = the **principal**, which is the original amount borrowed or saved

R = the interest rate

T = the time (in years)

Per annum means each year or annually. It is often abbreviated to p.a.

Worked example 5

\$500 is invested at 10% per annum simple interest. How much interest is earned in three years?

10% of \$500 = $\frac{10}{100} \times 500 = \$50$	The interest rate is 10% per annum.
The interest every year is \$50. So after three years, the interest is: $3 \times \$50 = \$150$	Multiply by the number of years.

Worked example 6

Sam invested $400 at 15% per annum for three years. How much money did he have at the end of the period?

At the end of the period he would have P + I (the principal plus the interest paid).

$I = \frac{PRT}{100}$ and P = 400, so:

$$P + I = 400 + \frac{(400 \times 15 \times 3)}{100}$$
$$= 400 + 180$$
$$= \$580$$

Worked example 7

How long will it take for $250 invested at the rate of 8% per annum simple interest to amount to $310?

Amount = principal + interest
Interest = amount − principal
∴ Interest = $310 − $250 = $60

Rate = 8% per annum $= \frac{8}{100} \times 250 = \$20$

So the interest per year is $20.
Total interest (60) ÷ annual interest (20) = 3
So it will take three years for $250 to amount to $310 at the rate of 8% per annum simple interest.

Worked example 8

Calculate the rate of simple interest if a principal of $250 amounts to $400 in three years.

Interest paid = $400 − $250 = $150

$I = \frac{PRT}{100}$

Change the subject of the formula to R to find the rate.

$100I = PRT$

$R = \frac{100I}{PT} = \frac{100 \times 150}{250 \times 3} = 20$

So, the interest rate = 20%

Remember

You can manipulate the formula to find any of the values:

$I = \frac{PRT}{100}$

$P = \frac{100I}{RT}$

$R = \frac{100I}{PT}$

$T = \frac{100I}{PR}$

Exercise 17.4

1 For each of the following savings amounts, calculate the simple interest earned.

Principal amount ($)	Interest rate (%)	Time invested
500	1	3 years
650	0.75	$2\frac{1}{2}$ years
1000	1.25	5 years

Principal amount ($)	Interest rate (%)	Time invested
1200	4	$6\frac{3}{4}$ years
875	5.5	3 years
900	6	2 years
699	7.25	3.75 years
1200	8	9 months
150 000	$9\frac{1}{2}$	18 months

2 Calculate how much would have to be repaid in total for the following loans.

Principal amount ($)	Interest rate (%)	Time invested
500	4.5	2 years
650	5	2 years
1000	6	2 years
1200	12	18 months
875	15	18 months
900	15	3 years
699	20	9 months
1200	21.25	8 months
150 000	18	$1\frac{1}{2}$ years

3 $1400 is invested at 4% per annum simple interest. How long will it take for the amount to reach $1624?

4 The simple interest on $600 invested for five years is $210. What is the rate percentage per annum?

Living maths

5 If you invest a sum of money at a simple interest rate of 6%, how long will it take for your original amount to treble?

6 Jessica spends $\frac{1}{4}$ of her income from odd jobs on books, $\frac{1}{3}$ on transport and $\frac{1}{6}$ on clothing. The rest she saves.

(a) If she saves $8 per month, how much is her income each month?
(b) How much does she save in a year at a rate of $8 per month?
(c) She deposits one year's savings into an account that pays 8.5% interest for five years.
  (i) How much interest would she earn?
  (ii) How much would she have altogether in the end?

7 Mrs MacGregor took a personal loan of £8000 over three years. She repaid £325 per month in that period.

(a) How much did she repay in total?
(b) How much interest did she pay in pounds?
(c) At what rate was simple interest charged over the three years?

Hire purchase

Many people cannot afford to pay cash for expensive items like television sets, furniture and cars so they buy them on a system of payment called hire purchase (HP).

On HP you pay a part of the price as a deposit and the remainder in a certain number of weekly or monthly instalments. Interest is charged on outstanding balances. It is useful to be able to work out what interest rate is being charged on HP as it is not always clearly stated.

In HP agreements, the deposit is sometimes called the down-payment. When interest is calculated as a proportion of the amount owed it is called a flat rate of interest. This is the same as simple interest.

Worked example 9

The cash price of a car was \$20 000. The hire purchase price was \$6000 deposit and instalments of \$700 per month for two years. How much more than the cash price was the hire purchase price?

Deposit = \$6000
One instalment = \$700
24 instalments = \$700 × 24 = \$16 800 (once per month over two years = 24 monthly instalments)

Total HP price = deposit + 24 instalments
= \$6000 + \$16 800
= \$22 800

The hire purchase price was \$2800 more than the cash price.

Worked example 10

A man buys a car for \$30 000 on hire purchase. A deposit of 20% is paid and interest is paid on the outstanding balance for the period of repayment at the rate of 10% per annum. The balance is paid in 12 equal instalments. How much will each instalment be?

Cash price = \$30 000

Deposit of 20% = $\frac{20}{100} \times 30000 = \$6000$

Outstanding balance = \$30 000 − \$6000 = \$24 000

Interest of 10% = $\frac{10}{100} \times 24000 = \$2400$

Amount to be paid by instalments = outstanding balance + interest
= \$24 000 + \$2400
= \$26 400

Each instalment = $\frac{26400}{12} = \$2200$ (divide by total number of instalments)

Exercise 17.5

1 A shopkeeper wants 25% deposit on a bicycle costing \$400 and charges 20% interest on the remaining amount. How much is:

(a) the deposit (b) the interest (c) the total cost of the bicycle?

2 A person pays 30% deposit on a fridge costing \$2500 and pays the rest of the money in one year with interest of 20% per year. How much does she pay altogether for the fridge?

3 A student buys a laptop priced at \$1850. She pays a 20% deposit and 12 equal monthly instalments. The interest rate is charged at 15% per annum on the outstanding balance.

(a) How much is each monthly instalment?
(b) What is the total cost of buying the laptop on HP?

4 A large flat screen TV costs \$999. Josh agrees to pay \$100 deposit and 12 monthly payments of \$100.

(a) Calculate the total amount of interest Josh will pay.
(b) What rate of interest was he charged?

5 A second-hand car is advertised for \$15 575 cash or \$1600 deposit and 24 monthly payments of \$734.70.

(a) What is the difference between the cash price and the HP price?
(b) What annual rate of interest is paid on the HP plan?

Compound interest

Simple interest is calculated on the original amount saved or borrowed. It is more common, however, to earn or to be charged **compound interest**. With a loan where you are charged compound interest, the interest is added to the amount you owe at regular intervals so the amount you owe increases for the next period. When you invest money for a fixed period, you can earn compound interest. In this case, the interest earned is added to the amount each period and you then earn interest on the amount plus the interest for the next period.

One way of doing compound interest calculations is to view them as a series of simple interest calculations. This method is shown in the following worked example.

When the principal, rate and time are the same, compound interest will be higher than simple interest. The exception is when the interest is only calculated for one period (for example one year), in that case, the compound interest and the simple interest will be the same.

Worked example 11

Priya invests $100 at a rate of 10%, compounded annually. How much money will she have after three years?

Year 1 $I = \frac{PRT}{100} = \frac{100 \times 10 \times 1}{100} = \$10$ $P + I = \$100 + \$10 = \$110$	Use the formula for simple interest.
Year 2 $I = \frac{PRT}{100} = \frac{110 \times 10 \times 1}{100} = \$11$ $P + I = 110 + 11 = \$121.00$	P for year two is $110; T is one year as you are only finding the interest for year two.
Year 3 $I = \frac{PRT}{100} = \frac{121 \times 10 \times 1}{100} = \$12.10$ $P + I = \$133.10$	P for year three is $121; T remains one year.

This table and graph compare the value of two $100 investments. The first is invested at 10% simple interest, the second at 10% compound interest.

Year (T)	Total $ 10% simple interest	Total $ 10% interest compounded annually
1	110	110
2	120	121
3	130	133.10
4	140	146.41
5	150	161.05
6	160	177.16
7	170	194.87
8	180	214.36
9	190	235.79
10	200	259.37

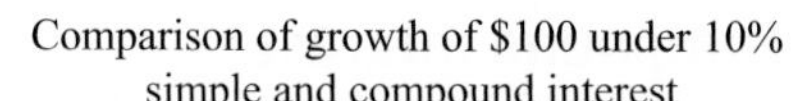

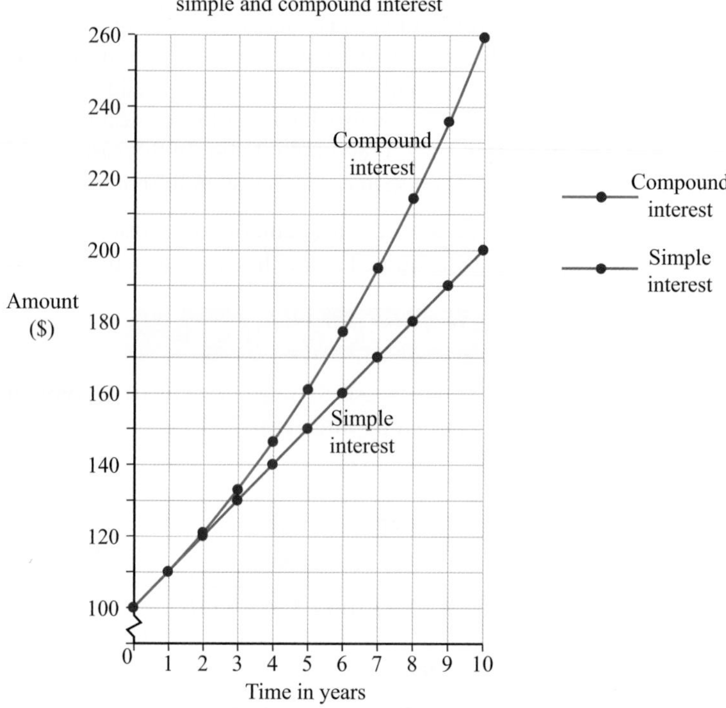

It is clear that choosing a compound interest rate is to the advantage of the investor. Remember though, that the same effect is felt with borrowing – the outstanding debt increases each period as the interest is compounded.

It takes a long time and lots of calculation to work out compound interest as a series of simple interest calculations. But there is a quicker method. Look at the calculations in the third column of the table.

REWIND

Indices were covered in chapter 2. ◀

Year (T)	Total $ 10% interest compounded annually	Working using a multiplier
1	110	$100 \times 1.1 = 110$
2	121	$100 \times 1.1 \times 1.1 = 121$
3	133.10	$100 \times 1.1 \times 1.1 \times 1.1 = 133.10$
4	146.41	$100 \times (1.1)^4 = 146.41$
5	161.05	$100 \times (1.1)^5 = 161.05$
6	177.16	$100 \times (1.1)^6 = 177.16$
7	194.87	$100 \times (1.1)^7 = 194.87$
8	214.36	$100 \times (1.1)^8 = 214.36$
9	235.79	$100 \times (1.1)^9 = 235.79$
10	259.37	$100 \times (1.1)^{10} = 259.37$

Multiply the decimal by itself the same number of times as the number of years. For three years it would be $1.1 \times 1.1 \times 1.1$ or $(1.1)^3$ not 1.1×3!

Can you see the rule?

- Add the annual interest rate to 100 to get a percentage increase (subtract for a decrease): $100\% + 10\% = 110\%$
- Express this as a decimal: $\frac{110\%}{100} = 1.1$
- Multiply the principal by a power of the decimal using the number of years as the power. So, for five years: $100 \times (1.1)^5$

You can also insert values into a formula to calculate the value of an investment when it is subject to compound interest.

$V = P\left(1+\frac{r}{100}\right)^n$, *where*

P is the amount invested

r is the percentage rate of interest

n is the number of years of compound interest.

Worked example 12

1 $1500 is invested at 5% p.a. compound interest. What will the investment be worth after 5 years?

$V = P\left(1+\frac{r}{100}\right)^n$ $= 1500\,(1+0.05)^5$ $= \$1914.42$	Insert values in the formula and then use your calculator.

2 A sum of money invested for 5 years at a rate of 5% interest, compounded yearly, grows to $2500. What was the initial sum invested?

$V = P\left(1+\frac{r}{100}\right)^n$ So, $P = A\left(1+\frac{r}{100}\right)^n$ $= \frac{2500}{(1+0.05)^5}$ $= \$1958.82$	Change the subject of the formula to make P the subject.

Exercise 17.6

1 Calculate the total amount owing on a loan of $8000 after two years at an interest rate of 12%:

(a) compounded annually (b) calculated as a flat rate.

2 How much would you have to repay on a credit card debt of $3500 after two years if the interest rate is:

(a) 19.5% compounded annually?
(b) 19.5% compounded half-yearly (the interest rate will be half of 19.5 for half a year)?

3 Calculate the total amount owing on a housing loan of $60 000 after ten years if the interest rate is 4% compounded annually.

Living maths

4 Jessica bought an apartment in Hong Kong for HK$3 200 000 as an investment. If the value of her apartment appreciates at an average rate of 3.5% per annum, what would it be worth in five years' time?

5 The human population of Earth in August 2010 was estimated to be 6.859 billion people. In August 2009, the population grew at a rate of 1.13%. Assuming this growth rate continues, estimate the population of the world in August of:

(a) 2015 (b) 2020 (c) 2025.

6 In 2010 there were an estimated 1600 giant pandas in China. Calculate the likely panda population in 2025 if there is:

(a) an annual growth in the population of 0.5%
(b) an annual decline in the population of 0.5%.

7 A population of microbes in a laboratory doubles every day. At the start of the period, the population is estimated to be 1 000 000 microbes.

(a) Copy and complete this table to show the growth in the population.

Time (days)	0	1	2	3	4	5	6	7	8
Total number of microbes (millions)	1	2	4						

(b) Draw a graph to show growth in the population over 8 days.

(c) Use the graph to determine the microbe population after:

i 2.5 days **ii** 3.6 days

(d) Use the graph to determine how long it will take the microbe population to reach 20 million.

8 This graph shows how a radio-active substance loses its radioactivity over time.

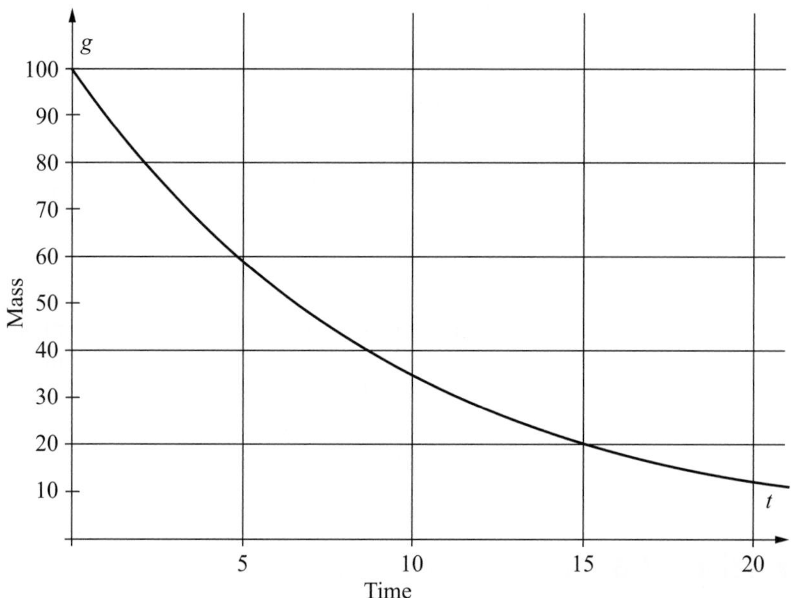

(a) The half life of the substance is how long it takes to decay to half its original mass. What is the half life of this substance?

(b) What mass of the substance is left after 20 minutes?

This is essentially the same as the compound interest formula above.

FAST FORWARD

When financial investments increase or decrease in value at an exponential rate we talk about appreciation (growth) and depreciation. When the number of individuals in a population increase or decrease exponentially over time, we usually talk about growth or decay. ▶

FAST FORWARD

You will deal with exponential curves in more detail in chapter 18. ▶

Exponential growth and decay

When a quantity increases (grows) in a fixed proportion (normally a percentage) at regular intervals, the growth is said to be exponential. Similarly, when the quantity decreases (decays) by a fixed percentage over regular periods of time, it is called exponential decay.

Increasing exponential functions produce curved graphs that slope steeply up to the right. Decreasing exponential functions produce curved graphs that slope down steeply to the right.

Exponential growth and decay can be expressed using formulae.

For growth: $y = a(1 + r)^n$

For decay: $y = a(1 - r)^n$

Where a is the original value or principal, r is the rate of change expressed as a decimal and n is the number of time periods.

Worked example 13

$100 is invested subject to compound interest at a rate of 8% per annum. Find the value of the investment correct to the nearest cent after a period of 15 years.

Value $= a(1 + r)^n$ — Use the formula for exponential growth and substitute the given values.

$= 100(1 + 0.8)^{15}$
$= 100(1.08)^{15}$
$= 317.2169114$

Value of investment is $317.22 (correct to the nearest cent).

Worked example 14

The value of a new computer system depreciates by 30% per year. If it cost $1200 new, what will it be worth in two years' time?

Value $= a(1 - r)^n$ — Use the formula for exponential decay and substitute the given values.

$= 1200(1 - 0.3)^2$
$= 1200(0.7)^2$
$= 588$

Value after two years is $588.

Exercise 17.7

1. Ms Singh owns a small business. She borrows $18 500 from the bank to finance some new equipment. She repays the loan in full after two years. If the bank charged her compound interest at the rate of 21% per annum, how much did she repay after two years?
2. The value of a car depreciates each year by 8%. A new small car is priced at $11 000. How much will this car be worth in:

   (a) 1 year **(b)** 3 years **(c)** 8 years **(d)** n years?
3. Nils invests his savings in an account that pays 6% interest compounded half yearly. If he puts $2300 into his account and leaves it there for two years, how much money will he have at the end of the period?
4. The total population of a European country is decreasing at a rate of 0.6% per year. In 2014, the population of the country was 7.4 million people.
   (a) What is the population likely to be in 2020 if it decreases at the same rate?
   (b) How long will it take for the population to drop below 7 million people?
5. A colony of bacteria grows by 5% every hour. How long does it take for the colony to double in size?

17.3 Buying and selling

When people trade they buy goods, mark them up (decide on a price) and then sell them.

The price the trader pays for goods is called the **cost price**.

The price the goods are sold at is called the **selling price**.

If the selling price is higher than the cost price, the goods are sold at a **profit**.

If the selling price is lower than the cost price, the goods are sold at a **loss**.

profit = selling price − cost price

loss = cost price − selling price

Percentage profit and loss

REWIND

Notice the similarity with percentage increases and decreases in chapter 5. ◀

Profit and loss are normally calculated as percentages of the cost price.

The following formulae are used to calculate percentage profit or loss:

$$\text{percentage profit} = \frac{\text{actual profit}}{\text{cost price}} \times 100\%$$

$$\text{percentage loss} = \frac{\text{actual loss}}{\text{cost price}} \times 100\%$$

Worked example 15

A shopkeeper buys an article for \$500 and sells it for \$600. What is the percentage profit?

Profit = selling price − cost price
= \$600 − \$500
= \$100

$$\text{Percentage profit} = \frac{\text{profit}}{\text{cost}} \times 100\%$$
$$= \frac{\$100}{\$500} \times 100\%$$
$$= 20\%$$

Worked example 16

A person buys a car for \$16 000 and sells it for \$12 000. Calculate the percentage loss.

Loss = cost price − selling price
= \$16 000 − \$12 000
= \$4000

$$\text{Percentage loss} = \frac{\text{loss}}{\text{cost}} \times 100\%$$
$$= \frac{\$4000}{\$16\,000} \times 100\%$$
$$= 25\%$$

Exercise 17.8

1 Find the actual profit and percentage profit in the following cases (use an appropriate degree of accuracy where needed):

(a) cost price \$20, selling price \$25
(b) cost price \$500, selling price \$550
(c) cost price \$1.50, selling price \$1.80
(d) cost price 30 cents, selling price 35 cents.

2 Calculate the percentage loss in the following cases (use an appropriate degree of accuracy where needed):

(a) cost price \$400, selling price \$300
(b) cost price 75c, selling price 65c
(c) cost price \$5.00, selling price \$4.75
(d) cost price \$6.50, selling price \$5.85.

3 A market trader buys 100 oranges for \$30. She sells them for 50 cents each. Calculate the percentage profit or loss she made.

Calculating the selling price, cost price and mark up

The cost price is always 100%. If you add 10% mark up, the selling price will be 110%.

People who sell goods have to decide how much profit they want to make. In other words, they have to decide by how much they will mark up the cost price to make the selling price.

cost price + % mark up = selling price

Worked example 17

A trader sells her product for \$39. If her mark up is 30%, what is the cost price of the product?

Cost price + mark up = selling price
Selling price = 130% of the cost price
So, \$39 = 130% × selling price
To find 100%:

$\frac{39}{130} \times 100 = \$30$

The cost price was \$30

Worked example 18

At a market, a trader makes a profit of \$1.08 on an item selling for \$6.48. What is his percentage profit?

Cost price + mark up = selling price Selling price − mark up = cost price \$6.48 − \$1.08 = \$5.40 $\text{Percentage profit} = \frac{\text{actual profit}}{\text{cost price}} \times 100$ $\frac{1.08}{5.40} \times 100 = 20\%$	Express the mark up as a percentage of cost price.

Worked example 19

Find the selling price of an article bought for \$400 and sold at a loss of 10%.

Cost price = \$400
Loss = 10% of \$400
$= \frac{10}{100} \times 400$
= \$40
Selling price = cost price − loss
= \$400 − \$40
= \$360

Exercise 17.9

1 Find the cost price of each of the following items:
  (a) selling price \$130, profit 20%
  (b) selling price \$320, profit 25%
  (c) selling price \$399, loss 15%
  (d) selling price \$750, loss $33\frac{1}{3}$%.

2 Find the selling price of an article that was bought for \$750 and sold at a profit of 12%.

3 Calculate the selling price of a car bought for \$3000 and sold at a profit of 7.5%.

4 Josh bought a computer for \$500. Two years later he sold it at a loss of 28%.
What was his selling price?

5 An article costing \$240 is sold at a loss of 8%. Find the selling price.

6 Sally makes jewellery and sells it to her friends. Her costs to make 10 rings were \$377. She wants to sell them and make a 15% profit. What should she charge?

7 Tim sells burgers for \$6.50 and makes a profit of \$1.43 on each one. What is his percentage profit on cost price?

Living maths

8 VAT at a rate of 17% is added *each* time an item is sold on. The original cost of an item is \$112.00. The item is sold to a wholesaler, who sells it on to a retailer. The retailer sells it to the public.

(a) How much tax will the item have incurred?
(b) Express the tax as a percentage of the original price.

Discount

If items are not being sold as quickly as a shop would like or if they want to clear stock as new fashions come out, then goods may be sold at a **discount**. Discount can be treated in the same way as percentage change (loss) as long as you remember that the percentage change is always calculated as a percentage of the original amount.

Worked example 20

During a sale, a shop offers a discount of 15% on jeans originally priced at \$75. What is the sale price?

$$\begin{aligned}\text{Discount} &= 15\% \text{ of } \$75\\ &= \frac{15}{100} \times 75\\ &= \$11.25\end{aligned}$$

$$\begin{aligned}\text{Sale price} &= \text{original price} - \text{discount}\\ &= \$75 - 11.25\\ &= \$63.75\end{aligned}$$

You can also work out the price by considering the sale price as a percentage of 100%. 100 − 15 = 85, so the sale price is 85% of \$75:

$$\frac{85}{100} \times 75 = \$63.75$$

Exercise 17.10

1 Copy and complete the following table.

Original price (\$)	% discount	Savings (\$)	Sale price (\$)
89.99	5		
125.99	10		
599.00	12		
22.50	7.5		
65.80	2.5		
10 000.00	23		

2 Calculate the percentage discount given on the following sales. Give your answer rounded to the nearest whole per cent.

Original price ($)	Sale price ($)	% discount
89.99	79.99	
125.99	120.00	
599.00	450.00	
22.50	18.50	
65.80	58.99	
10 000.00	9500.00	

Summary

Do you know the following?

- People in employment earn money for the work they do. This money can be paid as wages, salaries, commission or as a fee per item produced (piece work).
- Gross earnings refers to how much you earn before deductions. Gross earnings – deductions = net earnings. Your net earnings are what you actually receive as payment.
- Companies are obliged by law to deduct tax and certain other amounts from earnings.
- Simple interest is calculated per time period as a fixed percentage of the original amount (the principal). The formula for finding simple interest is $I = \frac{PRT}{100}$.
- Compound interest is interest added to the original amount at set intervals. This increases the principal and further interest is compounded. Most interest in real life situations is compounded.
- Hire purchase (HP) is a method of buying goods on credit and paying for them in instalments which include a flat rate of interest added to the original price.
- When goods are sold at a profit they are sold for more than they cost. When they are sold at a loss they are sold for less than they cost. The original price is called the cost price. The price they are sold for is called the selling price. If goods are sold at a profit, selling price – cost price = profit. If they are sold at a loss, cost price – selling price = loss.
- A discount is a reduction in the usual price of an item. A discount of 15% means you pay 15% less than the usual or marked price.

Are you able to …?

- use given information to solve problems related to wages, salaries, commission and piece work
- read information from tables and charts to work out deductions and tax rates
- calculate gross and net earnings given the relevant information
- use the formula to calculate simple interest
- manipulate the simple interest formula to calculate the principal amount, rate of interest and time period of a debt or investment
- solve problems related to HP payments and amounts
- calculate compound interest over a given time period and solve problems related to compound interest
- calculate the cost price, selling price, percentage profit or loss and actual mark up using given rates and prices
- work out the actual price of a discounted item and calculate the percentage discount given the original and the new price.

Examination practice

Exam-style questions

1 Sayed is paid \$8.50 per hour for a standard 36-hour week. He is paid 'time-and-a-half' for all overtime worked. Calculate:

(a) his gross weekly earnings if he works $4\frac{3}{4}$ hours overtime
(b) the hours overtime worked if he earns \$420.75 for the week.

2 Ahmed bought a DVD for \$15. He sold it to Barbara, making a 20% loss.

(a) How much did Barbara pay for it?
(b) Barbara later sold the DVD to Luvuyo. She made a 20% profit. How much did Luvuyo pay for it?

Tip

Questions on profit and loss may include calculations from other areas of mathematics.

3 Last year, Jane's wages were \$80 per week. Her wages are now \$86 per week. Calculate the percentage increase.

4 What is the simple interest on \$160 invested at 7% per year for three years?

5 Senor Vasquez invests \$500 in a Government Bond, at 9% simple interest per year. How much will the Bond be worth after three years?

6 Simon's salary has increased by 6% p.a. over the past three years. It is now £35 730.40 p.a.

(a) What did he earn per year three years ago?
(b) What is his gross monthly salary at the present rate?
(c) His deductions each month amount to 22.5% of his gross salary. What is his net pay per month?

7 A new car cost \$14 875. Three years later, the insurance company valued it at \$10 700. Calculate the percentage reduction in value over the three years.

8 Exercise equipment advertised at \$2200 is sold on sale for \$1950. What percentage discount is this?

Past paper questions

1 At 05:06, Mr Ho bought 850 fish at a fish market for \$2.62 each. 95 minutes later he sold them all to a supermarket for \$2.86 each.

(a) What was the time when he sold the fish? [1]
(b) Calculate his total profit. [1]

[Cambridge IGCSE Mathematics 0580 Paper 21 Q03 May/June 2009]

2 In January, Sunanda changed £25 000 into dollars when the exchange rate was \$1.96 = £1. In June she changed the dollars back into pounds when the exchange rate was \$1.75 = £1. Calculate the profit she made giving your answer in pounds (£).

[Cambridge IGCSE Mathematics 0580 Paper 21 Q11 May/June 2009]

3 (a) Ankuri lends her brother \$275 for four years at a rate of 3.6% per year **simple** interest. Calculate the total amount her brother owes after four years. [3]

(b) Monesh invests \$650 in a bank which pays 4% per year **compound** interest. Calculate the amount Monesh will have after two years. [3]

(c) Theresa and Ian have 400 euros (€) each.

(i) Theresa changes her €400 for pounds (£) when the exchange rate is €1 = £0.7857. Calculate the amount she receives. [2]

(ii) Ian changes his €400 for dollars (\$) when the exchange rate is \$1 = €0.6374. Calculate the amount he receives. [3]

[Cambridge IGCSE Mathematics 0580 Paper 31 Q08 May/June 2010]

18 Curved graphs

Key words

- Quadratic
- Parabola
- Axis of symmetry
- Turning point
- Minimum
- Maximum
- Reciprocal
- Hyperbola
- Intersection
- Exponential
- Gradient
- Tangent

In this chapter you will learn how to:

- construct a table of values to draw graphs called parabolas
- construct a table of values to draw graphs called hyperbolas
- interpret curved graphs
- use graphs to find the approximate solutions to quadratic equations

EXTENDED

- construct tables of values to draw graphs in the form of ax^n and $\frac{a}{x}$
- estimate the gradients of curves by drawing tangents
- use graphs to find the approximate solutions to associated equations.

The water arcs from this fountain form a curved shape which is called a parabola in mathematics.

In chapter 10 you saw that many problems could be represented by linear equations and straight line graphs. Real life problems, such as those involving area; the path of a moving object; the shape of a bridge or other structure; the growth of bacteria; and variation in speed, can only be solved using non-linear equations. Graphs of non-linear equations are curves.

In this chapter you are going to use tables of values to plot a range of curved graphs. You will also learn how to interpret curved graphs and how to find the approximate solution of equations from graphs.

18.1 Plotting quadratic graphs (the parabola)

In chapter 10 you learned that **quadratic** equations have an x^2 term as their highest power. The simplest quadratic equation for a quadratic graph is $y = x^2$.

Here is a table showing the values for $y = x^2$ from $-3 \leq x \leq 3$.

x	−3	−2	−1	0	1	2	3
$y = x^2$	9	4	1	0	1	4	9

You can use these points to plot and draw a graph just as you did with linear equations. The graph of a quadratic relationship is called a **parabola**.

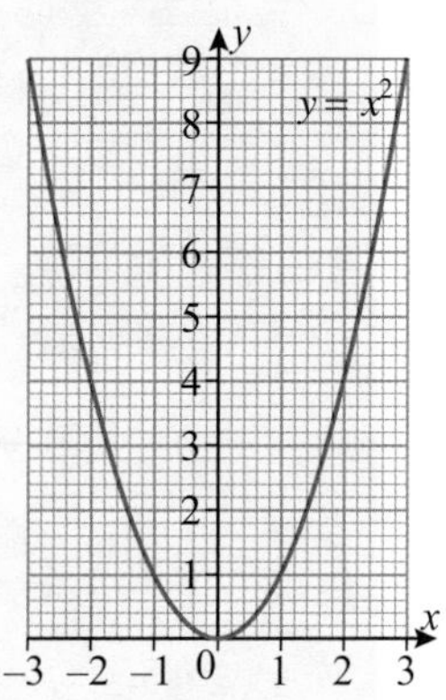

Here is the table of values for $y = -x^2$ from $-3 \leq x \leq 3$.

x	−3	−2	−1	0	1	2	3
$y = -x^2$	−9	−4	−1	0	−1	−4	−9

When you plot these points and draw the parabola you can see that the negative sign in front of the x^2 has the effect of turning the graph so that it faces downwards.

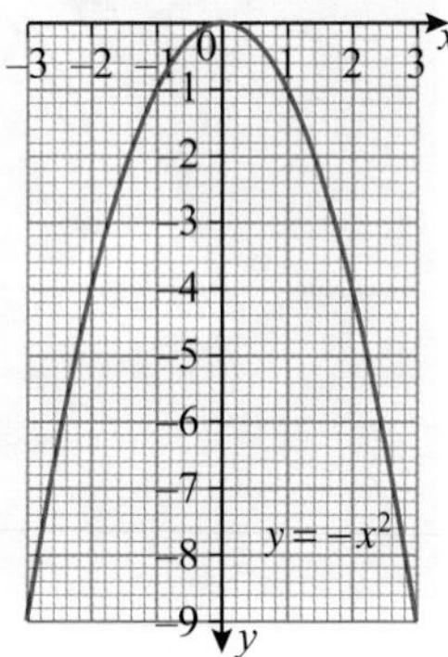

If the coefficient of x^2 in the equation is positive, the parabola is a 'valley' shaped curve.

If the coefficient of x^2 in the equation is negative, the parabola is a 'hill' shaped curve.

For most graphs, a turning point is a local **minimum** or **maximum** value of y. For a parabola, if the x^2 term is positive the turning point will be a minimum. If the x^2 term is negative, the turning point will be a maximum.

The axis of symmetry and the turning point

The **axis of symmetry** is the line which divides the parabola into two symmetrical halves. In the two graphs above, the y-axis ($x = 0$) is the axis of symmetry.

The **turning point** or vertex of the graph is the point at which it changes direction. For both of the graphs above, the turning point is at the origin (0, 0).

Exercise 18.1

Remember that if you square a negative number the result will be positive. If using your calculator, place brackets round any negatives.

1 Complete the following tables of values and plot the graphs on the *same* set of axes. Use values of −8 to 12 on the y-axis.

(a)

x	−3	−2	−1	0	1	2	3
$y = x^2 + 1$							

(b)

x	−3	−2	−1	0	1	2	3
$y = x^2 + 3$							

(c)

x	−3	−2	−1	0	1	2	3
$y = x^2 - 2$							

(d)

x	−3	−2	−1	0	1	2	3
$y = -x^2 + 1$							

(e)

x	−3	−2	−1	0	1	2	3
$y = 3 - x^2$							

(f) What happens to the graph when the value of the constant term changes?

These equations are all in the form $y = -x^2 + c$, where c is the constant term. The constant term is the y-intercept of the graph in each case.

2 Match each of the five parabolas shown here to its equation.

(a) $y = 4 - x^2$
(b) $y = x^2 - 4$
(c) $y = x^2 + 2$
(d) $y = 2 - x^2$
(e) $y = -x^2 - 2$

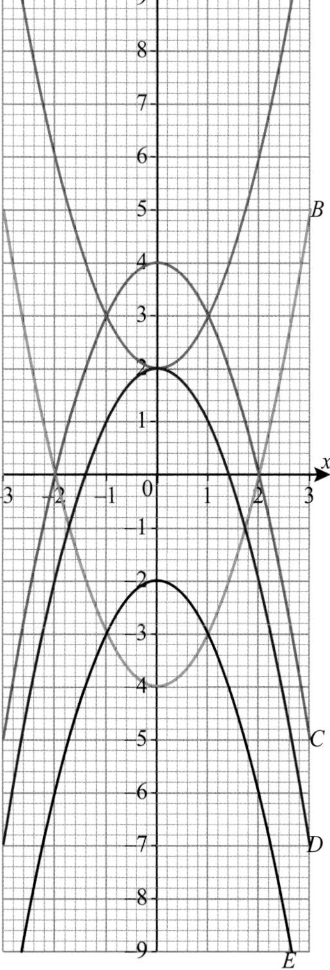

Equations in the form of $y = x^2 + ax + b$

You have seen how to construct a table of values and then plot and draw a parabola from simple quadratic equations. Now you are going to see how to draw up a table of values for more usual quadratic equations with an x^2 term, an x term and a constant term. In these cases, it is easiest if you work out each term on a separate row of the table and then add them to find the value of y. Read through the two worked examples carefully to make sure you understand this.

Worked example 1

Construct a table of values for $y = x^2 + 2x - 1$ for values $-4 \leq x \leq 2$.
Plot the points to draw the graph.

x	-4	-3	-2	-1	0	1	2
x^2	16	9	4	1	0	1	4
$2x$	-8	-6	-4	-2	0	2	4
-1	-1	-1	-1	-1	-1	-1	-1
$y = x^2 + 2x - 1$	7	2	-1	-2	-1	2	7

In this table, you work out each term separately.
Add the terms of the equation in each column to get the totals for the last row (the y-values of each point).

To draw the graph:

- plot the points and join them to make a smooth curve
- label the graph with its equation.

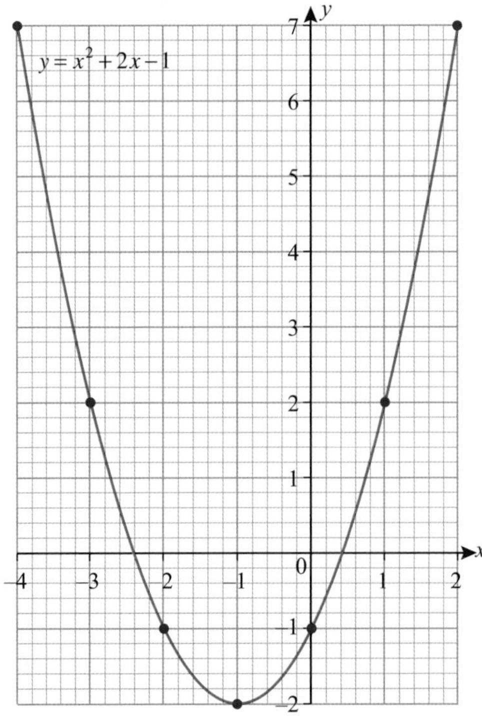

Worked example 2

Draw the graph of $y = 6 + x - x^2$ for values of x from –3 to 4.

x	–3	–2	–1	0	1	2	3	4
6	6	6	6	6	6	6	6	6
$+x$	–3	–2	–1	0	1	2	3	4
$-x^2$	–9	–4	–1	0	–1	–4	–9	–16
$y = 6 + x - x^2$	–6	0	4	6	6	4	0	–6

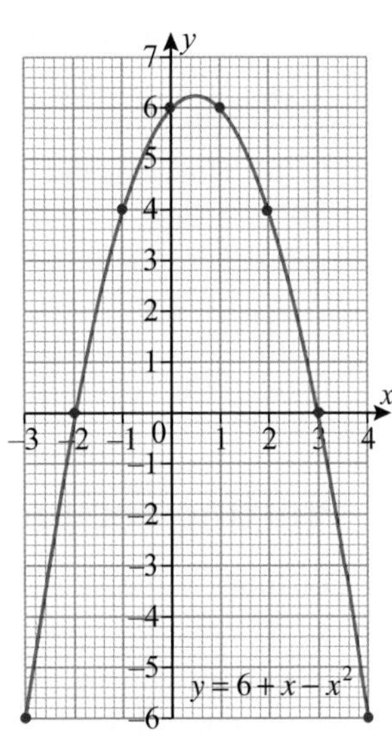

Some calculators have an in-built function to create tables of values. These can help you avoid errors provided you use them correctly. However, make sure that you can still do the calculations without the table function.

To plot the graph of a quadratic relationship:

- complete a table of values (often some of the values will be given)
- rule the axes and label them
- plot the (x, y) values from the table of values
- join the points with a smooth curve.

Exercise 18.2

1 Construct a table of values of $y = x^2 - 2x^2 + 2$ for $-1 \leq x \leq 3$ and use the (x, y) points from the table to plot and draw the graph.

2 Copy and complete this table of values and then draw the graph of $y = x^2 - 5x - 4$.

x	–2	–1	0	1	2	3	4	5	6
x^2	4								
$-5x$	10								
–4	–4	–4	–4	–4	–4	–4	–4	–4	–4
y									

3 Construct a table of values of $y = x^2 + 2x - 3$ from $-3 \leq x \leq 2$. Plot the points and join them to draw the graph.

4 Using values of x from 0 to 4, construct a table of values and use it to draw the graph of $y = -x^2 - 4x$.

5 Using values of x from –6 to 0, construct a table of values and use it to draw the graph of $y = -x^2 - 6x - 5$.

Living maths

6 People who design water displays (often set to music) need to know how high water will rise from a jet and how long it will take to return to the pool. This graph shows the height of a water arc from a fountain (in metres) over a number of seconds.

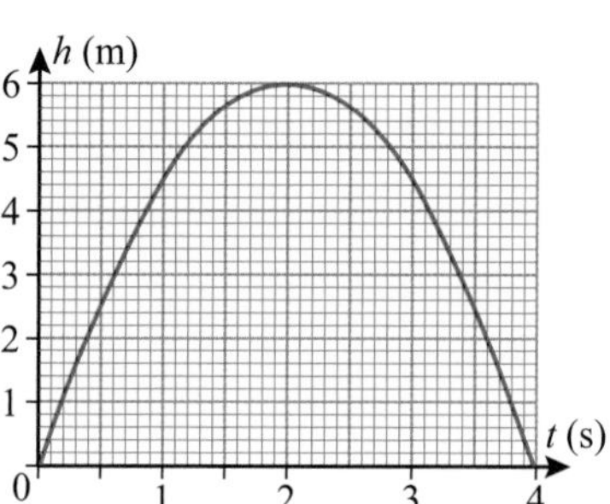

(a) What was the greatest height reached by the water arc?

(b) How long did it take the water to reach the greatest height?

(c) For how long was the water arc above a height of 2.5 m?

(d) How far did the water rise in the first second?

(e) Why do you think this graph shows only positive values of height?

18.2 Plotting reciprocal graphs (the hyperbola)

Reciprocal equations have a constant product. If $y = \frac{6}{x}$ then $xy = 6$. There is no value of y that corresponds with $x = 0$ because division by 0 is meaningless. Similarly, if x was 0, then xy would also be 0 for all values of y and not 6, as it should be in this example. This is what causes the two parts of the curve to be disconnected.

Equations in the form of $y = \frac{a}{x}$ (where a is a whole number) are called **reciprocal** equations. Graphs of reciprocal equations are called **hyperbolas**. These graphs have a very characteristic shape. Although it is one graph, it consists of two non-connected curves that are mirror images of each other, drawn in opposite quadrants.

Here is a table of values for $y = \frac{6}{x}$.

x	−6	−5	−4	−3	−2	−1	1	2	3	4	5	6
$y = \frac{6}{x}$	−1	−1.2	−1.5	−2	−3	−6	6	3	2	1.5	1.2	1

Include at least five negative and five positive values in the table of values to draw a hyperbola because it has two separate curves.

When you plot these points, you get this graph.

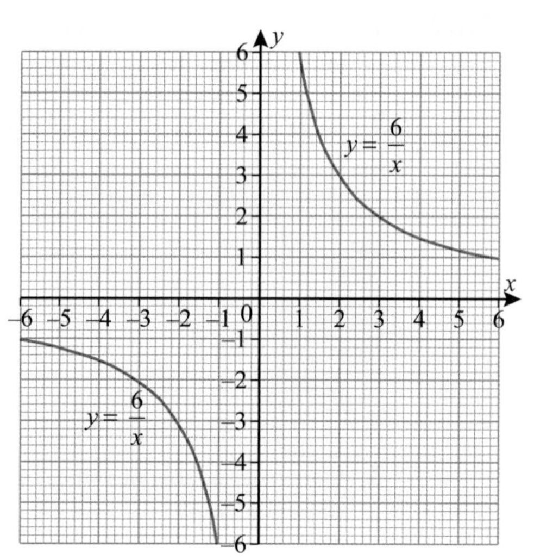

Notice the following about the graph:

- it has two parts which are the same shape and size, but in opposite quadrants
- the curve is symmetrical
- the curve approaches the axes, but it will never touch them
- there is no value of y for $x = 0$ and no value of x for $y = 0$.

Worked example 3

Construct a table of values and then draw a graph of $xy = -12$ ($x \neq 0$) for $-12 \leq x \leq 12$.

$xy = -12$ is the same as $y = \frac{-12}{x}$.

In this case, you can work out every second value as you will not need all 24 points to draw the graph.

x	−12	−10	−8	−6	−4	−2	2	4	6	8	10	12
$y = \frac{-12}{x}$	1	1.2	1.5	2	3	6	−6	−3	−2	−1.5	−1.2	−1

Plot the points to draw the graph.

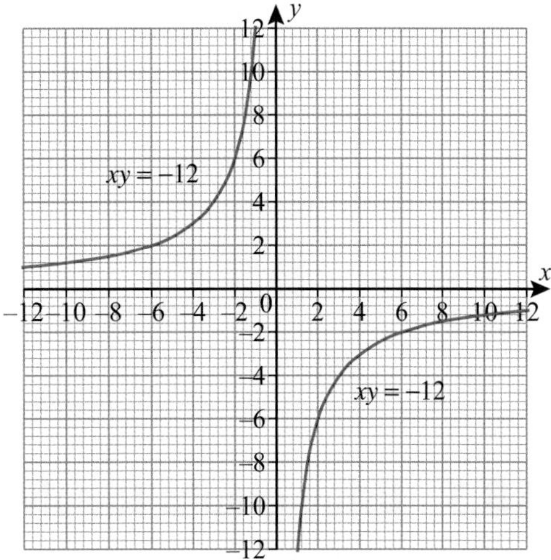

Notice that the graph of $xy = -12$ is in the top left and bottom right quadrants. This is because the value of the constant term (a in the equation $y = \frac{a}{x}$) is negative. When a is a positive value, the hyperbola will be in the top right and bottom left quadrants.

The quadrants are labelled in an anti-clockwise direction. The co-ordinates of any point in the first quadrant will always be positive.

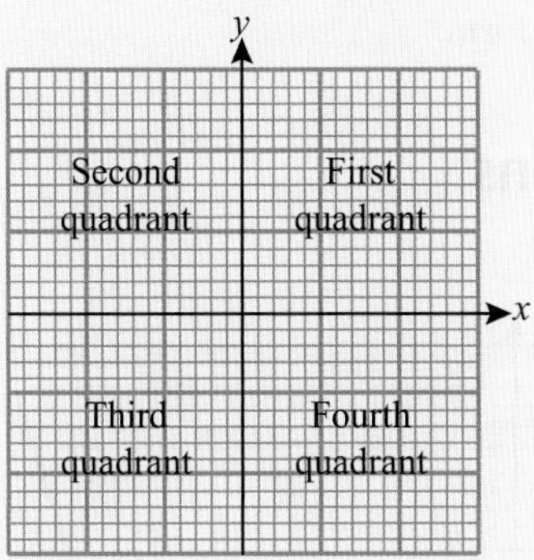

To plot the graph of a reciprocal relationship:

- complete a table of values (often some of the values will be given)
- rule the axes and label them
- plot the (x, y) values from the table of values
- join the points with a smooth curve
- write the equation on both parts of the graph.

Exercise 18.3

1 Copy and complete the following tables giving values of y correct to 1 decimal place. Use the points to plot each graph on a separate set of axes.

(a)

x	−6	−4	−3	−2	−1	1	2	3	4	6
$y=\frac{2}{x}$										

(b)

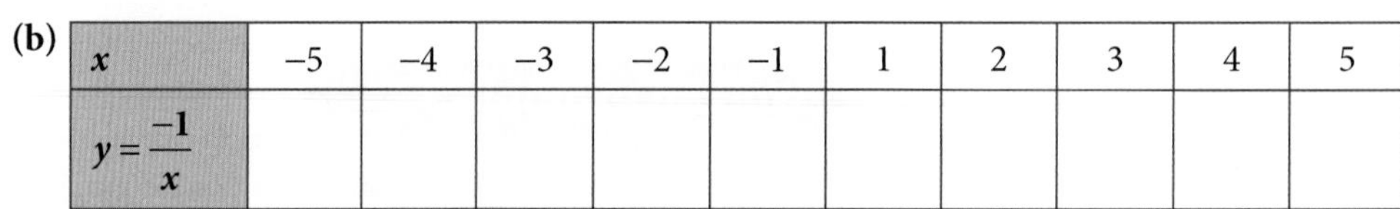

x	−5	−4	−3	−2	−1	1	2	3	4	5
$y=\frac{-1}{x}$										

(c)

x	−6	−4	−3	−2	−1	1	2	3	4	6
$y=\frac{-6}{x}$										

(d)

x	−6	−4	−3	−2	−1	1	2	3	4	6
$y=\frac{4}{x}$										

Living maths

2 A person makes a journey of 240 km. The average speed is x km/h and the time the journey takes is y hours.

(a) Complete this table of corresponding values for x and y:

x	20	40	60	80	100	120
y	12		4			2

(b) On a set of axes, draw a graph to represent the relationship between x and y.
(c) Write down the relation between x and y in its algebraic form.

18.3 Using graphs to solve quadratic equations

Suppose you were asked to solve the equation $x^2 - 3x - 1 = 0$.

To do this, you would need to find the value or values of x that make $x^2 - 3x - 1$ equal to 0.

You can try to do this by trial and error, but you will find that the value of x you need is not a whole number (in fact, it lies between the values of 3 and 4).

It is much quicker and easier to draw the graph of the equation $y = x^2 - 3x - 1$ and to use that to find a solution to the equation. Here is the graph:

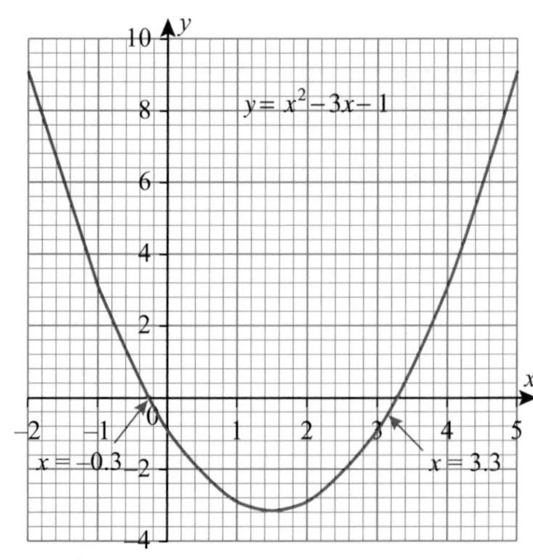

Use a sharp pencil. You will be able to correct your work more easily and it will be more accurate when looking at intersections.

The solution to the equation is the point (or points) where $y = 0$, in other words you are looking for the value of x where the graph crosses the x-axis.

If you look at the graph you can see that it crosses the x-axis in two places. The value of x at these points is 3.3 and –0.3.

These two values are sometimes referred to as the roots of the equation $x^2 - 3x - 1 = 0$.

You can use the graph to find the solution of the equation for different values of x. Work through the worked example carefully to see how to do this.

Worked example 4

This is the graph of $y = x^2 - 2x - 7$. Use the graph to solve the equations:

(a) $x^2 - 2x - 7 = 0$ **(b)** $x^2 - 2x - 7 = 3$ **(c)** $x^2 - 2x = 1$

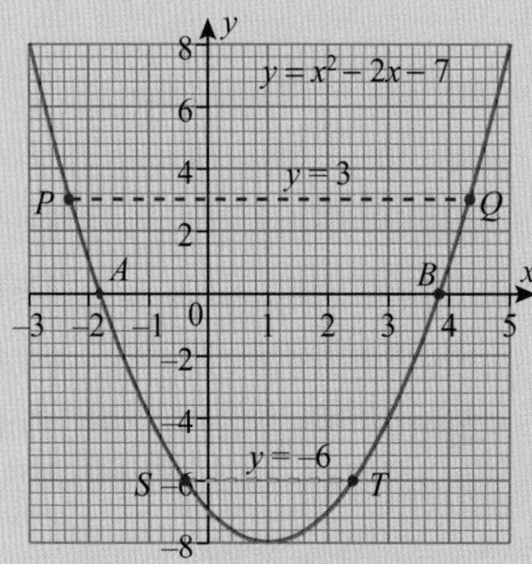

(a) Since this is the graph of $y = x^2 - 2x - 7$, simply find the points on the curve that have a y co-ordinate of 0 (i.e. where the curve cuts the x-axis).
There are two such points, marked A and B on the graph.
The x co-ordinates of these points are –1.8 and 3.8, so the solutions of the equation $x^2 - 2x - 7 = 0$ are $x = -1.8$ and $x = 3.8$

(b) Find the points on the curve that have a y co-ordinate of 3. (Draw in the horizontal line $y = 3$ to help with this.)
There are two such points, marked P and Q, on the graph.
The x co-ordinates of these points are –2.3 and 4.3, so the solutions of the equation $x^2 - 2x - 7 = 3$ are $x = -2.3$ and $x = 4.3$

(c) Rearrange the equation $x^2 - 2x = 1$ so that the left-hand side matches the equation whose graph you are using.
Subtracting 7 from both sides, you get $x^2 - 2x - 7 = 1 - 7$, that is $x^2 - 2x - 7 = -6$.
You can now proceed as you did in parts (a) and (b).
Find the points on the curve that have a y co-ordinate of –6; they are marked S and T on the graph.
The x co-ordinates of S and T are –0.4 and 2.4
The solutions of the equation $x^2 - 2x = 1$ are $x = -0.4$ and $x = 2.4$

In summary, to solve a quadratic equation graphically:

- read off the x co-ordinates of any points of intersection for the given y-values
- you may need to rearrange the original equation to do this.

Exercise 18.4

1 Use this graph of the relationship $y = x^2 - x - 2$ to solve the following equations:

(a) $x^2 - x - 2 = 0$
(b) $x^2 - x - 2 = 6$
(c) $x^2 - x = 6$

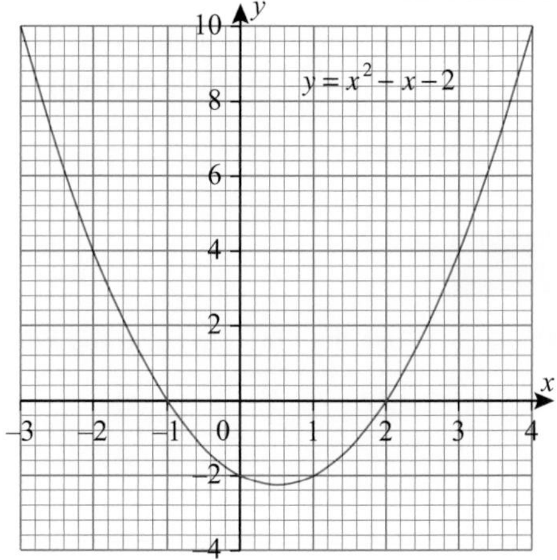

2 (a) Construct a table of values for $y = -x^2 - x + 1$ for values $-3 \leq x \leq 2$.
(b) Plot the points on a grid and join them with a smooth curve.
(c) Use your graph to solve the equation $-x^2 - x + 1 = 0$. Give your answer correct to 1 decimal place.

3 Solve the following equations by drawing suitable graphs over the given intervals.

(a) $x^2 - x - 3 = 0 \ (-3 \leq x \leq 4)$
(b) $x^2 + 3x + 1 = 0 \ (-4 \leq x \leq 1)$

4 (a) Use an interval of $-2 \leq x \leq 4$ to draw the graph $y = 4 - x^2 + 2x$.
(b) Use the graph to solve the following equations:

(i) $0 = 4 - x^2 + 2x$
(ii) $0 = -x^2 + 2x$

5 (a) Draw the graph of $y = x^2 - 2x - 4$ for values of x from –3 to 5.
(b) Use your graph to find approximate solutions to the equations:

(i) $x^2 - 2x - 4 = 0$
(ii) $x^2 - 2x - 4 = 3$
(iii) $x^2 - 2x - 4 = -1$

18.4 Using graphs to solve simultaneous linear and non-linear equations

As you did with linear equations, you can use graphs to solve a linear and a non-linear equation, or two non-linear equations simultaneously.

REWIND

In chapter 14 you learned how to use the point of **intersection** of two straight lines to find the solutions to simultaneous linear equations. Revise that section now if you cannot remember how to do this. ◀

Worked example 5

The graphs of $y = 2 + x$ and $y = x^2 - 3x + 4$ have been drawn on the same set of axes. Use the graphs to find the x-values of the points of intersection of the line and the curve.

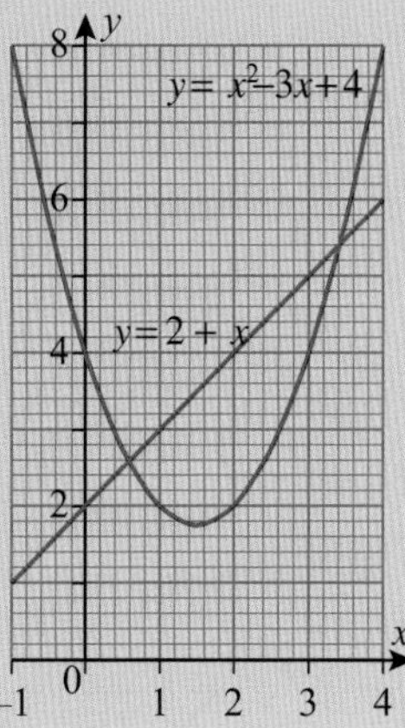

The co-ordinates of the two points of intersection are approximately (0.6, 2.6) and (3.4, 5.4), so the x-values of the points of intersection are $x = 0.6$ and $x = 3.4$

Tip

You might also be asked for the y-values, so it is important to pair up the correct x-value with the correct y-value. When $x = 0.6$, $y = 2.6$ and when $x = 3.4$, $y = 5.4$.

Worked example 6

The diagram shows the graphs of $y = \frac{8}{x}$ and $y = x$ for positive values of x.

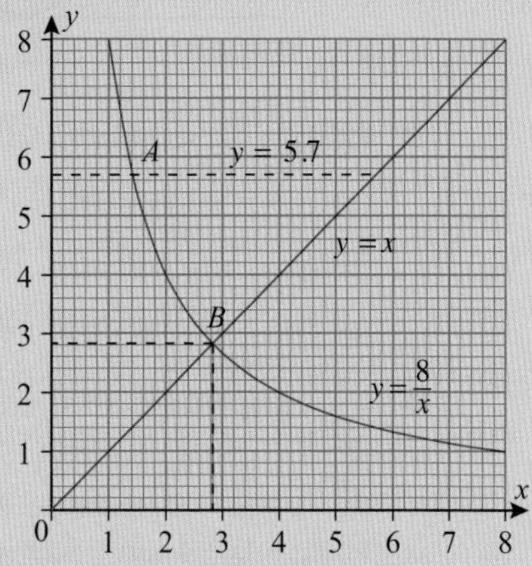

(a) Use the graph of $y = \frac{8}{x}$ to solve the equation $\frac{8}{x} = 5.7$

(b) Find a value of x such that $\frac{8}{x} = x$.

(a) You have to find a point on the curve that has a y co-ordinate of 5.7. Draw the line $y = 5.7$ to help find this it will be where the line cuts the curve.
The point is marked A on the diagram. Its x co-ordinate is 1.4, so the solution of the equation $\frac{8}{x} = 5.7$ is $x = 1.4$

(b) The straight line $y = x$ crosses the curve $y = \frac{8}{x}$ at the point B, with x co-ordinate is 2.8. Hence, a value of x such that $\frac{8}{x} = x$ is 2.8

Exercise 18.5

1 Find the points of intersection of the graphs and thus give the solution to the simultaneous equations.

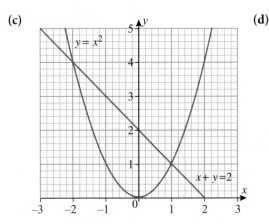

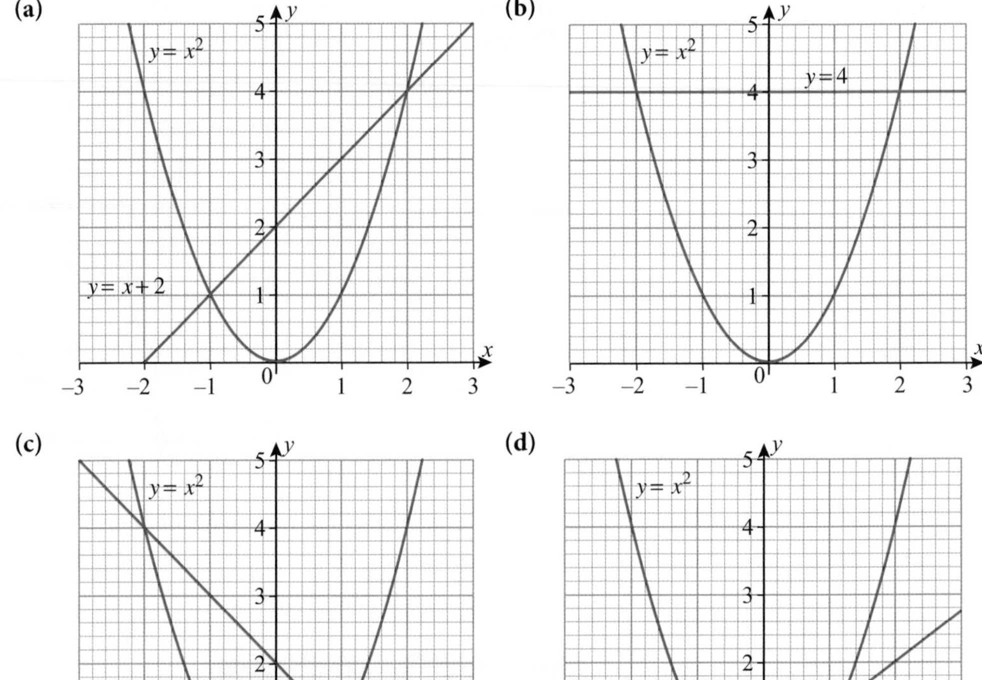

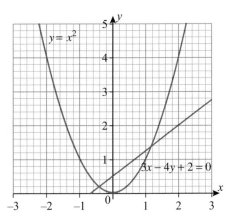

2 Find the points of intersection of the following graphs by drawing the graphs.

(a) $y = x^2$ and $y = 3x$

(b) $y = x$ and $y = \frac{2}{x}$

(c) $y = 2 - x$ and $y = x^2 - 5x + 6$

3 Use a graphical method to solve each pair of simultaneous equations:

(a) $y = x^2 - 8x + 9$ and $y = 2x + 1$
(b) $y = x^2 - x - 6$ and $y = 2 + x$
(c) $y = 4x + 4$ and $y = 2x - 3 + x^2$

4 Show graphically that there is no value of x which satisfies the pair of equations $y = -4$ and $y = x^2 + 2x + 3$ simultaneously.

18.5 Other non-linear graphs

So far you have learned how to construct a table of values and draw three different kinds of graphs:

- linear graphs (straight lines of equations in form of $y = mx + c$)
- quadratic graphs (parabolas of equations in the form of $y = x^2 + ax + b$)
- reciprocal graphs (hyperbolas of equations in the form of $y = \frac{a}{x}$)

> **Tip**
> You are expected to deal with equations that have terms with indices that can be any whole number from −2 to 3. When you have to work with higher order equations, they will not contain more than three terms.

In this section you are going to apply what you already know to plot and draw graphs formed by higher order equations (cubic equations) and those formed by equations that have combinations of linear, quadratic, reciprocal and cubic terms.

Plotting cubic graphs

A cubic equation has a term with an index of three as the highest power of x. In other words, one of the terms is ax^3. For example, $y = 2x^3$, $y = -x^3 + 2x^2 + 3$ and $y = 2x^3 - 4x$ are all cubic equations. The simplest cubic equation is $y = x^3$.

Cubic equations produce graphs called cubic curves. The graphs you will draw will have two main shapes:

If the coefficient of the x^3 term is positive, the graph will take one of these shapes.

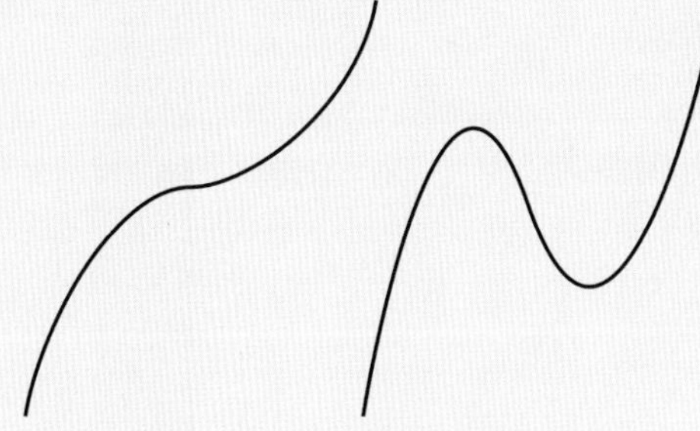

If the coefficient of the x^3 term is negative, the graph will be take one of these shapes.

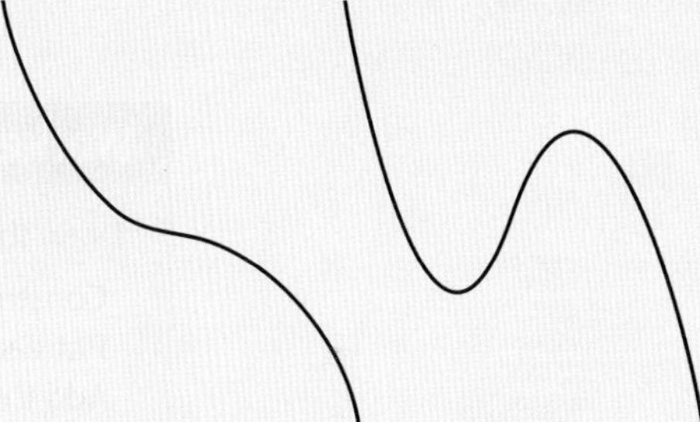

If x is positive, then x^3 is positive and $-x^3$ is negative.
If x is negative, then x^3 is negative and $-x^3$ is positive.

You can construct a table of values and plot the points obtained to draw a cubic graph.

Worked example 7

Complete the table of values and plot the points to draw the graphs on the same set of axes.

(a)

x	−2	−1	0	1	2
$y = x^3$					

(b)

x	−2	−1	0	1	2
$y = -x^3$					

As the value of x increases, the values of x^3 increase rapidly and it becomes difficult to fit them onto the graph. If you have to construct your own table of values, stick to low numbers and, possibly, include the half points (0.5, 1.5, etc.) to find more values that will fit onto the graph.

(a)

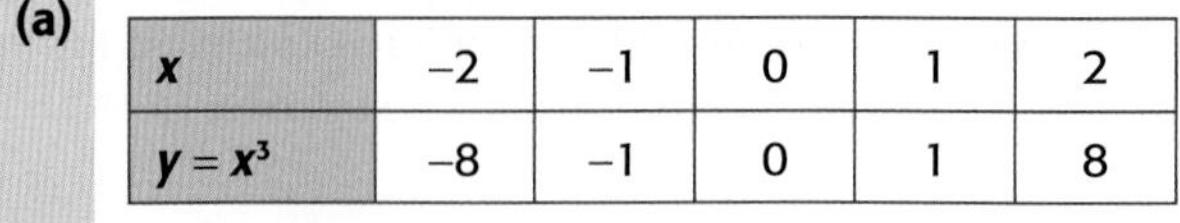

x	−2	−1	0	1	2
$y = x^3$	−8	−1	0	1	8

(b)

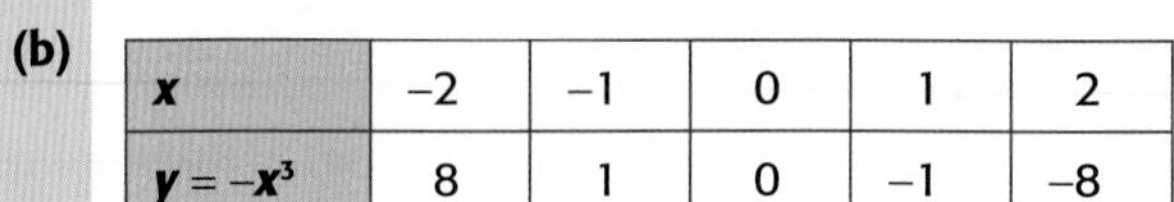

x	−2	−1	0	1	2
$y = -x^3$	8	1	0	−1	−8

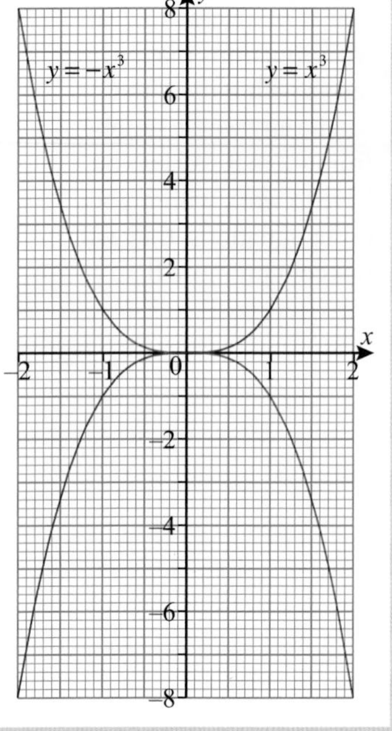

Worked example 8

Draw the graph of the equation $y = x^3 - 6x$ for $-3 \leq x \leq 3$.

Construct a table of values for whole numbers values of x first.
Put each term in a separate row.
Add the columns to find $y = x^3 - 6x$. (Remember not to add the top row when calculating y.)

x	−3	−2	−1	0	1	2	3
x^3	−27	−8	−1	0	1	8	27
$-6x$	18	12	6	0	−6	−12	−18
$y = x^3 - 6x$	−9	4	5	0	−5	−4	9

Construct a separate table for 'half values' of x.

x	−2.5	−1.5	−0.5	0.5	1.5	2.5
x^3	−15.625	−3.375	−0.125	0.125	3.375	15.625
$-6x$	15	9	3	−3	−9	−15
$y = x^3 - 6x$	−0.625	5.625	2.875	−2.875	−5.625	0.625

Plot the points against the axes and join them with a smooth curve.

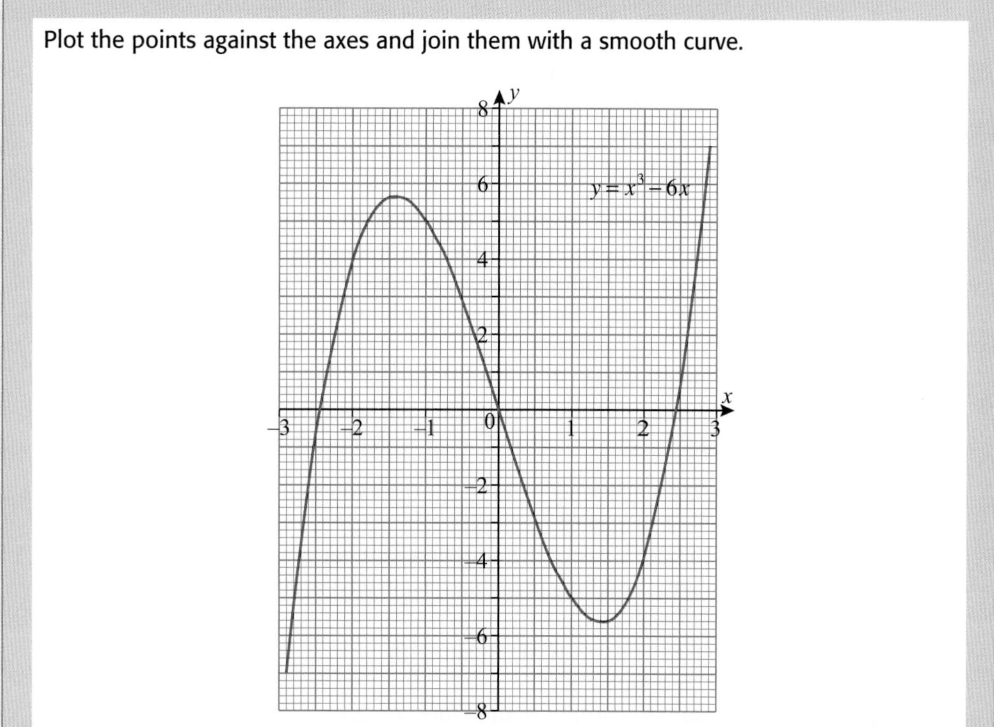

Using graphs to solve higher order equations

You can use cubic graphs to find approximate solutions to equations. The following worked example shows how to do this.

Worked example 9

(a) Draw the graph of the equation $y = x^3 - 2x^2 - 1$ for $-1 \leq x \leq 3$.

(b) Use the graph to solve the equations:

(i) $x^3 - 2x^2 - 1 = 0$

(ii) $x^3 - 2x^2 = -1$

(iii) $x^3 - 2x^2 - 5 = 0$.

(a) Construct a table of values of y for whole and half values x.

x	−1	−0.5	0	0.5	1	1.5	2	2.5	3
x^3	−1	−0.125	0	0.125	1	3.375	8	15.625	27
$-2x^2$	−2	−0.5	0	−0.5	−2	−4.5	−8	−12.5	−18
−1	−1	−1	−1	−1	−1	−1	−1	−1	−1
$y = x^3 - 2x^2 - 1$	−4	−1.625	−1	−1.375	−2	−2.125	−1	2.125	8

(b) Plot the points on the axes to draw the curve.

(i) To solve $x^3 - 2x^2 - 1 = 0$, find the point(s) on the curve that have a y co-ordinate of 0 (i.e. where the curve cuts the x-axis).
There is only one point (A on the graph).
The x co-ordinate of A is 2.2, so the solution of $x^3 - 2x^2 - 1 = 0$ is $x = 2.2$

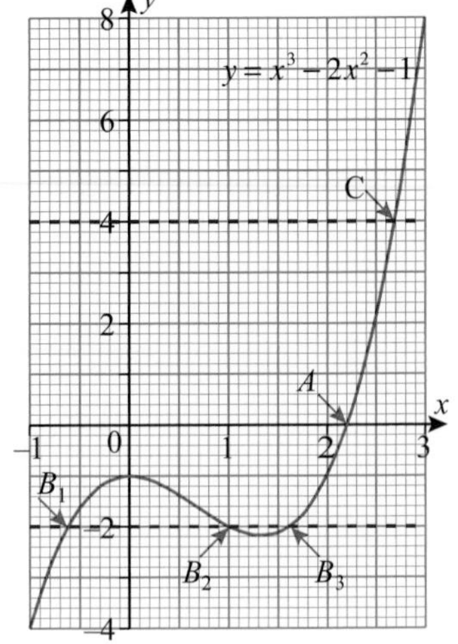

(ii) To solve $x^3 - 2x^2 = -1$, rearrange the equation so that the left-hand side is the same as the equation you have just drawn the graph for.
Subtracting 1 from both sides gives $x^3 - 2x^2 - 1 = -2$.
Now find the point(s) on the curve that have a y co-ordinate of -2 (draw the line $y = -2$ to help with this).

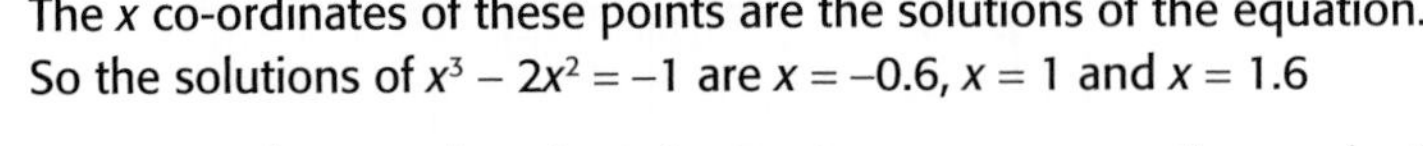

There are three points (B_1, B_2 and B_3 on the graph).
The x co-ordinates of these points are the solutions of the equation.
So the solutions of $x^3 - 2x^2 = -1$ are $x = -0.6$, $x = 1$ and $x = 1.6$

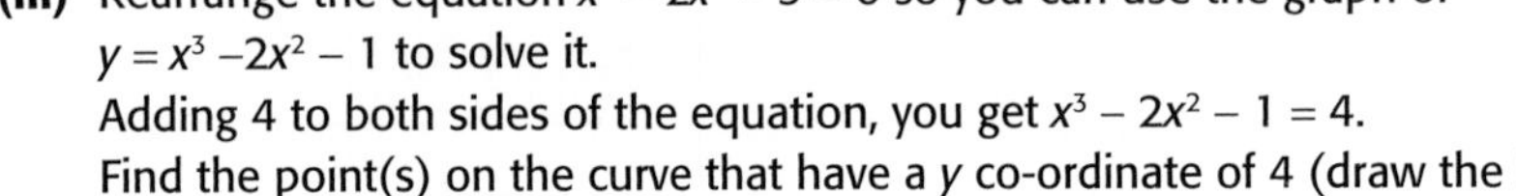

(iii) Rearrange the equation $x^3 - 2x^2 - 5 = 0$ so you can use the graph of $y = x^3 - 2x^2 - 1$ to solve it.
Adding 4 to both sides of the equation, you get $x^3 - 2x^2 - 1 = 4$.
Find the point(s) on the curve that have a y co-ordinate of 4 (draw the line $y = 4$ to help with this).
There is only one point (C on the graph).
At C the x co-ordinate is 2.7.
The approximate solution is, therefore, $x = 2.7$

Exercise 18.6

Before drawing the axes, check the range of y-values required from your table.

1 Construct a table of values from $-3 \le x \le 3$ and plot the points to draw graphs of the following equations.

(a) $y = 2x^3$ **(b)** $y = -3x^3$ **(c)** $y = x^3 - 2$ **(d)** $y = 3 + 2x^3$
(e) $y = x^3 - 2x^2$ **(f)** $y = 2x^3 - 4x + 1$ **(g)** $y = -x^3 + x^2 - 9$ **(h)** $y = x^3 - 2x^2 + 1$

2 **(a)** Copy and complete the table of values for the equation $y = x^3 - 6x^2 + 8x$. (You may want to add more rows to the table as in the worked examples.)

x	−1	−0.5	0	0.5	1.5	2	2.5	3	3.5	4	4.5	5
$y = x^3 - 6x^2 + 8x$	−15	−5.6										

(b) On a set of axes, draw the graph of the equation $y = x^3 - 6x^2 + 8x$ for $-1 \le x \le 5$.
(c) Use the graph to solve the equations:

(i) $x^3 - 6x^2 + 8x = 0$
(ii) $x^3 - 6x^2 + 8x = 3$

3 **(a)** Draw the graphs of $y = \frac{x^3}{10}$ and $y = 6x - x^2$ for $-4 \le x \le 6$.
(b) Use the graphs to solve the equation $\frac{x^3}{10} + x^2 - 6x = 0$

Graphs of equations with combinations of terms

When you have to plot graphs of equations with a combination of linear, quadratic, cubic, reciprocal or constant terms you need to draw up a table of values with at least eight values of x to get a good indication of the shape of the graph.

Worked example 10

Complete this table of values for the equation $y = 2x + \frac{1}{x}$ for $0.5 \leq x \leq 7$ and draw the graph.

x	0.5	1	2	3	4	5	6	7
$2x$	1	2	4	6	8	10	12	14
$\frac{1}{x}$								
$y = 2x + \frac{1}{x}$								

x	0.5	1	2	3	4	5	6	7
$2x$	1	2	4	6	8	10	12	14
$\frac{1}{x}$	2	1	0.5	0.33	0.25	0.2	0.17	0.14
$y = 2x + \frac{1}{x}$	3	3	4.5	6.33	8.25	10.2	12.17	14.14

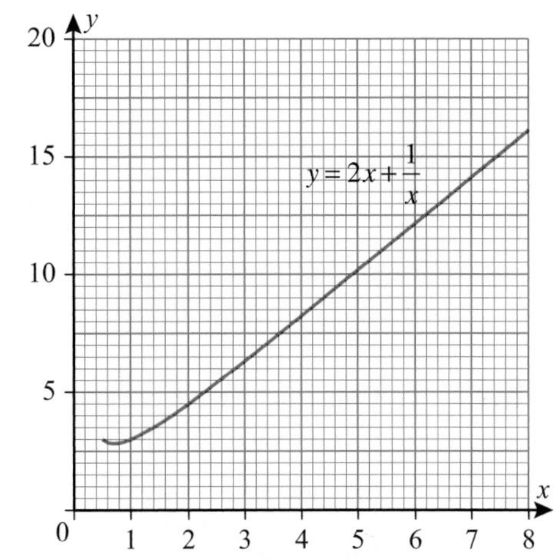

Worked example 11

Complete this table of values and plot the graph of $y = x^3 - \frac{1}{x}$ for $0.2 \leq x \leq 3$.

x	0.2	0.5	1	1.5	2	2.5	3
x^3	0.008		1		8		27
$-\frac{1}{x}$							
$y = x^3 - \frac{1}{x}$	−5.0						

x	0.2	0.5	1	1.5	2	2.5	3
x^3	0.008	0.125	1	3.375	8	15.625	27
$-\frac{1}{x}$	−5	−2	−1	−0.667	−0.5	−0.4	−0.33
$y = x^3 - \frac{1}{x}$	−5.0	−1.9	0	2.7	7.5	15.2	26.7

Round the y-values in the last row to 1 decimal place or it will be difficult to plot them.

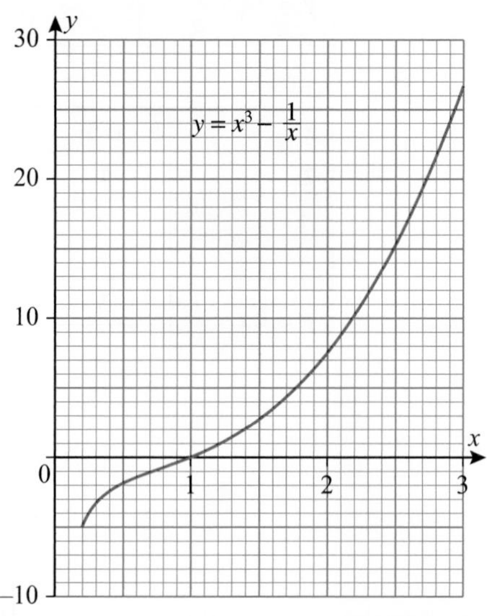

Exercise 18.7

REWIND

You learned about exponential growth and decay and applied a formula to calculate growth in chapter 17. ◀

1 Construct a table of values for $-3 \le x \le 3$ (including negative and positive values of 0.5 and 0.2) for each equation and draw the graph.

(a) $y = 3 + x^2 - \frac{2}{x}$

(b) $y = 3x - \frac{1}{x}$

(c) $y = -x + x^2 + \frac{2}{x}$

(d) $y = -x^3 - 2x + 1$ (omit the fractional values in this case)

Exponential graphs

An exponential graph in the form of $y = a^x$ will always intersect the y-axis at the point (0, 1) because $a^0 = 1$ for all values of a.

(You should remember this from the laws of indices.)

Euler's number, e = 2.71. . . , is so special that $y = e^x$ is known as *the* exponential function rather than *an* exponential function.

Exponential growth is found in many real life situations where a quantity increases by a constant percentage in a particular time: population growth and compound interest are both examples of exponential growth.

Equations in the general form of $y = a^x$ (where a is a positive integer) are called exponential equations.

The shape of $y = a^x$ is a curve which rapidly rises as it moves from left to right; this is exponential growth. As x becomes more negative, the curve gets closer and closer to the x-axis but never crosses it.

The shape of $y = a^{-x}$ is a curve which falls as it moves from left to right; this is exponential decay.

Worked example 12

(a) Complete the table of values for $y = 2^x$ for $-2 \leq x \leq 4$ and draw the graph.

x	−2	−1.5	−1	−0.5	0	1	2	3	4
$y = 2^x$									

(b) Use the graph to find the value of $2^{2.5}$ and check your result using the fact that $2^{2.5} = 2^{\frac{5}{2}} = \sqrt{2^5}$.

(a)

x	−2	−1.5	−1	−0.5	0	1	2	3	4
$y = 2^x$	0.25	0.35	0.5	0.71	1	2	4	8	16

Plot the points to draw the graph.

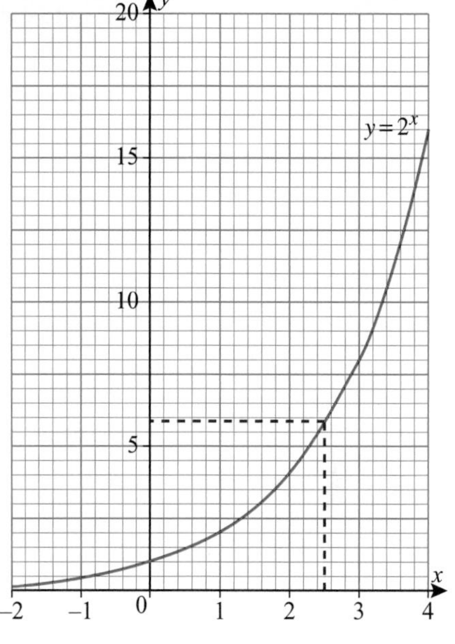

(b) From the graph you can see that when $x = 2.5$ the value of y is 5.7, so, $2^{2.5} \approx 5.7$

Check: $2^{2.5} = 2^{\frac{5}{2}} = \sqrt{2^5} = \sqrt{32} = 5.656...$

Exercise 18.8

1 (a) Draw the graph of $y = 3^x$ for x-values between −2 and 3. Give the values to 2 decimal places where necessary.

(b) On the same set of axes draw the graph of $y = 3^{-x}$ for x-values between −3 and 2. Give the values to 2 decimal places where necessary.

(c) What is the relationship between the graph of $y = 3^x$ and $y = 3^{-x}$?

2 The graph of $y = 10^x$ for $-0.2 \leq x \leq 1.0$ is shown here.

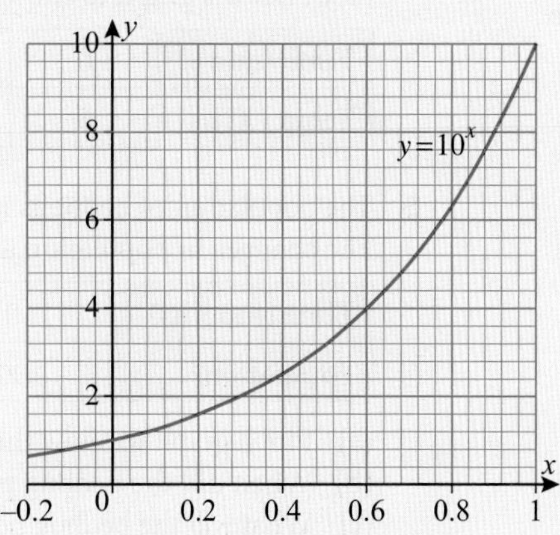

Use the graph to find the value of:

(a) $10^{0.3}$
(b) $10^{-0.1}$
(c) Copy the diagram using tracing paper and draw a straight line graph that will allow you solve the equation $10^x = 8 - 5x$.

Living maths

3 Bacteria multiply rapidly because a cell divides into two cells and then those two cells divide to each produce two more cells and so on. The growth rate is exponential and we can express the population of bacteria over time using the formula $P = 2^t$ (t is the period of time).

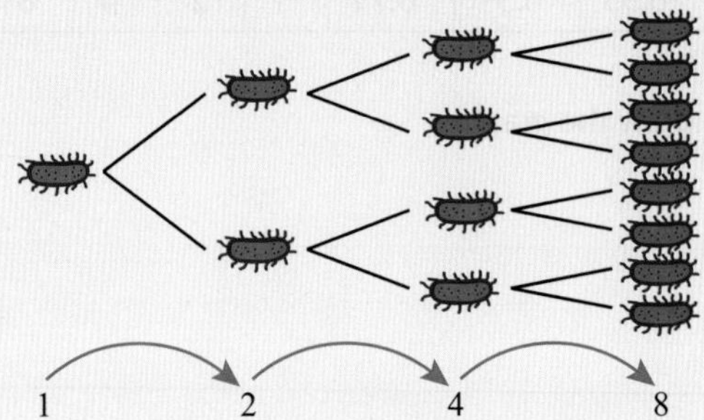

The graph shows the increase in bacteria numbers in a six-hour period.

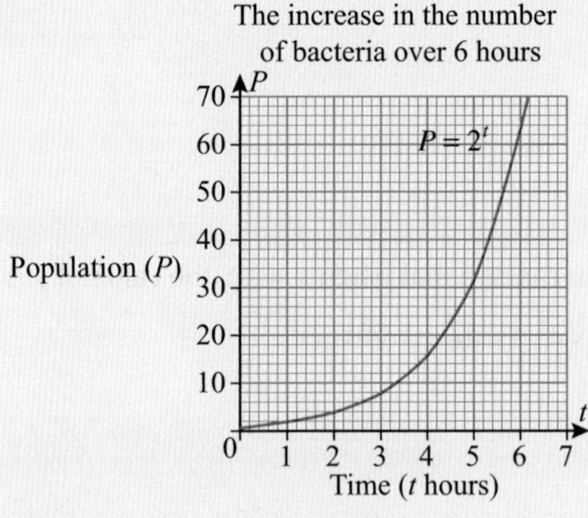

(a) How many bacteria are there after one hour?
(b) How long does it take for the number of bacteria to exceed 40 cells?
(c) How many cells will there be after six hours?
(d) When would you expect the population to exceed one million bacteria if it continued to grow at this rate?

These figures look different to the ones you are used to because the equation describing the temperature in terms of time is $T = 5 \times 3^t$; where T is the temperature and t is the time in minutes.

4 The temperature of metal in a smelting furnace increases exponentially as indicated in the table. Draw a graph to show this data.

Time (min)	0	1	2	3	4
Temp (°C)	5	15	45	135	405

5 The population of bedbugs in New York City is found to be increasing exponentially. The changes in population are given below.

Time (months)	0	1	2	3	4
Population	1000	2000	4000	8000	16 000

(a) Plot a graph to show the population increase over time.
(b) When did the bedbug population reach 10 000?
(c) What will the bedbug population be after six months if it continues to increase at this rate?

Recognising which graph to draw

You need to be able to look at equations and identify which type of graph they represent. This table summarises what you have learned so far.

Type of graph	General equation	Shape of graph
Straight line (linear)	$y = mx + c$ Highest power of x is 1. When $x = a$ the line is parallel to the y-axis and when $y = b$ the line is parallel to the x-axis.	
Parabola (quadratic)	$y = x^2$ $y = ax^2 + bx + c$ Highest power of x is 2.	
Hyperbola (reciprocal)	$y = \frac{a}{x}$ or $xy = a$	
Cubic curve	$y = x^3$ $y = ax^3 + bx^2 + cx + d$ Highest power of x is 3.	
Exponential curve	$y = a^x$ or $y = a^{-x}$	
Combined curve (linear, quadratic, cubic and/or reciprocal)	Up to three terms of: $y = ax^3 + bx^2 + cx + \frac{d}{x} + e$	

18.6 Finding the gradient of a curve

REWIND

Look again at calculating gradients from chapter 10. Make sure you understand how to do this before moving onto this section. ◀

This simple graph of height against distance shows the route followed by a mountain biker on a trail.

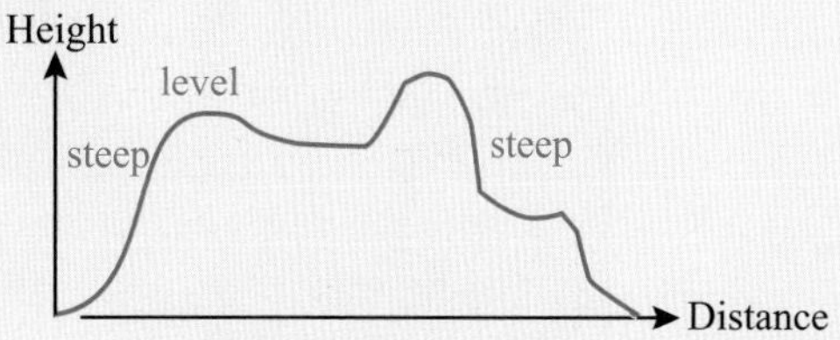

Some parts of the trail have a steep positive **gradient**, some have a gradual positive gradient, some parts are level and other parts have a negative gradient. It should be clear from this graph, that a curved graph never has a single gradient like a straight line has.

You cannot find the gradient of a whole curve but you can find the gradient of a point on the curve by drawing a **tangent** to it.

The gradient of a curve at a point is the gradient of the tangent to the curve at that point. Once you have drawn the tangent to a curve, you can work out the gradient of the tangent just as you would for a straight line $\left(\text{gradient} = \frac{y\text{-change}}{x\text{-increase}}\right)$.

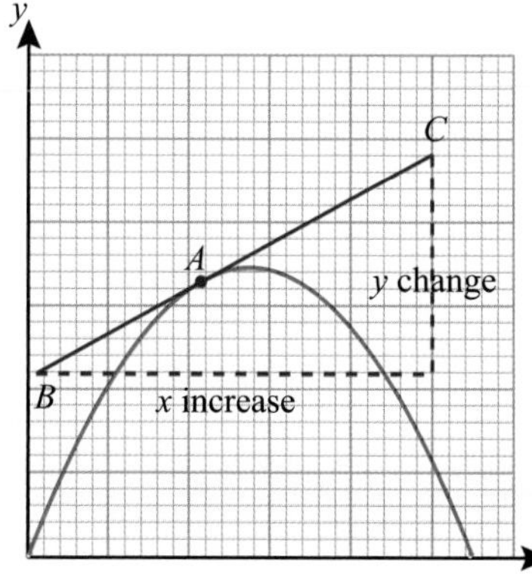

Look at the graph in the margin to see how this works. BC is the tangent to the curve.

How to draw the tangent

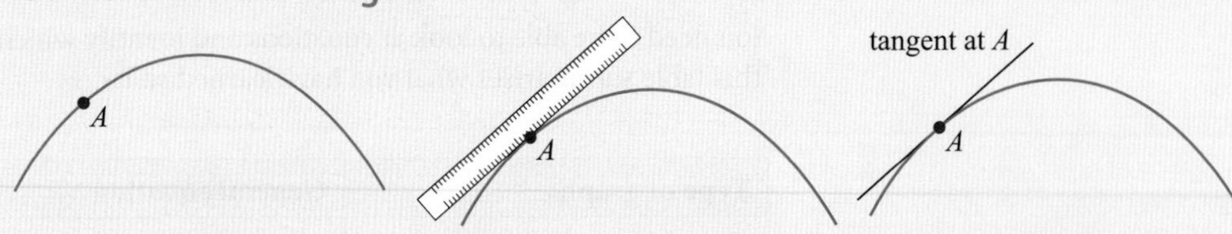

Mark a point on the curve (A).

Place your ruler against the curve so that it touches it only at point A.

Position the ruler so that the angle on either side of the point is more or less equal. Use a pencil to draw the tangent.

If you extend your tangent, it may touch your curve again at a completely different point but this is not a problem.

Calculating the gradient to a tangent

Mark two points, P and Q, on the tangent. Try to make the horizontal distance between P and Q a whole number of units (measured on the x-axis scale).
Draw a horizontal line through P and a vertical line through Q to form a right-angled triangle PNQ.

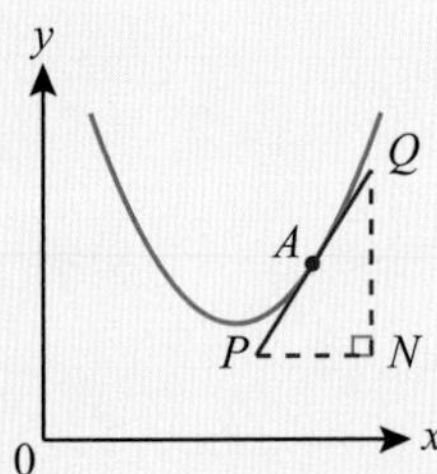

If the tangent is rising from left to right, its gradient is positive. If the tangent is falling from left to right, its gradient is negative.

Upwards = positive

Downwards = negative

$$\text{Gradient of the curve at } A = \text{Gradient of the tangent } PAQ = \frac{\text{distance } NQ \text{ (measured on the } y\text{-axis scale)}}{\text{distance } PN \text{ (measured on } x\text{-axis scale)}}$$

Tip

You must measure NQ and PN according to the scales on the y-axis and x-axis respectively. One of the most common mistakes is not doing this!

Worked example 13

The graph of the equation $y = 5x - x^2$ is shown in the diagram. Find the gradient of the graph:

(a) at the point (1, 4)
(b) at the point (3, 6).

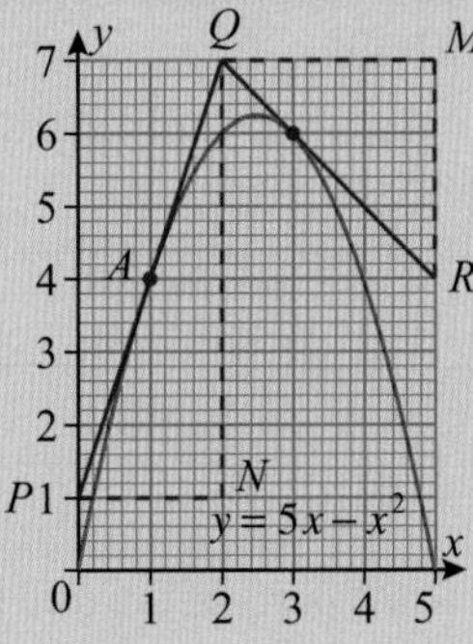

(a) At the point $A(1, 4)$, gradient $= \frac{NQ}{PN} = \frac{6}{2} = 3$

(b) At the point $B(3, 6)$, gradient $= \frac{MR}{QM} = \frac{-3}{3} = -1$

Tip

When estimating the gradient of a curve at a given point, it is sensible to use as long a tangent as possible on your diagram. The longer the tangent the more accurate the result.

Worked example 14

The graph shows the height of a tree (y metres) plotted against the age of the tree (x years). Estimate the rate at which the tree was growing when it was four years old.

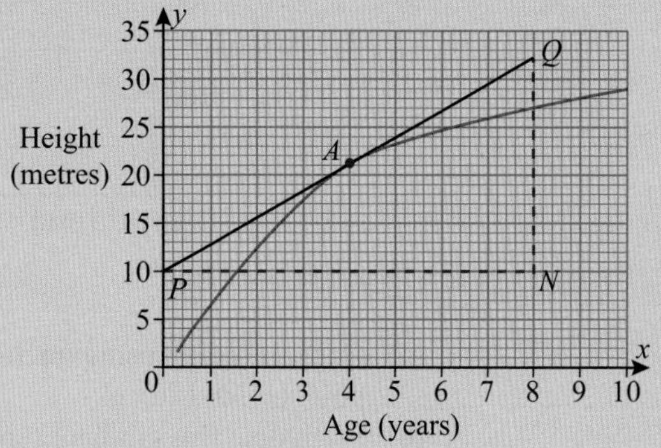

The rate at which the tree was growing when it was four years old is equal to the gradient of the curve at the point where $x = 4$.

Draw the tangent at this point (A).

Gradient at $A = \frac{NQ}{PN} = \frac{22.5}{8} = 2.8$

The tree was growing at a rate of 2.8 metres per year.

Exercise 18.9

1 The graph of $y = x^2$ is shown in the diagram.

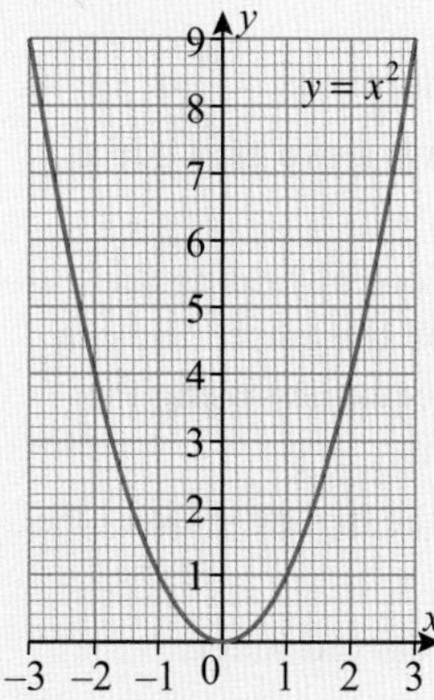

(a) Copy the graph using tracing paper and find the gradient of the graph at the point:

(i) (2, 4) (ii) (−1, 1).

(b) The gradient of the graph at the point (1.5, 2.25) is 3. Write down the co-ordinates of the point at which the gradient is −3.

2 The graph shows how the population of a village has changed since 1930.

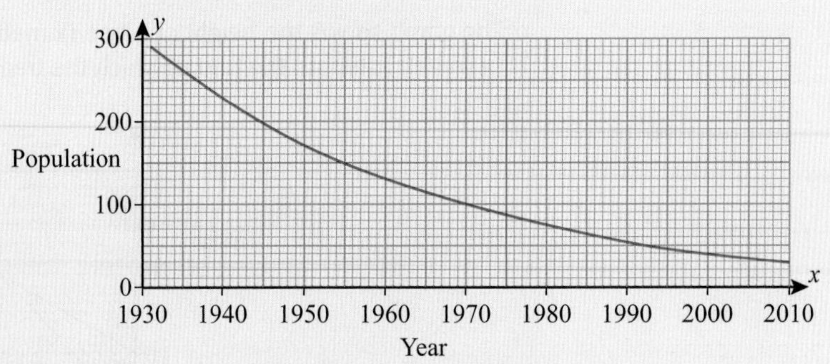

(a) Copy the graph using tracing paper and find the gradient of the graph at the point (1950, 170).

(b) What does this gradient represent?

3 **(a)** Draw the graph of the curve $y = x^3 + 1$ for values $-2 \leq x \leq 2$.

(b) Find the gradient of the curve at point $A(1, 2)$

Summary

Do you know the following?

- A quadratic equation is one in which the highest power of x is 2 (x^2).
- The graph of a quadratic equation is a recognisable curve called a parabola.
- A reciprocal equation is one in the form of $y = \frac{a}{x}$ or $xy = a$.
- The graph of a reciprocal equation is a two-part curve called a hyperbola.
- You can use graphs to solve equations by finding the value of x or y at different points on the graph. You can find the solution to simultaneous equations using the points of intersection of two graphs.
- A cubic equation is one in which the highest power of x is 3 (x^3).
- The graph of a cubic equation is a curved shape.
- Linear, quadratic, cubic and reciprocal terms can occur in the same equation. It is possible to graph these curves by constructing a table of values and then plotting the points.
- An exponential equation has the form $y = a^x$. These equations produce steep curved graphs.
- You can draw a tangent to a curve and use it to find the gradient of the curve at the point where the tangent touches it.

Are you able to …?

- construct a table of values for quadratic and reciprocal equations
- plot the graph of a parabola from a table of values
- plot the graph of a hyperbola from a table of values
- interpret straight line and quadratic graphs and use them to solve related equations
- construct tables of values and draw graphs for cubic equations and simple sums of linear and non-linear terms
- construct a table of values and draw the graph of an exponential equation
- interpret graphs of higher order equations and use them to solve related equations
- estimate the gradient of a curve by drawing a tangent to the curve.

Examination practice

Exam-style questions

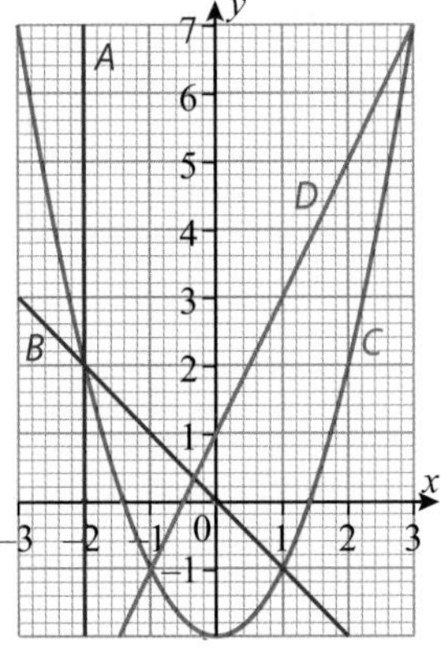

1 **(a)** Write the equation for each of the graphs *A*, *B*, *C* and *D*.

(b) Write down the co-ordinates of the intersection of:

(i) *A* and *B*

(ii) *C* and *D*

(c) What co-ordinates satisfy the equations of *B* and *D* at the same time?

(d) Which graph has an x-intercept of $-\frac{1}{2}$?

(e) Which graph is symmetrical about the y-axis?

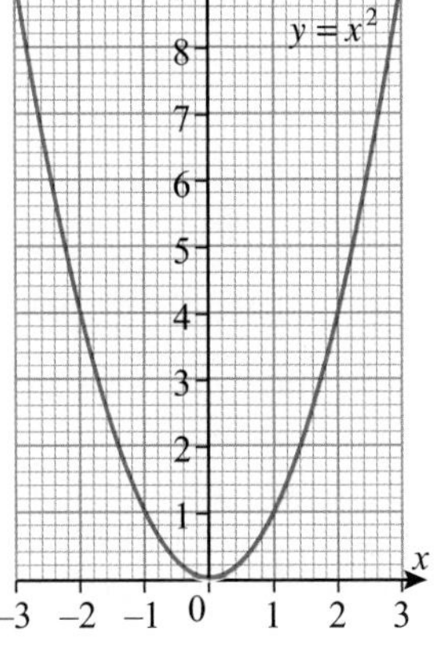

2 The graph of $y = x^2$ is drawn on the grid.

(a) The table shows some corresponding values of $y = x^2 + 3$. Copy and complete the table by filling in the missing values.

x	−2	−1.5	−1	−0.5	0	0.5	1	1.5	2
y		5.25	4	3.25	3		4	5.25	7

(b) Plot the graph of $y = x^2$ and the graph of $y = x^2 + 3$ for $-2 \le x \le 2$ on a grid.

(c) Will the two curves ever meet? Explain your answer.

(d) By drawing a suitable straight line on the same grid, solve the equations:

(i) $x^2 = 6$

(ii) $x^2 + 3 = 6$

3 Answer the whole of this question on graph paper.

x	0.6	1	1.5	2	2.5	3	3.5	4	4.5	5
y	f	−5.9	−3.7	−2.3	−1.1	0.3	1.9	3.8	q	r

Some of the values of $y = \frac{x^3}{12} - \frac{6}{x}$ are shown in the table above. Values of y are given correct to 1 decimal place.

(a) Find the values of p, q and r.

(b) Using a scale of 2 cm to represent 1 unit on the x-axis and 1 cm to represent 1 unit on the y-axis, draw the graph of $y = \frac{x^3}{12} - \frac{6}{x}$ for $-0.6 \le x \le 5$.

(c) From the graph, find the value of x (correct to 1 decimal place) for which $\frac{x^3}{12} - \frac{6}{x} = 0$.

(d) Draw the tangent to the curve at the point where $x = 1$, and estimate the gradient of the curve at that point.

4 Six sketch graphs are shown here.

(i)

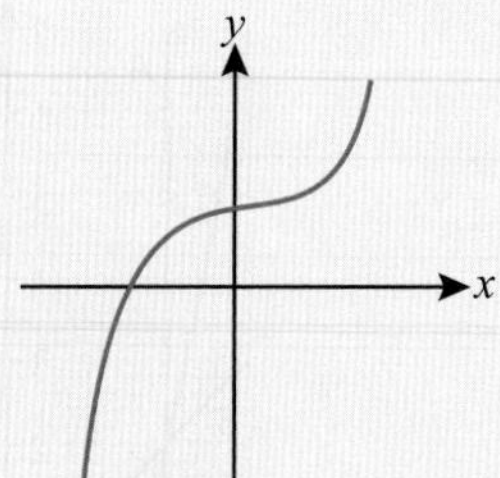

(ii)

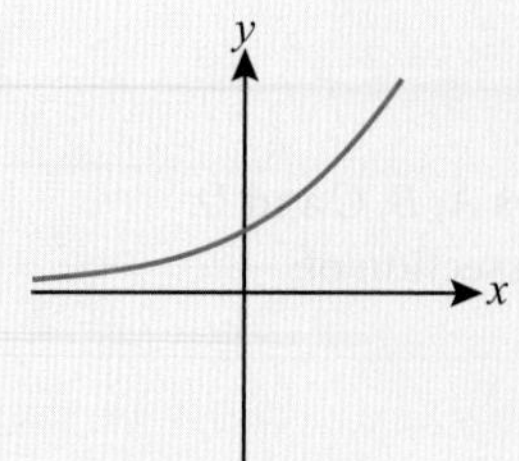

(iii)

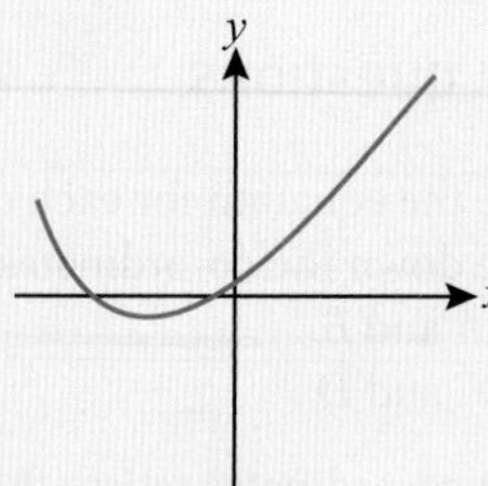

(iv)

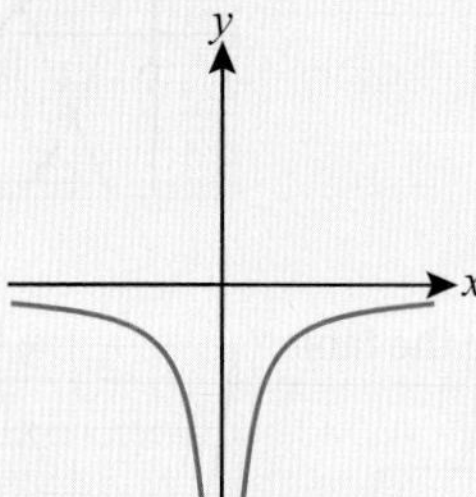

(v)

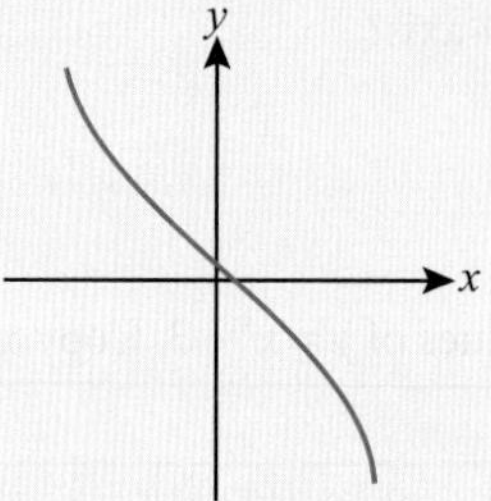

(vi)

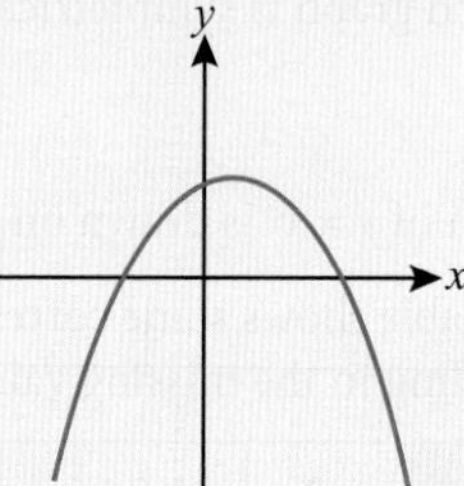

Match the graphs to the following equations.

(a) $y = 1 + x - 2x^2$

(b) $y = 3^x$

(c) $y = x^3 + x^2 + 1$

(d) $y = -\dfrac{16}{x^2}$

5 **(a)** In a chemical reaction, the mass, M grams, of a chemical is given by the formula $M = \dfrac{160}{2^t}$ where t is the time, in minutes, after the start.

A table of values for t and M is given below.

t (min)	0	1	2	3	4	5	6	7
M (g)	p	80	40	20	q	5	r	1.25

(i) Find the values of p, q and r.

(ii) Draw the graph of M against t for $0 \le t \le 7$. Use a scale of 2 cm to represent one minute on the horizontal t-axis and 1 cm to represent 10 grams on the vertical M-axis.

(iii) Draw a suitable tangent to your graph and use it to estimate the rate of change of mass when $t = 2$.

(b) The other chemical in the same reaction has mass m grams, which is given by $m = 160 - M$. For what value of t do the two chemicals have equal mass?

Past paper questions

1 **(a)**

(i) Complete the table for $y = 5 + 3x - x^2$. [3]

x	−2	−1	0	1	2	3	4	5
y	−5		5	7		5		−5

(ii) On the grid, draw the graph of $y = 5 + 3x - x^2$ for $-2 \le x \le 5$. [4]

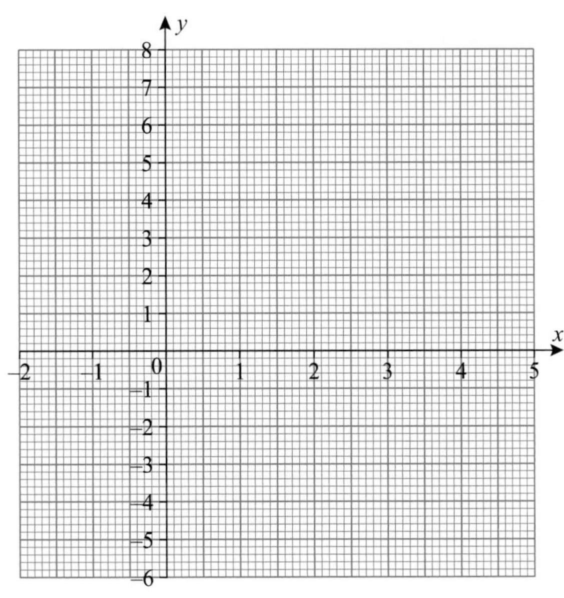

(b) Use your graph to solve the equation $5 + 3x - x^2 = 0$. [2]

(c)

(i) On the grid, draw the line of symmetry of $y = 5 + 3x - x^2$. [1]

(ii) Write down the equation of this line of symmetry. [1]

(d)

(i) On the grid, draw a straight line from (−1, 1) to (3, 5). [1]

(ii) Work out the gradient of this line. [2]

(iii) Write down the equation of this line in the form $y = mx + c$. [1]

[Cambridge IGCSE Mathematics 0580 Paper 33 Q05 October/November 2013]

2 **(a)** Complete the table of values for the equation $y = \frac{3}{x}, x \neq 0$.

x	−3	−2.5	−2	−1.5	−1	−0.5	−0.3	0.3	0.5	1	1.5	2	2.5	3
y	−1	−1.2		−2	−3	−6				3	2	1.5		1

[5]

(b) On a grid like the one below, draw the graph of $y = \frac{3}{x}$ for $-3 \le x \le -0.3$ and $0.3 \le x \le 3$.

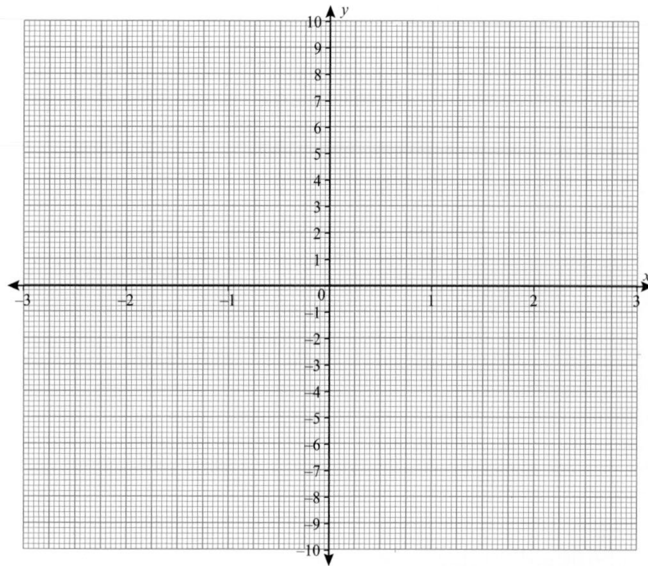

Tip

You will be given a grid, so you are unlikely to have to draw your own.

(c) Use your graph to solve the equation $\frac{3}{x} = 7$. [1]

(d) Complete the table of values for $y = \frac{2x}{3} - 1$. [2]

x	−3	0	3
y			

(e) On the grid, draw the straight line $y = \frac{2x}{3} - 1$ for $-3 \le x \le 3$. [2]

(f) Write down the co-ordinates of the points where the line $y = \frac{2x}{3} - 1$ intersects the graph of $y = \frac{3}{x}$. [2]

[Cambridge IGCSE Mathematics 0580 Paper 31 Q06 May/June 2010]

19 Symmetry and loci

Key words

- Symmetry
- Line symmetry
- Rotational symmetry
- Symmetrical
- Order of rotational symmetry
- Centre of rotation
- Plane symmetry
- Axis of symmetry
- Tangent
- Perpendicular bisector
- Chord
- Equidistant
- Subtend
- Arc
- Cyclic quadrilateral
- Locus
- Loci

In this chapter you will learn how to:

- identify line symmetry of two-dimensional shapes
- find the order of rotational symmetry of two-dimensional shapes
- recognise and use symmetrical properties of triangles, quadrilaterals and circles

EXTENDED

- recognise symmetry properties of prisms and pyramids
- apply symmetry properties of circles to solve problems

- understand that a locus describes the path of a set of points that obey a rule
- construct a locus for different sets of points in two-dimensions.

The front of this museum in Ho Chi Minh City in Vietnam, is symmetrical. If you draw a vertical line through the centre of the building (between the two red flags), the left side will be a mirror image of the right side.

The front of the building in the photograph is symmetrical. One half of the front of the building is the mirror image of the other. The line dividing the building into two halves is called the mirror line, or line of symmetry.

Shapes or objects that can be divided into two or more parts which are identical in shape and size are said to be symmetrical. Symmetry is found in both two-dimensional shapes and three-dimensional objects. In this chapter you are going to learn more about symmetry about a line, and turning, or rotational symmetry, in both two-dimensional shapes and three-dimensional objects.

19.1 Symmetry in two dimensions

There are two types of **symmetry** in two-dimensional shapes:

- **Line symmetry**
- **Rotational symmetry**

Line symmetry

If a shape can be folded so that one half fits exactly over the other half, it has line symmetry (also called reflection symmetry).

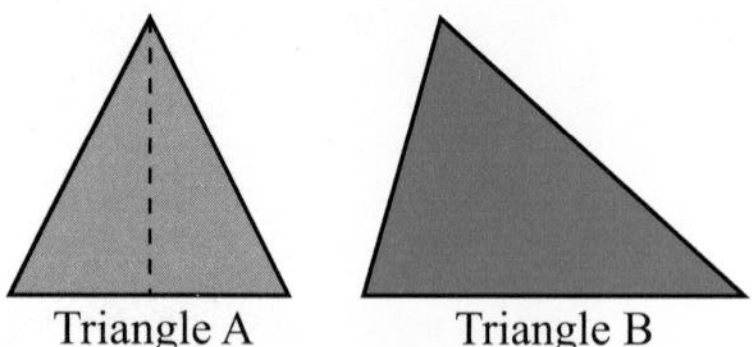

Triangle A is symmetrical. The dotted line divides it into two identical parts. Triangle B is not symmetrical. You cannot draw a line which will divide it into two identical halves.

If you place a mirror on the dividing line on shape A, the view in the mirror will be that of the whole triangle. The line is called the line of symmetry or mirror line of the shape.

Shapes can have more than one line of symmetry:

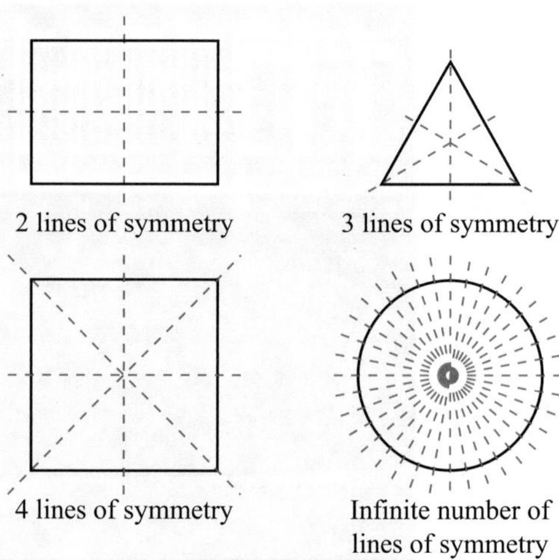

Exercise 19.1

1 Which of the broken lines in these figures are lines of symmetry? Check with a small mirror or trace and fold the shape if you are not sure.

Another name for an 'oval' is an 'ellipse'.

(a) Parallelogram

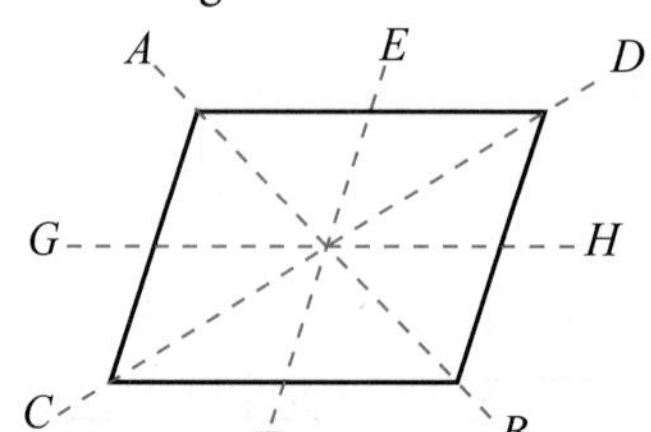

(b) Oval

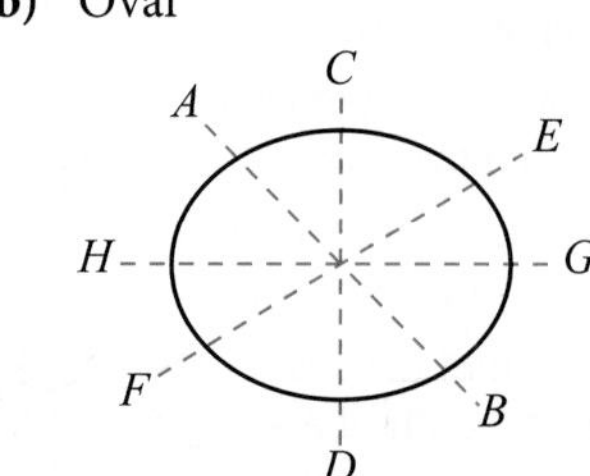

(c) Rectangle

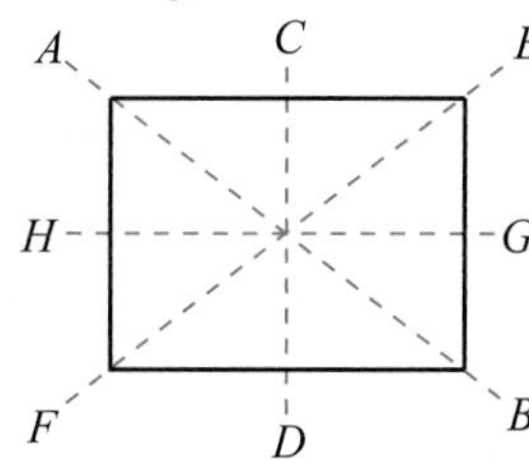

(d) Isosceles trapezium

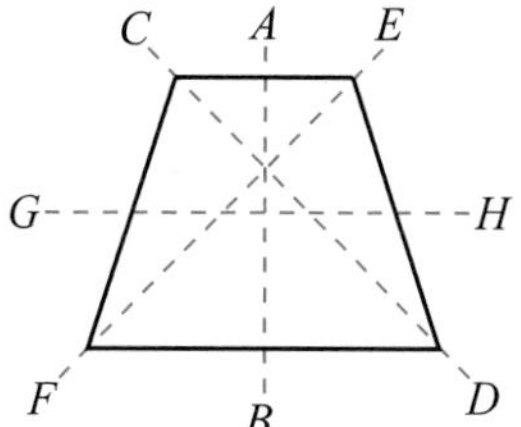

(e) Rhombus

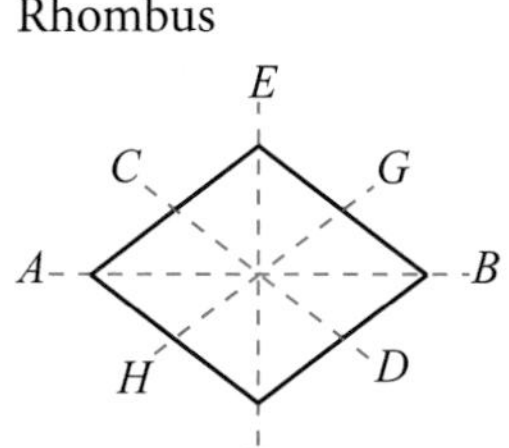

(f) Torus

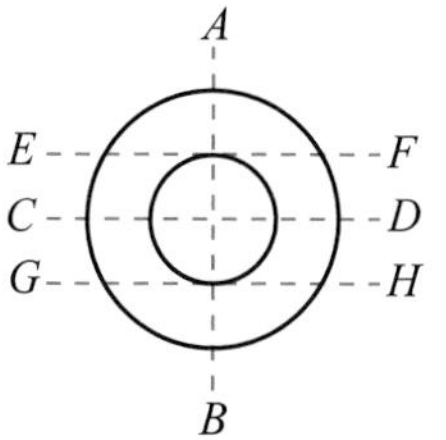

(g) L-shape

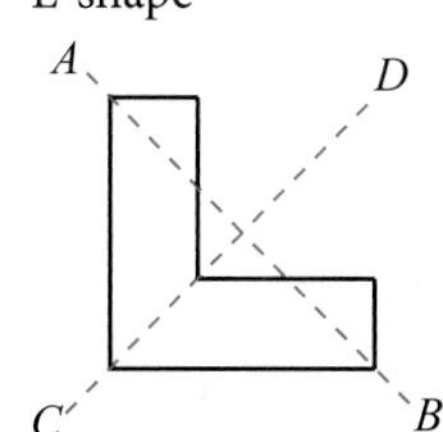

(h) Regular pentagon

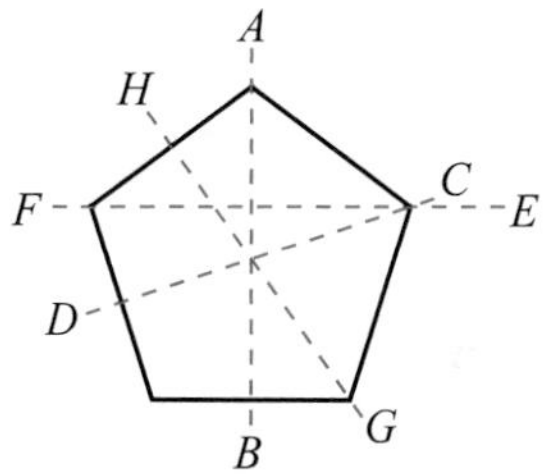

2 Sketch the following polygons and investigate to see how many lines of symmetry each one has. Copy and complete the table to summarise your results.

Shape	Number of lines of symmetry
Square	
Rectangle	
Equilateral triangle	
Isosceles triangle	
Scalene triangle	
Kite	
Parallelogram	
Rhombus	
Regular pentagon	
Regular hexagon	
Regular octagon	

3 Copy these figures and draw in all possible lines of symmetry.

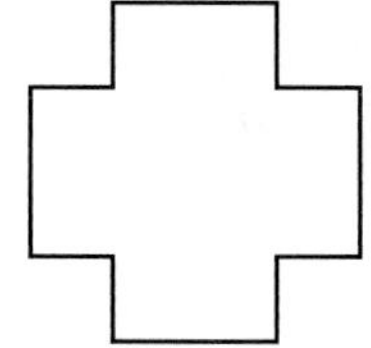

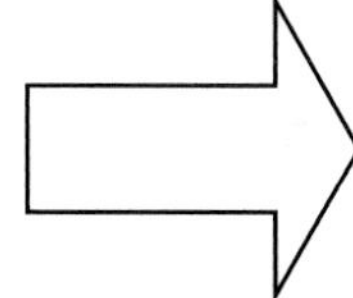
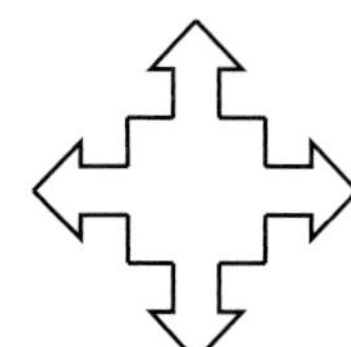

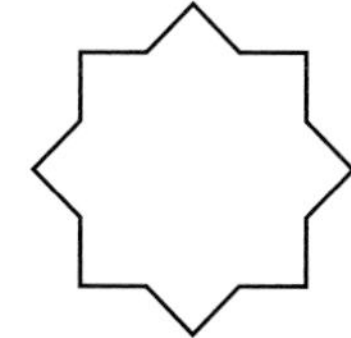

FAST FORWARD

You will deal with line symmetry on the Cartesian plane when you deal with reflections about a line in chapter 23. ▶

Think carefully about how the paper is folded. The diagram shows that it's folded into four.

Living maths

4 The children in a primary school class make shapes for a class pattern by cutting out a design drawn on the corner of a folded piece of paper.

(a) Draw the shapes that will be produced by each of these cut outs.
(b) Show the lines of symmetry on each shape by means of dotted lines.

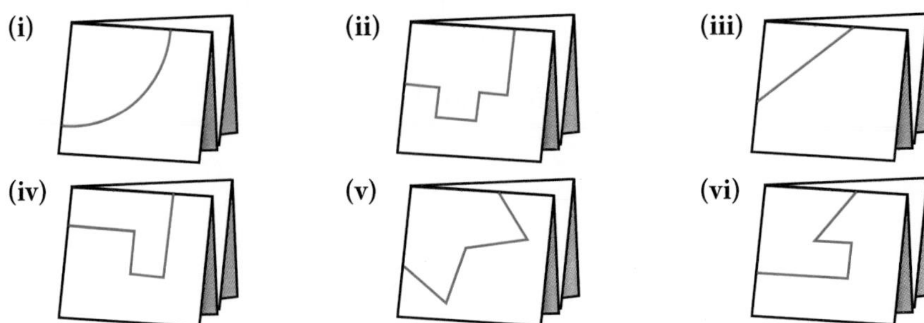

5 Find and draw the badges of five different makes of motor vehicle. Indicate the lines of symmetry on each drawing.

FAST FORWARD

You will deal with rotational symmetry on the Cartesian plane when you deal with rotations in chapter 23. ▶

Rotational symmetry

A rotation is a turn. If you rotate a shape through 360°, keeping its centre point in a fixed position, and it fits onto itself exactly at various positions during the turn, then it has rotational symmetry. The number of times it fits onto itself during a full revolution is its **order of rotational symmetry.**

The diagram shows how a square fits onto itself four times when it is turned through 360°. The dot in the centre of the square is the **centre of rotation.** This is the point around which it is turning. The star shows the position of one corner of the square as it turns.

If you have to turn the shape through a full 360° before its fits onto itself then it does *not* have rotational symmetry. Be careful though, because every shape will fit back onto itself after a whole revolution.

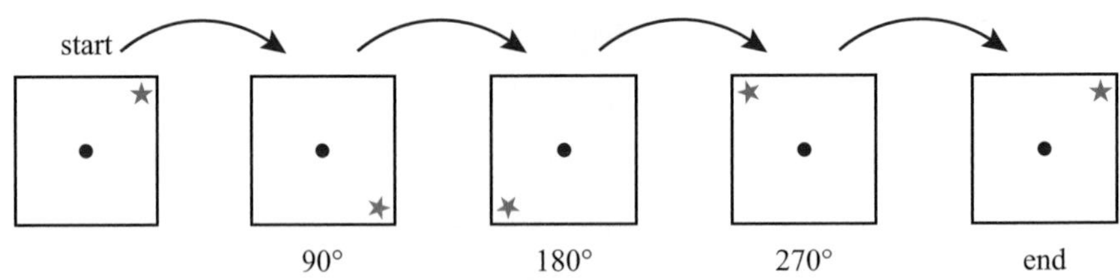

The square fits exactly onto itself four times in a rotation, when it has turned through 90°, 180°, 270° and 360°, so its order of rotational symmetry is 4. Remember it has to turn 360° to get back to its original position.

Exercise 19.2

1 State the order of rotational symmetry of each of the following polygons. The dot represents the centre of rotation in each.

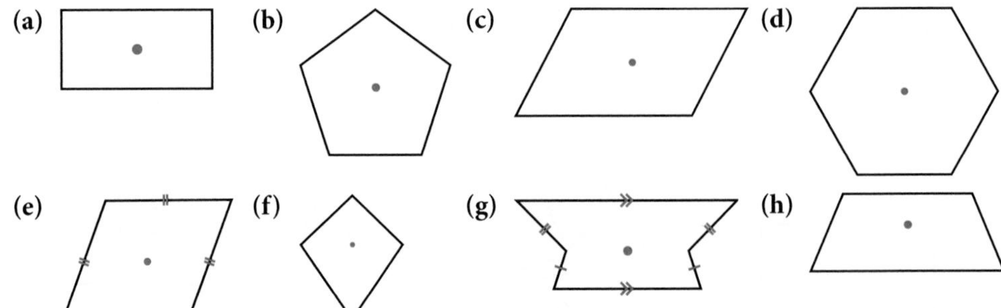

2 This table shows how many lines of symmetry there are in six regular polygons.

Regular polygon	Lines of symmetry	Order of rotational symmetry
Triangle	3	
Quadrilateral	4	
Pentagon	5	
Hexagon	6	
Octagon	8	
Decagon	10	

(a) Draw each shape and investigate its rotational symmetry. Sometimes it helps to physically turn the shape to see how many times it fits onto itself in a revolution.
(b) Copy and complete the table by filling in the order of rotational symmetry for each polygon.
(c) Describe how line symmetry and rotational symmetry are related in regular polygons.
(d) What pattern can you see relating line symmetry, order of rotational symmetry and number of sides in a regular polygon?

Living maths

3 Refer back to the motor vehicle badges you drew in Exercise 19.1. For each one, state its order of rotational symmetry.

4 Using a computer, print out the capital letters of the alphabet. (You can choose whichever font you like). Which letters have:

(a) only one line of symmetry?
(b) two or more lines of symmetry?
(c) rotational symmetry of order 2 or more?

5 Alloy rims for tyres are very popular on modern cars. Find and draw five alloy rim designs that you like. For each one, state its order of rotational symmetry.

19.2 Symmetry in three dimensions

REWIND

Three-dimensional figures (solids) were covered in chapter 7. ◀

There are two types of symmetry in three-dimensional shapes:

- **Plane symmetry**
- Rotational symmetry

Plane symmetry

A plane of symmetry in a three-dimensional solid is similar to a line of symmetry in a two-dimensional shape.

A plane is a flat surface. If you can cut a solid in half so that each half is the mirror image of the other, then the solid has plane symmetry.

This diagram of a cuboid shows that it can be cut three different ways to make two identical halves. The shaded area on each diagram represents the plane of symmetry (this is where you would cut it).

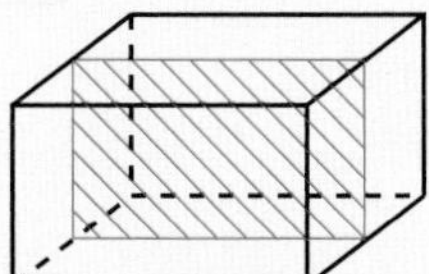
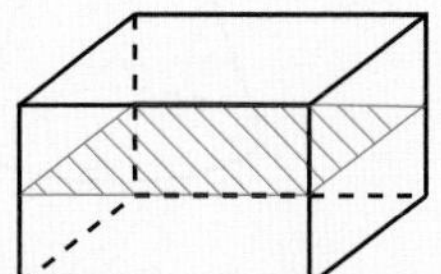
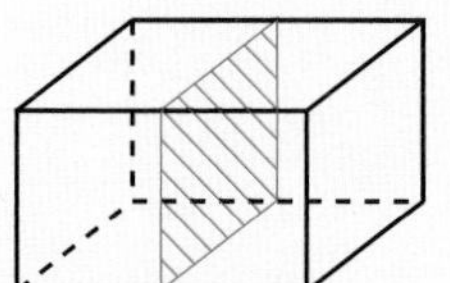

There are three planes of symmetry in a rectangular cuboid.

This diagram shows two possible cuts through a sphere that produce two identical halves.

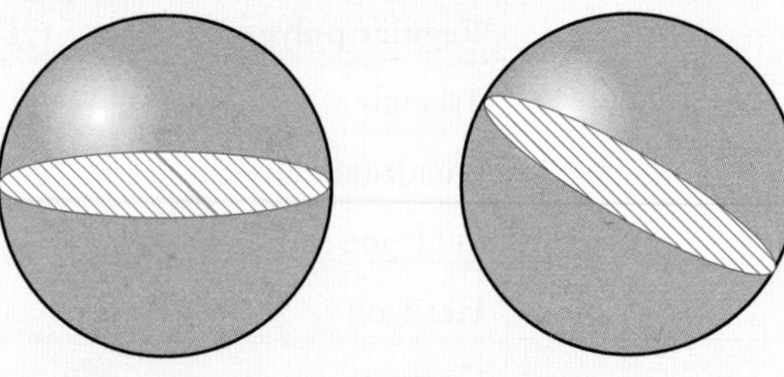

A sphere has an infinite number of planes of symmetry. It is symmetrical about any plane that passes through its centre.

Exercise 19.3

1 Here are two of the planes of symmetry in a cube:

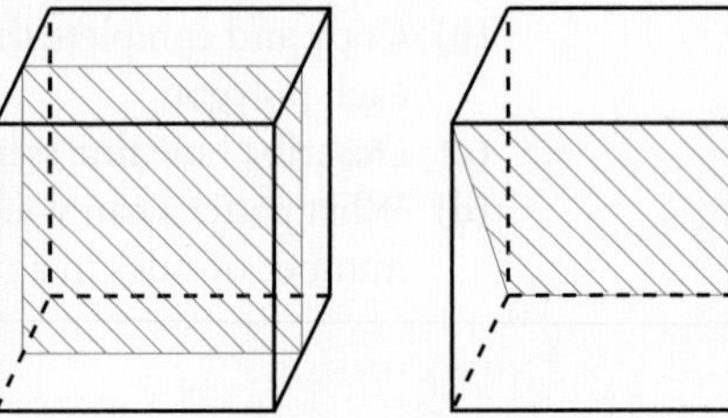

A cube has nine possible planes of symmetry. Make sketches to show the other seven planes.

2 How many planes of symmetry does each of the following solids have?

(a) (b)

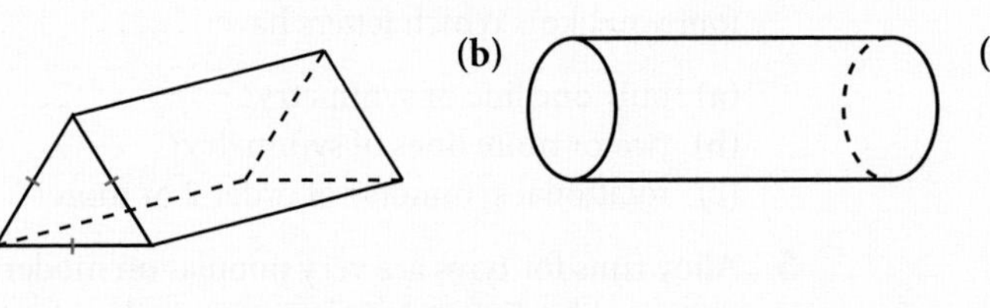

(c)

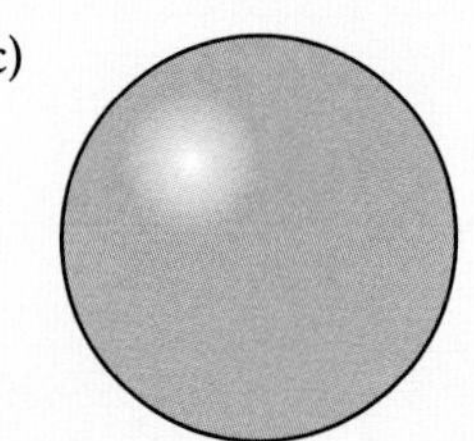

(d)

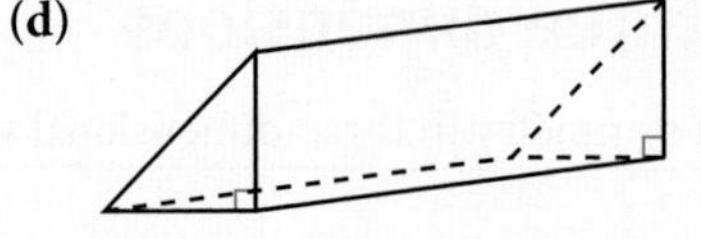

(e)

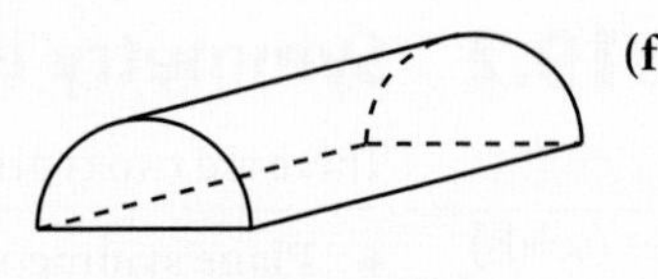

(f)

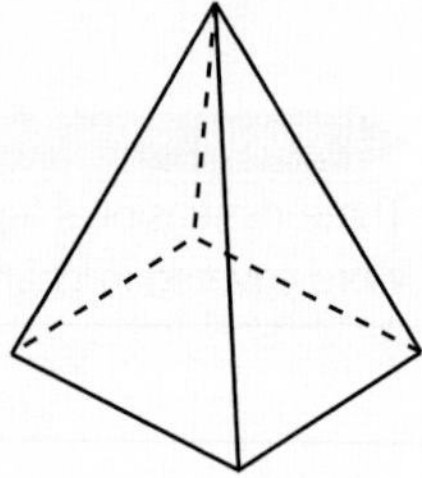

(g)

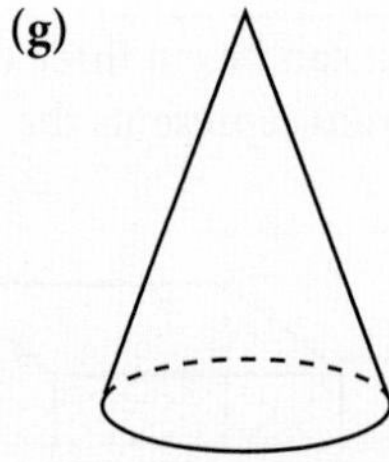

(h)

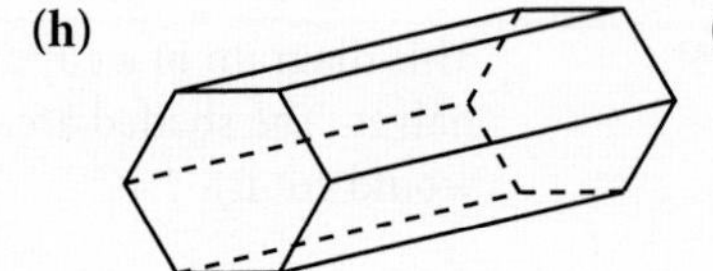

(i)

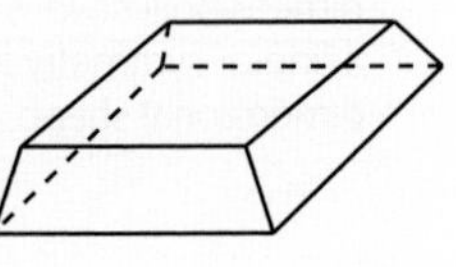

Rotational symmetry

Imagine a rod through a solid shape. The rod forms an axis for the shape to turn around. If you rotate the shape around the axis and it looks the same at different points on its rotation, then the shape has rotational symmetry. The rod is then the **axis of symmetry**.

This triangular prism has rotational symmetry of order 3 around the given axis.

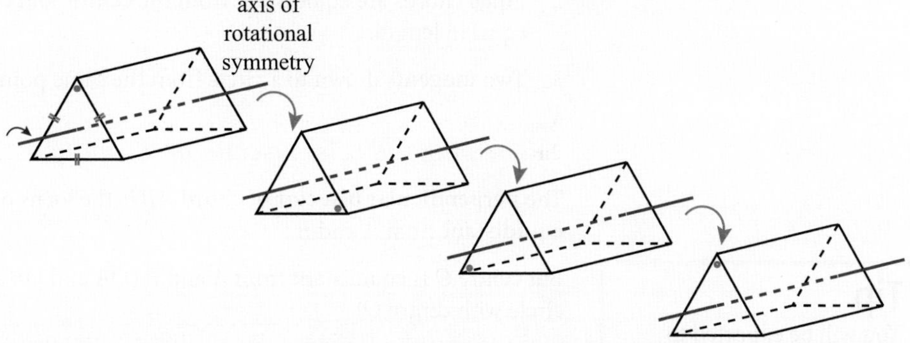

The triangular prism looks the same in three positions during a rotation, as it turns for rotation about 120°, 240° and 360°. The dot shows the position of one of the vertices during the turn.

Exercise 19.4

1 This diagram shows three possible axes of symmetry through a cuboid. For each one, state the order of rotational symmetry clockwise through 360°.

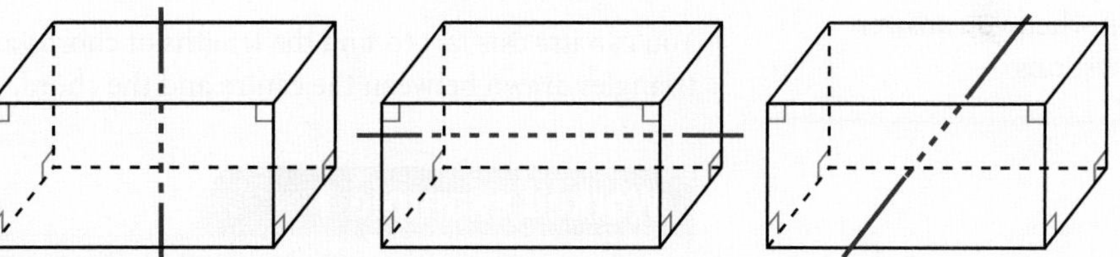

2 For each solid shown, determine the order of rotational symmetry for rotation about the given axis.

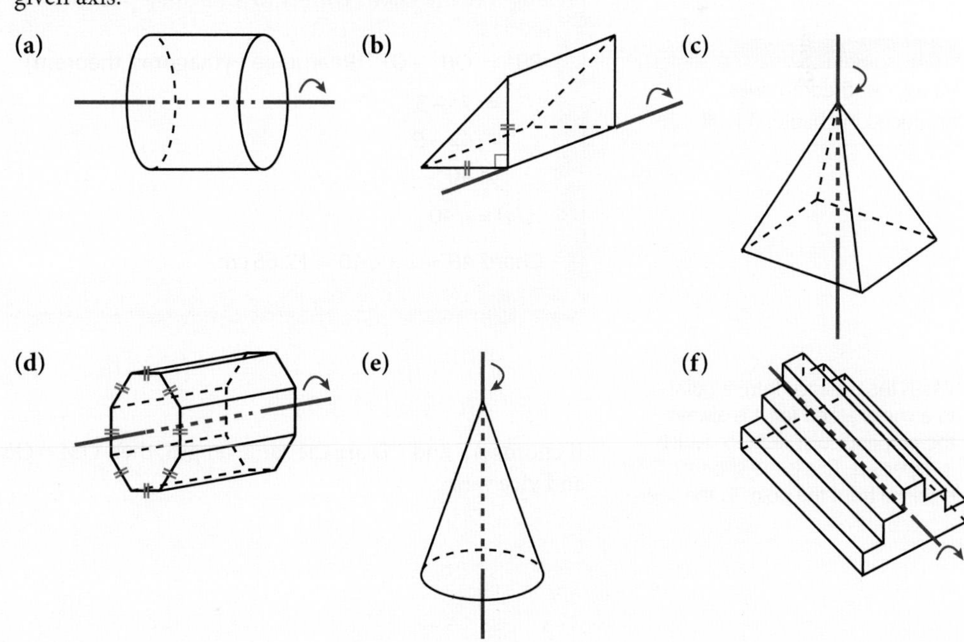

19.3 Symmetry properties of circles

REWIND

You were introduced to chords in chapter 3. ◀

A circle has line symmetry about any diameter and it has rotational symmetry about its centre. From these facts a number of results can be deduced:

1. The perpendicular bisector of a chord passes through the centre.
2. Equal chords are equidistant from the centre, and chords equidistant from the centre are equal in length.
3. Two **tangents** drawn to a circle from the same point outside the circle are equal in length.

1. The perpendicular bisector of a chord passes through the centre

The **perpendicular bisector** of **chord** *AB* is the locus of points **equidistant** from *A* and *B*.

But centre *O* is equidistant from *A* and *B* (*OA* and *OB* are radii of circle with centre *O*).

∴ *O* must be on the perpendicular bisector of *AB*.

Tip

You will be expected to state all symmetry and angle properties 'formally'. Learn the statements as they appear throughout the coming pages and be prepared to write them out when you answer questions.

This result can be expressed in other ways:

- The perpendicular from the centre of a circle to a chord meets the chord at its mid-point.
- The line joining the centre of a circle to the mid-point of a chord is perpendicular to the chord.

You can use this fact to find the lengths of chords and the lengths of sides of right-angled triangles drawn between the centre and the chord.

Worked example 1

Chord *AB* is drawn in a circle with a radius of 7 cm.
If the chord is 3 cm from the centre of the circle, find the length of the chord correct to 2 decimal places.

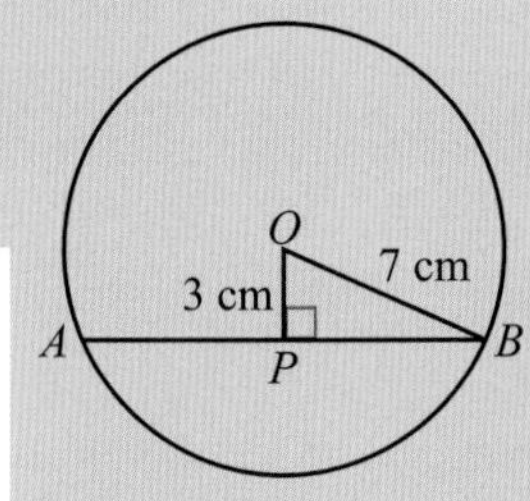

$PB^2 = OB^2 - OP^2$ (Rearrange Pythagoras' theorem)

$= 7^2 - 3^2$

$= 49 - 9$

$= 40$

$\therefore PB = \sqrt{40}$

Chord $AB = 2 \times \sqrt{40} = 12.65$ cm

REWIND

Pythagoras' theorem was introduced in chapter 11. ◀

When the distance from a point to a line is asked for, it is always the perpendicular distance which is expected. This is the shortest distance from the point to the line.

2. Equal chords are equidistant from the centre and chords equidistant from the centre are equal in length

If chords *AB* and *CD* are the same length, then *OM* = *ON*, and vice versa.

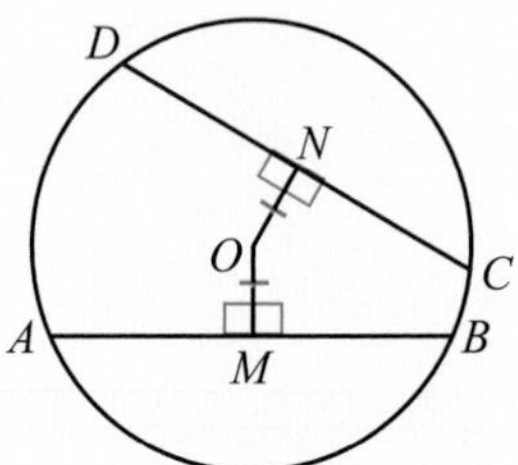

Think about how you could you prove $\Delta OAM \equiv \Delta ODN$; remember *OA* and *OD* are radii of the circle.

This is true because triangle *OAM* is congruent to triangle *ODN* and because the circle has rotational symmetry about its centre, *O*.

Worked example 2

O is the centre of the circle, radius 11 cm.
AB and CD are chords, $AB = 14$ cm.
If $OX = OY$, find the length of OY correct to 2 decimal places.

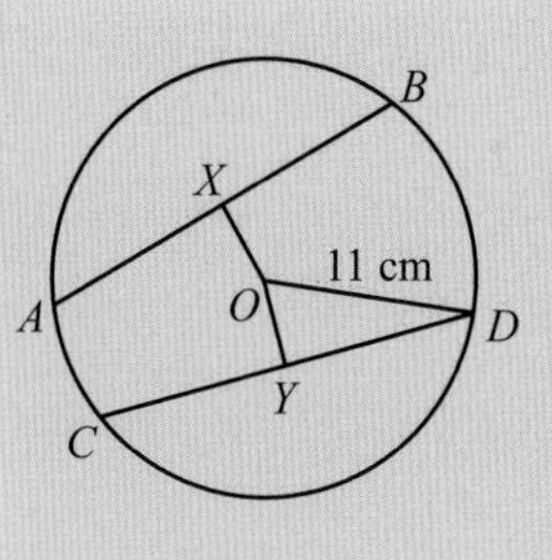

Since $OX = OY$, chords are equidistant so, $AB = CD = 14$ cm
$CY = YD = 7$ cm (OY is perpendicular bisector of CD)
$\angle OYD = 90°$

$$OY^2 = OD^2 - YD^2 \text{ (Pythagoras)}$$
$$= 11^2 - 7^2$$
$$= 121 - 49$$
$$= 72$$

$\therefore OY = \sqrt{72} = 8.49$ cm

3. Two tangents drawn to a circle from the same point outside the circle are equal in length

A and B are the points of contact of the tangents drawn from P.

The result is $PA = PB$.

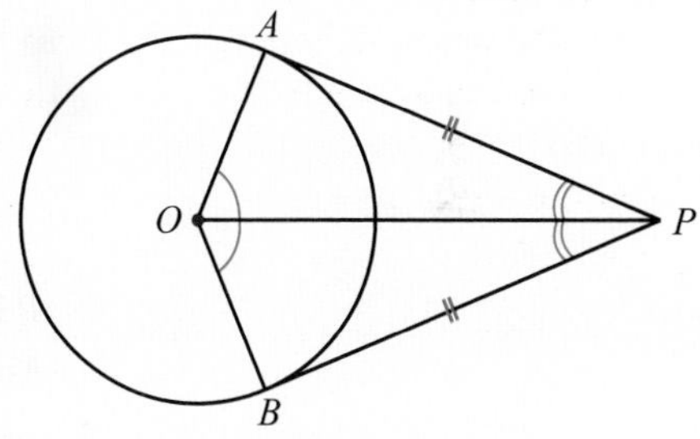

In addition:

- the tangents **subtend** equal angles at the centre (i.e. $\angle POA = \angle POB$)
- the line joining the centre to the point where the tangents meet bisects the angle between the tangents. (i.e. $\angle OPA = \angle OPB$)

This is true because the figure is symmetrical about the line OP. It can also be shown by proving that ΔOAP is congruent to ΔOBP. You need to use the 'tangent perpendicular to radius' property for this.

Worked example 3

Find the length of x and y in this diagram correct to 2 decimal places where appropriate.

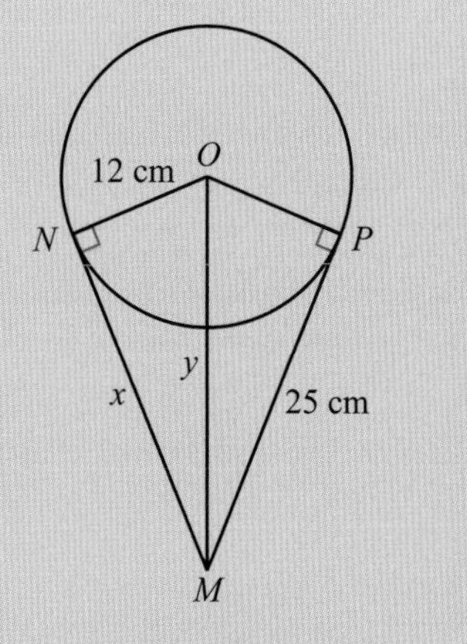

$NM = PM = 25$ cm (equal tangents)
$\therefore x = 25$ cm

$$y^2 = x^2 + NO^2 \text{ (Pythagoras)}$$
$$= 25^2 + 12^2$$
$$= 625 + 144$$
$$= 769$$

$y = \sqrt{769} = 27.73$ cm

Worked example 4

Find the size of angles x and y in this diagram.

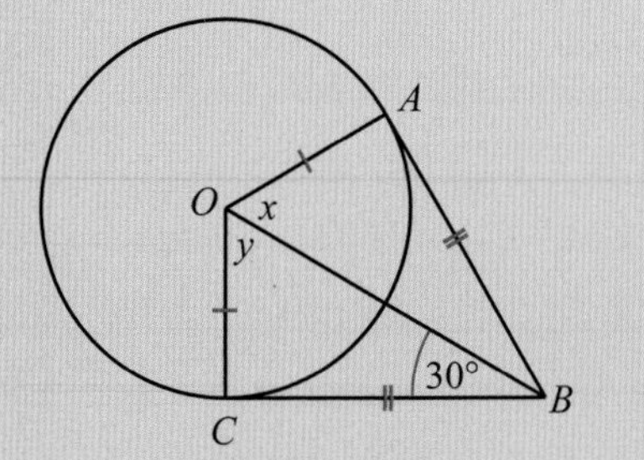

$\angle OCB = 90°$ (OC perpendicular to tangent CB)

$\therefore y = 180° - 90° - 30°$ (angle sum of triangle)

$y = 60°$

$y = x = 60°$ (tangents subtend equal angles at centre)

Exercise 19.5

1 Calculate the length of the chord AB in each of the following circles. (In each case, X is the mid-point of AB.)

(a) (b) 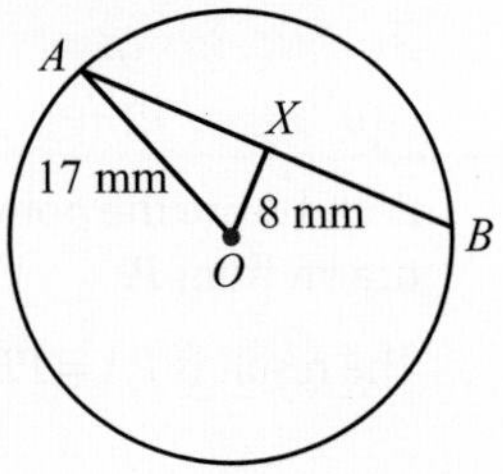 (c)

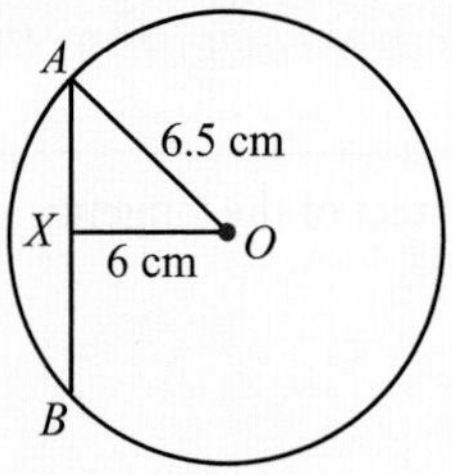

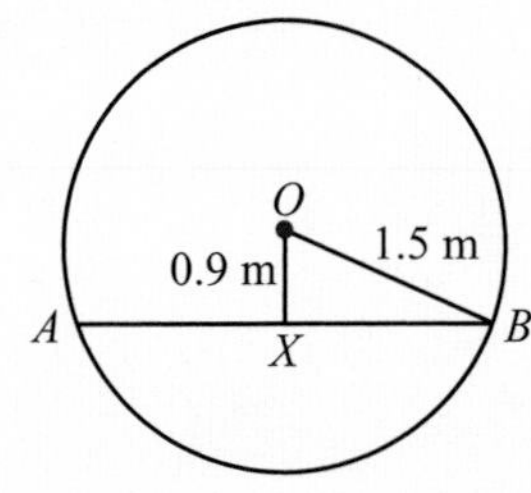

2 P is a point inside a circle whose centre is O. Describe how to construct the chord that has P as its mid-point

Concentric circles are circles with different radii but the same centre.

3 A straight line cuts two concentric circles at A, B, C and D (in that order).

Prove that $AB = CD$.

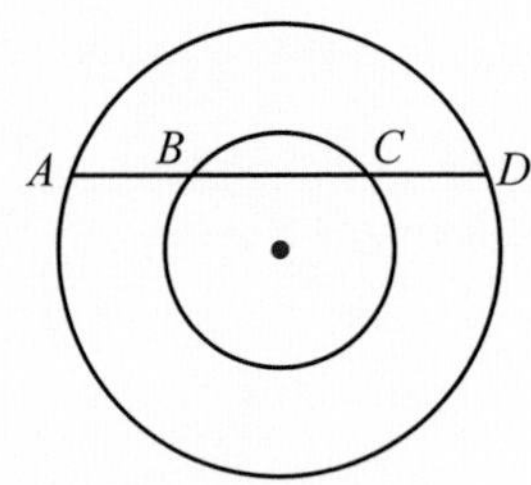

4 Apply what you have learned about circle properties to calculate the diameter of each circle. Give approximate answers to 3 significant figures. Show all your working and give reasons for any deductions.

(a)

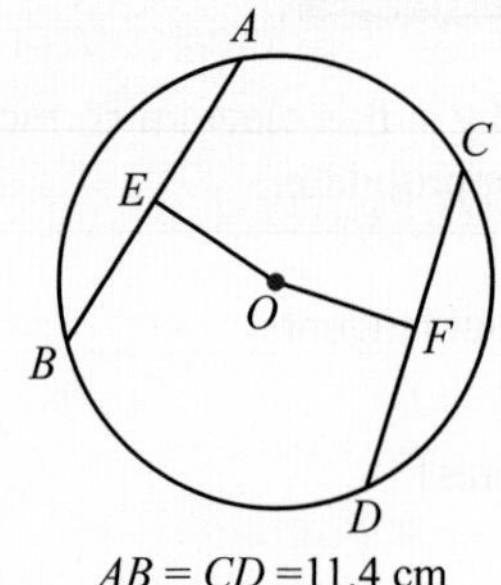

$AB = CD = 11.4$ cm

$OF = 6.5$ cm

(b)

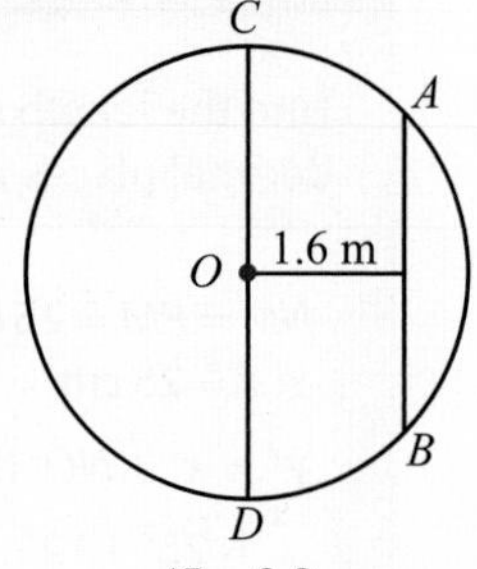

$AB = 2.8$ m

(c)

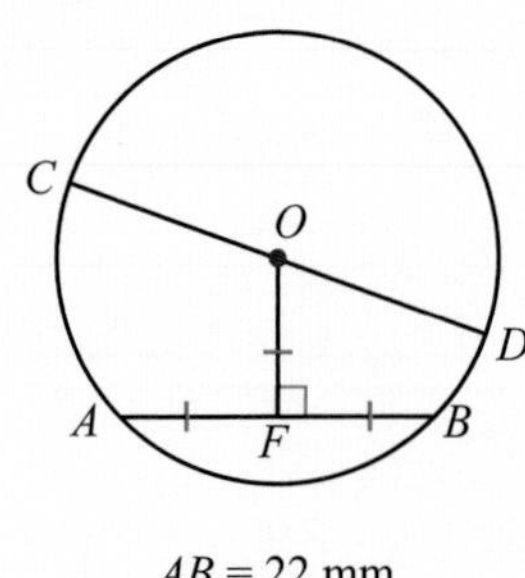

$AB = 22$ mm

5 A circle with a radius of 8.4 cm has a chord 5 cm from its centre. Calculate the length of the chord correct to 2 decimal places.

6 In this diagram, find the length of AO and the area of quadrilateral $AOCB$.
BA and BC are tangents to the circle.

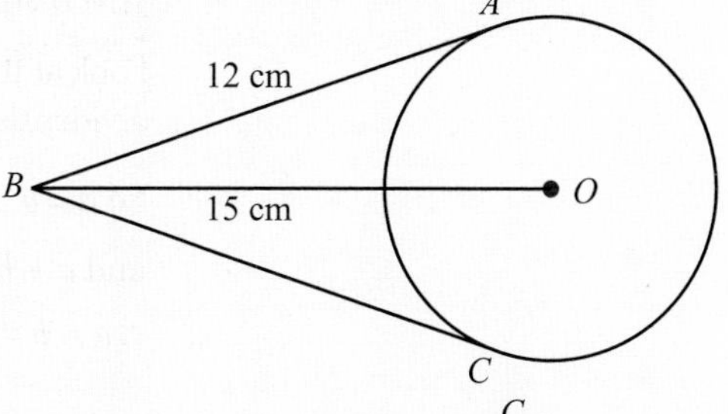

7 In the diagram, AB and AD are tangents to the circle. ABC is a straight line.
Calculate the size of angle x.

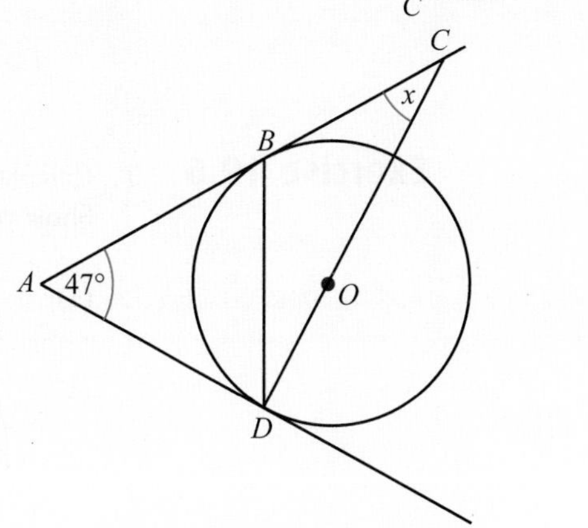

19.4 Angle relationships in circles

Circles have many useful angle properties that can be used to solve problems.

You will now explore more of these properties. The following examples and theorems will help you to solve problems involving angles and circles.

The angle in a semi-circle is a right angle (90°)

Read through the worked example to see how to work out the size of an angle in a semi-circle.

Worked example 5

AB is the diameter of a circle. C is the centre. D is any point on the circumference. Remember that all radii of a circle are equal. Work out the size of angle ADB.

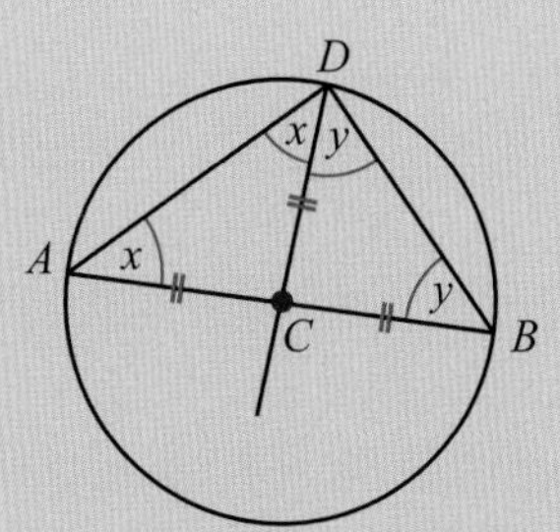

$AC = CB = CD$ (radii of circle)

$\therefore \Delta ACD$ and ΔBCD are isosceles.

$\therefore C\hat{A}D = A\hat{D}C = x$

and $C\hat{D}B = D\hat{B}C = y$

But $2x + 2y = 180°$ (sum angles ΔABD)

$\therefore x + y = 90°$

so $A\hat{D}B = 90°$

The angle between the tangent and radius is 90°

Look at the diagram carefully. You already know that the diameter divides the circle evenly into two equal parts.

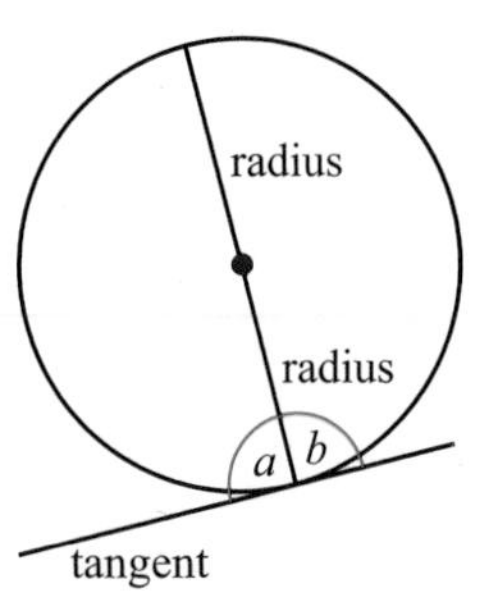

So $a = b$

and $a + b = 180°$ (angles on a straight line)

$\therefore a = b = 90°$

Exercise 19.6

1 Calculate the size of the lettered angles in each diagram. Show your working and give reasons for any deductions.

(a)

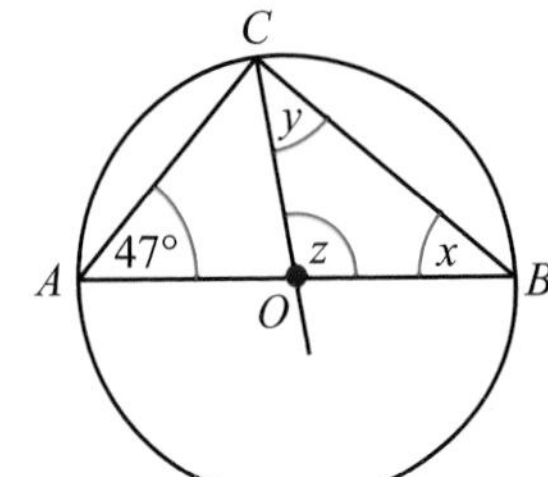

(b)

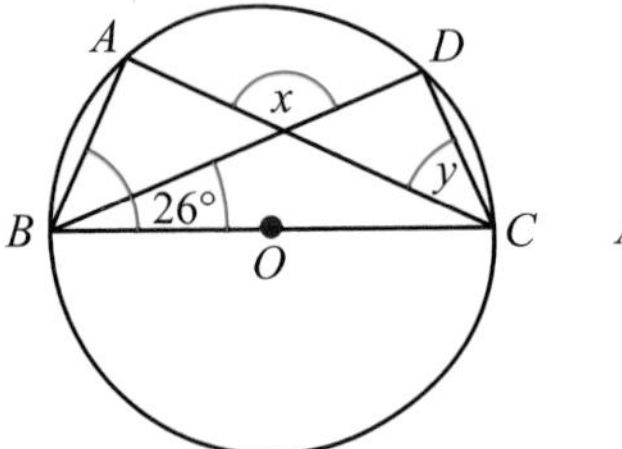

$A\hat{B}C = 60°$

(c)

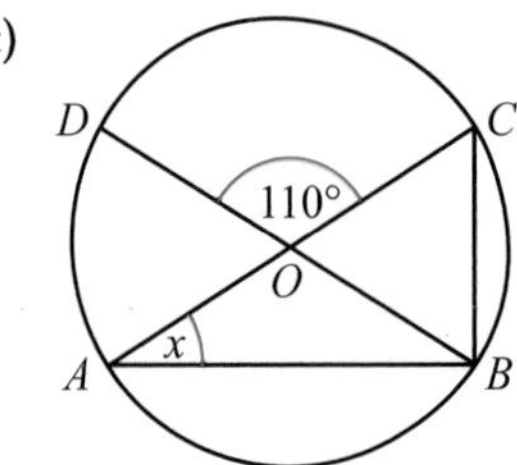

(d)

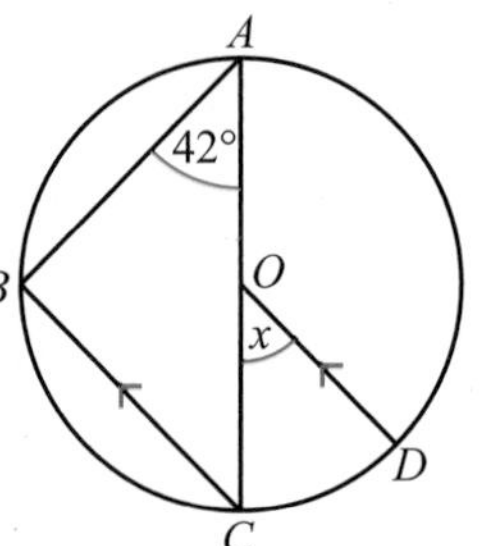

2 Calculate the value of x in each diagram. Show your working and give reasons for any deductions.

(a)

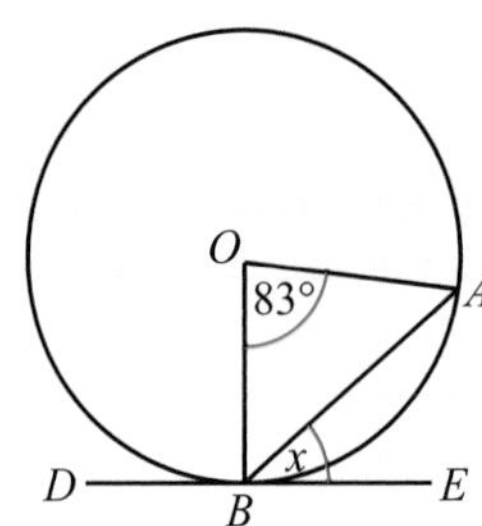

(b)

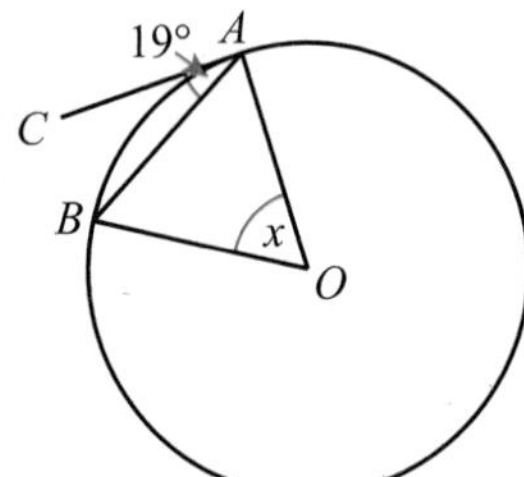

3 In the diagram, BCF and BAE are the tangents to the circle at C and A respectively.

AD is a diameter and $A\hat{B}C = 40°$.

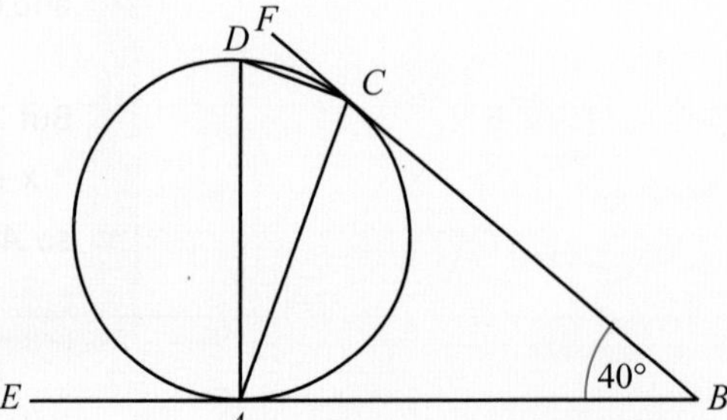

(a) Explain why ΔABC is isosceles.
(b) Calculate the size of:

(i) $C\hat{A}B$
(ii) $D\hat{A}C$
(iii) $A\hat{D}C$.

Further circle theorems

The angle at the centre of a circle is twice the angle at the circumference

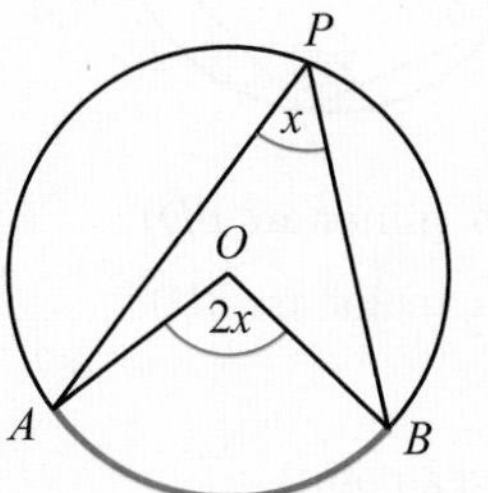

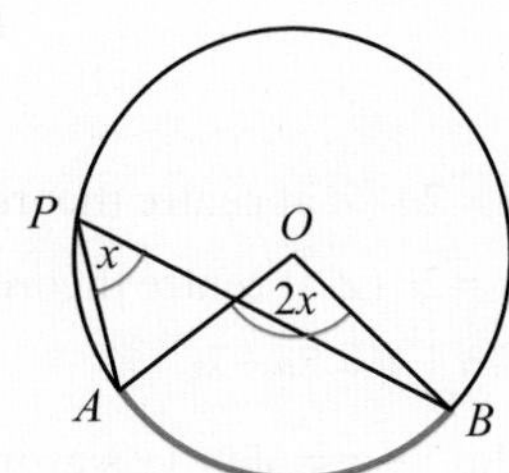

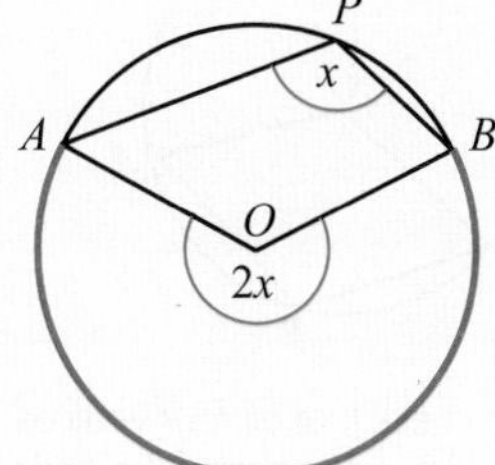

AB is an **arc** of a circle with centre O. P is a point on the circumference, but not on the arc AB. The angle at the centre theorem states that

$$A\hat{O}B = 2 \times A\hat{P}B$$

As you saw before, this is also true when AB is a semi-circular arc. The angle at the centre theorem states that the angle in a semi-circle is 90°. This is because, in this case, AOB is a straight line (180°).

Angles in the same segment are equal

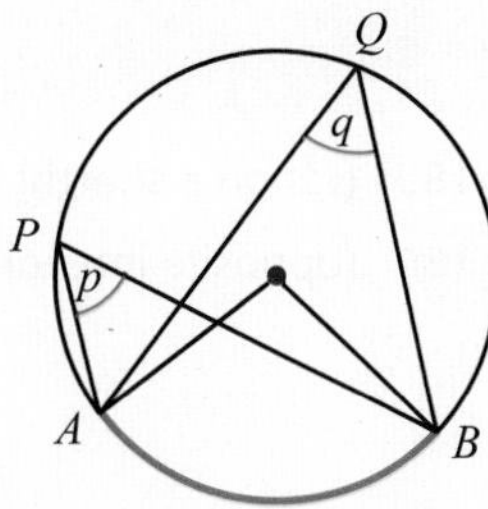

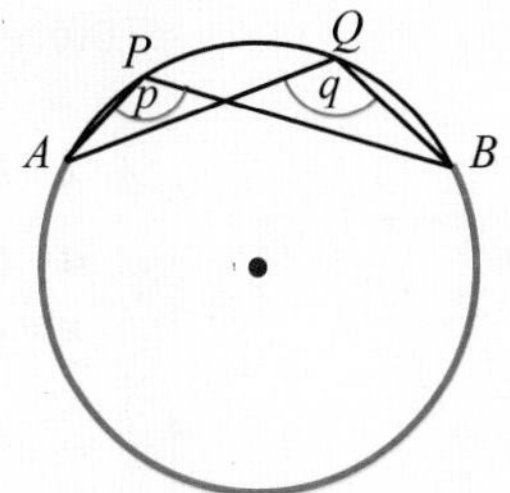

In these two diagrams, $p = q$. Each of the angles p and q is half the angle subtended by the arc AB at the centre of the circle.

The opposite angles of a cyclic quadrilateral add up to 180°

You may sometimes see 'cyclic quadrilateral' written as 'cyclical quadrilateral'.

A common error is to see the following as a cyclic quadrilateral:

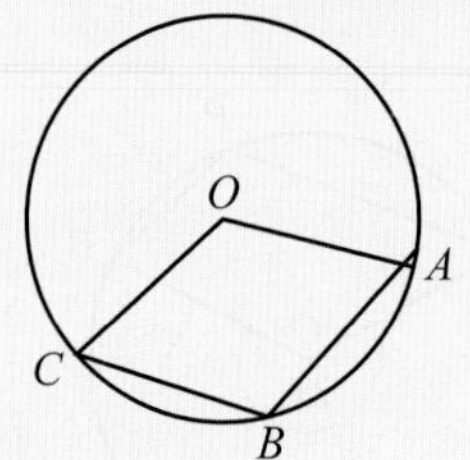

You must check that *all four* vertices sit on the circumference of the circle.

A **cyclic quadrilateral** is one that has all four vertices touching the circumference of a circle.

Look at the diagram and follow the working to see why this is the case.

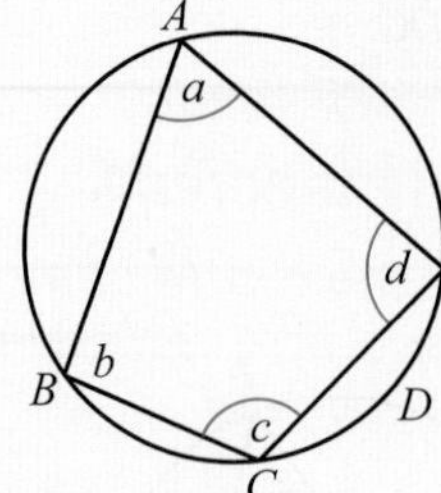

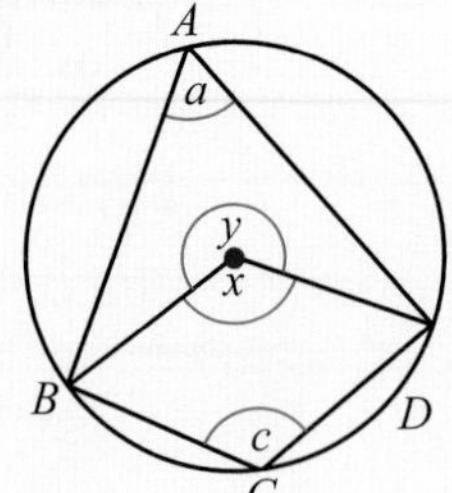

$x = 2a$ ($\angle$ at centre theorem, minor arc BD)

$y = 2c$ ($\angle$ at centre theorem, major arc BD)

$\therefore x + y = 2a + 2c$

But $x + y = 360°$ ($\angle$s around a point)

$\therefore a + c = 180°$ (opposite $\angle$s sum of a cyclic quadrilateral)

By a similar argument:

$b + d = 180°$

Each exterior angle of a cyclic quadrilateral is equal to the interior angle opposite to it

The worked example shows why this is the case.

Worked example 6

Prove that $x = a$.

$x + B\hat{C}D = 180°$ ($\angle$s on a straight line)

$a + B\hat{C}D = 180°$ (opposite interior $\angle$s of a cyclic quadrilateral)

$x = a$

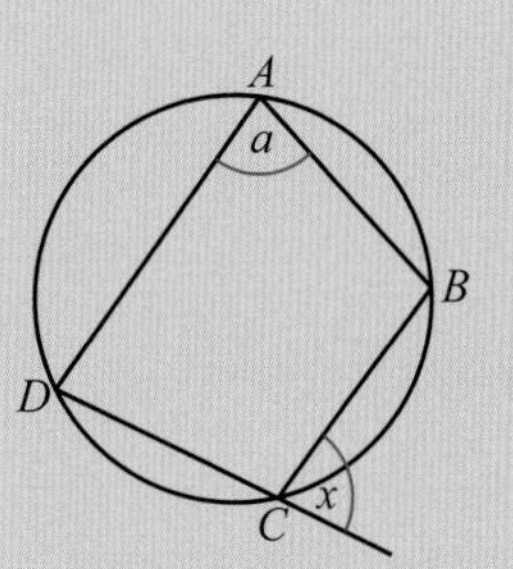

Exercise 19.7

1 Find the size of each lettered angle in these sketches.
When it is marked, O is the centre of the circle.

(a)

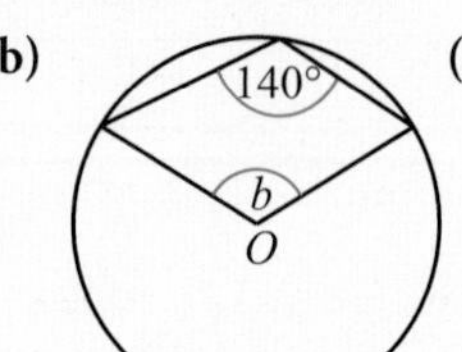

(b)

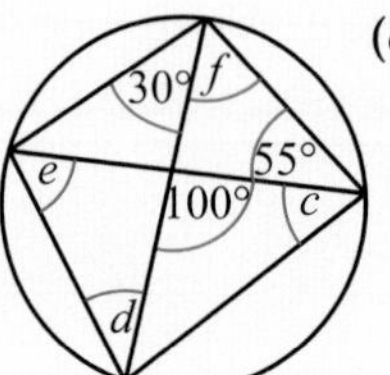

(c)

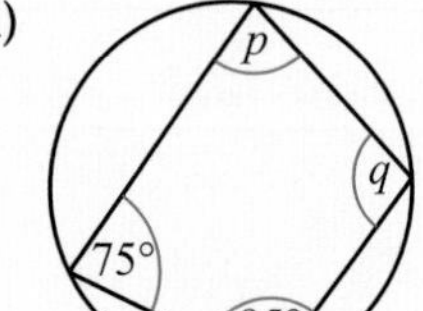

(d)

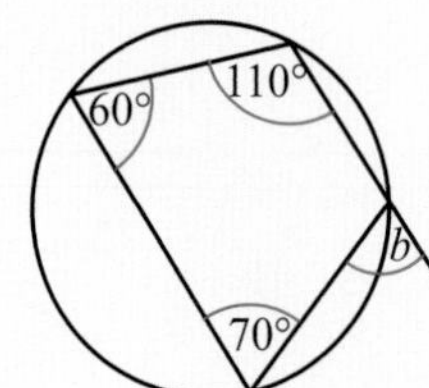

(e)

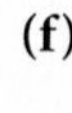

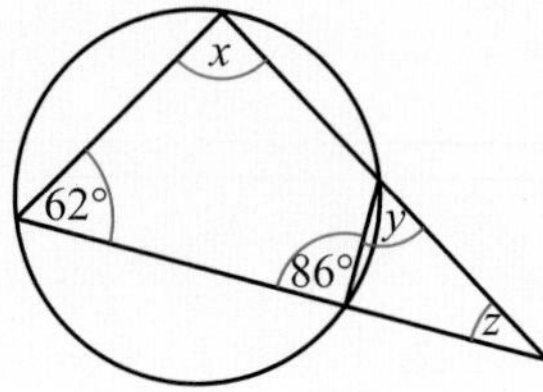

(f)

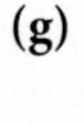

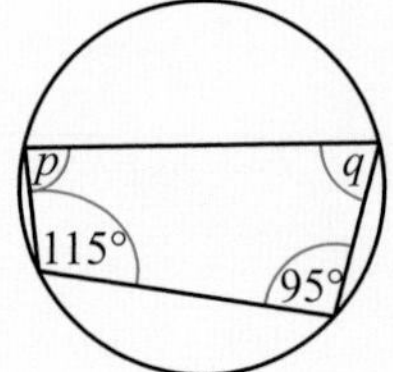

(g)

2 In the diagram SAT is the tangent to the circle at point A. The points B and C lie on the circle and O is the centre of the circle. If $A\hat{C}B = x$, express, in terms of x, the size of:

(a) $A\hat{O}B$
(b) $O\hat{A}B$
(c) $B\hat{A}T$.

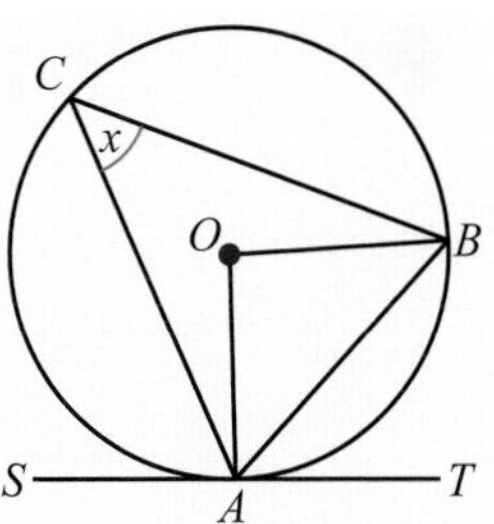

3 Find the size of each lettered angle in these sketches. When it is marked, O is the centre of the circle.

(a)

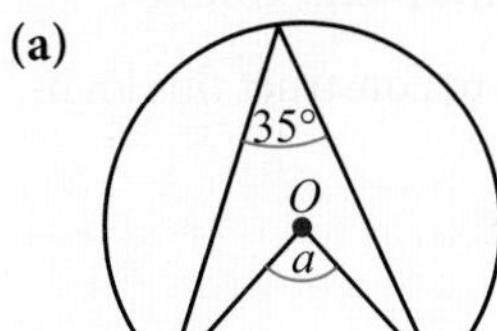

(b)

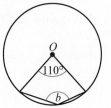

(c)

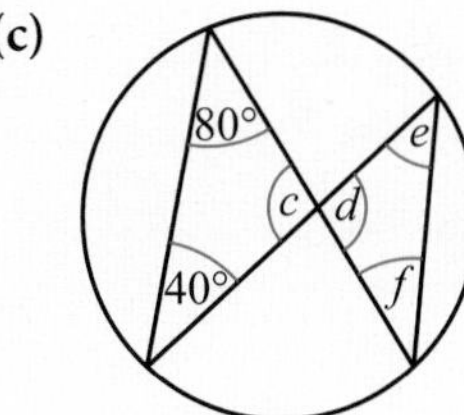

4 In the diagram, TA and TB are the tangents from T to the circle whose centre is O. AC is a diameter of the circle and $A\hat{C}B = x$.

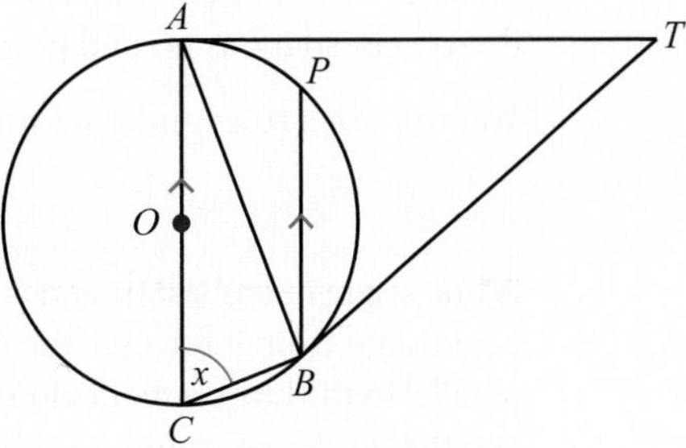

(a) Find $C\hat{A}B$ in terms of x.
(b) Find $A\hat{T}B$ in terms of x.
(c) The point P on the circumference of the circle is such that BP is parallel to CA. Express $P\hat{B}T$ in terms of x.

Living maths

5 The diagram shows a circular disc cut out of a square of silver sheet metal plate. The circle has a radius of 15 mm. O is the centre of the circle.

(a) Calculate the length of the sides and hence the area of the uncut metal square.
(b) What area of metal is left over once the circle has been cut from the square?

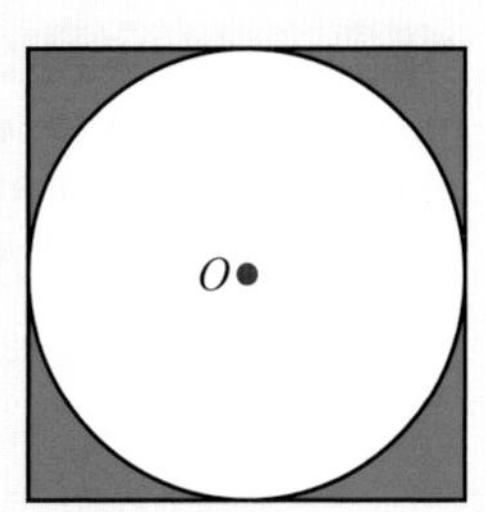

6 Mahindra makes badges by sticking an equilateral triangle onto a circular disc as shown. If the triangle has sides of 15 cm, find the diameter of the circular disc.

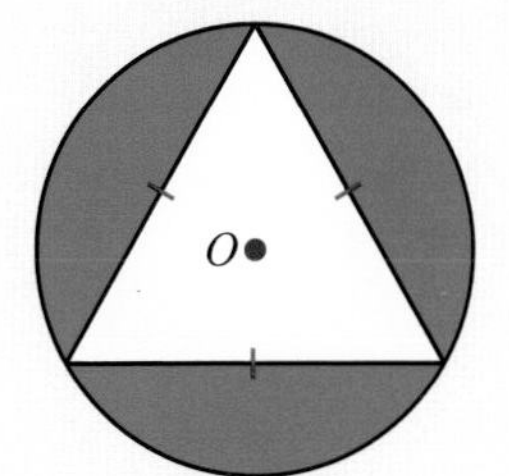

19.5 Locus

A **locus** is a set of points that obey a certain rule. The plural of locus is **loci**. You can think of a locus as the path followed by a moving point.

Some descriptions of loci produce shapes that you are already familiar with. Make sure you understand and recognise the following loci.

The locus of points at a given distance from a fixed point

The locus of points that are equidistant from a fixed point (O) is a circle. The centre of the circle is O and the radius of the circle is equal to the distance of the points from O.

You can use a pair of compasses to construct this locus.

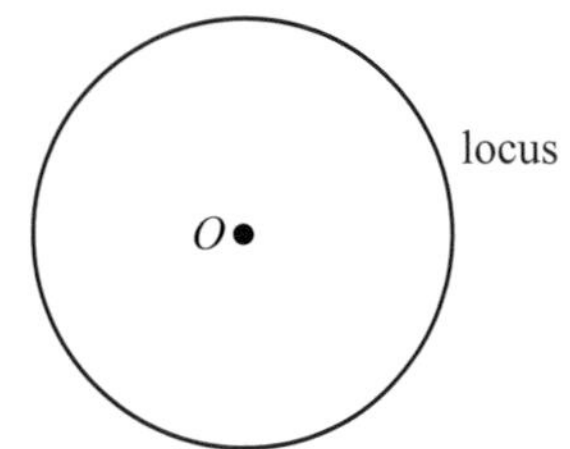

The locus of points at a given distance from a straight line

The locus of points equidistant to a straight line is parallel to it and the same distance from it. In other words, the path is two parallel lines on either side of the given line, the same distance from it. Remember, a line carries on to infinity in both directions, so it has no end points.

You can use a ruler and a set square to construct this locus.

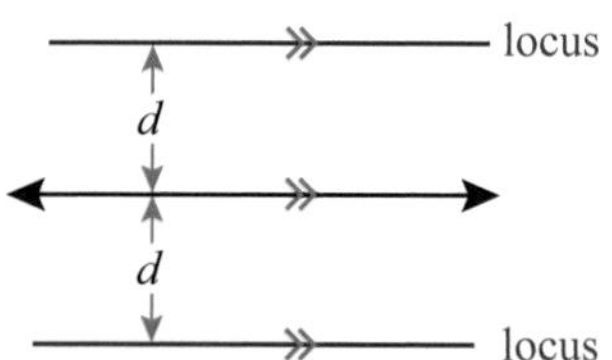

The locus of points at a given distance from a line segment

A line segment has a start and an end point so the locus of points equidistant from it forms a 'racing track' around it. The track is parallel to the line segment along both sides of straight section and these sides are equidistant from it. The locus curves around the end of the line segment to form two semi-circular end pieces. Each piece has the end of the line segment at its centre and the radius is equal to the distance of the point from the line segment.

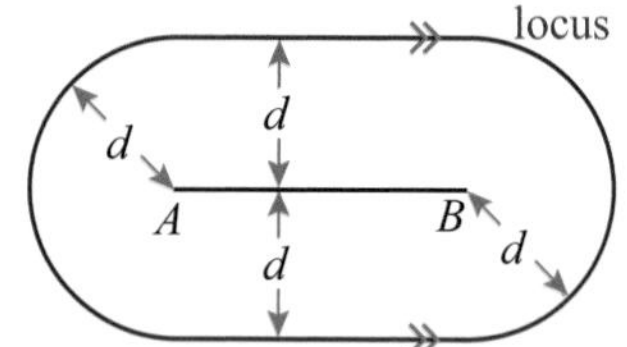

You can construct this locus using a ruler and set square and a pair of compasses.

REWIND

You can revise how to construct a perpendicular bisector and an angle bisector in chapter 3 if you have forgotten how. ◀

The locus of points equidistant from two given points

The locus of points that are equidistant from two fixed points is the perpendicular bisector of the line joining the points.

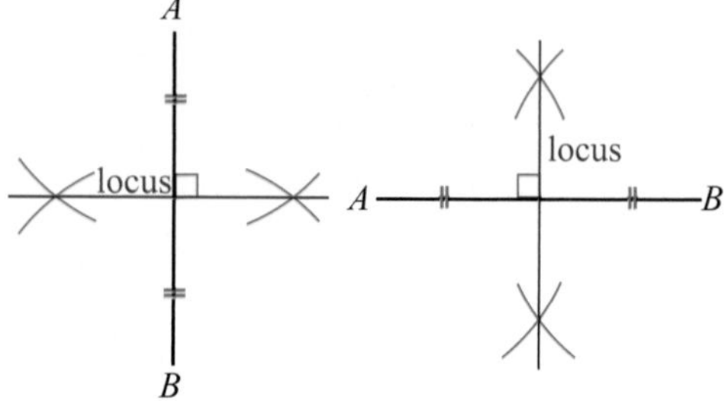

You can use a pair of compasses to construct this locus.

The locus of a point equidistant from two intersecting straight lines

The locus of the points that are equidistant from two intersecting straight lines is the bisector of the angle formed between the two lines.

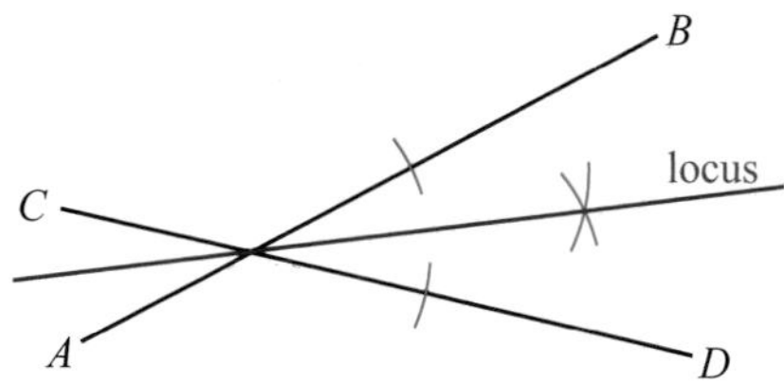

You can use a pair of compasses to construct this locus.

Worked example 7

Draw the locus of a point that moves so it is always 2.5 cm from a line 5 cm long.

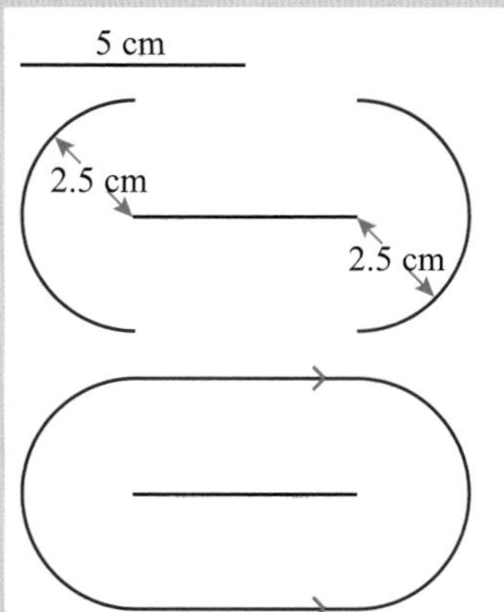

Draw a line 5 cm long.

Set your compasses to 2.5 cm. Draw two semi-circles with their centres at each end of the line.

Use a ruler and a set square to draw a parallel line at a distance of 2.5 cm above and below the given line.

Worked example 8

The positions of two points, *D* and *E*, are fixed. A point *P* is to be marked so that it is nearer to *D* than it is to *E*. Sketch the locus of possible positions of *P*.

The rule given is equivalent to the inequality $DP < EP$.

Because the rule is an inequality, the locus is a region of the plane.

The boundary of the region is the set of points that satisfy the equality $DP = EP$, that is, the set of points that are the same distance from *D* as they are from *E*.

The first diagram shows some of the points on the boundary. It is clear that the locus of these points includes the mid-point of *DE* and, by symmetry, it is perpendicular to *DE*. In other words, it is the perpendicular bisector of *DE*.

The shaded region in the second diagram is the locus of points that are nearer to *D* than they are to *E*. (The boundary is shown as a dashed line because it is not included in the region.)

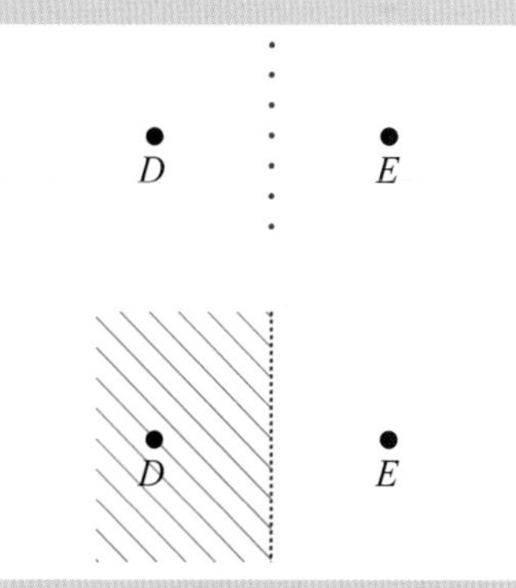

REWIND

Revise linear inequalities in chapter 14 if you find this difficult to understand. ◀

Exercise 19.8

1 Describe each of the following loci as a straight line, a curved line or a region.

(a) Points at 4 cm from a fixed point X.
(b) Points more than 4 cm but less than 6 cm from AB.
(c) Points which are 12 mm from line segment $AB = 2$ cm.
(d) Points which are equidistant from the two corners of a playing field.
(e) Points which are the same distance from the perpendicular sides of a rectangle.

Living maths

2 $ABCD$ is a rectangular plot of land 200 m by 500 m.

(a) Sketch and label the plot of land.
(b) The farmer wants to build a fence across the plot so that it is equidistant from point A and point C. Show on your diagram where this fence should be.

3 A monkey is in a rectangular enclosure which is 10 m by 17.5 m. It can reach outside the enclosure to a distance of 25 cm.

(a) Draw the locus of the points that the monkey can reach outside the enclosure.
(b) Where would you place the safety barrier to make sure that people cannot touch the monkey? Show this on your diagram and give a reason for your choice.

4 A pivot irrigation system on a farm turns in a 360° rotation from a fixed position to water the field. It can water to a distance of 40 m. Draw a diagram to show the locus of points watered by the irrigation system.

Use a scale drawing to help you solve these problems.

5 An engineer has to erect a mast for a mobile phone company. The area in which the mast is to be erected contains a park, an office block and a school. The office block is 80 m from the park and 180 m from the school. The mast is to be equidistant from the office block and the school and also 60 m from the park. Locate all the possible locations for the mast.

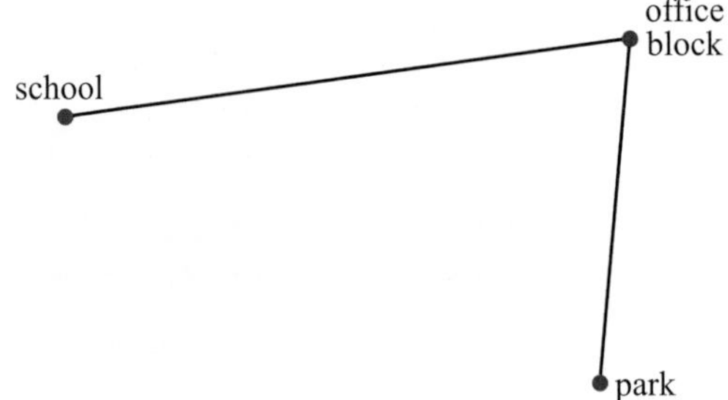

6 A, B and C represent three TV signal transmitter masts on a plan. B is 40 km away from both A and C. A is 50 km due north of C. Good signals from mast A are received up to 30 km away, from mast B you get a good signal up to 40 km away and from mast C you get a good signal up to 35 km away. Show, by shading, the region in which signals can be received from all three masts. Use a scale of 1 cm : 10 km.

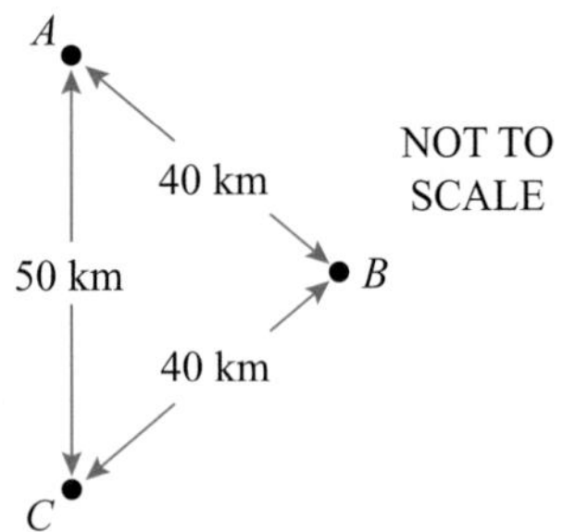

7 Three charity workers who live in Brazil want to arrange a weekend get-together at a convenient place. One person is based in Belem, one is based in Salvador and the other is based in Rio de Janeiro.

(a) Using the map and tracing paper, draw an outline map of Brazil and mark on the three cities. Draw a diagram showing what area of Brazil is equidistant from the three places.
(b) Is this a suitable place for a get-together? Explain why or why not.

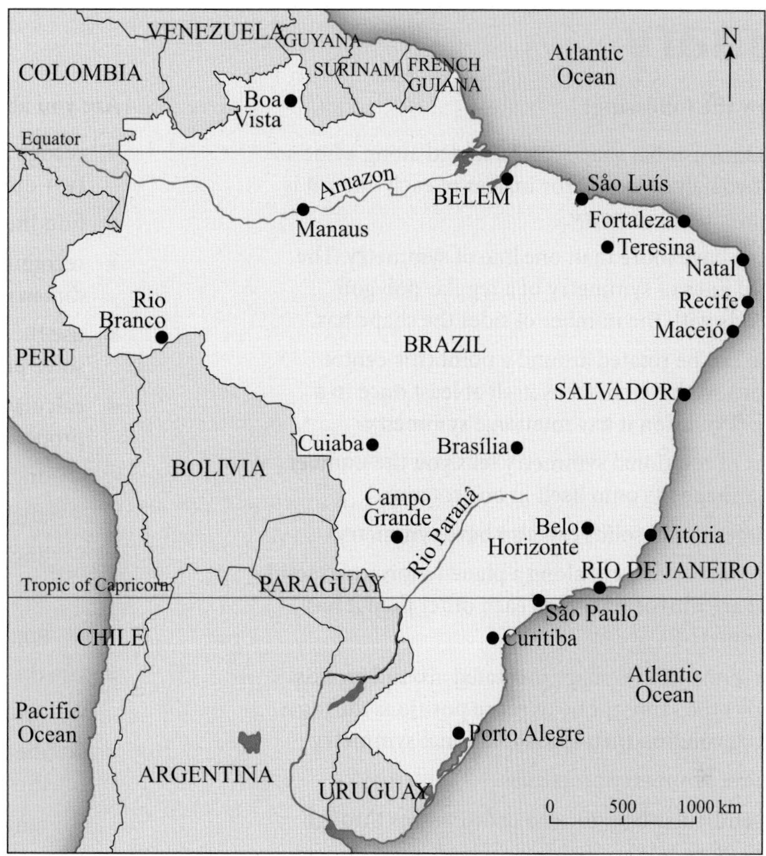

8 A farmer has a rectangular plot of land 140 m by 80 m.

(a) Using a scale of 1 cm to 20 m, construct an accurate plan of the field.
(b) The farmer has a circular irrigation system that waters in a radius of 50 m. Indicate where she should place this system to water the maximum possible area of the field.

9 X and Y are two points that are 4 cm apart. What is the locus of points that are 2 cm from X and 4 cm from Y?

10 Answer this question on a Cartesian plane numbered from –6 to 6 on both axes.

(a) Indicate the locus of points that are 4 units from the x-axis and write the equation for this locus.
(b) Indicate the locus of points that are 5 units from the origin and write the equation for this locus.
(c) How many points are there which satisfy the conditions of both loci?

Summary

Do you know the following?

- If a two-dimensional shape can be folded along a line so that the two halves are mirror images of each other it is said to have line symmetry.
- Shapes can have more than one line of symmetry. The number of lines of symmetry of a regular polygon corresponds with the number of sides the shape has.
- If a shape can be rotated around a point (the centre of rotation) so that it matches itself at least once in a complete revolution it has rotational symmetry.
- The order of rotational symmetry tells you the number of times a shape fits onto itself in one rotation.
- Three-dimensional solids can also have symmetry.
- When a shape can be cut along a plane to form two solid parts that are mirror images of each other then it has plane symmetry.
- If a three-dimensional shape is rotated around an axis and it looks the same at one or more positions during a complete revolution then it has rotational symmetry.
- Circles have symmetry properties.
- The perpendicular bisector of a chord passes through the centre of a circle.
- Equal chords are equidistant from the centre and chords equidistant from the centre are equal in length.
- Two tangents drawn to a circle from a point outside the circle are equal in length.
- The angle in a semi-circle is a right angle.
- The angle between a tangent and the radius of a circle is a right angle.
- The angle subtended at the centre of a circle by an arc is twice the angle subtended at the circumference by the arc.
- Angles in the same segment, subtended by the same arc, are equal.
- Opposite angles of a cyclic quadrilateral add up to 180°.
- Each exterior angle of a cyclic quadrilateral is equal to the interior angle opposite to it.
- A locus is a set of points that satisfy a given rule. A locus can be a straight line, a curve, a combination of straight and curved lines or a plane.

Are you able to ...?

- recognise rotational and line symmetry in two-dimensional shapes
- find the order of symmetry of a two-dimensional shape
- recognise rotational and line symmetry in three-dimensional shapes
- use the symmetry properties of polygons and circles to solve problems
- calculate unknown angles in a circle using its angle properties:
  - angle in a semi-circle
  - angle between tangent and radius of a circle
  - angle at centre of a circle
  - angles in the same segment
  - angles in opposite segments
- use the symmetry properties of circles:
  - equal chords are equidistant from the centre
  - the perpendicular bisector of a chord passes through the centre
  - tangents from an external point are equal
- construct loci around fixed points, lines and intersecting lines.

Examination practice

Exam-style questions

1 Which of the following figures have both line and rotational symmetry?

(a)

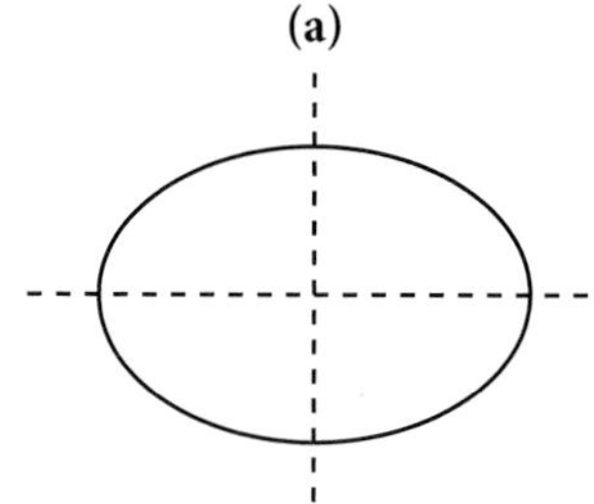

(b)

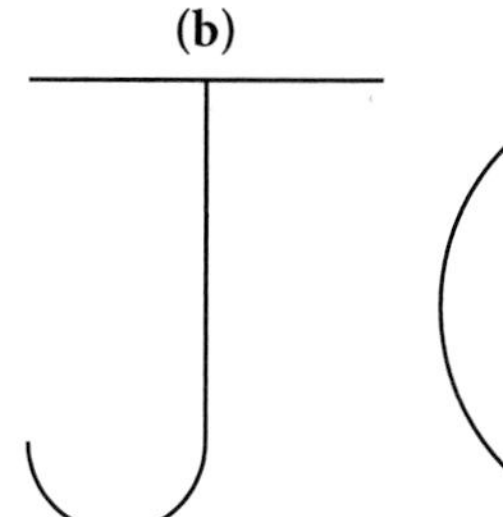

(c)

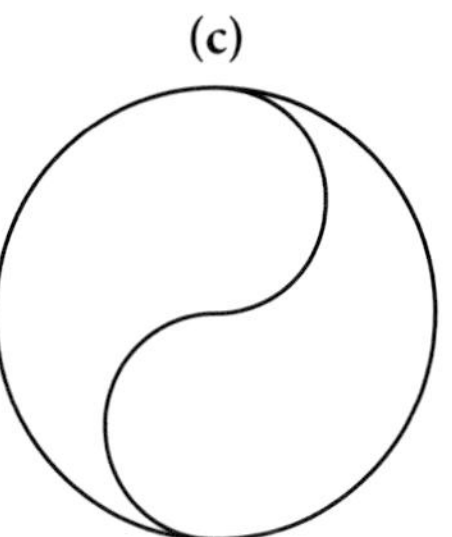

(d)

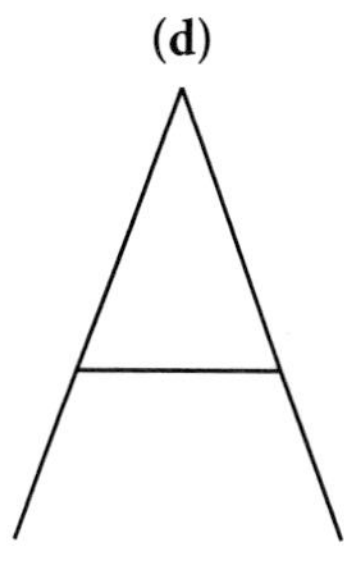

(e)

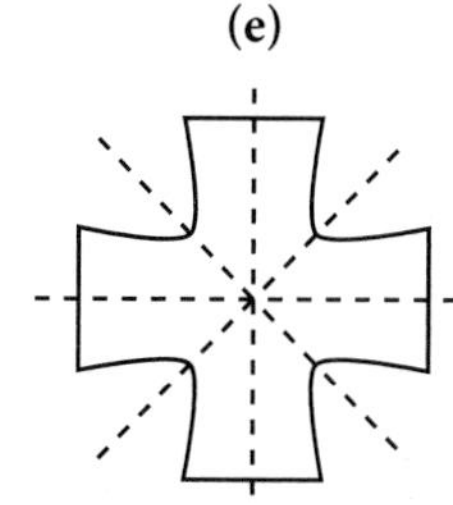

2 Using P as the centre of rotation, state the order of rotational symmetry in this figure.

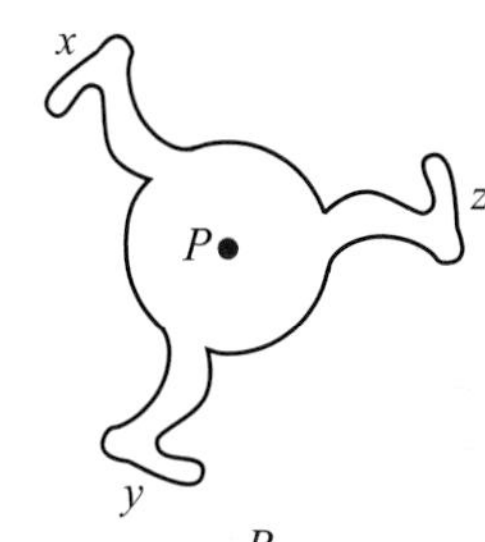

3 RST is a tangent to the circle with centre O. PS is a diameter. Q is a point on the circumference and PQT is a straight line.
$Q\hat{S}T = 37°$.
Write down the values of a, b, c and d.

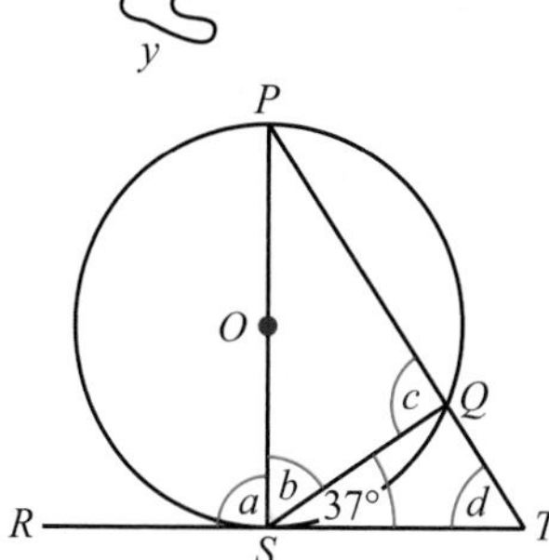

4 The diagram represents a garden $ABCDE$.
$AB = 2.5$ m, $AE = 7$ m, $ED = 5.2$ m,
$DC = 6.9$ m, $E\hat{A}B = 120°$, $D\hat{E}A = 90°$ and $E\hat{D}C = 110°$.

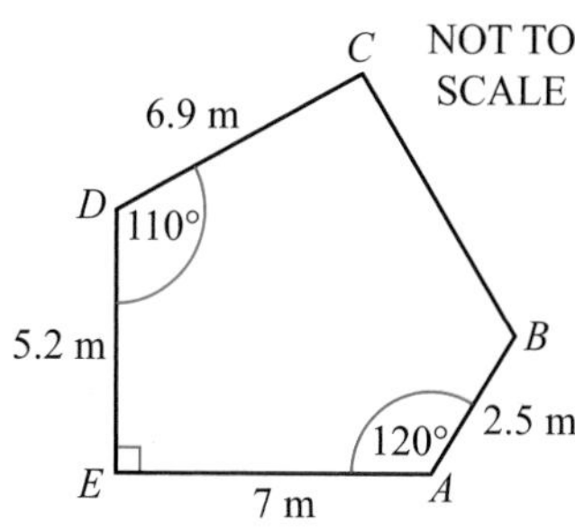

(a) **(i)** Using a scale of 1 cm to represent 1 m, construct an accurate plan of the garden.
(ii) Construct the locus of points in the garden equidistant from CD and CB.
(iii) Construct the locus of points in the garden 6 m from A.

(b) A fountain is to be placed nearer to CD than to CB and no more than 6 m from A. Shade and label R, the region within which the fountain could be placed in the garden.

Past paper questions

1 **(a)** Write down the order of rotational symmetry of this shape. [1]

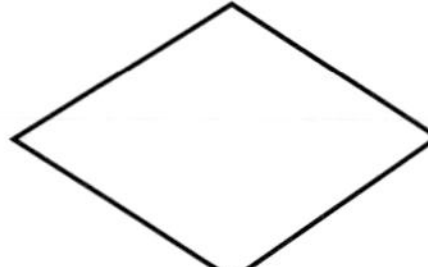

(b) Draw the lines of symmetry on this shape. [1]

[Cambridge IGCSE Mathematics 0580 Paper 11 Q05 October/November 2013]

2

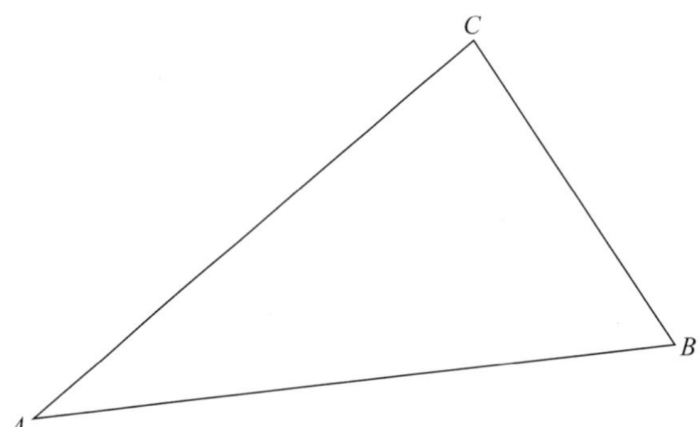

(a) On the diagram above, **using a straight edge and compasses only**, construct

(i) the bisector of angle ABC, [2]

(ii) the locus of points which are equidistant from A and from B. [2]

(b) Shade the region inside the triangle which is nearer to A than to B **and** nearer to AB than to BC. [1]

[Cambridge IGCSE Mathematics 0580 Paper 12 Q18 May/June 2011]

3

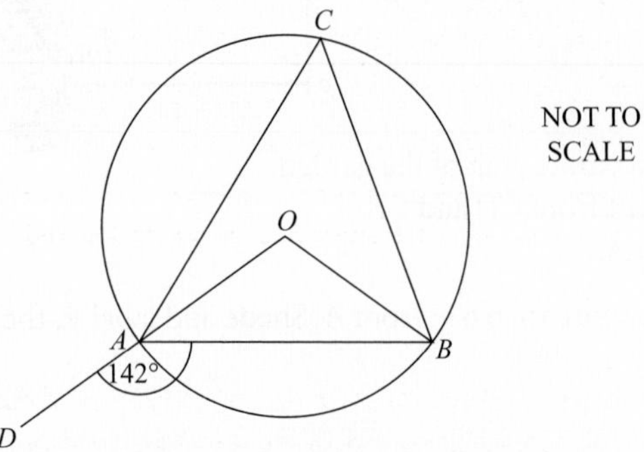

NOT TO SCALE

A, B and C are points on the circumference of a circle centre O.
OAD is a straight line and angle $DAB = 142°$.
Calculate the size of angle ACB. [3]

[Cambridge IGCSE Mathematics 0580 Paper 22 Q14 October/November 2013]

20 Histograms and frequency distribution diagrams

Key words

- Histogram
- Continuous
- Class interval
- Frequency
- Grouped
- Frequency tables
- Frequency density
- Modal class
- Cumulative frequency
- Cumulative frequency curve
- Quartiles
- Interquartile range
- Percentiles

In this chapter you will learn how to:

- construct and use histograms with equal intervals
- construct and use histograms with unequal intervals
- draw cumulative frequency tables
- use tables to construct cumulative frequency diagrams
- identify the modal class from a grouped frequency distribution.

EXTENDED

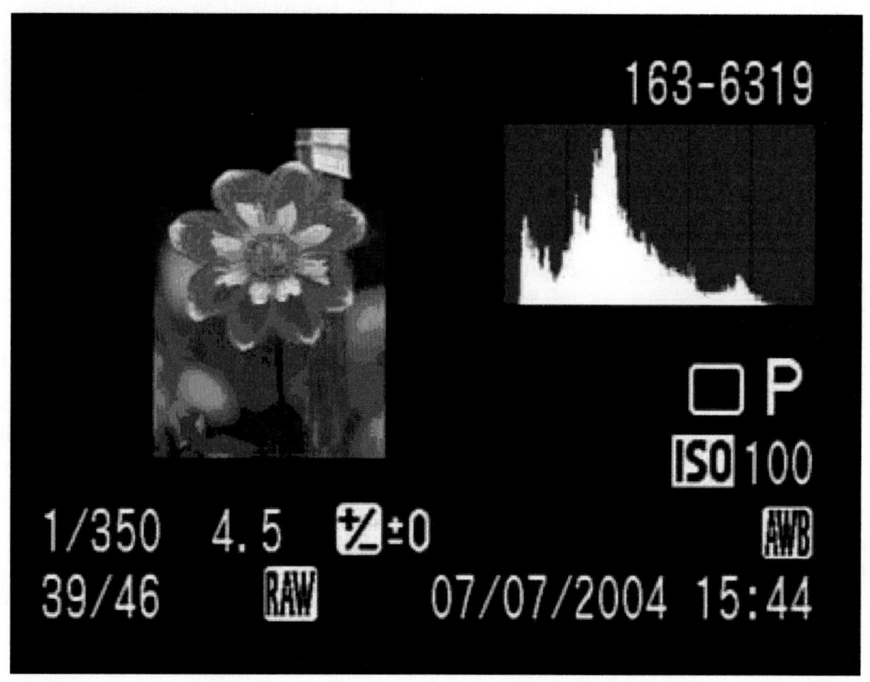

The diagram on the top right of this digital camera screen is a type of histogram which shows how light and shadows are distributed in the photograph. The peaks at the left show that this photo (the red flower) is too dark (underexposed).

You have already collected, organised, summarised and displayed different sets of data using pie charts, bar graphs and line graphs. In this section you are going to work with numerical data (sets of data where the class intervals are numbers) to learn how to draw frequency distribution diagrams called histograms and cumulative frequency curves.

Histograms are useful for visually showing patterns in large sets of numerical data. The shape of the graph allows you see where most of the measurements are located and how spread out they are.

20.1 Histograms

A **histogram** is a specialised graph that looks a lot like a bar chart but is normally used to show the distribution of continuous or grouped data.

Look at this histogram showing the ages of people visiting a gym.

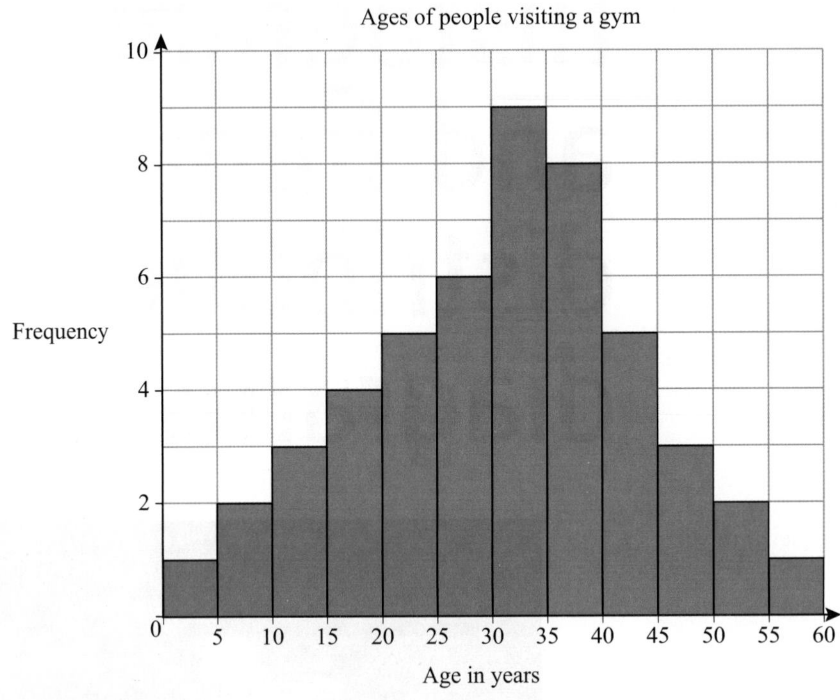

Notice that:

- The horizontal scale is **continuous** and each column is drawn above a particular **class interval**.
- The frequency of the data is shown by the *area* of the bars.
- There are no spaces between the bars on the graph because the horizontal scale is continuous. (If the **frequency** relating to a class interval is 0, you won't draw a bar in that class, so there will be a gap in the bars in that case.)

REWIND

Continuous data was introduced in chapter 4. ◀

REWIND

The grouping of data into classes was covered in chapters 4 and 12. ◀

Histograms with equal class intervals

When the class intervals are equal, the bars are all the same width. Although it should be the area of the bar that tells you the frequency of the class, it is common practice when class intervals are all equal to just let the vertical scale show the frequency per class interval (and so it is just labelled 'frequency', as in the diagram above).

Worked example 1

The table and histogram below show the heights of trees in a sample from a forestry site.

Height (h) of trees in metres	Frequency
$0 \le h < 5$	21
$5 \le h < 10$	18
$10 \le h < 15$	19
$15 \le h < 20$	29
$20 \le h < 25$	29
$25 \le h < 30$	30
$30 \le h < 35$	0
$35 \le h < 40$	2

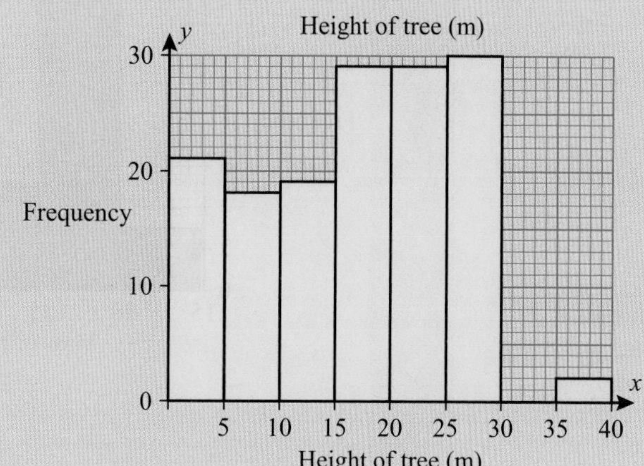

(a) How many trees are less than 5 m tall?
(b) What is the most common height of tree?
(c) How many trees are 20 m or taller?
(d) Why do you think the class intervals include inequality symbols?
(e) Why is there a gap between the columns on the right-hand side of the graph?

(a)	21	Read the frequency (vertical scale on the histogram) for the bar 0 – 5.
(b)	$25 \le h < 30$ m	Find the tallest bar and read the class interval from the horizontal scale.
(c)	61	Find the frequency for each class with heights of 20 m or more and add them together.

(d) The horizontal scale of a histogram is continuous, so the class intervals are also continuous. The inequality symbols prevent the same height of tree falling into more than one group. For example, without the symbols a tree of height 5 m could go into two groups and thus be counted twice.

(e) The frequency for the class interval $30 \le h < 35$ is zero, so no bar is drawn.

Worked example 2

Joy-Anne did an experiment in her class to see what mass of raisins (in grams) the students could hold in one hand. Here are her results.

18	18	20	22	22	22	22	23
23	24	24	25	25	25	25	25
25	26	26	27	30	30	31	35

REWIND

You learned how to draw **grouped frequency tables** in chapter 4. ◀

(a) Using the class intervals 16–20, 21–25, 26–30 and 31–35 draw a grouped frequency table.
(b) What is the modal class (the mode) of this data?
(c) Draw a histogram to show her results.

(a)

Mass of raisins	Frequency
16–20	3
21–25	14
26–30	5
31–35	2

Count the number in each class to fill in the table.

REWIND

You saw in chapter 12 that mode is the most frequent result. ◀

(b) The modal class is 21–25.

It is actually not possible to find the mode of grouped data because you do not have the individual values within each group. Instead, you find the class interval that has the greatest frequency. This is called the '**modal class**' (Extended students learned this in chapter 12).

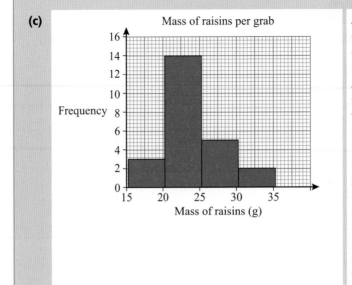

REWIND

You learned about upper and lower bounds in chapter 13. ◀

(c)

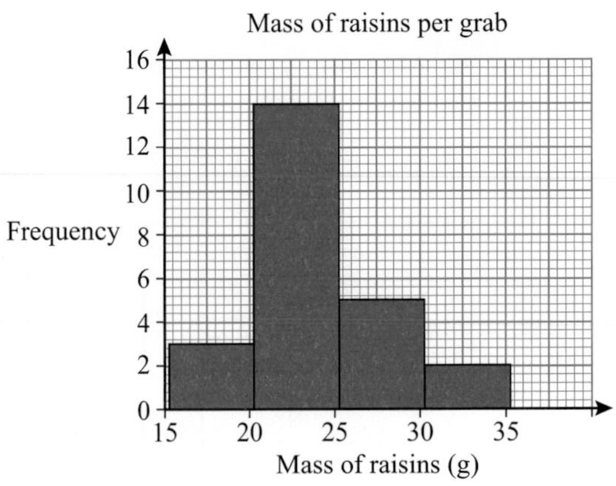

Although the data is in discrete groups, the raw data is actually continuous (it is mass). When Joy-Anne grouped the data, she rounded each mass to the nearest gram. This means that some raisins will have an *actual* mass that is between two of the discrete groups. To take this into account, each bar is plotted according to its upper and lower bound. So, the group 16 – 20 is drawn from 15.5 $\leq h < 20.5$ and so on, such that a handful of raisins with a mass of 20.56g, would be in the class interval 21 – 25 because the group's boundaries are 20.5 – 25.5g.

Exercise 20.1

Living maths

1 Maria is a midwife who recorded the mass of the babies she delivered in one month.

Mass (kg)	$0.5 \leq m < 1.5$	$1.5 \leq m < 2.5$	$2.5 \leq m < 3.5$	$3.5 \leq m < 4.5$	$4.5 \leq m < 5.5$
No. of babies	1	12	31	16	0

(a) What is the modal class?
(b) How many babies have a mass of 2.5kg or less?
(c) Draw a histogram to show this distribution.

2 Annike did a breakdown of the length of telephone calls (t) on her mobile phone account. These are her results.

Length of time (t) in minutes	**Frequency**
$0 \leq t < 2$	15
$2 \leq t < 4$	43
$4 \leq t < 6$	12
$6 \leq t < 8$	19
$8 \leq t < 10$	15
$10 \leq t < 12$	10
$12 \leq t < 14$	11
$14 \leq t < 16$	17

(a) How many calls did she make altogether?
(b) What is the most common length of a call?
(c) Draw a histogram to show this distribution.
(d) Make a new frequency table of these results using the class intervals given opposite.

Class interval	$0 \leq t < 4$	$4 \leq t < 8$	$8 \leq t < 12$	$12 \leq t < 16$
Frequency				

(d) Draw a histogram to show the new distribution.
(e) Write a few sentences comparing the distribution shown on the two histograms.

3 Shamiela cut 30 pieces of ribbon, which she estimated were each about 30 cm long. Her sister measured them and got the following actual lengths in centimetres:

29.1	30.2	30.5	31.1	32.0	31.3	29.8	29.5	31.6	32.4
32.1	30.2	31.7	31.9	32.1	29.9	32.1	31.4	28.9	29.8
31.2	31.2	30.5	29.7	30.3	30.4	30.1	31.1	28.8	29.5

(a) Draw a suitable frequency distribution table for this data. Use an equal class interval.
(b) Construct a histogram to show your distribution.
(c) How accurately did Shamiela estimate? Give a reason for your answer.

Be careful of discrete groups of continuous data; the raw data is continuous so can take any value between the groups.

4 The French Traffic Police recorded the number of vehicles speeding on a stretch of highway on a Friday night. Draw a histogram to show this data.

Speed over the limit (km/h)	1–10	11–20	21–30	31–40	41–50
Frequency	47	21	32	7	4

In other books, you might see histograms being used for grouped *discrete* data. Question 5 is a common example. In these cases, draw the histogram by extending the boundaries of each class interval to make them continuous, e.g. change 95 – 99 and 100 – 104 to $94.5 \leq m < 99.5$, $99.5 \leq m < 104.5$ etc. To draw a bar chart from this data, you would treat each group as a 'category' and draw the bar chart with gaps as normal.

5 Here are the IQ-test scores of a group of students.

IQ	Frequency
95–99	3
100–104	8
105–109	21
110–114	24
115–119	6
120–124	3
125–129	5
130–134	2
135–140	1

Draw a histogram to show this distribution.

Tip

Notice that $(f) = fd \times cw$ = area of a bar. You can use this to help you read frequencies from the histogram. Many questions are based on this principle.

Histograms with unequal class intervals

When the class intervals are not the same, using the height to give the frequency can be misleading. A class that is twice the width of another but with the same frequency covers twice the area. So, if the height is used to represent the frequency, the initial impression it gives is that it contains more values, which is not necessarily the case (see worked example 3). To overcome this, when the class intervals are unequal a new vertical scale is used called the **frequency density**.

$$\text{frequency density } (fd) = \frac{\text{frequency } (f)}{\text{class width } (cw)}$$

Frequency density takes into account the frequency relative to the size of the class interval, making it more fair when comparing different sized intervals.

Worked example 3

Here is a table showing the heights of 25 plants. Draw a histogram to show these results.

Height in cm	Number of plants
$5 \le h < 15$	4
$15 \le h < 20$	8
$20 \le h < 25$	7
$25 \le h < 40$	6

The heights in cm are the class intervals. The number of plants is the frequency.

First work out the frequency density by adding columns to your frequency distribution table like this:

Height (h) in cm	Number of plants (f)	Class width (cw)	Frequency density ($= f \div cw$)
$5 \le h < 15$	4	10	$\frac{4}{10} = 0.4$
$15 \le h < 20$	8	5	$\frac{8}{5} = 1.6$
$20 \le h < 25$	7	5	$\frac{7}{5} = 1.4$
$25 \le h < 40$	6	15	$\frac{6}{15} = 0.4$

If the data was plotted against frequency instead of frequency density (see below), it looks as though there are more plants in the class 25 – 40 compared to the class 5 – 10 but actually, their frequency densities are the same (see histogram in Worked example 3). The larger size of interval is misleading here, so we use frequency density as it is a fairer way to compare frequencies in classes of different sizes.

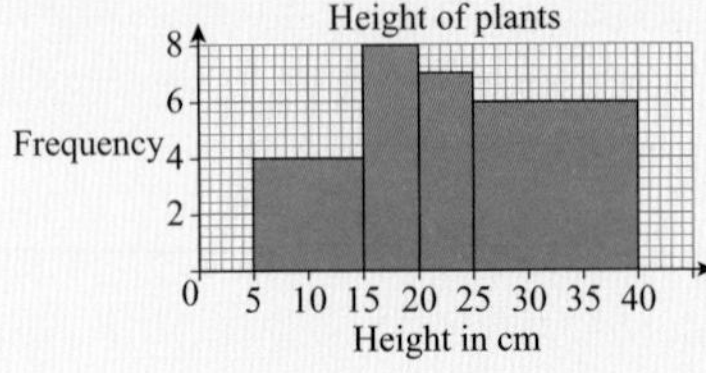

Next draw the axes. You will need to decide on a suitable scale for both the horizontal and the vertical axes. Here, 1 cm has been used to represent 10 cm on the horizontal axis (label height in cm) and 2 cm per unit on the vertical axis (label frequency density).

Once you have done this, draw the histogram, paying careful attention to the scales on the axes.

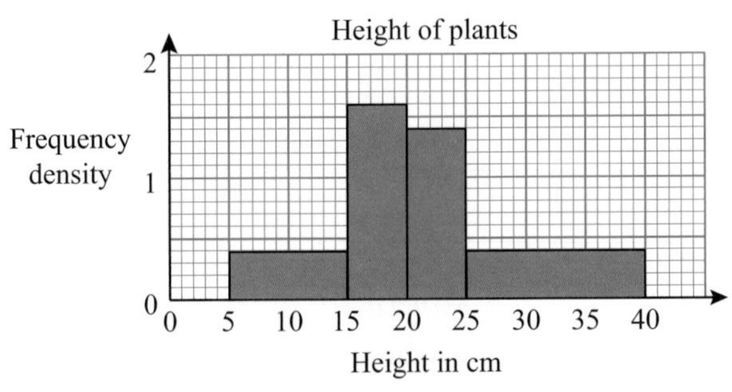

Exercise 20.2

1 140 people at a school fund-raising event were asked to guess how many sweets were in a large glass jar. Those who guessed correctly were put into a draw to win the sweets as a prize. The table shows the guesses.

No. of sweets (n)	Frequency (f)
$100 \leq n < 200$	18
$200 \leq n < 250$	18
$250 \leq n < 300$	32
$300 \leq n < 350$	31
$350 \leq n < 400$	21
$400 \leq n < 500$	20

(a) Use the table to calculate the frequency density for each class.
(b) Construct a histogram to display the results. Use a scale of 1 cm = 100 sweets on the horizontal axis and a scale of 1 cm = 0.2 units on the vertical axis.

2 The table shows the mass of young children visiting a clinic (to the nearest kg). Draw a histogram to illustrate the data.

Mass in kilograms (m)	Frequency
$6 \leq m < 9$	9
$9 \leq m < 12$	12
$12 \leq m < 18$	30
$18 \leq m < 21$	15
$21 \leq m < 30$	18

3 The table shows the distribution of the masses of the actors in a theatre group. Draw a histogram to show the data.

Mass in kilograms (m)	Frequency
$60 \leq m < 63$	9
$63 \leq m < 64$	12
$64 \leq m < 65$	15
$65 \leq m < 66$	17
$66 \leq m < 68$	10
$68 \leq m < 72$	8

Living maths

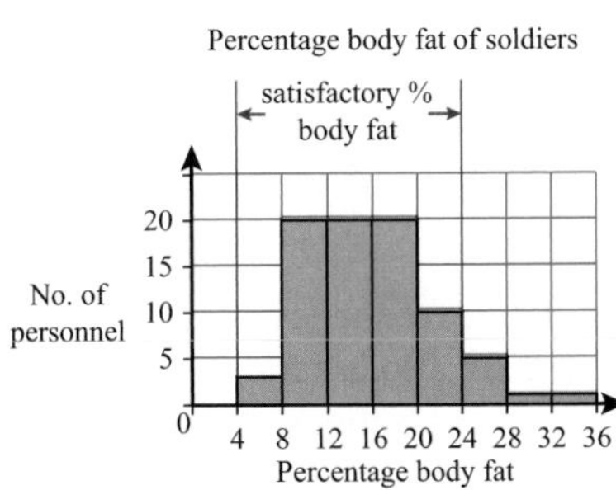

4 A group of on-duty soldiers underwent fitness tests in which their percentage body fat was calculated. The fitness assessor drew up this histogram of the results.

(a) How many soldiers were tested?
(b) How many soldiers had body fat levels within the healthy limits?
(c) How many soldiers had levels which were too high?
(d) Why do you think there no bar in the 0–4 category?
(e) Would you expect a similar distribution if you tested a random selection of people in your community? Give reasons for your answers.

5 A traffic officer used a computer program to draw this histogram showing the average speed (in km/h) of a sample of vehicles using a highway. The road has a minimum speed limit of 50 and a maximum speed limit of 125 km/h.

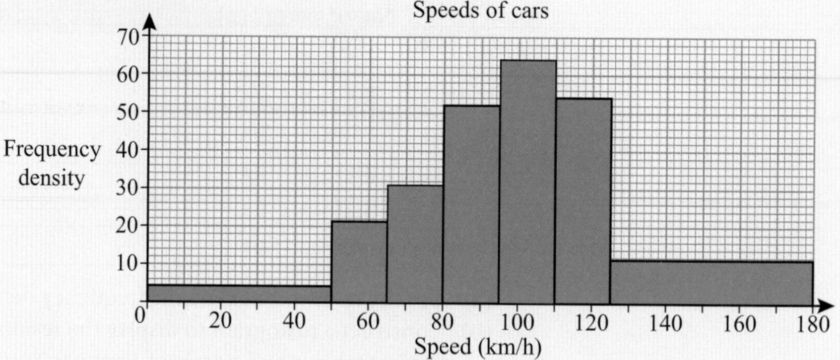

(a) Is it easy to see how many vehicles travelled above or below the speed limit? Give a reason for your answer.

(b) The traffic officer claims the graph shows that most people stick to the speed limit. Is he correct? Give a reason for your answer.

(c) His colleagues want to know exactly how many vehicles travel below or above the speed limit.

(i) Reconstruct this frequency table. Round frequencies to the nearest whole number.

Speed in km/h (s)	Frequency	Class width	Frequency density
$0 \le s < 50$			4.8
$50 \le s < 65$			21.3
$65 \le s < 80$			33.3
$80 \le s < 95$			52
$95 \le s < 110$			64
$110 \le s < 125$			54.6
$125 \le s < 180$			11.6

(ii) How many vehicles were below the minimum speed limit?

(d) What percentage of vehicles in this sample were exceeding the maximum speed limit?

20.2 Cumulative frequency

Sometimes you may be asked questions such as:

- How many people had a mass of less than 50 kilograms?
- How many cars were travelling above 100 km/h?
- How many students scored less than 50% on the test?

Cumulative means 'increasing as more is added'.

In statistics you can use a **cumulative frequency** table or a **cumulative frequency curve** to answer questions about data up to a particular class boundary. You can also use the cumulative frequencies to estimate and interpret the median and the value of other positions of a data set.

Cumulative frequency tables

Cumulative frequency is really just a 'running total' of the scores or results (the frequency in each group). The cumulative frequency gives the number of results which are less than, or equal to, a particular class boundary. This table shows how many students got a particular mark out of 10 (the frequency of each result) as well as the cumulative frequency.

Score out of 10	Frequency (f)	Cumulative frequency
3	4	4
4	5	$4 + 5 = 9$
5	3	$9 + 3 = 12$
6	3	$12 + 3 = 15$
7	5	20
8	7	27
9	2	29
10	1	30
Total	30	

- Each entry in the cumulative frequency column is calculated by adding the frequency of the current class to the previous cumulative frequency (or by adding all the frequencies up to and including the current class).
- The last figure in the cumulative frequency column must equal the sum of the frequencies because all results will be below or equal to the highest result.

Worked example 4

The heights of plants were measured during an experiment. The results are summarised in the table.

Height (h cm)	Frequency
$0 < h \leq 5$	20
$5 < h \leq 10$	40
$10 < h \leq 15$	60
$15 < h \leq 25$	80
$25 < h \leq 50$	50
Total	250

(a) Draw up a cumulative frequency table for this distribution.
(b) Determine which class interval contains the median height.

(a)

Height (h cm)	Frequency	Cumulative frequency
$0 < h \leq 5$	20	20
$5 < h \leq 10$	40	60
$10 < h \leq 15$	60	120
$15 < h \leq 25$	80	200
$25 < h \leq 50$	50	250
Total	250	

(b) $15 < h \leq 25$

The heights are given for 250 flowers, so the median height must be the mean of the height of the 125th and 126th flower. If you look at the cumulative frequency you can see that this value falls into the fourth height class (the 125th and 126th are both greater than 120 but less than 200).

REWIND

In chapter 12, median classes were introduced for grouped data. You will see that cumulative frequency curves will enable you to estimate the median when the number of data is large. ◀

Tip

You must plot the cumulative frequency at the upper end point of the class interval. Do not confuse this section with the mid-point calculations you used to estimate the mean in frequency tables.

Cumulative frequency curves

When you plot the cumulative frequencies against the upper boundaries of each class interval you get a cumulative frequency curve.

Cumulative frequency curves are also called ogive curves or ogives because they take the shape of narrow pointed arches (called ogees) like these ones on a mosque in Dubai.

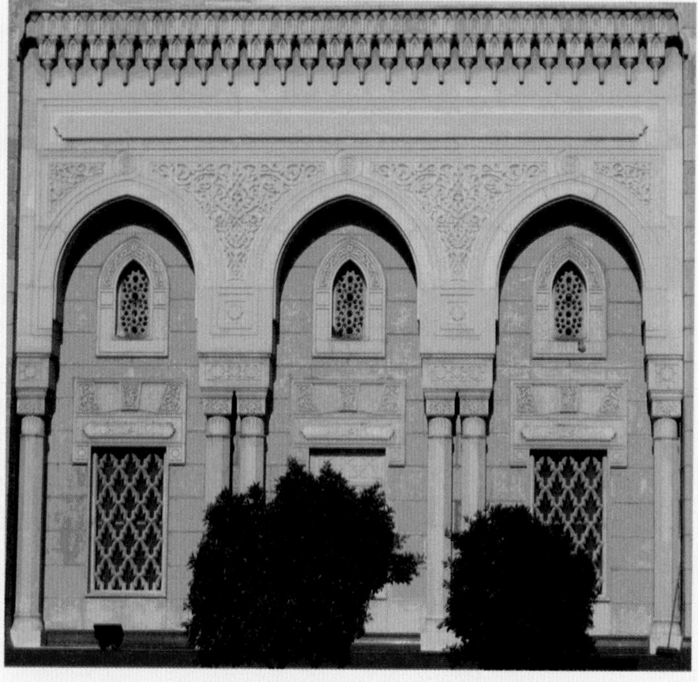

In mathematics, arches like these are seen as two symmetrical s-curves.

Worked example 5

The examination marks of 300 students are summarised in the table.

Mark	Frequency
1–10	3
11–20	7
21–30	13
31–40	29
41–50	44
51–60	65
61–70	70
71–80	49
81–90	14
91–100	6

(a) Draw a cumulative frequency table.
(b) Construct a cumulative frequency graph to show this data.
(c) Calculate an *estimate* for the median mark.

(a)

Mark	Frequency	Cumulative frequency
1–10	3	3
11–20	7	10
21–30	13	23
31–40	29	52
41–50	44	96
51–60	65	161
61–70	70	231
71–80	49	280
81–90	14	294
91–100	6	300

(b)

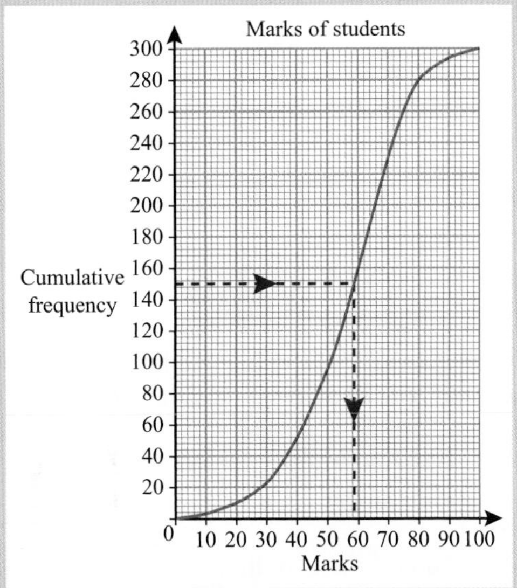

(c) The median is the middle value. For continuous data, the middle value can be found by dividing the total frequency by 2.

$\frac{300}{2} = 150$, so the median mark is the 150th result. Draw a line from the 150th student (on the vertical axis) parallel to the marks (horizontal) axis. Drop a perpendicular from where this line cuts the graph. Read the value from the horizontal axis.

The median mark is 58.

REWIND

You learned in chapter 12 how to work out the median for discrete data. Note that the cumulative frequency graph allows you to find an *estimate* for the actual value rather than a class interval. ◀

Worked example 6

This cumulative frequency curve shows the journey times to school of different students.

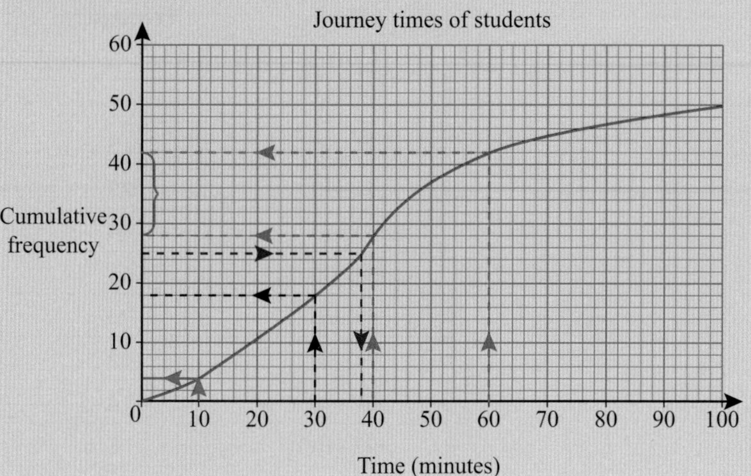

Use the curve to find:

(a) the total number of students
(b) an estimate of the median journey time
(c) the number of students who took less than 10 minutes to get to school
(d) the number of students who had journey times greater than 30 minutes
(e) the number of students who took between 40 minutes and one hour to get to school.

(a)	50	The top of the curve is at 50, so this is the total frequency.
(b)	38	$\frac{50}{2} = 25$ so its the 25th result; drop a perpendicular from where the line cuts the graph.
(c)	4	Read off the cumulative frequency at 10 minutes.
(d)	$50 - 18 = 32$	Subtract the cumulative frequency at 30 minutes, 18, from the total frequency.
(e)	$42 - 28 = 14$	Subtract the cumulative frequency at 40 minutes, 28, from that at 60 minutes, 42.

Worked example 7

Twenty bean seeds were planted for a biology experiment. The heights of the plants were measured after three weeks and recorded as below.

Heights (*h* cm)	$0 \le h < 3$	$3 \le h < 6$	$6 \le h < 9$	$9 \le h < 12$
Frequency	2	5	10	3

(a) Find an estimate for the mean height.
(b) Draw a cumulative frequency curve and find an estimate for the median height.

REWIND

You learned how to find an estimate for the mean of grouped data in chapter 12. Revise this now if you have forgotten it. ◀

(a) You will need the mid-points of the classes to help you find an estimate of the mean, and the cumulative frequency to help find an estimate of the median, so more columns need to be added to the table. Don't forget to label the new columns.

Heights (h cm)	Mid-point (x)	Frequency (f)	Frequency × mid-point (fx)	Cumulative frequency
$0 \leq h < 3$	1.5	2	3	2
$3 \leq h < 6$	4.5	5	22.5	7
$6 \leq h < 9$	7.5	10	75	17
$9 \leq h < 12$	10.5	3	31.5	20
Total		20	132	

Mean height $= \frac{132}{20} = 6.6\,\text{cm}$ $\left(\text{mean} = \frac{\text{total } fx}{\text{total } f}\right)$

(b)

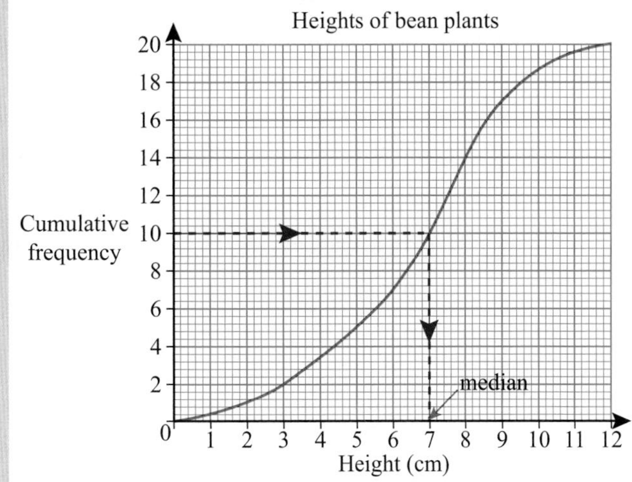

$\frac{20}{2} = 10$, so the median height is the 10th value.

Median height = 7.0 cm

Exercise 20.3

1 The heights of 25 plants were measured to the nearest centimetre.
The results are summarised in the table.

Height in cm	6–15	16–20	21–25	26–40
Number of plants	3	7	10	5

(a) Draw a cumulative frequency table for this distribution.
(b) In which interval does the median plant height lie?
(c) Draw the cumulative frequency curve and use it to estimate, to the nearest centimetre, the median plant height.

2 The table shows the amount of money, $\$x$, spent on books by a group of students.

Amount spent	No. of students
$0 < x \leq 10$	0
$10 < x \leq 20$	4
$20 < x \leq 30$	8
$30 < x \leq 40$	12
$40 < x \leq 50$	11
$50 < x \leq 60$	5

(a) Calculate an estimate of the mean amount of money per student spent on books.
(b) Use the information in the table above to find the values of p, q and r in the following cumulative frequency table.

Amount spent	≤ 10	≤ 20	≤ 30	≤ 40	≤ 50	≤ 60
Cumulative frequency	0	4	p	q	r	40

(c) Using a scale of 1 cm to represent 10 units on each axis, draw a cumulative frequency diagram.
(d) Use your diagram to estimate the median amount spent.

3 This cumulative frequency table shows the distribution of the masses of the children attending a clinic.

Mass in kilograms (M)	Cumulative frequency
$0 < m \leq 10.0$	12
$0 < m \leq 20.0$	26
$0 < m \leq 30.0$	33
$0 < m \leq 40.0$	41
$0 < m \leq 50.0$	46
$0 < m \leq 60.0$	50

(a) Draw a cumulative frequency diagram. Use a horizontal scale of 1 cm = 10 kg and a vertical scale of 0.5 cm = 5 children.
(b) Estimate the median mass.
(c) How many children had a mass higher than the median mass?

Quartiles

In chapter 12 you found the range (the biggest value – the smallest value) to see how dispersed various sets of data were. The range, however, is easily affected by outliers (extreme or unusual values), so it is not always the best measure of how the data is spread out.

The data shown on a cumulative frequency curve can be divided into four equal groups called **quartiles** to find a measure of spread called the **interquartile range**, which is more representative than the range because it is not affected by extremes.

The cumulative frequency curve on the next page shows the marks obtained by 64 students in a test. These are listed below:

- 48 students scored less than 15 marks. 15 marks is the upper quartile or third quartile Q_3.
- 32 students scored less than 13 marks. 13 marks is the second quartile Q_2, or median mark.
- 16 students scored less than 11 marks. 11 marks is the lower quartile or first quartile Q_1.

Whole number values are being used in this example to make it easier to understand. Usually your answers will be estimates and they will involve decimal fractions.

When finding the positions of the quartiles from a cumulative frequency curve you do not use the $\frac{(n+1)}{4}$, $\frac{(n+1)}{2}$ and $\frac{3}{4}(n+1)$ rules that you met for discrete data in chapter 12. Instead you use: $\frac{n}{4}$, $\frac{n}{2}$ and $\frac{3n}{4}$.

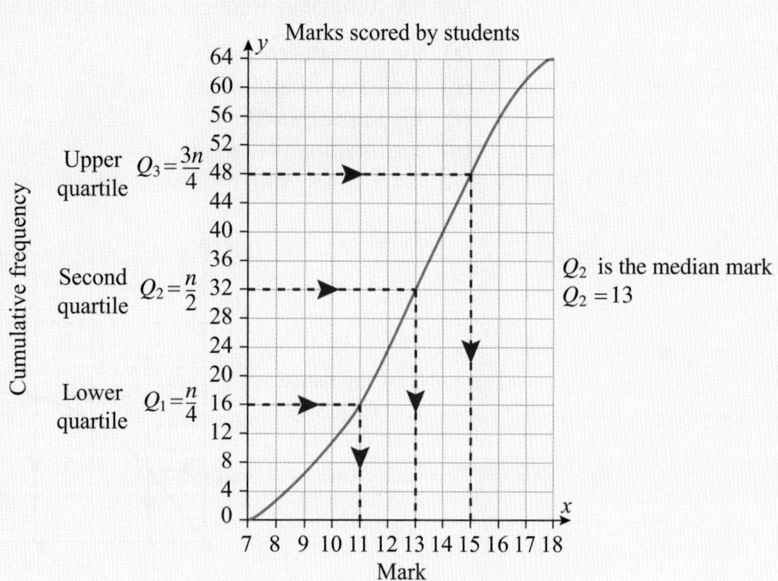

The interquartile range

The interquartile range (IQR) is the difference between the upper and lower quartiles: $Q_3 - Q_1$.

In effect, this is the range of the middle 50% of the scores, or the median of the upper half of the values minus the median of the lower half of the values.

In the example above, the IQR = 15 − 11 = 4

Because the interquartile range does not use any extreme small or large values it is considered a more reliable measure of spread than the range.

REWIND

The range was used to compare data sets in chapter 12. ◀

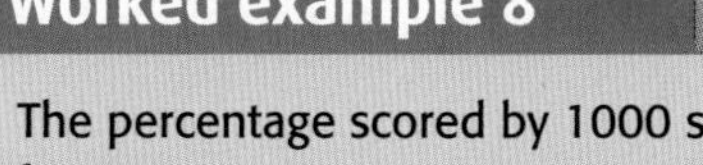

Worked example 8

The percentage scored by 1000 students on an exam is shown on this cumulative frequency curve.

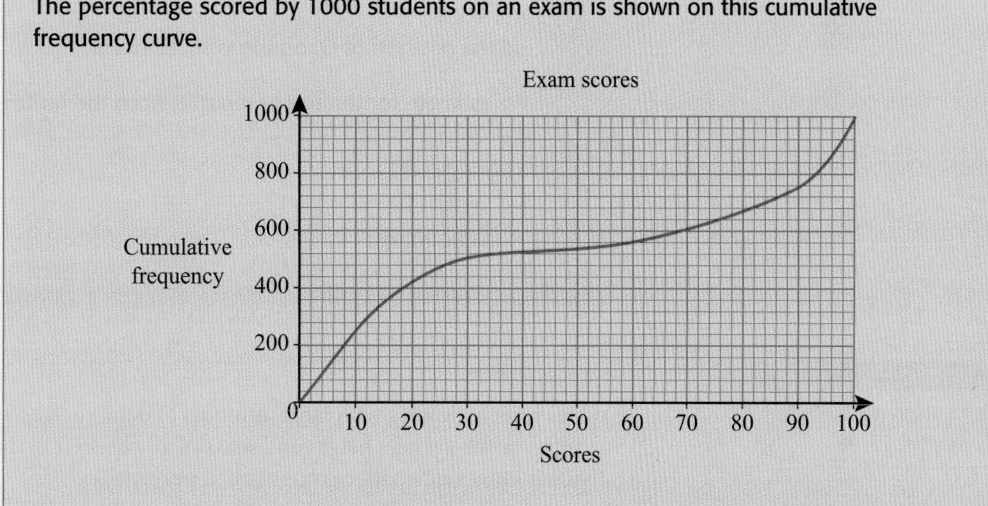

Use the cumulative frequency curve to find an estimate for:

(a) the median score
(b) the lower quartile
(c) the upper quartile
(d) the interquartile range.

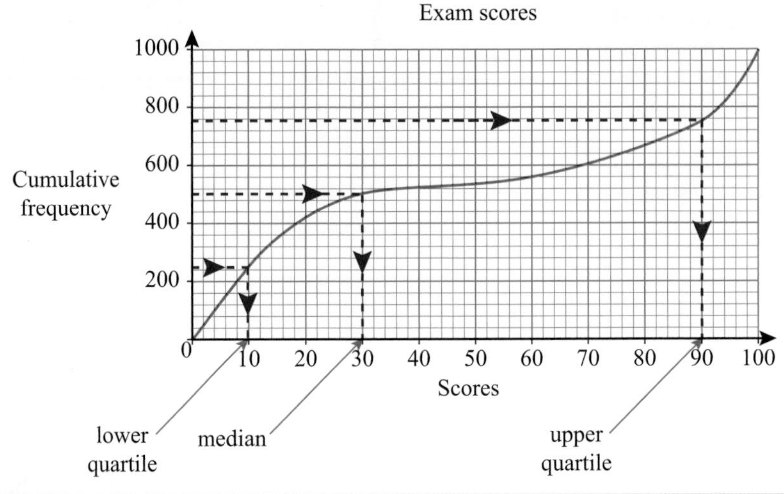

(a) $n = 1000$

So the position of Q_2 on the vertical axis is $\frac{n}{2} = \frac{1000}{2} = 500$

Draw the lines on the graph.
Estimate the median from the horizontal axis as 30 marks.

(b) $n = 1000$

So the position of Q_1 on the vertical axis is $\frac{n}{4} = \frac{1000}{4} = 250$

An estimate for the lower quartile, from the horizontal axis is 10 marks

(c) $n = 1000$

So the position of Q_3 on the vertical axis is $\frac{3n}{4} = \frac{3 \times 1000}{4} = 750$

An estimate for the upper quartile, from the horizontal axis is 90 marks.

(d)

$$\begin{aligned} \text{IQR} &= Q_3 - Q_1 \\ &= 90 - 10 \\ &= 80 \text{ marks} \end{aligned}$$

REWIND

Percentiles were briefly introduced in chapter 12. ◀

Percentiles

When you are dealing with large amounts of data, such as examination results for the whole country, or the average height and mass of all children in different age groups, it is useful to divide it into even smaller groups called **percentiles**.

Percentiles divide the data into 100 equal parts.

To find the position of a percentile use the formula $\frac{pn}{100}$, where p is the percentile you are looking for and n is how much data you have (the total frequency).

Using the data set in worked example 8:

The position of the 10th percentile on the cumulative frequency axis is $P_{10} = \frac{10 \times 1000}{100} = 100$

The position of the 85th percentile on the cumulative frequency axis is $P_{85} = \frac{85 \times 1000}{100} = 850$

(Don't forget that you need to move right to the curve and down to the horizontal axis to find the values of the percentiles.)

The percentile range is the difference between given percentiles. In the example above, this is $P_{85} - P_{10}$.

In chapter 12, percentiles were first introduced but only the 25th and 75th percentiles were used to introduce the interquartile range. A question was posed at the start of section 12.5 on page 244: 'All those candidates above the 80th percentile will be offered an interview. What does this mean?' The following worked example shows you how to answer this question.

Worked example 9

The cumulative frequency curve shows the test results of 200 candidates who have applied for a post at Fashkiddler's. Only those who score above the 80th percentile will be called for an interview. What is the lowest score that can be obtained to receive an interview letter?

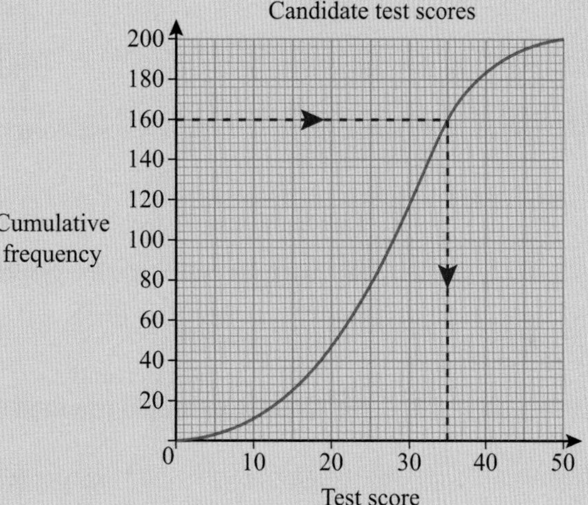

80% of 200 is 160.
So, the value of P_{80} is a test score of 35. (Read off the graph where the curve is 160)
Only those candidates who scored above 35 marks on the test will be called for an interview.

Exercise 20.4

1 The lengths of 32 metal rods were measured and recorded on this cumulative frequency curve. Use the graph to find an estimate for:

(a) the median
(b) Q_1
(c) Q_3
(d) the IQR
(e) the 40th percentile.

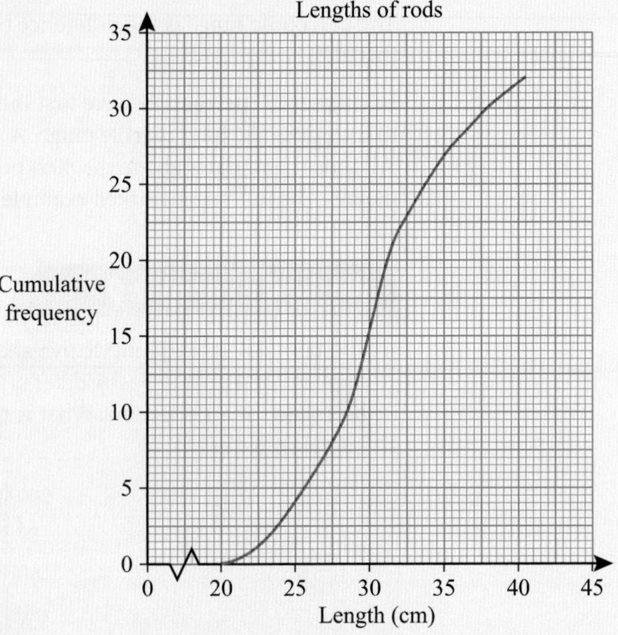

2 This cumulative frequency curve compares the results 120 students obtained on two maths papers.

(a) For each paper, use the graph to find:
  (i) the median mark
  (ii) the IQR
  (iii) the 60th percentile.
(b) What mark would you need to get to be above the 90th percentile on each paper?

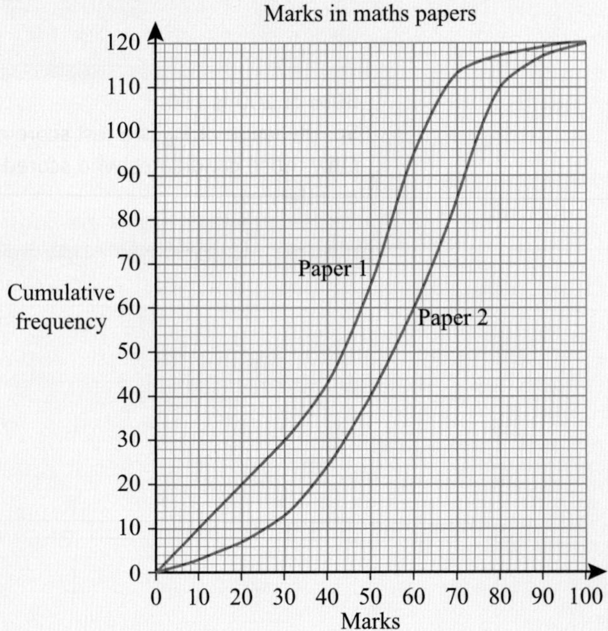

3 This cumulative frequency curve shows the masses of 500 12-year-old girls (in kg).

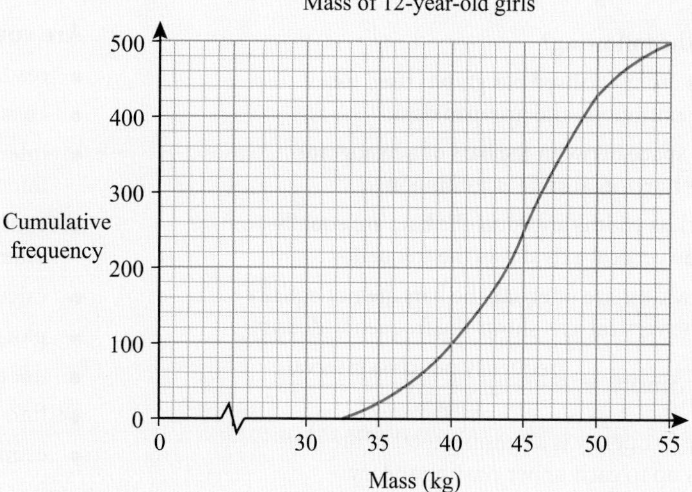

(a) Use the graph to work out:
(i) the median mass of the 12-year-olds
(ii) how many girls have a mass between 40 and 50 kg.
(b) What percentage of girls are unable to go on an amusement park children's ride if the upper mass limit for the ride is 51 kg?

4 This cumulative frequency table gives the speeds of 200 cars travelling on the highway from Kuala Lumpur International Airport into the city.

Speed in km/h (s)	Cumulative frequency
$s < 60$	2
$60 \leq s < 70$	8
$60 \leq s < 80$	24
$60 \leq s < 90$	45
$60 \leq s < 100$	96
$60 \leq s < 110$	123
$60 \leq s < 120$	171
$60 \leq s < 130$	195
$60 \leq s < 140$	200
Total	200

(a) Draw a cumulative frequency curve to show this data. Use a scale of 1 cm per 10 km/h on the horizontal axis and a scale of 1 cm per 10 cars on the vertical axis.
(b) Use your curve to estimate the median, Q_1 and Q_3 for this data.
(c) Estimate the IQR.
(d) The speed limit on this stretch of road is 120 km/h. What percentage of the cars were speeding?

Summary

Do you know the following?

- Histograms are specialised bar graphs used for displaying continuous and grouped data.
- There is no space between the bars of a histogram because the horizontal scale is continuous.
- When the class widths are equal the bars are equally wide and the vertical axis shows the frequency.
- If the class widths are unequal, the bars are not equally wide and the vertical axis shows the frequency density.
- Frequency density $= \dfrac{\text{frequency per class interval}}{\text{class width}}$
- Cumulative frequency is a running total of the class frequencies up to each upper class boundary.
- When cumulative frequencies are plotted they give a cumulative frequency curve or ogive.
- The curve can be used to estimate the median value in the data.
- The data can be divided into four equal groups called quartiles. The interquartile range is the difference between the upper and lower quartiles ($Q_3 - Q_1$).
- Large masses of data can be divided into percentiles which divide the data into 100 equal groups. They are used to compare and rank measurements.

Are you able to …?

- read and interpret histograms with equal intervals
- construct histograms with equal intervals
- interpret and construct histograms with unequal intervals
- construct a table to find the frequency density of different classes
- calculate cumulative frequencies
- plot and draw a cumulative frequency curve
- use a cumulative frequency curve to estimate the median
- find quartiles and calculate the interquartile range
- estimate and interpret percentiles.

Examination practice

Exam-style questions

1 After a morning's fishing Imtiaz measured the mass, in grams, of the fish he had caught. The partially completed histogram represents his results.

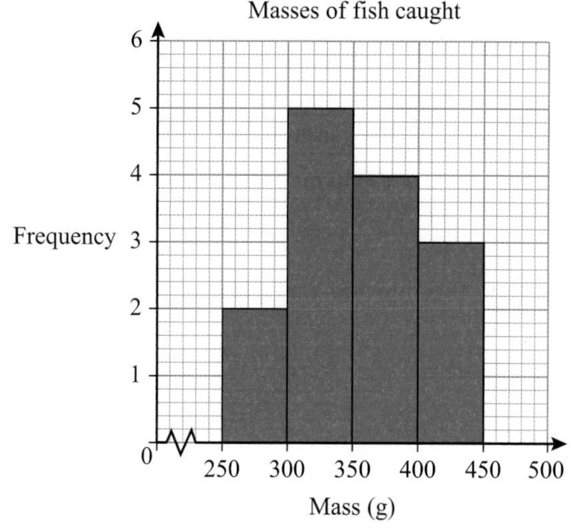

(a) Imtiaz also caught four other fish. Their masses were 225 g, 466 g, 470 g and 498 g. Add this data to a copy of the graph to complete it.

(b) Use the completed graph to complete this table.

Mass (m) in grams	Number of fish	Classification
$m < 300$		Small
$300 \leq m < 400$		Medium
$m \geq 400$		Large

(c) Represent the information in the table as a pie chart. Show clearly how you calculate the angle of each sector.

2 A researcher took a questionnaire to 64 households. The grouped frequency table shows the time taken (t minutes) by various home owners to complete a questionnaire.

Time taken (t) in minutes	No. of home owners
$0 \leq t < 2$	2
$2 \leq t < 3$	18
$3 \leq t < 4$	25
$4 \leq t < 6$	12
$6 \leq t < 9$	5
$9 \leq t < 15$	2

Using a scale of 1 cm to represent 2 minutes, construct a horizontal axis for $0 \leq t < 15$.
Using a vertical scale of 1 cm per 2 units, draw a histogram to represent this data.

Past paper questions

1 The table below shows the age and price of 20 used cars in a showroom.

Age (years)	6	5	4	5	4	5	1	6	3	8
Price ($)	1800	7600	9500	2500	4100	3100	5600	4700	4800	7900

Age (years)	1	2	9	10	3	7	1	8	2	3
Price ($)	6500	7000	1000	3800	1900	5200	3400	2100	4300	8200

(a) (i) Complete the frequency table for the price, $\$x$, of the cars.

Price ($)	$0 \leq x < 2000$	$2000 \leq x < 4000$	$4000 \leq x < 6000$	$6000 \leq x < 8000$	$8000 \leq x < 10\,000$
Frequency					

(ii) Draw a histogram to show this information.

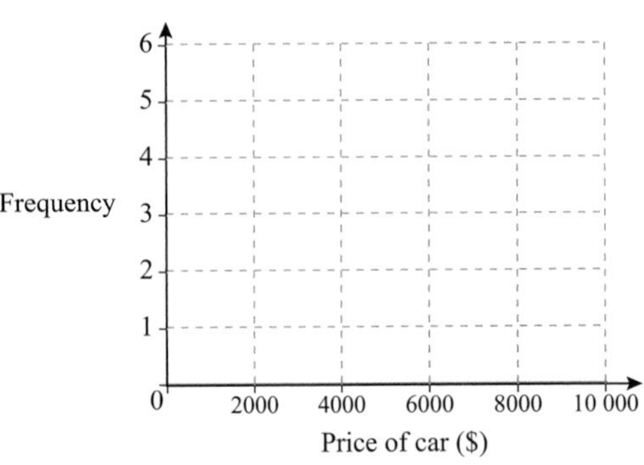

[Cambridge IGCSE Mathematics 0580 Paper 03 Q08 b May/June 2009]

2 The heights of 100 students are measured. The results have been used to draw this cumulative frequency diagram.

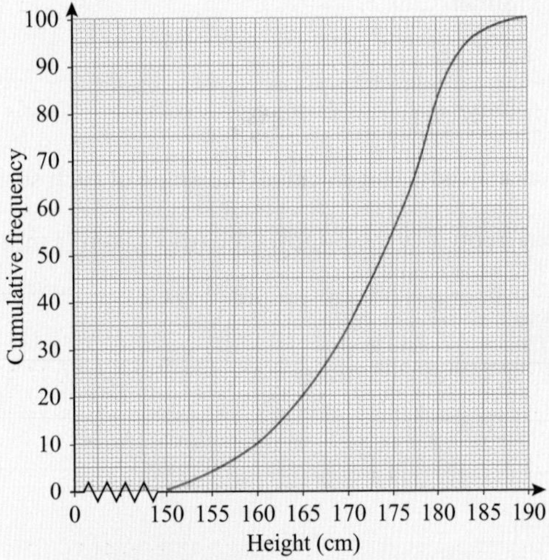

(a) Find

(i) the median height, [1]

(ii) the lower quartile, [1]

(iii) the inter-quartile range, [1]

(iv) the number of students with a height greater than 177 cm. [2]

(b) The frequency table shows the information about the 100 students who were measured.

Height (h cm)	$150 < h \leq 160$	$160 < h \leq 170$	$170 < h \leq 180$	$180 < h \leq 190$
Frequency			47	18

(i) Use the cumulative frequency diagram to complete the table above. [1]

(ii) Calculate an estimate of the mean height of the 100 students. [4]

[Cambridge IGCSE Mathematics 0580 Paper 21 Q03 May/June 2009]

21 Ratio, rate and proportion

Key words

- Ratio
- Scale
- Rate
- Speed
- Direct proportion
- Unitary method
- Ratio method
- Inverse proportion

In this chapter you will learn how to:

- record relationships using ratio notation
- find one quantity when the other is given
- divide amounts in a given ratio
- make sense of scales on maps, models and plans
- read and interpret rates
- calculate average speed
- EXTENDED: solve problems using distance–time and speed–time graphs
- understand what is meant by direct and inverse proportion
- solve problems involving proportionate amounts
- EXTENDED: use algebra to express direct and inverse proportion
- EXTENDED: increase and decrease amounts by a given ratio.

This is an architectural model of the Louvre Abu Dhabi Museum which is being built on Saadiyat Island; the man in the photo is the architect, Jean Nouvel. The model is approximately a 1 : 90 version of the real building, in other words, the real building will be 90 times larger than the model.

A ratio is a comparison of amounts in a particular order. The amounts are expressed in the same units and are called the terms of the ratio. A ratio is usually written in the form $a : b$. Actual measurements are not given in a ratio, what is important is the proportion of the amounts. Ratio is used when working with scale on maps, models and plans.

A rate is a comparison of two different quantities. Speed is a rate which compares distance travelled to the time taken. Other examples of rates in daily life are cost per kilogram of foods, beats per minute in medicine, runs per over in cricket, kilometres per litre of petrol and exchange rates of foreign currencies.

21.1 Working with ratio

When you speak out a ratio, you use the word 'to' so, 5 : 2 is said as '5 to 2'.

A **ratio** is a numerical comparison of two amounts. The order in which you write the amounts is very important. For example, if there is one teacher for every 25 students in a school, then the ratio of teachers to students is 1 : 25.

Ratios can also be written as fractions. A ratio of 1 : 25 can be written as $\frac{1}{25}$ and a ratio of 5 : 3 can be written as $\frac{5}{3}$.

When you write two quantities as a ratio, you must make sure they are both in the same units before you start. For example, the ratio of 20 c to \$1 is not 20 : 1, it is 20 : 100 because there are 100 cents in a dollar.

Writing ratios in simplest form

REWIND

If you have forgotten how to simplify fractions, look again at chapter 5. ◀

Ratios are in their simplest form when you write them using the smallest whole numbers possible. The ratio of 20 : 100 above is not in its simplest form. You can simplify ratios in the same way that you simplified fractions. $\frac{20}{100} = \frac{2}{10} = \frac{1}{5}$ so 20 : 100 = 1 : 5.

Worked example 1

Sanjita mixes eight litres of white paint with three litres of red paint to get pink paint. What is the ratio of:

(a) red paint to white paint?
(b) white paint to the total amount of paint in the mixture?
(c) red paint to the total amount of paint in the mixture?

(a) 3 litres to 8 litres = 3 : 8

(b) 8 litres white out of a total of 11 litres so 8 : 11 is the required ratio

(c) 3 litres red out of a total of 11 litres so 3 : 11 is the required ratio

Worked example 2

To make concrete, you mix cement, sand and gravel in the ratio 1 : 2 : 4.

(a) What is ratio of cement to gravel?
(b) What is the ratio of sand to gravel?
(c) What is the ratio of gravel to the total amount of concrete?
(d) What fraction of the concrete is cement?

(a) Cement to gravel is 1 : 4

(b) Sand to gravel is 2 : 4 = 1 : 2

(c) Concrete = 1 + 2 + 4 = 7 parts ∴ gravel is 4 parts out of 7, so 4 : 7 is the required ratio

(d) Concrete = 1 + 2 + 4 = 7 ∴ cement = $\frac{1}{7}$

Exercise 21.1

1 Write each of the following as a ratio.

(a) Nine men to nine women.
(b) One litre to five litres.
(c) 25 minutes to 3 minutes.
(d) 18 seconds out of every minute.
(e) 15 c out of every $1.
(f) two millimetres out of every centimetre.

2 A packet of sweets contains 12 red and five yellow sweets. What is the ratio of:

(a) red to yellow sweets
(b) yellow to red sweets?

3 Look at these two rectangles.

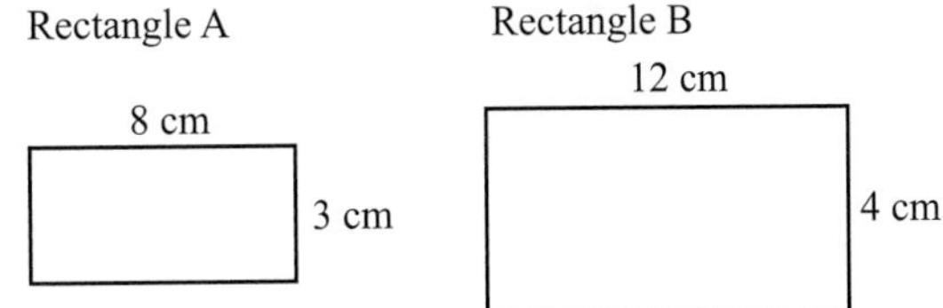

Express the following relationships as ratios:
(a) length of rectangle A to length of rectangle B
(b) width of rectangle A to width of rectangle B
(c) perimeter of rectangle A to perimeter of rectangle B
(d) area of rectangle A to area of rectangle B.

4 The table gives the mean life expectancy (in years) of some African animals.

Animal	Life expectancy (years)
Tortoise	120
Parrot	50
Elephant	35
Gorilla	30
Lion	15
Giraffe	10

Find the ratio of the life expectancies of:

(a) giraffe to tortoise
(b) lion to gorilla
(c) lion to tortoise
(d) elephant to gorilla
(e) parrot to lion
(f) parrot to tortoise.

5 What is the ratio of:

(a) a millimetre to a centimetre
(b) a centimetre to a metre
(c) a metre to a centimetre
(d) a gram to a kilogram
(e) a litre to a millilitre
(f) a minute to an hour?

6 Express the following as ratios in their simplest form.

(a) 25 litres to 50 litres
(b) 25 c to $2.00
(c) 75 cm to 2 m
(d) 600 g to five kilograms
(e) 15 mm to a metre
(f) 2.5 g to 50 g
(g) 4 cm to 25 mm
(h) 400 ml to 3 ℓ

REWIND

It may be useful to revise common factors from chapter 1. ◀

Equivalent ratios

Equivalent ratios are basically the same as equivalent fractions. If you multiply or divide the terms of the ratio by the same number (except 0) you get an equivalent ratio.

Worked example 3

For each of the following ratios find the missing value:

(a) $1:4 = x:20$
(b) $4:9 = 24:y$.

Method 1: multiplying by a common factor.

(a)	$1:4 = x:20$ $1:4 = 5:20$	$20 \div 5 = 4$, so $20 = 4 \times 5$ 1 must be multiplied by 5 as well.
(b)	$4:9 = 24:y$ $4:9 = 24:54$	$24 \div 4 = 6$, so $4 \times 6 = 24$ 9 must be multiplied by 6 as well.

Method 2: cross multiplying fractions.

(a)	$\frac{1}{4} = \frac{x}{20}$	Write the ratios as fractions.
	$x = \frac{1 \times 20}{4}$ $x = 5$	Solve the equation by multiplying both sides by 20.
(b)	$\frac{4}{9} = \frac{24}{y}$	Write each ratio as a fraction.
	$\frac{9}{4} = \frac{y}{24}$	Take the reciprocal of the fractions (turn them upside down) to get y at the top and make the equation easier to solve.
	$\frac{9 \times 24}{4} = y$ $\frac{216}{4} = y$ $y = 54$	Solve the equation by multiplying both sides by 24.

REWIND

You learned about the reciprocals of fractions in chapter 5. ◀

Equivalent ratios are useful when you need to solve problems involving a missing amount.

Exercise 21.2

1 Find the unknown values in the following equivalent ratios. Use whichever method you find easiest.

(a) $2:3=6:x$	**(b)** $6:5=y:20$	**(c)** $12:8=3:y$	**(d)** $27:x=9:2$
(e) $3:8=66:x$	**(f)** $1:5=13:y$	**(g)** $x:25=7:5$	**(h)** $40:9=800:y$
(i) $3:7=600:y$	**(j)** $2:7=30:x$	**(k)** $1.5:x=6:5$	**(l)** $\frac{1}{6}:\frac{1}{3}=2:y$

2 Use the equation (cross multiplying fractions) method to find the unknown values in the following equivalent ratios.

(a) $x:20=3:4$	**(b)** $12:21=x:14$	**(c)** $2:5=8:y$	**(d)** $3:5=x:4$
(e) $1:10=x:6$	**(f)** $8:13=2:y$	**(g)** $4:5=x:7$	**(h)** $5:4=9:y$

3 Say whether these statements are true or false. If a statement is false, explain why it is false.

(a) The ratio 1 : 6 is the same as the ratio 6 : 1.
(b) The ratio 1 : 6 is equivalent to 3 : 18.
(c) The ratio 20 : 15 can be expressed as 3 : 4.
(d) If the ratio of a mother's age to her daughter's age is 8 : 1, the daughter will be nine when her mother is 48 years old.
(e) If Mr Smith's wages are $\frac{5}{8}$ of Mr Jones' wages, then the ratio of their wages is 20 : 32.

Living maths

4 An alloy is a mixture of metals. Most of the gold used in jewellery is an alloy of pure gold and other metals which are added to make the gold harder. Pure gold is 24 carats (ct), so 18 carat gold is an alloy of gold and other metals in the ratio 18 : 6. In other words, $\frac{18}{24}$ parts pure gold and $\frac{6}{24}$ other metals.

(a) A jeweller makes an 18 ct gold alloy using three grams of pure gold. What mass of other metals does she add?
(b) An 18 ct gold chain contains four grams of pure gold. How much other metal does it contain?
(c) What is the ratio of gold to other metals in 14 ct gold?
(d) What is the ratio of gold to other metals in 9 ct gold?

5 An alloy of 9 ct gold contains gold, copper zinc and silver in the ratio 9 : 12.5 : 2.5.

(a) Express this ratio in simplest form.
(b) How much silver would you need if your alloy contained six grams of pure gold?
(c) How much copper zinc would you need to make a 9 ct alloy using three grams of pure gold?

6 An epoxy glue comes in two tubes (red and black), which have to be mixed in the ratio 1 : 4.

(a) If Petrus measures 5 ml from the red tube, how much does he need to measure from the black tube?
(b) How much would you need from the red tube if you used 10 ml from the black tube?

7 A brand of pet food contains meat and cereal in the ratio 2 : 9. During one shift, the factory making the pet food used 3500 kg of meat. What mass of cereal did they use?

Dividing a quantity in a given ratio

Ratios can be used to divide or share quantities. There are two ways of solving problems like these.

- Method 1: find the value of one part. This is the **unitary method**.

  1 Add the values in the ratio to find the total number of parts involved.

  2 Divide the quantity by the total number of parts to find the quantity per part (the value of one part).

  3 Multiply the values in the ratio by the quantity per part to find the value of each part.

- Method 2: express the shares as fractions. This is the **ratio method**.

  1 Add the values in the ratio to find the total number of parts involved.

  2 Express each part of the ratio as a fraction of the total parts.

  3 Multiply the quantity by the fraction to find the value of each part.

Worked example 4

Share \$24 between Jess and Anne in the ratio 3 : 5.

Method 1

$3 + 5 = 8$ $24 \div 8 = 3$ Jess gets \$9, Anne gets \$15.	There are 8 parts in the ratio. This is the value of 1 part. Jess gets 3 parts : $3 \times 3 = 9$ Anne gets 5 parts : $5 \times 3 = 15$

Method 2

$3 + 5 = 8$ Jess gets $\frac{3}{8}$ of \$24 $= \frac{3}{8} \times 24 = \$9$ Anne gets $\frac{5}{8}$ of \$24 $= \frac{5}{8} \times 24 = \$15$.	There are 8 parts in the ratio. Express each part as a fraction of the total parts and multiply by the quantity.

Exercise 21.3

1 Divide:

(a) 200 in the ratio 1 : 4
(b) 1500 in the ratio 4 : 1
(c) 50 in the ratio 3 : 7
(d) 60 in the ratio 3 : 12
(e) 600 in the ratio 3 : 9
(f) 38 in the ratio 11 : 8
(g) 300 in the ratio 11 : 4
(h) 2300 in the ratio 1 : 2 : 7.

2 Fruit concentrate is mixed with water in the ratio of 1 : 3 to make a fruit drink. How much concentrate would you need to make 1.2 litres of fruit drink?

3 Josh has 45 marbles. He shares them with his friend Ahmed in the ratio 3 : 2. How many marbles does each boy get?

4 \$200 is to be shared amongst Annie, Andrew and Amina in the ratio 3 : 4 : 5. How much will each child receive?

5 A line 16 cm long is divided in the ratio 3 : 5. How long is each section?

The capital letters N : P : K on fertiliser bags are the chemical symbols for the elements. The ratio of chemicals is always given on packs of fertiliser.

6 A bag of N : P : K fertiliser contains nitrogen, phosphorus and potassium in the ratio 2 : 3 : 3. Work out the mass of each ingredient if the bags have the following total masses:

(a) one kilogram (b) five kilograms (c) 20 kilograms (d) 25 kilograms.

7 The lengths of the sides of a triangle are in the ratio 4 : 5 : 3. Work out the length of each side if the triangle has a perimeter of 5.4 metres.

8 A rectangle has a perimeter of 120 cm. The ratio of its length to its breadth is 5 : 3. Sketch the rectangle and indicate what the lengths of each side would be.

9 In a group of 3200 elderly people, the ratio of men to women is 3 : 5. Calculate how many men there are in the group.

21.2 Ratio and scale

REWIND

Scale drawings were discussed in more detail in chapter 15. ◀

Scale drawings (maps and plans) and models such as the one of the Louvre Museum in Abu Dhabi (on page 453), are the same shape as the real objects but they are generally smaller.

Scale is a ratio. It can be expressed as 'length on drawing : real length'.

The scale of a map, plan or model is usually given as a ratio in the form of 1 : *n*. For example, the architects who designed the new Louvre building for Abu Dhabi made a 6 m wide scale model of the domed roof using aluminium rods to test how light would enter the dome. The scale of this model is 1 : 33.

A scale of 1 : 33 means that a unit of measurement on the model must be multiplied by 33 to get the length (in the same units) of the real building. So, if the diameter of the dome in the model was 6 m, then the diameter of the real dome will be 6 m × 33 = 198 m.

Expressing a ratio in the form of 1 : *n*

Some scale drawings, such as diagrams of cells in Biology, are larger than the real items they show. In an enlargement the scale is given in the form of *n* : 1 (where *n* > 1).

All ratio scales must be expressed in the form of 1 : *n* or *n* : 1.

To change a ratio so that one part = 1, you need to divide both parts by the number that you want expressed as 1.

Worked example 5

Express 5 : 1000 in the form of 1 : *n*

$5:1000$ $=\frac{5}{5}:\frac{1000}{5}$ $=1:200$	Divide both sides by 5, i.e. the number that you want expressed as 1.

Worked example 6

Express 4 mm : 50 cm as a ratio scale.

4 mm : 50 cm $= 4\text{mm} : 500\text{mm}$ $= 4 : 500$	Express the amounts in the same units first.
$=\frac{4}{4}:\frac{500}{4}$ $=1:125$	Divide by 4 to express in the form 1 : *n*.

Worked example 7

The form of 1 : *n* or *n* : 1 does not always the give a ratio with whole number parts.

Write 22 : 4 in the form of *n* : 1.

$22:4$ $=\frac{22}{4}:\frac{4}{4}$	Divide both sides by 4, i.e. the number that you want expressed as 1.
$= 5.5 : 1$	In this form you may get a decimal answer on one side.

Solving scale problems

There are two main types of problems involving scale:

- calculating the real lengths of objects from a scaled diagram or model,
  Real length = diagram length × scale
- calculating how long an object on the diagram will be if you are given the scale,
  Diagram length = real length ÷ scale

Worked example 8

The scale of a map is 1 : 25 000.

(a) What is real distance between two points that are 5 cm apart on the diagram?
(b) Express the real distance in kilometres.

(a)	Distance on map = 5 cm Scale = 1 : 25 000 ∴ Real distance = 5 cm × 25 000 = 125 000 cm The real distance is 125 000 cm.	Multiply the map distance by the scale. The units in your answer will the same units as the map distance units.
(b)	1 km = 100 000 cm 125 000 cm ÷ 100 000 = 1.25 km	From part (a) you know the real distance = 120 000 cm. You know that 1 km = 100 000 cm. So convert the real distance to km.

Worked example 9

A dam wall is 480 m long. How many centimetres long would it be on a map with a scale of 1 : 12 000?

Real length = 480 m
Scale = 1 : 12 000
Map length = real length ÷ scale
= 480 ÷ 12 000
= 0.04 m
1 m = 100 cm
0.04 × 100 = 4 cm
The dam wall would be 4 cm long on the map.

Exercise 21.4

1 Write each of the following scales as a ratio in the form

(i) $1 : n$ **(ii)** $n : 1$

(a) 1 cm to 2 m **(b)** 2 cm to 5 m **(c)** 4 cm to 1 km
(d) 5 cm to 10 km **(e)** 3.5 cm to 1 m **(f)** 9 mm to 150 km.

2 A scaled diagram of a shopping centre is drawn at a scale of 1 : 400. Find the real distance in metres of the following lengths measured on the diagram.

(a) 1 cm **(b)** 15 mm **(c)** 3.5 cm **(d)** 12 cm.

3 A map has a scale of 1 : 50 000. How long would each of these real lengths be on the map?

(a) 60 m **(b)** 15 km **(c)** 120 km **(d)** 75.5 km.

4 A rectangular hall is 20 m long and 50 m wide. Draw scaled diagrams of this hall using a scale of:

(a) 1 : 200 **(b)** 4 mm to 1 m.

Living maths

5 Use this map to find the straight line distance between:

(a) New Delhi and Bangalore **(b)** Mumbai and Kolkata **(c)** Srinagar and Nagpur.

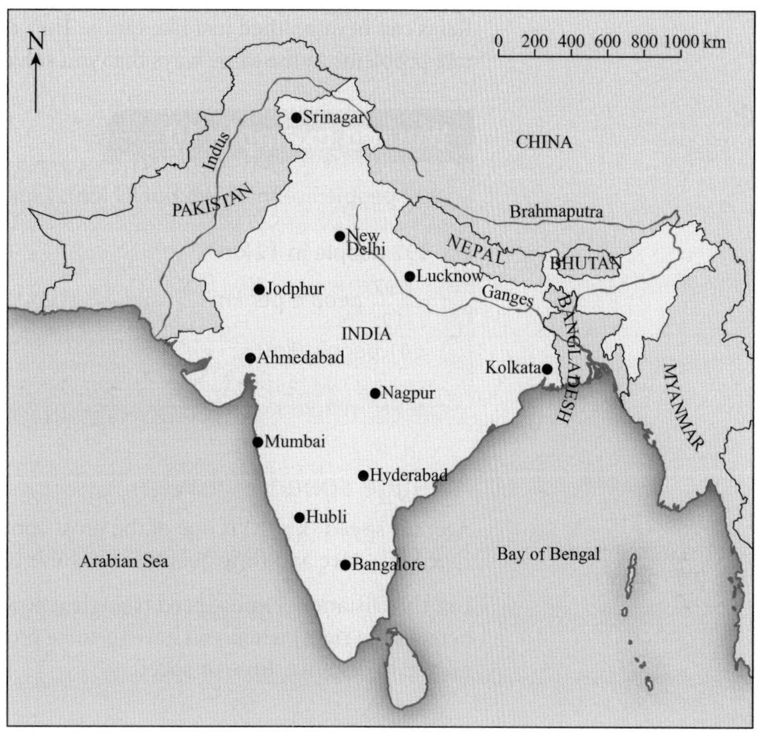

6 The scale used for this floor plan of a house is 1 : 150.

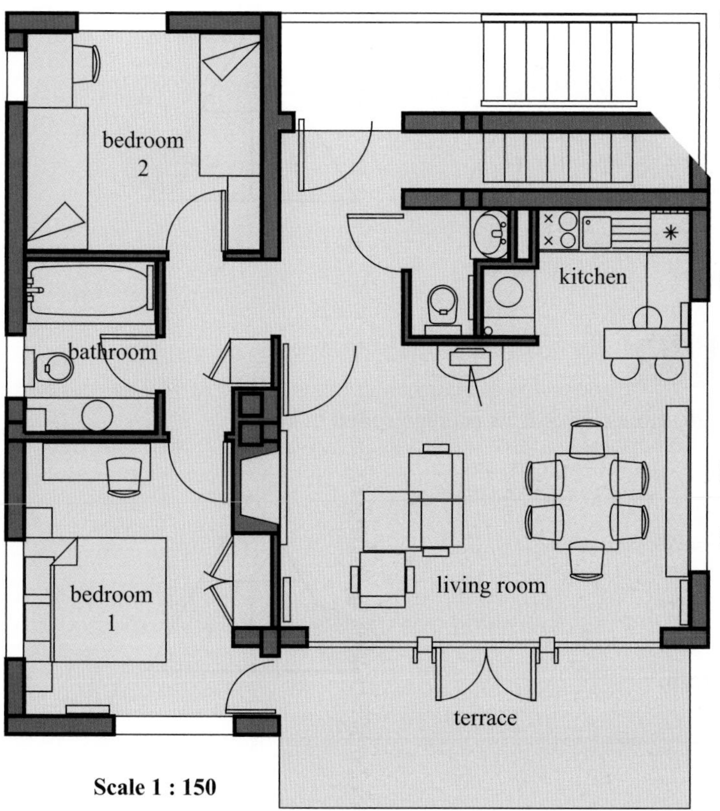

(a) What is real distance in metres is represented by 1 cm on the plan?

(b) Calculate the real length in metres of:

(i) the length of living room

(ii) the breadth of the living room

(iii) the length of the bath

(iv) the breadth of the terrace.

Remember to measure from inside wall to inside wall.

(c) What is the real area of:

(i) bedroom 1 **(ii)** bedroom 2 **(iii)** the terrace?

Work out the actual size of *each* length before you calculate the area.

(d) Calculate how much floor space there is in the bathroom (in m^2). (Include the toilet in the floor space.)

(e) Calculate the cost of tiling the bathroom floor if the tiles cost \$25.99 per square metre and the tiler charges \$15.25 per square metre for laying the tiles.

21.3 Rates

A **rate** is a comparison of two different quantities. In a rate, the quantity of one thing is usually given in relation to one unit of the other thing. For example, 750 ml per bottle or 60 km/h. The units of *both* quantities must be given in a rate.

Rates can be simplified just like ratios. They can also be expressed in the form of 1 : n. You solve rate problems in the same ways that you solve ratio and proportion problems.

Worked example 10

492 people live in an area of 12 km². Express this as a rate in its simplest terms.

492 people in 12 km²

$= \frac{492}{12}$ people per km² — Divide by 12 to get a rate per unit.

= 41 people/km² — Don't forget to write the units.

Average speed

A rate like km/h may sometimes be written kph (the 'p' stands for 'per').

Average **speed** (km/h) is one of the most commonly used rates. You need to be able to work with speed, distance and time quantities to solve problems.

Use the Distance–Time–Speed triangle (shown here on the right) when you have to solve problems related to distance, time or speed.

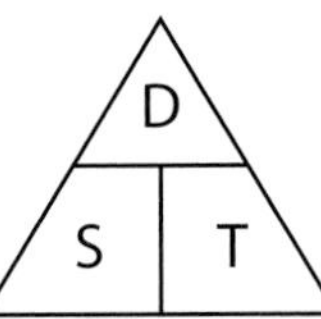

If you cover the letter of the quantity you need to find, then the remaining letters in the triangle give you the calculation you need to do (a multiplication or a division). For example:

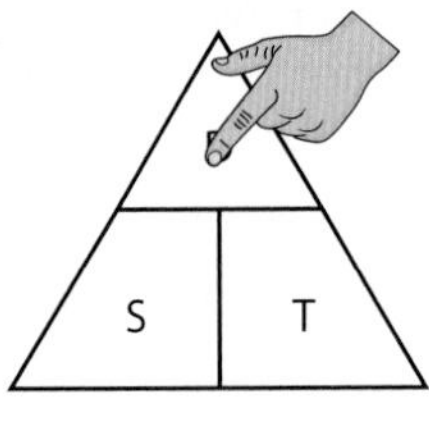

$D = S \times T$

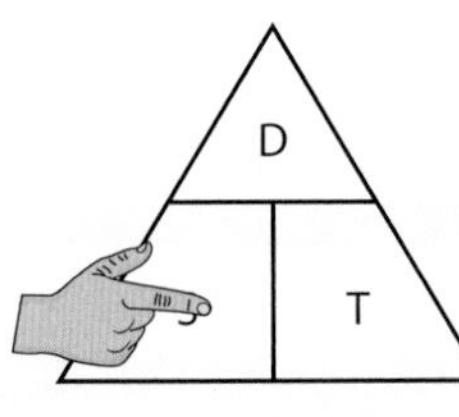

$S = \frac{D}{T}$

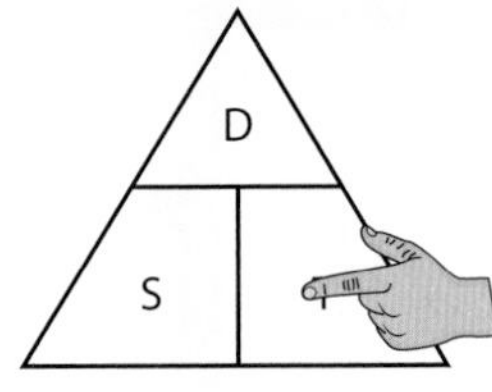

$T = \frac{D}{S}$

Worked example 11

A bus travels 210 km in three hours, what is its average speed in km/h?

$\text{Speed} = \frac{D}{T}$

Distance = 210 km, Time = 3 h,

$\therefore \text{speed} = \frac{210}{3}$

$= 70$ km/h

Its average speed is 70 km/h.

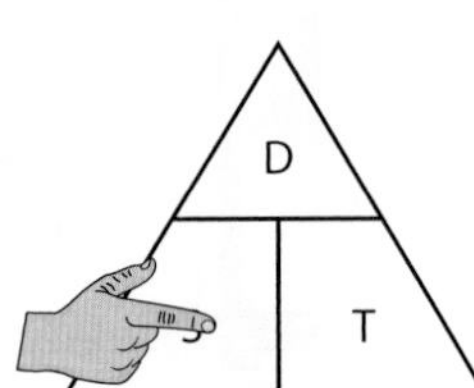

Tip

When you see the phrases 'how fast', 'how far' or 'for how long' you know you are dealing with a speed, distance or time problem.

Worked example 12

I walk at 4.5 km/h. How far can I walk in $2\frac{1}{2}$ hours at the same speed?

Distance = S × T
Speed = 4.5 km/h, T = 2.5 h,
∴ distance = 4.5 × 2.5 = 11.25 km
I can walk 11.25 km.

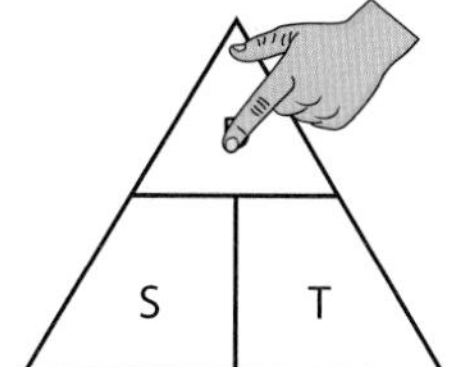

Worked example 13

How long would it take to cover 200 km at a speed of 80 km/h?

$$\text{Time} = \frac{D}{S}$$

Distance = 200 km, Speed = 80 km/h,

$$\therefore \text{time} = \frac{200}{80} = 2.5$$

It would take $2\frac{1}{2}$ hours.

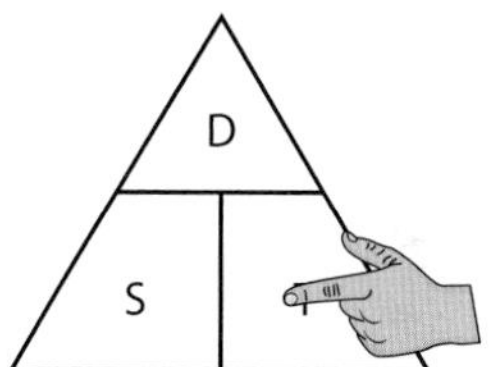

Exercise 21.5 *Living maths*

1 Express each of these relationships as a rate in simplest form.

(a) 12 kg for £5.
(b) 120 litres for 1000 km.
(c) \$315 for three nights.
(d) 5 km in 20 min.
(e) 135 students for five teachers.
(f) 15 hours spent per 5 holes dug.

2 A quarry produces 1200 t of crushed stone per hour. How much stone could it supply in:

(a) an eight-hour shift
(b) five shifts

3 Water leaks from a pipe at a rate of 5 ℓ/h. How much water will leak from the pipe in:

(a) a day
(b) a week?

4 A machine fills containers at a rate of 135 containers per minute. How long would it take to fill 1000 containers at the same rate?

5 Josh walks at 4.25 km/h. How far will he walk in three hours?

6 How far will a train travelling at 230 km/h travel in:

(a) $3\frac{1}{2}$ hours
(b) 20 minutes?

7 A plane flies at an average speed of 750 km/h. How far will it fly in:

(a) 25 minutes
(b) four hours?

8 A train left Cairo at 9 p.m. and travelled the 880 km to Aswan, arriving at 5 a.m. What was its average speed?

9 A runner completes a 42 km marathon in two hours 15 minutes. What was her average speed?

10 In August 2009, Usain Bolt of Jamaica set a world record by running 100 m in 9.58 seconds.

(a) Translate this speed into km/h.
(b) How long would it take him to run 420 m if he could run it at this speed?

21.4 Kinematic graphs

Distance–time graphs

Graphs that show the connection between the distance an object has travelled and the time taken to travel that distance are called distance–time graphs or travel graphs. On such graphs, time is normally shown along the horizontal axis and distance on the vertical. The graphs normally start at the origin because at the beginning no time has elapsed (passed) and no distance has been covered.

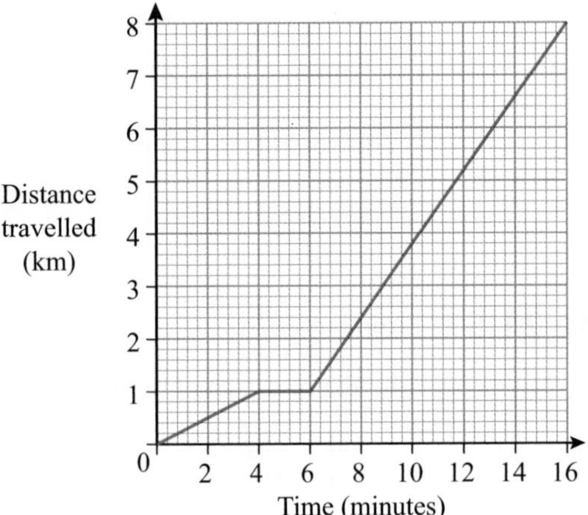

Look at the graph. Can you see that it shows the following journey:

- a cycle for 4 minutes from home to a bus stop 1 km away
- a 2 minute wait for the bus
- 7 km journey on the bus that takes 10 minutes.

The line of the graph remains horizontal while the person is not moving (waiting for the bus) because no distance is being travelled at this time. The steeper the line, the faster the person is travelling.

Worked example 14

Ashraf's school is 4 km from home and it takes him 40 minutes to walk to school. One morning he leaves at 7 a.m. After 15 minutes, he realises he has left his boots at home, so he runs back in 10 minutes. It takes him three minutes to find the boots. He runs at the same speed to school. The graph shows his journey.

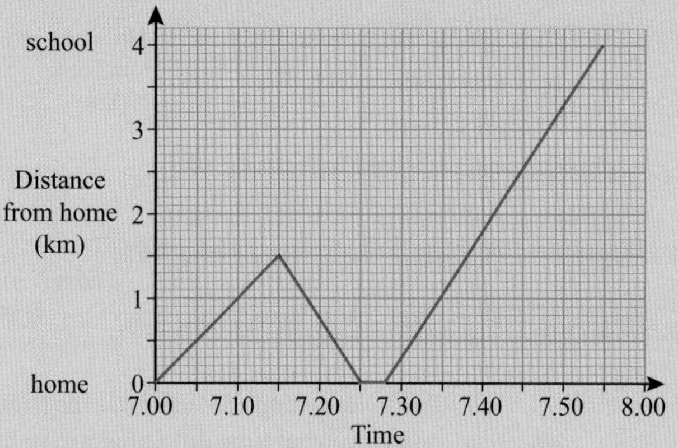

(a) How far had he walked before he remembered his boots?
(b) What happens to the graph as he returns home?
(c) What does the horizontal line on the graph represent?
(d) How fast did he run in m/min to get back home?

(a) Ashraf walked 1.5 km before he remembered his boots.

(b) The graph slopes downwards (back towards 0 km) as he goes home.

(c) The horizontal part of the graph corresponds with the three minutes at home.

(d) He runs 1.5 km in 10 minutes, an average speed 150 m/min.

Exercise 21.6 *Living maths*

1 This distance–time graph represents Monica's journey from home to a supermarket and back again.

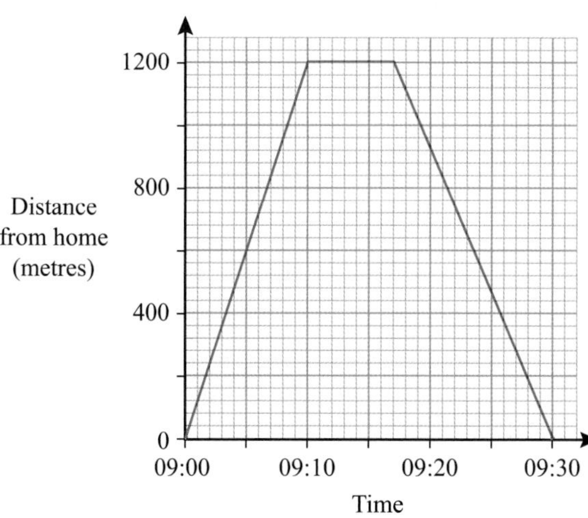

(a) How far was Monica from home at 09:06 hours?
(b) How many minutes did she spend at the supermarket?
(c) At what times was Monica 800 m from home?
(d) On which part of the journey did Monica travel faster, going to the supermarket or returning home?

2 Omar left school at 16.30. On his way home, he stopped at a friend's house before going home on his bicycle. The graph shows this information.

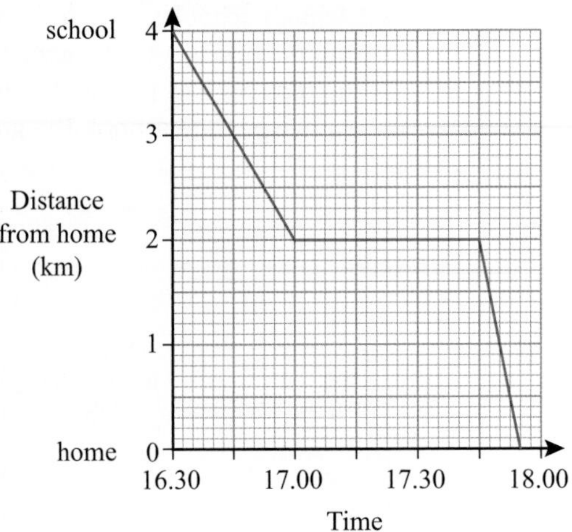

(a) How long did he stay at his friend's house?
(b) At what time did Omar arrive home?
(c) Omar's brother left school at 16.45 and walked home using the same route as Omar. If he walked at 4 km per hour, work out at what time the brother passed Omar's friend's house.

3 A swimming pool is 25 m long. Jasmine swims from one end to the other in 20 seconds. She rests for 10 seconds and then swims back to the starting point. It takes her 30 seconds to swim the second length.

(a) Draw a distance–time graph for Jasmine's swim.
(b) How far was Jasmine from her starting point after 12 seconds?
(c) How far was Jasmine from her starting point after 54 seconds?

Speed in distance–time graphs

The steepness (slope) of a graph gives an indication of speed.

- A straight line graph indicates a constant speed.
- The steeper the graph, the greater the speed.
- An upward slope and a downward slope represent movement in opposite directions.

The distance–time graph shown is for a person who walks, cycles and then drives for three equal periods of time. For each period, speed is given by the formula:

$$\text{speed} = \frac{\text{distance travelled}}{\text{time taken}}$$

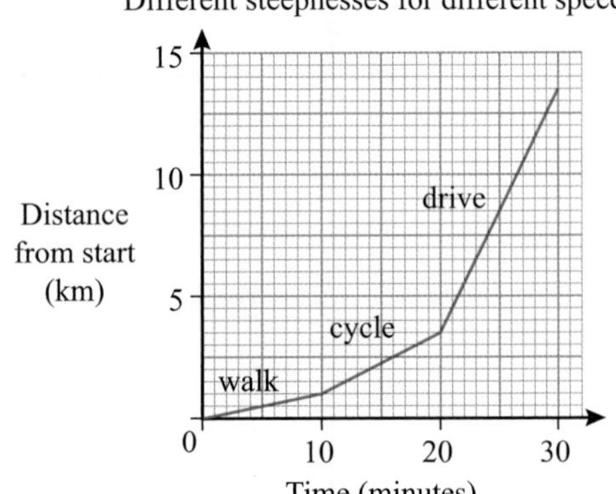

> **REWIND**
> You learned how to calculate the gradient of a straight line graph in chapter 10. ◀

> **REWIND**
> The gradient of a line is:
> - positive if the line slopes up from left to right,
> - negative if the line slopes down from left to right.
>
> See chapter 10 if you need a reminder. ◀

In mathematics, it is necessary to be more precise about what is meant by the steepness of a line. In the diagram, the steepness of line AB is measured by: $\frac{\text{increase in } y \text{ co-ordinate}}{\text{increase in } x \text{ co-ordinate}}$

This is the same as $\frac{\text{rise}}{\text{run}}$ or gradient of a straight line graph.

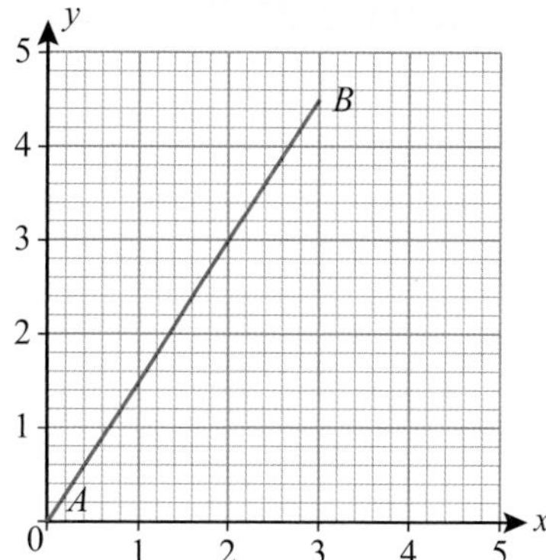

For a distance–time graph, a positive gradient indicates the object is moving in the direction of y, increasing, a zero gradient indicates the object is not moving and a negative gradient indicates the object is moving in the direction of y, decreasing.

For a distance–time graph:

$$\frac{\text{change in } y \text{ co-ordinate (distance)}}{\text{change in } x \text{ co-ordinate (time)}} = \frac{\text{time travelled}}{\text{time taken}} = \text{speed}$$

Thus, the gradient of the graph gives us the speed of the object and its direction of motion. This is known as the *velocity* of the object.

Here is another example:

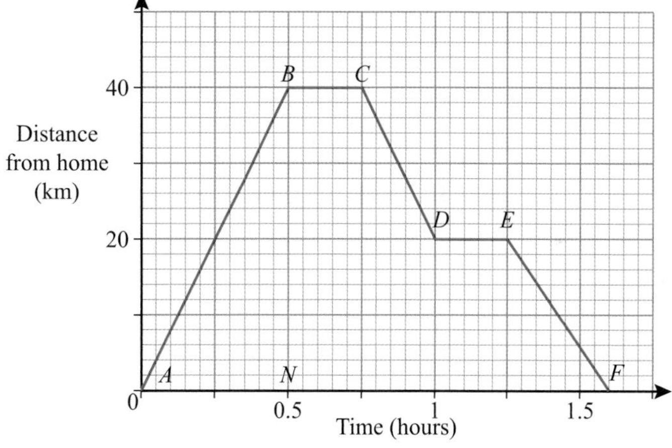

The travel graph represents a car journey. The horizontal sections have zero gradient (so the car was stationary during these times).

For section AB, the gradient is positive.

$$\text{Gradient} = \frac{NB}{AN} = \frac{40}{0.5} = 80\,\text{km/h}$$

For section CD, the gradient is negative.

$$\text{Gradient} = \frac{20-40}{0.25} = -80\,\text{km/h}$$

$\therefore$ the velocity was 80 km/h in the direction towards home.

For section EF the gradient is negative.

$$\text{Gradient} = \frac{0-20}{0.35} = -57.1\,\text{km/h}$$

$\therefore$ the velocity was 57.1 km/h in the direction towards home.

Exercise 21.7

1 (a) Clearly describe what is happening in each of the distance–time graphs below.
(b) Suggest a possible real life situation that would result in each graph.

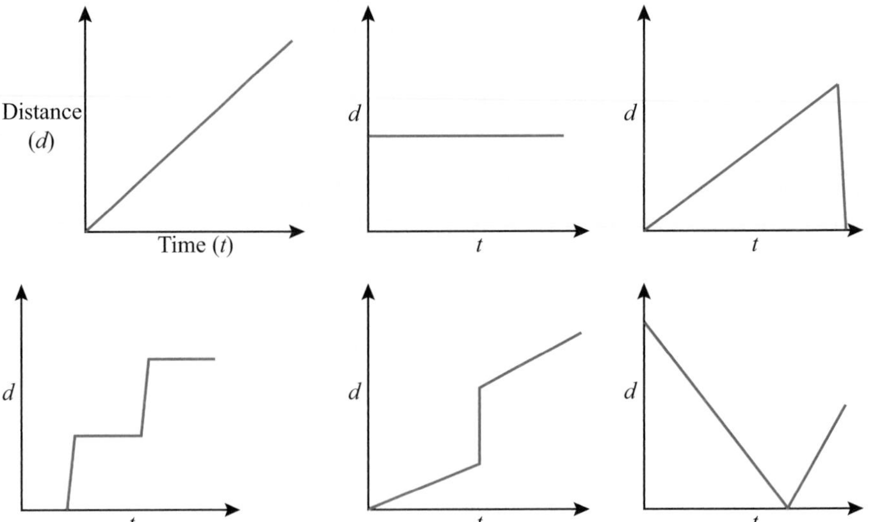

2 The graph shows Andile's daily run.

(a) For how many minutes does he run before taking a rest?
(b) Calculate the speed in km/h at which he runs before taking a rest.
(c) For how many minutes does he rest?
(d) Calculate the speed in m/s at which he runs back home.

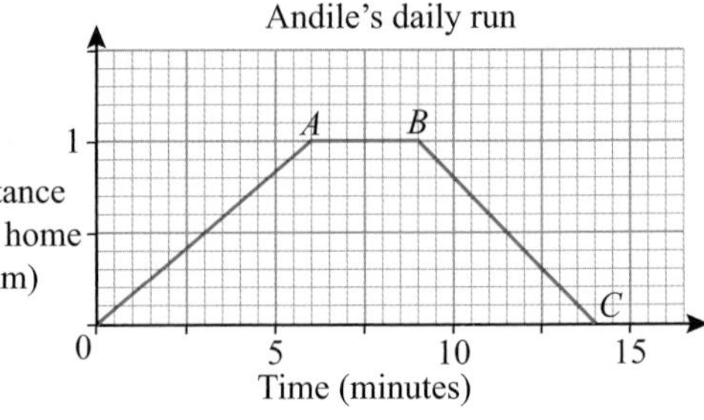

3 This graph shows the movement of a taxi in city traffic during a 4-hour period.

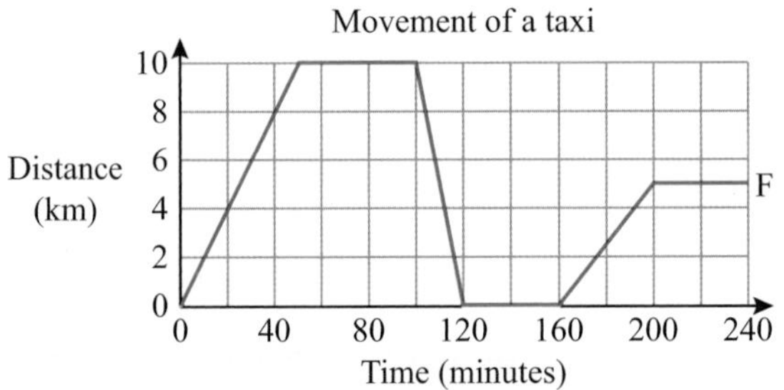

(a) Clearly and concisely describe the taxi's journey.
(b) For how many minutes was the taxi waiting for passengers in this period? How can you tell this?
(c) What was the total distance travelled?
(d) Calculate the taxi's average speed during:
(i) the first 20 minutes
(ii) the first hour
(iii) from 160 to 210 minutes
(iv) for the full period of the graph.

4 This is a real distance–time graph showing distance from the ground against time for a helicopter as it takes off and flies away from an airport.

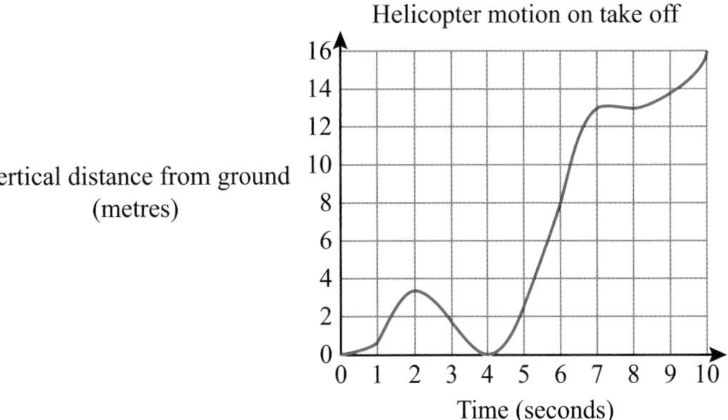

(a) Make up five mathematical questions that can be answered from the graph.
(b) Exchange questions with another student and try to answer each other's questions.

Speed–time graphs

In certain cases, the speed (or velocity) of an object may change. An increase in speed is called *acceleration*; a decrease in speed is called *deceleration*. A speed–time graph shows speed (rather than distance) on the vertical axis.

This graph shows a train journey between two stations.

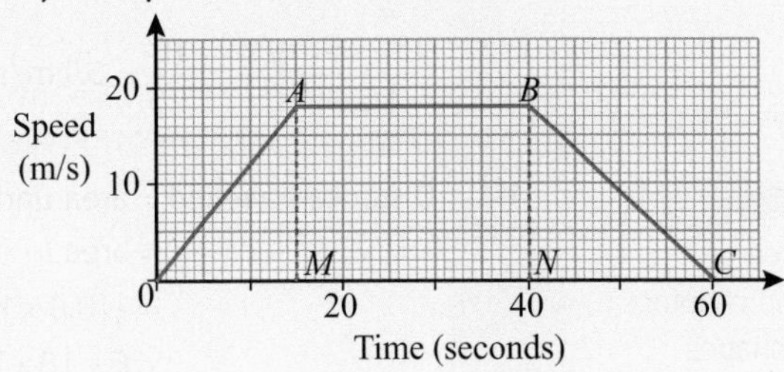

- The train starts at zero speed.
- The speed increases steadily reaching 18 m/s after 15 seconds.
- The train travels at a constant speed (horizontal section) of 18 m/s for 25 seconds.
- The train then slows down at a steady rate till it stops.
- The entire journey took 60 seconds.

Look at the first part of the journey again.

The speed increased by 18 m/s in 15 seconds.

$\frac{18\text{ m/s}}{15\text{ seconds}}$ is the gradient of the line representing the first part of the journey.

This is a rate of 1.2 m/s every second. This is the rate of acceleration. It is written as 1.2 m/s^2 (or m/s/s).

For a speed–time graph, the gradient = acceleration.

A positive gradient (acceleration) is an increase in speed.

A negative gradient (deceleration) is a decrease in speed.

You may sometimes see m/s written as m s^{-1} and m/s^2 as m s^{-2}.

Distance travelled in a speed–time graph

You already know that distance = speed × time. On a speed–time graph, this is represented by the area of shapes under the sections of graph. You can use the graph to work out the distance travelled.

REWIND

You worked with distance, time and speed earlier in this chapter. Refer back if you have forgotten the formulae. ◀

Worked example 15

This speed–time graph represents the motion of a particle over a period of five seconds.

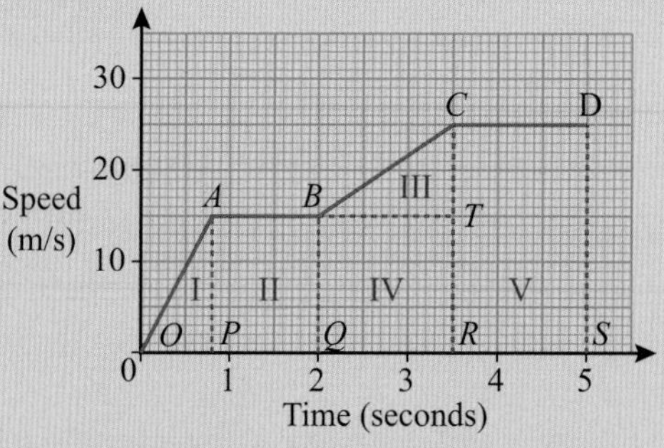

(a) During which periods of time was the particle accelerating?
(b) Calculate the particle's acceleration 3 seconds after the start.
(c) Calculate the distance travelled by the particle in the 5 seconds.

(a) The particle was accelerating in the period 0 to 0.8 seconds (section *OA*) and in the period 2 to 3.5 seconds (section *BC*).

(b)

$$\text{Acceleration} = \frac{\text{speed}}{\text{time}}$$

The acceleration was constant in the period 2 to 3.5 seconds, so the acceleration 3 seconds after the start is:

$$\frac{25-15(\text{m/s})}{3.5-2(\text{s})} = \frac{10}{1.5} = 6.7\,\text{m/s}^2$$

(c)

$$\begin{aligned}\text{Distance travelled} &= \text{area under graph}\\ &= \text{area I} + \text{area II} + \text{area III} + \text{area IV} + \text{area V}\\ &= \tfrac{1}{2}(0.8\times 15)+(1.2\times 15)+\tfrac{1}{2}(1.5\times 10)+(1.5\times 15)+(1.5\times 25)\\ &= 6+18+7.5+22.5+37.5\\ &= 91.5\end{aligned}$$

The distance travelled is 91.5 m.

REWIND

Apply the formulae for area of shapes that you learned in chapter 7 to find the area of the shapes under the graphs. ◀

Units are important

When calculating acceleration and distance travelled from a speed–time graph, it is essential that the unit of speed on the vertical axis involves the same unit of time as on the horizontal axis. In the example above the speed unit was metres per second and the horizontal axis was graduated in seconds. These units are compatible.

If the units of time are not the same, it is essential that the unit on one of the axes is converted to a compatible unit.

Worked example 16

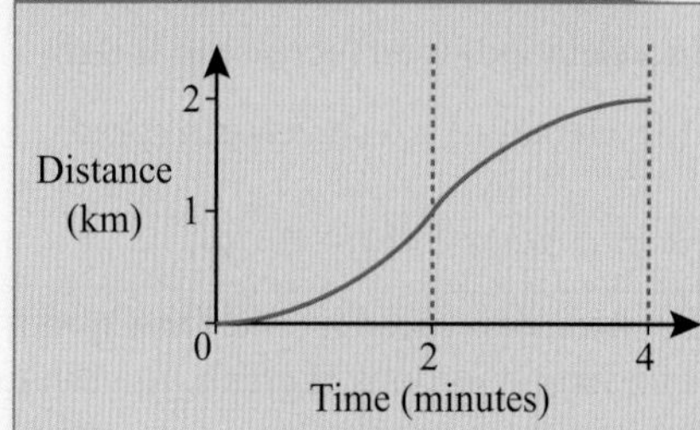

The diagram shown above is the distance–time graph for a short car journey. The greatest speed reached was 60 km/h. The acceleration in the first two minutes and the deceleration in the last two minutes are constant.

(a) Draw the speed–time graph of this journey.
(b) Calculate the average speed, in km/h, for the journey.

(a)	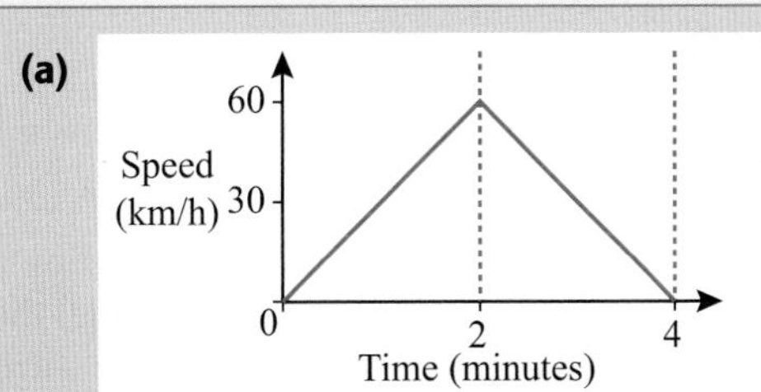	Since the acceleration and deceleration are both constant, the speed–time graph consists of straight lines. The greatest speed is 60 km/h.
(b)	Average speed $= \frac{2\text{ km}}{(4\text{ minutes})}$	Units of speed are more commonly m/s or km/h so the units need changing.
	$= \frac{2 \times 15}{60\text{ (minutes)}}$	Multiply top and bottom by 15 to get 60 minutes (= one hour) on the bottom.
	= 30 km/h	Calculate to give answer in km/h.

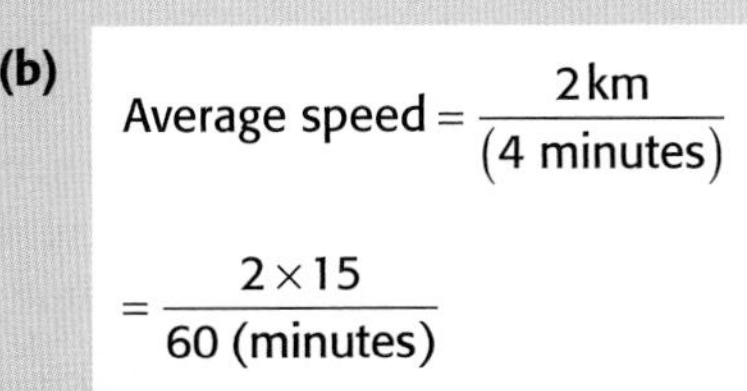

Exercise 21.8

1 The distance–time graph represents Ibrahim's journey from home to school one morning.

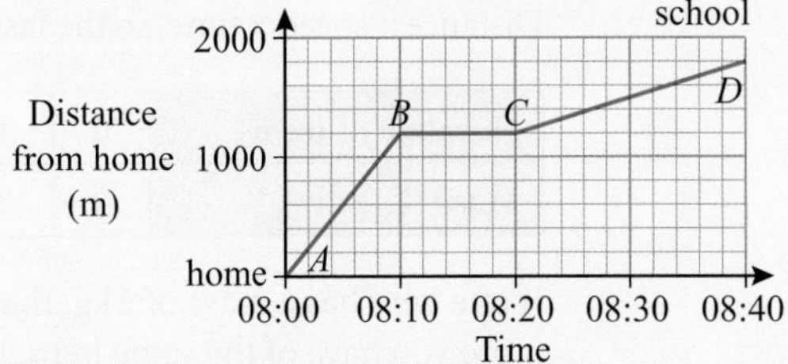

(a) How far was Ibrahim from home at 08:30 hours?
(b) How fast, in m/s, was Ibrahim travelling during the first 10 minutes?
(c) Describe the stage of Ibrahim's journey represented by the line *BC*.
(d) How fast, in m/s, was Ibrahim travelling during the last 20 minutes?

2 The graph below shows the speed, in m/s, of a car as it comes to rest from a speed of 10 m/s.

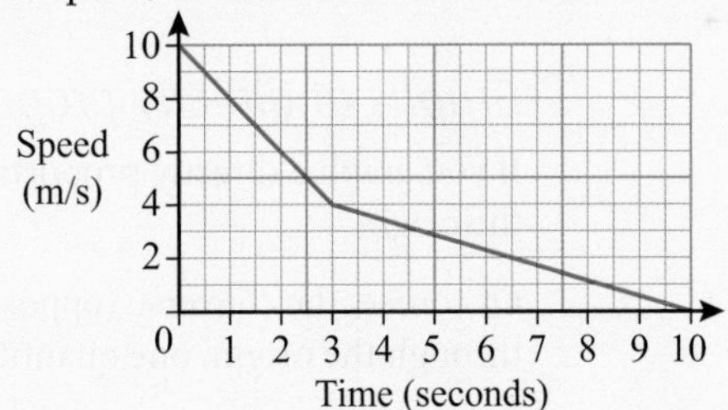

(a) Calculate the rate at which the car is slowing down during the first three seconds.
(b) Calculate the distance travelled during the 10 second period shown on the graph.
(c) Calculate the average speed of the car for this 10 second period.

3 The diagram below is the speed–time graph for a car journey.

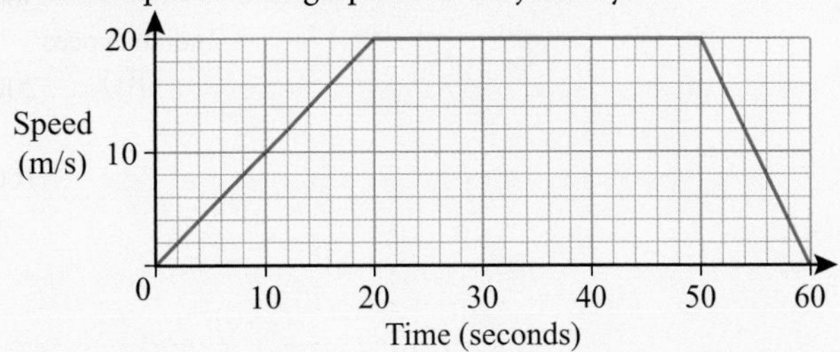

(a) Calculate the acceleration during the first 20 seconds of the journey.
(b) Calculate the distance travelled in the last 10 seconds of the journey.
(c) Calculate the average speed for the whole journey.

21.5 Proportion

In mathematics, proportion is an equation or relationship between two ratios. In general, $a : b = c : d$.

Quantities are said to increase or decrease in proportion if multiplying (or dividing) one quantity by a value results in multiplying (or dividing) the other quantity by the same value. In other words, there is a constant ratio between the corresponding elements of two sets.

Direct proportion

When two quantities are in **direct proportion** they increase or decrease at the same rate. In other words, the ratio of the quantities is equivalent. If there is an increase or decrease in one quantity, the other will increase or decrease in the same proportion.

Here are some examples of quantities that are in direct proportion:

Speed (km/h)	0	45	60	75	90	120
Distance covered in an hour (km)	0	45	60	75	90	120

Distance = speed × time, so the faster you drive in a set time, the further you will travel in that time.

Number of items	0	1	2	3	4
Mass (kg)	0	2	4	6	8

If one item has a mass of 2 kg, then two of the same item will have a mass of 4 kg and so on. The more you have of the same item, the greater the mass will be.

Number of hours worked	0	1	2	3
Amount earned ($)	0	12	24	36

The more hours you work, the more you earn.

Graphs of directly proportional relationships

If you graph a directly proportional relationship you will get a straight line that passes through the origin.

Of course, the converse (opposite) of this is also true. When a graph is a straight line that passes through the origin, one quantity is directly proportional to the other.

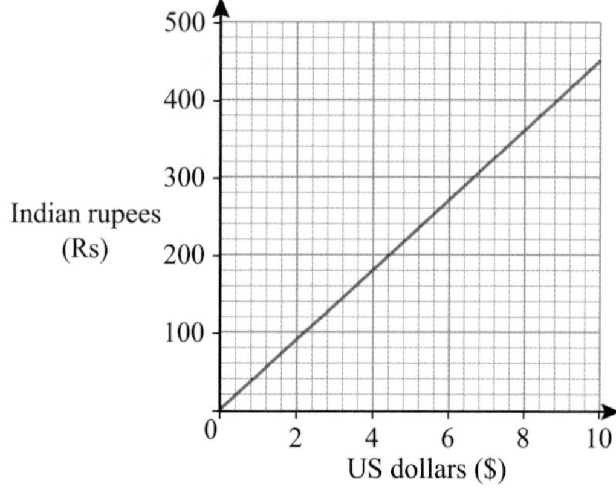

This graph shows the amount of Indian rupees you would get for different amounts of US dollars at an exchange rate of US$1 : Rs 45. Exchange rates are a good example of quantities that are in direct proportion.

Exercise 21.9

1 Which of these could be examples of direct proportion?

(a) The length of a side of a square and its area.
(b) The ages and heights of students.
(c) The amount of money collected in a sponsored walk if you are paid 5c per kilometre.
(d) The time it takes to cover different distances at the same speed.
(e) The heights of objects and the lengths of their shadows.
(f) The amount of petrol used to travel different distances.
(g) The number of chickens you could feed with 20 kg of feed.
(h) The height of the tree and the number of years since it was planted.
(i) The area of the sector of a circle and the angle at the centre.

The unitary method

The unitary method is useful for solving a range of problems to do with proportion. In this method, you find the value of one unit of the quantity. For example, the price of one cupcake or the amount of rupees you would get for one dollar.

REWIND

You have already used the unitary method to solve ratio problems earlier in this chapter. ◀

Worked example 17

Five bottles of perfume cost \$200. What would 11 bottles cost?

5 bottles cost \$200
1 bottle costs \$200 ÷ 5 = \$40
11 bottles cost 11 × \$40 = \$440

The same problem can be solved using the ratio method.

REWIND

You have already used the ratio method earlier in this chapter. ◀

Worked example 18

Using the problem from worked example 17, let x be the cost of 11 bottles.

$\frac{5}{200} = \frac{11}{x}$	Write out each part as a fraction.
$\frac{200}{5} = \frac{x}{11}$	Take the reciprocal both ratios (tum them upside down) to make it easier to solve the equation.
$\frac{200 \times 11}{5} = x$ $x = \$440$	

Exercise 21.10

1 Four soft drinks cost \$9. How much would you pay for three?

2 A car travels 30 km in 40 minutes. How long would it take to travel 45 km at the same speed?

3 If a clock gains 20 seconds in four days, how much does it gain in two weeks?

4 Six identical drums of oil weigh 90 kg in total. How much would 11.5 drums weigh?

5 An athlete runs 4.5 kilometres in 15 minutes. How far could he run in 35 minutes at the same speed?

Living maths

6 To make 12 muffins, you need:

240 g flour
48 g sultanas
60 g margarine
74 ml milk
24 g sugar
12 g salt

(a) How much of each ingredient would you need to make 16 muffins?
(b) Express the amount of flour to margarine in this recipe as a ratio.

7 A vendor sells frozen yoghurt in 250 g and 100 g tubs. It costs \$1.75 for 250 g and 80 cents for 100 g. Which is the better buy?

8 A car used 45 litres of fuel to travel 495 km.

(a) How far could the car travel on 50 ℓ of fuel at the same rate?
(b) How much fuel would the car use to travel 190 km at the same rate?

9 This graph shows the directly proportional relationship between lengths in metres (metric) and lengths in feet (imperial).

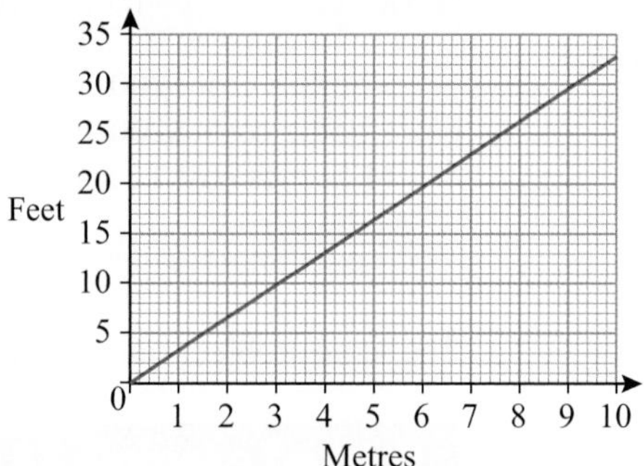

Feet is the plural of (one) foot.

(a) Use the graph to estimate how many feet there are in four metres.
(b) Given that 1 m = 3.28 feet and one foot = 0.305 m, calculate how many feet there are in 4 metres.
(c) Which is longer:
(i) four metres or 12 feet **(ii)** 20 feet or 6.5 metres?
(d) Mr Bokomo has a length of fabric 9 m long.
(i) What is its length to the nearest foot?
(ii) He cuts and sells 1.5 m to Mrs Johannes and 3 ft to Mr Moosa. How much is left in metres?
(e) A driveway was 18 feet long. It was resurfaced and extended to be one metre longer than previously. How long is the newly resurfaced driveway in metres?

Inverse proportion

In **inverse proportion**, one quantity decreases in the same proportion as the other quantity increases. For example, if work is to be done it can be done in less time if more people help. As the number of people who are working increases, the time it takes to get the job done decreases.

The graph of an inversely proportional relationship is a hyperbolic curve and not a straight line.

You can solve problems involving inverse proportion using either the ratio method or the unitary method.

Worked example 19

A person travelling at 30 km/h takes 24 minutes to get home from work.
How long would it take him if he travelled at 36 km/h?

30 km/h takes 24 minutes
So, 1 km/h would take 30×24 minutes

$\therefore$ at 36 km/h it would take $\frac{30 \times 24}{36}$

$= 20$ minutes.

Worked example 20

A woman working six hours per day can complete a job in four days.
How many hours per day would she need to work to complete the job in three days?

4 days takes 6 hours per day
$\therefore$ 1 day would take 4×6 hours $= 24$ hours per day

3 days would take $\frac{24}{3} = 8$ hours per day.

Exercise 21.11

1 A hurricane disaster centre has a certain amount of clean water. The length of time the water will last depends on the number of people who come to the centre. Calculate the missing values in this table.

No. of people	120	150	200	300	400
Days the water will last	40	32			

2 It takes six people 12 days to paint a building. Work out how long it would take at the same rate using:

(a) 9 people **(b)** 36 people

3 Sanjay has a 50 m long piece of rope. How many pieces can he cut it into if the length of each piece is:

(a) 50 cm **(b)** 200 cm **(c)** 625 cm?
(d) He cuts the rope into 20 equal lengths. What is the length of each piece?

4 An airbus usually flies from Mumbai to London in 11 hours at an average speed of 920 km/h. During some bad weather, the trip took 14 hours. What was the average speed of the plane on that flight?

5 A journey takes three hours when you travel at 60 km/h. How long would the same journey take at a speed of 50 km/h?

21.6 Direct and inverse proportion in algebraic terms

Tip
You might be asked to find a proportion equation and then find unknowns by solving. Recap how to solve equations from chapter 6.

Direct proportion

If the values of two variables are always in the same ratio, the variables are said to be in direct proportion. If the variables are P and Q, you write this as $P \propto Q$.

This is read as P is *directly* proportional to Q.

$P \propto Q$ means that $\frac{P}{Q}$ is constant. That is, $P = kQ$ where k is a constant.

If the constant is 2, then $P = 2Q$. This means that whatever P is, Q will be double that.

You can also write this as $\frac{P}{Q} = 2$.

Inverse proportion

If the product of the value of two variables is constant, the variables are said to be inversely proportional. If the variables are P and Q, you say $PQ = k$, where k is a constant. This means that P is inversely proportional to Q.

$PQ = k$ can also be written as $P = \frac{k}{Q}$.

So P is inversely proportional to Q can be written as $P \propto \frac{1}{Q}$.

The relationship between quantities is usually described in words and you will need to add the $\propto$ symbol in your working, as in these examples. The word 'direct' is not always used but if quantities are in inverse (or indirect) proportion this will be stated. Sometimes you will see, 'a varies with t', instead of 'a is in proportion to t.'

Worked example 21

y is directly proportional to x^3 and when $x = 2$, $y = 32$.

(a) Write this relationship as an equation.
(b) Find the value of y when $x = 5$.

(a) $y \propto x^3$ which means (as an equation) $y = kx^3$.
When $x = 2$, $x^3 = 2^3 = 8$
$\therefore 32 = 8k$
$\therefore k = \frac{32}{8} = 4$ and $y = 4x^3$

(b) If $x = 5$ then, $y = 4x^3 = 4 \times 5^3 = 500$

Worked example 22

F is inversely proportional to d^2 and when $d = 3$, $F = 12$.
Find the value of F when $d = 4$.

$F \propto \frac{1}{d^2}$ which means (as an equation) $F = \frac{k}{d^2}$.

When $d = 3$ and $F = 12$, $12 = \frac{k}{3^2} = \frac{k}{9}$

$\therefore k = 12 \times 9 = 108$ So, $F = \frac{108}{d^2}$

If $d = 4$ then, $F = \frac{108}{d^2} = \frac{108}{4^2} = 6.75$

Worked example 23

Some corresponding values of the variables p and q are shown in the table. Are p and q directly proportional?

p	2.8	7	11.2	16.8
q	2	5	8	12

Compare each pair in turn:

$\frac{2.8}{2} = 1.4$ $\frac{7}{5} = 1.4$ $\frac{11.2}{8} = 1.4$ $\frac{16.8}{12} = 1.4$

All the values are the same.
So, the values are directly proportional, $p = 1.4q$.

Worked example 24

x	3	4	5	6
y	12			

Copy and complete this table of values for:

(a) $y \propto x$

(b) $y \propto \frac{1}{x}$

(a) $y = kx$ Write the relationship as an equation

$12 = 3k$ Solve the equation for k

$\therefore k = 4$ and $y = 4x$. Substitute the value of k into original equation

x	3	4	5	6
y	12	16	20	24

(b) $y \propto \frac{1}{x}$ means $xy = k$ Write the relationship as an equation

$\therefore k = 3 \times 12 = 36$ and $y = \frac{36}{x}$. Use a value of x and corresponding value of y, to solve the equation for k

x	3	4	5	6
y	12	9	7.2	6

Worked example 25

The speed of water in a river is determined by a water-pressure gauge.
The speed (v m/s) is directly proportional to the square root of the height (h cm) reached by the liquid in the gauge. Given that $h = 36$ when $v = 8$, calculate the value of v when $h = 18$.

$v \propto \sqrt{h}$ means that $v = k\sqrt{h}$ where k is constant.
When $v = 8$, $h = 36$ and so $8 = k\sqrt{36} = 6k$.

It follows that $k = \frac{4}{3}$ and the formula connecting v and h is $v = \frac{4\sqrt{h}}{3}$.

When $h = 18$, $v = \frac{4\sqrt{18}}{3} = 5.66$ (to 3 s.f.)

Exercise 21.12

Sometimes you may see 'varies as' written instead of 'is directly proportional to'. Similarly, if $y \propto \frac{1}{x}$, then 'y varies inversely as x'.

1 For each of the following, y is inversely proportional to x. Write an equation expressing y in terms of x if:

(a) $y = 0.225$ when $x = 20$
(b) $y = 12.5$ when $x = 5$
(c) $y = 5$ when $x = 0.4$
(d) $y = 0.4$ when $x = 0.7$
(e) $y = 0.6$ when $x = 8$

2 y is inversely proportional to x^3. If $y = 80$ when $x = 4$, find:

(a) the constant of proportionality
(b) the value of y when $x = 8$
(c) the value y when $x = 6$
(d) the value of x when $y = 24$

3 Given that y is inversely proportional to x^2. Complete the table.

x	0.1	0.25	0.5	
y			1	64

4 Given that y is inversely proportional to $\sqrt{x}$. Complete the table.

x	25	100		
y	10		26	50

5 x and y are known to be proportional to each other. When $x = 20$, $y = 50$. Find k, if:

(a) $y \propto x$
(b) $y \propto \frac{1}{x}$
(c) $y \propto x^2$

6 A is directly proportional to r^2 and when $r = 3$, $A = 36$. Find the value of A when $r = 10$.

7 l is inversely proportional to d^3. When $d = 2$, $l = 100$. Find the value of l when $d = 5$.

8 Some corresponding values of p and q are given in the table. Are p and q inversely proportional? Justify your answer.

q	2	5	8	12
p	75	30	20	15

9 An electric current I flows through a resistance R. I is inversely proportional to R and when $R = 3$, $I = 5$. Find the value of I when $R = 0.25$.

10 Corresponding values of s and t are given in the table.

s	2	6	10
t	0.4	10.8	50

Which of the following statements is true?

(a) $t \propto s$ (b) $t \propto s^2$ (c) $t \propto s^3$.

11 It takes 4 people 10 hours to plaster a section of a building. How long will it take 8 people to do the same job working at the same rate?

12 In an industrial experiment it is found that the force, f, needed to break a concrete beam varies inversely with the length, l, of the beam. If it takes 50 000 newtons to break a concrete beam 2 metres long, how many newtons will it take to break a beam that is 6 metres long?

13 A submarine crew discovers that the water temperature (°C) varies inversely with the depth to which they submerge (km). When they were at a depth of 4 km, the water temperature was 6 °C.

(a) What would the water temperature be at a depth of 12 km?
(b) To what depth would they need to submerge for the water temperature to be −1 °C?

14 Variable P varies directly as variable m and inversely as variable n. If $P = 24$ when $m = 3$ and $n = 2$, find P when $m = 5$ and $n = 8$.

21.7 Increasing and decreasing amounts by a given ratio

In worked example 17 you found the cost of 11 bottles of perfume having been given the cost of five bottles. This is an example of increasing an amount in a given ratio. You could have been asked to increase $200 in the ratio 11 : 5.

Worked example 26

Increase $200 in the ratio 11 : 5

New value : original value = 11 : 5

New : 200 = 11 : 5

$$\frac{\text{New}}{200} = \frac{11}{5}$$

$$\text{New value} = \frac{11 \times 200}{5} = \$440$$

Worked example 27

Decrease 45 m in the ratio 2 : 3

New value : original value = 2 : 3

New : 45 = 2 : 3

$$\frac{\text{New}}{45} = \frac{2}{3}$$

$$\text{New value} = \frac{2 \times 45}{3} = 30\text{m}$$

Exercise 21.13

1 Increase 40 in the ratio 7 : 5.

2 Decrease 32 in the ratio 3 : 4.

3 Increase 84 in the ratio 5 : 4.

4 Decrease 57 in the ratio 2 : 3.

5 Nick has a picture of his dog that is 16 cm long and 10 cm wide. If he enlarges the picture in the ratio 5 : 2, what are the new dimensions?

Summary

Do you know the following?

- A ratio is a comparison of two or more quantities in a set order. Ratios can be expressed in the form $a : b$ or $\frac{a}{b}$. Ratios have no units.
- Ratios can be simplified by multiplying or dividing both quantities by the same number. This method produces equivalent ratios.
- Map scales are good examples of ratios in everyday life. The scale of a map is usually given in the form $1 : n$. This allows you to convert map distances to real distances using the ratio scale.
- A rate is a comparison of two different quantities. Usually a rate gives an amount of one quantity per unit of the other. Rates must include the units of the quantities.
- Speed is one of the most common rates. Speed = distance ÷ time.
- Kinematic graphs are used to show relationships between:
  - distance and time (distance–time graph)
  - speed and time (speed–time graph) and to solve problems in these areas.
- Proportion is a constant ratio between the corresponding elements of two sets.
- When quantities are in direct proportion they increase or decrease at the same rate.
- When quantities are inversely proportional, one increases as the other decreases.
- You can use algebraic expressions to represent direct and indirect (inverse) proportion and to solve problems related to these concepts. The symbol for proportion is $\propto$.
- You can increase and decrease amounts by a given ratio.

Are you able to …?

- simplify ratios and find the missing values in equivalent ratios
- divide quantities in a given ratio
- convert measurements on maps, plans and other scale diagrams to real measurements and vice versa
- express relationships between different quantities as rates in their simplest form and solve problems relating to rates
- read and interpret kinematic graphs
  - by calculating average speed
  - by calculating acceleration and deceleration from a graph and finding the distance travelled using the area under a linear speed–time graph
- solve problems involving direct and indirect proportion
- express direct and inverse proportion in algebraic terms
- solve direct and inverse proportion problems using algebraic methods
- increase and decrease amounts by a given ratio.

Examination practice

Exam-style questions

1 Sandra and Peter share a packet of 30 marshmallow eggs in the ratio 2 : 3. How many marshmallow eggs does Sandra receive?

2 Manos and Raja make $96 selling handcrafts. They share the income in the ratio 7 : 5. How much does Raja receive?

3 Silvia makes a scale drawing of her bedroom using a scale of 1 : 25. If one wall on the diagram is 12 cm long, how long is the wall in her room?

4 Mrs James bakes a fruit cake using raisins, currants and dates in the ratio 4 : 5 : 3. The total mass of the three ingredients is 4.8 kilograms. Calculate the mass of:

(a) the raisins
(b) the dates.

5 During an election, the ratio of female to male voters in a constituency was 3 : 2. If 2 400 people voted, how many of them were male?

6 A recipe for dough uses three parts wholemeal flour for every four parts of plain flour. What volume of wholemeal flour would you need if you used 12 cups of plain flour?

7 The speed–time graph below represents the journey of a train between two stations. The train slowed down and stopped after 15 minutes because of engineering work on the railway line.

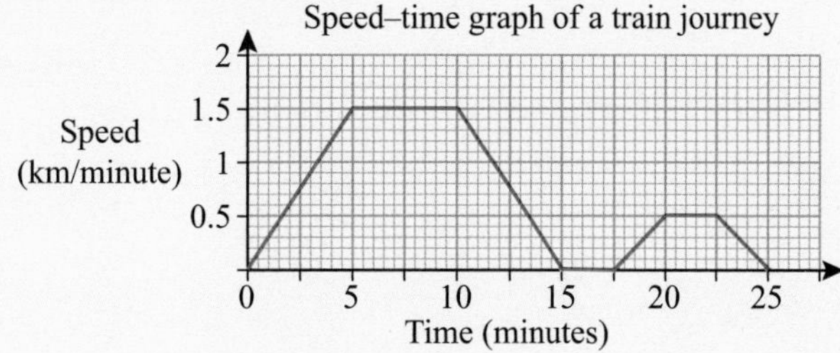

(a) Calculate the greatest speed, in km/h, which the train reached.
(b) Calculate the deceleration of the train as it approached the place where there was engineering work.
(c) Calculate the distance the train travelled in the first 15 minutes.
(d) For how long was the train stopped at the place where there was engineering work?
(e) What was the speed of the train after 19 minutes?
(f) Calculate the distance between the two stations.

Past paper questions

1 p varies directly as the square root of q.
$p = 8$ when $q = 25$.
Find p when $q = 100$. [3]

[Cambridge IGCSE Mathematics 0580 Paper 22 Q08 May/June 2011]

2 y varies inversely as the square of x, $y = 1.5$ when $x = 8$.
Find y when $x = 5$. [3]

[Cambridge IGCSE Mathematics 0580 Paper 21 Q14 May/June 2010]

3 A person in a car, travelling at 108 kilometres per hour, takes one second to go past a building on the side of the road.
Calculate the length of the building in metres. [2]

[Cambridge IGCSE Mathematics 0580 Paper 21 Q04 May/June 2010]

4 Two similar vases have heights which are in the ratio 3 : 2.

(a) The volume of the larger vase is $1080\,\text{cm}^3$. Calculate the volume of the smaller vase. [2]
(b) The surface area of the smaller vase is $252\,\text{cm}^2$. Calculate the surface area of the larger vase. [2]

[Cambridge IGCSE Mathematics 0580 Paper 21 Q18 May/June 2009]

5

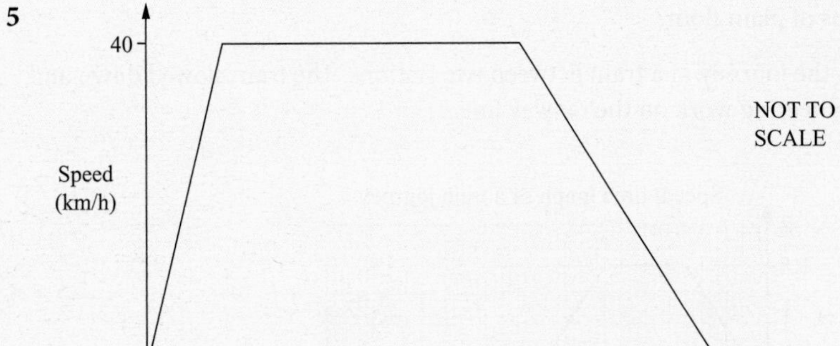

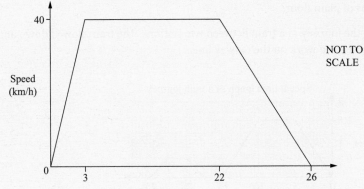

The diagram shows the speed-time graph of a train journey between two stations.
The train accelerates for 3 minutes, travels at a constant maximum speed of 40 km/h, then takes 4 minutes to slow to a stop.
Calculate the distance in kilometres between the two stations. [4]

[Cambridge IGCSE Mathematics 0580 Paper 22 Q16 May/June 2013]

22 More equations, formulae and functions

Key words

- Equation
- Subject
- Substitute
- Function
- Function notation
- Composite function
- Inverse function

In this chapter you will learn how to:

- make your own equations and use them to solve worded problems
- construct and transform more complex formulae
- use function notation to describe simple functions and their inverses
- form composite functions.

EXTENDED

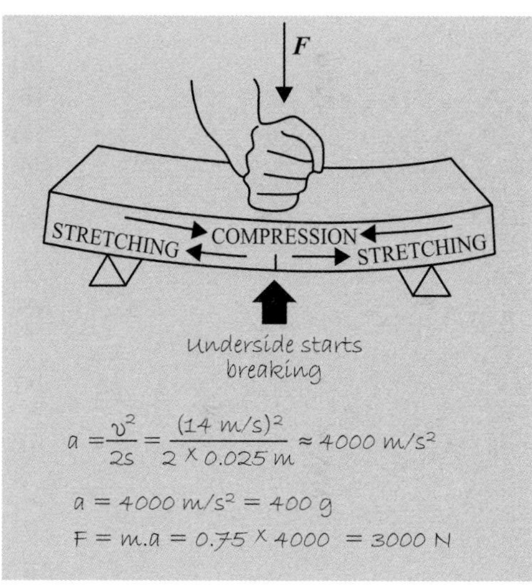

Formulae can be used to describe the very simple as well as the complex. They can be used to calculate the area of a shape, decide where best to strike a block to smash it or how to launch a rocket into space.

You have already worked with algebraic expressions and learned how to solve equations. Now you are going to apply what you know to solve worded problems by setting up your own equations.

You will also work with more complicated formulae and equations. You will need to be able to transform formulae to solve related problems.

Lastly, you will revise what you know about functions and learn how to use a more formal mathematical notation to describe functions and their inverses. You will also work with composite functions.

22.1 Setting up equations to solve problems

REWIND

You used algebra to write expressions and simple equations in chapter 2. Read through that section again if you have forgotten how to do this. ◀

You already know that you can translate worded problems (story sums) into **equations** using variables to represent unknown quantities. You can then solve the equation to find the solution to the problem.

Working through the simple problems in exercise 22.1 will help you remember how to set up equations that represent the sum, difference, product and quotient of quantities and use these to solve problems.

Exercise 22.1

1 For each statement, make an equation in terms of x and then and solve it.

(a) A number multiplied by four gives 32.
(b) If a certain number is multiplied by 12 the result is 96.
(c) A number added to 12 gives 55.
(d) The sum of a number and 13 is 25.
(e) When six is subtracted from a certain number, the result is 14.
(f) If a number is subtracted from nine the result is −5.
(g) The result of dividing a number by seven is 2.5.
(h) If 28 is divided by a certain number, the result is four.

2 Represent each situation using an equation in terms of y. Solve each equation to find the value of y.

(a) A number is multiplied by three, then five is added to get 14.
(b) When six is subtracted from five times a certain number, the result is 54.
(c) Three times the sum of a number and four gives 150.
(d) When eight is subtracted from half of a number, the result is 27.

3 Solve each problem by setting up an equation.

(a) When five is added to four times a certain number, the result is 57. What is the number?
(b) If six is subtracted from three times a certain number the result is 21. What is the number?
(c) Four more than a number is divided by three and then multiplied by two to give a result of four. What is the number?
(d) A number is doubled and then six is added. When this is divided by four, the result is seven. What is the number?

Solving more complex problems

The problems in exercise 22.1 are simple algebraic manipulations. You need to be able to set up equations to solve any problem. To do this, you need to read and make sense of the written problem, represent the situation as an equation and then solve it.

To solve problems by setting up equations:

- Read the problem carefully, paying attention to the words used.
- Decide what you need to find and what information is already given.
- Ask yourself if there is anything to be assumed or deduced from the given information. For example, if the problem mentions equal lengths and breadths of a room can you assume the room is a rectangle? Or, if you are working with a pack of cards, can you assume it is a standard pack with 52 cards?
- Consider whether there is a formula or mathematical relationship that you can use to connect the information in the problem. For example, if you are asked to find the distance around a round shape, you can use the formula $C = \pi d$, or if the problem involves time, distance and speed, you can use the time–distance–speed triangle to form an equation.

Worked example 1

My mother was 26 years old when I was born. She is presently three times as old as I am. What are our present ages?

Let my present age be x. $\therefore$ my mother's present age is $3x$.	She is 3 times as old as me.
The difference in ages is 26 years, so:	Mother will always be 26 years older.
$3x - x = 26$ $\therefore \quad 2x = 26$ $\therefore \quad x = 13$	
My present age is 13. My mother's present age is 39.	

Worked example 2

A parallelogram has its longest sides five times longer than its shorter sides. If it has a perimeter of 9.6 m, what are the lengths of the long and short sides?

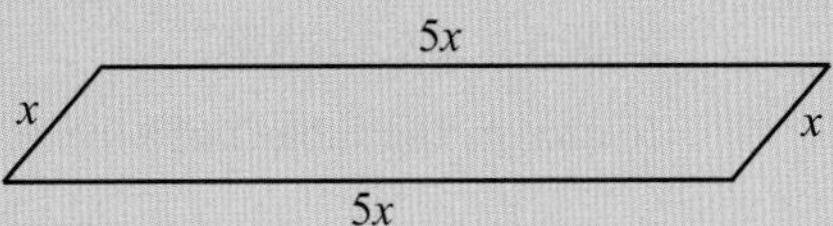

Always say what the variables you are using represent.

Let the shorter side be x metres. $\therefore$ the longer side is $5x$.	The longer side is five times the shorter side.
$5x + x + 5x + x = 9.6\,\text{m}$ $\therefore \quad 12x = 9.6\,\text{m}$ $\therefore \quad x = \frac{9.6}{12} = 0.8\,\text{m}$	Perimeter is the sum of the sides.
So, the shorter side is 0.8 m and the longer side is $5 \times 0.8 = 4\,\text{m}$.	

Exercise 22.2

1 A father is three times as old as his daughter. If the father is 31 years older than his daughter, what are their ages?

2 Jess and Silvia have 420 marbles between them. If Jess has five times as many marbles as Silvia, how many do they each have?

3 Soumik has \$5 less than his friend Kofi. If they have \$97.50 altogether, how much does each person have?

4 Two competition winners are to share a prize of \$750. If one winner receives twice as much as the other, how much will they each receive?

5 A grandfather is six times as old as his grandson. If the grandfather was 45 when his grandson was born, how old is the grandson?

6 A rectangle of perimeter 74 cm is 7 cm longer than it is wide. What is the length of each side?

7 Smitville is located between Jonesville and Cityville. Smitville is five times as far away from Cityville as it is from Jonesville. If the distance between Jonesville and Cityville is 288 km, how far is it from Jonesville to Smitville?

8 Amira is twice as old as her cousin Pam. Nine years ago, their combined age was 18. What are their present ages?

9 Jabu left town A to travel to town B at 6.00 a.m. He drove at an average speed of 80 km/h. At 8.30 a.m., Sipho left town A to travel to town B. He drove at an average speed of 100 km/h. At what time will Sipho catch up with Jabu?

10 Cecelia took 40 minutes to complete a journey. She travelled half the distance at a speed of 100 km/h and the other half at 60 km/h. How far was her journey?

22.2 Using and transforming formulae

REWIND

You have already seen basic transformations of formulae in chapter 6. The methods in this chapter are a little more involved. ◀

You already know that the variable which is written alone on one side of the '=' sign (usually the left) of a formula is called the **subject** of the formula. For example, in the formula for finding the circumference of a circle, $C = \pi d$, C is the subject of the formula. This means that it is very easy to find the value of C if you know the diameter of the circle.

In many cases, however, you know the value of the subject and you have to find the value of another variable. To do this, you need to transform the formula to make the other variable the subject of the formula.

To change the subject of a formula:

- expand to get rid of any brackets if necessary
- use inverse operations to isolate the variable required.

Inverse operations 'undo' the 'original'.

If you are told to solve for x, or find x, it means the same as 'make x the subject of the formula'.

Worked example 3

Given that $c = ax + b$, find x.

$ax + b = c$	Reorganise the formula so the term with the x is on the left-hand side of the '=' sign.
$ax = c - b$	Subtract b from both sides.
$x = \frac{c - b}{a}$	Divide both sides by a.

Worked example 4

Given that $m = \frac{1}{2}(x + y)$, solve this formula for x.

$m = \frac{1}{2}(x + y)$	
$\therefore\ 2m = x + y$	Multiply both sides by 2 to remove the fraction.
$\therefore\ 2m - y = x$	Subtract y from both sides.
$x = 2m - y$	Rewrite the formula so x is on the left-hand side of the '=' sign.

Worked example 5

Solve for h if $A = 2\pi r(r + h)$.

$A = 2\pi r(r + h)$	
$\therefore A = 2\pi r^2 + 2\pi rh$	Expand to remove the brackets.
$\therefore A - 2\pi r^2 = 2\pi rh$	Subtract to isolate the term with h in it.
$\therefore \frac{(A - 2\pi r^2)}{2\pi r} = h$	Divide to get rid of $2\pi r$ on the right-hand side.
$\therefore h = \frac{(A - 2\pi r^2)}{2\pi r}$	Express the formula in terms of h.

Exercise 22.3

1 Make x the subject of each formula.

(a) $m = x + bp$ **(b)** $n = pr - x$ **(c)** $4x = m$ **(d)** $ax^2 - b = c$ **(e)** $d - 2b = mx + c$

(f) $\frac{x}{y} = 3b$ **(g)** $m = \frac{p}{x}$ **(h)** $\frac{mx}{n} = p$ **(i)** $m = \frac{2x}{k}$ **(j)** $p = \frac{20}{x}$

2 Solve for x.

(a) $m = 3(x + y)$ **(b)** $c = 4(t - x)$ **(c)** $y = 3(x - 5)$

(d) $r = 2r(3 - x)$ **(e)** $m = 4c(x - y)$ **(f)** $a = \pi r(2r - x)$

3 Express $E = mc^2$ in terms of m.

4 Express $I = \frac{PRT}{100}$ in terms of R.

5 Express $k = \frac{1}{2}mv^2$ in terms of m.

6 Express $A = \frac{h(a + b)}{2}$ in terms of b.

7 Express $V = \frac{Ah}{3}$ in terms of h.

8 Express $V = \frac{\pi r^2 h}{3}$ in terms of h.

In real life applications, you will often know the value of the subject of the formulae and some of the other values. In these examples, you need to change the subject of the formula and **substitute** the given values before solving it like an equation.

Living maths

9 If $V = LBH$, find B when $V = 600$, $L = 34$ and $H = 26$. Give your answer correct to 2 decimal places.

10 Given that $V = Ah$, find h if $V = 1.26$ and $A = 0.41$. Give your answer correct to 2 decimal places.

11 The formula for converting temperatures from Celsius to Fahrenheit is $F = 32 + \frac{9C}{5}$. Find the temperature in degrees C to the nearest degree when F is:

(a) 100 **(b)** 212 **(c)** 32

12 You can find the area of a circle using the formula $A = 2\pi r^2$. If $\pi = 3.14$, find the radius r, of circular discs of metal with the following areas (A):

(a) 14 **(b)** 120 **(c)** 0.5

The inverse of $\sqrt{x}$ is $(x)^2$ but note, '$\sqrt{x}$' means the positive square root. There is only one value. So, $\sqrt{9} = 3$ and 3 only. But, if $x^2 = 9$ then $x = \pm\sqrt{9} = \pm 3$. You only use $\pm$ when undoing a square.

Formulae containing squares and square roots

Some formulae have squared terms and square roots. You need to remember that a squared number has both a negative and a positive root when you solve these equations.

Worked example 6

Make x the subject of the formula $ax^2 = b$.

$ax^2 = b$	
$x^2 = \frac{b}{a}$	Divide both side by a.
$x = \pm\sqrt{\frac{b}{a}}$	Take square root of both sides to get x.

Worked example 7

Given $r = \sqrt{\frac{A}{\pi}}$ express the formula in terms of A.

$r = \sqrt{\frac{A}{\pi}}$	
$r^2 = \frac{A}{\pi}$	Square both sides to get rid of the square root.
$\pi r^2 = A$	Multiply each side by π.
$A = \pi r^2$	

REWIND

You learned how to factorise in chapter 6. ◀

Formulae where the subject appears in more than one term

When the variable that is to be the subject occurs more than once, you need to gather the like terms and factorise before you can express the formula in terms of that variable.

Worked example 8

Given that $m = 6 - \frac{12}{p}$, make p the subject of the formula.

$m = 6 - \frac{12}{p}$	
$mp = 6p - 12$	Multiply both sides by p to remove the fraction.
$mp - 6p = -12$	Gather like terms.
$p(m - 6) = -12$	Factorise.
$p = \frac{-12}{(m-6)}$	

Exercise 22.4

1 Make x the subject of each formula.

(a) $m = ax^2$ (b) $x^2 - y = m$ (c) $m = n - x^2$ (d) $\frac{x^2}{y} = a$

(e) $a = \frac{bx^2}{c}$ (f) $a = x^2 - b^2$ (g) $m = \frac{n}{x^2}$ (h) $\sqrt{xy} = m$

(i) $a = \sqrt{5x}$ (j) $y = \sqrt{x - z}$ (k) $y = \sqrt{x} - z$ (l) $a = b + \frac{c}{\sqrt{x}}$

(m) $a - b\sqrt{x} = m$ (n) $\sqrt{3x - 1} = y$ (o) $a = \sqrt{y - 2x}$ (p) $y = \frac{a}{\sqrt{4x - b}}$

2 Express each of these formulae in terms of a.

(a) $x + a = ax + b$ (b) $L = Ba + (1 + C)a$ (c) $b = \frac{a}{a - 5}$

(d) $y = \frac{a + x}{a - x}$ (e) $y = \frac{a + 3}{1 + a}$ (f) $ma^2 = na^2 + 2$

3 Einstein developed the formula $E = mc^2$ when he worked on relativity. Express this formula in terms of c.

4 Pythagoras' theorem can expressed as $a^2 + b^2 = c^2$. Express this in terms of a.

5 Given that $y = \frac{a}{a + 2}$, express this formula in terms of a.

6 Given that in a square, $A = s^2$, transform the formula to find the length of one side (s).

7 In each of these formulae, make y the subject.

(a) $\frac{x}{3} = \frac{y}{2} - 1$ (b) $x = \frac{y + c}{3}$ (c) $\frac{x + z}{3} = \frac{y + z}{4}$ (d) $a = b - \frac{3y}{2}$

Living maths

8 In physics, the kinetic energy (E) of a particle can be found using the formula $E = \frac{1}{2}mv^2$, where m is the mass, and v is the velocity of the particle.

(a) Find E when $m = 8$ and $v = 3.5$.
(b) Show how you could rearrange the formula to find v.

9 The volume (V) of a cylinder is found using the formula $V = \pi r^2 h$, where r is the radius and h is the height of the cylinder.

(a) Find the volume, correct to the nearest cm^3, of a cylinder with a radius of 0.8 m and height of 1 m.
(b) Rearrange the formula to make r the subject.

10 You can use the formula $A = \frac{\pi d^2}{4}$ to find the area (A) of a circle, where d is the diameter of the circle.

(a) Find the area of a circle of diameter 1.2 m.
(b) Use the formula $A = \pi r^2$ to find the area of the same circle.
(c) Express the formula $A = \frac{\pi d^2}{4}$ in a way that would allow you to find the diameter of the circle when the area is known.

REWIND

The word function is sometimes used interchangeably with equation (although this is not always strictly true). You met equations of this type, where a value of x led to a value of y, when you worked with straight lines and quadratics in chapter 10. It will help you to read through that chapter again before you do this work. ◀

22.3 Functions and function notation

A **function** is a rule or set of instructions for changing one number (the input) into another (the output). If y is a function of x, then the value of y depends on the values you use for x. In a function, there is only one possible value of y for each value of x.

Function notation

In function notation you leave out the y and replace it with the conventional notation f(x). So, if 'f' is a function and 'x' is an input then, f(x) is the output when f is applied to x.

Function notation is a mathematical way of writing equations (functions). Function notation is widely used in computer applications and also in technical fields.

Think about the equation $y = x + 2$.
When you write this in function notation it becomes $f(x) = x + 2$.
$f(x)$ is read as, 'the function of x' or 'f of x'.
If $f(x) = x + 2$, then f(5) means the value of the function when $x = 5$.
In other words, $f(5) = 5 + 2 = 7$.
Similarly $f(-2) = -2 + 2 = 0$.

Functions can also be written as, $f : x \rightarrow 6 - 3x$.
This is read as, 'f is the function that maps x onto $6 - 3x$'.
The number $6 - 3x$ is sometimes called the image of x (under function f).

Here are three ways of writing the SAME function using different letters.

$x \rightarrow 3x - 1$

$t \rightarrow 3t - 1$

$y \rightarrow 3y - 1$

When there are two or more functions involved in a problem, you use different letters to represent them. For example, you could have:

$g(x) = x^2 - 2x + 3$ and $h(x) = 5x - 3$.

The steps taken to work out the value of any function f(x) can be shown on a simple flow diagram. For example, the function $f(x) = 2x + 5$ can be represented as:

$x \rightarrow \boxed{\times 2} \rightarrow \boxed{+5} \rightarrow 2x + 5$

The function $g(x) = 2(x + 5)$ can be represented as:

$x \rightarrow \boxed{+5} \rightarrow \boxed{\times 2} \rightarrow 2(x + 5)$

Note that the flow charts show the same operations but, as they are done in a different order, they produce different results.

Worked example 9

Given that $f(x) = x^2 - 3x$ and $g(x) = 4x - 6$, find the value of:

(a) f(6) **(b)** f(–3) **(c)** $g\left(\frac{1}{2}\right)$ **(d)** g(6).

(a) $f(6) = 6^2 - 3(6) = 36 - 18 = 18$

(b) $f(-3) = (-3)^2 - 3(-3) = 9 + 9 = 18$

(c) $g\left(\frac{1}{2}\right) = 4\left(\frac{1}{2}\right) - 6 = 2 - 6 = -4$

(d) $g(6) = 4(6) - 6 = 24 - 6 = 18$

Worked example 10

Given $h : x \rightarrow 9 - x^2$,

(a) write down the expression for h(x).
(b) Find:

(i) h(0) **(ii)** h(3) **(iii)** h(9) **(iv)** h(–9)

(a) $h(x) = 9 - x^2$

(b) (i) $h(0) = 9 - (0)^2 = 9 - 0 = 9$

(ii) $h(3) = 9 - (3)^2 = 9 - 9 = 0$

(iii) $h(9) = 9 - (9)^2 = 9 - 81 = -72$

(iv) $h(-9) = 9 - (-9)^2 = 9 - 81 = -72$

Worked example 11

If $f(x) = 3 + 2x$ and $f(x) = 6$, find x.

$3 + 2x = 6$ $2x = 6 - 3$ $2x = 3$ $x = 1.5$	The functions are equivalent.

Worked example 12

Given the functions $f(x) = x^2$ and $g(x) = x + 2$,

(a) solve the equation $f(x) = g(x)$
(b) solve the equation $4g(x) = g(x) - 3$.

(a)

$f(x) = g(x)$	
$\therefore x^2 = x + 2$	The functions are equivalent.
$x^2 - x - 2 = 0$	
$(x - 2)(x + 1) = 0$	Factorise.
so, $x = 2$ or $x = -1$	

(b)

$4g(x) = g(x) - 3$	
$\therefore 3g(x) = -3$	Subtract $g(x)$ from both sides.
$g(x) = -1$	Divide both sides by three.
$x + 2 = -1$	Replace $g(x)$ with $x + 2$.
$x = -3$	

Exercise 22.5

1 For each function, calculate:

(i) $f(2)$ **(ii)** $f(-2)$ **(iii)** $f(0.5)$ **(iv)** $f(0)$

(a) $f(x) = 3x + 2$ **(b)** $f(x) = 5x - 2$ **(c)** $f(x) = 2x - 1$
(d) $f(x) = 2x^2 + 3$ **(e)** $f(x) = x^2 - 2x$ **(f)** $f(x) = x^3 - 2$

2 $f(x) = 4x - 1$, find:

(a) $f(-1)$ **(b)** $f(0)$ **(c)** $f(1.5)$ **(d)** $f(-4)$

3 $f: x \rightarrow x^2 - 4$, find:

(a) f(2) **(b)** f(0) **(c)** f(−3) **(d)** f(0.25)

4 Given the functions $f(x) = x^3 - 8$ and $g(x) = 3 - x$, find the value of:

(a) f(2) **(b)** f(−1) **(c)** g(5) **(d)** g(−2)

5 Given the function $h: x \rightarrow 4x^2$, find:

(a) h(2) **(b)** h(−2) **(c)** $h\left(\frac{1}{2}\right)$

6 If $f(x) = 3x - 1$ and $f(x) = 3f(x) = 3$, find x.

7 If $h(x) = \frac{1}{x} + 1$ and $h(x) = 4$, find the value of x.

8 If $g(x) = \sqrt{4x+1}$ and $g(x) = 5$, find the value of x.

9 Given the functions $f(x) = x^2 - x$ and $g(x) = x^2 - 3x - 12$,

(a) solve the equation $f(x) = 6$
(b) solve the equation $f(x) = g(x)$.

10 Given $f: x \rightarrow 2x$, find:

(a) $f(a)$ **(b)** $f(a + 2)$ **(c)** $f(4a)$ **(d)** $4f(a)$

11 $f(x) = \frac{4+x}{x}$ $(x \neq 0)$

(a) Calculate $f\left(\frac{1}{2}\right)$, simplifying your answer.

(b) Solve $f(x) = 3$.

12 $f(x) = (2x + 1)(x + 1)$, find:

(a) f(2) **(b)** f(−2) **(c)** f(0)

Composite functions

A **composite function** is a function of a function. You get a composite function when you apply one function to a number and then apply another function to the result.

Look at these two functions: $f(x) = 2x + 1$ and $g(x) = x^2$.

$f(4) = 2(4) + 1 = 8 + 1 = 9$ (9 is the result of the first function.)

$g(9) = 9^2 = 81$ (The function g has been applied to result.)

The order of the letters in a composite function is important.
$gf(4) \neq fg(4)$.
$gf(x)$ means do f first then g.
$fg(x)$ means do g first then f.
So, the function closest to the x is applied first.

You can write what has been done as $g[f(4)] = 81$. However, normally the square brackets are left out and you just write $gf(4) = 81$. $gf(x)$ is a composite function.

Worked example 13

Given the functions $f(x) = x^2 - 2x$ and $g(x) = 3 - x$, find the value of:

(a) gf(4) **(b)** fg(4) **(c)** ff(−1) **(d)** gg(100)

(a) $gf(4) = g[f(4)] = g[16 - 8] = g[8] = 3 - 8 = -5$

(b) $fg(4) = f[g(4)] = f[3 - 4] = f[-1] = (-1)^2 - 2(-1) = 1 + 2 = 3$

(c) $ff(-1) = f[f(-1)] = f[1 + 2] = f[3] = 9 - 6 = 3$

(d) $gg(100) = g[g(100)] = g[3 - 100] = g[-97] = 3 - (-97) = 3 + 97 = 100$

Exercise 22.6

1 For each pair of functions, evaluate fg(x) and gf(x).

(a) $f(x) = x + 6$
$g(x) = x - 3$

(b) $f(x) = 2x^2 - 3x + 1$
$g(x) = 5x$

(c) $f(x) = 3x^2 - 4x + 2$
$g(x) = 3x - 2$

(d) $f(x) = \frac{4x}{3}$
$g(x) = x^2 - 9$

2 Given $f(x) = 2x$ and $g(x) = -x$, find:

(a) fg(x) **(b)** fg(2) **(c)** ff(4) **(d)** gf(1)

3 $f(x) = 3x + 1$ and $h(x) = 6x^2$, find:

(a) ff(x) **(b)** fh(x) **(c)** hh(−2) **(d)** hf(−2) **(e)** $hf\left(\frac{2}{5}\right)$

4 Given the functions $g(x) = x^2 + 1$ and $h(x) = 2x + 3$, find the values of:

(a) gh(1) **(b)** hg(1) **(c)** gg(2) **(d)** hh(5)

5 Find gh(4) and hg(4) if $g(x) = \frac{1}{x}$ and $h(x) = \frac{1}{x+1}$.

6 Given $f(x) = 8 - x^2$ and $g(x) = x^2 - 8$, find:

(a) fg(x) **(b)** gf(x) **(c)** ff(x) **(d)** gg(x)

7 Given $f(x) = 2x - 5$ and $g(x) = \frac{1}{x}$, evaluate:

(a) f(−10) **(b)** $g(\frac{2}{3})$ **(c)** $gf(\frac{5}{70})$ **(d)** gf(4) **(e)** ff(0)

8 If $f(x) = x^4$ and $g(x) = \sqrt{(x^2 + 36)}$, evaluate:

(a) fg(x) **(b)** gf(x) **(c)** ff(0) **(d)** gg(−2)

9 Given that $f(x) = -x$, $g(x) = x - 1$ and $h(x) = \frac{1}{x+2}$, show why it is not possible to evaluate hgf(1).

> **REWIND**
> Inverse functions were met briefly with trigonometry in chapter 15. ◀

Inverse functions

The **inverse** of any function (f) is the function that will do the opposite of f. In other words, the function that will undo the effects of f. So, if f maps 4 onto 13, then the inverse of f will map 13 onto 4.

In effect, when f is applied to a number and the inverse of f is applied to the result, you will get back to the number you started with.

In simple cases, you can find the inverse of a function by inspection. For example, the inverse of $x \to x + 5$ must be $x \to x - 5$ because subtraction is the inverse of addition; to undo add five you have to subtract five.

Similarly, the inverse of $x \to 2x$ is $x \to \frac{x}{2}$, because to undo multiply by two you have to divide by two.

The inverse of the function (f) is written as f^{-1}.

So, if $f(x) = x + 5$, then $f^{-1}(x) = x - 5$

and, if $g(x) = 2x$, then $g^{-1}(x) = \frac{x}{2}$.

Some functions do not have an inverse. Think about the function $x \to x^2$. This is a function because for every value of x, there is only one value of x^2. The inverse (in other words, the square root) is not a function because a positive number has two square roots, one negative, and one positive.

Finding the inverse of a function

There are two methods of finding the inverse:

- Method 1: using a flow diagram.
  In this method you draw a flow diagram for the function and then work out the inverse by 'reversing' the flow to undo the operations in the boxes.

- Method 2: reversing the mapping.

  In this method you use the fact that if f maps x onto y, then f^{-1} maps y onto x. To find f^{-1} you have to find a value of x that corresponds to a given value of y.

The worked examples 14–17 show you the two methods of finding the inverse of the same functions.

Worked example 14

Find the inverse of $f(x) = 3x - 4$.

Let x be the input to f^{-1}

$\frac{x+4}{3} \leftarrow \boxed{\div 3} \leftarrow \boxed{+4} \leftarrow x$

$\therefore f^{-1}(x) = \frac{x+4}{3}$

Using Method 1, the flow diagram, you get:

$f: \text{input} \rightarrow \boxed{\times 3} \rightarrow \boxed{-4} \rightarrow \text{output}$

$f^{-1}: \text{output} \leftarrow \boxed{\div 3} \leftarrow \boxed{+4} \leftarrow \text{input}$

Worked example 15

Given $g(x) = 5 - 2x$, find $g^{-1}(x)$.

Let x be the input to g^{-1}

$\frac{x-5}{-2} \leftarrow \boxed{\div(-2)} \leftarrow \boxed{-5} \leftarrow x$

$\therefore g^{-1}(x) = \frac{x-5}{-2} = \frac{5-x}{2}$

Using Method 1, the flow diagram, you get:

$g: \text{input} \rightarrow \boxed{\times(-2)} \rightarrow \boxed{+5} \rightarrow \text{output}$

$g^{-1}: \text{output} \leftarrow \boxed{\div(-2)} \leftarrow \boxed{-5} \leftarrow \text{input}$

Worked example 16

Find the inverse of the function $f(x) = 3x - 4$.

$y = 3x - 4$

$y + 4 = 3x$

$x = \frac{y+4}{3}$

Using Method 2, reversing the mapping.
Suppose the function maps x onto y (y is the subject).
Make x the subject of the formula, so that y maps onto x.

You know that f^{-1} maps y onto x, so $f^{-1}(y) = \frac{y+4}{3}$

This is usually written in terms of x so, $f^{-1}(x) = \frac{x+4}{3}$

Worked example 17

Given $g(x) = 5 - 2x$, find $g^{-1}(x)$.

Let $y = 5 - 2x$ $2x = 5 - y$ $x = \frac{5-y}{2}$	This means g maps x onto y. Make x the subject of the formula, so that y maps onto x.

g^{-1} maps y onto x, so $g^{-1}(y) = \frac{5-y}{2}$

This is usually written in terms of x so, $g^{-1}(x) = \frac{5-x}{2}$

Exercise 22.7

1 Find the inverse of each function.

(a) $f(x) = 7x$ (b) $f(x) = \frac{1}{7x^3}$ (c) $f(x) = x^3$

(d) $f(x) = 4x + 3$ (e) $f(x) = \frac{1}{2}x + 5$ (f) $f(x) = \frac{x+2}{2}$

(g) $f(x) = 3(x - 2)$ (h) $f(x) = \frac{2x+9}{2}$ (i) $f(x) = \frac{2(x+1)}{4-x}$

(j) $f(x) = x^3 + 5$ (k) $f(x) = \sqrt{3x + 8}$ (l) $f(x) = \frac{x+1}{x-1}$

2 For each pair of functions, determine whether $g(x)$ is the inverse of $f(x)$.

(a) $f(x) = 2x - 6$, $g(x) = \frac{x}{2} + 3$ (b) $f(x) = 12x$, $g(x) = \frac{x}{12}$

(c) $f(x) = 3x + 2$, $g(x) = x + \frac{3}{2}$ (d) $f(x) = x^3 - 2$, $g(x) = \sqrt[3]{x+2}$

3 Given the function $g(x) = \frac{x}{3} - 44$, find $g^{-1}(x)$.

4 For each function, find:

(i) $f^{-1}(x)$ (ii) $ff^{-1}(x)$ (iii) $f^{-1}f(x)$

(a) $f(x) = 5x$ (b) $f(x) = x + 4$ (c) $f(x) = 2x - 7$

(d) $f(x) = x^3 + 2$ (e) $f(x) = \sqrt{2x-1}$ (f) $f(x) = \frac{9}{x}$

(g) $f(x) = x^3 - 1$

5 Given the function $h(x) = 2(x - 3)$, find the value of:

(a) $h^{-1}(10)$ (b) $hh^{-1}(20)$ (c) $h^{-1}h^{-1}(26)$

6 $f(x) = \frac{1}{2}x + 5$ and $g(x) = 4x - \frac{2}{5}$

(a) Solve $f(x) = 0$
(b) Find $g^{-1}(x)$
(c) Solve $f(x) = g(x)$ giving your answer correct to 2 decimal places.
(d) Find the value of:

(i) $gf^{-1}(-2)$ (ii) $f^{-1}f(3)$ (iii) $f^{-1}g^{-1}(4)$

Summary

Do you know the following?

- Algebraic expressions and equations are useful for representing situations and solving worded problems.
- When you set up your own equations to represent problems you need to state what the variables stand for.
- A formula is an equation that links variables. The subject of the formula is the variable on the left-hand side of the formula.
- You can rearrange formulae to make any of the variables the subject. This is called changing the subject of the formula. It may also be called solving the formula for (x) or expressing the formula in terms of (x).
- More complex formulae can be transformed, including:
  - formulae that contain squares and square roots
  - formulae where the subject appears in more than one term.
- A function is a rule for changing one variable into another.
- Functions are written using conventional notation of $f(x) = x + 2$ and $f : x \rightarrow 2 - 3x$.
- You can use a flow diagram to represent the steps in a function.
- A composite function is a function of a function. The order of a composite function is important $fg(x)$ means do g first then f.
- An inverse function is function that undoes the original function. The reverse of the function.

Are you able to ...?

- set up your own equations and use them to solve worded problems
- change the subject of formula
- set up and transform even more complicated formulae such as those that contain squares, square roots or where the subject appears in more than one term
- substitute values to find the given subject of a formula
- read, understand and use function notation to describe simple functions
- form composite functions such as $gf(x)$ and $ff(x)$
- find the inverse of a function using a flow diagram
- find the inverse of a function by reversing the mapping.

Examination practice

Exam-style questions

1 Six litres of white paint are mixed with three litres of blue paint that costs \$2 per litre more. The total price of the mixture is \$24. Find the price of the white paint.

2 A trader has a mixture of 5c and 10c coins. He has 50 coins in all, with a total value of \$4.20. How many of each coin does he have?

3 If $S = \frac{a}{1-r}$, find a when $S = 5.2$ and $r = 0.3$.

4 f and g are the functions $f: x \to x - 5$ and $g: x \to 5 - x$. Which of the following are true and which are false?

(a) $f^{-1} = g$

(b) $g^{-1}: x \to 5 - x$

(c) $fg: x \to -x$

(d) $fg = gf$

5 $f(x) = 3x^2 - 3x - 4$ and $g(x) = 4 - 3x$.

(a) State the value of $f(-2)$.

(b) Solve the equation $f(x) = -3$.

(c) Solve the equation $f(x) = 0$, giving your answer correct to 2 decimal places.

(d) Solve the equation $g(x) = 2g(x) - 1$.

(e) Find $g^{-1}(x)$.

6 $f: x \to 3 - 4x$.

(a) Find $f(-1)$

(b) Find $f^{-1}(x)$

(c) Find $ff^{-1}(4)$

7 If $f(x) = \frac{5}{2x-1}$ and $f(x) = -2$, find x.

Past paper questions

1 Rearrange the formula to make x the subject.

$y = x^2 + 4$ [2]

[Cambridge IGCSE Mathematics 0580 Paper 22 Q06 October/November 2013]

2 Make y the subject of the formula. $A = \pi x^2 - \pi y^2$ [3]

[Cambridge IGCSE Mathematics 0580 Paper 23 Q16 October/November 2012]

3 **(a)** The surface area, A, of a cylinder, radius r and height h, is given by the formula $A = 2\pi rh + 2\pi r^2$.

(i) Calculate the surface area of a cylinder of radius 5 cm and height 9 cm. [2]

(ii) Make h the subject of the formula. [2]

(iii) A cylinder has a radius of 6 cm and a surface area of 377 cm^2. Calculate the height of this cylinder. [2]

(iv) A cylinder has a surface area of 1200 cm^2 and its radius and height are equal. Calculate the radius. [3]

(b) **(i)** On Monday a shop receives $60.30 by selling bottles of water at 45 cents each. How many bottles are sold? [1]

(ii) On Tuesday the shop receives x **cents** by selling bottles of water at 45 cents each. In terms of x, how many bottles are sold? [1]

(iii) On Wednesday the shop receives $(x - 75)$ **cents** by selling bottles of water at 48 cents each. In terms of x, how many bottles are sold? [1]

(iv) The number of bottles sold on Tuesday was 7 more than the number of bottles sold on Wednesday. Write down an equation in x and solve your equation. [4]

[Cambridge IGCSE Mathematics 0580 Paper 04 Q08 October/November 2006]

4 $f(x) = x^2$ $g(x) = 2^x$ $h(x) = 2x - 3$

(a) Find g(3). [1]

(b) Find hh(x) in its simplest form. [2]

(c) Find fg($x + 1$) in its simplest form. [2]

[Cambridge IGCSE Mathematics 0580 Paper 22 Q19 May/June 2011]

23 Transformations and matrices

Key words

- Transformation
- Object
- Reflection
- Rotation
- Translation
- Enlargement
- Image
- Vector
- Magnitude
- Scalar
- Matrix
- Commutative
- Determinant
- Inverse

In this chapter you will learn how to:

- reflect, rotate, translate and enlarge plane shapes
- recognise and describe transformations
- use vectors to describe translations
- add and subtract vectors and multiply them by scalars

EXTENDED

- calculate the magnitude of a vector
- represent vectors in conventional ways
- use the sum and difference of vectors to express them in terms of coplanar vectors
- use position vectors
- recognise and use combined transformations
- precisely describe transformations using co-ordinates and matrices
- display information in the form of a matrix
- perform matrix calculations including the determinant and inverse of non-singular matrices.

This is a batik printed fabric from Ghana. The fabric designers repeat shapes by moving them and turning them in a regular ways. In Mathematics we call this a transformation.

Transformation geometry deals with moving or changing shapes in set ways. You are going to revise what you know about transformations, use vectors and work with more precise mathematical descriptions of transformations. If you are following the extended course you will also learn about matrices and perform matrix calculations.

23.1 Simple plane transformations

Transformation means change. In Mathematics, a transformation is a change in the position or size of an **object** (or point). In this section you will deal with four types of transformations:

- **Reflection** (a flip or mirror image)
- **Rotation** (a turn)
- **Translation** (a slide movement)
- **Enlargement** (making the object larger or smaller).

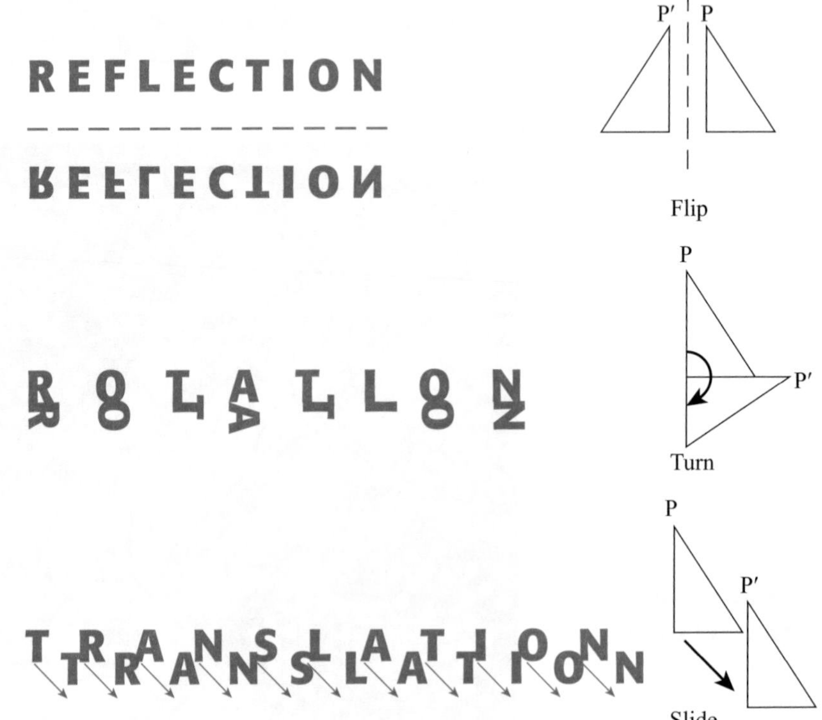

A transformation produces an **image** of the original object in a new position or at a different size. A point, P, on the object is labelled as P′ on the image.

REWIND

You learned about congruency and similarity in chapter 11. ◀

Reflections, rotations and translations change the position of an object, but they do not change its size. So, the object and its image are congruent. If you place the object and its image on top of each other, they coincide exactly.

When you enlarge an object, you change its size. The object and its image are similar. In other words, the lengths of corresponding sides on the image are in the same proportion as on the object.

Reflection

A reflection is a mirror image of the shape. The line of reflection is called the mirror line. Corresponding points on the object and the image are the same distance from the mirror line. These distances are always measured perpendicular to the mirror line. (In other words, the mirror line is the perpendicular bisector of the distance between any point and its image.) You can see this on the following diagrams.

Note that the mirror line tends to be drawn as a dashed line.

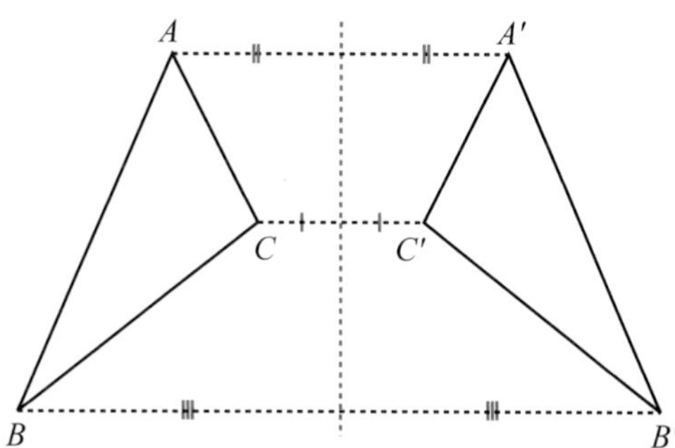

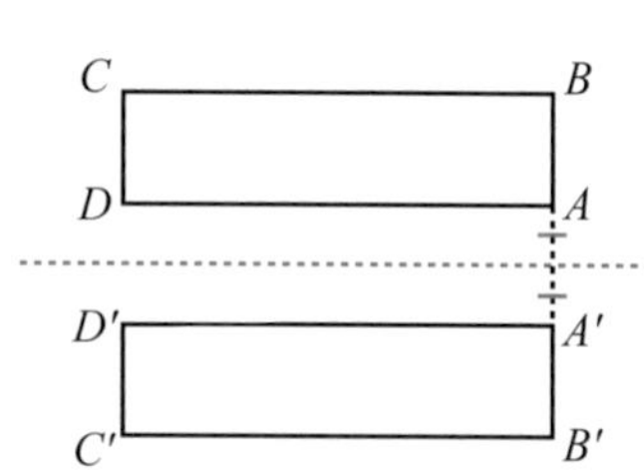

You need to be able to work with reflections in horizontal and vertical lines only.

To fully define a reflection, you need to give the equation of the mirror line.

Properties of reflection

- A point and its image are equidistant from the mirror line (m) after reflection about the line m.

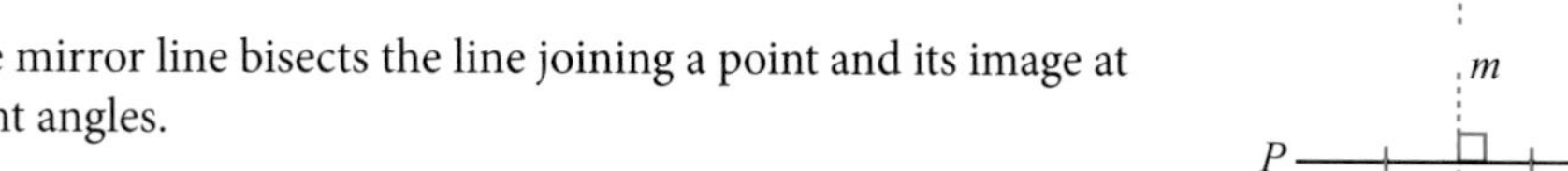

- The mirror line bisects the line joining a point and its image at right angles.

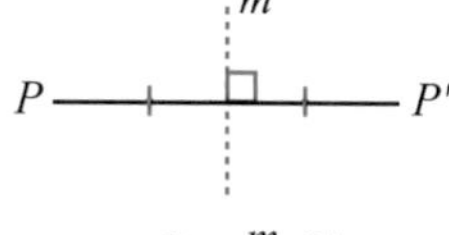

- A line segment and its image are equal in length. $AB = A'B'$.

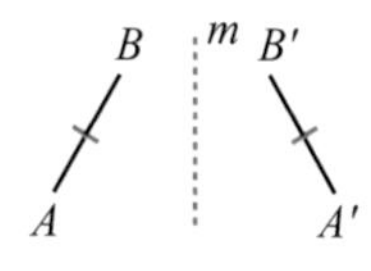

- A line and its image are equally inclined to the mirror line. $A\hat{O}M = A'\hat{O}M$.

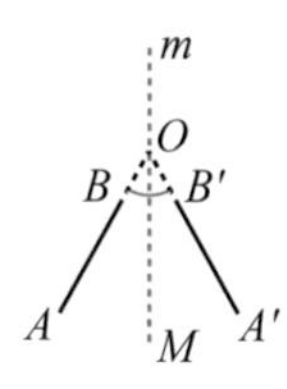

Invariant means a point, or a line, remains unchanged in its position and size.

- Points on the mirror line are their own images and are invariant.

- Under reflection, a figure and its image are congruent.

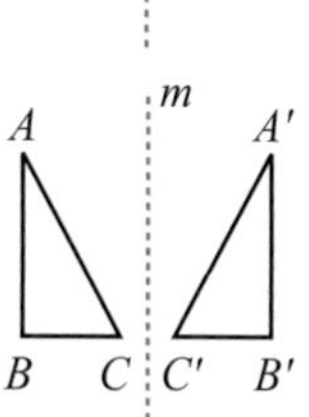

Worked example 1

When the mirror line is one of the grid lines this makes it easy to reflect any point. You simply count the squares from the point to the mirror line and the reflection is the same distance the other side of the mirror line.

Reflect $\triangle ABC$ about the mirror line.

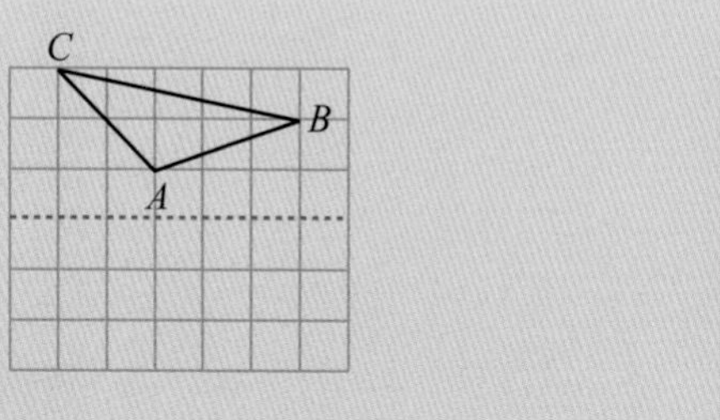

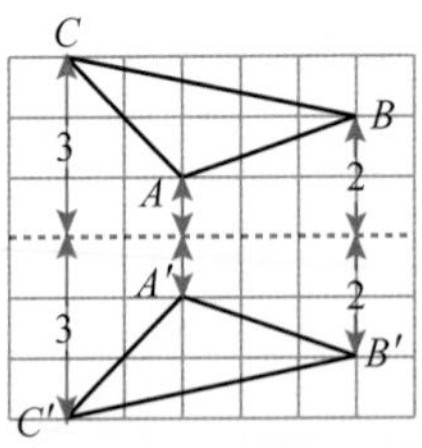

In the diagram, A is 1 unit from the mirror line, so its image A' is also 1 unit from the mirror line. Point B is 2 units from the mirror line, so its image B' is also 2 units from the mirror line. This is also true for C and its image C'.

The reflection of a straight line is a straight line. So, to obtain the reflection of ΔABC, join A' to B', B' to C' and C' to A'.

Worked example 2

A shape and its reflection are shown on the grid.

(a) Draw the mirror line.
(b) What is the equation of the mirror line?

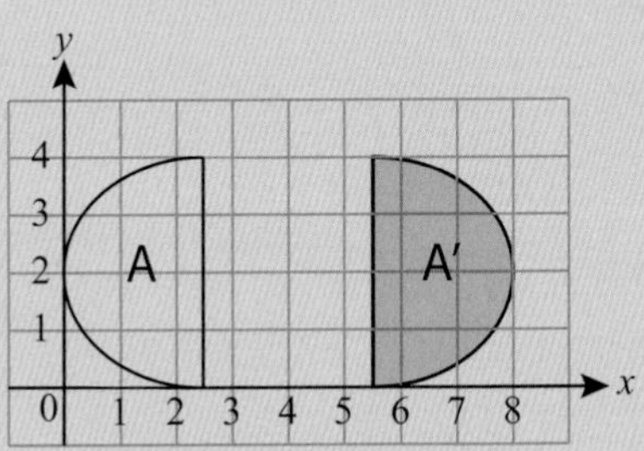

The mirror line is the perpendicular bisector of the line joining any point and its image.

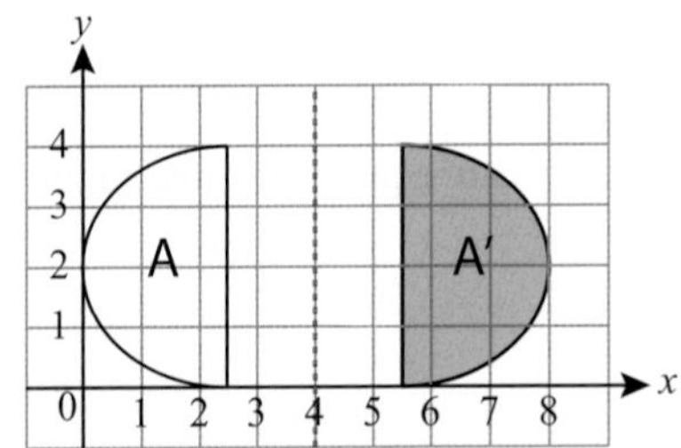

(a) The mirror line must be the same distance from corresponding points on A and A′.

(b) The mirror line is parallel to the y-axis. The x values of any point on it is 4, so the equation of the line is $x = 4$.

Worked example 3

Shape A is the object.

(a) Reflect shape A in the y-axis. Label the image B.
(b) Reflect shape A and shape B in the x-axis. Label the images A′ and B′ respectively.

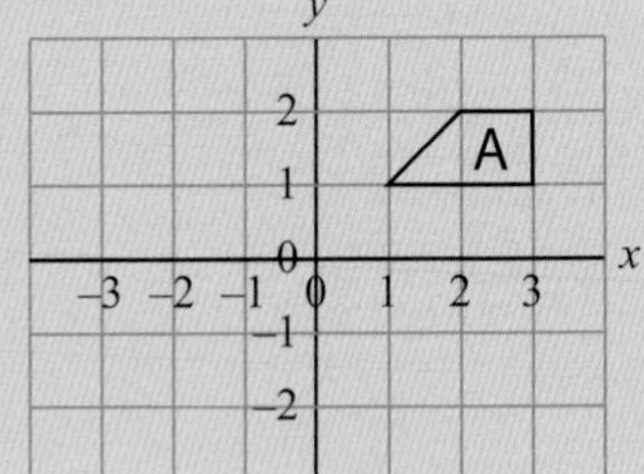

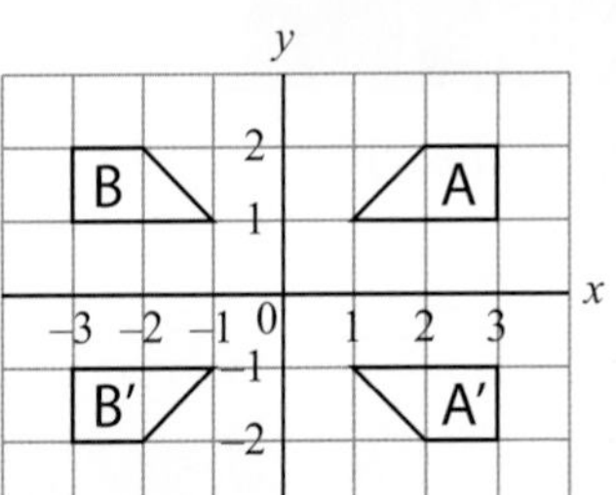

(a) The y-axis ($x = 0$) is the mirror line.

(b) The x-axis ($y = 0$) is the mirror line.

Exercise 23.1

1 Copy the shapes and the mirror lines onto squared paper.
Draw the image of each object.

(a) 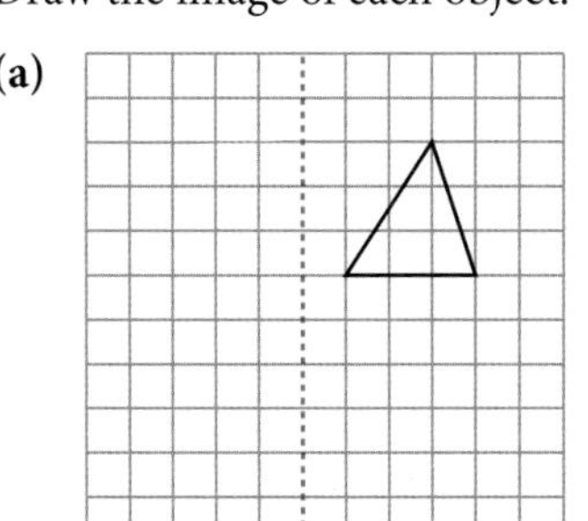

(b) 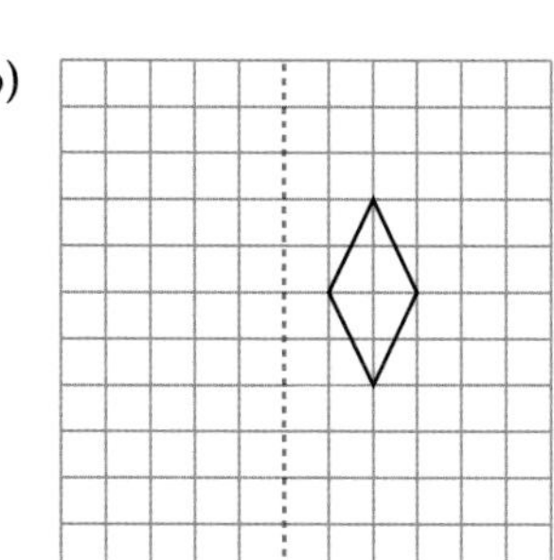

(c) 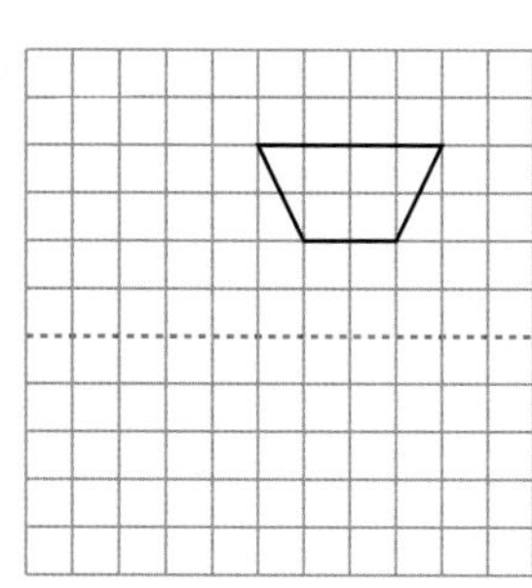

2 Copy the axes and shapes onto squared paper.

For each diagram:

(i) draw in the mirror line
(ii) give the equation of the mirror line.

(a)

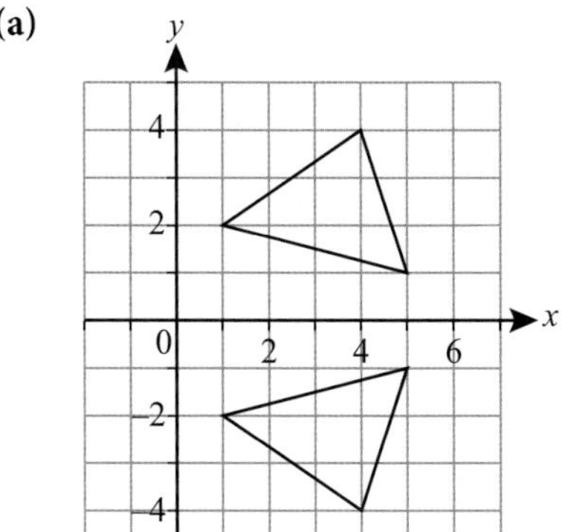

(b)

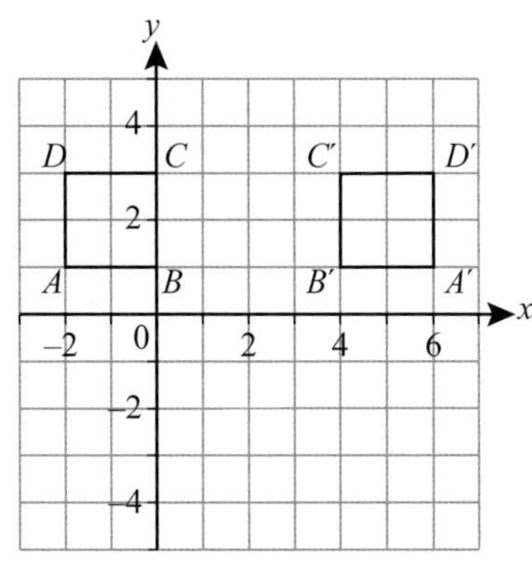

(c)

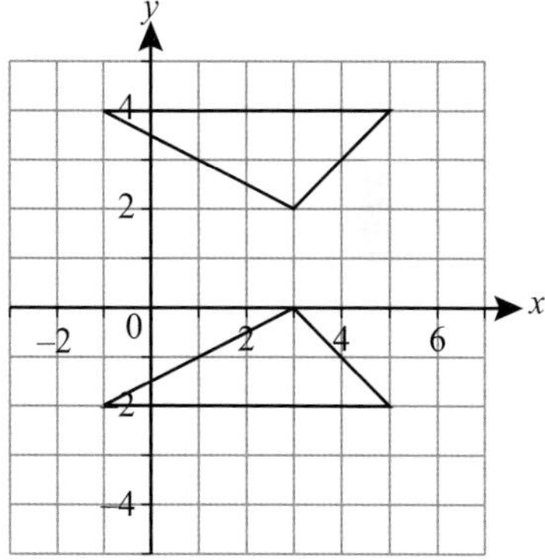

3 Copy the axes and the shape onto squared paper.

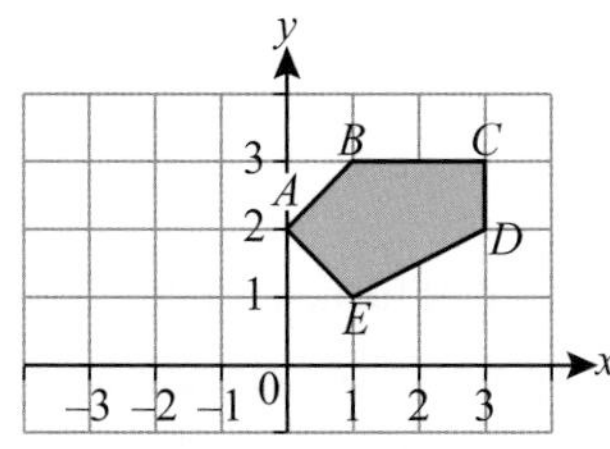

(a) Reflect polygon $ABCDE$ in the y-axis.
(b) Give the co-ordinates of point B after reflection (B').
(c) Which point on the shape $ABCDE$ is invariant? Why?

4 Copy the axes and the shape onto squared paper.

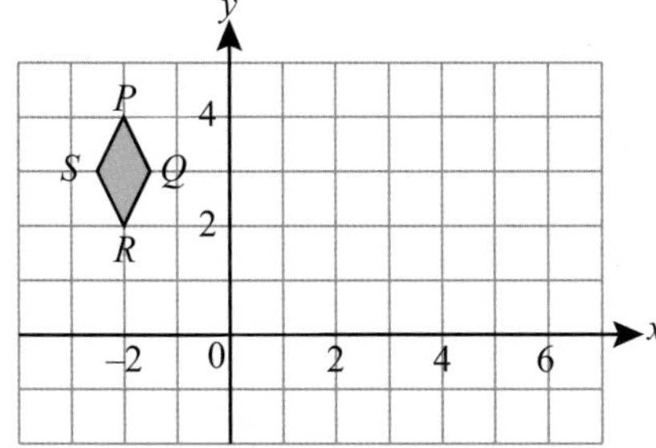

(a) Reflect the shape in the line $x = 1$. Label the image $P'Q'R'S'$.
(b) Reflect $P'Q'R'S'$ in the line $y = 2$. Label the image $P''Q''R''S''$.

5 Copy the axes and the diagram onto squared paper.

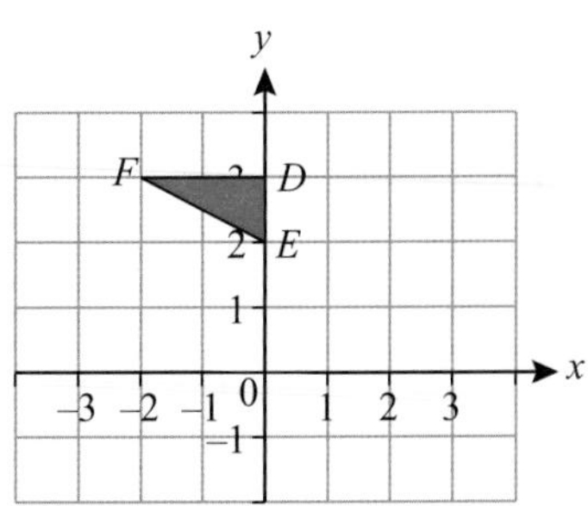

(a) Draw the image of ΔDEF when reflected in the y-axis. Label it $D'E'F'$.
(b) Give the co-ordinates of point F before and after reflection.
(c) Reflect ΔDEF in the line $y = 1$. Label the image $D''E''F''$.

Rotation

REWIND

You dealt with rotation when you studied rotational symmetry in chapter 19. ◀

A rotation is a turn around a fixed point. Rotation occurs when an object is turned around a given point. Rotation can be clockwise or anti-clockwise. The fixed point is called the centre of rotation and the angle through which the shape is rotated is called the angle of rotation.

In this diagram, the object has been rotated 90° clockwise about the centre of rotation (a vertex of the object).

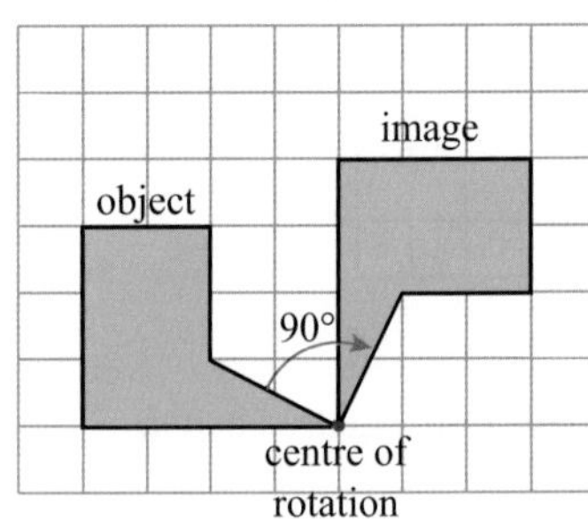

Properties of rotation

REWIND

You learned in chapter 19 that concentric circles have differ radii but the same centre. ◀

- A rotation through 180° is a half turn; a rotation through 90° is a quarter turn.
- Anti-clockwise rotation is positive and clockwise rotation is negative.
- A point and its image are equidistant from the centre of rotation.
- Each point of an object moves along the arc of a circle whose centre is the centre of rotation. All the circles are concentric:

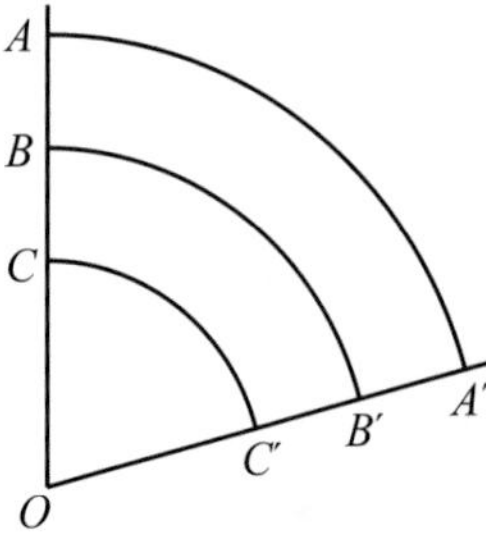

- Only the centre of rotation is invariant.

- The object and the image are congruent after rotation.

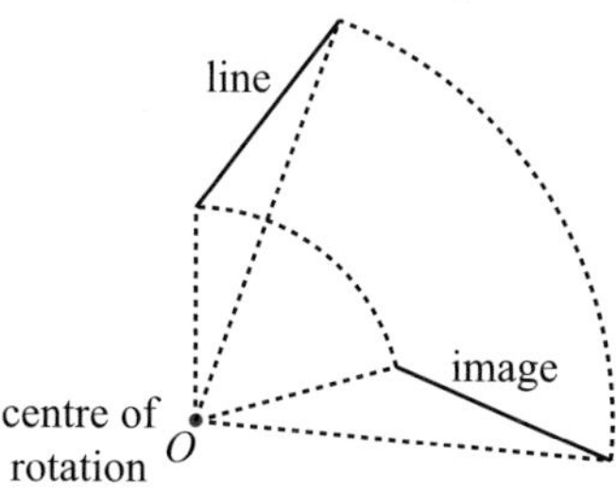

- The perpendicular bisector of a line joining a point and its image passes through the centre of rotation.

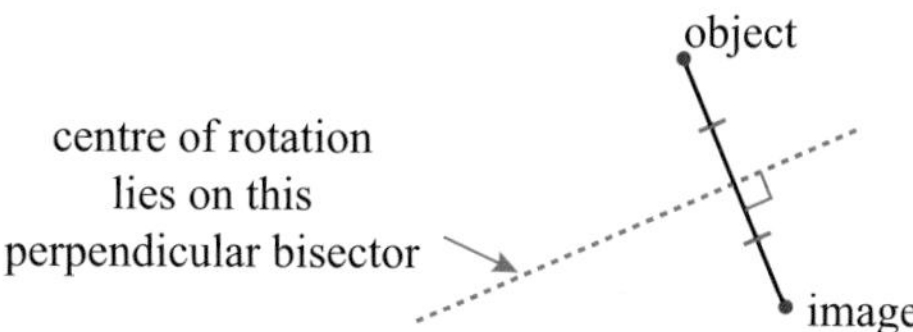

- A line segment and its image are equal in length.

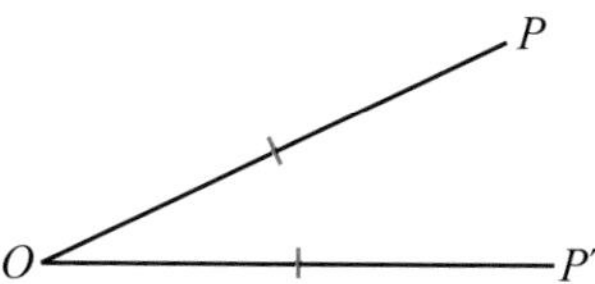

Tip

The centre of rotation will normally be the origin (0, 0), a vertex of the shape or the midpoint of a side of the shape. The amount of turn will normally be a multiple of 90°.

To describe a rotation you need to give:

- the centre of rotation
- the amount of turn (90°, 180° or 270°)
- the direction of the turn (clockwise or anti-clockwise).

You can use thin paper or tracing paper to help you do rotations:

1. Trace the shape and label the vertices.
2. Place the tracing over the object.
3. Use the point of a pair of compasses or pen to hold the paper at the point of rotation.
4. Turn the paper through the given turn.
5. The new position of the shape is the image.

Worked example 4

Rotate this shape 90° clockwise about:

(a) the origin (label the image $A'B'C'D'$)
(b) point A (label the image $A''B''C''D''$).

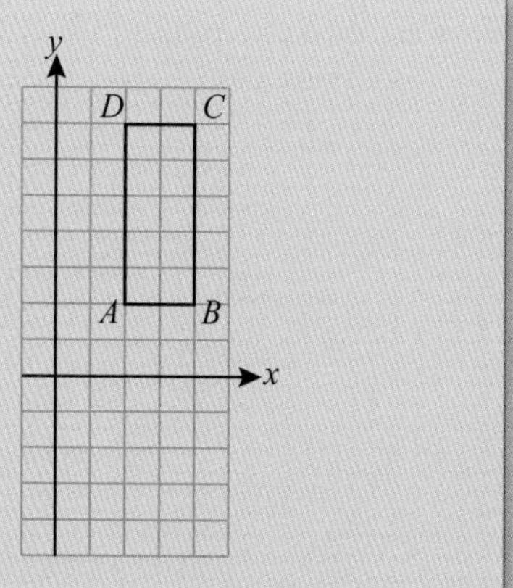

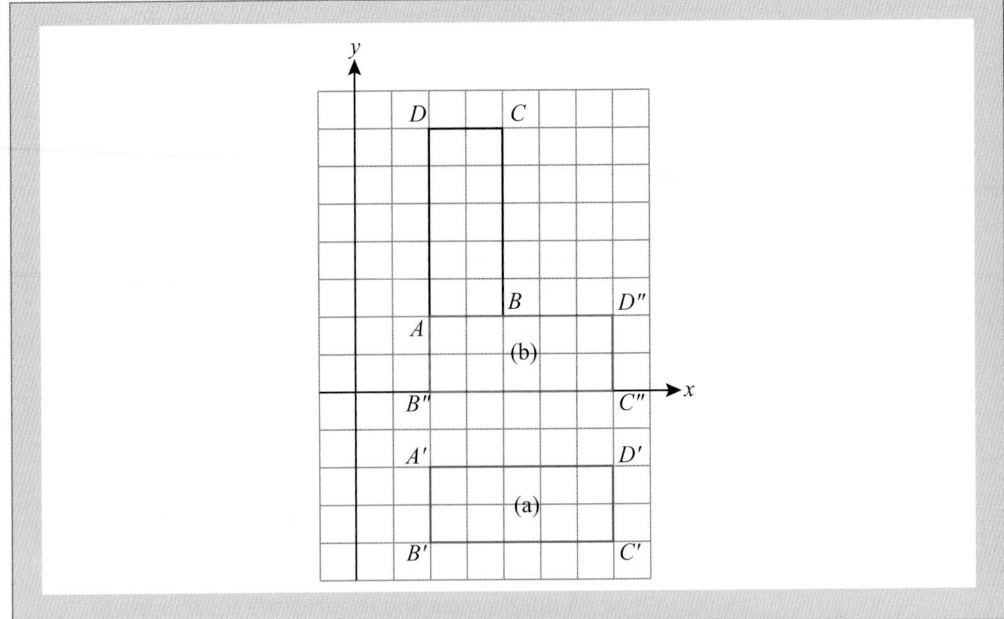

Exercise 23.2

1 Copy the diagrams in parts (**a**) to (**c**).
Draw the images of the given triangle under the rotations described.

(a) Centre of rotation (0, 0); angle of rotation 90° anti-clockwise.

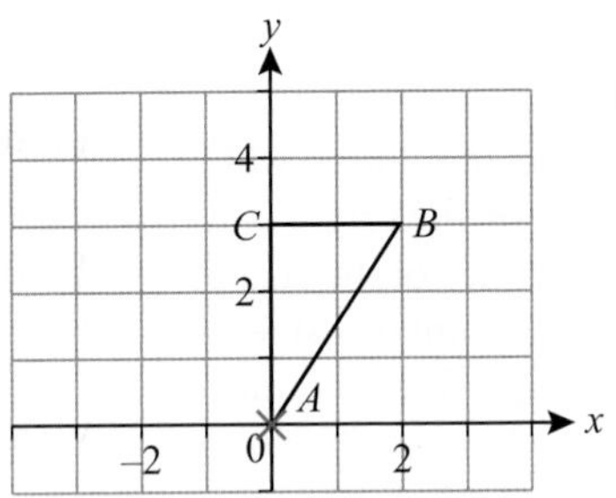

(b) Centre of rotation (3, 1); angle of rotation 180°.
(Note that (3, 1) is the midpoint of *AB*.)

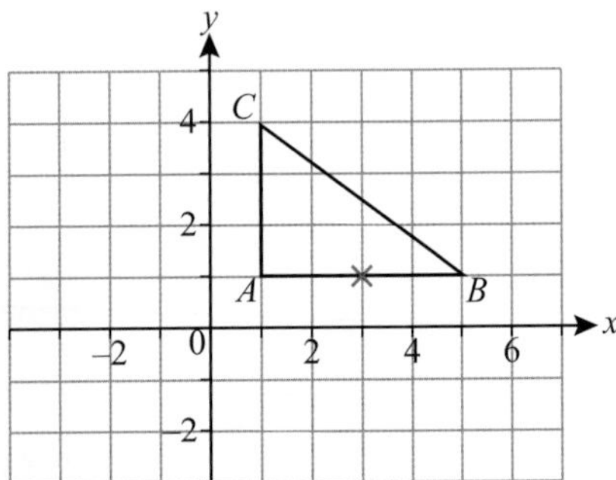

(c) Centre of rotation (−1, 0); angle of rotation 180°.

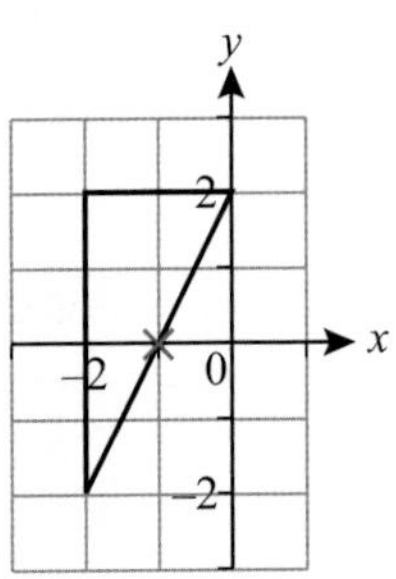

2 Fully describe the rotation that maps ΔABC onto $\Delta A'B'C'$ in each case.

(a)

(b)

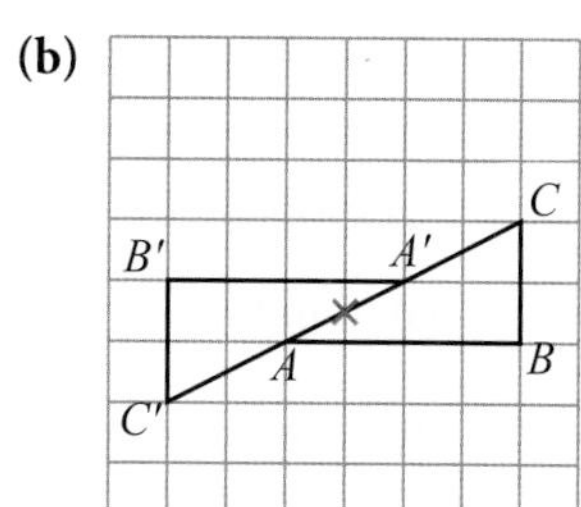

(c)

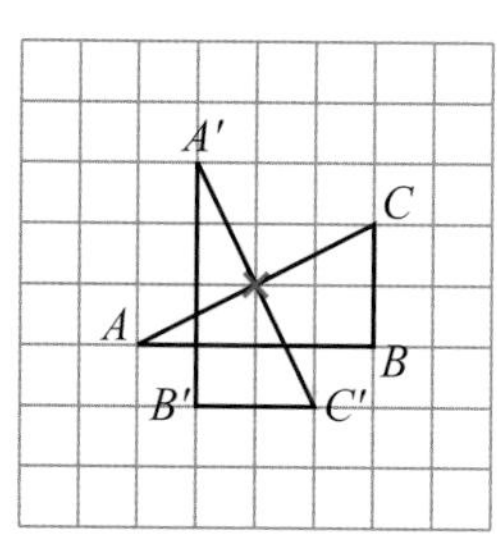

Living maths

3 Nick wants to rearrange the furniture in his living room. He drew this scale diagram showing the original layout of the room.

Is it possible for him to rotate all the furniture through point (0, 0) by the following amounts and still have it fit into the room?

(a) 90° clockwise?
(b) 90° anti-clockwise?
(c) 180° clockwise?

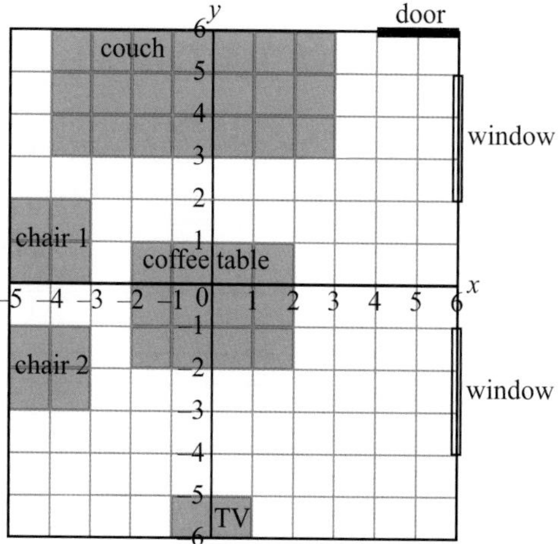

Translation

A translation, or slide, is the movement of an object over a specified distance along a line. The object is not twisted or turned. The movement is indicated by positive or negative signs according to the direction of movement along the axes of a plane. For example, movements to the left or down are negative and movements to the right or upwards are positive.

FAST FORWARD
You will deal with vectors in more detail later in this chapter. ▶

A translation should be described by a **column vector**: $\begin{pmatrix} x \\ y \end{pmatrix}$. This means a movement of x units in the x-direction (left or right) and a movement of y units in the y-direction (up or down).

In other words, a translation of $\begin{pmatrix} 2 \\ -3 \end{pmatrix}$ means the object moves two units to the right and three units downwards.

Be careful when writing column vectors. There is no dividing line, so they should *not* look like fractions. Write $\begin{pmatrix} 3 \\ 8 \end{pmatrix}$ rather than $\left(\frac{3}{8}\right)$; they mean different things.

In this diagram, the triangle T is translated to five positions. Each translation is described below:

Position 1 $\begin{pmatrix} 7 \\ 0 \end{pmatrix}$

Position 2 $\begin{pmatrix} 0 \\ 4 \end{pmatrix}$

Position 3 $\begin{pmatrix} -7 \\ 0 \end{pmatrix}$

Position 4 $\begin{pmatrix} 0 \\ -8 \end{pmatrix}$

Position 5 $\begin{pmatrix} 7 \\ -8 \end{pmatrix}$

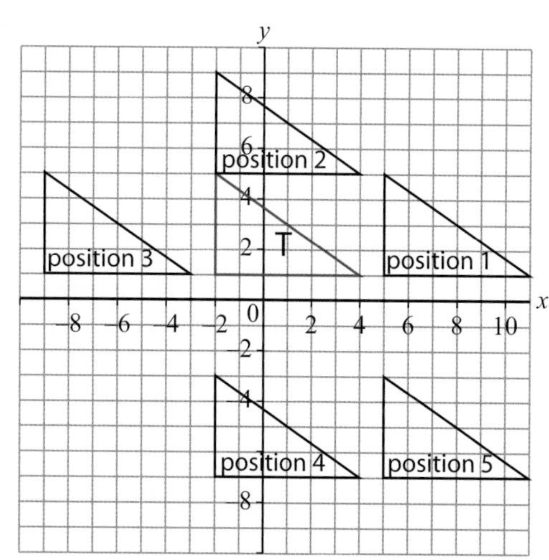

Properties of translation

- A translation moves the entire object the same distance in the same direction.
- Every point moves through the same distance in the same direction.
- To specify the translation, both the distance and direction of translation must be given by a column vector $\begin{pmatrix} x \\ y \end{pmatrix}$.
- The translation of an entire object can be named by specifying the translation undergone by any one point.
- No part of the figure is invariant.
- The object and the image are congruent.

Exercise 23.3

1 Draw sketches to illustrate the following translations:

(a) a square is translated 6 cm to the left
(b) a triangle is translated 5 cm to the right.

2 Write a column vector to describe the translation from A to B and from A to C in each of the following sets of diagrams.

(a)

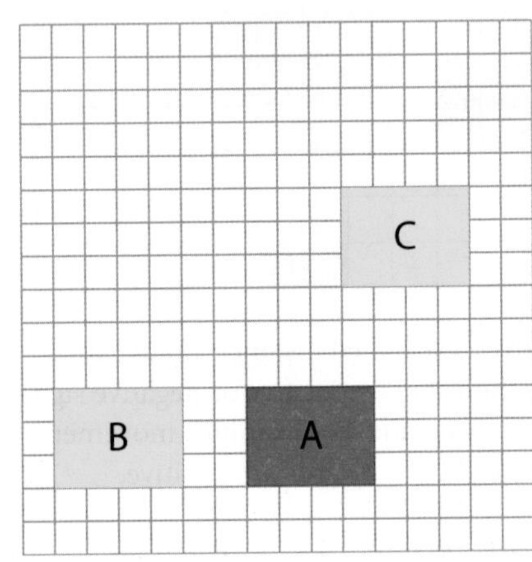

(b)

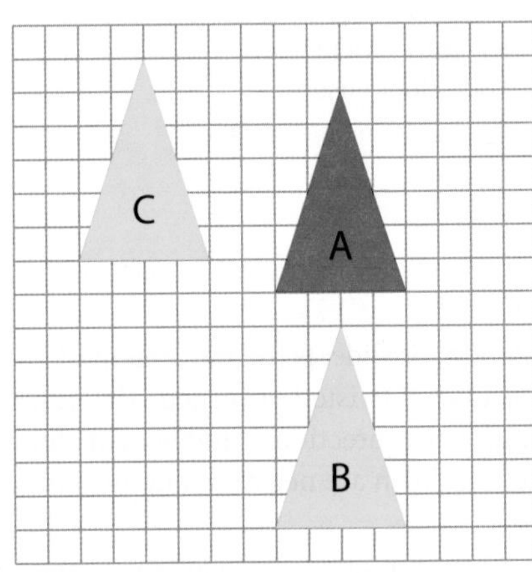

(c)

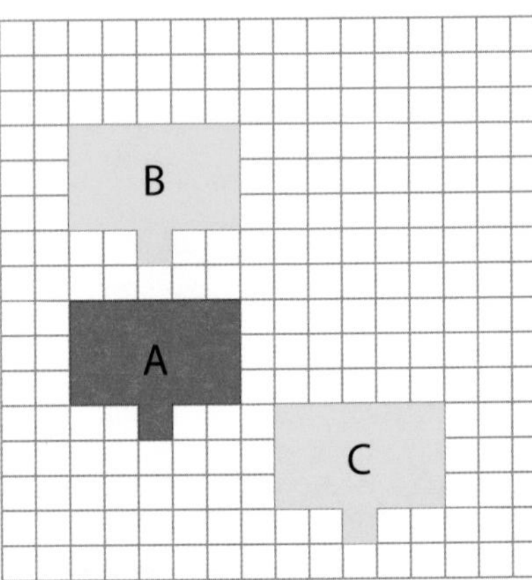

3 Copy the diagram onto squared paper. Translate the triangle ABC:

(a) three units to the right and two units down
(b) three units to the left and two units down
(c) three units upwards and one unit to the left
(d) three units downwards and four units right.

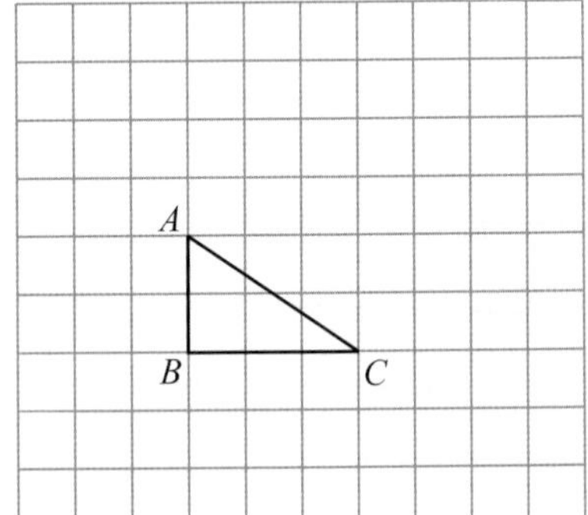

4 On squared paper, draw x- and y-axes and mark the points $A(3, 5)$, $B(2, 1)$ and $C(-1, 4)$.

(a) Draw $\Delta A'B'C'$, the image of ΔABC under the translation $\begin{pmatrix} 2 \\ -3 \end{pmatrix}$.

(b) Draw $\Delta A''B''C''$, the image of ABC under the translation $\begin{pmatrix} 4 \\ 1 \end{pmatrix}$.

5 ΔXYZ with $X(3, 1)$, $Y(2, 6)$ and $Z(-1, -5)$ is transformed onto $\Delta X'Y'Z'$ by a translation of $\begin{pmatrix} 4 \\ -2 \end{pmatrix}$. Determine the co-ordinates of X', Y' and Z'.

6 A rectangle $MNOP$ with vertices $M(1, 6)$, $N(5, 6)$, $O(5, 3)$ and $P(1, 3)$ is transformed by the translation $\begin{pmatrix} -3 \\ 2 \end{pmatrix}$ to produce rectangle $M'N'O'P'$.

(a) Represent this translation accurately on a set of axes.
(b) Give the co-ordinates of the vertices of the image.

Enlargement

REWIND

'Scale factor' was introduced in chapter 11. It is the multiplier that tells you how much one shape is larger than another. ◀

When a shape is enlarged it is made bigger. In an enlargement the lengths of sides on the object are multiplied by a scale factor (k) to form the image. The sizes of angles do not change during an enlargement, so the object and its image are similar. The scale factor can be a whole number or a fraction. To find the scale factor, you use the ratio of corresponding sides on the object and the image:

$$\text{Scale factor} = \frac{\text{image length}}{\text{original length}}$$

If the scale factor is given, you can find the lengths of corresponding sides by multiplication.

This diagram shows a square which has been enlarged by a scale factor of 1.5. This means that

$$\frac{\text{side } B}{\text{side } A} = 1.5$$

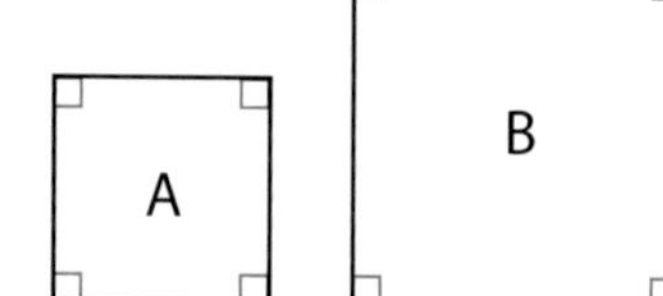

When an object is enlarged from a fixed point, it has a centre of enlargement. The centre of enlargement determines the position of the image. Lines drawn through corresponding points on the object and the image will meet at the centre of enlargement. You can see this on the following diagram.

The scale factor can be determined by comparing any two corresponding sides, for example:

$$\frac{A'B'}{AB} = \frac{2}{1} = 2,$$

or by comparing the distances of two corresponding vertices from the origin, for example:

$$\frac{OC'}{OC} = 2$$

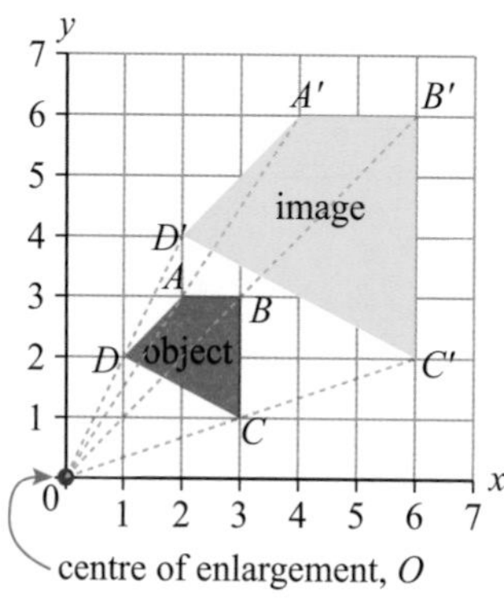

Properties of enlargement

- The centre of enlargement can be anywhere (inside the object, outside the object or on a vertex or line).
- A scale factor greater than 1 enlarges the object whilst a scale factor smaller than 1 reduces the size of the object, although this is sometimes still described as an enlargement.
- An object and its image are similar (not congruent) with sides in the ratio $1:k$ where k is the scale factor.
- The areas of the object and its image are in the ratio $1:k^2$.

- Angles and orientation of the object are invariant.
- If a point and its image are on opposite sides of the centre of enlargement, then the scale factor is negative.

Worked example 5

The figure shows quadrilateral *ABCD* and its image *A′B′C′D′* under an enlargement. Find the centre of enlargement and the scale factor.

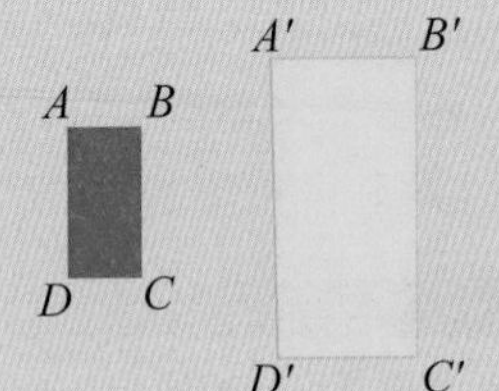

Join the point *A* and its image *A′*.
Extend *AA′* in both directions. Similarly, draw and extend *BB′*, *CC′* and *DD′*.
The point of intersection of these lines is the centre of enlargement, *O*.

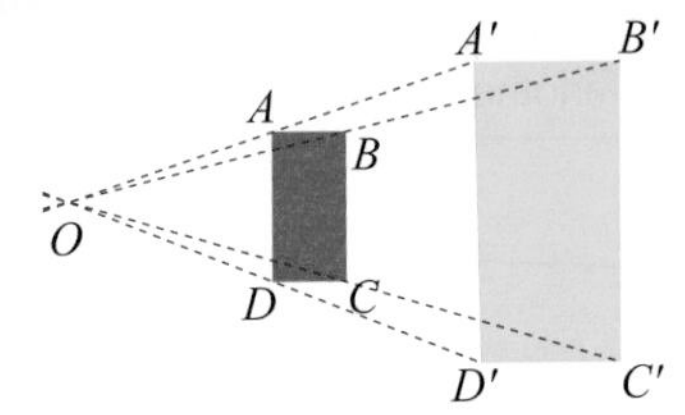

$OA = 25\,\text{mm}$
$OA' = 50\,\text{mm}$

Scale factor $= \frac{50}{25} = 2$

Measure *OA* and *OA′*.

The ratio *OA* : *OA′* gives the scale factor.

Worked example 6

Draw the image of rectangle *ABCD* with *O* as the centre of enlargement and a scale factor of two.

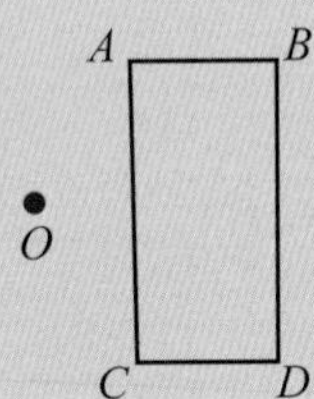

Join *OA*. Continue (produce) the line beyond *A*. Measure *OA*.

Multiply the length of *OA* by 2.

Mark the position of *A′* on the produced line so that $OA' = 2OA$.

Repeat for the other vertices.
Join *A′B′C′D′*.

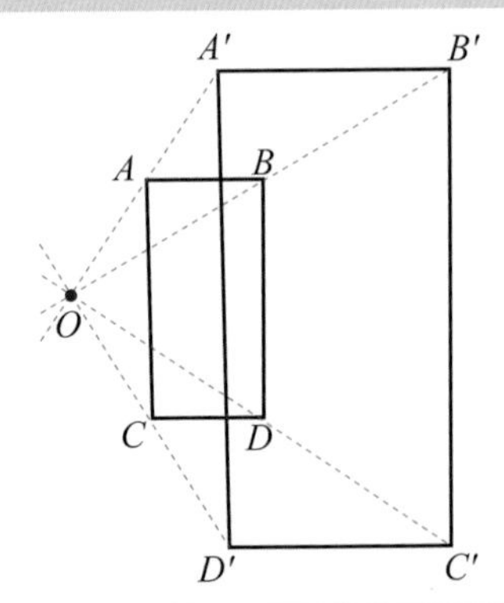

Exercise 23.4

1 For each enlargement, give the co-ordinates of the centre of enlargement and the scale factor of the enlargement.

(a)

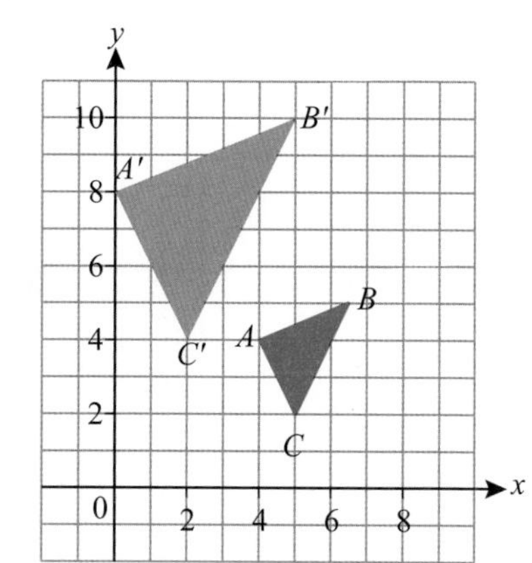

(b)

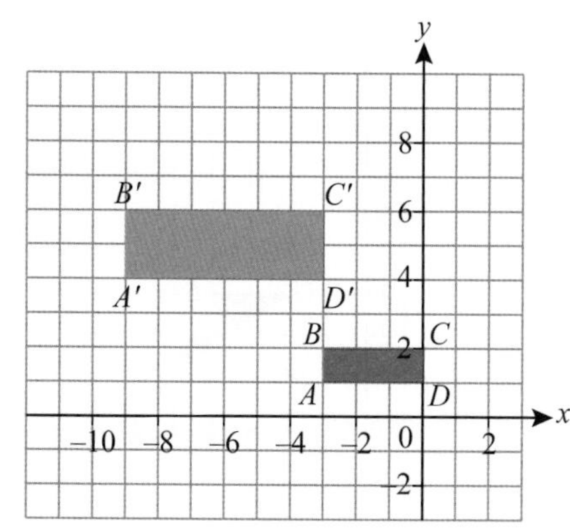

(c)

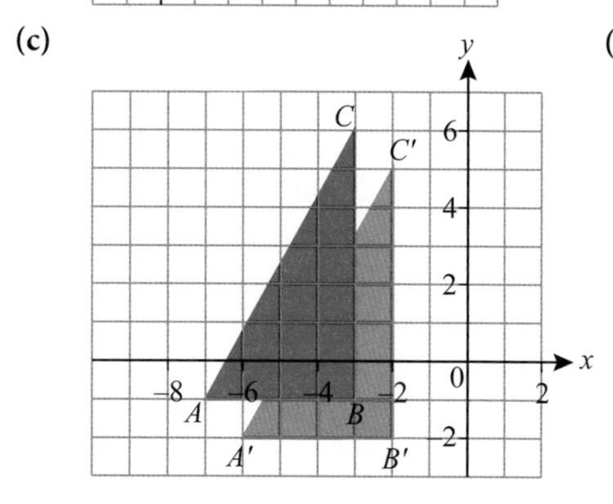

(d)

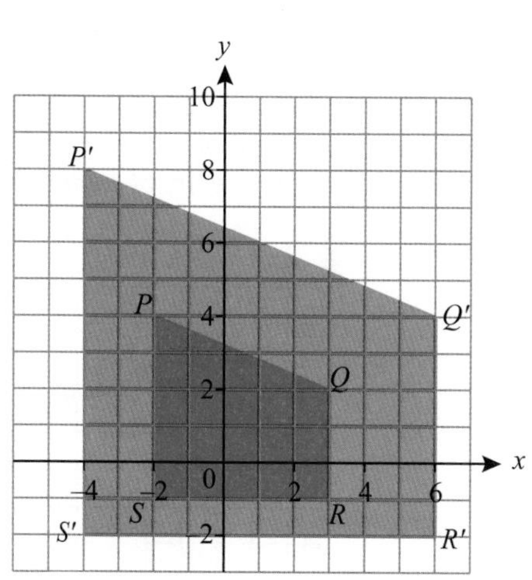

2 Copy the axes and shapes onto squared paper. Using the origin as the centre of enlargement, and a scale factor of three, draw the image of each shape under enlargement.

(a)

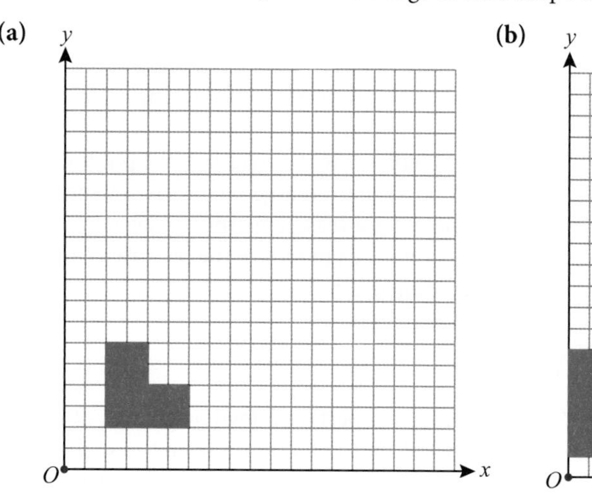

(b)

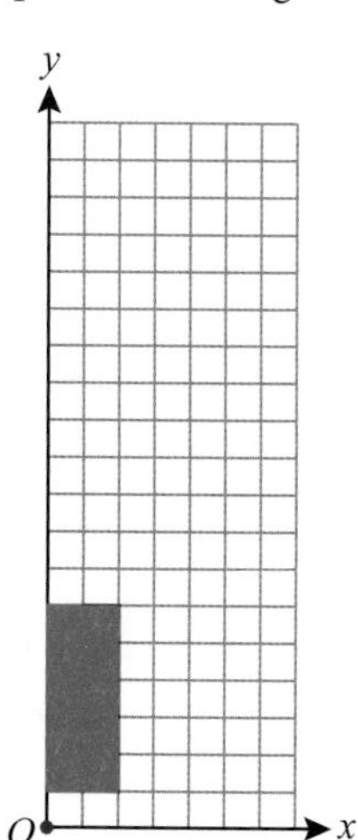

3 Copy the axes and shape onto squared paper. Draw the image of ΔABC under an enlargement of scale factor 2 and centre of enlargement $P(2, 1)$.

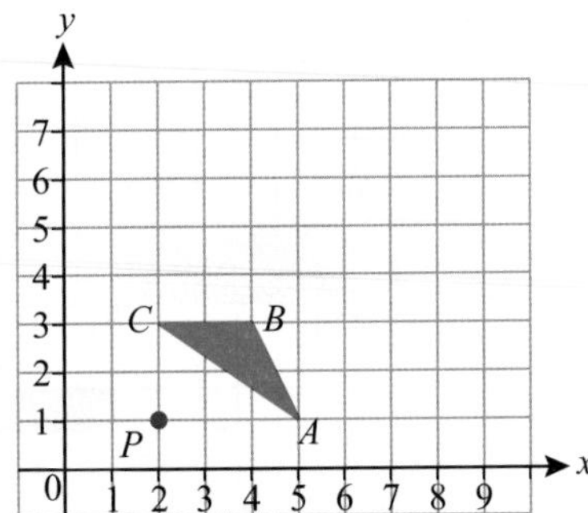

4 Copy the axes and shape onto squared paper. Draw the image of ΔDEF under an enlargement with scale factor -3 and centre of enlargement $P(2, 0)$.

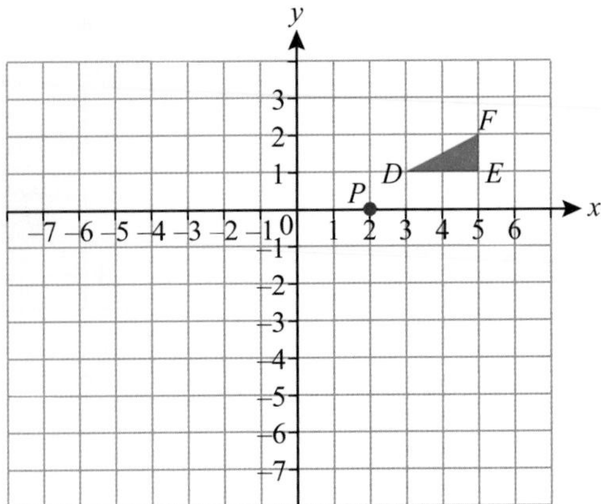

5 $\Delta G'H'I'$ is the image of ΔGHI under an enlargement. Find the scale factor of the enlargement and the co-ordinates of the centre of enlargement.

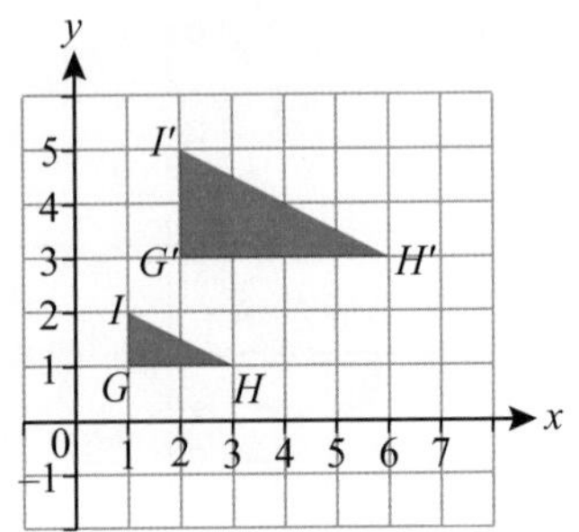

6 In the diagram, square $P'Q'R'S'$ is the image of square $PQRS$ under an enlargement. Find the scale factor of the enlargement and the co-ordinates of the centre of enlargement.

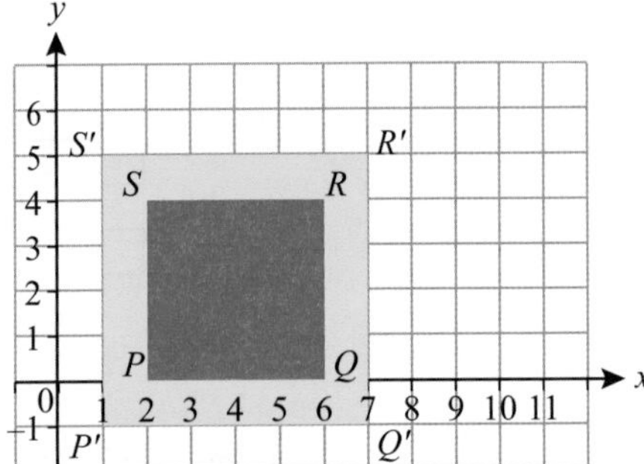

Living maths

7 Sheldon uses his computer software to enlarge and reduce pictures.

(a) He has a picture that is 10 cm long and 6 cm wide. If he enlarges it to be 16 cm long, how wide will it be?

(b) If Sheldon triples the width of the photograph, what will happen to its length?

(c) Is it possible to enlarge the picture by increasing the length and leaving the width the same? Give a reason for your answer.

(d) Sheldon needs to reduce the picture so it is a quarter of its original size. What will the new dimensions be?

23.2 Vectors

Some quantities are best described by giving both a **magnitude** (size) and a direction. For example, a wind speed of 35 km/h from the southeast or an acceleration upwards of 2 m/s^2. Force, velocity, displacement and acceleration are all **vector quantities**.

Other quantities such as time, temperature, speed, mass and area can be described by only giving their magnitude (they don't have a direction). In Mathematics, these quantities are called **scalars**.

In Mathematics, a vector is an ordered pair of numbers that can be used to describe a translation. The ordered pair gives both magnitude and direction.

Vector notation

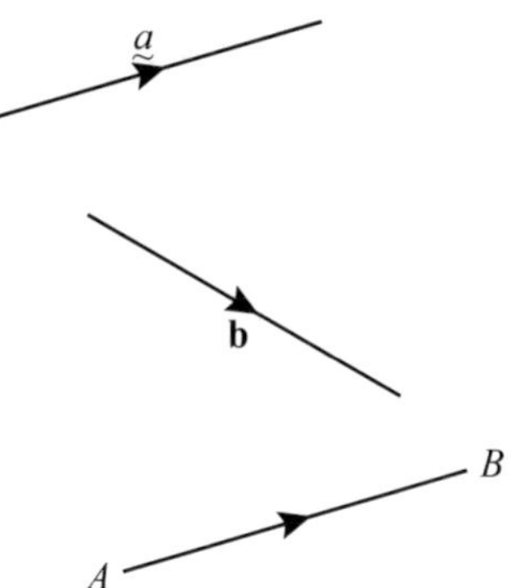

Vectors can be represented by a directed line segment as shown in the diagrams on the right. Note that the notation is either a small letter with a wavy line beneath it or a bold letter: e.g. $\underset{\sim}{a}$ or ***a***.

Vectors can also be represented by a named line such as *AB*. In such cases, the vector is denoted by **AB** or $\overrightarrow{AB}$. The order of letters is important because they give the direction of the line. $\overrightarrow{AB}$ is not the same as $\overrightarrow{BA}$.

Writing vectors as number pairs

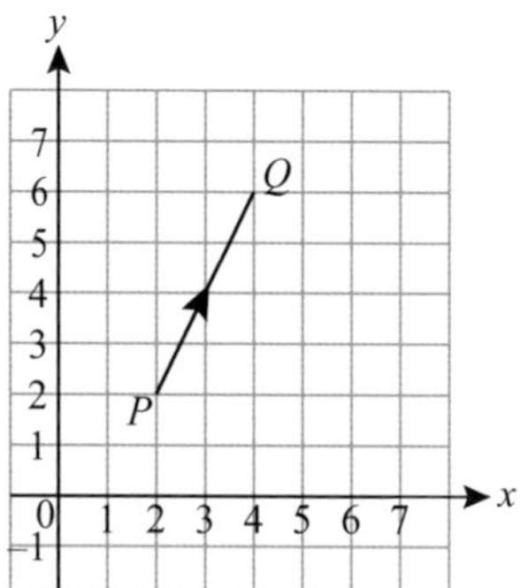

Vectors can also be written as a **column vector** using number pair notation. Look at line *PQ* on the diagram.

This line represents the translation of *P* to *Q*. The translation is two units in the positive *x*-direction and four units in the positive *y*-direction. This can be written as the ordered pair $\begin{pmatrix} 2 \\ 4 \end{pmatrix}$.

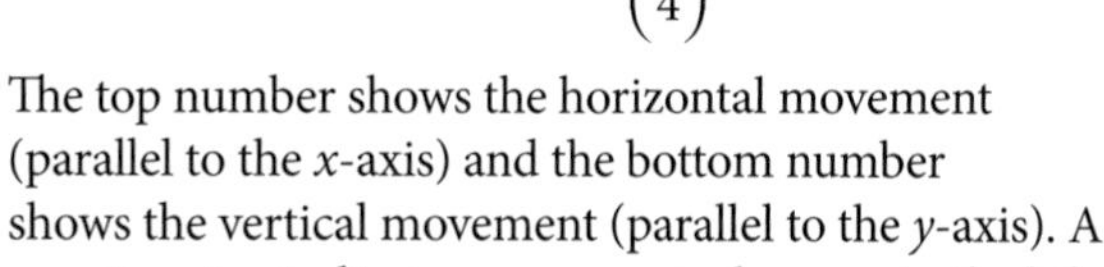

The top number shows the horizontal movement (parallel to the *x*-axis) and the bottom number shows the vertical movement (parallel to the *y*-axis). A negative sign indicates movements down or to the left.

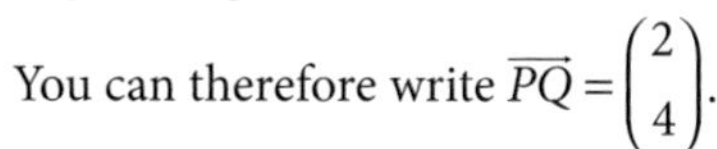

You can therefore write $\overrightarrow{PQ} = \begin{pmatrix} 2 \\ 4 \end{pmatrix}$.

Worked example 7

Express $\overrightarrow{RS}$ and $\overrightarrow{LM}$ as column vectors.

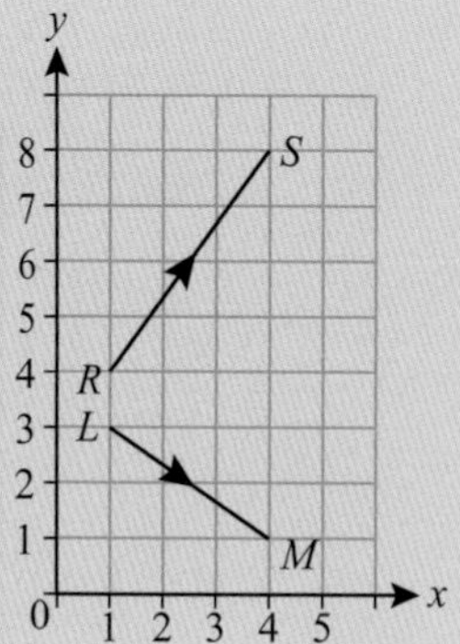

$\overrightarrow{RS} = \begin{pmatrix} 3 \\ 4 \end{pmatrix}$	Translation from *R* to *S* is three units right and four up.
$\overrightarrow{LM} = \begin{pmatrix} 3 \\ -2 \end{pmatrix}$ 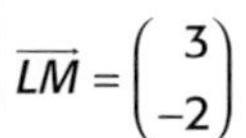	Translation from *L* to *M* is three units right and two down.

Worked example 8

Draw the column vectors $\begin{pmatrix} 1 \\ 3 \end{pmatrix}$ and $\begin{pmatrix} -2 \\ -4 \end{pmatrix}$.

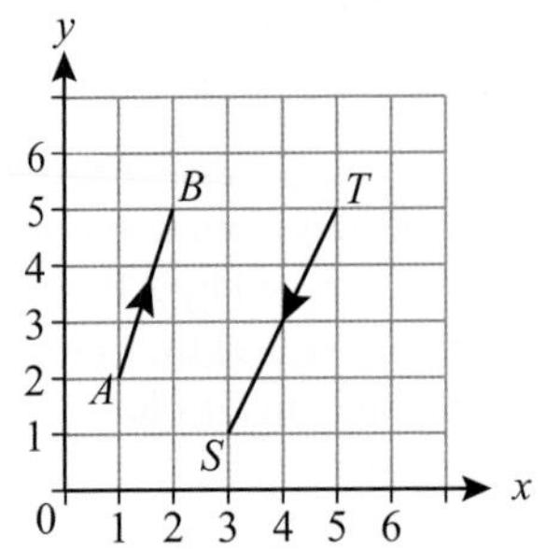

Start at any point, for example A, and move one right and three up to B. Join the points and indicate the direction using an arrow.

Start at any point, for example T, and move two left and then four down to S. Join the points and indicate the direction using an arrow.

Using vectors to describe a translation

You have already seen that column vectors can be used to describe translations.

In the diagram, ΔABC is translated to $\Delta A'B'C'$. All points on the object have moved two units to the right and three units upwards, so the column vector that describes this translation is $\begin{pmatrix} 2 \\ 3 \end{pmatrix}$.

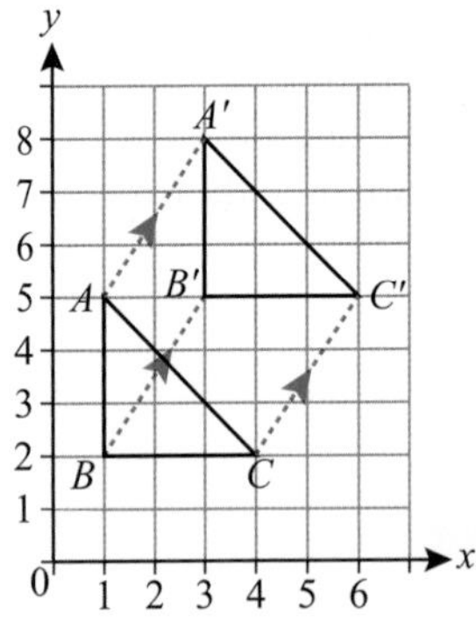

Worked example 9

Square R is to be translated to square S.
Find the column vector for the translation.

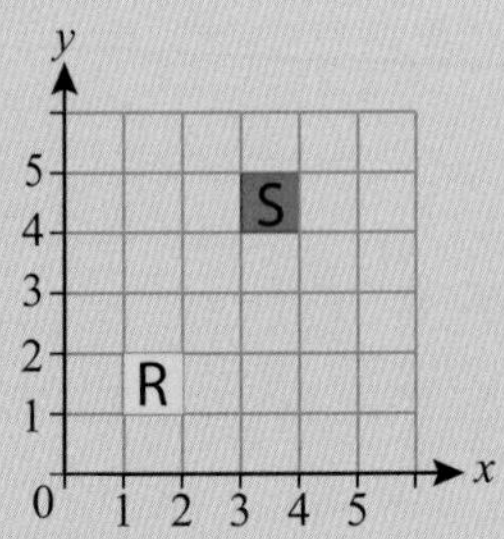

The column vector is $\begin{pmatrix} 2 \\ 3 \end{pmatrix}$.

Use one vertex of the object and the same vertex in its image to work out the translation.

Exercise 23.5

1 Write a column vector for each of the vectors shown on the diagram.

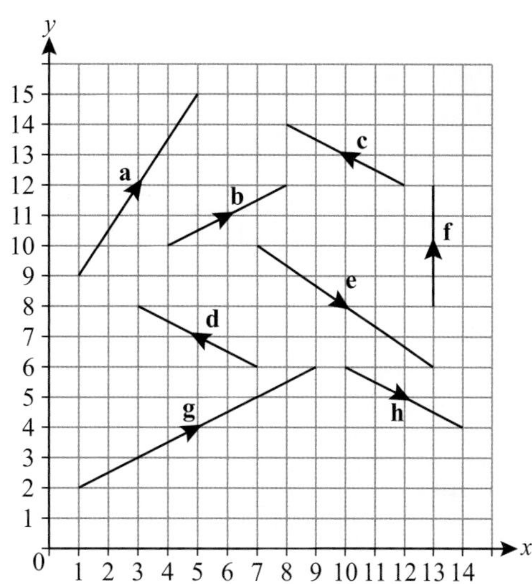

2 Represent these vectors on squared paper.

(a) $\overrightarrow{AB} = \begin{pmatrix} 5 \\ 2 \end{pmatrix}$ (b) $\overrightarrow{CD} = \begin{pmatrix} 2 \\ 2 \end{pmatrix}$ (c) $\overrightarrow{PQ} = \begin{pmatrix} -1 \\ 3 \end{pmatrix}$ (d) $\overrightarrow{RS} = \begin{pmatrix} 0 \\ 3 \end{pmatrix}$

(e) $\overrightarrow{TU} = \begin{pmatrix} -2 \\ 0 \end{pmatrix}$ (f) $\overrightarrow{MN} = \begin{pmatrix} -2 \\ -4 \end{pmatrix}$ (g) $\overrightarrow{KL} = \begin{pmatrix} 0 \\ -5 \end{pmatrix}$ (h) $\overrightarrow{VW} = \begin{pmatrix} -3 \\ -3 \end{pmatrix}$

(i) $\overrightarrow{EF} = \begin{pmatrix} 4 \\ 0 \end{pmatrix}$ (j) $\overrightarrow{JL} = \begin{pmatrix} -3 \\ -2 \end{pmatrix}$ (k) $\overrightarrow{MP} = \begin{pmatrix} -5 \\ 0 \end{pmatrix}$ (l) $\overrightarrow{QT} = \begin{pmatrix} -4 \\ 2 \end{pmatrix}$

3 In the diagram, *ABCD* is a parallelogram. Write column vectors for the following:

(a) $\overrightarrow{AB}$ and $\overrightarrow{DC}$

(b) $\overrightarrow{BC}$ and $\overrightarrow{AD}$.

(c) What can you say about the two pairs of vectors?

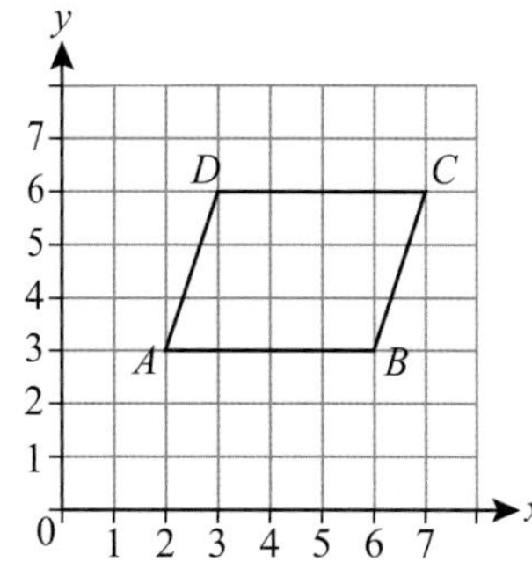

4 In the diagrams below, shapes *A*, *B*, *C*, *D*, *E* and *F* are mapped onto images *A'*, *B'*, *C'*, *D'*, *E'* and *F'* by translation. Find the column vector for the translation in each case.

(a)

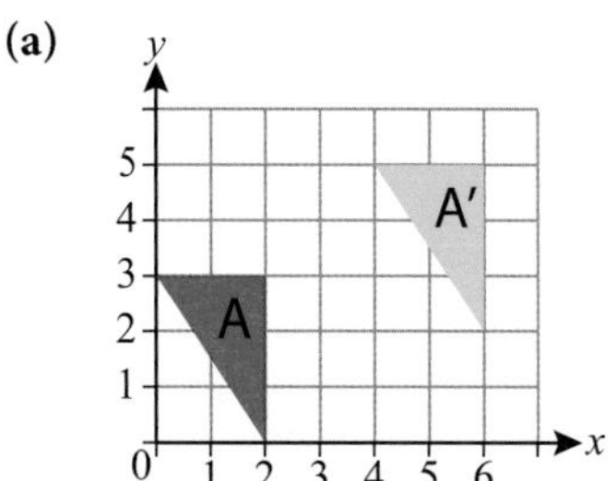

(b)

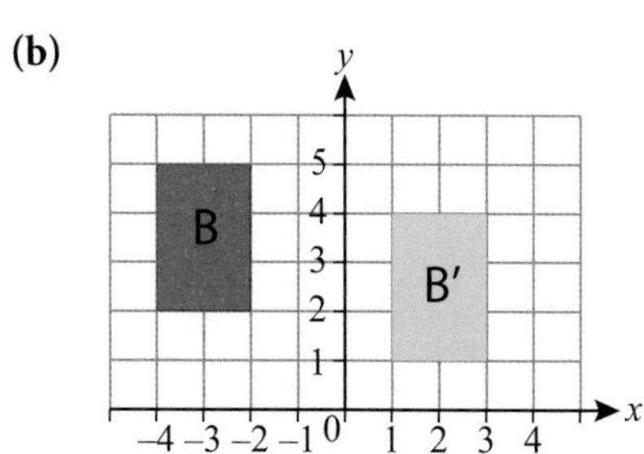

(c)

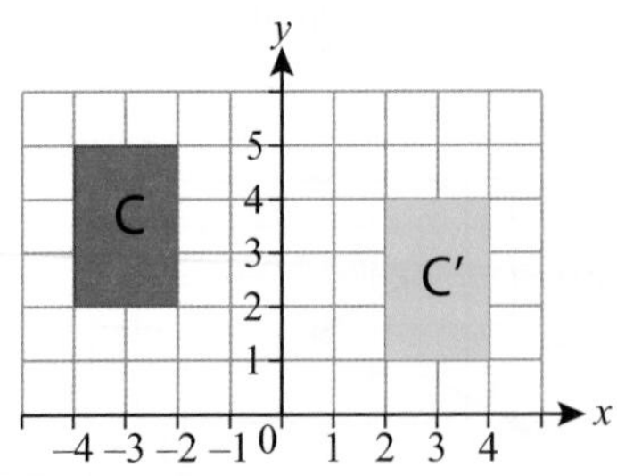

(d)

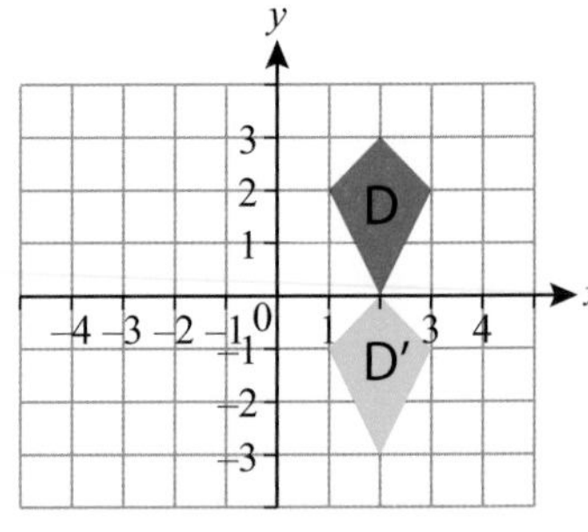

(e)

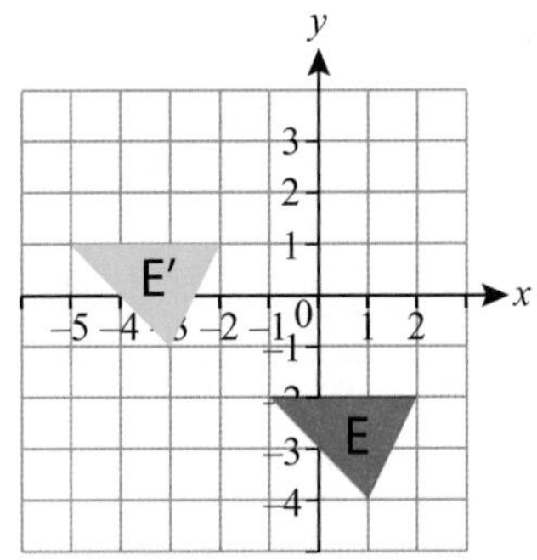

(f)

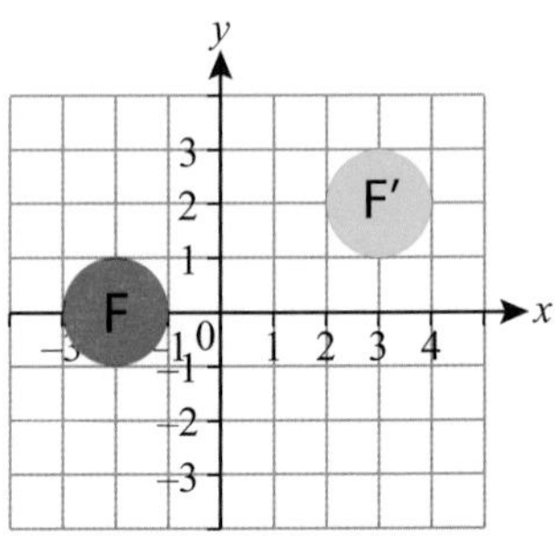

Equal vectors

Equal vectors have the same size (magnitude) and direction. As vectors are usually independent of position, they can start at any point. The same vector can be at many places in a diagram.

In the diagram, $\overrightarrow{AB}$, $\overrightarrow{CD}$, $\overrightarrow{XY}$, $\overrightarrow{LM}$ and $\overrightarrow{RS}$ are equal vectors.

$\overrightarrow{AB} = \overrightarrow{CD} = \overrightarrow{XY} = \overrightarrow{LM} = \overrightarrow{RS} = \begin{pmatrix} 1 \\ 2 \end{pmatrix}$

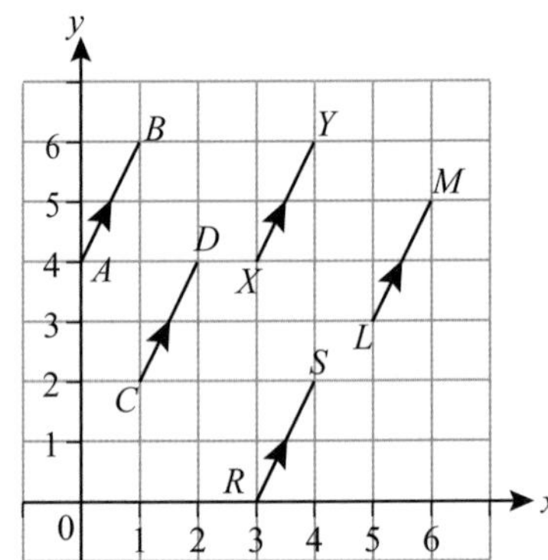

Multiplying a vector by a scalar

Remember a scalar is basically just a number. It has magnitude but no direction.

Look at this diagram. Vector $\overrightarrow{AC}$ is two times as long as vector $\overrightarrow{AB}$.

You can say:

$\overrightarrow{AC} = 2\overrightarrow{AB} = 2\begin{pmatrix} 2 \\ 1 \end{pmatrix} = \begin{pmatrix} 4 \\ 2 \end{pmatrix}$.

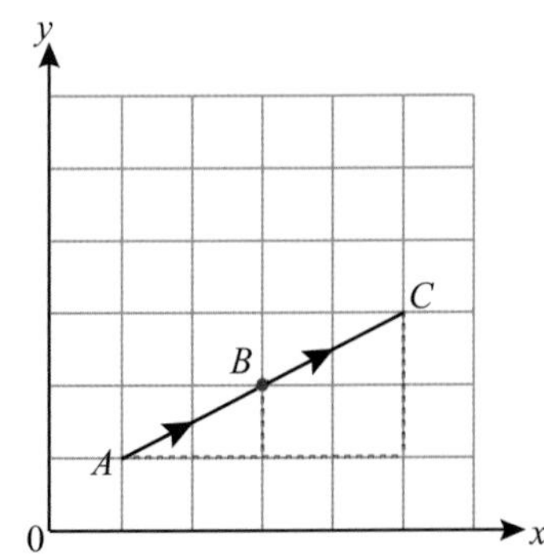

Here is another example.

A force, represented by vector **f**, is needed to move a 1 kg concrete block.

If you want to move a 2 kg concrete block, you would need to apply twice the force. In other words, you would need to apply **f** + **f** or 2**f**.

A force of 2**f** would have the same direction as **f**, but it would be twice its magnitude.

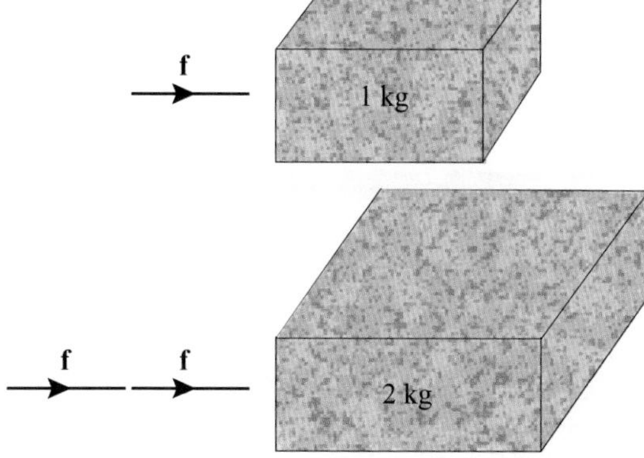

Multiplying any vector $\begin{pmatrix} x \\ y \end{pmatrix}$ by a scalar k, gives $k\begin{pmatrix} x \\ y \end{pmatrix} = \begin{pmatrix} kx \\ ky \end{pmatrix}$.

Vectors cannot be multiplied by each other, but they can be multiplied by a constant factor or scalar.

Vector **a** multiplied by 2 is the vector 2**a**. Vector 2**a** is twice as long as vector **a**, but they have the same direction. In other words, they are either parallel or in a straight line.

If $\mathbf{a} = \begin{pmatrix} 3 \\ 2 \end{pmatrix}$ then $2\mathbf{a} = 2\begin{pmatrix} 3 \\ 2 \end{pmatrix} = \begin{pmatrix} 6 \\ 4 \end{pmatrix}$.

Vector **a** multiplied by –1 is the vector –**a**, opposite in direction to **a**, but with the same magnitude as **a**.

*k***a** (where *k* is positive [+]) is in the same direction as **a** and *k* times as long. When *k* is negative [–], then *k***a** is opposite in direction to **a** but still *k* times as long.

Worked example 10

If $\mathbf{u} = \begin{pmatrix} 8 \\ -4 \end{pmatrix}$, find $\frac{1}{4}\mathbf{u}$.

$$\frac{1}{4}\mathbf{u} = \frac{1}{4}\begin{pmatrix} 8 \\ -4 \end{pmatrix} = \begin{pmatrix} \frac{1}{4} \times 8 \\ \frac{1}{4} \times -4 \end{pmatrix} = \begin{pmatrix} 2 \\ -1 \end{pmatrix}$$

Worked example 11

If $\mathbf{v} = \begin{pmatrix} -3 \\ 2 \end{pmatrix}$, find $-5\mathbf{v}$.

$$-5\mathbf{v} = -5\begin{pmatrix} -3 \\ 2 \end{pmatrix} = \begin{pmatrix} -5 \times -3 \\ -5 \times 2 \end{pmatrix} = \begin{pmatrix} 15 \\ -10 \end{pmatrix}$$

Exercise 23.6

1 If $\mathbf{a} = \begin{pmatrix} 3 \\ -7 \end{pmatrix}$, calculate:

(a) $3\mathbf{a}$ (b) $\frac{1}{2}\mathbf{a}$ (c) $-2\mathbf{a}$ (d) $-\mathbf{a}$ (e) $-\frac{3}{4}\mathbf{a}$ (f) $1.5\mathbf{a}$

Living maths

2 The diagram shows a rectangular metal burglar bar. Each section of the burglar bar can be represented by a vector. Sections can also be compared in terms of vectors. So, for example, $\overrightarrow{AJ} = 3\overrightarrow{AD}$.

Copy and complete these comparisons:

(a) $\overrightarrow{DF} = \_\_\overrightarrow{JK}$ (b) $\overrightarrow{JQ} = \_\_\overrightarrow{JF}$ (c) $\overrightarrow{HP} = \_\_\overrightarrow{HF}$
(d) $2\overrightarrow{GO} = \_\_\overrightarrow{GC}$ (e) $3\overrightarrow{DG} = \_\_\overrightarrow{CL}$ (f) $6\overrightarrow{BE} = \_\_\overrightarrow{CL}$

3 If $\mathbf{a} = \begin{pmatrix} -1 \\ -4 \end{pmatrix}$ and $\mathbf{b} = \begin{pmatrix} 3 \\ 7 \end{pmatrix}$ calculate:

(a) $-2\mathbf{a}$ (b) $3\mathbf{b}$ (c) $\frac{3}{2}\mathbf{b}$ (d) $-\frac{3}{4}\mathbf{a}$ (e) $-1.5\mathbf{a}$

(f) $-12\mathbf{b}$ (g) $-\frac{3}{2}\mathbf{a}$ (h) $-\frac{5}{9}\mathbf{b}$

Addition of vectors

In this diagram, point *A* is translated to point *B* and then translated again to end up at point *C*. However, if you translated the point directly from *A* to *C*, you end up at the same point. In other words, $\overline{AB} + \overline{BC} = \overline{AC}$.

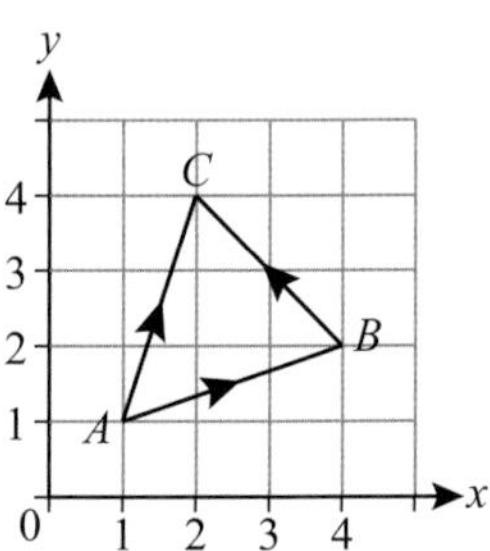

You can represent each translation as a column vector:

$$\overline{AB} = \begin{pmatrix} 3 \\ 1 \end{pmatrix}, \quad \overline{BC} = \begin{pmatrix} -2 \\ 2 \end{pmatrix}, \quad \overline{AC} = \begin{pmatrix} 1 \\ 3 \end{pmatrix}.$$

You know that $\overrightarrow{AB} + \overrightarrow{BC} = \overrightarrow{AC}$, so:

$$\begin{pmatrix} 3 \\ 1 \end{pmatrix} + \begin{pmatrix} -2 \\ 2 \end{pmatrix} = \begin{pmatrix} 1 \\ 3 \end{pmatrix}$$ Add the corresponding *x* (top) and *y* (bottom) values.

So, to add the vectors, you add the corresponding *x* and *y* co-ordinates.

$$\begin{pmatrix} x_1 \\ y_1 \end{pmatrix} + \begin{pmatrix} x_2 \\ y_2 \end{pmatrix} = \begin{pmatrix} x_1 + x_2 \\ y_1 + y_2 \end{pmatrix}$$

This is called the 'nose to tail' method or the triangle law.

Subtraction of vectors

Subtracting a vector is the same as adding its negative. So $\mathbf{a} - \mathbf{b} = \mathbf{a} + (-\mathbf{b})$.

Think about $\overrightarrow{AC} - \overrightarrow{AB}$:

adding the negative of $\overrightarrow{AB}$ is the same as adding $\overrightarrow{BA}$.

$\therefore\ \overrightarrow{AC} - \overrightarrow{AB} = \overrightarrow{AC} + \overrightarrow{BA}$

If you rearrange the vectors, you can apply the nose to tail rule and add them:

$\overrightarrow{AC} - \overrightarrow{AB} = \overrightarrow{BA} + \overrightarrow{AC} = \overrightarrow{BC}$

Any section of a line joining two points is called a line segment.

Worked example 12

In the figure, the various line segments represent vectors.

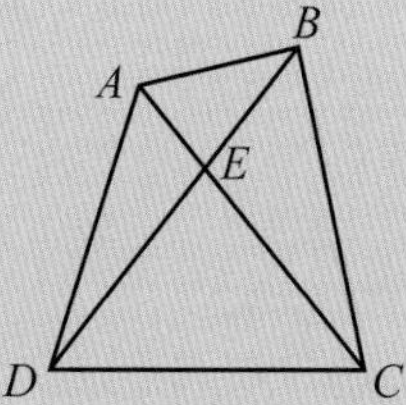

Find in the figure directed line segments equal to the following:

(a) $\overrightarrow{AE} + \overrightarrow{EC}$ **(b)** $\overrightarrow{DB} + \overrightarrow{BE}$ **(c)** $\overrightarrow{AD} + \overrightarrow{DB} + \overrightarrow{BC}$

(d) $\overrightarrow{CB} + \overrightarrow{BE} + \overrightarrow{EA} + \overrightarrow{AD}$

(a) $\overrightarrow{AE} + \overrightarrow{EC} = \overrightarrow{AC}$

(b) $\overrightarrow{DB} + \overrightarrow{BE} = \overrightarrow{DE}$ (If you travel from D to B and then from B to E, you have gone back on yourself and ended up at E, which is the same as travelling from D to E.)

(c) $\overrightarrow{AD} + \overrightarrow{DB} + \overrightarrow{BC} = \overrightarrow{AC}$ ($\overrightarrow{AD} + \overrightarrow{DB} = \overrightarrow{AB}$, and $\overrightarrow{AB} + \overrightarrow{BC} = \overrightarrow{AC} \therefore \overrightarrow{AD} + \overrightarrow{DB} + \overrightarrow{BC} = \overrightarrow{AC}$)

(d) $\overrightarrow{CB} + \overrightarrow{BE} + \overrightarrow{EA} + \overrightarrow{AD} = \overrightarrow{CE} + \overrightarrow{EA} + \overrightarrow{AD} = \overrightarrow{CA} + \overrightarrow{AD} = \overrightarrow{CD}$

Worked example 13

If $\mathbf{a} = \begin{pmatrix} 3 \\ 4 \end{pmatrix}$ and $\mathbf{b} = \begin{pmatrix} 2 \\ -1 \end{pmatrix}$, find the column vectors equal to:

(a) $\mathbf{a} + \mathbf{b}$ **(b)** $\mathbf{a} - \mathbf{b}$ **(c)** $3\mathbf{a}$ **(d)** $\mathbf{a} + 4\mathbf{b}$ **(e)** $2\mathbf{a} - 3\mathbf{b}$

(a) $\mathbf{a} + \mathbf{b} = \begin{pmatrix} 3 \\ 4 \end{pmatrix} + \begin{pmatrix} 2 \\ -1 \end{pmatrix} = \begin{pmatrix} 3+2 \\ 4-1 \end{pmatrix} = \begin{pmatrix} 5 \\ 3 \end{pmatrix}$

(b) $\mathbf{a} - \mathbf{b} = \begin{pmatrix} 3 \\ 4 \end{pmatrix} - \begin{pmatrix} 2 \\ -1 \end{pmatrix} = \begin{pmatrix} 3-2 \\ 4+1 \end{pmatrix} = \begin{pmatrix} 1 \\ 5 \end{pmatrix}$ $\left(\mathbf{a} - \mathbf{b} = \mathbf{a} + (-\mathbf{b}); -\mathbf{b} \text{ is same as } \begin{pmatrix} -2 \\ 1 \end{pmatrix}\right)$

(c) $3\mathbf{a} = 3\begin{pmatrix} 3 \\ 4 \end{pmatrix} = \begin{pmatrix} 3 \times 3 \\ 3 \times 4 \end{pmatrix} = \begin{pmatrix} 9 \\ 12 \end{pmatrix}$

(d) $\mathbf{a} + 4\mathbf{b} = \begin{pmatrix} 3 \\ 4 \end{pmatrix} + 4\begin{pmatrix} 2 \\ -1 \end{pmatrix} = \begin{pmatrix} 3+8 \\ 4+(-4) \end{pmatrix} = \begin{pmatrix} 11 \\ 0 \end{pmatrix}$

(e) $2\mathbf{a} - 3\mathbf{b} = 2\begin{pmatrix} 3 \\ 4 \end{pmatrix} - 3\begin{pmatrix} 2 \\ -1 \end{pmatrix} = \begin{pmatrix} 6 \\ 8 \end{pmatrix} - \begin{pmatrix} 6 \\ -3 \end{pmatrix} \begin{pmatrix} 0 \\ 11 \end{pmatrix}$

Worked example 14

If a question on vectors does not provide a diagram, you should draw one.

OACB is a parallelogram in which $\overrightarrow{OA} = \mathbf{a}$ and $\overrightarrow{OB} = \mathbf{b}$.
M is the midpoint of *BC* and *N* is the midpoint of *AC*.

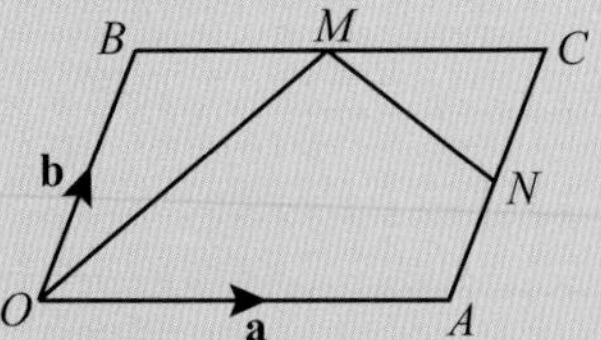

(a) Find in terms of **a** and **b**:

(i) $\overrightarrow{OM}$ **(ii)** $\overrightarrow{MN}$

(b) Show that $\overrightarrow{OM} + \overrightarrow{MN} = \overrightarrow{OA} + \overrightarrow{AN}$.

(a) **(i)** $\overrightarrow{OM} = \overrightarrow{OB} + \overrightarrow{BM}$

$\overrightarrow{OB} = \mathbf{b}$

M is the midpoint *BC*, so $\overrightarrow{BM} = \frac{1}{2}\overrightarrow{BC}$

$\therefore\ \overrightarrow{OM} = \mathbf{b} + \frac{1}{2}\mathbf{a}$

(ii) $\overrightarrow{MN} = \overrightarrow{MC} + \overrightarrow{CN} = \frac{1}{2}\overrightarrow{BC} + \frac{1}{2}\overrightarrow{CA}$

$= \frac{1}{2}\mathbf{a} + -\frac{1}{2}\mathbf{b}\ (\overrightarrow{CA} = -\overrightarrow{AC} = -\overrightarrow{OB})$

$= \frac{1}{2}\mathbf{a} - \frac{1}{2}\mathbf{b} = \frac{1}{2}(\mathbf{a} - \mathbf{b})$

(b) $\overrightarrow{OM} + \overrightarrow{MN} = (\mathbf{b} + \frac{1}{2}\mathbf{a}) + (\frac{1}{2}\mathbf{a} - \frac{1}{2}\mathbf{b})$

$= \mathbf{a} + \frac{1}{2}\mathbf{b}$

$\overrightarrow{OA} + \overrightarrow{AN} = \mathbf{a} + \frac{1}{2}\mathbf{b}$

$\therefore\ \overrightarrow{OM} + \overrightarrow{MN} = \overrightarrow{OA} + \overrightarrow{AN}$.

Exercise 23.7

1 $\mathbf{p} = \begin{pmatrix} 4 \\ -2 \end{pmatrix}$ and $\mathbf{q} = \begin{pmatrix} -1 \\ -3 \end{pmatrix}$.

Express in column vector form:

(a) $3\mathbf{p}$ (b) $\mathbf{p} + \mathbf{q}$

2 Given that $\mathbf{a} = \begin{pmatrix} 4 \\ -2 \end{pmatrix}$ and $\mathbf{b} = \begin{pmatrix} -4 \\ 3 \end{pmatrix}$, express $2\mathbf{a} - \mathbf{b}$ as a column vector.

3 If $\mathbf{a} = \begin{pmatrix} 8 \\ 10 \end{pmatrix}$, $\mathbf{b} = \begin{pmatrix} 4 \\ -2 \end{pmatrix}$ and $\mathbf{c} = \begin{pmatrix} 0 \\ -1 \end{pmatrix}$, calculate:

(a) $\mathbf{a} + \mathbf{b}$ (b) $2\mathbf{a} - 2\mathbf{b}$ (c) $\mathbf{b} - \mathbf{a}$

(d) $\frac{1}{2}\mathbf{b} - \mathbf{c}$ (e) $\mathbf{a} - 2(\mathbf{b} - \mathbf{c})$ (f) $2\mathbf{a} - \mathbf{c}$

(g) $\frac{1}{2}(2\mathbf{a} + \mathbf{b})$ (h) $\mathbf{c} + \frac{1}{2}(\mathbf{b} - \mathbf{a})$

4 In the diagram, BCE and ACD are straight lines. $\overrightarrow{AB} = 2\mathbf{a}$ and $\overrightarrow{BC} = 3\mathbf{b}$. The point C divides AD in the ratio 2 : 1 and divides BE in the ratio 3 : 1. Express in terms of **a** and **b**, the vectors:

(a) $\overrightarrow{AC}$ (b) $\overrightarrow{CD}$
(c) $\overrightarrow{CE}$ (d) $\overrightarrow{ED}$

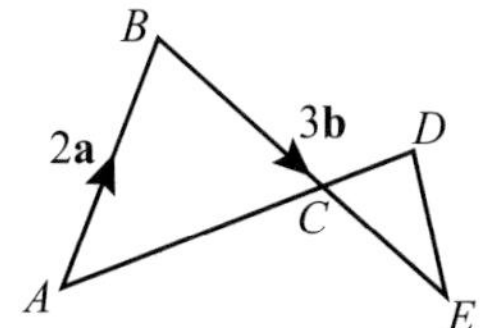

5 In ΔXYZ, $\overrightarrow{XY} = \mathbf{x}$ and $\overrightarrow{YZ} = \mathbf{y}$ and $WZ = \frac{1}{4}(XZ)$. Find in terms of **x** and **y**:

(a) $\overrightarrow{XZ}$ (b) $\overrightarrow{XW}$ (c) $\overrightarrow{YW}$

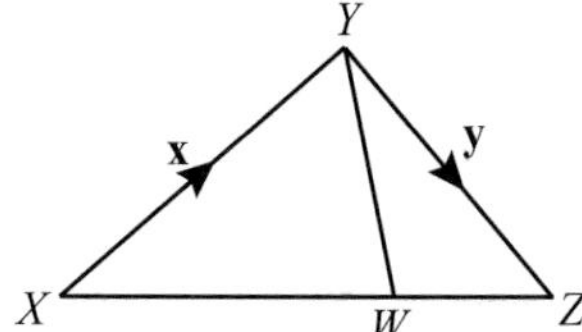

6 $OACB$ is a parallelogram in which $\overrightarrow{OA} = 2\mathbf{p}$ and $\overrightarrow{OB} = 2\mathbf{q}$.

M is the midpoint of BC and N is the midpoint of AC.

Find in terms of **p** and **q**:

(a) $\overrightarrow{AB}$ (b) $\overrightarrow{ON}$ (c) $\overrightarrow{MN}$.

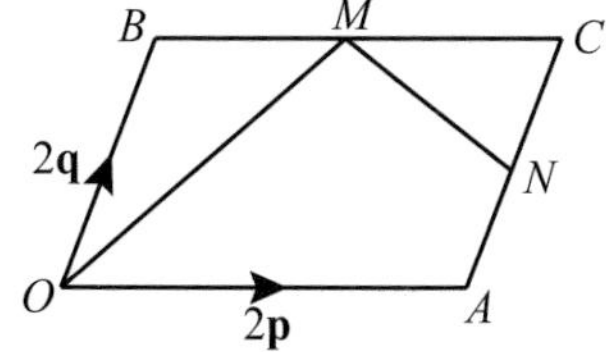

The magnitude of a vector

The magnitude of a vector is sometimes called the modulus.

The magnitude of a vector is its length. The notation $|\overrightarrow{AB}|$ or $|\mathbf{a}|$ is used to write the magnitude of a vector ($\overrightarrow{AB}$).

You use Pythagoras' theorem to calculate the magnitude of a vector.

In general, if $\overrightarrow{AB} = \begin{pmatrix} x \\ y \end{pmatrix}$ then $|\overrightarrow{AB}| = \sqrt{x^2 + y^2}$.

Worked example 15

Find the magnitude of the vector $\overrightarrow{AB} = \begin{pmatrix} 3 \\ -4 \end{pmatrix}$.

Draw $\overrightarrow{AB}$ as the hypotenuse of a right-angled triangle.

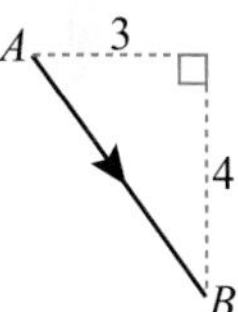

$AB^2 = 3^2 + 4^2$ (Pythagoras' theorem)
$AB^2 = 9 + 16$
$AB^2 = 25$
$AB = 5$

$\therefore |\overrightarrow{AB}| = 5$ units.

Worked example 16

If $\mathbf{a} = \begin{pmatrix} -5 \\ 12 \end{pmatrix}$ find $|\mathbf{a}|$.

$|\mathbf{a}| = \sqrt{(-5)^2 + (12)^2}$
$= \sqrt{169}$
$= 13$

Position vectors

A vector that starts from the origin (O) is called a position vector. On this diagram, point A has the position vector $\overrightarrow{OA}$ or **a**.

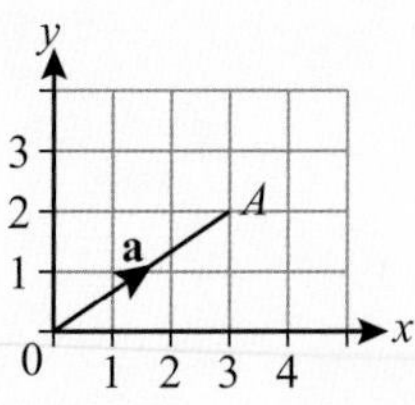

If $\mathbf{a} = \begin{pmatrix} 3 \\ 2 \end{pmatrix}$ then the co-ordinates of point A will be (3, 2).

Because the co-ordinates of the point A are the same as the components of the column vector $\begin{pmatrix} 3 \\ 2 \end{pmatrix}$ you can use position vectors to find the magnitude of any vector.

Worked example 17

The position vector of A is $\begin{pmatrix} 3 \\ 2 \end{pmatrix}$ and the position vector of B is $\begin{pmatrix} -2 \\ 4 \end{pmatrix}$.

Find the vector $2\overrightarrow{AB}$.

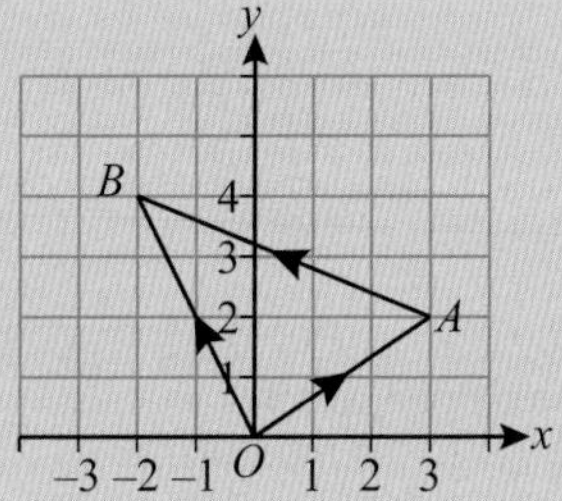

$\overrightarrow{OA} = \begin{pmatrix} 3 \\ 2 \end{pmatrix}$ and $\overrightarrow{OB} = \begin{pmatrix} -2 \\ 4 \end{pmatrix}$

$\overrightarrow{AB} = \overrightarrow{AO} + \overrightarrow{OB} = -\overrightarrow{OA} + \overrightarrow{OB} = \overrightarrow{OB} - \overrightarrow{OA}$

$= \begin{pmatrix} -2 \\ 4 \end{pmatrix} - \begin{pmatrix} 3 \\ 2 \end{pmatrix} = \begin{pmatrix} -5 \\ 2 \end{pmatrix}$

So, $2\overrightarrow{AB} = 2\begin{pmatrix} -5 \\ 2 \end{pmatrix} = \begin{pmatrix} -10 \\ 4 \end{pmatrix}$.

You could also find the column vector for $\overrightarrow{AB}$ by counting the movements parallel to the x-axis followed by those parallel to the y-axis.

Movement parallel to x-axis = −5 units. Movement parallel to the y-axis = 2 units

$\overrightarrow{AB} = \begin{pmatrix} -5 \\ 2 \end{pmatrix}$

so, $2\overrightarrow{AB} = 2\begin{pmatrix} -5 \\ 2 \end{pmatrix} = \begin{pmatrix} -10 \\ 4 \end{pmatrix}$.

Worked example 18

If A is point (−1, −2) and B is (5, 6), find $|\overrightarrow{AB}|$.

$\overrightarrow{OA} = \begin{pmatrix} -1 \\ -2 \end{pmatrix}$ and $\overrightarrow{OB} = \begin{pmatrix} 5 \\ 6 \end{pmatrix}$.

$\overrightarrow{AB} = \overrightarrow{AO} + \overrightarrow{OB} = -\overrightarrow{OA} + \overrightarrow{OB}$

$= \begin{pmatrix} -(-1) + 5 \\ -(-2) + 6 \end{pmatrix} = \begin{pmatrix} 6 \\ 8 \end{pmatrix}$

$|\overrightarrow{AB}| = \sqrt{6^2 + 8^2} = \sqrt{36 + 64} = \sqrt{100} = 10$

Exercise 23.8

1 Calculate the magnitude of each vector. Give your answers to 2 decimal places where necessary.

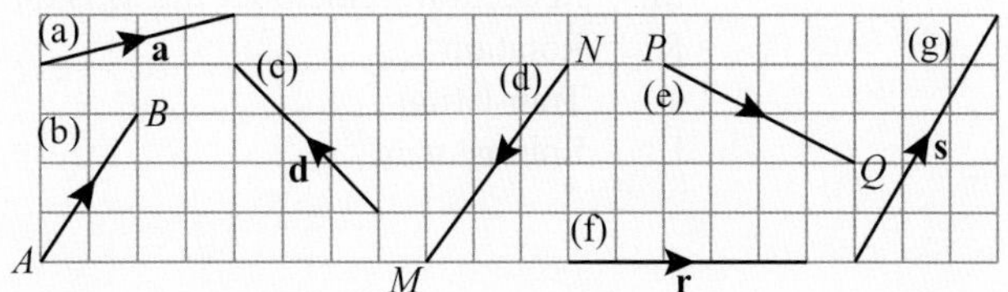

2 Find the magnitude of the following vectors. Give your answers to 2 decimal places where necessary.

(a) $\mathbf{a} = \begin{pmatrix} 5 \\ 9 \end{pmatrix}$ **(b)** $\overrightarrow{MN} = \begin{pmatrix} 7 \\ 11 \end{pmatrix}$ **(c)** $\mathbf{x} = \begin{pmatrix} -3 \\ 4 \end{pmatrix}$ **(d)** $\overrightarrow{PQ} = \begin{pmatrix} -6 \\ -8 \end{pmatrix}$

3 O is the point (0, 0), P is (3, 4), Q is (−5, 12) and R is (−8, −15).
Find the values of:

(a) $|\overrightarrow{OP}|$ **(b)** $|\overrightarrow{OQ}|$ **(c)** $|\overrightarrow{OR}|$

4 Points A, B and C have position vectors $\overrightarrow{OA} = \begin{pmatrix} 4 \\ 2 \end{pmatrix}$, $\overrightarrow{OB} = \begin{pmatrix} -1 \\ 3 \end{pmatrix}$ and $\overrightarrow{OC} = \begin{pmatrix} 6 \\ -2 \end{pmatrix}$.

(a) Write down the co-ordinates of A, B and C.
(b) Write down the vectors $\overrightarrow{AB}$, $\overrightarrow{CB}$ and $\overrightarrow{AC}$ in column vector form.

5 $OATB$ is a parallelogram. M, N and P are midpoints of BT, AT and MN respectively. O is the origin and the position vectors of A and B are **a** and **b** respectively. Find in terms of **a** and/or **b**:

(a) $\overrightarrow{MT}$ **(b)** $\overrightarrow{TN}$ **(c)** $\overrightarrow{MN}$
(d) the position vector of P, giving your answer in simplest form.

6 Find the magnitude of:

(a) the vector joining the points (−3, −3) and (3, 5)
(b) the vector joining the points (−2, 6) and (3, −1).

Living maths

7 Vector **b** shows the velocity (in km/h) of a car on a highway. The sides of each square on the grid represent a speed of 20 km/h. Find the speed at which the car was travelling.

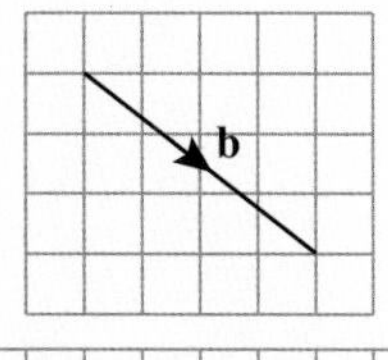

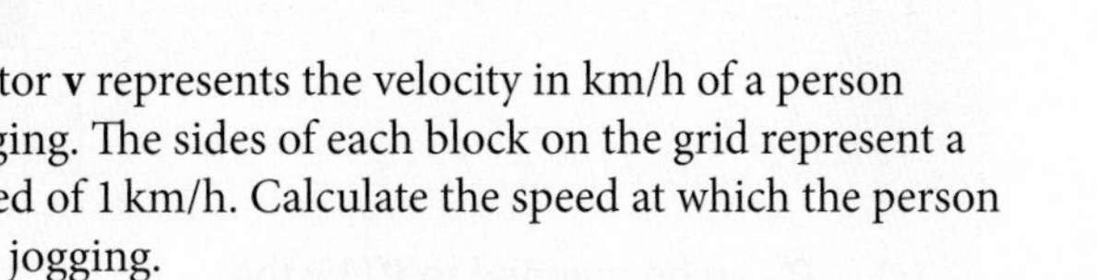

8 Vector **v** represents the velocity in km/h of a person jogging. The sides of each block on the grid represent a speed of 1 km/h. Calculate the speed at which the person was jogging.

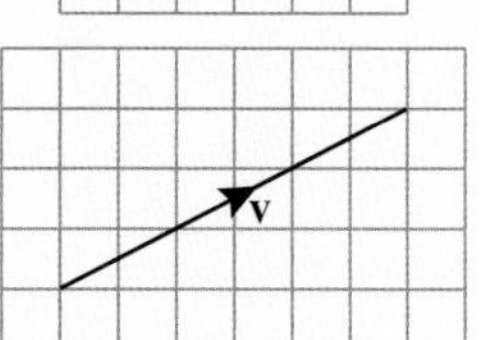

23.3 Combining transformations

You've already seen that an object can undergo a single transformation to map it to an image. An object can also undergo two transformations in succession. For example, it could be reflected in the x-axis and then rotated through a quarter turn, or it could be rotated and then reflected in the y-axis. Sometimes a combined transformation can be described by a single, equivalent transformation.

The following capital letters are conventionally used to represent different transformations:

M Reflection (remember the M is for mirror!)
R Rotation
T Translation
E Enlargement

Worked example 19

For the shape P shown in the diagram, let T be the translation $\begin{pmatrix} 2 \\ 1 \end{pmatrix}$ and M be the reflection in the y-axis.

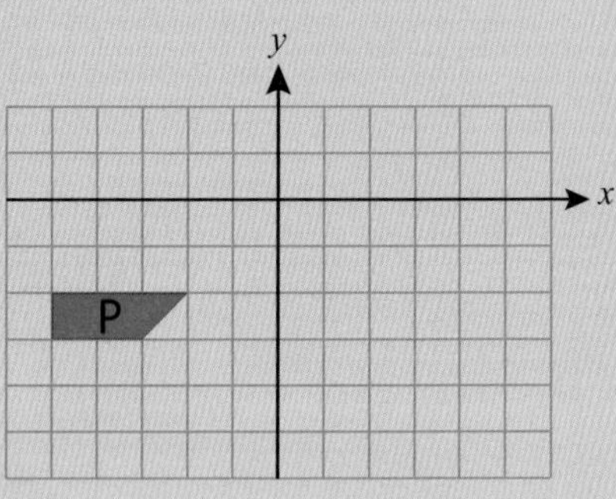

(a) Draw the image P' after the transformation TM(P).
(b) Draw the image P'' after the transformation MT(P).
(c) What single transformation maps P' onto P''?

(a) MT(P) means do T first then do M. Use a pencil. Do the first transformation and (faintly) draw the shape. Do the second transformation, draw the image. Label it correctly.

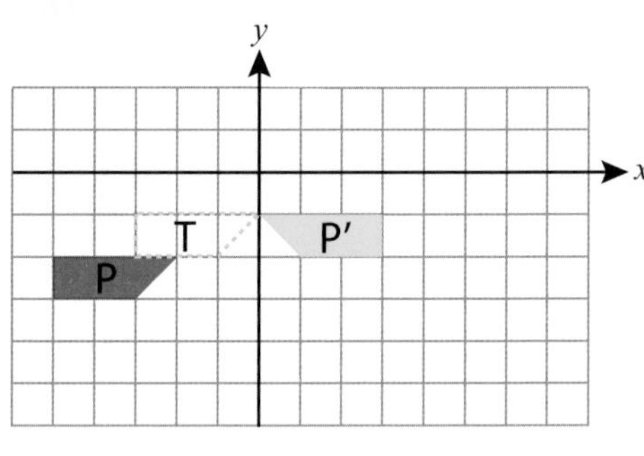

(b) TM(P) means do M first then do T. Use a pencil. Do the first transformation and (faintly) draw the shape. Do the second transformation, draw the image. Label it correctly.

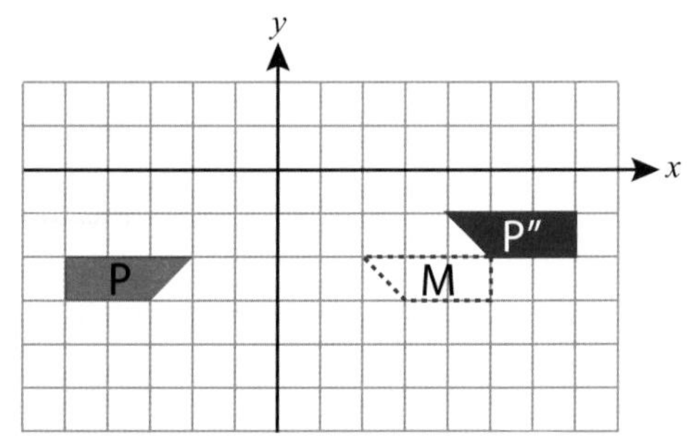

(c) P' can be mapped to P'' by the translation $\begin{pmatrix} 4 \\ 0 \end{pmatrix}$.

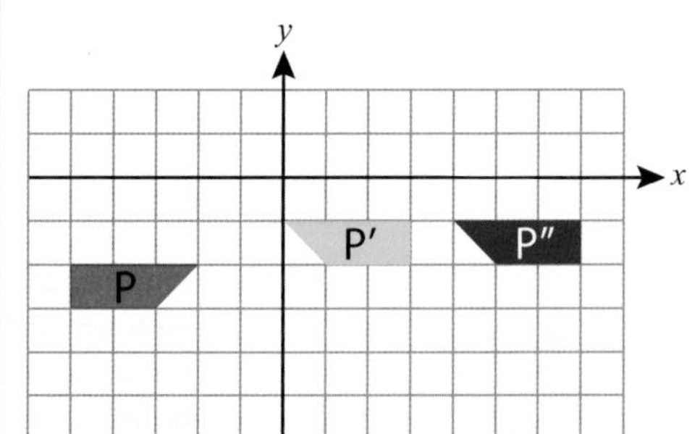

Exercise 23.9

1 ΔABC maps onto $A'B'C'$ after an enlargement of scale factor two from the centre of enlargement (2, 5). $A'B'C'$ is then mapped onto $A''B''C''$ by reflection in the line $x = 1$.

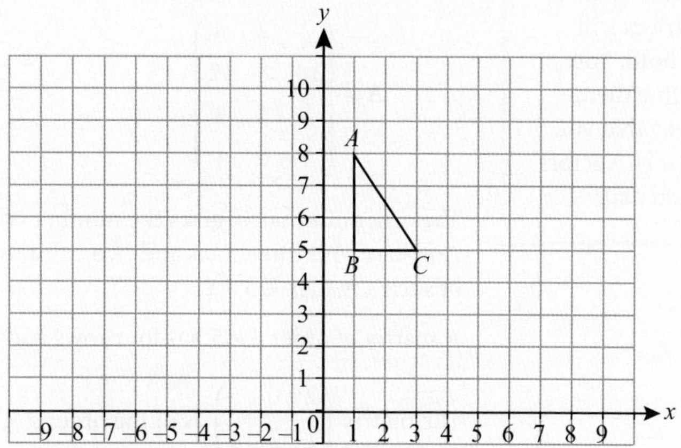

(a) Draw and label image $A'B'C'$.
(b) Draw and label the image $A''B''C''$.

2 A square $MNOP$ maps onto $M'N'O'P'$ after an enlargement of scale factor 1.5 with the centre of enlargement (3, 4). $M'N'O'P'$ is then rotated 180° about the point (0, 6) to give the image $M''N''O''P''$. Copy the diagram and show the position of both $M'N'O'P'$ and $M''N''O''P''$.

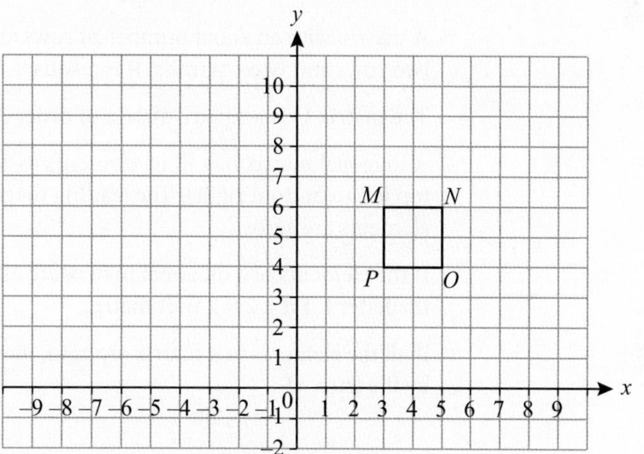

23.4 Matrices and matrix transformation

What is a matrix?

A set of numbers arranged in rows and columns enclosed in round or square brackets is called a **matrix**.

The matrix $\begin{pmatrix} 2 & 2 & 4 \\ 10 & 8 & 12 \\ 3 & 2 & 3 \\ 1 & 0 & 1 \end{pmatrix}$ has four rows and three columns.

Column 1, Column 2, Column 3

$$\begin{matrix} \text{Row 1} \rightarrow \\ \text{Row 2} \rightarrow \\ \text{Row 3} \rightarrow \\ \text{Row 4} \rightarrow \end{matrix} \begin{pmatrix} 2 & 2 & 4 \\ 10 & 8 & 12 \\ 3 & 2 & 3 \\ 1 & 0 & 1 \end{pmatrix}$$

> **Tip**
> All capital letters used to represent matrices will be printed in **bold**. You should underline them in the same way that you underline vectors. Vectors are matrices after all.

Each number in the array is called an entry or an element of the matrix.

A matrix is often denoted by a capital letter. For example, you can call the above matrix **A**.

$$\mathbf{A} = \begin{pmatrix} 2 & 2 & 4 \\ 10 & 8 & 12 \\ 3 & 2 & 3 \\ 1 & 0 & 1 \end{pmatrix}$$

The order of a matrix gives the number of rows followed by the number of columns in a matrix. A matrix with three rows and two columns is a three by two matrix or a 3×2 matrix. The order of such a matrix is 3×2.

A matrix of order 4×5 has four rows and five columns.

The matrix $\begin{pmatrix} 2 & 0 & 5 \\ 1 & 3 & 4 \end{pmatrix}$ is of the order 2×3. You say 'of the order two by three'.

Types of matrices

$$\mathbf{P} = \begin{pmatrix} 3 & 1 \\ 2 & 4 \end{pmatrix} \quad \mathbf{Q} = \begin{pmatrix} 4 & 1 & 0 \\ 5 & 3 & 1 \\ 1 & 2 & 5 \end{pmatrix} \quad \mathbf{C} = \begin{pmatrix} 4 & 0 & 0 \\ 0 & 3 & 0 \\ 0 & 0 & 5 \end{pmatrix} \quad \mathbf{I} = \begin{pmatrix} 1 & 0 \\ 0 & 1 \end{pmatrix} \quad \mathbf{O} = \begin{pmatrix} 0 & 0 \\ 0 & 0 \end{pmatrix}$$

A matrix with an equal number of rows and columns is called a square matrix. The matrix **P** has two rows and two columns. It is a square matrix of order 2×2.

The matrix **Q** is a square matrix of order 3×3.

A diagonal matrix has all its elements as zero except for those in the leading diagonal (from top left to bottom right). The leading diagonal elements in matrix **C** are 4, 3 and 5. All other elements are zeros.

If the elements of a diagonal matrix are all equal to one, it is called a unit matrix. It is denoted by the letter **I**. **I** is a 2×2 unit matrix.

If all the elements in a matrix are zero, then it is called a zero matrix or a null matrix. It is denoted by the letter **O**.

Equal matrices

Two matrices are equal if, and only if, they are identical. This means they must be of the same order and the respective elements must be identical.

$$\mathbf{A} = \begin{pmatrix} 4 & 1 \\ 3 & 5 \end{pmatrix} \quad \mathbf{B} = \begin{pmatrix} 4 & 1 \\ 3 & 5 \end{pmatrix} \quad \mathbf{C} = \begin{pmatrix} 5 & 3 \\ 2 & 4 \end{pmatrix} \quad \mathbf{D} = \begin{pmatrix} 5 & 2 \\ 3 & 4 \end{pmatrix}$$

Matrices **A** and **B** are equal matrices.

Matrices **C** and **D** are not equal.

Exercise 23.10

1 Write down the order of the following matrices.

(a) $\begin{pmatrix} 6 & 3 \\ 1 & 4 \end{pmatrix}$ (b) $\begin{pmatrix} 6 & 3 & 0 \\ 1 & 4 & 1 \end{pmatrix}$ (c) $\begin{pmatrix} 6 & 3 \\ 1 & 4 \\ 2 & 5 \end{pmatrix}$ (d) $\begin{pmatrix} 2 & 7 \end{pmatrix}$ (e) $\begin{pmatrix} 1 & 3 & 4 \end{pmatrix}$

(f) $\begin{pmatrix} 2 \end{pmatrix}$ (g) $\begin{pmatrix} 5 \\ 1 \end{pmatrix}$ (h) $\begin{pmatrix} 2 \\ 1 \\ 4 \end{pmatrix}$ (i) $\begin{pmatrix} 2 & 1 & -3 \\ 3 & 4 & 0 \\ 5 & 1 & 1 \end{pmatrix}$

2 Which of the following matrices are equal?

$\mathbf{A} = \begin{pmatrix} 4 & 5 \end{pmatrix}$ $\mathbf{B} = \begin{pmatrix} 5 & 4 \end{pmatrix}$ $\mathbf{C} = \begin{pmatrix} 4 & 5 & 6 \end{pmatrix}$ $\mathbf{D} = \begin{pmatrix} 4 \\ 5 \\ 6 \end{pmatrix}$ $\mathbf{E} = \begin{pmatrix} 4 & 5 & 6 \end{pmatrix}$

$\mathbf{F} = \begin{pmatrix} 6 & 5 & 4 \end{pmatrix}$ $\mathbf{G} = \begin{pmatrix} 6 & 3 \\ 1 & 4 \end{pmatrix}$ $\mathbf{H} = \begin{pmatrix} 6 & 3 \\ 1 & 4 \end{pmatrix}$

Addition and subtraction of matrices

You can only add or subtract matrices of the same order. To add, you simply add the corresponding elements in each matrix. To subtract, you subtract the corresponding elements in each matrix.

Worked example 20

Add $\begin{pmatrix} 3 & 2 & 1 \\ 0 & -4 & 5 \end{pmatrix}$ to $\begin{pmatrix} -1 & 1 & 3 \\ 2 & 4 & 0 \end{pmatrix}$.

$$\begin{pmatrix} 3 & 2 & 1 \\ 0 & -4 & 5 \end{pmatrix} + \begin{pmatrix} -1 & 1 & 3 \\ 2 & 4 & 0 \end{pmatrix} = \begin{pmatrix} 3+(-1) & 2+1 & 1+3 \\ 0+2 & (-4)+4 & 5+0 \end{pmatrix} = \begin{pmatrix} 2 & 3 & 4 \\ 2 & 0 & 5 \end{pmatrix}$$

Worked example 21

Subtract $\begin{pmatrix} 5 & 2 & 1 \\ 1 & -4 & 5 \end{pmatrix}$ from $\begin{pmatrix} 3 & 2 & 4 \\ 0 & -2 & 5 \end{pmatrix}$.

$$\begin{pmatrix} 3 & 2 & 4 \\ 0 & -2 & 5 \end{pmatrix} - \begin{pmatrix} 5 & 2 & 1 \\ 1 & -4 & 5 \end{pmatrix} = \begin{pmatrix} 3-5 & 2-2 & 4-1 \\ 0-1 & (-2)-(-4) & 5-5 \end{pmatrix} = \begin{pmatrix} 2 & 0 & 3 \\ -1 & 2 & 0 \end{pmatrix}$$

Scalar multiplication

You can multiply a matrix by a scalar (number). Each element of the matrix must be multiplied by the number.

Worked example 22

Multiply:

(a) $\begin{pmatrix} 6 & -1 \\ 3 & 2 \end{pmatrix}$ by 3 **(b)** $\begin{pmatrix} 3x & 2y \\ -5x & y \end{pmatrix}$ by 4.

(a) $$3\begin{pmatrix} 6 & -1 \\ 3 & 2 \end{pmatrix} = \begin{pmatrix} 3\times 6 & 3\times(-1) \\ 3\times 3 & 3\times 2 \end{pmatrix} = \begin{pmatrix} 18 & -3 \\ 9 & 6 \end{pmatrix}$$

(b) $$4\begin{pmatrix} 3x & 2y \\ -5x & y \end{pmatrix} = \begin{pmatrix} 4\times 3x & 4\times 2y \\ 4\times(-5x) & 4\times y \end{pmatrix} = \begin{pmatrix} 12x & 8y \\ -20x & 4y \end{pmatrix}$$

Exercise 23.11

Find:

1 $3(3\ -1)$

2 $3\begin{pmatrix}5\\-2\end{pmatrix}$

3 $2\begin{pmatrix}5 & -3\\0 & 1\end{pmatrix}$

4 $-4\begin{pmatrix}1 & -2\\3 & 0\end{pmatrix}$

5 $\frac{1}{2}\begin{pmatrix}4 & 0\\2 & 1\end{pmatrix}$

6 $3\begin{pmatrix}2a & -2b\\3a & 4b\end{pmatrix}$

7 $-2\begin{pmatrix}0 & 0\\0 & -1\end{pmatrix}$

8 $2\begin{pmatrix}4\\-1\end{pmatrix}-3\begin{pmatrix}1\\-2\end{pmatrix}$

Multiplication of matrices

You can multiply two matrices to get a product by following these rules:

- the number of columns in the first matrix must equal the number of rows in the second matrix
- the order of the product of the matrices is the number of rows in the first matrix multiplied by the number of columns in the second
- when multiplying, multiply the elements of a row of the first matrix by the elements in a column of the second matrix and add the products. For example, the sum of the products of the elements of the third row of the first matrix and the second column of the second matrix gives the elements in the third row and second column of the product matrix.

When we write two matrices next to each other we mean to multiply them.

Worked example 23

Find the product of $(2\ \ 5)\begin{pmatrix}4\\3\end{pmatrix}$.

Notice that the first matrix has two columns and the second matrix has two rows, so these *can* be multiplied. (See first bullet point in the list above.)

$2 \times 4 = 8$ (This is the first element in the row on the left × the first element in the column on the right.)

$5 \times 3 = 15$ (This is the second element in the row on the left × the second element in the column on the right.)

Add these two values to give 23.

∴ the product of the matrix is (23).

The first matrix had one row and the second matrix had one column, so the answer matrix has one row and one column. (See second bullet in the list.)

Worked example 24

Given that $\begin{pmatrix}x & 2\\3 & y\end{pmatrix}\begin{pmatrix}4\\-1\end{pmatrix}=\begin{pmatrix}8\\5\end{pmatrix}$, find the value of x and y.

Multiply the matrices first.

First row elements × first column elements give $(x \times 4 + 2 \times (-1)) = 4x - 2$
Second row elements × first column elements give $(3 \times 4 + y \times (-1)) = 12 - y$

So, $\begin{pmatrix}4x-2\\12-y\end{pmatrix}=\begin{pmatrix}8\\5\end{pmatrix}$.

The matrices are of the same order so corresponding elements are equal.
This means:

$4x - 2 = 8 \rightarrow x = 2.5$
and
$12 - y = 5 \rightarrow y = 7$

Worked example 25

Find the product of: $\begin{pmatrix} 2 & 3 \\ 1 & 0 \end{pmatrix}\begin{pmatrix} 3 & 1 \\ 6 & 4 \end{pmatrix}$.

$(2\ \ 3)\begin{pmatrix} 3 \\ 6 \end{pmatrix} = 2\times3+3\times6 = 6+18 = 24$	First row of left-hand matrix (LHM) × first column of right-hand matrix (RHM).
$(2\ \ 3)\begin{pmatrix} 1 \\ 4 \end{pmatrix} = 2\times1+3\times4 = 2+12 = 14$	First row of LHM × second column of RHM.
$(1\ \ 0)\begin{pmatrix} 3 \\ 6 \end{pmatrix} = 1\times3+0\times6 = 3+0 = 3$	Second row of LHM × first column of RHM.
$(1\ \ 0)\begin{pmatrix} 1 \\ 4 \end{pmatrix} = 1\times1+0\times4 = 1+0 = 1$	Second row of LHM × second column of RHM.

$\therefore$ the product is $\begin{pmatrix} 24 & 14 \\ 3 & 1 \end{pmatrix}$

Multiplication by a unit matrix

Because multiplication by 1 leaves the numbers unchanged, a square matrix is unchanged when multiplied by a unit matrix of the same order.

For example:

$$\begin{pmatrix} 1 & 0 \\ 0 & 1 \end{pmatrix}\begin{pmatrix} 3 & 2 \\ 5 & 4 \end{pmatrix} = \begin{pmatrix} 1\times3+0\times5 & 1\times2+0\times4 \\ 0\times3+1\times5 & 0\times2+1\times4 \end{pmatrix} = \begin{pmatrix} 3 & 2 \\ 5 & 4 \end{pmatrix}.$$

Order of matrices in multiplication

If A and B are two matrices, then AB is not generally equal to BA. We say that the multiplication of matrices is not **commutative**.

Commutative operations give the same result whatever order they are calculated in. Addition is commutative because $a + b = b + a$ but subtraction is not commutative because $a - b \neq b - a$.

Exercise 23.12

1 Find the following matrix products.

(a) $\begin{pmatrix} 4 & 5 \end{pmatrix}\begin{pmatrix} 3 \\ 2 \end{pmatrix}$ (b) $\begin{pmatrix} -2 & 1 \end{pmatrix}\begin{pmatrix} -3 \\ 0 \end{pmatrix}$ (c) $\begin{pmatrix} -3 & -2 \end{pmatrix}\begin{pmatrix} 3 \\ 4 \end{pmatrix}$

(d) $\begin{pmatrix} 3 & -2 \end{pmatrix}\begin{pmatrix} -2 \\ 3 \end{pmatrix}$ (e) $\begin{pmatrix} a & 3 \end{pmatrix}\begin{pmatrix} 1 \\ 3 \end{pmatrix}$

2 Carry out the following matrix multiplications.

(a) $\begin{pmatrix} 5 & 1 \\ 2 & 0 \end{pmatrix}\begin{pmatrix} 2 \\ 3 \end{pmatrix}$ (b) $\begin{pmatrix} -1 & -2 \\ -3 & 0 \end{pmatrix}\begin{pmatrix} -2 \\ -3 \end{pmatrix}$ (c) $\begin{pmatrix} 2 & 6 \\ 0 & 3 \end{pmatrix}\begin{pmatrix} 1 & 3 \\ 1 & 4 \end{pmatrix}$ (d) $\begin{pmatrix} 1 & -2 \\ 3 & 5 \end{pmatrix}\begin{pmatrix} 3 & -1 \\ -1 & 1 \end{pmatrix}$

3 Find the value of x in each of the following matrix equations.

(a) $\begin{pmatrix} x & 2 \end{pmatrix}\begin{pmatrix} 1 \\ 3 \end{pmatrix} = (10)$ (b) $\begin{pmatrix} 3 & x \end{pmatrix}\begin{pmatrix} 5 \\ 2 \end{pmatrix} = (17)$ (c) $\begin{pmatrix} x & -5 \end{pmatrix}\begin{pmatrix} 2 \\ 3 \end{pmatrix} = (-1)$

4 If $\mathbf{A} = \begin{pmatrix} 0 & 5 \\ 2 & -2 \end{pmatrix}$, $\mathbf{B} = \begin{pmatrix} 1 & 3 \\ -1 & 2 \end{pmatrix}$ and $\mathbf{I} = \begin{pmatrix} 1 & 0 \\ 0 & 1 \end{pmatrix}$, find:

(a) **AB** (b) **BA** (c) **AI** (d) **IA** (e) $\mathbf{B}^3$ (f) 2**A** + 3**B**

5 (a) Find the products of:

(i) $\begin{pmatrix} -1 & 2 \\ 2 & 1 \end{pmatrix}\begin{pmatrix} 3 & 0 \\ -1 & 2 \end{pmatrix}$ (ii) $\begin{pmatrix} 3 & 0 \\ -1 & 2 \end{pmatrix}\begin{pmatrix} -1 & 2 \\ 2 & 1 \end{pmatrix}$

(b) Is the multiplication of matrices commutative, according to your answers?
(c) Can you explain why or why not?

Determinant of a matrix

If $\mathbf{A} = \begin{pmatrix} 2 & 1 \\ 3 & 5 \end{pmatrix}$ then the number $(2 \times 5) - (1 \times 3)$ is the **determinant** of the matrix. In this case the determinant is 7.

The notation |**A**| is used to write the determinant.
In general:

If $\mathbf{A} = \begin{pmatrix} a & b \\ c & d \end{pmatrix}$, then $|\mathbf{A}| = ad - bc$.

|**A**| is the product of the elements in the leading diagonal minus the product of the elements in the other diagonal.

Caution: the |**A**| symbol is the same as that used for the magnitude of a vector earlier in this chapter. Take care not to confuse the two.

Worked example 26

If $\mathbf{M} = \begin{pmatrix} 5 & -2 \\ 1 & 3 \end{pmatrix}$, find |**M**|.

$5 \times 3 = 15$

$1 \times (-2) = -2$

M = 15 − (−2) = 15 + 2 = 17

Worked example 27

Find x if the determinant of $\begin{pmatrix} x & 3 \\ 4 & 1 \end{pmatrix} = 2$.

Determinant:

$(x \times 1) - (3 \times 4) = x - 12$

but this must $= 2$

$\therefore x - 12 = 2$

$\therefore x = 14$

Exercise 23.13

1 Find the determinants of the following matrices.

(a) $\begin{pmatrix} 4 & 1 \\ 3 & 5 \end{pmatrix}$ (b) $\begin{pmatrix} 6 & 8 \\ 3 & 4 \end{pmatrix}$ (c) $\begin{pmatrix} -3 & -2 \\ -1 & 1 \end{pmatrix}$ (d) $\begin{pmatrix} 2 & -1 \\ 3 & 9 \end{pmatrix}$ (e) $\begin{pmatrix} -1 & 0 \\ 0 & 1 \end{pmatrix}$

2 If $\mathbf{B} = \begin{pmatrix} x & 2 \\ 3 & 1 \end{pmatrix}$ and $|\mathbf{B}| = 3$, find the value of x.

3 Given that $\mathbf{C} = \begin{pmatrix} 1 & 4 \\ -2 & x \end{pmatrix}$ and $|\mathbf{C}| = 5$, find the value of x.

4 Find y if the determinant of the matrix $\begin{pmatrix} y & 2 \\ 3 & 2 \end{pmatrix} = 2$.

5 Given that $\mathbf{A} = \begin{pmatrix} -2 & p \\ -2 & 3 \end{pmatrix}$ and $|\mathbf{A}| = 12$, find the value of p.

REWIND

You learned earlier in the chapter that the order of multiplying matrices is important as you do not always obtain the same result. For a matrix and its inverse the order is not important as both ways will lead to a unit matrix. ◀

The inverse of a matrix

The **inverse** of a square matrix **A** is denoted by $\mathbf{A}^{-1}$. $\mathbf{A} \times \mathbf{A}^{-1} = \mathbf{A}^{-1} \times \mathbf{A} = \mathbf{I}$, where **I** is the unit matrix of the same order as **A**. (Remember that **I** denotes a unit matrix.)

Suppose there are two matrices **A** and **B** such that $\mathbf{A} = \begin{pmatrix} 5 & 2 \\ 7 & 3 \end{pmatrix}$ and $\mathbf{B} = \begin{pmatrix} 3 & -2 \\ -7 & 5 \end{pmatrix}$
$\mathbf{AB} = \begin{pmatrix} 1 & 0 \\ 0 & 1 \end{pmatrix}$ and $\mathbf{BA} = \begin{pmatrix} 1 & 0 \\ 0 & 1 \end{pmatrix}$. Therefore **B** is the inverse of **A**, or $\mathbf{A}^{-1}$.
Also, **A** is the inverse of **B**, or $\mathbf{B}^{-1}$.

Finding the inverse of a matrix

- Calculate the determinant of the matrix.
- If the determinant is one, swap the elements of the leading diagonal and change the signs of the elements of the other diagonal.
- If the determinant is not one or zero, swap the elements of the leading diagonal, change the signs of the elements of the other diagonal and divide each element by the determinant.
- If the determinant is zero, no division is possible. In such a case, the matrix has no inverse and is called a singular matrix.

Worked example 28

Find the inverse of $\begin{pmatrix} 2 & 1 \\ 4 & 2 \end{pmatrix}$.

Determinant is $(2 \times 2) - (4 \times 1) = 4 - 4 = 0$

Matrix is singular.

No inverse can be found.

Worked example 29

If $\mathbf{A} = \begin{pmatrix} 8 & 5 \\ 3 & 2 \end{pmatrix}$, find $\mathbf{A}^{-1}$.

$|\mathbf{A}| = (8 \times 2) - (3 \times 5) = 16 - 15 = 1$

$\mathbf{A}^{-1} = \begin{pmatrix} 2 & -5 \\ -3 & 8 \end{pmatrix}$

Worked example 30

Given that $\mathbf{A} = \begin{pmatrix} 5 & 7 \\ 6 & 9 \end{pmatrix}$, find $\mathbf{A}^{-1}$.

$|\mathbf{A}| = (5 \times 9) - (6 \times 7) = 45 - 42 = 3$

$$\mathbf{A}^{-1} = \frac{1}{3}\begin{pmatrix} 9 & -7 \\ -6 & 5 \end{pmatrix} = \begin{pmatrix} \frac{9}{3} & -\frac{7}{3} \\ -\frac{6}{3} & \frac{5}{3} \end{pmatrix} = \begin{pmatrix} 3 & -\frac{7}{3} \\ -2 & \frac{5}{3} \end{pmatrix}$$

Exercise 23.14

1 State whether each of the following matrices has an inverse. If the inverse exists, find it.

(a) $\begin{pmatrix} 4 & 6 \\ 1 & 2 \end{pmatrix}$ (b) $\begin{pmatrix} 2 & 3 \\ 5 & 8 \end{pmatrix}$ (c) $\begin{pmatrix} 3 & 2 \\ 6 & 4 \end{pmatrix}$ (d) $\begin{pmatrix} 3 & -2 \\ 2 & -1 \end{pmatrix}$ (e) $\begin{pmatrix} 3 & 4 \\ 5 & 6 \end{pmatrix}$

2 Show that I is its own inverse where $\mathrm{I} = \begin{pmatrix} 1 & 0 \\ 0 & 1 \end{pmatrix}$.

3 Show that each of the following matrices is its own inverse.

(a) $\begin{pmatrix} 1 & 0 \\ 0 & -1 \end{pmatrix}$ (b) $\begin{pmatrix} -1 & 0 \\ 0 & -1 \end{pmatrix}$ (c) $\begin{pmatrix} 0 & 1 \\ 1 & 0 \end{pmatrix}$ (d) $\begin{pmatrix} 0 & -1 \\ -1 & 0 \end{pmatrix}$

4 Given that $\mathbf{A} = \begin{pmatrix} 3 & 7 \\ 2 & 5 \end{pmatrix}$, find $\mathbf{A}^{-1}$.

23.5 Matrices and transformations

Matrices can be used to describe transformations in a plane.

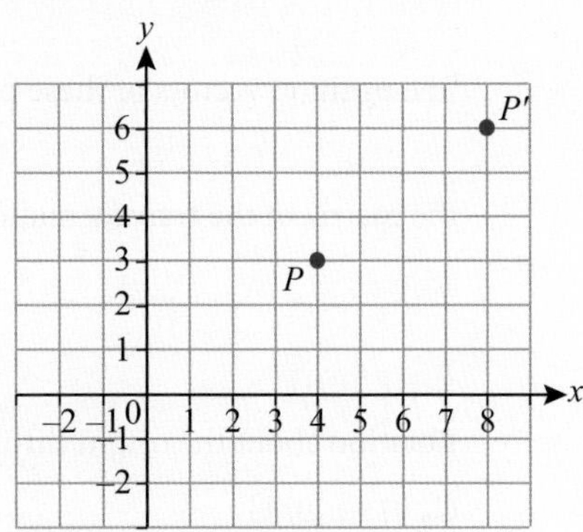

Suppose P is the point (4, 3), i.e. P is the point with position vector $\begin{pmatrix} 4 \\ 3 \end{pmatrix}$.

Multiply $\begin{pmatrix} 4 \\ 3 \end{pmatrix}$ by the matrix $\begin{pmatrix} 2 & 0 \\ 0 & 2 \end{pmatrix}$:

$\begin{pmatrix} 2 & 0 \\ 0 & 2 \end{pmatrix}\begin{pmatrix} 4 \\ 3 \end{pmatrix} = \begin{pmatrix} 8 \\ 6 \end{pmatrix}$.

$\begin{pmatrix} 8 \\ 6 \end{pmatrix}$ is another position vector; that is $P'(8, 6)$.

The matrix $\begin{pmatrix} 2 & 0 \\ 0 & 2 \end{pmatrix}$ transforms point $P(4, 3)$ into $P'(8, 6)$.

This principle can be used to describe some of the transformations you have worked with so far.

For the following transformations:

1. Select the points (1, 0) and (0, 1).
2. Find the images of these points under the given transformation.
3. Write down the position vectors of these images.
4. The position vector of the image of the first point becomes the first column and the position vector of the image of the second point is the second column of the required matrix.

Reflection

Reflection in the x-axis:

$(1, 0) \rightarrow (1, 0)$

$(0, 1) \rightarrow (0, -1)$

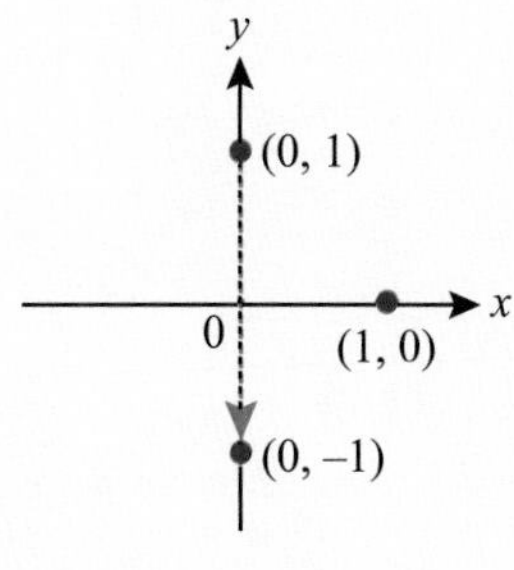

The position vectors of these points are $\begin{pmatrix} 1 \\ 0 \end{pmatrix}$ and $\begin{pmatrix} 0 \\ -1 \end{pmatrix}$,

so the matrix of the transformation is $\begin{pmatrix} 1 & 0 \\ 0 & -1 \end{pmatrix}$.

Reflection in the y-axis:

$(1, 0) \rightarrow (-1, 0)$

$(0, 1) \rightarrow (0, 1)$

The position vectors of these points are $\begin{pmatrix} -1 \\ 0 \end{pmatrix}$ and $\begin{pmatrix} 0 \\ 1 \end{pmatrix}$, so the matrix of the transformation is $\begin{pmatrix} -1 & 0 \\ 0 & 1 \end{pmatrix}$.

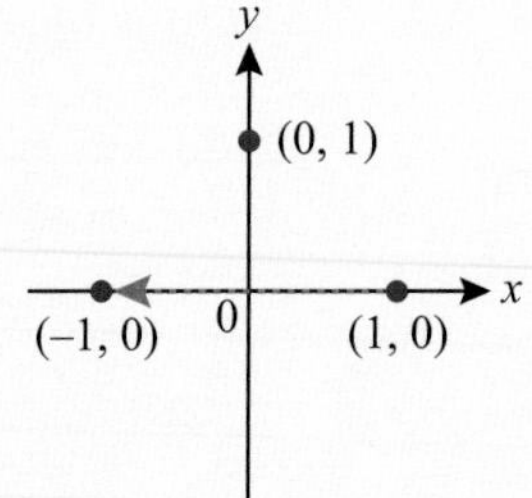

Rotation

Rotation about the origin through 90° anti-clockwise (+90°):

$(1, 0) \rightarrow (0, 1)$

$(0, 1) \rightarrow (-1, 0)$

The transformation matrix is $\begin{pmatrix} 0 & -1 \\ 1 & 0 \end{pmatrix}$.

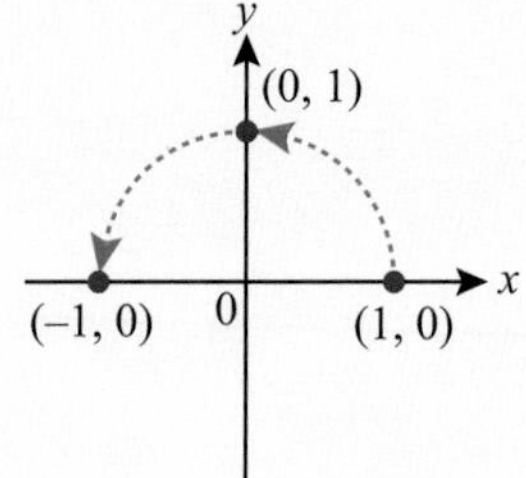

Rotation about the origin through 180° (a half turn):

$(1, 0) \rightarrow (-1, 0)$

$(0, 1) \rightarrow (0, -1)$

The transformation matrix is $\begin{pmatrix} -1 & 0 \\ 0 & -1 \end{pmatrix}$.

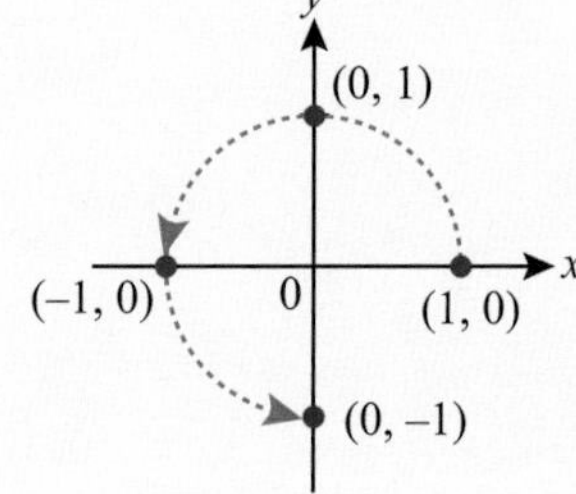

Enlargement

Enlargement with scale factor k, and centre of enlargement (0, 0):

$(1, 0) \rightarrow (k, 0)$

$(0, 1) \rightarrow (0, k)$

The transformation matrix is $\begin{pmatrix} k & 0 \\ 0 & k \end{pmatrix}$.

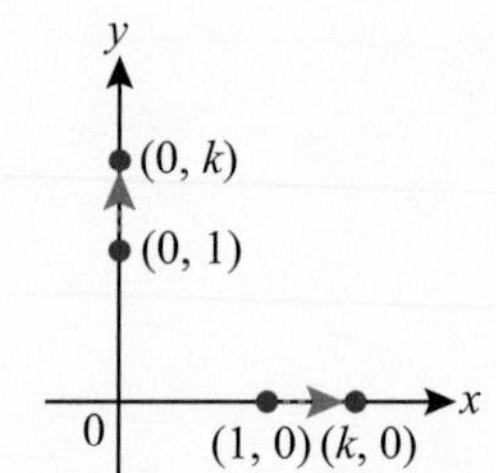

Translation

All the previous transformations are represented by a 2×2 matrix and, to find the image of a point, you have to pre-multiply (multiply on the left) the position vector $\begin{pmatrix} x \\ y \end{pmatrix}$ of the point by the appropriate matrix. It follows that the image of the origin (0, 0) is the origin; in other words, the origin is invariant. This is not the case for a translation because every point moves and there is no invariant point.

Translation is represented by a column vector or a column matrix of the order 2×1. To obtain the image of a point under translation you do not multiply by the matrix but you add the vector of the translation to the position vector $\begin{pmatrix} x \\ y \end{pmatrix}$ of the point.

Worked example 31

The diagram shows ΔPQR.
Show the new position of the triangle after the translation $\begin{pmatrix} -3 \\ 1 \end{pmatrix}$.

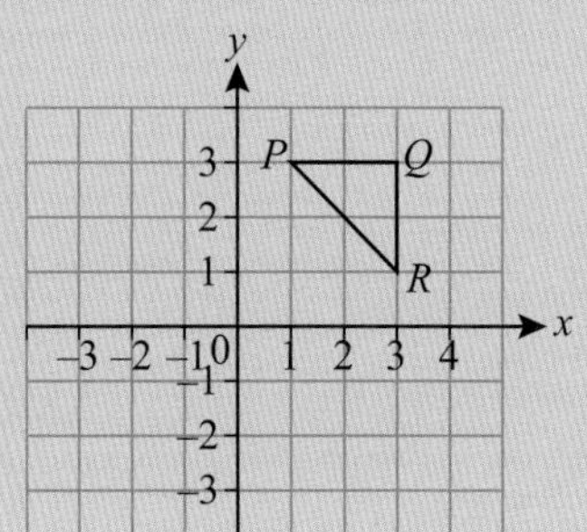

The position vector of P is $\begin{pmatrix} 1 \\ 3 \end{pmatrix}$.

The position vector of Q is $\begin{pmatrix} 3 \\ 3 \end{pmatrix}$.

The position vector of R is $\begin{pmatrix} 3 \\ 1 \end{pmatrix}$.

The image of P after translation is: $\begin{pmatrix} 1 \\ 3 \end{pmatrix} + \begin{pmatrix} -3 \\ 1 \end{pmatrix} = \begin{pmatrix} 1+(-3) \\ 3+1 \end{pmatrix} = \begin{pmatrix} -2 \\ 4 \end{pmatrix}$.

The image of Q after translation is: $\begin{pmatrix} 3 \\ 3 \end{pmatrix} + \begin{pmatrix} -3 \\ 1 \end{pmatrix} = \begin{pmatrix} 3+(-3) \\ 3+1 \end{pmatrix} = \begin{pmatrix} 0 \\ 4 \end{pmatrix}$.

The image of R after translation is: $\begin{pmatrix} 3 \\ 1 \end{pmatrix} + \begin{pmatrix} -3 \\ 1 \end{pmatrix} = \begin{pmatrix} 3+(-3) \\ 1+1 \end{pmatrix} = \begin{pmatrix} 0 \\ 2 \end{pmatrix}$.

The new position of ΔPQR is $\Delta P'Q'R'$.

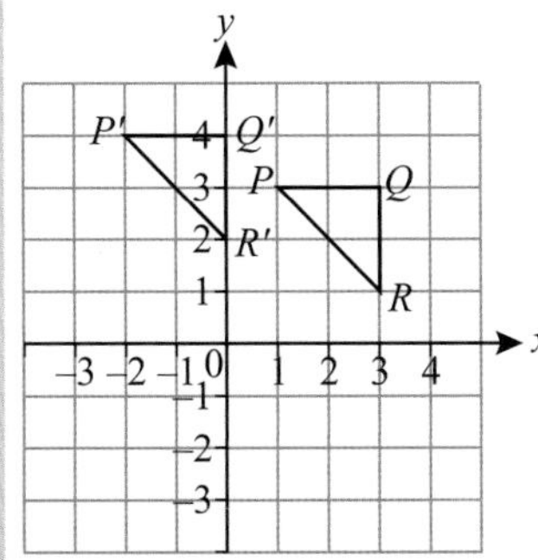

Exercise 23.15

1 Answer the whole of this question on a sheet of graph paper.

(a) **(i)** Draw x- and y-axes from –6 to +6, using 1 cm to represent 1 unit of x and y.
(ii) Draw ΔABC with vertices $A(2, 1)$, $B(5, 1)$ and $C(5, 5)$.

(b) **(i)** Draw the image of ΔABC under the transformation represented by the matrix $\begin{pmatrix} 0 & 1 \\ 1 & 0 \end{pmatrix}$ and label it $A'B'C'$.
(ii) Describe this single transformation.

(c) (i) Draw the image of ΔABC under reflection in the line $y = -x$ and label it $A''B''C''$.
(ii) Find the matrix that represents this transformation.
(d) (i) Describe fully the single transformation that maps ΔABC onto $\Delta A''B''C''$.
(ii) Find the matrix that represents this transformation.

2 Answer the whole of this question on a sheet of graph paper.

(a) Draw x- and y-axes from –6 to +6, using 1 cm to represent 1 unit on each axis.
Draw the triangle whose vertices are $A(2, 2)$, $B(5, 2)$ and $C(5, 3)$.

(b) **M** is the matrix $\begin{pmatrix} 0 & -1 \\ 1 & 0 \end{pmatrix}$ which represents the transformation T.
Draw accurately the image of triangle ABC under the transformation T, labelling it PQR.

(c) **N** is the matrix $\begin{pmatrix} 1 & 0 \\ 0 & -1 \end{pmatrix}$ which represents the transformation U.
Draw accurately the image of ΔABC under the transformation U, and label it XYZ.
(d) (i) Describe fully the single transformation that maps ΔPQR onto ΔXYZ.
(ii) Find the matrix that represents this transformation.
(e) (i) Calculate the matrix **NM**.
(ii) This matrix represents the transformation V. Draw accurately the image of ΔABC under transformation V, labelling it FGH.
(iii) State whether the transformation V is equivalent to transformation T followed by transformation U or to transformation U followed by transformation T.

3 The matrix $\mathbf{M} = \begin{pmatrix} 3 & 2 \\ -2 & -1 \end{pmatrix}$ describes a transformation on ΔABC. The co-ordinates of the image are $A'(2, 1)$, $B'(0, 1)$ and $C'(-3, 2)$. Find the following:
(a) the matrix $\mathbf{M}^{-1}$ that transforms $\Delta A'B'C'$ onto ΔABC.
(b) the co-ordinates of A, B and C.

Summary

Do you know the following?

- A transformation involves a change in the position and/or size of a shape.
- A reflection is a mirror image, a rotation is a turn, a translation is a slide and an enlargement is an increase in size.
- To fully describe a reflection you need to give the equation of the mirror line.
- To fully describe a rotation you need to give the angle and centre of rotation.
- To describe a translation you can use a column vector $\begin{pmatrix} x \\ y \end{pmatrix}$.
- To describe an enlargement you need to give the scale factor and the centre of enlargement.
- A vector has both magnitude and direction. You can add and subtract vectors but you cannot multiply or divide vectors. You can multiply a vector by a scalar.
- The magnitude of a vector $\begin{pmatrix} x \\ y \end{pmatrix} = \sqrt{x^2 + y^2}$. You write the magnitude as $|XY|$ or $|\mathbf{x}|$.
- A position vector is a vector that starts at the origin.
- A matrix is a set of numbers arranged in rows and columns. The order of the matrix gives the number of rows followed by the number of columns in the form r × c.
- Matrices of the same order can be added and/or subtracted.
- A matrix can be multiplied by a scalar. Matrices can also be multiplied by other matrices under certain conditions.
- The determinant of a matrix $\mathbf{A} = \begin{pmatrix} a & b \\ c & d \end{pmatrix}$ is $|\mathbf{A}| = (ad - bc)$.
- The inverse of a matrix **A** is $\mathbf{A}^{-1}$.
- Matrices can be used to describe transformations in a plane.

Are you able to …?

- reflect points and plane figures about horizontal and vertical lines
- rotate plane figures about the origin, vertices of the object and midpoints of the sides
- translate shapes using a column vector
- construct enlargements of simple shapes using the scale factor and centre of enlargement
- recognise and describe single and combined translations
- describe translations using column vectors
- add and subtract vectors and multiply vectors by a scalar
- calculate the magnitude of a vector
- use position vectors to find the magnitude of vectors
- display information in the form of a matrix
- calculate the sum and product of two matrices
- find the product of a matrix and a scalar
- work with zero matrices and identity matrices
- find the determinant and inverse of a non-singular matrix
- use combinations of transformations when working with shapes
- describe transformations using co-ordinates and matrices.

Examination practice

Exam-style questions

1 The diagram shows a triangle, labelled A.

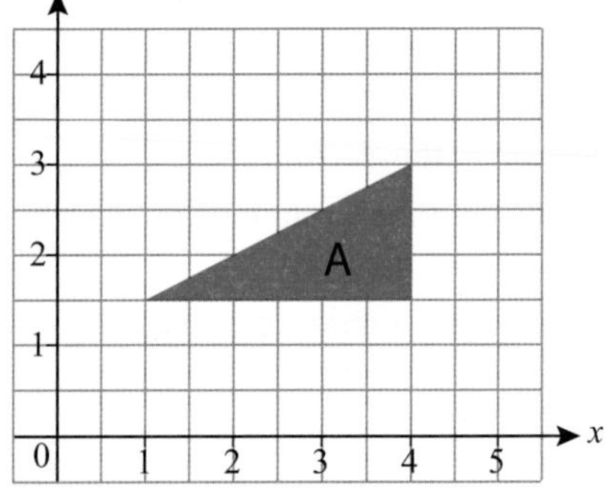

(a) On a grid of squared paper, draw accurately the following transformations:

(i) the reflection of ΔA in the y-axis, labelling it ΔB
(ii) the rotation of ΔA through 180° about the point (4, 3), labelling it ΔC
(iii) the enlargement of ΔA, scale factor two, centre (4, 5), labelling it ΔD.

2 Describe fully the transformations of the shaded triangle E onto triangles A, B, C and D in the diagram.

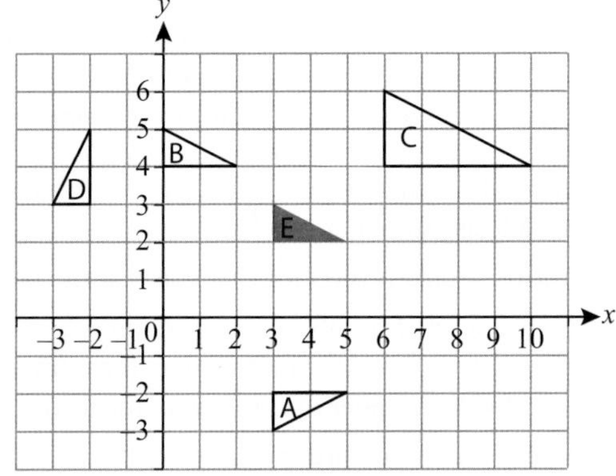

3 $\mathbf{m} = \begin{pmatrix} 3 \\ -4 \end{pmatrix}$ and $\mathbf{n} = \begin{pmatrix} -2 \\ 1 \end{pmatrix}$.

(a) Find:

(i) $\mathbf{m} + \mathbf{n}$
(ii) $3\mathbf{n}$

(b) Draw the vector **m** on a grid or on squared paper.

4 ΔABC is mapped onto $\Delta A'B'C'$ by an enlargement.

(a) Find the centre of the enlargement.
(b) What is the scale factor of the enlargement?

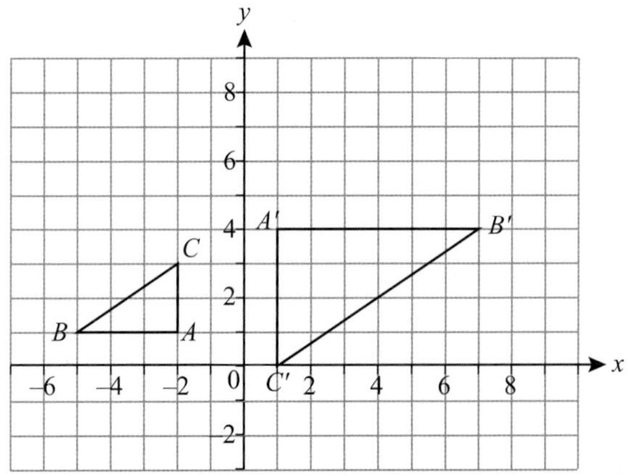

5 **(a)** Write down the column vector of the translation that maps rectangle R onto rectangle S.

(b) Describe fully another single transformation (not a translation) that would also map rectangle R onto rectangle S.

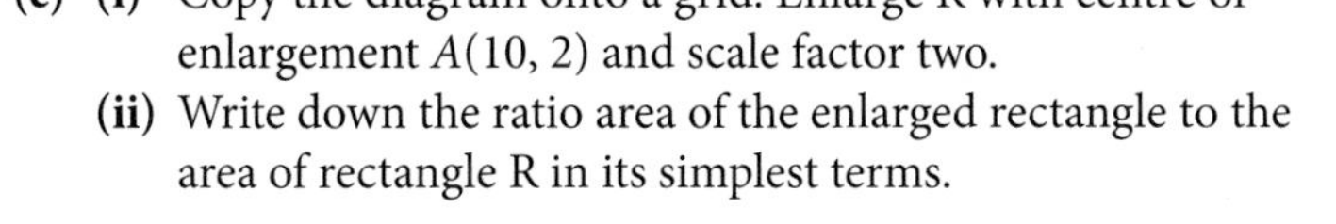

(c) **(i)** Copy the diagram onto a grid. Enlarge R with centre of enlargement $A(10, 2)$ and scale factor two.

(ii) Write down the ratio area of the enlarged rectangle to the area of rectangle R in its simplest terms.

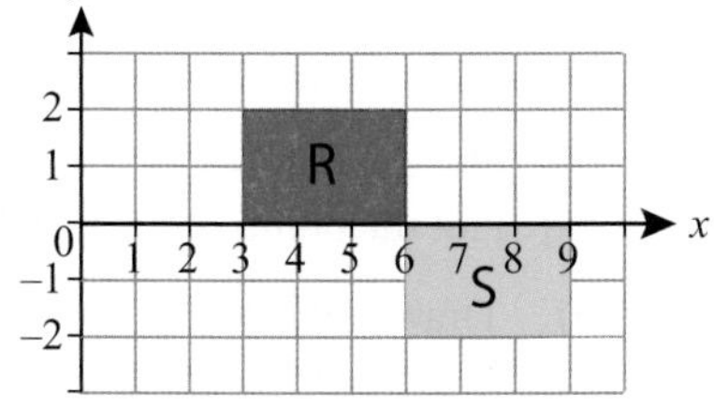

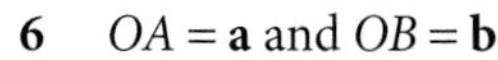

6 $OA = \mathbf{a}$ and $OB = \mathbf{b}$.

(a) $OC = \mathbf{a} + 2\mathbf{b}$. Make a copy of the diagram and label the point C on your diagram.

(b) $D = (0, -1)$. Write OD in terms of $\mathbf{a}$ and $\mathbf{b}$.

(c) Calculate $|\mathbf{a}|$ giving your answer to 2 decimal places.

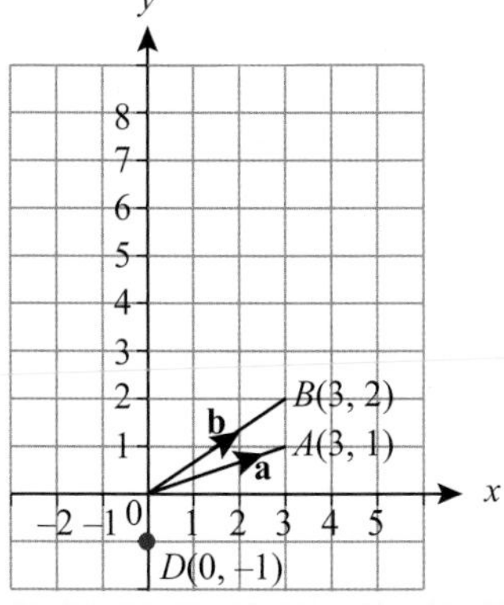

7 **(a)** In each case, describe fully the transformation that maps A onto:

(i) B
(ii) C
(iii) D

(b) State which shapes have an area equal to that of A.

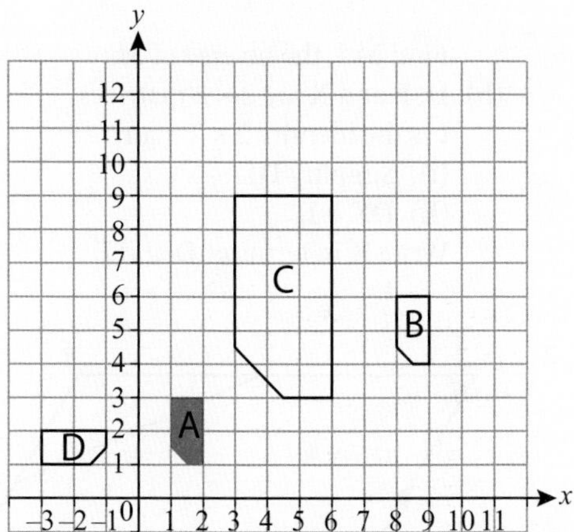

8 $\mathbf{A} = (1 \quad 2)$, $\mathbf{B} = \begin{pmatrix} -3 \\ 4 \end{pmatrix}$ and $\mathbf{C} = \begin{pmatrix} -2 & 5 \\ -3 & 6 \end{pmatrix}$.

(a) Which one of the following matrix calculations is possible?

(i) $\mathbf{A} + \mathbf{B}$ **(ii)** $\mathbf{AC}$ **(iii)** $\mathbf{BC}$

(b) Calculate $\mathbf{AB}$.

(c) Find $\mathbf{C}^{-1}$, the inverse of $\mathbf{C}$.

9 **(a)** Solve for x and y if $\begin{pmatrix} 3 & 2 \\ -1 & 6 \end{pmatrix}\begin{pmatrix} -3 \\ 2 \end{pmatrix} = \begin{pmatrix} x \\ y \end{pmatrix}$.

(b) Find the inverse of the matrix $\begin{pmatrix} 2 & -1 \\ 4 & 3 \end{pmatrix}$.

(c) Solve for t and u, $\begin{pmatrix} 3t & u \\ -t & 3u \end{pmatrix}\begin{pmatrix} 1 \\ 2 \end{pmatrix} = \begin{pmatrix} 10 \\ -10 \end{pmatrix}$.

10 Answer the whole of this question on a sheet of graph paper.

(a) Draw axes from –6 to +6, using a scale of 1 cm to represent 1 unit on each axis.

(i) Plot the points $A(5, 0)$, $B(1, 3)$ and $C(-1, 2)$ and draw ΔABC.
(ii) Plot the points $A'(3, 4)$, $B'(3, -1)$ and $C'(1, -2)$ and draw $\Delta A'B'C'$.

(b) (i) Draw and label the line l in which $\Delta A'B'C'$ is a reflection of ΔABC.
(ii) Write down the equation of the line l.

(iii) Find the values of p, q, r and s such that:

$$\begin{pmatrix} p & q \\ r & s \end{pmatrix}\overset{\begin{matrix}A & B & C\end{matrix}}{\begin{pmatrix} 5 & 1 & -1 \\ 0 & 3 & 2 \end{pmatrix}} = \overset{\begin{matrix}A' & B' & C'\end{matrix}}{\begin{pmatrix} 3 & 3 & 1 \\ 4 & -1 & -2 \end{pmatrix}}.$$

(iv) What transformation does the matrix $\begin{pmatrix} p & q \\ r & s \end{pmatrix}$ represent?

(c) Reflect $\Delta A'B'C'$ in the y-axis and label the new triangle $A''B''C''$.

(d) IF ΔABC is rotated about the origin it will map onto $\Delta A''B''C''$. What is the angle of rotation?

Past paper questions

1

(a) $\mathbf{M} = \begin{pmatrix} 3 & 2 \\ -1 & 1 \end{pmatrix}$

Find $\mathbf{M}^{-1}$, the inverse of **M**. [2]

(b) **D**, **E** and **X** are 2×2 matrices.
I is the identity 2×2 matrix.
(i) Simplify **DI**. [1]
(ii) **DX** = **E**.
Write **X** in terms of **D** and **E**. [1]

[Cambridge IGCSE Mathematics 0580 Paper 23 Q22 October/November 2012]

2

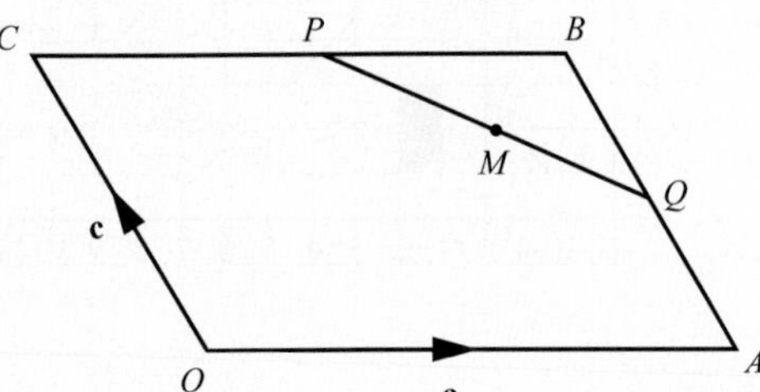

O is the origin and $OABC$ is a parallelogram.
$CP = PB$ and $AQ = QB$.

$\overrightarrow{OA} = \mathbf{a}$ and $\overrightarrow{OC} = \mathbf{c}$.
Find in terms of **a** and **c**, in their simplest form,

(a) $\overrightarrow{PQ}$, [2]
(b) the position vector of M, where M is the midpoint of PQ. [2]

[Cambridge IGCSE Mathematics 0580 Paper 22 Q16 May/June 2011]

24 Probability using tree diagrams

Key words

- Possible outcomes
- Sample space
- Independent events
- Mutually exclusive events
- Combined events
- Favourable combinations

EXTENDED

In this chapter you will learn how to:

- use tree diagrams to show all possible outcomes of combined events
- calculate the probability of simple combined events using tree diagrams.

The probability of getting heads when you toss one coin is 0.5. But what is the probability of getting heads only when you toss two, three or 15 coins at the same time?

In chapter 8 you used probability space diagrams to represent the sample space and all possible outcomes of an event. On these diagrams, outcomes are represented by points on a grid. When events are combined, you can think of them taking place in different stages. For example, when you toss two coins, you can look at the outcomes for the first coin, then the outcomes for the second coin. In experiments like this, it is convenient to use a tree diagram to list the outcomes of each stage in a clear and systematic way.

In this chapter you are going to learn how to use tree diagrams to represent outcomes of simple combined events. You are also going to learn how to use tree diagrams to calculate the probability of different outcomes.

24.1 Using tree diagrams to show outcomes

◀ REWIND

For **independent** events
P(A and then B) = P(A) × P(B).

For **mutually exclusive** events
P(A or B) = P(A) + P(B).

Read through chapter 8 again if you have forgotten this. ◀

A tree diagram is a branching diagram that shows all the **possible outcomes (sample space)** of one or more events.

To draw a tree diagram:

- make a dot to represent the first event
- draw branches from the dot to show all possible outcomes of that event only
- write the outcomes at the end of each branch
- draw a dot at the end of each branch to represent the next event
- draw branches from this point to show all possible outcomes of that event
- write the outcomes at the end of the branches.

The possible outcomes for the **combined events** of throwing a dice and tossing a coin at the same time:

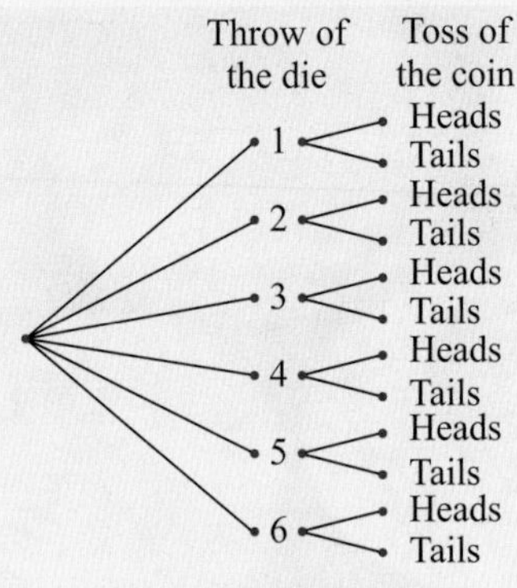

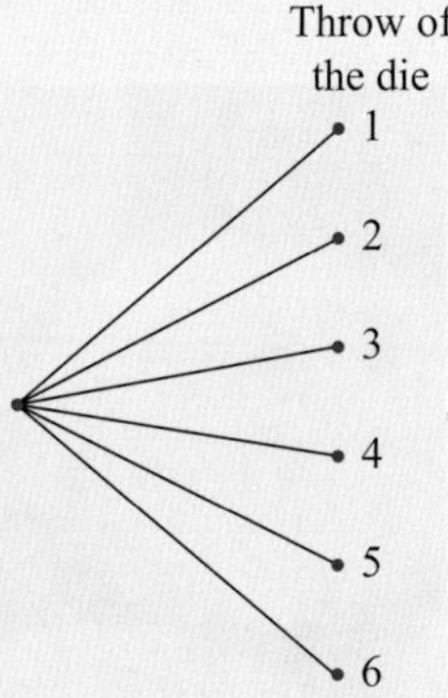

Worked example 1

When a woman has a child, she can have a girl or a boy. Draw a tree diagram to show the possible outcomes for the first three children born to a couple. Use B for boys and G for girls.

1st child	2nd child	3rd child	Possible combinations
B	B	B	B B B
		G	B B G
	G	B	B G B
		G	B G G
G	B	B	G B B
		G	G B G
	G	B	G G B
		G	G G G

Draw a dot for the first born child.
Draw and label two branches, one B and one G.
Repeat this at the end of each branch for the second and third child.

Note: this example assumes that a boy or a girl is equally likely at each stage, although this may not be the case in many families.

Exercise 24.1

1 Sandra has a bag containing three coloured counters: red, blue and green.

(a) Draw a tree diagram to show the possible outcomes when one counter is drawn from the bag at random, then returned to the bag before another counter is drawn at random.
(b) How many possible outcomes are there for the two draws?
(c) How many outcomes produce two counters the same colour?
(d) How many outcomes contain at least one blue counter?
(e) How many outcomes do not contain the blue counter?

2 Four cards marked A, B, C and D are in a container. A card is drawn, the letter noted, and then it is replaced. Another card is then drawn and the letter noted to make a two-letter combination.

(a) Draw a tree diagram to show the sample space in this experiment.
(b) How many outcomes are in the sample space?
(c) What is the probability of getting the letter combination BD?

24.2 Calculating probability from tree diagrams

Here is the tree diagram showing possible outcomes for throwing a dice and tossing a coin at the same time (H is used for head and T is used for tail).

This is the same diagram as in the previous section but now the probability of each outcome is written at the side of each branch.

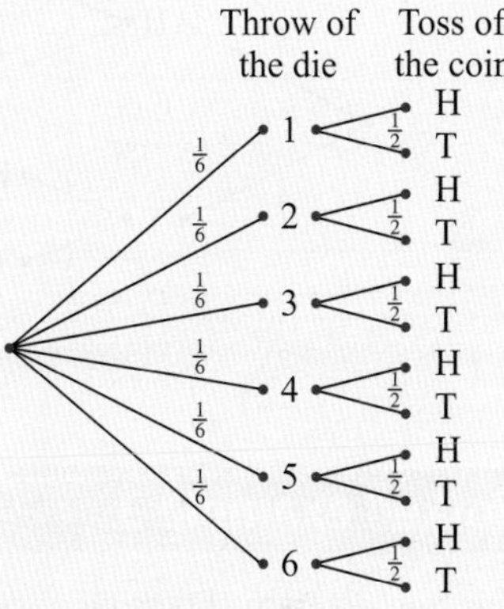

The probability of combined events on a tree diagram

To find the probability of one particular combination of outcomes:

- multiply the probabilities on consecutive branches, for example the probability of throwing a 5 and getting an H is $\frac{1}{6} \times \frac{1}{2} = \frac{1}{12}$.

REWIND

You learned in chapter 8 that mutually exclusive events cannot both happen together. ◀

To find the probability when there is more than one **favourable combination** or when the events are mutually exclusive:

- multiply the probabilities on consecutive branches
- add the probabilities (of each favourable combination) obtained by multiplication, for example, throwing 1 or 2 and getting an H is $\left(\frac{1}{6} \times \frac{1}{2}\right) + \left(\frac{1}{6} \times \frac{1}{2}\right) = \frac{1}{12} + \frac{1}{12} = \frac{2}{12} = \frac{1}{6}$

When you are interested only in specific probabilities, you can draw a tree diagram that only shows the favourable outcomes. For example, if you wanted to find the probability of getting a number < 5 and H in the above experiment, you might draw a tree diagram like this one:

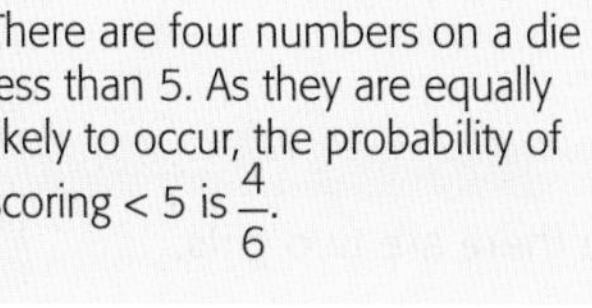

There are four numbers on a die less than 5. As they are equally likely to occur, the probability of scoring < 5 is $\frac{4}{6}$.

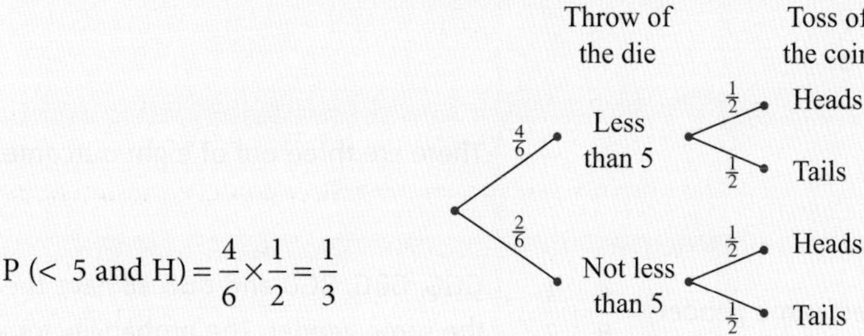

$$P(< 5 \text{ and } H) = \frac{4}{6} \times \frac{1}{2} = \frac{1}{3}$$

Worked example 2

Two coins are tossed together. Draw a tree diagram to find the probability of getting:

(a) two tails
(b) one head and one tail.

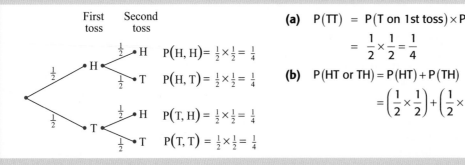

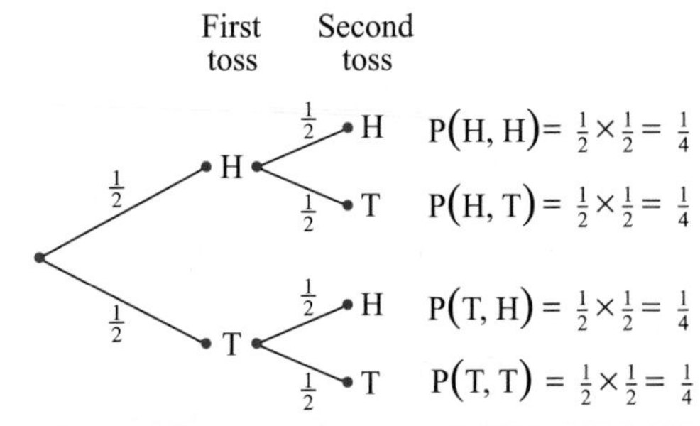

(a) $P(TT) = P(\text{T on 1st toss}) \times P(\text{T on 2nd toss})$

$= \frac{1}{2} \times \frac{1}{2} = \frac{1}{4}$

(b) $P(\text{HT or TH}) = P(HT) + P(TH)$

$= \left(\frac{1}{2} \times \frac{1}{2}\right) + \left(\frac{1}{2} \times \frac{1}{2}\right) = \frac{1}{4} + \frac{1}{4} = \frac{1}{2}$

Worked example 3

This tree diagram shows all possible combinations of boys and girls in a family of three children.

1st child, 2nd child, 3rd child, Possible combinations (every branch has probability $\frac{1}{2}$):

BBB
BBG
BGB
BGG
GBB
GBG
GGB
GGG

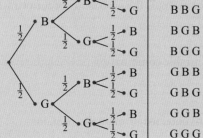

This assumes that the outcomes, boy or girl, are equally likely. A family with three children is chosen at random. Find the probability that:

(a) at least one child is a girl
(b) two of the children are girls
(c) the oldest and youngest children are the same gender.

(a)

$P(\text{at least one girl}) = 7\left(\frac{1}{2} \times \frac{1}{2} \times \frac{1}{2}\right)$

$= 7 \times \frac{1}{8}$

$= \frac{7}{8}$

All outcomes except BBB have at least one girl. This makes 7 outcomes. As each outcome is $\frac{1}{2} \times \frac{1}{2} \times \frac{1}{2}$ you can simply multiply this by 7.

(b)

$P(\text{two are girls}) = \frac{3}{8}$

There are three out of eight outcomes where there are two girls.

(c)

$P(\text{oldest and youngest same gender}) = \frac{4}{8} = \frac{1}{2}$

GGG, GBG, BGB and BBB all have the oldest and youngest of the same gender. The probability for each combination is $\frac{1}{8}$, so you can simply add the favourable combinations to give $\frac{4}{8}$.

Exercise 24.2

1 An unbiased coin is tossed twice. Draw a tree diagram to show the outcomes and use it to find the probability of the two tosses giving the same results.

2 A bag contains eight blue marbles and two red marbles. Two marbles are drawn at random. The first marble is replaced before the second is drawn.

(a) Draw a tree diagram to show all possible outcomes.
(b) What is the probability of getting:

(i) two red marbles
(ii) one red marble and one blue marble
(iii) two blue marbles?

3 A bag contains 12 beads. Five are red and the rest are white. Two beads are drawn at random. The first bead is replaced before the second is drawn.

(a) Represent the possible outcomes on a tree diagram.
(b) Find the probability that:

(i) both beads are red
(ii) both beads are white.

4 Harold wants to buy two new pets; he will buy them a week apart. He prefers birds to cats, but only slightly, and decides that so long as he buys them as chicks and/or kittens, it doesn't matter what combination he gets. The tree diagram below represents what combination of two pets he might buy.

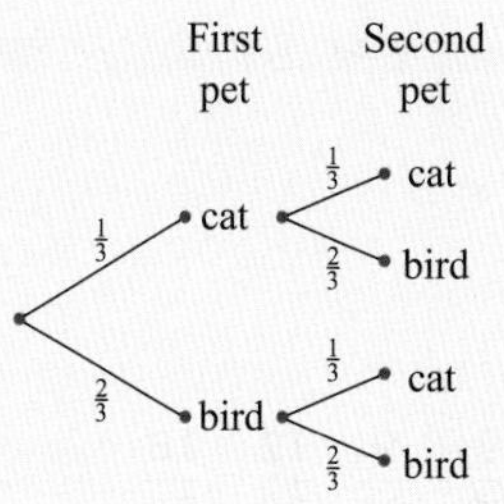

First pet
Second pet
$\frac{1}{3}$ cat
$\frac{1}{3}$ cat
$\frac{2}{3}$ bird
$\frac{2}{3}$ bird
$\frac{1}{3}$ cat
$\frac{2}{3}$ bird

(a) How many possible combinations of pet could be buy?
(b) What is the probability that he buys a cat and a bird?
(c) What is the probability that he buys two cats?
(d) Based on the probabilities above, what combination is he most likely to buy?

Conditional probability

The probability of an event may change depending on the outcome of an earlier event. For example, suppose you have an apple, an orange and a banana in front of you and you are only allowed to eat two fruits. Once you have chosen your first fruit, the options for the second choice depend on the first choice because you now only have two fruits left to choose from. If you eat the apple first, then you can only choose between the orange and the banana as your second fruit:

The probability of choosing an apple is $\frac{1}{3}$ because there are three fruits to choose from.

The probability of choosing the orange or the banana is $\frac{1}{2}$ because there are now only two fruits left to choose from.

In this example, the probability of the second event is conditional on the first event and we call this type of probability **conditional probability**. Worked example 3 shows you how to deal with this using a tree diagram.

When you are using a tree diagram always check whether the probability of an event changes because of the outcome of a previous event. Questions involving conditional probability often contain the instructions 'without replacement' or 'one after the other'.

Worked example 4

There are 21 students in a class, 12 are boys and 9 are girls. The teacher chooses two different students at random to answer questions.

(a) Draw a tree diagram to represent the situation.

(b) Find the probability that:

- **(i)** both students are boys (BB)
- **(ii)** both students are girls (GG)
- **(iii)** one student is a girl and the other is a boy.

(c) The teacher chooses a third student at random. What is the probability that:

- **(i)** all three students are boys
- **(ii)** at least one of the students is a girl?

(a)

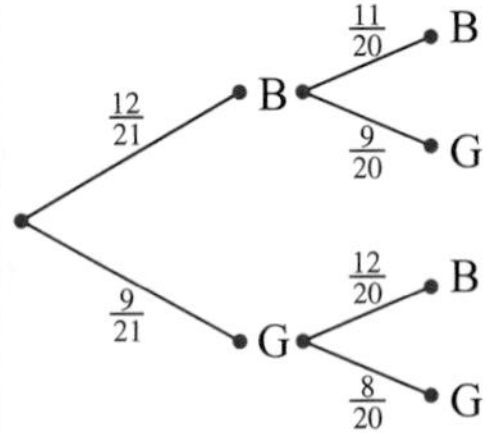

Notice that the second set of branches are conditional on the outcomes of the first set. This is an example of conditional probability. The teacher cannot choose the same student twice, so for the second set of branches there are only 20 students to choose from. Notice that if the first student is a boy, there are only 11 boys left for the second student but still 9 girls. If the first student is a girl then there are only 8 girls that could be chosen as the second student, but still 12 boys. In each case the numerator of one branch has changed but the numerators still add up to the value of the denominator (as this has also changed).

(b)

(i) $P(BB) = \frac{12}{21} \times \frac{11}{20} = \frac{11}{35}$

(ii) $P(GG) = \frac{9}{21} \times \frac{8}{20} = \frac{6}{35}$

(iii) $P(BG) + P(GB) = \frac{12}{21} \times \frac{9}{20} + \frac{9}{21} \times \frac{12}{20} = \frac{18}{35}$

The boy and girl can be chosen in either order.

(c)

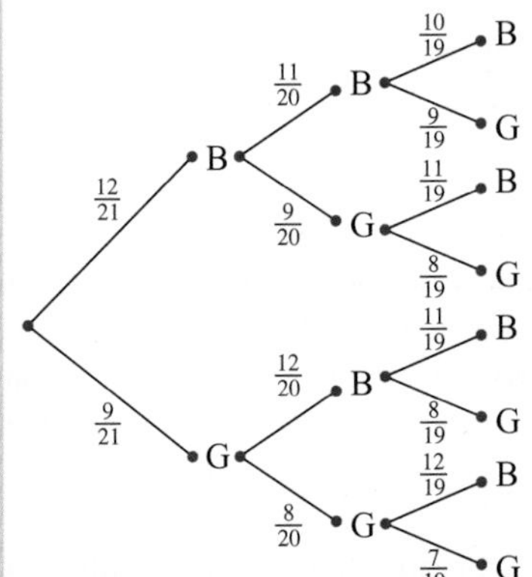

You may find it helpful to add a third set of branches to the diagram but, if you can see the pattern of the probabilities on the branches, you can just show the arithmetic as follows:

(i) $P(BBB) = \frac{12}{21} \times \frac{11}{20} \times \frac{10}{19} = \frac{22}{133}$

(ii) $P(\text{at least one } G) = 1 - P(\text{all boys})$

$= 1 - \frac{22}{133} = \frac{111}{133}$

(Sometimes it is faster to work out the probabilities that you don't want and subtract the result from 1.)

Exercise 24.3

A set of 52 playing cards contains 13 each of hearts, diamonds, clubs and spades. Diamonds and hearts are red. Clubs and spades are black. There are no jokers in a 52 card pack.

1 A card is randomly selected from a pack of 52 playing cards, and its suit is recorded. The card is not replaced. Then a second card is chosen.

(a) Draw a tree diagram to represent this situation.
(b) Use the tree diagram to find the probability that:

(i) both cards are hearts
(ii) both cards are clubs
(iii) the first card is red and the second card is black.

2 Mohammed has four scrabble tiles with the letters A, B, C and D on them. He draws a letter at random and places it on the table, then he draws a second letter and a third, placing them down next to the previously drawn letter.

(a) Draw a tree diagram to show the possible outcomes.
(b) What is the probability that the letters he has drawn spell the words:

(i) CAD (ii) BAD (iii) DAD?

(c) What is the probability that he won't draw the letter B?
(d) What is Mohammed's chance of drawing the letters in alphabetical order?

Living maths

3 Clarissa is having a baby. She knows that the baby will be a girl and she wants her to have a first and a second name. The names she is considering are Olga, Shirley, Karen and Anne.

(a) Draw a tree diagram to show all possible combinations of names for the baby.
(b) If Clarissa chooses two names at random, what are the chances that the baby will be called Karen Anne?
(c) What is the chance of the baby being named Anne Shirley?

4 Sindi, Lee, Marita, Roger, Bongile and Simone are the six members of a school committee. The committee needs to choose a chairperson and a treasurer. One person cannot fill both positions.

(a) Draw a tree diagram to show how many ways there are of choosing a chairperson and a treasurer.
(b) If the chairperson and treasurer are chosen at random, what is the probability of choosing Sindi as chairperson and Lee as treasurer?

5 A cleaner accidentally knocked the name labels off three students' lockers. The name labels are Raju, Sam and Kerry. The tree diagram shows the possible ways of replacing the name labels.

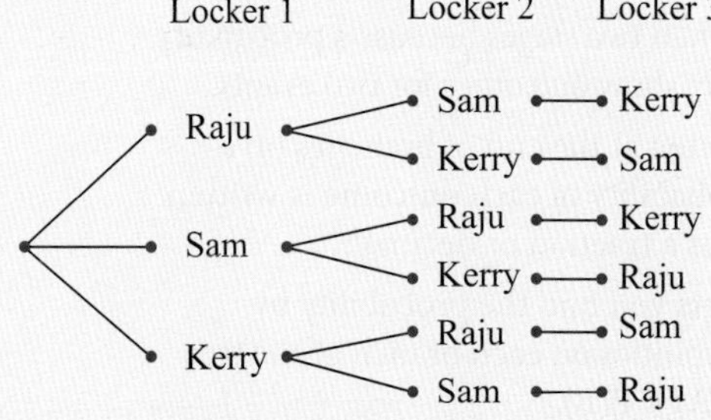

(a) Copy the diagram and write the probabilities next to each branch.
(b) Are these events conditional or independent? Why?
(c) How many correct ways are there to match the name labels to the lockers?
(d) How many possible ways are there for the cleaner to label the lockers?
(e) If the cleaner randomly stuck the names back onto the lockers, what are his chances of getting the names correct?

6 A climatologist reports that the probability of rain on Friday is 0.21. If it rains on Friday, there is a 0.83 chance of rain on Saturday, if it doesn't rain on Friday, the chance of rain on Saturday is only 0.3.

(a) Draw a tree diagram to represent this situation.
(b) Use your diagram to work out the probability of rain on:

(i) Friday and Saturday
(ii) Saturday.

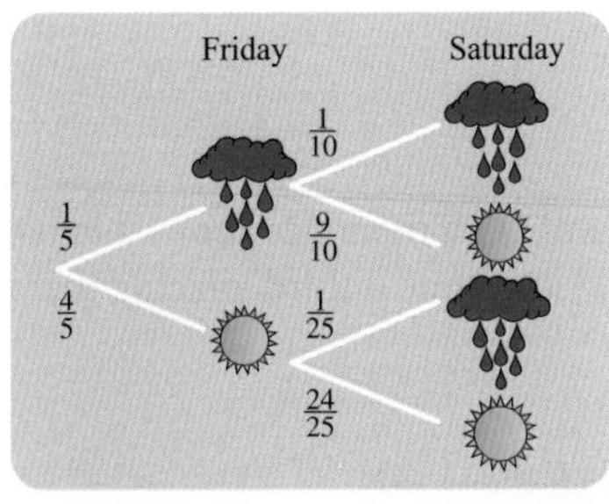

7 Look at this tree diagram sketched by a weather forecaster.

(a) Give the tree diagram a title.
(b) What does it tell you about the weather for the next two days in this place?
(Make sure you include probabilities as part of your answer).

8 Mahmoud enjoys flying his kite. On any given day, the probability that there is a good wind is $\frac{3}{4}$. If there is a good wind, the probability that the kite will fly is $\frac{5}{8}$. If there is not a good wind, the probability that the kite will fly is $\frac{1}{16}$.

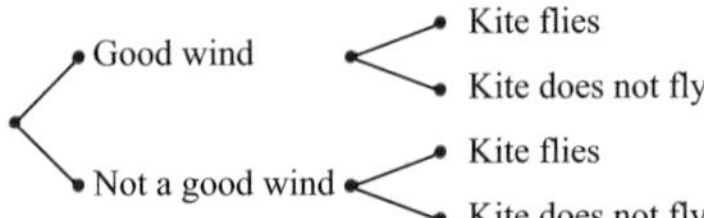

(a) Copy this tree diagram. Write the probabilities next to each branch.
(b) What is the probability of good wind and the kite flying?
(c) Find the probability that, whatever the wind, the kite does not fly.
(d) If the kite flies, the probability that it gets stuck in a tree is $\frac{1}{2}$. Calculate the probability that, whatever the wind, the kite gets stuck in a tree.

Summary

Do you know the following?

- The sample space of an event is all the possible outcomes of the event.
- When an event has two or more stages it is called a combined event.
- Tree diagrams are useful for organising the outcomes of different stages in an event. They are particularly useful when there are more than two stages because a probability space diagram can only show outcomes for two events.
- The outcomes are written at the end of branches on a tree diagram. The probability of each outcome is written next to the branches as a fraction or decimal.
- For independent events you find the probability by multiplying the probabilities on each branch of the tree. $P(A \text{ and then } B) = P(A) \times P(B)$.
- When events are mutually exclusive, you need to add the probabilities obtained by multiplication.

Are you able to ...?

- draw a tree diagram to organise the outcomes for simple combined events
- find the probability of each branch of a tree diagram
- calculate the probability of events using tree diagrams.

Examination practice

Exam-style questions

1 **(a)** Draw a tree diagram to show all possible outcomes when two unbiased dice are thrown at the same time.
(b) Find the probability, as a fraction in its lowest terms, that:

(i) the two dice will show a total score of eight
(ii) the two dice will show the same score as each other.

2 The tree diagram shows the possible outcomes when three number cards are placed in a container and then a card is drawn at random three times. Each time a card is drawn, it is placed on the table next to the previous card drawn.

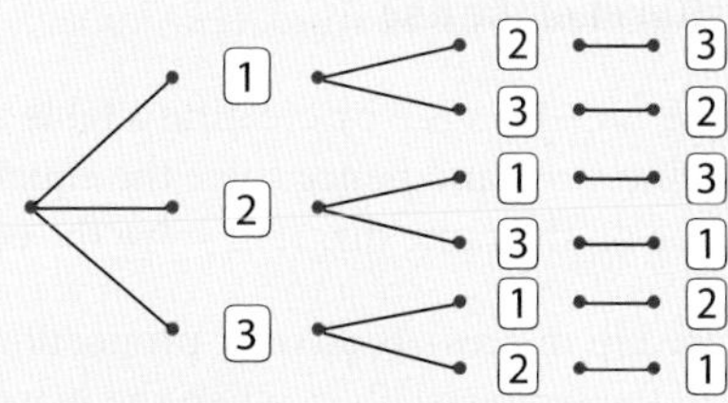

(a) Copy the diagram and fill in the probabilities on each branch.
(b) How many three-digit numbers can be formed in this experiment?
(c) What is the probability of the three-digit number being:

(i) 123 **(ii)** > 200 **(iii)** even **(iv)** divisible by three?

Past paper questions

1 Box A contains 3 black balls and 1 white ball.
Box B contains 3 black balls and 2 white balls.

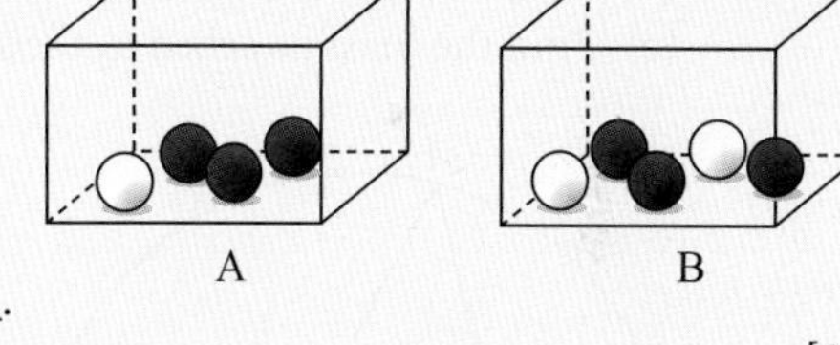

(a) A ball can be chosen at random from either box.
Copy and complete the following statement.
There is a greater probability of choosing a white ball from Box ______.
Explain your answer. [1]

(b) Abdul chooses a box and then chooses a ball from this box at random.
The probability that he chooses box A is $\frac{2}{3}$.

(i) Copy and complete the tree diagram by writing the four probabilities in the empty spaces. [4]

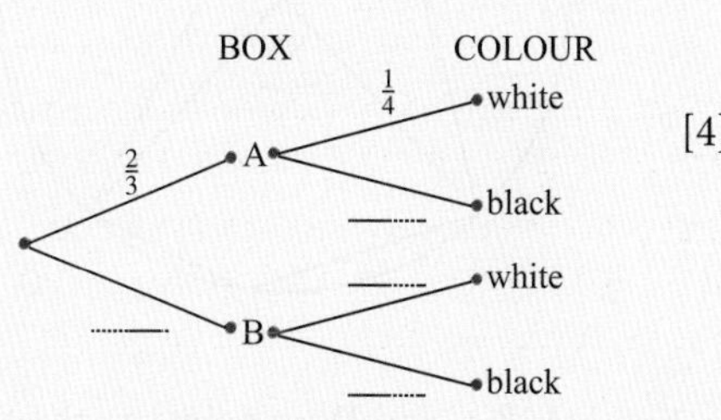

(ii) Find the probability that Abdul chooses box A and a black ball. [2]
(iii) Find the probability that Abdul chooses a black ball. [2]

(c) Tatiana chooses a box and then chooses **two** balls from this box at random (without replacement).
The probability that she chooses box A is $\frac{2}{3}$.
Find the probability that Tatiana chooses two white balls. [2]

[Cambridge IGCSE Mathematics 0580 Paper 41 Q4 a May/June 2010]

Examination practice: structured questions for Units 4–6

Exam-style questions

1 The diagram shows a staircase. The height of the staircase is 3.81 m, to the nearest centimetre, and the horizontal distance AB is 4.62 m to the nearest centimetre.

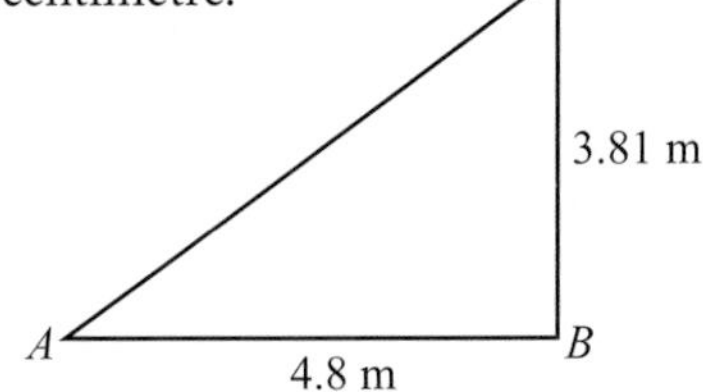

(a) Find upper and lower bounds for:

(i) the height BC

(ii) the horizontal distance AB.

(b) Find the maximum possible distance AC.

(c) Find the maximum possible gradient of the line AC.

2 (a) Draw the graph of $y = x^2 - 6x + 8$ for $-1 \leq x \leq 6$ by creating a table and plotting points.

(b) On the same diagram draw the line $y = 6$ and hence solve the equation $x^2 - 6x + 2 = 0$.

(c) By drawing a suitable straight line on the same diagram solve the equation $x^2 - 8x + 13 = 0$.

3 The extension of a spring, x (measured in metres), is directly proportional to the mass, m (measured in kilograms), attached to the end. The extension of the spring is 30 cm when the mass is 5 kg.

(a) Find an equation connecting x with m.

(b) Find x if $m = 12$ kg.

(c) Find m if $x = 0.54$ m.

You are now given that the potential energy stored, E (measured in joules), in the spring is proportional to the square of the extension, x. When the extension is h metres, the energy stored is P joules.

(d) Find an equation connecting E and x (your answer will contain terms in P and h).

(e) Find the mass attached to the spring if the potential energy is $49P$ joules.

4

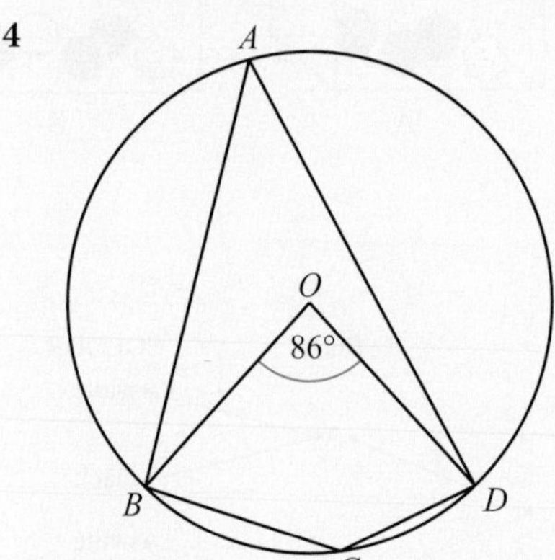

A, B, C and D are points on the circle, centre O. Angle $BOD = 86°$.

(a) (i) Work out the size of angle BAD.

(ii) Give a reason for your answer.

(b) (i) Work out the size of angle BCD.

(ii) Explain your answer fully.

5 (a) A pair of lines have equations:

$y = 2x - 1$ and $x + y = 5$.

Copy the axes shown below and draw both lines onto the same diagram.

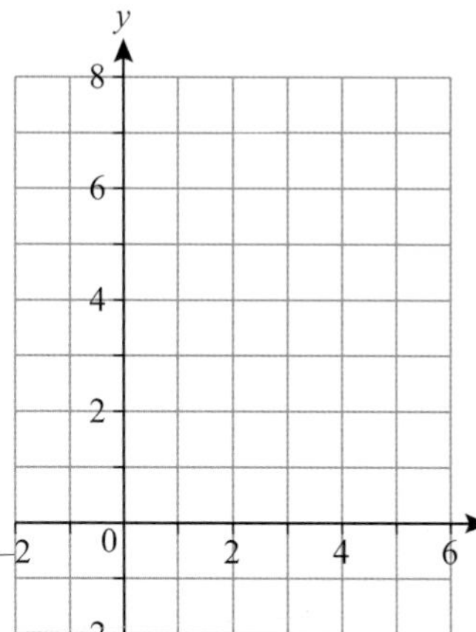

(b) Hence solve the pair of simultaneous equations:

$y = 2x - 1$
$x + y = 5$

(c) By shading the **unwanted** region, illustrate the region which satisfies the three inequalities:

$y > 2x - 1$

$x + y < 5$

$x > 0$

6 A bag contains n white tiles and five black tiles. The tiles are all equal in shape and size. A tile is drawn at random and is *not* replaced. A second tile is then drawn.

(a) Find:

(i) the probability that the first tile is white
(ii) the probability that both the first and second tiles are white.

(b) You are given that the probability of drawing two white tiles is $\frac{7}{22}$.

Show that:

$3n^2 - 17n - 28 = 0$

(c) Solve the equation, $3n^2 - 17n - 28 = 0$, and hence find the probability that exactly one white and exactly one black tile is drawn.

Past paper questions

1 A factory produces bird food made with sunflower seed, millet and maize.

(a) The amounts of sunflower seed, millet and maize are in the ratio
sunflower seed : millet : maize = 5 : 3 : 1 .
(i) How much millet is there in 15 kg of bird food? [2]
(ii) In a small bag of bird food there is 60 g of sunflower seed.
What is the mass of bird food in a small bag? [2]

(b) Sunflower seeds cost \$204.50 for 30 kg from Jon's farm or €96.40 for 20 kg from Ann's farm.
The exchange rate is \$1 = €0.718.
Which farm has the cheapest price per kilogram?
You must show clearly all your working. [4]

(c) Bags are filled with bird food at a rate of 420 grams per second.
How many 20 kg bags can be **completely** filled in 4 hours? [3]

(d) Brian buys bags of bird food from the factory and sells them in his shop for \$15.30 each. He makes 12.5% profit on each bag.
How much does Brian pay for each bag of bird food? [3]

(e) Brian orders 600 bags of bird food.
The probability that a bag is damaged is $\frac{1}{50}$.
How many bags would Brian expect to be damaged? [1]

[Cambridge IGCSE Mathematics 0580 Paper 42 Q01 October/November 2012]

2 (a)

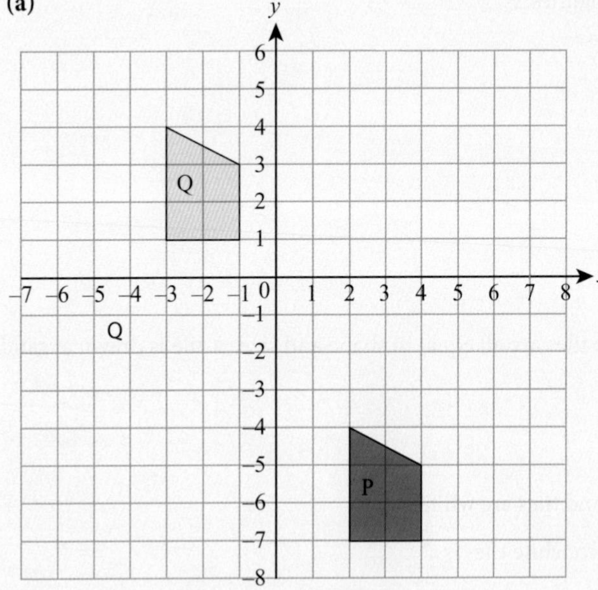

(i) Describe **fully** the single transformation which maps shape P onto shape Q. [2]

(ii) On the grid above, draw the image of shape P after reflection in the line $y = -1$. [2]

(iii) On the grid above, draw the image of shape P under the transformation represented by the matrix $\begin{pmatrix} 0 & -1 \\ 1 & 0 \end{pmatrix}$. [3]

[Cambridge IGCSE Mathematics 0580 Paper 42 Q02 a May/June 2013]

3 (a) Complete the table of values for $y = x^2 + 2x - 4$. [3]

x	−4	−3	−2	−1	0	1	2	3
y	4		−4		−4			11

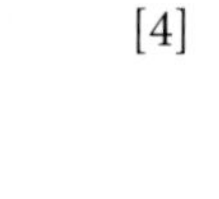

(b) On the grid, draw the graph of $y = x^2 + 2x - 4$ for $-4 \leq x \leq 3$. [4]

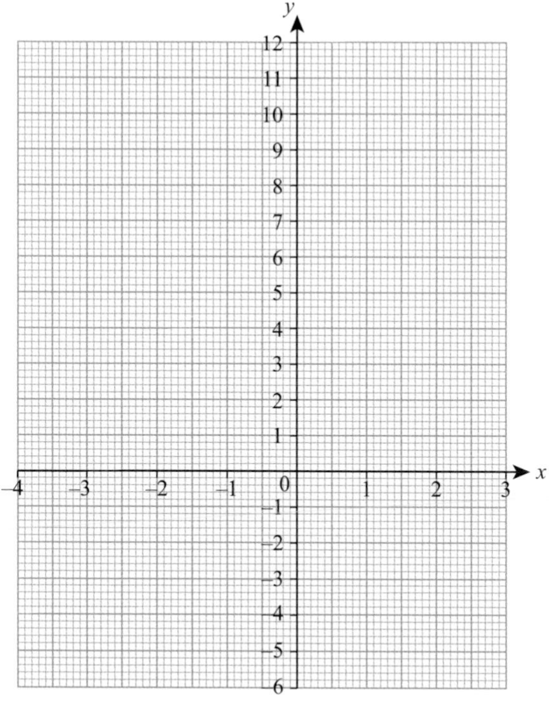

(c) **(i)** Draw the line of symmetry on the graph. [1]

(ii) Write down the equation of this line of symmetry. [1]

(d) Use your graph to solve the equation $x^2 + 2x - 4 = 3$ [2]

[Cambridge IGCSE Mathematics 0580 Paper 33 Q09 October/November 2012]

4 **(a)** The travel graph shows Helva's journey from her home to the airport.

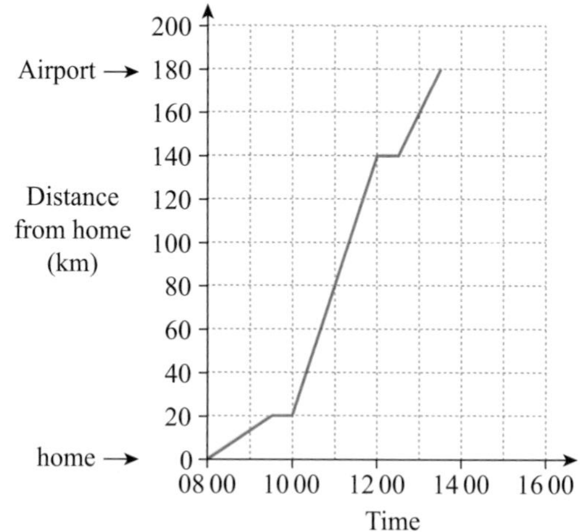

(i) What happened at 09 30? [1]

(ii) Work out the time taken to travel from home to the airport.
Give your answer in hours and minutes. [1]

(iii) Calculate Helva's average speed for the whole journey from home to the airport. [2]

(iv) Between which two times was Helva travelling fastest? [1]

(v) Helva's husband left their home at 11 00 and travelled directly to the airport.
He arrived at 15 30. Complete the travel graph for his journey. [1]

(b) Helva and her husband are flying from Finland to India.
Their plane takes off at 17 00 and arrives in India 7 hours 25 minutes later.

The time in India is $3\frac{1}{2}$ hours ahead of the time in Finland.

(i) What is the local time in India when the plane arrives? [2]

(ii) The temperature is -3°C in Finland and 23°C in India.
Write down the difference between these two temperatures. [1]

(c) Helva exchanged 7584 rupees for euros (€).
The exchange rate was 1€ = 56 rupees.
How many euros did Helva receive?
Give your answer correct to 2 decimal places. [2]

[Cambridge IGCSE Mathematics 0580 Paper 33 Q02 October/November 2012]

5 **(a)**

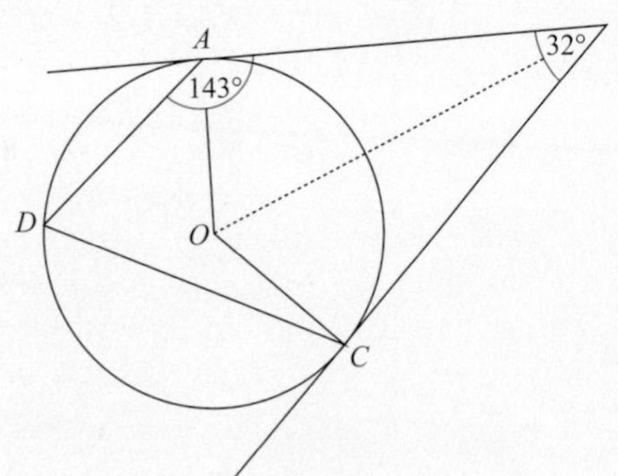

NOT TO SCALE

Points *A*, *C* and *D* lie on a circle centre *O*.
BA and *BC* are tangents to the circle.
Angle $ABC = 32°$ and angle $DAB = 143°$.

(i) Calculate angle *AOC* in quadrilateral *AOCB*. [2]

(ii) Calculate angle *ADC*. [1]

(iii) Calculate angle *OCD*. [2]

(iv) **(a)** $OA = 6$ cm.

Calculate the length of *AB*. [3]

[Cambridge IGCSE Mathematics 0580 Paper 42 Q04 a October/November 2012]

6 **(a)** **(i)** Factorise completely the expression $4x^2 - 18x - 10$. [3]

(ii) Solve $4x^2 - 18x - 10 = 0$. [1]

(b) Solve the equation $2x^2 - 7x - 10 = 0$.
Show all your working and give your answers correct to two decimal places. [4]

(c) Write $\frac{6}{3x-1} - \frac{2}{x-2}$ as a single fraction in its simplest form. [3]

[Cambridge IGCSE Mathematics 0580 Paper 42 Q03 October/November 2012]

Answers

Unit 1

Chapter 1

Exercise 1.1

1. (a) {3, 4, 6, 11, 16, 19, 25}
   (b) {4, 6, 16}
   (c) {3, 11, 19, 25}
   (d) {−4, −1, 0, 3, 4, 6, 11, 16, 19, 25}
   (e) {−4, −1}
   (f) $\{\frac{1}{2}, 0.75\}$
   (g) {4, 16, 25}
   (h) {3, 11, 19}
   (i) $\{-4, -1, 0, \frac{1}{2}, 0.75, 6\}$
2. (a) {109, 111, 113, 115}
   (b) Various, e.g. {2010, 2012, 2014, 2016} or {2020, 2022, 2024, 2026} etc.
   (c) {995, 997, 999, 1001, 1003, 1005}
   (d) {1, 4, 9, 16, 25}
   (e) Various, e.g. {0.49, 048, 0.47, 0.46, 0.45} or {0.4, 0.3, 0.2, 0.1}
   (f) Various, e.g. $\frac{11}{20}, \frac{3}{5}, \frac{13}{20}, \frac{7}{10}$ etc.
3. (a) even (b) even (c) odd
   (d) odd (e) even (f) even
4. (a) A perfect number is a number that is half of the sum of all of the positive numbers that will divide into it (including itself). For example, 6 is equal to half the sum of all the positive number that will divide into it $(1 + 2 + 3 + 6) \div 2 = 6$.
   (b) A palindromic number is a 'symmetrical' number like 16461 that remains the same when its digits are reversed.
   (c) A narcissistic number is one that is the sum of its own digits each raised to the power of the number of digits, e.g. $371 = 3^3 + 7^3 + 1^3$

Exercise 1.2

1. (a) $19 < 45$ (b) $12 + 18 = 30$
   (c) $0.5 = \frac{1}{2}$ (d) $0.8 \neq 8.0$
   (e) $-34 < 2 \times -16$ (f) $\therefore x = \sqrt{72}$
   (g) $x \leq -45$ (h) $\pi \approx 3.14$
   (i) $5.1 > 5.01$ (j) $3 + 4 \neq 3 \times 4$
   (k) $12 - (-12) > 12$
   (l) $(-12) + (-24) < 0$
   (m) $12x \approx -40$
2. (a) false (b) true (c) true
   (d) true (e) true (f) false
   (g) false (h) true (i) true
   (j) true (k) false (l) false
   (m) true (n) false
3. Students' own discussions.

Exercise 1.3

1. (a) 2, 4, 6, 8, 10
   (b) 3, 6, 9, 12, 15
   (c) 5, 10, 15, 20, 25
   (d) 8, 16, 24, 32, 40
   (e) 9, 18, 27, 36, 45
   (f) 10, 20, 30, 40, 50
   (g) 12, 24, 36, 48, 60
   (h) 100, 200, 300, 400, 500
2. (a) 29, 58, 87, 116, 145, 174, 203, 232, 261, 290
   (b) 44, 88, 132, 176, 220, 264, 308, 352, 396, 440
   (c) 75, 150, 225, 300, 375, 450, 525, 600, 675, 750
   (d) 114, 228, 342, 456, 570, 684, 798, 912, 1026, 1140
   (e) 299, 598, 897, 1196, 1495, 1794, 2093, 2392, 2691, 2990
   (f) 350, 700, 1050, 1400, 1750, 2100, 2450, 2800, 3150, 3500
   (g) 1012, 2024, 3036, 4048, 5060, 6072, 7084, 8096, 9108, 10 120
   (h) 9123, 18 246, 27 369, 36 492, 45 615, 54 738, 63 861, 72 984, 82 107, 91 230
3. (a) 32, 36, 40, 44, 48, 52
   (b) 50, 100, 150, 200, 250, 300, 350
   (c) 4100, 4200, 4300, 4400, 4500, 4600, 4700, 4800, 4900
4. 576, 396, 792, 1164
5. (c) and (e) not a multiple of 27

Exercise 1.4

1. (a) 10 (b) 40 (c) 12
   (d) 9 (e) 385 (f) 66
   (g) 18 (h) 60 (i) 72
   (j) 21 (k) 40 (l) 36
2. No – the common multiples are infinite.

Exercise 1.5

1. (a) $F_4 = 1, 2, 4$
   (b) $F_5 = 1, 5$
   (c) $F_8 = 1, 2, 4, 8$
   (d) $F_{11} = 1, 11$
   (e) $F_{18} = 1, 2, 3, 6, 9, 18$
   (f) $F_{12} = 1, 2, 3, 4, 6, 12$
   (g) $F_{35} = 1, 5, 7, 35$
   (h) $F_{40} = 1, 2, 4, 5, 8, 10, 20$
   (i) $F_{57} = 1, 3, 19, 57$
   (j) $F_{90} = 1, 2, 3, 5, 6, 9, 10, 15, 18, 30, 45, 90$
   (k) $F_{100} = 1, 2, 4, 5, 10, 20, 25, 50, 100$
   (l) $F_{132} = 1, 2, 3, 4, 6, 11, 12, 22, 33, 44, 66, 132$
   (m) $F_{160} = 1, 2, 4, 5, 8, 10, 16, 20, 32, 40, 80, 160$
   (n) $F_{153} = 1, 3, 9, 17, 51, 153$
   (o) $F_{360} = 1, 2, 3, 4, 5, 6, 8, 9, 10, 12, 15, 18, 20, 25, 30, 36, 40, 45, 60, 72, 90, 120, 270, 360$
2. (a) 4 (b) 45 (c) 14
   (d) 22 (e) 8
3. (a) false (b) true (c) true
   (d) true (e) true (f) true
   (g) true (h) false
4. The smallest factor is 1 and the largest factor is the number itself.

Exercise 1.6

1. (a) 3 (b) 8 (c) 5
   (d) 14 (e) 4 (f) 2
   (g) 22 (h) 6
2. (a) 3 (b) 3 (c) 11
3. (a) Any two from: 4, 6, 10, 14.
   (b) 12 and 18 are the only possible two, less than 20.
4. 1 because each prime number has only 1 and itself as factors
5. 18 m
6. 20 students
7. 150 bracelets

Exercise 1.7

1. 2
2. 14
3. (a) 6, 8, 9, 10, 12, 14, 15, 16, 18, 20, 21, 22, 24, 25, 26, 27, 28

(b) $6 = 3 + 3, 8 = 3 + 5,$
$9 = 2 + 7, 10 = 5 + 5,$
$12 = 5 + 7, 14 = 3 + 11,$
$15 = 2 + 13, 16 = 5 + 11,$
$18 = 5 + 13, 20 = 3 + 17,$
$21 = 2 + 19$ or $17 + 7$, $22 = 5 + 17,$
$24 = 5 + 19$ or $17 + 7$, $25 = 2 + 23,$
$26 = 3 + 23$ or $13 + 13$, $27 =$ not possible, $28 = 5 + 23$

4 3 and 5, 5 and 7, 11 and 13, 17 and 19, 29 and 31, 41 and 43, 59 and 61, 71 and 73

5 149 is prime. Determined by trial division by all integers from 2 to $\sqrt{149}$

6 (a) 233, 239, 293, 311, 313, 317, 373, 379
(b) 2333, 2339, 2393, 2399, 2939

Exercise 1.8

1 (a) $30 = 2 \times 3 \times 5$
(b) $24 = 2 \times 2 \times 2 \times 3$
(c) $100 = 2 \times 2 \times 5 \times 5$
(d) $225 = 3 \times 3 \times 5 \times 5$
(e) $360 = 2 \times 2 \times 2 \times 3 \times 3 \times 5$
(f) $504 = 2 \times 2 \times 2 \times 3 \times 3 \times 7$
(g) $650 = 2 \times 5 \times 5 \times 13$
(h) $1125 = 3 \times 3 \times 5 \times 5 \times 5$
(i) $756 = 2 \times 2 \times 3 \times 3 \times 3 \times 7$
(j) $9240 = 2 \times 2 \times 2 \times 3 \times 5 \times 7 \times 11$

Exercise 1.9

1 (a) 12 (b) 24 (c) 18
(d) 26 (e) 25 (f) 22
(g) 78 (h) 5

2 (a) 540
(b) 216
(c) 360
(d) 40
(e) 360
(f) 2850
(g) 270
(h) 360

3 (a) HCF = 36
LCM = 216
(b) HCF = 25
LCM = 100
(c) HCF = 5
LCM = 2280
(d) HCF = 12
LCM = 420

4 120 listeners

5 36 minutes

Exercise 1.10

1 (a) 65, 10, 70, 500
(b) 104, 64 (c) 21, 798

2 (a) true (b) false (c) false
(d) false (e) false (f) true
(g) false (h) false (i) true
(j) false

3 (a) no (b) no (c) no

4 (a) no (b) yes (c) no

5 (a) 2, 3, 4, 6
(b) 2, 3, 4, 6, 9, 12, 18
(c) Express the number as a product of its prime factors and then check that the prime factors of 12, 15 or 24 are included in the product.

Exercise 1.11

1 (a) 9 (b) 49 (c) 121
(d) 144 (e) 441 (f) 361
(g) 1024 (h) 10 000 (i) 196
(j) 4624

2 (a) 1 (b) 27 (c) 64
(d) 216 (e) 729 (f) 1000
(g) 1 000 000 (h) 5832
(i) 27 000 (j) 8 000 000

3 (a) $x = 5$ (b) $x = 2$
(c) $x = 11$ (d) $x = 9$
(e) $x = 18$ (f) $x = 20$
(g) $x = 20$ (h) $x = 15$
(i) $x = 1$ (j) $x = 81$
(k) $x = 1$ (l) $x = 6561$
(m) $x = 8$ (n) $x = 1$
(o) $x = 4$

4 (a) 3 (b) 8 (c) 1
(d) 2 (e) 10 (f) 0
(g) 9 (h) 20 (i) 36
(j) 42 (k) 2 (l) 1
(m) 3 (n) 4 (o) 10
(p) 6 (q) 8 (r) 9
(s) 12 (t) 18

5 (a) $324 = \underbrace{2 \times 2} \times \underbrace{3 \times 3} \times \underbrace{3 \times 3}$
$\sqrt{324} = 2 \times 3 \times 3$
$\sqrt{324} = 18$

(b) $225 = \underbrace{3 \times 3} \times \underbrace{5 \times 5}$
$\sqrt{225} = 3 \times 5$
$\sqrt{225} = 15$

(c) $784 = \underbrace{2 \times 2} \times \underbrace{2 \times 2} \times \underbrace{7 \times 7}$
$\sqrt{784} = 2 \times 2 \times 7$
$\sqrt{784} = 28$

(d) $2025 = \underbrace{3 \times 3} \times \underbrace{3 \times 3} \times \underbrace{5 \times 5}$
$\sqrt{2025} = 3 \times 3 \times 5$
$\sqrt{2025} = 45$

(e) $19\,600 = \underbrace{2 \times 2} \times \underbrace{2 \times 2} \times \underbrace{5 \times 5} \times \underbrace{7 \times 7}$
$\sqrt{19600} = 2 \times 2 \times 5 \times 7$
$\sqrt{19600} = 140$

(f) $250000 = \underbrace{2 \times 2} \times \underbrace{2 \times 2} \times \underbrace{5 \times 5}$
$\times \underbrace{5 \times 5} \times \underbrace{5 \times 5}$
$\sqrt{250000} = 2 \times 2 \times 5 \times 5 \times 5$
$\sqrt{250000} = 500$

6 (a) $27 = \underbrace{3 \times 3 \times 3}$
$\sqrt[3]{27} = 3$

(b) $729 = \underbrace{3 \times 3 \times 3} \times \underbrace{3 \times 3 \times 3}$
$\sqrt[3]{729} = 3 \times 3$
$\sqrt[3]{729} = 9$

(c) $2197 = \underbrace{13 \times 13 \times 13}$
$\sqrt[3]{2179} = 13$

(d) $1000 = \underbrace{2 \times 2 \times 2} \times \underbrace{5 \times 5 \times 5}$
$\sqrt[3]{1000} = 2 \times 5$
$\sqrt[3]{1000} = 10$

(e) $15\,625 = \underbrace{5 \times 5 \times 5} \times \underbrace{5 \times 5 \times 5}$
$\sqrt[3]{15\,625} = 5 \times 5$
$\sqrt[3]{15\,625} = 25$

(f) $32\,768 = \underbrace{2 \times 2 \times 2} \times \underbrace{2 \times 2 \times 2} \times$
$\underbrace{2 \times 2 \times 2} \times \underbrace{2 \times 2 \times 2} \times$
$\underbrace{2 \times 2 \times 2}$
$\sqrt[3]{32\,768} = 2 \times 2 \times 2 \times 2 \times 2$
$\sqrt[3]{32\,768} = 32$

7 (a) 25 (b) 49 (c) 64
(d) 32 (e) 7 (f) 5
(g) 14 (h) 10 (i) 8
(j) 4 (k) 10 (l) 10
(m) 6 (n) 6 (o) 3
(p) $\frac{3}{2}$

8 (a) 10 cm (b) 27 cm
(c) 41 mm (d) 40 cm

9 (a) 31 (b) 17
(c) 65 (d) 17
(e) 68 (f) 24
(g) 730 (h) 82
(i) 33 (j) 129

Exercise 1.12

1 (a) +$100 (b) −25 km
(c) −10 marks (d) +2 kg
(e) −1.5 kg (f) −8000 m
(g) −10 °C (h) −24 m
(i) −$2000 (j) +$250
(k) −2 h (l) +400 m
(m) +$450.00

Exercise 1.13

1 (a) $2 < 8$ (b) $4 < 9$
(c) $12 > 3$ (d) $6 > -4$
(e) $-7 < 4$ (f) $-2 < 4$
(g) $-2 > -11$ (h) $-12 > -20$
(i) $-8 < 0$ (j) $-2 < 2$
(k) $-12 < -4$ (l) $-32 < -3$
(m) $0 > -3$ (n) $-3 < 11$
(o) $12 > -89$

2 (a) −12, −8, −1, 7, 10
(b) −10, −8, −4, −3, 4, 9
(c) −12, −11, −7, −5, 0, 7
(d) −94, −90, −83, −50, 0

3 (a) 1 °C (b) −1 °C
(c) −3 °C (d) 12 °C
(e) −3 °C

4 $28.50

5 (a) −$420 (b) $920
(c) −$220

6 −11 m
7 −8 °C

8 (a) 7 p.m. (b) 12 p.m.
(c) 10 p.m. (d) 1 a.m.

Exercise 1.14

1 (a) $(4+7)\times 3 = 11\times 3 = 33$
(b) $(20-4)\div 4 = 16\div 4 = 4$
(c) $50\div(20+5) = 50\div 25 = 2$
(d) $6\times(2+9) = 6\times 11 = 66$
(e) $(4+7)\times 4 = 11\times 4 = 44$
(f) $(100-40)\times 3 = 60\times 3 = 180$
(g) $16+(25\div 5) = 16+5 = 21$
(h) $19-(12+2) = 19-14 = 5$
(i) $40\div(12-4) = 40\div 8 = 5$
(j) $100\div(4+16) = 100\div 20 = 5$
(k) $121\div(33\div 3) = 121\div 11 = 11$

2 (a) 108 (b) 72 (c) 3
(d) 10 (e) 32 (f) 9
(g) 5 (h) 1 (i) 140

3 (a) 13 (b) 8 (c) 58
(d) 192 (e) 12 000 (f) 1606
(g) 260 (h) 24 (i) 868

4 (a) 78 (b) 6 (c) 336
(d) 18 (e) 3 (f) 3
(g) 8 (h) 4 (i) 9

5 (a) $3\times(4+6)=30$
(b) $(25-15)\times 9=90$
(c) $(40-10)\times 3=90$
(d) $(14-9)\times 2=10$
(e) $(12+3)\div 5=3$
(f) $(19-9)\times 15=150$
(g) $(10+10)\div(6-2)=5$
(h) $(3+8)\times(15-9)=66$
(i) $(9-4)\times(7+2)=45$
(j) $(10-4)\times 5=30$
(k) $6\div(3+3)\times 5=5$
(l) BODMAS means that brackets are not needed
(m) $(1+4)\times(20\div 5)=20$
(n) $(8+5-3)\times 2=20$
(o) $36\div(3\times 3-3)=6$
(p) $3\times(4-2)\div 6=1$
(q) $(40\div 4)+1=11$
(r) BODMAS means that brackets are not needed

Exercise 1.15

1 (a) $5\times 10+3 = 50+3 = 53$
(b) $5\times(10+3) = 5\times 13 = 65$
(c) $2+10\times 3 = 2+30 = 32$
(d) $(2+10)\times 3 = 12\times 3 = 36$
(e) $23+7\times 2 = 23+14 = 37$
(f) $6\times 2\div(3+3) = 12\div 6 = 2$
(g) $\frac{15-5}{2\times 5} = \frac{10}{10} = 1$
(h) $(17+1)\div 9+2 = 18\div 9+2 = 2+2 = 4$
(i) $\frac{16-4}{4-1} = \frac{12}{3} = 4$
(j) $17+3\times 21 = 63+17 = 80$
(k) $48-(2+3)\times 2 = 48-5\times 2 = 48-10 = 38$
(l) $12\times 4-4\times 8 = 48-32 = 16$
(m) $15+30\div 3+6 = 15+10+6 = 31$
(n) $20-6\div 3+3 = 20-2+3 = 21$
(o) $10-4\times 2\div 2 = 10-4\div 1 = 10-4 = 6$

2 (a) 7 (b) 7 (c) 3
(d) 0 (e) 3 (f) 10

3 (a) false (b) true
(c) false (d) true

4 (a) $2-10\div 5=0$
(b) $13-18\div 9=11$
(c) $8\div(16-14)-3=1$
(d) $(9+5)-(6-4)=12$
or $(9+5)-(12-4)=6$

Exercise 1.16

1 (a) −10 (b) 8.86 (c) 13
(d) 29 (e) −22 (f) 8.75
(g) 20 (h) 0 (i) 4
(j) 70 (k) 12 (l) 20
(m) 8 (n) 15 (o) 20

2 (a) correct
(b) incorrect = 608
(c) correct
(d) correct
(e) incorrect = 368
(f) incorrect = 10

3 (a) $12\div(28-24)=3$
(b) $84-10\times 8=4$
(c) $3+7(0.7+1.3)=17$
(d) $23\times 11-22\times 11=11$

(e) $40 \div 5 \div (7-5) = 4$
(f) $9 + 15 \div (3+2) = 12$

4 (a) 0.5 (b) 2 (c) 0.183
(d) 0.5 (e) $\frac{1}{3} \approx 0.333$ (3sf)
(f) 1 (g) 2
(h) $\frac{2}{3} \approx 0.667$ (3sf)

5 correct to 3 significant figures
(a) 0.0112 (b) 0.0386
(c) −0.317 (d) 0.339

6 correct to 3 significant figures
(a) 89.4 (b) 20.8 (c) 7.52
(d) 19.6 (e) 2.94 (f) 1.45
(g) 0.25 or $\frac{1}{4}$ (h) 1.72

In questions 4, 5 and 6 you may find that your calculator gives an exact answer rather than a decimal. This may include a root or a fraction. Check your calculator manual to find out how to change this to a decimal.

Exercise 1.17

1 (a) 3.19 (b) 0.06 (c) 38.35
(d) 2.15 (e) 1.00 (f) 0.05
(g) 0.01 (h) 41.57 (i) 8.30
(j) 0.42 (k) 0.06 (l) 0.01
(m) 3.02 (n) 12.02 (o) 15.12

2 (a) (i) 4512 (ii) 4510
(iii) 5000
(b) (i) 12310 (ii) 12300
(iii) 10000
(c) (i) 65240 (ii) 65200
(iii) 70000
(d) (i) 320.6 (ii) 321
(iii) 300
(e) (i) 25.72 (ii) 25.7
(iii) 30
(f) (i) 0.0007650 (ii) 0.000765
(iii) 0.0008
(g) (i) 1.009 (ii) 1.01
(iii) 1
(h) (i) 7.349 (ii) 7.35
(iii) 8
(i) (i) 0.009980 (ii) 0.00998
(iii) 0.010
(j) (i) 0.02814 (ii) 0.0281
(iii) 0.03
(k) (i) 31.01 (ii) 31.0
(iii) 30
(l) (i) 0.006474 (ii) 0.00647
(iii) 0.006

3 (a) 2.556 (b) 2.56 (c) 2.6
(d) 2.56 (e) 2.6 (f) 3

Examination practice

Exam-style questions

1 (a) 3, 4, 6, 9, 15, 16, 19, 20
(b) 4, 9, 16 (c) −4, −1
(d) 3, 19 (e) 4, 6, 16, 20
(f) 4, 16, 20

2 (a) 1, 2, 3, 4, 6, 12
(b) 1, 2, 3, 4, 6, 8, 12, 24 (c) 12

3 16

4 (a) 12, 24, 36, 48, 60
(b) 18, 36, 54, 72, 90
(c) 30, 60, 90, 120, 150
(d) 80, 160, 240, 320, 400

5 72

6 2, 3, 5, 7, 11, 13, 17, 19, 23, 29, 31, 37

7 (a) $2^4 \times 5^2$
(b) $2^3 \times 3^3 \times 5$
(c) (i) $2^4 \times 3^3 \times 5^2 = 10\,800$
(ii) $2^3 \times 5 = 40$
(iii) $2^2 \times 5 = 20$
(iv) 1080 is not a cube number. Not all the factors are powers with indices that are multiples of 3.

8 (a) 676 (b) 79507

9 (a) 102 (b) 110 (c) 104

10 −4°C

11 (a) 32 (b) 340 (c) 25

12 $(7+14) \div (4-1) \times 2 = 14$

Past paper questions*

1 (a) 56, or any multiple of 56
(b) 3, 9, 27
(c) 3

2 (a) 0.001 (3sf)
(b) 0.002 (3sf) (0.00193... or 1.93×10^{-3} also fine)

Chapter 2

Exercise 2.1

1 (a) $6xy$ (b) $7ab$ (c) xyz
(d) $2y^2$ (e) $4ab$ (f) $12xy$
(g) $5ab$ (h) yz^2 (i) $\frac{6}{x}$
(j) $\frac{4x}{2y} = \frac{2x}{y}$ (k) $\frac{x+3}{4}$
(l) $\frac{m^3}{m^2} = m$
(m) $4x + 5y$ (n) $7a - 2b$
(o) $2x(x-4)$ (p) $\frac{3x(x+1)}{2}$
(q) $\frac{2(x+4)}{3}$ (r) $\frac{4x}{6x} = \frac{2}{3}$

2 (a) $m + 13$ (b) $m + 5$
(c) $25 - m$ (d) m^3
(e) $\frac{m}{3} + 3$ (f) $4m - 2m = 2m$

3 (a) $x + 3$ (b) $x - 6$ (c) $10x$
(d) $-8 + x$ (e) $x + x^2$ (f) $x + 2x$
(g) $\frac{2x}{x+4}$

4 (a) $\$(x - 10)$ (b) $\$\frac{x}{4}$ (c) \$15

5 (a) $m + 10$ years (b) $m - 10$ years
(c) $\frac{m}{2}$ years

6 (a) $\$\frac{p}{3}$ (b) $\$\frac{p}{5}$, $\$\frac{p}{5}$ and $\$\frac{3p}{5}$

Exercise 2.2

1 (a) 9 (b) 30 (c) 10
(d) 27 (e) 18 (f) 7
(g) 16 (h) 36 (i) 4
(j) 6 (k) 6 (l) 30
(m) 5 (n) 2

2 (a) 30 (b) 45 (c) 16
(d) 5 (e) 13 (f) 16
(g) 31 (h) 450 (i) 24
(j) 8 (k) 24 (l) 5
(m) $\frac{26}{3}$ (n) 10 (o) 4
(p) 3 (q) 6 (r) 225
(s) 12 (t) −10

3 (a) (i) $y = 0$ (ii) $y = 12$
(iii) $y = 16$ (iv) $y = 40$
(v) $y = 200$
(b) (i) $y = 1$ (ii) $y = 10$
(iii) $y = 13$ (iv) $y = 31$
(v) $y = 151$
(c) (i) $y = 100$ (ii) $y = 97$
(iii) $y = 96$ (iv) $y = 90$
(v) $y = 50$
(d) (i) $y = 0$ (ii) $y = \frac{3}{2}$
(iii) $y = 2$ (iv) $y = 5$
(v) $y = 25$
(e) (i) $y = 0$ (ii) $y = 9$
(iii) $y = 16$ (iv) $y = 100$
(v) $y = 2500$

(f) (i) 0 (or undefined)
(ii) $y = 33.3$ (3 sf)
(iii) $y = 25$ (iv) $y = 10$
(v) $y = 2$
(g) (i) $y = 4$ (ii) $y = 10$
(iii) $y = 12$ (iv) $y = 24$
(v) $y = 104$
(h) (i) $y = -6$ (ii) $y = 0$
(iii) $y = 2$ (iv) $y = 14$
(v) $y = 94$
(i) (i) $y = 0$ (ii) $y = 81$
(iii) $y = 192$ (iv) $y = 3000$
(v) $y = 375\,000$

4 (a) $\$(3x + 2y)$
(b) (i) \$18 (ii) \$100 (iii) \$350

5 (a) $P = 42$ cm (b) $P = 8$ m
(c) $P = 60$ cm (d) $P = 20$ cm

Exercise 2.3

1 (a) $6x, 4x, x$
(b) $-3y, \frac{3}{4}y, -5y$
(c) $ab, -4ba$
(d) $-2x, 3x$
(e) $5a, 6a$ and $5ab, ab$
(f) $-1xy, -yx$

2 (a) $8y$ (b) $7x$ (c) $13x$
(d) $22x$ (e) $5x$ (f) 0
(g) $-x$ (h) $-3y$ (i) $4x$
(j) $7xy$ (k) $4pq$ (l) $13xyz$
(m) $2x^2$ (n) $5y^2$ (o) $-y^2$
(p) $12ab^2$ (q) $5x^2y$ (q) $2xy^2$

3 (a) $5x + y$ (b) $4x + 2y$
(c) $7x$ (d) $4 + 4x$
(e) $6xy - 2y$ (f) $-x^2 + 2x$
(g) $-x + 4y$ (h) $3x + 3y$
(i) $8x + 6y$ (j) $8x - 2y$
(k) $14x^2 - 4x$ (l) $10x^2$
(m) $12xy - 2x$ (n) $8xy - 2xz$
(o) $-x^2 - 2y^2$ (p) $8x^2y - 2xy$
(q) $6xy - x$ (r) $6xy - 2$

4 (a) $2y - 8$ (b) $4x^2 - 5x$
(c) $7x + 4y$ (d) $y^2 + 5y - 7$
(e) $x^2 - 5x + 3$ (f) $x^2 + 5x - 7$
(g) $3xyz - 3xy + 2xz$
(h) $8xy - 10$ (i) $-3x^2 + 6x - 4$

5 (a) $P = 8x$
(b) $P = 4x + 14$
(c) $P = 6x + 3$
(d) $P = 5x + 4$
(e) $P = 12y - 6$
(f) $P = 8y^2 + 2y + 14$
(g) $P = 12y - 4$
(h) $P = 18x - 1$

Exercise 2.4

1 (a) $12x$ (b) $8y$ (c) $12m$
(d) $6xy$ (e) $8xy$ (f) $27xy$
(g) $24yz$ (h) $12xy$ (i) $8x^2y^2$
(j) $8x^2y$ (k) $27xy^2$ (l) $24xy^2$
(m) $8a^2b$ (n) $12ab^2c$
(o) $12a^2bc$ (p) $16a^2b^2c$
(q) $24abc$ (r) $72x^2y^2$

2 (a) $24x$ (b) $30x^2y$
(c) $12x^2y^2$ (d) x^3yz
(e) $48x$ (f) $24x^3y$
(g) $4x^2y^2$ (h) $12a^2bc$
(i) $60xy$ (j) $8xy$
(k) $9x^3y$ (l) $8x^3y^3$
(m) $42x^2y^2z^2$ (n) $56x^3y^2$
(o) $36x^2y^2z$ (p) $18x^4y^4$
(q) $54x^4y$ (r) $6x^3y^3$

3 (a) $5x$ (b) $4x$ (c) $3x$
(d) $6y$ (e) $7x$ (f) $2y$
(g) $\frac{y}{4}$ (h) $\frac{1}{4y}$ (i) $\frac{z}{2}$
(j) $6y$ (k) $\frac{1}{4}$ (l) $\frac{1}{9}$

4 (a) $4x$ (b) $6y$ (c) $\frac{4x}{y}$
(d) 8 (e) $\frac{7x^2}{y^2}$ (f) $3x$
(g) $\frac{x}{3}$ (h) $\frac{1}{4y}$ (i) $7y$
(j) $\frac{9y}{4}$ (k) $4xy$ (l) $\frac{4y}{x}$

5 (a) $\frac{xy}{6}$ (b) $\frac{x^2}{12}$ (c) $\frac{5x^2y}{6}$
(d) $\frac{10x}{3y}$ (e) $\frac{3xy}{8}$ (f) $\frac{25x^2}{4}$
(g) 2 (h) $\frac{x^2}{3}$ (i) $2xy$
(j) $\frac{8x}{3}$ (k) $\frac{1}{4}$ (l) x^2

Exercise 2.5

1 (a) $2x + 12$ (b) $3x + 6$
(c) $8x + 12$ (d) $10x - 60$
(e) $4x - 8$ (f) $6x - 9$
(g) $5y + 20$ (h) $24 + 6y$
(i) $9y + 18$ (j) $14x - 14y$
(k) $6x - 4y$ (l) $4x + 16y$
(m) $10x - 10y$ (n) $18x - 12y$
(o) $12y - 6x$ (p) $4y - 16x^2$
(q) $9x^2 - 9y$ (r) $28x + 7x^2$

2 (a) $2x^2 + 2xy$ (b) $3xy - 3y^2$
(c) $2x^2 + 4xy$ (d) $12x^2 - 8xy$
(e) $x^2y - xy^2$ (f) $12xy + 6y$
(g) $18xy - 8xy^2$ (h) $6x^2 - 4x^2y$
(i) $12x^2 - 12x^3$ (j) $36x - 8xy$
(k) $10y - 5xy$ (l) $12x - 3xy$
(m) $2x^2y^2 - 4x^3y$ (n) $12xy^2 - 8x^2y^2$
(o) $3x^2y^2 + 3xy^3$ (p) $2x^3y + x^2y^2$
(q) $81x^2 - 18x^3$ (r) $12xy^2 - 4x^2y^2$

3 (a) $A = x^2 + 7x$ (b) $A = 2x^3 - 2x$
(c) $A = 4x^2 - 4x$

Exercise 2.6

1 (a) $10 + 5x$ (b) $7y - 6$
(c) $4x - 8$ (d) $6x - 6$
(e) $2x^2 + 8x - 5$ (f) $4x + 1$
(g) $3x$ (h) $8x + 6$
(i) $6x + 9$ (j) $3x + 2$
(k) $8x + 6$ (l) $3y + xy - 4$
(m) $2x^2 + 8x - 8y$ (n) $-4y^2 + 4xy + 8y$
(o) $10y - 12y^2$ (p) $6x^2 + 12x - 9$
(q) $-y^2 + 6y$ (r) $6x - 6$

2 (a) $6x + 154$ (b) $4x + 2$
(c) $10x + 26$ (d) 92
(e) $2x^2 + 16$ (f) $6x^2 + 10x$
(g) $24xy + 4x$ (h) $2xy + 4x$
(i) $-3x - 18xy$
(j) $21x - 12y - 2xy$ (k) $22x^2 - 7x^3$
(l) $x^2 - xy + 6x - 3y$
(m) $16x - 3xy - 8$ (n) $2x^2$
(o) $4x^2 + 8xy$ (p) $2x^2 - 3x + 15$
(q) $9x - 17$ (r) $7xy + 9x$

Exercise 2.7

1 (a) 2^5 (b) 3^4 (c) 7^2
(d) 11^3 (e) 10^5 (f) 8^5
(g) a^4 (h) x^5 (i) y^6
(j) a^3b^2 (k) x^2y^4 (l) p^3q^2
(m) x^4y^3 (n) x^3y^4 (o) a^3b^3c

2 (a) 10 000 (b) 343
(c) 279 936 (d) 262 144
(e) 100 000 (f) 1
(g) 1024 (h) 6 561
(i) 64 (j) 648
(k) 164 025 (l) 65 536
(m) 5184 (n) 2304
(o) 30 375

3 (a) 2^6 (b) 3^5 (c) $2^4 \times 5^2$
(d) $2^6 \times 5^2$ (e) 2^{14} (f) $2^8 \times 3^4$
(g) 3^{10} (h) 5^8

4 $25 = 5^2$
$36 = 2^2 \times 3^2$
$64 = 2^6$
Power is always even.

Exercise 2.8

1 (a) 3^8 (b) 4^{11} (c) 8^2
(d) x^{13} (e) y^9 (f) y^7
(g) y^6 (h) x^5 (i) $6x^7$
(j) $9y^6$ (k) $2x^4$ (l) $6x^7$
(m) $15x^3$ (n) $8x^7$ (o) $8x^7$
(p) $4x^8$

2 (a) x^2 (b) x^9 (c) y
(d) x^2 (e) x^4 (f) x^2
(g) $3x^2$ (h) $3x^3$ (i) $4y$
(j) $\frac{x}{2}$ (k) 3 (l) $3x$
(m) $\frac{1}{3x}$ (n) $4xy$ (o) 1

3 (a) x^4 (b) x^6 (c) x^{12}
(d) y^6 (e) $32x^{10}$ (f) $9x^4y^4$
(g) 1 (h) $125x^6$ (i) x^6y^6
(j) $x^{10}y^{20}$ (k) x^3y^{12} (l) $16x^2y^4$
(m) $81x^8$ (n) x^4y^{24} (o) 1

4 (a) $12x^6$ (b) $24x^3y$
(c) $4x^4$ (d) $\frac{x^2}{4}$
(e) $44x^3a^4b^2$ (f) $4x^3 + 28x$
(g) $4x^3 - x^5$ (h) x^2
(i) $\frac{7}{x^4}$ (j) $2x^2$
(k) $\frac{x^{12}}{y^6}$ (l) $\frac{x^4y^8}{16}$
(m) 1 (n) $8x^5$ (o) $2xy^3$

Exercise 2.9

1 (a) $\frac{1}{4}$ (b) $\frac{1}{3}$ (c) $\frac{1}{8}$
(d) $\frac{1}{125}$ (e) $\frac{1}{1296}$ (f) $\frac{1}{32}$

2 (a) true (b) false
(c) false (d) false

3 (a) $\frac{1}{x^2}$ (b) $\frac{1}{y^3}$ (c) $\frac{1}{x^2y^2}$
(d) $\frac{2}{x^2}$ (e) $\frac{12}{x^3}$ (f) $\frac{7}{y^3}$
(g) $\frac{8x}{y^3}$ (h) $\frac{12}{x^3y^4}$

4 (a) x (b) $\frac{6}{x^6}$ (c) $\frac{1}{3x^4}$
(d) $\frac{1}{x^{11}}$ (e) $\frac{1}{8x^6}$ (f) $\frac{1}{x^6}$
(g) x (h) $\frac{1}{x^5}$

Exercise 2.10

1 (a) 2 (b) 2 (c) 16
(d) 36 (e) 64

2 (a) $x = 6$ (b) $x = \frac{1}{2}$
(c) $x = 16\,807$ (d) $x = 257$
(e) $x = 4$ (f) $x = 4$
(g) $x = 6$ (h) $x = 5$
(i) $x = 2$ (j) $x = -4$
(k) $x = \frac{1}{6}$ (l) $x = \frac{3}{4}$
(m) $x = 3$

3 (a) $x^{\frac{2}{3}}$ (b) $x^{\frac{7}{6}}$ (c) $\frac{1}{x^3}$
(d) $\frac{x^3}{y}$ (e) $x^{\frac{4}{7}}$ (f) $\frac{7x^2}{4}$
(g) $\frac{2}{x^2}$ (h) $\frac{3}{4x}$ (i) $\frac{1}{4x^{\frac{3}{2}}}$
(j) $\frac{x}{4}$ (k) $\frac{3x^{\frac{3}{4}}}{2}$ (l) $\frac{x}{8}$

Examination practice

Exam-style questions

1 (a) $n + 12$ (b) $2n - 4$
(c) $(nx)^2$ (d) $(n^2)^3$ or $(n^3)^2$

2 (a) $15xy + x$ (b) $5xy + 3y$

3 (a) a^2b (b) $2x^6$ (c) $6x^4y^2$
(d) 1 (e) $4x^5y^3$

4 (a) $x = 5$ (b) $x = -3$

5 (a) $8x - 4$ (b) $x^2 + 37xy$

6 (a) 10 (b) 10 (c) 10

7 (a) x^3 (b) $\frac{4}{x^2}$
(c) $\frac{1}{(2x-2)^3} = \frac{1}{8x^3 - 8}$

8 (a) $15x$ (b) $9y^3$ (c) $4x$

Past paper questions*

1 (a) $4x^{-24}$ or $\frac{4}{x^{24}}$ (b) $\frac{x^2}{16}$

Chapter 3

Diagrams provided as answers are NOT TO SCALE and are to demonstrate construction lines or principles **only**.

Exercise 3.1

1

	(a)	(b)	(c)
(i)	acute	Answers will vary	40°
(ii)	acute		70°
(iii)	obtuse		130°
(iv)	acute		30°
(v)	obtuse		170°
(vi)	right		90°
(vii)	acute		70°
(viii)	acute		60°
(ix)	obtuse		140°

(d) 290°

2 (a) This protractor is able to measure angles from 0° to 360°.
(b) Student's own answer. Something like: ensure that the 0°/360° marking of the protractor is aligned with one of the arms of the angle you are measuring, and the vertex of the angle is aligned with the centre of the protractor. Whether you use the inner or outer scale will be determined by what arm you aligned with 0 – use the scale that gives an angle < 180°.
(c) You would use the scale that gives you an angle > 180°.

Exercise 3.2

(a)

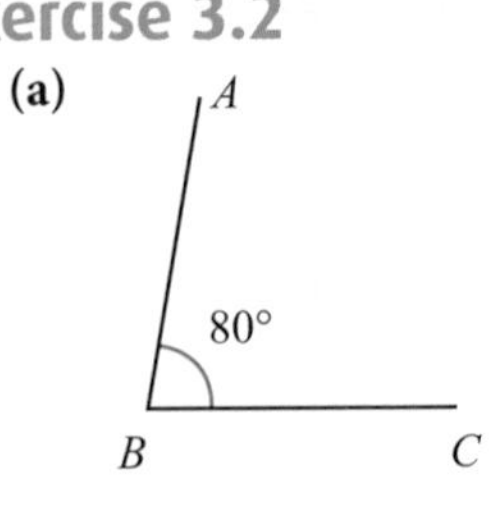

(b)

P
30°
Q
R

* Cambridge International Examinations bears no responsibility for the example answers to questions taken from its past question papers which are contained in this publication.

(c)

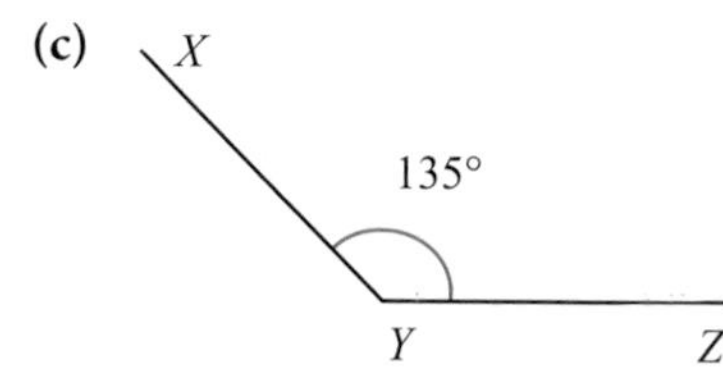

(d)

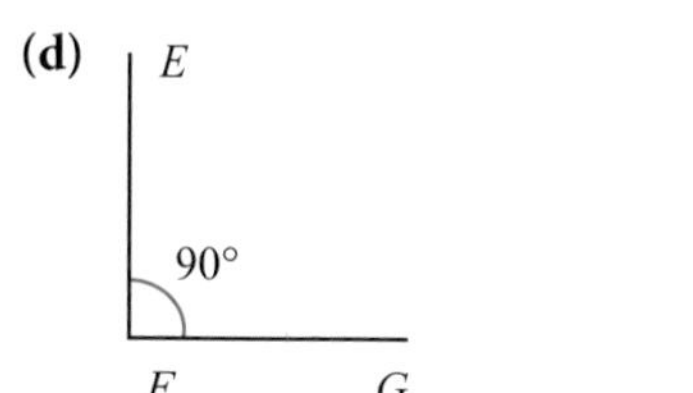

(e)

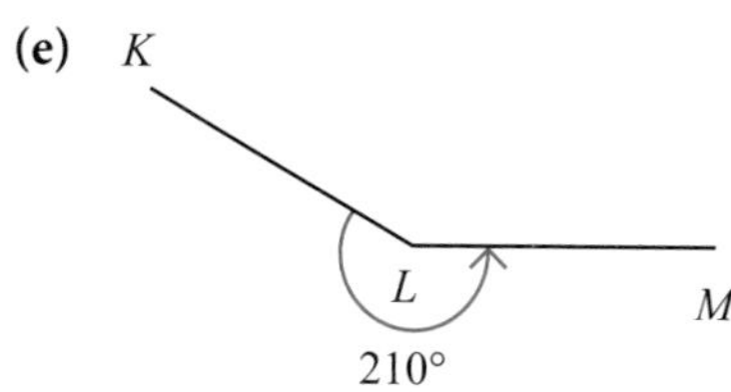

(f)

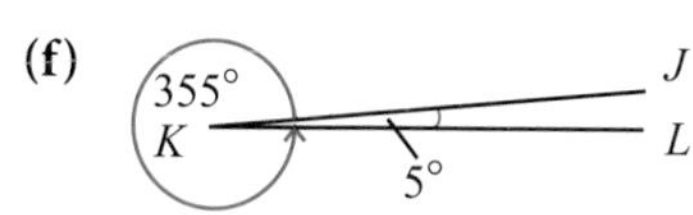

Exercise 3.3

1 (a) $E\hat{B}F$ and $F\hat{B}C$; or $A\hat{B}D$ and $D\hat{B}E$

(b) $A\hat{B}E$ and $E\hat{B}C$; or $D\hat{B}A$ and $C\hat{B}G$; or $D\hat{B}C$ and $A\hat{B}G$

(c) $A\hat{B}D$, and $D\hat{B}C$;
or $A\hat{B}E$ and $E\hat{B}C$;
or $A\hat{B}F$ and $F\hat{B}C$;
or $A\hat{B}G$ and $C\hat{B}G$;
or $D\hat{B}E$ and $E\hat{B}G$;
or $D\hat{B}F$ and $F\hat{B}G$;
or $D\hat{B}C$ and $C\hat{B}G$;
or $D\hat{B}A$ and $A\hat{B}G$;
or $A\hat{B}G$ and $G\hat{B}C$;

(d) $D\hat{B}E$, $E\hat{B}F$, $F\hat{B}C$ and $C\hat{B}G$
or $B\hat{D}A$ and $A\hat{B}G$
or $D\hat{B}F$, $F\hat{B}C$ and $C\hat{B}G$
or $D\hat{B}F$ and $F\hat{B}G$
or $D\hat{B}C$ and $C\hat{B}G$
(and combinations of these)

(e) $F\hat{B}C$ (f) $E\hat{B}A$

2 (a) $x = 68°$ (b) $x = 40°$
(c) $x = 65°$; $y = 115°$
(d) $x = 59°$; $y = 57°$
(e) $x = 16°$; $y = 82°$; $z = 16°$
(f) $x = 47°$; $y = 43°$; $z = 133°$
(g) $x = 57°$ (h) $x = 71°$
(i) $x = 38°$

3 (a) 30° (b) 15° (c) 30°

4 60° and 120°

5 53°, 127° and 27°.

Exercise 3.4

1 (a) $a = 112°$ alternate $\angle s$ equal
$b = 112°$ vertically opposite $\angle s$ equal

(b) $x = 105°$ alternative $\angle s$ equal
$y = 30°$ sum of triangle
$z = 45°$ alternate $\angle s$ equal

(c) $c = 40°$ vertically opposite $\angle s$ equal
$b = 72°$ corresponding $\angle s$ equal
$a = 68°$ $\angle s$ on a line
$d = 68°$ vertically opposite $\angle s$ equal
$e = 40°$ alternate $\angle s$ equal

(d) $a = 39°$ corresponding $\angle s$ equal
$b = 102°$ $\angle$ sum of triangle

(e) $x = 70°$ $\angle$ on a line
$y = 70°$ corresponding $\angle s$ equal
$z = 85°$ corresponding $\angle s$ equal
(180–95 = 85°, $\angle s$ on a line, z is corresponding $\angle$ equal to 85°)

(f) $x = 45°$ alternate $\angle s$ equal
$y = 60°$ Alternate $\angle s$ equal

(g) $x = 82°$ co-interior $\angle s$ supplementary
$y = 60°$ corresponding $\angle s$ equal
$z = 82°$ angles on a line

(h) $x = 42°$ alternate $\angle s$ equal
$y = 138°$ $\angle s$ on a line
$z = 65°$ alternate $\angle s$ equal

(i) $a = 40°$ alternate $\angle s$ equal
$b = 140°$ $\angle s$ on a line
$d = 75°$ $\angle s$ on a line
$c = 75°$ corresponding $\angle s$ equal
$e = 105°$ corresponding $\angle s$ equal

2 (a) $AB \parallel DC$ alternate $\angle s$ equal
(b) $AB \nparallel DC$ co-interior $\angle s$ not supplementary
(c) $AB \parallel DC$ co-interior $\angle s$ supplementary

Exercise 3.5

1 (a) $x = 54°$ $\angle$ sum of triangle
(b) $x = 66°$ base $\angle$ isosceles Δ
(c) $x = 115°$ $\angle$ sum of triangle
$y = 65°$ exterior $\angle$ of triangle equal to sum of the opposite interior $\angle s$ OR $\angle s$ on a line
$z = 25°$ $\angle$ sum of triangle

2 (a) $x = 60°$ exterior $\angle$ of Δ equal to sum of opposite interior $\angle s$, so $x + x = 120°$, $x = 60°$.

(b) $x = 44.\dot{3}°$
$4x = 86 + (180 - 2x)$
(exterior angle equals sum of opposite interior angles, and angle $\angle$ of triangle)
$6x = 266$
$x = 44.3°$

3 (a) $\angle B\hat{A}C = 180 - 95°$
($\angle s$ on a straight line)
$= 85°$
$\angle A\hat{C}B = 180° - 105°$
($\angle s$ on a straight line)
$= 75°$
$180 = x + 75 + 85$
($\angle$ sum of triangle)
$x = 180 - 160$
$x = 20°$

(b) $\angle CAB = 56°$
(vertically opposite angles equal)
$180 = 56 + 68 + x$
($\angle$ sum of triangle)
$x = 180 - 124$
$x = 56°$

(c) $\angle A\hat{C}E = 53°$ ($\angle s$ on straight line)
$x = 53°$ (comp $\angle s$ equal)
OR
$\angle CDE = 59°$ (comp $\angle s$ equal)
$180 = 68 + 59 + x$ ($\angle$ sum of Δ)
$x = 180 - 127$
$x = 53°$

(d) $180 = 58 + \angle ACB + \angle CBA$
($\angle$sum of triangle)
$\angle ACB = \angle CBA$ (isosceles Δ)
$\Rightarrow 180 = 58 + 2y$
$2y = 122$
$y = 61$
$x = 180 - 61$
(exterior $\angle s$ of a triangle equal to sum of opposite interior $\angle s$)
$x = 119°$

(e) $\angle AMN = 180 - (35 + 60)$
($\angle$ sum of Δ)
$\angle AMN = 85°$
$x = 85°$
(corresponding $\angle s$ equal)

(f) $\angle ACB = 360 - 295$
($\angle s$ around a point)
$\angle ACB = 65°$
$\angle ABC = 65°$ (isosceles Δ)
$x = 180 - (2 \times 65)$ ($\angle$ sum of Δ)
$x = 50°$

Exercise 3.6

1 (a) rhombus, kite or square
(b) square

2 (a) $\angle QRS = 112°$ (vertically opposite $\angle s$ equal)
$x = 112°$ (opposite $\angle s$ in ||gram)
(b) $x = 62°$ (isosceles Δ)
(c) $360 = 110 + 110 + 2x$
($\angle$ sum of quadrilateral)
$140 = 2x$
$x = 70°$
(d) $\angle MLQ = 180 - 110$
($\angle s$ on a straight line)
$\angle MN = 180 - 98$
($\angle s$ on a straight line)
$360 = 70 + 82 + 92 + x$
($\angle$ sum of quadrilateral)
$x = 116°$
(e) $360 = 3x + 4x + 2x + x$
($\angle$ sum of quadrilateral)
$360 = 10\,x$
$x = 36°$
(f) $360 = (180 - x) + 50 + 110 + 90$
($\angle s$ on a straight line, and $\angle$ sum of quadrilateral)
$360 = (180 - x) + 250$
$110 = 180 - x$
$x = 70°$

3 (a) $180 = 70 + 2y$ ($\angle$ sum on a Δ, isoscoles Δ to give $2y$)
$110 = 2y$
$y = 55$
$\therefore \angle PRQ = 55°$
$x = 180 - (55 + 55)$
($\angle s$ on a straight line, and isoscoles triangle)
$x = 70°$
(b) $\angle MNP = 98°$
(opposite $\angle s$ n ||gram)
$\angle RNM = 180 - 98$
($\angle s$ on a straight line)
$= 82°$
$180 = 2x + 82$ ($\angle$ sum of a triangle, and isoscoles triangle)
$2x = 98$
$x = 49°$

Exercise 3.7

1

Number of sides	5	6	7	8	9	10	12	20
Angle sum	540°	720°	900°	1080°	1260°	1440°	1800°	3240°

2 (a) 108° (b) 120° (c) 135°
(d) 144° (e) 150° (f) 165.6°

3 (a) 2340° (b) 360°
(c) 156° (d) 24°

4 24 sides

5 (a) $x = 135°$ (b) $x = 110°$
(c) $x = 72°$

Exercise 3.8

1 (a) diameter (b) major arc
(c) radius (d) minor sector
(e) chord (f) major segment

2 (a) (b)

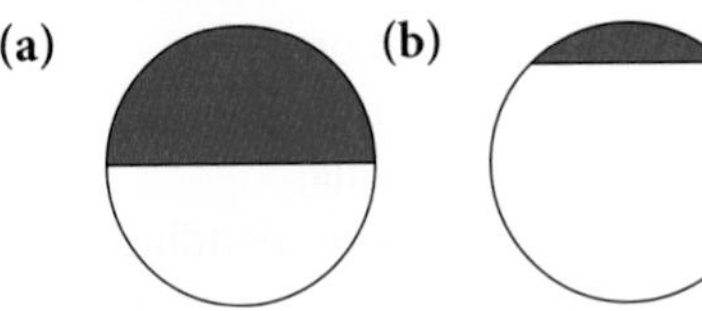

(c) (d)

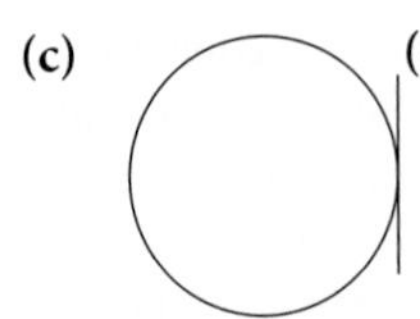

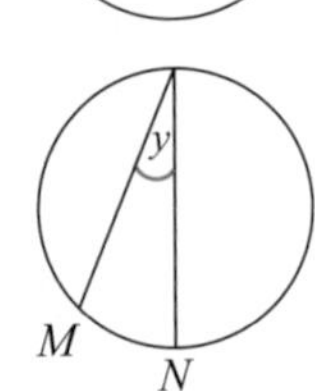

3 (a) radius (b) diameter
(c) minor arc
(d) DO, FO or EO
(e) major arc (f) sector

Exercise 3.9

NOT TO SCALE

1 (a)

(b)

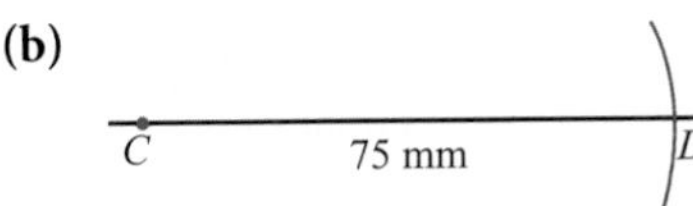

(c)

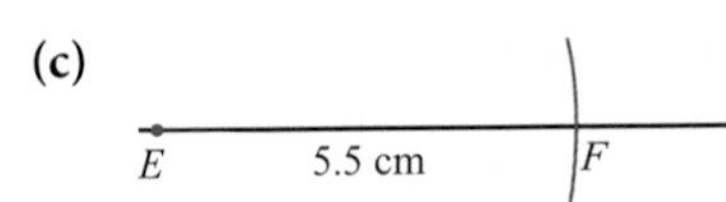

NOT TO SCALE

2 (a)

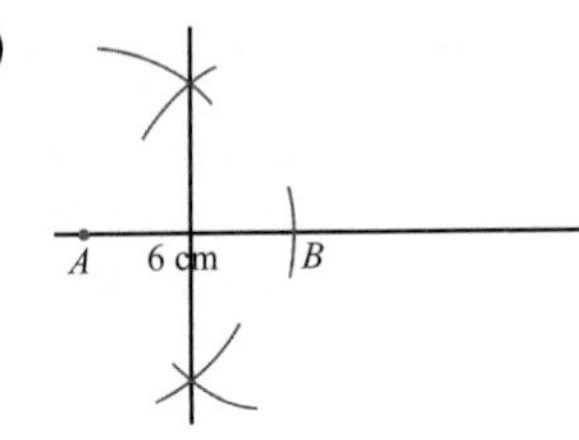

(b)

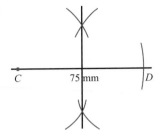

(c)

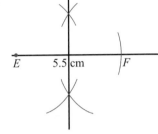

3 (a)–(b)

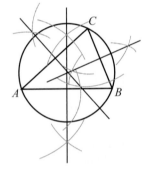

(c) The circle passes through each vertex of the triangle.

4 (a)

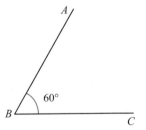

(b)

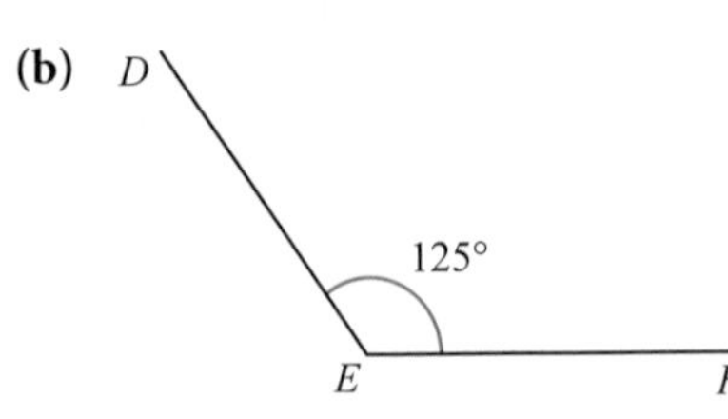

(c)

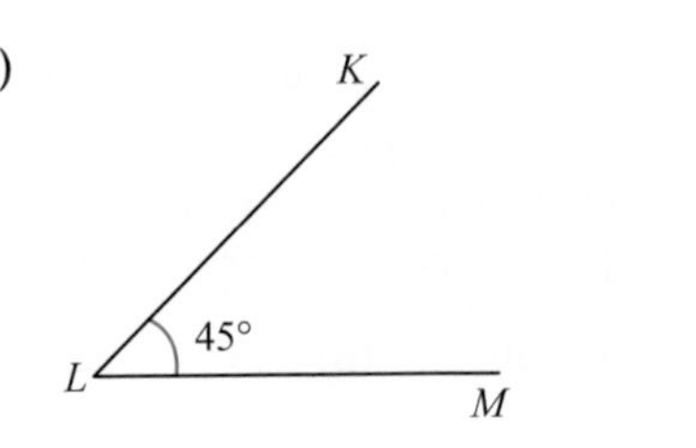

5 (a)

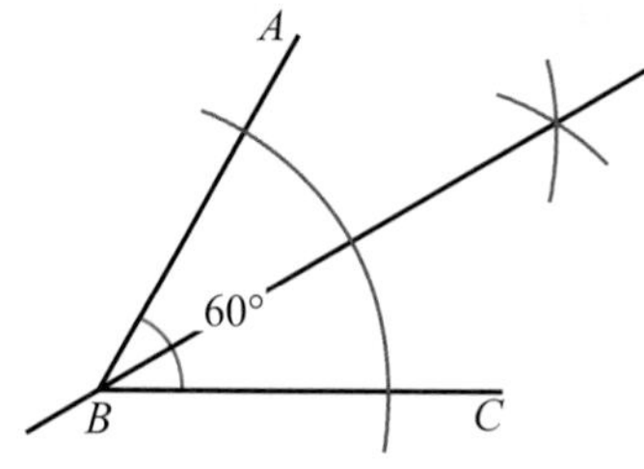

(b)

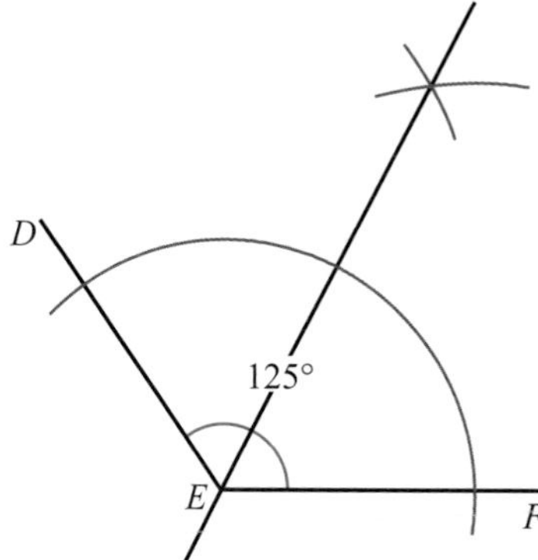

(c)

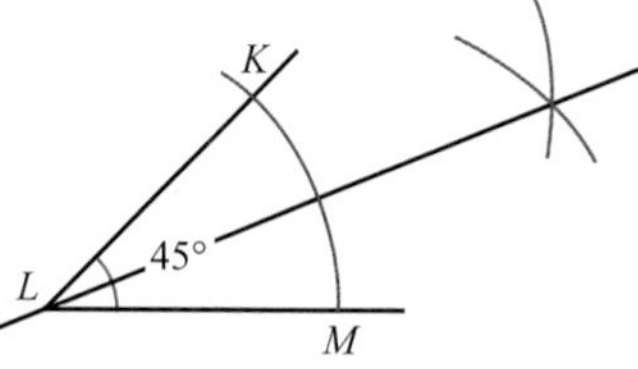

Exercise 3.10

NOT TO SCALE

1 (a)

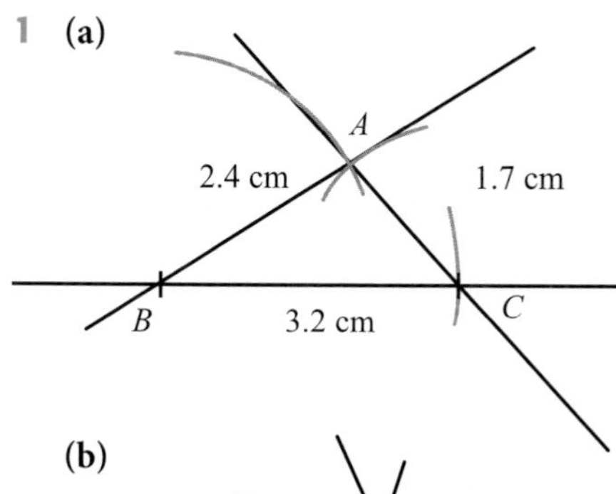

(b)

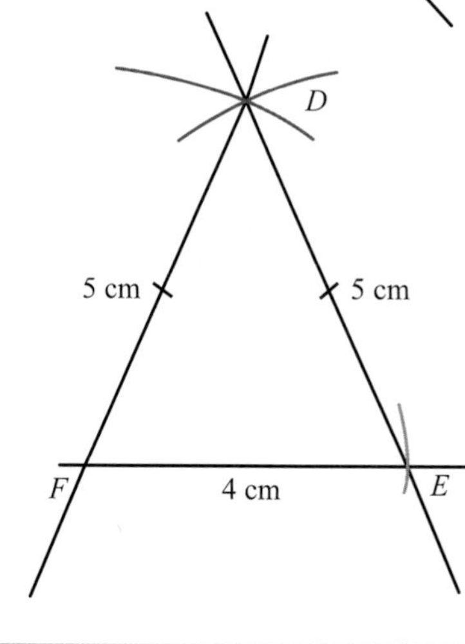

(c)

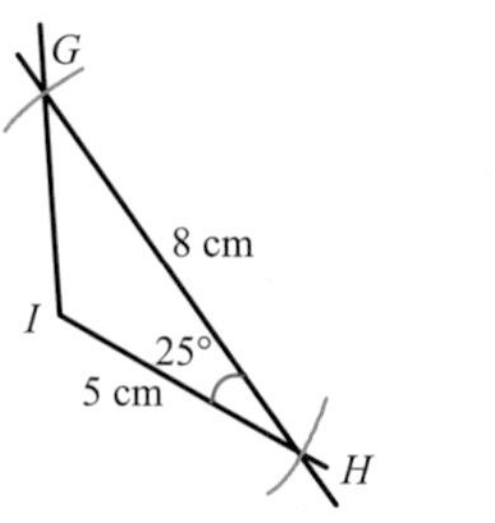

(d)

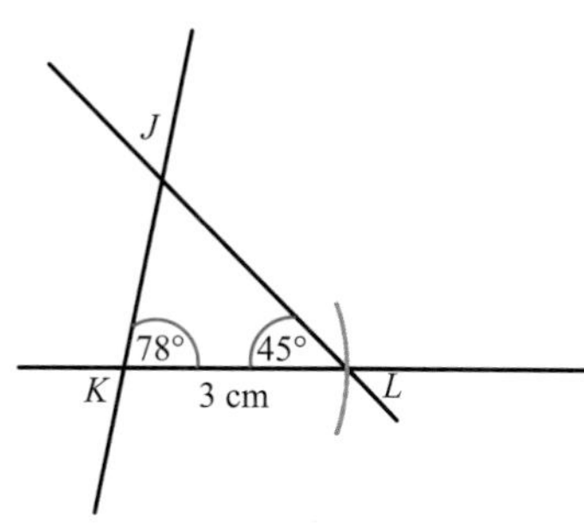

(e)

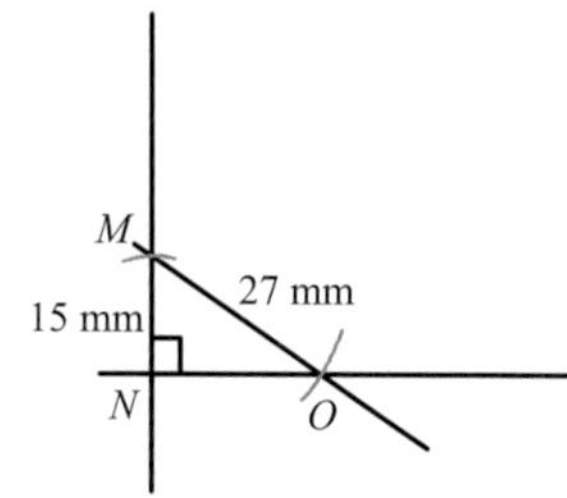

(f)

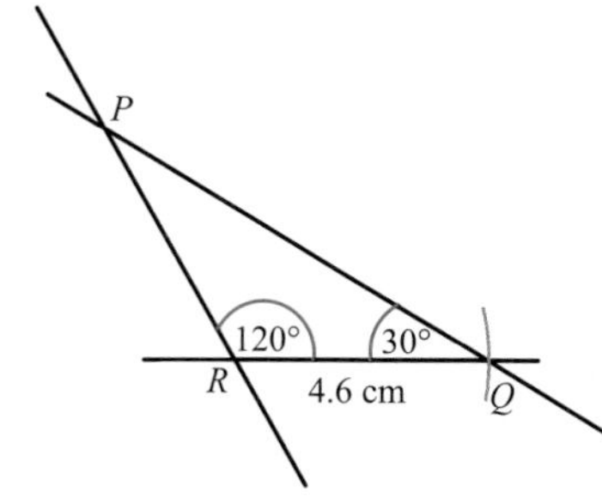

2 (a)

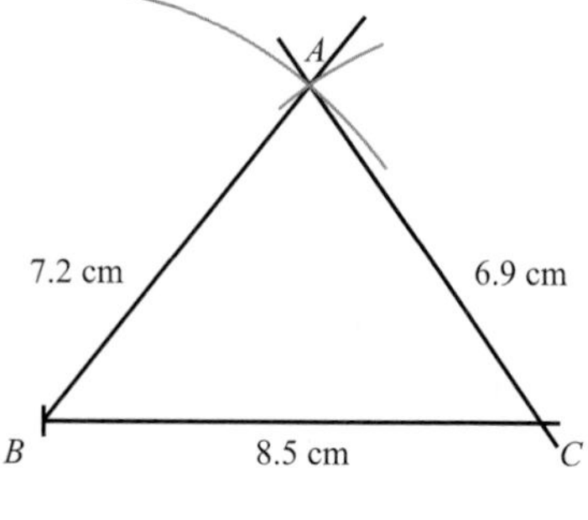

(b)

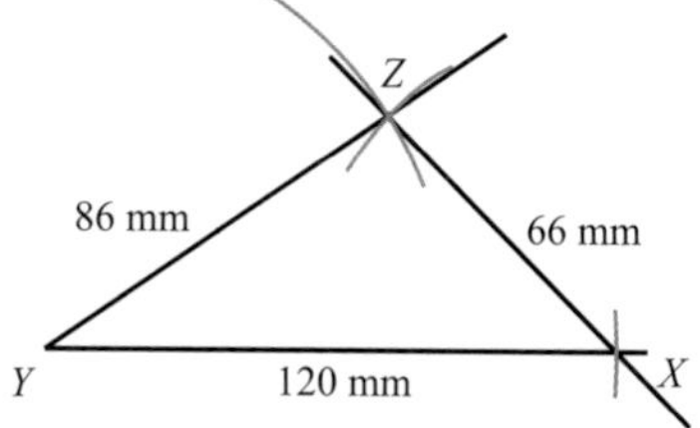

(c)

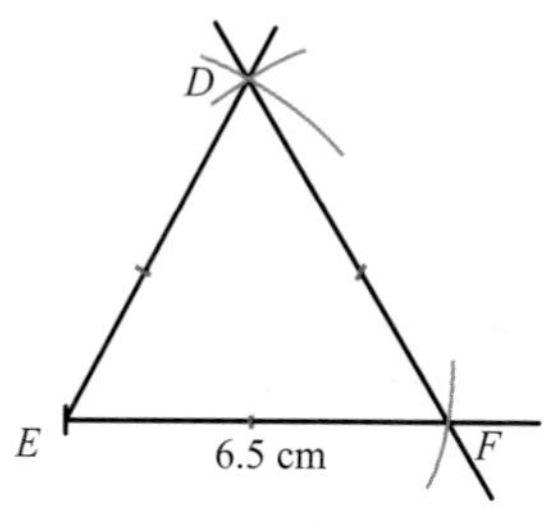

(d)

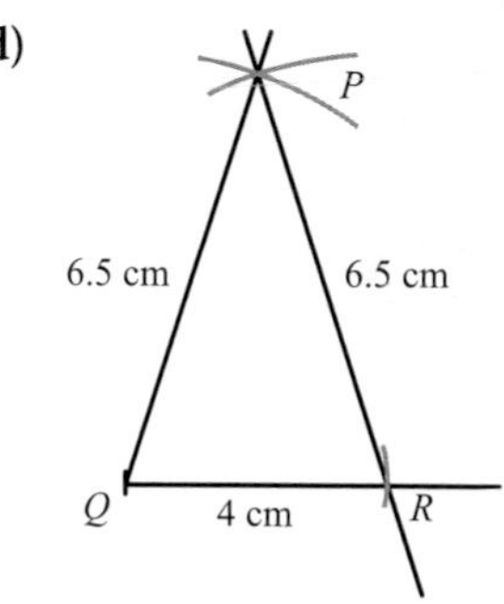

3 (a)

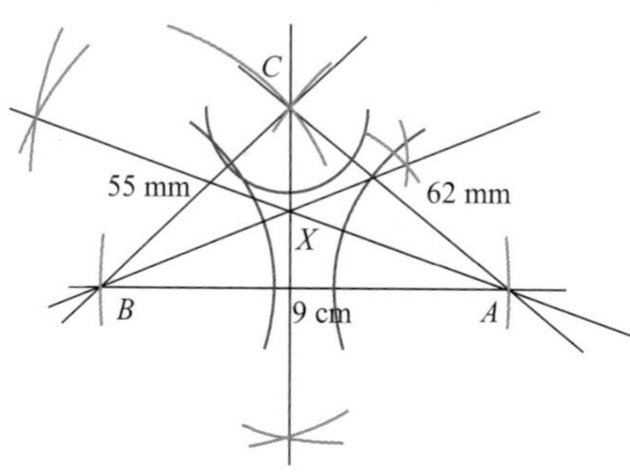

(b) $AX = 5\,\text{cm}$
$BX = 4.5\,\text{cm}$
$CX = 2\,\text{cm}$

4 (a)

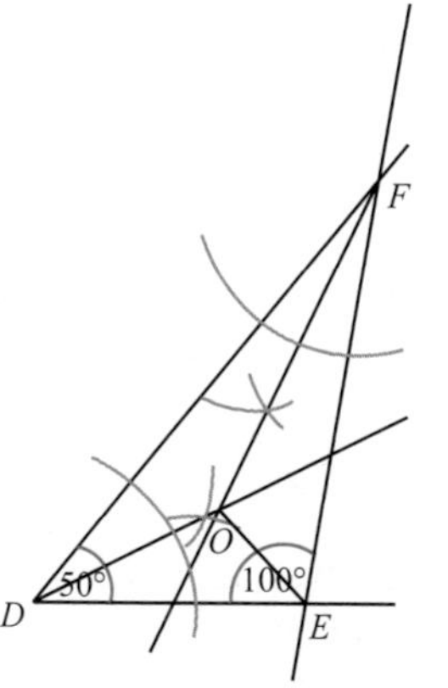

(b) $OE = 38\,\text{cm}$

5 (a)

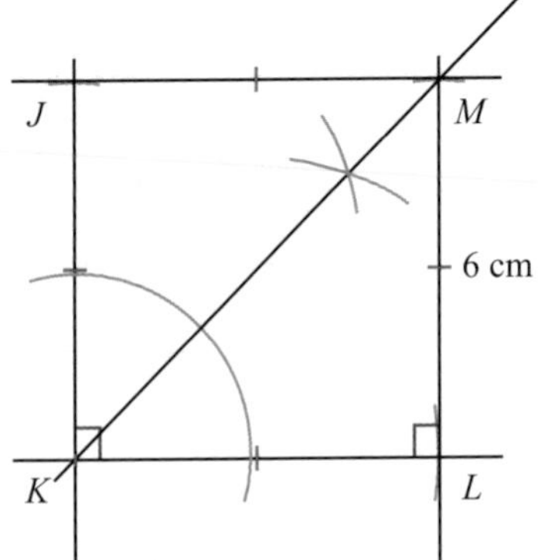

(b) By extending the bisector to see if it passes through M. As the diagonals of a square bisect the opposite angles, if it passes through M it will also be the bisector of M.

Exercise 3.11

NOT TO SCALE

(a)

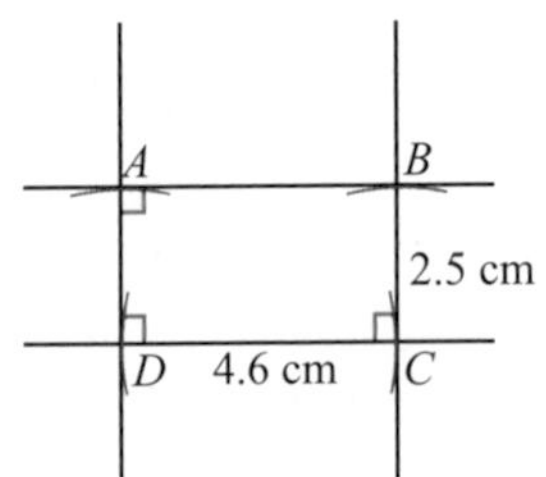

(b)

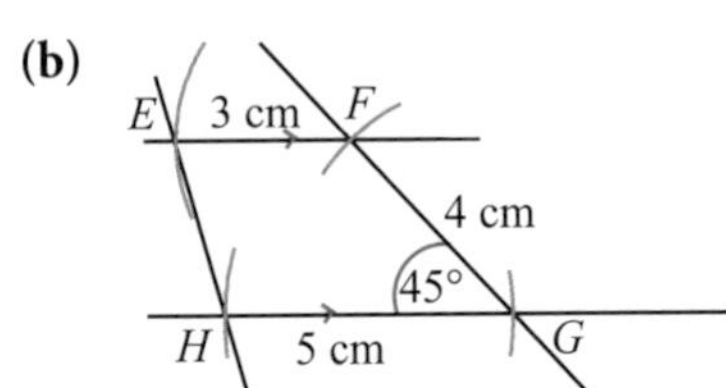

(c)

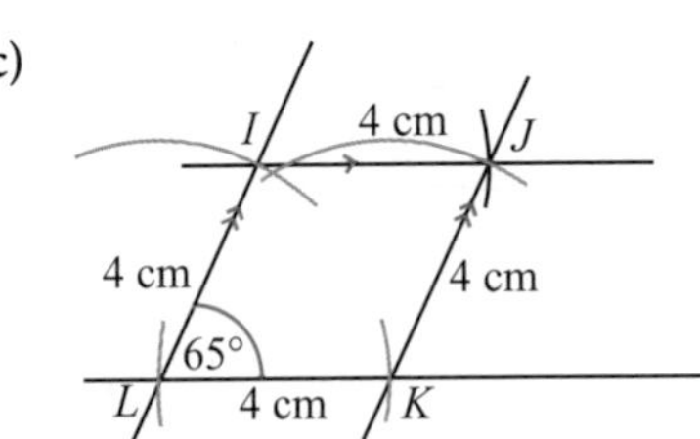

(d)

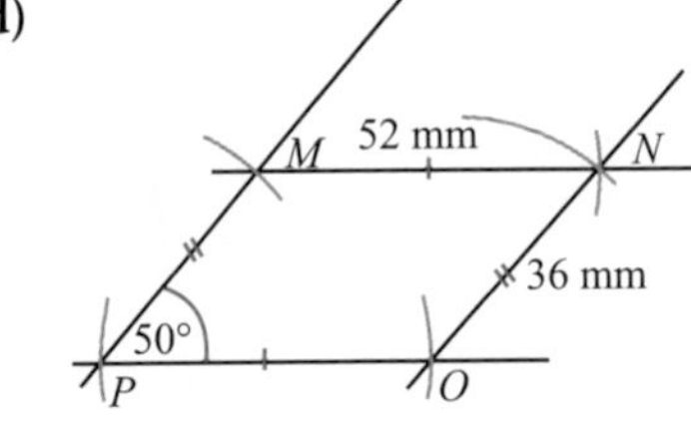

(e)

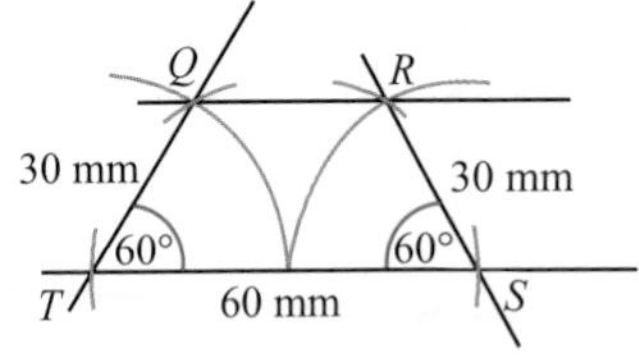

(f)

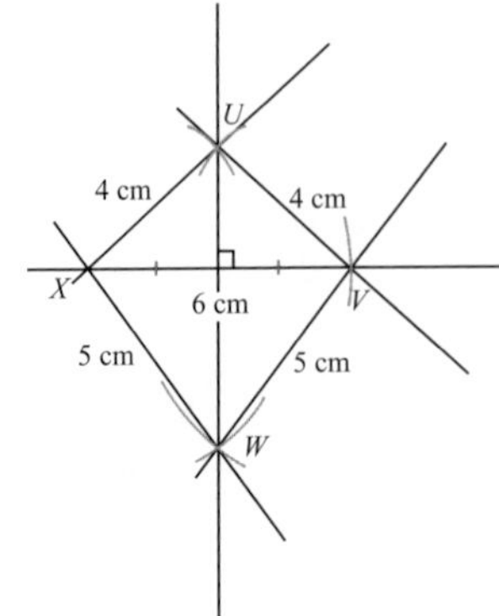

Examination practice

Exam-style questions

1 (a) $x = 99°$ co-interior $\angle s$ supplementary

(b) $x = 65°$ corresponding $\angle s$ equal

(c) $x = 75°$ $\angle$sum of isosceles Δ

(d) $x = 112°$ opposite $\angle s$ of ||gram

(e) $x = 110°$

If $y = \angle AEC$

$\Rightarrow 360 = 90 + 110 + 90 + y$

$y = 70°$

$\therefore \angle AEC = 70°$

$\angle ADE = 70°$ (isosceles triangle)

$x = 180 - 70$ ($\angle s$ on a line)

$x = 110°$

(f) $x = 72.5°$

Let y stand for base $\angle s$ of isosceles Δ.

$2y + 35 = 180$ (base $\angle s$ isosceles Δ and $\angle$ sum of Δ)

$y = 72.5°$

$\Rightarrow \angle QRP = 72.5°$

$\angle NRQ = 35°$ (alternate $\angle s$ equal)

$180 = x + 72.5 + 35$

$x = 72.5°$

2 (a) angle sum of triangle

(b) $y = 53°$

3 72°

4 (a) 360°

(b) 24° if a regular polygon

(c) 156°

5 (a) Exterior angle of triangle is equal to the sum of two opposite interior angles $\frac{x}{2} + \frac{x}{2} = x$.

(b) Opposite angles of parallelogram equal, and vertically opposite angles equal.

6 (a)–(c) NOT TO SCALE

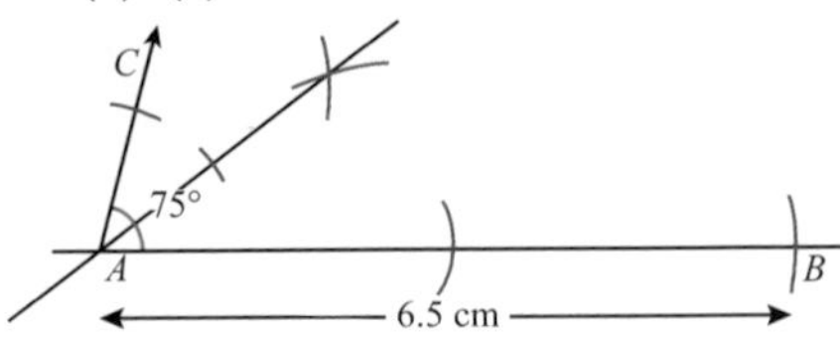

7 (a) NOT TO SCALE

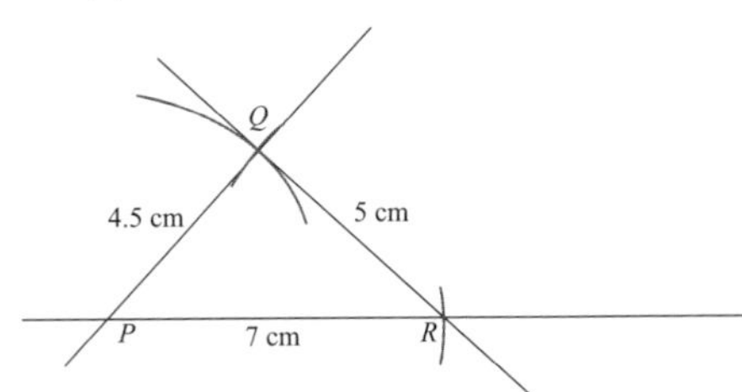

Past paper questions*

1 (a) $x = 20°$

(b) $y = 65°$

Chapter 4

Exercise 4.1

1 (a) (b) Students' answers will vary, below are possible answers.

Categorical data	Numerical data
Hair colour	*Number of brothers and sisters*
Eye colour	Hours spent doing homework
Gender	Hours spent watching TV
Mode of transport to school	Number of books read in a month
Brand of toothpaste used	Shoe size
Of cell phone	Test scores

* Cambridge International Examinations bears no responsibility for the example answers to questions taken from its past question papers which are contained in this publication.

2 (a) continuous (b) discrete
(c) continuous (d) continuous
(e) discrete (f) continuous
(g) continuous (h) discrete
(i) continuous (j) discrete
(k) discrete (l) discrete

3 (a) (i) Experiment
(ii) Primary
(iii) Numerical
(iv) Discrete

(b) (i) Survey
(ii) Primary
(iii) Categorical
(iv) Discrete

(c) (i) Use existing data
(ii) Secondary
(iii) Numerical
(iv) Continuous

(d) (i) Survey
(ii) Primary
(iii) Categorical
(iv) Discrete

(e) (i) Use existing data
(ii) Secondary
(iii) Numerical
(iv) Discrete

(f) (i) Experiment
(ii) Primary
(iii) Numerical
(iv) Discrete

(g) (i) Survey
(ii) Primary
(iii) Numerical
(iv) Continuous

(h) (i) Use existing data
(ii) Secondary
(iii) Categorical
(iv) Discrete

(i) (i) Use existing data
(ii) Secondary
(iii) Numerical
(iv) Discrete

(j) (i) Survey
(ii) Primary
(iii) Numerical
(iv) Discrete

Exercise 4.2

1

Score	Tally	Total
1	𝍸 III	8
2	𝍸 𝍸 II	12
3	𝍸 II	7
4	𝍸 III	8
5	𝍸 III	8
6	𝍸 II	7
		50

2 Students' own answers.

3 (a) 7 (b) 2 and 12
(c) Impossible with two dice.
(d) There are 3 ways of getting each of these scores.

Exercise 4.3

1 (a)

Number of coins	0	1	2	3	4	5	6	7	8
Frequency	6	2	6	4	4	2	4	1	1

(b) 8 (c) 2
(d) None or two coins
(e) 30: add column and total the frequencies.

2 (a)

Amount ($)	0–9.99	10–19.99	20–29.99	30–39.99	40–49.99	50–59.99
Frequency	7	9	5	2	1	1

(b) 16 (c) 1 (d) $10 – $19.99

3

Call length	Frequency
0–59 s	0
1 min–1 min 59 s	4
2 min–2 min 59 s	3
3 min–3 min 59 s	6
4 min–4 min 59 s	4
5 min–5 min 59 s	3

Exercise 4.4

1 (a) 9 (b) 33
(c) Mostly right-handed (d) 90

2 Student's own answers.

3 (a)

	Algebra	Geometry
Boys	4	2
Girls	2	4

(b) The boys prefer Algebra while the girls prefer Geometry.

Exercise 4.5

(a) (i) 3695 miles (ii) 8252 miles
(iii) 4586 miles
(b) Istanbul to Montreal
(c) 21 128 miles
(d) 4 hours
(e) Blanks match a city to itself so there is no flight distance.

Exercise 4.6

1 (a) 250 000 (b) 500 000
(c) 125 000 (d) 375 000

2 Answers may vary. Example:

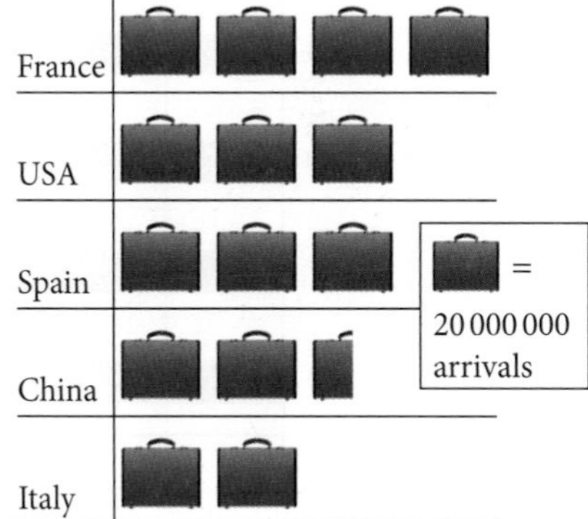

3 (a) Reel deal (b) Fish tales
(c) Golden rod – 210 fish;
Shark bait – 420 fish;
Fish tales – 140 fish;
Reel deal – 490 fish;
Bite-me – 175 fish

Exercise 4.7

1 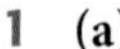

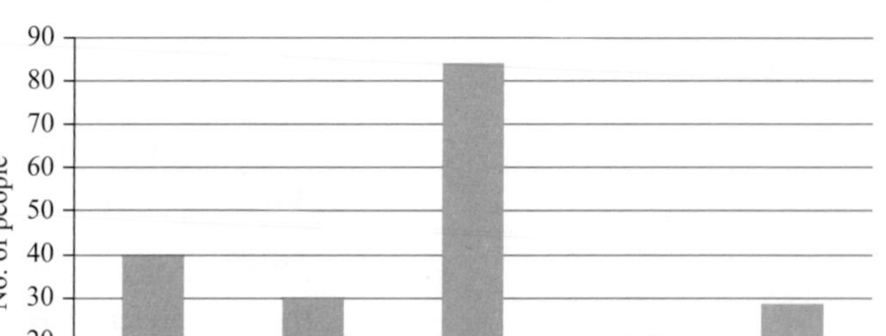

(b)

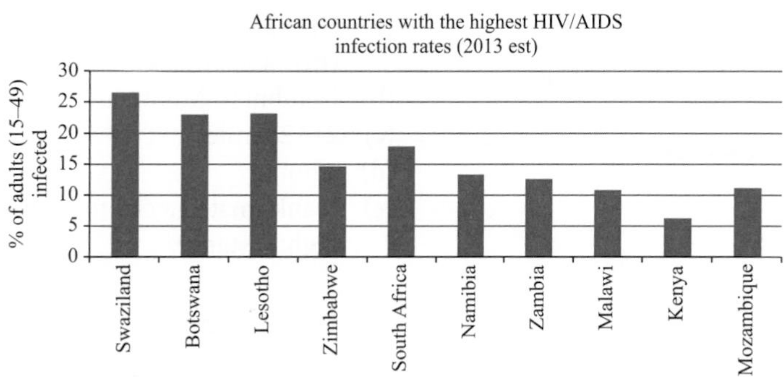

3 **(a)**

Temperature (°C)	32–34	35–37	38–40	41–43
Frequency	4	5	6	5

(b)

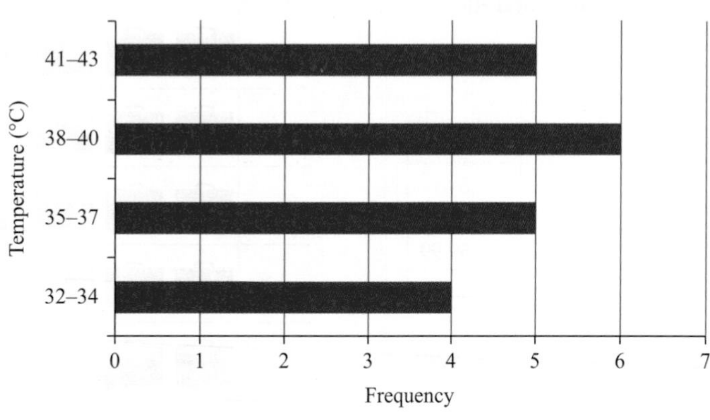

4

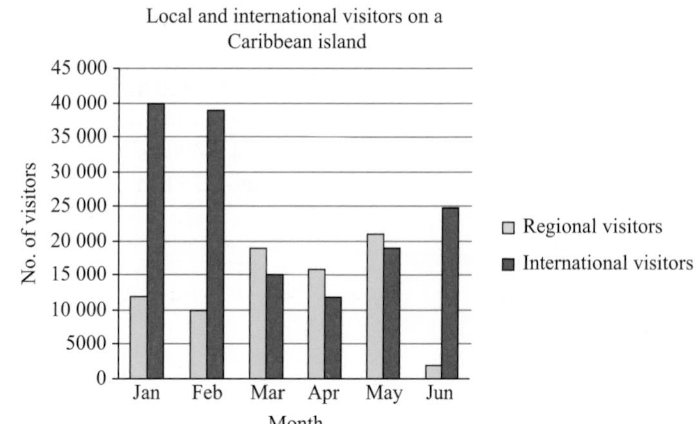

Exercise 4.8

1 Smoking habits among students

2 Home language of people passing through an international airport

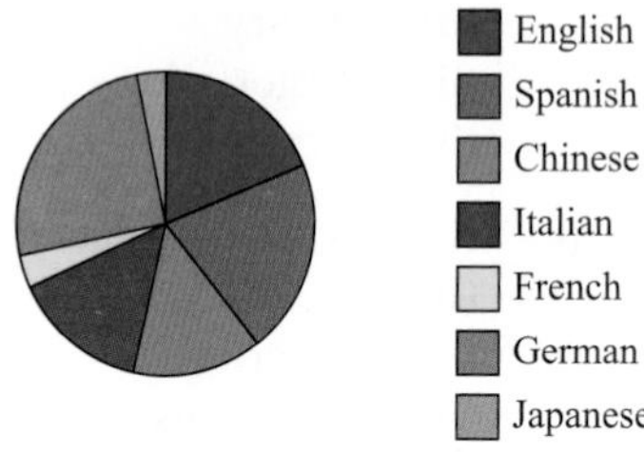

3 Land used on a farm to grow vegetables

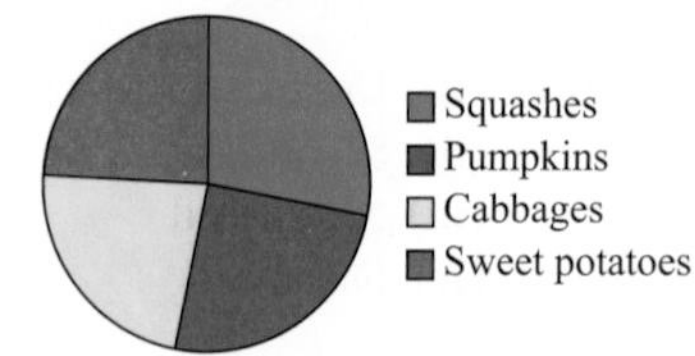

4 **(a)** $\frac{1}{4}$ **(b)** ≈11% **(c)** 0.25

(d) **(i)** 225 **(ii)** 100
(iii) 200 **(iv)** 150

Exercise 4.9

1 Answers may vary, examples include:

(a) Line graph – will show trends.

(b) Pie chart – most popular show will be clearly shown.

(c) Bar chart – different time slots will be displayed clearly.

(d) Pie chart – favourite subject will be clearly displayed.

(e) Bar chart – different reasons will be clearly displayed.

(f) Pie chart – will give a good pictorial representation of the different languages spoken.

(g) Bar chart – each car size will be shown clearly.

2 Students' own answers.

Examination practice

Exam-style questions

1 (a) Primary data – it is data collected by counting.

(b) Discrete data – the data can only take certain values.

(c)

No. of broken biscuits	Tally	Frequency
0	卌 卌 ||	12
1	卌 卌	10
2	卌 卌 |	11
3	卌 |	6
4	|	1
		40

(d) Bar chart – it will give a good representation of breakages.

2 (a) Heathrow

(b) 15 161

(c) Gatwick 25 000
Heathrow 41 000
London City 5 000
Luton 9 000
Stansted 15 000

(d)

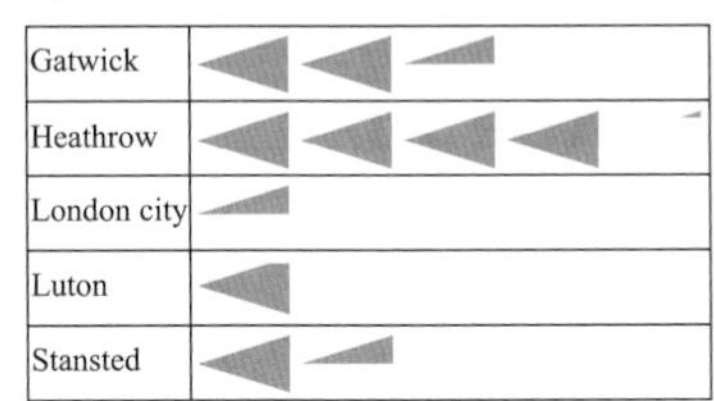

Key:
= 10 000 flights

3 (a) A two–way table.

(b) 4980

(c) District C – it has the highest percentage of laptops.

(d)

% of people in four districts who own a laptop and a mobile phone

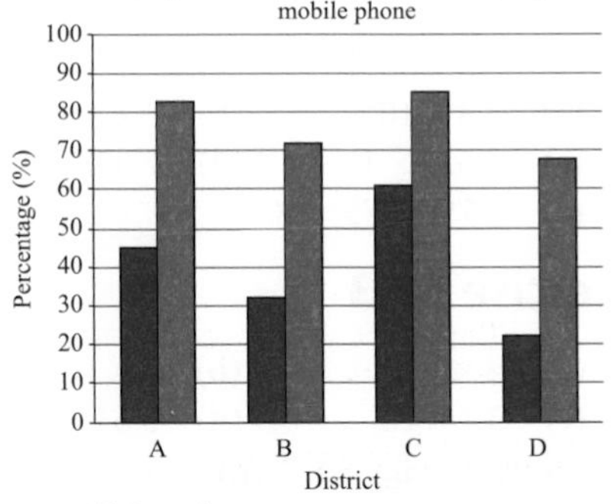

4 Mode of transport to work in Hong Kong

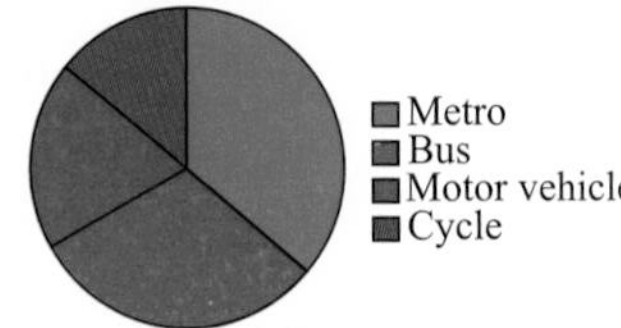

5 (a) Sport played by students.

(b) five

(c) baseball

(d) $\frac{1}{4}$

(e) 28 (to nearest whole number)

(f) 83 (to the nearest whole number)

Past paper questions*

1 (d)

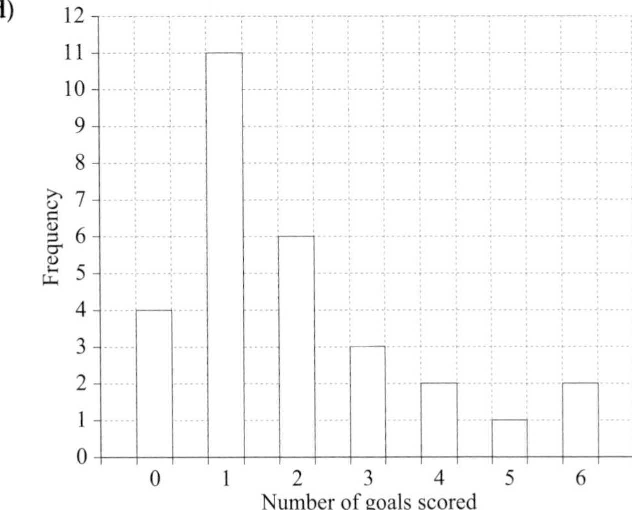

Unit 2

Chapter 5

Exercise 5.1

1 (a) $\frac{5}{9}=\frac{10}{18}=\frac{15}{27}=\frac{20}{36}$

(b) $\frac{3}{7}=\frac{6}{14}=\frac{9}{21}=\frac{12}{28}$

(c) $\frac{12}{18}=\frac{6}{9}=\frac{2}{3}=\frac{8}{12}$

(d) $\frac{18}{36}=\frac{1}{2}=\frac{2}{4}=\frac{3}{6}$

(e) $\frac{110}{128}=\frac{55}{64}=\frac{165}{192}=\frac{220}{256}$

2 (a) $\frac{1}{3}$ (b) $\frac{1}{3}$ (c) $\frac{3}{4}$

(d) $\frac{3}{5}$ (e) $\frac{1}{5}$ (f) $\frac{2}{3}$

(g) $\frac{3}{10}$

Exercise 5.2

1 (a) $\frac{10}{27}$ (b) $\frac{3}{14}$ (c) $\frac{2}{9}$

(d) $\frac{1}{4}$

2 (a) $\frac{1}{5}$ (b) $\frac{8}{21}$

(c) 2 (d) $\frac{92}{35}=2\frac{22}{35}$

(e) 32 (f) $\frac{319}{2}=39\frac{7}{8}$

(g) 180 (h) $80\frac{1}{2}$ or $\frac{161}{2}$

Exercise 5.3

1 (a) $\frac{2}{3}$ (b) $\frac{5}{7}$ (c) $\frac{1}{4}$

(d) $\frac{13}{9}=1\frac{4}{9}$ (e) $\frac{11}{30}$ (f) $\frac{1}{24}$

(g) $\frac{7}{8}$ (h) $2\frac{1}{16}$

* *Cambridge International Examinations bears no responsibility for the example answers to questions taken from its past question papers which are contained in this publication.*

2 (a) $3\frac{1}{3}$ (b) $6\frac{5}{11}$ (c) $18\frac{1}{4}$
(d) $3\frac{3}{4}$ (e) $-\frac{5}{6}$ (f) $12\frac{11}{16}$
(g) $6\frac{13}{16}$ (h) $2\frac{29}{60}$
(i) $1\frac{25}{42}$ (j) $\frac{1}{2}$
(k) $9\frac{5}{12}$ (l) $\frac{37}{60}$

3 (a) $\frac{1}{4}+\frac{1}{2}$ (b) $\frac{1}{2}+\frac{1}{6}$
(c) $\frac{1}{2}+\frac{1}{8}$ (d) $\frac{1}{16}+\frac{1}{8}$

Exercise 5.4

1 $\frac{3}{7}$
2 $\frac{14}{15}$
3 $\frac{4}{63}$
4 $\frac{2}{11}$
5 $\frac{147}{5}=29\frac{2}{5}$
6 $\frac{48}{85}$
7 $\frac{189}{122}=1\frac{67}{122}$
8 $\frac{13}{14}$

Exercise 5.5

1 $\frac{1}{40}$
2 $\frac{4}{5}$
3 $\frac{60}{7}=8\frac{4}{7}$
4 5
5 24
6 $\frac{1}{8}$
7 $\frac{3}{8}$
8 $9\frac{3}{5}$

Exercise 5.6

1 90 people
2 $\frac{4}{21}$
3 98
4 $\frac{3}{7}$
5 $\frac{1}{4}$

Exercise 5.7

1 (a) $\frac{7}{10}$ (b) $\frac{3}{4}$ (c) $\frac{1}{5}$
(d) $\frac{9}{25}$ (e) $\frac{3}{20}$ (f) $\frac{1}{40}$
(g) $\frac{43}{20}$ (h) $\frac{33}{25}$ (i) $\frac{47}{40}$
(j) $\frac{271}{250}$ (k) $\frac{1}{400}$ (l) $\frac{1}{50000}$

2 (a) 60% (b) 28% (c) 85%
(d) 30% (e) 4%
(f) $41.\dot{6}\% = 41\frac{2}{3}\%$

Exercise 5.8

1 40%
2 25%
3 27.0 (3sf)%
4 77.8%
5 79.2 (3sf)%
6 25%
7 0.025%

Exercise 5.9

1 4%
2 21%
3 7%
4 19%
5 25%
6 44%

Exercise 5.10

1 (a) 44 (b) 46 (c) 50
(d) 42 (e) 41.6

2 (a) 79.5 (b) 97.52
(c) 60.208 (d) 112.36
(e) 53.265

3 (a) 111.6 (b) 105.4
(c) 86.8 (d) 119.04
(e) 115.32

4 (a) 3.62 (b) 23.3852
(c) 36.0914 (d) 0
(e) 36.019

5 33 h
6 $13.44
7 26 199
8 126 990
9 10 h 34 min

Exercise 5.11

1 175
2 362.857
3 1960
4

Sale price ($)	% reduction	Original price ($)
52.00	10	57.78
185.00	10	205.56
4700.00	5	4947.37
2.90	5	3.05
24.50	12	27.84
10.00	8	10.87
12.50	7	13.44
9.75	15	11.47
199.50	20	249.38
99.00	25	132.00

5 (a) $20.49 (b) $163.93
(c) $11.89 (d) $19.66
(e) $12.95 (f) $37.54
(g) $24.39 (h) $105.90
(i) $0.81 (j) $0.66

6 (a) 40 students (b) 33 students
7 $20
8 80 kg
9 210 Litres (3sf)

Exercise 5.12

1 (a) 3.8×10^2 (b) 4.2×10^6
(c) 4.56×10^{10} (d) 6.54×10^{13}
(e) 2×10^1 (f) 1×10^1
(g) 1.03×10^1 (h) 5×10^0

2 (a) 2 400 000 (b) 310 000 000
(c) 10 500 000 (d) 9 900
(e) 71

3 (a) 8×10^{30} (b) 4.2×10^{12}
(c) 2.25×10^{26} (d) 1.32×10^9
(e) 1.4×10^{32} (f) 3×10^1
(g) 2×10^1 (h) 3×10^3
(i) 3×10^{42} (j) 1.2×10^3
(k) 5×10^{-4} (l) 1.764×10^{15}

4 (a) 3.4×10^4 (b) 3.7×10^6
(c) 5.627×10^5 (d) 7.057×10^9
(e) 5.7999973×10^9

Exercise 5.13

1 (a) 4×10^{-3} (b) 5×10^{-5}
(c) 3.2×10^{-5} (d) 5.64×10^{-8}

2 (a) 0.000 36 (b) 0.000 000 016
(c) 0.000 000 203 (d) 0.0088
(e) 0.71

3 (a) 8×10^{-20} (b) 6.4×10^{-12}
(c) 3.15×10^{-9} (d) 3.3×10^{-2}
(e) 2×10^{33} (f) 7×10^{-37}
(g) 5×10^{12} (h) 1.65×10^{1}

4 (a) 2.731×10^{-2} (b) 2.88×10^{-1}
(c) 7.01056×10^{3} (d) 1.207×10^{-5}

5 8.64×10^{4} seconds

6 (a) 3×10^{9} metres
(b) 6×10^{9} metres
(c) 3.06×10^{10} metres

7 (a) 1.07×10^{9} (b) 1.07×10^{12}

Exercise 5.14

1 Display will vary according to the calculator used.
(a) 4.2×10^{12} (b) 0.000018
(c) 2700000 (d) 0.0134
(e) 0.000000001 (f) 42300000
(g) 0.0003102 (h) 3098000000
(i) 2.076×10^{-23}

2 (a) (i) 1.09×10^{5}
(ii) 2.876×10^{-6}
(iii) 4.012×10^{9}
(iv) 1.89×10^{7}
(v) 3.123×10^{13}
(vi) 2.876×10^{-4}
(vii) 9.02×10^{15}
(viii) 8.076×10^{-12}
(ix) 8.124×10^{-11}
(x) 5.0234×10^{19}
(b) 8.076×10^{-12}
8.124×10^{-11}
2.876×10^{-6}
2.876×10^{-4}
1.09×10^{5}
1.89×10^{7}
4.012×10^{9}
3.123×10^{13}
9.02×10^{15}
5.0234×10^{19}

3 (a) 1.3607×10^{18} (b) 1.0274×10^{-15}
(c) 1.0458×10^{0} (d) 1.6184×10^{11}
(e) 5.2132×10^{19} (f) 3.0224×10^{-16}
(g) 2.3141×10^{12} (h) 1.5606×10^{17}

4 (a) 2.596×10^{6} (b) 7.569×10^{-5}
(c) 4.444×10^{-3} (d) 1.024×10^{-7}
(e) 3.465×10^{-4} (f) 2.343×10^{7}
(g) 5.692×10^{3} (h) 3.476×10^{-3}
(i) 1.604×10^{-3}

Exercise 5.15

1	2(1dp)
(a) $\frac{23.6}{6.3} \approx \frac{24}{6} \approx 4$	3.7
(b) $\frac{4}{0.09 \times 4} \approx \frac{4}{0.36} \approx 11$	12.7
(c) $\frac{7 \times 0.5}{9} \approx \frac{3.5}{9} \approx 0.38$	0.4
(d) $\frac{5 \times 6}{2.5+1} \approx \frac{30}{3.5} \approx 8.5$	8.0
(e) $\frac{\sqrt{49}}{2.5+4} \approx \frac{7}{6.5} \approx 1$	1.0
(f) $(0.5+2)(6.5-2) \approx (2.5)(4.5) \approx 10$	10.8
(g) $\frac{24+20}{5+6} \approx \frac{44}{11} \approx 4$	4.2
(h) $\frac{110-45}{19-14} \approx \frac{65}{5} \approx 13$	11.7
(i) $3^2 \times \sqrt{49} \approx 9 \times 7 \approx 63$	44.4
(j) $\sqrt{224 \times 45} \approx \sqrt{10080} \approx 100$	100.5
(k) $\sqrt{9} \times \sqrt{100} \approx 3 \times 10 \approx 30$	30.4
(l) $4^3 \times 2^4 \approx 64 \times 16 \approx 1024$	898.2

Examination practice

Exam-style questions

1 $\frac{5}{16}$

2 (a) 5% (b) $\frac{6}{25}$ (c) 17 822

3 29 975

4 7.5%

Past paper questions*

1 (a) $\frac{80}{20 - 4 \times 4}$ (b) 20 (c) 14.0

2 $(0.8)^2$

3 (a) $\frac{2}{3}$

(b) $\frac{2}{5}$

4 7.7 kg

5 $3\frac{7}{40}$

6 \$96

7 $\left(\frac{1}{10}\right)^2 + \left(\frac{2}{5}\right)^2$
$= \frac{1}{100} + \frac{4}{25}$
$= \frac{1}{100} + \frac{16}{100}$
$= \frac{17}{100} = 0.17$

8 \$88.20

9 \$461.25

Chapter 6

Exercise 6.1

1 (a) $-30p - 60$ (b) $-15x - 21$
(c) $-20y - 1$ (d) $-3q + 36$
(e) $-24t + 84$ (f) $-12z + 6$

2 (a) $-6x - 15y$ (b) $-24p - 30q$
(c) $-27h + 54k$ (d) $-10h - 10k + 16j$
(e) $-8a + 12b + 24c - 16d$
(f) $-6x^2 - 36y^2 + 12y^3$

3 (a) $-5x - 8$ (b) $-5x + 12$
(c) $10x - 38$ (d) $-13f$
(e) $-36g + 37$ (f) $12y - 20$

4 (a) $-26x^2 - 76x$ (b) $-x^2 + 77x$
(c) $-9x^2 + 30x$ (d) $24q$
(e) $-42pq + 84p$ (f) $-48m + 48n$

5 (a) $12x - 6$ (b) $13x - 6$
(c) $-2x + 17$ (d) $x + 13$
(e) $23 - 7x$ (f) $10x - 8$
(g) $7x - 5$ (h) $x^2 - 5x + 8$
(i) $3x^2 - 7x + 2$ (j) $2x^2 + 3x + 6$
(k) $2x - 18$ (l) $6x^2 + 6x - 6$

Exercise 6.2

1 (a) $x = 7$ (b) $x = -5$
(c) $x = 9$ (d) $x = -\frac{62}{7}$
(e) $x = 5$ (f) $n = 11$
(g) $q = 1.75$ (h) $t = 0.5$
(i) $x = 11.5$ (j) $x = 10.5$
(k) $x = 16.6$ (l) $x = 3$
(m) $x = -\frac{1}{7}$ (n) $x = 10$

* *Cambridge International Examinations bears no responsibility for the example answers to questions taken from its past question papers which are contained in this publication.*

2 (a) $x=2$ (b) $x=-10$
(c) $y=-3$ (d) $x=\frac{11}{15}$
(e) $p=1$ (f) $x=60$

3 (a) $x=2$ (b) $p=3$ (c) $t=1$
(d) $m=5$ (e) $n=10$ (f) $p=-\frac{5}{2}$
(g) $p=\frac{20}{13}$ (h) $x=-1$

4 (a) $x=2$ (b) $x=2$
(c) $x=12$ (d) $x=\frac{-13}{6}$
(e) $x=1$ (f) $x=\frac{15}{4}$

Exercise 6.3

1 (a) $3(x+2)$ (b) $3(5y-4)$
(c) $8(1-2z)$ (d) $5(7+5t)$
(e) $2(x-2)$ (f) $3x+7$
(g) $2(9k-32)$ (h) $11(3p+2)$
(i) $2(x+2y)$ (j) $3(p-5q)$
(k) $13(r-2s)$
(l) $2(p+2q+3r)$

2 (a) $7(3u-7v+5w)$
(b) $3x(y+1)$ (c) $3x(x+1)$
(d) $3p(5q+7)$ (e) $3m(3m-11)$
(f) $10m^2(9m-8)$
(g) $12x^3(3+2x^2)$ (h) $4pq(8p-q)$

3 (a) $2m^2n^2(7+2mn)$
(b) $abc(17+30b)$
(c) $m^2n^2(49m+6n)$
(d) $\frac{1}{2}(a+3b)$ (e) $\frac{1}{8}x(6x^3+7)$
(f) $8(x-4)$ (g) $(x+1)^2(1-4x)$
(h) $2x^3(3+x+2x^2)$
(i) $7xy(x^2-2x+3y)$
(j) $(y+3)(x+2)$

Exercise 6.4

1 (a) $a=c-b$ (b) $r=p-q$
(c) $h=\frac{g}{f}$ (d) $b=\frac{d-c}{a}$
(e) $a=bc$ (f) $n=\frac{t+m}{a}$

2 (a) $m=an-t$ (b) $a=\frac{t}{n-m}$
(c) $x=\frac{tz}{y}$ (d) $x=bc+a$
(e) $y=c-\frac{d}{x}$ (f) $b=a-c$

3 (a) $r=q(p-t)$ (b) $b=\frac{x-a}{c}$
(c) $m=n-\frac{t}{a}$ (d) $a=\frac{bc}{d}$
(e) $a=x-bc$ (f) $z=\frac{xy}{t}$

4 (a) $b=c^2$ (b) $b=\frac{c^2}{a}$
(c) $b=\left(\frac{c}{a}\right)^2$ (d) $b=c^2-c$
(e) $b=x-c^2$ (f) $y=\frac{x^2}{c}$

5 (a) $a=\frac{(v-u)}{t}$
(b) $s=\frac{\sqrt{n}(b-a)}{3}$
(c) $l=g\left(\frac{T^2}{4\pi^2}\right)$

Exercise 6.5

1 (a) Let $x=0.\dot{6}$
Then $10x=\boxed{6.\dot{6}}$
Subtracting:
$10x=\boxed{6.\dot{6}}$
$-x=0.\dot{6}$

$\boxed{9x}=6$
So $\boxed{9x}=6$
Simplify:
$x=\boxed{\frac{6}{9}=\frac{2}{3}}$

(b) Let $x=\boxed{0.\dot{1}\dot{7}}$
Then $100x=\boxed{17.\dot{1}\dot{7}}$
Subtracting:
$100x=\boxed{17.\dot{1}\dot{7}}$
$-x=\boxed{0.\dot{1}\dot{7}}$

$\boxed{99}\ x=\boxed{17}$
So $\boxed{99}\ x=\boxed{17}$
Simplify:
$x=\boxed{\frac{17}{99}}$

2 (a) $\frac{5}{9}$ (b) $\frac{1}{9}$
(c) $\frac{8}{9}$ (d) $\frac{8}{33}$
(e) $\frac{61}{99}$ (f) $\frac{32}{99}$
(g) $\frac{618}{999}$ (h) $\frac{233}{999}$
(i) $\frac{208}{999}$ (j) $\frac{1}{45}$
(k) $\frac{17}{90}$ (l) $\frac{31}{990}$
(m) $\frac{27}{11}$ (n) $\frac{1034}{333}$
(o) $\frac{23}{9}$ (p) 10
(q) 6 (r) $\frac{8}{9}$
(s) 1

3 (a) (i) 0.1
(ii) 0.01
(iii) 0.001
(iv) 0.000000001

(b) The answer is getting smaller because we are subtracting a larger number from 1 each time. The answer is approaching zero. No matter how small a number you think of, enough 9s can be added to the decimal subtracted from 1 to give an answer that is smaller than your chosen number. We would need an infinite number of 9s to get the answer zero, so no the answer can't arrive at zero.
(c) 6/9 = 2/3 and 2/9
(d) $4.\dot{8}$
(e) 8/9
(f) 4/9, 5/9,
$0.\dot{5}+0.\dot{4}=0.\dot{9}$

But $0.5+0.4=\frac{5}{9}+\frac{4}{9}=\frac{9}{9}=1.$

So $0.\dot{9}=1$
Parts a and b suggested that that the difference between 1 and 0.9999……decreased as more 9s were added. Here the recurring 9 is now the result of allowing the inclusion of more and more 9s to go on forever. Notice that the result finally arrives at the answer 1.

4 (a) 4.4 is indeed less than 4.5, but there are more numbers in between. For example 4.49 lies between 4.4 and 4.5, so 4.4 can't be the largest number smaller than 4.5.
(b) 4.49999 is indeed less than 4.5, but so is 4.4999999999, which is larger than 4.49999
(c) You can use algebra to show that $4.4\dot{9} = 4.5$. This means that $4.4\dot{9}$ is not *less* than 4.5 (because it is actually equal to it). There isn't actually an answer to the question. There is no largest number smaller than 4.5.

Examination practice

Exam-style questions

1 $T = 31$

2 (a) Temperature will be 19 °C
(b) You will need to climb to 1500 m.

3 (a) $n = \frac{e}{3}$ (b) $n = 7$

Past paper questions*

1 (a) $2x - 11y$
(b) $3x(2x - 3y)$

2 $a = \frac{4 + cb}{c}$

3 $3y - y^4$
4 $4y(x + 3z)$
5 $y = 14.5$
6 $x = 7$
7 $2y(3xy - 4)$

Chapter 7

Exercise 7.1

1 (a) 12.5 cm (b) 11.5 cm
(c) 9 cm (d) 9.6 cm

2 (a) 16 cm (b) 12 cm
(c) 25 cm (d) 38 cm
(e) 35 m (f) 23 km

3 (a) 55 cm^2 (b) 15 m^2
(c) 10 m^2 (d) 2.24 cm^2
(e) 16 m^2 (f) 7.84 cm^2
(g) 40 cm^2 (h) 42 m^2
(i) 8 cm^2 (j) 54 cm^2

4 (a) 50 m^2 (b) 52.29 m^2
(c) 33.1 cm^2 (3sf) (d) 37.8 cm^2
(e) 36 cm^2
(f) 145.16 cm^2
(g) 55.7 cm^2 (3sf)

5 (a) $h = 6$ cm (b) $b = 17$ cm
(c) $a = 2.86$ cm (3sf)
(d) $b = 5$ cm
(e) $h = 10.2$ cm (3sf)

6 183 tiles
7 14.14 cm × 14.14 cm

8 Students' answers will vary; the following are just examples.

(a)

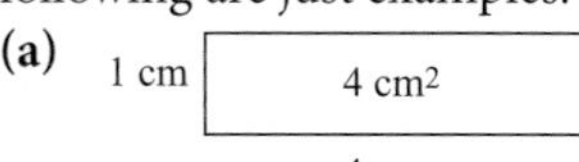

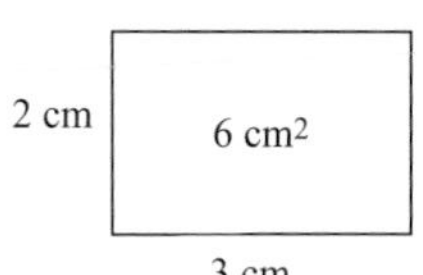

(b)

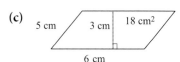

1 cm
6 cm²
6 cm

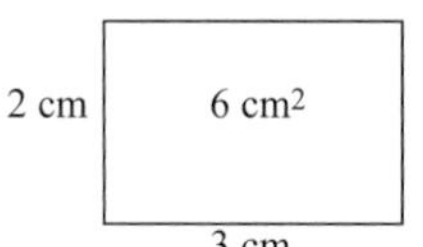

(c)

5 cm
3 cm
18 cm²
6 cm

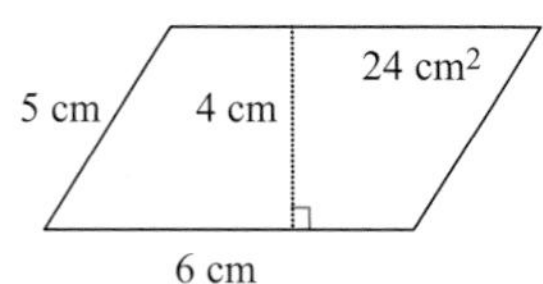

(d)

6.6 cm
4 cm
24 cm²
6 cm

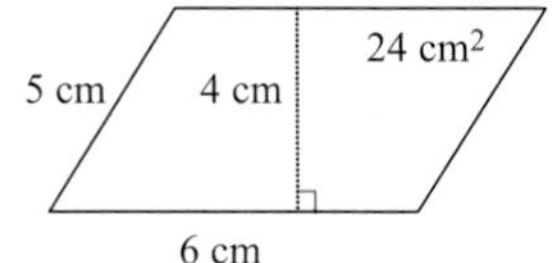

Exercise 7.2

1 Answers are correct to 3sf.
(a) $A = 50.3$ m^2 $C = 25.1$ m
(b) $A = 7.55$ mm^2 $C = 9.74$ mm
(c) $A = 0.503$ m^2 $C = 2.51$ m
(d) $A = 0.785$ cm^2 $C = 3.14$ cm
(e) $A = 1.57$ km^2 $C = 4.44$ km
(f) $A = 1.27$ m^2 $C = 4$ m (exact)

2 Answers correct 3sf.
(a) $A = 251$ cm^2
(b) $A = 13.7$ cm^2
(c) $A = 68.3$ m^2
(d) $A = 55.4$ cm^2
(e) $A = 154$ m^2
(f) $A = 149$ cm^2

3 23 bags
4 white = 0.1 m^2 red = 1.0 m^2
5 0.03 m^2

6 2 × 12 cm pizza ≈ 226.2 cm^2 and 24 cm pizza ≈ 452.4 cm^2, so two small pizzas is not the same amount of pizza as one large pizza.

Exercise 7.3

1 Answers correct to 3sf.
(a) $A = 198$ m^2 $l = 22.0$ m
(b) $A = 70.4$ cm^2 $l = 17.2$ cm
(c) $A = 94.7$ cm^2 $l = 29.6$ cm
(d) $A = 14.5$ m^2 $l = 9.68$ m

2 Answers correct to 3sf.
(a) $A = 12.6$ cm^2 $P = 16.2$ cm
(b) $A = 25.1$ cm^2 $P = 22.3$ cm
(c) $A = 1.34$ cm^2 $P = 7.24$ cm
(d) $A = 16.4$ m^2 $P = 16.5$ m
(e) $A = 116$ cm^2 $P = 44.2$ cm
(f) $A = 186$ m^2 $P = 55.0$ m
(g) $A = 0.185$ cm^2 $P = 1.88$ cm
(h) $A = 36.3$ cm^2 $P = 24.6$ cm
(i) $A = 244$ cm^2 $P = 62.5$ cm
(j) $A = 98.1$ m^2 $P = 43.4$ m

3 Answers correct 3sf.
(a) $A = 30.2$ cm^2 $P = 28.9$ cm
(b) $A = 77.4$ cm^2 $P = 31.3$ cm
(c) $A = 46.9$ m^2 $P = 39.2$ m
(d) $A = 15.1$ cm^2 $P = 43.2$ cm
(e) $A = 69.5$ m^2 $P = 56.5$ m

4 Answers correct to 3sf.
(a) $P = 144$ cm $A = 1400$ cm^2
(b) $P = 15.6$ cm $A = 17.0$ cm^2
(c) $P = 7.07$ cm $A = 3.63$ cm^2
(d) $P = 26.6$ cm $A = 32.6$ cm^2

* *Cambridge International Examinations bears no responsibility for the example answers to questions taken from its past question papers which are contained in this publication.*

Exercise 7.4

1

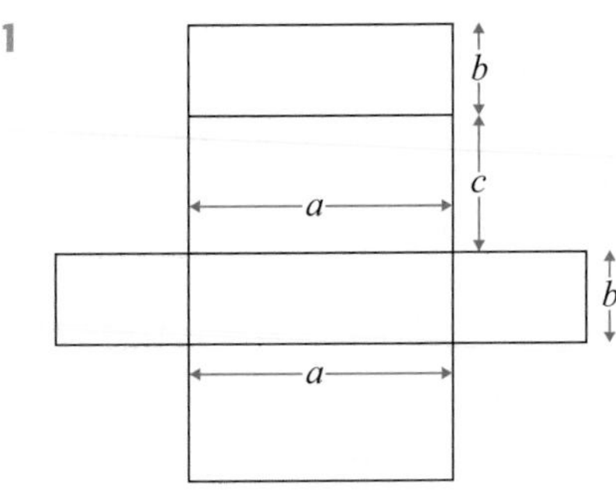

2 (a) Trapezium-based prism
(b) O and S
(c) $PQ = RQ = UV = VW$

3 (a)

4

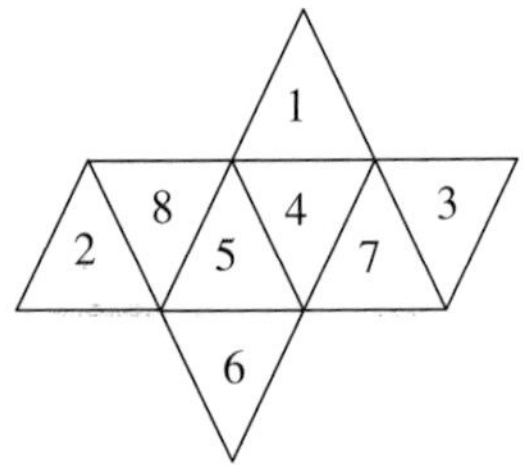

Exercise 7.5

1 volume = $66\,cm^3$
surface area = $144\,cm^2$

2 (a) (i) $720\,cm^3$
(ii) $548\,cm^2$
(b) (i) $13.8\,mm^3$ (3sf)
(ii) $40.3\,mm^2$ (3sf)

3 $432\,000\,cm^3$

4 (a) $768\,cm^3$
(b) $816\,cm^2$

5 $3.39\,m^3$ (3sf)
6 $76.7\,cm^2$ (3sf)
7 $241\,cm^3$ (3sf)

8 (a) $448\,m^3$
(b) 320 boxes
(c) $8.5\,m^2$

9 (a) $48\,m^3$ (b) Yes

Exercise 7.6

1 (a) $5030\,cm^2$ (3sf)
(b) $33500\,cm^3$ (3sf)

2 $5300\,cm^3$ (3sf)
3 $2570000\,m^3$ (3sf)

4 (a) $1070 = m^2$ (3sf)
(b) $2280 = m^3$ (3sf)

5 (a) $754 = cm^3$ (3sf)
(b) $415 = cm^2$ (3sf)

6 2.29 cm (3sf)

7 $\frac{R}{r} = \sqrt[3]{2}$

8 (a) $628\,cm^3$ (3sf)
(b) $542\,cm^2$ (3sf)

9 (a)

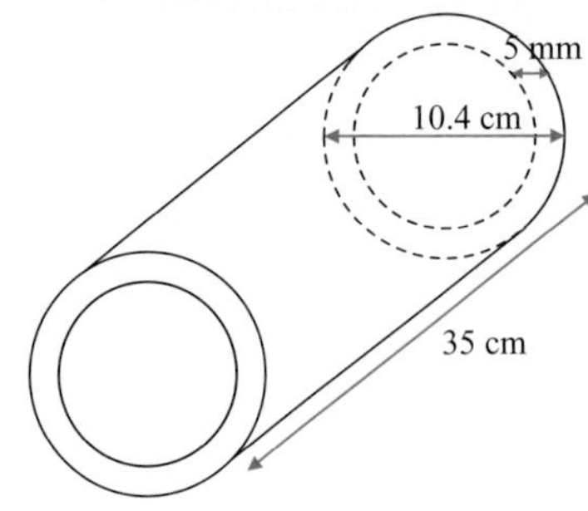

(b) volume of metal in the tube =

$$\left(\pi \times \left(\frac{10.4}{2}\right)^2 \times 35\right) - \left(\pi \times \left(\frac{10.4-1}{2}\right)^2 \times 35\right) cm^3$$

(c) $544\,cm^3$ (3sf)
(d) Total surface area of tube = $2 \times$ area of ring + area of outer tube + area of inner tube (Note 'ring' is the 5 mm thick end of the cylinder.)

$$2 \times \left[\pi \times \left(\frac{10.4}{2}\right)^2 - \pi\left(\frac{10.4-0.5}{2}\right)^2\right] + (\pi \times 10.4 \times 35) + [\pi \times (10.4-0.5) \times 35]\,cm^2$$

Examination practice

Exam-style questions

1 33 900 mm (3sf)
2 $P = 30.3$ cm (3sf) $A = 41.4\,cm^2$ (3sf)
3 $2.31\,m^3$ (3sf)

Past paper questions*

1 (d) 64 m
(e) $33.3\,m^3$

2 $170\,m^2$

3 $3620\,cm^2$ (3sf)

4 23 people

5 (a) $14.1\,cm^2$ (3sf)
(b) 28.4 cm (3sf)

Chapter 8

Exercise 8.1

1 $\frac{7}{50}$

2 (a) $\frac{1}{10}$ (b) $\frac{3}{20}$ (c) $\frac{131}{260}$ (d) $\frac{141}{260}$

3 (a) $\frac{1}{77}$ (b) $\frac{76}{77}$

4 (a) $\frac{4}{9}$ (b) $\frac{5}{9}$ (c) $\frac{0}{9}$ (d) 1

5 9 blue balls

6 (a) $\frac{1}{13}$ (b) $\frac{1}{4}$ (c) $\frac{1}{2}$ (d) $\frac{4}{13}$

Exercise 8.2

1 (a)

Second throw		First throw	
		H	T
	H	HH	TH
	T	HT	TT

(b) (i) $\frac{1}{2}$ (ii) $\frac{1}{4}$ (iii) $\frac{3}{4}$ (iv) $\frac{1}{4}$

2 (a)

Second die	×	First die 1	2	3	4	5	6
	1	1	2	3	4	5	6
	2	2	4	6	8	10	12
	3	3	6	9	12	15	18
	4	4	8	12	16	20	24
	5	5	10	15	20	25	30
	6	6	12	18	24	30	36

(b) (i) $\frac{1}{36}$ (ii) $\frac{0}{36}$ (iii) $\frac{2}{9}$
(iv) $\frac{7}{9}$ (v) $\frac{1}{6}$ (vi) $\frac{2}{9}$

3 (a)

Tetrahedral die		Spinner 1	2	3	4	5
	2	2	2	3	4	5
	4	4	4	4	4	5
	6	6	6	6	6	6
	8	8	8	8	8	8

(b) (i) $\frac{17}{20}$ (ii) $\frac{3}{20}$ (iii) $\frac{3}{10}$
(iv) $\frac{1}{4}$ (v) $\frac{7}{20}$

* Cambridge International Examinations bears no responsibility for the example answers to questions taken from its past question papers which are contained in this publication.

4 (a)

		First throw					
		4	6	10	12	15	24
Second throw	4	4	2	2	4	1	4
	6	2	6	2	6	3	6
	10	2	2	10	2	5	2
	12	4	6	2	12	3	12
	15	1	3	5	3	15	3
	24	4	6	2	12	3	24

(b) (i) $\frac{5}{18}$ **(ii)** $\frac{13}{18}$ **(iii)** 1

(iv) $\frac{17}{18}$ **(v)** $\frac{2}{9}$ **(vi)** $\frac{5}{18}$

Exercise 8.3

1 (a) $\frac{1}{36}$ **(b)** $\frac{1}{4}$ **(c)** $\frac{1}{6}$ **(d)** $\frac{5}{6}$

2 (a) red, red; red, blue; blue, red; blue, blue

(b) (i) $\frac{7}{12}$ **(ii)** $\frac{5}{12}$ **(iii)** $\frac{35}{144}$

(iv) $\frac{74}{144}$ **(v)** $\frac{70}{144}$ **(vi)** $\frac{49}{144}$

(vii) $\frac{95}{144}$

3 (a) $\frac{1}{169}$ **(b)** $\frac{1}{2704}$ **(c)** $\frac{1}{52}$

(d) $\frac{3}{8}$ **(e)** $\frac{1}{2}$ **(f)** $\frac{1}{2}$

4 (a) 0.24 **(b)** 0.24 **(c)** 0.36
(d) 0.72 **(e)** 0.48

Examination practice

Exam-style questions

1 (a) $\frac{8}{19}$ **(b)** $\frac{7}{18}$

2 (a) $\frac{2}{5}$ **(b)** 0

3 $\frac{7}{12}$

4 (a) red, black, black; black, red, black; black, black, red

(b) $\frac{2}{3}$

5 (a)

Face	1	2	3	4
Probability	$\frac{2}{9}$	$\frac{1}{3}$	$\frac{5}{18}$	$\frac{1}{6}$
	$\frac{4}{18}$	$\frac{6}{18}$	$\frac{5}{18}$	$\frac{3}{18}$

(b) 2 **(c)** 1 **(d)** $\frac{13}{18}$

6 (a)

		Josh						
	+	\$5	\$1	\$1	50c	20c	20c	20c
Soumik	\$5	\$10	\$6	\$6	\$5.50	\$5.20	\$5.00	\$5.20
	\$5	\$10	\$6	\$6	\$5.50	\$5.20	\$5.20	\$5.20
	\$5	\$10	\$6	\$6	\$5.50	\$5.20	\$5.20	\$5.20
	\$2	\$7	\$3	\$3	\$2.50	\$2.20	\$2.20	\$2.20
	50c	\$5.50	\$1.50	\$1.50	\$1	70c	70c	70c
	50c	\$5.50	\$1.50	\$1.50	\$1	70c	70c	70c
	50c	\$5.50	\$1.50	\$1.50	\$1	70c	70c	70c

(b) $\frac{6}{49}$ **(c)** $\frac{18}{49}$ **(d)** $\frac{27}{49}$

Past paper questions*

1 (a) 0.3

(b) 0

2 (a) (i)

Total	Tally	Frequency
2	||	2
3	𝍸	5
4	𝍸 𝍸	10
5	|||	3
6	𝍸 𝍸 𝍸 ||	17
7	𝍸 𝍸 |	11
8	𝍸 ||||	9
9	𝍸 |||	8
10	|||	3
11	|	1
12	|	1

(ii) $\frac{3}{70}$

3 (a) $\frac{2}{6}$ oe

(b) 200

Unit 3

Chapter 9

Exercise 9.1

1 (a) 5 → 7 → 9 → 11 → 13 → **15** → **17** → **19** → ...
+2 +2 +2 +2 +2 +2 +2 +2

(b) 3 → 8 → 13 → 18 → 23 → **28** → **33** → **38** → ...
+5 +5 +5 +5 +5 +5 +5 +5

(c) 3 → 9 → 27 → 81 → 243 → **729** → **2187** → **6561** → ...
×3 ×3 ×3 ×3 ×3 ×3 ×3 ×3

(d) 0.5 → 2 → 3.5 → 5 → 6.5 → **8** → **9.5** → **11** → ...
+1.5 +1.5 +1.5 +1.5 +1.5 +1.5 +1.5 +1.5

(e) 8 → 5 → 2 → −1 → −4 → **−7** → **−10** → **−13** → ...
−3 −3 −3 −3 −3 −3 −3 −3

(f) 13 → 11 → 9 → 7 → 5 → **3** → **1** → **−1** → ...
−2 −2 −2 −2 −2 −2 −2 −2

(g) 6 → 4.8 → 3.6 → 2.4 → 1.2 → **0** → **−1.2** → **−2.4** → ...
−1.2 −1.2 −1.2 −1.2 −1.2 −1.2 −1.2 −1.2

(h) 2.3 → 1.1 → −0.1 → −1.3 → **−2.5** → **−3.7** → **−4.9** → ...
−1.2 −1.2 −1.2 −1.2 −1.2 −1.2 −1.2

2 (a) 81, −243, 729
Rule = multiply previous term by −3.

(b) Fr, Sa, Su
Rule = days of the week.

(c) u, b, j = skip 1 extra letter of the alphabet each time.

(d) 5, 10, 6, 12
Rule = even position numbers increase by 2 and odd position numbers increase by 1. Rule.

Exercise 9.2

1 (a) (i) 33 **(ii)** $2n + 3$
(b) (i) 73 **(ii)** $5n - 2$
(c) (i) 14 348 907 **(ii)** 3^n
(d) (i) 21.5 **(ii)** $1.5n - 1$
(e) (i) −34 **(ii)** $-3n + 11$
(f) (i) −15 **(ii)** $-2n + 15$
(g) (i) −10.8 **(ii)** $-1.2n + 7.2$
(h) (i) 450 **(ii)** $2n^2$

2 (a) $4(2n - 1)$ **(b)** 3996 **(c)** 30

(d) Rule is $8n - 4$, so $8n - 4 = 154$ should give integer value of n if 154 is a term:

$8n - 4 = 154$
$8n = 150$
$n = 18.75$

* *Cambridge International Examinations bears no responsibility for the example answers to questions taken from its past question papers which are contained in this publication.*

OR
19th term = 108 and 20th term = 156 therefore 154 is not a term.

3 **(a)** $\frac{1}{2^n}$ **(b)** $\frac{4n-1}{3n+5}$

(c) $\frac{(4n-1)^2}{(3n+5)^2}$ **(d)** $\frac{n}{2}-\frac{7}{6}$

4 **(a)** $1, -2, -5, \ldots; -56$
(b) $1, 0, -1, \ldots; -18$
(c) $\frac{1}{2}, 2, 4.5, \ldots; 200$
(d) $0, 6, 24, \ldots; 7980$
(e) $\frac{3}{2}, 1, \frac{3}{4}, \ldots; \frac{1}{7}$
(f) $2, 16, 54, \ldots; 16\,000$

5 $x = -2$

6 x can take any value.

Exercise 9.3

(a)

Pattern number (n)	1	2	3	4	5	6	n	300
Number of matches (m)	4	7	10	13	16	19	$m = 3n + 1$	901

(b)

Pattern number (p)	1	2	3	4	5	6	p	300
Number of circles (c)	1	3	5	7	9	11	$c = 2p - 1$	599

(c)

Pattern number (p)	1	2	3	4	5	6	p	300
Number of triangles (t)	5	8	11	14	17	20	$t = 3p + 2$	902

(d)

Pattern number (p)	1	2	3	4	5	6	p	300
Number of squares (s)	5	10	15	20	25	30	$s = 5p$	1500

Exercise 9.4

1 $\frac{2}{3}$ **2** $\frac{2}{9}$

3 $\frac{23}{99}$ **4** $\frac{2}{11}$

5 $\frac{17}{90}$ **6** $\frac{43}{90}$

7 $\frac{284}{999}$ **8** 1

Exercise 9.5

1 **(a)** rational **(b)** rational
(c) rational **(d)** rational
(e) irrational **(f)** irrational
(g) rational **(h)** rational
(i) rational **(j)** rational
(k) rational **(l)** rational
(m) rational **(n)** irrational
(o) irrational **(p)** irrational

2 **(a)** $\frac{6}{1}$ **(b)** $\frac{19}{8}$ **(c)** $\frac{37}{33}$
(d) $\frac{8}{9}$ **(e)** $\frac{427}{1000}$ **(f)** $\frac{283}{90}$

3 Possible answers include:
(a) 2 **(b)** $\sqrt{5}$ **(c)** 1 **(d)** 2

4 The set of rational numbers and the set of irrational numbers are both infinite sets. But the set of rational numbers is 'countable' whereas the set of irrational numbers is 'uncountable'. This might suggest that there are more irrational numbers than rational numbers.

> The term 'countable' does not mean finite.
>
> In this context we mean that, if you tried to pair up every rational number with exactly one irrational number, you would have a lot of irrational numbers left over that you couldn't pair up but no rational numbers would be upaired.

5 Students' own answers. Example: An 'imaginary number' is a quantity of the form ix, where x is a real number and i is the positive square root of -1, e.g. $\sqrt{-3} = \sqrt{3}i$.

Exercise 9.6

1 **(a)** {Monday, Tuesday, Wednesday, Thursday, Friday, Saturday, Sunday}
(b) {Jan, Feb, Mar, Apr, May, Jun, Jul, Aug, Sep, Oct, Nov, Dec}
(c) {1, 2, 3, 4, 6, 9, 12, 18, 36}
(d) {Red, Orange, Yellow, Green, Blue, Indigo, Violet}
(e) {7, 14, 21, 28, 35, 42, 49}
(f) {2, 3, 5, 7, 11, 13, 17, 19, 23, 29}
(g) {TOY, OYT, YTO, YOT, OTY, TYO}

2 **(a)** hamster, rat
(b) peas, beans
(c) Dublin, Amsterdam
(d) Rhine, Yangtze
(e) redwood, palm
(f) soccer, rugby
(g) Italy, Spain
(h) Carter, Reagan
(i) Bach, Puccini
(j) lily, orchid
(k) 12, 15
(l) Labrador, Fox terrier
(m) Uranus, Neptune
(n) surprised, mad
(o) African, American
(p) pentagon, quadrilateral

3 **(a)** false **(b)** true **(c)** true
(d) false **(e)** true

4 **(a)** square numbers
(b) continents of the world
(c) even numbers less than 10
(d) multiples of 2
(e) factors of 12

Exercise 9.7

1 **(a)** **(i)** $A \cap B = \{6, 8, 10\}$
(ii) $A \cup B = \{1, 2, 3, 4, 5, 6, 8, 10\}$
(b) **(i)** 3 **(ii)** 8

2 **(a)** **(i)** $C \cap D = \{a, g, u, w, z\}$
(ii) $C \cup D = \{a, b, g, h, u, w, x, y, z\}$
(b) Yes, u is an element of C and D.
(c) No, g is an element of both sets and will be an element of the union of the sets.

3 **(a)** Equilateral triangles have two sides equal.
(b) F. Redefine G as triangles with two or three equal sides.

4 **(a)** **(i)** $T \cup W = \{1, 2, 3, 6, 7, 9, 10\}$
(ii) $T \cap W = \{1, 3\}$
(b) Yes; 5 is not listed in T.

5 **(a)** {cat, dog, turtle, aardvark}
(b) {rabbit, emu, turtle, mouse, aardvark}
(c) {rabbit, cat, dog, emu, turtle, mouse, aardvark}
(d) { } or ∅
(e) {rabbit, emu, mouse }
(f) {rabbit, cat, dog, emu, turtle, mouse, aardvark}

Exercise 9.8

1 **(a)** $A = \{6, 12, 18, 24\}$ and $B = \{4, 8, 12, 16, 20, 24\}$
(b) $A \cap B = \{12, 24\}$
(c) $A \cup B = \{4, 6, 8, 12, 16, 18, 20, 24\}$

2 **(a)** **(i)** $P = \{a, b, c, d, e, f\}$

(ii) $Q = \{e, f, g, h\}$
(b) $P \cap Q = \{e, f\}$
(c) (i) $(P \cup Q)' = \{i, j\}$
(ii) $P \cap Q' = \{a, b, c, d\}$

3 (a)

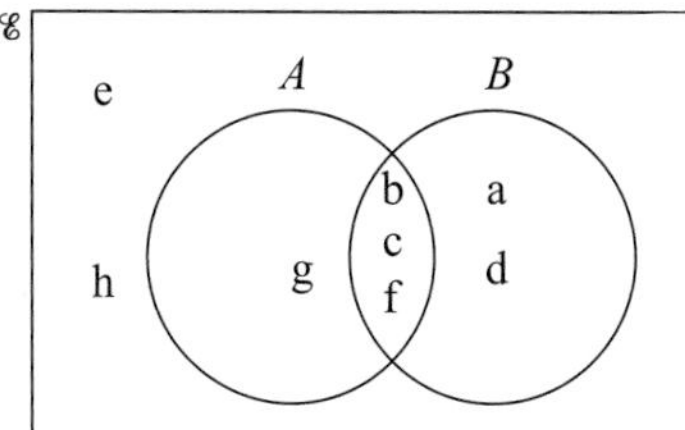

(b)

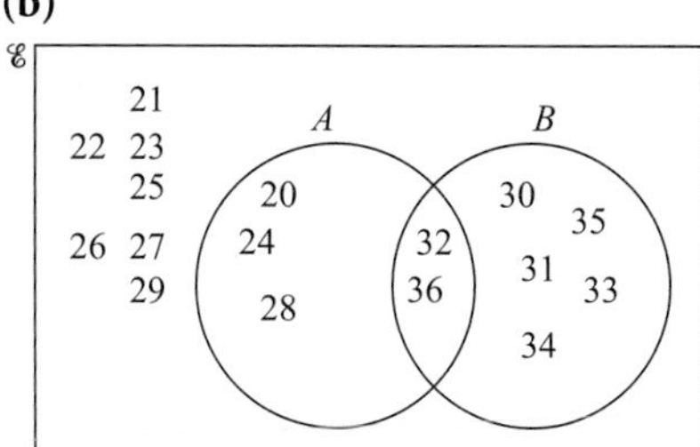

4 (a) $x = 6$
(b) $n(V) = 16$
(c) $n(S)' = 16$

5

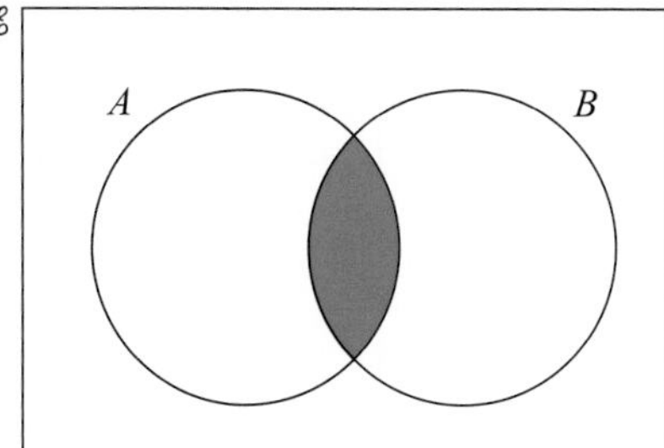

6 (a) 12 (b) 3 (c) 21
(d) 12 (e) $\frac{14}{24}$ or $\frac{7}{12}$ (f) $\frac{12}{19}$

Exercise 9.9

1 (a) {41, 42, 43, 44, 45, 46, 47, 48, 49}
(b) {equilateral triangle, square, regular pentagon, regular hexagon}
(c) {18, 21, 24, 27, 30}

2 (a) $\{x : x \text{ is an integer}, 1 < x < 9\}$
(b) $\{x : x$ is a letter of the alphabet, x is a vowel$\}$
(c) $\{x : x$ is a letter of the alphabet, x is a letter in the name Nicholas$\}$
(d) $\{x : x$ is an even number, $1 < x < 21\}$
(e) $\{x : x$ is a factor of 36$\}$

3 $\{x : x$ is a multiple of 3 and 5$\}$

4 (a) (i) {6, 7, 8, 9, 10, 11, 12, 13, 14, 15, 16, 17}
(ii) {1, 2, 3, 4, 5}
(iii) {1, 2, 3, 4, 5}
(iv) {16, 17}
(v) {1, 2, 3, 4, 5, 6, 7, 8, 9, 10, 11, 12, 13, 14, 15}
(b) $\mathscr{E}$
(c) {1, 2, 3, 4, 5, 6, 7, 8, 9, 10, 11, 12, 13, 14, 15, 16, 17}

Examination practice

Exam-style questions

1 (a)

Pattern number (n)	1	2	3	4
Number of dots (d)	5	8	11	14

(b) $d = 3n + 2$ (c) 182 (d) 29

2 (a)

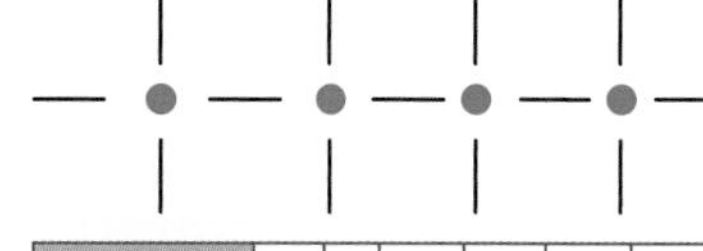

(b)

Dots (n)	1	2	3	4	5	6
Lines (l)	4	7	10	13	16	19

(c) 298 (d) $3n + 1$ (e) 28

Past paper questions*

1 (a) (i) 11
(ii) subtract 4 from previous term.
(b) 2, 6, 10 (c) $3n - 4$

2

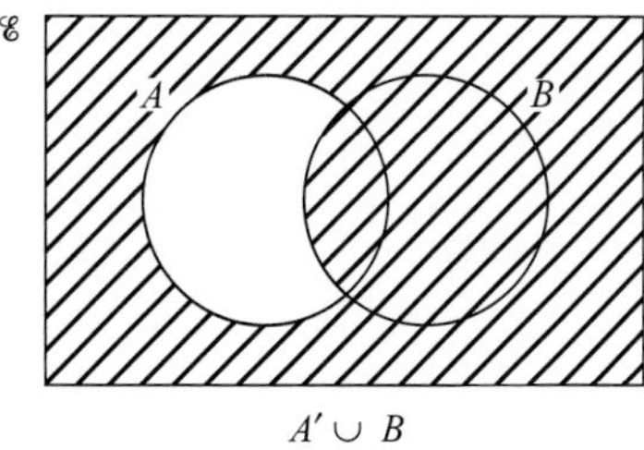

$A' \cup B$

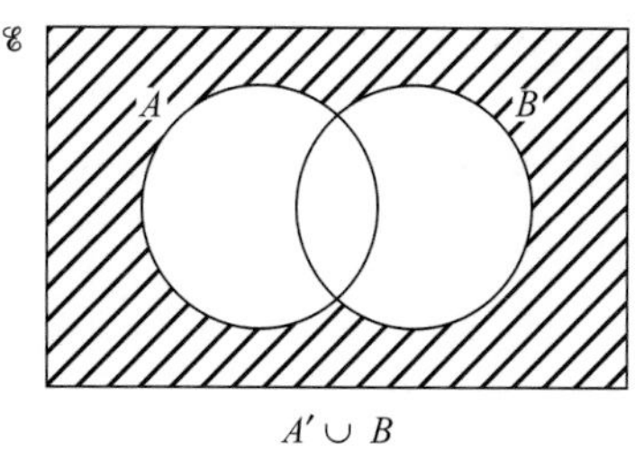

$A' \cup B$

3 $-4n + 17$

4

A'

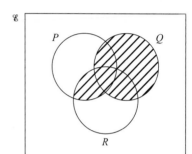

$(P \cap R) \cup Q$

5 (a) (i)

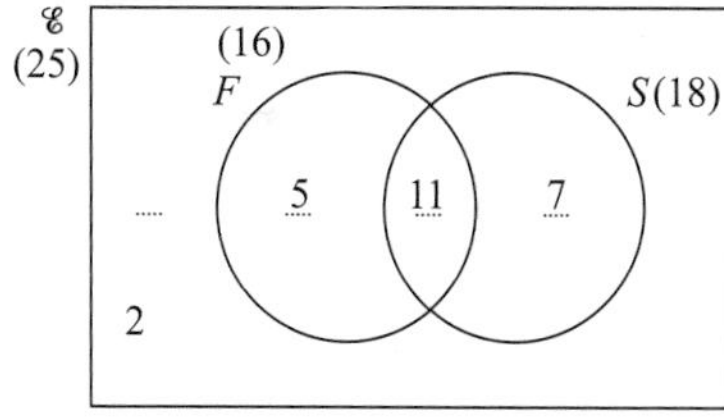

(ii) 9
(iii) 14
(iv) $\frac{11}{25}$
(v) $\frac{7}{100}$

(b) (i)

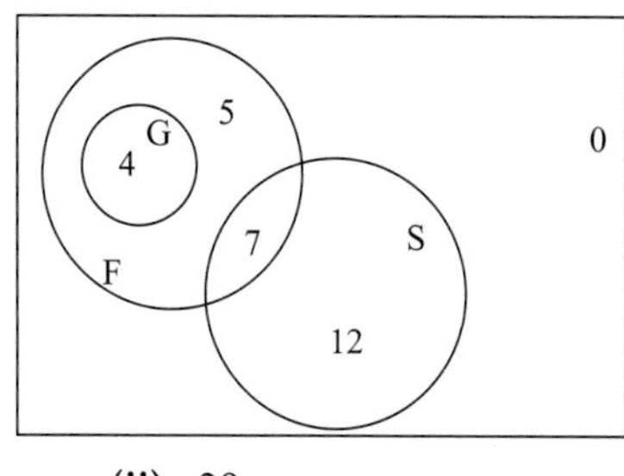

(ii) 28

* *Cambridge International Examinations bears no responsibility for the example answers to questions taken from its past question papers which are contained in this publication.*

Chapter 10

Exercise 10.1

1 (a)

x	−3	−2	−1	0	1	2	3
y	−7	−4	−1	2	5	8	11

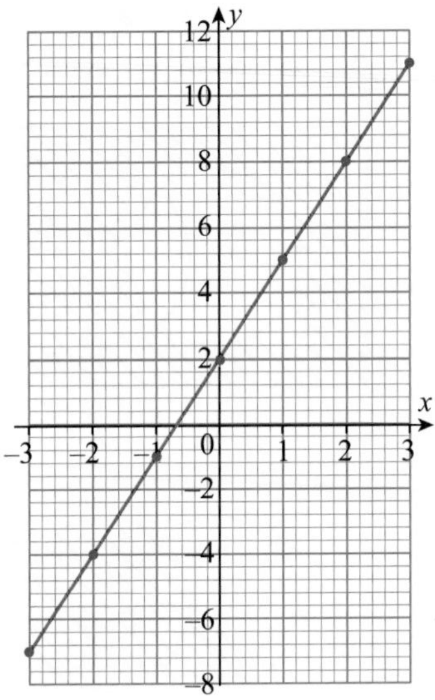

(b)

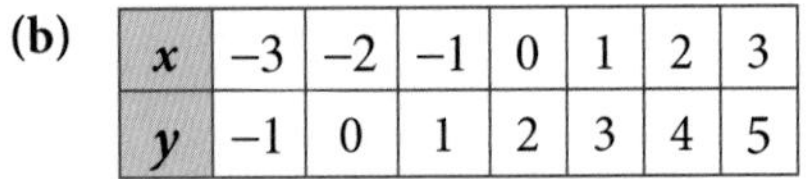

x	−3	−2	−1	0	1	2	3
y	−1	0	1	2	3	4	5

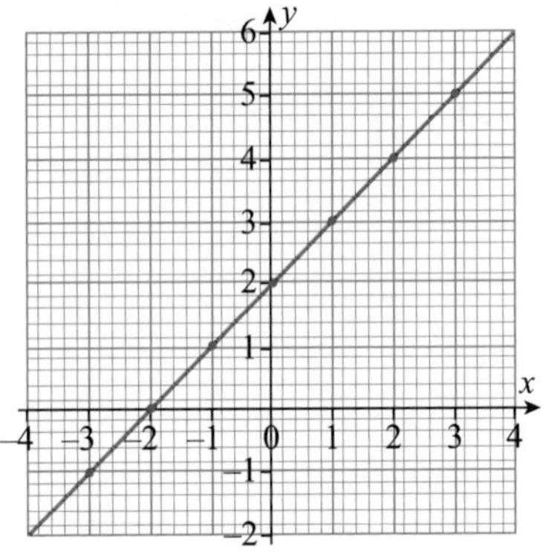

(c)

x	−3	−2	−1	0	1	2	3
y	−7	−5	−3	−1	1	3	5

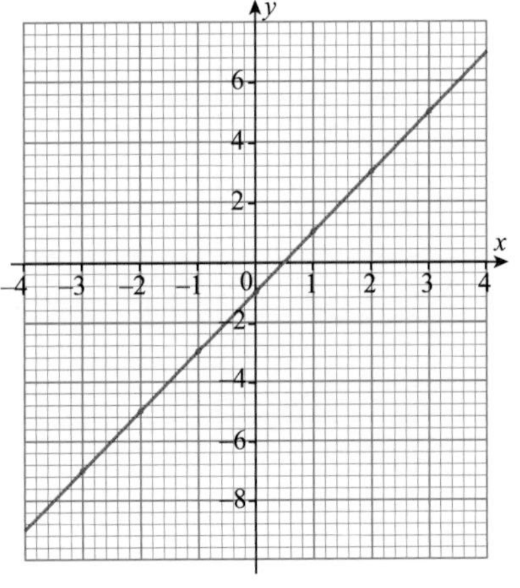

(d)

x	−3	−2	−1	0	1	2	3
y	−19	−14	−9	−4	1	6	11

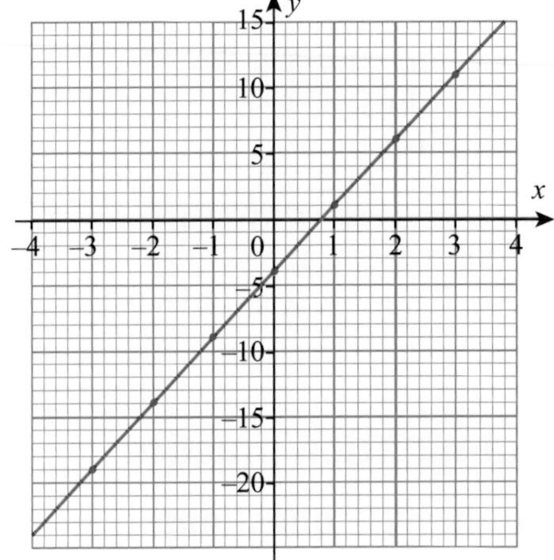

(e)

x	−3	−2	−1	0	1	2	3
y	7	5	3	1	−1	−3	−5

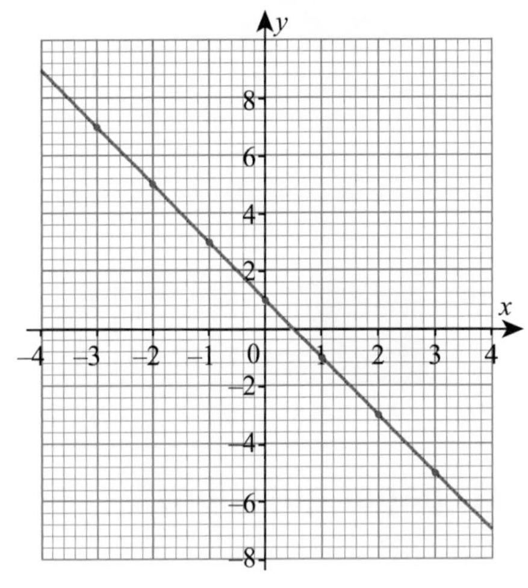

(f)

x	−3	−2	−1	0	1	2	3
y	1	0	−1	−2	−3	−4	−5

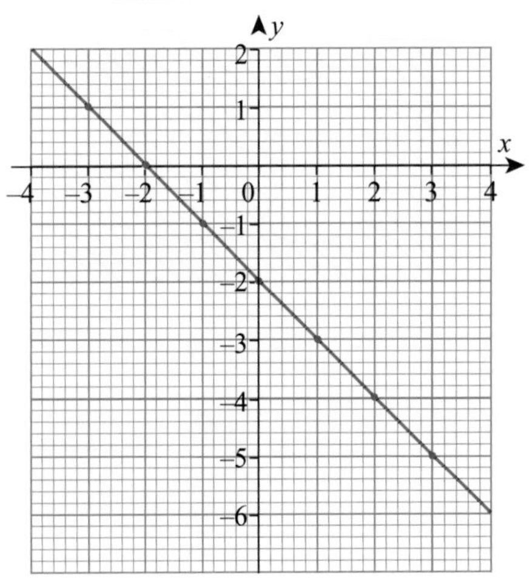

(g)

x	−3	−2	−1	0	1	2	3
y	9	8	7	6	5	4	3

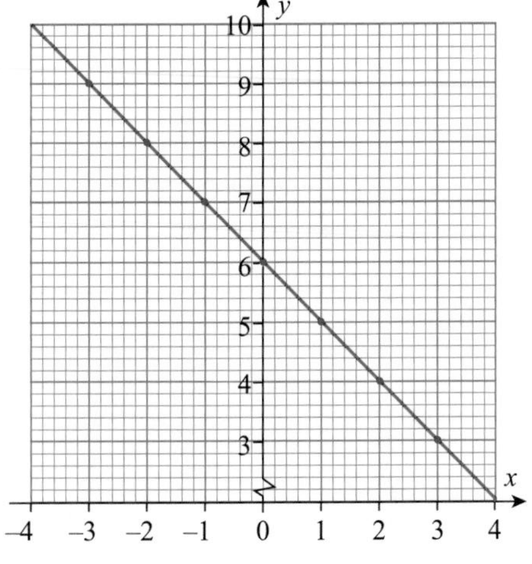

(h)

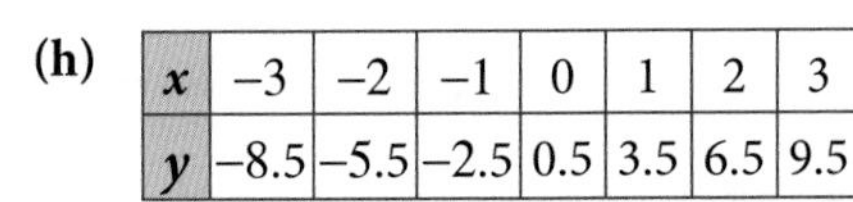

x	−3	−2	−1	0	1	2	3
y	−8.5	−5.5	−2.5	0.5	3.5	6.5	9.5

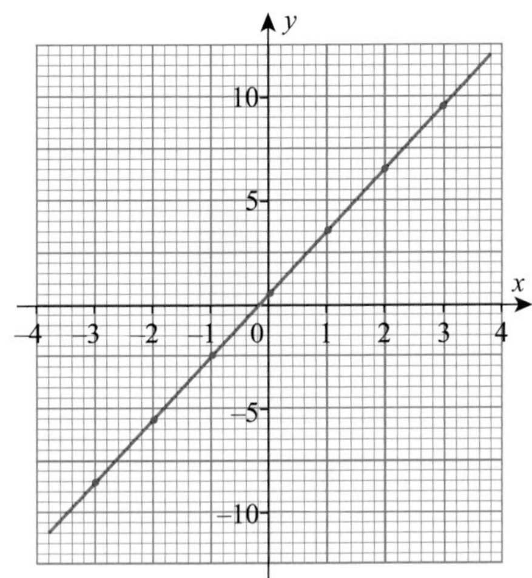

(i)

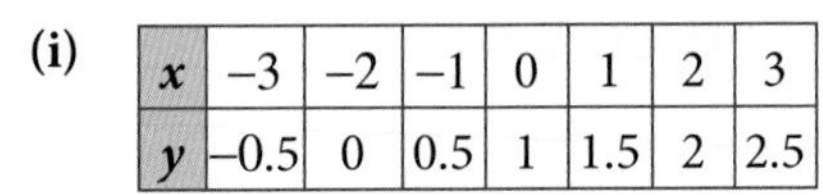

x	−3	−2	−1	0	1	2	3
y	−0.5	0	0.5	1	1.5	2	2.5

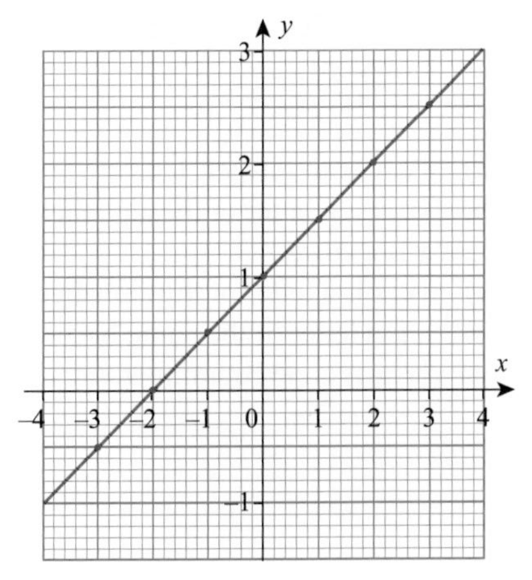

(j)

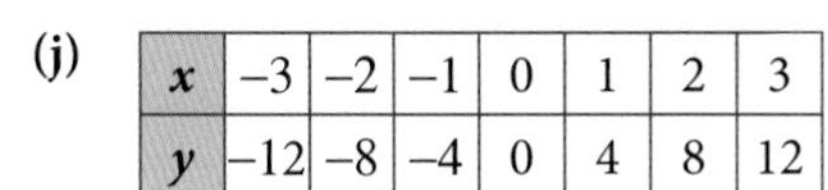

x	−3	−2	−1	0	1	2	3
y	−12	−8	−4	0	4	8	12

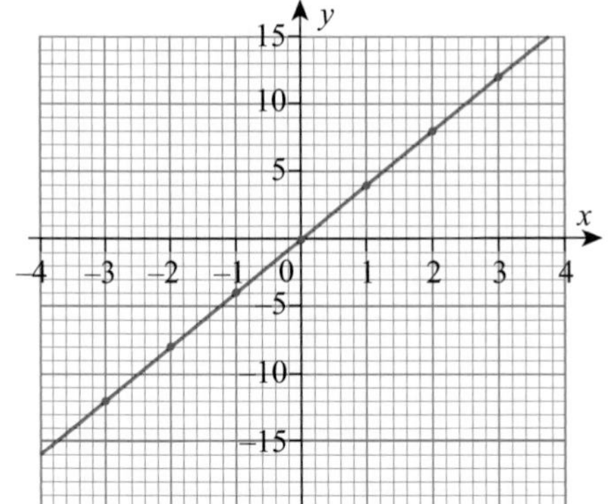

(k)

x	−3	−2	−1	0	1	2	3
y	−3	−3	−3	−3	−3	−3	−3

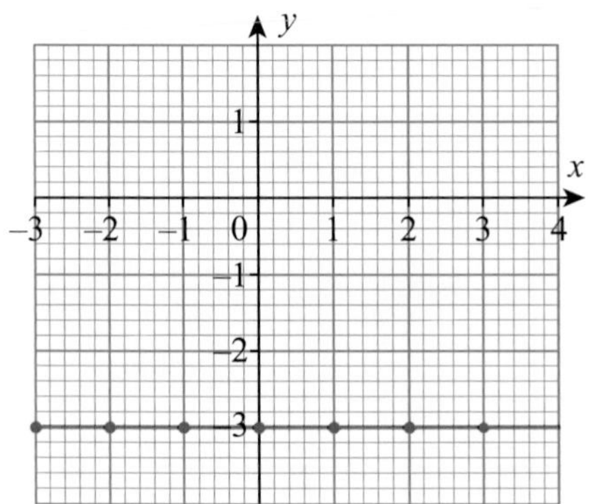

(l)

x	−3	−2	−1	0	1	2	3
y	2	1	0	−1	−2	−3	−4

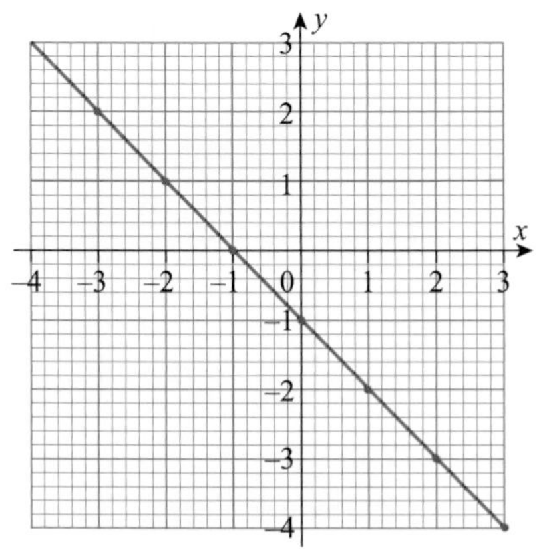

(m)

x	−3	−2	−1	0	1	2	3
y	7	6	5	4	3	2	1

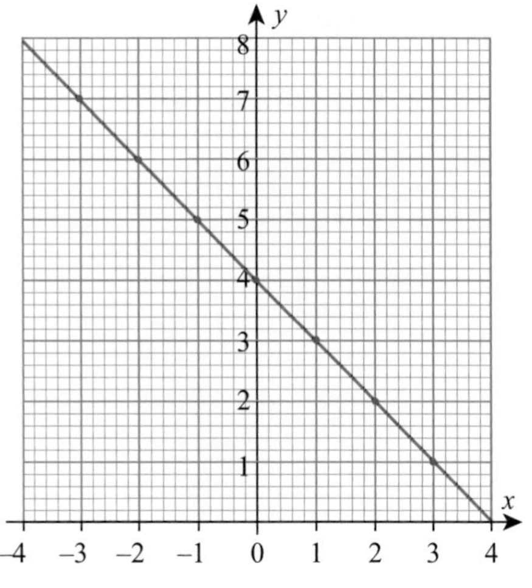

(n)

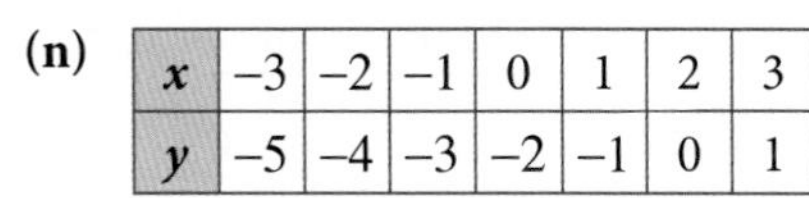

x	−3	−2	−1	0	1	2	3
y	−5	−4	−3	−2	−1	0	1

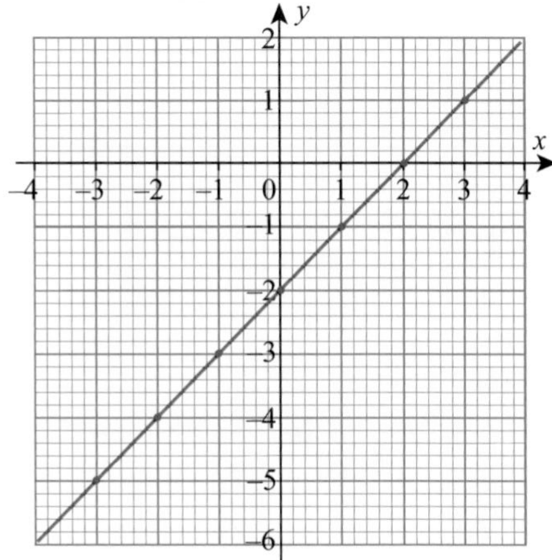

(o)

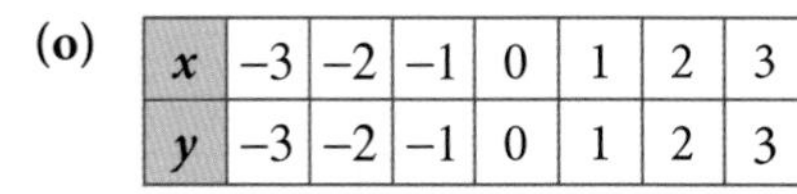

x	−3	−2	−1	0	1	2	3
y	−3	−2	−1	0	1	2	3

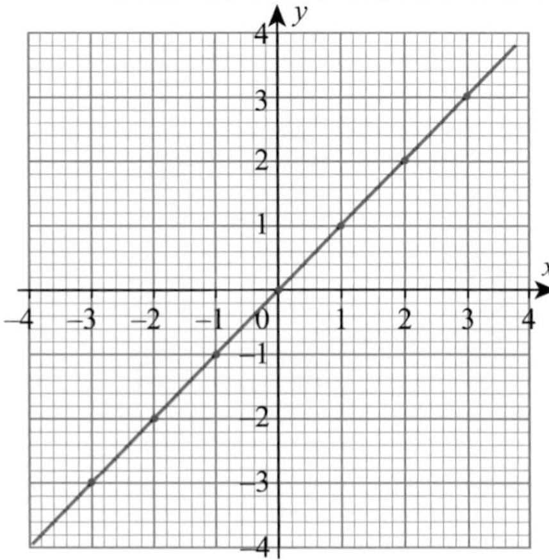

(p)

x	−3	−2	−1	0	1	2	3
y	3	2	1	0	−1	−2	−3

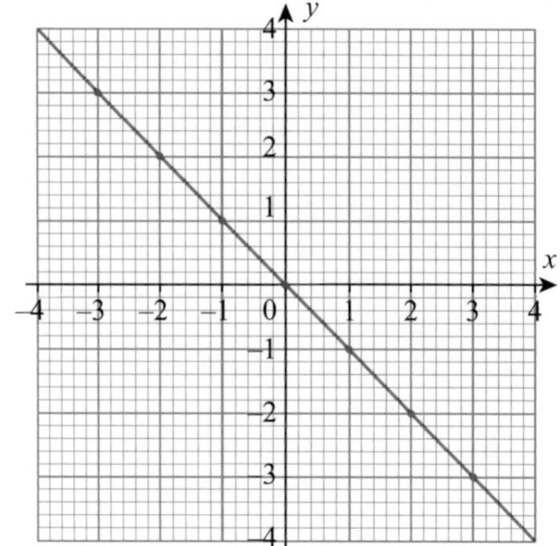

2

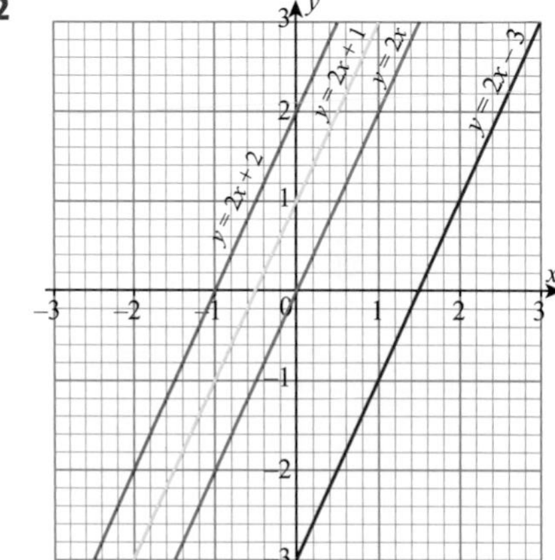

The lines are parallel.

3 (a)

x	−3	0	3
$y = x + 2$	−1	2	5

(b)

x	−3	0	3
$y = -x + 2$	5	2	−1

(c)

x	−3	0	3
$y = x - 2$	−5	−2	1

(d)

x	−3	0	3
$y = -x - 2$	1	−2	−5

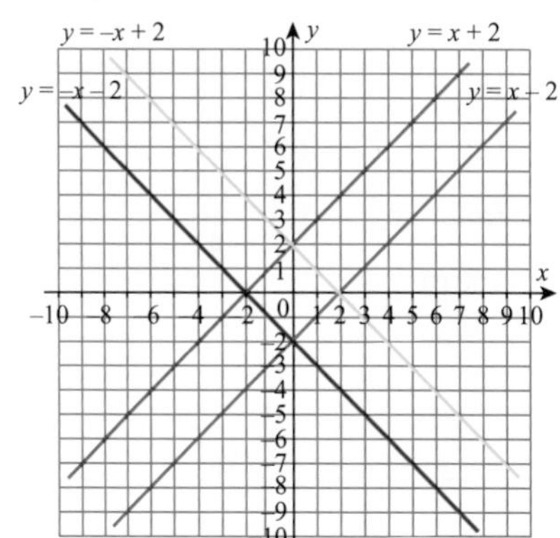

4 **(a)** $y = x + 2$ cuts the x-axis at $y = 2$
$y = -x + 2$ cuts the x-axis at $y = 2$
$y = x - 2$ cuts the x-axis at $y = -2$
$y = -x - 2$ cuts the x-axis at $y = -2$
(b) $y = x + 2$
(c) $-x + 2$ and $-x - 2$
(d) $y = x + 2$ and $y = -x + 2$
(e) $y = x - 2$ and $y = -x - 2$
(f) None of the graphs
(g) $y = x + 2$ is parallel to $y = x - 2$
$y = -x + 2$ is parallel to $y = -x - 2$
(h) Same coefficients of x but different constant values.

Exercise 10.2

1 $x = -4$
$x = 2$
$x = 7$
$y = 7$
$y = 3$
$y = -6$

2

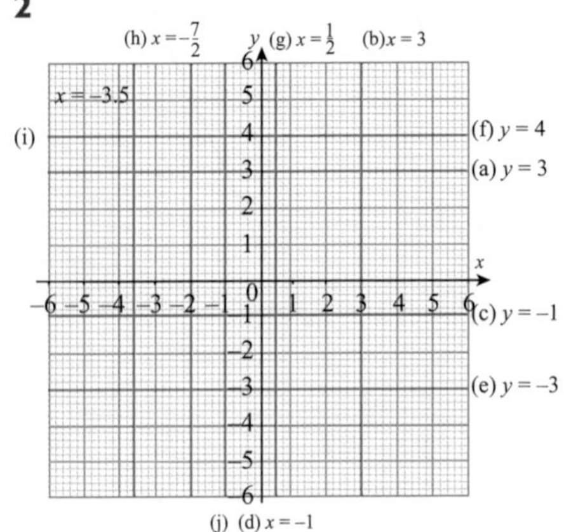

Exercise 10.3

1 **(a)** 3 **(b)** 2
(c) 5 **(d)** -3
(e) -2.5 **(f)** -1
(g) $\frac{1}{3}$ **(h)** $\frac{2}{3}$ **(i)** $-\frac{1}{4}$

2 **(a)** 3 **(b)** 1
(c) 2 **(d)** -3
(e) -3 **(f)** $\frac{17}{4}$

3 450 m

Exercise 10.4

1 **(a)**

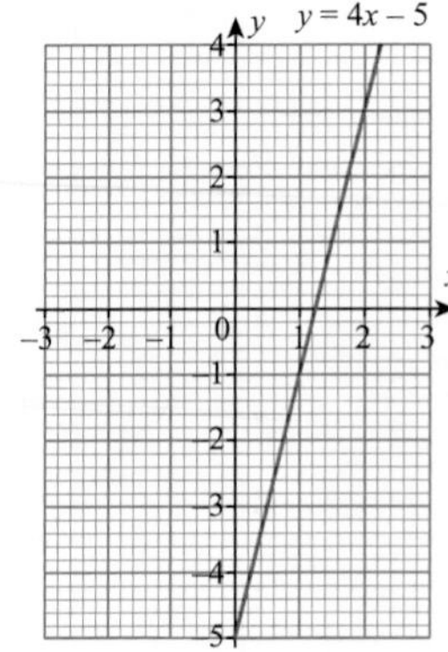

(b)

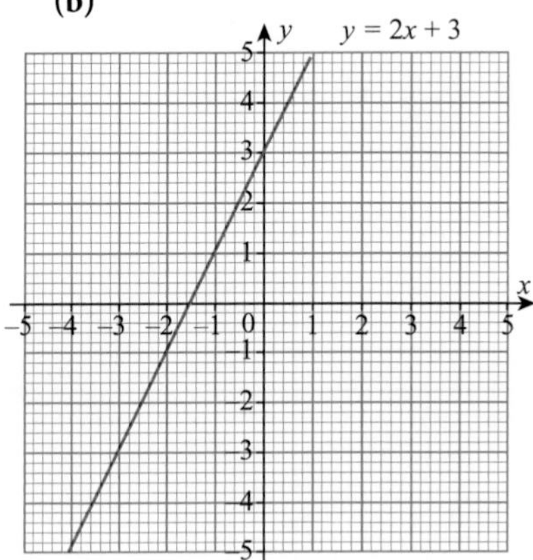

(c)

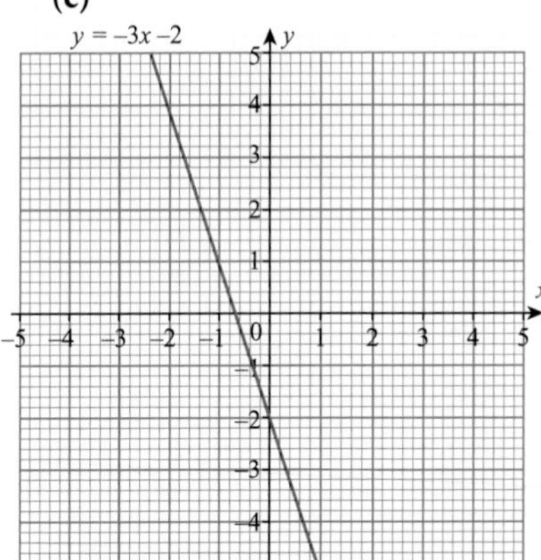

(d)

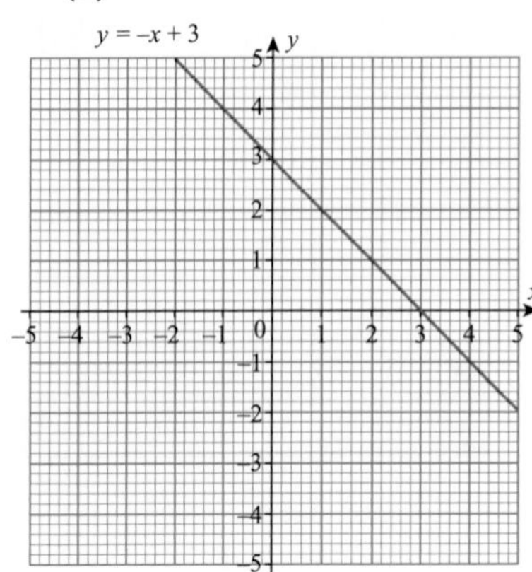

(e)

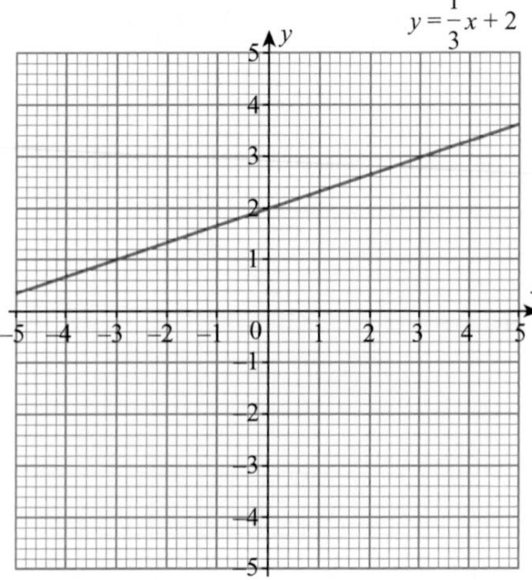

(f)

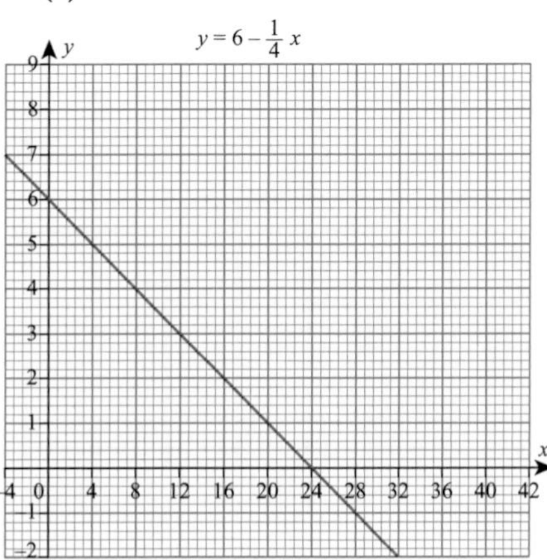

(g)

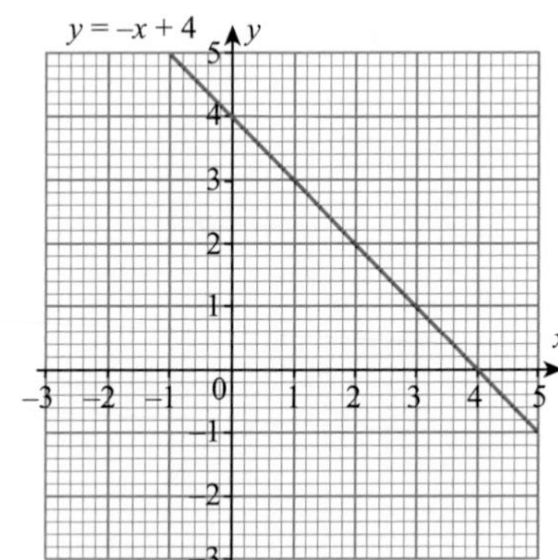

(h)

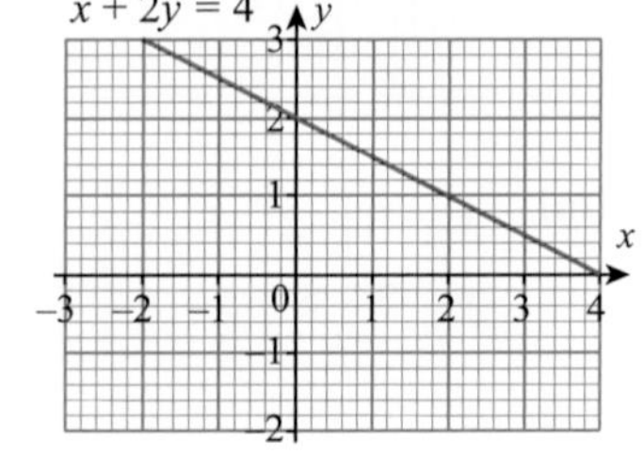

(i)

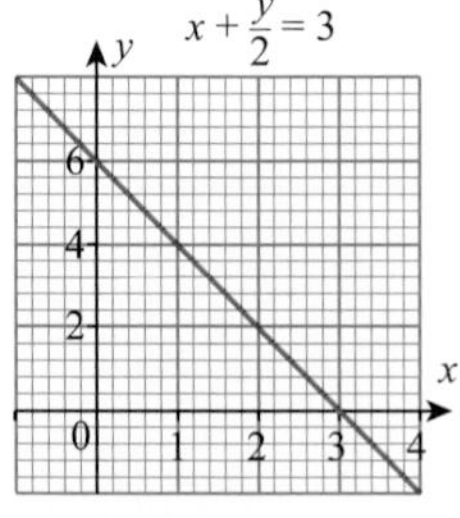

(j)

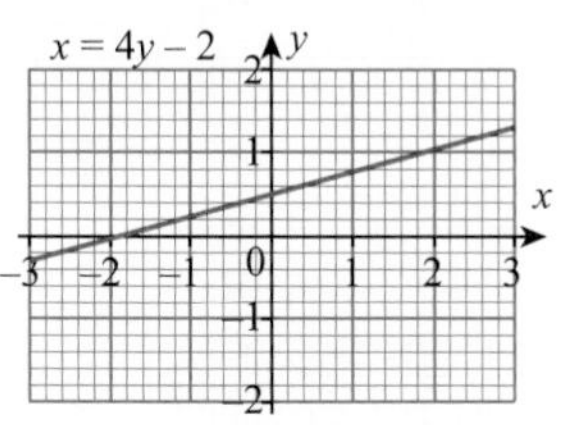

(k)

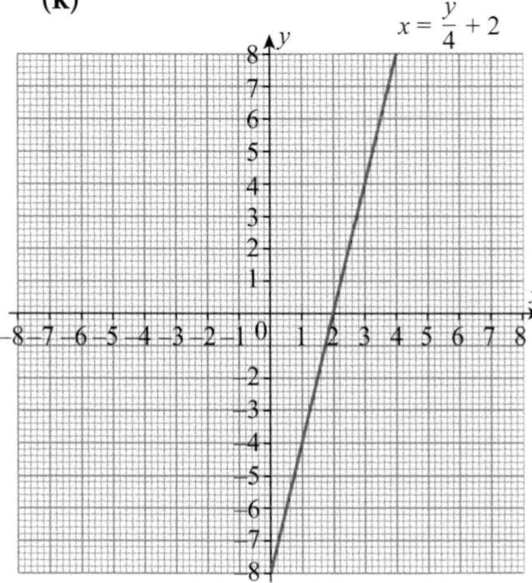

(l)

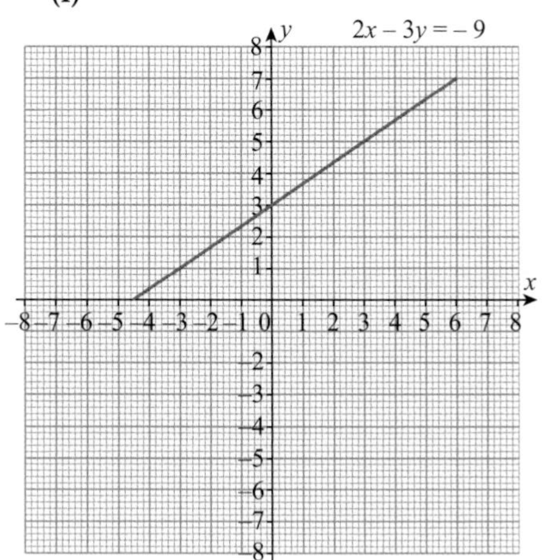

2

	$y = mx + c$	Gradient	y-intercept
(a)	$y = \frac{1}{2}x - 2$	$\frac{1}{2}$	-2
(b)	$y = -2x + 1$	-2	1
(c)	$y = 2x + 4$	2	4
(d)	$y = 2x - 5$	2	-5
(e)	$y = 2x + 5$	2	5
(f)	$y = \frac{-1}{3}x + 2$	$\frac{-1}{3}$	2
(g)	$y = 3x - 2$	3	-2
(h)	$y = -4x + 2$	-4	2
(i)	$y = 2x + 4$	2	4
(j)	$y = 6x - 12$	6	-12
(k)	$y = \frac{1}{8}x - 3$	$\frac{1}{8}$	-3
(l)	$y = -12x + 6$	-12	6

3 **(a)** $y = 2x + 3$ **(b)** $y = -3x - 2$
(c) $y = 3x - 1$ **(d)** $y = -\frac{3}{2}x - 0.5$
(e) $y = -\frac{3}{4}x + 2$ **(f)** $y = \frac{1}{2}x - 3$
(g) $y = 0.75x - 0.75$
(h) $y = -2$ **(i)** $y = 4$

4 **(a)** $y = -4x - 1$ **(b)** $y = \frac{1}{3}x + 1$
(c) $y = -3x + 2$ **(d)** $y = 5x + 2$
(e) $y = 3x + 1$ **(f)** $y = -x + 2$
(g) $y = 2x - 3$ **(h)** $y = \frac{2}{3}x - 1$
(i) $y = \frac{1}{4}x - 2$

5 **(a)** $y = 4x - 5$ **(b)** $y = -3x + 17$
(c) $y = \frac{9}{5}x - \frac{6}{5}$ **(d)** $y = \frac{17}{4}x - \frac{71}{4}$

6 Any line with the same gradient, e.g.
(a) $y = -3x - 5$ **(b)** $y = 2x + 13$
(c) $y = \frac{x}{2} - 3$ **(d)** $y = -x - 4$
(e) $x = -8$ **(f)** $y = 6$

7 (a), (c)

8 **(a)** $y = 2x - 2$ **(b)** $y = 2x$
(c) $y = 2x - 4$ **(d)** $y = 2x + \frac{1}{2}$

9 **(a)** Any line with gradient $\frac{2}{3}$, e.g. $y = \frac{2}{3}x - 5$
(b) Any line with same y-intercept, e.g. $y = 2x + 3$
(c) $y = 3$

Exercise 10.5

1 $y = -5x + 8$

2 **(a)** Gradient $AB = -2$; Gradient $PQ = \frac{1}{2}$; $-2 \times \frac{1}{2} = -1$, so AB is perpendicular to PQ
(b) Gradient $MN = \frac{1}{2}$; $\frac{1}{2} \times -2 = -1$, so MN is perpendicular to AB

3 $y = \frac{-1}{3}x + 5$

4 **(a)** $y = -\frac{1}{2}x + ½$ or $x + 2y - 1 = 0$
(b) $x + y + 1 = 0$

5 Gradient $A = -2$, Gradient $B = ½$ $-2 \times ½ = 1$, so A is perpendicular to B

6 $y = 5x - 18$

7 Gradient $AB = \frac{10}{9}$; Gradient $AC = ½$ so AB is not perpendicular to AC and figure cannot be a rectangle.

Exercise 10.6

1 **(a)**

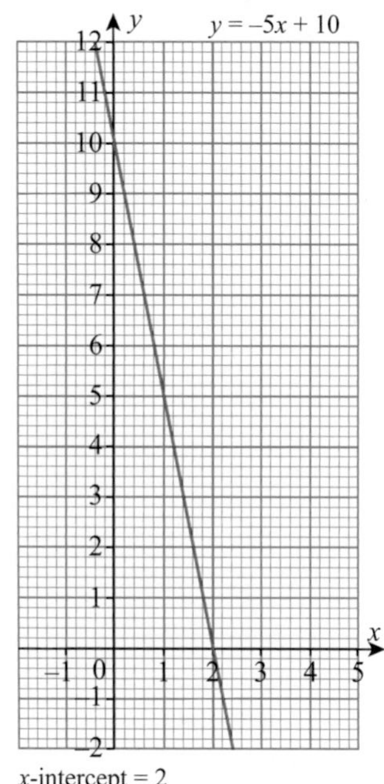

(b)

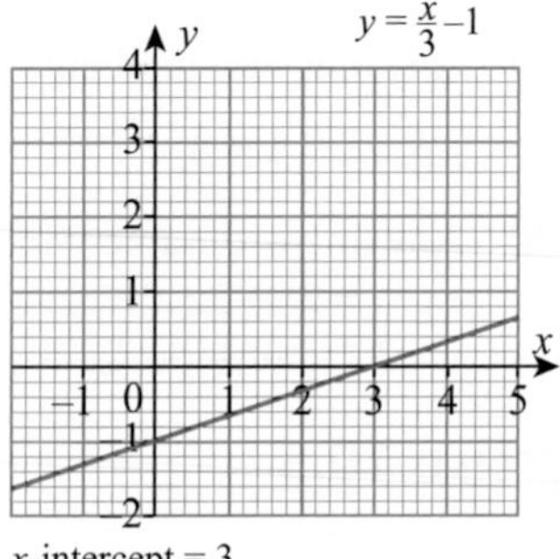

x-intercept = 3
y-intercept = –1

(c)

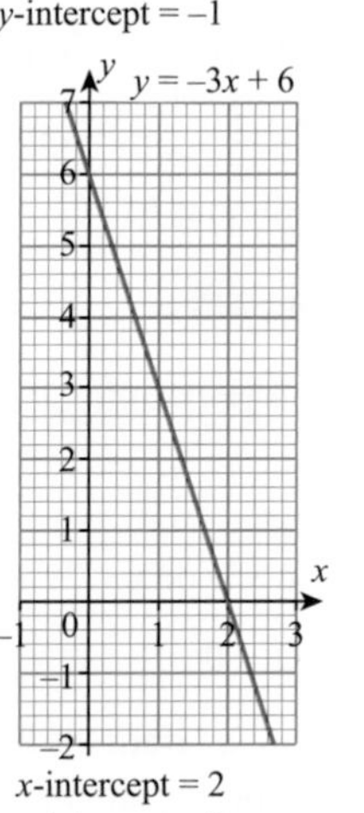

x-intercept = 2
y-intercept = 6

(d)

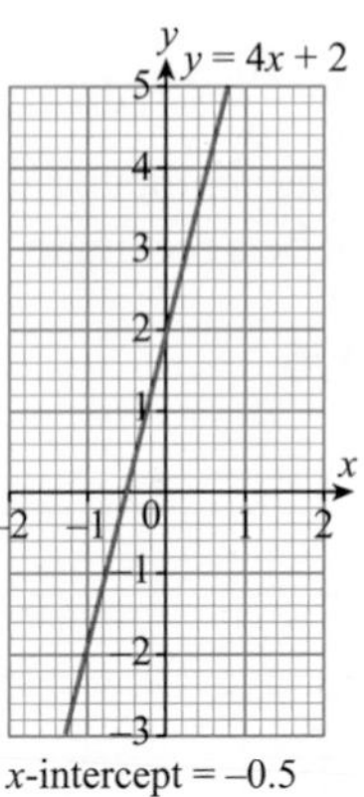

x-intercept = –0.5
y-intercept = 2

(e)

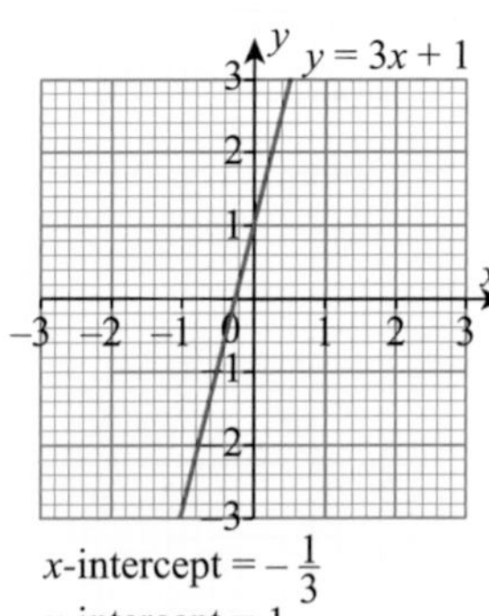

x-intercept = $-\frac{1}{3}$
y-intercept = 1

(f)

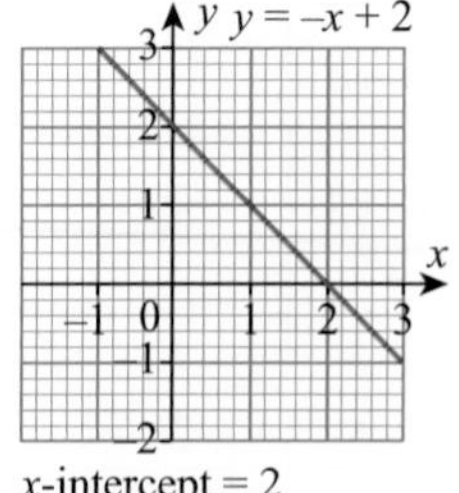

x-intercept = 2
y-intercept = 2

(g)

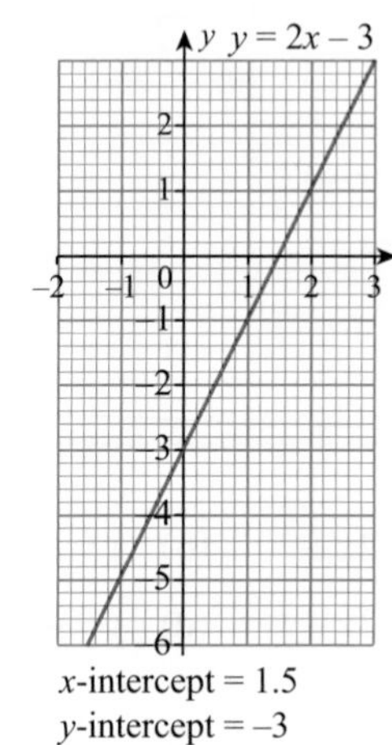

x-intercept = 1.5
y-intercept = –3

(h)

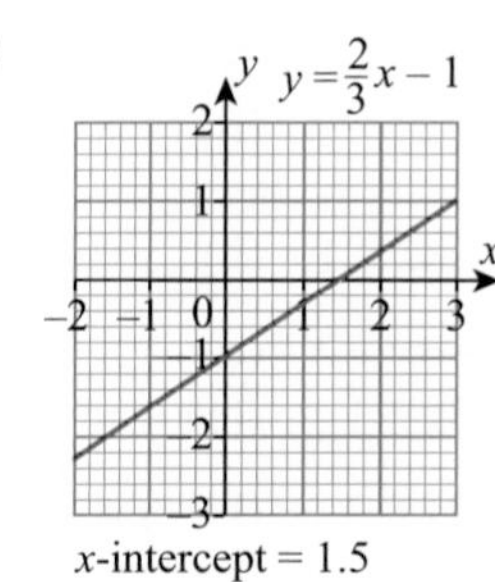

x-intercept = 1.5
y-intercept = –1

(i)

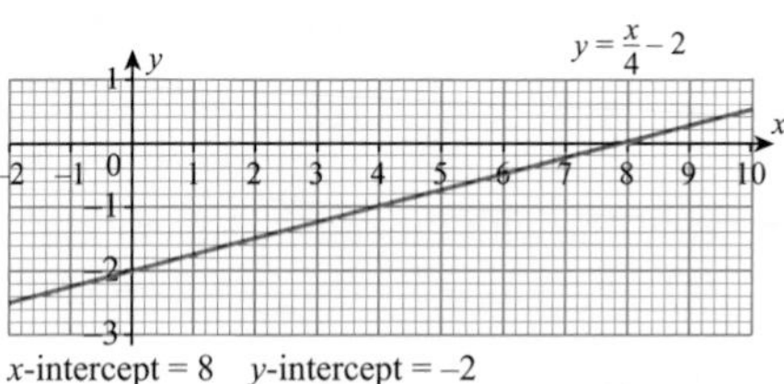

x-intercept = 8 y-intercept = –2

(j)

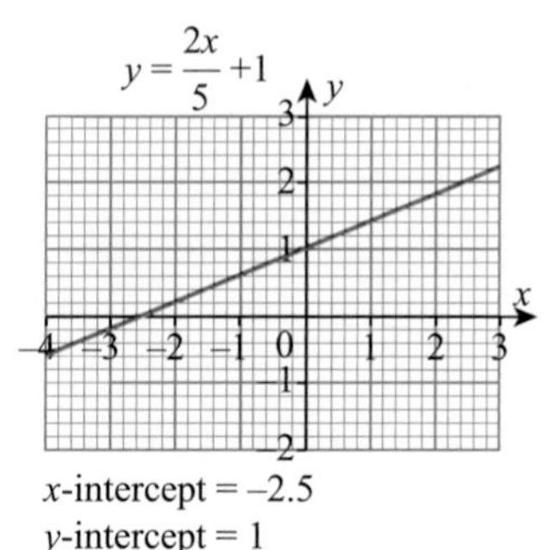

x-intercept = –2.5
y-intercept = 1

(k)

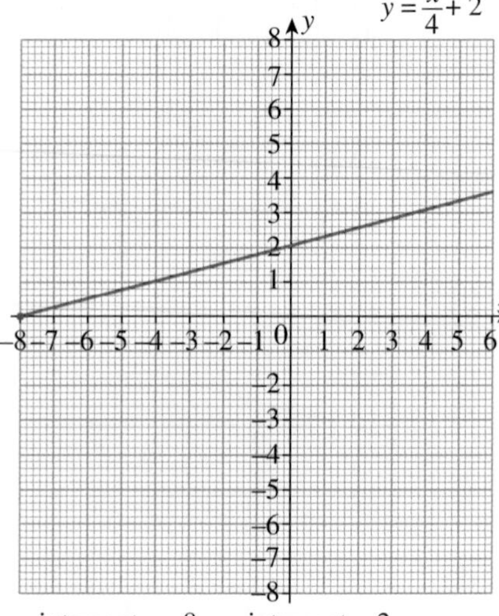

x-intercept = –8 y-intercept = 2

(l)

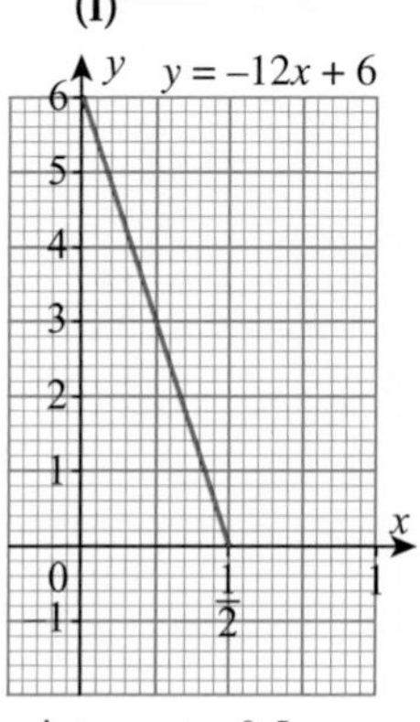

x-intercept = 0.5
y-intercept = 6

2 **(a)** $c = 2$ **(b)** $c = -4$
(c) $c = -9$ **(d)** $c = -8$
(e) $c = 4$ **(f)** $c = 3$
(g) $c = -2$ **(h)** $c = 2$

Exercise 10.7

1 **(a)** Length = 8.49 midpoint = (6, 9)
(b) Length = 4.47 midpoint = (3, 8)
(c) Length = 5.66 midpoint = (6, 5)
(d) Length = 3.16 midpoint = (4.5, 9.5)
(e) Length = 5 midpoint = (2.5, 5)
(f) Length = 1.41 midpoint = (11.5, 3.5)
(g) Length = 5 midpoint = (1, 3.5)
(h) Length = 6.08 midpoint = (4.5, 2)
(i) Length = 11.05 midpoint = (–2.5, 1.5)

2 $AB = 5.39$ midpoint $= (3, 4.5)$
$CD = 4.47$ midpoint $= (-4, 6)$
$EF = 8.60$ midpoint $= (-2.5, 2.5)$
$GH = 7.07$ midpoint $= (3.5, 0.5)$
$IJ = 5.10$ midpoint $= (2.5, -3.5)$
$KL = 12.65$ midpoint $= (1, -3)$
$MN = 5.39$ midpoint $= (-3.5, -2)$
$OP = 7.81$ midpoint $= (-4.5, -4)$

3 5.83
4 B
5 B

6 $AB = 6.40$
$AC = 4.24$
$BC = 7.28$

7 $a = 7$
8 $E = (-6, -2)$

Exercise 10.8

1 (a) $x^2 + 4x + 3$ (b) $x^2 + 10x + 24$
(c) $x^2 + 19x + 90$ (d) $x^2 + 15x + 36$
(e) $x^2 + 2x + 1$ (f) $x^2 + 9x + 20$
(g) $x^2 - 3x - 28$ (h) $x^2 + 5x - 24$
(i) $x^2 - 1$ (j) $x^2 - x - 72$
(k) $x^2 - 13x + 42$ (l) $x^2 - 9x - 52$
(m) $y^2 - 11y - 42$ (n) $z^2 - 64$
(o) $t^2 + 13t - 68$ (p) $h^2 - 6h + 9$
(q) $g^2 + 3\frac{1}{2}g - 2$ (r) $d^2 + \frac{3}{4}d - \frac{9}{8}$

2 (a) $12 - 7x + x^2$
(b) $3 + 7x - 6x^2$
(c) $6m^2 - 17m + 7$
(d) $-8x^2 + 2x + 3$
(e) $8a^2 - 2b^2$
(f) $-8m^2 - 2mn + 3n^2$
(g) $x^2 + \frac{3}{4}x + \frac{1}{8}$
(h) $2x^2 - \frac{2}{3}x - \frac{1}{6}$
(i) $-2x^4 + 6xy^2 - 4y^2$
(j) $-36b^2 - 26b + 42$
(k) $-4x^4 + 2xy^2 - 4x^3y + 2y^3$
(l) $6x^2 + 9x - 15$

3 (a) $2x^2 + 9x + 9$
(b) $3y^2 + 10y + 7$
(c) $7z^2 + 15z + 2$
(d) $4t^2 + 17t - 15$
(e) $2w^2 - 23w + 56$
(f) $16g^2 - 1$
(g) $72x^2 + 23x - 4$
(h) $360c^2 - 134c + 12$
(i) $-2m^2 + 10m - 12$

4 (a) $6x^3 + 9x^2 + 2x + 3$
(b) $15x^4 - 18x^2 + 3$
(c) $6x^3 + 9x^2y - 2xy - 3y^2$

Exercise 10.9

1 (a) $x^2 - 2xy + y^2$
(b) $a^2 + 2ab + b^2$
(c) $4x^2 + 12xy + 9y^2$
(d) $x^2 - 12xy + 4y^2$
(e) $x^2 + 4xy + 4y^2$
(f) $y^2 - 8x^2y + 16x^4$
(g) $x^4 - 2x^2y^2 + y^4$
(h) $4 + 4y^3 + y^6$
(i) $4x^2 + 16xy^2 + 16y^4$
(j) $\frac{1}{4x^2} - \frac{1}{4xy} + \frac{1}{16y^2}$
(k) $\frac{9x^2}{16} - \frac{3xy}{4} + \frac{y^2}{4}$
(l) $a^2 + ab + \frac{b^2}{4}$
(m) $a^2b^2 + 2abc^4 + c^8$
(n) $9x^4y^2 - 6x^2y + 1$
(o) $\frac{4x^2}{9} + \frac{16xy}{3} + 16y^2$
(p) $x^2 - 6x + 9$

2 (a) $4x - 12$
(b) $2x^2 + 2x - 19$
(c) $2y^2 + 8x^2$
(d) $\frac{x^2}{2} + \frac{8x}{3} - 2$
(e) $6x^2 + 13.8x + 3.6$
(f) $-16x^2 + 8xy + 2x - 2y^2$
(g) $-x^2 + 3x - 22$
(h) $4x^2 - 12xy - 19y^2$
(i) $-2x^3 - x^2 - 17x$
(j) $-4x^2 - 3x - 1$

3 (a) -49 (b) 4
(c) 66 (d) 64
(e) 0
(f) 241

Exercise 10.10

1 (a) $(x + 12)(x + 2)$
(b) $(x + 2)(x + 1)$
(c) $(x + 4)(x + 3)$
(d) $(x + 7)(x + 5)$
(e) $(x + 9)(x + 3)$
(f) $(x + 6)(x + 1)$
(g) $(x + 6)(x + 5)$
(h) $(x + 8)(x + 2)$
(i) $(x + 10)(x + 1)$
(j) $(x + 7)(x + 1)$
(k) $(x + 20)(x + 4)$
(l) $(x + 7)(x + 6)$

2 (a) $(x - 6)(x - 2)$
(b) $(x - 4)(x - 5)$
(c) $(x - 4)(x - 3)$
(d) $(x - 4)(x - 2)$
(e) $(x - 8)(x - 4)$
(f) $(x - 7)(x - 7)$
(g) $(x - 10)(x + 2)$
(h) $(x - 9)(x + 2)$
(i) $(x - 8)(x + 4)$
(k) $(x + 3)(x - 2)$
(l) $(x + 11)(x - 3)$
(m) $(x + 12)(x - 2)$

3 (a) $(y + 17)(y - 10)$
(b) $(p - 6)(p + 14)$
(c) $(x - 12)(x - 12)$
(d) $(t + 18)(t - 2)$
(e) $(v + 15)(v + 5)$
(f) $(x - 10)(x + 10)$

Exercise 10.11

1 (a) $(x + 6)(x - 6)$
(b) $(p + 9)(p - 9)$
(c) $(w + 4)(w - 4)$
(d) $(q + 3)(q - 3)$
(e) $(k + 20)(k - 20)$
(f) $(t + 11)(t - 11)$
(g) $(x + y)(x - y)$
(h) $(9h + 4g)(9h - 4g)$
(i) $4(2p + 3q)(2p - 3q)$
(j) $(12s + c)(12s - c)$
(k) $(8h + 7g)(8h - 7g)$
(l) $3(3x + 4y)(3x - 4y)$
(m) $2(10q + 7p)(10q - 7p)$
(n) $5(2d + 5e)(2d - 5e)$
(o) $(x^2 + y^2)(x^2 - y^2)$
(p) $x(y - x)(y + x)$

2 71
3 6

Exercise 10.12

1 (a) $x = 0$ or $x = 9$
(b) $x = 0$ or $x = -7$
(c) $x = 0$ or $x = 21$
(d) $x = 4$ or $x = 5$
(e) $x = -7$ or $x = -1$
(f) $x = -3$ or $x = 2$
(g) $x = -2$ or $x = -1$
(h) $x = -10$ or $x = -1$

(i) $x = 3$ or $x = 4$
(j) $x = 6$ or $x = 2$
(k) $x = 10$ or $x = -10$
(l) $t = -18$ or $t = 2$
(m) $y = -17$ or $y = 10$
(n) $p = -14$ or $p = 6$
(o) $w = 12$

Examination practice

Exam-style questions

1 (a) $x^2 + 20x + 36$ (b) $4x^2 - 9$
(c) $12y^4 - 5y^2 - 3$

2 (a) (i) $6x(2x - 1)$
(ii) $(y - 6)(y - 7)$
(iii) $(d + 14)(d - 14)$
(b) (i) $x = 0$ or $x = \frac{1}{2}$
(ii) $y = 6$ or $y = 7$
(iii) $d = 14$ or $d = -14$

Past paper questions*

1 (a)

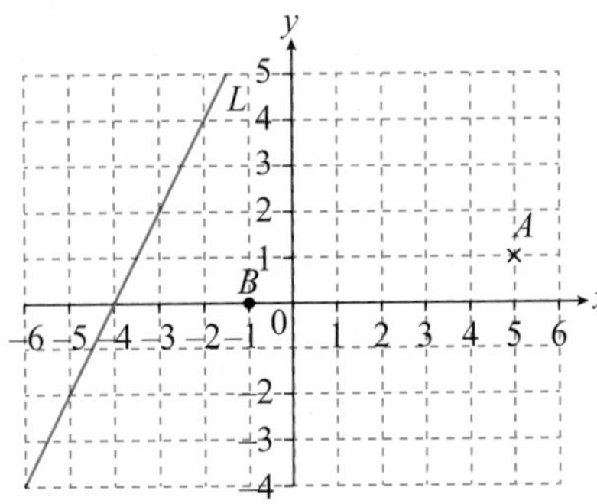

(b) $(-1, 0)$
(c) 2

Chapter 11

Exercise 11.1

1 (a) $x = 10$ cm (b) $y = 13.4$ cm
(c) $h = 2.59$ cm (d) $p = 1.62$ cm
(e) $t = 7.21$ m

2 (a) $x = 7.42$ m (b) $y = 3.63$ cm
(c) $t = 8.66$ cm (d) $p = 12$ m
(e) $a = 6$ cm

3 (a) $x = 2.80$ cm (b) $y = 4.47$ cm
(c) $h = 4.28$ cm (d) $p = 8.54$ km
(e) $k = 10.4$ cm (f) $h = 8.06$ cm
(g) $d = 6.08$ m (h) $f = 13$ m

4 (a) Right-angled
(b) Not right-angled
(c) Not right-angled
(d) Right-angled
(e) Right-angled

Exercise 11.2

1 53.2 inches
2 3.03 m
3 277 m
4 3.6 m
5 0.8 m

6 (a) 5.39 (b) 3.16
(c) 9.90 (d) 10.30

7 $P = 42.4$ cm

Exercise 11.3

1 (a) Similar; all angles equal.
(b) Similar; sides in proportion.
(c) Not similar; angles not equal.
(d) Not similar; sides not in proportion.
(e) Similar; angles equal.
(f) Similar; sides in proportion.
(g) Not similar; sides not in proportion.
(h) Similar; sides in proportion.
(i) Similar; angles equal.
(j) Similar; all angles equal.

2 (a) $x = 12$ (b) $y = 5$
(c) $p = 12$ (d) $a = 12$
(e) $b = 5.25$ (f) $c = 5.14$

3 $AC = 8.75$ cm
4 $CE = 4.51$ cm
5 $BC = 2.97$ m
6 lighthouse = 192 m
7 $r = 8$
8 $x = 60$

Exercise 11.4

1 (a) $\frac{4}{2} = 0.5$ $\frac{6}{5} = 1.2$

The ratio of corresponding sides are not the same so the shapes are not similar.

(b) All sides of shape 1 have length x and all sides of shape 2 have length y so the ratio of corresponding sides will be equal and the shapes are similar.

(c) $\frac{5}{4} = 1.25$ $\frac{4}{3} = 1.\dot{3}$

Ratios not equal, so not similar.

(d) $\frac{80}{60} = 1.\dot{3}$ $\frac{60}{45} = 1.\dot{3}$

Ratios of corresponding sides equal, therefore they are similar.

(e) $\frac{12}{8} = 1.5$ $\frac{9}{6} = 1.5$

Ratios of corresponding sides equal, therefore they are similar.

(f) They are not similar because not all corresponding angles are equal.

2 (a) $x = 9$ (b) $y = 14$
(c) $p = 3.30$ (d) $y = 7.46$
(e) $x = 50, y = 16$
(f) $x = 22.4, y = 16.8$
(g) $x = 7.5, y = 12.5$
(h) $x = 178$

Exercise 11.5

1 (a) 125 cm^2 (b) 36.43 m^2
(c) $2\,500\text{ m}^2$ (d) 225 cm^2

2 (a) $x = 18$ cm (b) $x = 54.55$ m
(c) $x = 3.125$ cm (d) $x = 10$ cm

3 (a) Area will be 4 times larger.
(b) Area will be 9 times larger.
(c) Area will be smaller by a factor of 4.

4 8 : 3

Exercise 11.6

1 $k^2 : k^3$

2 (a) 4 (b) 16 : 1 (c) 64 : 1

3 216 cm^2
4 172 cm^2

5 (a) 16 mm (b) 157.9 cm^2
(c) 83.2 cm^3

*Cambridge International Examinations bears no responsibility for the example answers to questions taken from its past question papers which are contained in this publication.

6 (a) $20.8\dot{3}$ cm³ (b) $21.\dot{3}$ mm³
(c) 0.75 m³ (d) 56.64 m³

7 (a) 525 cm² (b) 6860 cm³
(c) 36 cm (d) 14.15 cm

8

Height	13 cm	11 cm	9 cm
Surface area	x cm²	$\frac{121x}{169}$ cm²	$\frac{81x}{169}$ cm²
Volume	y cm³	$\frac{1331y}{2197}$ cm³	$\frac{729y}{2197}$ cm³

9 $x = 3.72$

Exercise 11.7

1 Triangles *ABC* and *PQR* are congruent because SSS is satisfied.
2 Triangles *ABC* and *PQR* are congruent because ASA is satisfied.
3 Triangles *ABC* and *PQR* are congruent because RSH is satisfied.
4 Triangles *ABC* and *PQR* are congruent because SSS is satisfied.
5 The triangles are congruent because SAS is satisfied.
6 Triangles *ABC* and *PQR* are congruent because RSH is satisfied. OR Triangles *ABC* and *PQR* are congruent because ASA is satisfied.
7 Triangles *ABC* and *PQR* are congruent because SAS is satisfied.
8 Triangles *ABC* and *PQR* are congruent because RHS is satisfied.

Examination practice

Exam-style questions

1 215 m further
2 4.21 m

3 (a) 35 cm (b) 37 cm

4 (a) $a^2 + b^2 = c^2$
$(7x)^2 + (24x)^2 = 150^2$
$49x^2 + 576x^2 = 22500$
$625x^2 = 22500$
$x^2 = 36$
(b) 336 cm

Past paper questions*

1 14.4 cm

Chapter 12

Exercise 12.1

1 (a) (i) Mode = 12
(ii) Median = 9
(iii) Mean = 8
(b) (i) Mode = 8
(ii) Median = 6
(iii) Mean = 5.7
(c) (i) Mode = 2.1 and 8.2
(ii) Median = 4.15
(iii) Mean = 4.79
(d) (i) Mode = 12
(ii) Median = 9
(iii) Mean = 11.7

3 (a) Andrew's median = 54
Barbara's median = 48.5
(b) Andrew's mean = 84.25
Barbara's mean = 98.875

4 For example, 1, 2, 3, 4, 15
5 Mode = none; mean = 96.4; median = 103
He will choose the median because it's the highest.
6 4451.6 cm
7 2.38 kg
8 $91.2\dot{6}$ °C
9 For example, 3, 4, 4, 6, 8
10 For example, 2, 3, 4, 7, 9
11 $\frac{mX + nY}{m + n}$

Exercise 12.2

1 (a) Ricky (i) mean = 0.152
(ii) range = 0.089
Oliver (i) mean = 0.139
(ii) range = 0.059
(b) Ricky
(c) Oliver

2 (a) Archimedes median = 13
Bernoulli median = 15
(b) Archimedes range = 16
Bernoulli range = 17
(c) Archimedes
(d) Archimedes

3 Backlights. Footlights has the best mean but the range is large, whereas Backlights and Brightlights have the same range but Backlights has a higher mean.

Exercise 12.3

1 (a) Mean = 4.48 (b) Median = 4
(c) Mode = 4 and 5 (d) Range = 8

2 (a)

Price	Frequency	Total
\$6.50	180	\$1170
\$8	215	\$1720
\$10	124	\$1240
		\$4130

(b) \$7.96

3 (a) Mode = no letters
(b) Median = 1 letter
(c) Mean = 0.85 letters
(d) Range = 5

4 (a) Mode = 1
(b) Median = 2
(c) Mean = 2.12

5 (a) Mode = 8
(b) Median = 6.5
(c) Mean = $6.0\dot{3}$
(d) If she wants to suggest the class is doing better than it really is, she would use the mode and say something like: most students got 8 of 10.

Exercise 12.4

1 Mean height = 141.7 cm

2 (a) 5.28 min (b) 5 min 17 s

3 Mean temperature = 57.36 °C

4 (a) Hawks mean mass = 76.4 kg
Eagles mean mass = 78 kg
(b) 45 kg for both (this is group range not *actual* data range)
(c) The range of masses of the players within each team is the same for both teams. So, one can say that on average, the Eagles have a larger mass than the Hawks.

5 Mean = 39.2 cm
6 Mean age = 42.23 years

Exercise 12.5

1 (a) Median = 6, $Q_1 = 4$, $Q_3 = 9$, IQR = 5
(b) Median = 17, $Q_1 = 12$, $Q_3 = 21$, IQR = 9
(c) Median = 14, $Q_1 = 5$, $Q_3 = 18$, IQR = 13

* *Cambridge International Examinations bears no responsibility for the example answers to questions taken from its past question papers which are contained in this publication.*

(d) Median = 3.4, $Q_1 = 2.45$, $Q_3 = 4.95$, IQR = 2.5
(e) Median = 15.65, $Q_1 = 14.1$, $Q_3 = 17.95$, IQR = 3.85

2 Median = 6, $Q_1 = 4$, $Q_3 = 8$, IQR = 4

3 (a) Summer: median = 18.5, $Q_1 = 16$, $Q_3 = 22$
Winter: median = 11.5, $Q_1 = 9.5$, $Q_3 = 12.5$
(b) Summer: IQR = 6
Winter: IQR = 3
(c) The lower IQR in winter shows that car numbers are more consistent. In poor weather people either use their own transport or take transport more consistently.

4 (a) Julian: median = 23, $Q_1 = 13$, $Q_3 = 24$
Aneesh: median = 18, $Q_1 = 14$ $Q_3 = 20$
(b) Julian: IQR = 11
Aneesh: IQR = 6
(c) The IQR for the *Algebraist* is more consistent than that for the *Statistician* and is therefore more likely to have a particular audience while the variation is greater for the *Statistician* and therefore could appeal to a varying audience.

Examination practice

Past paper questions*

1 (a) 4
(b) 7

2

Mark	Tally	Frequency
1	|||	3
2	||||	4
3	~~||||~~ |	6
4		0
5	||||	4
6	~~||||~~	5
7	|||	3
8	|||	3
9		0
10	||	2

(b) (i) 9 (ii) 3
(iii) 5 (iv) 4.8

3 (a) 137 g (3sf)
(b) (i)

Mass (*m* grams)	Frequency
$0 < m \le 80$	16
$80 < m \le 200$	126
$200 < m \le 240$	16

(ii)

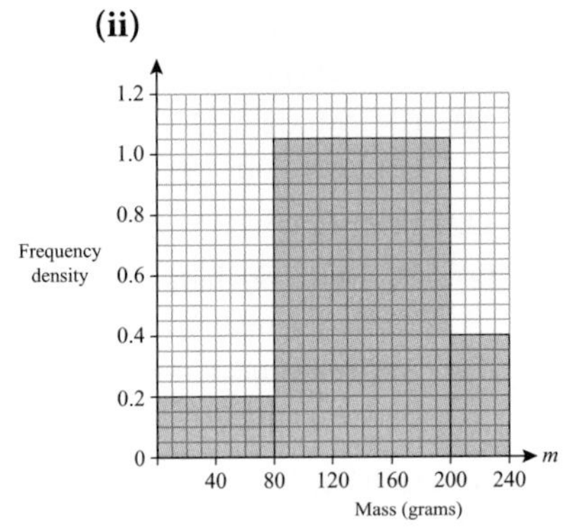

(b) 135 g

Unit 4

Chapter 13

Exercise 13.1

1 (a) 4000 g (b) 5000 m
(c) 3.5 cm (d) 8.1 cm
(e) 7300 mg (f) 5.760 t
(g) 210 cm (h) 2000 kg
(i) 1.40 m (j) 2.024 kg
(k) 0.121 g (l) 23 000 mm
(m) 35 mm (n) 8036 m
(o) 9.077 g

2 $32.4\text{ cm} < 3.22\text{ m} < 3\frac{2}{9}\text{ m}$

3 $125\text{ ml} < \frac{1}{2}\text{ litre} < 0.65\text{ litres} < 780\text{ ml}$

4 60

5 (a) 14230 mm, 0.01423 km
(b) 19 060 mg, 0.00001906 t
(c) 2750 ml, 275 cl
(d) 4 000 000 mm^2, 0.0004 ha
(e) 1300 mm^2, 0.000 000 13 ha
(f) 10 000 mm^3, 0.000 01 m^3

6 (a) 27 m^3 (b) 27 000 000 cm^3
(c) $2.7 \times 10^{10}\text{ mm}^3$

7 (a) $1.09 \times 10^{12}\text{ km}^3$
(b) $1.09 \times 10^{21}\text{ m}^3$
(c) $1.09 \times 10^{30}\text{ mm}^3$

8 (a) $1.13 \times 10^2\text{ cm}^3$
(b) $1.13 \times 10^5\text{ cm}^3$
(c) $1.13 \times 10^{-13}\text{ km}^3$

9 (a) 6 (b) 20 g

10 (a) No (b) No (c) Yes

Exercise 13.2

1 3 h 39 min

2 (a) 22.30 to 23.30
(b) 09.15 to 10.45
(c) 19.45 to 21.10

3 (a) 300 km (b) 120 km/h

4 9 min 47 s

5 Monday 10 February 02.30

6 (a)

Day	Mon	Tues	Wed	Thurs	Fri
Total time worked	7h 55min	7h 55min	7h 25min	7h 53min	8h 24min

(b) 39 h 32 min (c) $223.36

Exercise 13.3

1 (a) 20.02 (b) 45 min (c) 23 min

2 (a) 1 h 7 min
(b)

Aville	11:10
Beeston	11:45
Crossway	11:59
Darby	12:17

(c) 14:25

3 (a) 00:17 (b) 12 h 40 min
(c) 5 h 46 min
(d) (i) 01:29 or 13:34
(ii) Unlikely to be 01:29 because it is in the middle of the night – in the dark.
(e) (i) 1–6 February (Wed–Mon)
(ii) 1–4 February (Wed–Sat)

Exercise 13.4

1 (a) $11.5 \le 12 < 12.5$
(b) $7.5 \le 8 < 8.5$
(c) $99.5 \le 100 < 100.5$
(d) $8.5 \le 9 < 9.5$
(e) $71.5 \le 72 < 72.5$
(f) $126.5 \le 127 < 127.5$

2 (a) $2.65 \le 2.7 < 2.75$
(b) $34.35 \le 34.4 < 34.45$
(c) $4.95 \le 5.0 < 5.05$
(d) $1.05 \le 1.1 < 1.15$
(e) $-2.35 \le -2.3 < -2.25$
(f) $-7.25 \le -7.2 < -7.15$

3 (a) $131.5 \le 132 < 132.5$
(b) $250 \le 300 < 350$
(c) $402.5 \le 405 < 407.5$
(d) 14.5 million ≤ 15 million < 15.5 million
(e) $32.25 \le 32.3 < 32.35$
(f) $26.65 \le 26.7 < 26.75$
(g) $0.45 \le 0.5 < 0.55$
(h) $12.335 \le 12.34 < 12.345$
(i) $131.5 \le 132 < 132.5$
(j) $0.1335 \le 0.134 < 0.1345$

4 $250\,\text{kg} \le 300\,\text{kg} < 350\,\text{kg}$

5 (a) $99.5\,\text{m} \le 100\,\text{m} < 100.5\,\text{m}$
(b) 15.25 seconds ≤ 15.3 seconds < 15.35 seconds

6 $4.45\,\text{m} \le L < 4.55\,\text{m}$

Exercise 13.5

1 (a) $30.8 \le a^2 < 31.9$
(b) $13900 \le b^3 < 14100$
(c) $5.43 \le cd^3 < 5.97$
(d) $609 \le (a^2 + b^2) < 615$
(e) $0.248 < \frac{c}{b^2} < 0.251$
(f) $2.66 < \frac{ab}{cd} < 2.82$
(g) $-43.5 < \frac{c}{a} - \frac{b}{d} < -46.5$
(h) $2.74 < \left(\frac{a}{d} \div \frac{c}{b}\right) < 2.82$
(i) $48.9 < \left(dc + \sqrt{\frac{a}{b}}\right) < 50.7$
(j) $47.9 < \left(de - \sqrt{\frac{a}{b}}\right) < 49.7$

2 (a) 78.5 cm (b) 79.5 cm

3 $37\,\text{kg} \le \text{mass left} < 39\,\text{kg}$

4 (a) $3.605\,\text{cm} \le \text{Length} < 3.615\,\text{cm}$; $2.565\,\text{cm} \le \text{Width} < 2.575\,\text{cm}$
(b) $9.246825\,\text{cm}^2 \le \text{area} < 9.308625\,\text{cm}^2$
(c) $9.25\,\text{cm}^2 \le \text{area} < 9.31\,\text{cm}^2$

5 (a) $511105787\,\text{km}^2 \le$ Surface area $511266084\,\text{km}^2$
(b) $1.08652572 \times 10^{12}\,\text{km}^3 \le \text{Volume of Earth} < 1.087036906 \times 10^{12}\,\text{km}^3$

6 The smallest number of cupfuls is 426.4, and the largest is 433.6.

7 maximum gradient = 0.0739(3sf)
minimum gradient = 0.06

8 (a) $8.1\,\text{cm}^2 \le \text{area of } \Delta < 8.5\,\text{cm}^2$
(b) $5.76\,\text{cm} \le \text{hypotenuse} < 5.90\,\text{cm}$

9 $63.4° \le x° < 63.6°$

10 $45.2\% \le \left(\frac{45}{98} \times 100\right) < 46.7\%$

11 $332\,\text{kg} \le \text{mean mass} < 335\,\text{kg}$ (3sf)

12 $117.36 \le$ number of 5s, < 117.84

Exercise 13.6

1 (a) 140 °F (b) 60 °F
(c) −16 °C (d) 38 °C

2 (a) 4 lb (b) 4 kg
(c) 36 kg (d) 126 lbs
(e) (i) correct
(ii) 18 lb = 8 kg
(iii) 60 lb = 27 kg
(iv) correct

3 (a) \$40 (b) \$84
(c) £50 (d) £40

4 (a) 165 min (b) 4.8 kg
(c) $(40m) + 30 = 25$
$\Rightarrow m = -0.125$ kg
You cannot have a negative mass of meat. As the graph assumes it will always take at least 30 minutes to cook any piece of meat, you cannot use this graph for meat with a very small mass that will take less than 30 minutes to cook.

5 (a)

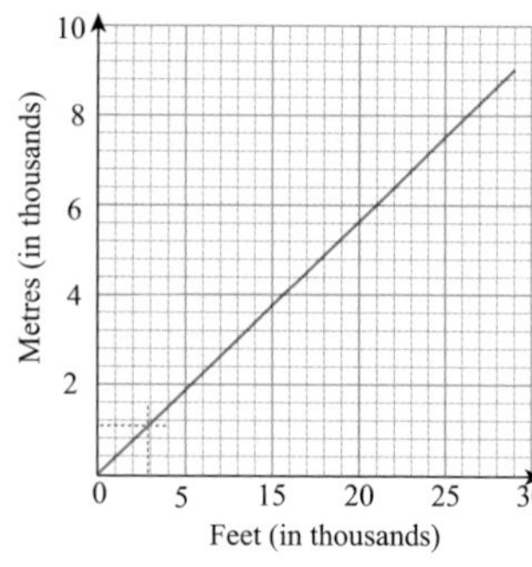

(b) 3600 ft (answer may vary +/– 100 foot.)
(c) 1050 ft (answer may vary slightly if answer to (b) varies from that shown.)

6 (a)

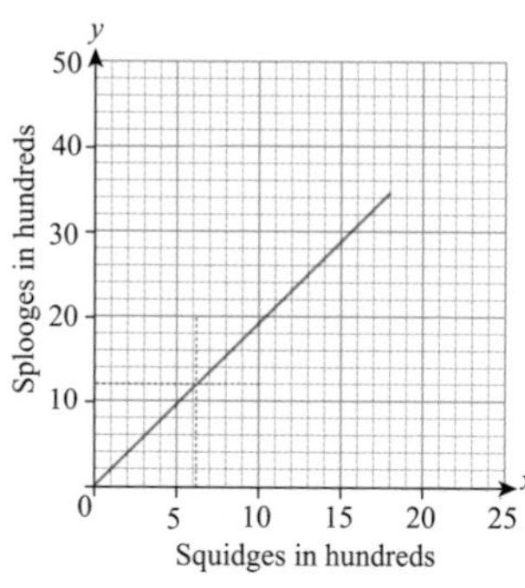

(b) 625 *Squidges* (answer may vary)
(c) 224 000 *Ploggs* (answer may vary: 220, 000 – 228, 000)

Exercise 13.7

1 \$18.50 2 \$4163.00
3 £8520 4 \$331.53
5 \$2218.18

Examination practice

Exam-style questions

1 (a) $4.116 \times 10^3\,\text{cm}^3 \le \text{Volume of cube} < 4.038 \times 10^3\,\text{cm}^3$
(b) $4.116 \times 10^6\,\text{mm}^3 \le \text{Volume of cube} < 4.038 \times 10^6\,\text{mm}^3$

2 (a) 104 km/h
(b) 69 mph

3 (a) $129 \le (a + b) < 130$
(b) $801 \le ab < 808$
(c) $0.0529 \le \left(\frac{a}{b}\right) < 0.0534$
(d) $122 \le \left(b - \frac{1}{a}\right) < 123$

Past paper questions*

1 $249.5 \le j < 250.5$
2 \$2.20
3 6.1 cm

* *Cambridge International Examinations bears no responsibility for the example answers to questions taken from its past question papers which are contained in this publication.*

Chapter 14

Exercise 14.1

1 (a)

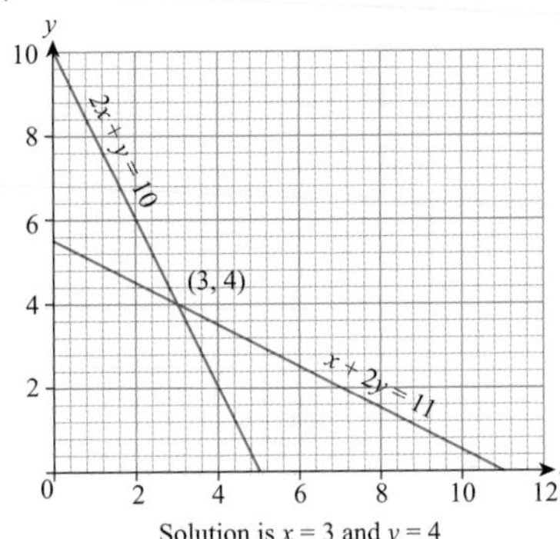

Solution is $x = 3$ and $y = 4$

(b)

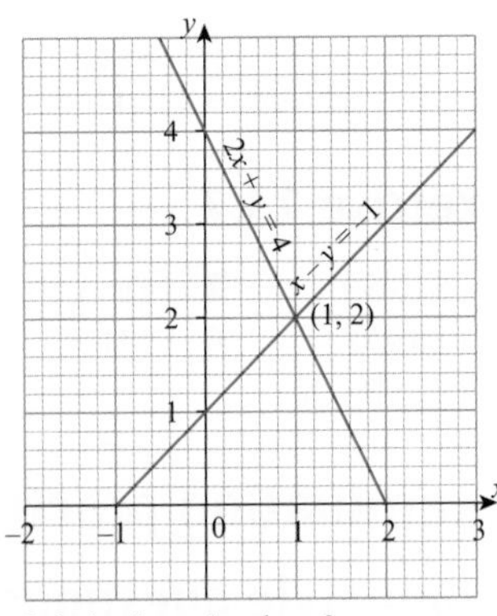

Solution is $x = 1$ and $y = 2$

(c)

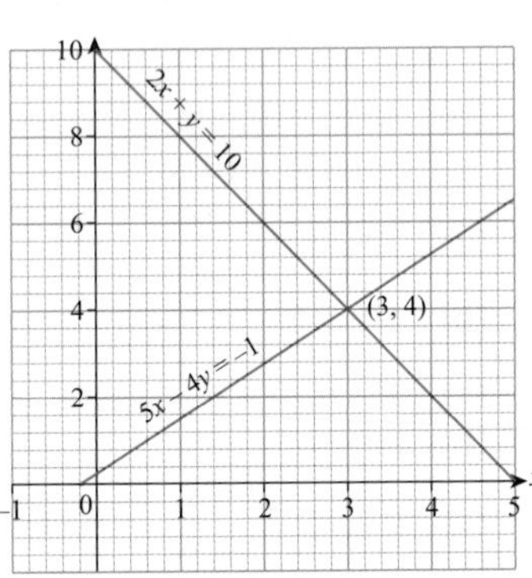

Solution is $x = 3$ and $y = 4$

2 (a) $x = -2, y = -2$ (b) $x = 3, y = 3$

(c) $x = 3, y = -2$ (d) $x = -1, y = 6$

(e) $x = \frac{1}{2}, y = -2$ (f) $x = \frac{4}{3}, y = \frac{4}{3}$

3 (a) $x = \frac{9}{11}, y = \frac{-1}{11}$ (b) $x = \frac{5}{4}, y = \frac{-3}{4}$

(c) $x = \frac{7}{4}, y = 1$ (d) $x = \frac{25}{17}, y = \frac{22}{17}$

4 (a) The scale can sometimes make it difficult to read off certain values, such as fractions, accurately.

(b) The equations must be solved algebraically.

Exercise 14.2

1 (a) $x = 2, y = 5$ (b) $x = 4, y = 3$

(c) $x = -10, y = 6$ (d) $x = \frac{4}{3}, y = \frac{-10}{3}$

(e) $x = -2, y = 4$ (f) $x = \frac{1}{11}, y = \frac{63}{11}$

(g) $x = \frac{1}{2}, y = \frac{1}{2}$ (h) $x = \frac{19}{17}, y = \frac{10}{17}$

2 (a) $x = 4, y = 4$ (b) $x = 2, y = 6$

(c) $x = 1, y = 2$ (d) $x = 5, y = -1$

(e) $x = 3, y = 4$ (f) $x = 1, y = 3$

(g) $x = 6, y = 3$ (h) $x = 5, y = 4$

(i) $x = 4, y = 3$ (j) $x = 4, y = 6$

(k) $x = 6, y = 6$ (l) $x = 4, y = 2$

3 (a) $x = 2, y = 4$ (b) $x = 4, y = 3$

(c) $x = -5, y = -10$ (d) $x = 5, y = 5$

(e) $x = \frac{3}{2}, y = 2$ (f) $x = 5, y = 3$

(g) $x = \frac{6}{5}, y = \frac{9}{10}$ (h) $x = \frac{7}{3}, y = \frac{-6}{13}$

(i) $x = \frac{-118}{55}, y = \frac{-5}{11}$ (j) $x = \frac{29}{4}, y = \frac{35}{12}$

(k) $x = 1, y = -4$ (l) $x = -1, y = -4$

(m) $x = 5, y = -7$ (n) $x = \frac{-7}{3}, y = \frac{3}{2}$

(o) $x = \frac{3}{5}, y = \frac{29}{5}$

4 (a) $x = 3, y = 4$ (b) $x = 2, y = 4$

(c) $x = -3, y = 5$ (d) $x = 6, y = 3$

(e) $x = 3, y = 5$ (f) $x = 3, y = -4$

(g) $x = 5, y = 3$ (h) $x = 2, y = 4$

(i) $x = 2, y = 3$ (j) $x = -2, y = 1$

(k) $x = -3, y = -2$ (l) $x = \frac{1}{2}, y = 2$

(m) $x = \frac{-1}{2}, y = 3$ (n) $x = -3, y = 4$

(o) $x = 5, y = 8$

5 (a) $x = \frac{209}{12}, y = \frac{-301}{80}$

(b) $x = -6.087, y = -23.652$ (3dp)

(c) $x = 0.015, y = -0.006$ (3dp)

(d) $x = \frac{112}{25}, y = \frac{504}{25}$

(e) $x = 3, y = -2$ (f) $x = -8, y = -2$

(g) $x = 6, y = -18$ (h) $x = 11, y = 27$

(i) $x = 5.928, y = -15.985$ (3dp)

6 (a) 90 and 30 (b) −14.5 and −19.5

(c) 31.5 and 20.5

(d) 14 and 20

7 Pen drive \$10 and hard drive \$25

8 48 blocks (36 of 450 seats and 12 of 400 seats)

Exercise 14.3

1 (a)

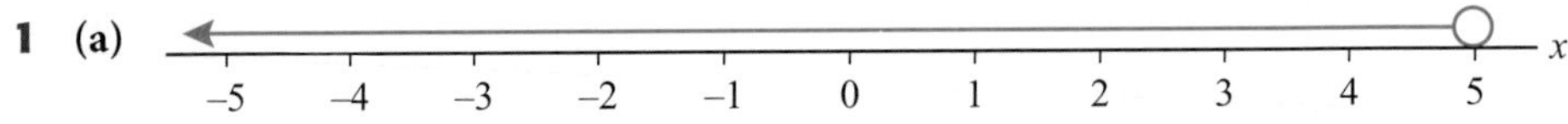

(b)

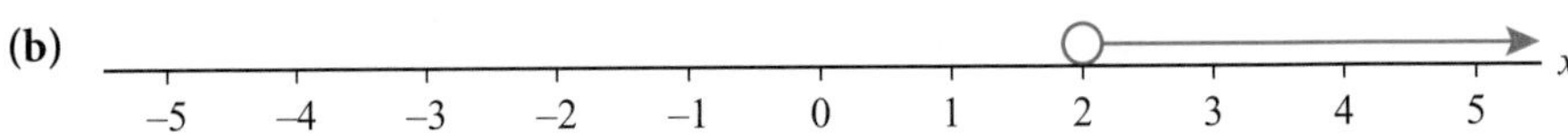

(c)

(d)

(e)

(f)

(g) 1.0 1.1 1.2 1.3 3.4 3.5 3.6 3.7 x

(h) −3.4 −3.3 −3.2 −3.1 2.8 2.9 3.0 x

(i) − −4.6 −4.5 −4.4 −3.2 −3.1 −3.0 r

2 (a) $\{4, 5, \ldots\ldots 31, 32\}$
(b) $\{8, 9, \ldots\ldots 18, 19\}$
(c) $\{18, 19, \ldots\ldots 26, 27\}$
(d) $\{-3, -2, -1\}$
(e) $\{-3, -2, -1, 0\}$
(f) $\{3, 4, \ldots\ldots 10, 11\}$
(g) $\{-6, -5, -4\}$
(h) $\{4, 5, 6\}$
(i) $\{3, 4\}$

Exercise 14.4

1 (a) $x < 2$
(b) $x > 3$
(c) $y \leq \frac{14}{5}$
(d) $y > -2$
(e) $c \geq 2$
(f) $x < 4$
(g) $x < 6$
(h) $p > 3$
(i) $x > -15$
(j) $g \geq 4$
(k) $w < 8$
(l) $k < \frac{7}{10}$

2 (a) $y > 30$ (b) $q < 12$
(c) $g \leq \frac{11}{2}$ (d) $h < 19$
(e) $y \leq 30$ (f) $x \leq -1$
(g) $h \geq -\frac{3}{2}$ (h) $y \geq \frac{-44}{3}$
(i) $n < 48$ (j) $v \leq \frac{-13}{6}$
(k) $z > 62$ (l) $k > 33$
(m) $e > \frac{31}{28}$

3 (a) $t > 9\frac{1}{4}$ (b) $t > \frac{109}{4}$
(c) $t > \frac{763}{4}$ (d) $r < \frac{10}{3}$
(e) $d \geq -139$

Exercise 14.5

1

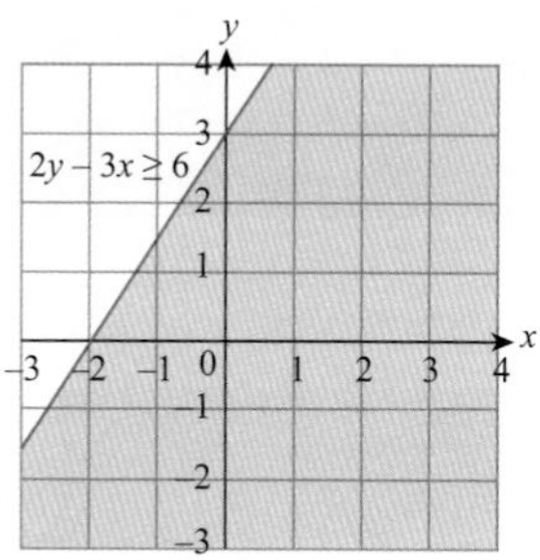

2

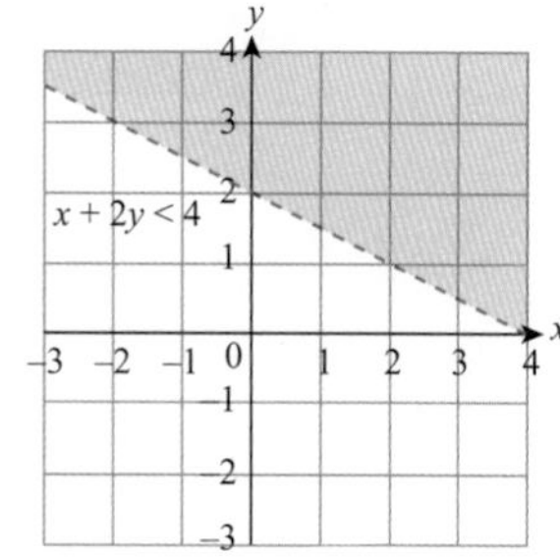

3

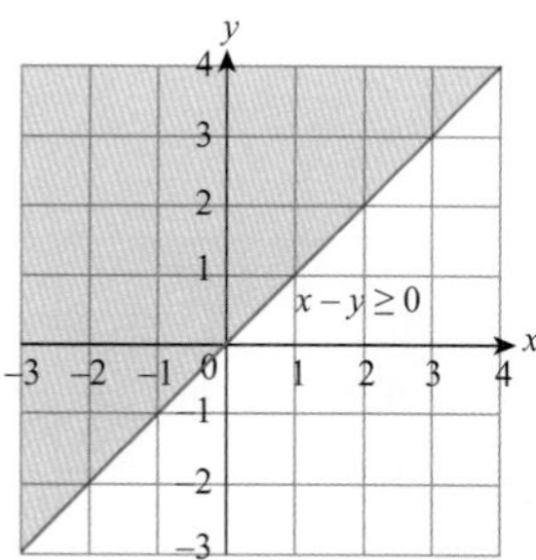

4 (a)

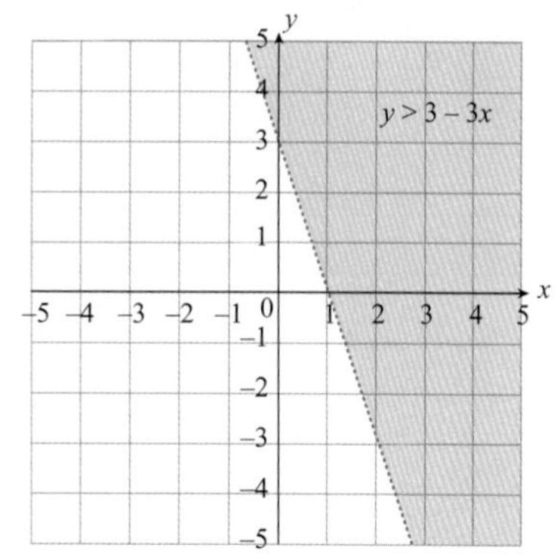

(b)

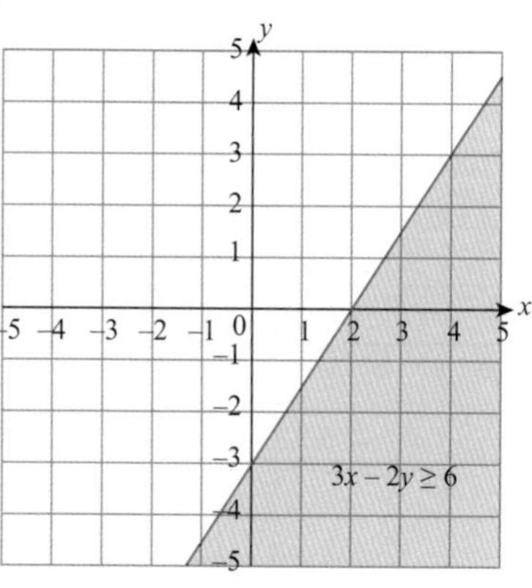

(c)

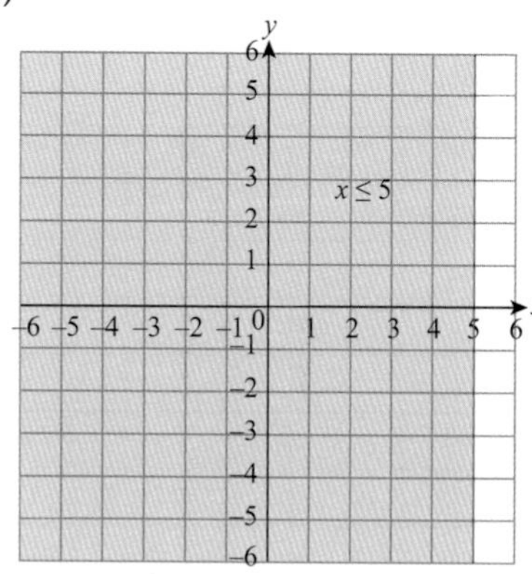

(d)

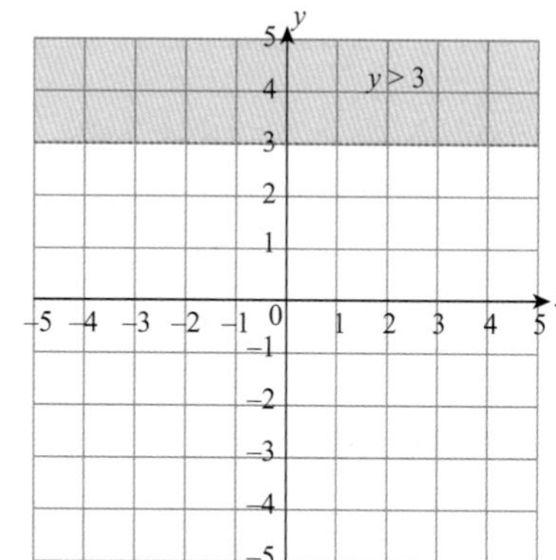

(e)

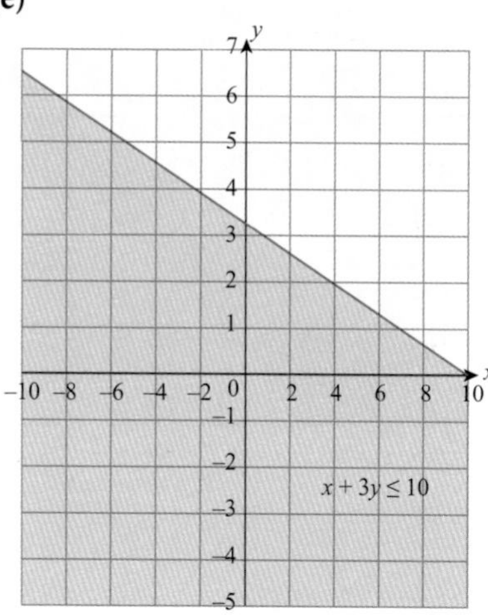

(f)

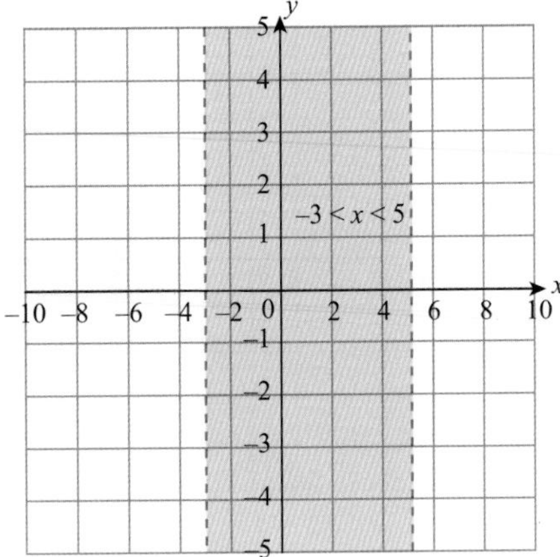

(g)

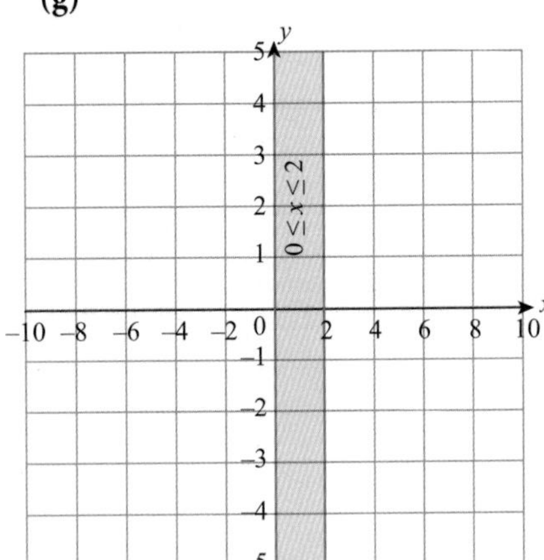

5 (a) above (b) below
(c) above and below

6 (a) $y \ge 3x + 3$ (b) $x + y < 3$
(c) $y \ge \frac{1}{3}x + 1$ (d) $y \le \frac{-3}{2}x$

Exercise 14.6

1

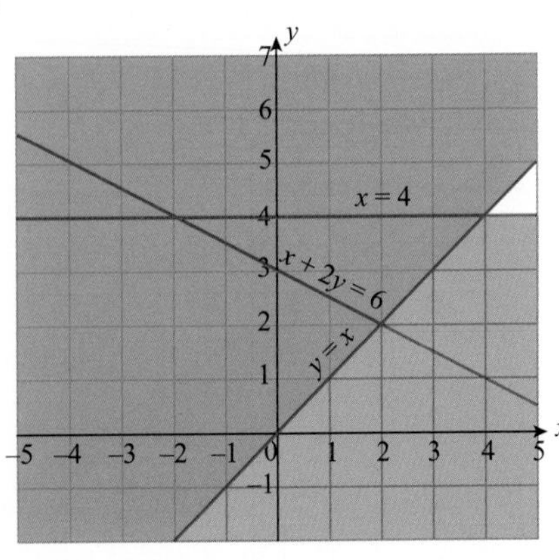

2

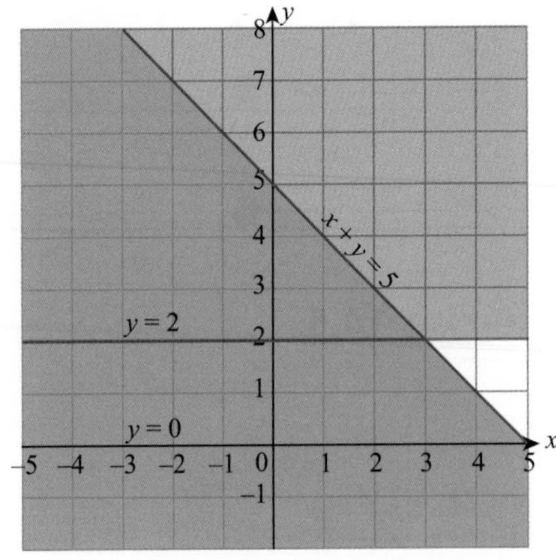

3

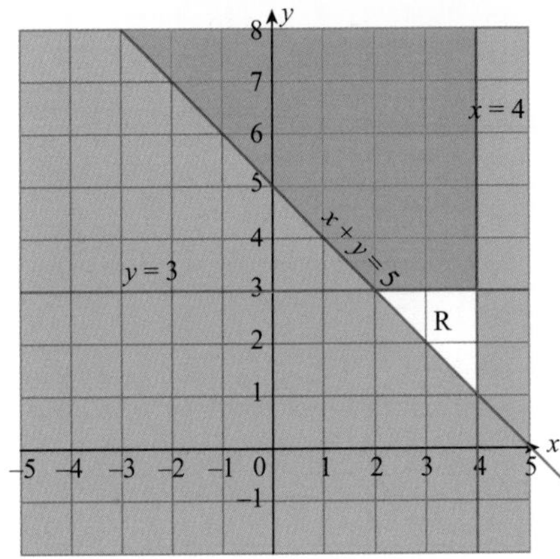

4 $y \le -x + 4$, $y > 2x + 1$, $x \le 2$

5 (3, 0), (2, 0), (2, 1), (1, 1), (1, 2), (1, 0), (0, 3), (0, 2)

6

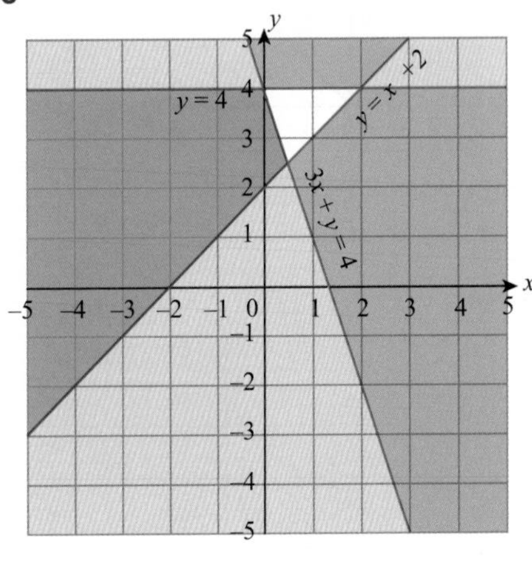

(0, 4) (1, 4) (2, 4) (1, 3)

Exercise 14.7

1 Greatest value: $3(6) + 2(6) = 30$
Least value: $3(-2) + 2(6) = 6$

2 (a)

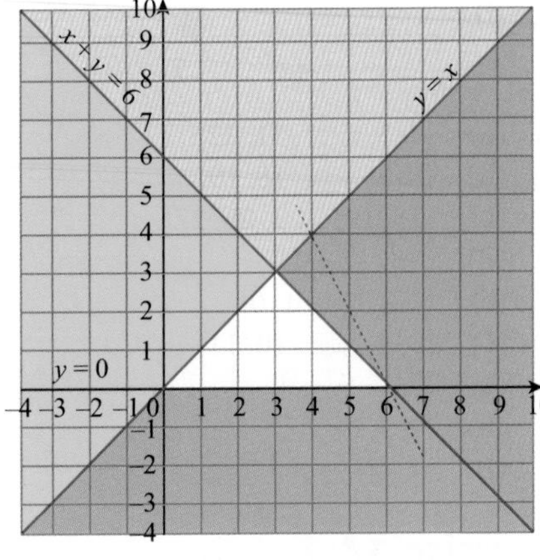

(b) $2(6) + 0 = 12$

3

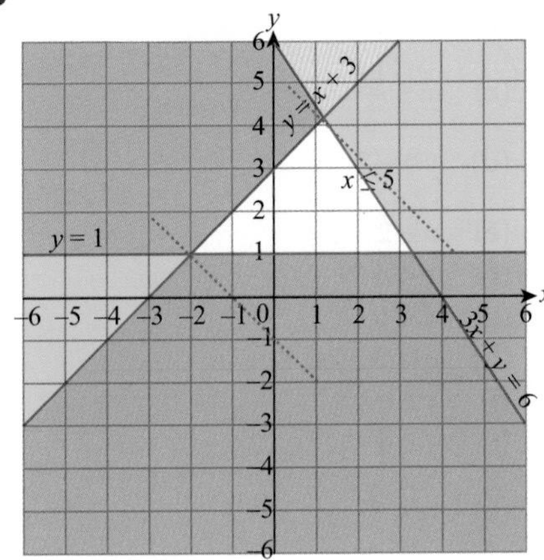

Greatest value = 5
Least value = −1

4

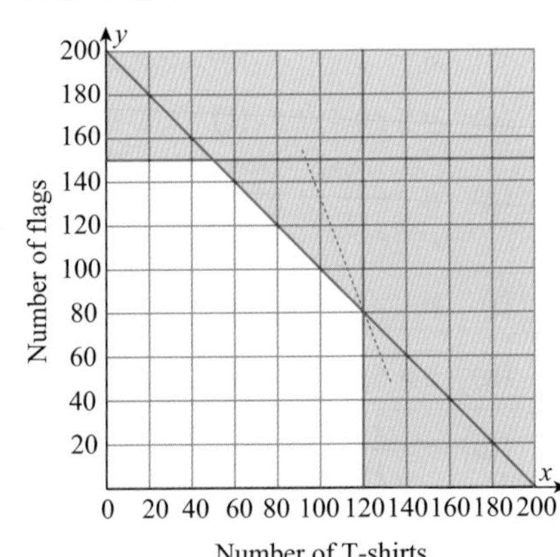

120 T-shirts and 80 flags will maximise income.

5

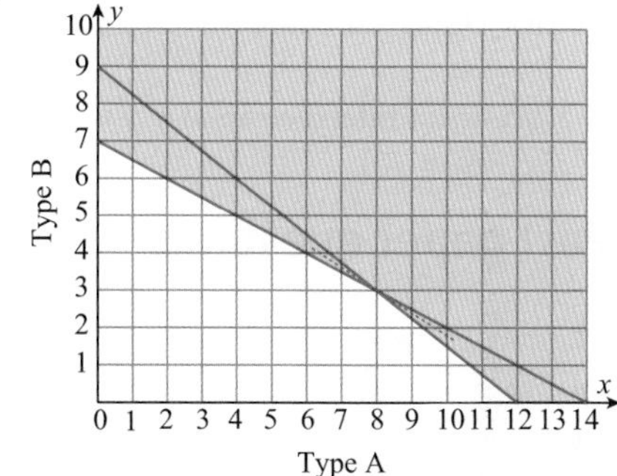

8 type A and 3 type B give 10 m³ storage

Exercise 14.8

1 **(a)** $(x+3)^2+5$ **(b)** $(x+4)^2-15$
(c) $(x+6)^2-16$ **(d)** $(x+3)^2-4$
(e) $(x-2)^2+8$ **(f)** $(x-)^2-18$
(g) $(x+\frac{5}{2})^2-\frac{21}{4}$ **(h)** $(x+\frac{7}{2})^2-\frac{57}{4}$
(i) $(x-\frac{3}{2})^2-\frac{21}{4}$
(j) $(x+\frac{7}{2})^2-\frac{81}{4}$
(k) $\left(x-\frac{13}{2}\right)^2-\frac{165}{4}$
(l) $(x-10)^2+300$

2 **(a)** $x=0.74$ or -6.74
(b) $x=-0.13$ or -7.87
(c) $x=3.41$ or 0.59
(d) $x=1.14$ or -6.14
(e) $x=2$ or 1
(f) $x=11.92$ or 0.08

3 **(a)** $x=3.70$ or -2.70
(b) $x=1.37$ or -4.37
(c) $x=0.16$ or -6.16
(d) $x=1.77$ or -2.27
(e) $x=1.89$ or 0.11
(f) $x=5.37$ or -0.37
(g) $x=1.30$ or -2.30
(h) $x=3$ or -1
(i) $x=1.61$ or -0.61

Exercise 14.9

1 **(a)** $x=-3$ or -4
(b) $x=-6$ or -2
(c) $x=-7$ or -4
(d) $x=-5$ or 1
(e) $x=-8$ or 2
(f) $x=8$ or -20
(g) $x=4$ or 2
(h) $x=7$ or -4
(i) $x=8$ or -3
(j) $x=8$ or 4
(k) $x=11$ or -9
(l) $x=12$ or -3
(m) $x=6$ or 4
(n) $x=5$ or 7
(o) $x=-3$ or 12

2 **(a)** $x=0.162$ or -6.16
(b) $x=-1.38$ or -3.62
(c) $x=-2.38$ or -4.62
(d) $x=-0.586$ or -3.41
(e) $x=3.30$ or -0.303
(f) $x=3.41$ or 0.586
(g) $x=7$, or 1 (this does factorise!)
(h) $x=2.73$ or -0.732
(i) $x=6.61$ or -0.606
(j) $x=8.24$ or -0.243
(k) $x=8.14$ or -0.860
(l) $x=-0.678$ or -10.3

3 **(a)** $x=1.71$ or 0.293
(b) $x=1.26$ or -0.264
(c) $x=0.896$ or -1.40
(d) $x=-0.851$ or 2.35
(e) $x=-1.37$ or 0.366
(f) $x=0.681$ or -0.881

4 **(a)** $x=2.28$ or 0.219
(b) $x=0.631$ or 0.227
(c) $x=0.879$ or -0.379
(d) $x=1.35$ or -2.95
(e) $x=-2.84$ or -9.16
(f) $x=6.85$ or 0.146

5 $x=1.61$ cm (-5.61 is not a solution because length cannot be negative)

Exercise 14.10

1 **(a)** $(3x+2)(x+4)$
(b) $(2x+3)(x-1)$
(c) $(3x+2)(2x-1)$
(d) $(3x+8)(x+2)$
(e) $(2x-5)(x+2)$
(f) $(4x-1)(4x+9)$
(g) $(3x+1)(x+5)$
(h) $(4x-1)(2x+1)$
(i) $(2x+3)(x-2)$
(j) $(2x+3)(x+3)$
(k) $(3x+8)(x-2)$
(l) $(5x-3)(2x+1)$
(m) $(5x+1)(x+1)$
(n) $(2x-1)(x-9)$
(o) $(6x-5)(2x+3)$

Exercise 14.11

1 As Exercise 14.10

2 **(a)** $(3x-7)(2x+3)$
(b) $-(2x+3)(x+5)$
(c) $(2x+3y)(2x+3y)$
(d) $(3x+y)(2x-7y)$
(e) $(x^2-9)(x^2-4)=(x-3)(x+3)(x-2)(x+2)$
(f) $2(3x-4y)(x-5y)$
(g) $(3x+2)(2x+1)$
(h) $(3x-4)(x-3)$
(i) $3(x-5)(x-8)$
(j) $(x-1)(x-2)$
(k) $4(x-1)(x-1)$
(l) $(2x)(6x+13)$

Exercise 14.12

1 **(a)** $\frac{x}{2}$ **(b)** $\frac{y}{4}$
(c) 5 **(d)** 10
(e) $\frac{t}{6}$ **(f)** $\frac{u}{3}$
(g) $\frac{t}{10}$ **(h)** $\frac{y}{2}$
(i) $\frac{3z}{4}$ **(j)** $\frac{4t}{3}$

2 **(a)** $\frac{xy}{3}$ **(b)** $\frac{x}{4y}$
(c) $\frac{1}{2}$ **(d)** $\frac{y}{2}$
(e) $5x$ **(f)** $3b$
(g) $\frac{2x}{3y}$ **(h)** $3b$
(i) $\frac{2}{3de}$ **(j)** $\frac{1}{4b^2}$

3 **(a)** $\frac{a}{5b}$ **(b)** ab
(c) $\frac{b}{2}$ **(d)** $\frac{ac}{4}$
(e) $\frac{abc}{2}$ **(f)** $\frac{9b}{4c}$
(g) $(abc)^2$ **(h)** $\frac{3y}{4x}$
(i) $\frac{4x^2z}{3y}$ **(j)** 9

4 **(a)** $\frac{1}{z^3}$ **(b)** $\frac{x^3z}{2y}$
(c) $\frac{3v}{7u^2w^4}$ **(d)** $\frac{x+3}{x+4}$
(e) $\frac{x}{x+4}$ **(f)** $\frac{y^3}{y+1}$
(g) $\frac{x-6}{x-4}$ **(h)** $\frac{x+5}{x-3}$

(i) 8 (j) $\dfrac{3x+2}{3x-2}$

(k) $\dfrac{x+3}{x+8}$ (l) $\dfrac{2x-3}{x+1}$

(m) $\dfrac{7x-1}{x-4}$ (n) $\dfrac{5y-4}{y-7}$

(o) $\dfrac{3x-7}{5x-4}$

5 (a) $\dfrac{3x-4}{7x+1}$ (b) x^2+y^2

(c) $\dfrac{1}{x}$ (d) x^2+1

(e) 1 (f) $\sqrt{x^3+y^3}$

Exercise 14.13

1 (a) $\dfrac{x^2}{4}$ (b) $\dfrac{3y^2}{14}$

(c) $\dfrac{3z^2}{14}$ (d) $\dfrac{t^2}{3}$

(e) 1 (f) $\dfrac{1}{6}$

(g) $\dfrac{3f}{2e}$ (h) $\dfrac{gh^2}{32}$

(i) 2 (j) $\dfrac{1}{2y^2}$

(k) $\dfrac{2d}{7c}$ (l) $\dfrac{r}{2pq}$

2 (a) $\dfrac{3z^2t^2}{x^3}$ (b) $\dfrac{2xt}{3}$

(c) $\dfrac{3}{4xy}$ (d) $\dfrac{64t^4y^4}{27}$

(e) $\dfrac{3}{4(x+y)^5(x-y)}$ (f) $\dfrac{1}{4(a-b)}$

(g) $\dfrac{\left(\sqrt{z^2+t^2}\right)^3}{144\,(x^2+y^2)}$ (h) $\dfrac{z-t}{z-y}$

Exercise 14.14

1 (a) $\dfrac{3y}{4}$ (b) $\dfrac{8t}{15}$

(c) $\dfrac{12u}{35}$ (d) $\dfrac{z}{14}$

(e) $\dfrac{5(x+y)}{12}$ (f) $\dfrac{3x}{2}$

(g) $\dfrac{11y}{8}$ (h) $\dfrac{a}{40}$

(i) $\dfrac{a}{2}$ (j) $\dfrac{7x+18y}{63}$

2 (a) $\dfrac{19(x+1)^2}{56}$ (b) $\dfrac{29pqr}{136}$

(c) $\dfrac{93p}{70}$ (d) $\dfrac{71x}{84}$

(e) $\dfrac{62x^2}{63}$ (f) $\dfrac{33-5x}{18}$

3 (a) $\dfrac{x+3}{a}$ (b) $\dfrac{23}{12a}$

(c) $\dfrac{19x}{6y}$ (d) $\dfrac{3a+2}{a^2}$

(e) $\dfrac{17}{6x}$ (f) $\dfrac{7}{5e}$

4 (a) $\dfrac{2x+5}{(x+1)(x+4)}$ (b) $\dfrac{5x-7}{(x-1)(x-2)}$

(c) $\dfrac{7x+39}{(x+2)(x+7)}$ (d) $\dfrac{5}{2x}$

(e) $\dfrac{7}{6xy}$ (f) $\dfrac{2+x^2}{x}$

(g) $\dfrac{x^2+2x+5}{2(x+1)}$

(h) $\dfrac{(x^2-1)(27y-14)}{63y^2}$

(i) $\dfrac{2y-x^3}{2x^2y}$

(j) $\dfrac{4x^2y+4xy-yz^2-z^3}{12xyz^2}$

(k) $\dfrac{1}{x+3}$ (l) $\dfrac{2}{x+2}$

Examination practice

Exam-style questions

1 (i) $\sqrt{37}$ (ii) 5

2 (a)

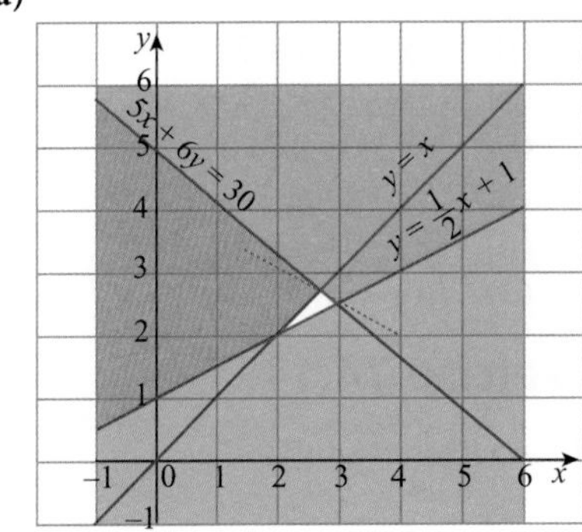

(b) Greatest value for $x+2y=8\frac{2}{11}$

(occurs at intersection of $x=y$ and $5x+6y=30$)

Past paper questions*

1 $x=1, y=\frac{1}{5}$

2 (8, 2)

3 1, 2, 3, 4

4 $\dfrac{23-2x}{12}$

5 (a) (i) $x \geq 5, y \leq 8, x+y \leq 14,$ $y \geq 0.5x$

(ii)

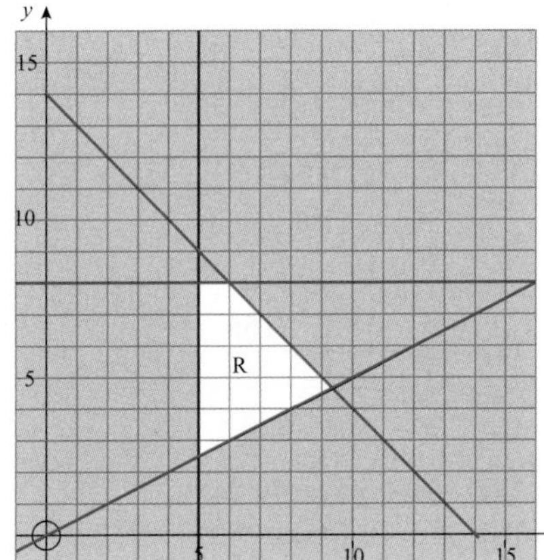

(b) (i) \$480

(ii) 6 small boxes, 8 large boxes

6 $\dfrac{h+4}{h+5}$

Chapter 15

Exercise 15.1

1 6.8 m × 5.2 m

2 (a) 3 cm

(b) 2.4 cm

3 (a) 5.6 cm

(b) 15°

*Cambridge International Examinations bears no responsibility for the example answers to questions taken from its past question papers which are contained in this publication.

Exercise 15.2

1 (a)

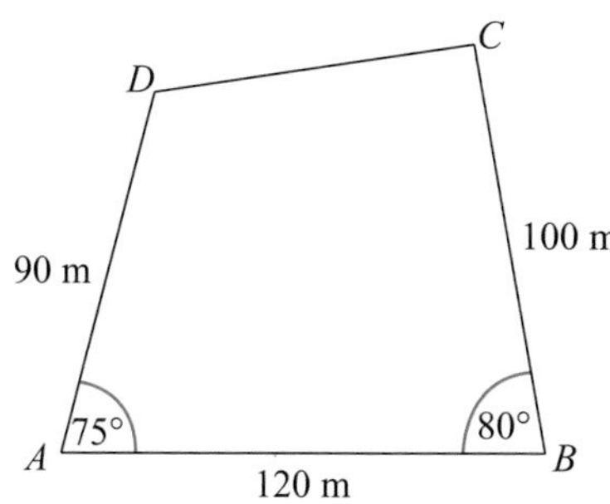

(b) $B\hat{C}D = 92°$; $A\hat{D}C = 113°$

(c) 80 m

2 (a) 20° (b) 3.4 m

3 (a) 20 m (b) 34.8 m (c) 35°

Exercise 15.3

1 (a) 270° (b) 135° (c) 045°

2 (a) 262° (b) 135°

3 (a) 110° (b) 050° (c) 230°
(d) 025° (e) 280°

4 (a) 108° (b) 288° (c) 147 km

5 (a) 9.6 km (b) 090°

Exercise 15.4

1

	Hypotenuse	Opposite *A*	Adjacent *A*
(a)	c	a	b
(b)	y	z	x
(c)	p	q	r
(d)	l	n	m
(e)	c	d	e
(f)	e	f	g

2 (a) opp (30°) = 5.7 cm
(b) opp(40°) = x cm
adj(50°) = x cm
(c) opp(65°) = q m or adj(250°)
opp(25°) = p m or adj(650°)
hypotenuse = r m

Exercise 15.5

1 (a) 0.700 (b) 1.04
(c) 0.325 (d) 1
(e) 0.279 (f) 0.323
(g) 0.00873 (h) 0

2 (a) $\tan A = \frac{1}{2}$ (b) $\tan A = \frac{3}{2}$
(c) $\tan A = \frac{1}{4}$ (d) $\tan x = \frac{3}{2}$
$\tan B = 4$
(e) $\tan x = \frac{n}{m}$ (f) $\tan C = a$
$\tan y = \frac{m}{n}$ (g) $\tan D = p^2$

3 (a) 5.20 cm (b) 4.62 m
(c) 35.7 m (d) 3.54 km
(e) 18 cm (f) 10.3 cm

4 (a) 20.8 cm (b) 16.1 cm
(c) 9.17 cm (d) 7.85 cm
(e) 40.6 cm (f) 115 m
(g) 2.61 m (h) 95.8 km
(i) 39.8 m

5 (a) 1.0724 (b) 32.8 m

6 32.3 m

7 (a) 1.73 (b) 2

8 0.45 m

9 Adi is correct, the pole is 4.34 m tall.

Exercise 15.6

1 (a) 40.4° (b) 60.0°
(c) 74.3° (d) 82.3°

2 (a) 22° (b) 38°
(c) 38° (d) 70°

3 (a) $a = 35.0°$ (b) $b = 77.5°$
(c) $c = 38.7°$
$d = 51.3°$
(d) $e = 18.4°$ (e) $f = 30°$

4 71.8° (1dp)

5 21.2° (1dp)

6 (a) 13.3 (3sf) (b) 26.7 (3sf)

7 $AB = 6.32$ (3sf)
$A\hat{C}B = 64.6°$ (1dp)

Exercise 15.7

1

	(a)	(b)	(c)	(d)	(e)	(f)	(g)
sin *A*	$\frac{4}{5}$	$\frac{7}{25}$	$\frac{12}{13}$	$\frac{20}{29}$	$\frac{8}{17}$	$\frac{4}{5}$	$\frac{13}{85}$
cos *A*	$\frac{3}{5}$	$\frac{24}{25}$	$\frac{5}{13}$	$\frac{21}{29}$	$\frac{15}{17}$	$\frac{3}{5}$	$\frac{84}{85}$
tan *A*	$\frac{4}{3}$	$\frac{7}{24}$	$\frac{12}{5}$	$\frac{20}{21}$	$\frac{8}{15}$	$\frac{4}{3}$	$\frac{13}{84}$

2 (a) 0.0872 (b) 0.9962
(c) 0.5000 (d) 0.8660
(e) 0.8660 (f) 0.5000
(g) 0.9962 (h) 0.0872

3 (a) $\cos 42° = \frac{g}{e}$ (b) $\sin 60° = \frac{c}{a}$
(c) $\cos 25° = \frac{RQ}{RP}$ (d) $\sin\theta = \frac{y}{r}$
(e) $\cos 48° = \frac{q}{r}$ (f) $\sin 30° = \frac{e}{f}$
(g) $\cos 35° = \frac{HI}{JI}$ (h) $\cos\theta = \frac{x}{r}$

4 (a) 0.845 m (b) 4.50 m
(c) 10.6 km (d) 4.54 cm
(e) 10.6 cm (f) 9.57 cm
(g) 14.1 cm (h) 106 cm
(i) 4.98 cm (j) 42.9 m
(k) 2.75 m (l) 137 m

5 (a) 81.9° (b) 57.1°
(c) 22.0° (d) 30°

6 (a) 25.9° (b) 44.9°
(c) 69.5° (d) 79.6°
(e) 26.9° (f) 11.5°

7 1.93 m (2 d.p.)

8 (a) 10.1 km (3sf)
(b) 14.9 km (3sf)

9 (a) 14.1 m (3sf)
(b) 5.13 m (3sf)

10 552 m (3sf)

11 (a) $x = 14.82$ cm
(b) $y = 10.09$ cm
(c) AΔ = 44.99 m
(d) $a = 29.52$ cm
$b = 52.80$ cm

12 (a) (i) 0.577 (ii) 0.577
(b) (i) 1.11 (ii) 1.11
(c) (i) −1.73 (ii) −1.73
(d) (i) 0.249 (ii) 0.249
$\therefore \tan x = \frac{\sin x}{\cos x}$

13 (a) 1 (b) 1 (c) 1
(d) $\sin^2 x + \cos^2 x = 1$

14 (a) $A\hat{C}B = 45°$ (b) $\sqrt{2}$ m
(c)

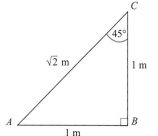

C
45°
$\sqrt{2}$ m
1 m
A
B
1 m

(d) $\sin 45° = \frac{1}{\sqrt{2}}$

$\cos 45° = \frac{1}{\sqrt{2}}$

$\tan 45° = 1$

(e) $y = 60°$ (f) $z = 30°$

(g) $EG = \sqrt{3}$ m

(h)

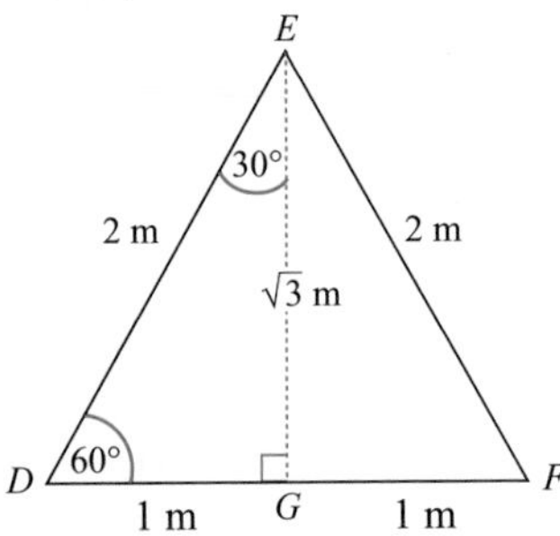

(i) $\sin 30° = \frac{1}{2}$

$\cos 30° = \frac{\sqrt{3}}{2}$

$\tan 30° = \frac{1}{\sqrt{3}}$

$\sin 60° = \frac{\sqrt{3}}{2}$

$\cos 60° = \frac{1}{2}$

$\tan 60° = \sqrt{3}$

(j)

Angle x	$\sin x$	$\cos x$	$\tan x$
30°	$\frac{1}{2}$	$\frac{\sqrt{3}}{2}$	$\frac{1}{\sqrt{3}}$
60°	$\frac{\sqrt{3}}{2}$	$\frac{1}{2}$	$\sqrt{3}$
45°	$\frac{1}{\sqrt{2}}$	$\frac{1}{\sqrt{2}}$	1

Exercise 15.8

1 (a) $A\hat{B}C = 16.2°$
(b) $BC = 17.9$ m

2 $AB = 13.856$ cm (3dp)

3 (a) $A\hat{B}C = 59.0°$
(b) $AB = 1.749$ (3dp)
(c) Capacity = 4.05 m^3

4 $A\hat{B}C = A\hat{C}B = 38.9°$ and $B\hat{A}C = 102.2°$

5 (a) 020° (b) 281.9 m
(c) 98 665 m^2

6 (a) 3.5 m (1dp)
(b) $DE = 6.1$ m (1dp)

7 $QT = 20$ cm (1sf)

8 (a) $A\hat{O}E = 72°$
(b) $A\hat{O}M = 36°$
(c) $OM = 1.376$ cm (3dp)
(d) 1.376 cm^2
(e) 6.882 cm^2 (3dp)

9 77.255 cm^2

10 $6.882a^2$ cm^2

11 $\dfrac{na^2}{\tan\left(\dfrac{360°}{2n}\right)}$

Exercise 15.9

1 (a) −cos 60° (b) sin 145°
(c) −cos 44° (d) sin 10°
(e) −cos 92° (f) cos 40°
(g) sin 59° (h) sin 81°
(i) cos 135° (j) cos 30°

2 (a) 45° (b) 135°
(c) 30° and 150° (d) 19° and 161°
(e) 145° (f) 55°
(g) 20° (h) 40° and 140°
(i) 90°
(j) 0° and 180° not possible in a triangle

Exercise 15.10

1 (a) 11.2 (b) 8.6
(c) 25.3 (d) 38.8°

2 (a) 10.6 cm (b) 5.73 cm
(c) 4.42 cm (d) 5.32 cm
(e) 6.46 cm (f) 155 mm

3 (a) 54.7° (b) 66.8° or 113.2°
(c) 69.8° or 110.2° (d) 25.3°
(e) 52.7° or 127.3° (f) 50.5°

4 $\hat{C} = 63°$
$AC = 15.9$ cm
$CB = 21.3$ cm

5 $\hat{F} = 25°$
$DE = 9.80$
$EF = 14.9$ cm

6 $\hat{R} = 32.2°$
$\hat{P} = 27.8°$
$QR = 7.0$ cm

7 (a) $\hat{Y}$ is opposite a side shorter than $\hat{X}$, so $\hat{Y} < \hat{X}$ and therefore <40°.
(b) $\hat{Y} = 30.9°$ and $\hat{Z} = 109.1°$
(c) $XY = 22.1$ cm

8 (a) $\angle ACB = 51°$
(b) $\angle ABC = 52°$
(c) $AC = 32.35$ mm

Exercise 15.11

1 $AC = 8.62$ cm

2 $DE = 22.3$ cm

3 $\hat{P} = 53.8°$

4 (a) 18.7 m
(b) $\hat{U} = 32.1°$ $\hat{T} = 52.9°$

5 (a) $\hat{X} = 60°$ (b) $\hat{Y} = 32.2°$
(c) $\hat{Z} = 87.8°$

6 (a) Return = 14.4 km (b) 296°

Exercise 15.12

1 (a) 10.0 cm^2 (b) 15.0 cm^2
(c) 52.0 cm^2 (d) 17.2 cm^2
(e) 22.7 cm^2 (f) 24.2 cm^2

2 108 cm^2

3 0.69 m^2

4 42.1 cm^2

5 (a) 30.6 cm^2 (b) 325.9 cm^2
(c) 1.74 m^2

6 (a) 174 cm^2
(b) 8.7 cm and 21.5 cm

7 (a) $\hat{Q} = 22.6°$ (b) $\hat{P} = 53.1°$

Exercise 15.13

1 (a) $AC = 25$ cm (b) $EC = 13.0$ cm
(c) 27.5°

2 (a) $EG = \sqrt{50}$ m
(b) $AG = \sqrt{75}$ m
(c) $A\hat{G}E = 35.3°$

3 (a) $A\hat{C}B = 53.1°$ (b) $BC = 5$ m
(c) $CD = 4.2$ m (d) $BM = 4.5$ m
(e) $B\hat{C}D = 65°$

4 (a) 14.9 cm (b) 15.2 cm
(c) $\theta = 11.4°$

5 (a) $AC = \sqrt{AB^2 + BC^2}$
(b) $DA = \sqrt{DC^2 - AC^2}$
(c) $DC = \sqrt{AD^2 + AC^2}$
(d) $D\hat{A}B = 90°$
(e) $B\hat{D}C = \cos^{-1}\left(\dfrac{BD^2 + DC^2 - BC^2}{2 \times BD \times DC}\right)$
(f) $A\hat{D}C = \cos^{-1}\left(\dfrac{AD}{CD}\right)$ or $\sin^{-1}\left(\dfrac{AC}{CD}\right)$

Examination practice

Exam-style questions

1 $AC = 9.8$ m, $BC = 6.9$ m
2 $D\hat{A}B = 47.9°$
3 9.9 m
4 (a) $X = 10.1$ m (to 3sf) (b) $Y = 20.6°$
5 (a) (i) $QX = 60 \tan 4° = 50.3$ m
(ii) 78.3 m
(b) (i) 250.3 m (ii) 257.4 m
(iii) 077°
6 (a) 5.16 m (b) 3.11 m^2
7 (a) 7 cm (b) 51.1°
8 (a) (90°, 1) (b) −1
(c)

(d) 2 solutions
9 (a) (i) $AB = 107.3$ km
(ii) $P\hat{A}B = 66.6°$ (iii) 143.4°
(b) (i) 5 h (ii) 12 km/h

Past paper questions*

1 6.6 m
2 (a) 17.5 m
(b) 20.4°
3 (a) 37.2°
(b) 11.7 cm^2
4 (a) 12.7 cm
(b) 28.2°
5 (a) (i) 14.6 km
(ii)

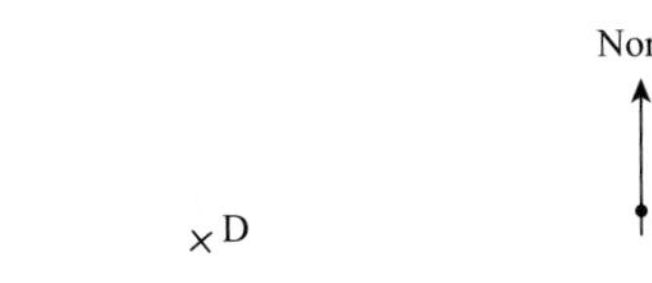

(iii) 260-264

Chapter 16

Exercise 16.1

1 (a) Positive; weak
(b) No correlation
(c) Negative; weak
(d) Negative; strong

2 (a) + (c)
Relationship between width and length of leaves

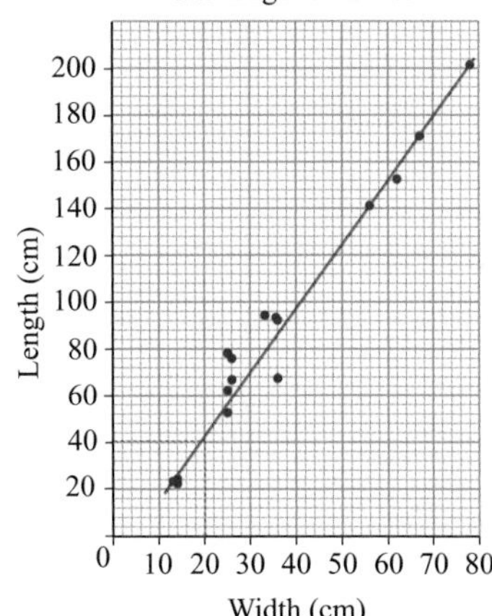

(b) Strong positive correlation.
(d) 40 cm

3 (a) Relationship between mass of dog and duration of morning walk

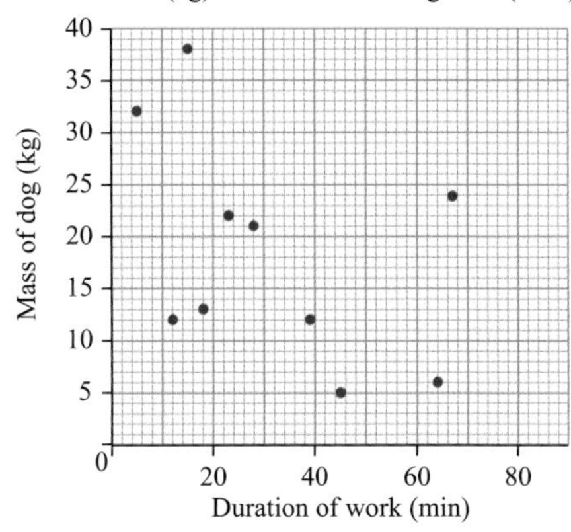

(b) No correlation
(c) The dogs are not a specific breed.

4 (a) + (c)

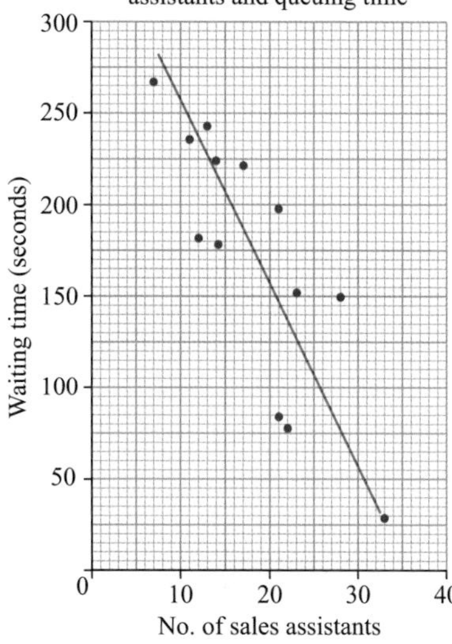

(b) Strong negative correlation.
(d) Value is outside the range of the collected data and waiting time will be negative time!

5 (a)

TV watching (min)	122	34	215	54	56	78	224	236	121	74	63	200
Maths score (%)	64	92	30	83	76	78	41	28	55	91	83	27

(b) Strong negative correlation.
(c)

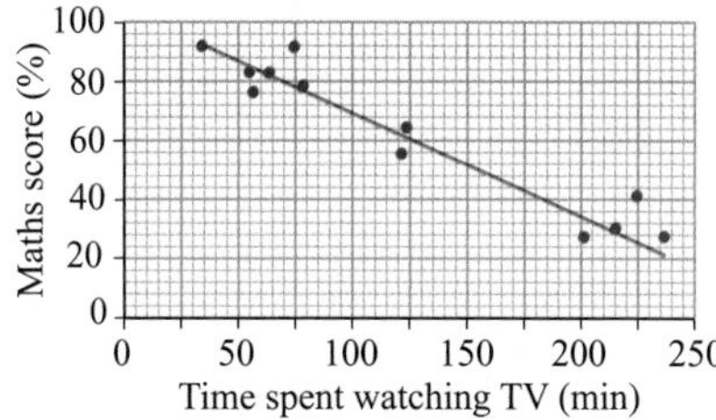

(d) 85 min
(e) No way of knowing how accurate the estimate is as performance in test is affected by many factors.

* *Cambridge International Examinations bears no responsibility for the example answers to questions taken from its past question papers which are contained in this publication.*

Examination practice

Exam-style questions

1 (a) + (c)

Relationship between price (£) and area

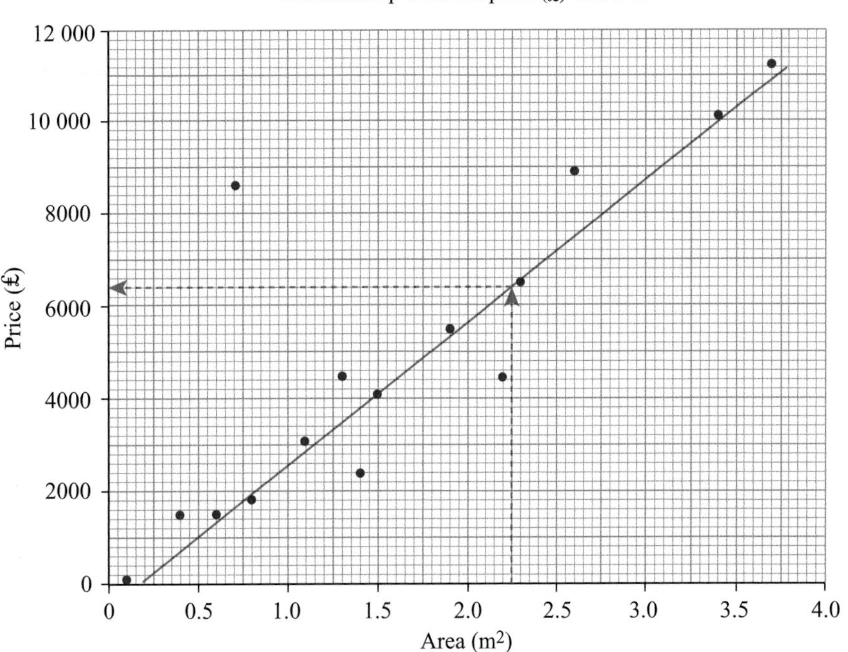

(b) Painting E because other paintings of a similar size are much cheaper.
(d) £6400
(e) Value is outside the range of the collected data.

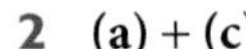

2 (a) + (c)

Comparison of 1st and 2nd year maintenance

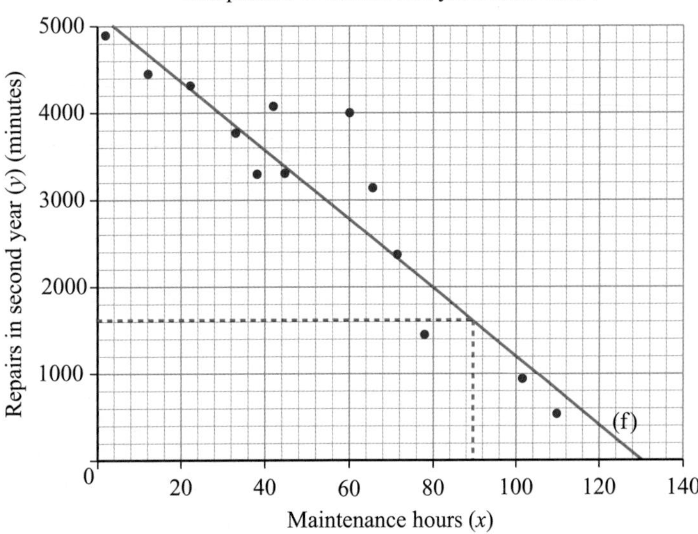

(b) Strong negative correlation.
(d) 1 800 minutes
(e) Repair time is a negative number – value is outside the range of the collected data.
(f) Approximately 130 hours – this is an extrapolated value so might not be accurate.

Past paper questions*

1 (a) and (b)

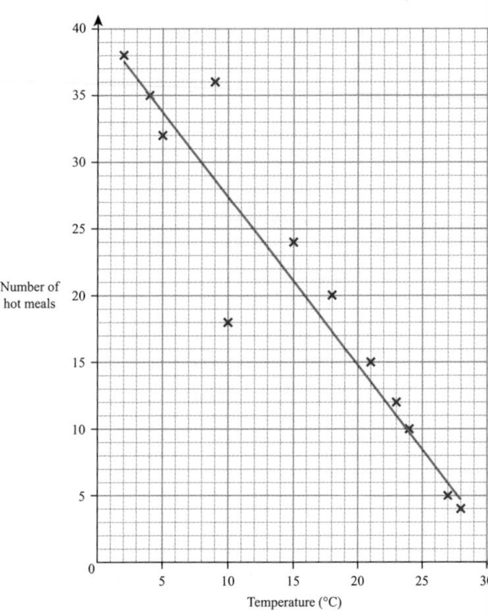

(c) strong negative

Unit 5

Chapter 17

Exercise 17.1

1 $49.50
2 $332.50
3 (a) $13.50 (b) £6.45
(c) 9.35 (d) $12.5
(e) $13.68
4 $2085.75
5 $474.30
6 $7125
7

Annie	$319.20
Bonnie	$315.00
Connie	$300.30
Donny	$403.20
Elizabeth	$248.85

* *Cambridge International Examinations bears no responsibility for the example answers to questions taken from its past question papers which are contained in this publication.*

8 All amounts in R million (3sf).

per year	per month (a)	35% tax per year (b)	per month after tax (c)
63.1	5.26	22.1	3.42
58.1	4.84	20.3	3.15
54.4	4.53	19	2.95
47.4	3.95	16.6	2.57
44	3.67	15.4	2.38
41.1	3.43	14.4	2.23
41.1	3.43	14.4	2.23
41	3.42	14.4	2.22
37.2	3.1	13	2.02
32.3	2.69	11.3	1.75

(d) Pine pienaar earned 1.12×10^{-2} million R (3sf) and Julion Roberts earned 6.00×10^{-3} million R(3sf).

Exercise 17.2

1

Employee	(a) Net income ($)	(b) % $\left(\frac{\text{net}}{\text{gross}}\right)$
B Willis	317.00	47
M Freeman	158.89	35
J Malkovich	557.20	43
H Mirren	383.13	42
M Parker	363.64	43

2 (a) Mean weekly earnings: $836.63
(b) Median weekly earnings: $853.30
(c) Range of earnings: $832.50

3 (a) Difference between gross and net income:
M Badru: 3954.52
B Singh: 724.79
(b) Percentage of gross income that each takes home as net pay:
M Badru: 70%
B Singh: 57%

Exercise 17.3

1

Taxable income	Annual tax	Monthly tax
(a) $98 000.00	$17 640.00	$1470.00
(b) $120 000.00	$21 600.00	$1800.00
(c) $129 000.00	$23 220.00	$1935.00
(d) $135 000.00	$24 510.00	$2042.50
(e) $178 000.00	$35 260.00	$2938.33

2 (a) (i) Yes
(ii) No – he pays $6181.25
(iii) $\$6181.25 = \$4681.25 + (40\,000 - 34\,000) \times 0.25$
(b) $67 616.75
(c) (i) She owes additional tax.
(ii) $238.25

3 (a) Value-Added-Tax:
VAT is paid at each step in the business chain. For the buyer it is the tax on the purchase price but for the seller it is the tax on the 'added value' part of the price. Rate/s at which charged vary from country to country.
(b) General sales tax:
Sales tax is paid only at the end of the consumer chain by the consumer. Rate/s at which charged vary from country to country.
(c) Customs and Excise duties:
Customs duties are taxes on imported goods. Excise duties are taxes on goods produced for sale, or sold, within a country. Rate/s at which charged vary from country to country.
(d) Capital Gains Tax:
Capital gains tax is paid on the profit made on the sale of assets. Rate/s at which charged vary from country to country.
(e) Estate duties:
These are taxes levied on people who inherit money, property, etc. Rate/s at which charged vary from country to country.

Exercise 17.4

1

Principal amount ($)	Interest rate (%)	Time invested	Interest earned ($)
500	1	3	15.00
650	0.75	2.5	12.19
1000	1.25	5	62.50
1200	4	6.75	324.00
875	5.5	3	144.38
900	6	2	108.00
699	7.25	3.75	190.04
1200	8	0.75	72.00
150 000	9.5	1.5	21 375.00

2

Principal amount ($)	Interest rate (%)	Time invested	Amount repay ($)
500	4.5	2	545.00
650	5	2	715.00
1000	6	2	1120.00
1200	12	1.5	1416.00
875	15	1.5	1071.88
900	15	3	1305.00
699	20	0.75	803.85
1200	21.25	0.67	1370.85
150 000	18	1.5	190 500.00

3 4 years

4 7% p.a.

5 33 years 4 months

6 (a) $32 (b) $96
(c) (i) $40.80 (ii) $136.80

7 (a) £11 700 (b) £3700
(c) 15.4% (1dp)

Exercise 17.5

1 (a) $100 (b) $60 (c) $460

2 $2850

3 (a) $141.83 (b) $2072

4 (a) £301 (b) 33.5% (1dp)

5 (a) $3657.80 (b) 13.09% (2dp)

Exercise 17.6

1 (a) $10 035.20 (b) $9920.00

2 (a) $4998.09 (b) $5077.92

3 $88 814.66

4 HK $3 800 596.18

5 (a) 7.337 billion × 7.255
(b) 7.761 billion × 7.675
(c) 8.210 billion × 8.118

6 (a) 1724 pandas
(b) 1484 pandas

7 (a)

Time (days)	0	1	2	3	4	5	6	7	8
Total number of microbes (millions)	1	2	4	8	16	32	64	128	156

(b)

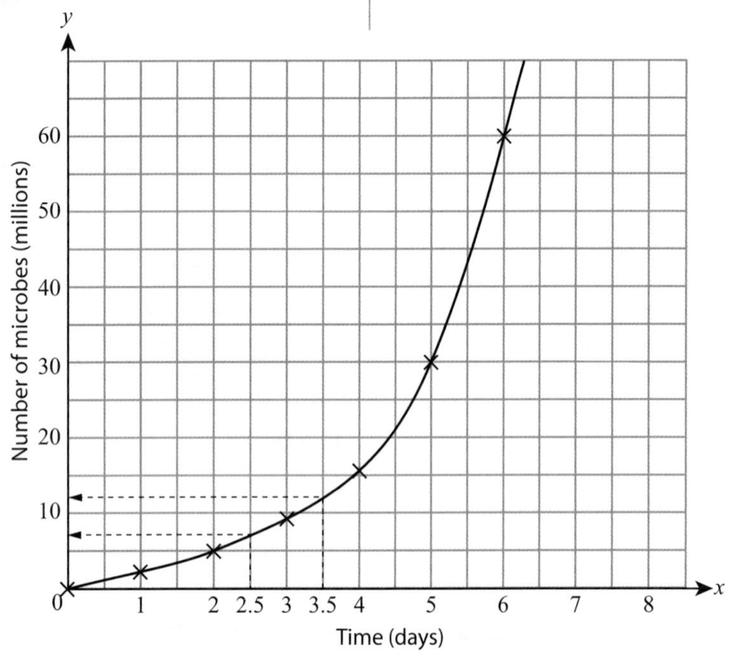

(c) (i) approximately 5.5 million
(ii) approximately 12 million
(d) just over 4 days

8 (a) 6.5 minutes (b) 12 grams

Exercise 17.7

1 $27 085.85

2 (a) $10 120 (b) $8565.57
(c) $5645.41 (d) $11 000(0.92)$n$

3 $2903.70

4 (a) 7 137 564
(b) 10 years

5 15 hours

Exercise 17.8

1

	Cost price ($)	Selling price ($)	Profit ($)	Profit (%)
(a)	20.00	25.00	5.00	25.00
(b)	500.00	550.00	50.00	10.00
(c)	1.50	1.80	0.30	20.00
(d)	0.30	0.35	0.05	16.67

2

	Cost price ($)	Selling price ($)	Loss ($)	Loss %
(a)	400.00	300.00	100.00	25.00
(b)	0.75	0.65	0.10	13.33
(c)	5.00	4.75	0.25	5.00
(d)	6.50	5.85	0.65	10.00

3 Percentage profit = 66.67%

Exercise 17.9

1 (a) $108.33 (b) $256.00
(c) $469.41 (d) $1125.00

2 $840
3 $3225
4 $360
5 $220.80
6 $433.55 for 10 and $43.36 each
7 28%
8 (a) $67.38 (b) 60%

Exercise 17.10

1

Original price ($)	% discount	Savings ($)	Sale price ($)
89.99	5	4.50	85.49
125.99	10	12.60	113.39
599.00	12	71.88	527.12
22.50	7.5	1.69	20.81
65.80	2.5	1.65	64.15
10 000.00	23	2300.00	7700.00

2

Original price ($)	Sale price ($)	% discount
89.99	79.99	11
125.99	120.00	5
599.00	450.00	25
22.50	18.50	18
65.80	58.99	10
10 000.00	9500.00	5

Examination practice

Exam-style questions

1 (a) $366.56 (b) 9 hours

2 (a) $12 (b) $14.40

3 7.5%
4 $33.60
5 $635

6 (a) £30 000.00 (b) £2 977.53
(c) £2 307.59

7 9.36%
8 11%

Past paper questions*

1 (a) 06:41 (6.41 (am), 6:41 and 06 41 also fine) (b) $204

2 £3000

3 (a) $314.60 (b) $703.04
(c) (i) $314.28 (ii) 627.55 (627.54)

* *Cambridge International Examinations bears no responsibility for the example answers to questions taken from its past question papers which are contained in this publication.*

Chapter 18

Exercise 18.1

1

	x	−3	−2	−1	0	1	2	3
(a)	$y=x^2+1$	10	5	2	1	2	5	10
(b)	$y=x^2+3$	12	7	4	3	4	7	12
(c)	$y=x^2-2$	7	2	−1	−2	−1	2	7
(d)	$y=-x^2+1$	−8	−3	0	1	0	−3	−8
(e)	$y=3-x^2$	−6	−1	2	3	2	−1	−6

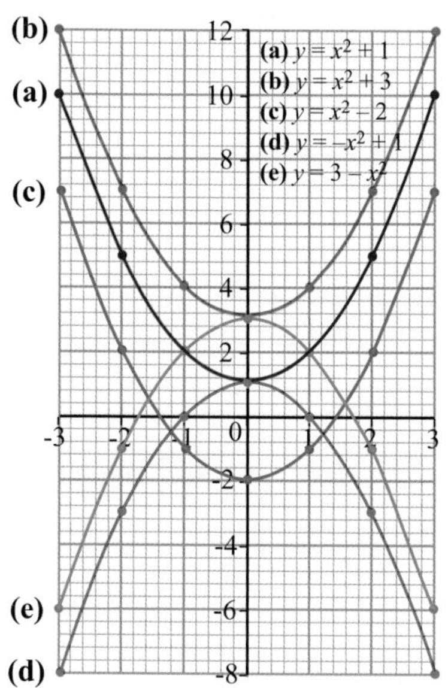

(f) When the value of the constant term changes the graph moves up or down the y-axis.

2 (a) C
(b) B
(c) A
(d) D
(e) E

Exercise 18.2

1

x	−1	0	1	2	3
$y=x^2-2x+2$	5	2	1	2	5

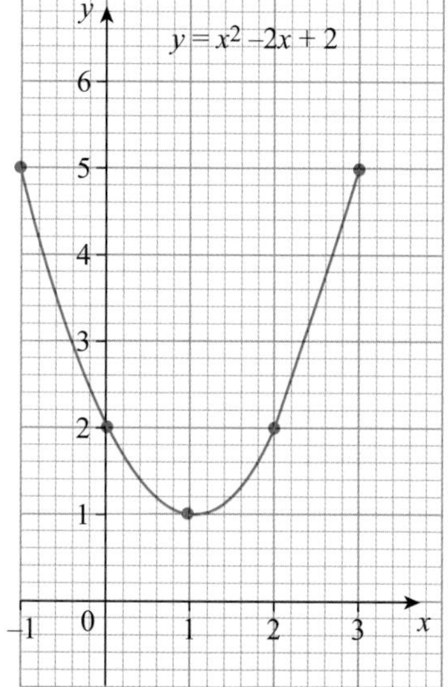

2

x	−2	−1	0	1	2	3	4	5	6
x^2	4	1	0	1	4	9	16	25	36
$-5x$	10	5	0	−5	−10	−15	−20	−25	−30
-4	−4	−4	−4	−4	−4	−4	−4	−4	−4
$y=x^2-5x-4$	10	2	−4	−8	−10	−10	−8	−4	2

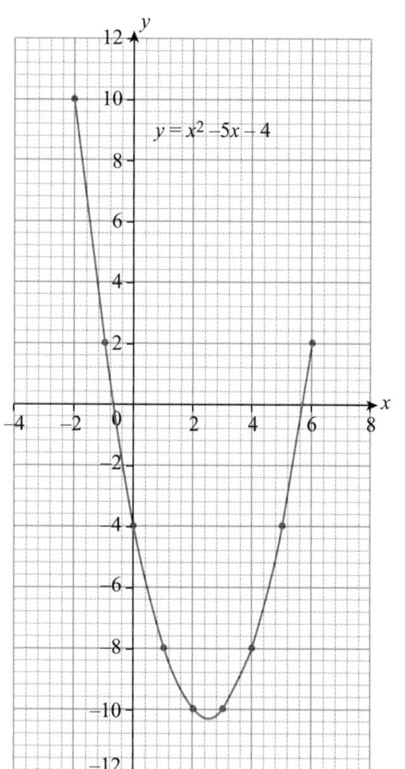

3

x	−3	−2	−1	0	1	2
$y=x^2+2x-3$	0	−3	−4	−3	0	5

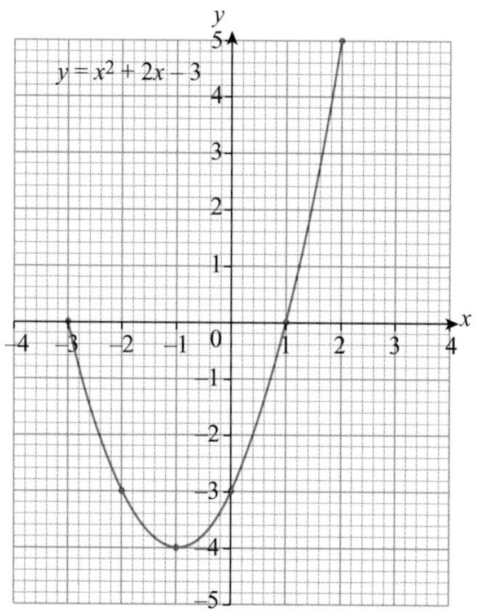

4

x	0	1	2	3	4
$y=-x^2-4x$	0	−5	−12	−21	−32

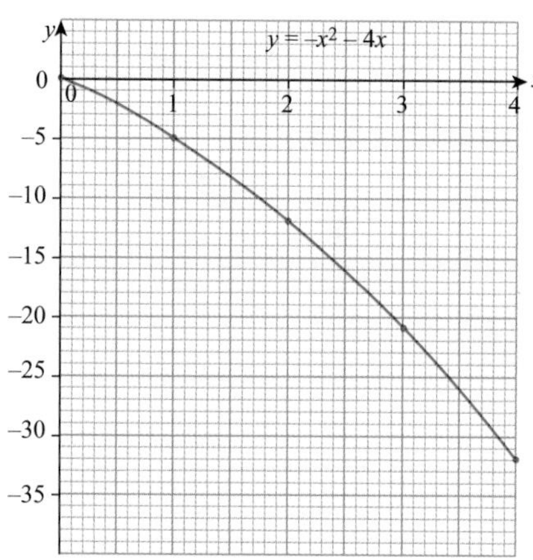

5

x	−6	−5	−4	−3	−2	−1	0
$y = -x^2 - 6x - 5$	−5	0	3	4	3	0	−5

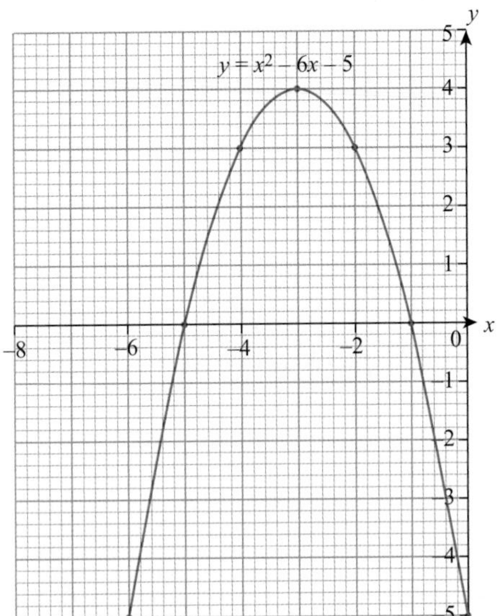

6 (a) 6 m
(b) 2 seconds
(c) 3 seconds
(d) 4.5 m
(e) The water surface is at $h = 0$.

Exercise 18.3

1 (a)

x	−6	−4	−3	−2	−1	1	2	3	4	6
$y = \frac{2}{x}$	$\frac{-1}{3}$	−0.5	$\frac{-2}{3}$	−1	−2	2	1	$\frac{2}{3}$	0.5	$\frac{1}{3}$

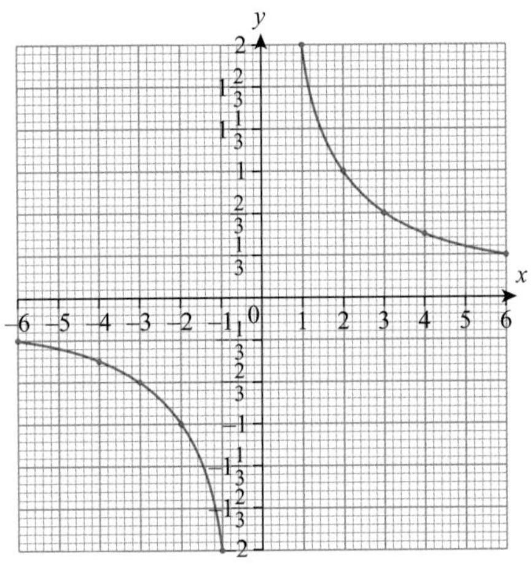

(b)

x	−5	−4	−3	−2	−1	1	2	3	4	5
$y = \frac{-1}{x}$	0.2	0.25	$\frac{1}{3}$	0.5	1	−1	−0.5	$\frac{-1}{3}$	−0.25	−0.2

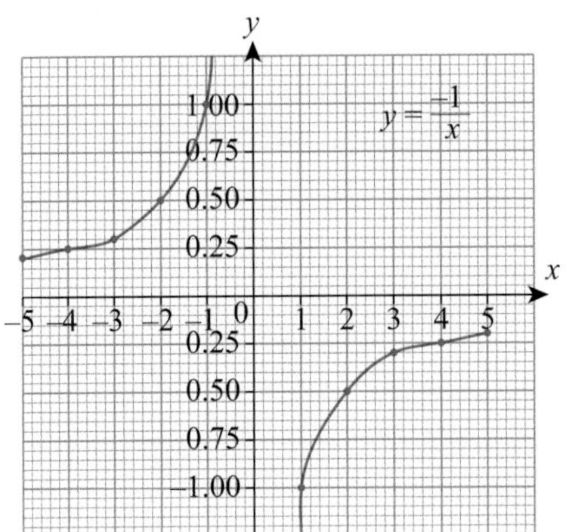

(c)

x	−6	−4	−3	−2	−1	1	2	3	4	6
$y = \frac{-6}{x}$	1	1.5	2	3	6	−6	−3	−2	−1.5	−1

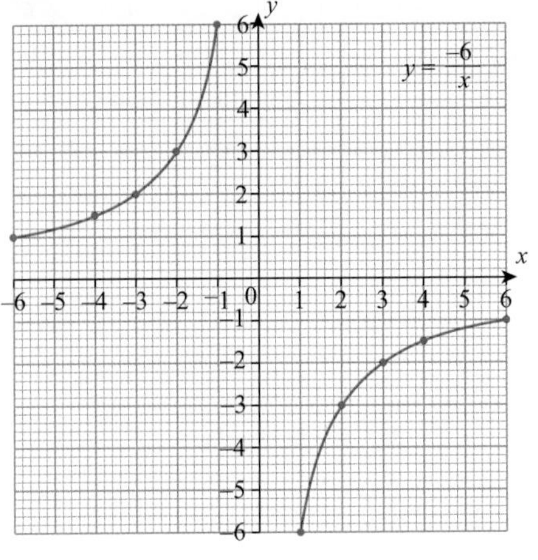

(d)

x	−6	−4	−3	−2	−1	1	2	3	4	6
$y = \frac{4}{x}$	$\frac{-2}{3}$	−1	$-1\frac{1}{3}$	−2	−4	4	2	$1\frac{1}{3}$	1	$\frac{2}{3}$

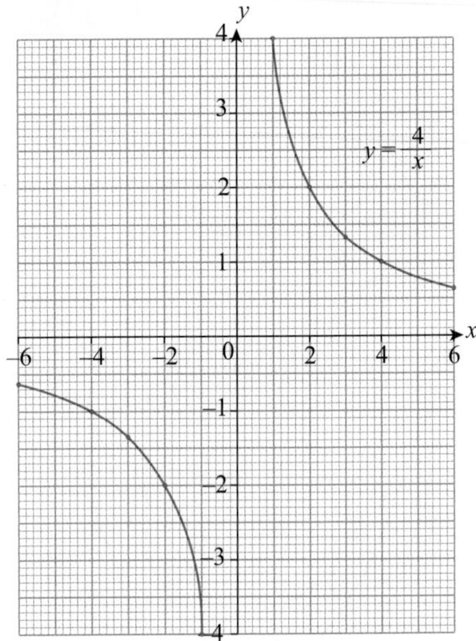

2 (a)

x	20	40	60	80	100	120
y	12	6	4	3	2.4	2

(b)

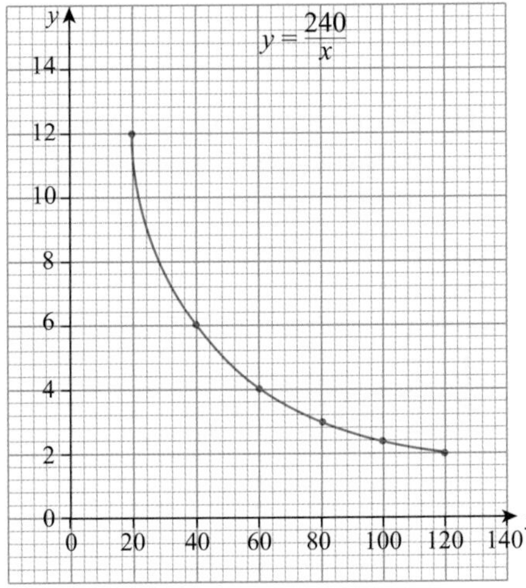

(c) $y = \frac{240}{x}$

Exercise 18.4

1 (a) $x = -1$ and $x = 2$
(b) $x = -2.4$ and $x = 3.4$
(c) $x = -2$ and $x = 3$

2 (a)

x	−3	−2	−1	0	1	2
$y = -x^2 - x + 1$	−5	−1	1	1	−1	−5

(b)

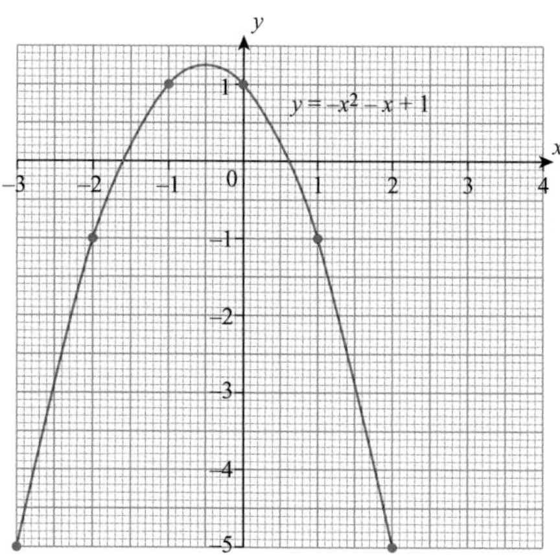

(c) $x = -1.6$ and $x = 0.6$

3 (a) $x = -1.3$ and $x = 2.3$

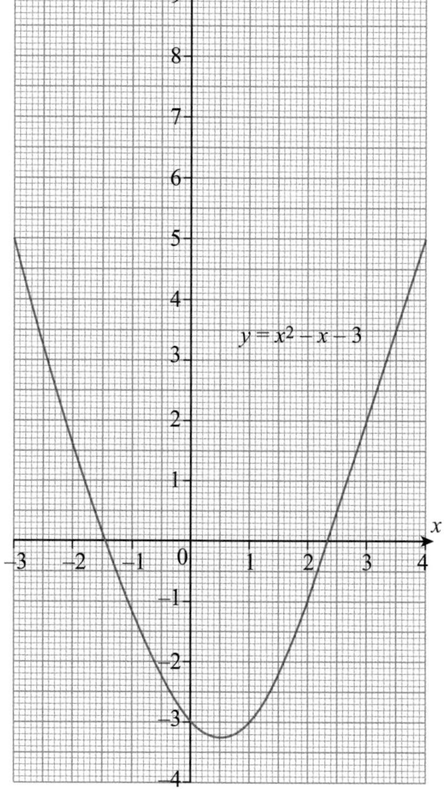

(b) $x = -2.6$ and $x = -0.4$

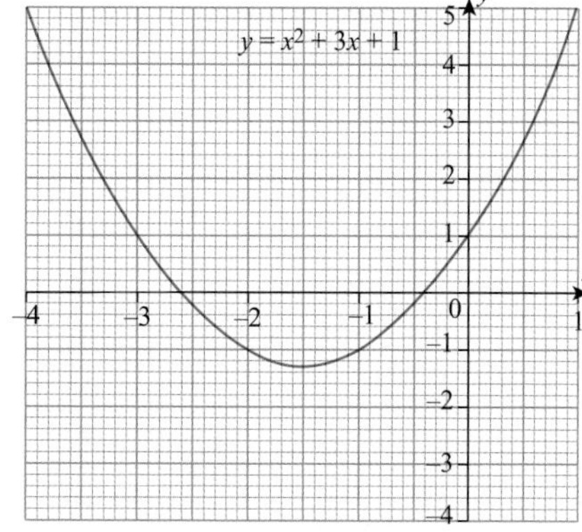

4 (a)

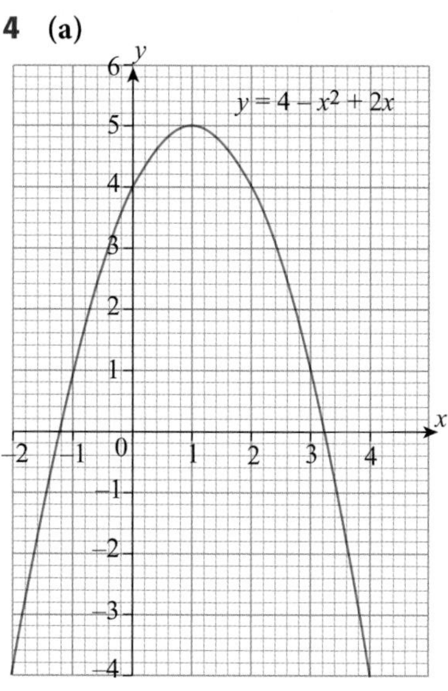

(b) (i) $x = -1.2$ and $x = 3.2$
(ii) $x = 0$ or $x = 2$

5 (a)

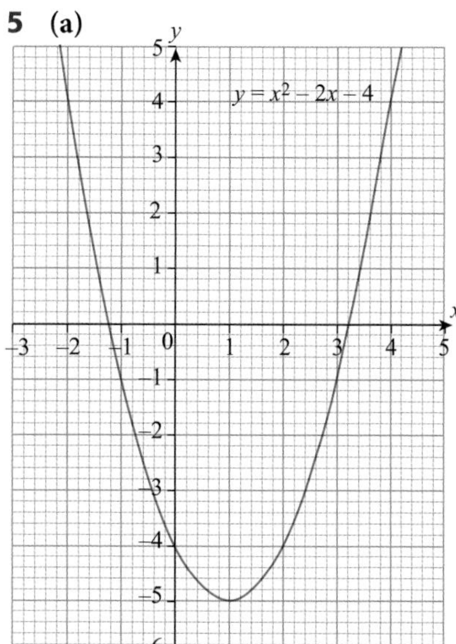

(Students, graph should also include the points (−3, 11) and (5, 11)

(b) (i) $x = -1.2$ and $x = 3.2$
(ii) $x = -1.8$ and $x = 3.8$
(iii) $x = -1$ and $x = 3$

Exercise 18.5

1 (a) $x = 2$ and $x = -1$
(b) $x = 2$ and $x = -2$
(c) $x = -2$ and $x = 1$
(d) $x = 1.2$ and $x = -0.4$

2 Students' own graphs
(a) (0, 0) and (3, 9)
(b) (−1.4, −1.4) and (1.4, 1.4)
(c) (2, 0)

3 (a) $x = 9.1$ and $x = 0.9$
(b) $x = -2$ and $x = 4$
(c) $x = 3.8$ and $x = -1.8$

4

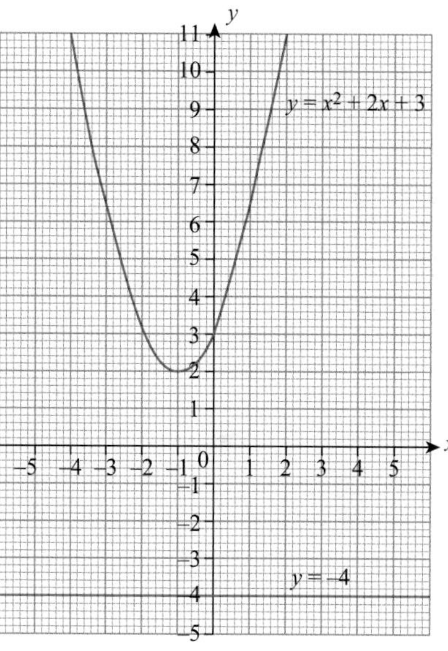

There are no points of intersection.

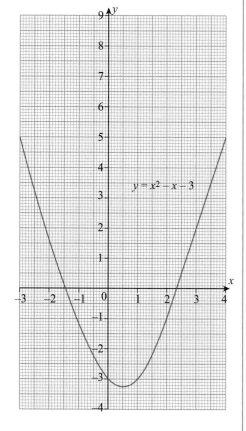

Exercise 18.6

1

	x	−3	−2	−1	0	1	2	3
(a)	$y = 2x^3$	−54	−16	−2	0	2	16	54
(b)	$y = -3x^3$	81	24	3	0	−3	−24	−81
(c)	$y = x^3 - 2$	−29	−10	−3	−2	−1	6	25
(d)	$y = 3 + 2x^3$	−51	−13	1	3	5	19	57
(e)	$y = x^3 - 2x^2$	−45	−16	−3	0	−1	0	9
(f)	$y = 2x^3 - 4x + 1$	−41	−7	3	1	−1	9	43
(g)	$y = -x^3 + x^2 - 9$	27	3	−7	−9	−9	−13	−27
(h)	$y = x^3 - 2x^2 + 1$	−44	−15	−2	1	0	1	10

(a)

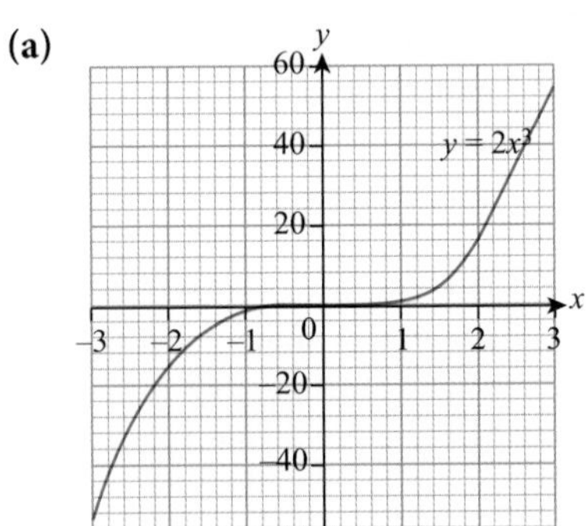

(b)

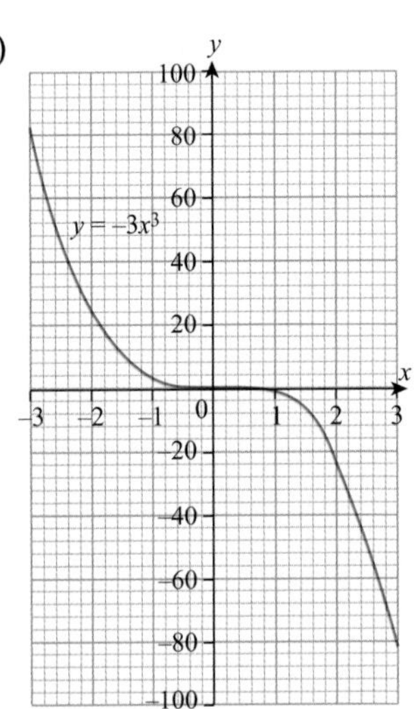

(c)

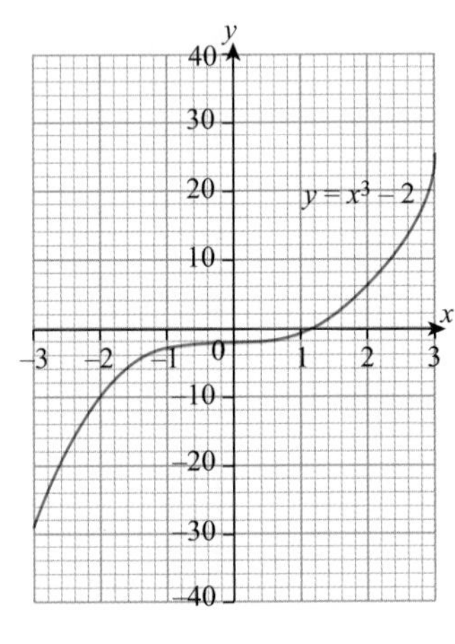

(d)

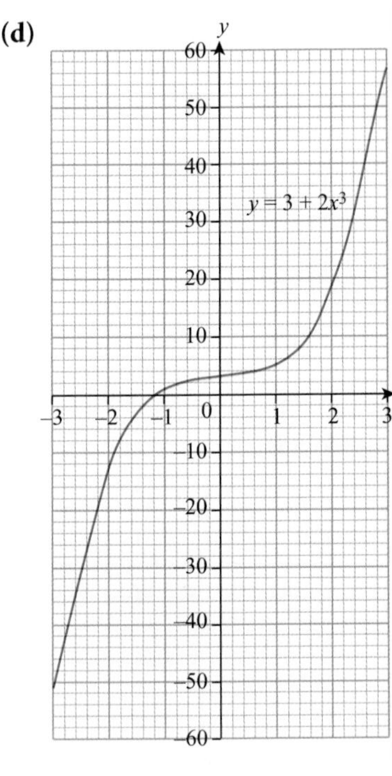

(e)

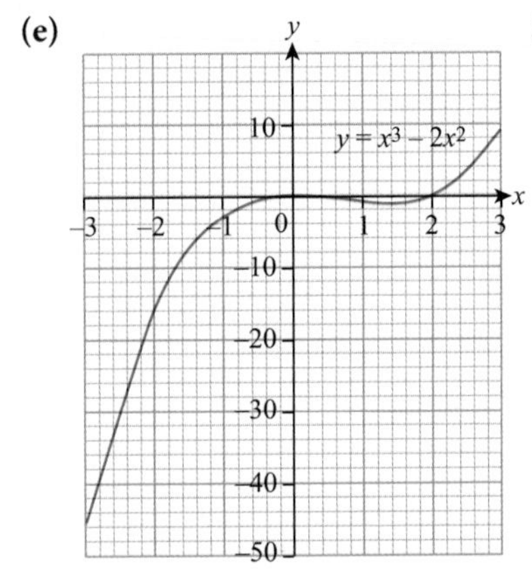

(f)

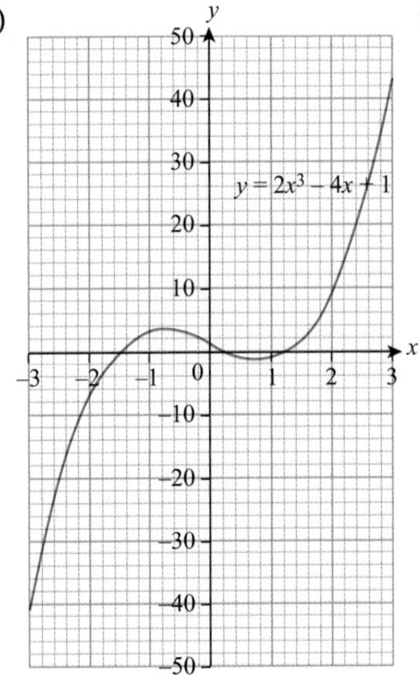

(g)

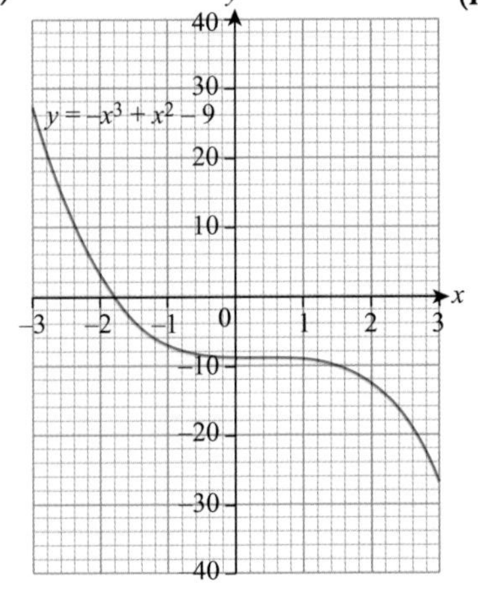

(h)

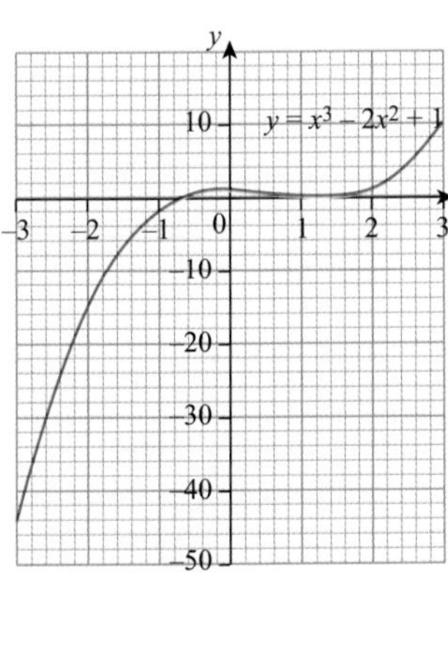

2 (a)

x	−1	−0.5	0	0.5	1	1.5	2	2.5	3	3.5	4	4.5	5
$y = x^3 - 6x^2 + 8x$	−15	−5.6	0	2.6	3	1.9	0	−1.9	−3	−2.6	0	5.6	15

(b)

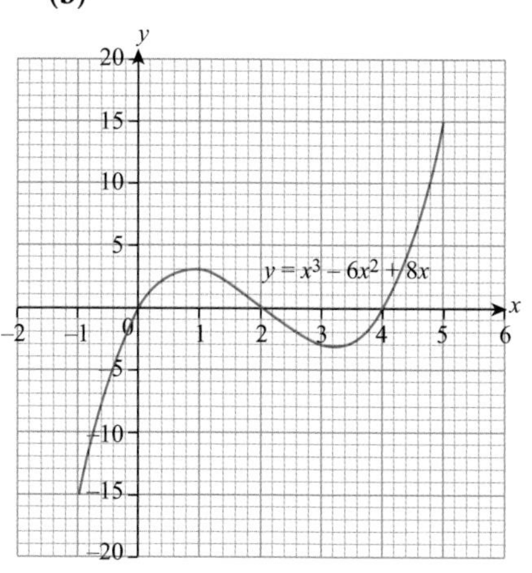

(c) (i) $x = 0$, $x = 2$ and $x = 4$

(ii) $x = 1$, and $x = 4.3$

3 (a)

x	−4	−3	−2	−1	0	1	2	3	4	5	6
$y = \frac{x^3}{10}$	−6.4	−2.7	−0.8	−0.1	0	0.1	0.8	2.7	6.4	12.5	21.6
$y = 6x - x^2$	−55	−27	−16	−7	0	5	8	9	8	5	0

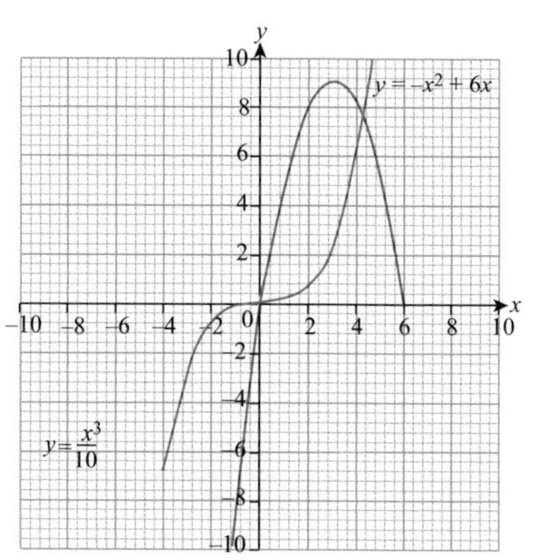

(Please note, only part of the graph is shown here).

(b) $x = 0$ and $x = 4.2$

Exercise 18.7

1

	x	−3	−2	−1	−0.5	−0.2	0	0.2	0.5	1	2	3
(a)	$y = 3 + x^2 - \frac{2}{x}$	12.7	8	6	7.3	13.0	N/A	7.0	−0.8	2	6	11.3
(b)	$y = 3x - \frac{1}{x}$	−8.7	−5.5	−2	0.5	4.4	N/A	−4.4	−0.5	2	5.5	8.7
(c)	$y = -x + x^2 + \frac{2}{x}$	11.3	5	0	−3.3	−9.8	N/A	9.8	3.8	2	3	6.7
(d)	$y = -x^3 - 2x + 1$	34	13	4	N/A	N/A	1	N/A	N/A	−2	−11	−32

Note: The y-values are rounded to 1 decimal place.

(a) $y = 3 + x^2 - \frac{2}{x}$

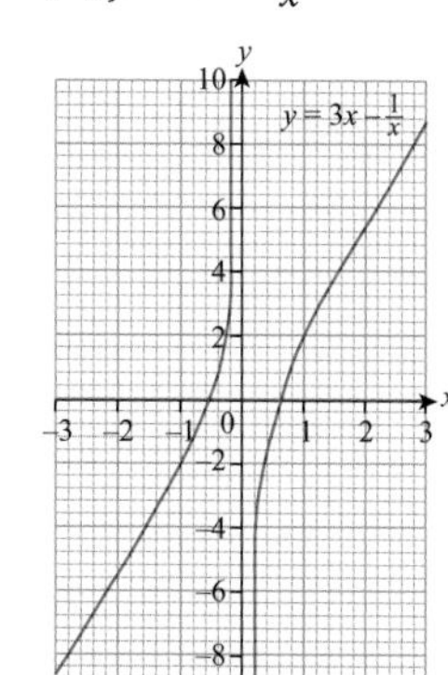

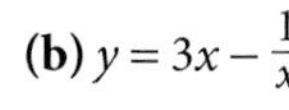

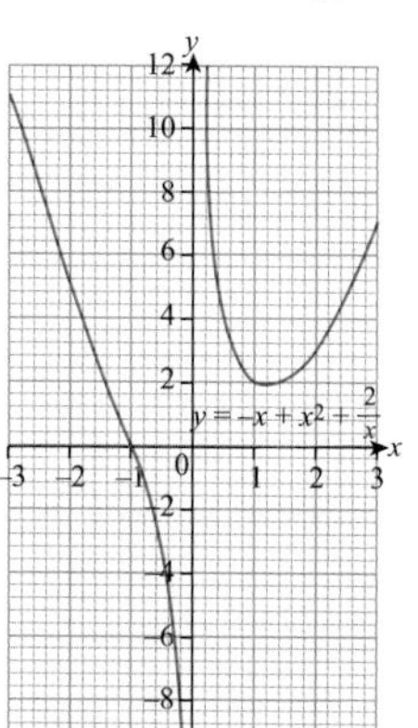

(c) $y = -x + x^2 + \frac{2}{x}$

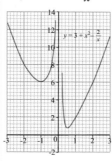

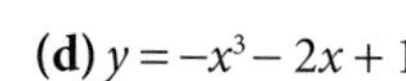

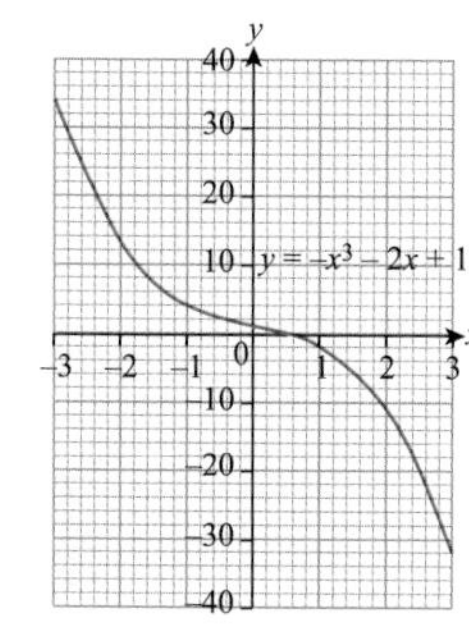

Exercise 18.8

1 (a) (b)

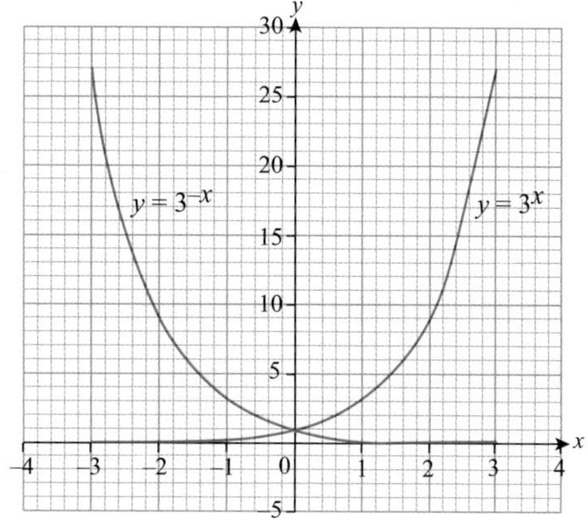

(c) The two graphs are symmetrical about the y-axis.

2 (a) 2 **(b)** 0.6

(c)

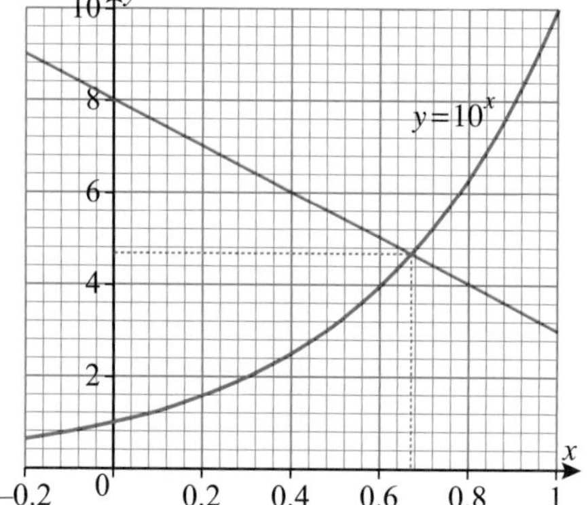

$10^x = 8 - 5x$ when $x = 0.67$
(0.66 – 0.68 also fine)

3 (a) 2 **(b)** 5.3 yrs

(c) 64 **(d)** 20 yrs

4

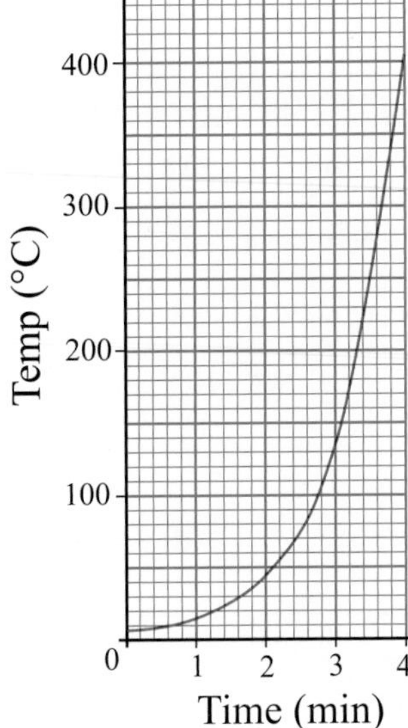

5 (a)

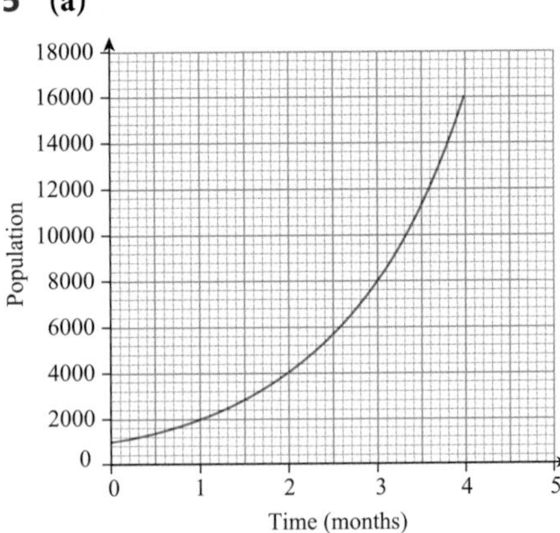

(b) 3.25 months
(c) 64 000

Exercise 18.9

1 (a)

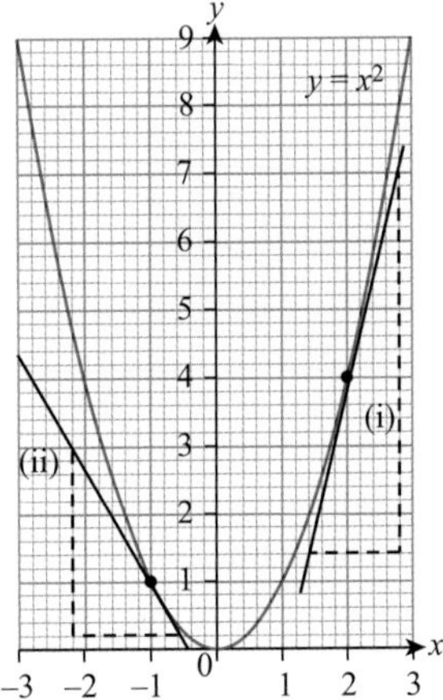

(i) 4
(ii) −2

(b) (−1.5, 2.25)

2 (a)

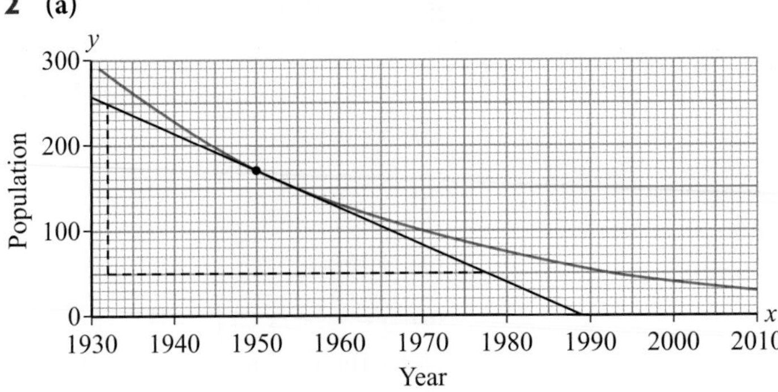

The gradient at point (1950, 170) is −4.3 people per year.

(b) Rate of change of population in the village in 1950.

3 (a)

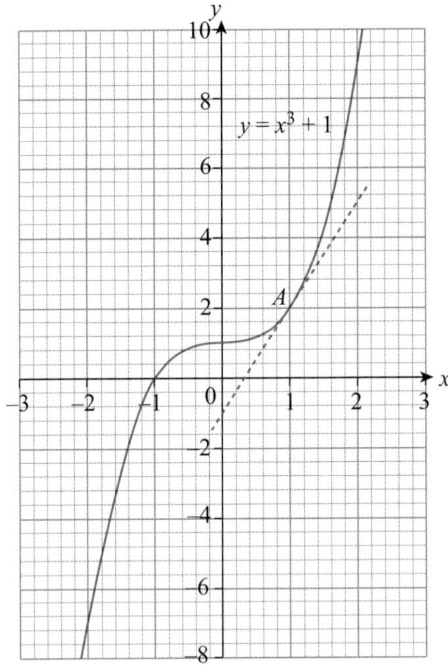

(b) 3

Examination practice

Exam-style questions

1 (a) A: $x = -2$
B: $y = -x$
C: $y = x^2 - 2$
D: $y = 2x + 1$

(b) (i) (−2, 2)
(ii) (3, 7) and (−1, −1)

(c) (−0.35, 0.35)

(d) $\left(-\frac{1}{3}, \frac{1}{3}\right)$ (e) D (f) C

2 **(a)**

x	−2	−1.5	−1	−0.5	0	0.5	1	1.5	2
y	7	5.25	4	3.25	3	3.25	4	5.25	7

(b)

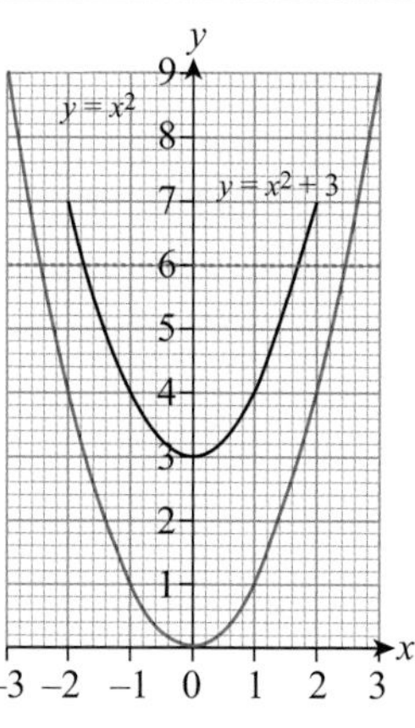

(c) No, x^2 will never equal $x^2 + 3$

(d) **(i)** $x = +2.4$ or -2.4

(ii) $x = +1.7$ or -1.7

3 **(a)** **(i)** $p = -10.$

(ii) $q = 6.3$

(iii) $r = 9.2$

(b)

x	0.6	1	1.5	2	2.5	3	3.5	4	4.5	5
y	−10	−5.9	−3.7	−2.3	−1.1	0.3	1.9	3.8	6.3	9.2

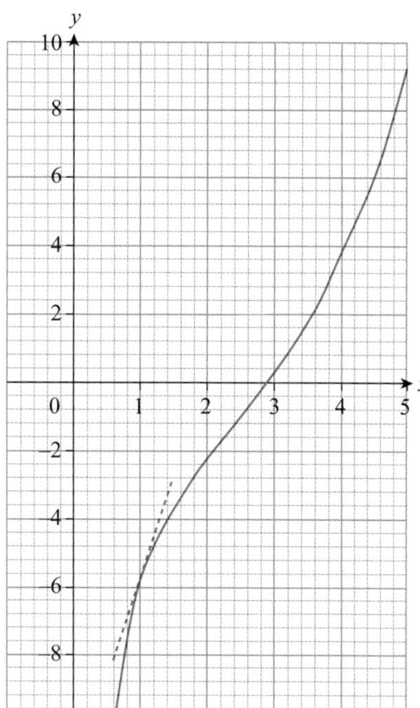

(c) $x = 2.9$

(d) Gradient = 6

4 **(a)** (vi) **(b)** (ii) **(c)** (i)

(d) (iv)

5 **(a)** **(i)** $p = 160, q = 10, r = 2.5$

(ii)

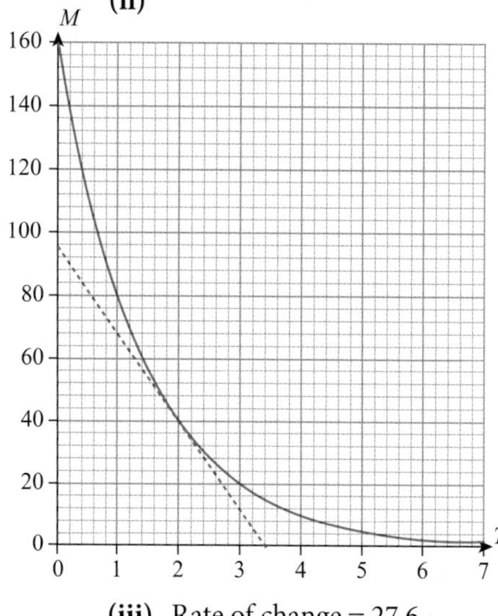

(iii) Rate of change = 27.6

(b) $t = 1$

Past paper questions

1 **(a)** **(i)**

x	−2	−1	0	1	2	3	4	−5
y	−5	1	5	7	7	5	1	5

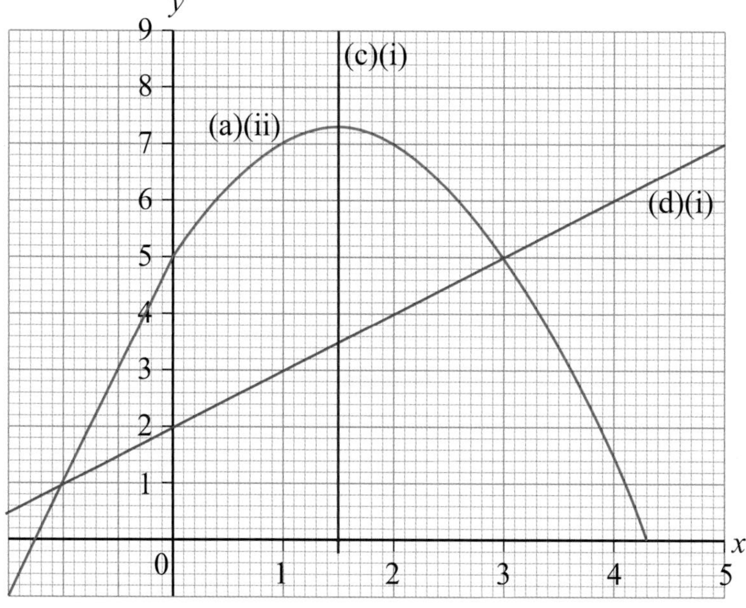

(b) $x = -1.2, x = 4.2$

(c) **(ii)** $x = 1.5$

(d) **(ii)** 1

(iii) $y = x + 2$

* *Cambridge International Examinations bears no responsibility for the example answers to questions taken from its past question papers which are contained in this publication.*

2 **(a)**

x	−3	−2.5	−2	−1.5	−1	−0.5	−0.3	0.3	0.5	1	1.5	2	2.5	3
y	−1	−1.2	−1.5	−2	−3	−6	−10	10	6	3	2	1.5	1.2	1

(b)

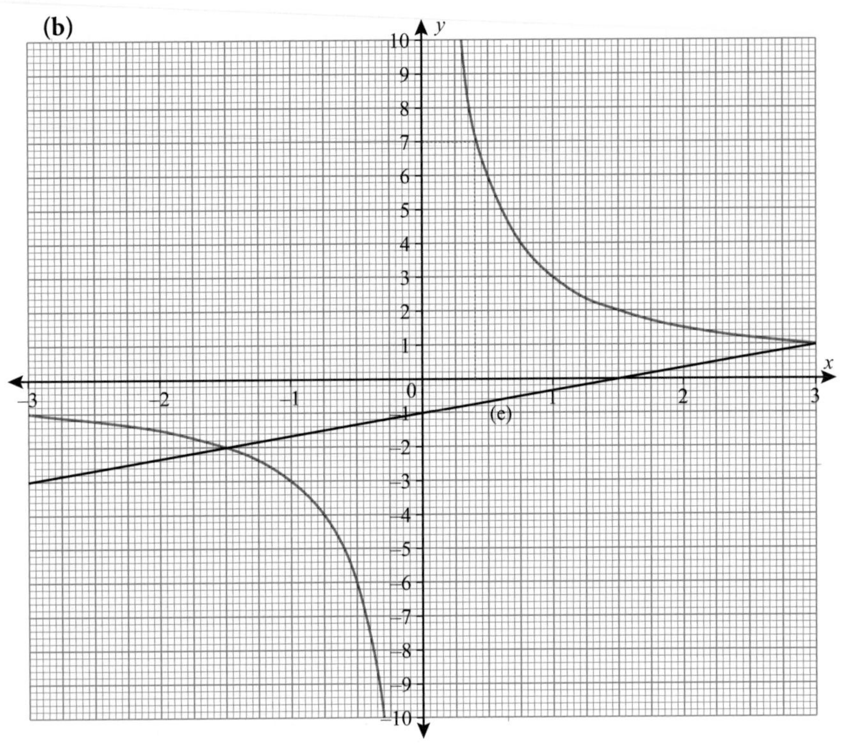

(c) $x = 0.4$ (0.4 – 0.5 fine)

(d)

x	−3	0	3
y	−3	−1	1

(e) (on graph)

(f) $x = -1.5$ and $x = 3$
(−1.5, 2) and (3, 1)

Chapter 19

Exercise 19.1

1 **(a)** None **(b)** *CD*, *HG*
(c) *CD*, *HG* **(d)** *AB*
(e) *AB*, *EF* **(f)** *AB*, *CD*
(g) *CD* **(h)** *AB*, *CD*, *GH*

2

Shape	Number of lines of symmetry
Square	4
Rectangle	2
Equilateral triangle	3
Isosceles triangle	1
Scalene triangle	0
Kite	1
Parallelogram	0
Rhombus	2
Regular pentagon	5
Regular hexagon	6
Regular octagon	8

3

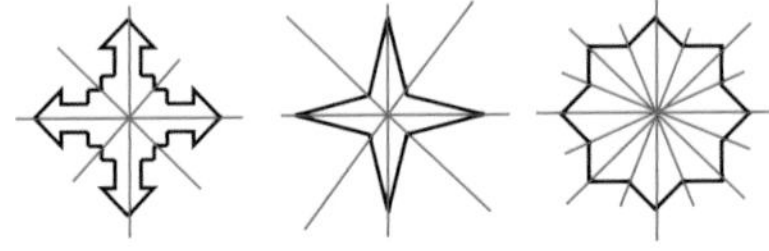

4

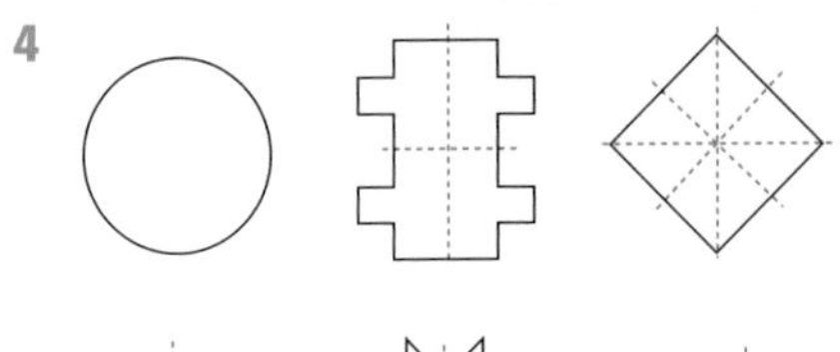

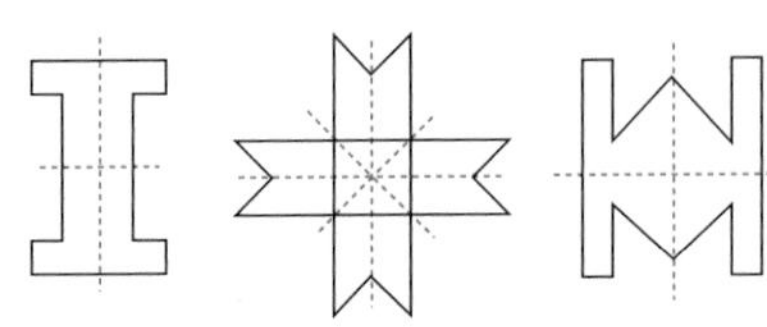

5 Students' own answers but might include names such as Audi, Citroën, Suzuki, Honda and Toyota.

Exercise 19.2

1 **(a)** 2 **(b)** 5 **(c)** 1
(d) 6 **(e)** 2 **(f)** 1
(g) 1 **(h)** 1

2 **(b)**

Regular polygon	Lines of symmetry	Order of rotational symmetry
Triangle	3	3
Quadrilateral	4	4
Pentagon	5	5
Hexagon	6	6
Octagon	8	8
Decagon	10	10

(c) Lines of symmetry = order of rotational symmetry in regular polygons

(d) Number of sides = lines of symmetry = order of rotational symmetry in regular polygons

3 Audi = 1
Citroën = 1
Suzuki = 2
Honda = 1
Toyota = 1

Students' own answers, this is an example.

4 ABCDEFGHIJKLMNOPQRST UVWXYZ
(a) ABCDEMQYUVWY
(b) HIOX (c) HIOSX

5 Students' answers will vary.

Exercise 19.3

1

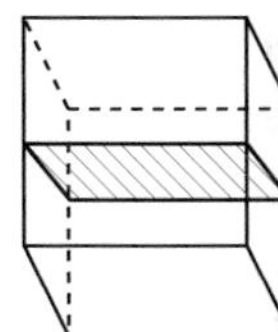

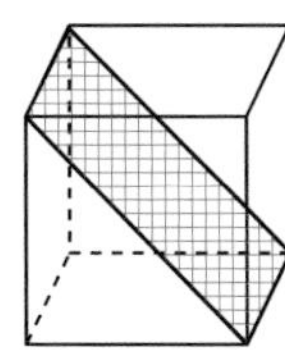

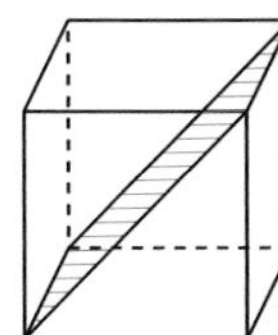

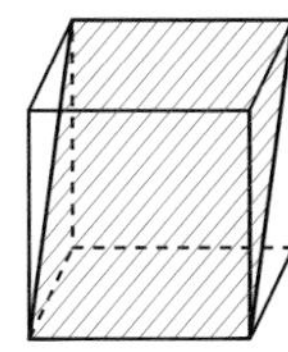

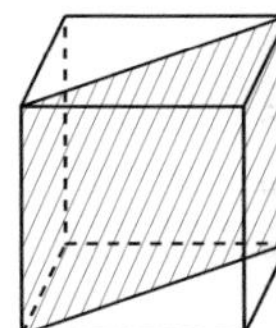

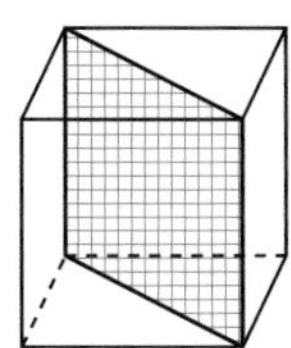

2 (a) 4
(b) infinite
(c) infinite
(d) 12 if base is a right-angled; isosceles triangle
(e) 2
(f) 2
(g) infinite
(h) 7
(i) 2

Exercise 19.4

1 Each has a rotational symmetry of 2

2 (a) Infinite (b) 4
(c) 2 (d) 8
(e) Infinite (f) 1

Exercise 19.5

1 (a) $AB = 5\text{ cm}$ (b) $AB = 30\text{ cm}$
(c) $AB = 2.4\text{ m}$

2 Join OP and construct a line at right angles to OP that will be the chord.

3 O is the centre of both concentric circles.
Construct OX perpendicular to AD.
$\therefore X$ is the mid-point of AD and BC
$\therefore BX = XC$ and $AX = XD$
$AB = AX - BX = XD - XC = CD$

4 (a) 17.3 cm (b) 4.25 m
(c) 31.1 mm

5 13.5 cm

6 $AO = 9\text{ cm}$
Area $AOCB = 108\text{ cm}^2$

7 $x = 43°$

Exercise 19.6

1 (a) $x = 43°, y = 43°, z = 94°$
(b) $x = 124°, y = 34°$
(c) $x = 35°$ (d) $x = 48°$

2 (a) $x = 41.5°$ (b) $x = 38°$

3 (a) Tangents subtended from the same point are equal in length.
(b) (i) $C\hat{A}B = 70°$
(ii) $D\hat{A}C = 20°$
(iii) $A\hat{D}C = 70°$

Exercise 19.7

1 (a) $p = 50°, q = 65°, r = 65°$
(b) $b = 80°$
(c) $c = 30°, d = 55°, e = 45°, f = 45°$
(d) $p = 85°, q = 105°$
(e) $b = 60°$
(f) $x = 94°, y = 62°, z = 24°$
(g) $p = 85°, q = 65°$

2 (a) $A\hat{O}B = 2x$ (b) $O\hat{A}B = 90° - x$
(c) $B\hat{A}T = x$

3 (a) $a = 70°$ (b) $b = 125°$
(c) $c = 60°, d = 60°, e = 80°, f = 40°$

4 (a) $90° - x$ (b) $180° - 2x$
(c) $2x - 90°$

5 (a) Length of side = 30 mm; area = 900 mm^2
(b) 193 mm^2

6 $10\sqrt{3} \approx 17.3\text{ cm}$

Exercise 19.8

1 (a) Curved line (a circle)
(b) a region
(c) a straight and curved line
(d) a straight line
(e) a straight line

2

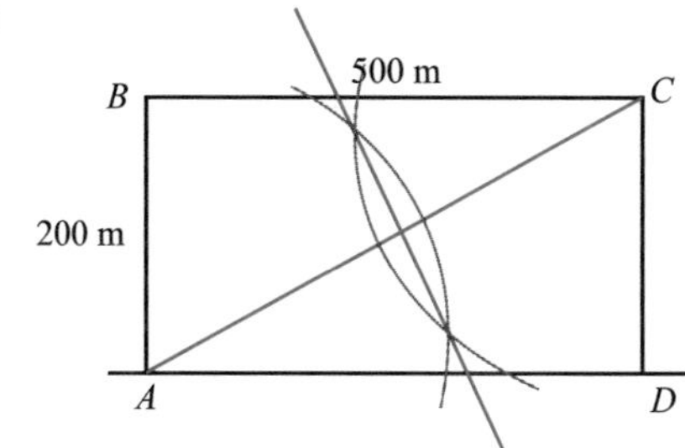

3 (a)

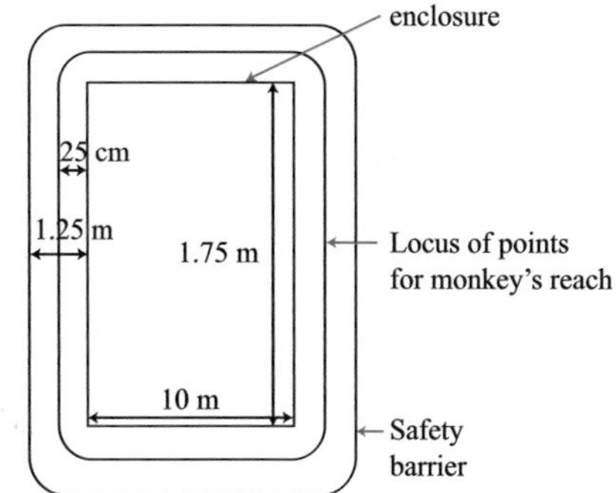

(b) If you consider a very tall human, their reach might be as much as 1 m. So, the barier should be at least 1m from the monkey's reach, which means 1.25 m from the enclosure.

4

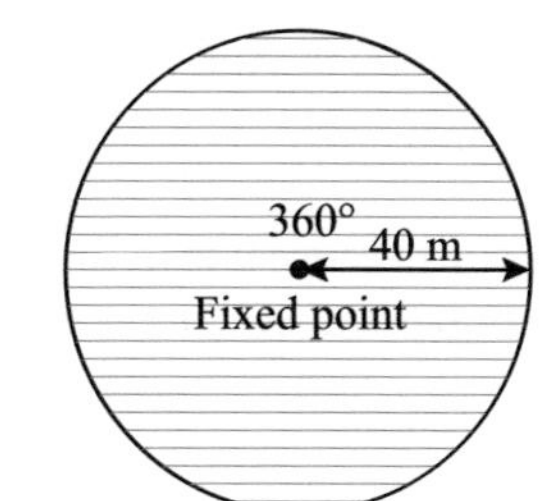

5

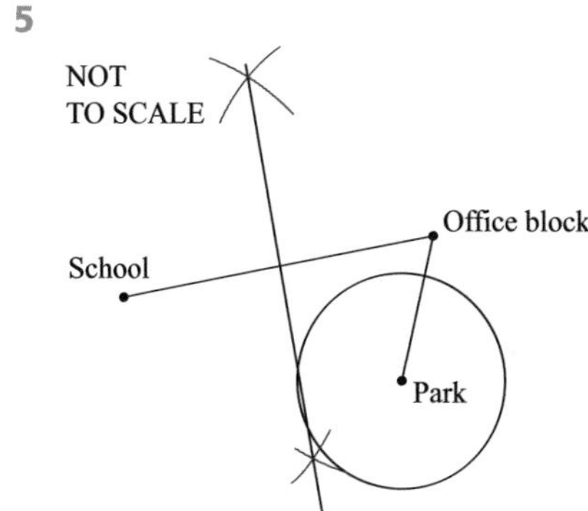

6

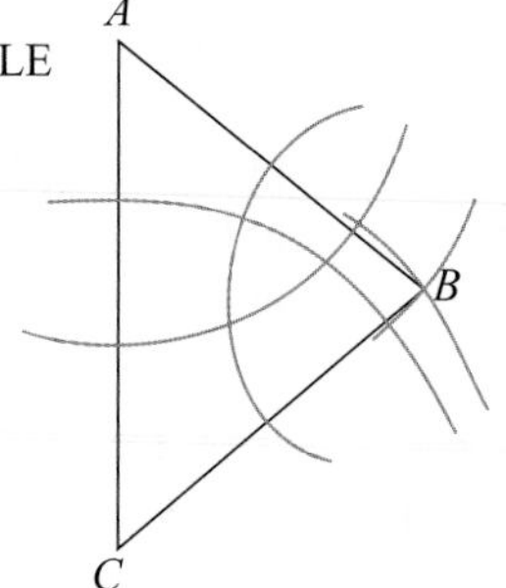

7 (a)

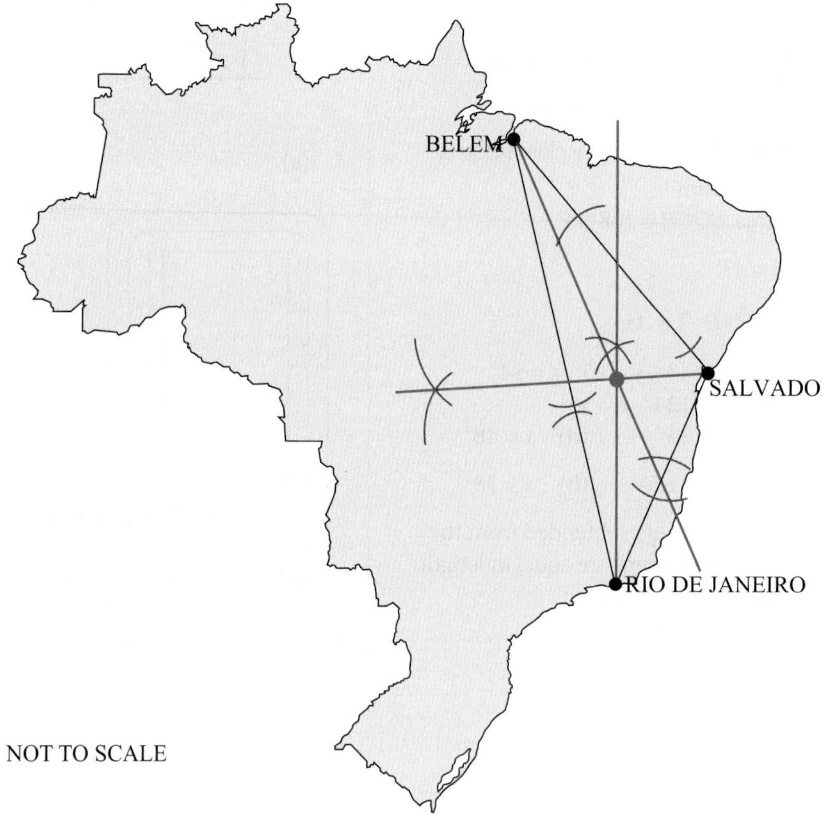

(b) No, because it is in the middle of brazil.

8 NOT TO SCALE

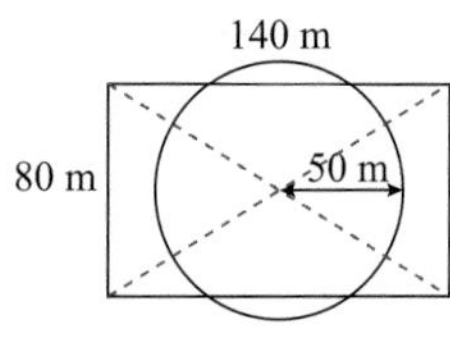

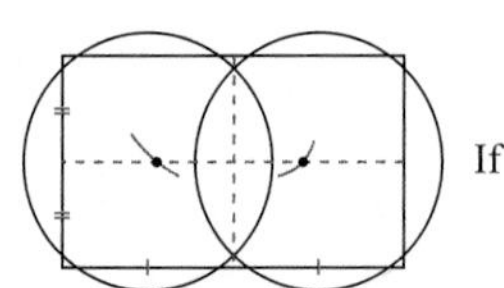

9 NOT TO SCALE

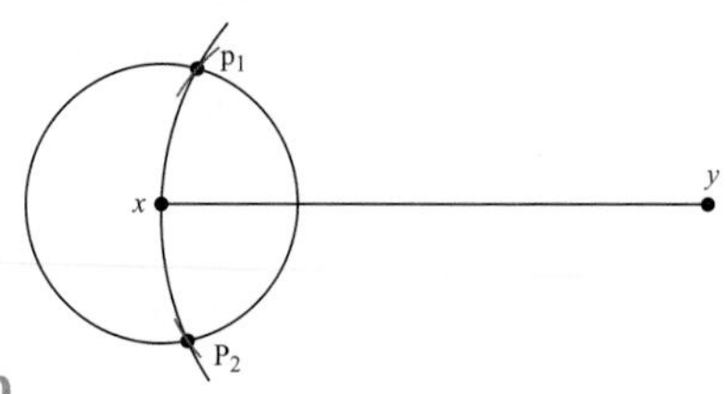

10

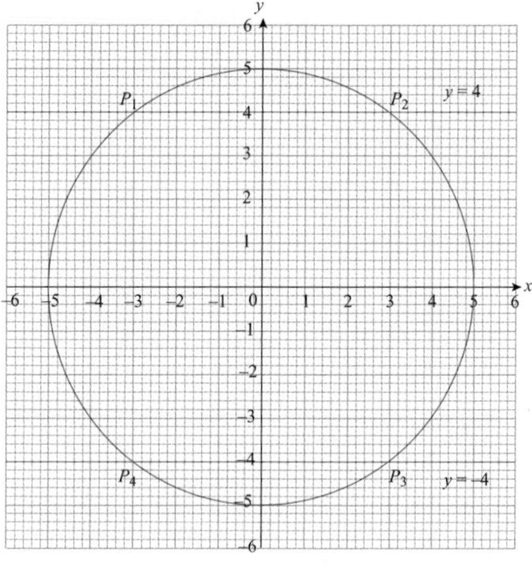

(a) $y = 4, y = -4$

(b) $\sqrt{x^2 + y^2} = 5$

(c) Four

Examination practice

Exam-style questions

1 **(a)** and **(e)**

2 Order 3

3 $a = 90°, b = 53°, c = 90°, d = 53°$

4 **(a) (i)**

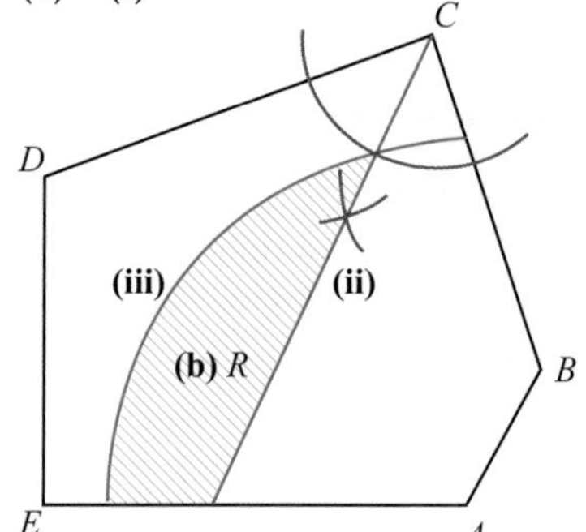

Past paper questions*

1 (a) 2

(b)

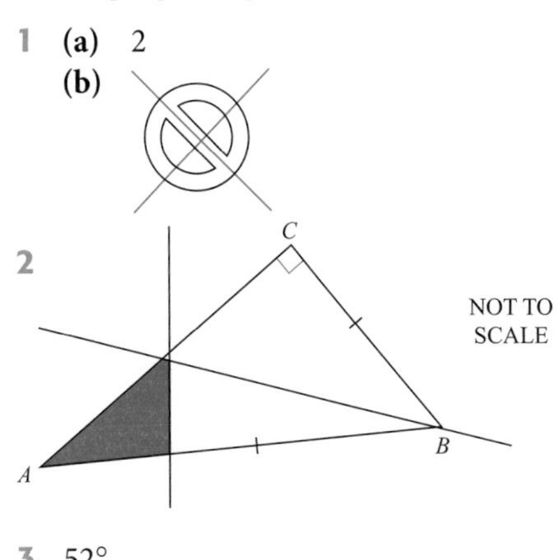

2

3 52°

Chapter 20

Exercise 20.1

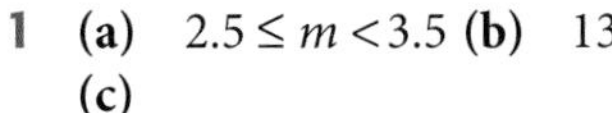

1 (a) $2.5 \le m < 3.5$ (b) 13

(c)

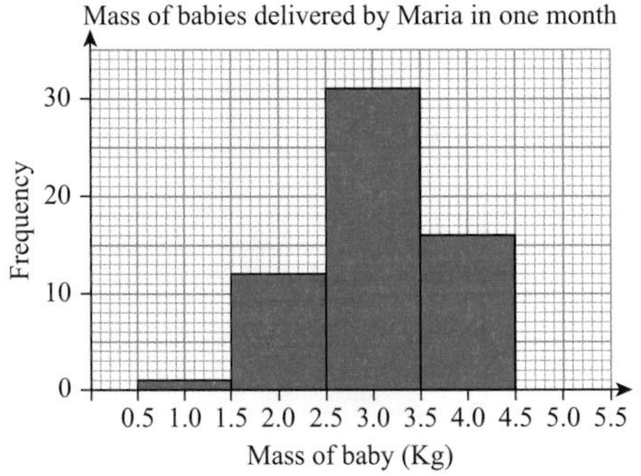

2 (a) 142 (b) $2 \le t < 4$ min

(c)

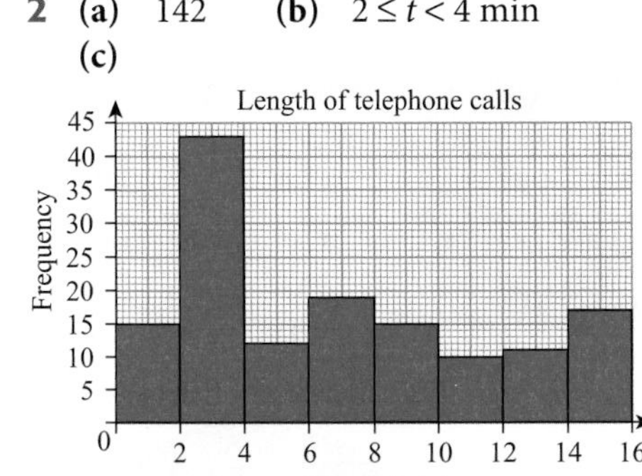

(d)

Class interval	$0 \le t < 4$	$4 \le t < 8$	$8 \le t < 12$	$12 \le t < 16$
Frequency	58	31	25	28

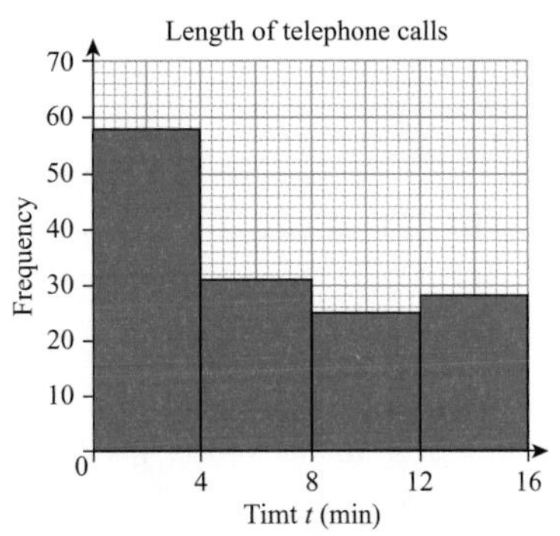

(e) The smaller the class intervals the more detailed the information represented. The larger class intervals give a good general picture of the data.

3 (a)

Class interval	Frequency
$28.5 \le l < 29.0$	2
$29.0 \le l < 29.5$	1
$29.5 \le l < 30.0$	6
$30.0 \le l < 30.5$	5
$30.5 \le l < 31.0$	2
$31.0 \le l < 31.5$	6
$31.5 \le l < 32.0$	3
$32.0 \le l < 32.5$	5

(b)

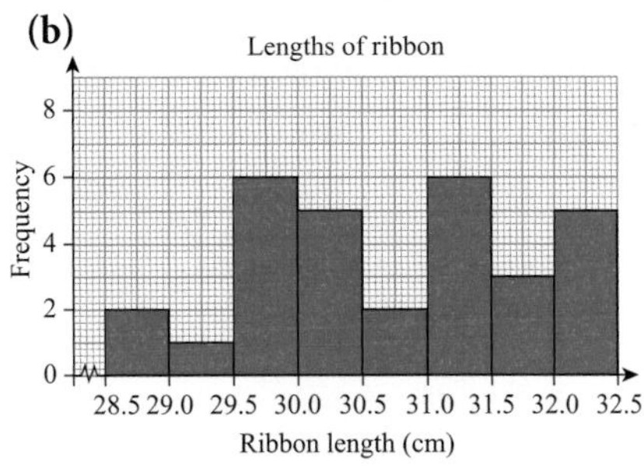

(c) Not very accurate; only 11 out of 30 were within 0.5 cm of 30 cm.

4

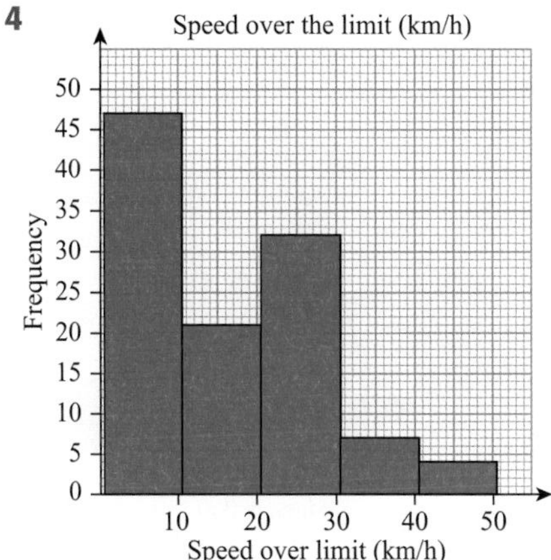

5

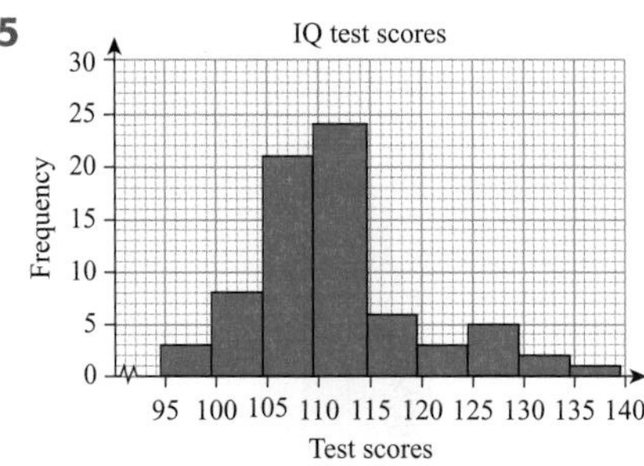

Exercise 20.2

1 (a)

No. of sweets (n)	Frequency (f)	Class width	Frequency density
$100 \le n < 200$	18	100	0.18
$200 \le n < 250$	18	50	0.36
$250 \le n < 300$	32	50	0.64
$300 \le n < 350$	31	50	0.62
$350 \le n < 400$	21	50	0.42
$400 \le n < 500$	20	100	0.2

(b)

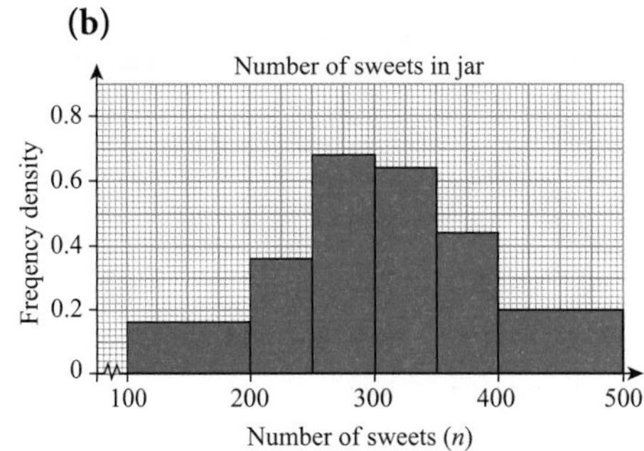

* *Cambridge International Examinations bears no responsibility for the example answers to questions taken from its past question papers which are contained in this publication.*

2

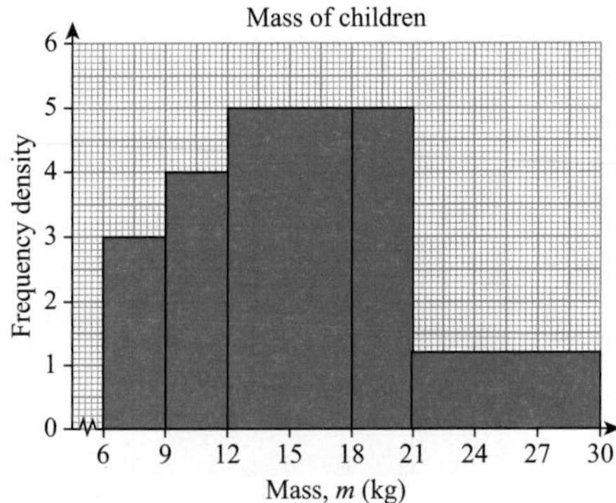

3

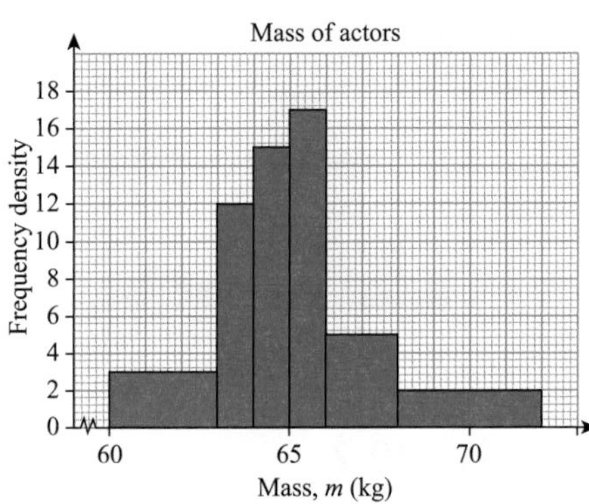

4 (a) 80 (b) 73 (c) 7
(d) Body fat is too low for intense physical activity.
(e) No – the expectation is that soldiers are physically active and therefore keep their body fat at a satisfactory level.

5 (a) No – frequency density and not frequency given.
(b) Yes – one can see most of the bars are with the boundaries of the speed limits.
(c) (i)

Speed (km/h)	Frequency	Class width	Frequency density
$0 \le s < 50$	240	50	4.8
$50 \le s < 65$	320	15	21.3
$65 \le s < 80$	500	15	33.3
$80 \le s < 95$	780	15	52
$95 \le s < 110$	960	15	64
$110 \le s < 125$	819	15	54.6
$125 \le s < 180$	638	55	11.6

(ii) 240 below the minimum speed limit
(d) 15%

Exercise 20.3

1 (a)

Height in cm	6–15	16–20	21–25	26–40
Number of plants	3	7	10	5
Cumulative frequency	3	10	20	25

(b) 21–25 cm
(c)

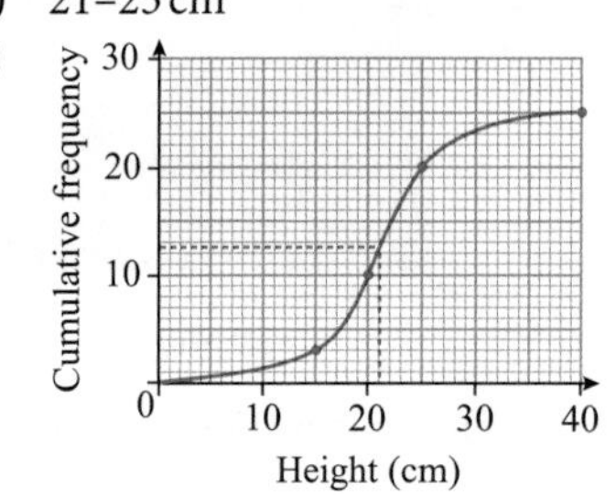

Median = 21 cm

2 (a) \$36.25
(b) $p = 12, q = 24, r = 35$
(c)

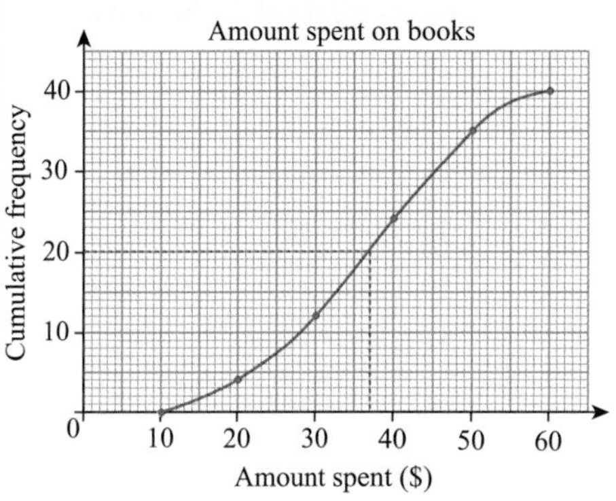

(d) Median amount spent \$37

3 (a)

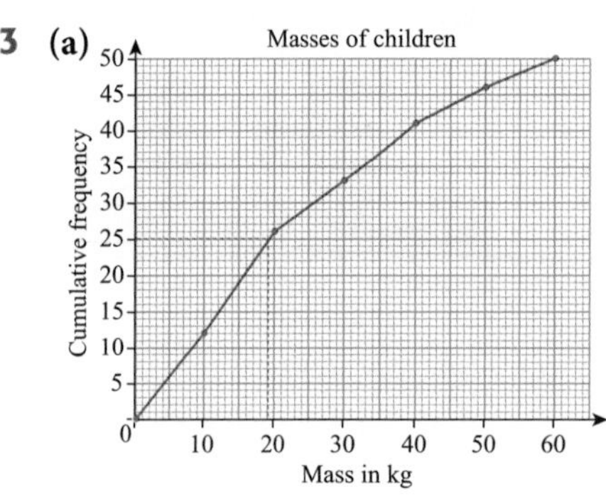

(b) 19 kg (c) 24

Exercise 20.4

1 (a) 30.0 cm (b) 27.5 cm (c) 33.5 cm
(d) 6 cm (e) 29.5 cm

2 (a) (i) Paper 1: 48% Paper 2: 60%
(ii) Paper 1: 28% Paper 2: 28%
(iii) Paper 1: 52% Paper 2: 66%
(b) Paper 1: >66% Paper 2: >79%

3 (a) (i) 45 kg (ii) 330 girls
(b) 10%

4 (a)

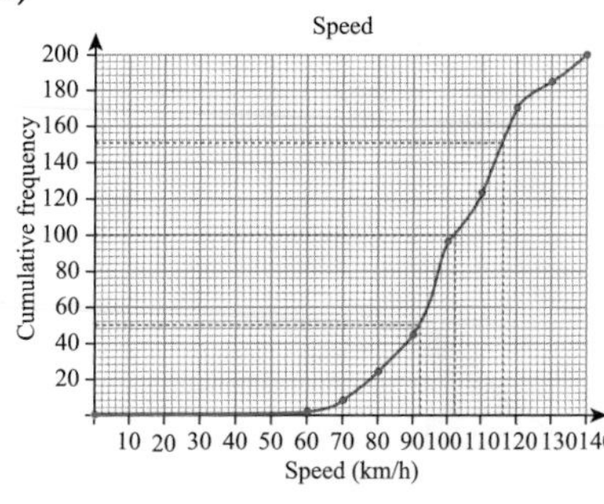

(b) Median = 102 km/h
$Q_1 = 92$ Speed km/h
$Q_3 = 116$
(c) IQR = 24 km/h (d) 7.5%

Examination practice

Exam-style questions

1 (a)

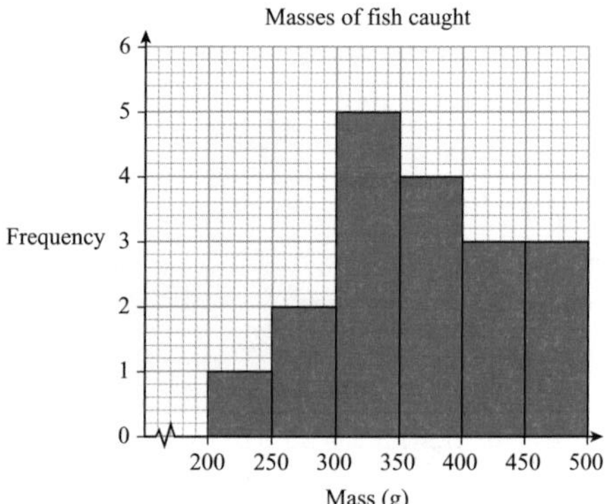

(b)

Mass (m) in grams	Number of fish	Classification
$m < 300$	3	Small
$300 \le m < 400$	9	Medium
$m \ge 400$	6	Large

(c) Classification of fish caught

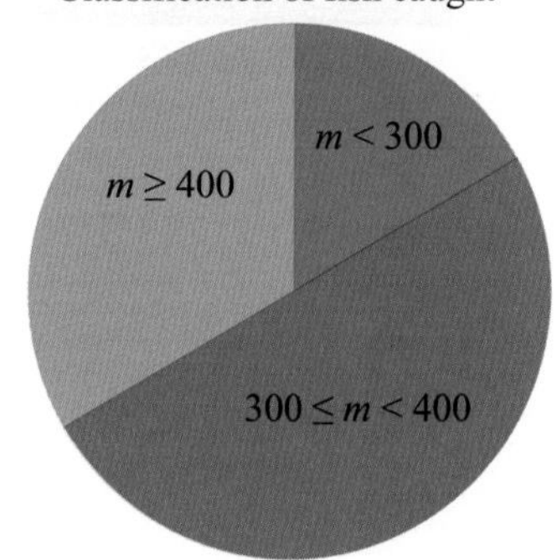

Total number of fish caught = 18

$$\frac{3}{18}\times 360° = 60°$$

$$\frac{9}{18}\times 360° = 180°$$

$$\frac{6}{18}\times 360° = 120°$$

2

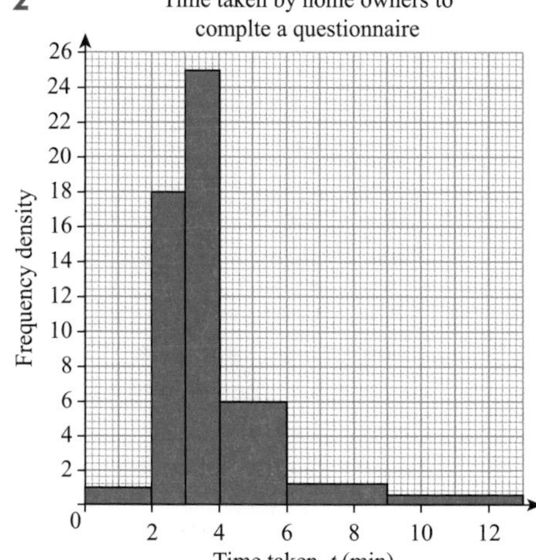

Past paper questions

1 **(a)** **(i)**

Price ($)	Frequency
$0 \le x < 2000$	3
$2000 \le x < 4000$	5
$4000 \le x < 6000$	6
$6000 \le x < 8000$	4
$8000 \le x < 10\,000$	2

(ii)

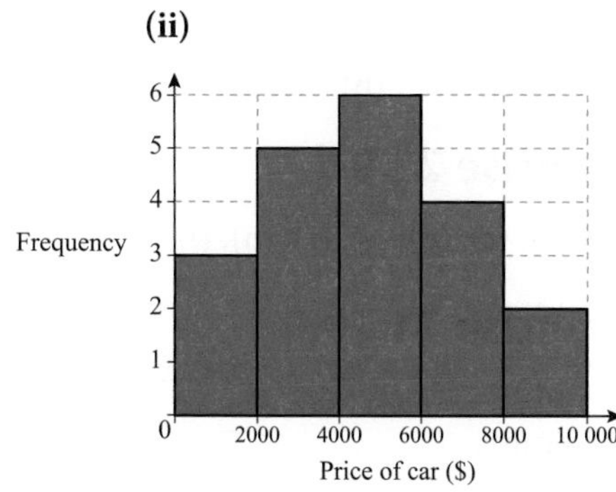

2 **(a)**

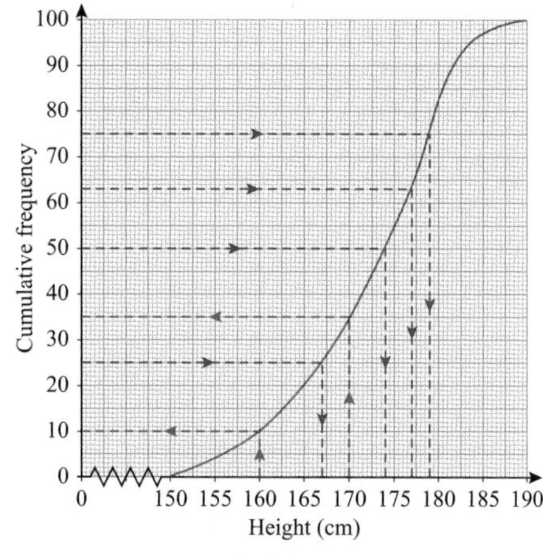

(i) 174 cm (174–174.25 is acceptable)
(ii) 167 cm
(iii) 12 cm
(iv) 37

(b) **(i)**

Height (h cm)	Frequency
$150 < h \le 160$	10
$160 < h \le 170$	25
$170 < h \le 180$	47
$180 < h \le 190$	18

(ii) 172.3 cm (172 cm would be acceptable)

Unit 6

Chapter 21

Exercise 21.1

1 **(a)** 1 : 1 **(b)** 1 : 5 **(c)** 25 : 3
(d) 3 : 10 **(e)** 3 : 20 **(f)** 1 : 5

2 **(a)** 12 : 5 **(b)** 5 : 12

3 **(a)** 2 : 3 **(b)** 3 : 4
(c) 11 : 16 **(d)** 1 : 2

4 **(a)** 1 : 12 **(b)** 1 : 2 **(c)** 1 : 8
(d) 7 : 6 **(e)** 10 : 3 **(f)** 5 : 12

5 **(a)** 1 : 10 **(b)** 1 : 100
(c) 100 : 1 **(d)** 1 : 1 000
(e) 1 000 : 1 **(f)** 1 : 60

6 **(a)** 1 : 2 **(b)** 1 : 8 **(c)** 3 : 8
(d) 3 : 25 **(e)** 3 : 200 **(f)** 1 : 20
(g) 8 : 5 **(h)** 2 : 15

Exercise 21.2

1 **(a)** $x = 9$ **(b)** $y = 24$
(c) $y = 2$ **(d)** $x = 6$
(e) $x = 176$ **(f)** $y = 65$
(g) $x = 35$ **(h)** $y = 180$
(i) $y = 1\,400$ **(j)** $x = 105$
(k) $x = 1.25$ **(l)** $y = 4$

2 **(a)** $x = 15$ **(b)** $x = 8$
(c) $y = 20$ **(d)** $x = 2.4$
(e) $x = 0.6$ **(f)** $y = 3.25$
(g) $x = 5.6$ **(h)** $y = 7.2$

3 **(a)** false **(b)** true
(c) false **(d)** false
(e) true

4 **(a)** 1 g **(b)** 1.33 g **(c)** 7 : 5
(d) 3 : 5

5 **(a)** 18 : 25 : 5 **(b)** 1.67 g
(c) 4.17 g

6 **(a)** 20 ml **(b)** 2.5 ml

7 15 750 kg

Exercise 21.3

1 **(a)** 40 : 160 **(b)** 1 200 : 300
(c) 15 : 35 **(d)** 12 : 48
(e) 150 : 450 **(f)** 22 : 16
(g) 220 : 80 **(h)** 230 : 460 : 1 610

2 0.3 l = 300 ml
3 Josh gets 27 Ahmed gets 18
4 Annie gets $50, Andrew gets $66.67 and Amina gets $83.33
5 Students should draw a 16 cm line with 6 cm marked and 10 cm marked.

6

	N (kg)	P (kg)	K (kg)
(a)	0.25	0.375	0.375
(b)	1.25	1.875	1.875
(c)	5	7.5	7.5
(d)	6.25	9.375	9.375

7 1.8 m : 2.25 m : 1.35 m

8 37.5 cm (length) by 22.5 cm (width) rectangle

37.5 cm
22.5 cm

9 1200 men

** Cambridge International Examinations bears no responsibility for the example answers to questions taken from its past question papers which are contained in this publication.*

Exercise 21.4

1

	(i)	(ii)
(a)	1 : 200	0.005 : 1
(b)	1 : 250	0.004 : 1
(c)	1 : 250 000	0.000 004 : 1
(d)	1 : 200 000	0.000 0005 : 1
(e)	1 : 28.6	0.035 : 1
(f)	1 : 16 700 000	0.000 000 06 : 1

2 (a) 4 m (b) 6 m
(c) 14 m (d) 48 m

3 (a) 0.0012 m = 0.12 cm = 1.2 mm
(b) 0.0003 km = 300 mm
(c) 0.0024 km = 2400 mm
(d) 0.00151 km = 1510 mm

4 (a) 100 mm × 250 mm
(b) 80 mm × 200 mm

5 (a) 1740 km (b) 1640 km
(c) 1520 km

6 (a) 1 cm = 150 cm = 1.5 m
Answers will vary due to measuring variations.
(b) (i) 8.4 m
(ii) 5.85 m
(iii) 2.7 m
(iv) 3.15 m
(c) (i) 27.92 m^2
(ii) 20.88 m^2
(iii) 26.46 m^2
(d) 3.94 m^2
(e) $162.49

Exercise 21.5

1 (a) 2.4 kg/£ (b) 0.12 l/km
(c) $105/night (d) 0.25 km/min
(e) 27 students/teacher
(f) 3 hours/hole dug

2 (a) 9600 t (b) 48 000 t

3 (a) 120 l (b) 840 l

4 7.4 minutes
5 12.75 km

6 (a) 805 km (b) 76.67 km

7 (a) 312.5 km (b) 3000 km

8 110 km/h
9 18.7 km/h

10 (a) 37.578 km/h (b) 40.236 s

Exercise 21.6

1 (a) 700 m (b) 7 min
(c) 09:07 and 09:21
(d) Going to the supermarket

2 (a) 45 min (b) 17:54 (c) 17:00

3 (a)

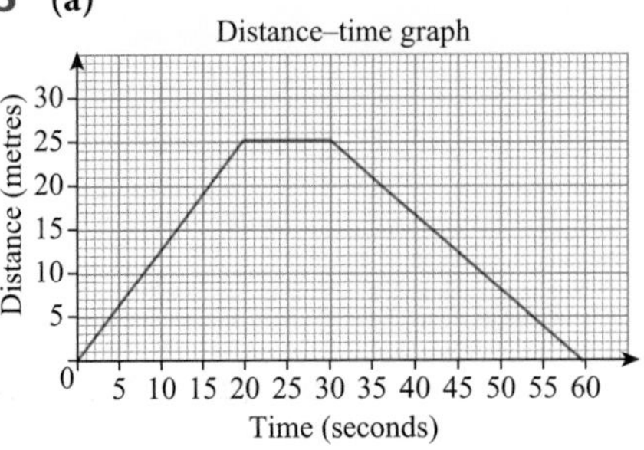

(b) 15 m (c) 5 m

Exercise 21.7

1 (a) and (b)
Answers will vary, examples:
(from left to right)
- The object is moving in the direction of y at a constant speed. Example: a helium-filled children's balloon released in a large hall (with no breeze).
- The object is stationary. Example: a parked car.
- The object is moving in the direction of y at a constant speed, then suddenly changes direction, moving at a much faster speed. Example: a squash ball travelling towards the court wall, hitting it then bouncing back.
- The object is moving very quickly in the direction of y at a constant speed, then stops and is stationary for a while, then continues in the same direction at the same speed as before, then stops and is stationary again. Example: a train travelling from Valladolid to Madrid, stopping at Segovia on the way.
- The object travels slowly at first, then very quickly, then slowly again in the direction of y. Example: an Olympic runner doing interval training.
- The object is moving at a constant speed in the opposite direction to y then it suddenly changes direction and travels at a slightly faster speed in the direction of y.

2 (a) 6 min (b) 10 km/h
(c) 3 min (d) 3.33 m/s

3 (a) For the first 50 minutes the taxi travelled a distance of 10 km at 12 km/h, then was stationary for 50 minutes then took 20 minutes to return to starting point at 30 km/h. The taxi was then stationary for 40 minutes, then travelled 5 km in 40 minutes at a speed of 7.5 km/h and was then stationary for 40 minutes.
(b) 130 minutes – the graph is horizontal.
(c) 25 km
(d) (i) 12 km/h (ii) 10 km/h
(iii) 6 km/h (iv) 6.25 km/h

4 (a) Other questions are possible, these are just examples: What is the total time taken to attain a height of 16 m?
When was the helicopter descending?
When was the helicopter ascending?
During what time period was the vertical speed the greatest?
At what speed was the helicopter travelling between 2 and 4 seconds?

Exercise 21.8

1 (a) 1 500 m
(b) 2 m/s
(c) He was stationary.
(d) 0.5 m/s

2 (a) 2 m/s^2 (b) 35 m (c) 3.5 m/s

3 (a) 1 m/s^2 (b) 100 m (c) 15 m/s

Exercise 21.9

1 (a), (c), (d), (e), (f), (h), (i)

Exercise 21.10

1 $6.75
2 60 min
3 70 s
4 172.5 kg
5 10.5 km

6 (a) 320 g flour, 64 g sultanas, 80 g margarine, 99 ml milk, 32 g sugar, 16 g salt
(b) 4 : 1

7 250 g

8 (a) 550 km (b) 17.31

9 (a) 13 ft (b) 13.12 ft
(c) (i) 4 m (ii) 6.5 m
(d) (i) 30 ft (ii) 6.59 m
(e) 6.49 m

Exercise 21.11

1

Number of people	120	150	200	300	400
Days the water will last	40	32	24	16	12

2 (a) 8 days (b) 2 days

3 (a) 100 (b) 25 (c) 8
(d) 250 cm

4 722.86 km/h

5 3 h 36 min

Exercise 21.12

1 (a) $y = \frac{4.5}{x}$ (b) $y = \frac{62.5}{x}$
(c) $y = \frac{2}{x}$ (d) $y = \frac{0.28}{x}$
(e) $y = \frac{4.8}{x}$

2 (a) $k = 5120$ (b) $y = 10$
(c) $y = 23.70$ (d) $x = 5.98$

3

x	0.1	0.25	0.5	0.0625
y	25	4	1	64

4

x	25	100	3.70	1
y	10	5	26	50

5 (a) 2.5 (b) 1000 (c) 0.125

6 400

7 6.4

8 p and q are not inversely proportional because $p \times q$ is not constant.

9 60

10 (a) false (b) false (c) true

11 5 h

12 16 666.7 N (16.7 kN to 3sf)

13

m	3	5
P	24	40

n	2	8
P	24	6

Exercise 21.13

1 56

2 24

3 105

4 38

5 40 cm long and 25 cm wide

Examination practice

Exam-style questions

1 Sandra receives 12 marshmallows

2 Raja receives $40

3 300 cm = 3 m

4 (a) 1.6 kg raisins (b) 1.2 kg dates

5 960 males

6 9 cups

7 (a) 90 km/h (b) 18 km/h^2
(c) 15 km (d) $2\frac{1}{2}$ min
(e) 18 km/h (f) 17.5 km

Past paper questions*

1 $p = 16$

2 $y = 3.84$ ($3\frac{21}{25}$ also fine)

3 30 m

4 (a) 320 cm^3 (b) 567 cm^2

5 15 km

Chapter 22

Exercise 22.1

1 (a) $4x = 32$, $x = 8$ (b) $12x = 96$, $x = 8$
(c) $x + 12 = 55$, $x = 43$ (d) $x + 13 = 25$, $x = 12$
(e) $x - 6 = 14$, $x = 20$ (f) $9 - x = -5$, $x = 14$
(g) $\frac{x}{7} = 2.5$, $x = 17.5$ (h) $\frac{28}{x} = 4$, $x = 7$

2 (a) $y = 3$ (b) $y = 12$
(c) $y = 46$ (d) $y = 70$

3 (a) $x = 13$ (b) $x = 9$
(c) $x = 2$ (d) $x = 11$

Exercise 22.2

1 Daughter = 15.5 years and father = 46.5 years

2 Silvia has 70 marbles; Jess has 350 marbles.

3 Kofi has $51.25 and Soumik has $46.25

4 $250 and $500

5 9 years

6 Width = 15 cm and length = 22 cm

7 48 km

8 Pam = 12 years and Amira = 24 years

9 6.30 p.m.

10 50 km

Exercise 22.3

1 (a) $x = m - bp$ (b) $x = pr - n$
(c) $x = \frac{m}{4}$ (d) $x = \sqrt{\frac{c+b}{a}}$
(e) $x = \frac{d - 2b - c}{m}$
(f) $x = 3by$ (g) $x = \frac{p}{m}$
(h) $x = \frac{np}{m}$ (i) $x = \frac{mk}{2}$
(j) $x = \frac{20}{p}$

2 (a) $x = \frac{m - 3y}{3}$ (b) $x = \frac{4t - c}{4}$
(c) $x = \frac{y + 15}{3}$ (d) $x = \frac{5}{2}$
(e) $x = \frac{m}{4c} + y$ (f) $x = 2r - \frac{a}{\pi r}$

3 $m = \frac{E}{c^2}$

4 $R = \frac{100I}{PT}$

5 $m = \frac{2k}{v^2}$

6 $b = \frac{2A}{h} - a$

7 $h = \frac{3V}{A}$

8 $h = \frac{3V}{\pi r^2}$

9 $B = 0.68$

10 $h = 3.07$

11 (a) 38 °C
(b) 100 °C
(c) 0 °C

12 (a) 1.49
(b) 4.37
(c) 0.28

* *Cambridge International Examinations bears no responsibility for the example answers to questions taken from its past question papers which are contained in this publication.*

Exercise 22.4

1 (a) $x=\sqrt{\frac{m}{a}}$ (b) $x=\sqrt{m+y}$
(c) $x=\sqrt{n-m}$ (d) $x=\sqrt{ay}$
(e) $x=\sqrt{\frac{ac}{b}}$ (f) $x=\sqrt{a+b^2}$
(g) $x=\sqrt{\frac{n}{m}}$ (h) $x=\frac{m^2}{y}$
(i) $x=\frac{a^2}{5}$ (j) $x=y^2+z$
(k) $x=(y+z)^2$ (l) $x=\left(\frac{c}{a-b}\right)^2$
(m) $x=\left(\frac{m-a}{-b}\right)^2$ (n) $x=\frac{y^2+1}{3}$
(o) $x=\frac{y-a^2}{2}$ (p) $x=\frac{(a-y)^2+b}{4}$

2 (a) $a=\frac{b-x}{1-x}$ (b) $a=\frac{L}{B+1+C}$
(c) $a=\frac{5b}{b-1}$ (d) $a=\frac{x(y+1)}{y-1}$
(e) $a=\frac{3-y}{y-1}$ (f) $a=\sqrt{\frac{2}{m-n}}$

3 $c=\sqrt{\frac{E}{m}}$

4 $a=\sqrt{c^2-b^2}$

5 $\frac{2y}{1-y}$

6 $s=\sqrt{A}$

7 (a) $y=\frac{2x}{3}+2$ (b) $y=3x-c$
(c) $\frac{4x+z}{3}$
(d) $y=\frac{2(b-a)}{3}$

8 (a) $E=49$ (b) $v=\sqrt{\frac{2E}{m}}$

9 (a) $V=2\,010\,619\text{ cm}^3$
(b) $r=\sqrt{\frac{V}{\pi h}}$

10 (a) $A=1.13\text{ m}^2$ (b) $A=1.13\text{ m}^2$
(c) $d=\sqrt{\frac{4A}{\pi}}$

Exercise 22.5

1

	(i) f(2) =	(ii) f(−2) =	(iii) f(0.5) =	(iv) f(0) =
(a)	8	−4	3.5	2
(b)	8	−12	0.5	−2
(c)	3	−5	0	−1
(d)	11	11	3.5	3
(e)	0	0	−0.75	0
(f)	6	−10	−1.875	−2

2 (a) −5 (b) −1
(c) 5 (d) −17

3 (a) 0 (b) −4
(c) 5 (d) −3.9375

4 (a) 0 (b) −9
(c) −2 (d) 5

5 (a) 16 (b) 16 (c) 1

6 $x=\frac{4}{3}$

7 $x=\frac{1}{3}$

8 $x=6$

9 (a) $x=-2$ or 3 (b) $x=-6$

10 (a) $2a$ (b) $2a+4$
(c) $8a$ (d) $8a$

11 (a) 9 (b) $x=2$

12 (a) 15 (b) 3 (c) 1

Exercise 22.6

1 (a) $fg(x)=x+3$; $gf(x)=x+3$
(b) $fg(x)=50x^2-15x+1$;
$gf(x)=10x^2-15x+5$
(c) $fg(x)=27x^2-48x+22$;
$gf(x)=9x^2-12x+4$
(d) $fg(x)=\frac{4x^2-36}{3}$;
$gf(x)=\frac{16x^2}{9}-9$

2 (a) $-2x$ (b) −4
(c) 16 (d) −2

3 (a) $9x+4$ (b) $18x^2+1$
(c) 3456 (d) 150
(e) $\frac{726}{25}$

4 (a) 26 (b) 7
(c) 26 (d) 29

5 $gh(4)=5$ $hg(4)=\frac{4}{5}$

6 (a) $-56+16x^2-x^4$
(b) $56-16x^2+x^4$
(c) $-56+16x^2-x^4$
(d) $56-16x^2+x^4$

7 (a) −25 (b) $\frac{3}{2}$ (c) $-\frac{7}{34}$
(d) $\frac{1}{3}$ (e) −15

8 (a) $(x^2+36)^2$ (b) $\sqrt{x^8+36}$
(c) 0 (d) $\sqrt{76}$

9 $hgf(1)=\frac{1}{0}$ which is undefined.

Exercise 22.7

1 (a) $\frac{x}{7}$
(b) $\sqrt[3]{\frac{1}{7x}}$
(c) $\sqrt[3]{x}$
(d) $\frac{x-3}{4}$ (e) $2(x-5)$ (f) $2x-2$
(g) $\frac{x}{3}+2$ (h) $\frac{2x-9}{2}$ (i) $\frac{4x-2}{2+x}$
(j) $\sqrt[3]{x-5}$ (k) $\frac{x^2-8}{3}$
(l) $f^{-1}(x)=\frac{x+1}{x-1}$

2 (a) $f^{-1}(x)=g(x)$
(b) $f^{-1}(x)=g(x)$
(c) $f^{-1}(x)\neq g(x)$
(d) $f^{-1}(x)=g(x)$

3 $g^{-1}(x)=3(x+44)$

4 (a) (i) $f^{-1}(x)=\frac{x}{5}$
(ii) $ff^{-1}(x)=x$
(iii) $f^{-1}f(x)=x$
(b) (i) $f^{-1}(x)=x-4$
(ii) $ff^{-1}(x)=x$
(iii) $f^{-1}f(x)=x$
(c) (i) $f^{-1}(x)=\frac{x+7}{2}$
(ii) $ff^{-1}(x)=x$
(iii) $f^{-1}f(x)=x$
(d) (i) $f^{-1}(x)=\sqrt[3]{x-2}$
(ii) $ff^{-1}(x)=x$
(iii) $f^{-1}f(x)=x$

(e) (i) $f^{-1}(x)=\frac{x^2+1}{2}$
(ii) $ff^{-1}(x)=x$
(iii) $f^{-1}f(x)=x$
(f) (i) $f^{-1}(x)=\frac{9}{x}$
(ii) $ff^{-1}(x)=x$
(iii) $f^{-1}f(x)=x$
(g) (i) $f^{-1}(x)=\sqrt[3]{x+1}$
(ii) $ff^{-1}(x)=x$
(iii) $f^{-1}f(x)=x$

5 (a) 8 (b) 20 (c) 11

6 (a) −10 (b) $\frac{5x+2}{20}$
(c) $x=1.54$
(d) (i) $-28\frac{2}{5}$ (ii) 3
(iii) $-7\frac{8}{10}$

Examination practice

Exam-style questions

1 \$2
2 16 5c coins and 34 10c coins
3 $a=3.64$
4 (a) false (b) true
(c) true (d) true
5 (a) 14 (b) $x=1.26$ or -0.26
(c) $x=1.76$ or -0.76
(d) $x=1$ (e) $\frac{4-x}{3}$
6 (a) 7 (b) $\frac{3-x}{4}$ (c) 4
7 $-\frac{3}{4}$

Past paper questions*

1 $x=\pm\sqrt{y-4}$

2 $y=\pm\sqrt{\frac{\pi x^2-A}{\pi}}$
or
$y=\pm\sqrt{x^2-\frac{A}{\pi}}$

3 (a) (i) 439.8 cm² (440 also fine)
(ii) $\frac{A-2\pi r^2}{2\pi r}=h$
(iii) $h=4.00$ cm (3.99–4.01 fine)
(iv) $r=9.77$ cm (9.77–9.78 fine)
(b) (i) 134 bottles
(ii) $\frac{x}{45}$ bottles
(iii) $\frac{x-75}{48}$
(iv) $\frac{x}{45}-7=\frac{x-75}{48}$
$48x-15120=45x-3375$
$x=3915$

4 (a) 8
(b) $4x-9$
(c) $2^{2(x+1)}$ or 2^{2x+2} or 4^{x+1} or 4×2^{2x}

Chapter 23

Exercise 23.1

1 (a)

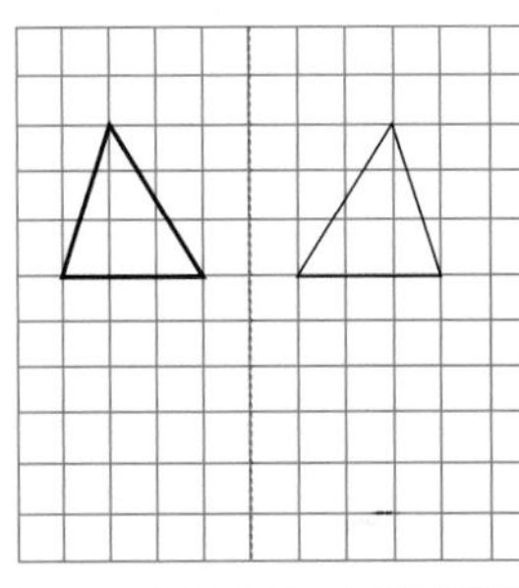

(b)

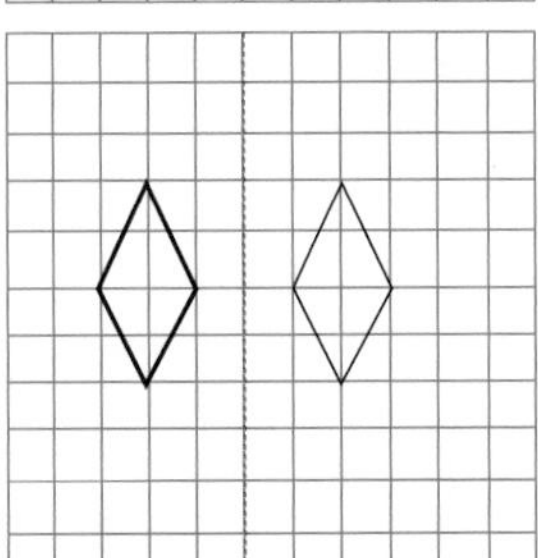

(c)

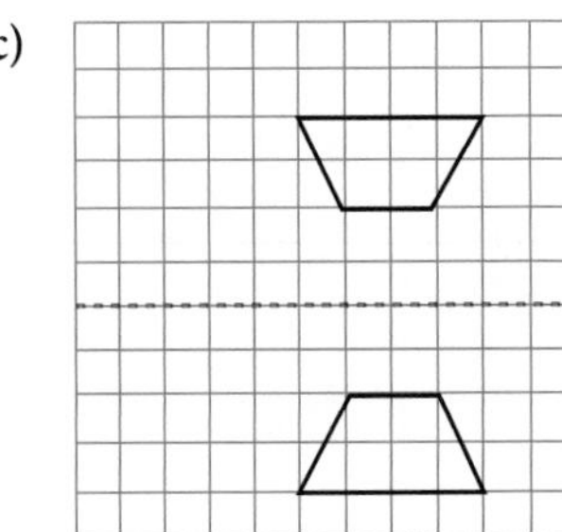

2 (a)

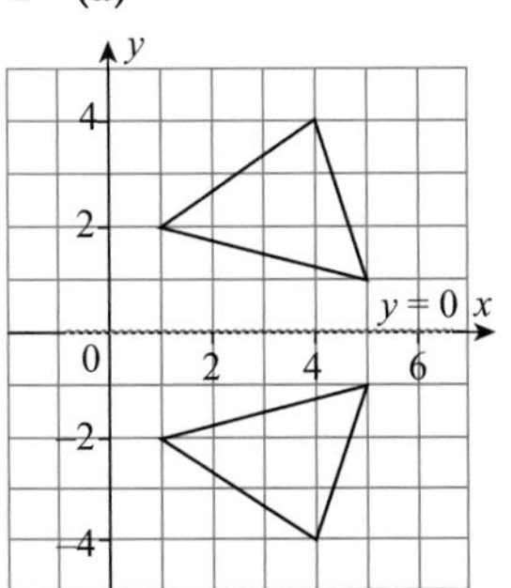

(b)

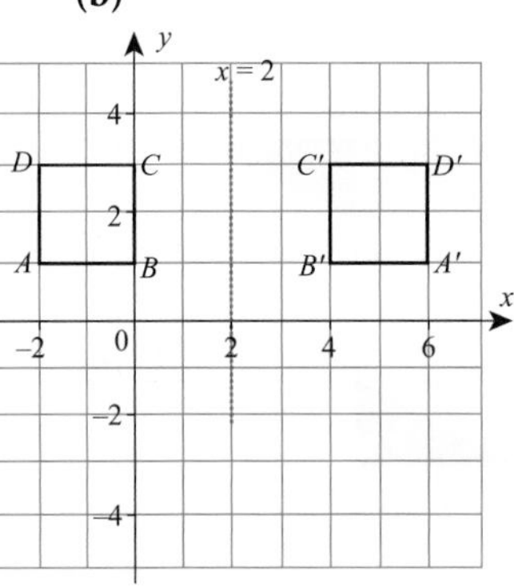

(c)

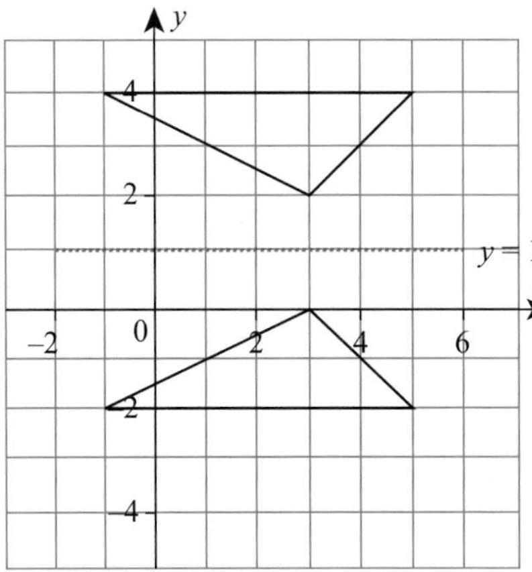

3 (a)

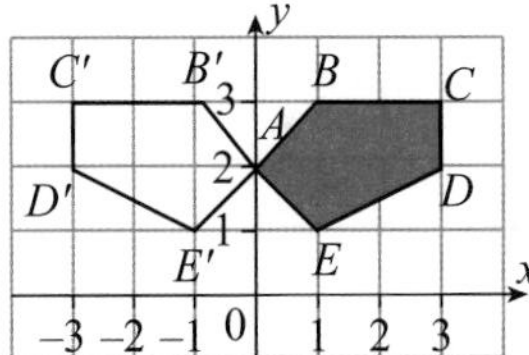

(b) $B'=(-1, 3)$
(c) A and A' are invariant – they are the same point.

4 (a) and (b)

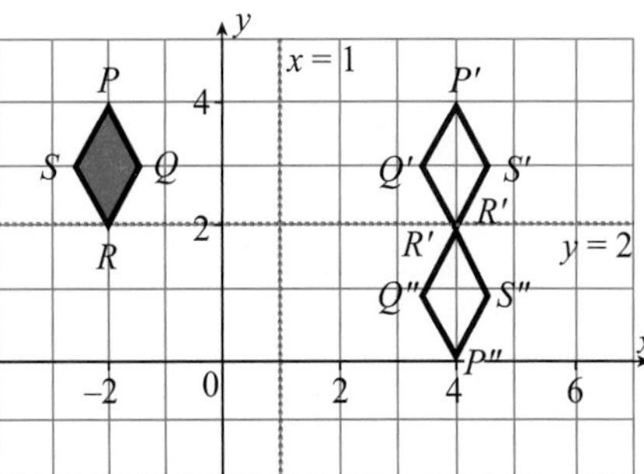

* *Cambridge International Examinations bears no responsibility for the example answers to questions taken from its past question papers which are contained in this publication.*

5 **(a)**

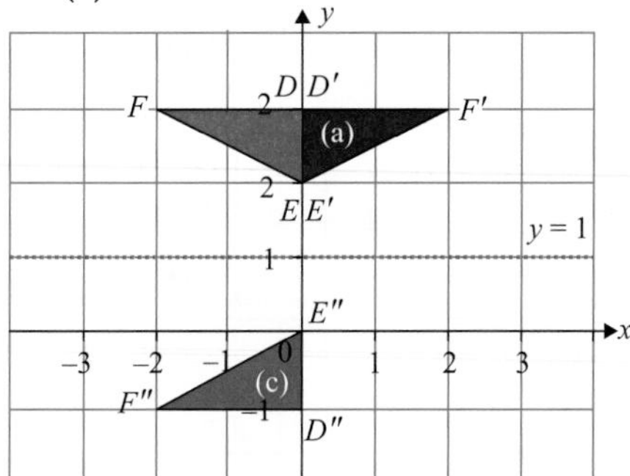

(b) F is at (–2, 3)
F′ is at (2, 3)

Exercise 23.2

1 **(a)**

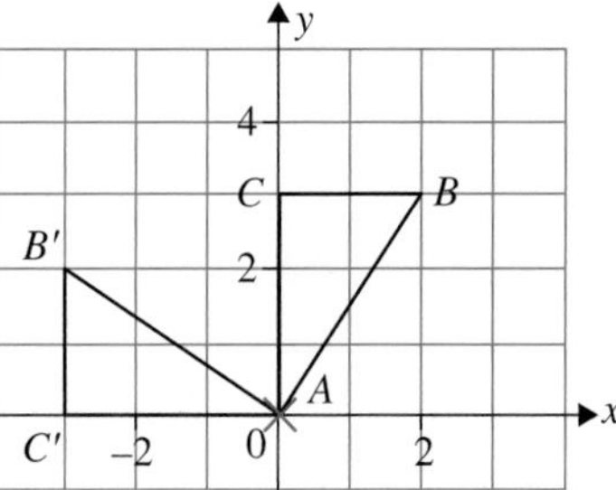

(b)

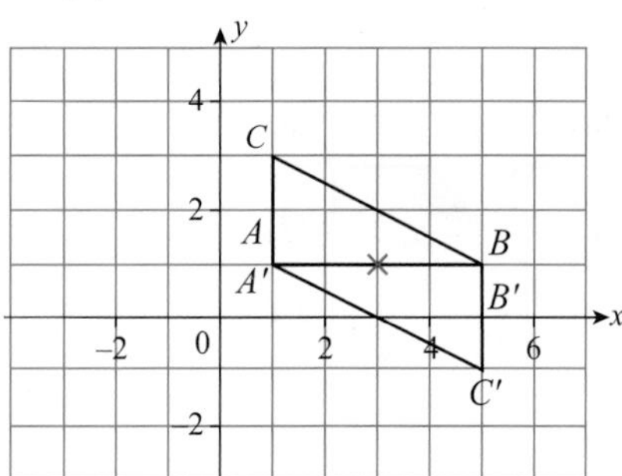

(c)

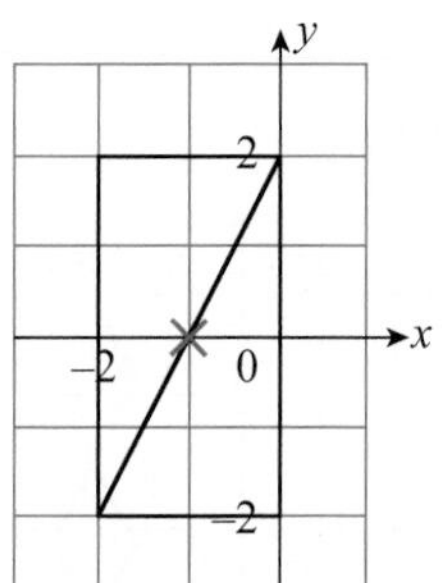

2 **(a)** Centre of rotation *A*; angle of rotation 90° clockwise.

(b) Centre of rotation point on line *AC*; angle of rotation 180°.

(c) Centre of rotation point on line *AC*; angle of rotation 90° clockwise.

3 **(a)** no **(b)** no **(c)** yes

Exercise 23.3

1

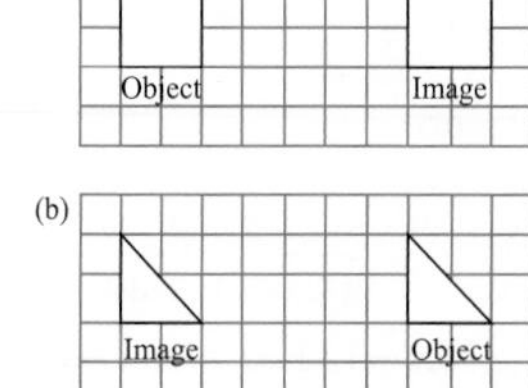

2 **(a)** $A \to B\begin{pmatrix}-6\\0\end{pmatrix}$ $A \to C\begin{pmatrix}3\\6\end{pmatrix}$

(b) $A \to B\begin{pmatrix}0\\-7\end{pmatrix}$ $A \to C\begin{pmatrix}-6\\1\end{pmatrix}$

(c) $A \to B\begin{pmatrix}0\\5\end{pmatrix}$ $A \to C\begin{pmatrix}6\\-3\end{pmatrix}$

3

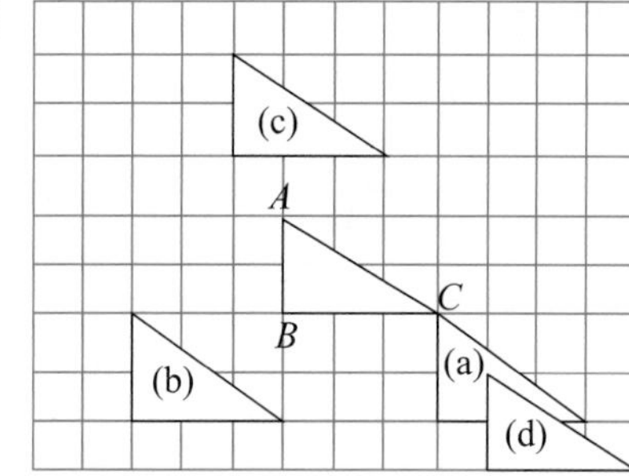

4 **(a)** and **(b)**

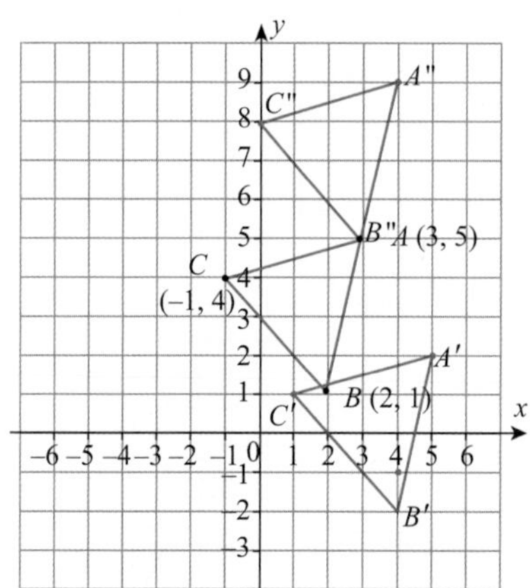

5 X' (7, –1)
Y' (6, 4)
Z' (3, –7)

6 **(a)** and **(b)**

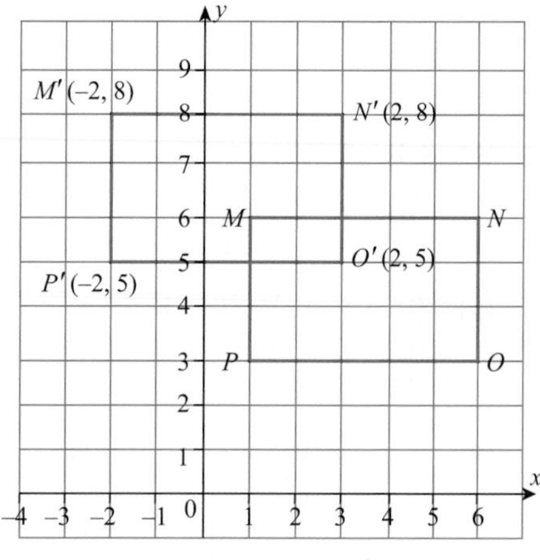

Exercise 23.4

1 **(a)** Scale factor 2; centre of enlargement = (8, 0)

(b) Scale factor 2; centre of enlargement = (3, –2)

(c) Scale factor 1 (not an enlargement), this is a translation of $\begin{pmatrix}-1\\-1\end{pmatrix}$.

(d) Scale factor 2; centre of enlargement (0, 0)

2 **(a)**

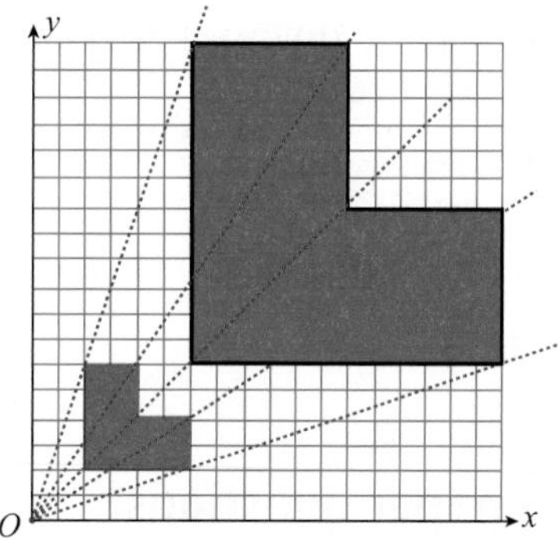

(b)

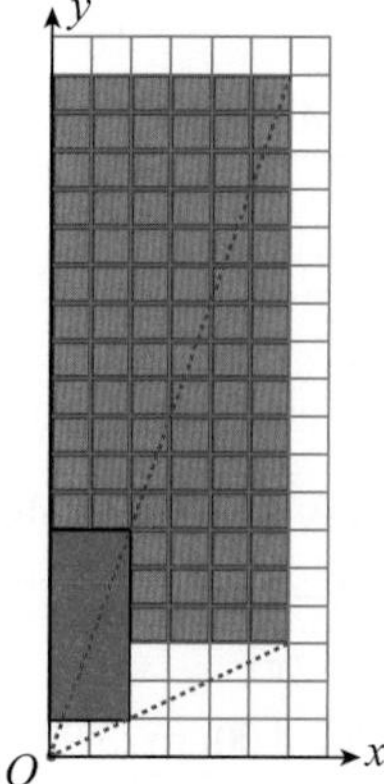

3

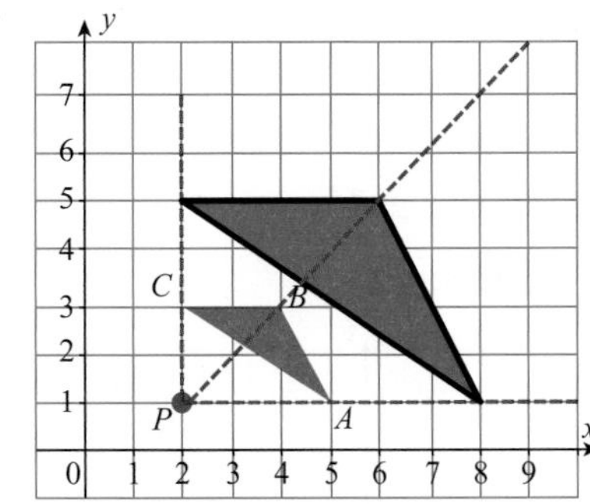

4

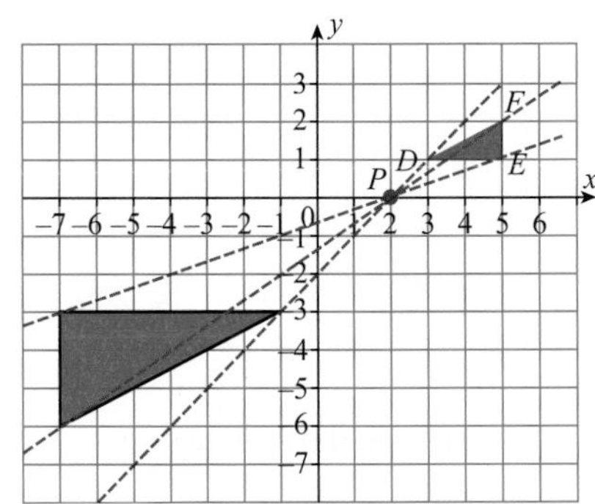

5 Scale factor 2; centre of enlargement (0, −1)

6 Scale factor 1.5; centre of enlargement (4, 2)

7 **(a)** 9.6 cm wide
(b) Length will be tripled.
(c) No; the image will not be in proportion.
(d) 2.5 cm long and 1.5 cm wide

Exercise 23.5

1 **(a)** $\begin{pmatrix}4\\6\end{pmatrix}$ **(b)** $\begin{pmatrix}4\\2\end{pmatrix}$ **(c)** $\begin{pmatrix}-4\\2\end{pmatrix}$
(d) $\begin{pmatrix}-4\\2\end{pmatrix}$ **(e)** $\begin{pmatrix}6\\-4\end{pmatrix}$ **(f)** $\begin{pmatrix}0\\4\end{pmatrix}$
(g) $\begin{pmatrix}8\\4\end{pmatrix}$ **(h)** $\begin{pmatrix}4\\-2\end{pmatrix}$

2

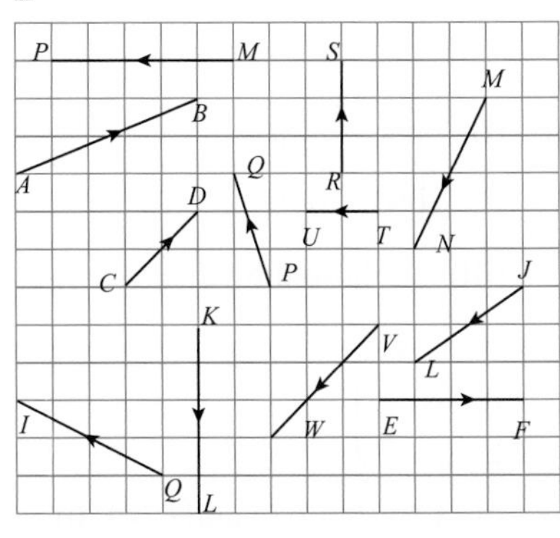

3 **(a)** $\overrightarrow{AB} = \begin{pmatrix}4\\0\end{pmatrix}$ $\overrightarrow{DC} = \begin{pmatrix}4\\0\end{pmatrix}$
(b) $\overrightarrow{BC} = \begin{pmatrix}1\\3\end{pmatrix}$ $\overrightarrow{AD} = \begin{pmatrix}1\\3\end{pmatrix}$
(c) They are equal.

4 **(a)** $\begin{pmatrix}4\\2\end{pmatrix}$ **(b)** $\begin{pmatrix}5\\-1\end{pmatrix}$ **(c)** $\begin{pmatrix}6\\-1\end{pmatrix}$
(d) $\begin{pmatrix}0\\-3\end{pmatrix}$ **(e)** $\begin{pmatrix}-4\\3\end{pmatrix}$ **(f)** $\begin{pmatrix}5\\2\end{pmatrix}$

Exercise 23.6

1 **(a)** $\begin{pmatrix}9\\-21\end{pmatrix}$ **(b)** $\begin{pmatrix}\frac{3}{2}\\\frac{-7}{2}\end{pmatrix}$ **(c)** $\begin{pmatrix}-6\\14\end{pmatrix}$
(d) $\begin{pmatrix}-3\\7\end{pmatrix}$ **(e)** $\begin{pmatrix}\frac{-9}{4}\\\frac{21}{4}\end{pmatrix}$ **(f)** $\begin{pmatrix}4.5\\-10.5\end{pmatrix}$

2 **(a)** $\overrightarrow{DK} = 2\overrightarrow{JK}$ **(b)** $\overrightarrow{JQ} = \frac{1}{4}\overrightarrow{JF}$
(c) $\overrightarrow{HP} = \frac{1}{2}\overrightarrow{HF}$ **(d)** $2\overrightarrow{GO} = \frac{1}{2}\overrightarrow{GC}$
(e) $3\overrightarrow{DG} = 1\overrightarrow{CL}$ **(f)** $6\overrightarrow{BE} = 2\overrightarrow{CL}$

3 **(a)** $\begin{pmatrix}2\\8\end{pmatrix}$ **(b)** $\begin{pmatrix}9\\21\end{pmatrix}$
(c) $\begin{pmatrix}4.5\\10.5\end{pmatrix}$ **(d)** $\begin{pmatrix}0.75\\3\end{pmatrix}$
(e) $\begin{pmatrix}1.5\\6\end{pmatrix}$ **(f)** $\begin{pmatrix}-36\\-84\end{pmatrix}$
(g) $\begin{pmatrix}1.5\\6\end{pmatrix}$ **(h)** $\begin{pmatrix}-\frac{5}{3}\\-\frac{35}{9}\end{pmatrix}$

Exercise 23.7

1 **(a)** $\begin{pmatrix}12\\-6\end{pmatrix}$ **(b)** $\begin{pmatrix}3\\-5\end{pmatrix}$

2 $\begin{pmatrix}12\\-7\end{pmatrix}$

3 **(a)** $\begin{pmatrix}12\\8\end{pmatrix}$ **(b)** $\begin{pmatrix}8\\24\end{pmatrix}$
(c) $\begin{pmatrix}-4\\-12\end{pmatrix}$ **(d)** $\begin{pmatrix}2\\0\end{pmatrix}$
(e) $\begin{pmatrix}0\\12\end{pmatrix}$ **(f)** $\begin{pmatrix}16\\21\end{pmatrix}$
(g) $\begin{pmatrix}10\\9\end{pmatrix}$ **(h)** $\begin{pmatrix}-2\\-7\end{pmatrix}$

4 **(a)** $2\mathbf{a} + 3\mathbf{b}$ **(b)** $\mathbf{a} + \frac{3\mathbf{b}}{2}$
(c) $\mathbf{b}$ **(d)** $\mathbf{a} + \frac{\mathbf{b}}{2}$

5 **(a)** $\mathbf{x} + \mathbf{y}$ **(b)** $\frac{3}{4}(\boldsymbol{x} + \boldsymbol{y})$
(c) $-\frac{1}{4}\mathbf{x} + \frac{3}{4}\mathbf{y}$

6 **(a)** $2q - 2p$ **(b)** $2p + q$ **(c)** $p - q$

Exercise 23.8

1 **(a)** 4.12 **(b)** 3.61 **(c)** 4.24
(d) 5 **(e)** 4.47 **(f)** 5
(g) 5.83

2 **(a)** 10.30 **(b)** 13.04
(c) 5 **(d)** 10

3 **(a)** 5 **(b)** 13 **(c)** 17

4 **(a)** $A(4, 2)$ $B(-1, 3)$ $C(6,-2)$
(b) $\overrightarrow{AB} = \begin{pmatrix}-5\\1\end{pmatrix}$ $\overrightarrow{CB} = \begin{pmatrix}-7\\5\end{pmatrix}$ $\overrightarrow{AC} = \begin{pmatrix}2\\-4\end{pmatrix}$

5 **(a)** $\frac{\mathbf{a}}{2}$ **(b)** $-\frac{\mathbf{b}}{2}$
(c) $\frac{\mathbf{a} - \mathbf{b}}{2}$ **(d)** $\frac{3\mathbf{a} + 3\mathbf{b}}{4}$

6 **(a)** 10 **(b)** 8.60

7 **(a)** 100 km/h **(b)** 6.71 km/h (3sf)

Exercise 23.9

1

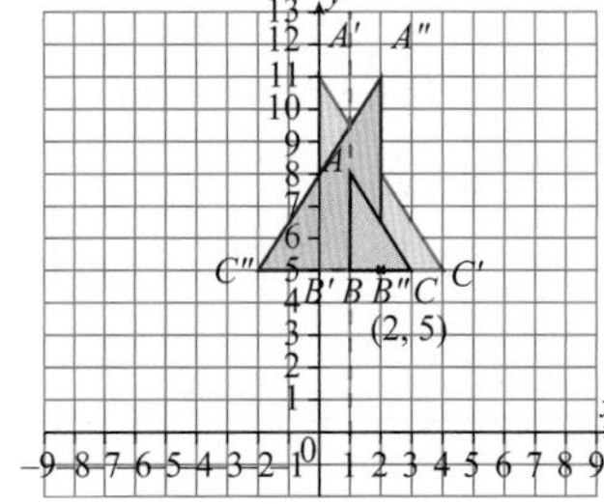

2

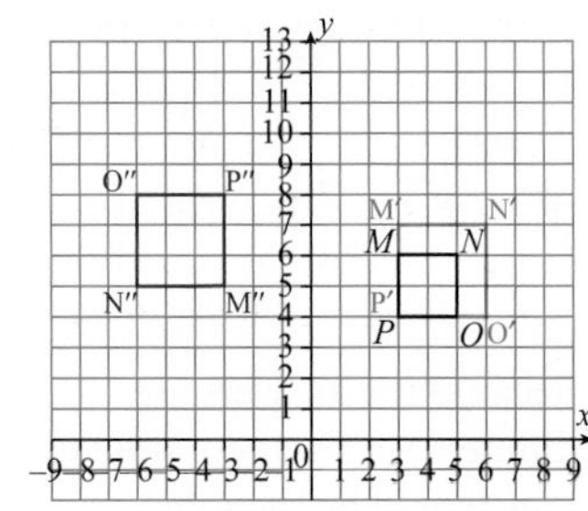

Exercise 23.10

1 **(a)** 2×2 **(b)** 2×3 **(c)** 3×2
(d) 1×2 **(e)** 1×3 **(f)** 1×1
(g) 2×1 **(h)** 3×1 **(i)** 3×3

2 C = E and G = H

Exercise 23.11

1 $\begin{pmatrix} 9 & -3 \end{pmatrix}$

2 $\begin{pmatrix} 15 \\ -6 \end{pmatrix}$

3 $\begin{pmatrix} 10 & -6 \\ 0 & 2 \end{pmatrix}$

4 $\begin{pmatrix} -4 & 8 \\ -12 & 0 \end{pmatrix}$

5 $\begin{pmatrix} 2 & 0 \\ 1 & 0.5 \end{pmatrix}$

6 $\begin{pmatrix} 6a & -6b \\ 9a & 12b \end{pmatrix}$

7 $\begin{pmatrix} 0 & 0 \\ 0 & 2 \end{pmatrix}$

8 $\begin{pmatrix} 5 \\ 4 \end{pmatrix}$

Exercise 23.12

1 **(a)** (22) **(b)** (6) **(c)** (-17)
(d) (-12) **(e)** $(a+9)$

2 **(a)** $\begin{pmatrix} 13 \\ 4 \end{pmatrix}$ **(b)** $\begin{pmatrix} 8 \\ 6 \end{pmatrix}$

(c) $\begin{pmatrix} 8 & 30 \\ 3 & 12 \end{pmatrix}$ **(d)** $\begin{pmatrix} 5 & -3 \\ 4 & 2 \end{pmatrix}$

3 **(a)** $x=4$ **(b)** $x=1$ **(c)** $x=7$

4 **(a)** $\begin{pmatrix} -5 & 10 \\ 4 & 2 \end{pmatrix}$ **(b)** $\begin{pmatrix} 6 & -1 \\ 4 & -9 \end{pmatrix}$

(c) $\begin{pmatrix} 0 & 5 \\ 2 & -2 \end{pmatrix}$ **(d)** $\begin{pmatrix} 0 & 5 \\ 2 & -2 \end{pmatrix}$

(e) $\begin{pmatrix} -11 & 12 \\ -4 & -7 \end{pmatrix}$ **(f)** $\begin{pmatrix} 3 & 19 \\ 1 & 2 \end{pmatrix}$

5 **(a)** **(i)** $\begin{pmatrix} -5 & 4 \\ 5 & 2 \end{pmatrix}$ **(ii)** $\begin{pmatrix} -3 & 6 \\ 5 & 0 \end{pmatrix}$

(b) no
(c) Because the answers are different, if it was commutative they would be the same.

Exercise 23.13

1 **(a)** 17 **(b)** 0 **(c)** −5
(d) 21 **(e)** −1

2 $x=9$
3 $x=-3$
4 $y=4$
5 $p=9$

Exercise 23.14

1 **(a)** $\begin{pmatrix} 1 & -3 \\ -\frac{1}{2} & 2 \end{pmatrix}$ **(b)** $\begin{pmatrix} 8 & -3 \\ -5 & 2 \end{pmatrix}$

(c) Singular matrix so no inverse.

(d) $\begin{pmatrix} -1 & 2 \\ -2 & 3 \end{pmatrix}$ **(e)** $\begin{pmatrix} -3 & 2 \\ \frac{5}{2} & -\frac{3}{2} \end{pmatrix}$

2

$$\begin{pmatrix} 1 & 0 \\ 0 & 1 \end{pmatrix}\begin{pmatrix} 1 & 0 \\ 0 & 1 \end{pmatrix} = \begin{pmatrix} 1\times1+0\times0 & 1\times0+0\times1 \\ 0\times1+1\times0 & 0\times0+1\times1 \end{pmatrix} = \begin{pmatrix} 1 & 0 \\ 0 & 1 \end{pmatrix}$$

3 **(a)**

$$\begin{pmatrix} 1 & 0 \\ 0 & -1 \end{pmatrix}\begin{pmatrix} 1 & 0 \\ 0 & -1 \end{pmatrix} = \begin{pmatrix} 1\times1+0\times0 & 1\times0+0\times-1 \\ 0\times1+-1\times0 & 0\times1+-1\times-1 \end{pmatrix} = \begin{pmatrix} 1 & 0 \\ 0 & 1 \end{pmatrix}$$

(b)

$$\begin{pmatrix} -1 & 0 \\ 0 & -1 \end{pmatrix}\begin{pmatrix} -1 & 0 \\ 0 & -1 \end{pmatrix} = \begin{pmatrix} -1\times-1+0\times0 & -1\times0+0\times-1 \\ 0\times-1+-1\times0 & 0\times0+-1\times-1 \end{pmatrix} = \begin{pmatrix} 1 & 0 \\ 0 & 1 \end{pmatrix}$$

(c)

$$\begin{pmatrix} 0 & 1 \\ 1 & 0 \end{pmatrix}\begin{pmatrix} 0 & 1 \\ 1 & 0 \end{pmatrix} = \begin{pmatrix} 0\times0+1\times1 & 0\times1+1\times0 \\ 1\times0+0\times1 & 1\times1+0\times0 \end{pmatrix} = \begin{pmatrix} 1 & 0 \\ 0 & 1 \end{pmatrix}$$

(d)

$$\begin{pmatrix} 0 & -1 \\ -1 & 0 \end{pmatrix}\begin{pmatrix} 0 & -1 \\ -1 & 0 \end{pmatrix} = \begin{pmatrix} 0\times0+-1\times-1 & 0\times-1+-1\times0 \\ -1\times0+0\times-1 & -1\times-1+0\times0 \end{pmatrix} = \begin{pmatrix} 1 & 0 \\ 0 & 1 \end{pmatrix}$$

4 $\begin{pmatrix} 5 & -7 \\ -2 & 3 \end{pmatrix}$

Exercise 23.15

1 NOT TO SCALE

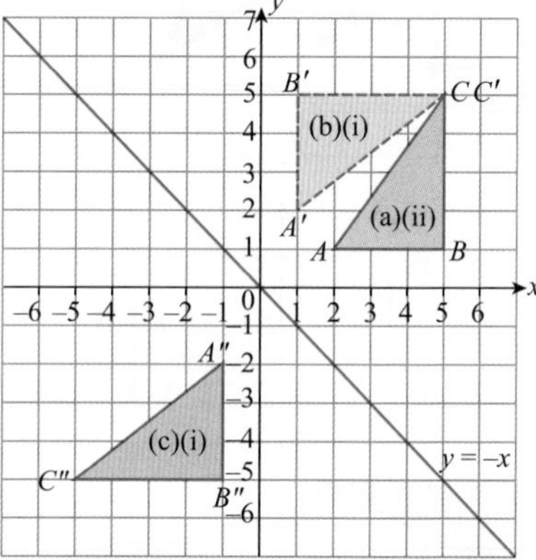

(b) **(ii)** Reflection in $y=x$

(c) **(ii)** $\begin{pmatrix} 0 & -1 \\ -1 & 0 \end{pmatrix}$

(d) **(i)** Reflection in the line $y=-x$.
(ii) $\begin{pmatrix} 0 & -1 \\ -1 & 0 \end{pmatrix}$

2

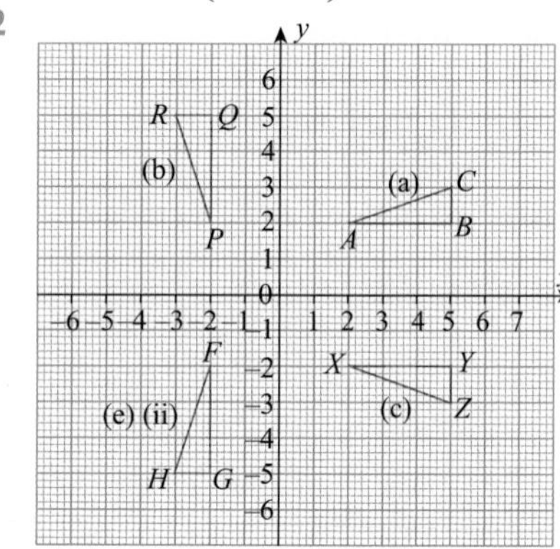

(d) **(i)** Reflection in the line $y=x$.
(ii) $\begin{pmatrix} 0 & 1 \\ 1 & 0 \end{pmatrix}$

(e) **(i)** $\begin{pmatrix} 0 & -1 \\ -1 & 0 \end{pmatrix}$

(iii) T followed by U.

3 **(a)** $\begin{pmatrix} -1 & -2 \\ 2 & 3 \end{pmatrix}$

(b) $A(-4, 5)$, $B(-2, 3)$ and $C(-1, 0)$

Examination practice

Exam-style questions

1 (a) NOT TO SCALE

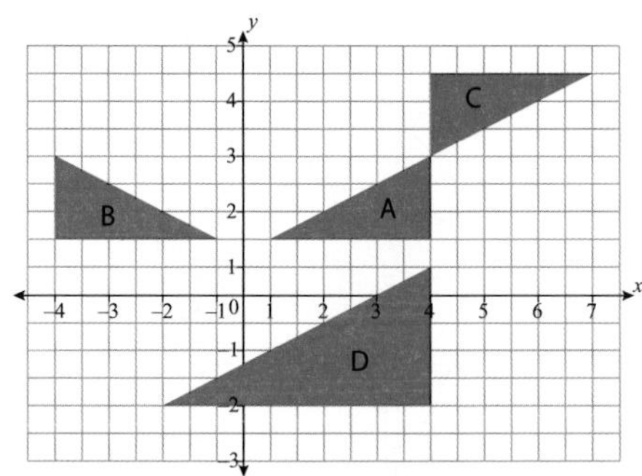

2 A: reflection about $y = 0$ (x-axis).

B: translation $\begin{pmatrix} -3 \\ 2 \end{pmatrix}$.

C: enlargement scale factor 2.

D: rotation + 90° about the origin.

3 (a) (i) $\begin{pmatrix} 1 \\ -3 \end{pmatrix}$ (ii) $\begin{pmatrix} -6 \\ 3 \end{pmatrix}$

(b)

4 (a) (−1, 2)

(b) Scale factor −2

5 (a) $\begin{pmatrix} 3 \\ -2 \end{pmatrix}$

(b) Rotation 180° about centre (6, 0).

(c) (i)

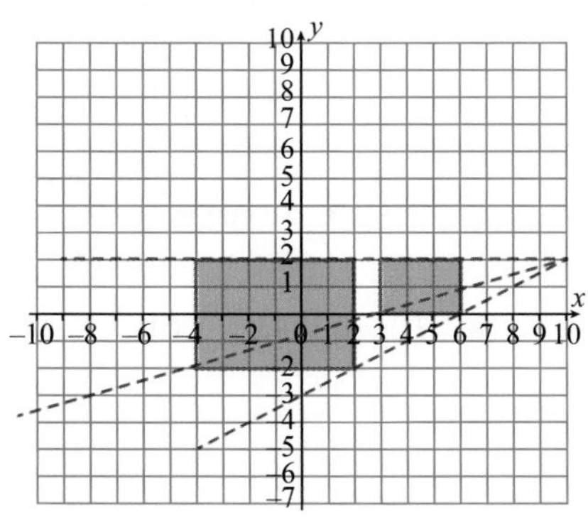

(ii) 4 : 1

6 (a)

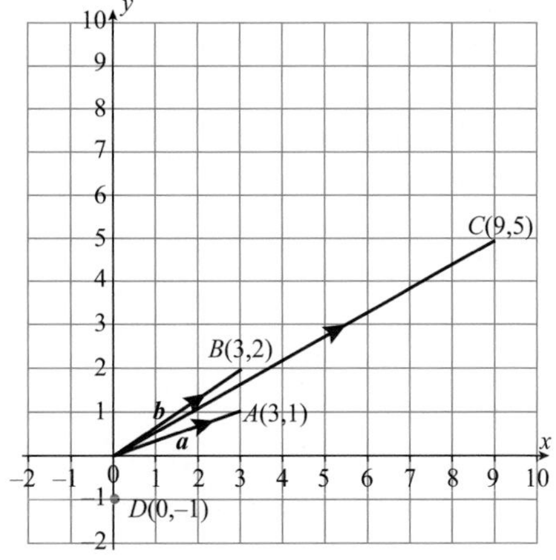

(b) **a** − **b** (c) $|\mathbf{a}| = 3.16$

7 (a) (i) Translation $\begin{pmatrix} 7 \\ 3 \end{pmatrix}$

(ii) Enlargement scale factor 3

(iii) Rotation 90° centre (2, 1) and translation $\begin{pmatrix} -3 \\ 1 \end{pmatrix}$

(b) Shapes B, D and F.

8 (a) (ii)

(b) (5) (c) $\begin{pmatrix} 2 & -\frac{5}{3} \\ 1 & -\frac{2}{3} \end{pmatrix}$

9 (a) $x = -5$ and $y = 15$

(b) $\begin{pmatrix} \frac{3}{10} & \frac{1}{10} \\ -\frac{2}{5} & \frac{1}{5} \end{pmatrix}$ (c) $t = 4$ and $u = -1$

10

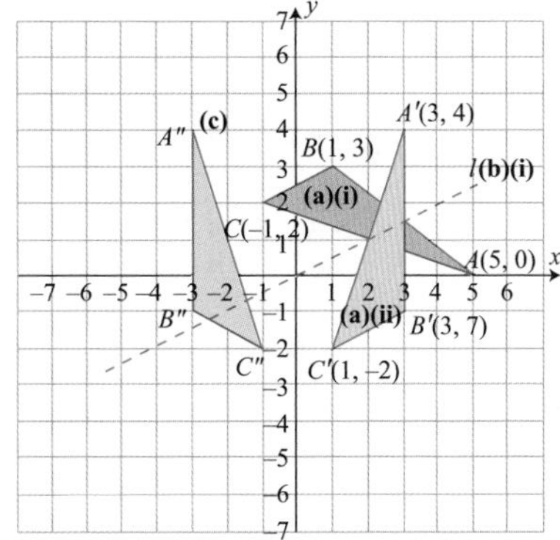

(b) (ii) $y = \frac{x}{2}$

(iii) $p = \frac{3}{5}, q = \frac{4}{5}, r = \frac{4}{5}, s = \frac{3}{5}$

(iv) Reflection about the line $y = \frac{x}{2}$

(d) 90° anti-clockwise

Past paper questions*

1 (a) $\frac{1}{5}\begin{pmatrix} 1 & -2 \\ 1 & 3 \end{pmatrix}$

(b) (i) **D**

(ii) $\mathbf{D}^{-1}\mathbf{E}$

2 (a) $\frac{1}{2}\boldsymbol{a} - \frac{1}{2}\boldsymbol{c}$

(b) $\frac{3}{4}\boldsymbol{a} + \frac{3}{4}\boldsymbol{c}$

Chapter 24

Exercise 24.1

1 (a)

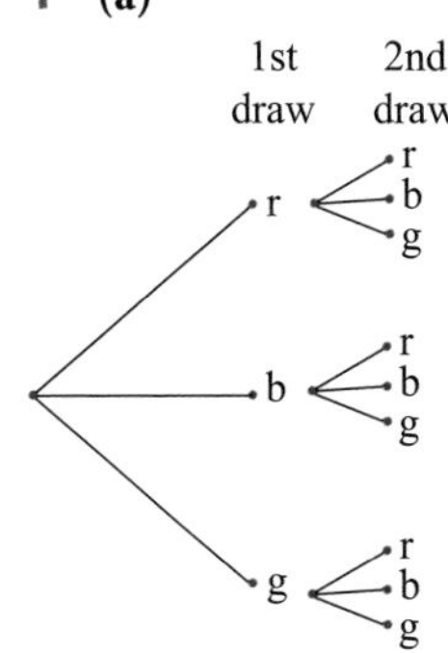

(b) 9 possible outcomes

(c) 3

(d) 5

(e) 4

2 (a)

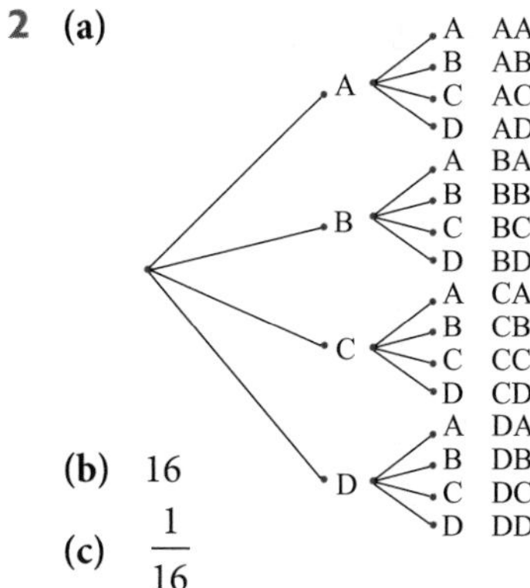

(b) 16

(c) $\frac{1}{16}$

Exercise 24.2

1

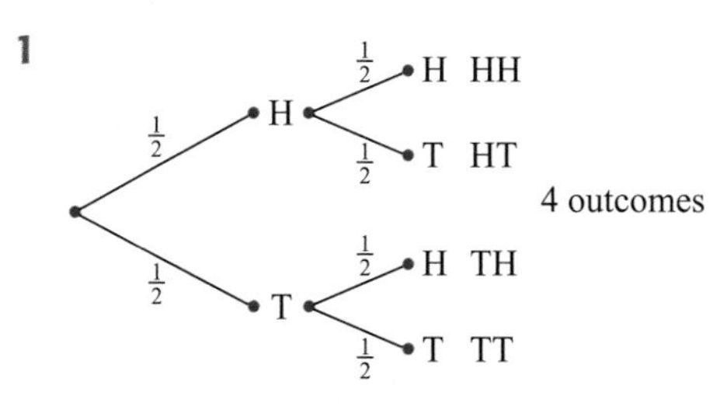

P(TT or HH) = $\frac{2}{4} = \frac{1}{2}$

* *Cambridge International Examinations bears no responsibility for the example answers to questions taken from its past question papers which are contained in this publication.*

2 (a)

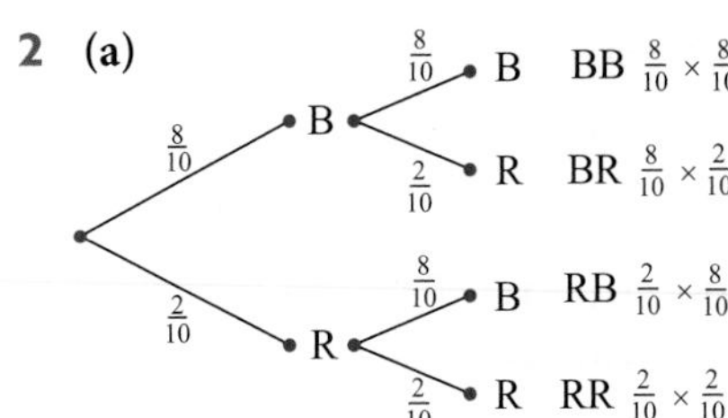

(b) (i) $P(RR) = \frac{1}{25}$

(ii) $P(RB) + P(BR) = \frac{8}{25}$

(iii) $P(BB) = \frac{16}{25}$

3 (a)

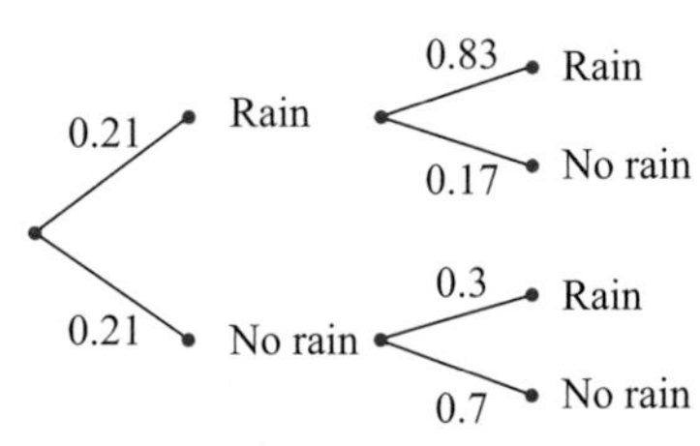

(b) (i) $P(RR) = \frac{25}{144}$

(ii) $P(WW) = \frac{49}{144}$

4 (a) 4

(b) $\frac{4}{9}$

(c) $\frac{1}{9}$

(d) He is equally likely either to buy two birds, or to buy one of each.

Exercise 24.3

1 (a)

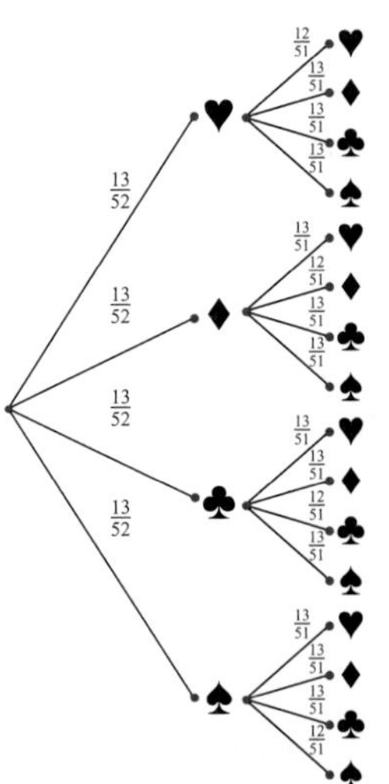

(b) (i) $P(\heartsuit\heartsuit) = \frac{13}{52} \times \frac{12}{51} = \frac{3}{51}$

(ii) $P(\clubsuit\clubsuit) = \frac{13}{52} \times \frac{12}{51} = \frac{13}{51}$

(iii) $P(\text{red, black}) = \frac{26}{52} \times \frac{26}{51} = \frac{13}{51}$

2 (a)

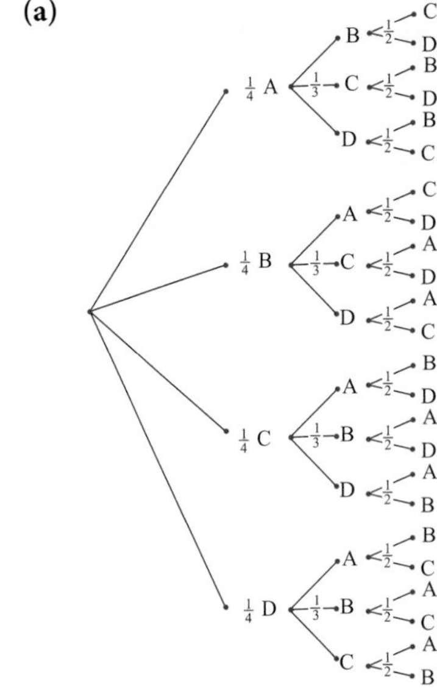

(b) (i) $\frac{1}{24}$ (ii) $\frac{1}{24}$

(iii) 0

(c) $\frac{1}{4}$ (d) $\frac{1}{24}$

3 (a) 12 outcomes

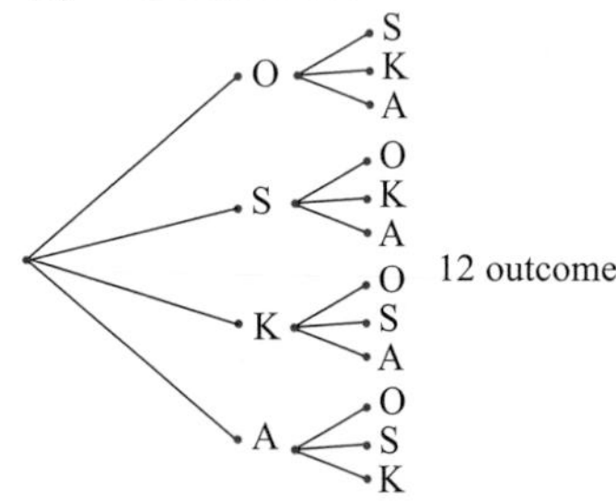

(b) $\frac{1}{12}$ (c) $\frac{1}{12}$

4 (a)

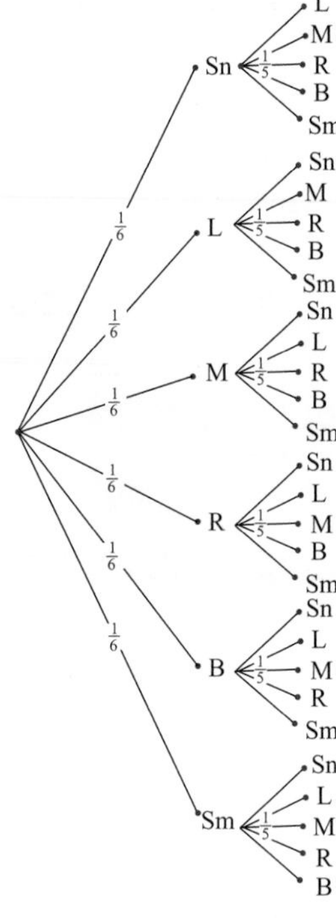

(b) $\frac{1}{30}$

5 (a)

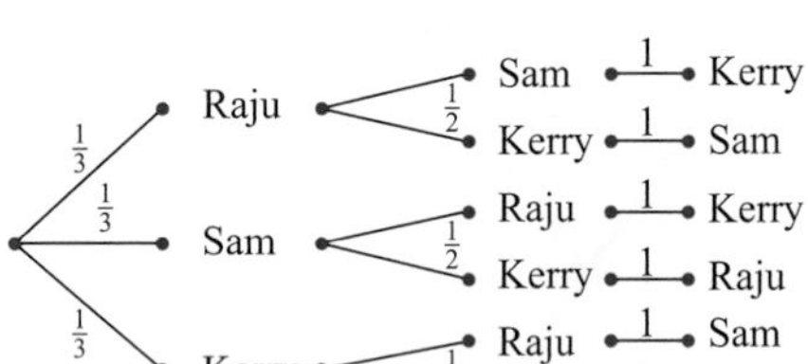

(b) Conditional – once the first name is chosen it cannot be chosen again, so the second choice depends on the first, and so on.

(c) 1 ways (d) 6 ways (e) $\frac{1}{6}$

6 (a) Friday Saturday

0.21	Rain	0.83	Rain
		0.17	No rain
0.21	No rain	0.3	Rain
		0.7	No rain

(b) (i) 0.1743 (ii) 0.4113

7 (a) weather forecast over the next 2 days

(b) $P(\text{rain both days}) = \frac{1}{50}$

$P(\text{sun both days}) = \frac{96}{125}$

$P(\text{1 fine day and 1 rain}) = \frac{53}{250}$

8 (a)

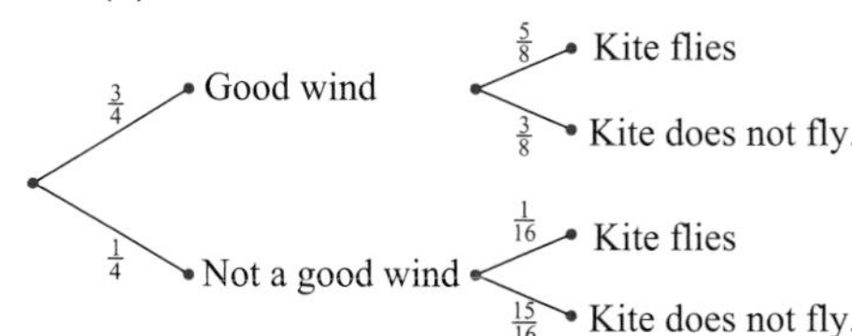

(b) $\frac{15}{32}$ **(c)** $\frac{33}{64}$ **(d)** $\frac{31}{128}$

Examination practice

Exam-style questions

1 (a)

(b) (i) $\frac{5}{36}$ **(ii)** $\frac{1}{6}$

2 (a)

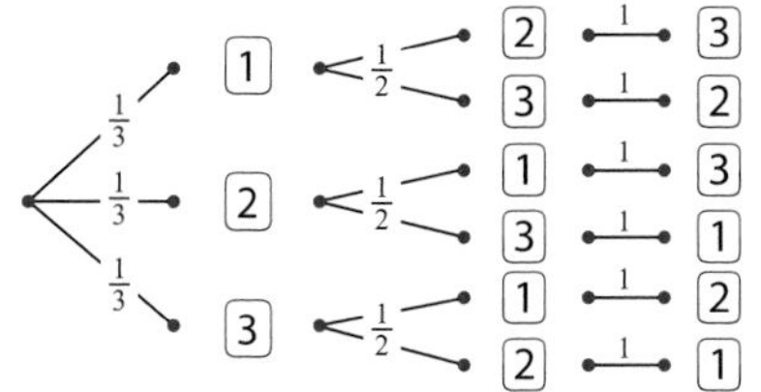

(b) 6

(c) (i) $\frac{1}{6}$ **(ii)** $\frac{2}{3}$

(iii) $\frac{1}{3}$ **(iv)** 1

Past paper questions*

1 (a) There is a greater probability of choosing a white ball from Box B.

P (white ball for Box B) $= \frac{2}{5}$,

whereas P (white ball for

Box A) $= \frac{1}{4}$.

When asked to explain your answer in a probability question, it is better to include the probabilities as the evidence to support your statement. You would have still scored the marks if you said that '1 out of 4 is smaller than 2 out of 5' because you are still providing evidence; if you had simply said 'box B contains more white balls' you would not have scored the marks.

(b) (i)

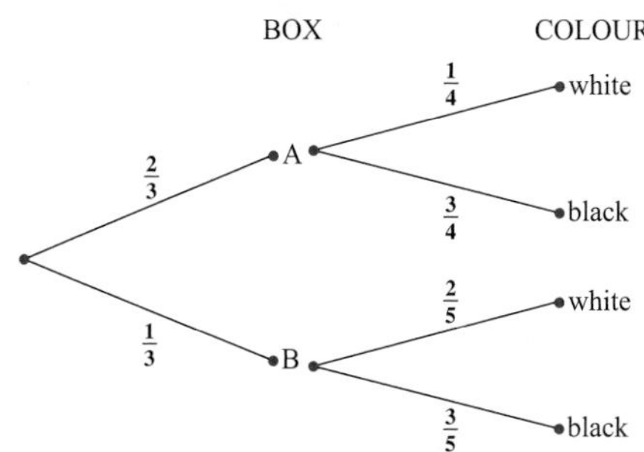

(ii) $\frac{1}{2}$ ($\frac{6}{12}$ or 0.5 also fine)

(iii) $\frac{7}{10}$ ($\frac{42}{60}$ or 0.7 also fine)

(c) $\frac{1}{30}$ ($\frac{2}{60}$ or 0.0333(3...)also fine)

* *Cambridge International Examinations bears no responsibility for the example answers to questions taken from its past question papers which are contained in this publication.*

Glossary

A

Acute An angle greater than 0° but less than 90°.

Adjacent A "shorter" side of a right-angled triangle that is "next to" an angle other than the right-angle.

Algebra The use of letters and other symbols to write mathematical information.

Alternate A pair of equal angles formed between two parallel lines and on opposite sides of the transversal (a line that crosses both parallel lines).

Angle A measure of the amount of turning between two lines that meet at a point.

Apex In a pyramid, the apex is the point, above the base, at which all the sloping sides meet.

Arc Part of the circumference of a circle.

Area A measure of the amount of space contained within a plane shape.

Average A single value used to represent a set of data. (A measure of the central tendency of the data.)

Axis of symmetry A line that divides a plane shape into two symmetrical halves or a "rod" about which a solid can rotate and still look the same in different positions.

Bar graph A diagram used to display discrete data.

Base When working with indices, the base is the number that is being raised to a power.

Bearing An angle indicating the direction of travel between two points. The bearing begins from the "North" direction and is measured clockwise round to the line joining start point and destination.

B

Bias Something that affects the chance of an event occurring in favour of a desired outcome.

Bivariate data Two measurements, relating to an investigation, taken at the same time.

BODMAS When more than one arithmetic operation appears in a sum, this mnemonic indicate the order in which the operations should take place. Brackets, Of, Divide, Multiply, Add, Subtract.

C

Categorical data Non-numerical data.

Centre of rotation The point around which a plane shape can rotate and show the same shape in different positions.

Chord A straight line joining one point on the circumference of a circle to another point on the circumference.

Circle A set of (joined) points that are the same distance (radius) from a given fixed point (the centre).

Class interval The difference between the upper and lower limits of groups of data.

Coefficient In a term which is a mixture of numbers and letters, the coefficient is the number that is multiplying the letters.

Column vector Number pair notation used to describe a vector as the movement between two points: x units in the x-direction (left or right) and y units in the in the y-direction (up or down) e.g. $\begin{pmatrix} x \\ y \end{pmatrix}$. See also vector.

Combined events One event followed by another event.

Commission Pay based on a percentage of sales made.

Common Denominator A common value that two or more fractions need to be converted to in order to be able to add and/or subtract fractions.

Common Factor A term that can be divided exactly into two or more other terms.

Complement The elements that are in the universal set but not in a given set.

Composite function Applying a function to a value and then another function to that result.

Composite number Integer with more than two factors i.e. it has more factors than just 1 and itself.

Compound interest Interest paid on interest already earned and not just the original capital.

Congruent Shapes that are identical in both shape and size.

Constant term A term in an equation or expression that has a fixed numerical value.

Continuous Data that can take any value in a range, such as height or weight.

Conversion Changing one quantity or unit into its equivalent in another unit.

Correlation The relationship between bivariate data.

Corresponding angles A pair of equal angles formed in the "same manner". These occur with parallel lines and transversals, in similar and congruent triangles and other similar shapes.

Corresponding sides Sides that occupy the same relative position in similar or congruent shapes.

Cosine ratio For a given angle (other than the right-angle) in a right-angled triangle, the cosine ratio is the length of the side adjacent to the angle divided by the hypotenuse of the triangle.

Cosine rule A formula connecting the three sides of a triangle and one of the angles.

Cost price The price that a trader pays for goods.

Co-interior angles The two angles formed on the same side of a transversal when it cuts two parallel lines. Co-interior angles add up to 180° (they are supplementary).

Cube A cube is the result obtained when a number is multiplied by itself and then multiplied by itself again.

Cumulative frequency A "running total" of the frequencies.

Cumulative frequency curve A curve formed using the cumulative frequencies as the vertical axis value.

Cyclic quadrilateral A quadrilateral whose vertices all exactly touch the circumference of a circle.

D

Data A set of facts, numbers or other information.

Deductions Money that is subtracted from income before tax is calculated.

Denominator The number on the bottom of a fraction.

Dependent variable A variable whose value depends on the value of another variable.

Determinant In a two by two matrix, the product of the elements in the leading diagonal minus the product of the elements in the other diagonal.

Difference between two squares A method of factorising (putting into brackets) one squared term subtracted from another.

Directed numbers Numbers that have a (positive or negative) direction; once a direction is taken to be positive, the opposite direction is negative e.g. $-4°c$ is a directed number.

Direct proportion When two quantities increase or decrease at the same rate.

Discount The amount by which an original selling price is reduced.

Discrete Data that can only take certain (usually integer) values.

E

Earnings The amount earned for work done. (See commission, salary and wages.)

Element A member of a set.

Empty set A set that contains no elements.

Enlargement A transformation of a shape that keeps the ratio of corresponding sides the same but increases or decreases the lengths of the sides.

Equation A mathematical "sentence" involving the use of the "=" sign.

Equation of a line A formula that shows how the x coordinate is related to the y coordinate.

Equidistant The same distance from.

Equivalent Fraction The result of multiplying (or dividing) the top and bottom of a fraction by the same value.

Estimate An approximate solution to a sum found by using rounded values.

Estimated mean A calculated approximation for the mean of grouped data.

Event The outcome that is being tested for in a probability "experiment".

Exchange rate The value to convert from one currency to another.

Expansion Multiplying out the terms inside a bracket by the term multiplying the bracket. (This includes multiplying one bracket by another.)

Experimental probability The chance of an event happening, calculated by running an "experiment" many times.

Exponent Another word for power or index, indicating how many times a base number is multiplied by itself.

Exponential A function formed when the variable is in the index.

Expression A group of terms linked by operation signs.

Extrapolation A value determined by continuing a line of best fit beyond the plotted data.

F

Face A plane shape that forms part of a solid.

Factor A number that divides exactly into another number with no remainder.

Factorisation To re-write an expression using brackets.

Favourable combinations Combinations of outcomes that mean a desired event has occurred.

Favourable outcomes Any outcomes that mean a desired event has occurred.

FOIL A mnemonic for the order of multiplying out terms in a double bracket expansion. First, Outside, Inside, Last.

Formula A general "rule" expressed algebraically (such as how to find the area of a shape).

Fraction Part of a whole.

Frequency The number of times a particular value occurs.

Frequency density The frequency of a class divided by the width of the class.

Frequency table A method of summarising data when values or classes occur more than once.

Function A set of rules or instructions for changing one number (an input) into another (an output).

Function notation An alternative mathematical way of writing equations.

G

Gradient The steepness of a line (or the steepness of a tangent drawn at a point on a curve).

Gross income Amount earned before deductions and tax.

Grouped The collection of individual data values into convenient groups. Used especially for continuous data.

H

Histogram A specialised graph used to illustrate grouped continuous data.

Hyperbola A graph where the variable is in the denominator of a fraction. (Also called reciprocal graphs.)

Hypotenuse The longest side of a right-angled triangle.

I

Image The new position of a point after a transformation.

Imperial A non-metric system of measurement.

Included angle In congruency, an angle that is formed by the meeting of two given sides.

Included side In congruency, a side that connects two given angles.

Independent An event whose outcome is not affected/influenced by what has occurred before.

Index Another word for power or exponent, indicating how many times a base number is multiplied by itself.

Integer Any of the negative and positive whole numbers, including zero.

y-intercept The point at which a line or curve crosses the y-axis.

x-intercept The point at which a line or curve crosses the x-axis.

Interest The amount charged for borrowing, or earned for investing, money.

Interest rate The percentage charged for borrowing, or earned for investing, money. (Usually an annual rate.)

Interquartile range The difference between the upper and lower quartiles.

Intersection In sets, the elements that are common to two or more sets. In algebra, the point where two lines or curves cross.

Inverse For a square matrix, a matrix that multiplies the original matrix to give the appropriate unit matrix.

Inverse functions A function that does the opposite of the original function.

Inverse proportion When one quantity decreases in the same proportion as another quantity increases.

Irrational number A (decimal) number that does not terminate or recur and cannot be written as a fraction.

L

Line A straight, one dimensional figure that extends to infinity in both directions. See "line segment".

Line graph A chart where numerical values are plotted against 'number lines' on vertical and horizontal axes. Points are plotted and joined to form a line.

Line of best fit A trend line drawn onto a scatter graph that passes as close to as many data points as possible.

Line segment A section of a line that is the shortest distance between two points.

Line symmetry A line that divides a plane shape into two halves so that one half is the mirror image of the other. (See also axis of symmetry.)

Linear Equation A linear equation has no terms with a power in x greater than one.

Linear inequalities Similar to linear equations but using $<$, $>$, $\leq$ or $\geq$.

Linear programming A method for finding region in a plane that satisfies a set of constraints defined as linear inequalities.

Loci The plural of locus.

Locus A set of points that obey a certain rule.

Loss When goods are sold for less than they were bought, the loss is the cost price – selling price.

Lower bound The exact smallest value that a number (given to a specified accuracy) could be.

Lower quartile The value of data at the 25th percentile.

Lowest Terms An equivalent fraction where the numerator and denominator are the smallest allowable whole numbers. Also called simplest form.

M

Magnitude The size (of a vector) irrespective of direction.

Matrix A set of numbers arranged in rows and columns.

Maximum A turning point or vertex on a graph whose y-coordinate is greater than points immediately to its left and right.

Mean An average that uses all the data.

Median An average, the middle value of data when it is arranged in increasing order.

Metric A measuring system based on multiples of ten.

Midpoint Exactly half way between the ends of a line segment.

Minimum A turning point or vertex on a graph whose y-coordinate is lower than points immediately to its left and right.

Mixed Number A number with a whole number part and a fraction part.

Modal class For grouped data, a class that has the highest frequency.

Mode An average, the most frequently occurring value in a set of data.

Multiple The result of multiplying a number by an integer.

Multiply out Multiplying out the terms inside a bracket by the term multiplying the bracket. (This includes multiplying one bracket by another.) See also expansion.

Mutually exclusive Events that cannot happen at the same time.

N

Natural number Any whole number from 1 to infinity, sometimes called "counting numbers". 0 is not included.

Negative correlation A trend, in bivariate data, where, as one value increases, the other value decreases.

Net The plane shape formed from the faces of a solid when it is "unfolded".

Net income Income from earnings after deductions and tax have been subtracted.

No correlation No apparent linear relationship between tow sets of data.

***n*th term** The value in the nth position in a sequence.

Numerator The number on the top of a fraction.

Numerical data Data that is in the form of numbers.

O

Object The original position of a point before a transformation.

Obtuse An angle greater than 90° but less than 180°.

Opposite A "shorter" side of a right-angled triangle that is "opposite" an angle other than the right-angle.

Order of rotational symmetry The number of times a shape fits onto itself in one rotation.

Outcome The possible results of an "experiment".

P

Parabola The graph of a quadratic relationship.

Parallel Lines that "never meet". The shortest distance between a pair of parallel lines remains the same.

Percentage A fraction with a denominator of 100.

Percentage decrease The amount that something has decreased as a percentage of the original value.

Percentage increase The amount that something has increased as a percentage of the original value.

Percentiles The value of data at a specified position (the data must be arranged in increasing order).

Perimeter The distance around the edges of a plane shape.

Periodic Repeats at regular intervals.

Perpendicular At right angles to. When the angle between two lines is 90°, the lines are perpendicular to each other.

Perpendicular bisector A line that cuts exactly through the middle of another line, making an angle of 90° with it.

Pictogram A diagram that uses symbols or small pictures to represent data.

Pie chart A circular chart which uses slices or sectors of the circle to show the data.

Plane symmetry A flat surface that cuts a solid into two halves so that one half is the mirror image of the other.

Polygon A plane (two-dimensional) shape with three or more sides.

Positive correlation A trend in bivariate data where as one value increase, so does the other.

Possible outcomes The possible results from an event.

Power Another word for exponent or index, indicating how many times a base number is multiplied by itself.

Primary data Data collected by the person who is going to use it.

Prime factor A prime number that divides exactly into another number with no remainder.

Prime number A whole number greater than 1 which has only two factors: the number itself and 1.

Principal The initial amount of money invested or borrowed.

Probability A measure of how likely an event is to happen

Probability scale The range of values from zero to one.

Possibility diagram A list or diagram that shows all the equally likely outcomes of an "experiment".

Profit When goods are sold for more than they were bought, the profit is the selling price – cost price.

Projection The image of a line on a plane such that the angle between the angle and the image is the smallest possible.

Q

Quadratic equation An equation that contains a quadratic expression.

Quadratic expression An expression where one term has a variable squared (and no variable with a higher power).

Quadrilateral Polygons with four sides.

Qualitative Another name for categorical data.

Quantitative Another name for numerical data.

Quartiles The values one quarter and three quarters through a set of data when arranged in ascending order.

R

Range A measure of the spread of data. The largest value – the smallest value.

Rate A comparison of two different quantities.

Ratio A comparison of amounts in a particular order.

Rational number A number that can be expressed as a fraction in its lowest terms.

Reciprocal The fraction obtained when the values of the numerator and denominator are interchanged. (See also hyperbola.)

Recurring decimals A decimal that continues forever, repeating itself at regular intervals.

Reflection A transformation that creates an image by reflecting points in a given line.

Reflex An angle greater than 180° but less than 360°.

Region A region in a plane that satisfies a set linear inequalities.

Relative frequency The experimental probability of an event happening.

Reverse percentage Finding the original value of an item before a percentage change has been applied.

Right-angle An angle that is exactly 90°.

Rotation A transformation that creates an image by rotating points by a given angle about a fixed point.

Rotational symmetry Symmetry by turning a shape about a fixed point so that it looks the same in different positions.

S

Salary Earnings based on a fixed yearly amount, usually paid in monthly instalments.

Sample space A list or diagram that shows the possible outcomes of two or more events.

Scalar A quantity that has size (magnitude) but not direction.

Scale A ratio that indicates how much smaller (or larger) a drawing is from the original object.

Scale drawing A representation of an object, either bigger or smaller than the original, whose corresponding sides remain in the same proportion.

Scale factor of areas The multiplying factor for the area of a shape that is enlarged from an original. (This is the square of the multiplying factor for sides.)

Scale factor of lengths The multiplying factor for the sides of a shape that is enlarged from an original.

Scale factor of volumes The multiplying factor for the volume of a shape that is enlarged from an original. (This is the cube of the multiplying factor for sides.)

Scatter diagram A diagram that plots pairs of bivariate data to help determine if there is any correlation between them.

Secondary data Data used for statistical purposes that has not been collected by the person performing the statistical analysis.

Sector Part of a circle defined by the angle that two radii make at the centre of the circle.

Selling price The price that a trader sells goods for.

Semi-circle Half of a circle.

Sequence A set whose elements have been listed in a particular order, with some connection between the elements.

Set A list or collection of objects that share a characteristic.

Set builder notation A means of describing the elements of a set without having to write them all down.

Similar Plane objects that have the same shape and proportion but are different in size.

Simple interest Interest that is calculated only on the original amount borrowed or invested.

Simplest Form An equivalent fraction where the numerator and denominator are the smallest allowable whole numbers. Also called lowest terms.

Simultaneous At the same time (or in the same position).

Sine ratio For a given angle (other than the right-angle) in a right-angled triangle, the sine ratio is the length of the side opposite to the angle divided by the hypotenuse of the triangle.

Sine rule In any triangle, the ratio of the sine of an angle to the length of the side opposite the angle is always the same.

Slant Height In a cone, the slant height is the shortest distance from a point on the circumference of the base to the apex.

Solid A three-dimensional object.

Solution The value obtained from solving an equation.

Speed A rate that compares distance travelled in a given time.

Spread A measure such as range or interquartile range.

Square The product obtained when a number is multiplied by itself.

Square root A number that, multiplied by itself gives a square.

Standard Form A shorthand method of writing very large or very small numbers.

Subject The variable written by itself (usually to the left of the "=" sign).

Subset A set whose elements are all also members of another (usually larger) set.

Substitute To replace one value with another (usually a letter with a number).

Substitution The replacement of a letter in a formula or expression with a number.

Subtended An angle formed at the meeting of two given lines.

Surface Area The total area of the faces of a three-dimensional solid.

Symbol A short way of writing mathematical information, such as "=" which means is equal to.

Symmetrical A shape that has a property of symmetry.

Symmetry Having the same shape in different positions either through reflection in a line or rotation about a point.

T

Tangent A straight line that just touches a curve at one point.

Tangent ratio For a given angle (other than the right-angle) in a right-angled triangle, the tangent ratio is the length of the side opposite to the angle divided by the side adjacent to the angle.

Tax threshold The amount of money that can be earned before any tax becomes payable.

Term Part of an expression or the individual numbers, letters, objects etc in a sequence.

Terminating decimals A decimal that does not continue forever.

Theoretical probability The chance of an event happening, calculated if it is known that the possible outcomes are equally likely.

Transformation A change in the position of a point or line following a given rule.

Translation A transformation that creates an image of a point by "sliding" it along a plane.

Trend The general direction of the line of best fit for bivariate data.

Trial An "experiment" to determine the value of an outcome.

Triangle A polygon with three sides.

Turning point A point on a graph where it changes direction. Usually a maximum or minimum point.

Two-way table A table that summarises the data from two or more sets of data.

U

Union A set that contains all the elements of two or more sets but without any repeats.

Unitary method A method for solving proportion problems.

Universal set For a given problem, all the elements that could possibly be included.

Unknown angle An angle whose value is to be calculated.

Unknown side A side whose length is to be calculated.

Upper bound The largest value that a number (given to a specified accuracy) could be.

Upper quartile The value of data at the 75th percentile.

V

Variable A letter in a formula or equation that can have different values.

Vector A quantity that has direction as well as size.

Venn diagram A pictorial method for illustrating the elements and interconnections of sets.

Vertically opposite A pair of equal angles formed when two straight lines cross.

Vertices The points where two or more edges of a plane shape meet.

Volume The amount of space contained inside a solid object.

Vulgar Fraction Another name for "common" fractions that have a numerator and denominator.

Wages Pay based on the number of hours worked, usually paid weekly.

Index

D

E